THE CAMBRIDGE HISTORY OF
THE POLAR REGIONS

The Cambridge History of the Polar Regions is a landmark collection drawing together the history of the Arctic and Antarctica from the earliest times to the present. In this book, structured as a series of thematic chapters, an international team of scholars offer a range of perspectives from environmental history, the history of science and exploration, cultural history, and the more traditional approaches of political, social, economic, and imperial history. The volume considers the centrality of Indigenous experience and the urgent need to build action in the present on a thorough understanding of the past. Using historical research based on methods ranging from archives and print culture to archaeology and oral histories, these essays provide fresh analyses of the discovery of Antarctica, the disappearance of Sir John Franklin, the fate of the Norse colony in Greenland, the origins of the Antarctic Treaty, and much more. This is an invaluable resource for anyone interested in the history of our planet.

ADRIAN HOWKINS is Reader in Environmental History at the University of Bristol.

PEDER ROBERTS is Associate Professor of Modern History at the University of Stavanger and Researcher at KTH Royal Institute of Technology.

THE CAMBRIDGE
HISTORY OF
THE POLAR REGIONS

*

Edited by

ADRIAN HOWKINS
University of Bristol

PEDER ROBERTS
University of Stavanger

CAMBRIDGE
UNIVERSITY PRESS

University Printing House, Cambridge CB2 8BS, United Kingdom

One Liberty Plaza, 20th Floor, New York, NY 10006, USA

477 Williamstown Road, Port Melbourne, VIC 3207, Australia

314–321, 3rd Floor, Plot 3, Splendor Forum, Jasola District Centre,
New Delhi – 110025, India

103 Penang Road, #05–06/07, Visioncrest Commercial, Singapore 238467

Cambridge University Press is part of the University of Cambridge.

It furthers the University's mission by disseminating knowledge in the pursuit of education, learning, and research at the highest international levels of excellence.

www.cambridge.org
Information on this title: www.cambridge.org/9781108429931
DOI: 10.1017/9781108555654

© Cambridge University Press 2023

This publication is in copyright. Subject to statutory exception and to the provisions of relevant collective licensing agreements, no reproduction of any part may take place without the written permission of Cambridge University Press.

First published 2023

Printed in the United Kingdom by TJ Books Limited, Padstow Cornwall

A catalogue record for this publication is available from the British Library.

Library of Congress Cataloging-in-Publication Data
NAMES: Howkins, Adrian, editor. | Roberts, Peder, editor.
TITLE: The Cambridge history of the polar regions / Edited by Adrian Howkins, Colorado State University, Peder Roberts, KTH Royal Institute of Technology, Stockholm.
DESCRIPTION: New York, NY : Cambridge University Press, [2022]
IDENTIFIERS: LCCN 2022007774 (print) | LCCN 2022007775 (ebook) | ISBN 9781108429931 (hardback) | ISBN 9781108555654 (ebook)
SUBJECTS: LCSH: Polar regions – History. | Polar regions – Climate. | BISAC: HISTORY / World
CLASSIFICATION: LCC G580 .C36 2022 (print) | LCC G580 (ebook) | DDC 910.911–dc23/eng20220528
LC record available at https://lccn.loc.gov/2022007774
LC ebook record available at https://lccn.loc.gov/2022007775

ISBN 978-1-108-42993-1 Hardback

Cambridge University Press has no responsibility for the persistence or accuracy of URLs for external or third-party internet websites referred to in this publication and does not guarantee that any content on such websites is, or will remain, accurate or appropriate.

Contents

List of Figures   page viii
List of Contributors   x
Acknowledgements   xvii

1 · Introduction: The Problems of Polar History   1
(PEDER ROBERTS AND ADRIAN HOWKINS)

2 · 'I Watch to See How the Land Is Changing': An Inuit Perspective on Changing Environments and Cultural Resilience in the Western Canadian Arctic   32
(GEORGE ANGOHIATOK, BRYAN VANDENBRINK, IAN HOGG, AND THOMAS MCILWRAITH)

3 · Evolution of the Antarctic Continent and Its Ice Sheet   55
(MARTIN SIEGERT AND ANDREW FOUNTAIN)

4 · The Initial Peopling of the Circumpolar North   79
(BJARNE GRØNNOW)

5 · Archaeology, Politics, and Sámi Heritage   106
(CARL-GÖSTA OJALA)

6 · The Norse Settlement of Greenland   129
(JETTE ARNEBORG)

7 · Russia, the First Arctic Empire, 1000–1917   153
(RYAN TUCKER JONES, ALEXEI KRAIKOVSKI, AND JULIA LAJUS)

8 · The Discovery of Antarctica from Ptolemy to Shackleton   181
(ERKI TAMMIKSAAR AND CORNELIA LÜDECKE)

Contents

9 · Sir John Franklin and the Northwest Passage in Myth and Memory 207
(RUSSELL A. POTTER)

10 · The Heroic Age of Antarctic Exploration, 1890 to the Present 229
(STEPHANIE BARCZEWSKI)

11 · Representing the Polar Regions through Historical Fiction 252
(ELIZABETH LEANE)

12 · Geography, Anthropology, and Arctic Knowledge-Making 279
(RICHARD C. POWELL)

13 · Britain's Polar Empire, 1769–1982 302
(DANIELLA MCCAHEY)

14 · Canada and the High Arctic Islands, 1880–1950 325
(JANICE CAVELL)

15 · The Genesis of the Spitsbergen/Svalbard Treaty, 1871–1920 354
(ROALD BERG)

16 · Industrial Whaling in the Arctic and Antarctic 378
(BJØRN L. BASBERG AND LOUWRENS HACQUEBORD)

17 · A Historical Archaeology of the First Antarctic Labourers (Nineteenth Century) 407
(MELISA A. SALERNO, M. JIMENA CRUZ, AND ANDRÉS ZARANKIN)

18 · Mining and Colonialism in the Circumpolar North 430
(HENRIK KNUDSEN, ARN KEELING, AND JOHN SANDLOS)

19 · Creating the Soviet Arctic, 1917–1991 462
(ANDY BRUNO AND EKATERINA KALEMENEVA)

20 · Greenland: From Colony to Self-government, 1721–2021 487
(JENS HEINRICH)

21 · Cold War Environmental Knowledge in the Polar Regions 510
(STEPHEN BOCKING AND PEY-YI CHU)

Contents

22 · The International Geophysical Year and the
Antarctic Treaty System 536
(KLAUS DODDS)

23 · The First Century of US Militarization in Alaska, 1867–1967 563
(MATTHEW FARISH)

24 · Petroleum Development and the State in Arctic
North America, 1919–1977 593
(PHILIP A. WIGHT)

25 · The Rise of Circumpolar Political Movements 621
(MARK NUTTALL)

26 · The History of Polar Environmental Governance 648
(ALESSANDRO ANTONELLO AND JUSTIINA DAHL)

27 · The Antarctic Extension of Latin America 672
(PABLO FONTANA)

28 · Moving Muskoxen as an Arctic Resource in the Twentieth Century 702
(DOLLY JØRGENSEN)

29 · Boundaries of Place and Time at the Edge of the Polar Oceans 726
(HAYLEY BRAZIER AND MARK CAREY)

30 · Re-storying from Within: Renewing Relationships Beyond the
Shadows of Polar History 749
(JACKIE PRICE, REBECCA MEARNS, AND EMILIE CAMERON)

31 · Conclusion: Time, and the Future of Polar History 770
(LIZA PIPER AND LIZE-MARIÉ HANSEN VAN DER WATT)

Index 789

Figures

x.1	Overview map of the Arctic (1).	page xix
x.2	Overview map of the Arctic (2).	xx
x.3	Overview map of the Antarctic (1).	xxi
x.4	Overview map of the Antarctic (2).	xxii
1.1	The circumpolar north including the Arctic treeline and the 10 degrees Celsius isotherm for July.	4
1.2	Louis-Edmond Hamelin's gradations of nordicity in Canada.	5
2.1	Map of important places in George Angohiatok's life.	33
2.2	Mabel and George Angohiatok.	36
3.1	Location map and surface elevation of Antarctica.	56
4.1	Archaeological sites related to early *Homo sapiens* in Siberia and modern-day Russia.	81
4.2	The earliest art in the Arctic. Objects from the Yana site.	83
4.3	Archaeological sites in modern-day Alaska and Yukon related to the earliest migrants across Beringia.	85
4.4	Significant early archaeological sites in Fennoscandia.	88
4.5	Excavation of the mid-passage in a dwelling of the Saqqaq Culture at the Qeqertasussuk site, West Greenland.	94
4.6	Location of the Qajaa and Qeqertasussuk archaeological sites in modern-day Greenland.	95
4.7	Three types of harpoon heads for sealing made of caribou antler, Saqqaq Culture.	98
5.1	The approximate area of Sápmi.	107
6.1	Location of the western and eastern Norse settlements in Greenland, and the northern hunting grounds.	132
6.2	Animal bone collection from farms V48 (Niaquusat), V51 (Sandnæs Kilaarsarfik), and GUS (The Farm Beneath the Sand) in the Western Settlement, and Ø17a (Narsaq) and Ø29a (Brattahlid Qassiarsuk) in the Eastern Settlement.	135
6.3	The church in Hvalsey fjord, farm Ø83 in the Eastern Settlement from around 1250/1300.	137
6.4	Woman's dress found at the churchyard at farm Ø111, Herjolfsnæs Ikigaat, in the Eastern Settlement.	139
7.1	Northern Eurasian treeline zone and monthly surface air temperature for July and January.	154

List of Figures

8.1	Philippe Buache, *Hemisphere Meridional où l'on voit les Parties inconnues du Globe qu sont à découvrir autour du Pôle Antarctique et les vastes étendues de Terres que peuvent renfermer ces espaces inconnus*. Paris, 1770.	184
8.2	*Méridional plus distinctement Australes et Philippe Buache et de l'Académie Royale des Sciences*. Paris, 1782.	188
8.3	August Petermann, *Karte der arktischen & antarktischen regionen zur Übersicht des geographischen Standpunktes im J. 1865, der Meeresströmungen*.	194
8.4	Overview map showing cumulative sightings of subsequently confirmed Antarctic territory based on maps published from 1825–1909.	199
9.1	Route of Franklin's final expedition, 1845–1847.	215
14.1	Districts in northern Canada, 1895.	332
14.2	Districts in northern Canada, 1897.	334
16.1	Historical whaling stations in Spitsbergen.	382
16.2	Historical whaling stations in the Antarctic.	394
16.3	Trends in Arctic, Antarctic, and global whaling.	398
17.1	Number of sealing vessels bound to the South Shetland Islands per sealing cycle and nationality.	410
17.2	Some spaces clearly defined in a nineteenth-century schooner.	417
17.3	Sealing sites in the South Shetland Islands.	419
17.4	Three-dimensional modelling of Cerro Negro sealing site on Livingston Island.	421
18.1	Notable mining sites in northern North America and Greenland.	431
18.2	Notable mining sites in northern Russia, Svalbard, and northern Scandinavia.	432
24.1	Long-distance hydrocarbon pipelines in Arctic and Sub-Arctic North America, 1942–1977.	603
27.1	Overlapping Argentine and Chilean claims in the Antarctic.	673
27.2	The President of Chile, Carlos Ibánez del Campo, with the President of Argentina, Juan Domingo Perón, 6 July 1953.	686
28.1	Overview of muskox movements discussed in this chapter.	703
29.1	Icebergs and fishing in the Ilulissat Icefjord, Greenland.	728
29.2	Ice-rafted debris embedded in icebergs recently calved from a Greenland ice sheet outlet glacier.	734

Contributors

GEORGE ANGOHIATOK is an Inuk elder and knowledge keeper from Ekaluktutiak (Cambridge Bay), Nunavut, Canada. A hunter and community provider, he has had a long-term association with the Ekaluktutiak Hunter and Trappers Organization and is currently serving as Vice-Chair. He is passionate about environmental protection and the wellbeing of Arctic peoples and wildlife.

ALESSANDRO ANTONELLO is Senior Research Fellow in History at Flinders University, Adelaide, Australia. He is the author of *The Greening of Antarctica: Assembling an International Environment* (Oxford University Press, 2019) and has published extensively on the environmental and international history of Antarctica, the global cryosphere, and the world ocean.

JETTE ARNEBORG, PhD, is a Senior Researcher at the Danish National Museum in Copenhagen. Arneborg is a trained archaeologist specializing in the Norse North Atlantic, especially Norse Greenland, where she has conducted archaeological investigations since 1982. Her research has focused on human ecodynamics and social relations and structures.

STEPHANIE BARCZEWSKI is Professor of Modern British History and Carol K. Brown Scholar in the Humanities at Clemson University in the United States. She is the author of *Antarctic Destinies: Scott, Shackleton and the Changing Face of Heroism* (Continuum, 2008) and, most recently, *Heroic Failure and the British* (Yale University Press, 2016).

BJØRN L. BASBERG is Professor in Economic History at the Norwegian School of Economics in Bergen. His main research interests are within the history of technology and economic history relating to nineteenth- and twentieth-century maritime industries, especially whaling and shipping, and the economic history of the Antarctic region in general.

ROALD BERG is Emeritus Professor of History at the University of Stavanger. He has been Visiting Fellow at Cambridge (Scott Polar Research Institute), where he wrote his latest book, *Norsk utanrikspolitikk etter 1814* (2016). His recent publications include "The Svalbard 'Channel', 1920–2020", in J. Weber, ed., *Handbook on Geopolitics and Security in the Arctic* (Springer, 2020).

List of Contributors

STEPHEN BOCKING is with the School of the Environment at Trent University, Peterborough, Ontario. He teaches courses on science and politics, environmental history, and global political ecology. He has a special interest in the history of environmental knowledge, in the Arctic and elsewhere.

HAYLEY BRAZIER is a PhD candidate in the Department of History at the University of Oregon and the Donald M. Kerr Curator of Natural History at the High Desert Museum. Her research examines the historical development of seafloor technologies in the Pacific Ocean's mysterious depths.

ANDY BRUNO teaches at Northern Illinois University and is the author of *The Nature of Soviet Power: An Arctic Environmental History* and *Tunguska: A Siberian Mystery and Its Environmental Legacy*. His contribution to this volume was supported by a Russian Science Foundation grant (project no. 20-68-46044), "Imaginary Anthropocene: Environmental Knowledge Production and Transfers in Siberia in the 20th and 21st Centuries," at Tyumen State University.

EMILIE CAMERON is Associate Professor in the Department of Geography and Environmental Studies at Carleton University. Her current research focuses on geographies of resource extraction, empire, and labour in the contemporary North.

MARK CAREY is Professor of Environmental Studies and Geography at the University of Oregon. He specializes in environmental history and does interdisciplinary work, particularly related to climate, glaciers, water, and disasters in the Andes and Arctic. He runs the Glacier Lab for the Study of Ice and Society, collaborating closely with students.

JANICE CAVELL works in the Historical Section, Global Affairs Canada, and is an Adjunct Research Professor of History and Northern Studies at Carleton University. She has published widely on exploration history and Arctic sovereignty issues.

PEY-YI CHU is a historian of Russia and the Soviet Union based at Pomona College in Claremont, California. Her first book, *The Life of Permafrost: A History of Frozen Earth in Russian and Soviet Science*, was published by University of Toronto Press in 2020.

MARÍA JIMENA CRUZ is a Postdoctoral Fellow of the Multidisciplinary Institute of History and Human Sciences, at the National Council of Scientific and Technical Research in Argentina. She is a member of the Landscapes in White research project. Her main research interests include archaeology of alimentation, Antarctic archaeology, archaeology of the modern world, and zooarchaeological studies.

JUSTIINA DAHL is a Senior Research Officer at the Swedish Research Council. Her PhD dissertation in International Relations from the European University Institute explored the role of science and technology in seven historical attempts to expand territorial sovereignty over previously unknown lands in the Arctic through, in hindsight, failed, new settlements.

List of Contributors

KLAUS DODDS is Professor of Geopolitics at Royal Holloway, University of London and a Fellow of the Academy of Social Sciences (UK). He is author and editor of many books, including *Ice Humanities: Living, Thinking and Working in a Melting World* (co-edited with Sverker Sörlin, Manchester University Press, 2022) and author of *Ice: Nature and Culture* (Reaktion, 2018). He is an Honorary Fellow of the British Antarctic Survey and a Trustee of the Royal Geographical Society.

MATTHEW FARISH is Associate Professor and Associate Chair, Undergraduate in the Department of Geography and Planning at the University of Toronto. He is the author of *The Contours of America's Cold War* (University of Minnesota Press, 2010) and is working on a book about US military survival schools, climate laboratories, and proving grounds.

PABLO FONTANA is a PhD Researcher at the Argentine Antarctic Institute (IAA) and at the CONICET (National Scientific and Technical Research Council). He is head of the Social Sciences Area in the IAA and has participated in Antarctic campaigns working on historical heritage.

ANDREW G. FOUNTAIN is Professor Emeritus of Geology and Geography at Portland State University, Portland, Oregon. He has studied glacial hydrology and mass balance processes on glaciers in both polar regions and in the western United States. For his scientific contributions, a glacier in Antarctica has been named in his honour.

BJARNE GRØNNOW is Research Professor in Arctic Archaeology at the National Museum of Denmark in Copenhagen, specializing in the prehistoric archaeology of Greenland. He has previously been Head of SILA – the Greenland Research Centre at the National Museum – and Associate Professor the University of Copenhagen.

LOUWRENS HACQUEBORD is Emeritus Professor in Arctic and Antarctic Studies at the University of Groningen, the Netherlands. He was Council member and Vice-President of the International Arctic Science Committee (IASC). His research focuses on exploration and exploitation of polar areas, in which context he has led several archaeological surveys and excavations, the best-known being the excavation of the seventeenth-century Dutch whaling settlement Smeerenburg on Svalbard.

JENS HEINRICH has an MA (2004) and PhD (2010) from Ilisimatusarfik/University of Greenland, and is of Greenlandic and Danish descent. Jens has worked at museums, universities and participated in the Greenlandic Reconciliation Commission and is currently at the Greenland Representation in Copenhagen. He lives with the biologist Eva Garde and has four children.

IAN HOGG is a biologist and Team Lead of Ecosystem and Cryosphere Research at Polar Knowledge Canada, as well as Adjunct Professor at the University of Waikato, New Zealand. He has maintained a long-term interest in polar regions and worked extensively in both the Arctic and Antarctic.

List of Contributors

ADRIAN HOWKINS is Reader in Environmental History at the University of Bristol. He is author of *The Polar Regions: An Environmental History* (Polity Press, 2015) and *Frozen Empires: An Environmental History of the Antarctic Peninsula* (Oxford University Press, 2017). He is a co-PI on the McMurdo Dry Valleys Long Term Ecological Research site in Antarctica, funded by the National Science Foundation.

RYAN TUCKER JONES is Ann Swindells Professor at the University of Oregon. He is the author of *Empire of Extinction: Russians and the North Pacific's Strange Beasts of the Sea, 1741–1867* (Oxford University Press, 2014) and *Red Leviathan: The Secret History of Soviet Whaling* (University of Chicago Press, 2022), as well as a co-editor of the *Cambridge History of the Pacific Ocean* (2022).

DOLLY JØRGENSEN is Professor of History, University of Stavanger, Norway. Her current research focuses on cultural histories of animal extinction. Her monograph *Recovering Lost Species in the Modern Age: Histories of Longing and Belonging* was published with MIT Press in 2019. She is co-editor-in-chief of the journal *Environmental Humanities*.

EKATERINA KALEMENEVA is Senior Lecturer at the Department of History, National Research University Higher School of Economics (HSE), Moscow, and Research Fellow at the Laboratory for Environmental and Technological History. Her academic interests include urbanization of the Soviet Arctic, and the role of architects in the formation of a new conception of the North in the Soviet Union.

ARN KEELING is Professor in the Department of Geography at Memorial University in St John's, Newfoundland, Canada. His research focuses on the history and contemporary legacies of extractive industries in northern Canada, as well as mine closure and remediation. Along with John Sandlos, he is co-author of *Mining Country: A History of Canada's Mines and Miners* (Lorimer, 2021).

HENRIK KNUDSEN is an Archivist and Senior Researcher at the Danish National Archives. He studied history of science and technology, receiving his PhD from Aarhus University in 2005. His field of interest covers science and technology in the global Cold War, science diplomacy, Arctic history, nuclear energy, and natural resources.

ALEXEI KRAIKOVSKI was born in 1972. He started exploration of the Early Modern Russian North while a student at St Petersburg University. Since then, he has taken part in a variety of research projects while working in the European University at St Petersburg and the Higher School of Economics.

JULIA LAJUS is Head of Laboratory for Environmental and Technological History and Associate Professor at the Department of History, HSE, St Petersburg, Russia. In 2011–2015 she served as Vice-President of the European Society of Environmental History. Her research focuses on the history of field sciences, such as fisheries science, oceanography and climatology, and environmental history of biological resources, especially in marine and polar areas.

List of Contributors

ELIZABETH LEANE is Professor of English in the College of Arts, Law and Education, University of Tasmania. She is Arts and Culture Editor of *The Polar Journal* and a former Australian Antarctic Arts Fellow. Her publications include *Antarctica in Fiction* (Cambridge, 2012), *South Pole* (Reaktion, 2016) and *Anthropocene Antarctica* (Routledge, 2019).

CORNELIA LÜDECKE is a retired Professor of History of Natural Sciences, founder of the History of Antarctic Research Expert Group within SCAR (2004), and President of the International Commission on History of Meteorology (2006–2009). She has published 19 monographs and over 180 articles on the history of meteorology, geography, and polar research.

DANIELLA MCCAHEY is Assistant Professor in British History at Texas Tech University. She has published research on a variety of topics, ranging from masculinity at Antarctic research stations to Southern Ocean whaling. She received her PhD in 2018 from the University of California, Irvine.

THOMAS MCILWRAITH is a cultural anthropologist at the University of Guelph, in Ontario, Canada. His interests include the oral histories, land uses, and harvesting practices of Indigenous peoples in the Sub-Arctic regions of western Canada, particularly in the contexts of industrial development.

REBECCA MEARNS currently resides in Iqaluit, Nunavut where she works as President of Nunavut Arctic College. Although she was born in what is now known as Nunavut, she spent her childhood in rural Scotland. Rebecca then moved back to Nunavut with her family and has lived there or been connected to Nunavut ever since. Rebecca left Nunavut to pursue her university education, where her research interest always brought her back to thinking about her land, language, and culture. Since returning to Nunavut she spends her time with family and friends, enjoying time on the land, picking berries, harvesting seals, sewing, baking, and learning the lessons that come along with each of these activities.

MARK NUTTALL is Professor and Henry Marshall Tory Chair of Anthropology at the University of Alberta and Fellow of the Royal Society of Canada. He is also Adjunct Professor in the Department of Arctic Social Sciences and Economics at Ilisimatusarfik/University of Greenland and the Greenland Climate Research Centre in Nuuk.

CARL-GÖSTA OJALA is a researcher in archaeology at Uppsala University, Sweden, and Associate Professor, Global Institution for Collaborative Research and Education, Hokkaido University, Japan. His research focuses on archaeology and heritage in Northern Fennoscandia, especially Sámi history and heritage, and the politics and ethics of archaeology. His publications include *Sámi Prehistories: The Politics of Archaeology and Identity in Northernmost Europe* (Uppsala University, 2009) and *Archaeologies of 'Us' and 'Them': Debating History, Heritage and Indigeneity* (Routledge, 2017, co-edited with Charlotta Hillerdal and Anna Karlström).

LIZA PIPER is Professor of History at the University of Alberta. A specialist in the histories of northern and western Canada, they are author of *The Industrial Transformation of*

List of Contributors

Subarctic Canada (UBC Press, 2009) and the forthcoming *When Disease Came to this Country: Epidemics and Colonialism in Northern North America* (Cambridge University Press).

RUSSELL A. POTTER is Professor of English at Rhode Island College. He has written extensively about the nineteenth-century fascination with the Arctic, particularly the 1845 expedition led by Sir John Franklin. His most recent book, *Finding Franklin: The Untold Story of a 165-Year Search*, was published in 2016 by McGill-Queen's University Press.

RICHARD POWELL is Professor of Arctic Studies at the University of Cambridge, where he teaches at the Scott Polar Research Institute and Department of Geography. He is author of *Studying Arctic Fields: Cultures, Practices, and Environmental Sciences* (McGill-Queen's University Press, 2017) and editor (with Klaus Dodds) of *Polar Geopolitics? Knowledges, Resources and Legal Regimes* (Edward Elgar, 2014).

JACKIE PRICE (she/her) currently lives in Iqaluit, Nunavut with her family. Having been raised and grown in what is now known as Nunavut, she has been engaged in the making, exploring, and defence of polar history for the majority of her life. She has explored these dynamics from various vantage points, most notably through the lens of political science, governance, and Indigenous governance. She has explored these ideas in a range of environments, including her own life, and the various homes she has had and shared with family and others in different settings and communities. She has also thought about the layers of tension and players at universities in Victoria, British Columbia, and Cambridge, UK.

PEDER ROBERTS works at the University of Stavanger and KTH Royal Institute of Technology. He is the author of *The European Antarctic: Science and Strategy in Scandinavia and the British Empire* (Palgrave Macmillan, 2011) and was leader of the European Research Council-funded project, Greening the Poles: Science, the Environment, and the Creation of the Modern Arctic and Antarctic.

MELISA A. SALERNO is a Researcher at the Multidisciplinary Institute of History and Human Sciences at the National Council of Scientific and Technical Research in Argentina. She is a member of the Landscapes in White research project. Her main research interests include Antarctic archaeology, archaeological theory, and body and embodiment.

JOHN SANDLOS is Professor of History at Memorial University of Newfoundland. He has written extensively on mining in northern regions and is the author, with Arn Keeling, of *Mining Country: A History of Canada's Mines and Miners* (Lorimer, 2021).

MARTIN SIEGERT is Co-Director of the Grantham Institute for Climate Change at Imperial College London. He is a glaciologist who uses geophysics to quantify the flow and form of ice sheets, both now and in the past. He was awarded the 2013 Muse Prize in Antarctic Science and Policy.

List of Contributors

ERKI TAMMIKSAAR is Senior Research Fellow of the Estonian University of Life Sciences and of the University of Tartu, Estonia. He has published five monographs and over 250 articles on the history of polar research, geography, and history of science in Russia and Estonia in the nineteenth and twentieth centuries.

BRYAN VANDENBRINK is from Ekaluktutiak (Cambridge Bay), Nunavut, and is a Science Ranger at the Canadian High Arctic Research Station, Polar Knowledge Canada. He is also working on a Master's degree in Integrative Biology at the University of Guelph, studying insect biodiversity and Inuit *Qaujimajatuqangit* (IQ) in the Canadian Arctic.

LIZE-MARIÉ HANSEN VAN DER WATT is a historian of the environment, heritage, and science, with a focus on the polar regions. She was co-editor of *Antarctica and the Humanities* (Palgrave Macmillan, 2016) and, in addition to her historical publications, conducted research with interdisciplinary teams on matters related to environmental change. As project leader and rapporteur, she has also worked at the science–policy interface in polar research and governance. Currently, she is leading a major research project, Decay Without Mourning: Future Thinking Heritage Practices, funded by the Riksbanken Jubileumsfond, and she is based at the Division for History of Science, Technology, and Environment at KTH Royal Institute of Technology, Sweden.

PHILIP A. WIGHT is Assistant Professor of History and Arctic & Northern Studies at the University of Alaska Fairbanks. He is an energy and environmental historian, focusing on infrastructure, mobility, and climate, and is currently finalizing his book manuscript, "Arctic Artery: The Trans-Alaska Pipeline System and the World It Made".

ANDRÉS ZARANKIN is Professor of Archaeology at the University of Minas Gerais, Brazil, and Director of the Laboratory of Antarctic Studies in Human Sciences (LEACH-UFMG). His main research interests include Antarctic archaeology, archaeological theory, archaeology of dictatorship, and historical archaeology.

Acknowledgements

Putting together an edited collection on the history of the polar regions has incurred far more debts of gratitude than we can acknowledge here. We owe thanks to all of the authors in the volume, especially knowing that our requests invariably came on top of already busy lives and heavy workloads, exacerbated by the coronavirus pandemic. Several of our original contributors were particularly badly impacted, and our thoughts continue to be with them.

We feel tremendously fortunate to be part of the scholarly communities that study the Arctic and Antarctica. As might be expected, these communities span a wide geographical range, and one of the great pleasures of editing this volume has been working with colleagues from many different parts of the world. A central point we hope to get across is that there is no single correct way to view the histories of the Arctic and Antarctica, and that viewpoints assumed in the past to be self-evidently privileged ought to be examined more critically. But even where there are quite significant differences among the contributors in terms of perspectives and approaches, we have been struck throughout this project by the warmth and generosity practised by the scholars working on the coldest places on Earth.

As editors, we have both benefited enormously from the scholarly community created by what is now the Standing Committee on Humanities and Social Sciences of the Scientific Committee on Antarctic Research (SC-HASS). Special thanks go to Cornelia Lüdecke, Daniela Liggett, Elizabeth Leane, and everyone else who has contributed to the group's growth over the years. Several organizations have provided financial support that has made possible our own work in the polar regions. The project has received funding from the European Research Council (ERC) under the European Union's Horizon 2020 research and innovation programme (grant agreement no. 716211 – GRETPOL). In addition, we would like to thank the US National Science Foundation, the McMurdo Dry Valleys Long Term Ecological Research Site, the British Academy, Colorado State University, KTH Royal Institute of Technology, and the University of Bristol.

An especially big thank you goes to Hans van der Maarel and Inge van Daelen at Red Geographics. The quality of their work reflects their professionalism – which was in abundant evidence also during their many interactions with the authors. Financial support for the maps was generously provided by the University of Stavanger. Lucy Rhymer and the team at Cambridge University Press have been wonderful to work with. We would like to thank Tina Adcock and Alessandro Antonello for reading and commenting on our introduction. The anonymous reviewers of our initial proposal offered some very helpful suggestions. All mistakes, of course, remain our own.

Finally, we would like to thank our families, colleagues, and friends for their support and encouragement throughout this project.

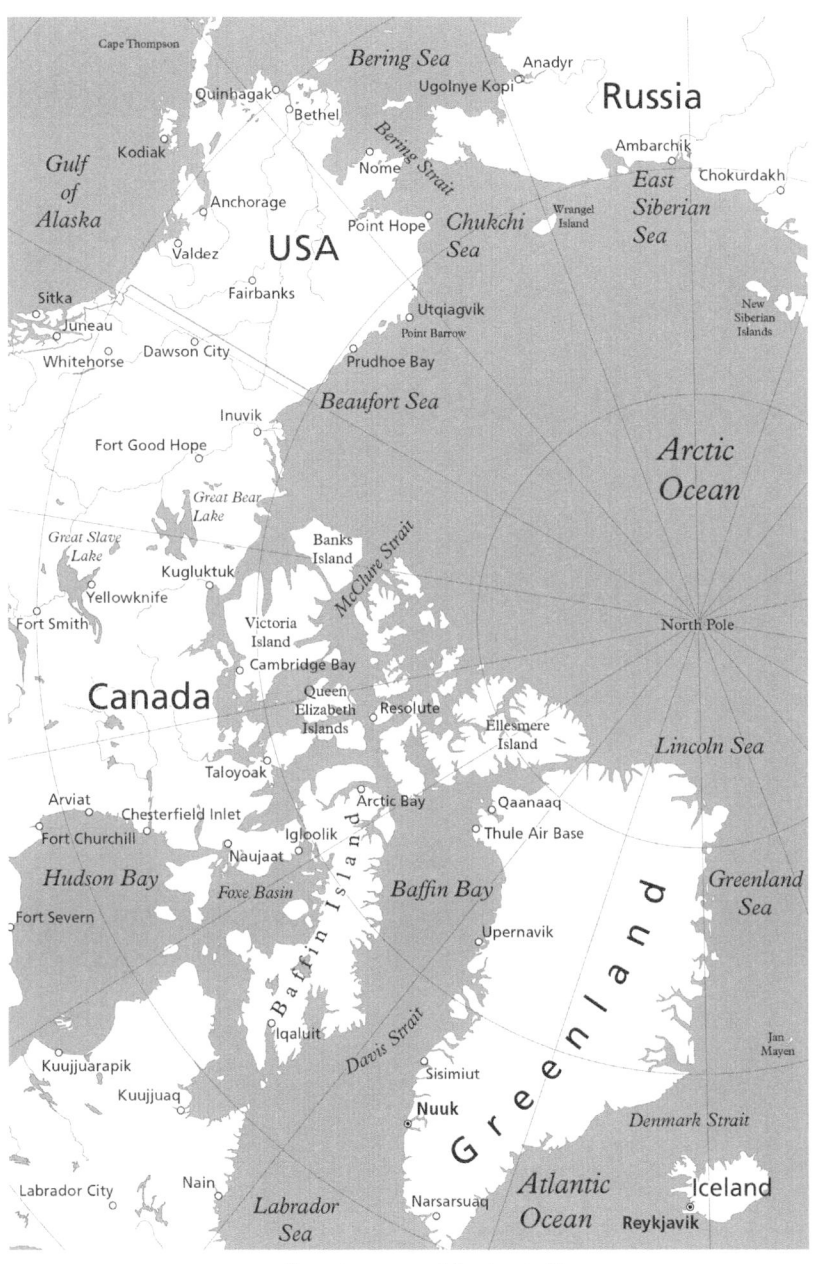

x.1 Overview map of the Arctic (1).

x.2 Overview map of the Arctic (2).

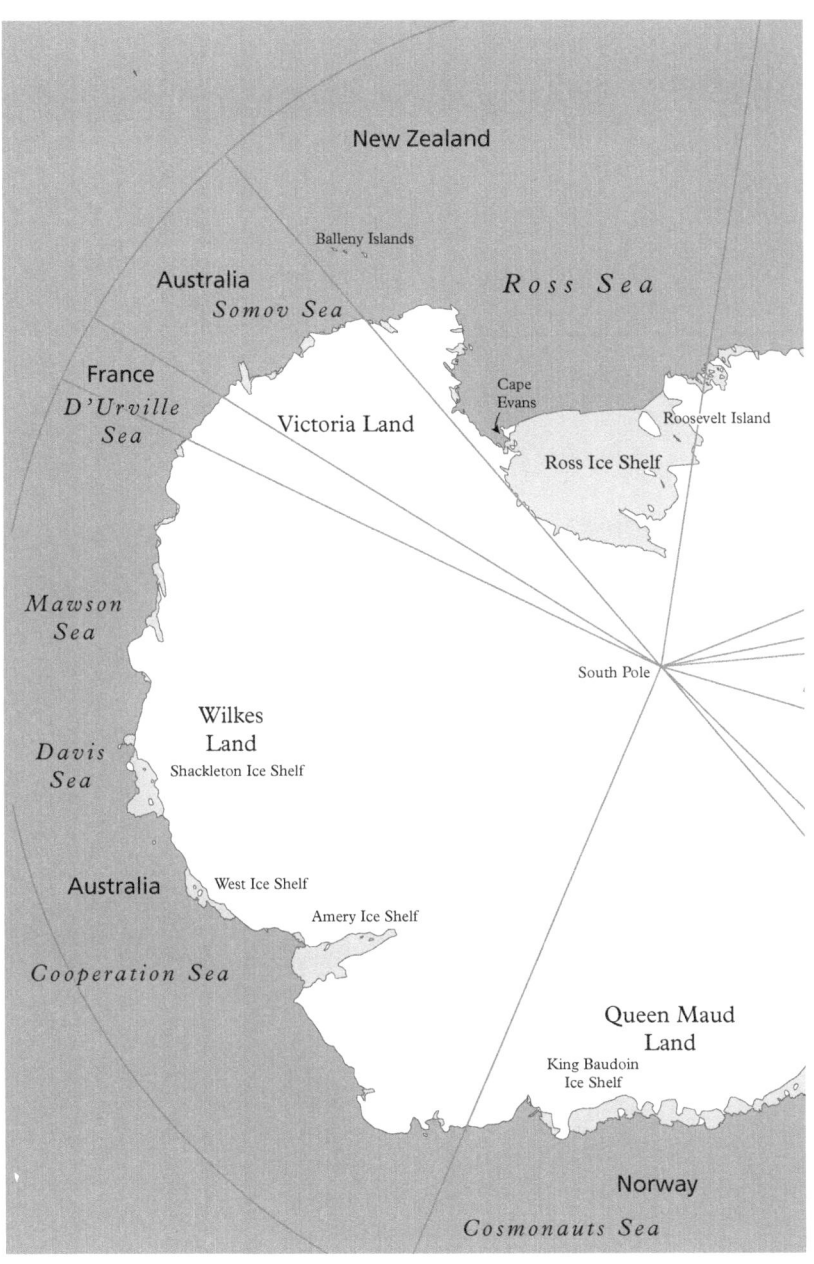

x.3 Overview map of the Antarctic (1).

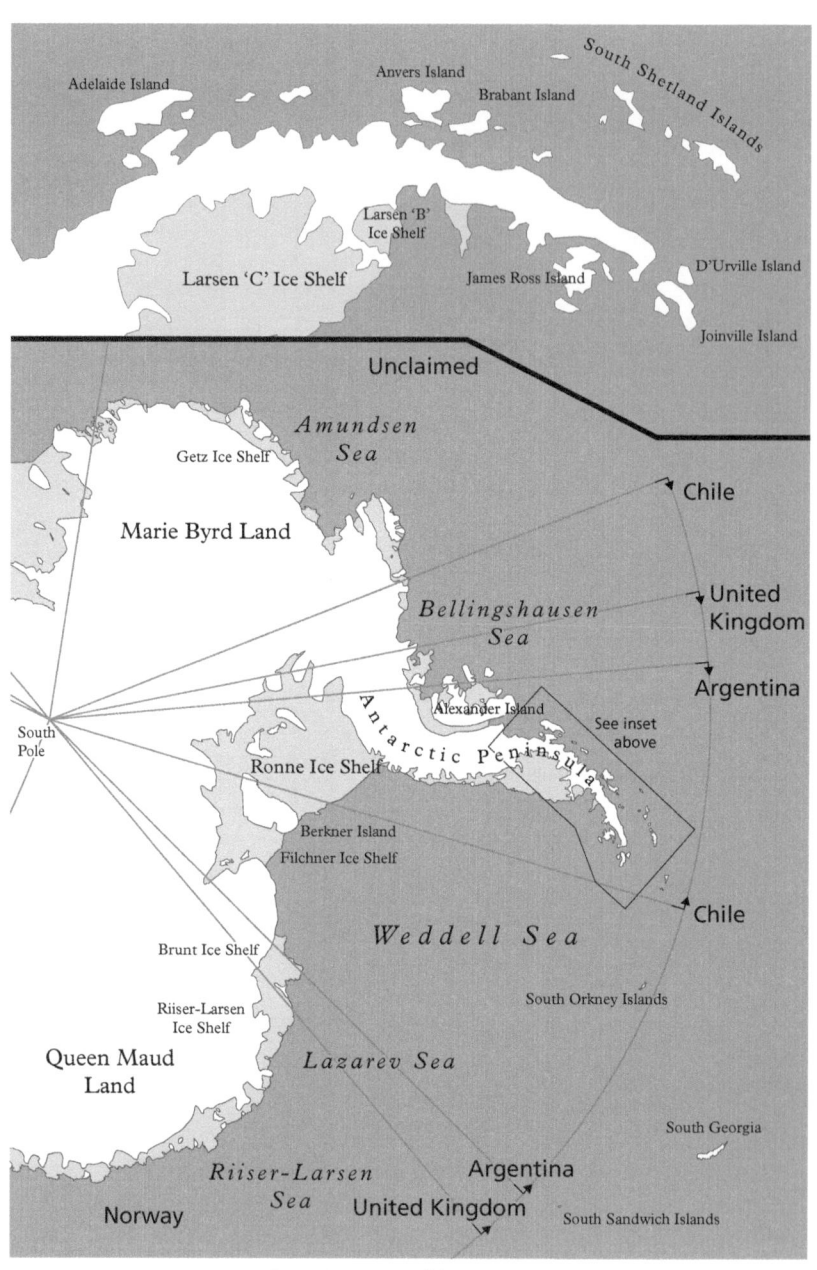

x.4 Overview map of the Antarctic (2).

I

Introduction: The Problems of Polar History

PEDER ROBERTS AND ADRIAN HOWKINS

Almost 100 years ago, the American Geographical Society (AGS) published an edited volume titled *Problems of Polar Research*, which started with the assumption that much remained to be learned about the Arctic and Antarctica. Edited by the geographer W. L. G. Joerg, an employee of the AGS, the volume contained chapters by many of the leading polar authorities of the day, most of whom were active participants in exploration and science.[1] 'Problems' had a double meaning: the authors referred to inadequacies and gaps in the contemporary state of knowledge, but also to the excitement of the potential for advancing understanding in difficult conditions. The volume sought to inspire its readers to think further and address the challenges. We approached this present volume with a similar view. To examine the history of the polar regions within a single volume is to take on a difficult task that not only brings together different histories and geographies, but also different conceptions of history and geography.

It is easy to take the existence of polar history for granted. To borrow the famous quote attributed to George Mallory about climbing Mount Everest, it often seems like we study polar history simply 'because it's there'.[2] To physical geographers, the north and south geographic poles exist as exceptional geographic entities characterized by extreme seasonal variation in daylight hours. Several countries have polar research institutes, there are polar-themed academic journals, and educational programmes exist in polar studies. In popular consciousness,

---

We are grateful to Tina Adcock and Alessandro Antonello for incisive and immensely helpful comments on the text. This project has received funding from the European Research Council (ERC) under the European Union's Horizon 2020 research and innovation programme (grant agreement no. 716211 – GRETPOL). Support also came from National Science Foundation awards 1637708 and 1443475, and a British Academy Knowledge Frontiers grant.

1 Joerg, *Problems of Polar Research*.
2 The quote appears in *New York Times*, "Climbing Mount Everest Is Work for Supermen", 151.

the 'polar regions' frequently connote visions of ice, cold, penguins, and polar bears. These visions are created and reinforced by representations of the Arctic and Antarctic in popular media. If there are polar regions, then surely there is polar history, its contents defined by their connection to specific geographic areas?

Problems start to emerge when we begin to ask questions about whether the polar regions should be regarded as quite the self-evident entities they might first appear. What exactly is the Arctic? What is Antarctica? How are these two regions connected? Adding a historical dimension further complicates our understanding. Who has defined the polar regions? Who benefits when we take the existence of polar history for granted? An important 'insider–outsider' theme permeates the history of the polar regions, especially in relation to the ways in which the Indigenous peoples of the Arctic understand their histories. But while being an insider or an outsider is often starkly binary, there are also times when it seems more of a continuum, especially in Antarctica where nobody is a permanent resident. In the spirit of *Problems of Polar Research*, this volume seeks both to challenge and to enthuse. But where *Problems of Polar Research* served to stabilize a field of inquiry with the weight of scientific gravitas, we hope to prompt critical reflection on whether writing polar history reifies as much as it edifies.

Geographical Definitions

Mallory's quip has become legendary because it affirms that geographical exceptionality creates its own reason. But although Everest gained its exceptional height above sea level from the collision of tectonic plates, it was just as much constructed as exceptional by a cultural context in which value was attributed to conquering high peaks.[3] Similarly, the polar regions as a concept have been constructed as exceptional in popular and scientific consciousness. In recent times it has become more common to hear mention of the 'third pole', a term that asserts the commonality of polar and alpine extremes, especially the Himalayas.[4] There is a pleasing veneer of certainty to the most northerly, the most southerly, and the highest point on the Earth's surface. But certain by what measure? A compass will point to magnetic north and not 'true' north – itself a linguistic distinction that betrays a preference for the permanently rooted over the transitory. The problem is only accentuated by

---

3 Indeed, even within the Himalayas, local residents attached greater reverence to another mountain – Nanda Devi – while K2 in the Karakorams is widely acknowledged as a sterner test of mountaineering skill.
4 See, for example, Synnott, *Third Pole*.

1 Introduction: The Problems of Polar History

the difficulty of finding appropriate boundaries for each polar region – let alone boundaries that are symmetrical between north and south.

The provocative title of a book by the geographer Mark Monmonier – *How to Lie with Maps* – captures a deeper truth that a map is an active creation rather than a passive transcription.[5] Consider the polar circles, the areas of the Earth in which there is at least one day a year when the Sun does not rise and one day a year when the Sun does not set, thereby defining the Arctic and Antarctic by their intense seasonality. A cartographically based gaze that demarcates each polar region as half of a logical pair derives its power from a global perspective that minimizes local difference to maximize global descriptive power.

The circles certainly have the benefit of being easy to represent – for cartographers, at least. But using this seasonal boundary in the north can lead to the inclusion of regions that may not fit other common definitions of the polar. Aklavik in the Northwest Territories of Canada, well above the Arctic Circle, has a record summer temperature of 33.9 degrees Celsius, higher than the record for St John's, Newfoundland, over 20 degrees of latitude further south.[6] The Arctic isotherm – a line above which average temperatures in July are below 10 degrees Celsius – produces a rather different and less uniform line from the neat polar circle (Figure 1.1). But is the isotherm any more accurate or authoritative? Certainly it is different, but the choice of the round number ten should prompt reflection on how natural it is. Another frequently used definition for the Arctic is based on the northern treeline. Aklavik is nestled within boreal forest, which, like the great *taiga* forests that cover much of Siberia, are in stark contrast with the treeless landscapes of Tasiilaq, eastern Greenland – which lies *below* the Arctic Circle, despite featuring both a climate and a suite of fauna that most would regard as stereotypically Arctic.

While a boundary based on average temperature could be applied to the Antarctic, the treeline is an almost entirely useless definition in treeless Antarctica. In contrast to the Arctic, Antarctica's continentality has often informed definitions. But this is complicated by the fact that significant portions of the continent are situated to the north of the Antarctic Circle. Thinking of Antarctica as a continent raises questions about the status of the surrounding islands and constitutes a key reason for the Antarctic Treaty zone being defined as the lands below 60 degrees south rather than simply the continent itself. One of the most interesting recent definitions of Antarctica is the ecosystem

---

5 Monmonier, *How to Lie with Maps*. See also the work of J. Brian Harley, especially Harley ed. Laxton, *New Nature of Maps*.
6 Temperature records obtained from Almanac Averages and Extremes at https://climate.weather.gc.ca.

Figure 1.1 The circumpolar north including the Arctic treeline and the 10 degrees Celsius isotherm for July.

definition of the Antarctic Convergence used by the Convention for the Conservation of Antarctic Marine Living Resources (CCAMLR), which encompasses the whole of the Southern Ocean. But there remains a distinction between the continent and the surrounding islands. When Argentina, Britain, and Chile were actively contesting the sovereignty of the Antarctic Peninsula region in the mid-twentieth century, a 'continental' base was often deemed of more political value than an island base; today's tourists demand a continental landing to 'bag' the continent.[7] By raising questions about where the land ends and the ocean begins, ice shelves, icebergs, and sea ice further complicate a definition of Antarctica based on continentality.[8]

At a time of rapid climate heating in large parts of both the Arctic and Antarctica, definitions of the polar regions based on any kind of physical

---

7 The geopolitics of Antarctic station building is discussed extensively in Howkins, *Frozen Empires*. For a discussion of the importance of continental landings in Antarctic tourism, see for example Zlotnicki, "For the Purists!".
8 On the history of ice as territory to be owned or conquered in Antarctica, see for instance Dodds, *Ice: Nature and Culture*, especially 114–119.

1 Introduction: The Problems of Polar History

geographical parameters are undermined by shifting boundaries. While the prospect of trees growing in Antarctica is still (probably) a long way off, climate-driven ecosystem change is allowing plants and other forms of vegetation to grow in places they previously did not.[9] There is something quite poignant in the idea of the polar regions themselves 'shrinking' as a result of climate heating: not only is there less ice or more vegetation, but in a sense less Arctic and less Antarctica as well, in the eyes of both scientists and (in the Arctic) Indigenous communities for whom detailed environmental knowledge may not translate reliably into the future.

It is humans that make the polar. The Canadian geographer Louis-Edmond Hamelin (1923–2020) recognized that in order to hold meaning, the Arctic must be viewed as a human creation. His great contribution was the concept of 'nordicity' (Figure 1.2), an index that combined physical and

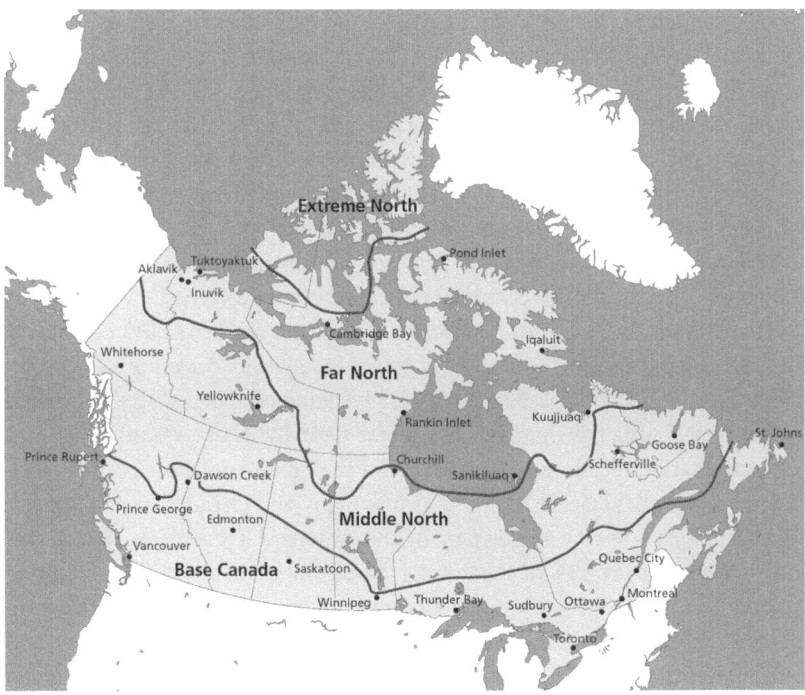

Figure 1.2 Louis-Edmond Hamelin's gradations of nordicity in Canada. (Adapted from Hamelin, "Espaces touristiques".)

9 McGeoch et al., "Monitoring Biological Invasion".

human geographical indices, '*valeurs polaires* (VAPO)' to express the 'state or level of being polar in the northern hemisphere'.[10] Climate played a central role in this scheme, as did distance. Hamelin's 'extreme north' dipped south into Manitoba and Saskatchewan, while his more hospitable 'middle north' encompassed Dawson City in Yukon.[11] But communications infrastructure was more important than distance as the crow flies. And temperature was only one factor along with others such as population size, population density, and economic development. 'No development, none foreseen' earned 100 VAPO; being an 'interregional centre with multiple services' and 'heavy investment' earned zero.[12] Hamelin's scheme lacked the simplicity of demarcations derived from a single cartographically derived variable. But nordicity captured something more important. Instead of boundaries between Arctic and non-Arctic, he saw gradations of more or less Arctic.

While integrating a welcome human dimension into the definition of the Arctic, Hamelin's nordicity is a highly Eurocentric concept. The label of 'no development, none foreseen' presumes the centrality of a set of activities associated with lifeways from further south. It takes little account of whether the sea ice in a particular region might be good for sledging, or whether a region might have a reputation for good hunting at a particular time of the year. Precise definitions of 'the Arctic' can actually be dangerous, implying a misleading uniformity that overlooks the specific factors important to particular communities, and flattening the deep pockets of Indigenous knowledge and attachment to place.

Unsurprisingly, no equivalent concept of australicity has emerged for Antarctica. Practically the entire landmass would be assigned a score of 100 on Hamelin's index, the scattered islands of human presence sustained entirely through resupply from the north. Without Indigenous communities or permanent settlements, the island continent of Antarctica appears a stable artefact in terms of human geography. Yet even here there are questions. Many Antarctic stations are located on islands off the continent's coast. Some, such as Marambio, are adjacent. Others, such as Signy and Orcadas, are halfway to South Georgia – which is not part of the Antarctic Treaty area, but which surely has some degree of australicity based on both physical and human geographies. Moreover, the state or level of being polar in the southern hemisphere is hardly uniform even on the continent itself. Transport and communication infrastructures vary greatly from base to base. And having overwintered on the continent remains a badge of honour that veterans point

10 Hamelin, *Canadian Nordicity*, xi.   11 Map X.1, above.
12 Hamelin, *Canadian Nordicity*, 21.

1 Introduction: The Problems of Polar History

to proudly as a fundamental distinction between themselves and those who have merely spent a summer on the continent, or not been there at all.[13]

Political gradations are even clearer in the north. The eight full member states of the Arctic Council – Canada, Denmark (Greenland), Finland, Iceland, Norway, Sweden, Russia, and the United States – share a common privilege of sovereignty over territory north of the Arctic Circle. But in other contexts the term 'Arctic Five' is used, based on having coastlines on the Arctic Ocean, thereby excluding Finland and Sweden, and, perhaps more controversially, Iceland.[14] Squabbles over who deserves observer status on the Council have echoes of Hamelin's arguments. China has declared itself a 'near-Arctic' state based not on cartographic proximity but on the fact that its political and economic interests make it a stakeholder in the region.[15] Other states with economies substantially involving maritime commerce, such as Singapore and South Korea, have similarly argued that their interests warrant observer status. Today, thirteen non-Arctic states are recognized as observers. One might ask whether we are headed for a future where every state in the world is Arctic to some degree.

Is this situation replicated in the Antarctic? To a point: notably, Brazil has claimed a kind of Antarctic status by dint of its southern coastline having an uninterrupted oceanic connection to Antarctica, following the 'frontage theory' developed by the political geographer Therezinha de Castro.[16] Membership of the Antarctic Treaty System (ATS) hinges on a state declaring itself willing to abide by the rules of the system. But there is an important element here, namely that the upper tier of ATS decision-making membership (status as a consultative party) depends upon active participation in Antarctic science. To have a voice at the Antarctic table means being active in Antarctica, wherever that state may be located. Being Antarctic is thus a right that is earned rather than inherited – even if the founding twelve consultative parties earned that status (and the right to define the values of the system) through differing degrees of activity.[17]

---

13 Howkins, "Have You Been There?".
14 The most striking example is perhaps the 2008 Ilulissat Declaration, in which the Arctic Five asserted that existing legal mechanisms (including the UN Convention on the Law of the Sea) were sufficient to administer the Arctic. The full text is available at www.regjeringen.no/globalassets/upload/ud/080525_arctic_ocean_conference-_outcome.pdf.
15 See for instance Dams et al., *Presence Before Power*.
16 Cardone, *Antarctic Politics of Brazil*.
17 See for instance Hemmings, "Considerable Values in Antarctica". On the implications of this for the legitimacy of the Antarctic Treaty see Yermakova, "Governing Antarctica".

The Power of Practice

Following an argument advanced by Michael Bravo in *North Pole: Nature and Culture*, we wish to make a claim that may strike some readers as bold: that elements of tradition, of lived practice, created the polar more powerfully than a line on a map. Polar history, like the concept of the polar regions, emerged from the desire of individual practitioners to stabilize and legitimize traditions, to give them life and meaning. 'The very idea of seeking the North Pole', writes Bravo, 'so beguiled these explorers that they felt compelled to search for a deeper history of the poles in which their own polar endeavours would make sense.'[18] Those who practised and endorsed 'polar exploration', 'polar geography', and 'polar science' created 'polar history' as the label for their achievements.

Conceptions of Arctic and Antarctic research as linked enterprises date back to at least the nineteenth century. The Earth's two magnetic poles functioned as the focal point for the 'Magnetic Crusade' of the 1830s and 1840s, a quest to construct a magnetic map of the Earth as a whole that was widely associated with the British Empire.[19] Several individuals were involved in both the Arctic and Antarctic during this period, most famously James Clark Ross, who participated in expeditions to both magnetic poles. Later in the century, the first International Polar Year of 1882–83 helped further establish the polar regions as a paired legitimate subject of scientific study, even if its activities were focused almost exclusively on the Arctic.[20] When exploration of the Antarctic continent began in earnest from the last years of the nineteenth century, both individuals and techniques travelled from north to south – from the Sámi men who accompanied the *Southern Cross* expedition in 1899–1901 to the many explorers for whom the poles constituted fungible, if not wholly identical fields of operation. The most well-known example is, of course, Roald Amundsen. Having been on the very first party to overwinter beneath the Antarctic Circle in 1898 in the ship *Belgica*, he subsequently completed the first traverse of the Northwest Passage and set his sights on being the first to the North Pole, only to be forestalled by the rival claims of the US explorers Robert E. Peary and Frederick A. Cook (the latter having also been one of Amundsen's shipmates on the *Belgica*). Famously, Amundsen announced his intention to proceed

---

18 Bravo, *North Pole*, 7.
19 Cawood, "Magnetic Crusade"; Enebakk, "Hansteen's Magnetometer".
20 On the first International Polar Year see Barr and Lüdecke, eds., *History of International Polar Years*.

1 Introduction: The Problems of Polar History

instead to the South Pole while at sea, setting up a race with the Briton Robert Falcon Scott – himself a protégé of Sir Clements Markham, an old Arctic hand.[21]

In the wake of the explorers and the scientists came institutions and professional structures. After Scott's death en route back from the Pole, the public collection in memory of this tragedy was so successful that it established the Scott Polar Research Institute (SPRI) in 1920.[22] From the start, SPRI had a mandate to cover both the Arctic and the Antarctic, reflecting Britain's self-image as a global empire capable of ordering and categorizing the rest of the world. In the United States, the AGS programme in geography of the polar regions that emerged later in the 1920s aimed to solidify the scientific foundations of a field – polar exploration – that AGS supremo Isaiah Bowman saw as dominated still by sensationalism.[23] The American Antarctic Society was founded in the United States in 1934 in the wake of Richard Byrd's expeditions, changing its name to the American Polar Society (APS) a year later to expand its pool of potential members among US expeditions in both polar regions.[24] With increasing numbers working in both polar regions, logistical skills and technical competence proved just as susceptible to being classified as 'polar' as expertise in specific scientific disciplines. Even when it became clear from the late 1930s that much of the world had entered a warmer period, and glacial recession in both the Arctic and the Antarctic became linked in the minds of physical geographers, the key ties between north and south were human as much as intellectual.[25]

Definitions of the 'polar regions' as a coherent category have almost always been developed by outsiders to these regions. The polar regions are only 'natural' categories within a worldview that privileges commonalities in climate, geomorphology, or the presence of marine mammals over the specific connections to place denoted by an Indigenous homeland. Consequently, polar institutions have always had a geopolitical function, in

---

21 On Amundsen see most notably Bomann-Larsen, *Roald Amundsen*; Huntford, *Scott and Amundsen*.
22 On the early history of SPRI see Roberts, *European Antarctic*, 78–81.
23 Joerg spearheaded this initiative despite his knowledge of the Arctic and Antarctic coming entirely from the maps and accounts of others. Wright, "Obituary: W. L. G. Joerg", 486.
24 https://americanpolar.org/about/our-history/. Byrd himself premised Operation *High Jump* – a massive 1947–48 US military exercise in Antarctica – as a means of building capacity in cold-weather warfare, despite the potential theatre being Arctic rather than Antarctic.
25 Roberts, *European Antarctic*, 105–110; Sörlin, "Narratives and Counter-narratives".

the sense of inscribing nationally inflected meanings upon and attachments to particular spaces. The hard power of projecting logistical capacity was one dimension, but so too was the softer-power mission of the APS and SPRI – to validate a connection with distant spaces, a mission that SPRI founder Frank Debenham regarded as essential for establishing polar exploration as a living tradition.[26]

A contrast here might be instructive. There is no *Cambridge History of the Tropical Regions*, despite the tropics being similarly capable of demarcation by climatic parameters and cartographic lines. And indeed, the mere thought feels uncomfortable. We suspect that for many readers it conjures up uncomfortable images of European imperialism and geographies defined by deviations from a temperate norm. And anyway, why would proximity to the Equator be the thing that binds together Rwanda, the Galapagos Islands, and East Timor? An answer lies in Denis Cosgrove's argument for the existence of 'ontological tropics', the (European) intellectual frames through which tropical regions were represented and understood, and which held greatest purchase when the tropics were marked by exotic difference.[27] Is it not the same for European visions of the polar regions, spaces constructed as distant in space and culture?[28] We suggest that there are similar 'ontological poles' marked by exteriority and otherness, constructed by a gaze that must be distant in order to mark differentiation.

Our claim is that polar history aggregates and indeed magnifies inherent problems with Arctic history or Antarctic history by per definition privileging explorers and scientists – the categories of practitioner for whom the polar regions have meaningful commonalities. The need to identify that which both polar regions have in common necessarily marginalizes that which is particular or unique. Such an approach can erase Indigenous cultures and undermine local ways of knowing. It also tends to overlook histories of work, especially domestic labour. Even the history of logistical operations in the polar regions is substantially skewed toward the heroic – expedition ships, feats of engineering, and epic traverses – rather than the infrastructures that annually support sealifts to northern communities or field operations in Antarctica, routine acts of maintenance rather than spectacles of conquest.[29] The fact that the 'polar

---

26 See Frank Debenham, "The Scott Polar Research Institute", undated draft (1922). SPRI uncatalogued letters (1919–1922), MS Folder 3 'Rough Notes for S.P.R.I. by Frank Debenham (1922).'
27 Cosgrove, "Tropic and Tropicality", 198.   28 See also Pálsson, "Arcticality".
29 We draw inspiration here from the manifesto of The Maintainers, who advocate for a greater focus on the often unseen and unappreciated agents who 'keep our world from falling apart.' See https://themaintainers.org/about-us.

1 Introduction: The Problems of Polar History

regions' label feels less uncomfortable than the 'tropical regions' attests to the ongoing dominance of explorers and their chroniclers in defining the field, and perhaps also to a lack of sustained critical analysis.

In a sense, our discontent echoes trends in the so-called New Western History of the US west (which at the time of writing is no longer quite so new), which has placed greater emphasis on Indigenous communities, racial minorities, gender and sexuality, and environments – and thus revised the older image of the west as a frontier space where agency rested primarily with white men.[30] In replacing process with place, the New Western History reveals that the wildness of the west was constitutive rather than incidental, and that the frontier between civilization and wildness was widely mythologized. It is instructive that the 1945 report by Vannevar Bush that led to the creation of the US National Science Foundation (NSF) was titled *Science: The Endless Frontier*.[31] Such a framing strengthened the categorization of regions such as the Arctic and Antarctica – both of which have seen extensive NSF activity – not as places to be engaged on their own terms, but spaces of difference to be tamed and conquered through the ongoing process of scientific research.

Much like the American west, both the Arctic and the Antarctic were framed by Europeans as spaces of difference and wildness. Explorers created each region through voyages and expeditions that produced maps and narratives alike; polar geography shaded easily into polar history.[32] The authority of the explorer to pronounce on the Arctic or the Antarctic relied on an implicit presumption of otherness, the agency of the explorer contrasted with the stasis of the places encountered, provided that the explorer continued to maintain critical distance from their subjects – bringing the sensibilities of home to the field. Even those who sought to deny that the Arctic was quite as alien as usually thought – most notably the Canadian Vilhjalmur Stefansson – persisted in regarding it as a frontier to be conquered from the south. There was no contradiction between the titles of two of Stefansson's most famous books, *The Friendly Arctic* and *The Northward Course of Empire*: the former only emphasized the desirability of getting on with the inevitable business of the latter.[33] Stefansson's views never gained widespread support, but the fact they gained any traction at all was due to his personal experience, which he parlayed into a career as a polar authority with the most

30 Limerick, *Legacy of Conquest*; White, *'It's Your Misfortune'*.
31 Bush, *Science: The Endless Frontier*.
32 We thank Alessandro Antonello for this observation.
33 Stefansson, *Friendly Arctic*; Stefansson, *Northward Course of Empire*.

extensive polar library in North America.³⁴ Stefansson's progression is a telling example of a wider trend, namely that the authority of the explorer to tell a story of polar exploration developed into a wider institutional authority about one (or both) polar regions. The authority of practice – of having lived in the north himself – was the bedrock of an enterprise that grew to encompass an enormous library and a staff who augmented his claim to polar expertise.³⁵

For states with traditions of polar exploration and polar science there was (and is) a clear incentive to perpetuate the polar regions as a category. This is especially the case for states with strong interests in both the Arctic and Antarctica, such as the United States, Russia, Britain, and Norway. The geopolitical value of exploration and science tends to work best when the geopolitics goes unstated, and when the focus remains on the polar practitioners themselves. By designating Antarctica as a 'continent for peace and science', the twelve original signatories of the Antarctic Treaty sought to depoliticize the continent for highly political motives. The fact that the Antarctic Treaty is frequently held up as a model for international governance (and even used as a potential model for Arctic governance) highlights how successful its members have been in keeping the focus on science, and, more recently, environmental protection. When the British Antarctic Survey had to explicitly state its geopolitical value to avoid merger with the National Oceanographic Institute, this might be seen as something of a failure of polar statecraft.³⁶ Asserting the unproblematic existence of the polar as a category is a means of perpetuating a particular form of politics – one that presumes that capacity to investigate and pronounce upon the polar regions is equally an unproblematic way of contributing to global knowledge.

We suggest that this centrality of the polar practitioner extended to the creation of polar history. Arctic and Antarctic exploration alike were a form of spectacle – and like all spectacles, they were meaningless without audience approval.³⁷ Those audiences were located not in the north or the south, but in the more temperate sites from where the expeditions were organized. They were eager for tales of drama, danger, and perhaps even death in the quest to conquer the unknown. When the race for the North and South Poles became

---

34 On Stefansson see for instance Diubaldo, *Stefansson and the Canadian Arctic*.
35 Forthcoming work by Tina Adcock will cast valuable light on how Stefansson created and operated his library.
36 See Daniella McCahey, Chapter 13 in this volume.
37 On the performative element, see most notably Robinson, *Coldest Crucible*; on exploration as media spectacle, see Riffenburgh, *Myth of the Explorer*.

1 Introduction: The Problems of Polar History

linked in the public mind, the concept of the polar explorer became real. And thus was a tradition invented.

Yet expeditions did not automatically become part of a historical tradition. Expeditions became popularized through media coverage and stabilized through official accounts, often in the name of the expedition leader, that recounted the trials and achievements of the venture. Good prose could heighten an expedition's fame – and when that prose became last words, the effect was only magnified. Robert Falcon Scott had already shown a talent for writing in the official volume from his first Antarctic expedition in 1901–04.[38] When his body and those of two companions were found in 1913, having died on their return journey from the South Pole, Scott's pathos-filled diary became a relic as much as a historical record.[39] Scott became a martyred saint within a secular tradition of polar exploration that perhaps reached its apotheosis in Britain, its path eased by a cultural predisposition to conquest of distant and different lands. Murals on the domed ceilings in the SPRI building commemorated voyages of polar discovery while its library amassed holdings on both polar regions. The Polar Medal recognized British achievement in either the Arctic or the Antarctic (or sometimes both), each in a sense an arena with common properties.

If maps constituted the Arctic and the Antarctic within geography, narratives constituted these regions within history – and that history was largely the province of the practitioners and those who shared their commitment to that tradition. Explorers such as Stefansson and Fridtjof Nansen published historical works about the Arctic that went beyond their own first-hand experiences.[40] Early historians of Antarctic exploration such as Hugh Robert Mill and Bjarne Aagaard took pains to ensure that the explorers endorsed their texts, and often viewed themselves as part of the same milieu to the point of sharing common goals.[41] History could be weaponized as a validation of a nation or an individual's accomplishments, but the sword was double-edged: when Aagaard's third volume on Norwegian hunting and research in the Antarctic failed to please his patron, the whaling baron and patron of exploration Lars Christensen, it resulted in a sudden withdrawal of support.[42] The first works explicitly dedicated to polar history placed

---

38 This point is recognized more or less universally, although Scott's sternest critic – Roland Huntford – mentioned it almost as a backhanded compliment in *Scott and Amundsen*.
39 On the memorialization of Scott see in particular Jones, *Last Great Quest*.
40 See for instance Stefansson, *Unsolved Mysteries*; Nansen, *In Northern Mists*.
41 Mill, *Siege*; Aagaard, *Fangst og forskning i Sydishavet*.   42 Roberts, *European Antarctic*, 70.

explorers firmly in the role of protagonists upon icy canvases. G. Firth Scott's 1921 *Daring Deeds of Polar Explorers: True Stories of Bravery, Resource, Endurance and Adventure at the Poles* was an early example of the genre.[43] In 1930 Joerg followed *Problems of Polar Research* with a history of polar aviation.[44]

Over time the institutions of polar research, polar governance, and polar science have also attracted their own historians. But although there is certainly some blurring of boundaries, histories of polar science and governance regimes are not nearly as popular as histories of polar exploration. Drawing, not incidentally, on a British expression, the most obvious reason is that histories of science can lack the '*Boy's Own*' excitement of exploration histories. Men around conference tables (and until surprisingly recently they have invariably been men) make less arresting subjects than heroes battling the elements. Polar research projects, and polar scientists, are more interesting and diverse than the public stereotype might suggest. Despite efforts by journalists such as the *New York Times* reporter Walter Sullivan to translate polar science into popular consciousness during the International Geophysical Year (IGY) of 1957–58, using the metaphor of an 'assault on the unknown', the frontier of knowledge has largely proved less striking than the frontier of cartography.[45]

Following a small flurry of polar-themed research publications and histories in the 1920s and 1930s, very little work that was explicitly polar was published in the years that followed. Among the rare exceptions was *A History of Polar Exploration* (1960) by Laurence Kirwan, the director and secretary of the Royal Geographical Society.[46] Again, the book was a history of exploration and endeavour that focused on acts of geographical conquest. The perspective was of an insider at a body that remained one of the more important patrons of British polar exploration – even if Kirwan himself was an archaeologist of Arabia and northeast Africa. Studies of polar exploration certainly did not disappear during this period, but they tended to focus on one pole or another. This allowed armchair explorers to revel in the details, without worrying too much about overarching context, as narratives of polar exploration continued to be a form of nostalgic escapism.

By the mid-twentieth century, the polar was sufficiently established as a category of analysis that it needed little ongoing support. Cold War geopolitics in both north and south continued to draw strongly on science and exploration, and there were incentives to keep the focus on explorers and

---

43 Scott, *Daring Deeds*.   44 Joerg, *Brief History*.   45 Sullivan, *Assault on the Unknown*.
46 Kirwan, *History of Polar Exploration*.

scientists as practitioners, and increasingly on the science itself. Sponsoring states, rather than the heroic individuals, increasingly became the focus in the age of Big Science. As the IGY showed, the polar had helped to provide a foundation for the planetary, with the Earth as a whole increasingly conceived as a set of geophysical systems. In turn, as demonstrated by the prominence of Antarctica in NASA's iconic 1972 'Blue Marble' image, the ability to view the Earth from space in turn reinforced the importance of the polar regions.[47]

In recent years, interest in the polar as a unit for description and analysis has frequently been driven by growing environmental concern. By presenting both the Arctic and Antarctica as vulnerable to climate heating, atmospheric scientists demonstrate both the transferability of their skills and the global scale of the problem. While the consequences of melting ice in the Arctic might be different from the consequences of melting ice in Antarctica, climate-driven ecosystem change threatens environments in both polar regions, the twin canaries in the coal mine of climate change. These global-scale anthropogenic threats are largely driven by activities on regional and local scales in locations closer to the Equator.

But there are concrete dangers to taking a polar perspective on many questions, of both science and institutional politics. A polar perspective must per definition struggle to recognize Indigenous knowledge traditions with deep roots in specific lands and seas. The success of the ATS has on occasion produced calls for some kind of analogous arrangement in the Arctic, which would erase or at least decentre Indigenous authority, even if the arrangement were kept to coordination of science.[48] Bodies such as the International Arctic Science Committee (IASC) may have drawn loose inspiration from the Antarctic, but they are ultimately bespoke instruments for a particular political and cultural situation. We suspect that Antarctic histories are far more amenable to being classified as polar histories, a label that Arctic-focused historians would be more hesitant to adopt, because it is so much easier to presume a uniform language of description and meaning when thinking first about a continent without its own permanent population.

Like the concept of the tropics, the concept of the polar regions is frequently connected to a global, scientific and often imperial vision of the world. To take a polar perspective is to see from the outside, perhaps even necessarily to minimize differences to see commonalities. This is the problem

---

47 See for instance Poole, *Earthrise*, especially 120.
48 See for instance Bones, "SCAR as Healing Process?"; van der Watt and Roberts, "Voicing Bipolar Futures".

of polar history. It is a serious and, on the surface, perhaps a fatal problem. Why, then, does this volume exist?

The Promise of the Polar

We contend that a new polar history is both possible and desirable. The value of the polar as a frame for scholarship will be a function of the value it can add, either through comparison or contrast – while also recognizing that the polar will often be a complementary rather than an exclusive or even a primary frame for analysis. In certain cases, the frame of the polar serves as a logical frame for a common story – for instance in logistics or the atmospheric sciences – but in very many other cases it provides a foil for local histories, their particularity a constant reminder that between (and within) the Antarctic and the Arctic lie tremendous differences. Imperial and colonial power structures must be recognized as fundamental and not incidental, and historians must ask why certain voices have authority and not others.

The polar was (and is) a category used by particular actors, and asking why they chose to use that category, and how they acted within it, can illuminate cultural as well as scientific worlds. Why has there been a Scott Polar Research Institute since 1920 (and not a Scott Antarctic Research Institute)? Why does France have an organization called Expéditions Polaires Françaises (founded in 1947)? Why did the US National Science Foundation change the name of its Office of Antarctic Programs to an Office of Polar Programs in the late 1960s? In each of these cases following the money, the individuals, and the equipment leads to histories that would be hamstrung without both an Arctic and an Antarctic perspective. But even here we must be attentive to who exactly counts as a practitioner. The singular importance of specific individuals such as Frank Debenham, Paul-Émile Victor, or Richard Byrd must be balanced by histories that recognize the maintenance of polar organizations as a continuous process. This is particularly true of logistics.[49] The US McMurdo Station in Antarctica employs hundreds of staff to allow a much smaller number of scientists to do their research. Even in Arctic locations with communities that pre-date the research station, such as Utqiagvik (formerly Barrow) in Alaska, there are frequently larger numbers of logistics staff than scientists. Many of these individuals forged careers based

---

49 On the dynamics of an important piece of Canadian research infrastructure – the Polar Continental Shelf Program – see Powell, *Studying Arctic Fields*.

1 Introduction: The Problems of Polar History

on the transferability of their practical knowledge, and it is not uncommon for support staff to work summer seasons in the Arctic and Antarctica in a single year. We might even think of logistics as the submerged nine-tenths of the iceberg, the scientific programs that make possible the small portion gleaming above the surface.

The promise of histories of polar logistics is tied in part to the polar regions as places of work. Environmental historian Richard White's argument that environments can be known through labour is a reminder both that the human and the non-human are entangled, and also that knowledge of environments is learned through living and working and not simply through studying.[50] Many of the knowledge traditions that link Arctic and Antarctic research have common roots, especially those from the geophysical sciences. Nonetheless, as historians, sociologists, and anthropologists have long argued, cultures and traditions of knowledge production are locally specific in terms of structure as well as content. This is most clearly the case with Indigenous knowledge of northern environments. Drawing on a study of the Burwash Landing region of the southern Yukon, anthropologist Paul Nadasdy has persuasively argued that traditional environmental knowledge (TEK) as described by non-Indigenous scientists constitutes an attempt to distill singular units of knowledge from a seamless body of learned experience from which isolated data points are not easily extracted.[51] Similar points might be made of Inuit *Qaujimajatuqangit* (IQ), another body of orally transmitted environmental knowledge that includes cultural and social elements.[52] This is contextually produced knowledge – how to live and thrive in a manner appropriate for a specific community within a specific environment. Living, working, and knowing are intimately and perhaps inextricably connected. Pondering this connection can also help illuminate the central place of labour in non-Indigenous knowledge production.

Another important factor is the overarching logic of capitalism, and the degree to which it has framed (and does frame) systems of knowledge production. Indigenous Arctic communities have long had extensive trade networks. Nevertheless, capitalism injected new elements into white–Indigenous relations in the Arctic that became permanently changed with more formal processes of colonialism. In the Antarctic, capitalism underpinned two processes of boom and bust: sealing in the nineteenth century and whaling in the twentieth. The peril of the polar perspective is that it can

50 See for instance White, "Are You an Environmentalist?".
51 Nadasdy, *Hunters and Bureaucrats*.
52 See for instance Karetak et al., eds., *Inuit Qaujimajatuqangit*.

erase Indigenous agency by focusing solely on the common elements in harvesting marine living resources, which by including the Antarctic force a reduction in the relevant variables. But perhaps perspectives from both polar regions can sometimes reveal a common story. Profits from Norwegian Antarctic whaling underwrote mapping in East Greenland, while Britain settled a sovereignty dispute over Bouvet Island in the Southern Ocean in part through extracting a concession from Norway over sovereignty in the High Arctic islands of Canada. The bodies of knowledge developed to regulate commercial whaling emerged in concert with the industry itself, aimed at benefiting the whaler more than the whale. Concepts of sustainability and equilibrium were invoked as early as the 1930s by marine biologists such as Johan Hjort.[53] Yet these models of economic units swimming in distant oceans were very different from the locally grounded knowledge of Iñupiat whalers on the Alaskan North Slope, for whom equilibrium was a matter of balance between people and whales rather than between economic inputs and outputs.[54]

A further complication involves the categories of actors that a particular scale makes visible, and the structural connection between where the historian looks and what (and whom) the historian sees. It is a well-established trope in Arctic and particularly Antarctic history that whalers and sealers travelled further and experienced more than commonly realized, but that the commercial necessity of secrecy precluded their full entry into the pantheon of explorers. Earthly and heavenly (or historical) rewards were thus kept separate. But how much is lost by fetishizing the written record, or indeed by identifying exploration as the primary justification for being remembered? The lived experiences of individuals who came to know the Arctic and the Antarctic through work should not be reduced to a numerically expressed impact upon the destruction of marine mammal populations. Indigenous and non-Indigenous whalers may have hunted the same animals, but they made sense of the environments of which they and the animals were a part in different ways.[55] While Antarctic expeditions of the Heroic Age are among the most over-documented events in human history, thanks to a profusion of diaries buttressed by logbooks, letters, and official accounts, many of the sealers who worked on the Antarctic islands in the early nineteenth century left few or no written records. Archaeological research of the sort conducted by the South American 'Landscapes in White' project can reveal the ways

53 Burnett, *Sounding of the Whale*; Roberts, *European Antarctic*.
54 Lowenstein, *Ancient Land: Sacred Whale*. 55 See in particular Routledge, *Do You See Ice?*.

1 Introduction: The Problems of Polar History

these individuals lived and worked, recovering experiences invisible to the textual record.[56] Local histories challenge the structural invisibility of those who did not leave textual records of their lives and work, even when that work took them to the Antarctic.

Whaling and sealing took both humans and capital far from European and American shores, and distributed products from polar animals to markets around the world. We applaud histories that emphasize the regional and global dimensions of these industries while suggesting that the polar can remain a useful frame of reference by emphasizing capital, labour, and colonialism in contexts still dominated by heroic explorers.[57] These trends have been most fully fleshed out in the Arctic, but as labour historian Ben Maddison has pointed out, this extends even to the sailors and labourers on early voyages of Antarctic exploration, who were more directly exposed to the environments in which they worked than the officers and scientists who produced the artefacts of cartographic knowledge.[58] To place such stories in the same context as narratives of heroic discovery is to challenge the primacy of exploration and explorers, and to undermine the centrality of the explorer to polar history.

Such challenges are warranted given the persistence of exploration as the dominant theme within histories that take a polar rather than a regional perspective – reinforced by a sense that the experience of explorers is so unique and singular that they define as well as star in this tradition. Consider Sir Ranulph Fiennes, whose own career as a professional explorer and adventurer has embraced both geographic poles as well as other extreme environments such as the Himalayas.[59] Having traversed both geographic poles during his 1979–82 Transglobe expedition, Fiennes subsequently crossed Antarctica on foot with the medical doctor Mike Stroud and then turned his hand to history, writing a biography of Robert Falcon Scott that drew heavily on his own experiences of unsupported sledging in Antarctica. Fiennes's target was the revisionist interpretation of Scott as a well-meaning

---

56 Zarankin and Senatore, *Historias*. See also Melisa A. Salerno, M. Jimena Cruz, and Andrés Zarankin, Chapter 17 in this volume.
57 Avango et al., "Between Markets and Geo-politics"; Qikiqtani Truth Commission, *Official Mind*; Demuth, *Floating Coast*; Tester and Kulchyski, *Tammarniit (Mistakes)*; Bruno, *Nature of Soviet Power*; Grant, *Polar Imperative*; Rud, *Colonialism in Greenland*; Grant, "State, Company, and Community Relations"; Priebe, "Greenland's Future"; Ojala and Nordin, "Mining Sápmi"; Fraser, "T'aih k'iighe' tth'aih zhit diidich'ùh".
58 Maddison, *Class and Colonialism*.
59 Of his many published works, see in particular Fiennes *Mad, Bad, and Dangerous to Know* and *To the Ends of the Earth*.

but inadequate amateur – an interpretation championed by the journalist Roland Huntford, whose experience of Nordic skiing made him far from competent in Fiennes's eyes to judge an Antarctic hero. To write about Hell, Fiennes wrote trenchantly, it helps to have been there.[60]

The image of Antarctica as Hell may be appropriate for an explorer battling a set of elements against which they can measure their courage and competence through feats of travel. To downplay the continent's harshness is to downplay Scott's achievements – not to mention those of Fiennes himself. Hell remains a frontier to be conquered and not a homeland to be lived in. Tropes of this kind are thus deeply unhelpful in understanding the lives of sheep farmers near Narsaq, residential school survivors in the Northwest Territories, or homemakers in Norilsk. But they may yet have value in focusing attention on how concepts of hostility and friendliness have proven surprisingly flexible, particularly in the Arctic. Stefansson's 1913–18 Canadian Arctic Expedition and subsequent attempt to colonize Wrangel Island ended in multiple deaths. Despite having apparently been to Hell, he returned convinced that its fires were cosy, and spent the remainder of his life trying with mixed success to argue that the Arctic was ripe for development and colonization, if only it were done properly. Raymond Priestley, who spent three winters in Antarctica during the Heroic Age – including one in an improvised ice cave – told students at Cambridge in the 1920s that he looked forward to a day when Antarctica featured sanatoria and facilities for tourists.[61]

Priestley never felt that Antarctica would become colonized and settled in an analogous manner to Stefansson's dream of a Canadianized Arctic. But others, most notably Chile and Argentina, have attempted to make Antarctica a homeland rather than an outpost. Following the birth of the first baby in Antarctica in 1978 to Argentine military parents, Chile responded by having their own births at Antarctic stations and setting up schools to teach the children of the military personnel and other staff serving there. Chile's 'housewives at the end of the world' served a distinctly geopolitical function.[62] The vision in the 1980s, which has not entirely gone away, was to turn the conglomeration of stations and logistics infrastructure surrounding Chile's Villa de las Estrellas station on King George Island into something of an Antarctic version of Longyearbyen, the administrative capital of Svalbard in the Arctic, a town with over 2,000 residents, complete with a kindergarten

---

60 Fiennes, *Race to the Pole*, xiii. 61 Roberts, "Frozen Field of Dreams", 217.
62 Llanos, "Housewives".

1 Introduction: The Problems of Polar History

and a school. The Latin American and Norwegian projects share an important characteristic: an attempt to demonstrate that a polar territory is part of the national geo-body, in the sense used by Thongchai Winichakul – holding a place in the heart of the national community in addition to being represented on its maps.[63] Such a territory cannot by definition be a frontier: it is an integral part of the homeland. Whether the attachment to place experienced by residents of Longyearbyen is analogous to that of Indigenous residents of traditional lands in the Arctic is doubtful (not least because famously neither births nor deaths are supposed to take place on Svalbard). Perhaps this is incidental, given that the real purpose of such communities is to create bonds of belonging in Oslo and Santiago.

The difference between Indigenous homelands and non-Indigenous homes is a real one because the depth of connection is so much greater and more all-embracing in the former. But does this also mean that only the latter can be explorers? The British–Canadian archaeologist and Arctic administrator Graham Rowley recalled being challenged by an Inuk student at Carleton University while teaching a course on the history of exploration in Canada. Seen from Europe, the discoverer of new lands and peoples was an explorer; seen from the lands themselves, he was an 'exotic visitor'.[64] This led Rowley not to abandon the category of the explorer – indeed, his author biography for the chapter described his own feats of exploration around the Eastern Arctic – but rather to expand it so as to include the first settlers in northern North America as agents of exploration and discovery rather than simply occupants of a space. The Inuit were perhaps the greatest of the Arctic explorers, making their homes in new lands and developing and mastering new techniques of travel, to the point where Rowley wondered if Sir John Franklin's famously disastrous expedition might have met a happier fate had they taken an Inuk guide.[65] It was unjust, Rowley felt, for Inuit to be denied their place in the first rank of explorers simply because they made the lands they reached their homes. Does this open the door for a polar history that is more inclusive of Indigenous peoples? Priscilla Wehi and her colleagues have recently used the term 'explorers' to describe the Polynesians who travelled deep in the Southern Ocean as early as the seventh century, possibly even sighting the Antarctic continent.[66] Their point is to emphasize that Māori should be recognized as part of a larger history of human engagement with

---

63 Winichakul, *Siam Mapped*.   64 Rowley, "Original Native Explorers", 40.
65 Rowley, "Original Native Explorers", 45.   66 Wehi et al., "Short Scan".

the Antarctic – and as holders of knowledge relevant to understanding and acting within the Antarctic today. They too were explorers.

But the most important message of Rowley's essay is the danger of the Eurocentric 'God' perspective. The view from above is not always better than the view from the ground, even if such a view can be found. One person's unknown frontier is another person's cherished homeland. Even if the category of the explorer were to be broadened to encompass more than just the Europeans who build a historical edifice around that label, it would privilege encounter over habitation. We argue that attention to scale breeds attention to diversity. Histories of the Arctic and Antarctica, especially when written at national or local scales, are often more attuned to nuance and difference, and less inclined to simplistic stories of progress. Master narratives from 'development' to 'conservation' and even 'law and order' are significantly complicated by local histories of Indigenous northern communities. For the peoples of the Arctic, the history of their parts of that region has been understood in ways that are both distinctive and similar to the histories of other parts of the world. Historical understanding is embedded in written texts, oral tradition, practices, and the landscape – all of which vary in form as well as content. Frank Tester and Peter Kulchyski have referred to a totalizing vision through which the Canadian state projected its will upon diverse Arctic communities.[67] As historians we must be wary of any analytic framework focused on a specific category of actor into which the diversity of human experience in diverse environments must be fitted. No matter how noble the intent, we suspect that a polar history centred on exploration will remain stuck in that trap.

Histories of actions by governments and companies are increasingly complicated by the more complex realities of how those decisions were resisted (and on some occasions embraced). Local dynamics among Inuit communities coalesced into a regional political action, and ultimately the 1977 creation of the Inuit Circumpolar Council (ICC).[68] The view of Svalbard from Oslo and Moscow is one of international power politics, but local histories reveal tensions, from the proliferation of anarcho-syndicalist unions in the early days of coal mining to the contradiction between the official myth of Pyramiden as a communist utopia and the near-veneration that its workers came to accord to non-Soviet consumer culture.[69] Something similar might

67 This is a theme in both Tester and Kulchyski, *Tammarniit (Mistakes)*, and Kulchyski and Tester, *Kiumajut (Talking Back)*.
68 Shadian, *Politics of Arctic Sovereignty*.
69 Avango, "Sveagruvan"; Andreassen et al., *Persistent Memories*.

even be said of Antarctica. Recent scholarship has devoted less attention to exploration, starting to move the history of the continent from being the history of a process to the history of a place. Such a trend is welcome not only for the focus it brings on Antarctica as a space of work and lived experience, in many cases representing in microcosm the overarching political structures of the sponsoring states, including racial and gender discrimination.[70]

Space remains for historical studies that take a regional focus, and these can often benefit from the wider perspectives of the sort offered by a polar framing. The negotiations that led up to the 1973 Agreement on the Conservation of Polar Bears involved both research and diplomacy, the former conducted largely within national frames, but developing into a transnational community of experts who were able to leverage action from their governments. The growing industry of scientific support for polar research, from Cape Chelyuskin and Cambridge Bay to McMurdo and Mawson, has created openings for states with Arctic interests to regard themselves as relevant to the Antarctic through provision of icebreakers or other cold climate technology.[71]

Thus we reach a somewhat paradoxical conclusion. The flowering of scholarship in the past two decades on the history of polar spaces has provided rich and important new studies of many aspects of the Arctic and the Antarctic, bringing critical perspectives on everything from Greenlandic/Danish mixed marriages to Antarctic wildlife management; and from energy regimes and environmental history in Beringia to visions of Antarctica as a productive Australian colony.[72] But we wonder if some historians of the Arctic and the Antarctic might not learn as much from works on the history of high-altitude research or on the emergence of the global climate.[73] The irony of polar history is that often it is done best precisely by *not* being polar history – by ushering in the era of what Michael Bravo has termed the 'post-polar'.[74]

The Chapters

This volume has been commissioned at a historical moment when there is both a renewed interest in the polar regions and an increased awareness of

[70] van Sittert, "'Ironman'"; van der Watt and Swart, "The Whiteness of Antarctica"; McCahey, "'Last Refuge'"; Bloom, *Gender on Ice*.
[71] Dahl et al., "Is There Anything Natural?", 326–329.
[72] Seiding, "'Married to the Daughters'"; Antonello, *Greening of Antarctica*; Demuth, *Floating Coast*; Hains, *Ice and Inland*.
[73] Heggie, *Higher and Colder*; Dry, *Waters of the World*.
[74] Bravo, "Preface. Legacies of Polar Science".

the problems of linking the Arctic and Antarctica. Climate change and the associated geopolitics of the far north and the far south have created an interest in the Arctic and Antarctica. At the same time, efforts to decentre and decolonize polar history are largely pulling in the opposite direction. In bringing together the thirty-one chapters in this volume on histories of the Arctic and Antarctica, we are challenging in addition to affirming the unity, and even the validity, of polar history. While highlighting this might be seen as an effort to 'have our cake and eat it', we would suggest that exposing these tensions is the most honest, the most exciting, and perhaps the only sustainable way of doing polar history.

We do not claim that this volume decolonizes polar history. As two middle-aged white men with permanent academic positions in northern Europe, our positionality as editors is in many ways identical to that of the scholars we critique and seek to move beyond. Yet we recognize that times have changed, and for the better. Twenty-five years ago, in the late twentieth century, it might still have been possible to aspire to write a comprehensive history of the polar regions. In the early 2020s such an aspiration appears not only almost impossible, but also misplaced. The quality, quantity, and diversity of scholarship on both the Arctic and Antarctic means that any pretence of comprehensive coverage can only be an expression of hubris. We may not be able to decolonize polar history with this volume, but we hope to have destabilized it, opening space for others to build in new directions.

This volume has no rigid definition of the 'polar regions' and instead relies on individual authors to define their subject of study. Our aim has been to assemble a set of chapters that make arguments about an aspect of polar history rather than attempting the futile task of comprehensive coverage. Quite a few chapters make no mention of the polar scale at all. While we as editors made no effort to commission a chapter on the 'Third Pole' of the Himalayas, it is nevertheless interesting that no authors have chosen to highlight this concept despite some tendency to do this in both popular and scientific literature. Relatively few of the authors in this collection would define themselves primarily as historians of the polar regions. Some might be historians of the Arctic, historians of Antarctica, historians of the Soviet Union, or historians of science. Several authors do not identify as historians at all. The perspectives offered in the different chapters do not always fit together neatly, and in fact there are sometimes tensions and disconnects among different chapters.

The volume opens with two chapters that illustrate very different approaches to the history of polar environments. George Angohiatok and his collaborators use George's description of his life's experiences to draw connections between the arc of a human life and the arc of environmental change in an Arctic region. Martin Siegert and Andrew Fountain centre a different knowledge tradition to paint a picture of how Antarctica came to be known through the earth and environmental sciences. Bjarne Grønnow then considers the great Inuit migrations from eastern Siberia across Beringia and ultimately as far as Greenland. Carl-Gösta Ojala contributes a study of the history of the Sámi people that emphasizes the political power of controlling not only narratives of the past, but the classification of material objects (and even human remains) as cultural property and not simply specimens for research. Jette Arneborg continues with the story of another settlement of Greenland, that of the Norse colonizers whose disappearance remains a source of mystery to the present – but which perhaps detracts from the equally fascinating story of how they lived in a land very different from those they had previously settled. Ryan Tucker Jones, Alexei Kraikovski, and Julia Lajus then describe how Imperial Russia attempted to create an Arctic empire that stretched as far as Alaska.

As the Arctic and Antarctica came into wider consciousness, practitioners began to categorise, map, and claim the polar regions through acts of exploration and 'discovery'. Cornelia Lüdecke and Erki Tammiksaar make the intriguing suggestion that the more interesting historical question is not who discovered Antarctica, but how it came to be defined as a continent in the first place, given its icy character. Russell Potter explores how and why the disappearance of Sir John Franklin has attained such cultural resonance, including in the northern communities near where his expedition was lost. Stephanie Barczewski focuses on the cultural importance of the 'Heroic Age' of Antarctic exploration as a phenomenon that has come to symbolize the history of the region for many. Elizabeth Leane follows with a chapter on historical fiction and biography as literary forms of representing and in some cases cementing polar knowledge. Richard Powell uses the history of Arctic geography and anthropology as a means of exploring how ideas about the peoples of the Arctic and their cultures have changed through time. Daniella McCahey makes a case for refocusing the history of the British Empire in the polar regions away from land and toward the seas. Janice Cavell explores the history of Canadian sovereignty claims over its High Arctic islands and the role those claims have played in both domestic and international political projects. Roald Berg offers a detailed explanation both of how the archipelago of Spitsbergen became the Norwegian territory of Svalbard, and of the tensions between national and international dimensions.

Ordering and exploiting frequently accompanied and followed exploration and discovery, as polar practitioners sought to make sense of what they were doing. Bjørn Basberg and Louwrens Hacquebord consider the long and diverse history of commercial whaling in both the Arctic and Antarctic, making a case for both connections and important differences. Melisa Salerno, Jimena Cruz, and Andrés Zarankin continue with an important examination of how archaeological fieldwork, combined with close study of written records, can illuminate the lives of the first Antarctic sealers. Henrik Knudsen, Arn Keeling, and John Sandlos analyse the history of mining in the Arctic – an industry that has touched many corners of the circumpolar north and continues to have important consequences today. Andy Bruno and Ekaterina Kalemeneva make an important argument for regarding the Soviet-era Arctic less as a monolithic expression of central ideology and more as a series of practices and projects that reflected negotiation with local conditions as well as individual initiative. Jens Heinrich argues that the political history of modern Greenland is one of a progression from Danish domination to Greenlandic autonomy, while emphasizing the agency of Indigenous Greenlanders in choosing the options they have in the past felt offered best prospects for improving their lives. Stephen Bocking and Pey-Yi Chu also take up links between militaries, states, and environmental knowledge-making in the Cold War. Klaus Dodds explores two of the defining events in the modern history of Antarctica – the International Geophysical Year and the Antarctic Treaty negotiations. Matt Farish uses the lens of militarization to explore the first century of United States rule over Alaska, while Phil Wight similarly uses a military perspective to shed new light on the history of Alaskan resource development and politics since World War II.

The final set of essays offer different perspectives, all of which highlight, in different ways, the promise of the polar. Mark Nuttall charts the history of both national and international Indigenous political movements in the Arctic, showing how Indigenous voices have created spaces within a range of political structures. Alessandro Antonello and Justiina Dahl explore the history of environmental management as both concept and practice in the Arctic and Antarctic. Pablo Fontana examines the history of Latin America and Antarctica as a story of competition but also on occasion cooperation. Dolly Jørgensen foregrounds animal history and considers another way through which humans sought to manipulate Arctic environments, through moving muskoxen between and within northern regions. Hayley Brazier and Mark Carey examine the many meanings of ice in the polar regions in both

1 Introduction: The Problems of Polar History

past and present. Jackie Price, Rebecca Mearns, and Emilie Cameron offer a thought-provoking and original set of thoughts on how the history of Arctic spaces is made, and what meaning it holds as elements in their lives today. Liza Piper and Lize-Marié Hansen van der Watt conclude the volume with a reflection on the state of polar history today – and where it might go in the future.

The American theologian Reinhold Niebuhr wrote a famous book titled *The Irony of American History* in which he questioned the role of virtue in the history of the United States.[75] By trying too hard to do good, he argues, the country has too often ended up doing harm. A similar sense of irony can be found in the history of the polar regions. The irony here is perhaps even more fundamental: the best way to do polar history is to *not* do polar history, and instead to rely on the individually crafted parts adding up to a whole that, if not coherent, is at least illuminating. Polar history only makes sense as a collection of historical studies of individual places and themes that correspond to our conception of the polar regions. It is possible that this will be the first and last *Cambridge History of the Polar Regions*, but there is nevertheless, we believe, real value in the exercise.

Bibliography

Aagaard, Bjarne, *Fangst og forskning i Sydishavet* (Sandefjord: Commander Chr. Christensen's Whaling Museum, 1930; 1934).

Andreassen, Elin, Hein Björck, and Bjørnar Olsen, *Persistent Memories: Pyramiden – A Soviet Mining Town in the High Arctic* (Trondheim: Tapir, 2010).

Antonello, Alessandro, *The Greening of Antarctica: Assembling an International Environment* (New York: Oxford University Press, 2019).

Avango, Dag, "Sveagruvan: svensk gruvhantering mellan industry, diplomati och geovetenskap", PhD diss. (KTH Royal Institute of Technology, 2005).

Avango, Dag, Louwrens Hacquebord, Ypie Aalders, et al., "Between Markets and Geo-politics: Natural Resource Exploitation on Spitsbergen from 1600 to the Present Day", *Polar Record* 47 (2011): 29–39, https://doi.org/10.1017/S0032247410000069.

Barr, Susan, and Cornelia Lüdecke, eds., *The History of the International Polar Years (IPYs)* (Heidelberg: Springer, 2010).

Bloom, Lisa, *Gender on Ice: American Ideologies of Polar Expeditions* (Minneapolis: University of Minnesota Press, 1993).

Bones, Stian, "SCAR as a Healing Process? Reflections on Science and Politics in the Cold War and Beyond: The Case of Norway", in Peder Roberts, Lize-Marié van der Watt, and Adrian Howkins, eds., *Antarctica and the Humanities* (New York: Palgrave Macmillan, 2016), pp. 231–249.

---

75 Niebuhr, *Irony of American History*.

Bravo, Michael, *North Pole: Nature and Culture* (London: Reaktion Books, 2019).
Bravo, Michael, "Preface. Legacies of Polar Science," in Jessica Shadian and Monica Tennberg, eds., *Legacies and Change in Polar Sciences. Historical, Legal and Political Reflections on the International Polar Year* (Farnham: Ashgate, 2009), pp. 13–16.
Bruno, Andy, *The Nature of Soviet Power: An Arctic Environmental History* (Cambridge: Cambridge University Press, 2017).
Burnett, D. Graham, *The Sounding of the Whale: Science and Cetaceans in the Twentieth Century* (Chicago: University of Chicago Press, 2012).
Bush, Vannevar, *Science: The Endless Frontier: A Report to the President* (Washington, DC: National Science Foundation, 1945).
Cardone, Ignacio Javier, *The Antarctic Politics of Brazil: Where the Tropic Meets the Pole* (Cham: Springer International, 2021).
Cawood, John, "The Magnetic Crusade: Science and Politics in Early Victorian Britain", *Isis* 70 (1979): 492–518.
Cosgrove, Denis, "Tropic and Tropicality", in Felix Driver and Luciana Martins, eds., *Tropical Visions in an Age of Empire* (Chicago: University of Chicago Press, 2005), pp. 197–216.
Dahl, Justiina, Peder Roberts, and Lize-Marié van der Watt, "Is There Anything Natural About the Polar?", *Polar Record* 55 (2019): 326–329.
Dams, Ties, Louise van Schaik, and Adája Stoetman, *Presence Before Power: China's Arctic Strategy in Iceland and Greenland* (The Hague: Clingendael Institute, 2018).
Demuth, Bathsheba, *Floating Coast: An Environmental History of Beringia* (New York: W. W. Norton, 2019).
Diubaldo, Richard, *Stefansson and the Canadian Arctic* (Montreal: McGill-Queen's University Press, 1999).
Dodds, Klaus, *Ice: Nature and Culture* (London: Reaktion Books, 2018).
Dry, Sarah, *Waters of the World: The Story of the Scientists Who Unravelled the Mysteries of Our Seas, Glaciers, and Atmosphere – and Made Our Planet Whole* (Scribe, 2019).
Enebakk, Vidar, "Hansteen's Magnetometer and the Origin of the Magnetic Crusade", *British Journal of the History of Science* 47 (2014): 587–608.
Fiennes, Ranulph, *Mad, Bad, and Dangerous to Know* (London: Hodder and Stoughton, 2008).
Fiennes, Ranulph, *Race to the Pole: Tragedy, Heroism and Scott's Antarctic Quest* (New York: Hyperion, 2004).
Fiennes, Ranulph, *To the Ends of the Earth* (London: Hodder and Stoughton, 1983).
Fraser, Crystal, "'T'aih k'iighe' tth'aih zhit diidìch'ùh (By Strength, We Are Still Here): Indigenous Northerners Confronting Hierarchies of Power at Day and Residential Schools in Nanhkak Thak (the Inuvik Region, Northwest Territories), 1959–1982", PhD diss. (University of Alberta, 2019).
Grant, Heather, "State, Company, and Community Relations at the Polaris Mine (Nunavut)", *Études/Inuit/Studies* 37 (2013): 37–57.
Grant, Shelagh, *Polar Imperative: A History of Arctic Sovereignty in North America* (Vancouver: Douglas & McIntyre, 2010).
Hains, Brigid, *The Ice and the Inland: Mawson, Flynn and the Myth of the Frontier* (Melbourne: University of Melbourne Press, 2002).
Hamelin, Louis-Edmond, *Canadian Nordicity: It's Your North Too*, trans. William Barr (Montreal: Harvest House, 1979).

Hamelin, Louis-Edmond, "Espaces touristiques en pays froides", *Teoros* 18 (1999): 4–9.
Harley, J. Brian, ed. Paul Laxton, *The New Nature of Maps: Essays in the History of Cartography* (Baltimore: Johns Hopkins University Press, 2001).
Heggie, Vanessa, *Higher and Colder: A History of Extreme Physiology and Exploration* (Chicago: University of Chicago Press, 2020).
Hemmings, Alan, "Considerable Values in Antarctica", *Polar Journal* 2 (2012): 139–156.
Howkins, Adrian, *Frozen Empires: An Environmental History of the Antarctic Peninsula* (Oxford: Oxford University Press, 2017).
Howkins, Adrian, "Have You Been There? Some Thoughts on (Not) Visiting Antarctica", *Environmental History* 15 (2010): 514–519.
Huntford, Roland, *Scott and Amundsen* (London: Hodder and Stoughton) 1979.
Joerg, W. L. G., *A Brief History of Polar Exploration Since the Introduction of Flying*, American Geographical Society Special Publication 11 (New York: American Geographical Society, 1930).
Joerg, W. L. G., *Problems of Polar Research: A Series of Papers by 31 Authors* (New York: American Geographical Society, 1928).
Jones, Max, *The Last Great Quest: Captain Scott's Antarctic Sacrifice* (Oxford: Oxford University Press, 2003).
Karetak, Joe, Frank Tester, and Shirley Tagalik, eds., *Inuit Qaujimajatuqangit: What Inuit Have Always Known to Be True* (Black Point, Nova Scotia: Fernwood, 2017).
Kirwan, Laurence, *A History of Polar Exploration* (New York: W. W. Norton, 1960).
Kulchyski, Peter and Frank Tester, *Kiumajut (Talking Back): Game Management and Inuit Rights 1900–1970* (Vancouver: University of British Columbia Press, 2007).
Limerick, Patricia Nelson, *The Legacy of Conquest: The Unbroken Past of the American West* (New York: Norton, 1987).
Llanos, Nelson, "Housewives at the End of the World: Chilean Women Living in Antarctica, 1984–1986", *Polar Journal* 9 (2019): 358–370.
Lowenstein, Tom, *Ancient Land: Sacred Whale: The Inuit Hunt and Its Rituals* (New York: Farrar, Straus and Giroux, 1993).
Maddison, Ben, *Class and Colonialism in Antarctic Exploration, 1750–1920* (London: Pickering and Chatto, 2014).
McCahey, Daniella, "'The Last Refuge of Male Chauvinism': Print Culture, Masculinity, and the British Antarctic Survey (1960–1996)", *Gender, Place and Culture* (2021), https://doi.org/10.1080/0966369X.2021.1873746.
McGeoch, Melodie, Justine D. Shaw, Aleks Terauds, and Jennifer E. Lee, "Monitoring Biological Invasion Across the Broader Antarctic: A Baseline and Indicator Framework", *Global Environmental Change* 32 (2015): 108–125.
Mill, Hugh Robert, *The Siege of the South Pole: The Story of Antarctic Exploration* (London: Alston Rivers, 1905).
Monmonier, Mark, *How to Lie with Maps*, 3rd edition (Chicago: University of Chicago Press, 2018).
Nadasdy, Paul, *Hunters and Bureaucrats: Power, Knowledge, and Aboriginal–State Relations in the Southwest Yukon* (Vancouver: University of British Columbia Press, 2003).
Nansen, Fridtjof, *In Northern Mists: Arctic Exploration in Early Times* (London: Heinemann, 1911).

New York Times, "Climbing Mount Everest Is Work for Supermen", *New York Times* (18 March 1923).

Niebuhr, Reinhold, *The Irony of American History* (New York: Charles Scribner's Sons, 1952).

Ojala, Carl-Gösta and Jonas M. Nordin, "Mining Sápmi: Colonial Histories, Sámi Archaeology, and the Exploitation of Natural Resources in Northern Sweden", *Arctic Anthropology* 52 (2015): 6–21.

Pálsson, Gisli, "Arcticality: Gender, Race, and Geography in the Writings of Vilhjalmur Stefansson", in Michael Bravo and Sverker Sörlin, eds., *Narrating the Arctic: A Cultural History of Nordic Scientific Practices* (Canton, MA: Science History Publications, 2002), pp. 275–308.

Poole, Robert, *Earthrise: How Man First Saw the Earth* (New Haven: Yale University Press, 2008).

Priebe, Janina, "Greenland's Future: Narratives of Natural Resource Development in the 1900s until the 1960s", PhD diss. (Umeå University, 2017).

Qikiqtani Truth Commission, *The Official Mind of Canadian Colonialism* (Iqaluit: Inhabit Media, 2014).

Riffenburgh, Beau, *The Myth of the Explorer: The Press, Sensationalism, and Geographical Discovery* (New York: Belhaven, 1993).

Roberts, Peder, "A Frozen Field of Dreams: The Construction of Antarctic Science in Norway, Sweden, and the British World, 1912–1952", PhD diss. (Stanford University, 2010), p. 217.

Roberts, Peder, *The European Antarctic: Science and Strategy in Scandinavia and the British Empire* (New York: Palgrave Macmillan, 2011).

Robinson, Michael, *The Coldest Crucible: Arctic Exploration and American Culture* (Chicago: University of Chicago Press, 2006).

Rowley, Graham, "The Original Native Explorers of the Arctic", in Walter O. Kupsch and Shirley Milligan, eds., *Living Explorers of the Canadian Arctic: The Historic Symposium of Arctic Scientists, Explorers, and Adventurers, Toronto 1978* (Outcrop: Yellowknife, 1986), pp. 40–46.

Rud, Søren, *Colonialism in Greenland: Tradition, Governance, and Legacy* (Cham: Springer, 2017).

Scott, G. Firth, *Daring Deeds of Polar Explorers: True Stories of Bravery, Resource, Endurance and Adventure at the Poles* (Philadelphia: J. B. Lippincott, 1922).

Seiding, Inge, "'Married to the Daughters of the Country': Intimacy and Intermarriage in Northern Greenland ca. 1750 to 1850", PhD diss. (Ilisimitusarfik – University of Greenland, 2013).

Shadian, Jessica, *The Politics of Arctic Sovereignty: Oil, Ice, and Inuit Governance* (Oxford: Routledge, 2014).

Sörlin, Sverker, "Narratives and Counter-narratives of Climate Change: North Atlantic Glaciology and Meteorology, c. 1930–1955", *Journal of Historical Geography* 35 (2009): 237–255.

Stefansson, Vilhjalmur, *The Friendly Arctic: The Story of Five Years in Polar Regions* (New York: Macmillan, 1921).

Stefansson, Vilhjalmur, *The Northward Course of Empire* (New York: Harcourt, Brace and Company, 1922).

1 Introduction: The Problems of Polar History

Stefansson, Vilhjalmur, *Unsolved Mysteries of the Arctic* (London: Harrap, 1939).

Sullivan, Walter, *Assault on the Unknown: The International Geophysical Year* (London: Hodder and Stoughton, 1962).

Synnott, Mark, *The Third Pole: My Everest Climb to Find the Truth about Mallory and Irvine* (London: Headline, 2021).

Tester, Frank and Peter Kulchyski, *Tammarniit (Mistakes): Inuit Relocation in the Eastern Arctic 1939–1963* (Vancouver: University of British Columbia Press, 1994).

van der Watt, Lize-Marié and Peder Roberts, "Voicing Bipolar Futures: The Antarctic Treaty System and Arctic Governance in Historical Perspective", in Nina Wormbs, ed., *Competing Arctic Futures: Historical and Contemporary Perspectives* (Cham: Palgrave Macmillan, 2018), pp. 139–164.

van der Watt, Lize-Marié and Sandra Swart, "The Whiteness of Antarctica", in Peder Roberts, Lize-Marié van der Watt, and Adrian Howkins, eds., *Antarctica and the Humanities* (Basingstoke: Palgrave Macmillan, 2016), pp. 125–156.

van Sittert, Lance, "'Ironman': Joseph Daniels and the White History of South Africa's Deep South", *Polar Record* 51 (2015): 501–512.

Wehi, Priscilla M., Nigel J. Scott, Jacinta Beckwith, et al., "A Short Scan of Māori Journeys to Antarctica", *Journal of the Royal Society of New Zealand* (2021), https://doi.org/10.1080/03036758.2021.1917633.

White, Richard, "Are You an Environmentalist or Do You Work for a Living?": Work and Nature in William Cronon, ed., *Uncommon Ground: Toward Reinventing Nature* (New York: W. W. Norton, 1995), pp. 171–185.

White, Richard, *'It's Your Misfortune and None of My Own': A New History of the American West* (Norman: University of Oklahoma Press, 1991).

Winichakul, Thongchai, *Siam Mapped: A History of the Geo-body of a Nation* (Honolulu: University of Hawaii Press, 1994).

Wright, John K., "Obituary: W. L. G. Joerg 1885–1952", *Geographical Review* 42 (July 1952): 482–488.

Yermakova, Yelena, "Governing Antarctica: Assessing the Legitimacy of the Antarctic Treaty System", PhD diss. (University of Oslo, 2021).

Zarankin, Andrés and M. Ximena Senatore, *Historias de un pasado en blanco: Arqueología histórica antártica* (Belo Horizonte: Argumentum, 2007).

Zlotnicki, Anna, "For the Purists! Our Continental Landing!", www.adventure-life.com/antarctica/stories/deep-south-small-ship-antarctica-expedition/for-the-purists-our-continental-landing.

2

'I Watch to See How the Land Is Changing': An Inuit Perspective on Changing Environments and Cultural Resilience in the Western Canadian Arctic

GEORGE ANGOHIATOK, BRYAN VANDENBRINK, IAN HOGG, AND THOMAS MCILWRAITH

Introduction

George Angohiatok (pronounced 'ano-HI-tok') is a keen observer of Arctic landscapes, animals, and peoples. Raised on the land by his parents and grandparents in the western Canadian Arctic, George talks easily about his deep appreciation for the land and his significant concerns for the future of the Arctic and Inuit. George shares his observations of changes to the physical and social environments – changes he calls overwhelming – through richly detailed personal narratives. In the conversations presented in this chapter, George deftly weaves together changes to both settings, and illustrates the importance of considering our two worlds holistically. George's story and words are transcribed here with minimal interruption from the other authors. Conventional academic reflections on methodology and literature are found within George's story and afterwards.

George is quick to acknowledge that he prefers winter to summer. When the land and water are frozen in the winter, travel everywhere is possible. In the summer, the sea is open and the land is strewn with lakes and rivers. Summer travel is much more complicated. And the differences between seasons, like the passage of time through one's life, hint at the themes of environmental, technological, and societal changes that George reveals in his recollections of Arctic history and community at Ekaluktutiak (Cambridge Bay, also spelled Iqaluktuuttiaq) in Nunavut, Canada (Figure 2.1). Born in 1955, George remembers winters with more sea ice than today. He describes the slow greening of the

2 An Inuit Perspective on Changing Environments

Figure 2.1 Map of important places in George Angohiatok's life.

Ekaluktutiak landscape as rains and warm temperatures have become commonplace. He reflects sensitively on the joy of his first snowmobile and the pain of alcohol and its pervasive use. Regardless of the elements in his stories, George insists that Inuit traditions have value. They endure and guide Inuit and non-Inuit alike towards a sustainable future. It is the relationships between family members and with strangers that support a hopeful narrative in which young people eventually take over his role as mentor, guide, historian, and tundra traveller.

Centring George's story in this volume reminds us that Inuit have always observed Arctic environments and they recognize their own positions in the recent history of the Arctic. George is an expert, taught and trained by knowledgeable people – experts in their own rights – and he is sought out for that expertise by government representatives, natural scientists, and social scientists. He is also looked to by community and family to share his wisdom and to ensure that his view of a world in which people, land, and animals are intertwined informs future generations of land-based experts, government officials, and scientists. This chapter shares some of George's extensive Arctic knowledge. It is an expression of the responsibility he carries to share what he knows and to encourage younger Inuit to participate in enduring practices.

George's Story

I was born west of Kugluktuk at a little place called Bernard Harbour [Nulahokyok] where a DEW Line [distant early warning] site was erected while we were living there, explains George Angohiatok during an interview session with Inuk biologist Bryan Vandenbrink. Bryan works with Ian Hogg at the Canadian High Arctic Research Station (CHARS) in Cambridge Bay. Tad McIlwraith is a southern anthropologist. Through the interviews and visits to his home, as well as time spent on the land while guiding for CHARS researchers, George is teaching us about changing social and natural environments at Ekaluktutiak, Nunavut.

George continues by introducing himself and his family. My Inuk name is Pamiok. My father's name was Sam Angohiatok. My mother's name was Doris Kikpak. And we grew up in Bernard Harbour with both our grandparents, mother and father's side. We were all together there. My father came from Prince Albert Sound on Victoria Island. And my mother and grandparents on my mother's side are from the western side of Victoria Island. So they met in Kugluktuk years ago and then started to live together and when they got together they moved out on the land with my grandparents. They had kids. I was the second eldest. I had an older sister, but she passed on from an illness. I wasn't sure what kind of illness, but her name was Alice. And I had two other siblings, Sam and Gary, in that order. And two other brothers that passed on, Timothy and Larry. And then the youngest, MJ, is my youngest sibling. So we lived in Bernard Harbour pretty well all my young life. And in wintertime we went to Read Island [Kikiktanayok] on Victoria Island and out on the sea ice. My father and grandparents harvesting seals, and that's what we survived on. Basically it's a supply of fish and seal in the winter. And they did harvest some caribou in the summertime.

So I grew up at Bernard Harbour until I was five or six, then they sent me off to residential school in Inuvik. That was really, really traumatizing for me personally, being the only person on the plane. My father was working on the DEW Line at the time, a place called Camp 5, and they put me on a plane to come to Cambridge Bay. And I was the only passenger on that big airplane. And then we picked up other students and went on to residential school at Inuvik. And that's a part of my life that really, really discouraged me, was that residential school. In the sense that there were so many things that happened in that school in a negative way to myself and my colleagues. And, being all alone without parents and people we're close to. We just accepted everything that they did, they said, and ordered us to do. We had no choice.

I went to school in Inuvik until my parents settled here in Cambridge Bay in 1966. I finished off what little school I had. They had to grade 8 here in Cambridge Bay. I completed that, grade 8, then I tried going south for further education. But I couldn't stand being in the hostel. My roots were on the land. I grew up on the land. And being in school was a struggle for me and my siblings. We were used to living on the land and surviving on the land. School, I just couldn't handle it. So I gave up after a couple months. Came back home and started work and started purchasing my own equipment.

And we moved on. Our father started work on the DEW Line and we started seeing modern life in the city or in the towns. We called them cities at the time cause there was more than ten people in one place. And life went on. We started seeing snowmobiles. Everybody in town had dog teams when we settled here. Very few snowmobiles, but dog teams helped us over the wintertime, at least to Christmas. Then we started seeing things like bikes [all-terrain vehicles; ATVs] and snowmobiles, and outboard motors, motorized tools to get around in. Then the people traded their dog teams for snowmobiles. The older people didn't change. They were stubborn. They drove their dog teams until they couldn't go anymore. The younger people, my father included, he started buying snowmobiles. Buying ATVs or three-wheelers in the summertime. A dirt bike was one of the first things we ever bought, two-wheelers. A little 3-horsepower outboard motor for the boat. Went from 3-horse to 18-horse to 30-horse and so on as the years progressed. And those changes were really an eye opener from living alone with no equipment to seeing these changes in our people.

I met my wife Mabel in 1969 (Figure 2.2). She was going out to school in another place, Fort Simpson, and then she came here. She moved into a hostel here in town and went to school and that's when we met. We got close and dated and then we got married. Really short, about five or six months from the time that we met that we became mister and missus. It was 1974 when we got married.

Grandmother and the Teachings of Previous Generations

One of the people that really stuck out in my young days was my maternal grandmother. Her name was Nellie Akana and I was really close to her and

Figure 2.2 Mabel and George Angohiatok.

used to spend a lot of time with her. My father would be out a lot with my grandfather, and my siblings were too small to understand what my Granny was trying to teach me at the time, they were just little kids. But when they left, and now I'm talking about in summertime, to go out seal hunting or caribou hunting, she was always busy. She was never idle and she always had a story. And I loved to be with her just because of that. I loved to hear the stories. I was always curious about how she grew up and where she grew up. And you could see it in her eyes when I asked her, when I questioned her. How did you grow up when you were my size? And she explained to me a lot of it was the same as it was when she was telling me the story.

But the hunting was different. There were different animals that they depended on. And she explained at length so many different times that the animals we see aren't going to be around forever. And she's the first person that I learned that from – about the caribou. She spoke of the muskox because we had never seen any. We had seen a lot of caribou but we had never ever seen muskox. So I was curious to what she meant by *umingmak* [muskox]. Umingmak means the 'bearded one'. She said it was much bigger than a caribou. Standing about the same size as a polar bear, on four feet. I first saw one when I was about five or six. I remember running back to the camp and telling my grandmother that I had just seen the devil, which is what it seemed like to me at the time. She asked me to describe what I had seen and then she quickly realized that I had just seen my first muskox. And she always had that little look in her eyes, that little smile. Brings a tear to my eye when I remember her. She, she was really caring and she really wanted to pass on what she knew. That was evident from day one. When my father, my mother, grandfather, couldn't do anything when they were out trying to get food for us so we could survive and my mother was looking after my siblings. So, a lot of free time with my grandmother and I treasured those moments.

I learned a lot about life from my grandmother. Story time in the winter, and story time in the iglu, was different than the summertime stories that she told because in the wintertime it was all of us in the iglu, everybody there. But in the summertime it was just her and me, and she would never stop talking. She was always explaining something. And if I questioned her about anything, she would spend a lot of time explaining. I miss her. I can hear her voice as I'm speaking, see her face, her smile. And all this was in our language, in her native language. She couldn't speak a word of English. Maybe she would say no or yes, that was about it, not being educated in the modern day. But very evident that she was a natural survivor on the land. And she knew and understood. And she passed on what she knew. That was special to me.

And having my own grandchildren growing up today, and trying to share with them what I know and what Mabel knows. Being in a community. It's painful too, to think back about different family members and what they meant and the teaching and what they taught me. But from my grandmother's mouth, most of what I know today was by word of mouth from her, all the physical aspects of doing things like how to harvest an animal was the man's side, of course, and I learned that, I picked that up as I grew. But I learned what to expect from my grandmother's words. The first time you harvest an animal, she explained, you're going to be shaky, and that's what we call buck fever. And she was right. When I harvested my first animal, a caribou, I was shaking like a leaf, excited. And I couldn't understand why

I was shaking. She told me it's excitement, the adrenaline. There's no word for adrenaline, in our language, but she explained it. Every child goes through that state when they harvest their first animal. It's just a natural part of life and the body reacts it seems for most people that do this for the first time and, yeah, I love my grandmother and I miss her.

The Changing Environment

Bryan and Ian appreciate George's observations that the colour palette of the Arctic environment has changed in George's lifetime. Speaking about his early life at Cambridge Bay, George says back then, in the early days when we first start spending summers here, the summers were very cold. A hot day would be 8 degrees, 10 degrees Celsius. That was a really hot day. You would average maybe 2 to 3 degrees every day. All summer. We never ever got rain. You never saw rain. The ground was all brown, dull. No vegetation. Now, you see willows everywhere. There was no such thing. There was some heather, very small growth. Roots, there were some roots we ate on the island. They were edible, very little colour, really cold.[1]

The memories continue, and George turns to sea ice, and his words echo the concerns of Arctic scientists.[2] The sea ice would form in early October and I could cross the strait to the mainland by 10th of October, 15th of October, on average during the year and that was earliest I could get across. And then summer, summer was short. The sea ice would hang around and not go. Some years it wouldn't all go, with that really low 2 degrees, 5 degrees, all summer. No rain. We couldn't travel by sea until the end of August. When the commercial fishing became a big thing in the early days, trying to reach the commercial fishing site through the ice was a bit tricky. A lot of times, quite a few years, we never made it to the site from ice, too much ice. So ice stayed around till the end of August and a few times the pack ice from the north would come right in and just fill the whole strait with multi-year ice, so the season was really short for boating.

And then you started noticing over the years that the temperatures started coming up. In our early marriage life, probably about five years into our marriage, it really warmed up. I tried to go swimming at the river. It was probably a 15 degree day, but it seemed so hot. The water was cold, really cold. Then we saw [. . .] more heat, more sun, earlier spring. Spring was a lot

1 See also ReelYouth, "Tundra Buster".   2 Perovich et al., "Sea Ice".

earlier than in my younger life. We'd do our fishing well into July. We were still on the ice, snowmobiling on the ocean in July. We had ice safe enough to get around. You could go Wellington Bay or Anderson Bay, across Coronation Gulf, on the ice. My birthday is 14th of July so I always use that date, measuring how far the ice is from the shore on the ocean. You know that date in the middle of July. In the early days, it will still be right fast to the land. And then as the years progressed, the ice got a little further by that time. The ice started floating a little earlier every year. And we started getting 15, 20 degree days and we started getting rain and the heat. Holy cow, it became a different place. So that change in temperature. Our boating time became stretched, got longer.

We found less need for long clothing. In the early days you needed a parka all the time. You always needed it, an extra large parka. All summer. We wore them all summer. Two to five degrees. And then I would say 1980 we started seeing the need for less clothing in the wintertime. It started warming up. Getting warmer earlier and warmer temperatures. By the time the 1990s came around, Mabel and I lived in town and we'd look back at the community. We'd go, 'Holy crap, look, we have colour', just the vegetation. We could see green. From a distance you could see that change was really visible. From 1960s to 1980s, first like night and day now. From cool summers, 2 to 5 degrees, to summers that now, are in excess of 20 degrees even 30 degrees a few times.

Ian asks about the relationship between traditional knowledge and science and George does not miss a beat. Well, my people are people, people that lived in north, they weren't educated in modern-day-like civilization. No education on numbers and all the things they teach in school. But their education is on survival skills. On the land. Staying alive is what I'm trying to get at. And that's what they organized their life around, living day-to-day and preparing for tomorrow. I enjoy it every time I'm out on the land. When I go out too, it's not always a goal to harvest something. I go out to see, to watch, and to see how the animals are doing, how the land is doing. And I try and detect any changes that are out there. And sharing that information with my fellow hunters and they share their experiences with me, I share with them where the animals are so we've got a better chance of successful harvest. Just to be out there. Recording either in my mind or more recently with a camera the changes that I see, whether negative or positive. There's a lot of both going on right now, negative and positive things. Positive things that I see are there are a few more people and a few more faces. Faces that I see out there that I've never seen before. And it's young people and that makes me feel proud. You know, I'll shake hands. Welcome to my lifestyle!

Watching Animals

Building on our interest in the relationship between biology and Inuit *Qaujimajatuqangit* (pronounced "caaw-ee-mah-ye-too-khang-eet"; also IQ or Inuit Knowledge),[3] George draws on his skills as a hunter and talks passionately about the role of animals in his life. Bryan asks about polar bears and the role of rifles. George responds, quick to share the importance of updated technology.[4]

Oh yeah, with rifles it was like night and day when we went to hunt polar bears. Not all hunts were successful without the rifle. Some of the bears are quicker. Some people do get injured. A few casualties that I know of. My grandfather ended up being dragged around by a polar bear. When they're on foot they follow the tracks. We had runners back then that like a marathon runner can run many miles tirelessly, and my grandfather was like that. He could run. He caught up to the bear and tried to keep it from getting into the rough ice. Rough ice is hard to run on for humans. Bears have no problem. They can jump from ice block to ice block. But, he tried to cut it off getting onto the big ice, the rough ice pack, and the bear got him. Grabbed his leg and you could see the four holes on his leg. He said it dragged him around for maybe a mile, mile and a half? And that's all it did. Bit him and just dragged him, dragged him around. And by then, the rest of the hunting crew caught up so he was safe. Big hole in his pants. His leg was bleeding badly from the four canine holes. Later on and at night time I spent a lot of time too looking at his leg. You could stick a finger inside the holes. You could see they were really deep, indented, all the holes on his leg. I'd sit there playing with them and make him explain to me how he got it again. And so, yeah, knowing the posture of the bear, understanding what the bear is going to do, and only armed with knives and lances. You know it just amazes me when I listen to their stories. You wouldn't have to be a part of the hunt, but when they explained it and what they did, it makes me shake and shiver! They would talk about where they hunt the polar bears. They always had a keen interest in getting that first bear. And I got my first bear with a rifle and I wouldn't even think about going up to one on foot without a rifle.

3 Karetak et al., eds., *Inuit Qaujimajatuqangit*; Wenzel, "From TEK to IQ", 238–250.
4 CBC News, "Inuit Hunters".

Or, wolves, yeah, when the wolfpack really started booming, really growing and, and people like myself being a harvester, we targeted the wolf for income. And a lot of wolves we started to see. When the caribou population came back, the muskox population boomed. We really started seeing lots of wolf. Big wolves, I mean all of them, all of them were huge. Even the orange coloured ones [a mixed breed with an escaped sled dog]. Big, big wolves, so when we see those we always went after the whitest, the biggest, the alphas, and we got more money for the big wolf. And, from the very first day, my grandparents were still alive, I started harvesting the big wolves. Big pack leaders, the alpha male and female, and they would ask where I got it. 'You see anymore?' I told them, 'Yeah, biggest pack I'd ever seen, twenty wolves.' Managed to get the biggest ones. Passed by the small ones or the slow ones and go to the fast white ones.

And my grandfather would explain that wolves are just like a pack of dogs. The alphas were the only ones that would mate in a pack. If you take an alpha male or female away, it will break that pack up. They have no more leaders. They have no main babymakers, so that pack most times will split into ten or more different pairs. Those pairs will start to breed and then they start bringing up their pups and the smaller animals will bring up smaller pups. And it is now very evident, anywhere on the island we see dog-sized wolves. You know, small. But they're still wolves, still predators, and very effective predators even though they're smaller. So yeah, when you take away the alphas of a big pack, that pack will break apart and they'll start their own families. So instead of just one pair breeding, you'll get a really big boom of wolf pups from all those females from different mates. So we had a really big boom of wolves, twenty years ago must be, just so many. I mean you'd be coming by in town and I'd be hunting wolves at the river in the dark. I'd be hunting wolves just across the bay. You'd get a call from a friend or family saying 'You still at work?' and I'm watching couple of wolves on the ice. You know, so many of them and smaller. I mean the colours all vary, but you start to notice that. You still get the odd ones that are big, big timber wolf, but very few of those now. Majority are about half the size of the big wolf.

Everything that's up here goes in cycles. At a certain point in time, animals will produce thousands of offspring. When those numbers get too big the explanation was that they move off. Some will starve, some will fall prey to predators. And the people on the land understood that – I'll use lemmings as an example for foxes and owls. On a good year when there's really lots of lemmings, the fox population booms. So it's similar with big prey like caribou and muskox and you get a pack of wolves. If there's no food, they'll hold their breeding down because they know that the little food they have is just enough for them to survive. So, when you get a boom, caribou and muskox, then they go, yeah, let's make some babies. So they do it and you see everything at that point in time, the numbers are just incredible. Numbers of muskox, number of caribou, number of predators at their peak for a few years. And then you start to see the decline and you know what's going to happen. It's been explained to me by my people. The animals come and go.

The government people understand that it's a cycle too, but still they make a great big deal about having to shut off hunters from harvesting the caribou. It's not our fault if the numbers come and go. It's something that Mother Nature does on her own. I've explained that so many times at the meetings with the government people, with the higher ups that make the decisions as to whether they should cease hunting altogether. And I've tried to help them understand. I've explained this is part of the cycle. Right now we're enjoying hundreds of them, thousands. Tomorrow they'll be gone. They didn't understand that. I mean, you could have a person working in here, wildlife, for next number of years and they do understand it. But then somebody else takes over and that knowledge is gone when somebody else takes over, so you have to explain it again.

Today the government is all gung ho about shutting down the hunting. And you know I'm trying to explain it. Humans are not the main impact on the caribou. They don't impose an impact where the caribou are going to die off. Two hundred caribou a year average for Cambridge Bay is not going to have any direct impact on the herd. But, see a pack of 100 wolves, each wolf, one wolf will take 30 caribou maybe, 30 to 40 caribou for that one wolf. Multiply that by 500 wolves on the island. That's a lot of caribou. I mean, you look at those numbers. And then we witnessed over the years at their peak, we've seen hundreds and hundreds of baby calves, caribou, killed in the spring. A lot of them eaten, a lot of them just killed. And then in the fall time, after the rut, the bull caribou expend all that they have into making sure that they breed with the females and sire their offspring. Their main goal is to make a baby, nothing else. They fight with each other. They don't eat for a month, so, and the wolves? The wolves are teaching their offspring, their babies, how to make a kill. And the male, bull caribou, even for his size, his size, doesn't matter to a wolf. I understand that to most predators size doesn't really matter. They'll kill anything. So, when they get all those caribou in the fall time, it's easy prey, I've seen that. I've witnessed that.

Societal Change

A careful observer of the natural environment, George is also highly attuned to the changing Arctic social environment. The interconnections between the natural and the social – with land at the centre – are striking.

When you look at society, remarks George, it's like night and day from my childhood days to today. In the early days you didn't have to know a person to help them. You recognize that look of hunger, that look of fear, and you help them. That's what we did. That's what we learned to do. Today, same thing. You see people hungry. You see people with no clothes, no bed. But nobody will lend a hand. I mean it's so different now. Greed, greed has set in. You know, on the land money means nothing.[5] On the land, your survival skills determine how good or how well your family and you do. But in a society like this, I get choked up thinking about it.

And then you get modern society. Today's just the most uncaring people. I mean I watch people struggle outside. People drive by. They don't care. There's no concern for fellow humans anymore today. No, fifty years ago, you didn't have to know somebody, you just recognized that they were in need. And you acted. That part is painful. I mean it hurts me today to see the people suffering like that. People with no food. People with no house. People with no families. In my day, people with no families that lost their families – man, we took people like that in that we didn't know. When we moved in town, we had a little matchbox house. There was eleven of us in that little matchbox house. It's a 12 by 20 foot house. Eleven people in there. And, distant relatives from the land came. They were living in iglus. We made room for them so they could go inside our house. And their distant relatives. You don't see that anymore today, I mean, you could knock on a door and nobody will answer the door. I mean it's night and day.[6]

The powerful observations, emotional and raw, hit Bryan, who pauses. George continues. Hard, society, I could see the change from living my lifestyle, caring, caring for people I don't know. It's painful. Family members moving away. And, even in our early days, even when you were away from your family, when you get back, you're a close knit family. And today I see a lot of the families are no longer families. They're apart. Same mother and father with another sibling but like two different worlds. In a modern society.

---

5 See also Wenzel, "Inuit Culture".
6 On the impact of permanent houses on Inuit identity, see Graburn, "Culture as Narrative". On the 'unannounced entrance' as a marker of trust and community, see Kulchyski, "Six Gestures".

A society that only looks after number one. Me, I get worked up, I feel the pain.

From 'Nothing Modern' to Town Life

George sees that the land-based skills are disappearing in the current generation. He reflects on way-finding and the importance of a sense of direction. George says:

I never got lost! I mean, people were always going great distances, but you never heard of anybody getting lost in those old days. Today you hear people getting lost all the time. I mean, it's one thing that when I started on my solo trips. After all the teaching, my father, grandfather, grandparents, everything that they taught me, I put into effect. And before I made that first solo trip, my father would jump on the *kamotik* [sled], and I would drive and he wanted to see. He wouldn't tell me which way to go, just tell me one day he might say go to this lake over that way and we'll go do some fishing. OK, I'd take him there, and take him back. Once he was satisfied I could get around without him, then I was free to roam. And you don't see that today, I was a twelve-year-old kid that started solo trips on my own.

Bryan weighs in, with his own understanding of life on the land. Nowadays, says Bryan, everybody is more reliant on GPSes. George responds. I mean there's people that don't know, you know. They get lost so easy, really poor sense of direction. And my grandkids are prime example of being able to know where you are. Brody [George's six-year-old grandson], oh my God, we go hundreds of miles stop. And just for the hell of it, I say ah, I'm gonna go home maybe tomorrow, maybe that way. He looks at me: 'Papa that's not home, home is that way.' He has a really, really good sense of direction. It's just the fact that nobody goes out anymore. I mean anything you do, from a very young age, you could do that, eh? You know, practice makes perfect and the thing is understanding. You have to understand what you are doing. And today, we are scared to see young people go out on their own you know. They don't know traditional navigation, they only know how to use that . . . GPS!

Despite his preference for traditional navigation techniques, George is often quick to embrace new technologies. He adds new items to his toolkit while adhering to the environmental principles with which he was raised. George likes to talk about the differences between old and new, and the nostalgia and admiration for his ancestors and teachers is audible. So in the early days, George says, we had nothing modern, nothing from modern civilization. It was just ourselves. What my parents and grandparents made with their bare hands, the tools that they needed to survive. And that's how it started. Simple things that you take for granted every day like toilet tissue. Things like that. How we wiped our butts. You know, in wintertime we used snow. In summertime, rocks or moss. It was all natural style of living. We depended on the land to sustain us for food and shelter. Everything we took from the land. Our shelter was made from snow in the wintertime to skin in the summer in the form of sealskin tent or caribou-skin tent, our sleds, and boats. And we'd never seen any manmade, modern-style things that we see today until the DEW Line was erected at Bernard Harbour. And that's when we started seeing equipment, big equipment and airplanes. We'd seen a few movies on the projector screen, picture screen there. And that was all new to us. In summer, my father would be using oars to get around on the water. We never owned outboard motors of any kind. No snowmobile. So travel around in the summertime was very slow. Oars and a little sail made up in a homemade *umiak*, we call them. Skin boats. There were no rifles. Nothing modern at the time. I remember there was absolutely nothing like we have today. So the hunting methods were really different. Especially when you start hunting the predators, the big predators like the polar bear without a rifle.

George continues, thinking about the changes to living conditions. There were people all over, away from town. Wellington Bay was one community (Figure 2.1). There was about, I would say, five to ten families there all year. And then you have Palik [Surrey River] just across. Everybody from the Perry Island side [Enakhakvik] moved across there. And in the wintertime when we went around with the dog team at first and skidoos later, we always ran into people out on the sea ice. There were always iglus and families living on the sea ice harvesting seals. And then when we go inland there'd be families at Ferguson Lake. I'd say there was about four different families along Ferguson Lake until you got to Wellington Bay. Wellington Bay was like a big busy place all the time. A lot of people. Almost as big as Cambridge Bay back then in the early days for numbers of people.

Then people started moving into town. They found out they don't have to freeze outside in the wintertime. They can stay in a comfortable matchbox house with an oil stove. When you were out there, there was no Coleman stove, no lanterns, there was just seal oil lamps. So people saw it as an easier life in town. It was easier!

And that created a lot of different hardships. People came in and didn't want to work when they moved in town. So, Social Services, or whatever it was called back then, it wasn't called Social Services, helping people that can't work and make their own money. So the town grew. Within about two years, it went from about 150 people to 400 people in town. Everybody was coming into town from the outskirts, settling in, warmer. Life was stable. You didn't risk your life out on the land.

But not everybody was able to work. So a lot of the people still depended on the land. There became a lot of people that trapped, usually foxes and seals that had fur, you know. Wolf and polar bear, as income. Trading power, I guess you'd call it. Back then they did a lot of trading. Go and bring that fur to the store and you wanted a rifle, you stacked up the fur until it was the same height of the rifle. The rifle was yours. Or anything that you wanted. That was their way of doing it back then, pile up the furs, same height as what you want to buy. The town was all about numbers . . . money! Money started floating around and it was just paper and to a lot of us it meant nothing. We didn't understand what money meant until you started needing to get gas and get equipment. And then you started to understand, yeah you've got to work to make some money to buy your rifle and ammo and survive. So in that short time our lifestyle changed from life on the land, peaceful and in harmony with nature, to living in a community where a lot of times I didn't know if we were going to survive the week.

But people started getting rifles. It became easier for them to harvest big game or any game for that matter, with a rifle. A little .22 calibre. The .22 short bullet was a lot more accurate and longer range than a traditional bow or lance. So, a little .22 did a lot back then. They would harvest muskox without putting their lives in jeopardy, or polar bears, the big game. A lot of those changes when I was growing were exciting. Exciting in the sense that we could get around quicker. I fell in love with the snowmobile in my young days. I was driving them hard. They were little 6- and 8-horsepower, single-cylinders. And in my young days when I'd go flat out I was maybe going 15 miles an hour, 20 miles an hour with an 18-horse. Just adapted from dog team to snowmobile and homemade sealskin, fish sleds to a wooden *kamotik* with steel runners. The runners back then were just soil coated over with water to freeze and have a smooth running surface. And that type of sled always demanded attention. It broke. If it hit a piece of ice, if it hit a rock. It would chip the running surface and make it really heavy. Unload the little sleigh. Tip it over and repair the sleigh and continue. And in the modern style you build a wooden *kamotik* and they were a lot bigger and longer with steel runners and you never have to do any repairs to the steel runners, but the towing part of it, you notice, would be a lot heavier than dragging the sealskin fish sleigh. They lasted a long time. You could use them for years compared to a sled you could pull apart and eat, winter to summer.

All those changes were pretty exciting for myself and my siblings as we learned to adapt our lifestyle with that change of getting around really quick and being able to, being able to harvest animals from long distance with the rifles. That was really exciting. The only thing about that was you needed money. It cost money to buy a snowmobile. It cost money to buy a sled. A rifle cost money. Everything cost money, so you noticed the change from my father being gung ho on going out and harvesting food to survive. We shifted from that, from the need to get out and survive, to going to work, bring in money to purchase modern-style food and modern-style equipment like the rifle and snowmobiles and boats and ATVs. And without that money you couldn't buy those. A lot of the old-timers I know were just trying to discourage us to use the modern stuff. And we'd seen it too when you go a long ways, you breakdown. You know, it's a long walk back. The dog teams never broke down.

I remember my father's first outboard motor was a little, something like a 3-horse. A really small motor. And it didn't cost an arm and a leg. It was like $100. But $100 back in that day was like thousands today. And I made a point that a snowmobile only lasted a season at best, so every year I continued working and I met up with Mabel later on in my life and then we started a family. Settled here in Cambridge Bay with her, got our own place. Had our own children. Then the phones came in the community. They were 'party lines'. When somebody dialed somebody's number, everybody's phone would ring. But you get a certain tone that you know it's yours. So you pick up the phone and you could hear people all the time. Party line, eh.

And that's what's missing nowadays, that need to ensure the safety and health of your fellow humans. The people that you share the land with. All of that is gone now. Just only a few people that I see nowadays, like myself, help the people. Help the needy. Now everybody's just only concentrating on what is mine. I gotta look after my family. I can't lend you my boat because my family needs it. Back then, it didn't matter who, if somebody was going out hunting, they let you know. You're welcome to go along and hop on the boat or hop on the *kamotik*. And that's so different today. You don't hear people nowadays saying 'I'm going out. You want to come?' Now, just 'I'm going out. I'm going to be out for so long and I don't need anybody to help me. I'm going alone.' I might have my friend with me, but ... see the changes, the negative part of today and yesterday. Just the people's willingness to interact with each other. That's missing today. Unless it's your immediate family or close friends, you don't get that kind of help there any more, you know. Even people that you don't really know or don't get along with all the time. They need help, you help them. Today you see people struggling to do something and just watch, you won't even lift a hand to help. That's a difference I see. Today's society compared to the early days. We went from caring people, from caring about everyone and everyone's needs, your needs included, to today it is maybe just your immediate family and that's all you help, your really close friends. That's the only people. And that's the really sad part of it. The change from caring.

My people were brought up on land. Caring. Loving. Enter society, modern society, and just become a totally different nation. Uncaring. Unforgiving. That hurts. Damn that hurts big time. But even without the education that modern society has today, you know, our generations from the past understood and lived the laws of the land. That's why we're here today.

Residential Schools and Alcohol

George attended residential school in Inuvik and, like so many Inuit, the experience was devastating.[7] I know that had I not gone to residential school, says George, I would be a totally different person. I guarantee that. It messed up my life big time, my train of thought. Imprinted really negative things in my lifetime, in my early life, in a negative way, residential school. Sometimes I ponder and think about what would have been had we not been sent to residential school. Over my lifetime it has affected me in a negative way all the time, always negative, and the things that happened in there made me who I became as an adult. And that happened to a lot of colleagues that ended up in the same situation. My wife Mabel was one of them too. She went to residential school, but she never experienced what I went through, and I'm not going to put in detail what happened in school. That is something that really upsets me even today.

George also points to alcohol as a catalyst for the challenges faced by Inuit. Weekends were the scariest times, he says. One really bad thing when growing up throughout the whole north I guess, probably in the world too

---

7 Truth and Reconciliation Commission, *Inuit and Northern Experience*.

for that matter, was alcohol and the effects of alcohol on people and communities that had no education around the effects of over-drinking. There was no education around what's going to happen if you keep drinking. Nobody was warned. Nobody was taught. They just got the alcohol and of course our generation, our people back then got hooked on it. Not everybody mind you, but the majority of the northerners got hooked on alcohol. That was really, really hard. I was the eldest of five of us so at six years old I was a mother, a father. I fed, clothed, washed, bathed, looked after my siblings at a very young age because there was nobody to do it. Everybody was drunk.

Weekends. They worked on weekdays but come weekends, that was the worse time. We hated the weekends. You know, it's supposed to be family time. Get out with the family. My father quit going out. For a long time he would binge drink. Those were very upsetting times for me and my siblings. I would ask my grandparents, 'How come my father's doing this?' And they'd have no explanation. They couldn't tell me. So, that was a really negative part of my life. Being neglected. Growing up on our own, basically, on the weekends. And that was the whole community pretty well that did this thing. Everybody drank. The whole town drank. Lots and lots of kids sitting together in one place or another. Just to get away from drunkards. There wasn't a lot of police like the RCMP.

So, it's affected me my whole life, alcohol. And up until a few years ago, when I finally gave it up, my wife gave me an ultimatum. She said, 'Alcohol or your family. It's your choice.' So thank goodness I made the right choice.

Share Everything

George is an optimistic and hopeful person. He acknowledges change and usually embraces it. As he tells Bryan, so many really big changes in our world. You see the change in people too. In the early days, the people, because we were nomadic, when you met another family, man it was joyful to meet with people. Share your hunting stories. Share your life story. Share everything. Share the food. If people were having a hard time, they were never left unattended. People looked after people. I mean it was a caring nation. Nobody was left out to freeze or starve, you know. If somebody had no home, there was always somebody who took them in. Like you're sitting in a house, eleven people in a little tiny matchbox. And we'd still let other people in. Because it was so much bigger than the iglu and skin tents.

George has a specific message for young people, too. Young people, like I said, people are all different. They're like snowflakes. No two people are the same. There's a lot of both negative and positive feelings that I see in this and again the cold being a big factor in some of their decisions as to what they are going to decide, how they're going to be up here. So, again, a word of encouragement to them to try it. Don't shake it until you try it. Unless you experience a little portion of my lifestyle, you know only yours.

Persistence, Resilience, and Change

George Angohiatok's interest in history and culture revolves around an ongoing commitment to land-based harvesting and the resilience of Inuit traditions in a changing world. Culturally, George is Copper Inuit, a widely used ethnonym for the Inuit of the central Canadian Arctic and based on the use of local copper in tools.[8] The history of Indigenous peoples on Kiilliniq [Victoria Island] is well-documented by Inuit oral history as well as by archaeologists and anthropologists. The Kitikmeot Heritage Society has written about ancient caribou hunting and char fishing practices by Inuit and their predecessors going back 4,000 years near Ekaluktutiak [Cambridge Bay]. Richard Condon and the Elders at Ulukhaktok note that the Copper Inuit were 'among the very the last Canadian Inuit groups to be contacted by the outside world'.[9] Encounters with explorers, back to the mid-nineteenth century, are etched in the oral history of Ulukhaktok Elders, immediate neighbours of Inuit at Kugluktuk and Ekaluktutiak. The ancestors guided and supported the exploring expeditions.

George describes the more recent history of this region, post-dating the trading post era and emphasizing the construction of the DEW Line, a project on which his father worked, and the impact of residential schools.[10] DEW Line construction began in the mid-1950s as part of Canada's commitment to the protection of North America during the Cold War. The timing of DEW Line construction corresponds with increasing consolidation of Inuit at Ekaluktutiak. Beyond the work provided by the construction and maintenance of the DEW Line, Damas suggests that declining numbers of caribou and a similar decline in the fur trade contributed to the growing community at Ekaluktutiak. Damas describes Ekaluktutiak in terms that evoke George's descriptions of matchbox houses:

> In the beginning housing was comprised mainly of shacks constructed from scrap lumber from dumps of DEW-line sites, but by 1965 nearly all Copper

---

8 Condon et al., *Northern Copper Inuit*; Damas, "Copper Eskimo".
9 See Condon et al., *Northern Copper Inuit*, 22.
10 See Condon et al., *Northern Copper Inuit*, 128–129.

2 An Inuit Perspective on Changing Environments

Eskimo who were living in the centralized communities had been supplied with insulated, oil-heated, frame houses by the government.[11]

George moved to Ekaluktutiak with his family in 1966.

George attended residential school in Inuvik. There were two large hostels there, Grollier Hall (Catholic) and Stringer Hall (Anglican), to which children were brought from many parts of the western Arctic. The system of large hostels was established by 1961, although smaller hostels and residentials schools go back to the late nineteenth century.[12] While George does not identify which school he attended, his disdain for his experiences at the school is palpable. As summarized in the Truth and Reconciliation Commission of Canada's report into residential schools:

> The [Arctic] hostels replicated the problems that had characterized the residential school system in southern Canada. They were large, regimented institutions, run by missionaries whose primary concern was winning and keeping religious converts. They employed a curriculum that was culturally and geographically inappropriate. While a number of schools developed admirable reputations, most students did not do well academically. Sexual abuse was a serious problem in a number of these institutions. The abuse was coupled with a failure on the part of the government and the residence administrations to properly investigate and prosecute it. Institutional interests were placed before those of the children.[13]

In his story, George highlights residential schooling as a major, negative force in his life. He also points briefly to the negative effects of alcohol and the cruelties of outsiders who sought the removal of Inuit from the land. Always the optimist, however, George offers that an enduring commitment to the land was his antidote for the misery associated with the worst of the newcomers to the north.

This chapter extends a long tradition of Inuit sharing life histories and making recordings of them. Rasmussen documented Inuit life stories in the contact era.[14] More recent scholarly and local efforts to document the experiences of Inuit Elders come from Wachowich, and MacDonald and Wachowich, working under the auspices of the Igloolik Oral History Project.[15] The Kitikmeot Heritage Society has also documented

---

11 Damas, "Copper Eskimo", 409.
12 Truth and Reconciliation Commission, *Inuit and Northern Experience*, 3.
13 Truth and Reconciliation Commission, *Inuit and Northern Experience*, 101.
14 Brumble, *Annotated Bibliography*.
15 Wachowich, *Saqiyuq*; MacDonald and Wachowich, *Hands' Measure*.

stories of Elders from the Kitikmeot region, which includes the areas central to George's life.[16] The motivation for this chapter comes from George himself. He is a noted storyteller who is known in the community and in the Canadian press for sharing his memories and his passion for the protection of animals and the physical environment. In doing so, he has encouraged northern and southern academics and scientists to piece his accounts together. A main function of CHARS in Ekaluktutiak [Cambridge Bay] is to facilitate this sharing of local knowledge as well as the co-development of new knowledge to help Inuit and Northerners to adapt to a changing climate. George plays a significant role in this work.

George's words convey the relationship between one's life story and environmental knowledge of the Arctic environment. The words bring together cultural history and environmental change. In doing so, they demonstrate the enduring value of local observations to scientific inquiry. Indeed, as Elders from the Kitikmeot region state: 'Inuit *Qaujimajatuqangit* [IQ] is . . . more than just knowledge [because it] includes a finely tuned awareness of the ever-changing relationship between Inuit and *nuna* (the land), *hila* (the weather), wildlife and the spiritual world.'[17] The Kitikmeot Elders continue in their discussion of IQ. They remind us that IQ is based on repeated and local observations. IQ is a multigenerational system of knowing about the work and is applicable to the changes observed in the physical and political environments.[18] Through George's eyes, our understanding of climate change, and its political and social consequences, is enhanced by the teachings of George's parents and grandparents, by intergenerational understanding and the wisdom George applies to those teachings for the future. George's sophisticated analysis of changing environments instructs us, as scientists and social scientists, to prioritize local observations over time. His accounts remind us of the parallels between assimilative social history and environmental degradation. Yet, in his optimistic way, George also helps us to see that with care, awareness, a willingness to share, and collaboration, the answers to the challenges to Inuit Culture and Arctic environments are not insurmountable.

By sharing his story, George draws important connections between the physical environment and the social environment. He reminds us that the two are intimately and inexorably linked, and that changes to the physical

---

16 Kitikmoet Heritage Society, *Iqaluktuurmiutat*.
17 Thorpe et al., *Thunder on the Tundra*, 4.   18 Thorpe et al., *Thunder on the Tundra*, 4–5.

environment – including the continuing effects of global climate change – have had troubling effects on Inuit. The land, the animals, and the people are indivisible in George's world despite the best efforts of visiting scientists and lingering government and industry officials from the South to divide the world into smaller and isolated chunks. As George notes, families separate into matchbox houses, greed sets in, and people are less likely to help each other. Money allows for continued access to the land and yet 'money means nothing on the land'.[19] But in these dire observations of social isolation and retreat from the places outside the hamlets are hopeful words. Young people are interested in Inuit land-based practices, George says. There are more people on the land than in recent generations. And in that renewed interest comes care and a resurgence of Inuit traditions and values. With that, there is hope that the northern regions of our planet are well-positioned to endure changes, too.

Bibliography

Brumble, H. D., III, *An Annotated Bibliography of American Indian and Eskimo Autobiographies* (Lincoln, NB: University of Nebraska Press, 1981).
CBC News, "Inuit Hunters Use New Radar Maps to Navigate Rough Ice", *CBC News* (14 February 2019), www.cbc.ca/news/canada/north/hunters-radar-maps-ice-navigation-1.5018722.
Condon, Richard G., Julia Ogina, and Holman Elders. *The Northern Copper Inuit: A History* (Norman, OK: University of Oklahoma Press, 1996).
Damas, David, "Copper Eskimo", in David Damas, ed., *Handbook of North American Indians*, Vol. 5: *Arctic* (Washington, DC: Smithsonian Institution Press, 1984), pp. 397–414.
Graburn, Nelson, "Culture as Narrative", in Pamela Stern and Lisa Stevenson, eds., *Critical Inuit Studies: An Anthology of Contemporary Arctic Ethnography* (Lincoln, NB: University of Nebraska Press, 2006), pp. 139–154.
Inuit Heritage Trust, Place Names Program: Traditional Place Names in the Kitikmeot (n.d.), http://ihti.ca/eng/place-names/pn-goog.html.
Karetak, Joe, Frank Tester, and Shiley Tagalik, *Inuit Qaujimajatuqangit: What Inuit Have Always Known to Be True* (Black Point, NS: Fernwood, 2017).
Kitikmoet Heritage Society, *Iqaluktuurmiutat: Life at Iqaluktuuq* (Cambridge Bay, NU: Kitikmoet Heritage Society, n.d.).
Kitikmeot Heritage Society, Kitikmeot Place Name Atlas (n.d.), https://atlas.kitikmeotheritage.ca/index.html (accessed 6 January 2021).
Kulchyski, Peter, "Six Gestures", in Pamela Stern and Lisa Stevenson, eds., *Critical Inuit Studies: An Anthology of Contemporary Arctic Ethnography* (Lincoln, NB: University of Nebraska Press, 2006), pp. 155–167.

19 Wenzel, "Inuit Culture", 50–51.

MacDonald, John and Nancy Wachowich, *The Hands' Measure: Essays Honouring Leah Aksaajuq Otak's Contribution to Arctic Science* (Iqaluit: Nunavut Arctic College Media, 2018).

Perovich, D., W. Meier, M. Tschudi, et al., "Sea Ice", in R. L. Thoman, J. Richter-Menge, and M. L. Druckenmiller, eds., *NOAA Arctic Report Card 2020* (2020), https://doi.org/10.25923/n170-9h57.

ReelYouth, "Tundra Buster: George Angohiatok (Pamiok)", Iqaluktuuttiaq (Cambridge Bay), Nunavut (ca. 2020), https://youtu.be/JOoAPzeR9qs (accessed 4 January 2021).

Thorpe, Natasha, Naikak Hakongak, Sandra Eyegetok, and Kitikmeot Elders, *Thunder on the Tundra: Inuit Qaujimajatuqangit of the Bathurst Caribou* (Ikaluktutiak, NU: Tuktu and Nogak Project/Generation Printing, 2001).

Truth and Reconciliation Commission of Canada, *Canada's Residential Schools*, Vol. 2: *The Inuit and Northern Experience. The Final Report of the Truth and Reconciliation Commission of Canada* (Winnipeg: Truth and Reconciliation Commission of Canada, 2015).

Wachowich, Nancy, *Saqiyuq: Stories from the Lives of Three Inuit Women* (Montreal: McGill-Queens University Press, 1999).

Wenzel, George W., "From TEK to IQ: Inuit *Qaujimajatuqangit* and Inuit Cultural Ecology", *Arctic Anthropology* 41 (2004): 238–250.

Wenzel, George W., "Inuit Culture: To Have and Have Not; or, Has Subsistence Become an Anachronism?", in Brian F. Codding and Karen L. Kramer, eds., *Why Forage? Hunters and Gatherers in the Twenty-First Century* (Albuquerque: University of New Mexico Press, 2016), pp. 43–54.

3

Evolution of the Antarctic Continent and Its Ice Sheet

MARTIN SIEGERT AND ANDREW FOUNTAIN

Introduction

Antarctica (Figure 3.1) is at the forefront of the climate change crisis. We know that it is an important player in global circulations of the atmosphere and the ocean, and that the gain/loss of ice on the continent exerts a major control on sea level. We are also aware that Antarctica has been pivotal in modulating past climate change and sea levels. This appreciation has only been achieved through scientific research over the past fifty years – a remarkable evolution in understanding, considering it was a remote and unknown continent in the early 1900s. Indeed, the first expeditions in which targeted scientific discovery was the sole focus date only to the late 1950s. Considering the rapid evolution in our understanding of Antarctica's ice sheet, and the continent on which it flows, it is worth taking time to review briefly how we arrived at this point. Geological field studies on the 2 per cent of ice-free area on the continent show that Antarctica was once part of the ancient Gondwana supercontinent that included South America, South Africa, India, and Australia. They also reveal how the development of the Antarctic ice sheet was influenced by the breakup of Gondwana and subsequent tectonic movement between 180 million and 35 million years ago, in conjunction with declining concentrations of atmospheric greenhouse gases. Over the past fifty years, through geophysical investigations, we have come to realize that this featureless, desolate ice mass is tattooed by dynamic and quickly accelerating processes that belie its apparently unchanging character. The flow and form of the Antarctic ice sheet is controlled to a large degree by its underlying geology, which will modulate how Antarctica responds to the warmth caused by continued emission of greenhouse gases. In this chapter, we provide a very brief history of Antarctic geoscience and, building on knowledge to date, point the way to future research goals that will lead to a better comprehension of Antarctic processes and change.

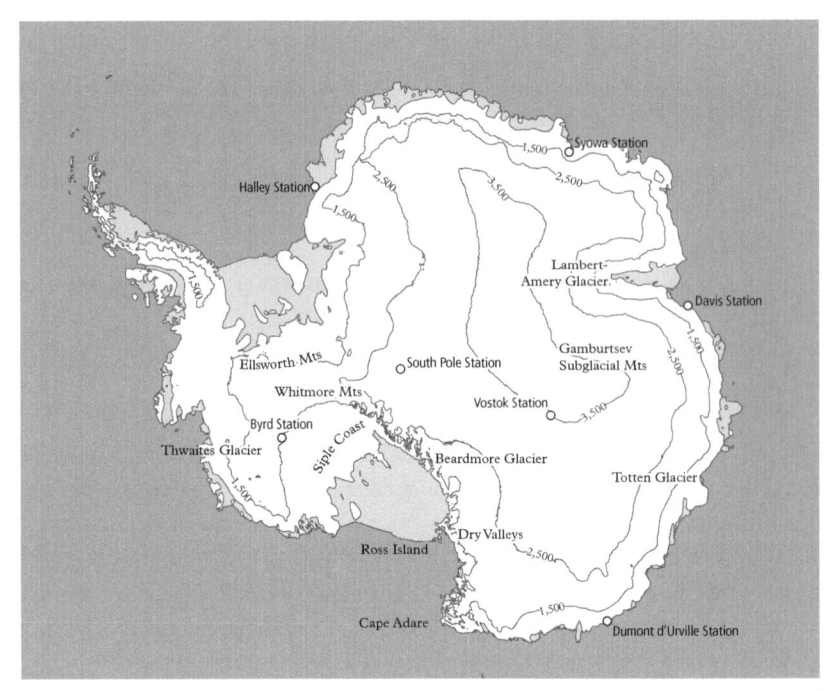

Figure 3.1 Location map and surface elevation of Antarctica with place names mentioned in the text. Contours are at 1,000 m intervals.

Early Ideas and Initial Exploration

The first known discovery of the Antarctic continent was in 1820/21 through three independent expeditions, led by Estonian and Russian naval officer Fabian von Bellingshausen; US sealer Nathaniel Palmer; and British sailors Edward Bransfield and William Smith.[1] The discovery was, like much in Antarctica, a consequence of technological advance, which in this case allowed ships to voyage south across the icy Southern Ocean in search of seals, whales, and other marine resources. Despite this discovery, the first documented and substantiated landing on Antarctica did not occur until 1895, when Norwegian Carsten Borchgrevink and New Zealander Alexander von Tunzelmann disembarked at Cape Adare, due south of New Zealand.[2] This event seems to have triggered a flurry of Antarctic expeditions, now known as the Heroic Age of Antarctic exploration. A mere six years later, the first serious attempt to reach the South Pole was organized: the 1901–04 *Discovery*

---

1 Headland, *Chronological List*.   2 Maddison, *Class and Colonialism*.

3 Evolution of Antarctic Continent and Ice Sheet

Expedition, led by Robert Falcon Scott with Edward Wilson and Ernest Shackleton.[3] Sailing about as far south as they could go in the Ross Sea, ~78° S, they dragged sleds across the Ross Ice Shelf, reaching 82° S, 724 km from the Pole. Three years later, Shackleton set off on the *Nimrod* Expedition (1907–09) and established a route to the Pole from the Ross Ice Shelf (at sea level) through the Transantarctic Mountains up on to the plateau of the ice sheet (at over 2,500m above sea level). He managed to trek to within 156 km of the South Pole before returning.[4] The South Pole was finally reached on 14 December 1911 by Roald Amundsen's Norwegian expedition, which had pioneered a new path to the plateau.[5] Scott's ill-fated *Terra Nova* campaign (1911–13) followed Shackleton's route and reached the South Pole 34 days after Amundsen, tragically perishing on the return journey.[6] Soon after, Douglas Mawson, who had earlier collaborated with Shackleton on the *Nimrod* Expedition, led a party under extreme conditions to explore the Antarctic coast south of Australia.[7] In 1914, Shackleton again headed for Antarctica, this time to be the first to traverse coast-to-coast across the continent. The Imperial Trans-Antarctic Expedition was ultimately unsuccessful owing to its ship, the *Endurance*, becoming locked into thick sea ice, which eventually sank it. Famously, Shackleton's team voyaged north to Elephant Island offshore of the extreme end of the Antarctic Peninsula, from which a small team sailed across the Southern Ocean in a small boat to South Georgia (where a whaling station existed), arranging a rescue mission to successfully recover the entire field party.[8] The rescue occurred in August 1916 and the world was at war. This was, as a consequence, the last of the major 'heroic' era campaigns.

Although the Heroic Age of exploration was characterized by attempts to reach the Pole, and advance into 'terra incognita', the numerous scientific discoveries, particularly by the British expeditions, laid the foundation for much of our scientific understanding in Antarctica. For example, Douglas Mawson, as part of Shackleton's *Nimrod* expedition, was the first to reach the geomagnetic South Pole in 1909. A few years later, Scott's *Terra Nova* expedition, in addition to the trek to the Pole, conducted field studies to describe the meteorology, marine and terrestrial biology, glaciology, and geology of Ross Island, the McMurdo Dry Valleys, and the Royal Society Range. Scott's *Terra Nova* party included two geologists, Frank Debenham and Raymond Priestley, and geographer T. Griffith Taylor. They conducted two geological field surveys to map the mountainous region on the western shore of

3 Wilson, *Diary of 'Discovery'*. 4 Riffenburgh, *'Nimrod'*.
5 Grochowicz, *Amundsen's Way*. 6 Ellis and Dell'Amore, *South Pole 1910–1913*.
7 Fitzsimons, *Mawson and Ice Men*. 8 Shackleton, *South!*.

McMurdo Sound (including the Dry Valleys) between January and March 1911, and then between November 1911 and February 2012. Even the ill-fated Scott party stopped to gather over 15 kg of fossils from upper Beardmore Glacier on their return through the Transantarctic Mountains.[9] That these samples were found with the bodies of the party is testament to the seriousness of Scott's attention to the wider scientific mission of the expedition. The fossils, including beech leaves from ~250 million years ago (Ma), were evidence of Antarctica's warm pre-glacial environment.

Years prior to these expeditions, and before any surface observations were made, James Croll – a self-taught Scottish mathematician and naturalist – made a remarkable theoretical prediction about the Antarctic ice sheet.[10] In 1879, having hypothesized that glaciers were able to flow, a controversial subject at that time, he produced the first numerical model of the ice sheet, in which he predicted the ice thickness at the centre of the continent to be between 4.6 km and 38 km, depending on the rheology (stiffness) of ice, which was unknown at the time.[11] The smaller estimate is relatively close to modern measurements of the thickest part of the ice sheet (4,897 m). As to the origin of the ice sheet, he earlier predicted that the Earth's orbital variations were responsible for pacing ice-age cycles[12] and made careful calculations of the variation of solar radiation over the last few hundred thousand years. His calculations were updated by Milutin Milankovitch in the mid-twentieth century,[13] forming the basis of our current understanding of long-term global climate change and ice-age cycles.[14]

The IGY and the Rise of Continental Measurements

Although science became an increasingly international endeavour after World War II, Antarctic science across the first half of the twentieth century was influenced by national efforts to establish sovereignty over the continent. From the 1920s to the 1940s, Britain (and the Commonwealth, including Australia and New Zealand), France, Norway, Germany, Chile, and Argentina each established claims.[15] World War II, the creation of the United Nations, and the International Geophysical Year (IGY) of 1957–58 changed this dynamic. Patterned on the first (1882–83) and second (1932–33) International Polar Years, which were mostly devoted to studies of the

---

9 Crane, *Scott of the Antarctic*. 10 Sugden, "James Croll (1821–1890)".
11 Croll, "On Thickness".   12 Croll, "On Physical Cause".
13 Milankovitch, "Kanon der Erdbestrahlung".
14 Berger, "Milankovitch Theory and Climate".   15 Howkins, "Frozen Empires".

3 Evolution of Antarctic Continent and Ice Sheet

Arctic,[16] the IGY (also known as the 3rd Polar Year)[17] coordinated scientists from sixty-seven countries and about 4,000 stations to study geophysical processes (e.g. ionosphere, earthquakes, ocean currents) worldwide. Antarctica was an important focus of the IGY because so little was known about its effects on atmospheric and oceanic circulation. IGY activities led to the establishment of new stations in Antarctica, increasing the number from twenty to forty-eight,[18] including permanent bases in the interior of East Antarctica (US South Pole Station and Russian Vostok Station) and at the coast (e.g. Japanese Syowa Station; Australian Davis Station; British Halley Station; and the French Dumont d'Urville Station). Although the IGY was a scientific enterprise, it had an important political dimension; only countries with robust economies and logistical capabilities could maintain a strong presence in Antarctica, and so Antarctic research became a hallmark of global power.

The IGY was notable for its use of overland traverses across the continent, plumbing the depth of the ice sheet using seismic geophysics, and taking atmospheric and stratospheric measurements, among other studies. Three major overland Antarctic expeditions traversed the continent: the Commonwealth Trans-Antarctic Expedition led by a joint British/New Zealand team; a US team that trekked across West Antarctica; and a Russian group that drove across East Antarctica. The seismic-sounding ice thickness profiles obtained were revolutionary, revealing that the ice is regularly thicker than 2.5 km and that in West Antarctica the ice is resting more than 2 km below sea level in places. Unknowingly, these results vindicated Croll's theoretical prediction.

Shortly after the IGY, the United States proposed that Antarctica be reserved for scientific, non-economic, activities, arguing that international access to all of Antarctica would serve the interests of science better than working within territorial sectors.[19] The result was the Antarctic Treaty, the object of which was to promote the peaceful use of Antarctica – military activity and atomic testing was banned, and internationally collaborative research promoted. The Treaty did not deprive any country of claims to territory but proposed a freezing of claims for the duration of the Treaty. The Scientific Committee on Antarctic Research (SCAR), the secretariat of which is based in the Scott Polar Research Institute (SPRI), Cambridge, UK, has advised the Treaty organization on scientific matters

---

16 Barr and Lüdecke, eds., *History of International Polar Years*.
17 Korsmo, "Genesis of International Geophysical Year".
18 Headland, "Antarctic Winter Stations". 19 Walton, *Antarctica*.

since its establishment. SCAR formed permanent working groups to deal with specific topics such as biology, geology, glaciology, geodesy, cartography, upper atmosphere physics, and solid earth geophysics.

Geology of Antarctica

Determining the geology of Antarctica is a daunting challenge considering that only about 2 per cent of the continent is ice-free.[20] This, with the obvious extreme conditions, has made scientific studies more difficult than in most other regions of the planet. However, Antarctic geological research also attracts great interest, partly because the continent is so poorly understood and also because of the mystique surrounding its exploration. Most of the expeditions prior to the IGY collected rocks, but this allowed for only a skeletal geologic understanding (see Anderson,[21] who provides an excellent review of early work). One expedition that focused on studying the geology of Antarctica was led by Douglas Mawson (the Australasian Antarctic Expedition, 1911–14), but the survey of the Antarctic Coast due south of Australia was beset with numerous problems, and the tragic loss of two of Mawson's field party (Belgrave Ninnis and Xavier Mertz).[22]

After World War II, British IGY explorations of the geology of the Antarctic Peninsula, combined with geologic surveys elsewhere including the McMurdo Dry Valleys and the Bunger and Vestfold Hills, led to a rudimentary depiction of Antarctic geology.[23] Later, when the continental drift of the southern continents was understood in terms of plate tectonics, the previously adjacent landmasses in Gondwanaland provided important geologic context for Antarctica. Antarctic geological investigations were challenging, pioneering, and fraught with dangers,[24] especially with the use of aircraft that provided access to remote locations.[25] Increased international cooperation, including through collaborative logistics, following the Antarctic Treaty, and improved technology for deep-field investigations, increased the access to exposed bedrock across the continent and reduced hazards. This allowed major collaborative international research programmes to take place that have accelerated our knowledge of Antarctica.

---

20 Drewry, *Antarctica*.   21 Anderson, "Bedrock Geology of Antarctica".
22 Riffenburgh, *Racing with Death*.   23 Fogg, *History of Antarctic Science*.
24 Behrendt, *Ninth Circle*.   25 Siegert, "Technology".

Summary of Antarctic Geology

As a consequence of twentieth-century field studies, which have sampled and analysed the bulk of exposed rocks, and more recent investigations that have used geophysical remote-sensing methods to infer structures beneath the ice, we now have a basic understanding of Antarctic geology. Summarizing from Jordan,[26] the oldest rocks in Antarctica are of Archaean age (>2.5 billion years (Ga)) and outcrop in a number of places such as Dronning Maud Land.[27] At this time much of East Antarctica was connected to southern Australia. By ~500 Ma, the Pan-African and Ross orogenies (the process of mountain building) involved the growth of the Gondwanan supercontinent by collision between South America, South Africa, and Dronning Maud Land in East Antarctica on one side, and Australia, the remaining bulk of East Antarctica, and India on the other. During this event, large volumes of magmatic material and terrain were accreted to Northern Victoria Land. Thick sequences of continental sediments from Gondwana were deposited on the continent, resulting in Devonian (420–360 Ma) to Triassic (250–200 Ma) sandstones and coals of the 'Beacon group', which extend from Dronning Maud Land to Northern Victoria Land.

The long-lived Gondwana supercontinent began to break up in Jurassic times (around 180 Ma). The precursor to this breakup was the emplacement of the Ferrar Large Igneous Province (LIP), which includes the intrusive basaltic Ferrar sills, extending along the entire length of the Transantarctic Mountains. This is thought to be evidence of upwelling of a plume of mantle material and has been studied to understand subsurface magmatic/volcanic processes.[28] The Antarctic Peninsula was subject to a period of intense magmatism at about the same time, possibly linked to the proximity of a mantle plume.

Continental separation of Antarctica from Gondwana started about 165 Ma as the other continents rifted from Antarctica in an approximately clockwise manner: Sri Lanka and India (127 and 118 Ma); Australia (~95 to ~45 Ma); and New Zealand (~100–72 Ma). Around 50 Ma, westward-directed subduction that began beneath the South Sandwich Islands led to oceanic spreading between South America and the Antarctic Peninsula, opening up fully by ~35 Ma.

---

26 Jordan, "Geological Histories".   27 Fitzsimons, "Proterozoic Basement Provinces".
28 Elliot and Fleming, *Ferrar Large Igneous Province*, 41–58; Marsh, "Magmatic Mush Column".

Today, while most faults, sutures, and rifts are no longer active in Antarctica, geological processes continue in the form of low-level volcanism,[29] modest rifting in West Antarctica that gently pulls it from East Antarctica,[30] and widespread glacier erosion. In some areas in central East and West Antarctica, very slow ice flow and extreme polar desert conditions have acted to preserve the Antarctic landscape, potentially for millions of years.[31] In other areas, glacial erosion, exploiting pre-existing geological structures, has cut deep ice-filled basins over 1.5 km below sea level. This incision potentially contributed to the uplift of both the Transantarctic and Gamburtsev Subglacial Mountains, and has generated and transported vast volumes of sediment onto the continental margins. The resulting marginal sediments preserve key records of the continent's glacial history.[32]

Antarctic Glacial History

Glaciation in Antarctica is linked to the concentration of atmospheric greenhouse gases and tectonics.[33] In the early Eocene, around 55 Ma, global carbon dioxide levels were over 1,000 parts per million (ppm), global air temperatures were more than 10 °C warmer than today, and no major volume of ice existed anywhere on the planet. Antarctica at this time was heavily vegetated. As global carbon dioxide levels decreased, so too did global temperatures, resulting in the formation of ice caps in Antarctica over the highlands of the Gamburtsev Mountains.[34] At ~35 Ma, the opening of the Drake Passage led to the formation of the circumpolar ocean current and the isolation of Antarctica climatically. This plunged the continent into the deep freeze, leading to the formation of large ice sheets. While the East Antarctic ice sheet is likely to have existed in some form for the past 14 million years, the Pliocene (around 5.4–2.4 Ma) saw ice lost periodically from parts of East Antarctica and most of West Antarctica, leading to global sea levels around 20 m higher than today. For the past 2 million years, the ice sheets have grown and shrunk over orbitally paced but greenhouse-gas-driven glacial cycles; the level of carbon dioxide varied from 180 ppm in full glacial

---

29 van Wyk de Vries et al., "New Volcanic Province". 30 Dalziel, "Extent of Rift System".
31 Rose et al., "Ancient Pre-glacial Erosion Surfaces". 32 Barrett et al., "Cenozoic Climate".
33 Florindo and Siegert, eds., *Antarctic Climate Evolution*; Noble et al., "Sensitivity of the Antarctic".
34 Bo et al., "Gamburtsev Mountains".

conditions to 280 ppm in interglacial periods. The future of the Antarctic ice sheet is in doubt because humans have pushed carbon dioxide levels to over 400 ppm since mid-nineteenth-century industrialization – a level not seen on Earth since the Pliocene. If humans keep emitting greenhouse gases at rates similar to now, the concentration could return to ~1,000 ppm by the end of this century, with likely long-term consequences for planetary habitability.[35] Predicting the future contribution of Antarctica to anthropogenic global warming is, thus, an international imperative.[36]

Geological Controls on the Biology of Antarctica

Being plunged into the deep freeze at ~35 Ma, and isolated from the rest of the planet by the Southern Ocean and its circumpolar current, a unique biology developed in and around Antarctica. As mentioned previously, it was the abundance of marine life that drove early explorers toward the southern continent in search of seals and whales. On the continent itself, the terrestrial ecosystems of vertebrate fauna are largely limited to seafaring species including penguins and seals, as no native terrestrial mammals, reptiles, or amphibians exist, and only one species of non-marine birds is resident.[37] Indeed, most life is found around the 'green fringe' of Antarctica – where the marine-dependent species are resident, and limited plant life such as mosses and lichens occur. In the continental interior, the broad expanse of ice and snow is largely devoid of lifeforms except for some bacteria, which can metabolize at cold temperatures.[38] Under the ice, in contact with the sediments or bedrock, water is relatively plentiful owing to geothermal heat slowly melting the ice. Within this melt, microbial life is evident.[39] Most of the inland terrestrial biodiversity is concentrated along the Transantarctic Mountains,[40] which divide the continent into East and West ice sheets. Though predominantly microbial, this biodiversity also includes metazoans such as arthropods (mites and springtails), flatworms, nematodes, tardigrades, and rotifers. Interestingly, the dispersal and speciation of these animals can be linked to the ice sheet history of growth and decay over the past ~15 million years based on phylogeography and

---

35 Siegert et al., "What Ancient Climates Tell Us".
36 Rintoul et al. "Antarctica and Southern Ocean"; Siegert et al., "21st Century Sea-Level Rise".
37 Convey et al., "Antarctic Terrestrial Life".   38 Carpenter et al., "Bacterial Activity".
39 Priscu et al., "Antarctic Subglacial Water".   40 Convey et al., "Spatial Structure".

molecular clock estimates.[41] The biology of Antarctica is unique in many ways and has developed as a direct consequence of its tectonic and climate evolution.

Surveying the Ice Sheet with Geophysics

In the early 1950s, very little was known about the thickness and flow of the Antarctic ice sheet. The first good measurements of the ice thickness were collected by Gordon Robin, then a PhD student and later to be Director of the SPRI for over thirty years, who designed and undertook pioneering seismic experiments as part of the Norwegian-British-Swedish Expedition (1949–52).[42] During the IGY, seismic traverses were carried out across sections of the continent by teams from Australia, Belgium, France, Japan, UK, USA, and the USSR.[43] Dynamite is exploded at the surface, and the emitted seismic waves travel through the ice, reflect off the bottom and return to the surface. Knowing the travel time of the wave and wave velocity through ice, the depth can be calculated. Through these efforts the immense thickness of the ice sheet and buried topography began to emerge, most notably through the work of Charles Bentley from the University of Wisconsin. However, seismic surveys were slow and laborious, requiring long sledging journeys, stopping to deploy equipment, explode the dynamite, packing up, and traversing to the next location. It became clear that continuing these kinds of surveys to map the ice sheet was not feasible in the long run, and new technology has since replaced seismic methods. However, seismics remain incredibly useful for site-specific applications. For example, they are used to determine the physical characteristics of the substrate under the ice[44] as well as the structure within the ice itself.[45] Because the seismometers have become so sensitive, and signal processing so adept, they can detect natural ice quakes, caused by ice cracking or sudden motion at the base, from which internal ice-sheet structure, basal ice motion and the hydrological/mechanical characteristics of the substrate under the ice can be deduced.[46]

---

41 Collins et al., "Genetic Diversity".
42 Holtzscherer and Robin, "Depth of Ice Caps"; Robin, *Glaciology. III.*
43 Bentley et al., "Structure of West Antarctica"; Robin and Swithinbank, "Fifty Years of Progress".
44 Blankenship et al., "Seismic Measurements"; Anandakrishnan et al., "Influence of Subglacial Geology".
45 Blankenship and Bentley, "Crystalline Fabric"; Smith et al., "Ice Fabric".
46 Aster and Winberry, "Glacial Seismology", 126801.

3 Evolution of Antarctic Continent and Ice Sheet

The technology that replaced long-distance seismic surveys and revolutionized thickness mapping was realized after a series of fatal aircraft accidents.[47] By the 1950s, military aircraft were using radar altimeters, whereby the height to the ground was measured by the travel time of radio waves. This technology was crucial for night and bad weather landings. However, over ice sheets the radar could not be trusted, sometimes indicating safe altitudes of more than a kilometre when the aircraft was within metres of the surface. Later investigations determined that at some radar frequencies the ice was transparent, and the measured reflections were coming from the bottom of the ice sheet rather than from the ice surface.[48]

The utility of aerial radar was quickly recognized, and by the late 1960s, methods for mapping ice depth had been developed.[49] The first airborne radar campaign was a unique international collaboration involving Robin's glacier geophysics group at SPRI, Preben Gudmundsen and his team at the Technical University of Denmark (DTU), and the US National Science Foundation (NSF) with the US Navy. SPRI supplied the scientists to plan the campaign and process the data, the DTU helped build the radar, and the NSF financed the aerial campaign using US Navy C-130 Hercules aircraft. Further international collaboration was required to use various stations across the continent for refuelling. These stations included Vostok (USSR), South Pole (US), Byrd (US), and Dome C (France). In the 1970s, over 400,000 km of radar lines were flown across the ice sheet. The survey covered about 40 per cent of the ice sheet and probably ranks as the greatest non-oceanographic exploratory campaign of the twentieth century. Results were published as the *Antarctica Glaciological and Geophysical Folio*.[50] The data acquired provided critical input for computer models of the ice sheet.[51] As models improve and spatial resolution increases, and new physical insights emerge from field and remote campaigns, they require better resolution of the ice thickness and bed topography. Continual collection and collation of new data services this need.[52]

---

47 Turchetti et al., "Accidents and Opportunities".
48 Waite and Schmidt, "Gross Errors in Height"; Walford, "Radio Echo Sounding"; Bogorodsky et al., *Radioglaciology*.
49 Robin et al., "Interpretation of Radio Echo Sounding". 50 Drewry, *Antarctica*.
51 McInnes and Budd, "Cross-sectional Model"; MacAyeal, "Irregular Oscillations"; Fastook and Mike, "Finite-Element Model".
52 See for instance Lythe et al., "BEDMAP"; Fretwell et al., "Bedmap2"; Morlighem et al., "Deep Glacial Troughs".

Radar data have led to a number of continent-wide surprises. The ice sheet was thought to be frozen to the bed, but results showed that only half was frozen – the rest was at the melting temperature and wet. Indeed, over 600 subglacial lakes with liquid water are known to exist.[53] An interface of water and ice produces a radar reflection much brighter than ice/rock or ice/sediment. A bright reflection combined with a flat surface suggests a subglacial lake.[54] Radar has also revealed subglacial mountains that appear alpine in character; the Gamburtsev Mountains[55] and the Ellsworth Subglacial Highlands[56] are both considered foci for ice sheet initiation in East and West Antarctica, respectively. Moreover, deep subglacial fjord-like features, discovered in interior East Antarctica, may be evidence of a former ice sheet margin upstream of the present location.[57]

By the mid-1990s, it was common for aerial radio-echo sounding surveys to include a suite of geophysical sensors, principally magnetic and gravity,[58] which allowed the tectonic settings of a variety of subglacial terrains (e.g. Lake Vostok, West Antarctic Rift System, Wilkes Subglacial Basin) to be identified.[59] Such work also made it possible to link the exposed geology to that hidden subglacially, to improve our understanding of Antarctic tectonic history, described previously. For example, Jordan and colleagues[60] discovered a prominent shear-zone (like the San Andreas Fault Zone) in West Antarctica near the Weddell Sea; and Aitken and others[61] detailed the ice-covered geology in Wilkes Land in East Antarctica, allowing an assessment of relative rates of subglacial erosion from which the long-term dynamic history of Totten Glacier was derived. A recent mapping[62] of Antarctica's magnetic anomaly (differences from the mean trend) has provided a continent-wide picture of geological structures. Future work using airborne and satellite-borne magnetics and gravity data is promising.

---

53 Siegert et al., "Recent Advances"; Livingstone et al., "Global Synthesis".
54 Siegert et al., "Inventory".   55 Ferraccioli et al., "East Antarctic Rifting".
56 Ross et al., "The Ellsworth Subglacial Highlands".
57 Young et al., "Dynamic Early East Antarctic Ice Sheet".
58 Behrendt et al., "CASERTZ Aeromagnetic Data"; Blankenship et al., "Active Volcanism".
59 Studinger et al., "Mesozoic and Cenozoic Extensional Tectonics"; Studinger et al., "Ice Cover"; Ferraccioli et al., "Aeromagnetic Exploration".
60 Jordan et al., "Inland Extent".
61 Aitken et al., "Subglacial Geology"; Aitken et al., "Repeated Large-scale Retreat".
62 Golynsky et al., "New Magnetic Anomaly Map".

The Unstable Ice Sheet: Ice Streams, Geology, and Global Warming

The seismic surveys of Robin, Bentley, and others, followed by the aerial radar surveys, demonstrated that the bottom of the West Antarctic Ice Sheet was well below sea level. Most of East Antarctica, by contrast, sits on bedrock above sea level. By the 1970s, it was realized that West Antarctica is potentially unstable as a glacial system.[63] If sea level were to rise, or if the ice sheet were to thin, increased buoyancy around the margin of the ice sheet would reduce basal friction, causing increased ice flow to the ocean. The increased flow would thin the ice sheet further and increase its instability. If the sea level were to rise enough, the entire West Antarctic ice sheet could destabilize, flowing into the ocean and raising sea level by about 3.5 m. But it was John Mercer,[64] a Cambridge geographer and Research Associate at the Byrd Polar Research Centre at Ohio State University, who first linked the possible collapse of the ice sheet to climate warming induced by anthropogenic greenhouse gases. He understood that melting at the grounding line, the zone between floating ice shelves and grounded ice, would increase as the ice sheet retreated into deeper topography, leading to further retreat and accelerated, unstoppable ice loss. These insights triggered a series of projects to understand the bathymetry of West Antarctica, its past climate and glacial history, and its dynamic behaviour.[65] Antarctica was no longer a static immobile ice mass isolated in the polar South, but a dynamic structure with the potential for rapid change with global implications.

By the early 1970s another new tool was available to study Antarctic earth science: satellite remote sensing. The size of the continent made surface-based methods of assessing ice sheet characteristics too slow and costly, relegating them to site-specific studies. Although aerial geophysical methods were a major improvement in data acquisition and spatial coverage, they too were costly and subject to the ever-changing weather conditions on the continent. But constantly orbiting satellites covered large swaths of Antarctica. They were also sponsored by national programmes that made the data available to scientists at little to no cost. One of the earliest useful satellites was Landsat, launched in 1972.[66] Other satellites followed, with greater spatial coverage (e.g. AVHRR in 1979), and higher spatial resolution

63 Weertman, "Stability of Junction"; Thomas and Bentley, "Model for Holocene Retreat".
64 Mercer, "West Antarctic Ice Sheet".
65 Alley and Bindschadler, eds., *West Antarctic Ice Sheet*.
66 Bindschadler, "Future of West Antarctic".

(e.g. SPOT in 1986). Mapping accuracy of the interior of the continent improved dramatically because maps based on aerial photography were subject to large errors due to the lack of bedrock landmarks necessary for ground control. Also, the ice flow direction and speed could be estimated from displacement of surface features. New kinds of sensors were developed for satellites, including laser altimetry,[67] which measures elevation, and interferometric synthetic aperture radar (InSAR),[68] which can be used to measure elevation and motion. InSAR is particularly useful because it has day/night and all-weather capability, a great advantage for a continent that is dark for about half the year and where weather is often cloudy. The GRACE satellites measure gravity over time, which changes owing to the gain or loss in the ice sheet mass.[69] All these satellites afforded a view of the continent that was previously impossible, yielding amazing insights into the dynamics of the ice sheet that could only be guessed at a few decades earlier.

Differences in flow rates within the Antarctic ice sheet have long been recognized. Before the IGY, Charles Swithinbank,[70] a British glaciologist working at SPRI, coined the name 'ice streams' for rivers of ice, within the ice sheet, that flow fast (>1 km per year) compared with the slowly moving surrounding ice, 1–20 m per year. Despite their relatively small area, ice streams discharge most of the ice from the continent, commonly draining to the ocean by floating over the sea surface as an ice shelf. If the ice sheet were to lose mass and decay, ice streams would play a pivotal role in that change. Their number and distribution were not apparent until satellite imagery mapped the continent, however.[71] Such data, in combination with targeted field measurements, have shown that the ice streams feeding the Ross Ice Shelf can turn on and off, and that their rapid speed is due to wet sediment at the bottom[72] that makes the ice stream base effectively frictionless.[73] The supply of sedimentary material to ice stream beds is therefore crucial to sustaining ice flow and is often controlled by local geology, as is evident from examples in both West and East Antarctica. In other situations, ice stream boundaries are dictated by faults and geologically driven topography: for example, Möller Ice Stream in West Antarctica is bounded by a series of

---

67 Brooks et al., "Ice Sheet Topography", 539–543.   68 Joughin et al., "Tributaries", 283–286.
69 Velicogna et al., "Continuity".   70 Swithinbank, "Ice Streams".
71 Bindschadler and Vornberger, "AVHRR Imagery"; Jezek, "RADARSAT-1".
72 Conway et al., "Switch of Flow Direction"; Engelhardt et al., "Physical Conditions".
73 Alley et al., "Till".

shear faults.[74] Indeed, Bingham and colleagues[75] used geophysical methods to note that thinning of the West Antarctic ice sheet has been steered along geological rift features beneath the ice. Thus, geology exerts an important control on ice sheet dynamics, and it is likely to affect how the ice sheet reacts to future warming.

The destabilization of West Antarctica is not thought likely to occur any time soon and may require several thousand years to complete, but large uncertainties plague these future projections. A more immediate concern is Pine Island Glacier and adjacent Thwaites Glacier, both in West Antarctica.[76] Warm, deep, ocean water is flowing under the ice shelves formed by these two glaciers and is melting the ice from the bottom[77]. Ice shelves typically exert some back pressure (buttressing) against the flowing ice due to side drag along the shoreline or to islands shrouded by the ice shelf that act as pinning points. The melt-thinning of the ice shelf reduces its buttressing effect against the glacier, accelerating its flow. Because the bases of the glaciers are below sea level, and become deeper inland, buoyancy at the glacier front increases as the glacier retreats, further increasing glacier flow. This feedback process, already under way, is probably past the point of no return and, alone, is expected to raise global sea level by at least 1 cm over the next two decades.[78] Initial concern regarding the stability of the Ronne and Ross Ice Shelves has abated, although watchful studies continue.

Ice shelf stability can also be threatened from an entirely different source. Increasingly warm temperatures and surface melt weaken the ice shelves, causing them to calve icebergs more readily.[79] Recent studies[80] suggest that accumulation of surface meltwater in crevasses increases the pressure at the crevasse tip, causing it to propagate further into the ice. Once it reaches the bottom, the seaward part of the ice shelf breaks off. Thus, as air temperatures warm to the melting point, the ice shelves become less stable, and the northernmost shelves on the Antarctic Peninsula are the most vulnerable.[81] Sequential calving of large icebergs has been observed, but more catastrophic

---

74 Siegert et al., "Controls".   75 Bingham et al., "Inland Thinning".
76 Rignot, "Fast Recession"; Shepherd, "Inland Thinning".
77 Jacobs et al., "Antarctic Ice Sheet Melting"; Jacobs et al., "Stronger Ocean Circulation".
78 Favier et al., "Retreat of Pine Island".   79 Doake and Vaughan, "Rapid Disintegration".
80 Banwell et al., "Direct Measurements".
81 Vaughan and Doake, "Recent Atmospheric Warming".

events have occurred. Over a period of fifty days in 1995, the Larsen A Ice Shelf, on the eastern side of the peninsula near its northern tip, catastrophically disintegrated into thousands of icebergs.[82] For some reason, that event did not capture the attention and imagination of the scientific community in the same way as the breakup of the Larsen B Ice Shelf in March 2002, when 3,320 km^2 of ice disintegrated over about three weeks, sending a plume of icebergs hundreds of kilometres into the ocean. Examination of satellite imagery prior to the event revealed that extensive surface melt on the ice shelf had drained into pre-existing crevasses over a number of years. Eventually, the strength of the shelf failed, and the shelf broke apart in a slow-motion explosion. Once the ice shelves were gone, the tributary glaciers feeding the shelves were no longer buttressed, and their flow accelerated.[83] The vulnerability of ice shelves is now clear: melting from warm air above or warm water below can weaken and cause them to fail. This failure does not directly result in sea level rise because the shelves are already floating. Instead, it is the subsequent response of the land-based glaciers, which fed the shelves, that accelerate and transport more ice into the ocean, thus increasing the sea level.

Summary and Future Work

Work over the past half-century has changed our view of Antarctica from a white, featureless mass of quiescent ice to one with myriad surface features that point to dynamical complexity. Theoretical insight supported by observational evidence shows that parts of the continent are unstable now, and that other parts may become unstable in future. And there is a new twist – changes to the ice sheet are not occurring in isolation. Rather, ocean temperatures and deep-water circulation are affecting the ice and its stability in important ways.

Much progress has been made in developing our understanding of Antarctica's geology and ice cover. Notably, we have a strong appreciation for how the ice sheets are responding to climate and ocean warming, and how this may progress in future. To guide future Antarctic research, SCAR, led by its former President, Chuck Kennicutt from Texas A&M University, launched an effort in 2014 to form international consensus on the top eighty scientific questions requiring answers within twenty years. A group of seventy-five scientists, drawn from across the world and across disciplines,

---

82 Gammie, "Breakaway Iceberg"; Rott et al., "Rapid Collapse".
83 Rott et al., "Northern Larsen Ice Shelf".

met to distil the questions solicited from the scientific community into the most necessary eighty. Some of the questions related to geology and ice sheet evolution include: (1) How does the bedrock geology under the Antarctic ice sheet inform our understanding of supercontinent assembly and breakup through Earth's history? (2) What are the thresholds that lead to irreversible loss of all or part of the Antarctic ice sheet? and (3) How do tectonics, dynamic topography, ice loading, and isostatic adjustment affect the spatial pattern of sea level change on all timescales?[84]

Five years after the results were first announced, and therefore a quarter of the way into its twenty-year period of investigation, Kennicutt and a group of international experts undertook a review of the scientific advances that had been made toward answering each of these questions.[85] The exercise stated that while "Progress has been made on a few of the questions … most remain largely unanswered due to several factors." This inability to answer most of the questions was caused primarily by incomplete remote data coverage at the scale and resolution necessary and a lack of access to the subglacial environment to allow sampling of bedrock. In conclusion, while there is a long history of scientific discovery concerning the geological evolution of the Antarctic continent, prominent scientific questions remain unanswered. We are, thus, still at the very early stages of understanding the geology of Antarctica.

In this short account of the historic evolution of our understanding of Antarctica's geology and its ice sheet, we have not discussed gender and diversity. Clearly, the early explorers were entirely white privileged men from the richest nations, and little had changed by the time of the IGY in 1957. Only in the past few decades have women, to any substantial degree, participated in or led geoscientific studies in Antarctica. Moreover, many more countries now have a permanent presence in Antarctica. To its credit, SCAR has been a champion for inclusion and diversity at all levels of Antarctic research. Looking to the future, geoscientific research can only benefit from the application of great minds, irrespective of race, class, sex, or nationality.

Bibliography

Aitken, A. R. A., J. L. Roberts, T. Van Ommen, et al., "Repeated Large-scale Retreat and Advance of Totten Glacier Indicated by Inland Bed Erosion", *Nature* 533 (2016): 385–389, https://doi.org/10.1038/nature17447.

---

84 Kennicutt et al., "Roadmap". 85 Kennicutt et al., "Sustained Antarctic Research".

Aitken, A. R. A., D. A. Young, F. Ferraccioli, et al., "The Subglacial Geology of Wilkes Land, East Antarctica", *Geophysical Research Letters* 41 (2014): 2390–2400, https://doi.org/10.1002/2014GL059405.

Alley, R. B., and R. A. Bindschadler, eds., *The West Antarctic Ice Sheet: Behaviour and Environment* (Washington, DC: American Geophysical Union, 2001).

Alley, R. B., D. D. Blankenship, S. T. Rooney, and C. R. Bentley, "Till Beneath Ice Stream B.4: A Coupled Ice-Till Flow Model", *Journal of Geophysical Research* 92 (1987): 8931–8940.

Anandakrishnan, S., D. D. Blankenship, R. B. Alley, and P. L. Stoffa, "Influence of Subglacial Geology on the Position of a West Antarctic Ice Stream from Seismic Observations", *Nature* 394 (1998): 62–65.

Anderson, J. J., "Bedrock Geology of Antarctica: A Summary of Exploration, 1831–1962", in *American Geophysical Union Antarctic Research Series*, Vol. 6: *Geology and Palaeontology of the Antarctic* (American Geophysical Union, 1965), pp. 1–70.

Aster, R. C., and J. P. Winberry, "Glacial Seismology", *Reports on Progress in Physics* 80, (2017): 126801, https://doi.org/10.1088/1361-6633/aa8473.

Banwell, A. F., I. C. Willis, G. J. Macdonald, et al., "Direct Measurements of Ice-Shelf Flexure Caused by Surface Meltwater Ponding and Drainage", *Nature Communications* 10 (2019): 730, https://doi.org/10.1038/s41467-019-08522-5.

Barr, S., and C. Lüdecke, eds., *The History of the International Polar Years (IPYs)* (Berlin, Heidelberg: Springer, 2010), https://doi.org/10.1007/978-3-642-12402-0.

Barrett, P., M. Hambrey, P. Christoffersen, N. Glasser, and B. Hubbard, "Cenozoic Climate and Sea Level History from Glacimarine Strata off the Victoria Land Coast, Cape Roberts Project, Antarctica", in M. J. Hambrey, P. Christoffersen, N. F. Glasser, and B. Hubbard, eds., *Glacial Sedimentary Processes and Products*, International Association of Sedimentologists Special Publication 39 (Oxford: Blackwell, 2007), pp. 259–287.

Behrendt, J. C., *Ninth Circle: A Memoir of Life and Death in Antarctica, 1960–1962* (University of New Mexico Press, 2005).

Behrendt, J. C., D. D. Blankenship, C. A. Finn, et al., "CASERTZ Aeromagnetic Data Reveal Late Cenozoic Flood Basalts(?) in the West Antarctic Rift System", *Geology* 22 (1994): 527–530.

Bentley, C. R., "Rapid Sea-Level Rise Soon from West Antarctic Ice-Sheet Collapse?", *Science* 275 (1997): 1077–1078.

Bentley, C. R., A. P. Crary, N. A. Ostenso, and E. C. Thiel, "Structure of West Antarctica", *Science* 131 (1960): 131–136, https://doi.org/10.1126/science.131.3394.131.

Berger, A., "Milankovitch Theory and Climate", *Reviews of Geophysics* 26 (1988): 624–657.

Bindschadler, R., "Future of the West Antarctic Ice Sheet", *Science* 282 (1998): 428, https://doi.org/10.1126/science.282.5388.428.

Bindschadler, R. A., and P. L. Vornberger, "AVHRR Imagery Reveals Antarctic Ice Dynamics", *Eos Transactions American Geophysical Union* 71 (1990): 741–742.

Bingham, R., F. Ferraccioli, E. King, et al., "Inland Thinning of West Antarctic Ice Sheet Steered Along Subglacial Rifts", *Nature* 487 (2012): 468–471, https://doi.org/10.1038/nature11292.

Blankenship, D. D., and C. R. Bentley, "The Crystalline Fabric of Polar Ice Sheets Inferred from Seismic Anisotropy", in Joseph Walder, ed., *The Physical Basis of Ice Sheet Modelling*, IAHS-AISH Publication 170 (Wallingford: IAHS Press, 1987), pp. 17–28.

3 Evolution of Antarctic Continent and Ice Sheet

Blankenship, D. D., R. E. Bell, S. M. Hodge, et al., "Active Volcanism Beneath the West Antarctic Ice Sheet and Implications for Ice-Sheet Stability", *Nature* 361 (1993): 526–529.

Blankenship, D. D., C. R. Bentley, S. T. Rooney, and R. B. Alley, "Seismic Measurements Reveal a Saturated Porous Layer Beneath an Active Antarctic Ice Stream", *Nature* 322, (1986): 54–57.

Bo, S., M. J. Siegert, S. M. Mudd, et al., "The Gamburtsev Mountains and the Origin and Early Evolution of the Antarctic Ice Sheet", *Nature* 459 (2009): 690–693, https://doi.org/10.1038/nature08024.

Bogorodsky, V., C. R. Bentley, and P. Gudmandsen, *Radioglaciology* (Dordrecht: Reidel, 1985).

Brooks, R., W. J. Campbell, R. O. Ramseier, H. R. Stanley, and H. J. Zwally, "Ice Sheet Topography by Satellite Altimetry", *Nature* 274 (1978): 539–543.

Carpenter, E. J., S. Lin, and D. G. Capone, "Bacterial Activity in South Pole Snow", *Applied and Environmental Microbiology* 66 (2000): 4514–4517, https://doi.org/10.1128/AEM.66.10.4514-4517.2000.

Collins, G. E., I. D. Hogg, P. Convey, et al., "Genetic Diversity of Soil Invertebrates Corroborates Timing Estimates for Past Collapses of the West Antarctic Ice Sheet", *Proceedings of the National Academy of Sciences* 117 (2020): 22293–22302, https://doi.org/10.1073/pnas.2007925117.

Convey, P., S. L. Chown, A. Clarke, et al., "The Spatial Structure of Antarctic Biodiversity", *Ecological Monographs* 84 (2014): 203–244, https://doi.org/10.1890/12-2216.1.

Convey, P., J. A. E. Gibson, C.-D. Hillenbrand, et al., "Antarctic Terrestrial Life: Challenging the History of the Frozen Continent?", *Biological Reviews* 83 (2008): 103–117, https://doi.org/10.1111/j.1469-185X.2008.00034.x.

Conway, H., G. Catania, C. Raymond, et al., "Switch of Flow Direction in an Antarctic Ice Stream", *Nature* 419 (2002): 465–467.

Crane, D., *Scott of the Antarctic* (Glasgow: Harper, 2012).

Croll, J., "On the Thickness of the Antarctic Ice, and Its Relations to that of the Glacial Epoch", *Quarterly Journal of Science* 1879 (January 1879).

Croll, J., "XIII. On the Physical Cause of the Change of Climate During Geological Epochs", *The London, Edinburgh, and Dublin Philosophical Magazine and Journal of Science* 28 (1864): 121–137, https://doi.org/10.1080/14786446408643733.

Cui, X., H. Jeofry, J. S. Greenbaum, et al., "Bed Topography of Princess Elizabeth Land in East Antarctica", *Earth System Science Data* 12 (2020): 2765–2774.

Dalziel, I. W. D., "On the Extent of the Active West Antarctic Rift System", *Terra Antartica Reports* 12 (2006): 193–202.

Doake, C. S. M., and D. G. Vaughan, "Rapid Disintegration of the Wordie Ice Shelf in Response to Atmospheric Warming", *Nature* 350 (1991): 328–330, https://doi.org/10.1038/350328a0.

Drewry, D. J., *Antarctica: Glaciological and Geophysical Folio* (Cambridge: Scott Polar Research Institute, 1983).

Elliot, D. H., and T. H. Fleming, *The Ferrar Large Igneous Province: Field and Geochemical Constraints on Supra-Crustal (High-Level) Emplacement of the Magmatic System*, Geological Society of London Special Publication 463 (Geological Society, 2018), pp. 41–58.

Ellis, T., and C. Dell'Amore, *South Pole 1910–1913: The British Antarctic Expedition* (London: Assouline, 2011).

Engelhardt, H., N. Humphrey, B. Kamb, and M. Fahnestock, "Physical Conditions at the Base of a Fast Moving Antarctic Ice Stream", *Science* 248 (1990): 57–59.

Fastook, J. L., and P. Mike, "A Finite-Element Model of Antarctica: Sensitivity Test for Meteorological Mass–Balance Relationship", *Journal of Glaciology* 40 (1994): 167–175.

Favier, L., Durand, G., Cornford, S. L., et al., "Retreat of Pine Island Glacier Controlled by Marine Ice-Sheet Instability", *Nature Climate Change* 4 (2014): 117–121, https://doi.org/10.1038/nclimate2094.

Ferraccioli, F., E. Armadillo, T. Jordan, E. Bozzo, and H. Corr, "Aeromagnetic Exploration Over the East Antarctic Ice Sheet: A New View of the Wilkes Subglacial Basin", *Tectonophysics* 478 (2009): 62–77.

Ferraccioli, F., Finn, C., Jordan, T. et al. "East Antarctic rifting triggers uplift of the Gamburtsev Mountains." *Nature* 479, 388–392 (2011).

Fitzsimons, I. C. W., "Proterozoic Basement Provinces of Southern and Southwestern Australia and Their Correlation with Antarctica", in M. Yoshida and B. F. Windley, eds., *Proterozoic East Gondwana: Supercontinent Assembly and Breakup*, Geological Society of London Special Publication 206 (London: Geological Society, 2003), pp. 93–130.

Fitzsimons, P., *Mawson and the Ice Men of the Heroic Age: Scott, Shackleton and Amundsen* (North Sydney: William Heinemann Australia, 2014).

Florindo, F., and M. J. Siegert, eds., *Antarctic Climate Evolution: Developments in Earth & Environmental Science*, Vol. 8 (Amsterdam: Elsevier, 2008).

Fogg, G. E., *A History of Antarctic Science* (Cambridge: Cambridge University Press, 2008).

Fretwell, P., H. D. Pritchard, D. G. Vaughan, et al., "Bedmap2: Improved Ice Bed, Surface and Thickness Datasets for Antarctica", *The Cryosphere* 7 (2013): 375–393.

Gammie, F., "Breakaway Iceberg 'Due to Warming'", *Nature* 374 (1995): 108.

Golynsky, A. V., F. Ferraccioli, J. K. Hong, et al., "New Magnetic Anomaly Map of the Antarctic", *Geophysical Research Letters* 45 (2018): 6437–6449, https://doi.org/10.1029/2018gl078153.

Greenbaum, J. S., D. D. Blankenship, D. A. Young, et al., "Ocean Access to a Cavity Beneath Totten Glacier in East Antarctica", *Nature Geoscience* 8 (2015): 294–298, https://doi.org/10.1038/NGEO2388.

Grochowicz, J., *Amundsen's Way: The Race to the South Pole* (Allen & Unwin, 2019).

Headland, R. K., *Chronological List of Antarctic Expeditions and Related Historical Events* (Cambridge: Cambridge University Press, 1989).

Headland, R. K., "Antarctic Winter Stations Operating During the International Geophysical Year (1957 Winter)" (Cambridge: Scott Polar Research Institute, University of Cambridge, 2017), www.spri.cam.ac.uk/resources/infosheets/igy57-58stations.pdf.

Holtzscherer, J. J., and G. de Q. Robin, "Depth of Polar Ice Caps", *Geographical Journal* 120 (1954): 193–202.

Howkins, A. J., "Frozen Empires: A History of the Antarctic Sovereignty Dispute Between Britain, Argentina and Chile: 1939–1959", PhD diss. (University of Texas at Austin: ProQuest Dissertations Publishing, 2008).

Jacobs, S. S., H. H. Hellmer, and A. Jenkins, "Antarctic Ice Sheet Melting in the Southeast Pacific", *Geophysical Research Letters* 23 (1996): 957–960.

3 Evolution of Antarctic Continent and Ice Sheet

Jacobs, S. S., A. Jenkins, C. F. Giulivi, and P. Dutrieux, "Stronger Ocean Circulation and Increased Melting Under Pine Island Glacier Ice Shelf", *Nature Geoscience* 4 (2011): 519–523.

Jezek, K. C., "RADARSAT-1 Antarctic Mapping Project: Change-Detection and Surface Velocity Campaign", *Annals of Glaciology* 34 (2002): 263–268, https://doi.org/10.3189/172756402781818030.

Jordan, T.A., F. Ferraccioli, N. Ross, et al., "Inland Extent of the Weddell Sea Rift Imaged by New Aerogeophysical Data", *Tectonophysics* 585 (2013): 137–160, https://doi.org/10.1016/j.tecto.2012.09.010.

Jordan, Tom A., "Geological histories of polar environments," Nuttall, Mark, Christensen, Torben R., Siegert, Martin (eds) *The Routledge Handbook of the Polar Regions*, (Abingdon: Routledge, 2018) 149–157.

Joughin, I., L. Gray, R. Bindschadler, et al., "Tributaries of West Antarctic Ice Streams Revealed by RADARSAT Interferometry", *Science* 286 (1999): 283–286.

Kennicutt, M. C., II, David Bromwich, Daniela Liggett, et al., Sustained Antarctic Research: A 21st Century Imperative. *One Earth* 1 (2019): 95–113, https://doi.org/10.1016/j.oneear.2019.08.014.

Kennicutt, M. C., II, S. L. Chown, J. J. Cassano, et al., "A Roadmap for Antarctic and Southern Ocean Science for the Next Two Decades and Beyond", *Antarctic Science* 27 (2015): 3–18, https://doi.org/10.1017/S0954102014000674.

Korsmo, F. L., "The Genesis of the International Geophysical Year", *Physics Today* 60 (2007): 38–43, https://doi.org/10.1063/1.2761801.

Livingstone, S. J., Li, Y., Rutishauser, A., et al., "Global Synthesis of Subglacial Lakes and Their Changing Role in a Warming Climate", *Nature Reviews Earth and Environment* 3 (2022): 106–124, https://doi.org/10.1038/s43017-021-00246-9.

Lythe, M. B., and David G. Vaughan, "BEDMAP: A New Ice Thickness and Subglacial Topographic Model of Antarctica", *Journal of Geophysical Research: Solid Earth* 106 (2001): 11335–11351.

MacAyeal, D. R., "Irregular Oscillations of the West Antarctic Ice Sheet", *Nature* 359 (1992): 29–32.

Maddison, B., *Class and Colonialism in Antarctic Exploration, 1750–1920* (London: Pickering & Chatto, 2014).

Marsh, B., "A Magmatic Mush Column Rosetta Stone: The McMurdo Dry Valleys of Antarctica", *Eos Transactions American Geophysical Union* 85 (2004): 497–502.

McInnes, B., and W. Budd, "A Cross-sectional Model for West Antarctica", *Annals of Glaciology* 5 (1984): 95–99.

Mercer, J. H., "West Antarctic Ice Sheet and CO_2 Greenhouse Effect: A Threat of Disaster", *Nature* 271 (1978): 321–325, https://doi.org/10.1038/271321a0.

Milankovitch, M., "Kanon der Erdbestrahlungen und seine Anwendung auf das Eiszeitenproblem", Royal Serbian Academy special publications 132, *Section of Mathematical and Natural Sciences* 33 (Belgrade, 1941) ("Canon of Insolation and the Ice-Age Problem", English trans. Israel Program for Scientific Translations, Jerusalem, 1969).

Morlighem, M., E. Rignot, T. Binder, et al., "Deep Glacial Troughs and Stabilizing Ridges Unveiled Beneath the Margins of the Antarctic Ice Sheet". *Nature Geoscience* 13 (2020): 132–137, https://doi.org/10.1038/s41561-019-0510-8.

Noble, T. L., E. J. Rohling, A. R. A. Aitken, et al., "The Sensitivity of the Antarctic Ice Sheet to a Changing Climate: Past, Present, and Future", *Reviews of Geophysics* 58 (2020): e2019RG000663, https://doi.org/10.1029/2019RG000663.

Priscu, J. C., S. Tulaczyk, M. Studinger, et al., "Antarctic Subglacial Water: Origin, Evolution and Ecology", in W. F. Vincent and J. Laybourn-Parry, eds., *Polar Lakes and Rivers: Limnology of Arctic and Antarctic Aquatic Ecosystems* (Oxford: Oxford University Press, 2008), pp. 119–135.

Riffenburgh, B., *'Nimrod': The Extraordinary Story of the 1907–09 British Antarctic Expedition* (London: Bloomsbury, 2005).

Riffenburgh, B., *Racing with Death: Douglas Mawson: Antarctic* (London: Bloomsbury, 2009).

Rignot, E. J., "Fast Recession of a West Antarctic Glacier", *Science* 281 (1998): 549, https://doi.org/10.1126/science.281.5376.549.

Rintoul, S. R., S. L. Chown, R. DeConto, et al., "Antarctica and the Southern Ocean in 2070: What Future Will We Choose?", *Nature* 558 (2018): 233–241, https://doi.org/10.1038/s41586-018-0173-4.

Robin, G. de Q., *Glaciology. III. Seismic Shooting and Related Investigations: Norwegian–British-Swedish Antarctic Expedition, 1949–52. Scientific Results*, Vol. 5 (1958).

Robin, G. de Q. and C. Swithinbank, "Fifty Years of Progress in Understanding Ice Sheets", *Journal of Glaciology* 33 (1987): 33–47, https://doi.org/10.3189/S0022143000215803.

Robin, G. de Q., S. Evans, and J. T. Bailey, "Interpretation of Radio Echo Sounding in Polar Ice Sheets", *Philosophical Transactions of the Royal Society of London. Series A, Mathematical and Physical Sciences* 265 (1969): 437–505.

Rose, K. C., N. Ross, T. A. Jordan, et al., "Ancient Pre-glacial Erosion Surfaces Preserved Beneath the West Antarctic Ice Sheet", *Earth Surface Dynamics* 3 (2015): 139–152, https://doi.org/10.5194/esurf-3-139-2015.

Ross, N., T. A. Jordan, R. G. Bingham, et al., "The Ellsworth Subglacial Highlands: Inception and Retreat of the West Antarctic Ice Sheet", *Geological Society of America Bulletin* 126 (2014): 3–15, https://doi.org/10.1130/B30794.1.

Rott, H., W. Rack, P. Skvarca, and H. De Angelis, "Northern Larsen Ice Shelf, Antarctica: Further Retreat After Collapse", *Annals of Glaciology* 34 (2002): 277–282.

Rott, H., P. Skvarca, and T. Nagler, "Rapid Collapse of Northern Larsen Ice Shelf, Antarctica", *Science* 271 (1996): 788, https://doi.org/10.1126/science.271.5250.788.

Scambos, T., C. Hulbe, and M. Fahnestock, "Climate-Induced Ice Shelf Disintegration in the Antarctic Peninsula", in E. Domack, et al., eds., *Antarctic Peninsula Climate Variability: Historical and Paleoenvironmental Perspectives*, Vol. 79 (AGU, 2003), pp. 79–92.

Scambos, T. A., J. Bohlander, C. A. Shuman, and P. Skvarca, "Glacier Acceleration and Thinning After Ice Shelf Collapse in the Larsen B Embayment, Antarctica", *Geophysical Research Letters* 31 (2004): L18402, https://doi.org/10.1029/2004GL020670.

Shackleton, E., *South! The Story of Shackleton's Last Expedition 1914–1917* (first published 1920). Available from CreateSpace Independent Publishing Platform (25 October 2017).

Shepherd, A., "Inland Thinning of Pine Island Glacier, West Antarctica", *Science* 291 (2001): 862–864, https://doi.org/10.1126/science.291.5505.862.

3 Evolution of Antarctic Continent and Ice Sheet

Siegert, M. J., "Technology and the Discovery of Antarctic Subglacial Landscapes", in M. Nuttall, T. Christensen, and M. J. Siegert, eds., *Routledge Handbook of the Polar Regions* (Routledge, 2018), pp. 435–441.

Siegert, M. J., R. B. Alley, E. Rignot, J. Englander, and R. Corell, "Twenty-First Century Sea-Level Rise Could Exceed IPCC Predictions for Strong-Warming Futures", *One Earth* 3 (2020): 691–703, https://doi.org/10.1016/j.oneear.2020.11.002.

Siegert, M. J., J. A. Dowdeswell, M. R. Gorman, and N. F. McIntyre, "An Inventory of Antarctic Sub-Glacial Lakes", *Antarctic Science* 8 (1996): 281–286.

Siegert, M. J., A. Haywood, D. Lunt, T. van de Flierdt, and J. Francis, "What Ancient Climates Tell Us About High Carbon Dioxide Concentrations in Earth's Atmosphere", Grantham Institute Briefing Note 13 (Imperial College London, 2020), https://doi.org/10.25561/79292.

Siegert, M. J., N. Ross, and A. Le Brocq, "Recent Advances in Understanding Antarctic Subglacial Lakes and Hydrology", *Philosophical Transactions of the Royal Society of London, A* 374 (2016): 20140306, https://doi.org/10.1098/rsta.2014.0306.

Siegert, M. J., N. Ross, J. Li, et al., "Controls on the Onset and Flow of Institute Ice Stream, West Antarctica", *Annals of Glaciology* 57 (2016): 19–24, https://doi.org/10.1017/aog.2016.17.

Smith, E. C., A. F. Baird, J. M. Kendall, et al., "Ice Fabric in an Antarctic Ice Stream Interpreted from Seismic Anisotropy", *Geophysical Research Letters* 44 (2017): 3710–3718, https://doi.org/10.1002/2016GL072093.

Studinger, M., R. Bell, C. Finn, and D. Blankenship, "Mesozoic and Cenozoic Extensional Tectonics of the West Antarctic Rift System from High-Resolution Airborne Geophysical Mapping", *Royal Society of New Zealand Bulletin* 35 (2002): 563–569.

Studinger, M., R. E. Bell, G. D. Karner, et al., "Ice Cover, Landscape Setting, and Geological Framework of Lake Vostok, East Antarctica", *Earth and Planetary Science Letters* 205 (2003): 195–210.

Sugden, D. E., "James Croll (1821–1890): Ice, Ice Ages and the Antarctic Connection", *Antarctic Science* (2014): 604–613, https://doi.org/10.1017/S095410201400008X.

Swithinbank, C. W. M. "Ice Streams". Polar Record, 7. (1954) 185–186.

Thomas, R. H., and C. R. Bentley, "A Model for Holocene Retreat of the West Antarctic Ice Sheet", *Quaternary Research* 10 (1978): 150–170, https://doi.org/10.1016/0033-5894(78)90098-4.

Turchetti, S., K. Dean, S. Naylor, and M. Siegert, "Accidents and Opportunities: A History of the Radio Echo-Sounding of Antarctica, 1958–79", *The British Journal for the History of Science* 41 (2008): 417–444, https://doi.org/10.1017/S0007087408000903.

van Wyk de Vries, M., R. G. Bingham, and A. S. Hein, "A New Volcanic Province: An Inventory of Subglacial Volcanoes in West Antarctica", *Geological Society of London Special Publications* 461 (2018): 231–248.

Vaughan, D. G., "West Antarctic Ice Sheet Collapse: The Fall and Rise of a Paradigm", *Climatic Change* 91 (2008): 65–79, https://doi.org/10.1007/s10584-008-9448-3.

Vaughan, D. G., and C. S. M. Doake, "Recent Atmospheric Warming and Retreat of Ice Shelves on the Antarctic Peninsula", *Nature* 379 (1996): 328–331, https://doi.org/10.1038/379328a0

Velicogna, I., Yara Mohajerani, Geruo A, et al., "Continuity of Ice Sheet Mass Loss in Greenland and Antarctica from the GRACE and GRACE Follow-On Missions",

Geophysical Research Letters 47 (2020): e2020GL087291, https://doi.org/10.1029/2020GL087291.

Waite, A., and S. Schmidt, "Gross Errors in Height Indication from Pulsed Radar Altimeters Operating Over Thick Ice or Snow", *Proceedings of the IRE* 50 (1962): 1515–1520, https://doi.org/10.1109/JRPROC.1962.288195.

Walford, M., "Radio Echo Sounding Through an Ice Shelf", *Nature* 204 (1964): 317–319.

Walton, D., *Antarctica: Global Science from a Frozen Continent* (Cambridge: Cambridge University Press, 2012).

Weertman, J., "Stability of the Junction of an Ice Sheet and an Ice Shelf", *Journal of Glaciology* 13 (1974): 3–11, https://doi.org/10.3189/S0022143000023327.

Welch, B. C., and R. W. Jacobel, "Analysis of Deep-Penetrating Radar Surveys of West Antarctica, US-ITASE 2001", *Geophysical Research Letters* 30 (2003): 1444, https://doi.org/10.1029/2009jf001622.

Wilson, E., *Diary of the 'Discovery' Expedition to the Antarctic Regions 1901–1904* (London: Blandford, 1966).

Young, D. A., A. P. Wright, J. L. Roberts, et al., "A Dynamic Early East Antarctic Ice Sheet Suggested by Ice Covered Fjord Landscapes", *Nature* 474 (2011): 72–75.

4

The Initial Peopling of the Circumpolar North

BJARNE GRØNNOW

Introduction

When and why did the originally tropical being, *Homo sapiens*, enter the circumpolar north? What attracted human societies to this part of the Earth characterized by extreme seasonal variability, long periods of darkness, rough and cold weather, barren tundra, high mountains, ice caps, and vast areas of sea ice? Through analyses of ancient material remains such as stone-built structures, artefacts and bones preserved in cultural layers on dwelling sites, Arctic archaeology provides some insights into these basic questions about the expansion of human societies into the circumpolar north and how they managed to thrive there for millennia.

Drawing on a rich record from archaeological sites and finds of artefacts and faunal material, the first part of this chapter describes, on a very general scale, the initial peopling of the Old World Arctic (northern Siberia and northern Scandinavia) and the initial crossing of the Bering Strait into the New World – a process that took more than 100,000 years. The second part of the chapter highlights the spread of hunting societies from the Bering Strait to East Greenland – a stretch of thousands of kilometres along the New World's icebound northern coasts, bordering vast inland areas. This development is in fact quite recent on an archaeological timescale, beginning only about 3,500 BC, when the so-called pre-Inuit societies 'broke the code' to making a good life even in the High Arctic. They based their subsistence economy primarily on marine game and made the sea ice and coastal zones their primary hunting grounds and home. These pre-Inuit migrations across the New World Arctic were one of the last major 'geographical steps' made by humanity into a hitherto uninhabited part of the Earth.

In this chapter, dates before the Late Glacial Maximum (c. 25,000 years ago) are shown as 'years ago' (uncalibrated radiocarbon years before present

[BP]) following the general trend in the literature dealing with early Arctic Russian and Siberian prehistory. For this era, the chronological resolution is generally quite low. However, for the Late Glacial period and onwards, archaeological data and chronological resolution increase dramatically, and it is important to calibrate the radiocarbon dates into 'human years' or 'solar years' in order to understand the complex cultural history of this era. Thus, the related dates are shown as 'calibrated BC' (cal. BC).

Hunters of Megafauna: The Spread of Palaeolithic Hunting Societies into the Arctic

Sub-Arctic Neanderthals and Denisovans

While the ice caps of the last ice age (the Weichselian, c. 115,000–11,500 years ago) covered most of northern Europe, some refugia with quite productive ecosystems were present in southern and central Europe. These became starting points of the initial peopling of the Sub-Arctic.[1] Archaeological finds – stray finds and assemblages of lithic artefacts from dwelling and hunting sites of the Middle Palaeolithic Mousterian tradition – have been made on the plains and in caves south of the ice caps from Europe to the Ural and further southeast (Figure 4.1).[2] These assemblages are likely to represent the first expansions of the ranges of the Neanderthals and Denisovans from their temperate environments in Europe and Central Asia into colder zones, probably attracted by living resources in the river valleys, such as moose and beaver, or on the dry plains, such as steppe bison and horse. The artefacts in the lowermost layers dated to 200,000–50,000 years ago in the Denisova Cave, Altai Mountains, reflect such hunting excursions into the cool ecozones of Asia by the Neanderthals and the Denisovans.[3] Recent analyses of ancient DNA in human remains even indicate that the two human groups interbred in the Altai region. The lithic tool kit of these Middle Palaeolithic societies included multifunctional 'hand axes' and elaborate cutting tools. There is debate over whether assemblages of tooth pendants, beads, and discs of eggshells and other ornamental objects, recently excavated in the Denisova Cave, were crafted by the Denisovans or were made by the first *Homo sapiens* visiting the area around 45,000 years ago.[4]

1 Plumet, *Des mythes*, 153ff.
2 Derevyanko, "Transition"; Derevyanko, "Most Ancient"; Kotlyakov et al., eds., *Human Colonization*, 510f.
3 Zykin et al., "West Siberia", 179–180.
4 Douka et al., "Age Estimates"; Slon et al., "The Genome".

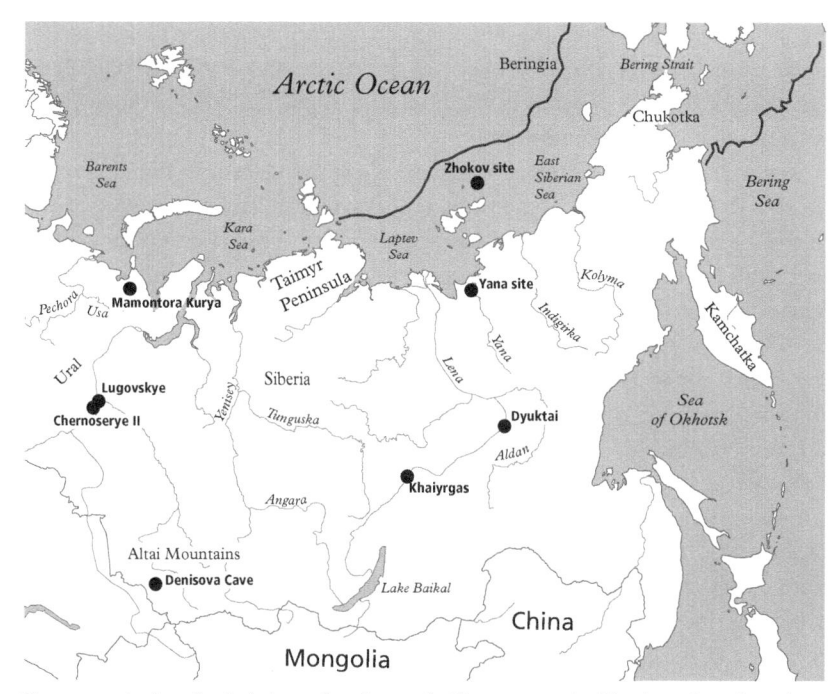

Figure 4.1 Archaeological sites related to early *Homo sapiens* in Siberia and modern-day Russia. The maximum extent of Beringia is marked by the solid black line.

The First Hunting Societies of Modern Humans in the Arctic

Warming episodes – the Karginsky Interglacial – during the last half of the Weichselian/Zyryansk Ice Age resulted in the formation of 'mosaic landscapes' in the mountains south of Siberia and in the river valleys leading north into the plains and tundra.[5] From this early period of modern *Homo sapiens sapiens*, the Upper Palaeolithic c. 50,000–25,000 years ago, archaeological sites have been recorded, some of them situated quite far north, both west of the Ural and in Siberia. Working from differences in lithic technology, artefact designs, and suites of radiocarbon dates, archaeologists have designated these first settlements of modern humans in the Arctic/Sub-Arctic zone the Ust'Karakol, Kara Bom, and Yana Cultures.[6]

The mosaic landscapes in the river valleys, with patches of forest containing populations of moose, red deer, and beaver, served as 'passages' for the

---

5 Volokitin and Gribchenko, "North"; Besprozvanny et al., "North of West Siberia", 189f. Pitulko and Pavlova, *Geoarchaeology*, 10–12.
6 Zykin et al., "West Siberia", 180; Pitulko and Pavlova, *Geoarchaeology*, 58f.

Upper Palaeolithic pioneer societies, which ultimately were attracted by the great hunting potentials further north: the megafauna of the steppe. Here thrived herds of steppe bison, caribou, and horse, as well as mammoth, woolly rhinoceros, and muskox.[7]

Mamontora Kurya, a site on the polar circle west of Ural on a river terrace in the Usa River valley and dated to 40,000–33,000 years ago, is an example of one of these earliest settlements in the true Arctic part of the circumpolar north.[8] Far east of the Urals, in northern central Siberia, well-preserved remains of a mammoth with probable hunting injuries and butchering marks dating from at least 45,000 years ago have recently been found,[9] but at the time of writing the earliest excavated Upper Palaeolithic settlement site is the Yana site. The cultural layers are encapsulated in deep permafrozen river terrace sediments that are now being exposed because of erosion by the Yana River.[10] Dated to about 30,000 years ago, the site shows a rich archaeological and faunal material left by hunting groups, who primarily subsisted on big game such as bison, caribou, and horse. Excavations have revealed hearths and 'work areas' where stone tools were made and artefacts of mammoth tusks and bone were produced, including foreshafts and projectile points for spears. At the Yana site some of the earliest ornamental and symbolic artefacts and 'art objects' in Siberia were found: beads, pendants, needles, dishes of ivory, and anthropomorphic designs carved in mammoth ivory pieces (Figure 4.2).[11] Yana is one of several Siberian Palaeolithic sites situated close to a mammoth 'cemetery' – a natural bone bed, which was exploited as a raw material outcrop. The earliest securely documented case of active hunting of mammoth is in fact much later: a vertebra penetrated by a projectile point of quartzite from Lugovskoye, dated to about 16,000 years ago.[12]

Human life conditions in the Arctic and Sub-Arctic changed with the onset of the Late Glacial Maximum around 25,000 years ago. Severe cooling during this Sartan Glaciation in Siberia made the northern ice caps expand, and arid, peri-glacial steppe replaced the former mosaic landscapes over vast areas in northern Asia. However, groups of Upper Palaeolithic humans still remained in the areas west of Ural even far north, for example along the Pechora River, and hunters still roamed the barren grounds south of the ice caps of Siberia.[13]

---

7 Gribchenko, "Environments".
8 Plumet, *Des mythes*, 180; Svendsen and Pavlov, "Mamontova Kurya".
9 Pitul'ko et al., "Early Human".   10 Pitul'ko and Pavlova, *Geoarchaeology*, 58ff.
11 Pitul'ko et al., "The Oldest Art".   12 Zykin et al., "West Siberia", 188.
13 Pitul'ko et al., "Revising the Archaeological"; Besprozvany et al., "North of West Siberia", 189.

4 Initial Peopling of the Circumpolar North

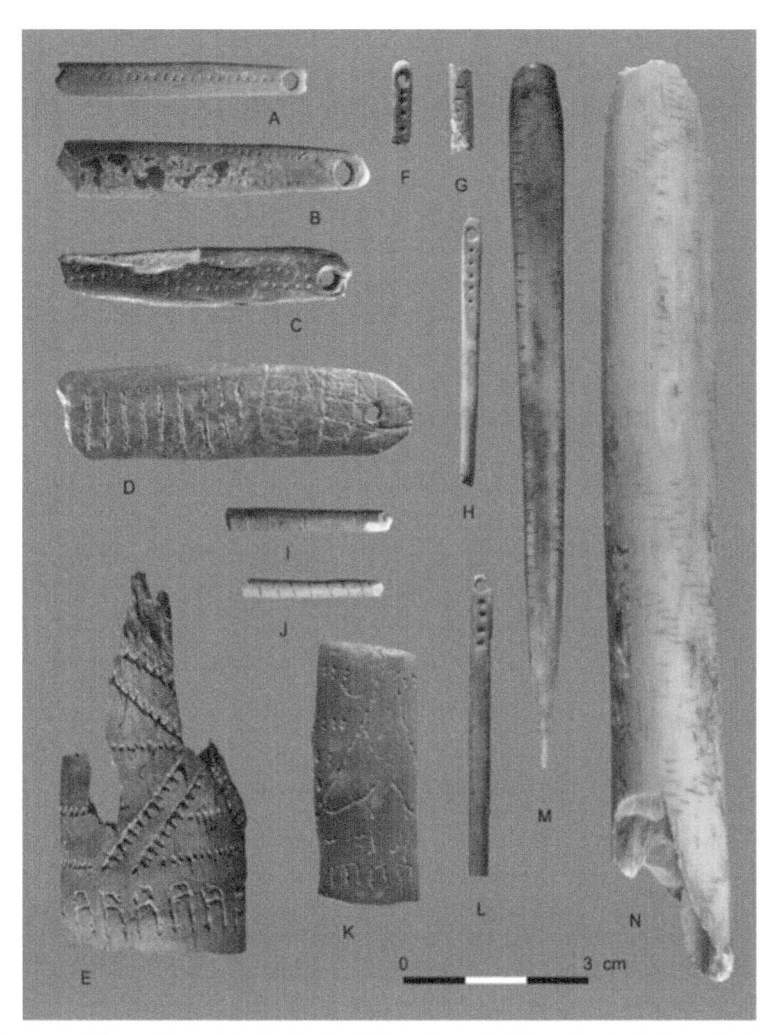

Figure 4.2 The earliest art in the Arctic. Objects from the Yana site. A–D, ivory diadems; E, fragment of a decorated object; F–H, L, needles and needle fragments; I, J, thin ivory shafts; K, ivory plaque with anthropomorphic image; M, awl with incisions; N, wolf(?) bone with spiral design. (Source: Pitul'ko et al., "The Oldest Art".)

By around 20,000 cal. BC, new groups began to move into these very cold and arid environments as societies of the Dyuktai Culture settled in the Aldan and Lena River valleys (e.g. the cave sites of Dyuktai and Khaiyrgas).[14] By the

14 Plumet, *Des mythes*, 248f.; Pitul'ko and Pavlova, *Geoarchaeology*, 38, 113.

Late Sartan Glaciation (around 16,000 cal. BC), severe climate fluctuations, including warm periods (interstadials), set in, resulting in various expansions and retractions of the ice caps and formation of more variate ecozones in the Old World Arctic. Thus, new potential resource spaces for human societies opened up.[15]

The subsequent Late Palaeolithic expansions of human societies into the Arctic can be traced via sites in the Pechora River basin, cave sites in the Ural Mountains, and sites in western Siberia (e.g. Chernoserye II and Lugovskye), as well as sites further east from the Berelekh tradition, named after a well-preserved site at the Indigirka River, dating to about 12,000–10,000 cal. BC.[16] Sites of the Dyuktai and the related Ushki Cultures have been located as far east as the Kolyma River basin and the Chukotka and Kamchatka peninsulas. The remarkably long-lasting Dyuktai Culture (c. 20,000–4,000 cal. BC)[17] introduced a new lithic technology – production of micro-blades for fine cutting and razor-sharp edges in projectile points – whereby their hunting tool kits became composite, lightweight, suited for long-distance transportation, and excellent for exploiting a wide spectrum of mammals, birds, and fish.[18] With the Dyuktai pioneer settlements in northeast Asia, humans had reached Beringia – the wide land bridge that then connected the Old and the New Worlds – a decisive geographical factor in the prehistory of the circumpolar north.

Beringia: The Land Bridge to Alaska

Beringia emerged as a result of the lowering of the sea level due to the formation of the huge ice caps of the last glacial period. This vast lowland steppe area dates back to about 40,000 years ago. It reached its maximum extent during the Sartan Glaciation due to a drop in the ocean level of more than 100 m. By this time, Beringia measured about 2,000 km north to south, and its 'mammoth steppe', which stretched from central Siberia far into Alaska, housed a rich and unparalleled megafauna consisting of herds of mammoth, steppe bison, horse, and caribou. However, during the Late Glacial and Early Holocene climate fluctuations, the rich steppe ecosystem was replaced by shrub tundra and finally deciduous forest before the land was completely transgressed by the rising seas. Already at the onset of the

---

15 Kuzmin, "Central Siberia", 213.
16 Zykin et al., "West Siberia", 184f., 188; Plumet, *Des mythes*, 250; Pitul'ko and Pavlova, *Geoarchaeology*, 92–109.
17 Pitul'ko and Pavlova, *Geoarchaeology*, 158; Kuzmin, "Central Siberia", 234–235.
18 Pitul'ko and Pavlova, *Geoarchaeology*, 141–142, 150.

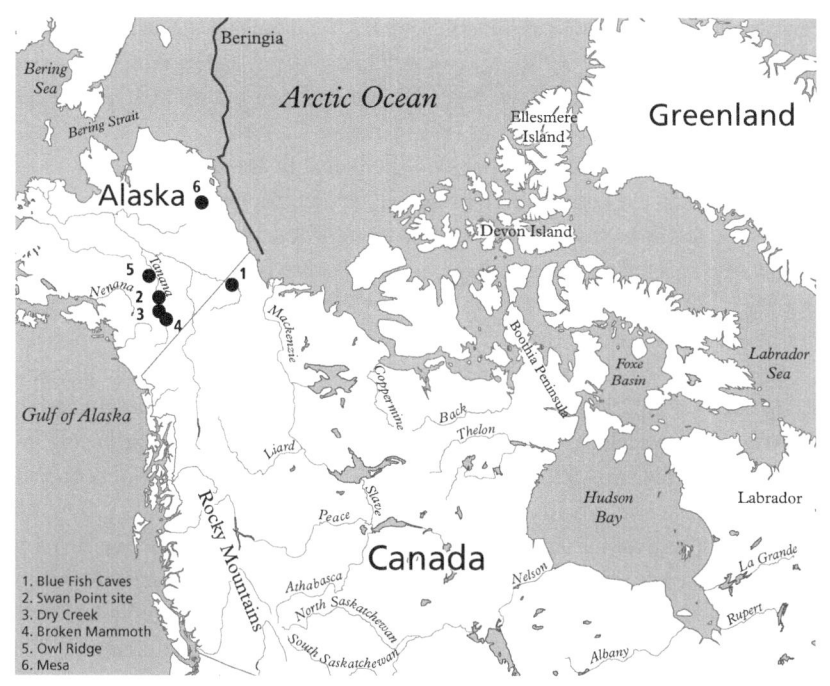

Figure 4.3 Archaeological sites in modern-day Alaska and Yukon related to the earliest migrants across Beringia.

Holocene warming around 9,500 cal. BC, the Bering Strait and the sea currents, almost as we know them now, were in place.[19]

The era of the mammoth steppe saw the first humans crossing Beringia on their way into the New World (Figure 4.3). The timing of these events is in dispute: most archaeologists believe that the peopling of Alaska and thus the North American continent was a process of multiple migrations by groups with different Siberian backgrounds, and that these events took place sometime during the Late Glacial periods of the Bølling–Allerød Interstadial (c. 12,700–10,900/10,600 cal. BC) and Younger Dryas (c. 10,600–9,500 cal. BC).[20] Designated the Palaeo-Arctic tradition and divided into the Denali and Nenana complexes (or cultures), the sites of these pioneers are found in central Alaska and Yukon.[21] It is assumed that an important part of the pioneer populations also utilized coastal resources, including marine

19 Anderson and Lozhkin, "Eastern Beringia"; Plumet, *Vers l'Esquimau*, 7.
20 Goebel and Potter, "First Traces"; Velichko et al., "Stages", 522f.
21 Goebel and Potter, "First Traces"; Graf and Goebel, "The Paleolithic".

mammals connected to kelp forests, as they spread quickly to the south along the Pacific by means of seagoing vessels. This is at least a plausible hypothesis for the spread of humans all the way to South America at a very early stage, as well as the formation of the palaeo-Indian pre-Clovis and Clovis Cultures, which, with remarkable pace, peopled the plains of North America south of the Cordilleran and Laurentian Ice Sheets.[22] From analyses of lithic artefacts it is possible to distinguish yet another characteristic early cultural tradition in Alaska: the Northern Palaeo-Indian complex, which might result from migrations from the Clovis ranges south of the ice caps through an ice-free corridor on the eastern side of the Rocky Mountains into northern and western Alaska.[23]

The earliest culture layers at the Swan Point site in the middle Tanana River valley represent the earliest securely dated settlement in Alaska. Dating to around 12,000 cal. BC (Early Bølling–Allerød Interstadial), the lithic assemblage from the site, with its wedge-shaped micro-blade cores (Yubetsu method) and micro-blades, clearly shows Siberian roots (the Dyuktai Culture). The Swan Point dwellers' fireplaces were fed with bones from the game they hunted: birds, horses, and cervids. The earliest assemblage from the site is interpreted as resulting from a short, single stay by hunters, repairing their tools and teaching apprentices the skills of flint knapping.[24]

It must be underlined that finds from the Blue Fish Caves as far east as the Yukon territory in Canada of worked bones – for instance a horse mandibula with cut marks and marrow split bones – are considered by some archaeologists to be the earliest traces of humans in North America. Recent studies support the excavators' original interpretation that humans were present in the caves and thus already in the easternmost Beringia area at the Glacial Maximum, c. 22,000 cal. BC, living in a kind of refugium until their world opened owing to the Late Glacial retreat of the ice caps.[25] Later, during the Allerød period (c. 11,500–10,600 cal. BC), sites like Dry Creek in the Nenana Valley and Broken Mammoth in the Tanana Valley were established, and these groups of the Denali and Nenana complexes also expanded their hunting ranges into the uplands of the valleys. During this period there were connections across the vanishing Beringia back to Siberia, among others to the Ushki Culture.[26] Finally, the very cold and arid finale of the ice age of

---

22 Fitzhugh, "The Origins", 254, 256.
23 Dixon, *Arrows*, 65f.; Graf and Goebel, "The Paleolithic", 337–338.
24 Gómez et al., "Knapping"; Graf and Goebel, "The Paleolithic", 319; Holmes et al., "Swan Point".
25 Cinq-Mars and Morlan, "Bluefish Caves"; Bourgeon et al., "Earliest Human".
26 Pitul'ko and Pavlova, *Geoarchaeology*, 117ff.; Graf and Goebel, "The Paleolithic", 321f.

the northern hemisphere, the Younger Dryas period, saw diversification of the pioneer societies in Alaska. Sites of the Denali complex, such as Owl Ridge, and of the palaeo-Indian complex, such as the Mesa site in northern Alaska, are characteristic of this Arctic period. Mesa was a highly specialized steppe-bison hunting location, with more than forty hearth features.[27]

The Holocene melting of the Laurentian Ice Sheet and the draining of the huge meltwater lakes south of it opened vast lowland plains and archipelagos in Arctic Canada. The Greenland Inland Ice also retreated, exposing a broad land zone intersected by deep fjords encircling the largest island on Earth. In the eastern New World Arctic, remarkably rich marine ecosystems developed sporadically at ice-free areas, polynyas, formed by intricate interplays between sea currents, seafloor topography, and prevailing winds.[28] However, throughout the first more than five millennia of climate optima following the ice age, no humans entered this huge eastern Arctic 'larder'. Its potential resources – marine and terrestrial game and raw materials – remained unexploited by human societies until the final expansion of the pre-Inuit cultures around 2,500 cal. BC.

The Early Holocene Human Colonization of the North

Into Arctic Scandinavia

Where the Fennoscandian Ice Sheet melted, open plains emerged, and already in the earliest interstadial, the Bølling period, herds of caribou and their top-predators, hunters of the Hamburgian Culture (probably originating in the Magdalenian Culture of central Europe), entered the tundra of the North European Plain and reached as far north as Jutland.[29] However it was only later, with the transition from Younger Dryas to Preboreal, at the onset of the Holocene around 9,500 cal. BC, that Early Mesolithic groups moved north from Doggerland (a landmass that was flooded by the North Sea around 6,500 years cal. BC) and via the Swedish west coast up along the now deglaciated coast of Norway and into northern Scandinavia (Figure 4.4).[30] This radical expansion of the hunting ranges seems – like other human expansions into the circumpolar

---

27 Kunz and Reanier, "Mesa Site".
28 Stirling, "Biological Importance"; Davidson et al., "History of Seabird Colonies"; Pedersen et al., "North East Greenland".
29 Riede and Tallavaara, eds., *Lateglacial and Postglacial Pioneers*.
30 Bjerck, "North Sea Continent".

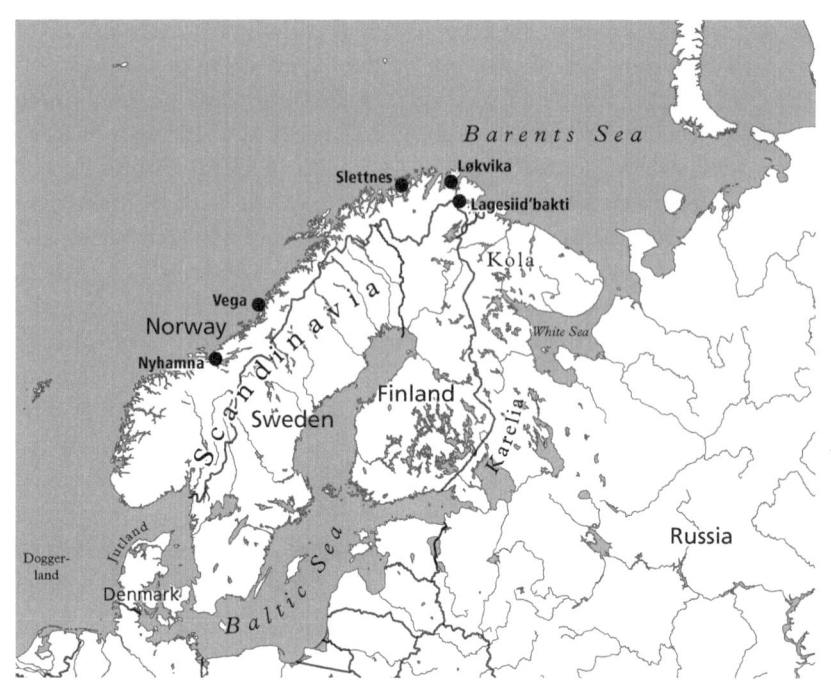

Figure 4.4 Significant early archaeological sites in Fennoscandia.

north – to have been remarkably fast, with a possible short delay in central Norway.[31] Archaeologically, these pioneer groups are designated the Fosna Culture, but a more neutral term, EM1 (Early Mesolithic 1), is often preferred.[32]

The driving forces behind this fast expansion into north Scandinavia are unknown, but the presence of 'virgin' ecosystems in the archipelagos, where fish and marine game attached to reefs and kelp forests thrived, no doubt attracted people. Exploitation of marine mammals demanded advanced technology, such as seagoing vessels and harpoons, and indeed the archaeological traces of EM1 sites along the Norwegian coast show a picture of highly mobile groups on the move. The sites are typically situated in the archipelago and consist of only a single or a few tent rings and fireplaces. The lithic technology was based on micro-blade production reflecting the use of composite, lightweight tools. The sites are interpreted as traces of families or

31 Kleppe, "Pioneer Colonization", 38–39.
32 Kleppe, "Pioneer Colonization"; Breivik and Bjerck, "Early Mesolithic".

4 Initial Peopling of the Circumpolar North

teams travelling in large skin boats resembling the *umiak* of the historic Inuit.[33] The EMI-period sites at Nyhamna and on the island of Vega on the west coast of Norway are characteristic of such pioneer 'travelling camps' in the coastal corridor to Arctic Scandinavia.[34] The hunting groups also made excursions into the fjords and inland, where they exploited caribou and fish.[35]

Analyses of the earliest lithic inventories in Sub-Arctic/Arctic Norway suggest that the arriving 'maritime' EMI groups from the west coast encountered more terrestrially oriented early Mesolithic groups, designated post-Swiderian, moving in from regions east of the glacial Yoldia Sea – present-day Karelia, Kola Peninsula, and Finland. Thus, the 'Komsa Culture' of the EMI phase in northernmost Norway is interpreted as resulting from the amalgamation of people from these two pioneer populations.[36] Among the earliest sites in northernmost Norway are Slettness, Løkvika, and Lagesiid'bakti, which were based on exploitation of coastal resources. However, the faunal material from Løkvika also included bones of reindeer, showing connections with the inland. Recent surveys have considerably increased the number of identified Early Mesolithic sites in the region.[37]

Mesolithic Coastal Hunters in Northern Siberia

The initial settlements at the White Sea, the Barents Sea, the Taimyr Peninsula, and further to the east along Siberia date to the Mesolithic period, when hunting societies of the Sumnagin, Uolba, and Siberdik traditions expanded their ranges from the northern forests into the vast plains.[38] Some groups settled, at least on a seasonal basis, on promontories and islands off the north Siberian coast, which at that time was situated several hundred kilometres north of the present-day coastline. From these vantage points people hunted both on the coastal plains and in the drift ice zone.

The finds from the permanently frozen layers at the remarkably large (8,000 m²) Zhokov site of the Sumnagin Culture, situated on one of the small New Siberian Islands, provide a unique window into a seasonal occupation at the Arctic Ocean dating to about 6,700 cal. BC. Traces of no fewer than thirteen dwellings were excavated, and the faunal material shows that subsistence on this site was based on a remarkable combined diet of meat and fat from caribou

---

33 Bjerck, "Colonizing Seascapes".   34 Bjerck, ed., *NTNU Vitenskapsmuseets*, 552–570.
35 Bang-Andersen, "First One Thousand Years".
36 Kleppe, "Pioneer Colonization", 34; Rankama and Kankaanpää, "From Russia with Love".
37 Hesjedal et al., *Arkeologi på Slettness*; Kleppe, "Desolate Landscapes"; Blankholm, "Macro-level".
38 Slobodin et al., "Western Beringia", 260f.

and polar bear, supplemented with a few seals, walrus, and geese. Large amounts of driftwood provided fuel and poles and planks for dwellings, and the wood also served as the raw material for tool shafts, ladles, dishes, hunting tools (including bows and arrows), and – for the first time – sledges. Bones of domestic dogs have been found, but the sledges were probably man-hauled as no toggles or traces from dog harnesses have been identified among the artefacts.[39]

Living in Icescapes: The Pre-Inuit Peopling of the New World Arctic

Finding the Key to Living in High Arctic Coastal Environments

Following the Mesolithic development in northeastern Siberia, where Arctic coastal resources were exploited, at least on a seasonal basis, Early Neolithic cultures – defined by their lithic technology and ceramic vessels – settled the coastal areas of the Kamchatka and Chukotka regions on a more permanent basis. The most generally accepted theory among archaeologists is that the first 'full-scale' Arctic societies, the pre-Inuit who entered the New World, developed out of these Siberian Neolithic roots in the Bering Strait area about 5,500 years ago. This is primarily based on comparative archaeological studies and ancient DNA traces in human remains. Earlier, these societies were designated 'palaeo-Eskimos', but archaeologists now prefer the terms 'Arctic Small Tool tradition' (ASTt), 'palaeo-Inuit', or 'pre-Inuit' for these pioneer societies.[40]

In the wake of the melting of the North American ice sheets and millennia of subsequent climate fluctuations, general warming, and formation of the Holocene sea currents and polar wind regimes, the New World Arctic developed into a vast landscape of tundra, mountains, fjords, archipelagos, and sea ice. As mentioned above, remarkably productive marine ecosystems formed in the apparently barren fields of sea ice. However, these *potential* resource spaces[41] were difficult to access and exploit: the ecological 'hot spots', like ice ledges, ice edges, and polynyas, are separated by great distances, and the animal populations migrate to and from these 'oases' according to the seasons. On top of this, the game populations fluctuate often drastically on an annual or decadal scale.[42]

---

39 Pitul'ko and Kasparov, *Ancient Arctic Hunters*; Slobodin et al., "Western Beringia", 263f.
40 Grønnow, *Frozen Saqqaq Sites*, 414ff.   41 Flora et al., "Present and Past Dynamics".
42 Schledermann, "Polynyas"; Meldgaard, *Ancient Harp Seal Hunters*, 32–35; Jeppesen et al., *Living in an Oasis*.

4 Initial Peopling of the Circumpolar North

The ability to trace such hot spots in the Arctic marine ecosystems, to evaluate their potential resources, to decode the fluctuations, to cope with the risks, and thus to turn such geographically delimited High Arctic areas into *realized* resource spaces was, as underlined before, a late achievement in human history. But around 3,500 cal. BC the code to living in the High Arctic was cracked, and as vast, hitherto unexploited areas from now on became hunting grounds, the pre-Inuit spread at a remarkable pace from Chukotka and Bering Strait via northern Alaska into the western Canadian Arctic. Following a relatively brief standstill there, the pre-Inuit continued their expansion by settling the entire Eastern Arctic within only a few generations.

A Cultural Historical Overview of the Initial Expansion

The initial spread of the pre-Inuit across the New World Arctic was, according to analyses of the radiocarbon dates, played out in two major stages. The first included the settling of northwestern and northern Alaska around 3,500 cal. BC. Archaeologists designate these people the Denbigh Flint complex, and their characteristic lithic tools, including advanced bifacial end blades, burins, scrapers, and micro-blades, are found on coastal sites as well as far inland along the rivers of northern Alaska, where caribou were hunted.[43] The earliest Denbigh Flint complex radiocarbon dates in Alaska are disputed.[44] However, it is a fact that traces of pioneer societies with a material culture resembling that of the Denbigh Flint complex are documented further east in the Canadian Arctic, where the pioneer groups are designated pre-Dorset. According to radiocarbon dates, this initial step from Alaska to Boothia Peninsula in the central Canadian Arctic took a maximum of four centuries, probably less.[45]

Subsequently the expansion stalled, probably within about five centuries. Either the archipelago further east did not offer attractive resources for the pre-Dorset pioneers at this time – much of the archipelago was still submerged – or it was a matter of demographic factors: the Eastern Arctic is huge, and the pioneer societies were 'small scale' and characterized by low population density. This is at least how these kind of societies are usually seen. Nevertheless, sometime between 2,470 and 2,290 cal. BC a fast spread of human societies into the hitherto uninhabited Eastern Arctic began. Archaeological evidence shows that in less than 180 years (about six

---

[43] Tremaine and Rasic, *Denbigh Flint Complex*. [44] Slaughter, *Radiocarbon Dating*.
[45] Grønnow, *Frozen Saqqaq Sites*, 381–382.

generations), vast areas were settled: from Foxe Basin in the Canadian archipelago to Labrador in the southeast, the High Arctic islands in the north, and ultimately the entire island of Greenland all the way to Scoresby Sound in East Greenland.[46] The processes behind this remarkable expansion are not fully understood. The coasts of the Greenland Sea and the North Atlantic formed the ultimate topographical eastern border of the pre-Inuit societies. After all, their transportation technology, sledges and skin boats, did not allow expansion across the formidable barrier that these oceans formed.

According to the archaeological analyses of differences in technologies, designs, subsistence, and settlement patterns, it is possible to distinguish between three pioneer pre-Inuit groups (or cultures) in the Eastern Arctic. Sites of the above-mentioned pre-Dorset have been found in the Canadian Arctic and at the 'Gateway to Greenland' – the North Water polynya, between Ellesmere Island and the Thule (Avernarsuaq) area – dating to c. 2,400 cal. BC. A specific group developed a strategy for living in the High Arctic based on muskox hunting in northernmost Canada and Greenland. This society, designated Independence I, coped with four to five months of winter darkness. The hunting ranges soon stretched south from Peary Land to the rich polynyas of northeast Greenland.[47]

Another group of the pre-Dorset found favourable living conditions around the North Water, from where they spread quickly to the extremely resource-rich environments of West Greenland. These people – designated the Saqqaq Culture – have left a very distinct archaeological 'fingerprint' through their extensive use of *killiaq* (silicified slate) for their lithic tools. With the subsequent spread of Saqqaq groups to South Greenland, around Cape Farewell and north along the east coast, and Independence I groups coming from the north into central East Greenland, the 'pre-Inuit circle' closed.[48]

Pre-Inuit Society, Material Culture, and Subsistence

Archaeological analyses of sites and finds provide at least some information on how the pioneering pre-Inuit societies lived their life constantly on the move and still managed to maintain a coherent society. Studies of settlement patterns show that the societies were egalitarian and organized in flexible family groups. Each group possessed seagoing vessels and probably sledges, and thus their gear, food, fuel, and other resources could be transported fast over long distances. The pioneer sites generally consist of the traces of a few, single-family tent dwellings

46 Grønnow, *Frozen Saqqaq Sites*, 377–380.
47 Schledermann, *Crossroads to Greenland*; Grønnow and Jensen, *The Northernmost Ruins*.
48 Grønnow, *Frozen Saqqaq Sites*.

(7–12 m²), but sites with either a few very large tent structures (up to 30 m²) or aggregations of dozens of single-family tents are known. They are interpreted as assemblage camps, where the normally separated families would gather regularly in order to exchange genes and information as well as to confirm social and spiritual connections, tell stories, and trade raw materials. Through activities in these aggregation camps, community spirit could be strengthened even during a state of constant migration into new lands.[49]

The archaeological traces of the family dwellings show that they were light, skin-covered tents, probably domes with frames of lashed, flexible poles of driftwood. These dwellings seem to be quite uniform all over the entire early pre-Inuit range: the same floor plans, layout of fireplaces, and an almost standard distribution of discarded artefacts and waste inside and around the tents. This also reinforced the coherence of the pre-Inuit society: during migrations into unknown land- and icescapes, their firmly structured dwellings formed a recognizable and predictable cosmos, providing order in the 'chaos' of the ever-changing environment.[50]

The hearth of the dwelling and the stone-built architecture framing it played an essential role. The fireplace provided both light in the dark season and indispensable heat. In the High Arctic, blubber and bones served as fuel in flagstone-framed box-hearths, often filled with fist-sized rocks ('cooking stones'), which accumulated heat and served as radiators in the dwellings (Figure 4.5). In areas where driftwood was an abundant resource, the archaeological record shows that large outdoor box-hearths were fed with firewood, and large quantities of cooking stones were heated. The hot stones were carried in wooden troughs into the dwelling and dumped in a stove compartment in the mid-passage inside the tent. Here the heaps of hot stones radiated smoke-free heating for hours. They were also used for boiling meat in water-filled skin bags and probably for rendering oil from seal and whale blubber. Transportable blubber lamps of sand- and soapstone were invented in the eastern Arctic at a later stage of the early pre-Inuit phase.[51]

Hearths as mentioned above, were often part of a so-called mid-passage or axial structure, dividing the floor of the tent into two halves. Typically, one half was an activity area whereas the opposite floor area served as a space for sleeping or resting. Careful excavation of an exceptionally well-preserved axial structure at the Saqqaq site, Qeqertasussuk, in Disko Bay, West Greenland, shows that this feature served practical purposes, acting for

---

49 Grønnow, *Frozen Saqqaq Sites*, 373–374; Savelle and Dyke, *Paleoeskimo Occupation*; Savelle et al., *Paleoeskimo Demography*.
50 Grønnow, *Frozen Saqqaq Sites*, 362–372.   51 Grønnow et al., *In Light of Blubber*.

Figure 4.5 Excavation of the mid-passage in a dwelling of the Saqqaq Culture at the Qeqertasussuk site, West Greenland. Framed by large flagstones, the mid-passage contained both a platform for food preparation (shown by student assistant Maria Steenholt in front) and a large heap of fire-cracked stones (in the back) for boiling meat in skin bags and for heating the dome-shaped tent. (Photo: Bjarne Grønnow, 1987.)

instance as a low table for processing and serving of food (finds of spoons, ladles, and wooden bowls) and for tool maintenance. However, ethnographic analogies suggest that the mid-passage feature also served as a symbolic entrance to spiritual worlds according to animistic/shamanistic cosmologies. A finely made, intact, hafted knife found below a mid-passage at Qeqertasussuk has been interpreted as a marker of the spiritual importance of this central feature.[52]

From the very beginning, the pre-Inuit possessed an advanced and light-weight material culture that formed the key to exploiting the resource spaces of the High Arctic. The finds from the two permanently frozen Early Saqqaq sites, Qajaa and Qeqertasussuk, in West Greenland (Figure 4.6) show that the pioneers used a wide range of light harpoons for hunting sea mammals, in

52 Grønnow, *Frozen Saqqaq Sites*, 286–291; Odgaard, *Hearth and Home*.

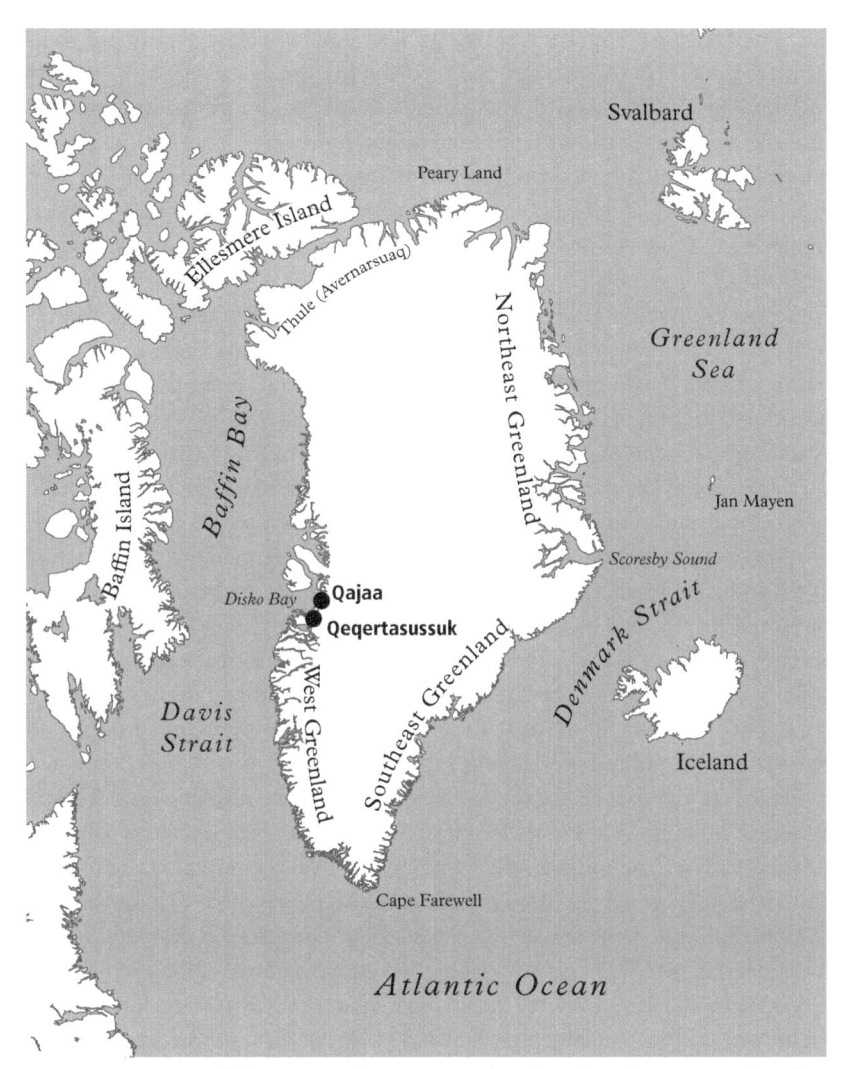

Figure 4.6 Location of the Qajaa and Qeqertasussuk archaeological sites in modern-day Greenland.

particular harp seals and ringed seals. Hunters in kayak-like, seagoing vessels would launch the harpoons by means of throwing boards and thus be able to hunt swimming animals at distances of up to 40 m. Other harpoons with toggling heads were used for hunting seals through breathing holes in the sea ice. The complex harpoon technology was supplemented by a broad spectrum of lances for killing harpooned marine mammals, as well as light darts for fowling and composite, reinforced bows and arrows for caribou and muskox hunting. Thus, with this diverse and lightweight tool kit, the hunter could select exactly the combination of gear to fit any kind of hunting opportunity. Tools for catching large whales have, however, not yet been found, even if whale bones, baleen, and ivory were used extensively as raw materials.[53]

Advanced raw material utilization and composite 'high tech' tools characterize the craftsmanship of the pre-Inuit. Most often, only the lithic components of tools have survived through millennia, but again the excellently preserved finds from frozen layers at the two Saqqaq sites in West Greenland open a unique window into this past technology. The butchering of seals and other game was done by means of a variety of knives with a bifacial end-blade of silicified slate mounted in a driftwood handle. Preparation of hides and working of wood, bone, ivory, baleen, and antler were made with specialized end- and side-scrapers and burins as well as razor-sharp micro-blades mounted in wooden hafts.[54] A few finds of sealskin pieces sewn with thin thread spun from sinew, along with fragments of skin stockings as well as sewing knives and tiny birdbone needles, indicate that pre-Inuit clothing must have been of the highest technological and aesthetic quality, like all parts of the pre-Inuit material culture.[55]

Faunal remains reflect the diversity of pre-Inuit resource exploitation. Whereas hunting in the northernmost High Arctic was obviously directed towards caribou and muskox, the faunal remains on sites around the polynyas and in the southern ranges show a wide variety of marine game, fish, and birds in combination with game from terrestrial hunting. The game was plentiful and, as mentioned above, had not yet adapted to the newly arrived top predator. At Qeqertasussuk, harp seals were the dominant game, but more than forty species are recorded in the faunal material, including Arctic fox, caribou, small whales, ringed seal, and a wide variety of sea birds and fish, as well as molluscs. Bones and baleen from large whales were frequently used raw materials, but it is an open question whether these whales were actively hunted.[56]

---

53 Grønnow, *Frozen Saqqaq Sites*, 47–115.
54 Grønnow, *Frozen Saqqaq Sites*, 115–182, 209–216.
55 Grønnow *Frozen Saqqaq Sites*, 182–185; Schmidt, *Catalogue of Worked Skin*.
56 Meldgaard, *Ancient Harp Seal Hunters*, 125–129.

Human Remains

Early pre-Inuit graves have not yet been identified, but some information on the treatment of the deceased can be gained from Qeqertasussuk, where a few human limb bones and tufts of human hair have been recovered in the lower midden layers (c. 2,400–2,200 cal. BC). The bones were weathered, and the proximal ends of the leg bones and both ends of the humerus showed irregular breaking patterns. The state of these bones suggests that before they were discarded they had gone through a skeletonization process, where the deceased had been de-fleshed.[57] The remains of a pre-Dorset infant have been uncovered under a flagstone inside a pre-Inuit dwelling structure on Devon Island, Canada, but neither a prepared burial pit nor grave goods were found in connection with these remains.[58] Results of ancient DNA analyses of the few early pre-Inuit remains from Greenland, including the human hair from Qeqertasussuk, and from Canada support the archaeologically based hypothesis that these people originated in Siberia and the Bering Strait region.[59]

The Non-Material World of the High Arctic Pioneers

Archaeological reasoning on prehistoric spiritual life is often based on interpretation of symbolic material culture – for instance decorated objects – as well as burials and architecture. However, in contrast to later pre-Inuit societies, the pioneers left only a handful of carved figurines and symbols engraved in antler and ivory artefacts.

The interpretation of the 'mid-passage' dwelling as reflecting a firmly structured cosmos of the pre-Inuit and the hearth as being an entrance to spiritual dimensions has been mentioned above. Some artefact designs seem to reflect an animistic world view, including the perception that all objects and beings have one or more souls. This is most obvious in the harpoon heads, where symbolic representations of different parts of animals – e.g. legs of caribou and muskox, and beaks of sea-birds – are integral parts of the design (Figure 4.7). Likewise, geometrical patterns and in rare cases symbolic spines or other simple skeletal elements, like ribs or 'breathing holes', are depicted by combinations of engraved lines and holes on lance foreshafts, needle cases, and tiny containers. A few finds of wooden rim fragments for large, circular drums indicate that shamanistic seances including drum

---

57 Frølich and Lynnerup, "Human Skeletal Remains".
58 Helmer and Kennedy, "Early Paleo-Eskimo Remains".
59 Gilbert et al., "Paleo-Eskimo mtDNA"; Rasmussen et al., "Ancient Human Genome"; Raghavan et al., "Genetic Prehistory".

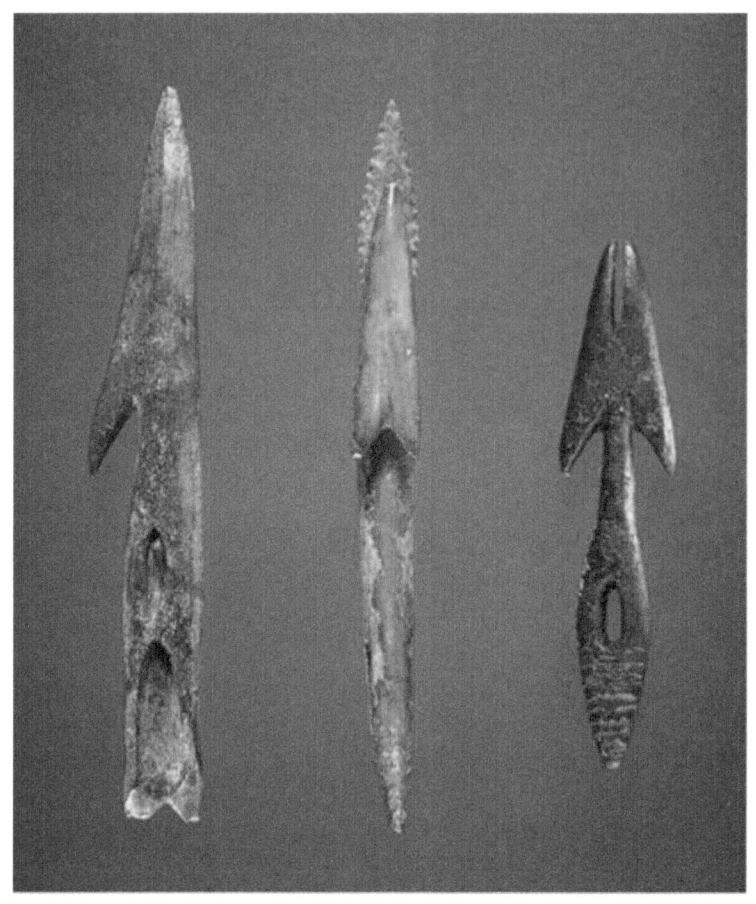

Figure 4.7 Three types of harpoon heads for sealing made of caribou antler, Saqqaq Culture. Elements inspired by animal anatomy like bird beaks and caribou or muskox cloven feet are characteristic for the design of the harpoons. The longest head is 80 mm long. (Photo: John Lee, The National Museum of Denmark.)

singing were part of the spiritual practices among the pre-Inuit.[60] Finally, a tiny mask carved from a piece of ivory and found on a pre-Dorset site on Devon Island in Canada shows the face of a tattooed individual. This figurine provides the only 'face-to-face' meeting with the very first people of the New World Arctic.[61]

60 Grønnow, "Backbone"; Grønnow, *Frozen Saqqaq Sites*, 341–343, 357–361.
61 Helmer, "Face from the Past".

Summary and Conclusions

We have seen that the spread of pioneer societies into the vast Arctic ecozone was often an abrupt or discontinuous process. Early Upper Palaeolithic human societies used the northern river valleys as hunting grounds and, not the least, as corridors providing access to the hunting grounds on the cold steppe and tundra of Siberia. This (probably seasonal) incorporation in the yearly hunting cycle of game like caribou, steppe bison, horse, muskox, mammoth, and woolly rhinoceros – the signature game of the arid steppes and the 'mammoth steppe' – demanded advanced subsistence strategies. The societies targeted hypermobile living resources – herds of migrating animals – which episodically yielded great amounts of food and raw materials. This drove both technological inventions and strategies for food storage and redistribution of resources in order to cope with significant seasonal fluctuations and some degree of unpredictability. Thirty thousand years ago, this strategy for the first time enabled hunter-gatherer societies to move into the major continental part of the circumpolar north, northern Siberia, on a more permanent basis.

The next major expansion into the north took place in the Late Palaeolithic around 14,000 cal. BC. The huge ice caps in North America and Scandinavia retreated, and vast inland areas as well as corridors along coasts opened up during the Late Glacial. Different migrations led humans across Beringia into the interior of Alaska and along the archipelago of the Pacific coast in a southerly direction. Later, around 9,500 cal. BC, a parallel process went on in the Old World, where the west coast of Norway was the scene of a remarkably fast migration from the south into Arctic Scandinavia during the early Pre-Boreal. This expansion was pre-conditioned by the late Palaeolithic/early Mesolithic societies' abilities to hunt marine mammals in the drift ice and open water, supplemented by fishing and gathering in the coastal zone as well as by seasonal hunting of caribou in the interior.

The final step in the peopling of the North consisted of the pre-Inuit expansion into the icescapes of the New World Arctic. Following the retreat of the ice caps due to the Holocene warming, sporadically distributed, biologically rich 'Arctic oases' like sea ice ledges, ice edges, and polynyas had developed over millennia along the Arctic coasts of Alaska, Canada, and Greenland, but it was as recently as around 3,500 cal. BC that humans broke the code for making a living out of these potential resources, so closely connected with the sea ice in all its forms. The invention of complex harpoon technologies for hunting seal, walrus, and other marine game was important in this respect. The initial spread of pre-Inuit groups from the Bering Strait eastwards to the central Canadian Arctic was fast, but then it paused for a few centuries. A second migration, around 2,400 cal. BC, brought these people into every part of the Eastern Arctic, including Greenland in the north and Labrador in the southeast. With our current knowledge, it is difficult to fully understand the demographic and cultural backgrounds and driving forces behind this rapid spread of small-scale pre-Inuit societies into such vast and diverse landscapes.

No doubt the character of the living resources of the northern ecozones played a decisive role in the initial peopling of the circumpolar north. The large herds of game on the steppe and tundra attracted people, the meat and fat of the game were nutritious, and when first tracked and encountered, the animals were easy prey as the pioneers moved into areas where the game had never encountered human hunters before. On the other hand, basic challenges in Arctic environments, such as land- and icescapes within difficult reach, protection against harsh weather conditions and darkness (housing and clothing), huge seasonal variations, sporadically distributed and fluctuating biotic resources, transportation, raw material procurement, and food storage, had to be met. Obviously, it was not a straightforward task for originally tropical beings like humans to move into the circumpolar north. Knowledge as well as experiences from millennia of successes and failures had to be accumulated and activated in order for human societies to thrive in the north. This might, at least on a macro-scale, explain the discontinuous and bumpy road to the initial peopling of this part of the world.

It is also obvious from this overview that considerations of subsistence strategies and technological inventions do not cover the entire story of the true pioneers of the north. As no direct analogues to these societies exist today, we can only infer from the archaeological sources that the driving forces behind the stepwise migrations must also have been embedded in a pioneer mindset. At least for the Late Palaeolithic and pre-Inuit pioneers, hypermobility – constant movement into unknown, uninhabited landscapes – became a way of life. Social, cultural, and spiritual coherence, even under constant travelling into new hunting ranges, was probably regularly reinforced when families from near and far met at aggregation camps. The firmly structured domestic spheres – for example, the mid-passage dwellings of the pre-Inuit, with all its symbolic aspects centred around the hearth or the blubber lamp – formed a counterweight to the constantly changing landscapes, environments and resources surrounding the people. The Arctic pioneers literally travelled with their cosmos as they settled the circumpolar north.

Bibliography

Anderson, Patricia M., and Anatoly V. Lozhkin, "Eastern Beringia: Climates and Environments During the Initial Peopling", in V. M. Kotlyakov, Andrey A. Velichko, and Sergey A. Vasil'ev, eds., *Human Colonization of the Arctic: The Interaction Between Early Migration and the Paleoenvironment* (London: Elsevier/Academic, 2017), pp. 299–310.

Bang-Andersen, Sveinung, "The First One Thousand Years: Human Colonization and Differentiated Landscape Use in South-Western Norway, 10,000–9,000 BC", in Hans Peter Blankholm, ed., *Early Economy and Settlement in Northern Europe: Pioneering, Resource Use, Coping with Change* (Bristol: Equinox, 2018), pp. 275–310.

Besprozvanny, Evgeniy M., Pavel A. Kosintsev, and Andrey A. Pogodin, "North of West Siberia", in V. M. Kotlyakov, Andrey A. Velichko, and Sergey A. Vasil'ev, eds., *Human Colonization of the Arctic: The Interaction Between Early Migration and the Paleoenvironment* (London: Elsevier/Academic, 2017), pp. 189–210.

Bjerck, Hein, "Colonizing Seascapes: Comparative Perspectives on the Development of Maritime Relations in Scandinavia and Patagonia", *Arctic Anthropology* 46 (2009): 118–131.

Bjerck, Hein, "The North Sea Continent and the Pioneer Settlement of Norway", in Anders Fischer, ed., *Man and Sea in the Mesolithic: Coastal Settlement Above and Below Present Sea Level*, Oxbow Monograph 53 (Oxford: Oxbow, 1995), pp. 131–144.

Bjerck, Hein, ed., *NTNU Vitenskapsmuseets arkeologiske undersøkelser, Ormen Lange Nyhamna* (Trondheim: Tapir Akademisk, 2008).

Blankholm, Hans Peter, "Macro-level Predictive Modelling of Early Stone Age Pioneer Settlement Locations in Varanger, Northern Norway", in Hans Peter Blankholm, ed., *Early Economy and Settlement in Northern Europe: Pioneering, Resource Use, Coping with Change* (Bristol: Equinox, 2018), pp. 77–101.

Bourgeon, Lauriane, Ariane Burke, and Thomas Higham, "Earliest Human Presence in North America Dated to the Last Glacial Maximum: New Radiocarbon Dates from Bluefish Caves, Canada", *PLoS ONE* 12 (2017), https://doi.org/10.1371/journal.pone.0169486.

Breivik, Heidi Melva, and Hein Bjerck, "Early Mesolithic in Central Norway: A Review of Research History, Settlements and Tool Tradition", in Hans Peter Blankholm, ed., *Early Economy and Settlement in Northern Europe: Pioneering, Resource Use, Coping with Change* (Bristol: Equinox, 2018), pp. 169–206.

Cinq-Mars, Jacques, and Richard E. Morlan, "Bluefish Caves and Old Crow Basin: A New Rapport", in Robson Bonnichsen and Karen L. Turnmire, eds., *Ice Age Peoples of North America: Environments, Origins, and Adaptations of the First Americans* (Corvallis: Oregon State University Press, 1999), pp. 200–212.

Davidson, Thomas A., Sebastian Wetterich, Kasper L. Johansen, et al., "The History of Seabird Colonies and the North Water Ecosystem: Contributions from Paleoecological and Archaeological Evidence", *Ambio* 47 (Supplement 2): *The North Water: Interdisciplinary Studies of a High Arctic Polynya under Transformation* (2018): 175–192.

Derevyanko, Antoly P., "The Most Ancient Migrations of Humans into Eurasia and the Problem of the Upper Paleolithic Formation", *Archaeology, Ethnography and Anthropology of Eurasia* 2 (2005): 22–36.

Derevyanko, Anatoly P., "Transition from Middle to Upper Paleolithic on the Altai", *Archaeology, Ethnography and Anthropology of Eurasia* 3 (2001): 70–103.
Dixon, James E., *Arrows and Atl Atls: A Guide to the Archaeology of Beringia* (National Park Service, Department of the Interior, 2013).
Douka, Katerina, Viviane Slon, Zenobia Jacobs, et al., "Age Estimates for Hominin Fossils and the Onset of the Upper Palaeolithic at Denisova Cave", *Nature* 565 (2019): 640–644, https://doi.org/10.1038/s41586-018-0870-z.
Fitzhugh, Ben, "The Origins and Development of Arctic Maritime Adaptations in the Subarctic and Arctic Pacific", in T. Max Friesen and Owen Mason, eds., *The Oxford Handbook of the Prehistoric Arctic* (Oxford: Oxford University Press, 2016), pp. 252–278.
Flora, Janne, Kasper L. Johansen, Bjarne Grønnow, Astrid O. Andersen, and Anders Mosbech, "Present and Past Dynamics of Inughuit Resource Spaces", in Kirsten Hastrup et al., eds., *Ambio* 47 (Supplement 2): *The North Water: Interdisciplinary Studies of a High Arctic Polynya under Transformation* (2018): 244–264.
Frølich, Bruno and Niels Lynnerup, "Human Skeletal Remains from Qeqertasussuk: The Anthropology", in Bjarne Grønnow, ed., *The Frozen Saqqaq Sites of Disko Bay, West Greenland: Qeqertasussuk and Qajaa (2400–900 BC). Studies of Saqqaq Material Culture in an Eastern Arctic Perspective*. Meddelelser om Grønland/Monographs on Greenland, Man and Society 356 (Copenhagen: Museum Tusculanum, 2017), pp. 464–474.
Gilbert, M. Thomas P., Toomas Kivisild, Bjarne Grønnow, et al., "Paleo-Eskimo mtDNA Genome Reveals Matrilineal Discontinuity in Greenland", *Science Express* (29 May 2008). Report and supporting online material, https://doi.org/10.1126/science.1159750.
Goebel, Ted, and Ben Potter, "First Traces: Late Pleistocene Human Settlement of the Arctic", in T. Max Friesen and Owen Mason, eds., *The Oxford Handbook of the Prehistoric Arctic* (Oxford: Oxford University Press, 2016), pp. 223–252.
Gómez Coutouly, Yan Axel, Angela K. Gore, Charles E. Holmes, et al., "Knapping, My Child, Is Made of Errors: Apprentice Knappers at Swan Point and Little Panguingue Creek, Two Prehistoric Sites in Central Alaska", *Lithic Technology* (2020), 2–26, https://doi.org/10.1080/01977261.2020.1805201.
Graf, Kelly E., and Ted Goebel, "The Paleolithic of Eastern Beringia from Western Alaska to Canadian Yukon", in V. M. Kotlyakov, Andrey A. Velichko, and Sergey A. Vasil'ev, eds., *Human Colonization of the Arctic: The Interaction Between Early Migration and the Paleoenvironment* (London: Elsevier/Academic Press, 2017), pp. 312–338.
Gribchenko, Yuriy N., "Environments of the Northeastern East European Plain at the Time of the Initial Human Colonization", in V. M. Kotlyakov, Andrey A. Velichko, and Sergey A. Vasil'ev, eds., *Human Colonization of the Arctic: The Interaction Between Early Migration and the Paleoenvironment* (London: Elsevier/Academic Press, 2017), pp. 105–133.
Grønnow, Bjarne, "The Backbone of the Saqqaq Culture: A Study of the Non-material Dimensions of the Early Arctic Small Tool Tradition", *Arctic Anthropology* 49 (2012): 58–71.
Grønnow, Bjarne, *The Frozen Saqqaq Sites of Disko Bay, West Greenland: Qeqertasussuk and Qajaa (2400–900 BC). Studies of Saqqaq Material Culture in an Eastern Arctic Perspective*. Meddelelser om Grønland/Monographs on Greenland, Man and Society 356 (Copenhagen: Museum Tusculanum, 2017).

4 Initial Peopling of the Circumpolar North

Grønnow, Bjarne, and Jens Fog Jensen, *The Northernmost Ruins of the Globe: Eigil Knuth's Archaeological Investigations in Peary Land and Adjacent Areas of High Arctic Greenland*. Meddelelser om Grønland/Monographs on Greenland, Man and Society 29 (Copenhagen: Museum Tusculanum, 2003).

Grønnow, Bjarne, Martin Appelt, and Ulla Odgaard, "In the Light of Blubber: The Earliest Stone Lamps in Greenland and Beyond", in Hans Christian Gulløv, ed., *Northern Worlds: Landscapes, Interactions and Dynamics*. Studies in Archaeology and History 22 (Copenhagen: National Museum, 2014), pp. 403–422.

Helmer, James W., "A Face from the Past: An Early Pre-Dorset Ivory Maskette from the Devon Lowlands, N.W.T.", *Inuit Studies* 10 (1986): 179–202.

Helmer, James W., and Brenda V. Kennedy, "Early Paleo-Eskimo Skeletal Remains from North Devon Island, High Arctic Canada", *Canadian Journal of Archaeology* 10 (1986): 127–143.

Hesjedal, Anders, Charlotte Damm, Bjørnar Olsen, and Inger Storli, *Arkeologi på Slettnes: Dokumentasjon av 11.000 års bosetning*. Tromsø Museums Skrifter 26 (Tromsø Museum, University of Tromsø, 1996).

Holmes, Charles E., Richard VanderHoek, and T. E. Dilley, "Swan Point", in F. H. West, ed., *American Beginnings: The Prehistory and Palaeoecology of Beringia* (Chicago: University of Chicago Press, 1996), pp. 319–323.

Jeppesen, Erik, Martin Appelt, Kirsten Hastrup, et al., "Living in an Oasis: Rapid Transformations, Resilience, and Resistance in the North Water Area Societies and Ecosystems", *Ambio* 47 (Supplement 2): *The North Water: Interdisciplinary Studies of a High Arctic Polynya under Transformation* (2018): 296–309.

Kleppe, Jan Ingolf, "Desolate Landscapes or Shifting Landscapes? Late Glacial/Early Post-Glacial Settlements of Northernmost Norway in the Light of New Data from Eastern Finnmark", in Felix Riede and Miikka Tallavaara, eds., *Lateglacial and Postglacial Pioneers in Northern Europe*. BAR International Series 2599 (Oxford: Archaeopress, 2014), pp. 121–145.

Kleppe, Jan Ingolf, "The Pioneer Colonization of Northern Norway", in Hans Peter Blankholm, ed., *Early Economy and Settlement in Northern Europe: Pioneering, Resource Use, Coping with Change* (Bristol: Equinox, 2018), pp. 13–58.

Kotlyakov, V. M., Andrey A. Velichko, and Sergey A. Vasil'ev, eds., *Human Colonization of the Arctic: The Interaction Between Early Migration and the Paleoenvironment* (London: Elsevier/Academic, 2017).

Kunz, Michael L., and Richard E. Reanier, "The Mesa Site: A Paleoindian Hunting Lookout in Arctic Alaska", *Arctic Anthropology* 32 (1995): 5–30.

Kuzmin, Yaroslav Y., "Central Siberia (the Yenisey-Lena-Yana Region)", in V. M. Kotlyakov, Andrey A. Velichko, and Sergey A. Vasil'ev, eds., *Human Colonization of the Arctic: The Interaction Between Early Migration and the Paleoenvironment* (London: Elsevier/Academic, 2017), pp. 213–237.

Meldgaard, Morten, *Ancient Harp Seal Hunters of Disko Bay: Subsistence and Settlement at the Saqqaq Culture Site Qeqertasussuk (2400–1400 BC), West Greenland*. Meddelelser om Grønland/Monographs on Greenland, Man and Society 30 (Copenhagen: Museum Tusculanum, 2004).

Odgaard, Ulla, "Hearth and Home of the Palaeo-Eskimos", *Études/Inuit/Studies* 27 (2003): 349–374.

Pedersen, Jørn, Bjarke Torp, Laura Hauch Kaufmann, Aart Kroon, and Bjarne Holm Jacobsen, "The North East Greenland Sirius Water Polynya Dynamics and Variability Inferred from Satellite Imagery", *Danish Journal of Geography* 110 (2010): 131–142.

Pitul'ko, Vladimir V., and Aleksey K. Kasparov, "Ancient Arctic Hunters: Material Culture and Survival Strategy", *Arctic Anthropology* 33 (1996): 1–36.

Pitul'ko, Vladimir V., and Elena Y. Pavlova, *Geoarchaeology and Radiocarbon Chronology of Stone Age Northeast Asia*. Peopling of the Americas Publications (College Station: Texas A&M University Press, 2016).

Pitul'ko, Vladimir, Alexei N. Tikhonov, Elena Y. Pavlova, et al., "Early Human Presence in the Arctic: Evidence from 45,000-Year-Old Mammoth Remains", *Science* 351 (2016): 260–263.

Pitul'ko, Vladimir V., Elena Y. Pavlova, Pavel A. Nikolsky, and V. Ivanova, "The Oldest Art of Eurasian Arctic: Personal Ornaments and Symbolic Objects from Yana RHS, Arctic Siberia", *Antiquity* 86 (2012): 642–659.

Pitulko, Vladimir, Elena Pavlova, and Pavel Nikolskiy, "Revising the Archaeological Record of the Upper Pleistocene Arctic Siberia: Human Dispersal and Adaptations in MIS 3 and 2", *Quaternary Science Reviews* 165 (2017): 127–148, https://doi.org/10.1016/j.quascirev.2017.04.004.

Plumet, Patrick, *Des mythes á la Préhistoire: Peuple du Grand Nord, Tome I* (Paris: Editions Errance, 2004).

Plumet, Patrick, *Vers l' Esquimau: Du mammouth á la baleine. Peuples du Grand Nord, Tome II* (Paris: Editions Errance, 2004).

Raghavan, Manasa, Michael DeGiorgio, Anders Albrechtsen, et al., "The Genetic Prehistory of the New World Arctic", *Science* 345 (2014), https://doi.org/10.1126/science.1255832.

Rankama, Tuija, and Jarmo Kankaanpää, "From Russia with Love: Eastern Intruders in North Norwegian Mesolithic", in Hans Peter Blankholm, ed., *Early Economy and Settlement in Northern Europe: Pioneering, Resource Use, Coping with Change* (Bristol: Equinox, 2018), pp. 139–167.

Rasmussen, Morten, Yingrui Li, Stinus Lindgren, et al., "Ancient Human Genome Sequence of an Extinct Palaeo-Eskimo", *Nature* 463 (2010): 757–762.

Riede, Felix, and Miikka Tallavaara, eds., *Lateglacial and Postglacial Pioneers in Northern Europe*. BAR International Series 2599 (Oxford: Archaeopress, 2014).

Savelle, James M., and Arthur Dyke, "Paleoeskimo Occupation History of Foxe Basin, Arctic Canada: Implications for the Core Area Model and Dorset Origins", *American Antiquity* 79 (2014): 249–276.

Savelle, James M., Arthur S. Dyke, Peter J. Whitridge, and Melanie Poupart, "Paleoeskimo Demography on Western Victoria Island, Arctic Canada: Implications for Social Organization and Longhouse Development", *Arctic* 65 (2012): 167–181.

Schledermann, Peter, *Crossroads to Greenland: 3000 Years of Prehistory in the Eastern High Arctic*. Komatik Series 2 (Calgary: Arctic Institute of North America, University of Calgary, 1990).

Schledermann, Peter, "Polynyas and Prehistoric Settlement Patterns", *Arctic* 33 (1980): 292–302.

Schmidt, Anne Lisbeth, "Catalogue of Worked Skin Fragments from Qeqertasussuk", in Bjarne Grønnow, ed., *The Frozen Saqqaq Sites of Disko Bay, West Greenland:*

4 Initial Peopling of the Circumpolar North

Qeqertasussuk and Qajaa (2400–900 BC). Studies of Saqqaq Material Culture in an Eastern Arctic Perspective. Meddelelser om Grønland / Monographs on Greenland, Man and Society 356 (Copenhagen: Museum Tusculanum, 2017), pp. 443–460.

Slaughter, Dale C., "Radiocarbon Dating the Arctic Small Tool Tradition in Alaska", Alaska Journal of Anthropology 3 (2005): 117–133.

Slobodin, Sergey B., Patricia M. Anderson, Olga Y. Glushkova, and Anatoly V. Lozhkin, "Western Beringia (Northeast Asia)", in V. M. Kotlyakov, Andrey A. Velichko, and Sergey A. Vasil'ev, eds., Human Colonization of the Arctic: The Interaction Between Early Migration and the Paleoenvironment (London: Elsevier / Academic, 2017), pp. 241–298.

Slon, Viviane, Fabrizio Mafessoni, Benjamin Vernot, et al., "The Genome of the Offspring of a Neanderthal Mother and a Denisovan Father", Nature 561 (2018): 113–116, https://doi.org/10.1038/s41586-018-0455-x.

Stirling, Ian, "The Biological Importance of Polynyas in the Canadian Arctic", Arctic 33 (1980): 303–315.

Svendsen, John I., and Pavel Y. Pavlov, "Mamontova Kurya: An Enigmatic Nearly 40,000 Years Old Palaeolithic Site in the Russian Arctic", in J. Zilhbo and F. D'Errico, eds., The Chronology of the Aurignacian and the Transitional Technocomplexes: Dating, Stratigraphies, Cultural Implications. Trabalhos de Archaeologia 33 (Lisboa: Direção-Geral do Património Cultural, 2003), pp. 109–120.

Tremaine, Andrew H., and Jeffrey T. Rasic, "The Denbigh Flint Complex of Northern Alaska", in T. Max Friesen and Owen Mason, eds., The Oxford Handbook of the Prehistoric Arctic (Oxford: Oxford University Press, 2016), pp. 349–370.

Velichko, Andrey A., Sergey A. Vasil'ev, Yuriy N. Gribchenko, and Elena I. Kurenkova, "Stages of the Initial Human Colonization of Arctic and Subarctic", in V. M. Kotlyakov, Andrey A. Velichko, and Sergey A. Vasil'ev, eds., Human Colonization of the Arctic: The Interaction Between Early Migration and the Paleoenvironment (London: Elsevier / Academic, 2017), pp. 509–530.

Volokitin, Alexander V., and Yuriy N. Gribchenko, "North of the East European Plain", in V. M. Kotlyakov, Andrey A. Velichko, and Sergey A. Vasil'ev, eds., Human Colonization of the Arctic: The Interaction Between Early Migration and the Paleoenvironment (London: Elsevier / Academic, 2017), pp. 75–152.

Zykin, Vladimir S., Valentina S. Zykina, Sergey V. Markin, and Liybov A. Orlova, "West Siberia," in V. M. Kotlyakov, Andrey A. Velichko, and Sergey A. Vasil'ev, eds., Human Colonization of the Arctic: The Interaction Between Early Migration and the Paleoenvironment (London: Elsevier / Academic, 2017), pp. 179–188.

5
Archaeology, Politics, and Sámi Heritage

CARL-GÖSTA OJALA

Introduction

Archaeology in Sápmi – the traditional core area of the Indigenous Sámi people in northern Norway, Sweden, Finland, and the Kola Peninsula in the Russian Federation – is a contested field of study, closely intertwined with issues of identity, ethnicity, and indigeneity, as well as conflicts over land and cultural rights. In recent decades, Sámi archaeology has emerged as a multidimensional and dynamic movement, engaged with the diversity of Sámi pasts and the complex interrelations between past and present. This chapter reviews current issues in Sámi archaeology and heritage management, and explores some of the political dimensions of archaeology in Sápmi and challenges that archaeologists and other researchers are facing in this field of tension.

One fundamental aspect characterizing Sámi archaeology as a field of study is the fact that Sápmi extends across the present-day state boundaries of northernmost Europe (see Figure 5.1). Therefore, Sámi archaeology by definition is cross-boundary archaeology, and needs to take into account the different histories and contemporary political and social conditions in the four countries. However, the modern state boundaries have played an important role in shaping the understanding of history and heritage in the Sámi areas, and they continue to play a fundamental role in archaeology and heritage management.

Another fundamental aspect is the colonial dimension, which is shared by all Sámi groups. Sámi archaeology is closely connected with the histories and legacies of Scandinavian/Nordic colonialism and Russian colonialism in the Arctic and Sub-Arctic, which have been contested topics. Sámi political and cultural revitalization movements, and Sámi struggles for self-determination, Indigenous rights, and decolonization have challenged traditional archaeology and heritage management in the Nordic countries. Therefore, Sámi archaeology also becomes an illustrative example of the politics of

5 Archaeology, Politics, and Sámi Heritage

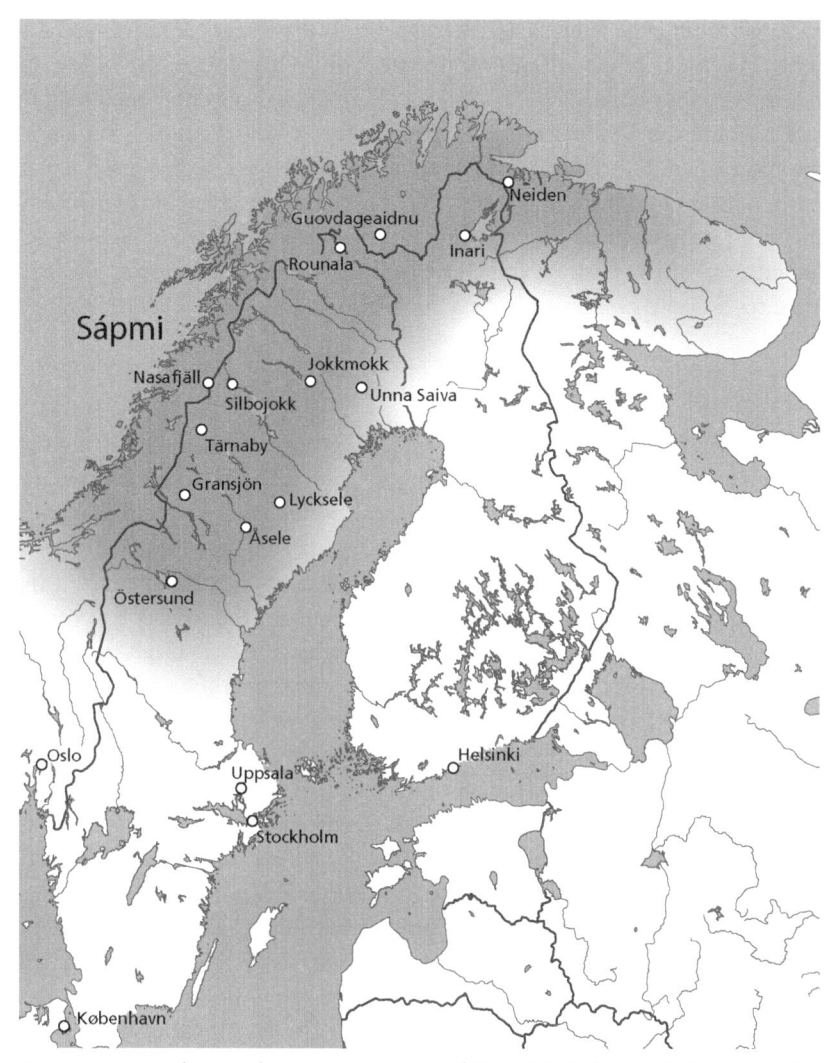

Figure 5.1 Map indicating the approximate area of Sápmi (shaded in grey), the present-day core settlement and cultural area of the Sámi people, with some of the sites mentioned in the chapter.

archaeology and heritage, and the challenges and possibilities of dealing with colonialism.

In the national imagination in Norway, Sweden, and Finland, Sáminess represents northernness (or extreme northernness), in contrast to the main national self-image. Seen in a research historical perspective, Sámi archaeology has been marginalized within national archaeologies. However, in recent times, aspects of Sámi history and heritage have become increasingly important in the national history-writing in the Nordic countries. Similarly, the colonial dimensions, earlier ignored or silenced, have been considered as more relevant to the national narratives. As such, Sámi archaeology points to the need to recognize and explore the northern, Arctic and Sub-Arctic, dimensions of the history and heritage of the Nordic countries, and the need to critically examine Nordic colonialism.

Archaeology, Indigeneity, and Politics

The border between 'North' and 'South' is one of the most fundamental borders in Nordic archaeology, affecting not only interpretations and understandings of prehistoric and early historical periods, but also structures of archaeological research and cultural heritage management. The North has recurrently been perceived as wilderness and periphery, characterized by relative primitiveness and retarded development. In the history of Nordic archaeology, northern archaeology has largely been marginalized and more or less excluded from the national narratives. Perceptions of North and South in archaeology have been, and still are, closely connected with notions of Sámi and Swedish, Norwegian, and Finnish history, culture, and identity, as well as notions of Nordic colonialism in Sápmi.

Archaeology is not only about the past. Every interpretation of the past is carried out in the contemporary world, with its socio-cultural and political contexts. Sámi struggles for self-determination and land and cultural rights are part of the international Indigenous movement. Sámi representatives have also participated actively, and played an important role, in international Indigenous fora. In archaeology and heritage studies, responding to the demands and challenges posed by Indigenous groups, a field of Indigenous archaeology has developed in the last decades.

Indigenous archaeology is a relatively new movement within critical archaeology, which has gained importance globally in recent years. It has been promoted, by its proponents, as a movement to challenge and transform traditional archaeology and heritage management, in order to work for decolonization and the empowerment of Indigenous groups. The most influential debates on Indigenous archaeology have taken place in English-speaking settler colonial nations – the USA, Canada, Australia, and New

5 Archaeology, Politics, and Sámi Heritage

Zealand – although discussions today take place in many other parts of the world.[1]

Indigenous archaeology is closely connected with issues of colonialism and decolonization – issues which are highly relevant in the contemporary Sámi context. The Native American archaeologist Sonya Atalay stresses that a decolonizing archaeology, encompassing a much wider field than 'traditional' archaeology 'must include topics such as the social construction of cultural heritage, concerns over revitalization of tradition and Indigenous knowledge, issues of ownership and authority, cultural and intellectual property, and the history and role of museums, collections and collecting'.[2] In Indigenous archaeology approaches, much focus has been placed on community-based and community-initiated research, with participatory and collaborative methodologies – ways of doing research that consider not only academic interests and standards, but also seriously involve the perspectives, interests, wishes, and priorities of local and Indigenous communities.[3]

As an example of collaborative community-based archaeology projects in the Arctic and Sub-Arctic regions, one can mention the excavations at Nunalleq in Alaska, conducted by researchers from the University of Aberdeen in collaboration with the local Yup'ik community of Quinhagak. In this project, an amazingly rich archaeological material at a pre-contact Yup'ik settlement site (sixteenth to seventeenth centuries) has been rescued from destruction due to coastal erosion and climate change, at the same time working to revitalize local Yup'ik knowledge and traditions.[4]

Recent decades have seen a growth of collaborative archaeology projects in Sápmi, based in and initiated from within local Sámi communities, especially in the South Sámi regions, where archaeology has been especially controversial, for instance in court cases dealing with land rights, and where Sámi (pre)history has earlier been invisibilized.[5] Collaborative projects have also taken place in other regions of Sápmi, for instance using Participatory GIS (geographic information systems) in collaborative projects with local Sámi communities, mapping landscapes and landscape resources.[6]

---

1 See e.g. Smith and Wobst, eds., *Indigenous Archaeologies*; Watkins, "Through Wary Eyes"; Atalay, "Indigenous Archaeology"; Atalay, *Community-Based Archaeology*; Bruchac et al., eds., *Indigenous Archaeologies*; Nicholas, ed., *Being and Becoming*; Hillerdal et al., *Archaeologies*.
2 Atalay, "Indigenous Archaeology".
3 See Atalay, *Community-Based Archaeology*; Colwell, "Collaborative Archaeologies".
4 Hillerdal et al., "Nunalleq"; Mossolova and Knecht, "Bridging Past and Present".
5 See e.g. Norberg and Fossum, "Traditional Knowledge"; Ljungdahl and Norberg, eds., *Ett steg*; Norberg and Winka, eds., *Sydsamer*.
6 E.g. Barlindhaug, *Cultural Sites*.

Another central theme in the development of the field of Indigenous archaeology concerns repatriation and reburial debates, which are also of great importance in Sápmi today. Today, there is a large body of literature dealing with repatriation and reburial claims and cases in different parts of the world, not least in settler colonial nations.[7] Although the field of Indigenous archaeology is highly relevant to debates on Sámi archaeology, it has seldom been discussed explicitly within Sámi archaeology, with some recent exceptions.[8]

Sámi Archaeology as a Field of Study

Sápmi covers a vast area in the northernmost part of Europe, with great variation in natural conditions, climate, and vegetation. Within the Sámi regions, there is great cultural, economic, and linguistic variation. The diversity and dynamics in Sápmi are especially important to emphasize in an archaeological context, as Sámi Culture and identity have often been represented as a homogeneous and static entity in earlier research. The borders of Sápmi in space and time have been debated and contested by different actors, and present a special problem for archaeological research dealing with long historical perspectives.

Sámi history and identity have, in many ways, been treated as 'the Other' in relation to national histories and identities in the nation states of Norway, Sweden, and Finland. Much within these national identities has been based on connections with the south, while the northern dimensions have been downplayed. The divide between north and south in Norwegian, Swedish, and Finnish identity and heritage is mirrored in the history of archaeology. In Swedish archaeology, for instance, there has been a clear divide between northern and southern spheres of archaeology, which has had great impact on interpretations of prehistoric and early historical periods.[9]

Much less archaeological research has taken place in the northern parts of the Nordic countries than in the southern parts of the countries. Fewer rescue excavations have taken place, owing to a lower exploitation pressure from, for instance, building of roads and housing. For example, in northern

---

7 See Fforde et al., eds., *The Dead*; Gabriel and Dahl, eds., *Utimut*; Colwell, *Plundered Skulls*; Fforde et al., eds., *Routledge Companion to Indigenous Repatriation*.
8 Ojala and Nordin, "Mining Sápmi"; Harlin, "Sámi Archaeology"; Knutson, *Conducting Archaeology*.
9 See discussions in Loeffler, *Contested Landscapes*; Hagström Yamamoto, *I gränslandet*; Ojala and Ojala, "Northern Connections"; cf. also Herva and Lahelma, *Northern Archaeology*.

5 Archaeology, Politics, and Sámi Heritage

Sweden, there are large areas which have not been archaeologically surveyed at all, while most areas in southern Sweden have been systematically surveyed, often several times. Many excavations were carried out in connection with the exploitation of water power in northern Sweden in the 1940s to 1970s, but covering only certain areas along the large rivers and lakes.[10] Inland and mountain surveys were conducted in the 1990s, but were stopped in the 2000s, leaving huge areas without any archaeological surveys. The lack of surveys, and resources to build expertise in Sámi archaeology, constitutes a great problem in today's Sámi heritage management.[11] At the same time, other acts of exploitation, such as large-scale forestry, threaten large parts of the archaeological heritage of Sápmi.

Scholarly interest in Sámi pasts has followed a number of central threads.[12] In earlier research, the 'origins' of the Sámi population has been a central theme in the interest of scholars – reflecting, it might be argued, a desire to define and delimit the national 'Other'. Changing views on Sámi origins and ethnogenesis have been put forth within different subjects, such as history, archaeology, ethnography, linguistics, and ancient DNA research.[13]

Since the earliest writings on Sámi Culture in the early modern period, Sámi religion and rituals have been at the centre of the interests of scholars.[14] Archaeological investigations and studies of Sámi offering sites have provided new knowledge about the development of Sámi religious traditions.[15] Archaeology has also presented new perspectives on the early missionary process, which complement studies on the early modern missionary and Christianization processes based on textual sources.[16]

In recent decades, archaeological research has also focused on aspects of landscape perspectives, settlement patterns, socio-economic relations, and human–animal relations, using new methods.[17] The emergence and development of reindeer husbandry has been a central topic in research. Another related example is the study of hearth sites from the Iron Age, and from the

---

10 Biörnstad, *Kulturminnesvård och vattenkraft*.   11 Knutson, *Conducting Archaeology*.
12 For more general overviews of the history of Sámi archaeology see Ojala, *Sámi Prehistories*; Halinen, "Arkeologia ja saamentutkimus"; Hansen and Olsen, *Hunters in Transition*.
13 Ojala, *Sámi Prehistories*; Aikio, "An Essay on Saami"; cf. also discussions on interrelations of archaeology and linguistics concerning South Sámi history in Piha, *Eteläsaamelaiset rautakautisessa Pohjolassa*.
14 See e.g. Schefferus, *Lappland*.
15 Schanche, *Graver*; Fossum, *Förfädernas land*; Äikäs, *From Boulders to Fells*.
16 Wallerström, *Kunglig*; Lidén et al., "Nya resultat"; cf. also Rydving, *End of Drum-Time*; Rydving, *Tracing Sami Traditions*; Rasmussen, "Post-Reformation Religious Practices".
17 Hedman, *Boplatser och offerplatser*; Bergman, *Kulturarv*; Fjellström, *Food Cultures*.

medieval and early modern periods, perhaps the most common category of archaeological remains in Sápmi.[18]

Archaeology in the South Sámi regions in Norway and Sweden has been an especially controversial field of study, with close connections with land rights conflicts.[19] Archaeologists have debated how to interpret archaeological remains from the Iron Age and the early medieval period in the South Sámi region, for instance graves and settlement sites, often interpreted as belonging either to early Scandinavian or Sámi groups. Archaeologists have also acted as expert witnesses in several court cases where the traditional rights of Sámi villages to reindeer grazing lands have been questioned. Part of the background to these conflicts over land rights stems from ideas formulated in the late nineteenth century that the Sámi were relatively late newcomers to this region, having immigrated to Scandinavia from somewhere in the east and gradually spreading further to the south, reaching today's South Sámi area only in the seventeenth century – a perspective that has been heavily criticized by archaeologists in recent decades, not least based on new archaeological discoveries in the region. In this context of contested South Sámi history and heritage, several research projects have been conducted in collaboration between archaeologists, museums, local communities, and Sámi tradition bearers, especially documentation and survey projects, aiming to trace and document the unwritten South Sámi (pre)history.[20]

In recent years, discussions on Sámi history outside the present-day core Sámi area, south of the current South Sámi region, have gained in importance. Several researchers have explored Sámi presence in central Norway and Sweden in the Iron Age, the Middle Ages and the early modern period, and the relationships between Sámi and Nordic groups.[21] New archaeological surveys and investigations have shed light on a part of Sámi – and Swedish and Norwegian – history that has not been acknowledged in the traditional national narratives. Archaeologists have also debated the relationship between Finnish and Sámi groups in present-day Finland in the Viking Age.[22]

18 Hedman, *Boplatser och offerplatser*; contributions in Halinen and Olsen, eds., *In Search of Hearths*.
19 Zachrisson et al., *Möten i Gränsland*; Zachrisson, "Arkeologi inför rätta"; Zachrisson, *Gränsland*; Ojala, *Sámi Prehistories*.
20 See further Norberg and Fossum, "Traditional Knowledge"; Ljungdahl and Norberg, *Ett steg*; Norberg and Winka, *Sydsamer*.
21 Zachrisson et al., *Möten i Gränsland*; Bergstøl and Reitan, "Samer på Dovrefjell"; Skalleberg Gjerde, *Sørsamisk eller førsamisk?*; Amundsen, "Changing Histories"; Skalleberg Gjerde and Bergstøl, "Sámi-Vikings?".
22 Ahola et al., eds., *Fibula, Fabula, Fact*.

5 Archaeology, Politics, and Sámi Heritage

However, the connections between archaeology and land rights conflicts, such as the court cases mentioned above, have also led to heated discussions over ethnic interpretations of the past, and to issues of 'who was first'. Several archaeologists have testified about the sometimes difficult situation for archaeologists in the context of local conflicts in different parts of Sápmi.[23]

Sápmi also stretches into the Kola Peninsula, in northwestern Russia. The border between the Nordic countries and Russia has been one of the most important within the Sámi region, and has played a fundamental role for the understanding of history in the region. Because of the political situation in the twentieth century, the border between 'East' and 'West' in Sápmi has had a great impact on the field of archaeology. During large parts of the Soviet period, contacts and collaboration between archaeologists in the Nordic countries and Soviet Russia were very limited. After the fall of the Soviet Union, archaeologists have worked to increase contacts and initiate collaborative cross-boundary projects.[24] However, the border continues to affect views on archaeology and heritage in Sápmi.

In Russia, the Sámi population is a small minority group, which legally belongs to the group of Indigenous peoples of northern Russia and Siberia, often named 'the small-numbered peoples of the north'.[25] Kola Sámi struggles for political rights and influence take place in often difficult circumstances, which is also the case with the larger Indigenous movement in Russia.[26]

Sámi archaeology in Russia is part of a research tradition which, especially during Soviet times, was in many ways different from that of the Nordic countries.[27] In recent decades, Russian archaeologists have also discussed issues concerning Sámi origins and the extent of the earlier settlement areas.[28] The debates have concerned, for instance, archaeological remains such as graves and stone constructions along the Karelian coast and on islands of the White Sea, and whether these remains should be considered as Sámi or not – a debate in several ways similar to those in central Sweden and

---

23 Wallerström, *Vilka var först?*; Hedman, "Vardagens arkeologi"; Zachrisson, *Gränsland*; Harlin, "Sámi Archaeology".
24 See further Ojala, "East and West".
25 See further Slezkine, *Arctic Mirrors*; Donahoe et al., "Size and Place".
26 Overland and Berg-Nordlie, *Bridging Divides*; Berg-Nordlie, *Fighting to Be Heard*; Vladimirova, "Nature Conservation".
27 Ojala, *Sámi Prehistories*.
28 Manjukhin, *Proiskhozjdenije saamov*; Kotjkurkina, *Narody Karelii*; Murashkin, "Arkheologitjeskije".

Norway.[29] Archaeological studies have also dealt with, for instance, hearth sites on the Kola Peninsula.[30]

Colonial Histories and Legacies in Sápmi

Colonial heritage in Sápmi has been a contested issue. The very notion of Nordic colonialism in the Sámi areas has been a controversial question, related to ideas about Nordic exceptionalism and Nordic colonialism as being less 'colonial' than that of other European colonial powers. However, in recent years, more intense discussions on Nordic colonialism in general, and Nordic colonial history in Sápmi in particular, have taken place, and several scholars have acknowledged and explored the impact and relevance of Nordic colonialism.[31]

The colonial dimension is also very relevant to the politics of identity in Sápmi. In Sweden, discussions have concerned Sámi identity criteria, in which the divisions between reindeer-herding Sámi and non-reindeer-herding Sámi, or between mountain Sámi and forest Sámi – both divisions imposed by the Swedish state in the late nineteenth and early twentieth centuries – have played an important role.[32] In Finland, there has been a very heated discussion on definitions and understandings of Sáminess, in particular the criteria for inclusion in the electoral roll of the Sámi Parliament. Which criteria should be used, and who should have the right to make the final decision, the Finnish state or the Sámi Parliament? This debate has also been played out in academic texts.[33]

The exploitation of natural resources in Sámi areas has deep historical roots and has over time been a very substantial source of economic revenue for the different states. The expanding mining industry in northern Sweden,

---

29 Manjukhin and Lobanova, "Archaeological Monuments"; Sjakhnovitj, "'Lop' i 'loparskije'"; Kosmenko, "Ekologitjeskaja i kulturnaja".
30 Murashkin and Kolpakov, "Liva 1".
31 See e.g. discussions in Fur, *Colonialism in the Margins*; Fur, "Colonialism and Swedish History"; Naum and Nordin, eds., *Scandinavian Colonialism*; Lehtola, "Sámi Histories"; Ojala and Nordin, "Mining Sápmi"; Höglund and Andersson Burnett, "Introduction: Nordic Colonialisms". In Denmark, a series of five collective volumes on the colonial history of Denmark has been published in 2017, under the name *Danmark og kolonierne*. Interestingly, the volumes do not include any extensive discussions on colonialism in relation to the Sámi people in Norway, which was under Danish rule in the early modern period.
32 Beach, "Self-determining the Self"; Åhrén, *Är jag en riktig same?*; cf. also Gaski, "Sami Identity".
33 See arguments and discussions in Sarivaara, *Statuksettomat saamelaiset*; Lehtola, "Sámi Histories"; Junka-Aikio, "Can the Sámi Speak?"; Valkonen, "Conceptual Governance"; Joona, "ILO Convention No. 169".

5 Archaeology, Politics, and Sámi Heritage

Norway, and Finland has been confronted by a growing protest movement in recent years, led partly by Sámi activists, partly by environmental activists.[34] There is also high pressure from extractive industries in the eastern Sámi areas on the Kola Peninsula, which is a highly industrialized region in the Russian Arctic.

One case of anti-mining protests, which has gained much attention in mass media and social media, concerns the planned iron mine at Gállok, outside Jokkmokk/Jåhkåmåhkke, northern Sweden, which has become a strong symbol of Sámi struggles for decolonization and Indigenous rights. Plans for a new mine in the vicinity of the early modern Nasafjäll mine in the mountains on the Norwegian side of the border have also sparked protests from the local Sámi communities. Silver was first discovered at Nasafjäll in the 1630s, and mining activities were started by the Swedish crown, which became the start of the still ongoing exploitation of mineral resources in Sápmi. Nasafjäll constitutes a powerful symbol for Swedish colonialism, forced labour, and forced conversion in Sápmi – a symbol that is reactivated in today's protest movement.

In these protests, the understanding of the colonial history in Sápmi and the relevance of Sámi Indigenous rights are central. There are several well-preserved early modern mining and metal works sites in Sápmi, which become important as part of heritage processes. Recent historical-archaeological research has addressed the history and heritage of early modern mining, and material culture at the mining and metal works sites.[35] How should these heritage sites be managed, and how should the history of mining in Sápmi be remembered and narrated?

Sámi Cultural Rights and Debates on Repatriation and Reburial

As part of the missionary work of the Swedish church in the seventeenth and eighteenth centuries, and the campaigns against non-Christian Sámi religious beliefs and practices, many Sámi sacred drums (which were of great importance in early modern Sámi Indigenous religion) were confiscated in different places in Sápmi, for instance during court sessions in Kemi Lappmark,

---

34 Ojala and Nordin, "Mining Sápmi"; Liliequist and Cocq, eds. *Samisk kamp*; cf. perspectives on resistance in Komu, *Pursuing the Good Life*.
35 Awebro et al., *Silvret från Nasafjäll*; Ojala and Nordin, "Mining Sápmi"; Nordin and Ojala, "Copper Worlds"; Nordin and Ojala, "Industrial Revolution"; Nurmi, "Clockwork Porridge".

northern Finland, in 1671 and in Åsele, northern Sweden, in 1725. Many of the confiscated drums were burned or otherwise destroyed. Missionaries and clergymen also destroyed many sacrificial sites, as well as sacred *sieidi*-stones and sacred wooden objects in the Sámi areas. The missionary activities, including the attacks on Sámi Indigenous religion and ritual sites and objects, were a central part of the colonial expansion of the Swedish state in Sápmi in the seventeenth and eighteenth centuries.[36]

However, at the same time, the sacred drums also attracted much attention and interest among scholars and collectors in the Scandinavian countries and other European countries. Closely connected with state and industrial colonial projects in Sápmi, a practice of colonial collecting also developed, driven by desire, curiosity, and interest in the Sámi material objects, as something exotic and different, and potentially powerful and dangerous. The sacred drums were especially sought-after, and many ended up in collections in Sweden and elsewhere in Europe.[37]

A similar process also took place in Norway, where many drums were confiscated or destroyed. The missionary Thomas von Westen played an important role, gathering a large number of drums in the early eighteenth century that were taken to Copenhagen, where many of them were destroyed in a fire later in the eighteenth century. The drums that today are kept at museums in different countries in Europe have become important symbols for Sámi Culture and identity, and Sámi actors have long demanded the repatriation of the drums.

However, in the debates on repatriation, the most discussed and contested issue has concerned the collections of Sámi human remains, which are kept at different institutions and museums in the Nordic countries.[38] This is a highly sensitive, symbolically and emotionally charged, issue. For many Sámi, and others, the collections of human remains represent a painful, traumatic, and unsettled colonial history.

The histories of collecting Sámi human remains – as well as Sámi drums – should be of importance for how these collections are treated today. It is important to take into account the ways in which the collecting took place and the motives behind the collecting, but also the larger contexts in which the collecting was conducted. These contexts include, for instance, racial

---

36 Rydving, *End of Drum-Time*; Ojala, "Encountering 'the Other'"; Nordin and Ojala, "Collecting, Connecting, Constructing"; Ojala and Nordin, "Mapping Land and People".
37 Snickare, "Kontroll"; Nordin and Ojala, "Collecting, Connecting, Constructing".
38 Harlin, *Recalling Ancestral Voices*; Mulk, "Conflicts"; Ojala, *Sámi Prehistories*.

5 Archaeology, Politics, and Sámi Heritage

anthropology, racial biological research, measuring of skulls, disrespectful and offensive excavation or plundering of graves, and international exchange and trade with Sámi skulls and skeletons during the nineteenth and the early twentieth centuries. There also exist contemporary accounts about local protests against the excavations or plundering of Sámi graves, and of the unethical ways in which many excavations were conducted.[39]

Today, there are collections of Sámi human remains at several museums and institutions in Sweden. Many of these human remains, in particular human skulls, come from collections gathered for anatomical and craniological research and later racial biological research in the nineteenth century and early twentieth century.[40] There are also old anatomical collections in Norway and Finland, which contain human remains collected and registered as being Sámi.[41] Furthermore, as a result of scientific exchange between scholars and collectors, as well as trade in human remains, there are collections of Sámi human remains at different institutions and museums in other parts of the world. However, knowledge about these collections outside the Nordic countries is currently very limited.

In 2007, the Sámi Parliament in Sweden decided, after demands from Sámi activists, to request, firstly, a complete survey of all Sámi human remains in state collections and how they had become part of these collections, and secondly, a repatriation and appropriate reburial of the remains.[42]

In recent years, a few cases of reburial of Sámi human remains have taken place in Norway, Sweden, and Finland, following demands from Sámi activists and local populations. One significant event was the reburial in northern Norway in 1997 of the skulls of Aslak Hætta and Mons Somby, who had been executed for participation in the violent Kautokeino/Guovdageaidnu uprising in northern Sápmi in 1852. After the execution, the skulls had been separated from their bodies and taken to the anatomical collections of the University of Oslo. Only after a long struggle by relatives were the skulls returned and reburied.[43]

In Sweden, the human remains from the so-called 'Soejvengeelle's grave' (the grave of the 'Shadow Man') in Tärna/Dearna parish in the county of Västerbotten were reburied in 2002.[44] The grave was excavated in 1950 by

---

39 See further Ojala, *Sámi Prehistories*; Ojala, "Svenska kyrkan".
40 Svanberg, *Människosamlarna*; Ojala, "Svenska kyrkan".
41 Harlin, *Recalling Ancestral Voices*.   42 Sametinget 2007.
43 Mathisen, "Three Burials". For more on the background and unfolding of the Kautokeino uprising, see Zorgdrager, *De rettferdiges strid*.
44 Stångberg, "Soejvengeelle"; Ojala, *Sámi Prehistories*.

Ernst Manker from the Nordiska museet in Stockholm. Manker had made a promise that the remains would be reburied after analyses, but this did not happen. After demands from the local Sámi community, the human remains were returned from the museum. In this case, new archaeological investigations and datings were carried out before the reburial, which showed that the grave was much older (from the fifteenth century) than earlier thought. This case is an example of the possibility of collaborating and reaching agreement, where scientific interests as well as the wishes and interests of local populations for the reburial of human remains can be respected. Another case in Sweden was the reburial in 2011 of human remains from a grave at Gransjön, near Frostviken in the northern part of the county of Jämtland, which had been excavated in the 1980s and had been kept at the County Museum of Jämtland. In this case, new analyses were also carried out before the reburial.[45]

In August 2019, the largest reburial of Sámi human remains in Sweden was conducted in Lycksele, Västerbotten County, when twenty-five skulls were reburied at the churchyard in the old marketplace. The churchyard had been used in the seventeenth and eighteenth centuries, mainly by the Sámi communities of the region, and was excavated in the 1950s. The repatriation process involved not only the return of the human remains, but also an exploration of the contexts of the excavation in the 1950s and the subsequent handling of the remains at museums and universities.[46] At the ceremony in Lycksele, representatives of the National Historical Museum in Stockholm and the Swedish church made public apologies for their roles in the excavation and handling of the remains.

In Neiden/Njauddâm, northern Norway, another important reburial case took place, when in 2011 the remains of almost 100 individuals, which had been stored in the Anatomical Institute at the University of Oslo, were reburied. The human remains had been excavated in 1915 at the Skolt Sámi Orthodox churchyard in Neiden, despite local protests. In this case, different opinions were raised among the local Skolt Sámi community members as to whether the human remains should be reburied without further study or whether they should first be analysed and researched to increase knowledge about the local Skolt Sámi history.[47] This case underlines the complexity of reburial cases and the importance of careful, inclusive dialogues with local communities.

45 Hansson, "En samisk återbegravning".
46 See description of the repatriation process, involving both archival and community work, in Aurelius, *Máhtsatiebmie likttemijne*.
47 Svestad, "What Happened in Neiden?"; Svestad, "Caring for the Dead?".

5 Archaeology, Politics, and Sámi Heritage

In Finland, a reburial of human remains from the anatomical collections at Helsinki University was carried out at an old cemetery island in Lake Inari in 1995.[48] In Norway and Finland, there are special agreements on how to handle the old anatomical collections of Sámi human remains, which is still not the case in Sweden.[49]

There are also several cases concerning Sámi human remains currently being discussed in the Nordic countries. One of the most debated and contested cases concerns the remains from the churchyard at Rounala in northernmost Sweden. The human remains were excavated in 1915, in order to collect genuine Sámi skulls for the collections of the Department of Anatomy at Uppsala University. Demands for reburial have been put forth by Sámi activists for many years. At the same time, research has been done on the remains, leading to new results that date the churchyard to the Middle Ages, a much earlier period than had been thought. These results are important for the understanding of the little-known medieval history of the region. Furthermore, they indicate very early influences from Christianity in the area, which call for a rethinking of the general missionary history. In recent years, the remains have been transferred to Ájtte – the Swedish Mountain and Sámi Museum in Jokkmokk. However, they are still considered the property of the Swedish state and the Sámi Parliament does not have the right to decide on a reburial. Recently, Ájtte has expressed the wish to rebury the remains. At present, it is unclear what will happen with these human remains, whether they will be available for future research or eventually reburied.[50]

Another current case concerns excavated human remains from the early modern churchyard at Silbojokk/Silbbajåhkå in Norrbotten County, Sweden, where a silver works was located in the seventeenth century, refining silver ore from the above-mentioned Nasafjäll mines. Owing to erosion from the damming of Lake Sädvvájávrre, rescue excavations have been carried out at the old churchyard by the Norrbotten County Museum.[51] Demands for a reburial of these bones have been put forth by Sámi activists. It is unclear how the human remains from Silbojokk will be handled and whether they will be reburied.

48 For more on this reburial case, see Lehtola, "Sámi Histories"; Harlin, *Recalling Ancestral Voices*.
49 Harlin, *Recalling Ancestral Voices*; Holand and Sommerseth, "Ethical Issues".
50 Ojala, *Sámi Prehistories*; Aronsson, "Research on Human Remains"; Lidén et al., "Nya resultat"; Fjellström, *Food Cultures*.
51 See Lindgren, "Silbojokk".

Besides collections with human remains, discussions on repatriation have also concerned archaeological artefacts from excavations of Sámi offering sites and ethnographic objects. In Sweden, a recent case concerns the artefacts from the Sámi offering site of Unna Saiva. Unna Saiva was excavated in the early twentieth century by the archaeologist Gustaf Hallström, and many metal objects were collected from the site at the time.[52] In Norway, a repatriation process called Bååstede has been ongoing in recent years, entailing the transfer of Sámi ethnographical objects from Norsk Folkemuseum in Oslo (about half of the museum's Sámi collection) to the different Sámi museums in Norway.[53] Another repatriation process is under way in Finland, concerning Sámi ethnographical objects at the National Museum in Helsinki which will be transferred to the Siida Sámi Museum in Inari/Aanaar.

Heritage management systems vary between the different states in Sápmi, with the Sámi Parliaments in Norway, Sweden, and Finland exercising different levels of power and influence in heritage issues (the Sámi Parliament in Norway having the strongest position), but similar pressing questions are posed: what are the practical implications of Sámi Indigenous rights, and how can national heritage management be decolonized?

Conclusion

Sámi archaeology is a complex field of study, illustrating the interrelations between archaeology, politics, and identity in the Arctic and Sub-Arctic. Archaeology in Sápmi is closely connected with ethnopolitical and cultural revitalization movements, as well as debates on and conflicts over land and cultural rights – for instance, as discussed in this chapter, relating to mining and other extractive industries, and heritage issues such as repatriation and reburial.

In debates on land and cultural rights in Sápmi, references are often made to discourses of human rights and international law. The United Nations Declaration on the Rights of Indigenous Peoples (UNDRIP), from 2007, is especially relevant in this context. Several articles in the Declaration deal with Indigenous cultural rights. Article 12.1 of the Declaration states that:

> Indigenous peoples have the right to manifest, practice, develop and teach their spiritual and religious traditions, customs and ceremonies; the right to maintain, protect, and have access in privacy to their religious and cultural

52 Salmi et al., "Animal Offerings".   53 Gaup et al., eds., *Bååstede*.

5 Archaeology, Politics, and Sámi Heritage

sites; the right to the use and control of their ceremonial objects; and the right to the repatriation of their human remains.[54]

The implementation, concerning Sámi cultural heritage, of these statements on Indigenous rights needs to be discussed in greater depth in the Nordic countries. Overall, there is a need to address the inequalities in heritage management and the lack of resources for Sámi heritage management in Sweden. Recently, the Swedish National Heritage Board has issued new guidelines for the handling of human remains in museum collections and the handling of repatriation claims, which recognize the relevance of UNDRIP in dealing with Sámi heritage. How this recognition will be implemented in practice is still unclear.

In Norway, there is an ongoing truth and reconciliation process concerning the state's treatment of the Sámi people and the Kven population (Finnish-speaking minority population in northern Norway). A similar process has been initiated in Finland concerning the policies and practices of the Finnish state in relation to the Sámi people.[55] In Sweden, the government has declared that a truth and reconciliation commission will be appointed. Currently, there is a process led by the Sámi Parliament and Sámi organizations to develop plans for the commission, following demands that it should be Sámi-led and firmly based in the Sámi communities. In 2020, a truth and reconciliation commission was appointed by the Swedish government to investigate relations between the Swedish state and the Tornedalian minority population in northern Sweden.[56]

In recent years, scholars and activists have emphasized the importance of promoting Sámi voices and perspectives in research, and engaging with Indigenous methodologies and research ethics in Sámi contexts – themes that are highly relevant for archaeology and heritage management.[57] Currently, the Sámi Parliament in Sweden is developing a policy for Sámi-related research. In Finland, the Sámi Parliament has recently declared its wish to have a stronger position concerning Sámi-related research.[58]

---

54 United Nations Declaration on the Rights of Indigenous Peoples, www.un.org/esa/socdev/unpfii/documents/DRIPS_en.pdf.
55 See critical perspectives on truth and reconciliation processes in Sámi contexts in Kuokkanen, "Reconciliation".
56 The Tornedalian minority population is an official minority population in northern Sweden within Sápmi and the Tornedalian language Meänkieli is an official minority language in Sweden.
57 See e.g. Porsanger and Guttorm, eds., *Working with Traditional Knowledge*; Drugge, ed., *Ethics in Indigenous Research*; Eriksen et al., eds., *Knowing from the North*.
58 Harlin, "Sámi Archaeology".

In dealing with these issues, it is important to recognize that Sápmi today is a multicultural and multi-ethnic region, also involving diversity within Sámi communities. It is also important to avoid over-simplified socio-cultural and ethnic classifications, which risk overshadowing the complexities and dynamics of the history of Sámi communities, interactions with other communities, and development of shared spaces in Sápmi.

The field of Sámi archaeology faces many future challenges, but also possibilities. There is great potential in more cross-border cooperation within the Sámi area, especially with Russia. There is a pressing need for discussions on power relations within archaeology and heritage management, including Sámi self-determination in heritage issues, the future structures of Sámi cultural heritage management, and the development of Sámi heritage institutions and expertise.

Furthermore, Sámi archaeology, with all its complexities, carries the potential to incorporate northern dimensions in Nordic archaeology and history-writing. In the Nordic context, it is important to critically examine the understanding of colonial history and heritage in Sápmi, as well as the conceptualization of indigeneity in archaeology and heritage management.

These discussions on archaeology, politics, and Sámi heritage raise many critical questions about the ethics and politics of archaeology, and the roles and responsibilities of archaeologists and heritage specialists working in colonial contexts – and more generally, about the role of archaeology, bridging past and present, in Arctic and Sub-Arctic societies.

Bibliography

Archival and Unpublished Sources

Sametinget 2007 = Sametinget, Sammanträdesprotokoll 2007:1, Sammanträdesdatum 2007–02–20–22, Lycksele. Kiruna: Sametingets kansli.

Published Sources

Ahola, Joonas, Frog, and Clive Tolley, eds., *Fibula, Fabula, Fact: The Viking Age in Finland* (Helsinki: Finnish Literature Society, 2014).
Åhrén, Christina, *Är jag en riktig same? En etnologisk studie av unga samers identitetsarbete* (Umeå: Umeå universitet, 2008).
Äikäs, Tiina, *From Boulders to Fells: Sacred Places in the Sámi Ritual Landscape* (Helsinki: Archaeological Society of Finland, 2015).

5 Archaeology, Politics, and Sámi Heritage

Aikio = Luobbal Sámmol Sámmol Ánte (Ante Aikio), "An Essay on Saami Ethnolinguistic Prehistory", in Riho Grünthal and Petri Kallio, eds., *A Linguistic Map of Prehistoric Northern Europe* (Helsinki: Finno-Ugrian Society, 2012), pp. 63–117.

Amundsen, Hilde R., "Changing Histories and Ethnicities in a Sámi and Norse Borderland", *Acta Borealia* 34 (2017): 178–197.

Aronsson, Kjell-Åke, "Research on Human Remains of Indigenous People: Reflections from an Archaeological Perspective (with an Example from Rounala)", in H. Fossheim, ed., *More Than Just Bones: Ethics and Research on Human Remains* (Oslo: Norwegian National Research Ethics Committees, 2013), pp. 65–79.

Atalay, Sonya, *Community-Based Archaeology: Research with, by, and for Indigenous and Local Communities* (Berkeley/Los Angeles: University of California Press, 2012).

Atalay, Sonya, "Indigenous Archaeology as Decolonizing Practice", *American Indian Quarterly* 30 (2006): 280–310.

Aurelius, Adriana, *Máhtsatiebmie likttemijne – Återbördande i försoning: En processbeskrivning över repatrieringen i Lycksele 2019* (Lycksele: Liksjuon Sámiensiäbrrie, 2019).

Awebro, Kenneth, Nils Björkenstam, Jan Norrman, et al., *Silvret från Nasafjäll. Arkeologi vid Silbojokk* (Stockholm: Riksantikvarieämbetet, 1989).

Barlindhaug, Stine, *Cultural Sites, Traditional Knowledge and Participatory Mapping: Long-term Land Use in a Sámi Community in Coastal Norway* (Tromsø: University of Tromsø, 2013).

Beach, Hugh, "Self-determining the Self: Aspects of Saami Identity Management in Sweden", *Acta Borealia* 24 (2007): 1–25.

Berg-Nordlie, Mikkel, *Fighting to Be Heard in Russia and in Sápmi: Russian Sámi Representation in Russian and Pan-Sámi Politics, 1992–2014* (Tromsø: Arctic University of Norway, 2017).

Bergman, Ingela, *Kulturarv, landskap och identitetsprocesser i norra Fennoskandien 500–1500 e.Kr* (Stockholm: Riksbankens Jubileumsfond, 2018).

Bergstøl, Jostein, and Gaute Reitan, "Samer på Dovrefjell i vikingtiden. Et bidrag til debatten omkring samenes sørgrense i forhistorisk tid", *Historisk Tidsskrift (Norsk)* 87 (2008): 9–27.

Biörnstad, Margareta, *Kulturminnesvård och vattenkraft 1942–1980: en studie med utgångspunkt från Riksantikvarieämbetets sjöregleringsundersökningar* (Stockholm: Kungl. Vitterhetsakademien, 2006).

Bruchac, Margaret M., Siobhan M. Hart, and H. Martin Wobst, eds., *Indigenous Archaeologies: A Reader on Decolonization* (Walnut Creek: Left Coast, 2010).

Colwell, Chip, "Collaborative Archaeologies and Descendant Communities", *Annual Review of Anthropology* 45 (2016): 113–127.

Colwell, Chip, *Plundered Skulls and Stolen Spirits: Inside the Fight to Reclaim Native America's Culture* (Chicago/London: University of Chicago Press, 2017).

Donahoe, Brian, Joachim Otto Habeck, Agnieszka Halemba, and István Sánta, "Size and Place in the Construction of Indigeneity in the Russian Federation", *Current Anthropology* 49 (2008): 993–1020.

Drugge, Anna-Lill, ed., *Ethics in Indigenous Research: Past Experiences – Future Challenges* (Umeå: Umeå University, 2016).

Eriksen, Thomas Hylland, Sanna Valkonen, and Jarmo Valkonen, eds., *Knowing from the North: Sámi Approaches to History, Politics and Belonging* (London and New York: Routledge, 2019).

Fforde, Cressida, Jane Hubert, and Paul Turnbull, eds., *The Dead and Their Possessions: Repatriation in Principle, Policy and Practice* (London and New York: Routledge, 2002).

Fforde, Cressida, C., Timothy McKeown, and Honor Keeler, eds., *The Routledge Companion to Indigenous Repatriation: Return, Reconcile, Renew* (London and New York: Routledge, 2020).

Fjellström, Markus, *Food Cultures in Sápmi: An Interdisciplinary Approach to the Study of the Heterogeneous Cultural Landscape of Northern Fennoscandia AD 600–1900* (Stockholm: Stockholm University, 2020).

Fossum, Birgitta, *Förfädernas land: En arkeologisk studie av rituella lämningar i Sápmi, 300 f. Kr.–1600 e.Kr* (Umeå: Umeå universitet, 2006).

Fur, Gunlög, "Colonialism and Swedish History: Unthinkable Connections?", in Magdalena Naum and Jonas Monié Nordin, eds., *Scandinavian Colonialism and the Rise of Modernity: Small Time Agents in a Global Arena* (New York: Springer, 2013), pp. 17–36.

Fur, Gunlög, *Colonialism in the Margins: Cultural Encounters in New Sweden and Lapland* (Leiden: Brill, 2006).

Gabriel, Mille, and Jens Dahl, eds., *Utimut: Past Heritage – Future Partnerships. Discussions on Repatriation in the 21st Century* (Copenhagen: International Work Group for Indigenous Affairs, 2008).

Gaski, Lina, "Sami Identity as a Discursive Formation: Essentialism and Ambivalence", in Henry Minde, Harald Gaski, Svein Jentoft, and Georges Midré, eds., *Indigenous Peoples: Self-determination, Knowledge, Indigeneity* (Delft: Eburon, 2008), pp. 219–236.

Gaup, Káren Elle, Inger Jensen, and Leif Pareli, eds., *Bååstede: The Return of Sámi Cultural Heritage* (Trondheim: Museumsforlaget, 2021).

Gjerde, Hege Skalleberg, *Sørsamisk eller førsamisk? Arkeologi og sørsamisk forhistorie i Sør-Norge: En kildekritisk analyse* (Oslo: University of Oslo, 2016).

Gjerde, Hege Skalleberg, and Jostein Bergstøl, "Sámi-Vikings?", in Hanne Lovise Aannestad, Unn Pedersen, Marianne Moen, Elise Naumann, and Heidi Lund Berg, eds., *Vikings Across Borders: Viking Age Transformations*, Vol. II (London and New York: Routledge, 2021), pp. 166–178.

Hagström Yamamoto, Sara, *I gränslandet mellan svenskt och samiskt: Identitetsdiskurser och förhistoria i Norrland från 1870-tal till 2000-tal* (Uppsala: Uppsala University, 2010).

Halinen, Petri, "Arkeologia ja saamentutkimus", in Irja Seurujärvi-Kari, Petri Halinen, and Risto Pulkkinen, eds., *Saamentutkimus tänään* (Helsinki: Suomalaisen Kirjallisuuden Seura, 2011), pp. 130–176.

Halinen, Petri, and Bjørnar Olsen, eds., *In Search of Hearths: A Book in Memory of Sven-Donald Hedman* (Helsinki: Finnish Antiquarian Society, 2019).

Hansen, Lars Ivar, and Bjørnar Olsen, *Hunters in Transition: An Outline of Early Sámi History* (Leiden: Brill, 2014).

Hansson, Anders, "En samisk återbegravning", *Historisk arkeologisk tidskrift* (2018): 111–125.

Harlin, Eeva-Kristiina, *Recalling Ancestral Voices: Repatriation of Sámi Cultural Heritage* (Inari: Siida Sámi Museum, 2008).

Harlin, Eeva-Kristiina, "Sámi Archaeology and the Fear of Political Involvement: Finnish Archaeologists' Perspectives on Ethnicity and the Repatriation of Sámi Cultural Heritage", *Archaeologies* 15 (2019): 254–284.

Hedman, Sven-Donald, *Boplatser och offerplatser: Ekonomisk strategi och boplatsmönster bland skogssamer 700–1600 AD* (Umeå: Umeå universitet, 2003).

5 Archaeology, Politics, and Sámi Heritage

Hedman, Sven-Donald, "Vardagens arkeologi i Norrbotten: en personlig betraktelse", in Inga Lundström, ed., *Historisk rätt? Kultur, politik och juridik i norr* (Stockholm: Riksantikvarieämbetet, 2007), pp. 193–207.

Herva, Vesa-Pekka, and Antti Lahelma, *Northern Archaeology and Cosmology: A Relational View* (London/New York: Routledge, 2020).

Hillerdal, Charlotta, Anna Karlström, and Carl-Gösta Ojala, eds., *Archaeologies of 'Us' and 'Them': Debating History, Heritage and Indigeneity* (London/New York: Routledge, 2017).

Hillerdal, Charlotta, Rick Knecht, and Warren Jones, "Nunalleq: Archaeology, Climate Change, and Community Engagement in a Yup'ik Village", *Arctic Anthropology* 56 (2019): 4–17.

Höglund, Johan, and Linda Andersson Burnett, "Introduction: Nordic Colonialisms and Scandinavian Studies", *Scandinavian Studies* 91 (2019): 1–12.

Holand, Ingegerd, and Ingrid Sommerseth, "Ethical Issues in the Semi-Darkness: Skeletal Remains and Sámi Graves from Arctic Northern Norway", in Hallvard Fossheim, eds., *More than Just Bones: Ethics and Research on Human Remains* (Oslo: Norwegian National Research Ethics Committees, 2013), pp. 21–47.

Joona, Tanja, "ILO Convention No. 169 and the Governance of Indigenous Identity in Finland: Recent Developments", *The International Journal of Human Rights* 24 (2020): 241–256.

Junka-Aikio, Laura, "Can the Sámi Speak Now? Deconstructive Research Ethos and the Debate on Who Is a Sámi in Finland", *Cultural Studies* 30 (2016): 205–233.

Knutson, Charina, *Conducting Archaeology in Swedish Sápmi: Policies, Implementations and Challenges in a Postcolonial Context* (Kalmar: Linnaeus University, 2020).

Komu, Teresa, *Pursuing the Good Life in the North: Examining the Coexistence of Reindeer Herding, Extractive Industries and Nature-Based Tourism in Northern Fennoscandia* (Oulu: University of Oulu, 2020).

Kosmenko, M. G., "Ekologitjeskaja i kulturnaja adaptatsija okhotnikov-rybolovov bronzovogo, zjeleznogo vekov i morskikh promyslovikov epokhi Srednevekovja v Karelii", in M. G. Kosmenko, ed. *Adaptatsija kultury naselenija Karelii k osobennostjam mestnoj prirodnoj sredy periodov mezolita – srednevekovja*, (Petrozavodsk: Karelian Research Center, 2009), pp. 135–168.

Kotjkurkina, S. I., *Narody Karelii: istorija i kultura* (Petrozavodsk: Karelija, 2004).

Kuokkanen, Rauna, "Reconciliation as a Threat or Structural Change? The Truth and Reconciliation Process and Settler Colonial Policy Making in Finland", *Human Rights Review* 21 (2020): 293–312.

Lehtola, Veli-Pekka, "'The Right to One's Own Past': Sámi Cultural Heritage and Historical Awareness", in Maria Lähteenmäki and Päivi Maria Pihlaja, eds., *The North Calotte: Perspectives on the Histories and Cultures of Northernmost Europe* (Inari: Puntsi, 2005), pp. 83–94.

Lehtola, Veli-Pekka, "Sámi Histories, Colonialism, and Finland", *Arctic Anthropology* 52 (2015): 22–36.

Lidén, Kerstin, Markus Fjellström, and Thomas Wallerström, "Nya resultat från Eskil Olssons Rounala-grävning 1915", in Per Moritz, ed., *Norrbotten 2018–2019: Arkeologi* (Luleå: Norrbottens Museum, 2019), pp. 235–261.

Liliequist, Marianne, and Coppélie Cocq, eds., *Samisk kamp: kulturförmedling och rättviserörelse* (Umeå: h:ström, 2017).

Lindgren, Åsa, "Silbojokk", in Per Moritz, ed., *Norrbotten 2018–2019: Arkeologi* (Luleå: Norrbottens Museum, 2019), pp. 263–279.

Ljungdahl, Ewa, and Erik Norberg, eds., *Ett steg till på vägen: Resultat och reflexioner kring ett dokumentationsprojekt på sydsamiskt område under åren 2008–2011* (Östersund: Gaaltije – sydsamiskt kulturcentrum, 2012).

Loeffler, David, *Contested Landscapes/Contested Heritage: History and Heritage in Sweden and Their Archaeological Implications Concerning the Interpretation of the Norrlandian Past* (Umeå: Umeå University, 2005).

Manjukhin, I. S., *Proiskhozjdenije saamov* (Petrozavodsk: Russian Academy of Sciences, 2002).

Manjukhin, I. S., and N. V. Lobanova, "Archaeological Monuments of the Kuzova Archipelago", in E. Ieshko and N. Mikhailova, eds., *Natural and Cultural Heritage of the White Sea Islands* (Petrozavodsk: Karelian Research Center, 2002), pp. 55–60.

Mathisen, Stein R., "The Three Burials of Aslak Hætta and Mons Somby: Repatriation Narratives and Ritual Performances", *Museum Worlds* 5 (2017): 22–34.

Mossolova, Anna, and Rick Knecht, "Bridging Past and Present: A Study of Precontact Yup'ik Masks from the Nunalleq Site, Alaska", *Arctic Anthropology* 56 (2019): 18–38.

Mulk, Inga Maria, "Conflicts over the Repatriation of Sami Cultural Heritage in Sweden", *Acta Borealia* 26 (2009): 194–215.

Murashkin, A. I., "Arkheologitjeskije pamjatniki Kolskogo Polyostrova i problema proiskhozhdenija Saamov", *Arkheologitjeskije Vesti* 12 (2005): 148–152.

Murashkin, Anton I., and Evgeniy M. Kolpakov, "Liva 1: The First Medieval Sámi Site with Rectangular Hearths in Murmansk Oblast (Russia)", in Petri Halinen and Bjørnar Olsen, eds., *In Search of Hearths: A Book in Memory of Sven-Donald Hedman* (Helsinki: Finnish Antiquarian Society, 2019), pp. 75–87.

Naum, Magdalena, and Jonas M. Nordin, eds., *Scandinavian Colonialism and the Rise of Modernity: Small Time Agents in a Global Arena* (New York: Springer, 2013).

Nicholas, George P., ed., *Being and Becoming Indigenous Archaeologists* (Walnut Creek: Left Coast, 2011).

Norberg, Erik, and Birgitta Fossum, "Traditional Knowledge and Cultural Landscape", in Jelena Porsanger and Gunvor Guttorm, eds., *Working with Traditional Knowledge: Communities, Institutions, Information Systems, Law and Ethics* (Kautokeino: Sámi allaskuvla, 2011), pp. 193–223.

Norberg, Erik, and Ulf Stefan Winka, eds., *Sydsamer – landskap och historia: ett dokumentationsprojekt på sydsamiskt område under åren 2012–2014* (Östersund: Gaaltije – sydsamiskt kulturcentrum, 2014).

Nordin, Jonas M., *The Scandinavian Early Modern World: A Global Historical Archaeology* (London and New York: Routledge, 2020).

Nordin, Jonas M., and Carl-Gösta Ojala, "Collecting, Connecting, Constructing: Early Modern Commodification and Globalization of Sámi Material Culture", *Journal of Material Culture* 23 (2018): 58–82.

Nordin, Jonas M., and Carl-Gösta Ojala, "Copper Worlds: A Historical Archaeology of Abraham and Jakob Momma-Reenstierna and Their Industrial Enterprise in the Torne River Valley, c. 1650–1680", *Acta Borealia* 34 (2017): 103–133.

Nordin, Jonas M., and Carl-Gösta Ojala, "An Industrial Revolution in an Indigenous Landscape: The Copper Extraction of the Early Modern Torne River Valley in a Global Context", *Fennoscandia Archaeologica* 37 (2020): 61–81.

5 Archaeology, Politics, and Sámi Heritage

Nurmi, Risto, "A Clockwork Porridge: An Archaeological Analysis of Everyday Life in the Early Mining Communities of Swedish Lapland in the Seventeenth Century", in Tiina Äikäs and Anna-Kaisa Salmi, eds., *The Sound of Silence: Indigenous Perspectives on the Historical Archaeology of Colonialism* (New York: Berghahn, 2019), pp. 90–118.

Ojala, Carl-Gösta, "East and West in Sápmi: Borders and Identities in Sámi Historical Archaeology", *Historiskarkeologisk tidskrift* (2021): 149–166.

Ojala, Carl-Gösta, "Encountering 'the Other' in the North: Colonial Histories in Early Modern Northern Sweden", in Magdalena Naum and Fredrik Ekengren, eds., *Facing Otherness in Early Modern Sweden: Travel, Migration and Material Transformations, 1500–1800* (Woodbridge: Boydell, 2018), pp. 209–228.

Ojala, Carl-Gösta, *Sámi Prehistories: The Politics of Archaeology and Identity in Northernmost Europe* (Uppsala: Uppsala University, 2009).

Ojala, Carl-Gösta, "Svenska kyrkan och samiska mänskliga kvarlevor", in Daniel Lindmark and Olle Sundström, eds., *De historiska relationerna mellan Svenska kyrkan och samerna* (Skellefteå: Artos & Norma, 2016), pp. 983–1018.

Ojala, Carl-Gösta, and Jonas M. Nordin, "Mapping Land and People in the North: Early Modern Colonial Expansion, Exploitation and Knowledge", *Scandinavian Studies* 92 (2019): 98–133.

Ojala, Carl-Gösta, and Jonas M. Nordin, "Mining Sápmi: Colonial Histories, Sámi Archaeology, and the Exploitation of Natural Resources in Northern Sweden", *Arctic Anthropology* 52 (2015): 6–21.

Ojala, Karin, and Carl-Gösta Ojala, "Northern Connections: Interregional Contacts in Bronze Age Northern and Middle Sweden", *Open Archaeology* 6 (2020): 151–71.

Overland, Indra, and Mikkel Berg-Nordlie, *Bridging Divides: Ethno-Political Leadership among the Russian Sámi* (New York: Berghahn Books, 2012).

Piha, Minerva, *Eteläsaamelaiset rautakautisessa Pohjolassa: Kielitieteellis-arkeologinen näkökulma* (Turku: University of Turku, 2020).

Porsanger, Jelena, and Gunvor Guttorm, eds., *Working with Traditional Knowledge: Communities, Institutions, Information Systems, Law and Ethics* (Guovdageaidnu/Kautokeino: Sámi allaskuvla/Sámi University College, 2011).

Rasmussen, Siv, "Post-Reformation Religious Practices among the Sámi", in Sigrun Høgetveit Berg, Rognald Heiseldal Bergesen, and Roald Ernst Kristiansen, eds., *The Protracted Reformation in the North*, Vol. III (Berlin: de Gruyter, 2020), pp. 265–285.

Rydving, Håkan, *The End of Drum-Time: Religious Change among the Lule Saami, 1670s–1740s*, 2nd edition (Uppsala: Uppsala University, 1995).

Rydving, Håkan, *Tracing Sami Traditions: In Search of the Indigenous Religion among the Western Sami During the 17th and 18th Centuries* (Oslo: Institute for Comparative Research in Human Culture, 2010).

Salmi, Anna-Kaisa, Tiina Äikäs, Markus Fjellström, and Marte Spangen, "Animal Offerings at the Sámi Offering Site of Unna Saiva: Changing Religious Practices and Human–Animal Relationships", *Journal of Anthropological Archaeology* 40 (2015): 10–22.

Sarivaara, Erika Katjaana, *Statuksettomat saamelaiset: Paikantumisia saamelaisuuden rajoilla* (Guovdageaidnu/Kautokeino: Sámi allaskuvla/Sámi University College, 2012).

Schanche, Audhild, *Graver i ur og berg: Samisk gravskikk og religion fra forhistorisk til nyere tid* (Karasjok: Davvi girji, 2000).
Schefferus, Johannes, *Lappland* (Uppsala: Gebers, 1956 [1673]).
Sjakhnovitj, M. M., "'Lop' i 'loparskije' pamjatniki Severnoj i Zapadnoj Karelii", in L. G. Sjajakhmetova, ed., *Kolskij sbornik* (St Petersburg: Institut istorii materialnoj kultury, 2007), pp. 228–246.
Slezkine, Yuri, *Arctic Mirrors: Russia and the Small Peoples of the North* (Ithaca and London: Cornell University Press, 1994).
Smith, Claire, and H. Martin Wobst, eds., *Indigenous Archaeologies: Decolonizing Theory and Practice* (New York: Routledge, 2005).
Snickare, Mårten, "Kontroll, begär och kunskap: Den koloniala kampen om Goavddis", *Rig* 97 (2014): 65–77.
Stångberg, Andreas, "Soejvengeelle: En samisk grav i Vapsten", in Åsa Virdi Kroik, ed., *Efter förfädernas sed: Om samisk religion* (Göteborg: Boska, 2005), pp. 40–56.
Svanberg, Fredrik, *Människosamlarna: Anatomiska museer och rasvetenskap i Sverige ca 1850–1950* (Stockholm: Historiska museet, 2015).
Svestad, Asgeir, "Caring for the Dead? An Alternative Perspective on Sámi Reburial", *Acta Borealia* 36 (2019): 23–52.
Svestad, Asgeir, "What Happened in Neiden? On the Question of Reburial Ethics", *Norwegian Archaeological Review* 46 (2013): 194–242.
UN Declaration on the Rights of Indigenous Peoples, www.un.org/esa/socdev/unpfii/documents/DRIPS_en.pdf.
Valkonen, Sanna, "Conceptual Governance on Defining Indigeneity: The Sámi Debate in Finland", in Thomas Hylland Eriksen, Sanna Valkonen, and Jarmo Valkonen, eds., *Knowing from the Indigenous North: Sámi Approaches to History, Politics and Belonging* (London/New York: Routledge, 2019), pp. 142–162.
Vladimirova, Vladislava, "Nature Conservation in Russia: The Case of Indigenous Sámi Rights in the Kola Peninsula", in Lars Elenius, Christina Allard, and Camilla Sandström, eds., *Indigenous Rights in Modern Landscapes: Nordic Conservation Regimes in Global Context* (London and New York: Routledge, 2017), pp. 94–110.
Wallerström, Thomas, *Kunglig makt och samiska bosättningsmönster: Studier kring Väinö Tanners vinterbyteori* (Oslo: Novus, 2017).
Wallerström, Thomas, *Vilka var först? En nordskandinavisk konflikt som historisk-arkeologiskt dilemma* (Stockholm: Riksantikvarieämbetet, 2006).
Watkins, Joe, "Through Wary Eyes: Indigenous Perspectives on Archaeology", *Annual Review of Anthropology* 34 (2005): 429–449.
Zachrisson, Inger, "Arkeologi inför rätta: Sydsamernas äldre historia", in Inga Lundström, ed., *Historisk rätt? Kultur, politik och juridik i norr* (Stockholm: Riksantikvarieämbetet, 2007), pp. 137–157.
Zachrisson, Inger, *Gränsland: Mitt arkeologiska liv* (Skellefteå: Ord & Visor, 2016).
Zachrisson, Inger, Verner Alexandersen, Martin Gollwitzer, et al., *Möten i Gränsland. Samer och germaner i Mellanskandinavien* (Stockholm: Statens Historiska Museum, 1997).
Zorgdrager, Nellejet, *De rettferdiges strid, Kautokeino 1852: Samisk motstand mot norsk kolonialisme* (Nesbru: Vett & Viten, 1997).

6

The Norse Settlement of Greenland

JETTE ARNEBORG

Introduction

Greenland has been peopled from the west by several different groups and only once – in the late tenth century AD – from the east, this time by Norse farmers from northern Europe. Unlike the mobile Arctic hunters, the Norse settlers were sedentary, and the society they established in southwest Greenland was based on the natural vegetation, hunting, and trade with their homelands. For almost 500 years the Norse population in Greenland thrived, and then it vanished for reasons not yet fully understood. Several explanations have been put forward: that the small Norse society failed because of inflexible social and economic strategies,[1] or fell victim to a combination of unfortunate circumstances,[2] or (as recently argued) suffered from organized and systematic violence by invading Inuit.[3]

Contact between the Norse Greenlanders and Scandinavia came to an end in the early 1400s, but, being subject to Norwegian kings from 1262 and Danish-Norwegian kings from 1380, Greenland was still considered Danish-Norwegian territory. It was in the name of the Danish-Norwegian king Frederik IV that the priest Hans Egede re-established contact with the far-away land in 1721 for the purpose of bringing the Protestant faith to the still Catholic Norse inhabitants. Egede did not find any Roman Catholics there; instead, he began his missionary work among the Inuit who were present. Having disappeared almost 300 years earlier, Greenland's Norse European inhabitants not only made their mark in history as the people who mysteriously disappeared, they were also determinative for the lives of their successors, the Inuit, for many years to come.

---

1 For example, Diamond, *Collapse*, 239.   2 Dugmore et al., "Cultural Adaptation".
3 Nedkvitne, *Norse Greenland*, 327–377.

Settlers from the East

According to Icelandic sagas, at the closing of the Viking Age era in the late tenth century the petty chieftain Eireki rauða and a group of farmers left Iceland with all their worldly possessions, domestic animals included, to settle the virgin lands west of Iceland. Two regions on the southern part of the west coast of the vast island met their requirements for good pasture lands.

The Norse settlement in Greenland was bound up with the settlement of Iceland in the late 800s A D. The increased sailings in the North Atlantic led to more ships being blown off course on their way to and from Iceland. The Icelander Gunnbjörn Úlfsson was one of those shipwrecked. On his way from Norway to Iceland, at some point in the beginning of the tenth century, Gunnbjörn discovered skerries (small rocky islands) in the distance which, according to the sagas, he named Gunnbjarnarsker.[4] The skerries were situated on the east coast of Greenland, perhaps somewhere around modern-day Tasiilaq. Still, it was not the east coast that Eireki rauða was heading for when, in the 980s, he set out to find the land Gunnbjörn had seen. Probably instructed by other sailors who knew it was crucial to escape the cold East Greenland Current and the dangerous polar ice that it brought, Eireki took a more southerly course, rounded Cape Farewell, and landed in southwest Greenland.

Eireki knew where to go. A few radiocarbon dates suggest possible Norse activity in the Eastern Settlement from before the official settlement, indicating that pioneers might have surveyed the land before the actual *landnam*.[5] At the head of Igaliku fjord, approximately 2 km northeast of the small settlement of Igaliku, circular turf-built structures might be the traces of provisional tent houses from the visits of some of Eireki's forerunners. One of the structures is radiocarbon dated within the period 776–976 (with 95.4 per cent probability).[6] However, the early dates are of charcoal from local birch (*Betula pubescens*), and gathering of dead and dry firewood at a much later time cannot be ruled out.[7] Two samples also of *Betula pubescens* from an unidentified wooden construction from the churchyard at a farm at Nunataaq (farm Ø1) are also dated within the periods 724–885 and 871–985, respectively.[8] They too may indicate pre-settlement visits.

---

4 GHM, Vol. I, 71–134.   5 Icelandic for 'taking land'.   6 KIA-13447, Gulløv, "Booths", 96.
7 Ólafsson, "New Evidence".
8 AAR-8295 charcoal, *Betula pubescens* 889 (with one sigma or 68 per cent probability 781–958) and AAR-8296 charcoal, *Betula pubescens* 779 (with one sigma or 68 per cent probability 724–885).

The Settlers and Their Motivations to Move to Greenland

Who were the settlers and where did they come from? Genetically, the immigrants to Greenland belonged to the same group of people who settled the Faroe Islands in the eighth to ninth centuries and Iceland in the late ninth century. Strontium analyses indicate that the settlers in Greenland originated in Iceland.[9] They were a genetic mixture of Celtic individuals from northern Britain Isles and Norwegians.[10] The motivations for leaving one's home country can be many. It could have been a response to social, political, economic, or cultural changes in the homeland, or it could have been the desire to achieve something new and conceivably better in the new land. In the case of Greenland, the latter seems a reasonable suggestion. Immigration to Iceland apparently had ended when the first Icelanders settled in Greenland, perhaps because Iceland was fully settled, and it was difficult to get land to establish your own farm. The new land was empty of people, and the prospect of large virgin landholdings could lead ambitious small chieftains like Eireki rauða to emigrate in the hope of gaining better social conditions and wealth. The fact that Eireki named the new land Greenland indicates the hopes and expectations of new productive land.

However, access to the High Arctic commodities, such as furs from polar bears and foxes, white falcons, and, not the least, walrus tusks, which were highly esteemed on the North European markets, were also pull factors. Recent archaeological finds of bones and fragments of teeth from walruses in early settlement layers in Iceland suggest Icelandic participation in the very profitable trade in walrus tusks that expanded rapidly in northern Europe during the Viking period. However, after a few centuries of hunting, the walrus colonies in Iceland became extinct, and to maintain the lucrative trade, it has been suggested that the Icelanders expanded their catchment area to include Greenland.[11] In Greenland, large colonies of obtainable walruses were to be found on the west coast around modern-day Sisimiut, in Disko Bay, and even further north (Figure 6.1). Due to the long distance, hunting directly from Iceland was not an option. The relatively warm and fertile fjord regions in the south were suitable for the pastoral economy the

---

9 Price and Arneborg, "Peopling of North Atlantic".
10 Margaryan et al., "Population Genomics".
11 Frei et al., "Was It for Walrus?"; Keighley et al., "Disappearance of Icelandic Walruses"; Star et al., "Ancient DNA".

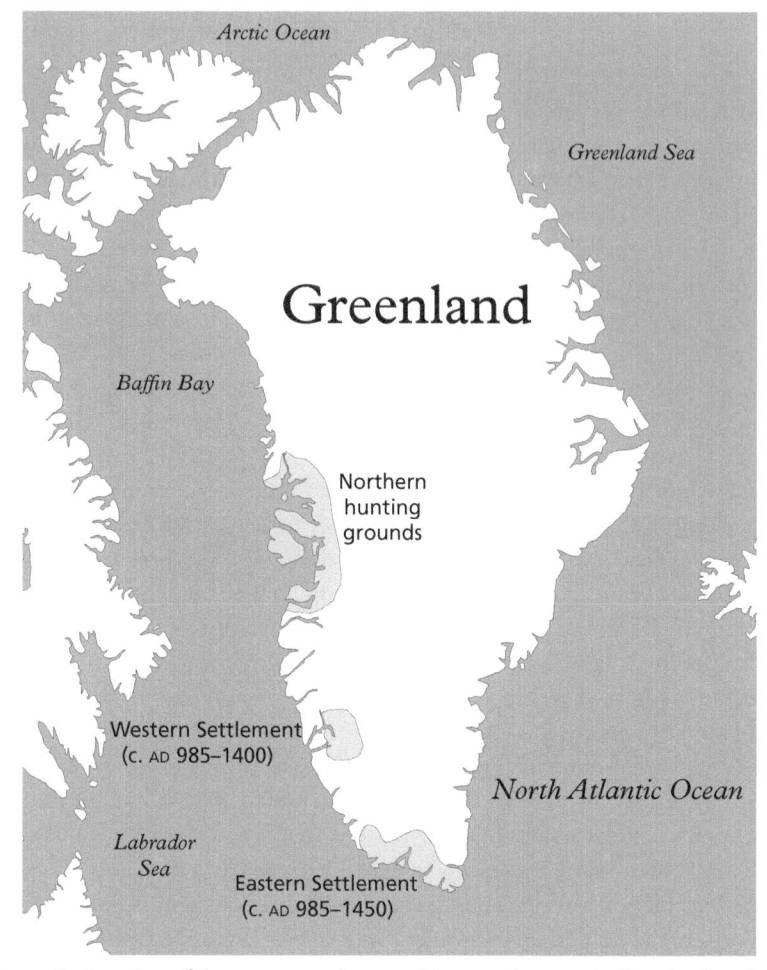

Figure 6.1 Location of the western and eastern Norse settlements in Greenland, and the northern hunting grounds.

immigrants brought with them from Iceland, and raw materials that they themselves could not get in Greenland could be obtained from Europe in exchange for sought-after Arctic resources. Local farming and long-distance hunting for foreign trade commodities were interconnected, and both were prerequisites for the Norse to thrive. With the settlement of Greenland, the Icelanders extended the boundaries of the Viking world to the west.

The first group of settlers was small. Based on the information in Grænlendiga saga, fourteen ships headed by Eireki rauða made it to

Greenland;[12] allowing for about thirty individuals per ship – men, women, and presumably also children, from all social groups – this adds up to about 420 individuals, which is close to 500 individuals and the accepted minimum level for a sustainable starting population. With a relatively slow increase in population and limited immigration, the population is estimated to have reached about 2,000–2,500 individuals around 1250/1300.[13] With an estimated average of 4.5 to 7.5 persons per household, the starting population in theory could settle about eighty to eighty-five farms.[14] However, considering the inequalities between the immigrants onboard the ships and the labour needed to establish a farm from scratch, we may envisage fewer farms and larger households that, besides the landowner and his family, also included servants or slaves.

Settlement and Subsistence

Settlement took place in the climatic Medieval Warm Period, and the grassland and dwarf shrub heaths of the boreal Sub-Arctic (>10 °C in the warmest month, July) inner fjord regions around Tunulliarfik and Igaliku fjords and the large Vatnahverfi region in South Greenland (60° N) attracted the first waves of settlers. Later newcomers settled in regions that were less attractive for agriculture and in the Low Arctic inner fjord regions in the present-day Nuuk area. The settlement in the Nuuk region (64° N) constituted the Western Settlement. The Norse Eastern Settlement covered the fjords from Cape Farewell in the south to Arsuk and Ivittuut in the north (60° N to 61° N). The farms were scattered across the landscape, on the fertile moraine plains along the fjords, next to lakes, and in the valleys. Access to pastureland and fresh water were determinants for the choice of site, but access to other resources such as firewood, driftwood for building material and woodworking, fishing lakes and rivers, soapstone to produce domestic utensils, and sandstone for hones and whetstones also determined where farms were built.

The immigrants introduced cattle, sheep, goats, horses, and, to a lesser degree, also pigs to Greenland, together with dogs, cats, and – unintentionally – mice, and the setup of the farms reflected the pastoral economy they brought with them from Iceland.[15] Grass for the grazing animals and grass for winter fodder was essential to the farming system, and the landscape was

12 Magnusson and Pálsson, *Vinland Sagas*, 50–51.
13 Lynnerup, "Endperiod Demographics", 18–19.   14 Madsen, "Pastoral Settlement", 213.
15 Smiarowski et al., "Zooarchaeology".

immediately turned into pasture. The most fertile spots were kept for growing grass for winter fodder, called the in- or homefield, where the most important farmhouses – dwelling, byre, and barn, and at some farms also the churches – were located. In Scandinavia, traditionally, the homefield was fenced in to keep out the grazing livestock. This, however, was only the case on the larger farms in Greenland, perhaps because the number of livestock was limited and therefore easy to control using either dogs or herdsmen. The livestock grazed in the less fertile outfields, and in the summertime the animals were brought to the summer grazing farms away from the main farms.[16]

The outfields and the commons were not reserved for the domestic animals only. In the Western Settlement large herds of reindeer roamed the landscape and were easily accessible for the farmers, to a much greater degree than in the Eastern Settlement. Fish were available in lakes and fjords, and in both settlements colonies of stationary harbour seals were present in the fjords. In spring and autumn, large populations of migratory harp and hooded seals passed the settlements on their way to and from their breeding grounds in the Gulf of Saint Lawrence area and off Newfoundland,[17] and wild fauna was crucial to the Norse subsistence economy. The distributions of animal bones in the early (c. 1000 to c. 1150) collections from the farms at Narsaq Ø17a in the Eastern Settlement, and The Farm Beneath the Sand (*Gården under Sandet*, or GUS) and Niaquusat V48, reflect the *landnam* (land-taking) situation. At both the coastal farm at Narsaq (Ø17a) and the inland farm GUS in the Western Settlement, domesticates made up between 30 and 40 per cent of the bone collection. At the two Western Settlement farms, Sandnes (V51) and Niaquusat (V48), it was less than 20 per cent.[18] The limited number of domesticates may reflect the numbers that the settlers were able to bring with them on the ships from Iceland. Still, the figures did not change significantly in the following period from around 1150 to approximately 1300. The share of domesticate did not go beyond 45 per cent at any of the farms (Figure 6.2). Including collections that have not been collected in chronological layers, farms situated in the central region of the Eastern Settlement, Tunulliarfik (Ø34), and in Vatnahverfi (Ø71 and Ø167) have about 50 to 60 per cent domesticates. Among the group of domesticates, sheep and goats dominated on all farms. Among the wild fauna, seals dominated, but reindeer were also an important source of meat, especially in the Western Settlement.[19]

16 Øye, "Farming Systems", 111–113; Madsen, "Pastoral Settlement", 198, 203–212, 243.
17 Smiarowski et al., "Zooarchaeology", 7.
18 McGovern, "Contributions"; Enghoff, *Hunting*.
19 McGovern, "Contributions"; Enghoff, *Hunting*, 89; Nyegaard, "Dairy Farmers".

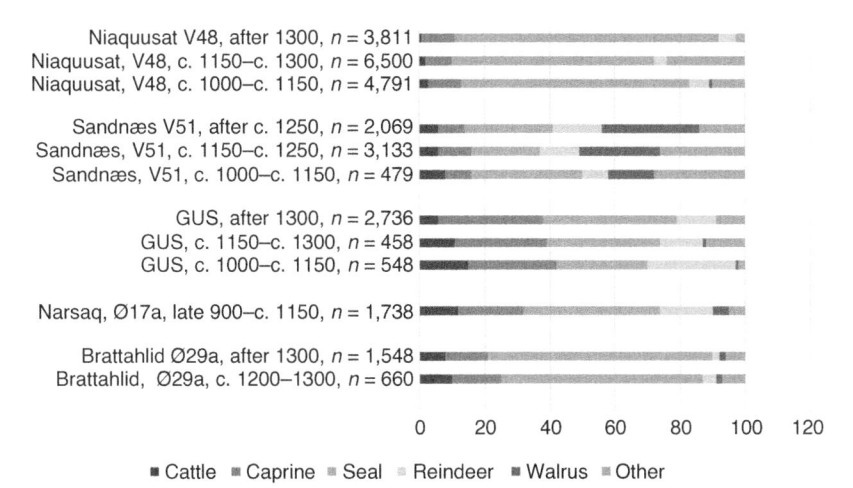

```
Niaquusat V48, after 1300, n = 3,811
Niaquusat, V48, c. 1150–c. 1300, n = 6,500
Niaquusat, V48, c. 1000–c. 1150, n = 4,791

Sandnæs V51, after c. 1250, n = 2,069
Sandnæs, V51, c. 1150–c. 1250, n = 3,133
Sandnæs, V51, c. 1000–c. 1150, n = 479

GUS, after 1300, n = 2,736
GUS, c. 1150–c. 1300, n = 458
GUS, c. 1000–c. 1150, n = 548

Narsaq, Ø17a, late 900–c. 1150, n = 1,738

Brattahlid Ø29a, after 1300, n = 1,548
Brattahlid, Ø29a, c. 1200–1300, n = 660

              0    20   40   60   80  100  120

■ Cattle  ■ Caprine  ■ Seal  ▫ Reindeer  ■ Walrus  ■ Other
```

Figure 6.2 Animal bone collection from farms V48 (Niaquusat), V51 (Sandnæs Kilaarsarfik), and GUS (The Farm Beneath the Sand) in the Western Settlement, and Ø17a (Narsaq) and Ø29a (Brattahlid Qassiarsuk) in the Eastern Settlement. Per cent of whole collection, NISP (number of identified specimen) counts. (Data from: McGovern, "Contributions"; McGovern et al., "Zooarchaeology of Ø17a"; McGovern and Palsdóttir, "Preliminary Report"; McGovern et al., "Vertebrate Zooarchaeology"; and Enghoff, *Hunting*.)

The farm buildings were built of local, accessible materials: turfs, stones, and driftwood. Dwellings, byres, and barns were thoroughly insulated with thick outer walls of turf to keep humans and domesticates warm. Provisions were stored in houses built with unsealed stone to allow the air to preserve the food.[20]

Influence from the East: Church and Crown

The Greenlanders had roots in the Scandinavian Viking Age societies, where there were great differences between rich and poor, between free and unfree, and where family and class affiliation were of great importance for the individual's position in society. Among the first Icelandic colonists in Greenland were both free peasants, like Eireki rauða, and the unfree and dependent, who for one reason or another, voluntarily or involuntarily, had taken the trip across the Atlantic. Everyone had their place in the social hierarchy, even before they landed in Greenland, and the society they founded was an imprint of what they brought with them from Iceland.

20 Roussell, *Farms and Churches*.

Ownership of land was the social measure of value, and the free peasants with the most and the best land were the socially and economically dominant. They were the leaders in political and religious life. Others owned larger or smaller farms, while many were landless and dependent on the landowners. Through time, the power in society was concentrated in fewer families and larger farms, and many probably became tenants and labourers on the larger farms.[21]

No heathen graves have to this day been recorded in the Norse settlements and many, if not all immigrants were Christians when they arrived in Greenland. At some *landnam* farms, churches surrounded by circular churchyards were built at the home field in close connection to the dwellings, signalling the unity between secular authority and religion. The church buildings were small, inside only about 10 m^2 on average, and the surrounding churchyards had diameters between 14 and 20 m. Considering the size of the churches, they may only have served the church owner and his household, whereas the churchyards were open to neighbours without a church, most probably for payment.

The number of the early *landnam* churches is uncertain, but at least seven were taken out of use during the first half of the 1200s. Perhaps as early as the beginning of the 1100s, larger two-cell Romanesque churches with a nave and a smaller chancel to the east appeared; at some places they succeeded the small *landnam* churches, at other farms they were the first church on the site. The two-cell churches and the later one-cell stone churches that appeared around 1250–1300 were surrounded by four-sided churchyards.[22]

In 1124, one of the largest farms in the Eastern Settlement, *Garðar*, became the residence of the Greenlandic bishop subjected to the Norwegian archbishop in Nidaros/Trondheim.[23] According to the sources, it was the Greenlanders themselves who approached the Norwegian king Sigurd *Jorsalfar* (the crusader) to request their own bishop. The King agreed and assigned the cleric Arnaldur. He and his successors were Norwegians. The bishop controlled all ecclesiastical affairs in his diocese, economic matters included, and it is noteworthy that – contrary to what happened in Iceland – Greenlandic bishops were not chosen from among the Greenlanders themselves. In Iceland, the most powerful families

---

21 Vésteinsson et al., "Dimensions of Inequality", 174–175, 180, 184–185.
22 Jette Arneborg, Jan Heinemeier, and Niels Lynnerup, work in progress, "Small Churches and Church Organisation in Norse Greenland".
23 Arneborg, "Roman Church".

6 The Norse Settlement of Greenland

maintained control over their dioceses until the beginning of the 1300s. Hereafter the bishops in Iceland were Norwegians and later Danish. Apparently in Greenland none of the church-owning families were powerful enough to seize power over the local church. Supporters of the Norwegian bishops quite likely profited, from the decisions of the bishops, and, as indicated in the stories, one or more families might have reached out to the Norwegians for support. The introduction of the two-cell churches might be an effect of the rapprochement with the Norwegians. The larger churches allowed for larger congregations, a parish system was introduced, and the old system of charging a usage fee was replaced by fixed tithe. Religious ceremonies were regulated, and liturgical ceremonies could be held according to current practices in Scandinavia. Norse Greenland was slowly but surely drawn closer into the Norwegian orbit. After around 1250/1300, one-cell stone churches were introduced in Greenland (Figure 6.3). The architecture was influenced by Norwegian church building, and the new one-cell churches were most

Figure 6.3 The church in Hvalsey fjord, farm Ø83 in the Eastern Settlement, from around 1250/1300. (Photo: Jette Arneborg 2004.)

probably built by master builders from the British Isles who were sent to Greenland by the Norwegian King.[24]

In 1261, Oddur of Sjölltum, Páll Magnússon, and Knarrar-Leifur arrived in Norway after having spent four winters in Greenland, bringing the news that the Greenlanders had agreed to pay taxes and fines to the Norwegian king. The decision must have been the result of an active political effort on the part of the Crown and supported by the Church. At the coronation of King Håkon IV in Bergen in 1247, the papal envoy Cardinal William of Sabina had declared that no people in the world should be without a king, and that same summer Bishop Ólafur was sent to Greenland with the task of urging the Greenlanders to recognize King Håkon's sovereignty over the country.[25] The Icelanders, too, submitted to the Norwegian king in the early 1260s after many years of resistance. The original agreement between the Icelanders and the king has been lost, but later agreements that are assumed to reflect the original deal include tax payments to the king and Norwegian guarantees for navigation of Iceland.[26] The Greenlanders may have had a similar agreement. Shipping and thus trade with Norway was crucial for the Greenlanders, and securing the maintenance of this trade must have been among their most important demands on the king. Only a few royal officials are mentioned in the written accounts, and royal power probably relied on the ecclesiastical administration, which already had more than 100 years of experience when the Crown entered the scene. In Ívar Bárðarsons Greenland Description from the late 1300s, only two farms in Greenland are ascribed to the Crown, and its income from land ownership must have been limited. The Crown introduced a monopoly on trade in the North Atlantic, and the main interests in Greenland were in collecting taxes on trade paid in walrus products and other Arctic goods.

Contacts with Norway presupposed access to large and expensive seagoing ships – the *knarr*. Whether the Greenlanders themselves ever owned ships that could cross the North Atlantic is doubtful. Certainly, after their subjection to the Norwegian Crown they depended on ships coming to them, and according to Icelandic annals years could pass between ship calls. In 1308, the bishop at Garðar received news from Bishop Árni, his colleague in Bergen, including the news of the death of King Erik. The King had died in Bergen in 1299.[27]

---

24 Roussell, *Farms and Churches*, 126; Bertelsen and Schnohr, "Muslingemørtel og megalitter", 9.
25 GHM, Vol. II, 774–775.   26 Imsen, "Introduction", 27.   27 GHM, Vol. III, 94–100.

6 The Norse Settlement of Greenland

Despite less frequent shipping and consequently the absence of contacts, innovations from Europe found footholds in Greenland, and not only in the political and ecclesiastical domain. Adapted to the environment, the available raw materials, and Greenlandic creativity, foreign influences on daily life on the farms can be traced in architecture, language, and personal belongings. The language was West Norse, a dialect of Old Norse which the Norse Greenlanders shared with Norwegians, Faeroese, and Icelanders, and even though runic inscriptions show that the Norse Greenlanders developed regional characteristics they also demonstrate that the Greenlanders followed the general linguistic currents around the North Atlantic.[28] The close-fitting dresses, pleated dresses, buttoned-up tunics, liripipe hoods, and details such as gussets that allowed the long dresses to hang elegantly were influenced by fashions from abroad, but made in accordance with what local resources allowed (Figure 6.4).[29] In many respects, the Norse Greenlanders developed

Figure 6.4. Woman's dress found at the churchyard at farm Ø111, Herjolfsnæs Ikigaat, in the Eastern Settlement. The buried were found wrapped in the robes. Length of dress: 120 cm. (Photo: National Museum of Denmark License: CC-BY-SA.)

28 Imer, *Peasants and Prayers*, 48–52.
29 Nørlund, *Buried Norsemen*; Fentz, "Dragter", 162–165.

their own identity, but the overall signal was clear. They belonged to the north European Christian civilization.

Life on the Farms

The farms were largely self-sufficient and were managed with the hands available. Small and medium-sized farms were family run with the help of a few servants. The large and rich farms had many servants and workers to run the farm. All routines on the farms followed the course of nature, adapted to the length of the days and the change of seasons. The year opened with the arrival of summer. The cattle came to pasture, and so did the sheep and goats that had spent the winter in the stables. Grasslands were fertilized with manure from byres and stables. The sheep were sheared, and the wool was washed for later processing. Like the byres and stables, the houses were also cleaned out. Towards the summer, people and animals went to the summer pastures and stayed there for months.[30] Milk production began after the animals had been on grass for a while, which meant daily milking and processing of the milk into butter and cheese that could be stored over the winter. Summer was also hunting time. The stationary harbour seal (*Phoca vitulina*) could be caught all year round, while the first migrations of the Greenland seal (*Pagophilus groenlandicus*) and the hooded seal (*Cystophora cristata*) passed the coasts of southwest Greenland in May–June. On the coast, in addition to seals, the hunters also caught seabirds, and they collected eggs, feathers, and down.[31] Summer was also the time when hunters headed for the northern hunting grounds to catch walruses and other Arctic animals. In the Western Settlement the hunt for reindeer began in late August–September, while reindeer hunting was sporadic in Østerbygden, where the population was limited. As winter approached, the free-ranging sheep and goats were gathered and moved closer to the farmhouses. This was slaughter time, and time to cut the grass for winter fodder and to get the remaining animals to byres and stables. This was followed by a time of daily feeding of the stabled animals and care of the animals that roamed freely throughout the winter. Firewood had to be collected and peat cut for house building and house repairs before winter set in, and fences and enclosures were inspected and repaired. The late migration of the harp seal passed the southwest coast of Greenland from October to February and again drew the

---

30 Albrethsen and Keller, "Use of *Saeter*". 31 Smiarowski et al., "Zooarchaeology", 6–8.

hunters from the farms to the coast, but not as many as in the spring, as the autumn catch was less intense than the spring catch. Winter was mostly spent indoors, and this was the time when household utensils and personal equipment were manufactured and repaired. Particularly important was the wool work, where the raw wool was spun into thread and woven into textiles for clothing and other useful things such as sails for their smaller, local ships and for packaging materials. The many tasks were distributed to everyone, men, women, and children, reflecting necessity in a working community. On the socially lowest-ranking farms, where few people lived, the work tasks were distributed among fewer people, and life was harder, while the farmers on the larger farms employed servants and tenants and could draw on a much larger workforce.

The women were responsible for all indoor activities, including everything that had to do with the food. They made sure that there was always a fire in the fireplace, and they took care of the wool work and babysitting, while the men were responsible for the outdoor work such as keeping the farm, maintaining the farm buildings, enclosures, and fences, and digging ditches and peat. It was also the men who were responsible for the hunt and the fishing. But men did not monopolize the outdoor work. Women also took their turn outside the house. They washed the clothes in the cold river, they milked the farm animals, and they were responsible for milk and butter production. They took part in farm life, and it was the women who gathered the hay after the men had cut the grass in the homefield. On farms where there was a shortage of manpower, the women probably also took care of the men's work to a certain extent. The children were trained for their future lives by following the adults; the girls followed the women, and the boys followed the men.[32] Several tasks were solved in collaboration with others. The roaming sheep and goats were collected in late summer, in collaboration with the neighbouring farms. The seal hunting on the outer coast was most likely regionally organized, as probably not all hunters owned ships they could take out. The trips to the northern hunting grounds were organized by the elites and the church, who owned both the ships and the equipment for the hunt in the north.

The layout of the farm buildings with the most important houses gathered centrally in the homefield did not change. However, as in Scandinavia, the Viking Age longhouses where most activities took place in the large central hall were replaced by room-divided dwellings. At some places, primarily

---

32 Jochens, *Women in Old Norse Society*.

inland in the Western Settlement at middle-sized and smaller farms, all buildings on the farm (dwelling, byre for cattle, stable for sheep and goats, barn, and workshops) were built close together and connected with openings and doors. Thus, in winter the farmers did not have to go outside when feeding the stabled domesticates. The layout has been named the centralized farm. It is only known in Greenland, and its appearance in the beginning of the 1200s may be due to deteriorating climate.[33]

Norse societies were ruled by the free farmers according to laws they themselves devised. Central to the system was the þing where they met and discussed and regulated matters of common interest.[34] At a lower level, this included issues such as when to gather the roaming sheep and goats and when to leave the farms for the seal hunt. At a higher level, it was at the þing that political decisions were made and where disagreements and enmity were mediated. Even though the influence of the Church increased in both political and personal matters, the Greenlandic farmers needed a regulatory legal system for internal and mutual matters. For instance, in proceedings in 1389 in Bergen, a group of Norwegian merchants pleaded their innocence of the crime of having traded with the Greenlanders without royal permission by stating that they acted in accordance with decisions taken by the Greenlandic farmers at their alþinge. A physical þing, the site where the farmers met, has not been located. Especially in the early settlement period it may have been on a neutral location out on the land and not associated with any individual's land, as in Iceland.[35] Later, when the influence of the Church increased, and a few magnates had taken over the power in society, the leading farmers may have met on their farms.

Hunting Trips to the North and Encounters with *Skrælings*

From the initial settlement the Norse sailed the north to catch walrus, polar bears, and other coveted animals in the Arctic. Walruses can be caught from around Sisimiut and further north to the Disko Bay and beyond (Figure 6.1). A small black slate with a runic inscription found on the small island of Kingittorsuaq off Upernavik shows Norse activities as far north as around 73° N, and Norse artefacts found in late Dorset and early Thule Inuit houses

---

33 Roussell, *Farms and Churches*, 159–190, 242.
34 Sanmark, "Greenlandic Assembly Sites", 178.   35 Vésteinsson, "What Is a Booth?".

north of the Melville Bay indicate possible Norse presence even further north.³⁶

Historia Norwegie from the late 1100s reports chance meetings between Norse hunters and small men that they named Skrælings. The Skrælings lacked iron completely and used whales' teeth for missiles and sharp stones for knives. The place of the meeting is described as *beyond the Greenlanders*, which is not informative, and who the Skrælings were is uncertain. In his Íslendingabók from the beginning of the same century, the Icelander Arí Þorgilsson used the same name for the people the Norse encountered in Vinland, and Historia Norwegie's *beyond the Greenlanders* may very well refer to a place on the American continent, meaning that the Skrælings could refer to either the pre-Inuit Late Dorset Culture or early Thule Inuit. North Greenland north of Melville Bay was inhabited by the Late Dorset people from the beginning of the 700s until the end of the 1200s. When the early Thule Inuit migrated into North Greenland from Canada is still debated, but most probably it was during the 1200s, at the same time that the Late Dorset disappeared from the area. Archaeological investigations in the Disko Bay suggest Thule Inuit winter settlement at Sermermiut close to modern-day Ilulissat in the 1200s.

In 1266, returning Norse hunters reported that although they had sailed further north than usual, they had not encountered any Skrælings.³⁷ How far north they had sailed, we do not know, but the narrative gives the impression that the Norse hunters were used to encountering Skrælings on their hunting trips. That they apparently wanted to seek them out is indicated from the fact that the priests – probably from the episcopal see at Garðar – subsequently, but in vain, sent new ships to the north. Assessed in a contemporary perspective, it is easy to see the benefits for both parties of mutual trade. The Norsemen could get coveted Arctic products in exchange for South Greenlandic and European products, which could have utility value and perhaps also be prestigious for the Inuit. Thus, the explanation for the Norsemen's interest in locating the Skrælings in 1266 may have been the desire to trade with them. On the other hand, it does not seem that the Skrælings were particularly interested. Accidental exchange may have occurred, but neither the 1266 account nor the archaeological finds at Inuit and Norse sites give the impression of formalized trade routines between the two population groups. Very few Norse artefacts found at the Inuit

36 McCullough, *Ruin Islanders*; Gulløv, "Inuit-European Interactions," 898.
37 GHM, Vol. III, 241.

settlements can with certainty be dated to the period from before the two Norse settlements were depopulated – hence not looted from the abandoned farms – and the few Inuit artefacts found at the Norse farms have more the character of souvenirs found on hunting trips to the north.[38] We have no evidence of genetic interaction between Norsemen on the one hand and Pre-inuit and Inuit on the other.[39]

Towards the End

The Norse settlements were thriving until the 1300s, when farms were gradually abandoned, beginning in the marginal areas where agriculture was less profitable. In the late 1300s the Western Settlement was depopulated, and about fifty to sixty years later the farms in the Eastern Settlement were also abandoned. The last bishop who resided at Garðar died in 1378. In a letter written at the bishop's see in 1409, the two priests Eindriði Andrésson and Páll Hallvarðsson confirmed the marriage of the Icelanders Þorstein Ólafsson and Sigriður Björnsdóttir, which had happened in Hvalseyfjorden's church the year before. The following year, in 1410, Sigriður and Þorstein left Greenland together with a larger group of stranded Icelanders, probably carrying with them the letter that confirmed their marriage. The Icelanders' departure from Greenland in 1410 is the last recorded voyage between Greenland and Norway, and the letter they had with them was to be the last written sign of life in the Norse Greenlandic settlements. What led to the depopulation is still debated.

Skrælings

The Norwegian clergyman Ívar Bárðarson was sent from Bergen in Norway to Greenland shortly after 1342 for reasons not known today, and during his stay he travelled to the Western Settlement, allegedly to throw out the *Skrælings* from the settlement, but when he arrived, he met neither Christians nor pagans.[40] Ívar's visit is assumed to have taken place between approximately 1350 and 1355, close to, but a little earlier than, the latest radiocarbon dates we have from the Western Settlement. The purpose of Ívar's mission does not suggest good relations between the two population groups. Nor does the information in the Icelandic annals from 1379: 'The Skrælings made hostile

38 Jensen et al., *Cultural Encounters*, 25–27.
39 Margaryan et al., "Population Genomics", 393.
40 Jónsson, *Det gamle Grønlands Beskrivelse*, 30.

attacks on the Greenlanders, killed 18 men of them, but captured two boys and made them slaves.' Where the 1379 raid took place is not mentioned. The mention of Ívar's travel to the Western Settlement in his Greenland Description gave rise to the theory, presented as early as the early 1700s, that the Inuit destroyed the Norse.[41] Since then, even the thinnest layers of charcoal found in archaeological excavations were – especially in the 1800s and the first decades of the 1900s – seen as evidence of bands of Inuit attacking the Norse Greenlanders and burning down their farms and churches. A critical review of the archaeological record, however, shows that these fires were limited to only a single room or two, and most likely they originated in and emanated from fireplaces. At a few places, the burnt room was rebuilt, and the fire cannot thus be dated to the time of depopulation. At other sites, layers of charcoal are from a time after the abandonment of the farms and probably caused by visiting Inuit. Thus, archaeology does not support the presumption that the Inuit systematically destroyed the Norse and their settlements,[42] but both the information about Ívar Bárðarson's vain journey to the Western Settlement and the attack in 1379 suggest encounters between the sedentary Norse farmers with their strong idea of personal rights to ownership and – probably – summer-visiting Inuit to whom resources were for all to utilize. Permanent Inuit settlement in the Norse settlements only seems to have taken place after the Norsemen had left their farms.[43]

Demography

The estimated population of 2,000–2,500 individuals in the late 1200s may be too low. Nevertheless, the population of the settlements was not large, and it was therefore vulnerable to events such as the confrontation with the Inuit in 1379, fatal accidents on the risky voyages to the north, and emigration. Based on the estimated 2,000 individuals in the late 1200s, a loss of just a few young individuals per year would have had a severe effect on the population and would have initiated a downward population curve, ultimately leading to extinction within a relatively short time span. Other reasons for a population to become extinct are exceptionally high mortality rates within a noticeably short period of time, usually related to war and epidemics. However, even rates up to 10 per cent of young adults killed in warfare or by epidemics would

---

41 Fyllingsnes, *Undergongen*, 31–62.   42 Contrary to Nedkvitne, *Norse Greenland*, 350–356.
43 Jensen et al., *Cultural Encounters*, 25.

not substantially decrease birth rates, and we have neither written nor archaeological evidence of mass death in Greenland caused by either war or disease.[44]

The Environment

In 1257, the volcano Samalas exploded on the island of Lombok, east of Java in the Indian Ocean, producing a vicious cooling effect on the globe's climate. Even the Norse farmers in Greenland were affected. Modelling of the climate in Greenland from the end of the 900s until the 1400s shows that a colder regime took over after the warm period at the time around settlement. Climate change meant more unstable weather, with winds, more storms, more rainfall, and more ice in the fjords. The snow on the ground and the ice in the fjords remained for longer in the summer, and this led to lower temperatures and consequently, shorter growing seasons. It became more difficult to navigate at sea, where ice and wind created problems for sailing both regionally and to Europe. Sea-level rise caused by isostatic movements in the Greenland ice cap, and coastal erosion, meant that valuable grazing areas were gradually flooded and lost to agriculture.[45] Also owing to the colder climate, advancing glaciers changed the landscapes, and lush green pastures in the inland were transformed into barren sand and gravel plains.[46]

Expansion and Withdrawal

Abandonment of farms in the marginal areas began in the 1300s,[47] and the church building activities show the same development. From the 1100s, perhaps earlier, the Romanesque stone and turf-built two-cell churches replaced the small *landnam* churches in the central regions, and they were increasingly also built at farms in the more marginal areas, while later only the farms in the central regions of the Eastern Settlement had the economy to build the prestigious large one-cell stone churches. This happened from the end of the 1200s, reflecting the increased Norwegian influence in Greenland. Two one-cell stone churches were built in areas that can be described as marginal. One was at Anavík farm (V7) – at what is now Ujarassuit – in the northern branches of Nuuk fjord in the Western Settlement; the other was at

---

44 Lynnerup, "Endperiod Demographics", 19.   45 Mikkelsen et al., "Norse in Greenland".
46 Schweger, "Geoarchaeology", 17.   47 Madsen, *Pastoral Settlement*, 255.

the nunnery in Uunartoq fjord in the southern part of the Eastern Settlement (Ø149). Both churches were built on farms whose economy did not rest solely on agriculture. Anavík was close to and probably controlled some of Greenland's best soapstone quarries. The convent, together with the Cathedral, controlled the therapeutic hot springs on Uunartoq island.[48] The individual farms seem to have undergone a similar development from expansion in the first centuries to contraction in the last period of settlement. The centralized farm known as The Farm Beneath the Sand in the Western Settlement was – measured in square metres and number of houses – at its largest from the late 1200s to around 1300.

Fewer Cows, More Sheep and Goats, and Many Seals

The Norse Greenlanders were farmers, and the social system was based on the ownership of land. Still, the composition of animal bones from the middens shows that the economy of the farms from the initial settlement rested on a combination of livestock farming and hunting, and that hunting throughout the settlement period contributed more than 50 per cent of many farms' economy. The cows were the most prestigious domestic animals, and the number kept on a farm was a measure of the farmer's social status. They were, both in need for grass of the best quality and the manpower required to keep the herd running, the most demanding of the domesticated animals. Over time, even on the richest farms, the cattle herd was reduced, while the number of sheep and goats increased. At the same time, the importance of livestock farming in general decreased in favour of hunting, especially of seals. On The Farm Beneath the Sand, the number of cattle bones fell from 15 per cent of all identified bones in the period 1000–1159 to 6 per cent in the period 1300–1400, while the proportion of sheep and goats increased from 27 to 32 per cent, the proportion of seal bones increased from 28 to 41 per cent, and that of reindeer fell from 27 to 12 per cent.[49] (Figure 6.2). The increasing dependence on marine resources can also be read in the bones of the Norse Greenlanders themselves. The contents of the carbon-13 isotopes measured in the skeletons reveal the content of digested marine protein, and in Norse Greenland the marine contents increased over time. Although there were both regional and social differences, right from the initial settlement the immigrants in Greenland digested more

48 Jónsson, *Det gamle Grønlands Beskrivelse*, 24.   49 Enghoff, *Hunting*, 89–91.

marine food than did their relatives back home in Iceland, and at the end of the settlement some lived on a 70–80 per cent marine diet.[50]

Deserted Settlements

The Norse settlement in Greenland was, from the starting point, vulnerable. Geographically, the settlements were far away from the world of which the Norse settlers saw themselves as a part, and on which they depended. At the subsistence level, the Greenlandic farmers had to fend for themselves, and from the beginning the subsistence economy was based on a combination of agriculture and hunting. Dependence on the marine resources, especially on seals, increased over time. Declining pastures and most probably also a diminishing labour force led to adjusting the number of the resource-intensive cattle. The number of sheep and goats increased at the expense of the cattle, and hunting increased at the expense of the domesticates.

Their willingness to adapt was great, but life in Greenland also depended on contacts with Europe, both economically and mentally. The Norse Greenlanders required, among other things, the import of iron, but mentally it was just as important that they could maintain their Nordic, Christian identity. The large farms with churches were the focal points of the social and economic system, and developments in church building suggest a shift from a more egalitarian society towards a centralization of power in fewer hands, centred in the best and most fertile agricultural regions. Even though the importance of seal hunting increased and became vital for physical survival to the very last, agriculture was maintained as the essential element of society. Control of land remained the social and economic measure of value, and as long as the farmers controlled society from their farms the increased hunting was not a threat to the social order; on the contrary, it supported the existing order and kept people alive. On the other hand, seal hunting also masked the fundamental problems that existed in agriculture, and seal hunting on the outer coast further introduced stress to the diminishing population. A single lost ship and possible loss of young human lives could, in the long run, have major consequences for the viability of the small population.

The elite managed to control internal development, but despite the established connections to Norway, it was difficult or almost impossible for the Greenlanders to act on developments in the world around them. They depended on the outside world but could not influence developments

50 Arneborg et al., "Human Diet".

outside their own borders. It seems that the established trade contacts ebbed away in the late 1300s. In 1349/1350, Icelandic annals reported that no ship came to Iceland from Norway, and the same most probably also applied to Greenland. In the year 1368, it is reported that Bishop Álfur – the last bishop to reside in Greenland – arrived in Greenland, and at that time the Greenlanders had been without a bishop for nineteen years. In the period from 1349 to 1368, there is only one record of the Greenland *knarr* in the annals, and that is from 1366, when it is announced that the *knarr* was equipped for the Greenland voyage. The following year, it was reported that it had sunk north of Bergen. After Álfur's arrival in Greenland in 1368, quite a few ship calls are reported, but none of them were planned. All were ships that had blown off course on travels between Norway and Iceland. The last known ship sailed from Greenland in 1410.[51]

Was the lost communication due to conditions in Greenland or events in Norway? Emigration, accidents, and hostile confrontations with the Inuit may have led to a decline in the number of inhabitants and a shortage of labour. Walrus tusks were a particular incentive for foreign merchants to travel to Greenland, but lack of supplies from Greenland or fall in demand and prices in Europe may have reduced the Norwegian merchants' desire to put ships and crews at risk to sail to Greenland.[52] Norway may no longer have had the resources to send ships there. Europe experienced terrible outbreaks of plague in the years 1347–52, and Norway, where the plague struck in 1349, was particularly hard hit. The Norwegian population was drastically reduced, and it took many years before the country recovered. A contributing factor to the lack of sailing from Norway may also be sought in the political changes that took place in the wake of the dynastic union between Norway and Denmark in 1380. The monarchy moved south, to Denmark, where interest in the North Atlantic and the less profitable tax-paying islands was smaller than it was in Norway.

Many factors come into play when the depopulation of the Norse settlements in Greenland is discussed. The source base is limited, in some cases even contradictory, and causes and reactions are intertwined. The Nordic settlement in Greenland in the late 900s was based on expectations that were no longer present in the early 1400s. Life had changed dramatically, and from having once been an important part of the Norwegian kingdom, Greenland was marginalized. Those who could might have moved away, leaving a small community that could no longer reproduce itself, and extinction took place.

51 GHM, Vol. III, 19–43.   52 Roesdahl, "Walrus Ivory", 187, 189.

Bibliography

Albrethsen, Svend Erik, and Christian Keller, "The Use of *Saeter* in Medieval Norse Farming in Greenland", *Arctic Anthropology* 23 (1986): 91–107.

Arneborg, Jette, "The Roman Church in Norse Greenland", *Acta Archaeologica* 61 (1991): 142–150.

Arneborg, Jette, Niels Lynnerup, and Jan Heinemeier, "Human Diet and Subsistence Patterns in Norse Greenland AD c.980 – AD c.1450: Archaeological Interpretations", *Journal of the North Atlantic* Special Volume 3 (2012): 119–133.

Bertelsen, Thomas, and Josephine Schnohr, "Muslingemørtel og megalitter", *Skalk* 3 (2019): 6–9.

Diamond, Jared, *Collapse: How Societies Choose to Fail or Succeed* (New York: Penguin, 2005).

Dugmore, Andrew J., Thomas H. McGovern, Orri Vésteinsson, Jette Arneborg, and Richard Streeter, "Cultural Adaptation, Compounding Vulnerabilities and Conjunctures in Norse Greenland", *Proceedings of the National Academies of Science* 109 (2012): 3658–3663. www.pnas.org/cgi/doi/10.1073/pnas.1115292109

Enghoff, Inge Bødker, *Hunting, Fishing and Animal Husbandry at the Farms Beneath the Sand, Western Greenland*. Meddelelser om Grønland/Monographs on Greenland, Man and Society 28 (Copenhagen: Museum Tusculanum, 2003).

Fentz, Mytte, "Dragter", in Else Roesdahl, ed., *Dagligliv i Danmarks middelalder* (Copenhagen, 1999), pp. 151–171.

Frei, Karin M., Ashley N. Coutu, Konrad Smiarowski, et al., "Was It for Walrus? Viking Age Settlement and Medieval Walrus Ivory Trade in Iceland and Greenland", *World Archaeology* (2015): 1–28, https://doi.org/10.1080/00438243.2015.1025912.

Fyllingsnes, Frode, *Undergongen til dei norrøne bygdene på Grønland i seinmellomalderen*. Skrifter 2 (Oslo: Middelalderforum, 1990).

GHM (Grønlands Historiske Mindesmærker), Vols. I–III (Kjøbenhavn: Det kongelige nordiske Oldskrift-Selskab, 1845).

Gulløv, Hans Christian, "Booths from Early Norse Greenland", in Caroline Paulsen and Helgi D. Michelsen, eds., *Símunarbók* (Tórshavn: Fróðskapur, 2008), pp. 90–105.

Gulløv, Hans Christian, "Inuit-European Interactions in Greenland", in Max Friesen and Owen Mason, eds., *The Oxford Handbook of the Prehistoric Arctic* (Oxford Handbooks Online, 2016), p. 898, https://doi.org/10.1093/9780199766956.013.44.

Imer, Lisbeth, *Peasants and Prayers: The Inscriptions of Norse Greenland*. Studies in Archaeology & History 25 (Copenhagen: Publications from the National Museum, 2017).

Imsen, Steinar, "Introduction", in Steinar Imsen, ed., *Rex Insularum: The King of Norway and His 'Skattlands' as a Political System c. 1250–c. 1450* (Bergen: Fagbokforlaget, 2014), pp. 13–31.

Jensen, Einar Lund, Kristine Raahauge, and Hans Christian Gulløv, *Cultural Encounters at Cape Farewell*. Monographs on Greenland 348 (Copenhagen: Museum Tusculanum, 2011).

Jochens, Jenny, *Women in Old Norse Society* (Ithaca and London: Cornell University Press, 1995).

Jónsson, Finnur, *Det gamle Grønlands Beskrivelse af Ívar Bárðarson udgiven efter Håndskrifterne* (København: Levin & Munksgaard, 1930).

Keighley, Xenia, Snæbjörn Pálsson, Bjarni F. Einarsson, et al., "Disappearance of Icelandic Walruses Coincided with Norse Settlement", *Molecular Biology and Evolution* 36 (2019): 2656–2667, https://doi.org/10.1093/molbev/msz196.

Lynnerup, Niels, "Endperiod Demographics of the Greenland Norse", *Viking Settlers of the North Atlantic: An Isotopic Approach. Journal of the North Atlantic* Special Volume 7 (2014): 18–24.

Madsen, Christian Koch, "Pastoral Settlement, Farming, and Hierarchy in Norse Vatnahverfi, South Greenland", PhD diss. (University of Copenhagen, 2014), www.nabohome.org/postgraduates/theses/ckm/.

Magnusson, Magnus, and Hermann Pálsson, *The Vinland Sagas: The Norse Discovery of America* (Baltimore: Penguin, 1965).

Margaryan, Ashot, Daniel J. Lawson, Martin Sikora, et al., "Population Genomics of the Viking World", *Nature* 585 (2020): 390–396.

McCullough, Karen M., *The Ruin Islanders: Thule Culture Pioneers in the Eastern High Arctic*. National Museum of Man Mercury Series 141 (Quebec: Canadian Museum of Civilization, 1989).

McGovern, Thomas H., "Contributions to the Paleoeconomy of Norse Greenland", *Acta Archaeologica* 54 (1985): 73–122.

McGovern, Thomas H., and A. Palsdóttir, *Preliminary Report of a Medieval Norse Archaeofauna from Brattahlið North Farm (KNK 2629), Qassiarsuk, Greenland*. NORSEC Zooarchaeology Laboratory Report no. 34 (New York: CUNY Northern Science and Education Center, 2006), www.nabohome.org/publications/labreports/Norsec34B rattahlidGreenlando5.pdf.

McGovern, Thomas H., Thomas Amorosi, Sophia Perdikatis, and James Woollett, "Vertebrate Zooarchaeology of Sandnes V51: Economic Change at a Chieftain's Farm in West Greenland", *Arctic Anthropology* 33 (1996): 92–121.

McGovern, Thomas H., Gerald F. Bigelow, Thomas Amorosi, James Woollett, and Sophia Perdikaris, "The Zooarchaeology of Ø17a", in Christen L. Vebæk, ed., *Narsaq: A Norse landnáma Farm*. Meddelelser om Grønland/Monographs on Greenland, Man and Society 18 (1993), pp. 58–72.

Mikkelsen, Naja, Antoon Kuijpers, and Jette Arneborg", The Norse in Greenland and Late Holocene Sea-Level Change", *Polar Record* 44 (2008): 45–50, https://doi.org/10.1017/S0032247407006948

Nedkvitne, Arnved, *Norse Greenland: Viking Peasants in the Arctic* (London/New York: Routledge, 2019).

Nørlund, Poul, *Buried Norsemen at Herjolfsnes*. Meddelelser om Grønland/Monographs on Greenland, Man and Society 67 (Copenhagen: Museum Tusculanum 1924).

Nyegaard, Georg, "Dairy Farmers and Seal Hunters: Subsistence on a Norse Farm in the Eastern Settlement, Greenland", *Journal of the North Atlantic* 37 (2018): 1–80.

Ólafsson, Guðmundur, "New Evidence for Dating of Iceland's *landnam*: Viking Age Finds in Cave Víðgelmir", in *Current Issues in Nordic Archaeology: Proceedings of the 21st Conference of Nordic Archaeologists, 6–9 September 2001, Akureyri, Iceland* (Reykjavík: Society of Icelandic Archaeologists, 2003), pp. 1–4.

Øye, Ingvild, "Farming Systems and Rural Societies ca. 800–1350", in Reidar Almås, ed., *Norwegian Agricultural History* (Trondheim: Tapir Academic Press, 2004), pp. 80–140.

Price, T. Douglas, and Jette Arneborg, "The Peopling of the North Atlantic: Isotopic Results from Greenland", Viking Settlers of the North Atlantic: An Isotopic Approach", *Journal of the North Atlantic* Special Volume 7 (2018): 164–185.

Roesdahl, Else, "Walrus Ivory: Demand, Supply, Workshops, and Greenland", in Andras Mortensen and Simun V. Arge, eds., *Viking and Norse in the North Atlantic: Select Papers from the Proceedings of the Fourteenth Viking Congress, Tórshavn, 19–30 July 2001* (Tórshavn: Annales Societatis Scientiarum Færoensis Supplementum XLIV, 2005), pp. 182–191.

Roussell, Aage, *Farms and Churches in the Mediaeval Norse Settlements of Greenland*. Meddelelser om Grønland/Monographs on Greenland, Man and Society 89 (Copenhagen: Museum Tusculanum, 1941).

Sanmark, Alexandra, "The Case of the Greenlandic Assembly Sites", *Journal of the North Atlantic* Special Volume 2 (2010): 178–192.

Schweger, Charles, "Geoarchaeology of the GUS Site: A Preliminary Framework", in Jette Arneborg and Hans Christian Gulløv, eds., *Man, Culture and Environment in Ancient Greenland* (Copenhagen: Danish National Museum and Danish Polar Center, 1998).

Smiarowski, Konrad, Ramona Harrison, Seth Brewington, et al., "Zooarchaeology of the Scandinavian Settlements in Iceland and Greenland: Diverging Pathways", in Umberto Albarella et al., eds., *The Oxford Handbook of Zooarchaeology* (Oxford Handbooks Online, 2017), https://doi.org/10.1093/10.1093/oxfordhb/9780199686476.013.9.

Star, Bastian, James H. Barrett, Agata T. Gondek, and Sanne Boessenkool, "Ancient DNA Reveals the Chronology of Walrus Ivory Trade from Norse Greenland", *Proceedings of the Royal Society B* 285 (2018): 20180978, https://dx.doi.org/10.1098/rspb.2018.0978.

Vésteinsson, Orri, "What Is a Booth? Material Symbolism at Icelandic Assembly Sites", *Journal of the North Atlantic* Special Volume 5 (2013): 111–124.

Vésteinsson, Orri, Michelle Hegmon, Jette Arneborg, Glen Rice, and Will G. Russell, "Dimensions of Inequality: Comparing the North Atlantic and the US Southwest", *Journal of Anthropological Archaeology* 54 (2019): 172–191.

7
Russia, the First Arctic Empire, 1000–1917

RYAN TUCKER JONES, ALEXEI KRAIKOVSKI, AND
JULIA LAJUS

Introduction

To claim Russia as an Arctic empire requires some consideration of both the concepts of Arctic and empire. First, despite the fact that little of Russia's imperial territory lies above the Arctic Circle, its rulers have nonetheless long governed predominantly cold lands and seas – colder, in fact, than many places north of the circle.[1] Therefore, this chapter will discuss Russian activities that sometimes occurred far outside a strict geographical understanding of the Arctic. These include the area known as the 'Russian North' (*Russkii Sever*) around the White Sea basin and to the south along the Northern Dvina River and its tributaries. It also includes the northern Urals and large portions of northern Siberia. Very little of Siberia lies above the Arctic Circle, but much of this part of Eurasia experiences Arctic conditions. Treeless permafrost predominates north of 60°. Air temperatures, declining as one moves eastward, are amongst the lowest in the world in the northeastern regions of Yakutia and Kolyma (Figure 7.1). There, the ocean is choked with ice in all but a short summer season. The period of Russian expansion came just after the conclusion of the Medieval Warm Period (the abnormally warm climatic conditions that prevailed in Northern Europe from c. 950 to 1250 AD), during which Siberian treelines moved south and temperatures fell even further, dramatically so in northern Siberia. Russians built a Siberian empire not only in one of the coldest regions on Earth, but in a place even colder than it is today.[2]

Second, the fact that the Russian state was an empire is widely accepted. But just as we argue for a wide definition of 'Arctic', in this chapter we assume a relatively expansive concept of empire. Russians not only exerted political control over large portions of the Arctic, but also rerouted its economic, social, and cultural life. In the northern conditions, these imperial

[1] Kollmann, *Russian Empire*, 22, 24. [2] Macdonald et al., "Climate Change", 2286.

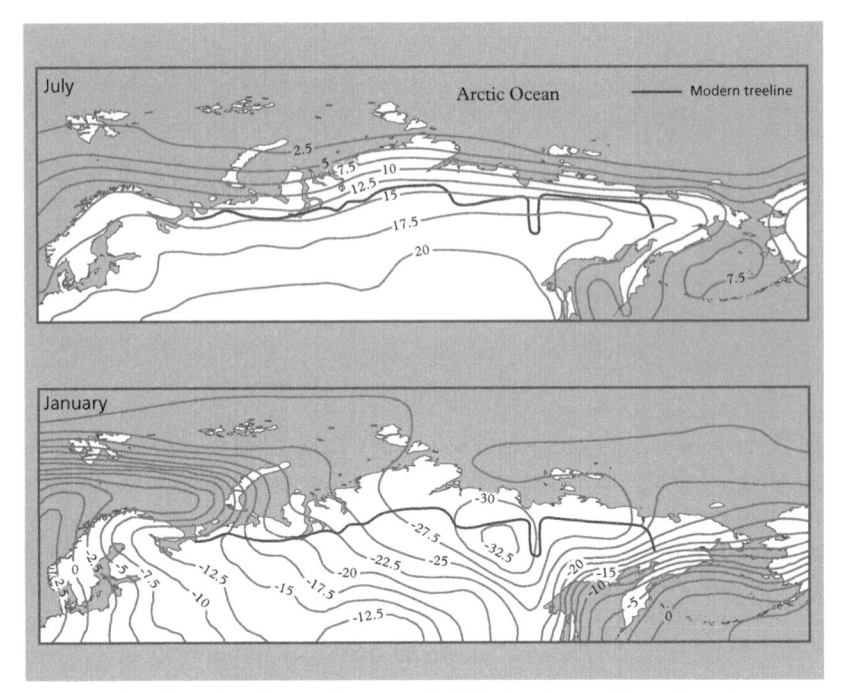

Figure 7.1 Northern Eurasian treeline zone (bold line) and monthly surface air temperature for (top) July and (bottom) January. (Data from MacDonald et al., "Climate Change".)

activities demanded special forms of expertise. Accordingly, we detail the production of knowledge about the Arctic, as well as the application and development of both traditional and new management techniques as crucial components of imperialism. We argue that the position of Russia as the first Arctic empire was based on the early development of specific skills necessary to propagate Russian culture into these severe regions and eventually incorporate them as core 'Russian' territories. We fully agree with the statement of historical geographers that the story of Russia is 'a story of how Russians adapted to, and also moulded to their needs, a series of rather different natural environments',[3] including Arctic ones.

Finally, this chapter examines the ambiguities of the Arctic's simultaneous remoteness from centres of human population and its importance for international commerce and science. Presenting an environment resistant to the

3 Shaw, "Russia's Geographical Environment", 43.

agricultural practices most significant for Russians, its liminality and the difficulty of its defence invited others in. At the same time, the Arctic's challenges and porosity encouraged Russians to invite international collaboration in its scientific study and the application of human technology. During most of the period under study, the Russian Arctic was attractive to explorers and, later, scientists from main centres of knowledge, especially German lands in the eighteenth century. Russian exploration in the nineteenth century was closely observed by British and then Scandinavian scientists. From the 1880s, international cooperation in the Arctic began with active participation and sometimes leadership from scientists who worked in the Russian Empire. Thus, even as Russia pioneered Arctic imperialism, the Russian Arctic developed into an arena of innovation, with practices emerging locally or adapted from abroad and then transferred across the vast northern spaces from the Kola Peninsula to Kamchatka. The reality for the Russian Arctic's local inhabitants, who were often considered impediments as much as assets to imperial desires, was far less innovative. Instead, they found themselves in a familiar colonial situation, as subjects of militarism, political and social experiment, and – when fortunate – neglect.

The Russian North and the Origins of the Russian Arctic Experience

The northern frontier of the core territory settled by Slavs, the predecessors of Russians, what we may call 'Northern Rus'', was situated on the watershed of the Upper Volga and the Northern Dvina water systems in the east and on the northern Novgorodian lands in the west. An ancient system of portages linked these riverine routes, therefore creating a transportation network between the Baltic, Black, Caspian, and White seas. The Finnish tribes that dominated this vast area in the Early Medieval time had diverse contacts with Slavs before the formation of the Russian state. The towns of Beloozero and Ladoga, founded under strong Viking influence, are probably the oldest existing urban centres in this area, appearing in the sources from 862 and predating the rise of Novgorod in the following century.[4]

From the 1030s, the chronicles mention among the Novgorod possessions the region 'beyond the portages' (*Zavoloch'e*), which means the land situated to the north and northeast. Those were the first steps from the Northern Rus'

---

4 Birnbaum, *Lord Novgorod the Great*, 15–16, 57; Curta, *Eastern Europe*, 283; Roslund, "Bringing 'the Periphery'", 181.

to the 'Russian North', the area situated outside Russians' original core territory. Russians began gradually moving northwards to the White Sea. The rivers were the major routes of travel, and water transport remained for centuries the central technology of mobility in the area. Most settlers came either from Novgorod or the Upper Volga Area and its urban centres of Rostov, Suzdal, and – later – Vladimir.

In the thirteenth century, before and after the Mongol invasion, both Novgorod and the princes of the Upper Volga region controlled dispersed possessions in the upper and middle course of the Northern Dvina. The Novgorodians founded the town of Olonets – which became the administrative centre of Karelia – and the town of Vologda, which controlled the Northern Dvina river system from its source.[5] To the northeast from Vologda, the settlers from the Upper Volga founded the town later known as Velikii Ustyug (Ustyug the Great) that became the base for further expansion in that direction.[6]

The unification of the Russian state in the late fifteenth century under Moscow – which rose to prominence after shrugging off Mongol control – meant a new political and economic reality for the Russian North. Large private landholdings, previously belonging to Novgorodian feudal nobility, became the property of the sovereign, and most of the rural population began to live on land owned by the state, making them members of the free peasant communities. Unlike the secular nobility, Novgorod church landowners managed to retain their possessions in the region. But even more important was the immigration of monks from central Russia, descendants of the monastic tradition established by St Sergius of Radonezh in the late fourteenth century. Looking for a place where monks could live an ideal Christian life, serving and glorifying God as members of disciplined and well-organized communities spending time in pious isolation and hard work, the monks moved further and further northwards.[7] By 1553, the Pechengsky monastery marked the northernmost point of the monastic movement, instantiating the power of Orthodox Christianity and the Russian state on the Barents Sea coast of the Kola Peninsula. By the sixteenth century, previous flows of settlers mixed in the coastal zone of the White Sea, giving origin to the distinct ethnic group known as the Pomors, 'People of the Sea', with strong economic and cultural links with the coastal fisheries especially on the Barents Sea coast.[8]

5 Makarov, "Traders".   6 Makarov, *Kolonizatsiia*, 6–7.
7 Kraikovski et al., "Between Piety".
8 Bernshtam, *Pomory*, 26–31; Lajus et al., "Sea Fisheries".

7 Russia, the First Arctic Empire, 1000–1917

Early Russian northern experience shaped the vision of the North as a vast area, requiring long-distance terrestrial and water mobility under harsh conditions. The area, though, was rich in natural resources with high value on the international market. Locals were exploiting a wide variety of environments. They harvested salt from seawater and underground brines, while the rivers, lakes, and seas provided a variety of marketable species of fish and marine mammals. From forest animals they took furs and other products. The Russian North also became one of Muscovy's centres of tar and potassium production.[9]

The Rise of the Eurasian Arctic Empire: The Russian North and Siberia in the Sixteenth and Seventeenth Centuries

The territorial expansion to the north and east from the White Sea led to new cross-cultural contacts. Moving to the east, towards the northern Urals, Russians encountered the Nenets and Komi people. The town of Pustozersk in the Pechora watershed, founded in the late fifteenth century, became the first Russian urban settlement north of the Arctic Circle, and directed Russian expansion in the area.[10] This opened the way for penetration further to the east, to the land of Khanty and Mansi in the Ob' River drainage.[11] Monastic colonization did not follow this direction, but the wealthy Stroganov family of salt-makers and merchants – who could not compete with the monasteries on the market of the Russian North – gradually moved out to exploit the natural resources of the Perm' area. The Stroganovs' possessions became the base for further Russian expansion into Siberia. In the 1550s, after the conquest of Kazan and Astrakhan, the Russian tsar Ivan the Terrible began receiving tribute from the ruler of the Sibir khanate that was conquered in 1580s by a Cossack expedition led by Yermak and supported by Stroganovs. Yermak's campaign resulted in the foundation of Tumen' and Tobolsk, the earliest Russian urban centres in Siberia. This success opened the way to further Russian expansion into Siberia towards the Pacific Ocean.[12]

In the White Sea area, Kola Peninsula, and the Barents Sea coast, Russians encountered the Sámi people, who became objects of Christian missionization. The state administration settled in the town of Kola at the southern end of the Kola Bay of the Barents Sea, controlling the area and the Sámi on behalf of the

---

9 Vdovina, "Dobyvaiushchie promysly". 10 Jasinski and Ovsiannikov, *Pustozersk*.
11 Pertsev, "Pohod moskovskih". 12 Forsyth, *History*, 25–34.

Tsar. Taking advantage of state infrastructure, the Pomors began to substantially exploit marine natural resources. The seasonal cod and halibut fisheries on the Murman coast of the Kola Peninsula were combined with hunting expeditions to the coastal areas and the islands of the Barents Sea. The monasteries took an active part in these activities.[13] Archaeological findings also suggest that at that time the Russian hunters reached Spitsbergen, although no documentary evidence to support this possibility has yet been found.[14]

At the same time, the North became an arena of multifaceted contacts between Russians and Europeans. The growing global maritime economy brought European traders to the Kola Peninsula and later to the White Sea. The international port of Arkhangelsk, founded in 1584 after the arrival of the English merchants to the Northern Dvina,[15] became the major administrative, commercial, and cultural centre of the Russian North.

The next century witnessed the transformation of the Moscow Tsardom into a Eurasian superpower dominating territory roughly equivalent to twenty-first-century Russia. The seventeenth century was a very significant period for the Russian North. After the period of political and social cataclysms known as Time of Troubles (1598–1613), the Sukhona–Dvina riverine route between Vologda and Arkhangelsk became the major communication line connecting the economy of the enormous country with the international market. The trade centres along this commercial artery played an important role in the production and distribution of highly valued products like salt, blubber, fur, and products of local craftsmen.

The complex economy of the Russian North was based on efficient methods of exploitation of the local natural resources. For instance, the development of marine harvesting depended on the development of salt production, shipbuilding, and smithery. The production of salt, in turn, was linked with the production and transportation of fuel timber. The monasteries took the position of the economic leaders of the area, controlling the most profitable markets and providing the necessary organizational and managerial skills. In general, the seventeenth-century economy of the Russian North looked rather modern, with a high level of bureaucratization and many important organizational innovations, including the participation of foreign – predominantly Dutch – merchants in local commercial life.[16]

13 Nikonov, 'Kto v more ne khodil'.   14 Dadykina et al., "Mastering the Arctic".
15 Mayers, North-East Passage.
16 Kotilaine, Russia's Foreign Trade; Jasinski and Ovsiannikov, Vzgliad na Evropeiskuiu Arktiku; Dadykina and Kraikovski, "Monks"; Kraikovski et al., "Water Management".

Shipping and shipbuilding deserve special discussion. Shipbuilders in the Russian North developed and utilized a variety of types of vessels well-suited to the specific conditions of the area. Some of them, like the *koch* (plural: *kochi*), small, single-masted sloops, became iconic in the history of Russian shipping. Not only did the *koch* facilitate growing international linkages in the Russian North, but it became essential for the history of another crucial part of Russia's Arctic empire – Siberia.

The lands east of the Urals, whose conquest was enabled by Yermak's expedition, then abounded in fur-bearing sables, which inhabited a wide, contiguous band of boreal forest stretching all the way to the North Pacific.[17] In summer, the sable's pelage is short and scruffy. However, in the long Siberian winter, the animal grows a deep brown coat that is, in the words of Soviet biologists, 'exceptionally fluffy and silky'.[18] The sable, once trapped and its fur peeled from its body, attracted buyers in Russia, but more importantly in Western Europe and China.[19] The fact that Arctic Siberia lay between these two poles of early modern global wealth, but still far distant from their commercial centres, shaped much of its colonial history.[20] After Russian explorers encountered sea otters in the North Pacific in the 1720s, this rarer but even more valuable animal helped bring those cold oceans into the world market as well.

Initial Russian advances into Siberia in the sixteenth and seventeenth century borrowed technologies developed in the course of northern colonization. Both government servitors and private entrepreneurs (*promyshlenniki*) navigated Siberia primarily along its rivers and coastline. Pomors from the Arkhangelsk region spearheaded oceanic exploration, using their *kochi*, which could be constructed on site if necessity dictated.[21] These techniques put a premium on skilled carpenters, a profession later dominated by Siberian Yakuts, who contributed vital expertise to North Pacific exploration.[22] But Muscovy found the Arctic sea route difficult to control, with several English voyagers also exploring this area, and the government forbade maritime voyages from 1617 until the early 1620s. After that time, however, Russians again pushed eastward along the coast, now from the fur trade and administrative centre of Mangazeia, founded near the mouth of the Taz River in Yamalo-Nenets land in 1600. Less than fifty years later, in 1647, a group of fur

---

17 Heptner and Naumov, eds., *Mammals*, 777–790; Krasheninnikov, "Sable Hunting".
18 Heptner and Naumov, eds., *Mammals*, 761.
19 Martin, *Treasures*; Fisher, *Russian Fur Trade*. 20 Monahan, *Merchants of Siberia*.
21 Lantzeff and Pierce, *Eastward to Empire*, 183. 22 Jones, *Empire of Extinction*, 77.

traders and servitors under the partial command of Semen Dezhnev launched *kochi* from the mouth of the Lena River and navigated past Siberia's eastern terminus (*Svyatoi Nos*, renamed Cape Dezhnev) and into the North Pacific.[23] Russians had explored nearly the entirety of Siberia's Arctic coast.

The speed of Russian exploration through Siberia, though, obscures the spottiness of their control. As Soviet historian S. V. Bakhrushin demonstrated, the Russians' main mode of procuring furs, the *yasak*, formally signified tribute taking from native Siberians, but in reality often indicated the establishment of voluntary trade relations. Russians possessed neither the personnel nor sufficient technologies of possession to enact any greater suzerainty. Until the eighteenth century, what power they exercised in Siberia consisted of their ability to terrorize scattered groups into submission by taking hostages, or *amanaty*.[24] Russian colonizers also often found themselves internally divided, as rival groups from different outposts battled for access to the next rich sable grounds.[25] As a servitor advised a fellow fur trader during one such contest, 'It is not proper to send the natives to kill Russians. You had better kill them yourself.'[26] When Muscovy's power waned, as it did during the Time of Troubles, of pretenders and foreign invasion in the 1620s, these feuds raged unabated. On the other hand, these internecine conflicts could impel the government into action. The important northern Siberian city of Yakutsk was founded in 1638 precisely to establish peace amongst feuding Russians, who, united, were then able to coordinate 'ruthless attacks' against the Yakuts living by the Lena River.[27]

The transfer of the Russian Arctic experience to Siberia was characterized by continuity and complexity. While moving eastwards, Russians developed several mechanisms of control over the vast territories. The experience of efficient and fast construction of fortified settlements under the general supervision of state experts helped to create a network of forts along the riverine routes. The major urban centres of the region, like Tobol´sk and Surgut in western Siberia, Irkutsk and Yakutsk in eastern Siberia, started as typical seventeenth-century Russian fortifications constructed in accordance with well-elaborated technologies of infrastructural control of the frontier zones.[28] This network of fortified centres was linked to the existing urban

23 Lantzeff and Pierce, *Eastward to Empire*, 128, 190.   24 Bakhrushin, "*Yasak* (Fur Tribute)".
25 Remnev, ed., *Sibir' v Sostave*, 7.
26 Quoted in Lantzeff and Pierce, *Eastward to Empire*, 138.
27 Lantzeff and Pierce, *Eastward to Empire*, 138, 139.
28 Gorbachev et al., *Gradostroitelstvo Sibiri*, 61–79.

infrastructure of the European North and formed a sort of unity from the White Sea to the Pacific Ocean. For instance, Ustyug in the seventeenth century became one of the major distribution centres for the goods delivered from Siberia, including furs.[29] No wonder that Siberia soon became an area of activities for the dwellers of the Russian North, with the Pomor newcomers active participants in the exploitation of resources of the Lena River basin.[30] Eventually, as Valerie Kivelson demonstrated, the Muscovian authorities incorporated Siberia intellectually into the empire, with its maps, for example, describing it as part of a larger Orthodox ecumene.[31] If these technologies of control long remained thin, they were resilient, and they formed the foundation of a much more intensive form of Arctic colonization in the next century.

The Challenge of Westernization in the Long Eighteenth Century

The radical transformation of Russia by Peter the Great and his successors is very well known.[32] If Peter in some ways steered the Russian ship of state towards the west, he also steered it northward. With the establishment of St Petersburg in 1703 as a new capital and port, Russia's northern maritime trade and power waxed.[33] Arkhangelsk and the Russian North in general undoubtedly lost their position as trade centres. However, Arkhangelsk became one of the most important centres of shipbuilding and recruiting of seamen for the newly founded Russian Navy, a role it played until the end of the age of sail.[34] Furthermore, like many other cities in Russia, by the late eighteenth century Arkhangelsk adapted the modern urban form patented in St Petersburg. The city was rebuilt along a regular plan, with buildings constructed in classical European style.[35]

The eighteenth century also saw further, significant innovations for imperial control in the Russian North. The empire looked for methods to involve private entrepreneurs in state-organized projects. Often, government efforts to transform life according to European examples were unsuccessful. Monopolistic companies, organized in 1703–1768 to market marine resources, and possibly develop whaling on Spitsbergen, achieved significant financial

---

29 Merzon and Tikhonov, *Rynok Ustiuga Velikogo*, 274–286.
30 Kraikovski, "'The Sea on One Side'". 31 Kivelson, "'Between All Parts'".
32 Lindsey, *Russia*; de Madariaga, *Russia*; Dixon, *Modernisation of Russia*.
33 Repin, *Vneshniaia torgovlia*. 34 Bespiatykh, *Arkhangelsk*.
35 Milchik and Popova, *Pervye vorota Rossiiskogo gosudarstva*.

success but failed to bring the government the strategic benefits they had hoped for.[36] As a result, the monasteries managed to remain the principal centres of organizational and managerial expertise in the region throughout the eighteenth century, despite the secularization of monastic lands in 1764. That year, the imperial treasury took possession of most of the monasteries' lands and fishing grounds, redistributing them to the peasants who had previously been dependent on the monasteries. In 1775 the government abolished duties on fishing and marine hunting. Soon, the Pomors began a profitable trade with Norway, exchanging Russian grain and timber for Norwegian fish.[37] However, efforts to force the Pomors to build and use European vessels instead of their traditional *kochi* mostly failed.[38] The same was true for projects aimed to improve the techniques of fish salting in the North in an attempt to raise their quality and compete with Western commodities.[39] Thus, economic activity largely proceeded along traditional lines.

For the Urals and Siberia, the eighteenth century was marked by unprecedented state activity in industrial and infrastructural development. The growing metal industry of the Urals became the basis for rapid urbanization, while Peter's plan to strengthen control over Siberian possessions and to establish the navy's permanent presence in the Pacific Ocean resulted in significant improvement of the transportation and urban infrastructure in the area. The cities received new development, including stone buildings in Tobolsk and new port premises in Okhotsk.[40] All this infrastructure facilitated further expansion to the east with the final aim of establishing stronger control over the area up to Kamchatka and Chukotka, which still remained problematic from the point of view of the imperial bureaucracy.

Perhaps the harshest limit to Russian power in the Siberian Arctic was eco-cultural. The short growing seasons, as much as the bitter winter cold, severely curtailed any prospect of growing the cereal grains upon which Russian culture had been built. Despite repeated experiments from the Yamal Peninsula to Kamchatka, no land in Arctic Siberia ever produced much of the foods Russians wanted. Of course, native Siberians survived on the abundant fish, reindeer, marine mammals, and antiscorbutic herbs found or tended in the Eurasian Arctic. But Russians judged this strange diet one of the chief

---

36 Kraikovski, "Good vs. Bad Fisheries"; Kraikovski, "Profits from under the Water".
37 Schrader, "Pomor Trade".   38 Bryzgalov, "Stroitelstvo".
39 Ovsiannikov and Jasinski, "Krestinin o promysle".
40 Gorbachev et al., *Gradostroitelstvo Sibiri*, 79–100.

markers of Siberians' otherness and inferiority, and in most cases refused or were unable to adapt to local foods.[41] Again, the Russian state came to its subjects' aid, providing a yearly grain salary for government servitors. But, given the distances and terrain involved, this solution rarely sufficed. Bags of grain sometimes took six years to go from Irkutsk to Kamchatka, by which time their price had risen thirty times. Malnutrition and disease reigned. When Captain Cook's explorers visited Kamchatka in 1779, they found that every inhabitant of the city of Petropavlovsk was scorbutic.[42] These problems persisted into the nineteenth century in Alaska, where Russian settlers often teetered on the edge of starvation amidst some of the world's best-fed people, blessed with nearly inexhaustible salmon runs.

Given these limitations, Russian power in Siberia depended, as did many European empires of the time, on local cooptation. The wealth introduced into Siberian societies through the fur trade raised the power of local leaders, whether they be Samoyed or Tlingit, and these new leaders had every reason to encourage continued engagement with Russians.[43] In partnership with *promyshlenniki*, Yakuts, with a pre-existing system of strong leadership, proved particularly 'energetic and adaptable colonisers' of other Siberians.[44] Similarly, the Chukchi of the far northeast never really submitted to imperial rule, but used their access to Russian trade goods to exert increased influence around the Bering Strait. Throughout Siberia, Indigenous people grew their domesticated reindeer herds, often in spectacular fashion, probably in response to new market opportunities offered by the influx of Russians.[45] As Andrei Golovnev and Gail Osherenko put it for the Nenets, in a statement that applies for many Siberians at the time: Russians represented nothing extraordinary, but were thought of as an unpredictable but manageable 'political nature ... not so different from the real arctic nature'.[46]

Of course, far from all Siberians were able to forge favourable relationships with the invaders. Everywhere, novel diseases rent holes in northern communities, to an extent still barely understood by historians.[47] The worst impacts came when illnesses were paired with reductions in food sources; this is well documented for the Chukchi, Yupik, and Iñupiat of the Bering Strait who died in large numbers when Americans decimated walrus herds in

---

41 Slezkine, *Arctic Mirrors*, 57.   42 Gibson, *Feeding the Russian Fur Trade*, 220, 221, 223.
43 Forsyth, *History*, 61.   44 Forsyth, *History*, 56.
45 Krupnik, *Arctic Adaptations*, 164–165; for details, see Lebedev, "Sem'ia" .
46 Golovnev and Osherenko, *Siberian Survival*, 3, 4.
47 Forsyth, *History*, 58; Zadonina, *Khronologiia*.

the late nineteenth century. One thousand Chukchi were estimated to have perished from Russian-introduced smallpox.[48] Similar, unrecorded tragedies must have occurred in earlier centuries throughout the Siberian north, even if the Russians did not directly destroy food sources. The failures of agriculture along with the impact of introduced diseases means that we can understand Russia's Arctic colonization as a limited form of ecological imperialism, similar to developments in the Canadian Arctic.[49] There is much research still to be done on this topic.

As Indigenous Siberians often responded to the new market for furs by moving out of productive hunting grounds in favour of the deeper forest frequented by sables, they – like the Russians – became increasingly dependent on grain imports.[50] Colonization could also occur in far more direct form. The Koryaks and Itelmen of Kamchatka rebelled in the early eighteenth century, nearly repelling the Russians, only to suffer bitter defeat, increased resource extraction, and slow cultural genocide.[51]

The impetus for the Kamchatkan revolts was connected to a major revolution in Russian attempts to comprehend and manage these distant and challenging lands and seas. From the early eighteenth century the Russian Empire increasingly turned to a new technology, natural history. That discipline, as practiced at the time, encompassed everything from the description of plants and animals of different regions of the globe, to general ethnography and comparative linguistics. While the term 'science' would not be fitted to these practices until the nineteenth century, natural history's remit overlapped with the modern conception of science, though it was then far more eclectic. Developed primarily in Europe's Royal Academies, natural history was well-suited to assist the voracious appetites of early modern European imperialism. Famously, James Cook employed the naturalist Joseph Banks on his 1769 voyage. In fact, the Russian Empire had preceded this pairing of science and empire by several decades.

This mechanism of imperial control was first applied in Siberia, not in the European North. Emperor Peter I had sent the German naturalist Daniel Gottlieb Messerschmidt to explore Siberia in 1719.[52] And while Messerschmidt's scientific work languished after his premature death, others fared better. The First Kamchatka Expedition started the scientific mapping of the North Pacific, while the Second Kamchatka Expedition (1733–43) resulted in the full-scale naturalistic description of Arctic Siberia. Serving with Vitus Bering's Second

48 Bockstoce, *Furs and Frontiers*, 319.   49 Piper and Sandlos, "Broken Frontier".
50 Jordan, ed., "Landscape and Culture", 29; Golovnev, *Istoricheskaia Tipologiia*.
51 Al'kov and Drezen, *Kolonial'naia politika*.   52 Messerschmidt, *Forschungreise*.

Kamchatka contingent, naturalist Georg Wilhelm Steller played a key advisory role during the voyage to Alaska and subsequent shipwreck in the Commander Islands. Though he failed to discover any valuable minerals, as had been hoped, Steller's travel journal and zoological writings from Alaska and Kamchatka attracted widespread European attention and acclaim. Amongst other accomplishments, Steller provided the only scientific description of the northern (later Steller's) sea cow, which would be driven to extinction by Russian hunters by 1768. Stepan Krasheninnikov, who served with Steller, provided descriptions of Kamchatka with the precise topographical and ethnographic material useful for administration, part of what Willard Sunderland has termed a turn towards 'territoriality' – a heightened concern with knowing and shaping territory – in Russian imperial practice.[53] Other eighteenth-century Russian explorers/naturalists of the north, such as Khariton Laptev, Semen Cheliuskin, and Aleksei Chirikov, made similar contributions to these practices, while leaving their names on the Arctic landscape.[54]

Unique among contemporaneous empires, Russia employed a large number of foreign naturalists, a situation stemming from the lack of domestic scholars. While St Petersburg tried to control the external flow of information, foreign naturalists often leveraged transnational linkages to evade restrictions. Their critical stance towards Russia's management of its northern colonies encouraged a developing European conception of Russia as backward, couched increasingly as part of a barbaric east, rather than 'northern', as earlier commentators had imagined it and its Siberian colonies.[55] This combination of serious scientific study and colonial criticism quickly became characteristic of the mostly German naturalists' contribution to Russian empire-building in the Siberian and Alaskan north. For instance, when Bering's demands that the Itelmen transport the expedition's effects across Kamchatka caused them extreme hardship, provoking another revolt, Steller harshly criticized Russian colonial oppression, adding another new concern to the naturalists' brief.

In the European North, the practice of imperial control through scientific knowledge appeared half a century later. The famous Russian polymath Mikhail Lomonosov, who was born near Arkhangelsk, maintained a lifelong interest in the Arctic, even as he spent most of his adult days in St Petersburg. Lomonosov often used Arctic imagery in his poems, and coined the slogan that 'Russian power will grow with Siberia and the Northern Ocean', words still referenced by Russian

53 Sunderland, "Imperial Space".
54 Okhotina-Lind, ed., *Vtoraia Kamchatskaia Ekspeditsiia*.
55 Jones, *Empire of Extinction*; Kusber, "Mastering the Imperial Space", 56.

authorities.[56] Lomonosov also postulated that there was ice-free water around the North Pole, and argued that navigation from Kola to Kamchatka was possible. To test these claims, two expeditions led by Admiral Vassily Chichagov, head of Arkhangelsk port, were organized in 1765 and 1766. But the ships found thick ice near Spitsbergen and were forced to return.

Lomonosov may have been wrong about an ice-free northern passage (at least in the eighteenth century), but he was correct that Russian power, in the Arctic and elsewhere, was to grow. Expeditions to the Russian Arctic organized by the St Petersburg Academy of Sciences in the 1760s and 1770s are among the best known scientific enterprises of the eighteenth century. In the European North, an expedition led by academic Ivan Lepekhin to the large spaces between Lake Ladoga and the Kola Peninsula brought the region to European attention. While Lepekhin's suggestion for more intensive exploitation of Arctic seas brought no direct results, it was probably the basis of the White Sea Fishing Company (*Belomorskaia Promyslovaia Kompaniia*) founded by Nikolai Rumiantsev, chancellor of the empire.[57] To the company's misfortune, it lost numerous ships to Arctic storms before the political uncertainty of the Napoleonic Wars ushered it into bankruptcy in 1813.[58]

Naturalists such as Lepekhin, Peter Simon Pallas, and Georg Heinrich von Langsdorff enjoyed close access to St Petersburg's halls of power, and thus their critiques helped both to form European opinion about the Russian Empire and to bring about significant reforms in colonial governance.[59] For example, Emperor Alexander I implemented Langsdorff's ideas for military-agricultural colonies in Kamchatka and his plans for smallpox inoculation of the Itelmen in 1812, even as Napoleon's armies threatened the western gates of empire.[60] Langsdorff's vision for Kamchatka represented well the broad contours of naturalists' advice – well-meaning if paternalistic concerns for native Siberian welfare, prescriptions for more consistent and intrusive state regulation, and a persistent overestimation of agriculture's potential in the Arctic. Their activities helped create a strong basis for increasing imperial control over the region.

Strategic Periphery: The Nineteenth-Century Arctic

In the first half of the nineteenth century the European North increasingly began to be understood as a periphery that could operate according to the

---

56 Ogorodov et al., "M. V. Lomonosov"; Lomonosov, "Kratkoe opisanie", 498.
57 *Puteshestviia Akademika Ivana Lepekhina*; Ozeretskovsky, *Opisanie*.
58 Skugarev, "V period zakata".   59 Jones, "'These Great Plains'".
60 Ordubadi, "Die Halbinsel Kamčatka", 107.

general rules of the country and thus did not need special care from the state.⁶¹ Just as trade began to run through the Baltic, St Petersburg turned to that region for the manpower to study and govern the Arctic. Baltic Germans formed the core of the Russian Imperial Navy.⁶² Their numbers included Admiral Adam von Krusenstern, who in 1815–18 piloted the brig *Rurik* in search of a northern passage between Eurasia and North America. Despite failing to reach the Arctic Ocean through the Bering Strait, the expedition seriously advanced the scientific study of the North Pacific part of the Arctic.⁶³

Baltic Germans also formed an increasingly important bloc at the Academy of Sciences. Talented and conscientious Baltic German administrator-intellectuals included such figures as Arctic explorer Admiral Friedrich (Fedor) Litke (Lütke) and Baron Ferdinand von Wrangell (also spelled Wrangel). The latter served as chief manager of Russian America and was an honorary member of the St Petersburg Academy of Sciences, making significant contributions to Arctic science.⁶⁴ In 1830 Wrangell also became one of the first to describe the phenomenon of permafrost, observing in Yakutsk a deep well that never filled with water because the ground remained frozen (the well is known as the Shergin well and became a standard point for permafrost measurement). Later, Gerhard Baron von Maydell helped establish that Verkhoyansk in northeastern Siberia was the world's coldest inhabited place.⁶⁵

Another Baltic-German, zoologist Karl Ernst von Baer, left a successful career in Königsberg to serve the Russian Academy of Sciences, following his dream to study the Arctic. In 1837 Baer became one of the first naturalists to study the geology, fauna, flora, and especially the climate of Novaya Zemlya.⁶⁶ Baer coined the word *Eiskeller* (ice-cellar) to describe the Kara Sea, and – most importantly – established permafrost as a scientific object and for the first time mapped its presence across the northern and eastern portions of the Russian Empire.⁶⁷ Baer advocated sending expeditions to eastern Siberia to measure permafrost, one of which was led by Alexander von Middendorff, who with Baer in summer 1840 explored the coasts of the Kola Peninsula. In 1842–45 Middendorff conducted pioneering studies of

---

61 Lajus, "Colonization", 170.   62 Kopelev, *Na sluzhbe Imperii*.
63 Bekasova, "Voyaging Towards the Future".
64 Wrangel, *Statistische und Ethnographische Nachrichten*.
65 Tammiksaar, "Gerhard Baron von Maydell", 260.
66 Tammiksaar, "Contributions".
67 Tammiksaar and Stone,"Karl Ernst von Baer"; Chu, *Life of Permafrost*, 25–42.

permafrost, climate, geomorphology, zoology, and the ethnography of Siberia, especially in the remote regions of the Taimyr Peninsula and Yakutia.[68]

The Russian Imperial Geographic Society (founded in 1845 by Baer and his scientific circle)[69] sent its first expedition to determine the northern terminus of the Ural Mountains at the Arctic Sea, work that shed light on Pallas's earlier supposition that the mountains extended underwater to the North Pole and would later buttress Russian claims to the Arctic Ocean.[70] Forging similar ties between science and empire, while adding commerce, the Swedish-Finnish whaler Otto Lindholm played a key role in establishing Russia's first successful whaling venture. The Russian-Finnish Whaling Company (created in 1851) caught whales primarily in the Sea of Okhotsk and the Gulf of Alaska, both with the hopes of profit and shoring up an official presence in those distant imperial reaches. After the Crimean War destroyed the company, Lindholm returned to the Far East, where he caught more whales and began a study of ocean currents.[71]

Russia's cooptation of Baltic German and Finno-Swedish subjects extended the practice of using Pomor knowledge and technology in the Siberian Arctic. Indeed, St Petersburg turned the empire's vast and expanding multiculturalism into a signature strength. In Alaska, it even created a deliberate form of ethnic hybridity, encouraging the marriage of Russian men with Unangan and Alutiiq women in order to create a class of Creole labourers who could combine detailed knowledge of local environments with familiarity of Russian culture in order to wring the greatest profit out of the colony.[72] In fact, native and creolized Siberians everywhere continued to do the bulk of the hard work of making empire function in these cold environments. After the reforms of administrator Mikhail Speranskii in 1822, Indigenous Siberian leaders were tasked with administering local and Russian laws in addition to collecting the taxes that had been regularized in the eighteenth century. Local law still predominated, as Russian laws only came into effect when subjects rebelled against imperial authority.[73]

Native Siberians did not always welcome the increasing Russian attempts to apply scientific methods to their region. In 1827, Samoyed leader Paigol

---

68 Sukhova and Tammiksaar, *Aleksandr Fedorovich Middendorf*; Chu, *Life of Permafrost*, 41–45.
69 Sukhova, "Ob osnovanii Russkogo".
70 Sukhova and Skrydlov, "Russian Geographical Society".
71 Lindholm, *Beyond the Frontiers*.   72 Vinkovetsky, *Russian America*.
73 Golovnev and Osherenko, *Siberian Survival*, 44–45, 65.

refused to assist the expedition of navigator V. Ivanov, since, as Paigol claimed, the Russians had come 'to measure the lands for the purpose of later taking these lands away'.[74] Other local leaders undercut him and worked with the Russians, but history vindicated Paigol. The application of science rendered Siberia far better known, and more thoroughly exploited and governed.

New technologies, especially in conjunction with fossil fuels, also re-routed Russia's Arctic empire. In the late 1800s, Russians began to settle in the lower Ob River for fishing, since, thanks to steam navigation, fish could now be brought profitably to market.[75] Soon, the newcomers encroached on Samoyed and Nenets land. That same steam navigation also brought foreign imperial powers back to the Russian Arctic in substantial numbers for the first time since the Time of Troubles. Norwegian and Austro-Hungarian expeditions surveyed the Siberian coastline in the 1870s. British steam whalers would work the Kara Sea in the 1890s.[76] Norwegians made several successful attempts to navigate the Kara Sea in the hopes of opening new shipping lanes. These hopes were fulfilled in 1894 by British Captain Joseph Wiggins, who received information and support from several Russian merchants in the region.[77] The famous Swedish polar scientist and explorer Adolf Erik Nordenskiöld, who knew Russian and corresponded with Russian scientists and polar enthusiasts, successfully navigated to the mouth of the Yenisei River in 1875–76. In 1878–80 his ship *Vega*, carrying an international team of scientists, became the first to travel the length of the northern passage from Norway to Japan.

International interest in the Russian Arctic was not always so benign from an imperial point of view. During the Crimean War (1853–56), the British Navy had burned the town of Kola, which lost its status as a centre of the region. After Russia's defeat, St Petersburg began to secure the vast but sparsely populated region's relative openness and vulnerability. In 1859–61 the Ministry of State Domains organized an expedition to the White and Barents Sea coasts under the leadership of Nikolai Danilevski, a disciple of Baer, who had studied Russian fisheries since the 1840s. The expedition hoped to provide an impetus for economic development, and it laid the foundations for the subsequent government programme for the colonization of the Murman coast of the Barents Sea. The nearby Finnmark coast (part of

---

74 Golovnev and Osherenko, *Siberian Survival*, 65.
75 Golovnev and Osherenko, *Siberian Survival*, 62–66.
76 Adams (collection), Scott Polar Research Institute Archives.
77 Armstrong, *Northern Sea Route*, 2–13; Saunders, "Captain Wiggins".

Norway, then in union with Sweden) offered a model for economic development as well as a source of settlers.[78] In 1868, St Petersburg introduced substantial privileges to settlers willing to come to the Russian Arctic. Significant numbers came during this period, with many staying until the 1930s, when they were forcibly removed from the strategically important coast by the Soviet authorities.[79]

Other strategies to link the Russian North to imperial governance and economic activity followed. From 1835, a Russian statistical committee began to work in Arkhangelsk, collecting and publishing detailed data on the region's population and economy. In 1875 the Arkhangelsk–Murman steamship company began connecting the region's coastal areas.[80] In the 1880s, the railway from St Petersburg to Arkhangelsk was completed and telegraph connections soon followed. Interest in the mineral resources of the European North grew from the 1860s when the wealthy Arkhangelsk merchant Mikhail Sidorov, who successfully developed gold mining at the Yenisei River, attempted to organize the extraction of iron, coal, and newly discovered oil in the Pechora region. Although a lack of infrastructure and labour doomed these plans, and Sidorov remained primarily a timber trader, he established himself as a well-known advocate of Arctic economic development based on scientific research. Sidorov was especially interested in the development of the Northern Sea Route along the Siberian coasts, and he helped support Nordenskiöld's exploration.[81]

However, Sweden's growing interest in Spitsbergen at the beginning of the 1870s awakened the concern of the Russian government. Patriotic indignation was fuelled by Sidorov and other public figures and was picked up by the press. In spite of the fact that Russian hunters had not visited Sptisbergen since 1851, access to its natural resources was considered vital to the Russian state and public, and thus Russia – together with Norway, but against Sweden – supported the archipelago's status as a *terra nullius*. To further Russian geopolitical goals in the Arctic, the state organized the resettlement of several Nenets families from the mainland tundra to Novaya Zemlya, a very concrete twinning of Siberian and Northern Russian development. In 1870, the Russian Imperial Navy organized a squadron of ships under the command of Vice-Admiral Konstantin Posiet to deliver the first settler and symbolically maintain power over these islands. Middendorff, who took part

78 Lajus, "In Search of Instructive Models". 79 Yurchenko and Nielsen, eds., *In the North*.
80 Owen, *Dilemmas of Russian Capitalism*.
81 Sidorov, *Besedy o Sever Rossii*; Sidorov, *Trudy dlia oznakomleniia*; Studitskii, *Istoriia otkrytiia morskogo*.

in this voyage as a naturalist, argued for attention to 'the enormous riches of the polar sea' and their rational exploitation. He was especially interested in deciphering the flow of warm waters of the Gulf Stream into the Arctic Ocean. However, Middendorff doubted that the North Pole could be reached by ship, instead proposing an expedition by dogs and sledges that never took place.[82]

Despite Russian reservations about foreign activities in the Arctic, by the 1880s it had become evident that international cooperation was essential for the region's exploration. Thus, the first major event of international scientific collaboration – the first International Polar Year (IPY) – occurred in the Arctic. Taking place from 1882 to 1883, the IPY saw the participation of eleven nations. While the main inspiration came from Karl Weyprecht, who together with Julius Payer discovered Franz Josef Land in 1873, Russians also played a significant role. In particular, Heinrich Wild, the director of Pulkovo Observatory near St Petersburg, was essential to the IPY's organization, when Russia established two meteorological stations, one at Novaya Zemlya and the other at the mouth of the Lena River.[83] This international enterprise became a model for subsequent polar years in the twentieth century.

The Interplay of Internationalism and Nationalism: The Beginning of the Twentieth Century

The Russian Arctic in the first two decades of the twentieth century saw a continued interplay of internationalism and nationalism. An important step in international scientific cooperation in the High Arctic was the Swedish-Russian Meridian Expedition's joint research in Spitsbergen in 1899–1901.[84] At the same time, marine and fisheries scientists also began collaboration, establishing the International Council for Exploration of the Seas (ICES). Russian scientists of the Murman Scientific Fisheries Expedition, funded by the philanthropic Committee for the Aid to Pomors, took responsibility for the bulk of oceanographic research in the northern region. The first research vessel in Europe went to the Barents Sea.[85] This cooperation allowed a substantial transfer of modern methodologies to Russian marine

82 Sukhova and Tammiksaar, *Aleksandr Fedorovich Middendorf*, 303.
83 Tammiksaar et al., "International Polar Year"; Tammiksaar and Sukhova, "Russian Polar Stations".
84 Pinkhenson, *Problema Severnogo morskogo puti*, 484–488.
85 Lajus, "Foreign Science"; Lajus, "Experts on Unknown Waters".

science.[86] From a technological standpoint, the crucial change was the introduction of the bottom trawl to the Arctic in the 1910s, which became the main fishing implement in the Barents Sea by the 1920s, with huge repercussions for the ocean environment.[87] Leading Russian scientist Dmitry Mendeleev used his professional power to lobby for studies on the Arctic Ocean, writing in 1901 that Russia's 'need to conquer the polar sea is absolute'.[88] Although imperial authorities rejected Mendeleev's ambitious research plans for the Arctic, the scientist assisted Admiral Stepan Makarov's programme of building powerful icebreakers. The first of these, the *Yermak* (named after the first 'conqueror' of Siberia), was built in Newcastle in 1898 and sailed to Spitsbergen in 1899.[89]

Siberian Arctic exploration at the same time went far more poorly. An Academy of Sciences expedition led by Eduard von Toll searching for new land in the East Siberian Sea turned tragic, with the entire crew perishing. Disaster struck again ten years later, when in 1912 two Russian polar expedition, led by Georgy Sedov and Georgy Brusilov – and encouraged in their venture by the success of American explorers and Roald Amundsen – failed to reach the North Pole, while suffering significant losses. A third expedition under the leadership of geologist Vladimir Rusanov disappeared in the Kara Sea after conducting research at Spitsbergen. But the Russian Empire at its sunset saw not only failures, but successes as well: two ships, the *Taimyr* and the *Vaigach*, performed the first successful navigations from Arkhangelsk to Vladivostok, linking the Russian Arctic's two poles. They also made the last significant geographical discovery in the Arctic, encountering several large islands now known as Severnaya Zemlya.

Noting that the Arctic was a zone of international interaction, Admiral Stepan Makarov described it as Russia's 'front door' (*fasad*), but a more appropriate metaphor for the relations with the Arctic at that period of time might have been the back door.[90] Through the end of the Russian Empire, authorities considered the region almost exclusively as a storehouse of resources to be used for St Petersburg's gains, or a prestigious field of scientific study. The well-being of local inhabitants held little or no interest for central authorities. The backyard needed to be useful, and it should be protected, but there was little need for local development or improvement.[91]

---

86 Lajus, "Linking People through Fish". 87 Finstad and Lajus, "Fisheries".
88 Mendeleev, *K poznaniiu Rossii*. 89 Saunders, "Captain Wiggins".
90 Levonevskii, *S. O. Makarov i zavoevanie Arktiki*, 47.
91 Eklund et al., "Imageries and Historical Change".

The outbreak of World War I immediately demonstrated the crucial importance of Russian access to the Arctic Ocean. The Murmansk railway was constructed in 1915–16, connecting Petrograd (as St Petersburg had been known since 1914) with the new port, Romanov-on-Murman, later to be renamed Murmansk. The Arctic's importance was also recognized through the establishment of the Polar Commission at the Academy of Sciences and the Committee of the North within the Russian Geographic Society. In December 1916, a special meeting was organized in Petrograd with the slogan 'reconstructing the northern periphery is a national task'.[92] Moreover, in a special diplomatic note, the Ministry of Foreign Affairs proclaimed Russian sovereignty over Arctic lands between Nordkapp and the Bering Strait. There was an attempt to put the Russian flag on Franz Josef Land, but it remained de facto *terra nullius* until 1929. Just before the war, several meteorological and radio stations opened at Novaya Zemlya and Yamal, with a station on Dickson Island at Yenisei Bay following in 1916.[93]

All of these developments, of course, were put on hold with the 1917 Bolshevik Revolution, many to be taken up with redoubled intensity thereafter (see Chapter 19). But, by that year, with nearly 900 years of sustained engagement, Russians had already established the earliest, and – still – the longest-tenured Arctic empire in human history.

Conclusion

Radiating north and east from the Slavic heartlands of the northern Eurasian plains, inhabitants of pre-Petrine Russia and then the Russian Empire had conquered and coopted hundreds of different peoples, whose own technologies of Arctic habitation assisted the Russian advance. With a complex of political, economic, social, and technological innovations developed in the Russian North, the colonizers swept with amazing speed eastward to the Bering Sea across some of the world's coldest lands and seas.

In the process of colonization, Russians became early adapters of the scientific techniques developing in Western Europe, allowing further intensification of colonial exploitation. Often in collaboration with other Europeans, Russians made signature advances in Arctic science and technology, including inaugurating the study of permafrost and constructing icebreakers.

---

92 Pinkhenson, *Problema Severnogo morskogo puti*, 645.   93 Lajus, "Field Stations".

Expanding, knowing, and directing the Arctic empire was one thing, but making it pay turned out to be another. When the furs ran out, so did the profits. And, despite repeated attempts, local inhabitants failed to develop the exports that St Petersburg hoped for. With no ability to develop traditional Russian forms of agriculture, and outcompeted by Baltic trade, much of the Russian North languished economically. So did northern Siberia, which remained essentially untouched by the construction of the trans-Siberian railroad. The many humans living in the Russian Arctic – native Siberians, Pomors, and the many Russian settlers less preoccupied with imperial projects – nonetheless constructed meaningful lives, below the view of empire, close to the ground, fusing with the *taiga*, the *tundra*, and the cold.

Bibliography

Adams (Collection), William, Jr, Scott Polar Research Institute Archives, University of Cambridge.
Al'kov, Ya. P. and A. E. Drezen, *Kolonial'naia politika tsarisma na Kamchatke i Chukotke v XVIII veke* (Leningrad: Izdatel'stvo Instituta Narodov Severa TSIKSSR, 1935).
Armstrong, Terence, *The Northern Sea Route: Soviet Exploration of the North East Passage* (Cambridge: Cambridge University Press, 1952).
Bakhrushin, S. V., "*Yasak* (Fur Tribute) in Siberia in the Seventeenth Century", trans. Ryan Tucker Jones and Andrian Vlakhov, *Alaska Anthropology* 14 (2016): 41–70.
Bekasova, Alexandra, "Voyaging Towards the Future: The Brig Rurik in the North Pacific and the Emerging Science of the Sea", *British Journal for the History of Science* 53 (2020): 469–495, https://doi.org/10.1017/S0007087420000448.
Bernshtam, T. A., *Pomory. Formirovanie gruppy i sistema khoziaistva* (Leningrad: "Nauka", Leningradskoe otd-nie, 1978).
Bespiatykh, Iu. N., *Arkhangelsk nakanune i v gody Severnoi voiny 1700–1721* (St Petersburg: BLITS; Istoricheskaia illiustratsiia, 2010).
Birnbaum, Henrik, *Lord Novgorod the Great: Essays in the History and Culture of a Medieval City-State* (Bloomington: Slavica, 1981).
Bockstoce, John R., *Furs and Frontiers in the Far North: The Contest among Native and Foreign Nations for the Bering Strait Fur Trade* (New Haven: Yale University Press, 2009).
Bryzgalov, V., "Stroitelstvo zapadnoevropeiskikh sudov v Pomor (pervaia polovina XVIII v", in Iu. N. Bespiatykh, Ja. V. Weluvenkamp, and L. D. Popova, eds., *Niderlandy i Severnaia Rossiia: Sbornik nauchnykh statei* (St Petersburg: BLITS, 2003), pp. 235–249.
Chu, Pey-Yi, *The Life of Permafrost: A History of Frozen Earth in Russian and Soviet Science* (Toronto/Buffalo/London: University of Toronto Press, 2020).
Curta, Florin, *Eastern Europe in the Middle Ages (500–1300)*, Vol. 1 (Leiden: BRILL, 2019).
Dadykina, Margarita, and Kraikovski Alexei, "Monks, Management and God's Mercy: The Russian Monasteries and the Environment of the Russian North in the Early Modern Age (16th–18th Centuries)", in Dario Canzian and Elisabetta Novello, eds. *Ecosystem Services in Floodplains* (Padova: Padova University Press, 2019), pp. 47–53.

7 Russia, the First Arctic Empire, 1000–1917

Dadykina, Margarita, Kraikovski Alexei, and Lajus Julia, "Mastering the Arctic Marine Environment: Organizational Practices of Pomor Hunting Expeditions to Svalbard (Spitsbergen) in the Eighteenth Century", *Acta Borealia* 1 (2017): 50–69.

de Madariaga, Isabel, *Russia in the Age of Catherine the Great* (New Haven: Yale University Press, 1981).

Dixon, Simon, *The Modernisation of Russia, 1676–1825* (Cambridge: Cambridge University Press, 1999).

Eklund, Niklas, Julia Lajus, Vassily Borovoy, et al., "Imageries and Historical Change in the European Russian Arctic", in E. Carina and H. Keskitalo, eds., *The Politics of Arctic Resources: Change and Continuity in the 'Old North' of Northern Europe* (New York: Routledge, 2019), pp. 200–220.

Finstad, Bjorn-Peter, and Julia Lajus, "The Fisheries in Norwegian and Russian Waters, 1850–2010", in David Starkey and Ingo Heidbrink, eds., *A History of the North Atlantic Fisheries*, Vol. 2: *From the 1850s to the Early Twentieth-First Century* (Bremen: Hauschild, 2012), pp. 226–237.

Fisher, Raymond H., *The Russian Fur Trade, 1550–1700* (Berkeley: University of California Press, 1943).

Forsyth, James, *A History of the Peoples of Siberia: Russia's North Asian Colony 1581–1990* (Cambridge: Cambridge University Press, 1992).

Gibson, James, *Feeding the Russian Fur Trade: Provisioning of the Okhotsk Seaboard and the Kamchatka Peninsula, 1639–1856* (Madison: University of Wisconsin Press, 1969).

Golovnev, Andrei, *Istoricheskaia Tipologiia Khoziaisva Narodov Severo-Zapadnoi Sibiri* (Novosibirsk: Izdatel'stvo Novosibirskogo Universiteta, 1993).

Golovnev, Andrei, and Gail Osherenko, *Siberian Survival: The Nenets and their Story* (Ithaca: Cornell University Press, 1999).

Gorbachev, V. T., N. N. Kradin, N. P. Kradin, et al., *Gradostroitelstvo Sibiri* (St Petersburg: Kolo, 2011).

Heptner, V. G., and N. P. Naumov, eds., *Mammals of the Soviet Union*, Vol. II, Part 1b (Moscow: Vysshaya Shkola, 1967).

Jasinski, M. E., and O. V. Ovsiannikov, *Pustozersk. Russkii gorod v Arktike* (St Petersburg: Peterburgskoe Vostokovedenie, 2003).

Jasinski, M. E., and O. V. Ovsiannikov, *Vzgliad na Evropeiskuiu Arktiku. Arkhangelskii Sever: problemy i istochniki*, Vols. 1, 2 (St Petersburg: Peterburgskoe Vostokovedenie, 1998).

Jones, Ryan Tucker, *Empire of Extinction: Russians and the North Pacific's Strange Beasts of the Sea, 1742–1867* (Oxford: Oxford University Press, 2014).

Jones, Ryan Tucker, "'These Great Plains Were Once the Bottom of the Sea': Peter Simon Pallas, Siberian Geohistory, and Empire", in Jane Hacking, Jeffrey Hardy, and Matthew Romaniello, eds., *Russia in Asia: Imaginations, Interactions, and Realities* (New York: Routledge, 2020).

Jordan, Peter, "Landscape and Culture in Northern Eurasia: An Introduction", in Peter Jordan, ed., *Landscape and Culture in Northern Eurasia* (Walnut Creek: Left Coast Press, 2011).

Kivelson, Valerie A., "'Between All Parts of the Universe': Russian Cosmographies and Imperial Strategies in Early Modern Siberia and Ukraine", *Imago Mundi* 60 (2008): 166–181.

Kollmann, Nancy Shields, *The Russian Empire 1450–1801* (Oxford: Oxford University Press, 2017).

Kopelev, Dmitrii N., *Na sluzhbe Imperii. Nemtsy i Rossiiskii flot v pervoi polovine XIX veka* (St Petersburg: Izdatel'stvo Evropeiskogo Universiteta v Sankt-Peterburge, 2010).

Kotilaine, Jarmo, *Russia's Foreign Trade and Economic Expansion in the Seventeenth Century: Windows on the World* (Leiden: Brill, 2005).

Kraikovski, Alexei, "Good Fisheries vs. Bad Fisheries: Ideological and Scientific Base for the Governmental Projects of Modernization of Russian System of Marine Harvesting in the 18th Century", in Joanaz de Melo et al., eds. *Environmental History in the Making*, Vol. II: *Acting* (Switzerland: Springer, 2017), pp. 49–70.

Kraikovski, Alexei, "Profits from under the Water: The International Blubber Market, Russian Monopolistic Companies and the Idea of Whaling Development in the Eighteenth Century", *International Journal of Maritime History* 31 (2019): 34–49.

Kraikovski, Alexei, "'The Sea on One Side, Trouble on the Other': Russian Marine Resource Use Before Peter the Great", *The Slavonic and East European Review* 93 (2015): 39–65.

Kraikovski, Alexei, Margarita Dadykina, Zoya Dmitrieva, and Julia Lajus, "Between Piety and Productivity: Monastic Fisheries of the White and Barents Sea in the 16th–18th Centuries", *Journal of the North Atlantic* 41 (June 2020): 1–21, https://doi.org/10.3721/037.006.4101.

Kraikovski, Alexei, Margarita Dadykina, and Ekaterina Kalemeneva, "Water Management in Russian Monasteries, 16th–18th cc", in *Gestione dell'acqua in Europa (XII–XVIII secc.)/Water Management in Europe (12th–18th Centuries)*, Vol. 49 (Firenze: Firenze University Press, 2018), pp. 319–336.

Krasheninnikov, Stepan P., "Sable Hunting in Eastern Siberia in the Early 18th Century", trans. James Gibson, *Polar Geography* 28 (2004): 147–161.

Krupnik, Igor, *Arctic Adaptations: Native Whalers and Reindeer Herders of Northern Eurasia*, trans. Marcia Levenson (Hanover: University Press of New England, 1993).

Kusber, Jan, "Mastering the Imperial Space: The Case of Siberia", *Ab Imperio* 4 (2008): 52–74.

Lajus, Julia, "Colonization of the Russian North: A Frozen Frontier", in Christina Folke-Ax, et al., eds., *Cultivating the Colony: Colonial States and their Environmental Legacies* (Athens, OH: Ohio University Press, 2011), pp. 164–190.

Lajus, Julia, "Experts on Unknown Waters: Environmental Risk, Fisheries Science and Local Knowledge in the Russian North", in Nicholas Breyfogle, ed., *Eurasian Environments: Nature and Ecology in Imperial Russian and Soviet History* (Pittsburg: University of Pittsburg Press, 2018), pp. 205–220.

Lajus, Julia, "Field Stations on the Coast of the Arctic Ocean in the European Part of Russia from the First to Second IPY", in Sverker Sörlin, ed., *Science, Geopolitics and Culture in the Polar Region: Norden beyond Borders* (Farnham: Ashgate, 2013), pp. 111–142.

Lajus, Julia, "'Foreign Science in Russian Context': Murman Scientific Fishery Expedition and Russian Participation in Early ICES Activity", *ICES Marine Science Symposia* 215 (2002): 64–72.

Lajus, Julia, "In Search of Instructive Models: The Russian State at a Crossroads to Conquering the North", in Dolly Jorgensen and Sverker Sorlin, eds., *Northscapes:*

7 Russia, the First Arctic Empire, 1000–1917

History, Technology, and the Making of Northern Environments (Vancouver: University of British Columbia Press, 2013), pp. 110–136.

Lajus, Julia, "Linking People through Fish: Science and Barents Sea Fish Resources in the Context of Russian-Scandinavian Relations", in Sverker Sörlin, ed., *Science, Geopolitics and Culture in the Polar Region: Norden beyond Borders* (Farnham: Ashgate, 2013), pp. 171–194.

Lajus, Julia, Alexei Kraikovski, and Alexei Yurchenko, "Sea Fisheries in the Russian North c. 1400–1850", in David J. Starkey, Jon Th. Thor, and Ingo Heidbrink, eds., *A History of the North Atlantic Fisheries*, Vol. 1: *From Early Times to the Mid-Nineteenth Century* (Bremerhaven: Deutsches Schiffahrtsmuseum, 2009), pp. 41–64.

Lantzeff, George, and Richard Pierce, *Eastward to Empire: Exploration and Conquest of the Russian Open Frontier to 1750* (Montreal: McGill-Queen's University Press, 1973).

Lebedev, Vladimir, "Sem'ia i proizvodstvennyi kolektiv u naseleniia pritundrovoi polosy severo-zapada Turukhanskogo kraia v XIX v", *Sovetskaia Etnografia* 2 (1980): 82–91.

Levonevskii, D. A., S. O. *Makarov i zavoevanie Arktiki: 'Ermak' vo l'dakh: materialy i dokumenty o S.O. Makarove i ledokole 'Ermak'* (Moscow: Izdatel'stvo Glavsevmorputi, 1943).

Lindholm, Otto, *Beyond the Frontiers of Imperial Russia* (Javea: Alexander de Haes Tyrthoff, 2008).

Lindsey, Hughes, *Russia in the Age of Peter the Great* (New Haven: Yale University Press, 1998).

Lomonosov, Mikhail V., "Kratkoe opisanie raznykh puteshestvii po severnym moriam i pokazanie vozmozhnogo prokhodu Sibirskim okeanom v Vostochnuiu Indiiu", in *Polnoe sobranie sochinenii*, Vol. 6 (Moscow: Izdatel'stvo AN SSSR, 1952), pp. 417–498.

MacDonald, G. M., K. V. Kremenetski, and D. W. Beilman, "Climate Change and the Northern Russian Treeline Zone", *Philosophical Transactions of the Royal Society* 363 (2008): 2285–2299.

Makarov, N. A., *Kolonizatsiia severnykh okrain Drevnei Rusi v XI–XIII vv. Po materialam arkheologicheskikh pamiatnikov na volokakh Belozeria i Poonezhia* (Moscow: NITc 'Skriptorii', 1997).

Makarov, N. A., "Traders in the Forest: The Northern Periphery of 'Rus' in the Medieval Trade Network", in Tracy, James D., Kathryn Reyerson, and Theofanis G. Stavrou, eds., *Pre-modern Russia and Its World: Essays in Honor of Thomas S. Noonan* (Wiesbaden: Otto Harrassowitz, 2006), pp. 115–134.

Martin, Janet, *Treasures of the Land of Darkness: The Fur Trade and Its Significance for Medieval Russia* (Cambridge: Cambridge University Press, 2004).

Mayers, Kit, *North-East Passage to Muscovy: Stephen Borough and the First Tudor Explorations* (Cheltenham: History Press, 2005).

Mendeleev, Dmitrii, *K poznaniiu Rossii* (St Petersburg: Izdanie A.S. Suvorina, 1907).

Merzon, A. Ts., and Iu. A. Tikhonov, *Rynok Ustiuga Velikogo v period skladyvaniia vserossiiskogo rynka (XVII vek)* (Moscow: AN SSSR, 1960).

Messerschmidt, D. G., *Forschungreise durch Sibirien, 1720–1727*, ed. E. Winter and N. A. Figurovskii, 5 vols (Berlin: Akademie-Verlag, 1962–77).

Milchik, M. I., and L. D. Popova, *Pervye vorota Rossiiskogo gosudarstva* (St Petersburg: 'Liki Rossii', 2002).

Monahan, Erika, *The Merchants of Siberia: Trade in Early Modern Eurasia* (Ithaca: Cornell University Press, 2016).

Nikonov, S. A., '*Kto v more ne khodil, tot Bogu ne malivalsia*': *Promyslovaia kolonizatsiia Murmanskogo berega i Novoi Zemli krestianami i monastyriami Pomor'ia v XVI–XVIII vv* (Moscow, St Petersburg: Nestor Istoriia, 2020).

Ogorodov, S. A., F. A. Romanenko, and V. I. Solomatin, "M.V. Lomonosov i osvoenie Severnogo morskogo puti", *Vestnik Moskovaskogo universiteta Ser. 5. Geografiia* 5 (2011): 11–17.

Okhotina-Lind, Natal'ia, ed., *Vtoraia Kamchatskaia Ekspeditsiia: Dokumenty, 1741–1742. Morskie Otriady* (St Petersburg: Nestor Istoriia, 2018).

Ordubadi, Diana, "Die Halbinsel Kamčatka in den Schriften des Leiters der Ersten Russischen Weltumsegulung (1803–1806) Adam Johann von Krusenstern und seines Naturforschers Georg Heinrich Freiherr von Langsdorff", in Erich Kasten, ed., *Reisen an den Rand des Russichen Reichs: Die Wissenschaftliche Erschließung der Nordpazifischen Küstengebiete im 18. und 19. Jahrhundert* (Fürstenburg/Havel: Kulturstiftung Sibrien, 2013).

Ovsiannikov, O. V., and M. E. V. V. Jasinski, "Krestinin o promysle i solenii belomorskikh seldei po norvezhskim i gollandskim retseptam vo vtoroi polovine XVIII v", in Iu. N. Bespiatykh, ed., *Russkii Sever i Zapadnaia Evropa* (St Petersburg: BLITS, 1999), pp. 401–426.

Owen, Thomas C., *Dilemmas of Russian Capitalism: Fedor Chizhov and Corporate Enterprise in the Railroad Age* (Harvard: Harvard University Press, 2005).

Ozeretskovsky, Nikolai, *Opisanie Koly i Astrakhani* (St Petersburg: Imperatorskaia Akademiia nauk, 1804).

Pertsev, N. V., "Pokhod moskovskikh voisk 1499 g. v Jugru v kontekste vneshnei i vnutrennei politiki Moskovskogo gosudarstva", *Genesis: istoricheskie issledovaniia* 2 (2018): 40–54.

Pinkhenson, D. M., *Problema Severnogo morskogo puti v epokhu kapitalizma. Istorria otkrytiia i osvoenia Severnogo morskogo puti*, Vol. 2 (Leningrad: Morskoi Transport, 1962).

Piper, Liza, and John Sandlos, "A Broken Frontier: Ecological Imperialism in the Canadian North", *Environmental History* 12 (October 2007): 759–795.

Puteshestviia Akademika Ivana Lepekhina v 1772 godu 4 (St Petersburg: Izdatel'stvo Imperatorskoi Akademii Nauk, 1805).

Remnev, Anatoly, ed., *Sibir' v Sostave Rossiiskoi Imperii* (Moscow: Novoe Literaturnoe Obozrenie, 2007).

Repin, N. N., *Vneshniaia torgovlia i sotsialno-ekonomicheskoe razvitie Rossii v XVIII v.* (Arkhangelogorodskii i Peterburgskii porty) (Omsk: Omskii gosudarstvennyi universitet, 1989).

Roslund, Mats, "Bringing 'the Periphery' into Focus: Social Interaction between Baltic Finns and the Svear in the Viking Age and Crusade Period (c.800 to 1200)", in Johan Callmer, Ingrid Gustin, and Mats Roslund, eds., *Identity Formation and Diversity in the Early Medieval Baltic and Beyond: Communicators and Communication. The Northern World*, Vol. 75 (Leiden/Boston: Brill, 2017), pp. 168–204.

Saunders, David, "Captain Wiggins and Admiral Makarov: Commerce and Politics in the Russian Arctic (1874–1904)", *Polar Record* 53 (2017): 427–435.

Schrader, Tatjana A., "Pomor Trade with Norway", *Acta Borealia* 5 (1988): 111–118.

Shaw, Denis, "Russia's Geographical Environment", in Maureen Perrie, ed., *The Cambridge History of Russia I: From Early Rus' to 1680* (Cambridge: Cambridge University Press, 2006), pp. 19–43.
Sidorov, Michail, *Besedy o Severe Rossii v 3 m otdelenii Imperatorskogo vol'nogo ekonomicheskogo obschestva* (St Petersburg, 1867).
Sidorov, Michail, *Trudy dlia oznakomleniia s Severom Rossii* (St Petersburg: tipografiia D. I. Shemetkina, 1882).
Skugarev, V. D., "V period zakata parusnogo flota (1801–1856)", in Iu. A. Mikhailov, A. L. Kolodkin, and A. Kontalev, eds., *Pod flagom Rossii: istoriia zarozhdeniia i razvitiia morskogo torgovogo flota* (Moscow: Soglasie, 1995), pp. 131–194.
Slezkine, Yuri, *Arctic Mirrors: Russia and the Small Peoples of the North* (Ithaca: Cornell University Press, 1996).
Studitskii, Fedor, *Istoriia otkrytiia morskogo puti iz Evropy v sibirskie reki i do Beringova proliva* (St Petersburg, 1883).
Sukhova, N. G., "Ob osnovanii Russkogo geograficheskogo obschestva", *Izvestiia Russkogo geograficheskogo obschestva* 150 (2018): 68–81.
Sukhova, N. G., and A. Yu. Skrydlov, "The Russian Geographical Society and the Polar Studies in the Second Half of the 19th Century", *IOP Conference Series: Earth and Environmental Science Arctic: History and Modernity* 180 (2018): 012001.
Sukhova, N. G., and E. Tammiksaar, *Aleksandr Fedorovich Middendorf. K 200-letiiu so dnia rozhdeniia* (St Petersburg: Nestor-Istoriia, 2015).
Sunderland, Willard, "Imperial Space: Territorial Thought and Practice in the Eighteenth Century", in Jane Burbank, Mark von Hagen, and Anatolyi Remnev, eds., *Russian Empire: Space, People, Power, 1700–1930* (Bloomington: Indiana University Press, 2007), 33–66.
Tammiksaar, Erki, "The Contributions of Karl Ernst von Baer to the Investigation of the Physical Geography of the Arctic in the 1830s–40s", *Polar Record* 38 (2002): 121–140.
Tammiksaar, Erki, "Gerhard Baron von Maydell (1835–1894) und die Bedeutung Seiner Forschungen in Nordost-Sibirien", in *Erschienen in Reisen an den Rand des Russischen Reiches: Die wissenschaftliche Erschließung der nordpazifischen Küstengebiete im 18. und 19. Jahrhundert*, herausgegeben von Erich Kasten, electronic ed. (Fürstenberg/Havel: Kulturstiftung Sibirien 2013), pp. 243–267.
Tammiksaar, Erki, and Ian R. Stone, "Karl Ernst von Baer and the Kara Sea 'Eiskeller'", *Polar Record* 33 (1997): 239–242.
Tammiksaar, Erki, and Natal'ya G. Sukhova, "The Russian Polar Stations", in Susan Barr and Cornelia Lüdecke, eds., *The History of the International Polar Years (IPYs)* (Heidelberg: Springer, 2010), pp. 76–89.
Tammiksaar, Erki, Natal'ya G. Sukhova, and Cornelia Lüdecke, "The International Polar Year 1882–1883", in Susan Barr and Cornelia Lüdecke, eds., *The History of the International Polar Years (IPYs)* (Heidelberg: Springer, 2010), pp. 7–33.
Vdovina, L. N., "Dobyvaiushchie promysly", in A. V. Arcihovskii, ed., *Ocherki russkoi kul'tury XVII v. Chast' pervaja. Material'naia kul'tura. Gosudarstvennyi stroi* (Moscow: Izdatel'stvo MGU, 1979), pp. 55–74.
Vinkovetsky, Ilya, *Russian America: An Overseas Colony of a Continental Empire, 1804–1867* (Oxford: Oxford University Press, 2011).

Wrangel, Ferdinand Petrovich, *Statistische und Ethnographische Nachrichten über die Russischen Besitzungen an der Nordwestkust von Amerika*, ed. K. E. von Baer (St Petersburg: Imperial Academy of Sciences, 1839).

Yurchenko, Alexei, and Jens Petter Nielsen, eds., *In the North My Nest Is Made: Studies of the History of Murman Colonization, 1860–1940* (St Petersburg: European University at St Petersburg and University of Tromso, 2005).

Zadonina, N. V., *Khronologiia prirodnykh i sotsial'nykh fenomenov v Sibiri i Mongolii* (Irkuts: Izdatel'stvo Irkutskogo Gosudarstvennogo Universiteta, 2008).

8

The Discovery of Antarctica from Ptolemy to Shackleton

ERKI TAMMIKSAAR AND CORNELIA LÜDECKE

Introduction

There is a wealth of literature on Antarctic research. Many overviews on the nature of Antarctica, cartography, its geology and glaciation, inhabitants and visitors, and cultural perspectives have been published recently.[1] The first history of polar exploration of Europeans was published in 1756.[2] Since then, many more Western historical overviews have been published, and we also have a chronological list of expeditions to Antarctica as well as good coverage in encyclopedias.[3] In addition to these publications, there are several studies of the significance of ice and the development of natural sciences in the understanding of the physical nature of Antarctica. There are also some important recents works on the history of science which have not been fully integrated with the histories of exploration and discovery.[4]

Today we know that the Antarctic continent consists mainly of ice, but this 'simple fact' was not known to the navigators and scientists who had been looking for a *'terra incognita'* in the south since the Renaissance. This unknown land was predicted in the world map of the ancient geographer Claudius Ptolemy, which appeared first in Latin in 1478.[5] Up to the beginning

---

This article was supported by Estonian University of Life Sciences P180276SPTL. Special thanks to Rip Bulkeley and Stéphane Schmitt for valuable comments and help with literature and archival sources. Many thanks to Rip and Helen Rohtmets-Aasa for the English revision.

1 Manzoni, *La nature dell' Antarctide*; Clancy et al., *Mapping Antarctica*; Kleinschmidt, ed., *Geology*; Arrebola and Jacobs, *Antarctica*; Crane et al., eds., *Imaging Antarctica*.
2 de Brosses, *Historie des navigations*.
3 cf. Fricker, *Antarktis*; Balch, *Antarctica*; Mill, *Siege*; Kirwan, *History of Polar Exploration*; Hatherton, ed., *Antarctica*; Bertrand, *Americans in Antarctica*; Day, *Antarctica*; Barr and Lüdecke, eds., *History of the International Polar Years*; Lüdecke, *Germans in the Antarctic*; Headland, *Chronology of Antarctic Exploration*; Riffenburgh, ed., *Encyclopedia of the Antarctic*.
4 Pyne, *The Ice*; Bulkeley, *Bellingshausen*, 53–61; Tammiksaar, "Russian Antarctic Expedition".
5 Brown, *Story of Maps*, 79; Christoph, "Vom Anfang des Kosmos", 161.

of the twentieth century, many navigators visited the southern hemisphere and discovered lands there, but not *Terra Incognita*, which the French mathematician Oronce Fine called *Terra Australis* on his map published in 1534 after Fernão Magalhães' voyage around the world.[6] But navigators brought back too little empirical evidence to prove the existence or non-existence of a southern continent. The complicated physical and climatic characteristics of Antarctica – especially in relation to ice, cold, and uncertainties about where the ice ends and the land begins – gave rise to many speculations on what the physical geography should look like. This makes the question of the discovery of Antarctica a difficult and interesting topic. We will argue in our chapter why it is unnecessary to determine who first sighted the Sixth Continent and should be honoured as the 'discoverer of Antarctica' in the way that Christopher Columbus is often seen as the 'discoverer of America'.

Vanishing Common Knowledge about an Existing Mainland in the South

Thanks to the authority of Ptolemy's map, the concept of *Terra Australis* was very strong in the European world. It can be seen in historical atlases like the *Typus Orbis Terrarium* drawn by Flemish and Dutch cartographers, such as Ortelius, Mercator, Janszoon, and Blaeu from the sixteenth and seventeenth centuries, or written in Bernhard Varenius's book *Geographia Generalis*, first published in 1650. Under Varenius's influence, eighteenth-century French scientists and philosophers of the Enlightenment such as Charles-Louis de Montesquieu, Jean-Jacques Rousseau, and Georges-Louis Leclerc de Buffon continued to believe that a large continent, *Terra Australis*,[7] existed in the south polar region.

At the end of June 1739, navigator Jean-Baptiste Charles Bouvet de Lozier returned to France after searching for *Terra Australis* in the South Atlantic, where he found '*glaces*' (icebergs).[8] Based on this information, the royal cartographer, Philippe Buache, a member of the French Academy of Sciences, compiled a map of the southern polar region. Although he was convinced of the existence of *Terres Australes ou Antarctiques*, he did not map the outlines of such a continent.

Buache's map had been examined by Buffon in September 1739, and in 1749, Buffon wrote 'those *glaces* [seen by Bouvet] were not very far from the [Antarctic] land'.[9] Before Bouvet, no navigator had found '*glaces*' at 47–48 degrees latitude in the southern polar waters, in contrast to the northern

6 Marr, ed., *Worlds of Oronce Fine*. 7 Varenius, *A Compleat System of Geography*, 100.
8 Delépine, "Jean-Baptiste Bouvet de Lozier".
9 Buffon and Fouchy, "Rapport des commissaires", folio 219.

8 Discovery of Antarctica

polar regions where icebergs had been met, for example by English navigators Martin Frobisher, John Davis, Henry Hudson, and William Baffin near Greenland's coasts, the 'Arctic Continent', as Varenius called it.[10] Thus, in 1749, Buffon was the first to declare that the physical geography of the northern and southern hemispheres had to be similar.[11] Thereupon, Buache thoroughly analysed the materials of the expeditions to the northern polar seas and published a map of the Arctic and Antarctic regions in 1754.[12] On the map of Antarctica compiled by Buache in 1757, as yet undiscovered rivers sent their ice to the Antarctic Ocean like the large Siberian rivers (Figure 8.1).[13] Given that rivers could not produce very much ice every spring (and any fresh ice in the ocean was assumed to originate from rivers), it was believed that an open polar sea must exist around the North Pole.[14]

During his second voyage around the world (1772–75), the British navigator James Cook attempted to solve the questions raised by Ptolemy, Flemish and Dutch cartographers, and French scientists, and to prove the presence of a continent in the south polar region. He was able to confirm that the huge icebergs seen by Bouvet in the south really did exist in great numbers, but he never saw land south of the Antarctic Circle, and 'never found any of the ice which we took up incorporated with earth, or any of its produce'.[15] Despite this, Cook concluded that

> the southern hemisphere [had now been] sufficiently explored; and a final end put to the searching after a southern continent, which has at times, ingrossed the attention of some of the maritime powers, for near two centuries past, and been a favourite theory amongst the geographers of all ages. That there may be a continent, or large tract of land, near the pole, I will not deny; on the contrary I am of opinion there is ..., the excessive cold, the many islands and vast floats of ice, all tend to prove that there must be land to the South.[16]

In consequence, Cook omitted the Antarctic continent from his expedition map, leaving the nature of the South Pole open. The result was a white spot at 90° S. Any mainland or islands remained to be searched for among the 'vast floats of ice' under 60° S, but without any benefit for mankind.[17] Referring to Cook's findings, Buffon changed his point of view.[18]

---

10 Headland, *Chronology of Antarctic Exploration*, 89; Varenius, *A Compleat System of Geography*, 100.
11 Buffon, *Histoire naturelle*, Vol. 1, 212–220; Buffon, *Œuvres complètes*, 420–431.
12 Buache, "Mémoire"; Buache, "Considérations géographiques"; Broc, "Un géographe".
13 Buache, "Idée de l'existence". 14 Buffon, *Histoire naturelle*, Vol. 1, 218–219.
15 Cook, *Voyage*, Vol. 2, 240. 16 Cook, *Voyage*, Vol. 2, 239. 17 Cook, *Voyage*, Vol. 2, 243.
18 Buffon, *Histoire naturelle*, 5 supplément, 609–610.

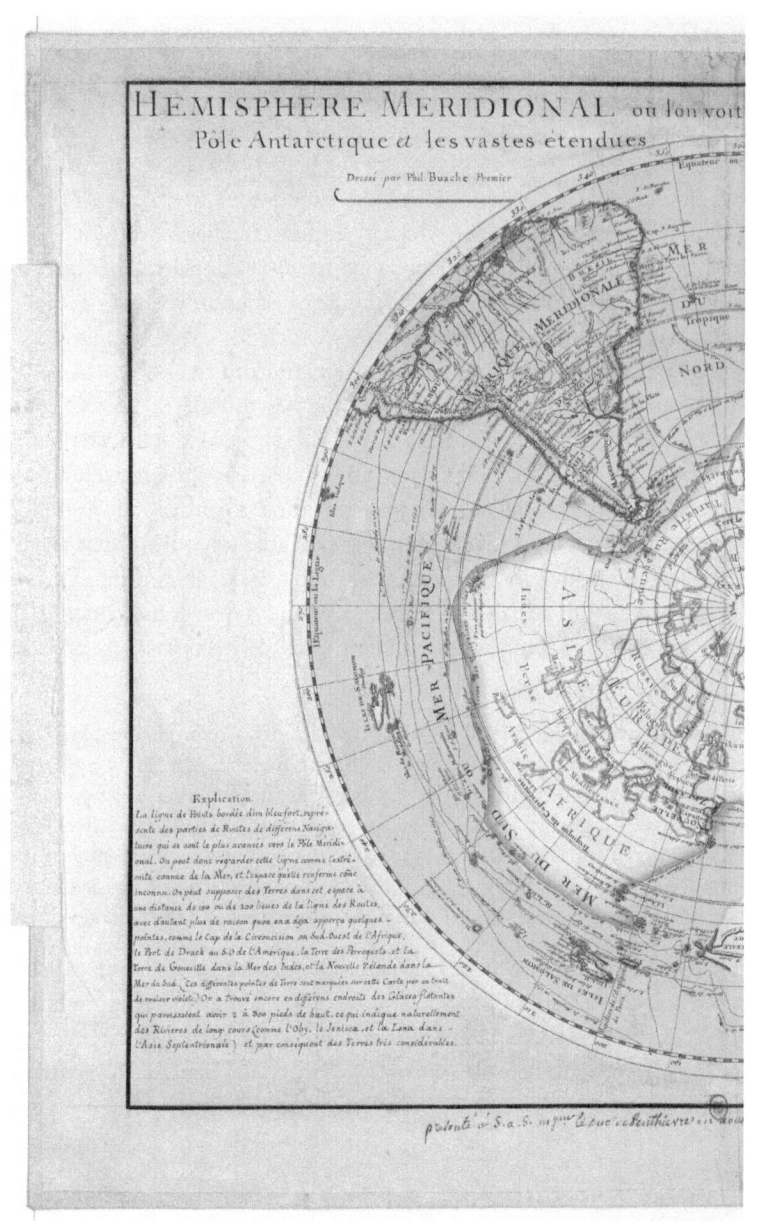

Figure 8.1 Philippe Buache, *Hemisphere Meridional où l'on voit les Parties inconnues du Globe qu sont à découvrir autour du Pôle Antarctique et les vastes étendues de Terres que peuvent renfermer ces espaces inconnus*. Paris, 1770. (Courtesy of the Bibliothèque Nationale France, Paris.)

8 Discovery of Antarctica

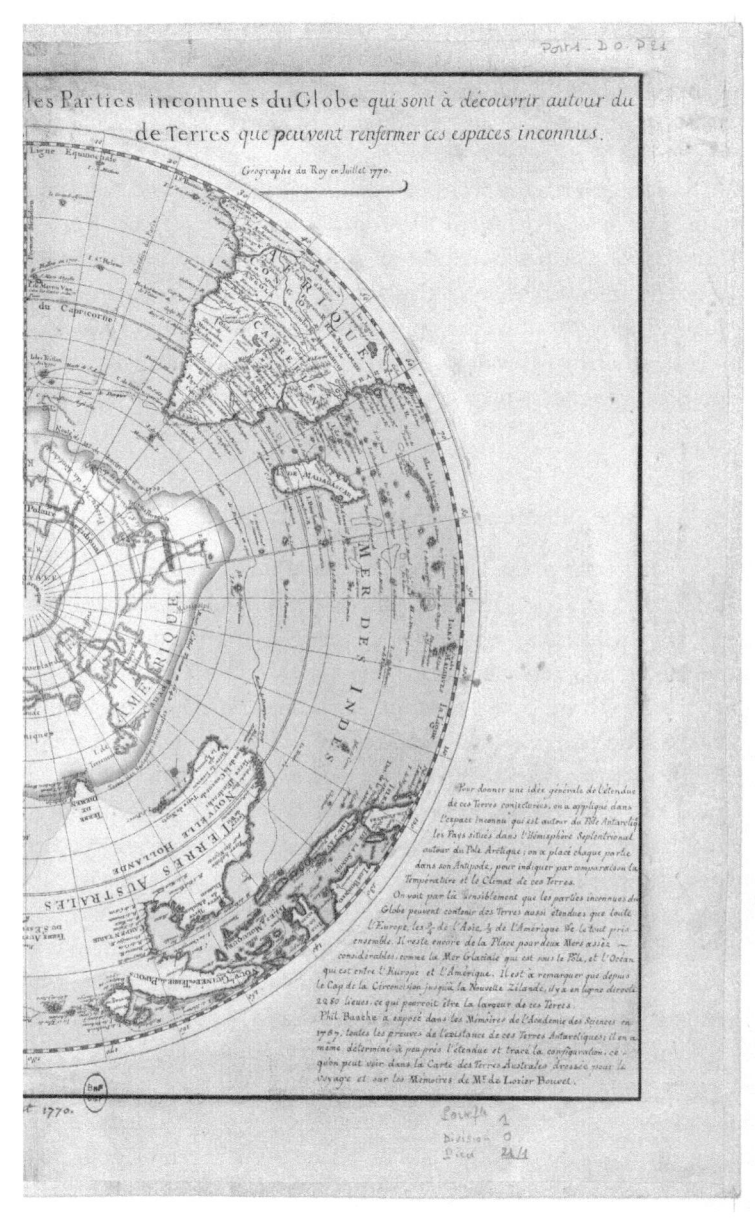

Figure 8.1 (cont.)

He wrote, 'if there is no benefit and the territories in the south and north are inaccessible for mankind, then it is irrelevant, if land(s) exist(s) there or not, because anyway all the precipitation and fog will become ice, covering more and more territories'.[19] *Terra Australis* was also deleted from Buache's original map in the version issued by the French Academy of Sciences in 1782. Instead, its location was simply marked with the word '*soupçonnées*' [suspected], and the Antarctic Ocean was marked with the word '*conjecturée*' [conjectured] (Figure 8.2).

In short: Cook's expedition caused more uncertainty in the minds of navigators and scientists than clarity about the physical geography of the south polar regions, and this ambiguity was caused by the huge masses of ice seen in the southern polar waters. As a result of Cook's expedition, the study of the physical geography near the South Pole was seen as an unimportant issue.

The Nineteenth Century: Cook's Legacy

The nineteenth century was a period of a rapid development in the natural sciences. Botany, zoology, geology, palaeontology, and physical geography, including geophysics and meteorology, emerged from natural history as a result of empirical observations made during new scientific investigations and expeditions to North and South America, Africa, and the interior parts of Asia.

Much less attention was paid to the study of the northern and southern poles. Exceptions were the British and Russian expeditions immediately after the Napoleonic Wars. In the British expeditions, John Franklin mapped the northern coast of North America, and new sailing routes were explored in the northwest and northeast; and the Russian expedition to northeast Siberia made the discovery that the connection between America and Asia, which had previously been assumed, did not exist.[20] At the same time, there was no interest in exploring Greenland beyond whaling and missionary work.[21]

However, there was no universal lack of interest towards the south polar area. Cook's three round-the-world trips brought to the fore that in the southern polar waters there were many whales and seals south of South Georgia, Australia and New Zealand, which meant high-income opportunities for private entrepreneurs who were not afraid of taking risks. According to Robert

---

19 Buffon, *Histoire naturelle*, Vol. 1, 604.
20 Savours, *Search*; Tammiksaar et al., "Hypothesis Versus Fact"; Tammiksaar, "Ferdinand von Wrangell"; Tammiksaar, "Peter Anjou".
21 Ellis, *Men and Whales*; Lüdecke, "East Meets West".

8 Discovery of Antarctica

H. Headland, English sealing trips to South Georgia began in 1786.[22] Ventures from other nations, primarily the USA, followed.

When the Englishman William Smith, captain of the brig *Williams*, accidentally discovered land, which he called 'New South Britain', on his way from Buenos Aires to Valparaiso in February 1819, it seemed incredible in the light of Cook's findings. Was it possible that Smith had confused earth and ice?[23] In 1820, Captain William Henry Shirreff, senior officer of the Royal Navy on the Pacific coast of South America, sent an Irish officer, Edward Bransfield, together with Smith on the *Williams* to inspect the latter's discovery. The expedition proved that 'New South Britain' did not exist. Instead, an archipelago was discovered, which was renamed 'New South Shetland'.[24] A year after Bransfield, Smith's discovery was also confirmed by the Russian expedition to Antarctica (1819–21) led by Fabian Gottlieb von Bellingshausen.[25]

When Bellingshausen returned to Kronstadt in early August 1821, European newspapers and geographical magazines reported that Cook's findings had been surpassed by Smith, who had found the Southern Continent.[26] The deputy leader of the Russian expedition, Captain Mikhail Lazarev, ironically wrote to a friend in October 1821 that South Shetland was still just an archipelago and added: 'so much for the South Continent there!'[27] But Bransfield and Smith together had indeed sighted new lands in 1820: Tower Island and Trinity Land at 62° S, heading south and east from New South Shetland. A midshipman on the *Williams*, Charles Poynter, wrote in his diary on 30 January 1820, 'Our theme of conversation was the idea of having by the direction the land took found what might possibly lead to the discovery of the long-contested existence of a Southern Continent.'[28] However, Bransfield's and Smith's new discovery no longer attracted widespread public attention, probably because the portion of land discovered was so small and did not seem to be of any value. Only three articles were published in London in 1821, but no discussion followed.[29] Moreover, articles and books by Ivan Simonov, astronomer of the Russian expedition, published in Europe in the early 1820s, showed that Cook's legacy about the ambiguity of the physical geography within the Antarctic Circle was still relevant.[30]

---

22 Headland, *Chronology of Antarctic Exploration*, 95.   23 Jones, *Antarctica Observed*, 66.
24 Jones, *Antarctica Observed*, 70.
25 Bellingshausen, *Voyage of Captain Bellingshausen*, Vol. 2, 421.
26 "Das neue antarktische Continent"; Campbell, *Discovery*, 203–213.
27 "Pis'ma Mikhaila Petrovicha Lazareva", 59.   28 Campbell, *Discovery*, 132.
29 Campbell, *Discovery*, 213; Bone, "Edgar Bransfield's Antarctic Voyage".
30 Cf. "Nähere Nachrichten"; Simonow, *Beschreibung einer neuen Entdeckungsreise*; Simonoff, "Nachricht von der Entdeckungsreise"; Simonoff, "Lettres XXVII, III, VIII, XIV".

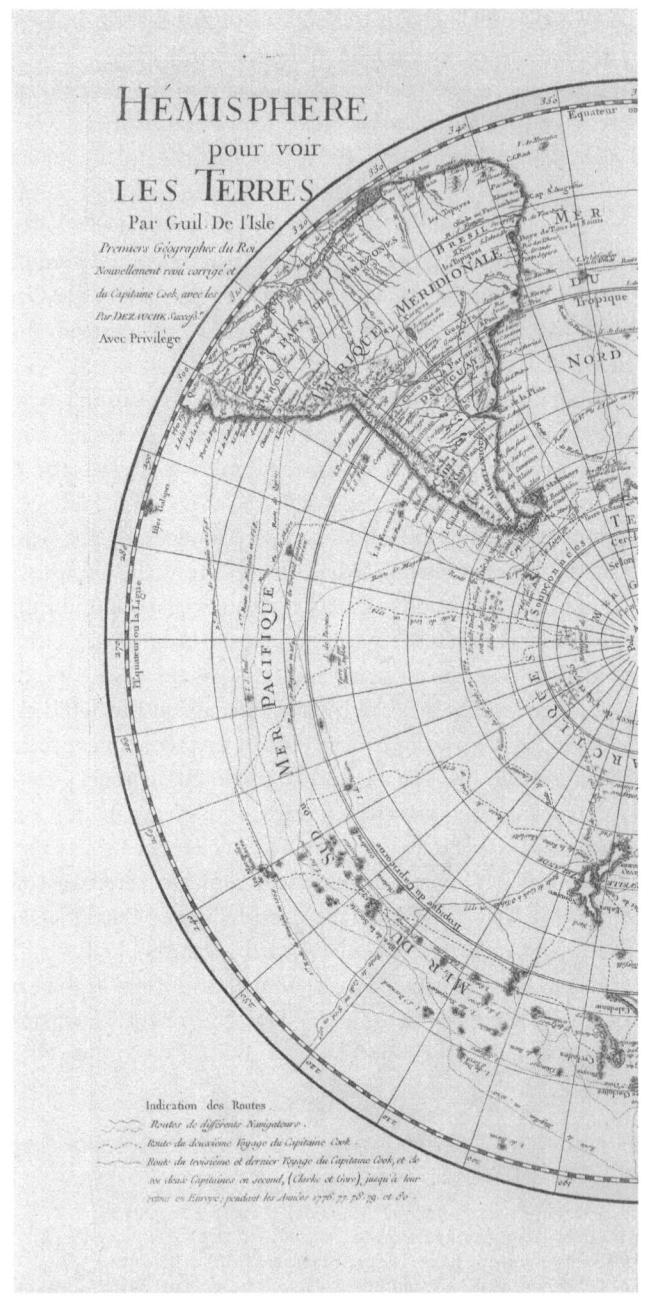

Figure 8.2 *Méridional plus distinctement Australes et Philippe Buache et de l'Académie Royale des Sciences*. Paris, 1782. (Courtesy of the Bibliothèque Nationale France, Paris.)

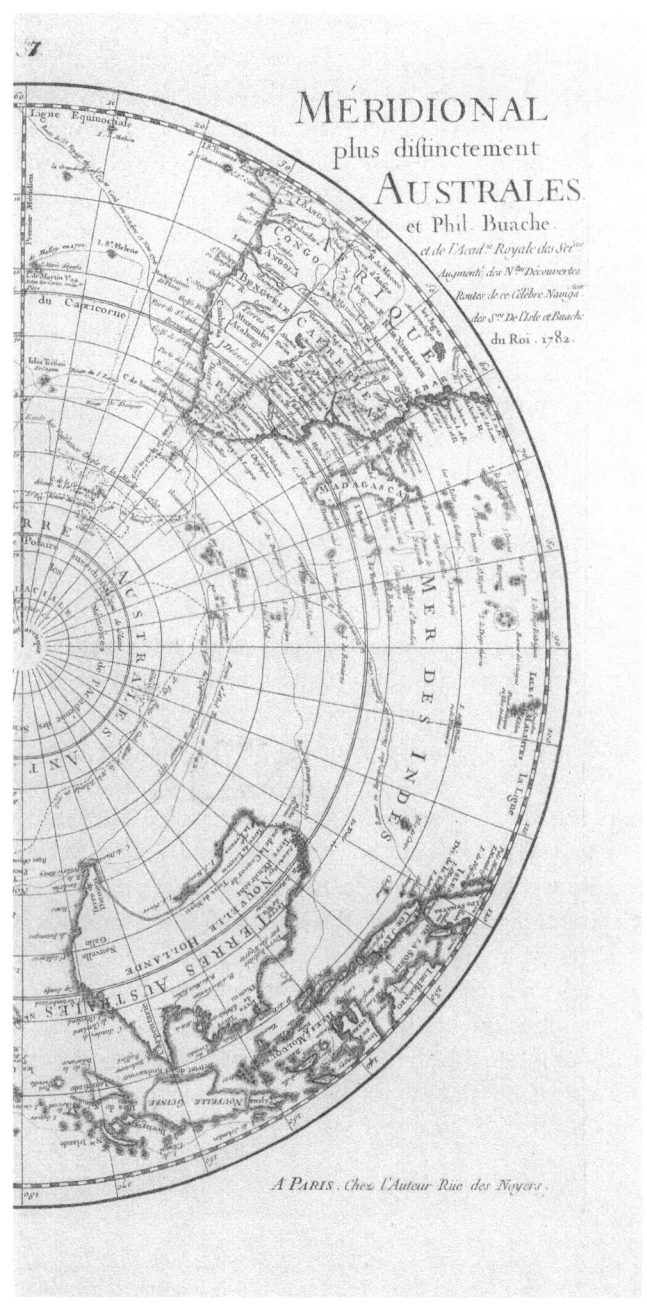

Figure 8.2 (cont.)

When the British sealer James Weddell was lucky enough to discover the sea 'perfectly clear of field ice' to the southeast of the South Shetland Islands in 1823, he confirmed Cook's conjecture 'that field ice is formed and proceeds from land, and is not formed in open sea' and 'ice islands are formed only in openings or recesses of land'.[31] The formation of ice-islands had been similarly described by Bellingshausen, who wrote that the pieces of ice not melting in the summer 'unite with other pieces formed farther out of sea, or with blocks, broken away from icebergs or other supporting points through the action of winds and currents, and form solid fields, which then ... afterwards produce immense floating icebergs'.[32]

A different picture of the physical geography near the South Pole was revealed by the 1830–33 expedition under the leadership of sealer John Biscoe.[33] In 1831, Biscoe discovered Enderby Land and Graham Land (today part of the Antarctic Peninsula) in 1833, which he believed 'to be of great extent'.[34] The first Russian circumnavigator in the years 1803–06 and prominent author of the *Atlas of the Pacific Ocean* (1824–27), Adam Johann von Krusenstern, wrote to Alexander von Humboldt in 1833: 'Bellingshausen's "discoveries" at 69 South Latitude [Peter I Island and Alexander Land in January 1821] awoke interest again in connection with the discoveries of Capt. Biscoe in the same region ... If that appears to be true, it makes for the extent [of this land] over 900 miles and, no doubt, deserves to be called a continent.'[35]

Humboldt did not agree with Krusenstern, writing in the first volume of his book *Kosmos*: 'Whether both poles are surrounded by hard earth or ice-filled ice ocean, we do not know.'[36] And there were enough reasons for the leading scientist of his time to leave this question open. Humboldt, who was intensely interested in discovering patterns of global climate and the magnetic field, had initiated expeditions in the second half of the 1830s to accurately determine the Earth's magnetic field in the southern hemisphere and especially to locate the South Magnetic Pole.[37] Humboldt's call became the 'Magnetic Crusade' and was followed by three nations: the United States of America, France, and Great Britain.

---

31 Weddell, *Voyage*, 13, 40, 42.
32 Bellingshausen, *Voyage of Captain Bellingshausen*, Vol. 2, 417.
33 Biscoe and Enderby, "Recent Discoveries"; Kirwan, *History of Polar Exploration*, 138–141.
34 Biscoe and Enderby, "Recent Discoveries", 110.   35 B.[erghaus], *Briefwechsel*, 11–12.
36 Humboldt, *Kosmos*, Vol. 1, 308.
37 Lüdecke, "Bedeutung", 178–180; Mawer, *South by Northwest*, 11–19.

8 Discovery of Antarctica

The United States Exploring Expedition (1838–42), led by the Navy Lieutenant Charles Wilkes, sailed about 2,400 km along the pack ice at about 65° S between 100° 31′ E and 136° 11′ E in early 1840.[38] They made many land sightings on route, leading Wilkes to announce that he had discovered an Antarctic continent (Wilkes Land) beyond the pack ice.[39] But the discoveries by the English captain John Balleny in 1839, by the French circumnavigator Jules Sebastién César Dumont d'Urville in the same region (Adélie Land and Claire Coast) in January 1840, and by the British Antarctic Expedition (1839–43), led by James Clark Ross, showed that the data on these discoveries were not enough to prove the existence of the Southern Continent.[40]

Taking into account the differences between the experience of his own expeditions and those of Balleny, d'Urville, and Wilkes, Ross wrote that the newest discoveries in the South

> do not appear to me sufficient grounds to justify the assertion that the various patches of land recently discovered by the American, French, and English navigators on the verge of the Antarctic Circle unite to form of a great Southern Continent ... [These discoveries] being mostly of inconsiderable extent, of somewhat uncertain determination, and channels between them, would lead rather to the conclusion that they form a chain of islands.[41]

On the other hand, Ross's expedition discovered the coast of Queen Victoria Land at about 71° S at the eastern side of an open sea (Ross Sea) in January 1841.[42] Ross found it even more difficult to assess the significance of his discoveries because he had, like Bellingshausen, seen a 'perpendicular cliff of ice, between one hundred and fifty and two hundred feet above the level of the sea perfectly flat and leveled at the top'.[43] In contrast to d'Urville, Ross concluded 'that the outer edge of the barrier was not resting upon the ground'.[44] D'Urville, however, had supported the idea that 'the formation of this enormous [ice] wall ... was a sort of envelope or crust of ice covering a solid base of either earth or rocks, or even of scattered shoals around big

---

38 Wilkes, *Narrative*, 2; Wilkes, in Murray, ed., *Antarctic Manual*, 360–435; Bertrand, *Americans in Antarctica*, 158–197; Wilkes, *Atlas to the Narrative*; Bertrand, *Americans in Antarctica*, 75, 183.
39 Bertrand, *Americans in Antarctica*, 179, 166.
40 d'Urville, *Account in Two Volumes*, Vol. 2, 479–488; d'Urville, in Murray, ed., *Antarctic Manual*, 441; Ross, *Voyage of Discovery*, Vol. 1, 273–276; Ross, *Ross in the Antarctic*.
41 Ross, *Voyage of Discovery*, Vol. 1, 274–275.   42 Ross, *Voyage of Discovery*, Vol. 1, 185.
43 Bellingauzen, "Donesenie kapitana", 212; Bellingshausen, *Voyage of Captain Bellingshausen*, Vol. 1, 128–129; [Novosil'skij], *Shestoj continent*, 10, 13; Ross, *Voyage of Discovery*, Vol. 1, 218; "Pis'ma Mikhaila Petrovicha Lazareva", 59; Bulkeley, *Bellingshausen*, 83, 168; Tammiksaar, "Russian Antarctic Expedition", 588–591.
44 Ross, *Voyage of Discovery*, Vol. 1, 222.

land mass'.[45] He also stated that 'I am reluctant to accept that such gigantic masses [of ice layers] could be the product of single year, and if otherwise, one should be able to distinguish there the deposits of successive years by the layers being horizontally inclined'.[46]

In d'Urville's view, natural processes like the formation of huge ice masses must have taken place very rapidly. But this idea was based on incorrect assumptions. Cook, Bellingshausen, Ross, and d'Urville carried out temperature measurements close to the Antarctic Circle only in summer, which did not give the slightest idea of the winter conditions. Besides, it was not advisable to compare the Antarctic with the Arctic, where the expeditions of William Edward Parry (1819–20), as well as John and James Clark Ross (1829–30), to the Strait of Boothia, of Ferdinand von Wrangell (1821–24) to the coast of northeastern Siberia, and of Petr Pakhtusov (1832–33 and 1834–35) to Novaya Zemlya had recorded very low winter temperatures (down to −36 °C).[47] Unlike the Arctic Ocean, which was surrounded by mainland, the South Pole area was surrounded by oceans and fog, and thus was not expected to have such low temperatures. When Humboldt wrote about the advances in climate research in 1845, systematic temperature observations to determine global patterns had only just begun to gain momentum (thanks to his efforts), and did not cover the Arctic areas until the International Polar Year of 1882–83.[48]

There were other gaps in knowledge. In the 1830s and 1860s it was still thought that during summer, river ice caused the abundance of ice in the polar sea, because this ice was not salty.[49] As early as 1683, Robert Boyle, natural scientist and fellow of the Royal Society, had proved on the basis of Willem Barents[z] and Thomas James's observations during their Arctic voyages that seawater also freezes, but this knowledge was not widespread.[50] In 1817, the freezing of seawater was described again and confirmed by the observations of William Scoresby, Wrangell, and Bellingshausen during their expeditions.[51] However, the understanding that

45 d'Urville, *Account in Two Volumes*, Vol. 2, 488.
46 d'Urville, *Account in Two Volumes*, Vol. 2, 488.
47 Parry, *Journal of a Voyage*; Ross and Ross, *Narrative of Second Voyage*; Parrot, ed., *Physikalische Beobachtungen*; Ritter, ed., *Reise*; Baer, "Ueber das Klima"; Tammiksaar, "Contributions", 133.
48 Humboldt, *Kosmos*, Vol. 1, 340; Humboldt, *Des lignes isothermes*; cf. Tammiksaar et al., "International Polar Year".
49 cf. Baer, "Ueber das Klima", 237; Petermann, "Nordpol und Südpol", 156; Tammiksaar and Stone, "Karl Ernst von Baer".
50 Boyle, *New Experiments and Observations*, 119–125.
51 Parrot, "Ueber das Gefrieren"; Scoresby, "On Greenland", 267–269, 271–274; Parrot, ed., *Physikalische Beobachtungen*, 29–46; Bellingshausen, *Voyage of Captain Bellingshausen*, Vol. 2, 417.

oceans could be a field of specific scientific research developed gradually, because there was considerable confusion about the salinity of polar seas, how much the polar ice melted in summer, and how much the ice breakup in the large Siberian and North American rivers in spring affected the formation of new ice in the Arctic Ocean.

Cook's Continued Influence

Because of the lack of empirical data, it remained impossible to determine whether a south polar continent existed until the middle of the nineteenth century, although speculation continued. In 1860, the American naval officer Matthew Fontaine Maury published his *Physical Geography of the Sea*, which analysed the wind directions observed by vessels moving across the world's oceans and seas (a total of nearly 1.16 million observations). These data indicated that humid winds prevailed between 40° S and the Antarctic region. Maury therefore predicted a permanent low-pressure system around the South Pole, concluding that the data 'indicate the existence of a mild climate – mild by comparison [with land surrounding the Arctic Ocean] – within the Antarctic Circle'.[52] He was convinced of the existence of a mountainous continent in the south polar region, where the moisture carried by the winds fell as rain or snow, causing the formation of large glaciers and the icebergs which hindered navigation in this area.[53]

In a slightly different way, the internationally respected German cartographer August Petermann tried to predict the physical geography of the Antarctic region on theoretical grounds. A hundred and ten years after Buache, he analysed the routes of all expeditions towards the North and South Poles and the observations of ice and temperatures from these expeditions, and visualized his results in a map (Figure 8.3).[54] Although Petermann's theoretical view of the physical geography of the Arctic met with wide interest, thanks to his world-famous geographical journal, his view on Antarctica was largely ignored.[55] Based on the routes of ten expeditions in the far south, Petermann proved that the southern boundary of the ice that was impenetrable to ships fluctuated greatly from year to year, allowing him to conclude that the South Pole was not a continent, but rather an ocean covered with a non-permanent ice cap.[56] Like Maury, Petermann emphasized

---

52 Maury, *Physical Geography*, 463. 53 Maury, *Physical Geography*, 477.
54 Petermann, "Nordpol und Südpol".
55 Tammiksaar et al., "Hypothesis Versus Fact".
56 Petermann, "Neue Karte der Süd-Polar-Regionen".

Figure 8.3 August Petermann, *Karte der arktischen & antarktischen regionen zur Übersicht des geographischen Standpunktes im J. 1865, der Meeresströmungen &&*). (Courtesy of the Library of the Estonian University of Life Sciences, Tartu.)

that only a few temperature measurements had been made in the southern polar areas, but he was convinced on the basis of the oceanic nature inside the Antarctic Circle that winter temperatures in the Antarctic were much higher than in the Arctic.[57] As a cartographer, Petermann also criticized those who, convinced of the existence of the Antarctic continent, boldly asserted their views by drawing its coastline, despite lacking information that would allow an accurate representation.[58]

57 Petermann, "Neue Karte der Süd-Polar-Regionen", 419, 425.
58 Petermann, "Neue Karte der Süd-Polar-Regionen", 415.

8 Discovery of Antarctica

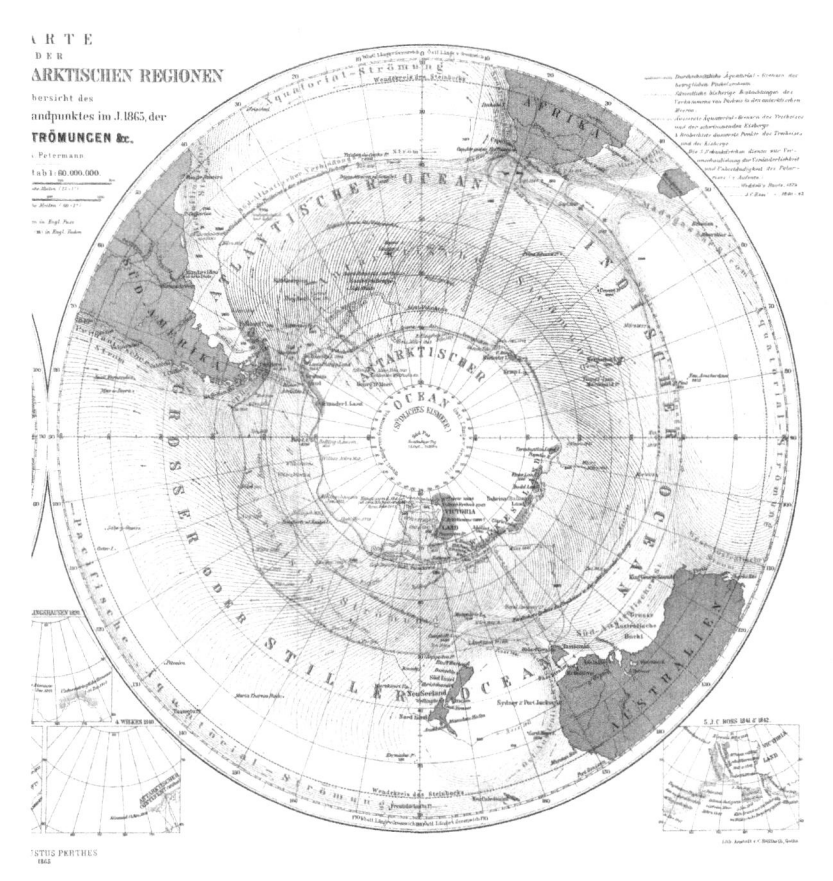

Figure 8.3 (cont.)

Like Petermann, the German geophysicist Georg Neumayer analysed the movement of ice to conclude that winter temperatures in the Southern Ocean were relatively high. Based on the results of Bellingshausen's expedition, he concluded that there was an ocean current flowing from the Kerguelen archipelago southwards, allowing ships to penetrate the South Pole region.[59]

In the mid-1860s, when Petermann was actively organizing expeditions to the Arctic, there was little interest in the scientific world for sending out expensive expeditions to explore the south polar areas.[60] Thus even a century

59 Neumayer, "Erforschung des Süd-Polargebietes"; cf. Clancy et al., *Mapping Antarctica*, 122–123.
60 Petermann, "Neue Karte der Süd-Polar-Regionen", 423; cf. Tammiksaar et al., "Hypothesis Versus Fact".

after Cook's expedition, his hesitant assumptions about the continent or the ocean in the south had neither been refuted nor substantiated by observations. There were still too few scientific data from the region. In such circumstances, James Clark Ross's statement from 1847 was still valid: 'Let each nation therefore be contented with its due share, and lay claim only to the discovery of those portions which they were the first to behold.'[61] Instead of following his advice, however, the scientific audience continued to indulge in speculation about the discoverer of Antarctica on the basis of inadequate data.[62] In Russia, for example, many natural scientists, such as Karl Ernst von Baer, were convinced that the Antarctic continent had been discovered by Ross, and the British took a similar viewpoint.[63] The French, however, supported d'Urville; and the Americans believed in Wilkes as the discoverer.

Blue (Ice) Continent at the South Pole

There was, however, a theory that could have made it easy to resolve the question of the existence of the icy Antarctic continent as early as the mid-nineteenth century. The Swiss geologists Ignatz Venetz, Jean de Charpentier, and Louis Agassiz promoted the idea of an ice age in which Europe had been covered by thick glaciers, rising in mountains like the Alps.[64] The first person to study the Greenland ice sheet was the Danish geologist Hinrich Rink, who visited Greenland many times from 1848 to study the physical laws of glacier movement.[65] In the mid-1850s, the American explorer Elisha Kent Kane also realized that Greenland might consist of a large ice sheet.[66] Nevertheless, the first direct proof of the huge ice cap in the interior of Greenland was obtained by Fridtjof Nansen's expedition, which crossed the island on skis in 1888.[67] This was important because proponents of the ice age theory required empirical data to convince others that glaciers could move and cover as large a territory as Europe or the northern part of Asia. Thomas Krüger and Natal'ya G. Sukhova have shown that it took four decades to prove there had

---

61 Ross, *Voyage of Discovery*, Vol. 1, 275.
62 Cf. Murray, "Exploration"; Markham, "Antarctic Expeditions"; Neumayer, "Die wissenschaftliche Erforschung".
63 Cf. "Otkrytie novogo materika"; Tammiksaar, "Russian Antarctic Expedition", 582; Smirnov, "Proekt M. F. Mori".
64 Venetz, "Abhandlung über die Veränderung"; Charpentier, *Sur la cause*; Agassiz, "Des glaciers"; Agassiz, "Discours"; Agassiz and Bettannier, *Études sur les glaciers*.
65 Rink and Shaw, "On the Supposed Discovery"; Rink, *Die Eisdecke Grönlands*; Rink, "Einige Bemerkungen".
66 Bolles, *Eiszeit*, 162, 181–182, 197.   67 Nansen, *First Crossing*.

been an ice age.[68] The first scientist to observe the indicators and principles of the moving inland ice of Greenland in nature was the German geographer Erich von Drygalski, during his expedition of 1892–93. He proposed to continue this work in south polar areas.[69]

A comparison with Greenland was one way to prove that there was a large continent consisting mainly of ice at the South Pole.[70] At the same time, Clements Markham, president of the Royal Geographical Society, was convinced that there was a strait between West and East Antarctica, because at the South Atlantic side and at the Pacific side of the South Pole region there were similar great embayments (the Ross Sea and Weddell Sea).[71] Another British scientist, John Murray, speculated about the existence of a southern continent from meteorological and oceanographic data, and also from rocks dredged in the far south during the *Challenger* expedition (1873–76).[72]

In the 1890s, there was more speculation about the physical geography of the South Pole than there were clear answers. Systematic research was needed to clarify the existence of a substantial body of land around the South Pole. This finally led to a thorough study of the south polar region. It was largely to Neumayer's credit; he had dreamed of exploring the South Pole ever since the 1860s.[73] In July 1895 he presented a detailed report on the tasks and importance of the study of the southern polar areas at the Sixth International Geographical Congress in London.[74] After Neumayer, the territory around the South Pole was the last large white spot on the globe, and thanks to his initative the assembled geographers finally launched an investigation.

In the closing years of the nineteenth century, temperature data were collected during the first wintering in Antarctic waters by the Belgian Antarctic expedition (1897–99) under the leadership of Adrien de Gerlache. He provided some evidence for the existence of an Antarctic continent covered with glaciers.[75] Meteorological observations during winter, especially wind observations connected with the position of the anticyclone, indicated 'that the Antarctic land area belongs chiefly to the Eastern Hemisphere, where most topographical indications of a continent are presented to us by Victoria Land and Wilkes Land'.[76]

---

68 Krüger, *Discovering the Ice Ages*; Sukhova, "Istoriya izucheniya".
69 Drygalski, *Verborgene Eiswelten*, 16–23; Drygalski, "Die Aufgaben".
70 Drygalski, "Die Südpolar-Forschung".   71 Filchner, *Zum sechsten Erdteil*, 3.
72 Murray, "Exploration"; Markham, "Antarctic Expeditions"; cf. Clancy et al., *Mapping Antarctica*, 124–125.
73 Neumayer, *Auf zum Südpol!*   74 Neumayer, "Die wissenschaftliche Erforschung".
75 Supan, "Das antarktische Klima".
76 Supan, "The First Meteorological Complete Year", 47.

In 1900, the German oceanographer Otto Krümmel summarized the findings of Arctic and Antarctic research, including Petermann's elongated shape for the northern coast of Greenland, Nansen's drift on board *Fram* across the Arctic Ocean (1893–96), and Neumayer's ocean current from Kerguelen, and posited in a confidential letter to Drygalski that the southern region was divided between a continent south of the Pacific Ocean and a huge ocean gyre, which entered the region from the Indian Ocean, crossed the South Pole, and flowed out into the Atlantic Ocean.[77]

Efforts to resolve the question of whether there was an Antarctic continent continued to serve as a motivation to send expeditions southward of the Antarctic Circle in the very beginning of the twentieth century. The German South Polar Expedition led by Drygalski, a British expedition led by Robert Falcon Scott, R.N., a Scottish expedition led by the natural scientist William Speirs Bruce, and a Swedish expedition led by geologist Otto Nordenskjöld additionally agreed on an international meteorological and magnetic cooperation that followed the goals of the First International Polar Year.[78] When Drygalski did not find any ocean current towards the South Pole, he devoted his efforts to the study of the inland ice of the Antarctic, while Scott penetrated an unknown area on the shelf ice as far as 82° S.[79]

After these expeditions had returned and evaluated their measurements, the German geographer Wilhelm Meinardus determined the presumed altitude of the Antarctic continent, mainly from measurements of atmospheric pressure, as 2,000 ± 200 m.[80] The existence of the southern continent was held to have been theoretically proved, contrary to the predictions of Maury, Petermann, and Neumayer. Finally, by progressing a considerable distance from the Ross Sea towards the South Pole, Ernest Shackleton's *Nimrod* expedition (1907–09) showed that the whole penetrated territory was a large, high ice sheet that rose into the interior of the continent, rather than an ice-covered ocean as previously presumed (Figure 8.4).[81]

Conclusion

There is probably no subject in the history of geographical exploration on which there have been as many different views in the literature as on the

77 Krümmel, *Letter to Drygalski*.
78 Tammiksaar et al., "International Polar Year"; Lüdecke, "International Cooperation"; cf. Schilling, *Der letzte weiße Flecken*.
79 Drygalski, *Zum Kontinent*; Scott, *Voyage of the 'Discovery'*.
80 Meinardus, "Die mutmaßliche Höhe".   81 Shackleton, *Shackleton in the Antarctic*.

8 Discovery of Antarctica

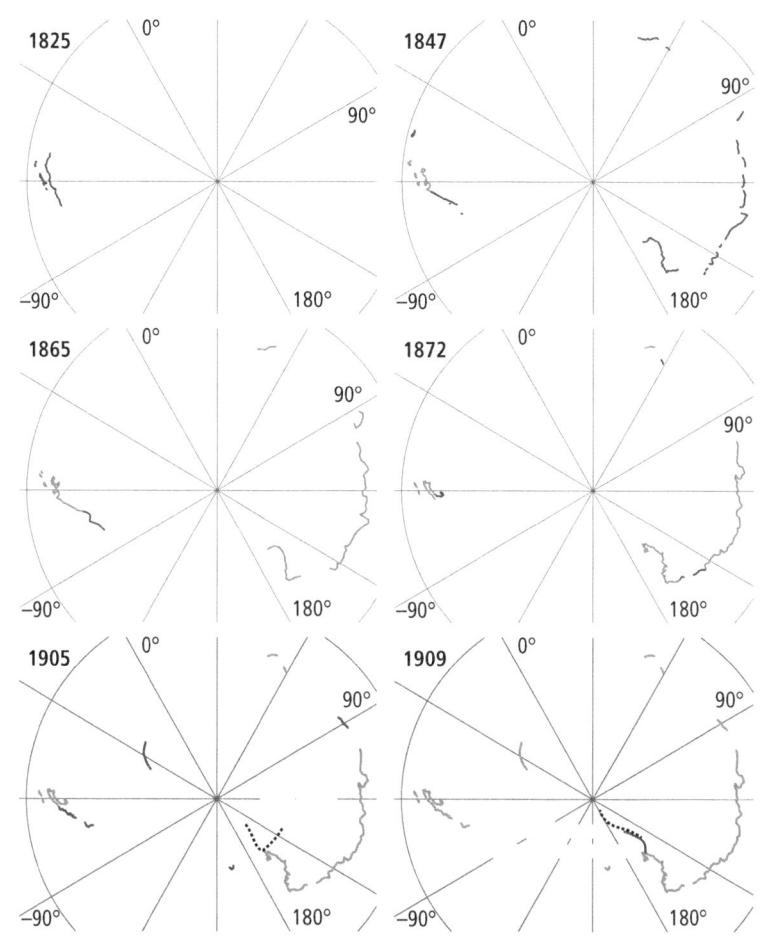

Figure 8.4 Overview map showing cumulative sightings of subsequently confirmed Antarctic territory based on maps published from 1825 to 1909. Dotted lines represent overland journeys.

existence or non-existence of a continent in the south polar region. From antiquity, the existence of a southern *Terra Incognita* was assumed. This idea persisted from the Renaissance to the eighteenth century, as various expeditions repeatedly searched for such a landmass. New lands were indeed discovered in the southern hemisphere, but again and again they turned out not to be part of *Terra Australis*, but separate islands or even new continents such as New Holland (Australia). There was no trace of the southernmost continent. Eventually, despite writing that there *was* a continent at the South Pole, James Cook omitted Antarctica from his maps. Different types of ice, from giant icebergs to ice slush, and the absence of *terra firma*, confused Cook as it did his followers, including Bellingshausen, Ross, Wilkes, and d'Urville. All of them discovered plots of land in the south, but were these ice walls interconnected? With no credible answers to that question, they could only speculate. The physical geography near the South Pole was compared with the physical geography near the North Pole. But proving the existence of the Antarctic continent required the existence of an innovative and empirically determined theory of the ice age, as well as the systematic collection of temperature and pressure observations throughout the year and all around the globe (including the south polar areas) in the nineteenth century.

A decisive set of observations from which to confirm the hypothesis of *Terra Australis* from antiquity was obtained by the Antarctic expeditions of the so-called "Heroic Age" in the early twentieth century. The existence of some form of icy Antarctic continent was no longer in doubt and the competition as to which nation had discovered Antarctica first came very much to the fore.[82] Americans, who had not joined in the cooperation, were concerned that the British would surely declare themselves to be the discoverers of the Antarctic continent, because Ross's discovery of Victoria Land had largely refuted Wilkes's findings. In 1901, Scott had just left for Antarctica when the American historian Edwin Swift Balch tried to diminish Ross's position by pointing out that the American sealer Nathaniel Palmer might have discovered the continent on 17 November 1820.[83] However, according to an article published by Rupert Thomas Gould in 1925, Bransfield, rather than Palmer, sighted Antarctica first on 30 January 1820.[84] From that point until 1941 there was a heated debate about who had been the first to see Antarctica between Balch and his supporters and Gould and his adherents. After World War II the Russians also intervened, claiming that the Antarctic continent was discovered on 28 January 1820 by Bellingshausen's expedition.[85] To some extent, the struggle from the Cold War era on whether Antarctica was discovered by Bransfield or Bellingshausen continues to our time.

From today's knowledge, we could consider either Bellingshausen, Palmer, or Bransfield as the discoverer of Antarctica, but we should not deliberately ascribe modern aspects of scientific knowledge to them or to

---

82 Shackleton, *Shackleton in the Antarctic*.   83 Balch, *Antarctica*, 72, 91, 174.
84 Gould, "First Sighting".   85 Tammiksaar, "Russian Antarctic Expedition".

other Antarctic explorers. It would be more correct to accept that our knowledge of the complicated physical geography of southern polar areas has slowly been transformed since the eighteenth century. We must acknowledge that at the beginning of the twentieth century, only thanks to the cumulation of observational data, the general development of scientific theories and different fields of natural sciences helped to solve the question about the icy continent existing around the South Pole. All navigators, explorers, and scientists from Cook to Shackleton provided single links to achieve this result. No person alone was able to solve the whole puzzle, as shown above. For that reason, there is no longer any basis to ask who discovered Antarctica first, because it was a result of common work.

Bibliography

Agassiz, Louis, "Des glaciers, des moraines, et des blocs erratiques", *Bibliothèque universelle de Gèneve* 12 (1837): 369–394.
Agassiz, Louis, "Discours prononcé à l'ouverture des séances de la Société Helvétique des Sciences naturelles", *Actes de la Société Helvétique des Sciences naturelles* 2 (1837): 5–32.
Agassiz, Louis, and Jean Bettannier, *Études sur les glaciers* (Neuchâtel: Nicolet, 1840).
Arrebola, Sebastián, and Shoshanah Jacobs, *Antarctica: Discovering the Last Continent* (Buenos Aires: Vazquez Mazzini, 2012).
Baer, Karl Ernst von, "Ueber das Klima von Nowaja-Semlja und die mittlere Temperatur insbesondere", *Bulletin scientifique publié par l'Academie Impériale des Sciences de Saint-Pétersbourg* 2 (1837): 225–238.
Balch, Edwin Swift, *Antarctica* (Philadelphia: Larv and Scott, 1902).
Barr, Susan, and Cornelia Lüdecke, eds., *The History of the International Polar Years (IPYs)* (Berlin, Heidelberg: Springer, 2010).
Bellingshausen, Faddej Fadeevich, *The Voyage of Captain Bellingshausen to the Antarctic Seas 1819–1821*, trans. Edward Bullough, 2 vols. (London: Hakluyt Society, 1945).
Bellinsgauzen, Faddej Fadeevich, "Donesenie kapitana 2 ranga Billinsgauzena iz Porta Zhaksona o svoem plavanii", *Zapiski, izdavaemyya gosudarstvennym admiral'teiskim departamentom otnosyashchiyasya i moreplevaniyu, naukam i slovestnosti* 5 (1823): 201–219.
B.[erghaus, Heinrich]. *Briefwechsel Alexander von Humboldt's mit Heinrich Berghaus aus den Jahren 1825 bis 1858*, Vol. 2 (Leipzig: Hermann Costenoble, 1863).
Bertrand, Kenneth J. *Americans in Antarctica, 1775–1948*, American Geographical Society Special Publication 3 (New York: American Geographical Society, 1971).
B.[ertuch], F.[riedrich] J.[ohann], "Südliches Polarland?", *Neue allgemeine geographische Ephemeriden* 9 (1821): 130.
Biscoe, John, and Messrs Enderby, "Recent Discoveries in the Antarctic Ocean", *Journal of the Royal Geographical Society of London* 3 (1833): 104–112.
Bolles, Edmund Blair, *Eiszeit. Wie ein Professor, ein Politiker und ein Dichter das ewige Eis entdeckten* (Berlin: Argon, 1999).

Bone, Thomas Maine, "Edgar Bransfield's Antarctic Voyage, 1819–20, and the Discovery of Antarctic Continent", *Polar Record* 4 (1947): 385–393.

Boyle, Robert, *New Experiments and Observations Touching Cold, or an Experimental History of Cold* (Oxford: Richard Davis, 1683).

Broc, Numa, "Un géographe dans son siècle, Philippe Buache (1700–1773)", *Dix-huitième Siècle* 3 (1971): 223–235.

Brown, Lloyd A., *The Story of Maps* (Boston: Little, Brown and Company, 1949).

Buache, Philippe, "Considérations géographiques et physiques sur les Terres Australes et Antarctiques," *Mémoires de mathématique et de physique, tirés des registres de l'Académie Royale des Sciences* 1755 (1761): 17–20.

Buache, Philippe, "Où l'on donne une idée de l'existence des Terres Antarctiques, et de leur Mer glaciale intérieure; Avec quelques Remarques sur un globe physique en relief, d'un pied de diamètre, qui sert de modèle pour celui de neuf pieds", *Mémoires de mathématique et de physique, tirés des registres de l'Académie Royale des Sciences* 1757 (1762): 190–203.

Buache, Philippe, "Mémoire sur les différentes idées qu'on a eues de la traversée de la mer Glaciale arctique et sur les communications ou jonctions qu'on a supposées entre diverses rivières", *Mémoires de mathématique et de physique, tirés des registres de l'Académie Royale des Sciences* 1754 (1759): 1–18.

Buffon, Georges-Louis Leclerc de, *Œuvres complètes*, ed. Stéphane Schmitt and Cédric Crémière (Paris: Honoré Champion, 2007), Vol. 1.

Buffon, Georges-Louis Leclerc de, and Grandjean de Fouchy, "Rapport des commissaires sur un ouvrage de M. Buache", *Procès-verbaux des séances de l'Académie Royale des Sciences* (Archives of the Parisian Academy of Sciences) (5 septembre 1739), folio 219.

Buffon, Georges-Louis Leclerc de, *Histoire naturelle, générale et particulière, avec la Description du cabinet du Roy* (Paris: Imprimerie Royale, 1749), Vol. 1.

Buffon, Georges-Louis Leclerc, comte de, *Histoire naturelle, générale et particulière* (Paris: De l'imprimerie Royale, 1778), 5 supplément.

Bulkeley, Rip, *Bellingshausen and the Russian Antarctic Expedition 1819–21* (Basingstoke: Palgrave Macmillan, 2014).

Campbell, R. J., *The Discovery of the South Shetland Islands: The Voyages of the Brig Williams 1819–1820 as Recorded in Contemporary Documents and the Journal of Midshipman C. W. Poynter* (London: Hakluyt Society, 2000), Series III, Vol. 4.

Charpentier, Jean de, *Sur la cause probable du transport des blocs erratiques de la Suisse* (Paris: Chez Carilian-Goeury, 1835).

Christoph, Ulf, "Vom Anfang des Kosmos bis zum Menschen: Antike Konzeptionen von Wasserräumen und Wasserformen", in Doris G. Eibl, Lorelies Ortner, Ingo Schneider, and Ulf Christoph, eds., *Wasser und Raum. Beiträge zu einer Kulturtheorie des Wassers* (Göttingen: V&R Unipress, 2008), pp. 143–181.

Clancy, Robert, Manning, John, and Henk Brolsma, *Mapping Antarctica: A Five Hundred Year Record of Discovery* (Dordrecht, Heidelberg, New York, London: Springer, 2014).

Cook, James, *A Voyage Towards the South Pole and Round the World; Performed in His Majesty's Ships the 'Resolution' and 'Adventure', in the Years 1772, 1773, 1774, and 1775*, 2 vols. (London: Strahan and Cadell, 1777).

Crane, Ralph, Elisabeth Leane and Mark Williams, eds., *Imaging Antarctica: Cultural Perspectives on the Southern Continent* (Hobart: Quintus, 2011).

8 Discovery of Antarctica

"Das neue antarktische Continent oder Neu-Schottland", *Neue allgemeine geographische Ephemeriden* 8 (1820): 81–83.

Day, David, *Antarctica: A Biography* (Sydney: Random House, 2012).

de Brosses, Charles, *Historie des navigations aux Terres Australes*, 2 vols. (Paris: Durand, 1756).

Delépine, Gracié, "Jean-Baptiste Bouvet de Lozier", in Beau Riffenburgh, ed., *Encyclopedia of the Antarctic* (New York: Routledge, 2007), Vol. 1, pp. 175–176.

Drygalski, Erich von, "Die Aufgaben der Forschung an Nordpol und Südpol", *Geographische Zeitschrift* 4 (1898): 121–133.

Drygalski, Erich von, "Die Südpolar-Forschung und die Probleme des Eises", in Georg Kollm, ed., *Verhandlungen des Elften Deutschen Geographentages zu Bremen am 17., 18. und 19. April 1895* (Berlin: Reimer, 1896), pp. 18–29.

Drygalski, Erich von, *Verborgene Eiswelten. Erich von Drygalskis Bericht über seine Grönlandexpeditionen 1891, 1892–1893*, ed. Cornelia Lüdecke (Munich: August Dreesbach, 2015).

Drygalski, Erich von, *Zum Kontinent des eisigen Südens* (Berlin: Reimer, 1904).

d'Urville, Jules Sebastién César Dumont, *An Account in Two Volumes of Two Voyages to the South Seas*, trans. Helen Rosemann, 2 vols. (Melbourne: Melbourne University Press, 1987).

Ellis, Richard, *Men and Whales* (New York: Knopf, 1991).

Filchner, Wilhelm, *Zum sechsten Erdteil. Die zweite deutsche Südpolar-Expedition* (Berlin: Ullstein, 1922), Vol. 3.

Fricker, Karl, *Antarktis* (Berlin: Schall, 1898).

Gould, R. T., "The First Sighting of the Antarctic Continent", *The Geographical Journal* 65 (1925), 220–225.

Hatherton, Trevor, ed., *Antarctica* (London: Buttler and Tunner, 1965).

Headland, Robert Keith, *A Chronology of Antarctic Exploration* (London: Quaritch, 2009).

Humboldt, Alexandre de, *Des lignes isothermes et de la distribution de la chaleur sur le globe* (Paris: Peronneau, 1817).

Humboldt, Alexander von, *Kosmos. Entwurf einer physischen Weltbeschreibung* (Stuttgart und Tübingen: Cotta'scher, 1845).

Jones, A. G. E., *Antarctica Observed: Who Discovered the Antarctic Continent?* (Whitby: Caedmon of Whitby, 1982).

Kirwan, Laurence P., *A History of Polar Exploration* (Harmondsworth: Penguin, 1962).

Kleinschmidt, Georg, ed., *The Geology of the Antarctic Continent*, Beiträge zur regionalen Geologie der Erde 33 (Stuttgart: Borntraeger Science, 2021).

Krüger, Thomas, *Discovering the Ice Ages: International Reception and Consequences for a Historical Understanding of Climate* (Leiden: Boston, 2013).

Krümmel, Otto, Letter to Drygalski (15 April 1900). Leibniz-Institut für Länderkunde, Leipzig, Drygalski estate: Box 61, No. 4755, lfd. 3.

Lüdecke, Cornelia, "Die Bedeutung Alexander von Humboldts für die wissenschaftliche Erforschung der Antarktis", *Studia Fribergensia*, Beiträge zur Alexander-von-Humboldt-Forschung 18 (1994): 177–187.

Lüdecke, Cornelia, "East Meets West: Meteorological Observations of the Moravians in Greenland and Labrador in the 18th Century", *History of Meteorology* 2 (2005): 123–132.

Lüdecke, Cornelia, *Germans in the Antarctic* (Cham: Springer Nature, 2021).

Lüdecke, Cornelia, "International Cooperation in Antarctica (1901–1904)", in Susan Barr and Cornelia Lüdecke, eds., *The History of the International Polar Years (IPYs)* (Berlin, Heidelberg: Springer, 2010), pp. 127–134.
Manzoni, Marcello, *La nature dell' Antarctide* (Milan: Springer, 2001).
Markham, Clements, "The Antarctic Expeditions", in Georg Kollm, ed., *Verhandlungen des Siebenten Internationalen Geographen-Kongresses, Berlin 1899* (Berlin: Kühl, 1899), Vol. 2, pp. 623–630.
Marr, Alexander, ed., *The Worlds of Oronce Fine: Mathematics, Instruments and Print in Renaissance France* (Donington: Shaun Tyas, 2009).
Maury, Matthew Fontaine, *The Physical Geography of the Sea and Its Meteorology* (London: Sampson, 1860).
Mawer, Granville Allen, *South by Northwest: The Magnetic Crusade and the Contest for Antarctica* (Kent Town: Wakefield Press, 2006).
Meinardus, Wilhelm, "Die mutmaßliche Höhe des antarktischen Kontinents", *Petermanns Geographische Mitteilungen* 9 (1909): no. 9, 304–309; no. 12, 355–360.
Mill, Hugh Robert, *The Siege of the South Pole: The Story of Antarctic Exploration* (London: Alston Rivers, 1905).
Murray, George, ed., *The Antarctic Manual for the Use of the Expedition 1901* (London: Royal Geographical Society, 1901).
Murray, John, "The Exploration of the Antarctic Regions", *The Scottish Geographical Magazine* 2 (1886): 527–547.
"Nähere Nachrichten von der Entdeckungsreise des Russischen Capitäns Bellingshausen (Aus dem 'Invalid' 100)", *Neue allgemeine geographische Ephemeriden* 9 (1821): 508–512.
Nansen, Fridtjof, *The First Crossing of Greenland*, 2 vols. (London: Longmans, 1890).
Neumayer, Georg von, *Auf zum Südpol! 45 Jahre Wirkens zur Förderung der Erforschung der Südpolar-Region 1855–1900* (Berlin: Vita Deutsches Verlagshaus, 1901).
Neumayer, Georg von, "Die Erforschung des Süd-Polargebietes", *Zeitschrift der Gesellschaft für Erdkunde zu Berlin* 7 (1872): 151–167.
Neumayer, Georg von, "Die wissenschaftliche Erforschung des Südpolar-Gebietes", in Georg Kollm, ed., *Verhandlungen des Elften Deutschen Geographentages zu Bremen am 17., 18. und 19. April 1895* (Berlin: Reimer, 1896), pp. 9–17.
[Novosil'skij, Pavel], *Shestoj Continent ili kratkoe obozrenie plavanij k yugu ot Kuka do Rossa* (St Petersburg: Veimar, 1854).
"Otkrytie novogo materika v Yuzhnom polusharii", *Syn Otechestva* 1 (1842): 24–32.
Parrot, Georg Friedrich, "Ueber das Gefrieren des Salzwassers mit Rücksicht auf die Entstehung des Polar-Eises", *Annalen der Physik* 57 (1817): 144–162.
Parrot, Georg Friedrich, ed. *Physikalische Beobachtungen des Captain-Lieutenant Baron v. Wrangel[l] während seiner Reisen auf dem Eismeere in den Jahren 1821, 1822 und 1823* (Berlin: Reimer, 1827).
Parry, Edward William, *Journal of a Voyage for the Discovery of a North-West Passage from the Atlantic to the Pacific; Performed in the years 1819–20, in His Majesty's ships Hecla and Griper* (London: Murray, 1821).
Petermann, August, "Der Nordpol und Südpol, die Wichtigkeit ihrer Erforschung in geographischer und kulturhistorischer Beziehung", *Mittheilungen aus Justus Perthes' Geographischer Anstalt über wichtige neue Erforschungen auf dem Gesammtgebiete der Geographie* 11 (1865): 146–160.

8 Discovery of Antarctica

Petermann, August, "Neue Karte der Süd-Polar-Regionen", *Mittheilungen aus Justus Perthes geographischer Anstalt über wichtige neue Erforschungen auf dem Gesammtgebiete der Geographie* 10 (1863): 407–428.

"Pis'ma Mikhaila Petrovicha Lazareva k Alekseyu Antonovichu Shestakovu v g. Krasnyj Smolenskoj gubernii", *Morskoj sbornik* CDIII (1918): 51–66.

Pyne, Stephen J., *The Ice: A Journey to Antarctica* (London: Arlington Books, 1987).

Riffenburgh, Beau, ed., *Encyclopedia of the Antarctic*, 2 vols. (New York: Taylor and Francis: 2007).

Rink, Hinrich Johannes, *Die Eisdecke Grönlands als ein Rest der Glacialzeit unserer nördlichen Erdhälfte* (Berlin: Wilhelm Gronau, 1891).

Rink, Hinrich Johannes, "Einige Bemerkungen über das Inlandeis Grönlands und die Entstehung der Eisberge", *Verhandlungen der Gesellschaft für Erdkunde zu Berlin* 19 (1892): 65–69.

Rink, Heinrich, and Norton Shaw, "On the Supposed Discovery, by Dr. E. K. Kane, U. S. N., of the North Coast of Greenland, and of an Open Polar Sea, &c.; As Described in 'Arctic Explorations in the Years 1853, 1854, 1855'", *Journal of the Royal Geographical Society of London* 28 (1858): 272–287.

Ritter, Carl, ed., *Reise des kaiserlich-russischen Flotten-Lieutenants Ferdinand v. Wrangel[l] längs der Nordküste von Sibirien und auf dem Eismeere in den Jahren 1820 bis 1824*, trans. Georg von Engelhardt, 2 vols. (Berlin: Voss'sche Buchhandlung, 1839).

Ross, Maurice James, *Ross in the Antarctic* (Whitby: Caedmon of Whitby, 1982).

Ross, James Clark, *A Voyage of Discovery and Research in the Southern and Antarctic Regions during the Years 1839–43*, 2 vols. (London: Murray, 1847).

Ross, John, and James Clark Ross, *Narrative of a Second Voyage in Search of North-West Passage and of a Residence in the Arctic Regions during the years 1829, 1830, 1831, 1832, 1833* (London: Webster, 1835).

Savours, Ann, *The Search for the North West Passage* (London: Palgrave Macmillan, 1999).

Schilling, Pascal, *Der letzte weiße Flecken. Europäische Antarktisreisen um 1900* (Göttingen: Wallstern, 2016).

Scoresby, William, "On the Greenland or Polar Ice", *Memoirs of the Wernerian Society* 2 (1818).

Scott, Robert Falcon, *The Voyage of the 'Discovery'* (London: Smith, Elder & Co., 1905).

Shackleton, Ernest, *Shackleton in the Antarctic: Being the Story of the British Antarctic Expedition, 1907–1909* (London: Heinemann, 1911).

Simonoff, Iwan, "Nachricht von der Entdeckungsreise, welche auf Befehl's der Russischen Regierung von dem Kapitain Bellingshausen, in den Jahren, 1819, 1820 und 1821 im stillen Ocean und in den südlichen Meeren gemacht ist", *Neue allgemeine geographische Ephemeriden* 14 (1824): 285–306.

Simonoff, Jean, "Lettres XXVII, III, VIII, XIV", *Correspondance astronomique, géographique, hydrographique et statistique* 9 (1823): no. 6, 556–574; 10 (1824): no. 1, 19–45; no. 2, 141–154; no. 3, 250–273.

Simonow, Iwan Michailowitsch, *Beschreibung einer neuen Entdeckungsreise in das südliche Eismeer* (Wien: Wallishausser, 1824).

Smirnov, Valentin G., "Proekt M. F. Mori ob issledovanii yuzhnykh polyarnykh stran", *Izvestiya Russkogo geograficheskogo obshchestva* 130, no. 5 (1998): 46–54.

Sukhova, Natal'ya Georgievna, "Istoriya izucheniya sledov lednikovogo perioda na territorii Rossii v XIX–nachale XX stoletiya", *Izvestiya Russkogo geograficheskogo obshchestva* 132, no. 6 (2000): 66–76.

Supan, Alexander, "Das antarktische Klima", in Georg Kollm, ed., *Verhandlungen des dreizehnten Deutschen Geographentages zu Breslau am 28., 29. und 30. Mai 1901* (Berlin: Reimer, 1901), pp. 45–53.

Supan, Alexander, "The First Meteorological Complete Year from the South Polar Regions", in George Murray, ed., *The Antarctic Manual for the Use of the Expedition in 1901* (London: Royal Geographical Society, 1901), pp. 45–50.

Tammiksaar, Erki, "The Contributions of Karl Ernst von Baer to the Investigation of the Physical Geography of the Arctic in the 1830s–1840s", *Polar Record* 38 (2002): 121–140.

Tammiksaar, Erki, "Ferdinand von Wrangell: White Spots on the Northeast Coast of Siberia Disappear", *Polar Record* 37 (2001): 151–153.

Tammiksaar, Erki, "Peter Anjou: The Contours of Novosibirskiye Ostrova Become More Precise", *Polar Record* 38 (2002): 359–360.

Tammiksaar, Erki, "The Russian Antarctic Expedition under Command of Fabian Gottlieb von Bellingshausen and Its Reception in Russia and the World", *Polar Record* 52 (2016): 578–600.

Tammiksaar, Erki, and Ian R. Stone, "Karl Ernst von Baer and the Kara Sea 'Eiskeller'", *Polar Record* 33 (1997): 239–242.

Tammiksaar, Erki, Natal'ya Georgievna Sukhova, and Ian R. Stone, "Hypothesis Versus Fact: August Petermann and Polar Research", *Arctic* 52 (1999): 237–243.

Tammiksaar, Erki, Natal'ya Georgievna Sukhova, and Cornelia Lüdecke, "The International Polar Year 1882–1883", in Susan Barr and Cornelia Lüdecke, eds., *The History of the International Polar Years (IPYs)* (Heidelberg: Springer, 2010), pp. 7–33.

Varenius, Bernhard, *A Compleat System of Geography* (London: Stephen Austen, 1734).

Venetz, Ignaz, "Abhandlung über die Veränderung der Temperatur in den Schweizer Alpen", *Denkschriften der allgemeinen schweizerischen Gesellschaft für die gesamte Naturwissenschaften* 1 (1833): 125–143.

Weddell, James, *A Voyage Towards the South Pole, Performed in the Years 1822–24, Containing an Examination of the Antarctic Sea*, 2nd edition (London: Longman, 1827).

Wilkes, Charles, *Atlas to the Narrative of the United States Exploring Expedition during the Years 1838, 1839, 1840, 1841, 1842* (London: Sherman, 1844).

Wilkes, Charles, *Narrative of the United States Exploring Expedition during the Years 1838, 1839, 1840, 1841, 1842* (Philadelphia: Sherman, 1844).

9
Sir John Franklin and the Northwest Passage in Myth and Memory

RUSSELL A. POTTER

Introduction

The European quest for a passage by water across North America long predates the nineteenth century, but it was to be then that it took on the urgency of national achievement, and it was to be one man – Sir John Franklin (1786–1847) – whose career came to symbolize the entire era. It may seem an ironic honour, given the disaster that his final expedition of 1845 became, but it must be remembered that the search for his ships was the spur for many more expeditions than had been launched before him. As Joseph Conrad noted in his 1924 essay "Geography and Some Explorers", 'This great navigator, who never returned home, served geography even in his death. The persistent efforts, extending over ten years, to ascertain his fate advanced greatly our knowledge of the polar regions.'[1] Indeed, the Franklin fascination long outlasted this initial search period, extending well into the twenty-first century, when his ships *Terror* and *Erebus* were finally located and dived on by archaeologists from Parks Canada. Moreover, the cultural legacies of his disappearance gave rise to dozens of novels, an Australian musical, a German opera, and most recently the 2018 AMC television series *The Terror*, itself based on Dan Simmons's novel of that name.[2]

The whole affair, until relatively recently, might be looked upon as yet another instance of a Eurocentric 'great explorer' narrative, and yet here again history has taken an unpredicted turn: Franklin's ships, which eluded searchers for a century and a half, were finally found only when Inuit oral

---

1 Conrad, "Geography and Some Explorers", 253.
2 The 1991 musical, *Franklin: Van Diemen's Land to the Northwest Passage*, was written by Tony Phipps and Ken Ferguson, and performed by the Frozen Assets ensemble. The opera, based on Sten Nadolny's *Die Entdeckung der Langsamkeit* [*The Discovery of Slowness*], was composed by Giorgio Battistelli and premiered in October 1997 at the Theater Bremen. The television series *The Terror* was developed and directed by David Kajganich and Soo Hugh and premiered on AMC in March 2018.

testimony – long disparaged, particularly in Britain – was trusted. The first find was HMS *Erebus*, discovered on the western coast of the Adelaide Peninsula, precisely where Inuit testimony recorded by nineteenth-century searchers had placed it; HMS *Terror* came two years later, although in this case it was a living Inuk whose account of having seen a mast above the ice led to its discovery.[3] After some initial acrimony, the government of Canada and that of the territory of Nunavut, in whose waters the ships lie, formed mutual agreements, with the cooperation of the Inuit Heritage Trust and other regional Inuit organizations.[4] Thus, the Franklin myth has become an intercultural one, even though the underlying issues of colonialism and Indigenous rights remain problematic. Inuit guardians are now paid to watch over the wrecks of both ships, and the continued interest in the Franklin story brings hundreds of tourists north each summer.

In this chapter, I hope to lay out the background and key points of these now intertwined histories, as well as noting the significant literary and cultural responses and productions that have formed and fostered the Franklin myth, and with it the myth of the 'fabled' Northwest Passage. The latter has now become an issue in a new era of geopolitics, with Canada claiming the passage as 'internal waters', while the United Nations Convention on the Law of the Sea regards it as an 'international strait'. In a time when climate change has also begun to become more evident in the Arctic, with less sea ice each year, the prospect of a passage that would be navigable year-round is no longer a distant one. Indeed, one of the most familiar Arctic obsessions of the nineteenth century, the 'open polar sea', may soon be what it never was before – a reality. In this and other ways, the name of Sir John Franklin has come to symbolize the peculiar confluence of history, ideology, cultural identity, and geopolitics that has framed the Canadian Arctic in modern times, even as the steady flow of artefacts and archaeological work has reshaped what we know about him.

Myths and Maps: The Pre-History of the Passage

The myth of a passage by water either through or around North America goes back at least to the sixteenth century, when several well-known cartographers – among them Gerardus Mercator (1512–94) – placed a 'Strait of Anián' athwart

---

3 This was Sammy Kogvik, a Canadian Ranger from Gjoa Haven; see Pringle, "Unlikely Tip".
4 See "Parks Canada".

9 Sir John Franklin and the Northwest Passage

the continent. In some versions, it connected either with the Gulf of California or (after 1611) Hudson's Bay, while in others its western entrance was further to the north. Indeed, one of its other names – the Strait of Juan de Fuca – remains attached to the sea route between Vancouver Island and Washington's Olympic Peninsula, which at least at the beginning followed the hoped-for direction. Later explorers, beginning with Manuel Quimper in 1789, showed that it bifurcated at its eastern end, opening to Puget Sound at the south, and a series of narrower straits to the north that eventually open back into the Pacific, not into the North Sea as de Fuca had claimed.[5]

The idea, however, proved to be a persistent one. Martin Frobisher (c. 1535–94), made three voyages to the southern end of Baffin Island in 1576, 1577, and 1578. Although he soon realized that the inlet he had found, 'Frobisher Bay', was not a passage, he conceived the idea of establishing a colony in the place Queen Elizabeth dubbed *meta incognita* (border unknown).[6] His third voyage included a flotilla of fifteen vessels, which brought equipment for establishing dwellings, building a smithy or forge, and conducting smelting operations on the glittering ore that Frobisher believed to contain gold. Perhaps fortunately – given that the growing season on South Baffin was far too short for any English crops – part of his flotilla was delayed by a storm, and discontent among the would-be colonists scuttled the idea of a settlement. The glittering rocks turned out to be only worthless pyrite stones, some of which have ended up incorporated into a stone wall in Dartford, Kent. Relations with the Inuit were poor, and there were armed conflicts associated with all three expeditions. Frobisher also took an Inuk hostage on his first voyage, purportedly to exchange for five of his own men who had gone missing, as well as a small family of three on his second; none survived long after their arrival in England.[7]

Afterwards, the passage was repeatedly sought from the east by British explorers, starting with Henry Hudson and continuing through multiple expeditions in the eighteenth century. Among these was that of James Knight in 1719; he and his two ships, the *Albany* and *Discovery*, were never

---

5 Beerman, "Manual Quimper".
6 Great Britain Hydrographic Department, *Arctic Pilot*, 364.
7 The first Inuk captive was brought to London, where he died not long afterwards. The second group, consisting of a woman (Arnaq), her infant child (Nutaaq), and a man (Kalicho) arrived in Bristol in September of 1577; by that November all three were dead. Two were buried at St Stephen's Church in Bristol, while the infant – who had been taken to London – was buried at St Olave's Church there. See Harper, "Abduction"; Harper, "Five Missing Men".

seen again, although archaeological evidence suggests the expedition may have met its end by starvation near Marble Island in Hudson Bay. Sir Francis Drake was the first English navigator to search for a western entrance in 1579, but claimed to have been turned back by adverse winds and 'the most vile, thick, and stinking fogs' – he did not even reach the opening of the Strait of Juan de Fuca.[8] Next in line was James Cook, on what was to be his final voyage. He too sought the passage from the west in 1776, trusting what turned out to be untrustworthy Russian maps; although he was able to enter the Bering Strait, impenetrable polar sea ice prevented any further progress. The era as a whole has been aptly chronicled by Glyn Williams, and the title of his book, *Voyages of Delusion: The Northwest Passage in the Age of Reason*, epitomizes the spirit of the quest.[9]

Land expeditions were the other element of the search for the passage; certainly, it seemed, the northern terminus of any north-flowing river would be a potential gateway, as well as eliminating the possibility of any continental passage to its south. The 1771 trek of Samuel Hearne reached the mouth of the Coppermine River, showing that it discharged into Arctic waters rather than the Pacific, and the 1789 expedition of Alexander Mackenzie down his eponymous river had just the same result. And, although the British generally referred to these northern waters as the 'Polar Sea', it was clear from many of their observations that it was not a wide and clear body of water, but rather a much more rambling series of shores, possibly constituting a passage, but none so direct as had been imagined by earlier cartographers. James Cook's invective against Jacob von Stählin, who first published the map that launched Cook's final wild goose chase, could serve as a closing apothegm of the role of mapmakers in this era: 'It is a map to which the most illiterate of [von Stählin's] illiterate seafaring countrymen would have been ashamed to set his name.'[10]

A Renewed Effort: The 'Barrow' Era

As has been often described, most engagingly in Fergus Fleming's 2001 book *Barrow's Boys*, the push for the passage – and the Pole – began in earnest in

---

8 Wood, *Elizabethan Sea-Dogs*, 138.   9 Williams, *Voyages of Delusion*.
10 Von Stählin was actually just the man who made the map public; it had been drawn up by Ivan Borisovich Sindt, charged by the Russian government with a 'careful surveying of all islands lying between Kamchatka and America'. Sindt apparently gave undue credence to (or simply misunderstood) maps made for him by fur traders. See Haycox et al., eds., *Enlightenment and Exploration*, 137.

1818.[11] There were many factors – the great numbers of idle ships and men available in the wake of Britain's final victory over Napoleon, new developments in the understanding of terrestrial magnetism and natural science, and commercial opportunities in terms of fisheries – but the role of Sir John Barrow as Second Secretary of the Admiralty was certainly the catalyst for them all. In 1817, having learned from a letter written by the whaling captain William Scoresby that ice conditions in the Arctic were unusually favourable, Barrow advocated for two expeditions – one to head directly toward the Pole, and one to re-survey Baffin's Bay, with an eye toward finding an opening that might lead to a passage west. John Franklin served as second-in-command of the first of these under Captain David Buchan; their two ships, the *Dorothea* and the *Trent*, were badly damaged by rough seas and ice north of Spitsbergen, and forced to limp home. The other, commanded by John Ross aboard the *Isabella* and *Alexander*, was – in terms of the area surveyed and the safe return of its vessels and men – a far greater success, re-establishing Baffin's Bay (which had scarcely been visited since the days of its eponymous discoverer), making first contact with the Inughuit of northwest Greenland, and locating what proved to be a very promising passage indeed in the form of Lancaster Sound. Unfortunately, perhaps because of some sort of temperature inversion or mirage, Ross believed it to be blocked at its head by a range of tall peaks, and so sailed home to public ridicule and condemnation by Barrow. Barrow was particularly irked by the fact that Ross had avoided risk – he called his a 'voyage of pleasure'[12] – and made it quite clear that, for any future such expedition, risk would be its very purpose, and the definition of success.[13]

The following year, Ross's second-in-command William Edward Parry was put in charge of a new expedition aboard *Hecla* and *Griper*; he sailed right through the mythical mountains and penetrated west nearly to 108 degrees of longitude. There, on Melville Island, he wintered over with his ships, setting a pattern for expeditions to come – but the heavy polar sea ice to his west proved unyielding, and he was left to sail home with the great quest unfulfilled. Twice he returned – in 1821 and 1824 – trying different routes, but without success.

Nevertheless, he had established the pattern: to penetrate as far as one could, winter over, and make a further attempt the following summer. The desolation of an Arctic winter and the crushing of Parry's ship the *Fury*, in

---

11 Fleming, *Barrow's Boys*.   12 [Barrow], "Ross's Voyage of Discovery", 252.
13 For a discussion of the role of risk in exploration, see Potter, "Exploration and Sacrifice".

1824, both lent a Romantic aura to the undertaking, and were taken up by poets (among them Franklin's first wife Eleanor Porden) and painters (Caspar David Friedrich's *Das Eismeer* [the Sea of Ice], 1824, was based in part on newspaper accounts of Parry's *Griper* being nipped in the ice in 1821).[14] The Arctic frame-narrative of Mary Shelley's *Frankenstein* (1818 and 1831) also owed something to this polar turn of the public imagination.

That imagination had its dark side, first foreshadowed when in 1819 John Franklin was sent on an overland expedition to trace the shores of what was then known as 'the Polar Sea' in the area near the outlet of the Coppermine River. This region, known as 'Rupert's Land', was essentially a vast private grant, and was not directly controlled by the British government. The lack of government infrastructure – the Hudson's Bay Company and the North West Company operated competing trading posts and supply lines – led the Admiralty to rely on a small party of four officers and one ordinary sailor; the bulk of the work of paddling and stowage was to be done by experienced *voyageurs* and Indigenous guides, with provisions contracted out to the fur companies. The rival companies stinted on supplies, each blaming the other; the *voyageurs* soon felt they were overworked and undersupplied. They knew the hazards of the land, and resented being ordered to descend the river late in the season and with inadequate provisions. Once they arrived, the canoes turned out to be poorly suited for coastal surveys; several were damaged, and morale grew even lower. Unfamiliar with the land or the climate, Franklin chose to return by what, on the map, seemed a short cut back to his base camp at Fort Enterprise; the result was an unmitigated disaster. The canoes had to be hauled, and were lost or destroyed at river crossings; eleven of the fourteen *voyageurs* died of starvation and exposure. There was at least one case of cannibalism among the guides, a murder (of one of the officers), and an execution (of the guide who was suspected of the murder). The hobbled, reduced party that reached the fort – really not much more than a drafty shack – lost two more men to starvation; only the timely arrival of food and care from the Indigenous Dene people – summoned by George Back after an epic trek on snowshoes – saved the lives of the remaining men. And yet, on his return in 1823, Franklin was not condemned, but rather hailed as 'the man who ate his boots', an exemplar of British pluck and persistence. His experience was seen as the willing embrace of unavoidable risk, as well as a sort of crucible for his character; he was dispatched the next season for a second land

---

14 An account of this appeared in the *Literarisches Conversationsblatt* in January of 1821; see Potter, *Arctic Spectacles*, p. 58.

expedition (1825-27), this time without loss of life, after which he wrote the expected book and accepted the expected laurels.

For a time, the Admiralty dispatched no new expeditions, leaving the door open – perhaps unintentionally – to private endeavours. The most notable of these came in 1829, when Sir John Ross, eager to refurbish his explorer's reputation, and his nephew James Clark Ross undertook a search for the passage under the sponsorship of gin magnate Sir Felix Booth. Booth had only one stipulation: that the Longitude Prize, which would otherwise offer a cash reward for each further degree west, be abolished; it was one thing to seek fame, apparently, quite another to seek money.[15] He need not, as things turned out, have worried; the Rosses' expedition aboard their ship *Victory* set no new record, although James Clark Ross did manage to locate the North Magnetic Pole via a sledging expedition from the ship. They also spent three long winters in the Arctic, with the essential assistance of the nearby Netsilik Inuit. Finally, having nearly been given up for dead, they were rescued by a passing whaler – which, of all ships, was John Ross's former *Isabella*, now converted for use as a whaler.[16] Here, as in many other areas, commerce came quickly in the footsteps of exploration.

The Rosses' return to universal acclaim was, in many ways, the high-water (or 'high-ice') mark of the era. It was clear from their experience, and from Parry's, that no navigable passage of commercial value existed; from a purely commercial viewpoint, the risks were far too high. When asked by a parliamentary inquiry whether the passage, if found, would be of value, John Ross was blunt: 'I believe it would be utterly useless.'[17] And yet, in a strange way, the uselessness of the passage only redoubled its symbolic value; it was from this moment onward a purely disinterested goal, freed from the overtones of commerce. Science gladly took its place – although, as was to be the case with the 'space race' of the 1960s, there were strong elements of nationalism as well; Barrow declared that Britain would suffer humiliation if, having 'opened the doors' at both ends of the passage, it was unable to traverse it. And yet, for twelve long years after the Rosses' return, the passage gave way to other goals, principally the multi-year Antarctic voyage commanded by James Ross from 1839 to 1843. In part, this reflected

---

15 Baigent, "Booth, Sir Felix".   16 Edinger, *Fury Beach*.
17 *Selection of Reports and Papers of the House of Commons*, Vol. 32, p. 235. Ross had been asked 'if [a further attempt to discover the Northwest passage were] successful, would it be attended with any public benefit?'.

a shift in priorities, with the 'Magnetic Crusade', led by Parry's former shipboard scientist Edward Sabine (1788–1883), taking increasing priority over purely geographical goals. Nevertheless, the search for the passage never entirely faded, least of all from the thoughts of Sir John Barrow.

The Franklin Era

After Ross's return from his largely successful circumnavigation of Antarctica, it was widely expected that he would set out again, either once more to the south, or to the north. Instead, he married and settled down, promising his new wife that he would give up voyages of discovery. Barrow, whose time at the Admiralty was drawing to a close, was eager to launch one last attempt on the Northwest Passage; after Ross declined the command, he turned to Franklin as a suitably experienced Arctic commander. Although often spoken of as the best-prepared expedition of its kind, this new foray was actually readied with some haste; Franklin was not offered the command until February of 1845, scarcely four months before its planned departure. Ross's same ships – the *Erebus* and *Terror* – were quickly refitted, with the one major change being the addition of ex-railway steam engines and propellers (steam power was gaining favour at the Admiralty, and its new champion Francis Pettit 'Propeller' Smith was to accompany one of the escort ships). Space limitations, though, meant that each ship carried only enough fuel to run its engine for roughly twelve days. Public interest was, alas, not quite as high as for previous Arctic voyages; although a visit from Queen Victoria was anticipated, she chose instead to inspect the nearby steam vessel *Great Britain* in the company of Smith.[18] Somewhat like a much slower-motion version of the Apollo 13 space mission, Franklin's expedition (Figure 9.1) was to gain its extraordinary fame only after it became clear that something had gone terribly wrong.

The outlook of Franklin and his officers and men was decidedly sanguine. After all, only a relatively modest portion of the passage – that between Cape Walker on Somerset Island and Cape Herschel on King William Island – remained uncharted. The *Erebus* and *Terror* were veterans of many polar voyages, as were both their captains; the 127 men under their command – though mostly new to the Arctic – were experienced seamen. A special 'ice master' familiar with the vagaries of northern navigation had been appointed

---

18 See "Her Majesty's Visit", 7. There is no record of her having visited *Erebus* and *Terror*, either in the daily 'Court Circulars' or in the Queen's personal diary.

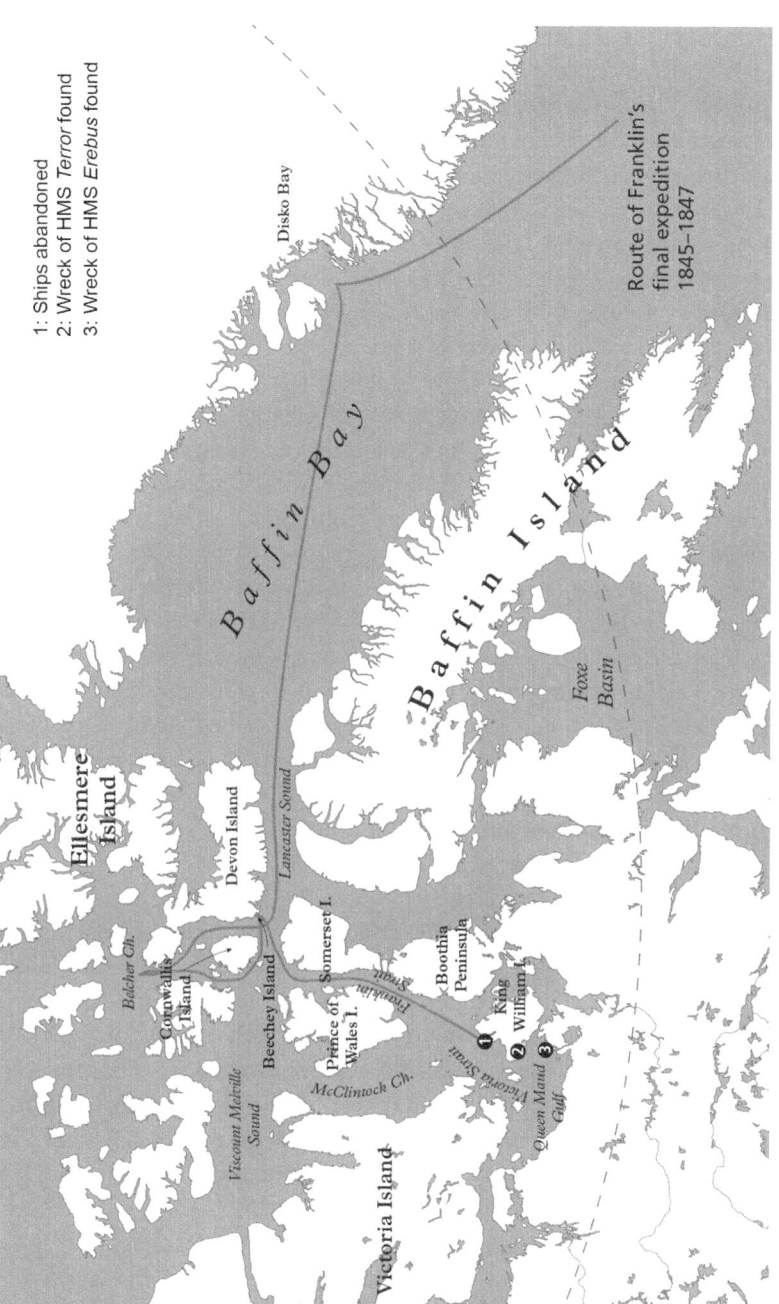

Figure 9.1 Route of Franklin's final expedition, 1845–1847.

to each vessel, and to ward off scurvy, that special scourge of polar voyagers, 930 gallons of lemon juice had been stowed aboard. A vast array of scientific instruments, including several different types of magnetometers, dredges for gathering biological specimens, 'dip circles' for measuring the Earth's horizontal magnetic deflection, and even a complete daguerreotype camera outfit were also on hand. And, should the hours grow long while the ships were in 'winter quarters', a library of 1,700 books was at the ready, along with props and costumes for staging plays, and a barrel organ on each ship that could play everything from a hymn to a jig at the turn of a crank.[19]

Anticipating at least one and possibly two 'winterings over', the ships were provisioned for three years. When nothing was heard of them in 1847, concerns began to grow, concerns that were only amplified when a search party, led by Franklin's friend John Richardson and Hudson's Bay Company surveyor John Rae in 1847, returned in 1849 having found no trace of them. Theirs turned out to be the first of more than thirty searches that would be mounted over the next twelve years, during which time the mystery of Franklin's disappearance was very widely covered in the press in Britain, Europe, and the United States. The year 1850 saw the discovery of Franklin's first winter harbour at Beechey Island; the graves of three of his men stood on its shore. Further traces were not found until 1854, when John Rae encountered a group of Inuit who had with them small personal items he realized must have come from Franklin's men. Trading with other Inuit, he acquired a large collection of material, including Franklin's own Guelphic Order of Hanover; these, on their return to Britain, were hailed as 'relics' of men who everyone now realized must be dead.

A final expedition led by Francis Leopold McClintock in 1857–59 at last found further evidence on King William Island – skeletons scattered along the shore, an abandoned whaleboat, and one lone written record, the so-called 'Victory Point' note. It proved to be the perfect 'last note', combining as it did an earlier record – which stated that the members of the expedition were 'All Well' – surrounded by a marginal addition made a year later, describing the death of Sir John Franklin and twenty-three of his men. It quickly became iconic; reproduced in facsimile on the cover of *Harper's Weekly* and the *Illustrated London News*, a similar version was included in every copy of

---

19 Particulars of all these materials supplied to the expedition are in Cyriax, *Franklin's Last Arctic Expedition*. The number of books brought varies considerably in secondary sources; the figure of 1,700 comes from a letter sent home from *Erebus* by Charles Hamilton Osmer, the ship's purser (1 July 1845), Scott Polar Research Institute SPRI MS 248/449/1–2.

9 Sir John Franklin and the Northwest Passage

McClintock's book about his search, *The Voyage of the Fox in Arctic Seas*, which sold more copies that year even than George Eliot's *The Mill on the Floss*, and was quickly translated into German, French, and other European languages. A copy in French later reached ten-year-old Józef Korzeniowski – the future Joseph Conrad – in 1867; in an essay published in 1924 a few months before his death, he credited the book with having started him on the 'romantic explorations' of his 'inner self' that led him to become a writer.[20] Other authors and artists were similarly stirred by the Franklin story, among them Wilkie Collins and Charles Dickens, who produced a play, *The Frozen Deep*, loosely based on the expedition; Jules Verne made his 'Captain Hatteras' a Franklin obsessive, and Algernon Charles Swinburne penned a florid elegy, "The Death of Sir John Franklin", in 1860. The American artist Frederic Church added a broken mast in tribute to Franklin to his magisterial 1861 painting "The Icebergs", and three years later Sir Edwin Landseer drew on the darker vein of Arctic disaster with his "Man Proposes, God Disposes". The painting depicts two polar bears beside a fallen mast; one tears at the 'red ensign' indicating a Royal Navy vessel, while the other crunches on what appears to be a human rib. 'A blanched bone – no need to ask what bone,' observed the *Times*.[21]

Landseer's bears, perhaps understandably, were scorned by Lady Franklin and the old cadre of Arctic officers. He had dared to allude to what was, at the time, the scandalous news, arriving in Inuit testimony brought home by Dr John Rae in 1854, that Franklin's men, in their desperation, had resorted to what Rae called 'the last resource' – cannibalism. Rae's report was widely denounced in the press, most stridently by Dickens himself in the pages of his own weekly magazine, *Household Words*. Denouncing the Inuit accounts as the 'vague babble of savages . . . with a domesticity of blood and blubber,' he declared that it must have been the 'Eskimos' themselves that had set upon and killed Franklin's brave sailors.[22] To the dark undertone of cannibalism, Dickens added the still darker tones of racism and ethnocentrism, which in a peculiar manner only amplified the story's attraction and longevity. Although many at the time shared Dickens's outrage, they too shared the inner shudder that accompanied even discussing such a matter. In 1991, a dig led by archaeologists Margaret Bertulli and Anne Keenleyside finally discovered decisive evidence that cannibalism had taken place at the Erebus Bay site on King William Island. Numerous elements of different bones

---

20 Conrad, "Geography and Some Explorers".   21 "Exhibition of the Royal Academy", 14.
22 Dickens, "The Lost Arctic Voyagers".

showed clear, sharp cut-marks, especially in the vicinity of the joints, which Dr Keenleyside has described as 'consistent with defleshing'.

The other shift that, as fate would have it, made the Franklin expedition vivid in the public's eye was the emergence of the illustrated press. The *Illustrated London News* was a pioneer, depicting the captain's cabin aboard *Erebus* in one of its earliest issues, and continuing to document every step of the Franklin search era, from the earliest searches in 1849 through to Schwatka's search in 1880. In the United States, periodicals such as *Gleason's Pictorial, Harper's Weekly*, and *Frank Leslie's Illustrated Newspaper* did the same. Other visual media, from moving panoramas to magic lantern shows to stereoview slides, made one or another 'Arctic Expedition' – some sets didn't specify *which* – classics of each medium, and nearly always depicted an ice-bound ship, a village of igloos, and a lonely grave.

Through these media the Franklin story continued to motivate further searches, and stir more people into 'romantic explorations'. Among these, the most prominent was the American journalist Charles Francis Hall, who in 1860, just when it seemed the fate of Franklin was known, was stirred by the conviction that some of his men might yet be alive. Hall's epiphany, in fact, seems to have had its origins in his attending a moving panorama, T. P. Failing's "Grand Panorama of Kane's Voyages", which had appeared in Cincinnatti in 1858.[23] Improbably, Hall managed to raise money and secure passage northward on a whaler in what was to be the first of three Arctic expeditions. On the first (1860–62), he ended up stuck in Cumberland Sound, hundreds of kilometres from any Franklin sites. Making the best of his circumstances, he gathered Inuit testimony about Frobisher's three Arctic incursions near that area from 1576 to 1578. The detailed nature of these accounts convinced Hall that he might learn more of the true fate of Franklin the same way. On his second expedition (1864–69) he reached an area far closer to where Franklin's ships were lost and, working with the Inuit translator Tookoolito, collected an enormous amount of written testimony about them. Yet even before this material was organized and published, Hall was off again, this time with the backing of the US government aboard a ship christened the *Polaris*. He reached a new furthest north, and had settled in for the winter on the coast of Greenland at a place known as Thank God Harbor, when he was poisoned, probably by the ship's doctor.[24]

---

23 See Potter, *Arctic Spectacles*, 219–220.
24 The ship's physician, Dr Emil Bessels, had long been among the suspects, the method used being arsenic poisoning (Bessels attended Hall during Hall's final illness, which began after he drank a cup of 'strangely sweet' coffee). His body was later exhumed

A second American searcher, Frederick Schwatka, went north in 1878 to follow up on Inuit accounts of written records having been found. He, like Hall, took up the Inuit method of travelling by dogsled and providing food by hunting, which enabled him to make one of the longest sledge journeys yet accomplished by a European. He did not discover any records, but collected additional Inuit testimony, some of it from eyewitnesses, which would later prove to be of great value. Echoing a choice made by Hall, he also brought back the skeleton of one of Franklin's men, identified by a medallion found at the grave as Lieutenant John Irving; Irving was interred in Edinburgh. The skeleton retrieved by Hall, initially misidentified, was deposited in the base of a large marble memorial to Franklin's men in Greenwich; in 2009, when the memorial was moved, the bones were analysed and are now believed to be those of Dr Harry Goodsir, the expedition's naturalist. These two, and the three men buried at Beechey Island, remain the only identified bodies of any of the expedition's 129 men.

The Modern Era

Franklin remained – and remains – an almost mythical figure. The twentieth and early twenty-first centuries saw well over 100 new searches, nearly all of them by private parties who had formed a personal connection to the story. The persistent draw of the Franklin 'mystery' derives in part from its unique combination of vast troves of potential evidence with a complete lack of closure – but it also owes something to the romantic visions of the north, which – though their origins can be found in the early nineteenth century – have continued to this day, imbuing the Franklin story with a tragic sensibility of the sublime and irresistible forces of nature.[25] Interest increased further in the 1980s, which saw the exhumation and autopsying of the three bodies at Beechey Island by the Canadian anthropologist Owen Beattie; the 1988 book he co-wrote with John Geiger, *Frozen in Time*, brought the Franklin story to renewed international attention.

In the 1990s, an amateur Canadian historian, David C. Woodman, began a close study of the Inuit evidence recorded by Hall, Schwatka, and others; his

from its grave in Greenland, and elevated levels of arsenic were found in his hair and fingernails. The final evidence came via recently unearthed letters, in which Bessels confessed his 'undying affection' for the young artist Vinnie Ream; Miss Ream had also dined with Hall in New York, and sent him numerous gifts at the time his last expedition sailed. See Barr, "Epilogue: Motive for Murder".

25 This aspect of the Franklin story was first articulated by Chauncey Loomis in his seminal essay, "The Arctic Sublime".

1991 book *Unravelling the Franklin Mystery: Inuit Testimony* offered a reconstruction of later events based primarily on this oral testimony. Woodman followed his book with a series of small-scale expeditions of his own, seeking to find one of Franklin's ships that the Inuit described as being off the western coast of the Adelaide Peninsula, south of King William Island. Other searchers also looked in this area, including Barry Ranford, a high-school teacher from Ontario, who located a significant site on King William Island near where McClintock had seen a whaleboat. The site, known by its Borden grid system coordinates as NgLj-2, was the location of the archaeological work of Keenleyside and Bertulli already mentioned. Ranford died in 1996, and although several of his colleagues from his earlier trips continued to search the area, no significant new finds were made.

It was only with the involvement of Parks Canada's underwater archaeologists, which began in 2009, that large-scale searches using side-scan sonar were mounted. In 2014, these searches finally yielded fruit: the sonar revealed the first image of HMS *Erebus*, whose wreck lay almost exactly between the two spots indicated by the Inuit to Hall and Schwatka. Almost exactly two years later, thanks to a tip from Canadian Ranger Sammy Kogvik, HMS *Terror* was found in, of all places, Terror Bay on King William Island. The bay had been named in 1859 by McClintock – for symmetry's sake, as he named the bay on the other side of the Gore Peninsula Erebus Bay – but he had no idea that its eponymous vessel lay shrouded in its depths. *Terror* was found in a far better state of preservation than *Erebus*, and for that reason most subsequent archaeological work has focused on *Erebus*, which is partly crushed and located in an area where currents have caused damage to her decks in the years since her rediscovery. From 2018 to 2019, an exhibit, "Death in the Ice", appeared at the National Maritime Museum in Greenwich (UK), the Canadian Museum of History in Ottawa, the Mystic Seaport Museum in Connecticut, and the Anchorage Museum in Alaska; relics retrieved from the *Erebus*, as well as those recovered in the nineteenth century, were both displayed. The Inuit story was pointedly included, not only because of their essential role in helping to locate the ships, but to put the land and the people in context with the explorers who encountered them.

In Canada, this period leading up to and following the discovery of Franklin's ships saw them become a powerful political symbol, albeit of shifting significance. The government of Conservative Prime Minister Stephen Harper regarded the search for the ships as a way to assert Canadian sovereignty over the Northwest Passage. When Liberal Prime Minister Justin Trudeau took his place in 2015, the focus shifted to seeing the ships as symbols of a shared history in which Inuit played a vital role. Inuit guardians are paid to watch the ships in the summer months, and monies have been earmarked for an expansion of the Nattilik Heritage Centre in Gjoa Haven, the Inuit hamlet closest to where the ships were found. The involvement of Inuit in decision-making about managing the sites has been established via a special Franklin advisory committee, as well as through the Inuit Heritage Trust. Louie Kamookak, a Gjoa Haven resident who for many years worked to keep the Franklin story alive and preserve its living history, was made an Officer of the Order of Canada for his work. At the same time, some Inuit leaders felt that their communities – faced with housing shortages, health issues, and food insecurity – had more immediate needs that the federal government of Canada was neglecting.

The Northwest Passage itself was forever associated with Franklin's name. When it was finally traversed by Roald Amundsen in 1903–06, he credited his boyhood reading of accounts of the Franklin expedition and its sufferings as the inspiration for him to seek the passage himself. Unlike Franklin, Amundsen spent a great deal of time living with the Inuit and learning their methods of dog driving and living off the land; he used many of those same techniques to help him become the first person to reach the geographical South Pole in 1911. The passage – in fact there are several possible routes through it – has been traversed many times since; among the more significant crossings was that of the RCMPV *St Roch*, piloted by Henry Larsen, which made the first crossing from west to east in 1940–42; the submarine USS *Seadragon*, which made the first underwater transit; the oil tanker SS *Manhattan*, which became the first full-size commercial ship to transit the passage in 1969; and the MV *Crystal Serenity*, which became the largest cruise ship ever to make the passage in 2016 – it repeated the journey in 2017. According to the Scott Polar Research Institute, as of 2019, 313 vessels had so far made full transits.[26]

The twenty-first century has also seen an increasing number of commercial vessels of all kinds, including not only passenger liners but foreign-flagged tankers and freighters. In 2017, the Chinese government sent its icebreaker *Xue Long* [Snow Dragon] through the passage; it was followed the next year by three specially built cargo ships owned by China's COSCO Shipping Corporation. There is some irony in the fact that the passage, which was once touted as the 'sea route to the Orient', has had its first commercial traffic from China. Global climate change has, indeed, made the passage more

---

26 See Robert Headland's list, "Transits of the Northwest Passage to End of the 2019 Navigation Season", maintained by the Scott Polar Research Institute: www.spri.cam.ac.uk/resources/infosheets/northwestpassage.pdf

passable, though it should be borne in mind that warmer water does not necessarily mean less ice in any given location; indeed, it may mean more loose ice and more icebergs calving, either of which could pose challenges for commercial ships. The increasing number of cruise ships may also pose a problem; while, so far, no such ship has required a full-scale search-and-rescue operation, there have been close calls, most recently when the *Akademik Ioffe* ran aground in 2018 while returning from a diversion to Kugaaruk, which itself was made because of ice conditions preventing it from making a scheduled passenger turnaround at Resolute Bay.

Yet even as the passage may be on its way to navigability, its reputation as a perilous waterway has continued. Part of this is due to the renewed interest in Franklin, which has made the story newly attractive to novelists. Since the publication of Nancy Cato's *North-West by South* in 1965, more than two dozen novels inspired in whole or in part by Franklin's expedition have been published. Among the more notable are German novelist Sten Nadolny's 1987 *Die Entdeckung der Langsamkeit* [The Discovery of Slowness]; it was the source for an opera by Giorgio Battistelli. John Wilson's *North With Franklin: The Lost Journals of James Fitzjames* used the device of extending the actual narrative that Fitzjames – Franklin's second-in-command aboard the *Erebus* – began in letters home to his sister-in-law. But it was to be Dan Simmons's horror-inflected *The Terror* in 2007 that cast the longest shadow; it was adopted as a ten-episode television series by David Kajganich and aired on AMC in 2018 to widespread critical acclaim. Among the show's more welcome breaks with entertainment industry practices was the casting of Inuit actors in Inuit roles, including Johnny Issaluk as a Netsilik hunter, and Greenlander Nive Nielsen as 'Lady Silence'.

From Swinburne onward, the Franklin saga has been a recurring subject of poetry, most notably the 1965 verse play *Terror and Erebus* by the Canadian poet Gwendolyn McEwen, which originally appeared as a radio drama on the CBC.[27] David Solway's poetic cycle *Franklin's Passage* included mash-ups of Franklin-oriented websites and press coverage; it won the 2004 Grand Prix du Livre de Montreal, the first anglophone book to receive this honour.[28] The tragic turn of the story was made for the ballad tradition, with various versions of "Lady Franklin's Lament" appearing from the 1850s onward; the version recorded by Martin Carthy in 1966, using the alternative title "Lord Franklin", has become the standard. But it was to be Stan Rogers' "Northwest Passage", first released in 1981, which would perhaps most powerfully evoke

27 In MacEwen, *Afterworlds*.   28 Solway, *Franklin's Passage*.

the heroic/mythic spirit of Franklin; new versions have been recorded in every style from rock to heavy metal, and some have even referred to it as almost a 'second Canadian national anthem'. All of these lyric forays have tended to cement both the myth of the 'ill-fated' and innocent Franklin, as well as that of his long-lamenting widow, Lady Jane Franklin (née Griffin), who funded and organized many of the early searches for her husband, as well as the one by McClintock which finally brought home definitive evidence of his death.

Scholars of Disaster

While the flurry of interest in the Franklin expedition certainly shaped the broader view of his legacy around the world, scholarly examinations of the nature of the failures that led to the loss of the expedition have, in many ways, taken up the darker side of the story since the 1980s. Owen Beattie's autopsies of the Beechey Island casualties pointed to high levels of lead as a potential contributing cause of death; the lead was traced to sloppily soldered cans provided by the low bidder for the Navy contract, Samuel Goldner. The human bones found at NgLj-2, studied by archaeologists Margaret Bertulli and Anne Keenleyside, also showed elevated lead levels, along with cutmarks that Keenleyside regarded as strong evidence of cannibalism – supporting once-scorned Inuit oral testimony – and this interpretation is now almost universally accepted. Cultural mores have shifted as well, such that the reality of such 'survival cannibalism' no longer seems to detract from the reputation of the expedition.

The lead-poisoning hypothesis, however, though it held sway for than two decades, eventually spurred additional research that weakened its case for being the primary cause of the expedition's failure. Improvements in technology, including higher-resolution X-ray fluorescence in studying skeletal remains, have shown that bones from later in the expedition's journey had not absorbed much more lead than those who died more than three years before at Beechey Island. More decisively, a study of the bones of Royal Navy sailors who were buried at English Harbour in Antigua – many of them very close contemporaries of Franklin's sailors – had comparable, even higher, levels of lead without the benefit of Goldner's tinned food.[29] The consensus today is that, while it surely did have some impact on the men – and a few individuals had very much higher levels than most – it can no longer be seen

---

29 Giffin et al., "Skeletal Lead Burden".

as the single decisive factor. Work based on looking at the medical records of other contemporary ships also suggests that the more common diseases of the day, particularly tuberculosis – evidence of which was seen on all three bodies at Beechey Island, and may well have been the cause of death of one of them – may have played a larger role. Lastly, the damage to the crew's health during its final period, when they were man-hauling sledges over land with almost certainly inadequate provisions, may have been decisive.

The Inuit testimony first examined by David Woodman has also received further attention. In a second book, *Strangers Among Us* (1995), he examined evidence that one party of Franklin's men may have made it as far east as the Melville Peninsula. In her 2008 book, *Encounters on the Passage: Inuit Meet the Explorers*, Dorothy Eber catalogued the distant echoes of the original testimony – most of it given between 1854 and 1880 – in the memory of living Inuit elders today. A second undertaking of this kind, based in Louie Kamookak's home town of Gjoa Haven, is currently in progress, and will compile accounts of the elders there of the stories told by their ancestors. The greater understanding of this body of material has contributed significantly to understanding of the final phase of the expedition, and has been used to help guide and interpret modern archaeological work in the area of King William Island. A number of land-based archaeologists, with Dr Douglas Stenton prominent among them, have continued to excavate and examine known Franklin sites; Dr Stenton has also managed to recover DNA from many of the remains, although no match has yet been made with a living individual.[30]

In the humanities, the cultural significance of the Franklin story has recently attracted additional attention. Some work has focused on the coverage of the story in magazines, newspapers, and the illustrated press,[31] as well as in popular visual depictions.[32] The understanding of existing relics of the expedition has been broadened[33] and their display investigated as a cultural practice.[34] The Franklin fascination itself, together with its role in the long history of searches from the Victorian era to the present, has been the subject of several books.[35] Finally, the entire historiographical approach to the Franklin story has been subject to question and analysis in Adriana Craciun's 2016 study *Writing Arctic Disaster*; Craciun argues that for too long we have experienced the Franklin story, along with others of explorers *in extremis*, in a manner rather too similar to that of our Victorian forebears; to

---

30 Stenton, "Finding the Dead".   31 Cavell, *Tracing the Connected Narrative*.
32 Potter, *Arctic Spectacles*.   33 Walpole, *Relics of the Franklin Expedition*.
34 Davis-Fisch, *Loss and Cultural Remains*.
35 Potter, *Finding Franklin*; Hutchinson, *Franklin's Erebus and Terror Expedition*.

her, this merely replicates the rituals of colonialism and empire.[36] The contemporary revival of Franklin interest, however, shows just how potent and persistent the tug of cultural nostalgia can be. Sir Michael Palin's 2018 book *Erebus: The Story of a Ship* perhaps best encapsulates this feeling, both in its positive form (the success of *Erebus* on Ross's Antarctic expedition) and its fascinating negative (the disaster aboard that same ship on Franklin's final voyage).[37] In the end, as with other great disasters – Pompeii, the charge of the Light Brigade, RMS *Titanic* – it seems that the cold glow of the cultural myth yet has a vital supporting role to play, as the public's fascination fuels the ongoing research and archaeological work.

The Future of the Past

Work in many areas continues to expand understanding of the history of the quest for the Northwest Passage, as well as the numerous cultural encounters and controversies that quest has engendered. The Parks Canada underwater archaeological team has returned to the ships each year (with the exception of the *annus horribilis* of 2020) and plans to continue its work. One indication of how long that may take is the earlier work of a similar team on a Basque shipwreck in Red Bay, Labrador – a project that took nearly a decade. The secrets contained within the better-preserved *Terror* await the completion of work aboard the more vulnerable *Erebus*, and it is entirely possible that there may be found written records, physical evidence, and even photographs (the expedition was sent with a complete daguerreotype apparatus supplied by the London firm of Richard Beard) that may well sweep away more than a century and a half of conjecture. If any number of recovered bones can be matched with the DNA of living descendants, that too may change our understanding of that final period after the ships were abandoned. At this moment, we still do not know for certain whether either vessel was in fact piloted – or merely drifted – into its present location.

For the Inuit, for whom the peculiar disaster of these strangers was only one event in many millennia of memory, it is a sometimes vexed inheritance. Yes, it brings shiploads of Franklin buffs to the north,[38] and those same people contribute to local economies through both direct payments to the communities they visit, and the purchase of locally made artwork and crafts – but as

---

36 Craciun, *Writing Arctic Disaster*.   37 Palin, *Erebus*.
38 In 2017, in addition to the expedition cruise ships that transited the passage (the *Bremen*, *Crystal Serenity*, and *Le Boreal*), the *Akademik Sergey Vavilov* and *Akdemik Ioffe* (both operated by One Ocean Expeditions), and the *Ocean Endeavour* (operated by Adventure Canada) made multiple ten-day excursions throughout the summer season.

the people of many a Caribbean island have found, dependence on tourism as a source of sustenance can be a curse. The hazards of this dependence were made starkly clear in 2020, when all ports in Nunavut were ordered closed, and expedition cruises suspended; what had been planned as the 'Year of Inuit Art' ended up as a season in which no art at all was sold in the communities. It has been a matter of pride for many Inuit who serve as guardians at the wreck sites that they are preserving places of great importance to people around the world; and yet, in their home communities, social and economic problems remain unsolved. Particularly in Gjoa Haven – the community best situated to benefit from such tourism – persistent issues such as suicide, substance abuse, domestic violence and crime make many feel that the newfound fame of their home has not yet brought with it tangible benefits to their families. It is possible, though, that those who visit and see these problems may also be motivated to find ways to help these communities.[39]

On the global economic stage, the Northwest Passage may indeed play a growing role in shipping and commerce, and whatever international conventions may be, it seems only right and proper that those who use this resource contribute something to the communities that live on its shores. Should there be a human or an ecological disaster along this route, a far more robust infrastructure – from ports to ice charts to search-and-rescue capabilities – would be needed to address it. The possibility of the melting of the polar ice cap could bring even more such issues – but with many rights tied to the continental shelf of neighbouring nations, including Denmark and Russia, it could also become a potential place of conflict. Ultimately, the Northwest Passage of the future is one that can only be remembered, respected, and protected via international cooperation. It is to be hoped that the interest in the many fascinating histories of this region – and not just those associated with Franklin or other Western explorers – will contribute to this possibility.

Bibliography

Baigent, Elizabeth, "Booth, Sir Felix, first baronet (1780–1850), distiller and promoter of Arctic exploration", in *Oxford Dictionary of National Biography* (23 September 2004).

---

39 One example of this is in Clyde River, Nunavut. I visited this community in 2019, and was given a tour of the Illisaqsivik Centre by one of the passengers on the ship where I served as a lecturer – he was one of the centre's major funders. Illisaqsivik provides general community services, as well as hosting a library and learning centre for children, stocked with books in both English and Inuktitut.

9 Sir John Franklin and the Northwest Passage

Barr, William (Ed.) and Bessels, Emil, "Epilogue: Motive for Murder", in *Polaris: The Chief Scientist's Recollections of the American North Pole Expedition, 1871–73* (Calgary: University of Calgary Press, 2016), 537–542.

[Barrow, Sir John], "Ross's Voyage of Discovery", *The Quarterly Review* 21 (January and April 1819): 252.

Beerman, Eric, "Manuel Quimper: un marino limeño en la costa oeste del Canadá", *Derroteros de la Mar del Sur* 4 (1996): 23–30.

Brannan, Robert Louis, *Under the Management of Mr. Charles Dickens: His Production of 'The Frozen Deep'* (Ithaca: Cornell University Press, 1966).

Cavell, Janice, *Tracing the Connected Narrative: Arctic Exploration in British Print Culture, 1818–1860* (Toronto: University of Toronto Press, 2008).

Conrad, Joseph, "Geography and Some Explorers", *National Geographic Magazine* 45 (March 1924): 253.

Craciun, Adriana, *Writing Arctic Disaster: Authorship and Exploration* (Cambridge: Cambridge University Press, 2016).

Cyriax, Richard J., *Sir John Franklin's Last Arctic Expedition* (London: Methuen, 1939).

Davis-Fisch, Heather, *Loss and Cultural Remains in Performance: The Ghosts of the Franklin Expedition* (Basingstoke: Palgrave Macmillan, 2012).

Dickens, Charles, "The Lost Arctic Voyagers", *Household Words* 245 & 246 (2 and 9 December 1854).

Eber, Dorothy Harley, *Encounters on the Passage: Inuit Meet the Explorers* (Toronto: University of Toronto Press, 2008).

Edinger, Ray, *Fury Beach: The Four-Year Odyssey of Captain John Ross and the Victory* (New York: Berkley Books, 2004).

Edinger, Ray, "Exhibition of the Royal Academy", *The Times* (30 April 1864): 14.

Fleming, Fergus, *Barrow's Boys: The Original Extreme Adventurers* (New York: Atlantic Monthly Press, 2000).

Geiger, John, and Owen Beattie, *Frozen in Time: Unlocking the Secrets of the Franklin Expedition* (Regina: Western Producer Prairie Books, 1988).

Geiger, John, and Alanna Mitchell, *Franklin's Lost Ship: The Historic Discovery of HMS Erebus* (Toronto: HarperCollins, 2017).

Giffin, K. L., T. Swanston, I. Coulthard, et al., "Skeletal Lead Burden of the British Royal Navy in Colonial Antigua", *International Journal of Osteoarchaeology* 27 (2017): 672–682.

Great Britain Hydrographic Department, *Arctic Pilot* 5 (1969): 364.

Harper, Kenn, "Abduction", *Nunatsiaq News* (3 October 2020).

Harper, Kenn, "Five Missing Men", *Nunatsiaq News* (16 October 2020).

Haycox, Stephen, James K. Barnett, and Caedmon Liburd, eds., *Enlightenment and Exploration in the North Pacific, 1741–1805* (Seattle, London: University of Washington Press, 1997), p. 137.

"Her Majesty's Visit to the Great Britain Steam-Ship", *Lloyd's Weekly Newspaper* (27 April 1845): 7.

Hutchinson, Gillian, *Sir John Franklin's Erebus and Terror Expedition: Lost and Found* (London, New York: Adlard Coles Nautical, 2017).

Keenleyside, Anne, Margaret Bertulli, and Henry C. Fricke, "The Final Days of the Franklin Expedition: New Skeletal Evidence", *Arctic* 50 (1997): 36–46.

Loomis, Chauncey, "The Arctic Sublime", in U. C. Knoepflmacher and G. B. Tennyson, eds., *Nature and the Victorian Imagination* (Berkeley: University of California Press, 1977), 95–112.

MacEwen, Gwendolyn, *Afterworlds* (contains "Terror and Erebus") (Toronto: McClelland and Stewart, 1987).

Martin, Ronald Richard, Steven Naftel, Sheila Macfie, Keith Jones, and Andrew Smith, "Pb Distribution in Bones from the Franklin Expedition: Synchrotron X-ray Fluorescence and Laser Ablation/Mass Spectroscopy", *Applied Physics A* 11 (2013): 23–29.

Millar, Keith, Adrian W. Bowman, William Battersby, and Richard R. Welbury, "The Health of Nine Royal Naval Arctic Crews, 1848 to 1854: Implications for the Lost Franklin Expedition", *Polar Record* 265 (2016): 423–441.

Nadolny, Sten, *The Discovery of Slowness* (New York: Viking, 1987).

Palin, Michael, *Erebus: The Story of a Ship* (London: Hutchinson, 2018).

"Parks Canada, Nunavut Heritage Trust Sign Deal on Franklin Artifacts", *Nunatsiaq News* (24 April 2019), https://nunatsiaq.com/stories/article/parks-canada-nunavut-heritage-trust-sign-deal-on-franklin-artifacts/.

Potter, Russell, *Arctic Spectacles: The Frozen North in Visual Culture, 1818–1875* (Seattle, London: University of Washington Press, 2007).

Potter, Russell, "Exploration and Sacrifice: The Cultural Logic of Arctic Discovery", in Frédéric Regard, ed., *The Quest for the Northwest Passage: British Narratives of Arctic Exploration, 1576–1874* (London: Pickering & Chatto, 2013), 1–18.

Potter, Russell, *Finding Franklin: The Untold Story of a 165-Year Search* (Montreal: McGill-Queen's University Press, 2016).

Pringle, Heather, "Unlikely Tip Leads to Discovery of Historic Shipwreck", *National Geographic* online (13 September 2016).

Selection of Reports and Papers of the House of Commons 32: *Literary and Scientific* (1836): 235.

Simmons, Dan, *The Terror: A Novel* (New York: Little, Brown, 2007).

Solway, David, *Franklin's Passage* (Montréal, Kingston: McGill-Queen's University Press, 2004).

Stenton, Douglas R., "Finding the Dead: Bodies, Bones and Burials from the 1845 Franklin Northwest Passage Expedition", *Polar Record* 54 (2018): 197–212.

Walpole, Garth, *Relics of the Franklin Expedition: Discovering Artifacts from the Doomed Arctic Voyage of 1845*, ed. Russell Potter (Jefferson: McFarland, 2017).

Williams, Glyn, *Voyages of Delusion: The Northwest Passage in the Age of Reason* (London: HarperCollins, 2003).

Wilson, John, *North with Franklin: The Lost Journals of James Fitzjames* (Markham: Fitzhenry & Whiteside, 1999).

Wood, William, *Elizabethan Sea-Dogs: A Chronicle of Drake and His Companions* (New Haven: Yale University Press, 1920).

Woodman, David C., *Strangers Among Us* (Montreal: McGill-Queen's University Press, 1995).

Woodman, David C., *Unravelling the Franklin Mystery: Inuit Testimony* 2nd edition (Montreal: McGill-Queen's University Press, 2015).

10

The Heroic Age of Antarctic Exploration, 1890 to the Present

STEPHANIE BARCZEWSKI

Introduction

No era of polar history has received more attention than the Heroic Age of Antarctic exploration. Its three most famous explorers – Robert Falcon Scott, Roald Amundsen, and Ernest Shackleton – have been the subjects not only of academic research, but also of novels, plays, films, television programmes, and exhibitions at major museums. Rather than retelling in detail a familiar story, this chapter will trace how the history of the Heroic Age has evolved over the past century or so. Its core argument is that the very features which made it so compelling in the first decades of the twentieth century have made its place in recent European and American culture more problematic. It will conclude by suggesting a new way of thinking about the Heroic Age.

The Conventional Narrative of the Heroic Age

In the mid-1890s, western European nations, along with Japan and the United States, began to focus on Antarctica for the purposes of territorial expansion, natural resource extraction and increased global prestige. Over the next two decades, eight countries sent sixteen expeditions south, beginning with the Belgian explorer Adrien de Gerlache's survey of Graham Land in 1897.[1] The

---

I am extremely grateful to John Moisson for editing this essay.
[1] The expeditions are: the Belgian Antarctic Expedition (led by de Gerlache, 1897–99); the British Antarctic Expedition (Carsten Borchgrevink, 1898–1900); the (British) National Antarctic Expedition (Robert Falcon Scott, 1901–04); the First German Antarctic Expedition (Erich von Drygalski, 1901–03); the Swedish Antarctic Expedition (Otto Nordenskjöld and Carl Anton Larsen, 1901–03); the Scottish National Antarctic Expedition (William Spiers Bruce, 1902–04); the Third French Antarctic Expedition (Jean-Baptiste Charcot, 1903–05); the British Antarctic Expedition (Ernest Shackleton, 1907–09); the Fourth French Antarctic Expedition (Charcot, 1908–10); the Japanese Antarctic Expedition (Nobu Shirase, 1910–12); the South Pole Expedition (Roald Amundsen, 1910–12); the British Antarctic Expedition (Scott, 1910–13); the Second

de Gerlache expedition achieved a deliberate first – the first sledging journey into the continent's interior – and an accidental one – the first overwinter, which became necessary after the expedition's ship became trapped in the ice of the Bellingshausen Sea. All nineteen men survived, although two went insane.

More misfortune and misery followed, but so did glory and achievement, culminating in the conquest of the South Pole in 1911. As they had been in the Arctic decades earlier, the British were the most determined participants, although they were once again denied the ultimate prize. In 1898, the magazine publisher Sir George Newnes funded an Anglo-Norwegian adventurer named Carsten Borchgrevink to overwinter at Cape Adare on the edge of the Ross Sea. Borchgrevink established a new farthest south, but his efforts were largely ignored by the British government and geographical establishment, as they were planning a larger-scale expedition. This became the British National Antarctic Expedition of 1901–04, led by the thirty-three-year-old naval officer Robert Falcon Scott.

Frequently referred to by the name of the purpose-built ship in which it sailed south, the *Discovery*, Scott's first expedition suffered from confusion over its objectives – scientific research or geographic discovery? – and methods of transport. 'Our ignorance was deplorable', wrote Scott in his published account.[2] Neither he nor any of his men had experienced living and working in a polar environment. The Royal Geographical Society's *Antarctic Manual* declared that 'a sandwich of frozen bear's blubber and biscuit is palatable enough', implying that polar bears inhabited Antarctica.[3] Their inexperience proved fatal when two men were lost in a blizzard and tumbled over the edge of a cliff. Even so, the southern journey began with high hopes, but the sledging party – Scott, the expedition's doctor Edward Wilson, and third officer Ernest Shackleton – discovered that Antarctic terrain was not smooth ice, but a series of ridges and crevasses. Scott's calculation of the calories needed to fuel the men was woefully inadequate. They struggled to 82° 17′ S, 482 km further south than anyone had ever been, but still 800 km from the Pole. Scott conceded that the result 'compares poorly with our hopes and expectations on leaving the ship'.[4]

German Antarctic Expedition (Wilhelm Filchner, 1911–13); the Australasian Antarctic Expedition (Douglas Mawson, 1911–14); the Imperial Trans-Antarctic Expedition (Shackleton, 1914–17); and the Shackleton–Rowett Expedition (Shackleton, 1921–22).
2 Scott, *Voyage of the Discovery*, Vol. I, 229.   3 Turney, 1912, 31.
4 Scott, *Voyage of the Discovery*, Vol. II, 87.

10 Heroic Age of Antarctic Exploration

The next few years saw the dispatch of German, Swedish, Scottish, and French expeditions, all of which concentrated on mapping and data collection. It was not until 1907 that Shackleton, determined to prove his mettle after having been invalided home from *Discovery*, resumed the quest for the Pole. Scott's sledging teams had not managed to use dogs successfully, but the failed southern journey proved that men could not drag their supplies over so great a distance. Shackleton therefore decided to use ponies. Accompanied by Boyd Adams, Eric Marshall, and Frank Wild, he set off on 29 October 1908. Because of their weight, the ponies sank deep into the snow, slowing their progress, but they pressed on, ascending the Transantarctic Mountains via a glacier that Shackleton named after his patron Sir William Beardmore. On the Polar Plateau, however, their food and endurance diminished rapidly. On 9 January 1909, they turned back at 88° 23′ S, 156 km from the Pole. Adams later wrote that 'if we'd gone on another hour, we shouldn't have got back'.[5]

Shackleton returned to a rapturous welcome. The Pole was now within reach, and it seemed likely that a Briton would get there first. Over the next two years, France and Japan dispatched scientific and geographical surveys, but the race for Antarctica's greatest prize was on. Scott announced his intention to try again, but he had a secret rival: the Norwegian explorer Roald Amundsen, who had served as first mate on de Gerlache's expedition and led the first expedition to sail through the Northwest Passage from 1903 to 1905. Amundsen had been planning to try for the North Pole, but after that was claimed in 1909 he turned his ambitions south. Thinking he had the field to himself, Scott departed in June 1911 on the *Terra Nova*. In Melbourne, he received Amundsen's terse telegram, 'Beg leave to inform you *Fram* proceeding Antarctic.'[6]

After an attempt in early September was abandoned because of bitterly cold temperatures, Amundsen set off again with four men and fifty-two dogs on 19 October. Covering an average of 37 km per day, they reached the Pole on 14 December and returned to their base on 26 January 1912, ten days ahead of schedule. 'We haven't got much to tell in the way of privation or great struggles,' Amundsen told the men who had remained at the base. 'The whole thing went like a dream.'[7]

Scott's southern journey began on 24 October 1911, five days after Amundsen's departure. Amundsen used the same five-man team, supported

---

5 Riffenburgh, *'Nimrod'*, 280.   6 Huntford, *Last Place on Earth*, 303.
7 Huntford, *Last Place on Earth*, 509.

by dogs, from start to finish, but Scott's complex plan utilized supporting parties, dogs, ponies, and untested motor-sledges. The last supporting party turned back with only 257 km to go, leaving the five-man team of Scott, Wilson, Lawrence Edward 'Titus' Oates, Henry Robertson 'Birdie' Bowers, and Edgar Evans with rations so abundant that they needed to average only 11 km a day. But on 16 January 1912, Bowers spotted a black flag fluttering in the wind which marked the remains of one of Amundsen's camps. The crestfallen men arrived at the Pole the next day.

The race to the Pole had been lost; the race was now, as Scott wrote, 'between the season and hard conditions and our fitness and good food'.[8] As their pace slowed, rations were stretched to the limit, and the weather was growing colder.[9] On 16 February, Evans collapsed in the snow and died in the tent that night. Oates struggled on for another month, but on 17 March, he told his companions, 'I am just going outside and may be some time.'[10] He walked out into the snow and was never seen again. Two days later, the three remaining men were trapped in their tent by a blizzard. On 29 March, Scott recorded the final entry in his diary: 'We shall stick it out to the end, but we are getting weaker, ... and the end cannot be far. It seems a pity, but I do not think I can write more.'[11]

Two years later, Shackleton decided to try again for polar glory. He planned to cross the Antarctic continent via the Pole from the Weddell Sea to the Ross Sea, covering a total of 2,400 km, with the first half of the journey over virtually unknown territory. The expedition departed on 1 August 1914, the day that Germany declared war on Russia. Whalers at the station at Grytviken on South Georgia Island warned Shackleton that it was one of the worst seasons on record for ice in the Weddell Sea, but he headed south nonetheless. They encountered their first pack ice 320 km north of where it was expected, but his ship, the *Endurance*, battered its way through. On 10 January 1915 they sighted Coats Land; the ship's captain Frank Worsley pressed Shackleton to land, but he refused, as it would add 320 km to the journey. Six days later, they were trapped in thick ice. They were only 96 km from land, but the intervening ice surface was covered by massive pressure ridges caused by the floes grinding against each other, rendering any effort to sledge across them futile.[12]

---

8 Scott, *Scott's Last Expedition*, 421.
9 For the deteriorating weather conditions that Scott faced on the return journey, see Solomon, *The Coldest March*.
10 Scott, *Scott's Last Expedition*, 430.   11 Scott, *Scott's Last Expedition*, 432.
12 Huntford, *Shackleton*, 378–379, 391, 399, 408–410.

Frustratingly, they were carried further from land every day, as the pack swirled around the Weddell Sea in a counter-clockwise direction. By June, they had drifted over 1,100 km from their original position and were now at the sea's far western edge, where the wind and current drove the pack against the peninsula of Graham Land. The *Endurance*'s v-shaped hull was intended to plough through loose ice floes rather than withstand the pressure of being trapped in the pack. The ship 'shrieks, groans and quivers in agony', wrote photographer Frank Hurley, 'but tighter and more relentless is the grip'.[13] On 27 October, after 281 days trapped in the ice, Shackleton gave the order to abandon ship; it sank a month later on 21 November. They were over 480 km from the nearest land, with nothing but unstable ice in between. Hoping to reach open water, they dragged the ship's boats, which weighed over a ton each, across the ice. After three days of back-breaking labour in which they covered less than 3 km in total, Shackleton ordered a halt. They would camp instead, hoping that the ice would break up and allow them to take to the boats. By late March 1916, the mountains of Graham Land were visible in the distance, but the ice remained stubbornly intact. Now their only hope was to reach Clarence or Elephant Island, 193 km to the north.

Finally, the ice began to crack, and Shackleton gave the order to launch the boats on 9 April 1916. After three days of picking their way through floes and bergs, the weather cleared sufficiently for Worsley to take a navigational reading. The result was disheartening: because of a strong easterly current, they were 35 km *further* from Clarence Island than they had been when they had started. A shift in the wind allowed them to make better progress, and after a week at sea they reached Elephant Island, the first land they had set foot on for 497 days. They camped on a strip of beach 182 m long and 27 m deep; 365 m cliffs blocked them from moving further into the island's interior. Food, in the form of penguins and seals, was relatively abundant, but there was little hope of rescue, as Elephant Island had not been visited in over a century. Eight days after they arrived, Shackleton, Worsley, and three other men set sail in the largest and sturdiest of the boats, the *James Caird*, for South Georgia Island, 1,287 km to the northeast.

The journey took them across the Drake Passage, which is in the only latitude on Earth where there is no land, so that massive waves sweep unimpeded around the globe. During the seventeen-day voyage, Worsley could only take four navigational readings owing to overcast skies. Battling sixty-knot winds, they constantly bailed water and chipped ice from the hull.

13 Hurley, *Diaries*, 29.

On 8 May, they sighted South Georgia and managed to slip through a narrow passage between the rocks that surround the island. They then traversed South Georgia's mountainous interior to Grytviken. After several failed attempts, Shackleton returned to Elephant Island in August 1916 and rescued the other men.[14]

The Evolution of Heroic Age Mythology

The above account focuses on the 'Big Three' figures of the Heroic Age – Scott, Amundsen, and Shackleton – but it would look much the same if lesser-known figures were incorporated. From 1911 to 1914, the Australian explorer Douglas Mawson led the Australasian Antarctic Expedition, the primary focus of which was a sledging journey by Mawson and two companions to the unexplored coastal territory around Cape Adare. On the way back, Belgrave Edward Ninnis fell into a crevasse and Xavier Mertz succumbed to an unknown illness (probably an overdose of Vitamin A resulting from eating the livers of their sledge dogs), leaving Mawson to complete the final 160 km alone. It was a remarkable feat, and after his return home, he became an Australian national hero: schools, streets, and even entire towns were named after him.[15]

Mawson's story is another version of the standard narrative of the Heroic Age, dominated by the exploits of individual explorers and the perspective of the Anglophone world. It is not neutral or objective, but instead reflects the predilections and prejudices of the time in which it was created.[16] Francis Spufford terms it a 'deliberately cultivated myth', while Rebecca Farley defines it as a 'narrative of adventure'.[17] The story was largely fashioned by the explorers themselves, as their diaries and published accounts served as its main sources; their priorities therefore shaped public perception.[18] But even as they were being written, these diaries and accounts were influenced by considerations as to how they would be received by contemporary audiences and by posterity. Prior to publication, anything that might cast the expedition

---

14 Three men died from the team which had been sent to the other side of Antarctica in order to lay supply depots for Shackleton and his men.
15 See Roberts, *Alone on the Ice*.
16 The argument that Antarctica represents a blank screen onto which humanity can project whatever values it chooses has been challenged by Elena Glasberg in *Antarctica as Cultural Critique*, ch. 5. It is, however, capable of producing a diverse range of mythological interpretations. See Roberts, "White (Supremacist) Continent".
17 Spufford, *I May Be Some Time*, 101; Farley, "'By Endurance We Conquer'", 235. As an example of this kind of narrative, see Larson, *Empire of Ice*.
18 'The expedition diary has been integral to histories of early twentieth century Antarctic exploration, both received and revisionist.' Leane, "Antarctic Diaries", 28.

in a negative light was removed.[19] Using these diaries as the most important record, the press presented the story of Antarctic exploration to an eager public. By the end of the nineteenth century

> the relationship between newspapers and explorers required more than ever that new lands be portrayed as tests for daring individuals who were willing to risk their lives to make gains for science, the flag, or mankind ... A demand developed for triumph over obstacles, and the greater the difficulty, the more the danger, the longer and harder the journey, the better the public liked it.[20]

Although the 'narrative of adventure' remained central to perceptions of the Heroic Age, over time other narratives emerged alongside it in collective memory. First came a 'narrative of tragedy', which lasted through World War II and which focused primarily on the deaths of Scott and his four companions. From the 1960s onwards, a more censorious view questioned the competency of some explorers, with Scott again taking the leading role. This 'narrative of incompetence' initially took an iconoclastic and comedic approach (e.g., Monty Python's famous 'Scott of the Antarctic' sketch in 1970), but as time went on it took more serious form, most obviously in Roland Huntford's dual biography *Scott and Amundsen* (1979).[21]

These attacks on the reputations of polar explorers were in keeping with a broader shift away from the celebration of conventional imperial and military heroes in post-1945 Western culture. This trend was particularly pronounced in a rapidly decolonizing Britain, where 'the metropolitan state's investment in imperial heroes through education, ceremonial and public monuments diminished after 1945'.[22] Antarctic explorers were better suited to survive in this altered cultural context than explorers of other parts of the world, since Antarctica had never been formally colonized and had no Indigenous population. Moreover, unlike Britain's former colonies, Antarctica remained 'a significant arena for British power projection'.[23] At the same time, the United States, reeling from the Vietnam War, the Iran Hostage crisis, and a sense that

---

19 'The ... desire to produce accurate and faithful accounts of exploration inevitably gave the explorers themselves a decisive role in determining which historical narratives became dominant, and what values ought to be encoded within them.' Roberts et al., "Antarctica: A Continent", 5–6.
20 Ryan, *Cartographic Eye*, 56. See Driver, *Geography Militant*; Riffenburgh, *Myth of the Explorer*.
21 David Day challenged Douglas Mawson's heroic reputation in *Flaws in the Ice* (2013), in which Day accused Mawson of deliberately starving Xavier Mertz to death in order to save himself.
22 Jones et al., "Introduction", 802. See also Roberts, "Heroes".
23 Jones, "'Truth about Captain Scott'", 857.

its global power was slipping, required new forms of heroism as well. What emerged as the main post-colonial narrative of the Heroic Age was a 'narrative of survival', in which the race for the Pole retreated further into the background, and a safe return became the gauge of leadership and success. The emergence of this new narrative was most obvious in the surge in popularity of Shackleton's *Endurance* expedition, which began with a blockbuster exhibition at the Natural History Museum in New York City in 1999. In the years that followed, Shackleton became the focus of numerous books, two IMAX films, and a British television miniseries. The essence of this narrative, with its emphasis on survival against obstacles and challenges, was no coincidence, as it suited two formerly powerful nations now worried about their global status.

I have written elsewhere about the evolution of Heroic Age narratives over time.[24] What is most relevant to point out in this context, however, is that these narratives are *stories*. This does not mean that they are completely fictional, for they contain elements of truth, but they have been shaped by their creators and their audiences to fit the times in which they appeared. The 'adventure' narrative was created by the explorers themselves, in order to emphasize their achievements and to ensure that their published accounts were profitable. The 'narrative of tragedy' came to dominate accounts of the Heroic Age between World War I and the 1960s because it made death meaningful and therefore consolatory in an era in which tens of millions of people suffered bereavement resulting from violent conflict. The 'narrative of incompetence' emerged in the 1960s, an iconoclastic and counter-cultural age when traditional forms of heroism came to be viewed more cynically. The 'narrative of survival' developed in an anxious post-colonial Britain and post-Vietnam America, in an attempt to extract reassurance from old stories of individual and national greatness.

These changes have kept the Heroic Age relevant to new audiences.[25] They have taken shape, however, in a context of changing attitudes towards empire, once seen as a source of national prestige in Western nations but now more often viewed as racist, brutally violent, politically oppressive, and morally indefensible.[26] The leading figures of the Heroic Age maintain a presence in collective memory – albeit not entirely unscathed, as the decline in Scott's

---

24 Barczewski, *Antarctic Destinies*.
25 'Narratives of imperial heroism have proved surprisingly flexible, reconfigured under a range of pressures not only in the metropole but also in former colonies.' Jones et al., "Introduction", 802.
26 The literature on violence and empire is large and growing. See Bailkin, "Boot and Spleen"; Gott, *Britain's Empire*; Kolsky, *Colonial Justice*; Sherman, *State Violence*; Tharoor, *Inglorious Empire*.

reputation illustrates – but the exclusively white male figures of that era are increasingly ill-suited to contemporary tastes, which demand a more diverse range of heroes.

Indeed, the emergence of the 'narrative of survival', although it provided a temporary respite, threatens to exacerbate the problems faced by Heroic Age heroes. Its dominant figure, Shackleton, has been recast as an aggressively masculine hero, in contrast to the 'effeminization' of Scott that has taken place since the 1960s. As Max Jones and I have both described elsewhere, the attacks on Scott's reputation have raised questions about his masculinity and sexuality. Both Huntford and Trevor Griffiths in his television adaptation *The Last Place on Earth* (ITV, 1985) depict Scott as dominated by his wife Kathleen, and Griffiths hints that he had difficulty consummating his marriage. Huntford implies that Scott chose Edgar Evans as a member of the party which made the final push to the Pole because he 'seemed infatuated by Evans' crude working-class animal muscularity'; in his screenplay – the notes of which refer to Scott's 'Nancy Boy qualities' – Griffiths also suggests that Scott admired Evans' muscular physique.[27]

Jones argues that Huntford and Griffiths portray Scott in this way because it suited their different political agendas.[28] The conservative Huntford endorsed the Thatcherite view of post-Suez British 'declinism', in which national decline was interpreted as a failure of will rather than the result of anti-colonial nationalism, increased economic competition, and the emergence of the United States and the Soviet Union (and later China) as global superpowers. He asserted that the celebration of Scott's failure was a symptom of the national malaise that Thatcher sought to eradicate. The Marxist Griffiths, in contrast, saw Scott's heroic reputation as an expression of Britain's longstanding tendency to embrace jingoistic nationalism, a tendency that was very apparent after the Falklands War in 1982. In a deliberate reference to Thatcher's declaration of victory in the Falklands, Griffiths sarcastically titled the final episode of *The Last Place on Earth* 'Rejoice!'[29]

Prior to the 1990s, Shackleton had not enjoyed nearly as lofty a reputation as Scott. Because the *Endurance* expedition took place during World War I, it did not have the same resonance as Scott's tragic death at a time when so many

---

27 Huntford, *Last Place on Earth*, 315.; Jones, '"Truth about Captain Scott"', p. 869. I find the use of such methods to undermine the status of a hero odious and archaic.
28 Jones, '"Truth about Captain Scott"', 867–869.
29 In an interview included in the print edition of the screenplay, Griffiths characterized both Scott's attempt on the Pole and the Falklands conflict as 'crazed, impossible, vainglorious' ventures. Griffiths, *Judgement over the Dead*, xxxi–xxxii.

people were looking for solace; death was the dominant cultural motif, not survival. 'Fancy that ridiculous Shackleton & his South Pole – in the crash of the world,' huffed Winston Churchill to his wife in 1916.[30] A century later, however, Shackleton had eclipsed Scott as the leading Antarctic hero in both Britain and the United States. His enhanced reputation resulted from a rejection of declinism in Britain during the Thatcher years and America's recovery from the trauma and divisiveness of the Vietnam War during the Reagan years. It was also, however, the product on both sides of the Atlantic of a 'crisis of masculinity', in which white male hegemony was perceived as being under threat due to a decline in industrial employment, an increasing number of non-white immigrants, and government policies intended to increase diversity in the workplace.[31] In this context, Shackleton was presented as a model for aspiring CEOs in the hyper-masculine corporate culture of the era.[32]

Seen in this light, the post-1990 version of Shackleton-as-hero contrasts with the post-1960 version of Scott-as-debunked-hero.[33] On the one hand, Shackleton's rise shows that explorer heroes were not condemned to irrelevance by the end of empire, but instead could be re-imagined for a postcolonial age. But on the other, it represented only a temporary respite from the shortcomings of traditional Antarctic heroism in present-day context. Shackleton's reconstruction as a conventionally masculine hero suited two nations undergoing crises of national confidence. His newfound heroic status emerged from the same cultural impulses that led to the installation of the National World War II Memorial in Washington in 2004 and the RAF Bomber Command Memorial in London in 2012. These two self-consciously patriotic memorials were deliberately intended as rebuttals of the more modern style of war memorial exemplified by Maya Lin's Vietnam Veterans Memorial in Washington, with its stark and sombre list of the dead. But to many observers, their overt nationalism seemed excessively bombastic.[34]

Defining New Forms of Antarctic Heroism

In recent years, traditional forms of heroism have been strongly criticized. The reputations not only of imperial conquerors, slave traders, and generals

---

30 Huntford, *Shackleton*, 488.
31 Farley, "'By Endurance We Conquer'", 246. See also DiPiero, *White Men Aren't*.
32 Morrell and Capparell, *Shackleton's Way*; Koehn et al., "Leadership in Crisis".
33 For the evolution of Mawson's reputation, see Hains, *Ice and Inland*; and Collis, "Mawson's Hut".
34 For a survey of the changing meaning of World War II memorials, see Lowe, *Prisoners of History*.

who fought for the Confederacy in the American Civil War, but also of 'great men' such as Winston Churchill and George Washington are now questioned. Explorers, including Captain James Cook and David Livingstone, have been specifically targeted because of their implicit support for colonialism. Although they have managed to avoid that sort of reputational revisionism, Antarctic heroes are also in danger of being condemned to obsolescence in a culture that increasingly celebrates a more diverse range of values. There has been discussion, for example, of removing the statue of Scott in Christchurch, New Zealand, because of objections – emanating primarily from the Māori community – that he was part of 'a colonising activity'.[35] Even if Antarctic history does not need to be – and perhaps cannot be – entirely 'decolonized', it thus may need to evolve further from its conventional form in order to ensure its continuing cultural relevance and appeal.

How, then, can traditional narratives of the Heroic Age be changed better to reflect current views? In the first place, these narratives are almost entirely about white men.[36] As the authors of a study of women's participation in Antarctic research wrote in 2019, Antarctica has traditionally been 'a site for heroic masculinity and leadership by men'.[37] The conventional method of overcoming male dominance of historical writing has been to write alternative versions that emphasize women's contributions.[38] Women, however, were not included in Antarctic expeditions until very recently, so there is no possibility of arguing that they were present but hidden, waiting to be rediscovered by historians willing to identify their faint traces in the archives.

There are, to be sure, a few examples of an early female presence in the Antarctic. Māori oral tradition suggests that women accompanied the Polynesian navigators Ui-te-Rangiora and Te Ara-tanga-nuku on their voyages in the Southern Ocean around 650 and 1000 AD respectively.[39] In the late 1760s, Jeanne Baret renamed herself 'Jean' and donned sailor's clothing in order to serve as an assistant to her lover Philibert Commerçon on Louis

---

35 www.stuff.co.nz/national/300033885/christchurch-statues-staying-put-despite-low-regard-from-local-iwi (accessed 17 April 2021).
36 Bloom, *Gender on Ice*; Collis, "Australian Antarctic Territory".
37 Nash et al., "'Antarctica'". An extreme example of this conception of Antarctica was the myth that the Nazis had established a secret base there to which Hitler fled after 1945. Peder Roberts writes, 'The idealized image of the Nazi regime – characterized by discipline, violent conquest, hyper-masculinization, technology and a fetishization of purity – could be distilled into a cultural essence suited to Antarctica.' Roberts, 'White (Supremacist) Continent', 117. See also Godwin, *Arktos*; Summerhayes and Beeching, "Hitler's Antarctic Base"; Summerhayes and Lüdecke, *Third Reich in Antarctica*.
38 Burns, *Just Tell Them*; Chipman, *Women on the Ice*; Land, *New Explorers*.
39 Dodds and Yusoff, "Settlement and Unsettlement".

Antoine de Bougainville's circumnavigation, which reached sub-Antarctic waters. Louise Seguin also disguised herself as a man in order to accompany her lover Captain Yves-Joseph de Kerguelen-Trémarec on his voyage into the southern Indian Ocean in 1772.[40] But these cases were exceptional and caused considerable consternation when they were discovered. Baret was subjected to a strip search in Papua New Guinea, and the discovery of Seguin's sex was one cause of Kerguelen's court-martial in 1776. The only other women in the Antarctic before World War II were the wives and female relatives who accompanied sealers and whalers. In 1935, Caroline Mikkelsen, the wife of a Norwegian sealing captain, became the first woman known to have set foot on the Antarctic continent.

These women were companions, not true Antarctic researchers, and none of them were involved in the expeditions of the Heroic Age. In 1914, three self-described 'strong, healthy girls' applied to join Shackleton's *Endurance* expedition, and five years later seven women applied to join John Lachlan Cope's expedition to Graham Land.[41] All were rejected.[42] The history of women in the Antarctic as something other than subordinates to men did not begin until 1956, when Maria Klenova joined a Soviet research expedition as a marine geologist. She was followed by female scientists from South Africa, Australia, Argentina, and the United States.[43] It was not until 1983 that the British Antarctic Survey permitted a woman to join a field programme.[44]

There was one way, however, in which women played a key role in the history of the Heroic Age. By the late nineteenth century, scientific and geographical societies faced pressure to admit women to their ranks, and in 1892 the RGS decided to allow twenty-two new female fellows. But when some of the male fellows objected, the decision was reversed the following year, though the already-admitted female fellows were grudgingly permitted to remain. Lord Curzon, who later became president of the RGS, wrote, 'We contest *in toto* the general capability of women to contribute to scientific geographic knowledge. Their sex and training render them equally unfitted for exploration; and the genus of professional female globe-trotters with which America has lately familiarized us is one of the horrors of the

---

40 Hulbe et al., "Women in Glaciology".
41 www.spri.cam.ac.uk/archives/shackleton/articles/1537,2,30,5-6.html (accessed 2 November 2020); Blackadder, "Frozen Voices", p. 171.
42 'On a physical level women were actively – in fact, strenuously – excluded from Antarctica in the first century of its history.' Blackadder, "Frozen Voices", 170.
43 The American military lifted the ban on women working in Antarctica in 1969.
44 Seag, "Women Need Not Apply", 319.

latter end of the nineteenth century.'⁴⁵ It was not until 1913 that women were once again admitted as fellows.

As a result, when the RGS elected a new president in 1893, a candidate who was broadly acceptable to both sides of the debate was required. The choice was Clements Markham, who as his first task sought to identify a project that would heal the bitter divisions caused by what he termed 'the Lady problem'. He later wrote to Curzon, 'You well remember the trouble about the admission of females ... I believed, rightly or wrongly, that the only way to restore the Society's credit was to undertake some great enterprise in the cause of geography.'⁴⁶ For this 'great enterprise', Markham chose Antarctica, and began formulating plans for what became the *Discovery* expedition. Women therefore played an important but indirect role in initiating the Heroic Age, which is one way of writing them into its history.

The story is similar for non-white people. Farley has written of how the literature of exploration contributes to a 'construction of hegemonic whiteness' which 'served the imperialist project'.⁴⁷ The absence of non-white persons from its best-known expeditions makes this interpretation applicable to the Heroic Age. There was at least one non-white participant in Antarctic exploration in the nineteenth century: in 1840 Te Atu (John Sac), whose mother was Māori, accompanied Charles Wilkes's United States Exploring Expedition as an interpreter.⁴⁸ So far as is known, the first non-white person to set foot on the Antarctic continent was Louis Potaka, a Māori doctor who served on Richard Byrd's second Antarctic expedition in 1934.⁴⁹ Next came George Washington Gibbs Jr, a mess attendant on Byrd's third expedition in 1939–40.⁵⁰ Gibbs's story confirms the existence of systemic racism in Antarctic exploration. He joined the American Navy as a mess attendant because it was the only position open to African Americans at the time, and was soon frustrated by the lack of opportunity for advancement. A month after he made that historic first step, he wrote in his diary:

> Was up at five-thirty this morning, as usual, to begin my daily routine as a mess attendant, which is monotonous, I am doing the same thing every day and at times I think I will go nuts, especially when I think about my race being limited to one branch of services, regardless of the many qualifications that members of my race have.

---

45 Turney, *1912*, 24.   46 Turney, *1912*, 27.   47 Farley, "'By Endurance We Conquer'", 236.
48 van der Watt and Swart, "The Whiteness of Antarctica", 151, n53.
49 van der Watt and Swart, "The Whiteness of Antarctica", 137.
50 Uenuma, "George Washington Gibbs Jr.".

Although he earned two citations for meritorious conduct on the expedition, he complained that the racism of his fellow servicemen 'at times make this cruise very hard for me'.[51] In 1948, Joseph Daniels, a black stevedore from Cape Town, sailed south on a naval voyage to claim Marion Island for South Africa. Daniels's experience was also shaped by institutional racism, in his case with fatal consequences: he drowned when a wave overturned a boat which was being used to ferry supplies ashore. His death, writes Lance van Sittert, was no accident, but rather the result of seeing 'black labour as expendable'.[52] The identity of the first black European to visit Antarctica, meanwhile, is unknown.[53]

A potential challenge to an exclusively white European narrative of the Heroic Age is posed by the Japanese Antarctic Expedition of 1910–12. Its leader, Nobu Shirase, wanted to prove that Japan was equal to its European rivals. 'The powers of the world ridicule the Empire of Japan,' he wrote in 1910 in a letter imploring the Japanese government to back his efforts, 'saying we Japanese are barbarians who are strong and brave in warfare, but timid and cowardly when it comes to the realm of science.'[54] But the government was not convinced, and Shirase was forced to seek private funding, resulting in a late start which prevented the expedition from reaching Antarctica in its first season. With the Pole now out of reach, he scaled back his plans and carried out a quick 'Dash Patrol' south and a survey of King Edward VII Land. Shirase was initially acclaimed in Japan, because his expedition was seen as confirming that the Japanese were equal to Europeans in their physical hardiness. The militarism and nationalism associated with the final years of the Meiji Restoration became more controversial over time, however, and Shirase faded into obscurity well before he died in 1946. In the West, Shirase's expedition, if it was noted at all, met with derision and relief that it had not accomplished more, as his efforts aroused suspicions of Japanese imperialist intentions in Antarctica. The Japanese expedition can thus be seen as the exception that proves the rule of a white European-dominated conception of the Heroic Age.[55]

51 In 2009, the US Board on Geographic Names designated as 'Gibbs Point' the northwest corner of Gaul Cove, located on Horseshoe Island off the west coast of Graham Land.
52 van Sittert, "'Ironman'", 509.
53 Today, less than 3 per cent of people working in polar science in the United Kingdom come from a BAME (Black, Asian, and Minority Ethnic) background, https://britishantarcticterritory.org.uk/blog-diversity-in-polar-science/ (accessed 19 May 2020).
54 Turney, 1912, 146.
55 For the complexity of Shirase's reception in Australia, see Howitt, "Japanese Antarctic Expedition".

The Heroic Age and the Modern Ideal of Antarctica as a 'Land of Science'

A further difficulty with the conventional history of the Heroic Age in the present day is its strongly nationalistic character.[56] The surging nationalism of pre-World War I Europe spread to Antarctica, where countries eagerly seized territory, much as they had previously done in Africa.[57] In 1908, Britain claimed South Georgia Island, the South Sandwich Islands, the South Orkney Islands, the South Shetland Islands, and Graham Land on the Antarctic Peninsula. When Edgeworth David, a member of Shackleton's *Nimrod* expedition, led a sledging foray to determine the location of the South Magnetic Pole in 1909, he declared, 'I hereby take possession of this area now containing the Magnetic Pole for the British Empire.'[58] Mawson raised funds for his expedition by promising to claim territory for the British Empire. During the inter-war years, British ambitions expanded; Leo Amery, Colonial Secretary from 1924 to 1929, wanted to incorporate the entire continent into the British Empire.[59] Nor were such impulses limited to explorers from Britain and its colonies. Shirase's 'Dash Patrol' claimed the vicinity of their furthest south for Japan and named it the 'Japanese Snow Field'.[60] By the late 1940s, spurred by the possibility of uranium deposits, seven countries (Argentina, Australia, Chile, France, New Zealand, Norway, and the United Kingdom) had made territorial claims in Antarctica. Of particular international concern was the potential for the Cold War to turn Antarctica into a zone of conflict between the United States and the Soviet Union. In 1946, the American military launched Operation Highjump, a training exercise intended to test men and materiel in extreme cold.

It was acknowledged at the time that the race to the Pole had become a contest among nations. The Scottish naturalist William Spiers Bruce was

---

56 Elena Glasberg refers to the race for the South Pole as 'the crowning achievement of western nationalism'. Glasberg, "Last Place on Earth", 65.
57 'When the rival Norwegian and British parties ... raced to the geographic South Pole in 1911, they epitomized an early-twentieth-century phenomenon that cannot be understood without reference to the bloom of European nationalisms.' Roberts, *European Antarctic*, 1.
58 Turney, *1912*, 59.
59 Roberts et al., "Antarctica: A Continent", 3. See also Beck, "Securing the Dominant 'Place'".
60 These territorial claims confirm Roger Launius's observation that 'the poles have repeatedly served as vehicle by which to focus national aspirations; competition among international rivals played out in these settings'. Launius, "Toward the Poles", 57. For Arctic exploration and its relationship to American national identity, see Robinson, *Coldest Crucible*.

invited to join Scott's *Discovery* expedition in 1899, but turned it down because he was planning his own expedition, which he pointedly referred to as 'Scottish'. Markham urged him to abandon such 'mischievous rivalry', but Bruce nonetheless went south on his own in 1902.[61] Coverage of his expedition in the English and Scottish press followed these nationalist lines. The English press barely credited Bruce's expedition for its impressive scientific achievements, but in Scotland he 'came to represent ... a particular facet of the Scottish character – self-reliant, resolute, dedicated and, crucially, independent of the authorities of London'.[62]

English explorers were not immune from such nationalism, though they tended to project it internationally rather than within Britain. After Shackleton came close to reaching the Pole, Scott declared, 'In whatever measure that remaining distance is computed, it is for England to cover it.'[63] After his accomplishment was only grudgingly recognized in Britain, Amundsen wrote in his memoir in 1928 that 'the British are a race of very bad losers'.[64] Wilhelm Filchner, the leader of the Second German Antarctic Expedition, were seen as a failure in his home country because, although he discovered the southern limit of the Weddell Sea and collected important scientific data, he did not achieve the success of his British and Norwegian counterparts.[65]

Such attitudes sit uneasily with the post-1945 conception of Antarctica as a site of international scientific cooperation. Proposed by the United States in 1959 in order to curb Soviet ambition, the Antarctic Treaty System reserved the continent as a site of international scientific research and prohibited military activities there. Today, although national competition certainly persists, Antarctica's place as a site of global scientific cooperation is more significant than ever.[66] Glasberg writes:

> The ice ... is under threat. It is no longer the enemy or the implacable outside force to be conquered. Nor is it an uncomplicated pure wilderness. It is no longer ... a blank backdrop for imperial posturing. Rather, the ice is fragile, melting, ever shifting – in need of rescue ... Especially as a sentimental object of anthropocentric panic – the ice is melting and we're all going to die! – Antarctica's ruin now prefigures and announces a more universal ruin.[67]

61 Turney, 1912, 31.   62 Keighren, "Poles, Pressmen", 215.   63 Turney, 1912, 70.
64 Turney, 1912, 142.   65 Murphy, *German Exploration*.
66 'Unlike the rest of the world, with its complicated relations between people and nature, Antarctica is governed by an enlightened political order that acts both through and for science.' Roberts et al., "Antarctica: A Continent", 2.
67 Glasberg, "'Living Ice'", p. 222.

But if the conventional history of the Heroic Age does not fit such an internationalist view, the potential exists to reconceive it yet again. Peder Roberts, Adrian Howkins, and Lize-Marié van der Watt write:

> Antarctica's present-day status as a continent for science and peace is merely the latest in a series of frames for understanding what kind of space Antarctica is – and what kind of space it ought to be ... To assume that the status quo of today is an ideal state rather than the consensus of a particular historical moment ... is to mistake the contingent for the necessary.[68]

A sense of the need for international cooperation in polar research existed long before the late twentieth century. The search for the Northwest Passage was 'sometimes coordinated' among the interested nations, and the first International Polar Year was held in 1882–83.[69] The 'Magnetic Crusade' of the nineteenth century was another example of 'a cooperative endeavour' in polar exploration.[70]

International cooperation was, however, rarer in the Antarctic than in the Arctic. There, 'nationalism dominated the scientific efforts ... from the beginning', as the competition for geographical prizes served as the main motivator for expeditions, not scientific cooperation.[71] Even so, the expeditions of the Heroic Age were not entirely lacking in global perspectives. The Shirase expedition took place at a time when Japan sought entry into the international scientific community. The Japanese government's reluctance to support Shirase stemmed not from isolationism, but rather from a sense that his lack of scientific expertise might embarrass his country on the global stage.[72] The British expeditions of the Heroic Age shared this mix of nationalist and internationalist motives. Max Jones has argued that the conventional view of Scott's last expedition as another entry in the nationalist and imperialist race to the Pole fundamentally misunderstands both Scott's own objectives and how the expedition was perceived in its time. Scott's scientific goals were real and not merely intended to conceal his ambition to reach the Pole first.[73] After his death, the British public viewed him as a 'martyr to science', and the global scientific and geographical community flooded the RGS with

---

68 Roberts et al., "Antarctica: A Continent", 3.
69 Launius, "Toward the Poles", 53; Cronenwett, "Publishing Arctic Science".
70 Launius, "Toward the Poles", 57. See also Carter, "Going Global".
71 Launius, "Toward the Poles", 61. See also Elzinga, "Antarctica"; Elzinga and Bohlin, "Politics of Science"; Headland, "Antarctic Odyssey".
72 Stevenson, "Polar Years and Japan", 127.   73 Jones, *Last Great Quest*, 9.

condolences.[74] A prominent strand of the criticism of Amundsen in Britain was that he had not attempted to carry out a serious programme of scientific research, but instead had merely dashed to the Pole. Some of this was undoubtedly sour grapes, but it nonetheless reveals that Antarctic expeditions were expected to contribute to global scientific knowledge. Mawson turned down Scott's offer to join the *Terra Nova* expedition because he was not interested in trying for the Pole, but rather wanted to investigate whether there had once been a land-bridge linking Antarctica to Australia.[75] John King Davis, the captain of Mawson's ship *Aurora*, wrote to William Spiers Bruce of his irritation that the race to the Pole was serving as a distraction from more important scientific tasks: 'If Scott or Amundsen reach the Pole, people will perhaps realise that nothing much can be learnt from this sort of thing and be more willing to help really useful work.'[76] Shackleton was not as highly regarded in his own time as he is today in part because he was seen as a 'trophy-bagger' rather than a man of science.

Placing these points in global context, Chris Turney reminds us that during the Heroic Age:

> A frozen continent shaped by climatic extremes, and inhabited by wildlife and vegetation hitherto unknown to science, was uncovered. Feats of endurance, self-sacrifice and technological innovation laid the foundations for contemporary scientific exploration. Regaled with tales of derring-do, the public became excited by what was being discovered in Antarctica ... The blend of research and exploration was a high point in science communication, as the different Antarctic teams strove to enthrall and educate those at home. Over the following decades, though, the tragic events of the era came to overshadow the amazing work accomplished, and much of this work was forgotten outside the small Antarctic scientific community.[77]

This is not to argue that that the 'true' Antarctica is a 'land of science' whereas the 'heroic' Antarctic is a land of myth, but rather to point out that many narratives about the Heroic Age are available to historians. Peder Roberts observes that the idea of Antarctica as a peaceful space where scientific interests predominate

---

74 Jones, *Last Great Quest*, ch. 5.
75 Mawson 'created a niche for his 1911–1914 expedition by depicting it as more scientific than Scott's through its disavowal of the geographic South Pole as a goal. The expedition was best remembered for Mawson's own remarkable survival after a sledging journey went catastrophically wrong, but this did not diminish his success in portraying himself as a serious scientific figure.' Roberts et al., "Antarctica: A Continent", 9.
76 Turney, *1912*, 232.   77 Turney, *1912*, 5.

rests on this notion that science is an almost transcendently benevolent force, an enlightened alternative to mineral prospecting or military fortification – even though the near-hegemony of science over engagement with today's Antarctic is itself a product of the social, political and economic forces that shaped the rest of the modern world.[78]

The conventional version of Heroic Age history, which not only offers compelling stories but reminders of the way that man and nature have interacted in one of the most challenging environments on Earth, may be combined with our contemporary interest in climate science to create a new, anthropocentric history that is very relevant to our present age. It will also help to de-romanticize our present-day conceptions of Antarctica and remind us that political motivations remain very significant.

Ample scope therefore exists for re-envisioning the conventional narrative of the Heroic Age in ways that would reduce its dependence on white male heroes and national rivalry.[79] Pre-World War II narratives of Antarctic history have tended to emphasize the human presence, whereas post-war narratives have tended to emphasize scientific research. A new narrative would combine the human and scientific histories of the Antarctic in a way that would tell the story of the Heroic Age more accurately and make it relevant for a new audience, who will be looking to Antarctica for answers to vital questions about the environmental challenges now facing humanity.

Bibliography

Bailkin, Jordanna, "The Boot and the Spleen: When Was Murder Possible in British India?", *Comparative Studies in Society and History* 48 (2006): 462–493.

Barczewski, Stephanie, *Antarctic Destinies: Scott, Shackleton and the Changing Face of Heroism* (London: Continuum, 2008).

Beck, Peter, "Securing the Dominant 'Place in the Wan Antarctic Sun' for the British Empire: The Policy of Extending British Control over Antarctica", *Australian Journal of Politics and History* 29 (1983): 448–461.

Blackadder, Jesse, "Frozen Voices: Women, Silence and Antarctica", in Bernadette Hince, Rupert Summerson, and Arnan Wiesel, eds., *Antarctica: Music, Sounds and Cultural Connections* (Acton: ANU Press, 2015), pp. 168–178.

Bloom, Lisa, *Gender on Ice: American Ideologies of Polar Expeditions* (Minneapolis: University of Minnesota Press, 1993).

Burns, Robin, *Just Tell Them I Survived! Women in Antarctica* (Crow's Nest, New South Wales: Allen & Unwin, 2001).

---

78 Roberts, *European Antarctic*, 2–3.   79 Howkins, "Emerging from the Shadow".

Carter, Christopher, "Going Global in Polar Exploration: Ninteenth-Century American and British Nationalism and Peacetime Science", in Roger D. Launius, James Rodger Fleming, and David H. DeVorkin, eds., *Globalizing Polar Science: Reconsidering the International Polar and Geophysical Years* (New York: Palgrave Macmillan, 2010), pp. 85–105.

Chipman, Elizabeth, *Women on the Ice: A History of Women in the Far South* (Melbourne: Melbourne University Press, 1987).

Collis, Christy, "The Australian Antarctic Territory: A Man's World?", *Signs* 34 (2009): 514–519.

Collis, Christy, "Mawson's Hut: Emptying Post-colonial Antarctica", *Journal of Australian Studies* 23 (1999): 22–29.

Cronenwett, Philip N., "Publishing Arctic Science in the Nineteenth Century: The Case of the First International Polar Year", in Roger D. Launius, James Rodger Fleming, and David H. DeVorkin, eds., *Globalizing Polar Science: Reconsidering the International Polar and Geophysical Years* (New York: Palgrave Macmillan, 2010), pp. 37–46.

Day, David, *Flaws in the Ice: In Search of Douglas Mawson* (Melbourne: Scribe, 2013).

DiPiero, Thomas, *White Men Aren't* (Durham, NC: Duke University Press, 2002).

Dodds, Klaus J., and Kathryn Yusoff, "Settlement and Unsettlement in Autearoa/New Zealand and Antarctica", *Polar Record* 41 (2005): 141–155.

Driver, Felix, *Geography Militant: Cultures of Exploration and Empire* (Oxford: Blackwell, 2001).

Elzinga, Aant, "Antarctica: The Construction of a Continent by and for Science", in Elisabeth Crawford, Terry Shinn, and Sverker Sörlin, eds., *Denationalizing Science* (Berlin: Springer, 1993), pp. 73–106.

Elzinga, Aant, and Ingemar Bohlin, "The Politics of Science in Polar Regions", in Aant Elzinga, ed., *Changing Trends in Antarctic Research* (Dordrecht: Kluwer, 1993), pp. 7–27.

Farley, Rebecca, "'By Endurance We Conquer': Ernest Shackleton and Performances of White Male Hegemony", *International Journal of Cultural Studies* 8 (2005): 231–254.

Glasberg, Elena, *Antarctica as Cultural Critique: The Gendered Politics of Scientific Exploration and Climate Change* (New York: Palgrave Macmillan, 2012).

Glasberg, Elena, "The Last Place on Earth: Antarctica and Virtual Capitalism", *Political and Legal Anthropology Review* 21 (1998): 65–76.

Glasberg, Elena, "'Living Ice': Rediscovery of the Poles in an Era of Climate Crisis", *Women's Studies Quarterly* 39 (2011): 221–246.

Godwin, Joscelyn, *Arktos: The Polar Myth in Science, Symbolism and Nazi Survival* (London: Thames and Hudson, 1993).

Gott, Richard, *Britain's Empire: Resistance, Repression and Revolt* (London: Verso, 2012).

Griffiths, Trevor, *Judgement over the Dead: The Screenplay to The Last Place on Earth* (London: Verso, 1986).

Hains, Brigid, *The Ice and the Inland: Mawson, Flynn and the Myth of the Frontier* (Carlton South: Melbourne University Press, 2002).

Headland, Robert K., "Antarctic Odyssey: Historical Stages in Development of Knowledge of Antarctica", in Aant Elzinga, T. Nordin, D. Turner, and U. Wråkberg, eds., *Antarctic Challenges: Historical and Current Perspectives on Otto*

Nordenskjöld's Antarctic Expedition 1901–1903 (Göteborg: Royal Society of Arts and Sciences in Gothenburgh, 2004), pp. 15–24.

Howitt, Rohan, "The Japanese Antarctic Expedition and the Idea of White Australia", *Australian Historical Studies* 49 (2018): 510–526.

Howkins, Adrian, "Emerging from the Shadow of Science: Challenges and Opportunities for Antarctic History", in Peder Roberts, Adrian Howkins, and Lize-Marié van der Watt, eds., *Antarctica and the Humanities* (London: Palgrave Macmillan, 2016), pp. 251–272.

Hulbe, Christina L., Weili Wang, and Simon Ommanney, "Women in Glaciology: An Historical Perspective", *Journal of Glaciology* 56 (2010). www-cambridge-org.libproxy.c lemson.edu/core/journals/journal-of-glaciology/article/women-in-glaciology-a-his torical-perspective/205304CE84CEFFCC59FA4BC83AB962AE/core-reader

Huntford, Roland, *The Last Place on Earth: Scott and Amundsen's Race to the South Pole* (New York: Modern Library, 1999).

Huntford, Roland, *Shackleton* (New York: Carroll & Graf, 1985).

Hurley, Frank, *The Diaries of Frank Hurley 1912–1941* (London: Anthem, 2011).

Jones, Max, *The Last Great Quest: Captain Scott's Antarctic Sacrifice* (Oxford: Oxford University Press, 2003).

Jones, Max, "'The Truth about Captain Scott': *The Last Place on Earth*, Debunking, Sexuality and Decline in the 1980s", *Journal of Imperial and Commonwealth History* 42 (2014): 857–881.

Jones, Max, Berny Sèbe, John Strachan, Bertrand Taithe, and Peter Yeandle, "Introduction: Decolonising Imperial Heroes: Britain and France", *Journal of Imperial and Commonwealth History* 42 (2014): 787–825.

Keighren, Innes M., "Of Poles, Pressmen and the Newspaper Public: Reporting the Scottish National Antarctic Expedition, 1902–1904", *Scottish Geographical Journal* 121 (2005): 203–218.

Koehn, Nancy F., Erica Helms, and Philip Mead, "Leadership in Crisis: Ernest Shackleton and the Epic Voyage of the Endurance", Harvard Business School Case 803–127 (April 2003; revised December 2010), www.hbs.edu/faculty/Pages/item.aspx?num=29815 (accessed 10 October 2020).

Kolsky, Elizabeth, *Colonial Justice in British India: White Violence and the Rule of Law* (Cambridge: Cambridge University Press, 2011).

Land, Barbara, *The New Explorers: Women in Antarctica* (New York: Dodd, Mead and Company, 1981).

Larson, Edward J., *An Empire of Ice: Scott, Shackleton and the Heroic Age of Antarctic Exploration* (New Haven: Yale University Press, 2011).

Launius, Roger D., "Toward the Poles: A Historiography of Scientific Exploration during the International Polar Years and the International Geophysical Year", in Roger D. Launius, James Rodger Fleming, and David H. DeVorkin, eds., *Globalizing Polar Science: Reconsidering the International Polar and Geophysical Years* (New York: Palgrave Macmillan, 2010), pp. 47–81.

Leane, Elizabeth, "Antarctic Diaries and Heroic Reputations: Changing the Subject", in Peder Roberts, Adrian Howkins, and Lize-Marié van der Watt, eds., *Antarctica and the Humanities* (London: Palgrave Macmillan, 2016), pp. 27–51.

Lowe, Keith, *Prisoners of History: What Our Memorials to World War II Tell Us about Our History and Ourselves* (New York: St Martin's, 2020).

Morrell, Margaret, and Stephanie Capparell, *Shackleton's Way: Leadership Lessons from the Great Explorer* (New York, London: Penguin, 2001).

Murphy, David Thomas, *German Exploration of the Polar World: A History, 1870-1940* (Lincoln, NE, London: University of Nebraska Press, 2002).

Nash, Meredith, Hanne E. F. Nielsen, Justine Shaw et al., "'Antarctica Just Has this Hero Factor': Gendered Barriers to Australian Antarctic Research and Remote Fieldwork", *PLoS One* (16 January 2019), https://journals.plos.org/plosone/article?id=10.1371/journal.pone.0209983.

Riffenburgh, Beau, *The Myth of the Explorer: The Press, Sensationalism, and Geographical Discovery* (New York: Belhaven, 1993).

Riffenburgh, Beau, *'Nimrod': Ernest Shackleton and the Extraordinary Story of the 1907-09 British Antarctic Expedition* (London: Bloomsbury, 2005).

Roberts, David, *Alone on the Ice: The Greatest Survival Story in the History of Exploration* (New York: W. W. Norton, 2014).

Roberts, Peder, *The European Antarctic: Science and Strategy in Scandinavia and the British Empire* (New York: Palgrave Macmillan, 2011).

Roberts, Peder, "Heroes for the Past and Present: A Century of Remembering Amundsen and Scott", *Endeavour* 35 (2011): 142-150.

Roberts, Peder, "The White (Supremacist) Continent: Antarctica and Fantasies of Nazi Survival", in Peder Roberts, Adrian Howkins, and Lize-Marié van der Watt, eds., *Antarctica and the Humanities* (London: Palgrave Macmillan, 2016), pp. 107-112.

Roberts, Peder, Adrian Howkins and Lize-Marié van der Watt, "Antarctica: A Continent for the Humanities", in Peder Roberts, Adrian Howkins, and Lize-Marié van der Watt, eds., *Antarctica and the Humanities* (London: Palgrave Macmillan, 2016), pp. 1-23.

Robinson, Michael F., *The Coldest Crucible: Arctic Exploration and American Culture* (Chicago: University of Chicago Press, 2014).

Ryan, Simon, *The Cartographic Eye: How Explorers Saw Australia* (Cambridge: Cambridge University Press, 1996).

Scott, Robert Falcon, *Scott's Last Expedition: The Journals* (New York: Carroll and Graf, 1996).

Scott, Robert Falcon, *The Voyage of the Discovery*, Vols. I and II (New York: Cooper Square Press, 2001).

Seag, Morgan, "Women Need Not Apply: Gendered Institutional Change in Antarctica and Outer Space", *Polar Record* 7 (2017): 319-335.

Sherman, Taylor, *State Violence and Punishment in India* (Abingdon, New York: Routledge, 2010).

Solomon, Susan, *The Coldest March: Scott's Fatal Antarctic Expedition* (New Haven and London: Yale University Press, 2002).

Spufford, Francis, *I May Be Some Time: Ice and the English Imagination* (London: Faber & Faber, 1996).

Stevenson, William R., III, "The Polar Years and Japan", in Roger D. Launius, James Rodger Fleming, and David H. DeVorkin, eds., *Globalizing Polar Science: Reconsidering the International Polar and Geophysical Years* (New York: Palgrave Macmillan, 2010), pp. 123-141.

Summerhayes, Colin, and Peter Beeching, "Hitler's Antarctic Base: The Myth and the Reality", *Polar Record* 43 (2007): 1-21.

Summerhayes, Colin, and Cornelia Lüdecke, *The Third Reich in Antarctica: The German Antarctica Expedition 1938–39* (Norwich: Erskine, 2012).

Tharoor, Shashi, *Inglorious Empire: What the British Did to India* (London: Hurst, 2017).

Turney, Chris, *1912: The Year the World Discovered Antarctica* (Berkeley: Counterpoint, 2012).

Uenuma, Francine, "George Washington Gibbs Jr. Defied Danger and Racism to Become the First African-American to Visit Antarctica", *Smithsonian* (27 February 2019). www.smithsonianmag.com/history/george-washington-gibbs-jr-defied-danger-and-racism-become-first-african-american-visit-antarctica-180971568/

van der Watt, Lize-Marié, and Sandra Swart, "The Whiteness of Antarctica: Race and South Africa's Antarctic History", in Peder Roberts, Adrian Howkins, and Lize-Marié van der Watt, eds., *Antarctica and the Humanities* (London: Palgrave Macmillan, 2016), pp. 125–156.

van Sittert, Lance, "'Ironman': Joseph Daniels and the White History of South Africa's Deep South", *Polar Record* 51 (2015): 501–512.

11

Representing the Polar Regions through Historical Fiction

ELIZABETH LEANE

Introduction

> Bill ... butted in with the comment that there was no such thing as purely reproductive recollection ... that the reputations of the remembered dead, from the insignificant mannikin to the most illustrious subject, underwent a change from the very moment of departure. Temporal existence ended, the imaginative faculty of posterity took over. The man who had died in battle, or in the pursuance of some purely personal goal, instantly became the brave hero who had perished for the glory of his country.[1]

In this passage from Beryl Bainbridge's 1991 novel *The Birthday Boys*, Robert Falcon Scott, leader of the *Terra Nova* Antarctic expedition, recalls the reflections of his fellow explorer and friend, the naturalist and physician Edward 'Bill' Wilson. The conversation occurs while the men are together in a tent during a depot-laying expedition in March 1911. Lawrence 'Titus' Oates and Apsley Cherry-Garrard listen in on the exchange, which is broken by the entrance of Henry 'Birdie' Bowers. Readers of Bainbridge's novel, well aware of the fate of the historical Scott and his polar party, including Wilson, Oates, and Bowers, would recognize multiple ironies in this scenario. When Scott and the other men died in or near a similar tent in March 1912, their reputations were indeed subject to exactly the process described in these lines. However, these words are themselves a recollection: whatever Bill said is transmitted and potentially distorted in Scott's reproduction. Moreover, the whole passage is spoken by literary characters – Bainbridge's fictionalized versions of the historical explorers – and the narrative of which they are a part is itself an example of 'the imaginative faculty of posterity', although a posterity that has moved beyond the celebration of polar heroes to a more complex and contested process of revision and remembrance.

---

1 Bainbridge, *Birthday Boys*, 96.

Occurring almost exactly halfway through the novel, this metafictional moment is the closest Bainbridge (one of the best-known twentieth-century British writers of literary historical novels) comes in *The Birthday Boys* to an explicit comment on the complex relationship between literature and history.

This chapter investigates the ways in which Anglophone writers have used fiction to explore, unpack, complicate, and challenge the history and historiography of expeditions to the polar regions. I begin by briefly outlining theoretical debates that circulate around historical fiction and its relationship to history before explaining the particular significance of the genre to the polar regions. I then identify some productive ways to group contemporary historical novels dealing with polar exploration, pointing to the insights enabled by particular stylistic and structural features. The remaining part of the chapter demonstrates some of these insights by examining four relatively recent novels: Bainbridge's *The Birthday Boys*; Irish-Canadian novelist Ed O'Loughlin's *Minds of Winter* (2016), which switches between multiple Arctic and Antarctic settings and periods as it traces the movements of a mysterious marine chronometer; US author Andrea Barrett's *The Voyage of the Narwhal* (1998), which focuses on a fictional 1850s Arctic journey in search of the lost Franklin expedition; and British writer Rebecca Hunt's *Everland* (2014), set on a fictional Antarctic island, in which the stories of a 1913 exploring party and a 2012 centenary expedition unfold in eerie parallel. My aim is not to be exhaustive or comprehensive but rather to use these texts to demonstrate the multiple ways in which imaginative writers trouble received exploration histories of the Arctic and Antarctic.

Dressing Skeletons: Writing the Past through History and Fiction

'Historical novelists take the bare bones of "history", some facts, some atmosphere, some vocabulary, some evidence, and weave a story within the gap.'[2] Jerome De Groot's anatomical metaphor for the technique of the historical novelist seems particularly apt for the Arctic and Antarctic, as the physical remains of Western explorers have played an outsized role in the way the history of the polar regions has been storified. Near the start of his analysis of the polar regions in the English imagination, Francis Spufford uses a similar metaphor to explain the ongoing survival of certain exploration stories, singling out another famously tragic explorer, Scott: 'Like any

2 De Groot, *The Historical Novel*, 9–10.

successful myth, [Scott's story] provides a skeleton ready to be dressed over and over in the different flesh different decades feel to be appropriate.'[3] And while histories and biographies undertake the majority of this costuming process, literature, particularly fiction, also has a part to play.

As De Groot explains, the relationship between these two forms of 'dressing' the past – fiction and history – has been the subject of ongoing debate since the form of the historical novel was consolidated in the early nineteenth century. Contemporary literary critics tend to be reluctant to offer firm definitions of the genre. Characterized by 'hybridity and flexibility', it stretches from literary fiction to popular novels such as the historical romance and the adventure story.[4] The most influential critic of the form, mid-twentieth-century Marxist critic Georg Lukács, argued that the key feature of the historical novel proper (exemplified and inaugurated, for Lukács, by Walter Scott) is 'not the retelling of great historical events ... [but] that we should re-experience the social and human motives which led men to think, feel and act just as they did in historical reality'.[5] As De Groot explains, for Lukács, 'The realism of the novel allows readers to engage with and empathise with historical individuals and thence gain a sense of their own historical specificity.'[6]

From the later twentieth century, however, a new form of the literary historical novel emerged in relation to debates about the relationship between fiction, history, and historiography. Because of the relative belatedness of human encounter with the high polar regions – the Antarctic continent had not even been sighted when Walter Scott began publishing the works he would become famous for – the majority of polar historical novels have been published in this recent period, so it is worth examining this newer form of the historical novel more closely.

The second half of the twentieth century saw a re-examination of history as representation and narrative construction, which was itself a result of post-structural literary and cultural theory. The most influential historian within this debate has been Hayden White, whose 1976 essay "The Fictions of Factual Representation" drew attention to the 'extent to which the discourse of the historian and that of the imaginative writer overlap, resemble or correspond with each other'. White argues that to produce a coherent account – to present events within a 'comprehensible totality' – 'historians must utilize precisely the same tropological strategies, the same modalities of

---

3 Spufford, *I May Be Some Time*, 4. 4 De Groot, *The Historical Novel*, 2.
5 Quoted in De Groot, *The Historical Novel*, 27. 6 De Groot, *The Historical Novel*, 29.

representing relationships in words, that the poet or novelist uses'.[7] The publication of titles such as Ann Curthoys and John Docker's *Is History Fiction?* (2006), Beverly Southgate's *History Meets Fiction* (2009), and Alexander Macfie's collection *The Fiction of History* (2015) shows that this conversation is far from settled.

During the same period, literary critics have been paying increasing attention to the historical novel: De Groot writes that 'the "literariness" of history has led to a resurgence of interest in fictional forms and the way they represent the past'.[8] While the traditional historical novel remained popular, writers also began to engage with historiographical debates, displaying increasing self-awareness of the limits of imaginatively recreating past periods, people, and events. Skepticism of grand narratives, metafictional elements in which the narrative draws attention to itself, deliberate anachronisms, multiple or unreliable narrators, pastiche, and political critique (particularly feminist and post-colonial) became characteristic of this approach. A range of terms with different nuances and emphases – such as 'historiographic metafiction' and 'the neo-historical novel' – have been coined to capture various aspects of this new form of historical fiction. Here, I use 'post-modernist historical novel' as a convenient if homogenizing catch-all. Novels of this kind ask, in Amy Elias's summary,

> what is history, exactly, and how does it enable both individual and collective agency? What is the difference between history and memory and fantasy? What events of the past have become lost to us in the present, why have they become lost, and why should we want to recuperate them? What political forces work against our understanding or even knowledge of the past?[9]

Such questions, I argue below, take on distinct forms when applied to the history of the polar regions.

Post-modern Historical Fiction and the Polar Regions

Anglophone literature of the Arctic and Antarctic has long been obsessed with not only the history of these regions but also the way in which this history is constructed and repeated. 'In seeking to put an end to the expansion of cultural fantasy around the last place on earth', writes Elena Glasberg, 'geographical attainments in fact only led to further attempts, arrivals,

---

7 White, *Tropics of Discourse*, 121, 125.   8 De Groot, *The Historical Novel*, 112.
9 Elias, "Historiographic Metafiction", 294.

gestures of closure, or newly extended limits that could not be contained by their own impetus'.[10] This urge to repeat and retell has focused on two expeditions in particular, both of which ended in tragedy and death: in the Arctic, the mid-nineteenth-century disappearance of the Franklin expedition while searching for the Northwest Passage, a loss which itself generated many further expeditions; and, in the Antarctic, Scott's *Terra Nova* expedition – a South Polar tragedy that acted as a counterbalance to Franklin's in the north. Russell Potter, in a review of O'Loughlin's *Minds of Winter*, suggests that the 'Franklin novel' might be considered a sub-genre in itself, counting at least twenty examples that together offer 'every version of Franklin one can imagine', as well as versions of his officers, his Inuit guides, and his wife. A similar argument could be made for the 'Scott novel'.

Human interaction with the polar regions, and particularly the Arctic, is of course vastly longer, richer, and more diverse than these and other Western expeditions, and Anglophone polar historical fiction to some extent reflects this wider history. Ian McGuire's *The North Water* (2016), for example, is set on a mid-nineteenth-century Arctic whaler, and Jesse Blackadder's very different *Chasing the Light* (2013) on an Antarctic whaling vessel in the 1930s. Michael Chabon's *The Amazing Adventures of Kavalier & Clay* (2000) includes an Antarctic episode set during World War II, and Favel Parrett's *When the Night Comes* (2014) involves a journey on a national expedition vessel during the 1980s. Tanya Tagaq's *Split Tooth* (2018) is set in a small town in Nunavut during the 1970s. Many other examples could be cited. The focus in this chapter is on a prominent subset of this literary engagement with the history of the polar region, comprising texts that might be termed 'expedition novels' – those that retell, challenge, subvert, or re-imagine well-known historical exploration efforts.

The novel is admittedly only one of the forms that literary responses to polar expeditions have taken, with writers also using poetry, drama, and other forms to explore historical events and figures. The *Terra Nova* expedition alone has been the subject of many examples. These include poems such as Derek Mahon's "Antarctica" (1985), Dorothy Porter's "Wilson's Diary" (1982), "Auroral Corona with Two Figures" (1983), and "Oates' Diary" (1989), Chris Orsman's *South: An Antarctic Journey* (1996), Anne Michaels' "Ice House" (1999), and various poems in Elizabeth Bradfield's collection *Approaching Ice* (2010). Drama, in particular, seems well-suited to re-imagining polar expeditions, which were themselves in many ways highly

---

10 Glasberg, *Antarctica as Cultural Critique*, 9.

performative undertakings. Despite the challenges of staging the Antarctic icescape, there is a growing a number of Scott expedition plays alone, including Douglas Stewart's verse drama for radio *The Fire on the Snow* (1944); Howard Brenton's *Scott of the Antarctic* (1972); Ted Tally's *Terra Nova* (1981); and Patricia Cornelius's *Do Not Go Gentle* (2012). These responses span the gamut of possible approaches, from the respectful through the excoriating, running in rough parallel with Scott historiography. The later three of these performance works employ formal counterparts to the techniques of the post-modern historical novel, eschewing realism and linearity, juxtaposing different times, places and points of view, and allowing contradictory narratives to coexist.

However, the historical novel – particularly in its post-modern form – remains the dominant genre through which imaginative writers engage with and interrogate polar expedition history and historiography. There are a number of reasons why writers often choose fiction as the form in which to respond to the history of polar exploration. To begin with, prose fiction has a particular resonance in dealing with historiographic questions because of its formal similarity to standard histories. As White observes, 'There are many histories that could pass for novels, and many novels that could pass for histories, considered in purely formal (or, I should say, formalist) terms.'[11] Historical novels exploit this formal likeness to historical documents by incorporating various kinds of real, modified or entirely imagined archival texts, with traditional historical novels usually doing so to shore up the sense of realism of the story, and post-modern examples more often highlighting the effort of trying to assimilate historical data.[12]

Early polar expeditions make particularly interesting historical subjects in this sense. These expeditions produced a huge range of written texts – the logbooks and records kept by leaders and scientists from which to write official narratives and reports; the less formal journals maintained by many expeditioners, eager to record an unusual and glamorous undertaking; letters to loved ones at home; lists, instructions, messages, and notes of all kinds; 'newspapers' and creative efforts produced to maintain good spirits in periods of leisure; and many more. In high-latitude environments where there were few or (in Antarctica) no outside observers to produce their own accounts, these expedition documents took on heightened significance as records of achievement. Polar historical fiction explores the gaps, contradictions, and subtexts of polar expedition records, thereby drawing attention to the fictive

---

11 White, *Tropics of Discourse*, 121–122.   12 Hutcheon, *Poetics of Postmodernism*, 114.

techniques that historical narratives must themselves employ to provide a coherent account.

While polar expeditions may have produced copious textual records, these records did not, of course, represent the points of view of all of those involved in or affected by the expedition. As Ben Maddison has observed with respect to Antarctic history, the majority or records were written by elites – 'leaders of expeditions, ships' captains, officers, scientists and artists'.[13] The voices of less privileged participants, such as crew members, cooks, dog-handlers, radio officers, and, in the north, Indigenous guides, are seldom heard. Maddison points to a related 'heroization' of Antarctic history – a process by which historians have placed 'prominent individuals such as [Roald] Amundsen at the centre of historical explanation', assessing successes or failures on the basis of these individuals' personal qualities and treating Antarctic exploration as 'a drama of self-contained survival in adversity'.[14] While this tendency is particularly visible in Antarctica, with its shorter and in some ways simpler exploration history, it is also evident in exploration of the north, which has proceeded via its own list of heroes (sometimes overlapping with those of the south). Shelagh D. Grant observes that Arctic historiography, at least until the mid-twentieth century, was primarily concerned with 'heroes, conquest and pride in achievement', marginalizing 'Inuit history, conserved through countless generations by the oral tradition'.[15] Novelists have provided two primary responses to this emphasis within polar history on heroic endeavours by white male middle-class individuals: on the one hand, de-reifying the hero figure by retelling his story with very different emphases, so that the whole ethos of individual achievement and conquest is questioned; and on the other, foregrounding or imagining the perspectives of those whose stories have not been told or widely heard, most often because of their class, race, or gender.

Another reason why historical novelists might be particularly drawn to narratives of exploration of the remote (for English speakers) polar regions is their ability to act as useful spatial metaphors for the exploration the novelist (as well as the historian) undertakes in guiding readers into a temporally unfamiliar world. Comparing the historical novel to science fiction, De Groot observes that 'fundamentally [the genre] entails an engagement on the part of the reader (possibly unconsciously) with a set of tropes, settings and ideas that are particular, alien and strange'.[16] The shifting and unfamiliar material

13 Maddison, *Class and Colonialism*, 1. 14 Maddison, *Class and Colonialism*, 3.
15 Grant, "Arctic Historiography", 145. 16 De Groot, *The Historical Novel*, 4.

characteristics of polar ice and atmosphere can stand in for the uncertainties of knowing the past. In O'Loughlin's *Minds of Winter*, for example, the Norwegian explorer Roald Amundsen dismisses some snow-covered mountains floating 'just over the horizon' as an Arctic atmospheric illusion, but notes that 'a mirage might once have had substance, might be the echo of some remote object or event – refracted, reflected, enlarged or inverted, a story distorted by ice and by light'.[17] The deceptive polar landscape reminds the reader that while stories told about the past may have a genuine relationship with actual events, there is no way of knowing what processes have shaped their transmission.

The polar regions are often represented in fiction as chronotopes in the purest sense: places that are *about* time. Their icescapes have a peculiarly close relationship to the past or future – they are points where one might easily slip between different time periods. The space of the 'heroic hut', remaining just as it was when the early expeditions exited, and the explorer's dead body, frozen where it fell, frequently function in Antarctic literature as the most obvious manifestation of the preserving power of ice, with its seeming ability to compress temporal intervals to almost nothing. Conversely, extreme diurnal changes near the poles, with days stretching out as long as seasons, create a sense of time passing slowly, or not at all. Watches and chronometers thus feature strongly in polar literature, such as Birdie Bowers' watch in French novelist Marie Darrieussecq's future-set *White* (2006; first published in French in 2003), or the strange marine chronometer from the Franklin expedition in *Minds of Winter*. Novels such as Hunt's *Everland* (2014) and Steven Heighton's *Afterlands* (2005) sport titles that yoke together time and space, their adverbs of unspecified or infinite futures bringing a mythic, otherworldly quality to the places where their action is set. Even the mundane title of *The Birthday Boys* suggests a narrative that is as much interested in time as in space or place. This sense of the polar regions as sites of anomalous temporality makes them favoured settings for genres that deal with the future – hence the numerous utopian, science fiction, and thriller novels set at the poles – but also with those interested in the past.

Polar Expedition Novels

Polar expedition novels are as heterogeneous in style and tone as the historical novel itself, varying from popular genre fiction, such as Dan

---

17 O'Loughlin, *Minds of Winter*, 323.

Simmons' Franklin horror *The Terror* (2007), to literary fiction, such as *The Birthday Boys*, and from fairly traditional historical narratives, such as Robert Ryan's *Death on the Ice* (2009), to self-consciously post-modern and metafictional approaches, such as *Minds of Winter*. In the following, I suggest some ways of grouping these novels according to their relationships with historical expeditions and their non-fiction narratives.

Perhaps the most straightforward form of polar historical fiction is the narrative that – to adopt the metaphor mentioned above – aims to put 'flesh on the bones' of a famous non-fiction expedition narrative – most often Scott's or Franklin's, but also those of Charles Francis Hall, Adolphus W. Greely, Roald Amundsen, Ernest Shackleton, Douglas Mawson, and others. Examples include Kåre Holt's *The Race* (1974; 1976 in English translation); Paxton Davis's *A Flag at the Pole* (1976), Robert Edric's *The Broken Lands* (1992), Bainbridge's *The Birthday Boys*, Adrian Caesar's *The White* (1999), Ryan's *Death on the Ice*, Tim Griffiths's *Endurance* (2015), Laura Waterman's *Starvation Shore* (2019), and Hélène Gaudy's *A World with No Shore* (2019; 2022 in English translation). Like most historical novels, these texts draw closely and sometimes explicitly on non-fiction narratives and source documents. For example, Ryan describes *Death on the Ice* as 'fiction based on fact', lists seventeen books that he found useful in its creation, and acknowledges his indebtedness to various museums and individuals.[18] However, as literary texts they are able to fill in gaps in the narrative and bring an intimacy that only the imagination makes available. While such novels can certainly be historically revisionist, in part or in whole, and draw on post-modern techniques, broadly speaking they tend to be more traditional, linear, and realist than others described here. And because of the tendency for polar history to be framed in terms of individual personalities and achievements, these novels often hold a conversation with biography as much as history, although some, such as *The Birthday Boys*, deliberately undermine this idea by offering multiple points of view which do not necessarily cohere.

These narratives are often told from the perspective, or in the voice, of the expedition leader and/or other prominent members of the expedition. Literary techniques such as free indirect discourse, changing focalization, first-person narration, and dialogue enable authors to represent imagined detail – particularly psychological – that a conventional historical (or biographical) account would at the very least need to signal as speculative. Reflecting on his prizewinning 'non-fiction novel' *The White: Last Days in*

---

18 Ryan, *Death on the Ice*, 497.

the Antarctic Journeys of Scott and Mawson 1911–1913, Australian novelist and poet Adrian Caesar answers critics who would have him write a purely factual biography by noting the impossibility of such an account: 'biographical "facts" are exceedingly hard to come by. And those that are yielded up would have to be presented in the form of a list, in order to avoid the shaping, and therefore interpreting, gestures of narrative form ... both history and biography have inescapable elements of fiction in them'. For Caesar, working on the cusp of biography and fiction enabled him 'fully to imagine the physical and emotional experiences of Scott and Mawson but also ha[ve] room for the non-fictional elements of the story and for analysis'.[19] Laura Waterman, whose *Starvation Shore* deals with the story of the Arctic Greely expedition, similarly argues that, where certain historical events are unknown and probably unknowable, 'telling the story ... through the novel form' can reach 'a kind of truth'.[20]

While writers such as Caesar and Bainbridge are interested in the hidden inner lives of well-known public figures such as Scott, others provide a more oblique approach by deliberately taking the point of view of marginalized, neglected, or excluded actors – especially women (those associated or, in the Arctic, involved with expeditions); working-class and African American expedition members; and Indigenous people who joined, guided, or encountered expeditions. Because these participants often did not leave written documents, the narratives that imagine their stories have a freer relationship with historical accounts, using their oblique perspective to challenge stereotypical representations of both explorers and the people and environments they encountered. Examples include Canadian writer Rudy Wiebe's prize-winning book *A Discovery of Strangers* (1995), which focuses on a relationship between a young midshipman on Franklin's first expedition and a Dene woman known to the Europeans as Greenstocking; Heighton's *Afterlands*, which recounts the experiences of the *Polaris* Arctic expedition members, a diverse multinational group who were marooned on an ice floe for many months; and O'Loughlin's *Minds of Winter*, discussed below. The marginalized actors in these texts are often real historical figures – Heighton's narrative, for example, is focalized alternately through the theoretical leader of the group, white American George Tyson; Inuit interpreter Tukulito (or 'Hannah'); and German immigrant Roland Kruger. However, this figure

---

19 Caesar, "Grey Areas in 'The White'", 99–100. The paradoxical term 'non-fiction novel' to describe *The White* comes from (among other sources) Pan Macmillan's webpage for the book, www.panmacmillan.com.au/9781743340356/.
20 Waterman, *Starvation Shore*, author's note.

may also be an imagined, historically impossible one, as in Mordecai Richler's *Solomon Gursky Was Here* (1989), in which a Gursky family member is discovered to be the sole survivor of the Franklin expedition.

The critical approach that an outsider perspective enables means that many (although not all) of these novels draw on the techniques of the postmodern historical novel, questioning received history and historiographical approaches. *Afterlands*, for example, has a complex narrative structure that – in addition to the triply focalized main narrative – incorporates images and extracts from actual non-fiction accounts (George Tyson's book *Arctic Experiences* [1874] and his field notes), contemporary broadsides, a map, epigraphs from famous writers such as Joseph Conrad, and Heighton's autobiographical reflections on his own search for the historical traces of his subjects. Far from seeking to find resolution about 'what happened' on the expedition, the narrative refuses to settle on a single perspective or reliable account. The characters live not in the present, but an 'afterland' of changing historical reputation.[21]

Other historical novelists choose to invent an entirely fictional expedition, although often one with metaphorical or metonymical parallels with historical ones. Thomas Keneally's *The Survivor* (1969), for example, which deals with the guilt experienced by the sole survivor of a famous sledging expedition, recalls both Apsley Cherry-Garrard of the *Terra Nova* expedition and Douglas Mawson, leader of the Australasian Antarctic Expedition. Keneally's later historical mystery novel, *Victim of the Aurora* (1977), similarly draws on elements of both expeditions.[22] Cormac James's *The Surfacing* (2014) and Barrett's *The Voyage of the Narwhal* deal with fictional expeditions in search of Franklin's men, and the explorers that populate Hunt's *Everland* closely resemble the men of Scott's second expedition. While these narratives are also often based on extensive research, the device of a fictional expedition divorces the novel from tired debates about or comparisons with what 'really' happened. James's author's note, for example, lists numerous published and unpublished sources that formed a historical 'template' for *The Surfacing*, but states bluntly that 'Where known facts have not suited my narrative, I have ignored them.'[23] The device of a fictional expedition, in which elements of various historical voyages can be combined and made visible, enables potentially stronger critiques of the underlying ideologies – personal and political – that drive polar exploration.

21 My observations here repeat points made in more detail in Leane, "Review of *Afterlands*".
22 See Ryan, "Antarctic Hoosh".   23 James, *The Surfacing*, 370–371.

11 The Polar Regions through Historical Fiction

A final form of polar exploration fiction worth highlighting here comprises juxtaposed narratives of a fictional contemporary expedition/quest and an earlier one, which may itself be historical or imagined. Again, the connection between the narrative may be metaphorical – one expedition echoes the other in its aims, power dynamics, or outcomes – and/or metonymic – the contemporary expedition is focused on memorializing the earlier one, collecting and analysing textual evidence to tell its story, or tracing family connections between past and present. Examples include *Minds of Winter* and *Everland*, discussed below; Robert Pierce's *Dead Men* (2012), in which an Antarctic arts residency holder who calls herself Birdie Bowers becomes obsessed with locating the tent in which Scott's men died; and Robyn Mundy's *Nature of Light* (2009), the story of a photographer who travels to Antarctica as a tribute to Frank Hurley's images, running parallel with an account of the 1911–14 expedition on which Hurley travelled. These novels tend to be the most explicitly metafictional and historiographically focused of those discussed here, as the discovery of various historical documents or insights enables the contemporary characters to directly reflect on the construction of received histories. The extent to which the characters' quest for historical information necessarily echoes the author's own research adds another layer of complexity.

In the remainder of this chapter, I focus closely on four relatively recent novels – two (primarily) Arctic, two Antarctic – in order to illustrate some of these features of contemporary polar expedition fiction.

'Mostly I Told the Story As It Happened': *The Birthday Boys*

Perhaps the best known of all Anglophone polar historical novels is Bainbridge's *The Birthday Boys*. Published in 1991, the book formed one of a series of acclaimed historical novels that Bainbridge produced around this time, including *An Awfully Big Adventure* (1990), set immediately after World War II, and *Every Man for Himself* (1996), which focused on the other famous icy tragedy of 1912, the *Titanic* disaster. In terms of the chronology of shifting approaches to Scott's reputation, *The Birthday Boys* appeared at the height of a period of critical revisionism spurred by the publication of Roland Huntford's polemical biography *Scott and Amundsen* (1978) and its television adaptation as *The Last Place on Earth* (1985).[24] However, while Bainbridge's

---

24 See Jones, "From 'Noble Example'".

book at times draws almost verbatim on Huntford's account,[25] her narrative is not primarily interested in debunking the Scott myth. In his analysis of Bainbridge's historical fiction, Brett Grubisic argues that she ignores the conventional historiographic significance of particular events in favour of domestic and personal details of the people involved and their relationships.[26] In a sense, Bainbridge's novel can be readily understood in terms of conventional historical fiction's ability to put 'flesh on the bones' of the skeletons of the past. However, as Grubisic notes, *The Birthday Boys* also shares elements of post-modern fiction in its tendency to unsettle any sense of a single, stable narrative.[27]

Structurally, *The Birthday Boys* comprises five long chapters, each told in the first-person voice of a different member of the polar party. Each speaker relates a different stage in the expedition – not only the attempt on the Pole, but also other ventures such as the winter journey to Cape Crozier – discontinuously and sporadically but in chronological order, covering the period from mid-June 1910, when the expedition departed, to the death of Oates (the final narrator) in mid-March 1912. While the multiple narrators are not normally recalling the same events, the use of flashbacks creates overlap. The order of speakers – Evans followed by Wilson, Scott, Bowers, and Oates – echoes the men's positioning in the famous image of Scott's polar party at the Pole, which graces the cover of the Penguin paperback edition of the novel.

Along with the reader's prior knowledge of historical events, the device of birthdays holds the different narratives together: one or more of the men's birthdays is narrated in each chapter, with Oates's famous departure from the tent occurring on his own birthday. Thematically, this device – as well as the novel's title – evokes ideas of childishness and Boy's Own adventures, which resonates with Bainbridge's explicit references to the children's story *Peter Pan* (a text with strong connections to Scott[28]) and, more broadly, her exploration of the men's imagined childhoods and relationships with their mothers.

Spoken in first person and mostly in the past tense, Bainbridge's chapters generically reference the quintessential polar genre of the expedition diary.

---

25 For example, compare Huntford, *Scott and Amundsen*, 352, with Bainbridge, *Birthday Boys*, 96. Bainbridge also draws on sources closer to the expedition itself, such as Scott's published and unpublished journals, and Cherry-Garrard's *The Worst Journey in the World*.
26 Grubisic, *Understanding Beryl Bainbridge*, 136.
27 Grubisic, *Understanding Beryl Bainbridge*, 134–136.
28 For a discussion of *The Birthday Boys* that deals with the intertextual relationship with Barrie's play, see Kucała, "Beryl Bainbridge's *Birthday Boys*".

However, rather than a series of dated entries with no knowledge of future events, these are intimate narratives told retrospectively from specific stages within the expedition (including, in Oates's case, the moment of death), and in this sense function more as miniature memoirs. Unlike fictionalized diary entries, the narratives are ambiguous in their purpose, motivation, and intended audience: too structured for interior monologues, but too intimate and confessional for self-vindications aimed at posterity. These differing and sometimes contradictory accounts distinguish *The Birthday Boys* from the traditional historical novel and bring it closer to historiographic metafiction. Instead of a single public history – a grand narrative – the reader is presented with merely a series of local or micro-narratives.

Moreover, the reliability of these local narratives is itself in question. Bainbridge begins her book from the perspective of 'Taff' Evans, the only working-class member of the polar party, and the only one who kept no diary of the journey, providing greater freedom of voice and perspective. Through Evans's own account, the reader quickly learns that he is often drunk, loves to embellish his stories, and admits to changing timelines and 'codding' (fooling or hoaxing).[29] Mentioning an incident when he and Scott fell into a crevasse together, he notes that 'Mostly I told the story as it happened.'[30] Like the historical novelist's classic 'author's note', in which the writer demonstrates knowledge of historical records while admitting to departure from them, Evans's confession of a tendency towards narrative embellishments paradoxically increases a sense of his honesty.

What Taff by his own admission leaves out of his public renditions of the crevasse tale is the erection he recalls experiencing while the two men were dangling 'close as sweethearts'. Taff reasons that this was a reaction to the closeness of death, 'the best of me, rising up in protest against extinction', but it is presumably the homoerotic implications that lead him to omit this detail from his public retellings.[31] This is one of several moments in the novel where the men's narratives touch obliquely or explicitly on questions of masculinity, homosociality, and homoeroticism. Yet while the characters – particularly Bowers – echo stereotypical nineteenth-century British assumptions about masculinity, race and class, at times they also anticipate the later demise of such assumptions. When Bowers insists that the use of dogs or motorized vehicles in polar travel is 'unsporting', Wilson suggests that he is 'perhaps clinging to the inappropriate chivalry of a bygone age'.[32] Bowers

---

29 Bainbridge, *Birthday Boys*, 10. 30 Bainbridge, *Birthday Boys*, 11.
31 Bainbridge, *Birthday Boys*, 11. 32 O'Loughlin, *Minds of Winter*, 142.

himself believes 'the world is changing ... and it's tremendous luck to have been born in the last few seconds of an epoch in which a man is still required to stand up and be counted'.[33] Bainbridge's Bowers sees himself as almost superseded, giving his narrative a sense of historical self-awareness. This feeling of outdatedness is even more explicit in Wilson's narrative, in the passage quoted at the beginning of this chapter, and at an earlier point when he reflects that 'Con and myself, Birdie and Oates, even Peter Pan Evans with his penchant for swinging one round by the seat of the trousers, are the misfits, victims of a changing world ... All the things we were taught to believe in, love of country, of Empire, of devotion to duty, are being held up to ridicule.'[34] Here Wilson seems to foresee how the late twentieth century will view him and his companions – he understands himself as a historical subject.

Thus while *The Birthday Boys*, in the words of critic Elisabeth Wennö, 'reveals and challenges the ideology of Antarctic heroism', exposing 'the turn-of-the-century ideology, or ethos, of empire, conquest and supremacy',[35] it does so in an ironic, self-conscious way that refuses simple retrospective judgement of the men whose voices it impersonates. Like many polar historical novels, it warns against holding onto any one reading of historical events as 'truth' for very long. The novel is a process of accepting competing and contradictory views simultaneously without having to fully accept or deny any. When it comes to a topic such as the 'race to the Pole', which historically has been characterized by ongoing, polarized, often finicky, and sometimes hostile debate about personality, leadership, logistics, and other details, fiction offers a circuit breaker and enables a new way of thinking about the polar past.

'Stories Converge at the Poles': *Minds of Winter*

Where Bainbridge narrows in on five men in a single polar expedition, O'Loughlin's *Minds of Winter* (2016) ranges widely across geographical and temporal settings. *Minds of Winter* follows the contemporary story of two strangers – Fay Morgan and Arthur 'Nelson' Nilsson – drawn together in the town of Inuvik in the Canadian Arctic as they search for traces of family members who have gone missing in the polar wilderness: Fay's grandfather Hugh, an officer in the Canadian Air Force, and Nelson's brother, Albert, a geographer and Antarctic researcher. Albert has left behind a cache of

---

33 O'Loughlin, *Minds of Winter*, 145.   34 O'Loughlin, *Minds of Winter*, 64.
35 Wennö, '"Encased in Ice"', 43.

puzzling documents – letters, memoirs, maps, and reports – that unexpectedly reference Hugh and in turn become part of the narrative. The action ranges across 180 years, beginning at Franklin's time as governor of Van Diemen's Land, and shifting geographically from the Antarctic to parts of the Scandinavian and Russian Arctic as well as Canada. Franklin's lost expedition and later journeys in search of it, Hall's *Polaris* expedition, Scott's *Terra Nova* expedition, Amundsen's Arctic explorations, the fiction of Jack London, the Northwest Territories legend of the enigmatic trapper Albert Johnson, and the Cold War Arctic Distant Early Warning (DEW) Line become intertwined. Connecting these polar narratives is a marine chronometer bought at auction by the National Maritime Museum in Greenwich, but originally listed among the equipment of the lost Franklin expedition – a non-fictional object described in an actual *Guardian* newspaper article reproduced as the story's prologue. While the clock acts as something of a McGuffin in the novel, tying together otherwise disparate stories, symbolically it signals the polar regions as landscapes intrinsically linked to ideas about time.

Many of the multiple stories that make up *Minds of Winter* are narrated by or from the point of view of characters on the sidelines of the famous expeditions they described. The first chapter follows Franklin's niece, Sophia Cracroft, as she attends a ball held aboard the Antarctic expedition ships *Erebus* and *Terror* after their return to Van Diemen's Land. Infatuated with the handsome Captain Ross, but romanced by the less glamorous Commander Crozier, Sophie herself longs to 'cut off her hair, dress as a boy and run off with the ships'.[36] An entrancing tune she hears called "The Girl I Left Behind Me" becomes a refrain in the novel, connecting Sophia to a later woman traveller and 'girl left behind', Amundsen's lover Bess Magids. Another chapter consists of a short autobiography narrated by Ipiirviq – known to English speakers as Joe Ebierbing or 'Eskimo Joe' – and transcribed by Amundsen in King William Island during the latter's famous journey through the Northwest Passage. Ipiirviq describes his own travels, together with his wife Taqulittuq (or Hannah), to Britain and the United States (where he meets Sophia) and on expeditions led by Charles Francis Hall – including the notorious *Polaris* expedition that is the focus of another polar historical novel, *Afterlands*. Linking many of the stories is the figure of Cecil Meares, a dog-handler with Scott's *Terra Nova* expedition, whose real-life activities in Antarctica, Manchuria, and Canada become the basis in the

---

36 O'Loughlin, *Minds of Winter*, 33.

novel for an extensive espionage career involving a secret organization called 'Room 38', the enigmatic clock, and a message cylinder from Franklin's expedition.

While these stories from the margins function at one level as ways to propel the mysterious clock through narrative time and space, they also enable a critique of the enterprise of polar exploration. The narrative of Magids' journey to meet her lover, only to find that he is lost forever in the Arctic, reveals many unheroic aspects of the Norwegian explorer's life. Reflecting on the obscurity of one of Amundsen's fellow Antarctic expeditioners, who fell out with his leader and later committed suicide, Bess reflects, 'That's what happens to the other men of history' – only the hero, the man who constructs the story, remains in the public eye.[37] Ipiirviq, who counts himself as a 'an explorer' and a 'great one', observes that 'The white men came to these regions and looked for all sorts of things that they dream of but they found only the ice and the islands and places so cold and dark that even the Inuit don't hunt there.' His and his wife's journeys to 'Orkney and Hull and New York and London', his narrative suggests, were just as bold and just as anti-climactic.[38]

The Arctic and Antarctic settings of these intertwined stories lead Fay, working her way through Albert's archive, to conclude that 'stories converge at the poles. Like lines on a map'.[39] However, while Fay's and Nelson's stories do converge, there is a sense in which the multiplying narratives confuse rather than clarify. Wondering what links all the stories in the archive, Fay notes that all of their protagonists 'were lost. They disappeared in the ice'. Immediately, however, she realizes that in the case of Meares, 'There was no mystery about his death. It was his life that was largely a blank space.' As the narrative continues, the identities of Fay and Nelson themselves become increasingly blank. Fay's credit card stops working, her bank believing that she is dead, and the reliability of her self-account is called into question. As Russell Potter notes in an interview with O'Loughlin, the character's name echoes the *fata morgana* mirage (named after Morgan Le Fay of Arthurian legend), suggesting illusion.[40] Nelson's last name, Nilsson, evokes nothingness, and his first name – a nickname – is merely a variant on this. As the narrative progresses, ambiguity grows over his identity and whether he is in fact his supposed brother Albert. Like the

---

37 O'Loughlin, *Minds of Winter*, 343.
39 O'Loughlin, *Minds of Winter*, 225.
38 O'Loughlin, *Minds of Winter*, 181–182.
40 Potter, "Interview with the Author".

men they have been researching – Meares, Ipiirviq, Albert Johnson – the identities of Fay and Nelson are multiple and their lives unknowable. The polar regions themselves become a metaphor for this unknowability. Late in the novel, Hugh, stationed at a DEW radar base and listening to the beeps of the Sputnik satellite just launched into space, reflects that the world has fundamentally changed. As long as the Earth's surface was represented as a Mercator-style map, he muses, the polar regions remained unpresentable, the lines of longitude 'march[ing] off the map in parallel lockstep, refusing to compromise, much less converge'. Unlike a globe – for Hugh, a totalizing object from which escape is impossible – a map is 'built on hacks and heuristics and mistakes and lies, cracks through which you might, just maybe, someday slip away'.[41] Not long after this insight, Hugh walks off into the polar night, with a line – 'I could be out there for a while' – reminiscent of the famous final departure of Oates (himself a character in the novel).[42] At the end of *Minds of Winter*, when the dead bodies of a man and a woman – presumably Nelson and Fay – are found in the snow outside Inuvik, the local police officer's observation that some people 'fall through the cracks' becomes, in the light of Hugh's statement, a victory rather than tragedy.[43] O'Loughlin states in his author's note that 'all good mysteries ... ought never to be solved', and the reader is duly left with no clear answers.[44] While in one sense stories converge at the poles, as on a globe, in another they resist the relentless drive for absolute knowledge of all parts of the planet. When cartographic mystery is removed, narrative mystery must be sustained.

Despite *Minds of Winter*'s thoroughly post-modern preference for gaps and contradictions over a coherent narrative, and for the pleasures of flawed representation over scientific precision, O'Loughlin's novel is in some ways the most traditional of those examined here. In a review of the book, Neta Gordon observes astutely that 'For all its emphasis on uncovering unofficial histories, *Minds of Winter* rests, to a large extent, on a kind of uncritical nostalgia for the myth of the "mysterious" Arctic and Antarctic.'[45] O'Loughlin critiques the polar hero, one might argue, only to replace him with another stereotype of masculine adventure, the international spy. In this sense *Minds of Winter* fails to meet the challenge of the Wallace Stevens poem that provides its title – to gaze on a winter landscape and see 'Nothing that is not there and the nothing that is'.[46]

41 O'Loughlin, *Minds of Winter*, 444   42 O'Loughlin, *Minds of Winter*, 448.
43 O'Loughlin, *Minds of Winter*, 475.   44 O'Loughlin, *Minds of Winter*, 481.
45 Gordon, "Ruining a Good Mystery", 175.
46 Quoted in O'Loughlin, *Minds of Winter*, epigraph.

Yet even here *Minds of Winter* makes the post-modern move of pre-empting criticism by rehearsing it within its own narrative. In a particularly convoluted chapter, Meares tells Hugh Morgan of his encounter at the Korea–Manchuria border with Jack London – a real-life author famous for his tales of the Canadian Arctic. The reader is then provided with a (fictional) unpublished short story by London, part of Albert Nilsson's archive, in which a writer character much like London recounts a meeting with a foreigner much like Meares. This story contains yet another one: the writer relates a macabre tale, set in the Northwest Territories during the Klondike gold rush, that has in turn been told to him by a Russian-born prospector. The doubly fictionalized Meares keeps calling out the writer's more romantic embellishments, eventually advising him to avoid 'that sort of Gothic' and to embrace a sparer style: 'Everything is very plain and modern now.'[47] However, this modernist advice is itself designed to throw London off the scent of a story Meares now knows to contain factual information related to the clock and message cylinder: the real import of the story is exactly in the details that seem most outlandish. *Minds of Winter* thus plays not only with the historiography of the polar regions but also their literary history, never arriving at a stable point that might allow readers to get their bearings.

'I Want My Name on the Map': *The Voyage of the Narwhal*

In comparison to *Minds of Winter*, Barrett's *The Voyage of the Narwhal* (1998), centring on a fictional journey in search of the lost Franklin expedition, initially feels far more like the traditional historical novel. While it contains many long excerpts of real nineteenth-century Arctic and scientific narratives (and copies of engravings), these take the conventional form of epigraphs rather than parts of the narrative itself. The story is told linearly in the third person, focalized primarily through the novel's central protagonist, naturalist and polar explorer Erasmus Darwin Wells. Nonetheless, as Erasmus's over-determined name might suggest, the novel is self-conscious in its approach to polar history and historiography, mounting a sustained critique of the white masculinist values and mindsets that drove polar exploration.

The story focuses on Erasmus's Arctic journey and its aftermath, including experiences overwintering in the ice and interacting with the Netsilik Inuit. The expedition is led by Zeke Vorhees, the young, charismatic son of

47 O'Loughlin, *Minds of Winter*, 283.

a wealthy shipping magnate who is engaged to Erasmus's sister, Lavinia. Erasmus is already a polar veteran, having travelled with the (historical) United States Exploring Expedition to Antarctica led by Charles Wilkes, during which he was frustrated with 'noxious Navy discipline', the constant downgrading of scientific work in favour of geographical survey and, in the journey's aftermath, Wilkes's smoothing over of his many failures in his published expedition narrative.[48] Hoping for a better experience on the *Narwhal* journey, he quickly discovers that Zeke is a self-aggrandizing egomaniac: '"I want my *name* on something," [Zeke] called. "Something *big* – is that so hard to understand? I want my name on the map."'[49] Obsessed with the idea of an open polar sea, Zeke deliberately orchestrates the expedition's entrapment in ice so that it is forced to overwinter. With his increasingly autocratic behaviour endangering and alienating the crew, he eventually mounts an ill-advised one-man expedition north. Zeke's failure to return at the end of summer forces the remaining men, led by a reluctant Erasmus, to leave the vessel and head south, where they are eventually rescued. Presumed dead, Zeke unexpectedly returns to America, having survived by living with the Netsilik, and brings back with him two members of this community – a woman he calls Annie and her son, known as Tom – whom he displays on the lecture circuit. Erasmus is publicly constructed as the villain of the expedition for supposedly abandoning his leader.

The Voyage of the Narwhal, then, stages a strong critique of the 'great man' narrative of polar exploration discussed earlier. Accordingly, the narrative is focalized through outsider figures: primarily Erasmus – like Zeke, a wealthy white man, but also a self-effacing scientist who finds himself increasingly at odds with the racist and dehumanizing views of his profession; to a lesser extent, Alexandra, Lavinia's companion in Zeke's absence, a skilful scientific illustrator who longs for a life beyond the domestic; and, briefly, Annie and Tom, who are equally contemptuous of Zeke, but whose inner life remains impervious to other characters' assumptions about their inferiority or their victimhood. Alert to the beauty and intricacy of the Arctic landscape, Erasmus is increasingly appalled by Zeke's inability to see beyond his own self-absorbed goals, particularly in his interactions with the Netsilik community. Annie in turn outlines an organic worldview completely at odds with a society that values heroic individual achievement:

> Her tribe was like one great person, each of them a limb, an organ, a bone. Onto the hand her family formed, Zeke had come like an extra finger . . . He

48 Barrett, *Voyage*, 33, 69–72.   49 Barrett, *Voyage*, 168 [original emphasis].

saw himself as a singular being, a delusion they'd found laughable and terrifying all at once. When he strutted around, it was as if one of the fingers of that hand had torn itself loose, risen up, and tottered over the snow.⁵⁰

For Annie, polar explorers are 'like children', dependent on others and determined to give 'their names to the landscape, pretending to discover places her people had known for generations'.⁵¹

Central to the construction of Zeke as polar hero is the narrative that he himself creates around the journey. As leader – the man who gives lectures and writes the official account – he holds the power to tell the story of the expedition. Prior reading of polar expedition literature has moulded Zeke's idea of what achievement means, and his contribution to the genre – entitled, like Barrett's novel, *The Voyage of the Narwhal* – emphasises his own exciting adventures. In the background of the action is the (historical) second Grinnell expedition led by Elisha Kent Kane. Kane's book, which in the world of the novel is released prior to Zeke's return, sells in huge numbers (as did its real-life counterpart⁵²). Although Zeke confiscates journals and makes all expedition members promise not to produce their own narratives for a year after their return – a fairly standard approach for polar expeditions of the time – Erasmus eventually considers countering Zeke's book with an alternative account. However, a conversation with a disgruntled and unpleasant member of Kane's expedition checks him: '*How can I write one word about the arctic when a person such as Godfrey is also writing a book, one that says me, me, me, me, me.*'⁵³ Erasmus does, in the end, produce a book. However, instead of an alternative but still individualistic tale, this new narrative is a team-based effort, with drawings by Erasmus's artist brother that are etched by Alexandra, and it focuses not on relics, journeys, and achievements, but on a place and its inhabitants. The novel concludes on a utopian note, with Erasmus and Alexandra (no longer a woman-left-behind) journeying to the Arctic together with and at the instigation of Tom, who longs for his home. *The Voyage of the Narwhal*, then, imagines a different kind of exploration history by imagining a new kind of polar expedition narrative.

'How Time Tricks Us': *Everland*

Hunt's *Everland* was published in 2014, just after the centenary of the 'race to the Pole' and its numerous re-enactments. Her novel responds to these

50 Barrett, *Voyage*, 319. 51 Barrett, *Voyage*, 344.
52 Kane's narrative, *Arctic Explorations* (1856), sold 65,000 copies. See Kitson, *Nineteenth-Century Travels*, 142.
53 Barrett, *Voyage*, 300 [original emphasis].

11 The Polar Regions through Historical Fiction

events, recounting the experiences of a disastrous 1913 three-person expedition to an imaginary Antarctic island alongside the eerily similar events of a memorial scientific expedition in 2012.[54] The earlier party – members of a larger expedition travelling in a ship called the *Kismet* and led by Captain Lawrence – is entirely fictional, and bears no straightforward one-to-one relationship with any historical expedition. However, characters and details of the *Kismet* expedition strongly reference Scott's, as does the title of the novel and its setting, the island of Everland. While the naming of the island is mundanely explained – the expedition's major sponsor is steel manufacturer Joseph Evelyn – the reference to the setting of *Peter Pan* – 'Never Never Land' – is clear, and reinforced by the modern characters' jokes about 'Lost Boys'.[55] The *Peter Pan* references also intertextually link *Everland* with Bainbridge's *The Birthday Boys*.[56]

Hunt's primary interest in *Everland* is the relationship between time, identity, history, and memory in a place where there are no outside witnesses. Reputation, the narrative suggests, depends on whose testimony is trusted. The novel's explicitly historiographic interest is evident early, when members of the (fictional) international Antarctic base Aegeus mark the departure of the modern scientific party to the largely unexplored island with a screening of the 'old sixties classic' *Everland* – a film which, like the historical 1948 *Scott of the Antarctic*, has a famous score.[57] Like the audience of a pantomime, the expeditioners happily boo the brutal actions of a man named Napps who abandons his companion, Dinners. The audience 'ham[s] along' as the on-screen Napps reflects ironically, 'How time tricks us . . . into seeing who we really are . . . And what choices we make.'[58] The remainder of the book unfolds these ideas of time, change, and identity in both the historical expedition and its centenary counterpart.

The 1913 narrative focuses on the capable first mate Napps, the large, tough Millet-Bass, and the Antarctic novice and scientist Dinners who, it transpires, is included in the expedition only because he is Evelyn's nephew. A storm leaves the men – especially Dinners – in a desperate condition from their moment of arrival, and they spend their time on the island trying to survive until the *Kismet* returns. As the interdependent men struggle to cope, alliances

---

54 The geography of the 1913 expedition is vague. The ship returns to Oamaru, suggesting a location in the Ross Sea or East Antarctica. However, the Sun goes beyond the horizon in mid-March, which puts the island at or near the South Pole, a geographical impossibility.
55 Hunt, *Everland*, 21.
56 For discussion of Everland in relation to *Peter Pan*, see Hewenn, "Legacies".
57 Hunt, *Everland*, 7–8.   58 Hunt, *Everland*, 10.

are formed and reformed, with Napps first infuriated by, then protective of Dinners, who is both pathetic and dangerously unhinged. While Napps initially appears gruff and unempathetic, in the end he sacrifices his own chances of survival to help Dinners, who in a state of semi-madness abandons his companions and shreds his diary, making their survival impossible and destroying firsthand evidence of their story. When the *Kismet* men arrive and find only the mute and dying Dinners, a retrospective version of events is quickly constructed which casts Napps as a heartless brute who left his companion to die. Lawrence uses his official narrative to consolidate this story, intimidating or blackmailing anyone who threatens to put forward an alternative account. Dinners's motto, given on his sledging flag and repeated on numerous occasions throughout the narrative, is 'The times are changing and we change with them.'[59] While the events on the island in one sense bear this out in the men's changing relationships and qualities, once history takes over this ability to change is removed from them: reputation becomes frozen in the Everland of posterity.

The 2012 party, who visit Everland to survey its animal populations while memorializing the original expedition, experience similar dynamics in which their alliances with each other, and parallels with the 1913 men, shift and change. The leader, Antarctic veteran Decker, structurally echoes Napps; the robust, uneducated field officer Jess recalls Millet-Bass; and the inexperienced and fragile scientist Brix – included only owing to personal connections – strongly resembles Dinners. Again, however, events undermine these easy equations, as Brix begins to show the positive character traits of Napps, and Decker, with his need to be the 'big hero' on his final Antarctic trip, betrays and abandons his companion like Dinners and then, like Lawrence, reports a fabricated story in order to protect his reputation.[60] Although she is found, like Dinners, in a bad condition beneath the upturned dinghy *Joseph Evelyn*, Brix takes on Napps's role as both the unrecognized hero and unacknowledged victim of the expedition.

Everland plays an active role in the events of both expeditions in the most literal sense. A small island dominated by an active volcano and a glacier, Everland is a place that cannot be trusted. For both parties, the island conjures a Gothic sense of foreboding from the outset: the modern expeditioners know it as a 'creepy place'; their forebears argue about its unlucky, 'supposedly haunted' quality. Its rumblings interrupt their excursions,

---

59 Repetitions of the phrase occur in Hunt, *Everland*, 119, 120, 191, 193, 204, 213.
60 Hunt, *Everland*, 142.

unsettle their equipment and damage their supplies; its geothermal heat means their buried food, normally preserved by the cold, is spoiled, or rather 'digested'.[61] Both parties experience an increasing sense of a menacing, almost satanic, presence, as landscape features come to resemble horned animals. For both parties their story ends when a blizzard renders the landscape unintelligible. Napps's insistence that the island 'isn't alive' and does not have 'macabre charisma' only reinforces the sense of its malicious intent.[62]

As its name suggests, Everland is also a place that speaks incessantly of time and of history: 'The natural metabolism of time was suspended in Antarctica ... In these places the past didn't linger but invaded with a clap of immediacy.'[63] The modern expeditioners keep finding unsettling remains of their Heroic Era counterparts – old tins, Dinner's sledging flag, and eventually Napps's preserved body. Each group hears strange shouts, voices, and noises that suggest they may be haunting each other, slipping inadvertently through time. Their experiences, and sometimes their conversations, unfold in uncannily close parallel. And they are constantly encountering non-human features that reinforce their sense of accumulating history. Both teams muse on the slow-growing lichen they discover, against which a human life is so short as to be barely measurable.[64] A seal tooth becomes through its carbon isotopes 'a transcript of a conversation between the seal and his environment ... a history which lived through the death of its speakers. What appeared, ultimately, was the story of Antarctica.'[65] Nonetheless, despite the evidence within material remains of both human and non-human artefacts, 'the past was a different world. It remained unknowable and evasive, even when you were holding solid proof of it in your hands.'[66]

Despite its 2014 publication, Antarctic setting, and concern with the material manifestation of time, there is little direct reference to climate change in *Everland*. There are certainly hints that all is not well with the Antarctic environment, either in 1913 or 2014. The Heroic Era team argue about the ethics of killing fur seals, given that they had been hunted to the brink of extinction. The later expeditioners are collecting data to enable better wildlife protections. The island's glacier has 'receded in modern times', shrinking back from its margins 'like a drought-stricken river'.[67] But a sense of the encroachment of the outside world on Antarctica is most

---

61 Hunt, Everland, 188.   62 Hunt, Everland, 87.   63 Hunt, Everland, 82–83.
64 Hunt, Everland, 83, 118.   65 Hunt, Everland, 158.   66 Hunt, Everland, 56.
67 Hunt, Everland, 226.

evident in the industrial urban metaphors used to described the landscape and its ice. The 1913 men, whose expedition is sponsored by a steel magnate, experience 'smog-coloured days'.[68] Instead of the stereotypical 'remote splendour' that newcomer Brix expects, Everland is 'a disappointment', a 'rubble moonscape that had all the charm of a builder's yard', its volcano a 'drab, slagheap-like mount', its low-clouded sky 'the colour of diesel fumes'.[69] Its glacier seems to have incorporated the qualities of the motor vehicles producing the exhaust gases that contribute to its demise: its ice, beginning as 'an ectoplasmic blue', arrives at sea level 'as stained as an underpass blackened by decades of traffic fumes'. Chunks of ice at its foot are 'as furrowed and dented as crushed cars' and are piled 'in dumper truck quantities'. The gorge it has 'bulldozed' is 'highway-wide'.[70] Although Hunt avoids the clichéd ice-core metaphor, Everland embodies the evidence of a collective human history of environmental impact that underlines the personal histories being formed in its icescape.

Conclusion

The novels discussed and analysed here demonstrate that, in the ongoing effort to produce histories of the polar regions, narrative fiction operates as both a partner and a provocateur. Historical fiction can flesh out the bare skeletons of documentary records, presenting possible versions of events without asking us to settle on any of them. At the same time, the genre acts as a reminder to the historian that 'facts' can never speak for themselves. Any historical novel must be engaged to some degree with documentary record to warrant this categorization, but it is equally the case that any historical account must draw to some extent on techniques of fictional storytelling in order to create a legible narrative. While this is true of historical fiction dealing with any place or period, it is particularly salient in the case of Anglo-European exploration of the polar regions, an endeavour in which records, figures, dates, lists, coordinates, and logbooks have been so important. Even more strikingly, in these imaginative narratives the ice regions of the planet, which (at least to low-latitude eyes) are unfamiliar, shape-shifting, and visually deceptive, act as unsettling metaphors for the inaccessible realms through which historians guide their readers.

68 Hunt, Everland, 188.   69 Hunt, Everland, 21, 35.   70 Hunt, Everland, 225.

Bibliography

Bainbridge, Beryl, *The Birthday Boys* (London: Penguin, 1991).
Barrett, Andrea, *The Voyage of the Narwhal* (London: Flamingo-HarperCollins, 1998).
Caesar, Adrian, "Grey Areas in 'The White'", *Meanjin* 61 (2002): 98–103.
Cherry-Garrard, A., *The Worst Journey in the World*. (London: Carroll & Graf, 1989).
De Groot, Jerome, *The Historical Novel* (London, New York: Routledge, 2010). Accessed through ProQuest Ebook Central.
Elias, Amy, "Historiographic Metafiction", in Brian McHale and Len Platt, eds., *The Cambridge History of Postmodern Literature* (Cambridge: Cambridge University Press, 2016), pp. 293–307.
Glasberg, Elena, *Antarctica as Cultural Critique: The Gendered Politics of Scientific Exploration and Climate Change* (New York: Palgrave Macmillan, 2012).
Gordon, Neta, "Ruining a Good Mystery", review of *Minds of Winter* by Ed O'Loughlin. *Canadian Literature* 235 (2017): 174–175.
Grant, Shelagh D., "Arctic Historiography: Current Status and Blueprints for the Future?", *Journal of Canadian Studies* 33 (1998): 145–153.
Grubisic, Brett Josef, *Understanding Beryl Bainbridge* (Columbia: University of South Carolina Press, 2008).
Hewenn, Jessica, "The Legacies and Frozen Time of Antarctica: Robert Falcon Scott, Peter Pan and Rebecca Hunt's *Everland*", *Australasian Journal of Victorian Studies* 21 (2016): 94–105.
Hunt, Rebecca, *Everland* (London: Fig Tree, Penguin, 2014).
Huntford, Roland, *Scott and Amundsen: The Last Place on Earth*. Revised and updated edition (London: Abacus-Time Warner, 2002).
Hutcheon, Linda, *A Poetics of Postmodernism: History, Theory, Fiction* (New York, London: Routledge, 1988).
James, Cormac, *The Surfacing* (Melbourne: Text Publishing, 2014).
Jones, Max, "From 'Noble Example' to 'Potty Pioneer': Rethinking Scott of the Antarctic, c.1945–2011", *Polar Journal* 1 (December 2011): 191–206.
Kane, Elisha Kent, *Arctic Explorations: The Second Grinnell Expedition in Search of Sir John Franklin, 1853, '54, '55*, (Philadelphia: Childs & Peterson, 1856).
Kitson, Peter, ed., *Nineteenth-Century Travels, Explorations and Empires: Writings from the Era of Imperial Consolidation 1835–1910*, Vol. 1: *North and South Poles* (London: Pickering and Chatto, 2003).
Kucała, Bozena, "Beryl Bainbridge's *The Birthday Boys*: Travelling Towards the Pole of Death", in Jacek Fabiszak, Ewa Urbaniak-Rybicka, and Bartosz Wolski, eds., *Crossroads in Literature and Culture* (Berlin, Heidelberg: Springer, 2013), 411–420.
Leane, Elizabeth, "Review of *Afterlands*, by Steven Heighton", *Polar Record* 43 (2007): 374–375.
Maddison, Ben, *Class and Colonialism in Antarctic Exploration, 1750–1920* (London: Pickering & Chatto, 2014).
O'Loughlin, Ed, *Minds of Winter* (London: Riverrun, Quercus, 2016).
Potter, Russell, "Interview with the Author, Ed O'Loughlin", *The Arctic Book Review*, https://arcticbookreview.blogspot.com/p/interview-with-author-ed-o.html (accessed 29 January 2021).

Ryan, John S., "Antarctic Hoosh: The Genesis of a Keneally Novel". Paper presented to the Scott Polar Research Institute, University of Cambridge, December 1989.

Ryan, Robert, *Death on the Ice* (London: Headline Review, 2009).

Spufford, Francis, *I May Be Some Time: Ice and the English Imagination* (London: Faber, 1996).

Waterman, Laura, *Starvation Shore* (Madison: University of Wisconsin Press, 2019).

Wennö, Elizabeth, "'Encased in Ice': Antarctic Heroism in Beryl Bainbridge's *The Birthday Boys*", in Heidi Hansson and Cathrine Norbert, eds., *Cold Matters: Cultural Perceptions of Snow, Ice and Cold* (Umeå: Umeå University and the Royal Skyttean Society, pp. 2009), 41–54.

White, Hayden, *Tropics of Discourse: Essays in Cultural Criticism* (Baltimore: Johns Hopkins University Press, 1976).

12

Geography, Anthropology, and Arctic Knowledge-Making

RICHARD C. POWELL

Introduction

The Arctic is a region that has been understood very much *through* its environment. Issues of nature and environment have been central themes investigated by both anthropologists and geographers. Much canonical work by geographers and anthropologists has focused on investigating environmental and cultural interactions, using concepts such as landscape, site, or place. The academic disciplines of geography and anthropology have therefore contributed to the process of *making Arctics*. This chapter examines these contentions.

Perhaps in consequence of these shared interests, Arctic anthropology and Arctic geography have had a contested, and at times uncomfortable, history. This has derived from competing institutional practices of canonicity and pedagogy between the respective parent disciplines. However, a number of *fin de siècle* Arctic anthropologists were initially trained as geographers, such as Franz Boas and Kaj Birket-Smith, and derived many common field practices and methods.

Through these shared intellectual objects, much research in both disciplines had a regional focus, in that it attempted to investigate the relations between environments and their inhabitants in particular *places*. This fell out of favour after 1945 in Anglo-American geography. Indeed, during the second half of the twentieth century, when much of Anglophone geography was preoccupied with attempts at quantification and spatial science,[1] historical geographers were some of the few remaining proponents of regionally based scholarship in the discipline. In anthropology, regionally based specialisms developed through fieldwork remained more popular in disciplinary initiation,[2] but this also came under pressure for greater theoreticism from the late 1950s.

1 Barnes, "Lives Lived". 2 Powell, "Sirens' Voices?".

In recent decades, intellectual historians in both disciplines have attempted to return to some of these central themes. However, insufficient attention is often paid to the legacies and imbrications between these areas of research. In the study of the Arctic, there has been limited investigation. In this chapter, I attempt to provide some thoughts around the emergence of deep themes in the fields of anthropology and geography, as well as outlining some of the consequences.

This chapter examines the reasons for these shared relationships and tensions and draws out some of the consequences for the enduring conceptualization of the northern circumpolar region. In order to exemplify the wider argument, I draw upon some of my own research into the understanding of 'Arctic cultures'.[3] In doing so, the chapter also begins to delineate the reasons for the contemporary state of Arctic/Northern studies and its disciplinary imbrications.

Fin de siècle Social Sciences

Many social science disciplines are hesitant over regional specialism, placing it in opposition to theory creation and circulation. In my work, I have tried to historicize this ambivalence and investigate its emergence during the very moment of modern, European disciplinarity in the late nineteenth century.[4] It argues that emergent framings of natural regions, evident for example in the work of the German and English 'new geographers', such as Theobald Fischer and Halford Mackinder, resulted from a certain vision of globalism that was critical to the *fin de siècle* delineation of both disciplines and areas.[5] Moreover, these imaginaries remain dominant in political understandings of the purposes and uses of regional knowledge today.

The International Relations scholar Karoline Postel-Vinay has argued that the second half of the nineteenth century was critical for the emergence of the notion of *globality*.[6] That is, this period was characterized by increasing centralization of geographical knowledges in European centres of power, or metropoles. As colonial empires learnt more about the world, and in

---

3 This chapter contributes to a larger attempt to think about how, and the ways in which, fieldwork in the Arctic moved from being canonical to anti-canonical in geography and anthropology, and the consequences this had for geographical, anthropological, and political imaginaries about the circumpolar region. It draws on research funded by the British Academy, the Leverhulme Trust, and the European Research Council.
4 Powell, "Echoes"; Powell, "Notes".
5 Powell, "Study of Geography?"; Powell et al., "Interventions".
6 Postel-Vinay, "European Power".

particular about difficult-to-access areas such as the interior of the African continent or the polar regions, new geographical or geopolitical imaginations began to arise. These knowledges included details and classifications of geographical patterns, as well as geographical processes. These understandings of the physicality of the Earth were to underpin a new political geography.[7] As Postel-Vinay puts it, there is therefore a need to understand 'how the physical finitude of the planet became the fundamental principle of regulation of a specific international order – the European one – and how that order aimed to planetary hegemony'.[8] This particular formation of the global, argues Postel-Vinay, is the most important imperial legacy of the nineteenth century. As intellectual historians have shown, though, this period was also about the emergence of disciplinarity.[9] Scholars were attempting to constitute new fields, but always in dialogue with other disciplines and other intellectual histories.

In recent years, historians of geography have tried to investigate these imperial histories to understand their connections with the institutionalization of disciplines. Further work is required to investigate relations between these histories and processes or region formation, particularly at the poles. Moreover, what has often been neglected in discussions by historians of geography is the importance of the First International Polar Year, 1882–83. There is evidence of widespread discussion about international collaboration in the field sciences from the early 1880s, notwithstanding wider colonial scrambles elsewhere at the same time (particularly in Africa).[10] This had various political and imperial ramifications, as well as disciplinary ones. In short, this meant that for geography to become a consolidated, institutionalized discipline in an era of university expansion in Europe, it needed to have a new, and coherent, intellectual project.[11] But it also required focus on specific regions of the newly constructed globe. Disciplines became institutionalized, and through that process, regions of globe were formed, even created, as objects of study.

Conceptions of 'Nature' and 'Environment' in the Study of Geography and Anthropology in the 1880s

It was within this milieu that the Oxford geographer Halford Mackinder sketched his vision for the future of geographical research and pedagogy in

7 Heffernan, "Mapping Schmitt".   8 Postel-Vinay, "European Power", 324.
9 Anderson and Valente, "Discipline and Freedom".   10 Barr, "Geographical Aspects".
11 Powell, "Notes".

the late 1880s. In his famous address before the Royal Geographical Society in 1886, entitled 'On the Scope and Methods of Geography', Mackinder outlined the tenets of his 'New Geography', focusing on classification, fieldwork, and imperial service.[12] Mackinder went on to play a key role at various important institutions in British geography, such as the RGS, the Geographical Association, LSE, and Reading University, as well as being holder of the first Readership in Geography at Oxford (in 1887), and later the founding Head of the School of Geography at Oxford (in 1899), the first in Britain and Ireland.

This account is well-known by geography undergraduates, as are Mackinder's later, and interrelated, forays into geopolitics.[13] This situation is frustrating, for historians at least, because it reduces complicated narratives into easily accessible founding myths and this reduces awareness of wider fields of connections. This is because as any historian of geography who has examined the 1880s is aware, Mackinder's programme for geography was only one of a number publicized at the time by scholars such as Peter Kropotkin in 1885 ("What Geography Ought to Be") and William M. Davis in 1887 ("The Study of Geography").[14]

In retrospect, by the far the most interesting of the plethora of statements about geography in the 1880s is that published by Franz Boas in *Science* in 1887 as "The Study of Geography".[15] In this statement, Boas drew from his reading in the German intellectual tradition and his field experiences in Baffin Island to present a wholly different vision for geography. In this section, I focus on the relations between nineteenth-century Arctic anthropology and Arctic geography using the lens of Franz Boas's fieldwork in Qikiqtaaluk (southern Baffin Island). In summary, I argue that Boas's fieldwork with the Inuit of Cumberland Sound in 1883–84 needs to be seen as a critical moment in the history of *geography*, because of the implications it had for the understanding of nature, environment, and region.

Boas travelled to Cumberland Sound in June 1883, on the ship *Germania* that was evacuating the German IPY station. He overwintered into 1884 with American and Scottish whalers at Kekerten, and then that summer visited various Inuit communities around the Sound. Although this was Boas's only episode of Arctic fieldwork, he continued to publish from it until 1927.[16]

---

12 Mackinder, "Scope and Methods".
13 Mackinder, "Geographical Pivot"; Mackinder, *Democratic Ideals*.
14 Kropotkin, "What Geography Ought to Be"; Davis, "Study of Geography".
15 Boas, "Study of Geography". 16 Powell, "Study of Geography?".

There has been lots of important work on Boas by historians of anthropology such as George Stocking and, more recently, by Julia Liss and Matti Bunzl.[17] Key figures in the International Arctic Social Sciences Association (IASSA), such as Igor Krupnik and, especially, Ludger Müller-Wille, as well as the late Douglas Cole, among many others, have done important work in demonstrating the centrality of Boas's Baffin Island fieldwork in inventing the specialism of 'Arctic Anthropology'.[18] However, despite their canonical status in anthropology, these research practices, and the vision of geography that they embodied, are very much neglected by historians of geography, and it is this neglect and its consequences that need to be stressed for our investigations.

In his *Science* paper, Boas summarized two origin positions of all sciences, which he claimed emerged from two different desires in the human mind. The first is that of physics, which stems from the 'aesthetic desire' for order in phenomena. This seeks explanation through the creation of laws. The second position is based on 'affective impulse' towards the need to understand particular phenomena.[19] This comes from the awe that humans feel in encountering the world around them. This, Boas claims after Alexander von Humboldt, is found in the science of cosmography.

This debate in Boas emerged from a contemporary debate in Germany inspired by neo-Kantians in the 1880s that emerged from the reception of the works of Alexander von Humboldt and Carl Ritter earlier in the century. By the early 1880s, this was being pursued in the work of Friedrich Ratzel in engagement with a wider circle of German geographers.[20] And, in a wider sense, this is a familiar debate from the history of the relationship between the natural and social sciences. What was important for Boas was the implication of this debate for the definition of geography: 'It is easily understood, therefore, why in geography the contest between these views is particularly lively. Here naturalists and historians meet in a common field of work.'[21]

Over the past century and a half, Boas's statement has received relatively little attention from geographers. In a short paper from fifty years ago, Roger Trindell claimed that Boas had been completely neglected in the geographical literature.[22] Ironically, Richard Hartshorne devoted two years of his life to

---

17 Stocking, "From Physics to Ethnology"; Stocking, *Ethnographer's Magic*; Liss, "Patterns of Strangeness"; Bunzl, "Franz Boas".
18 Examples include Krupnik, ed., *Early Inuit Studies*; Cole, *Franz Boas*; Cole and Müller-Wille, "Franz Boas' Expedition"; Müller-Wille, ed., *Franz Boas among the Inuit*; Müller-Wille, *Franz Boas Enigma*; Müller-Wille and Gieseking, *Inuit Whalers*.
19 Boas, "Study of Geography", 139. 20 Ratzel, *Anthropo-Geographie*.
21 Boas, "Study of Geography", 138. 22 Trindell, "Franz Boas".

learning German in order to uncover the German roots of the nature of geography, but in his landmark account of the nature of geography, published in 1939, Boas does not feature at all.[23] David Livingstone, in *The Geographical Tradition*, does devote a few pages to Boas, but his commentary focuses more on the race/environment debate in the 1930s, rather than the earlier origins of the professional discipline.[24] More recently, historical geographer Gerry Kearns's scholarly biography of Mackinder presented chapters that made successive, comparative examinations of Mackinder's views on geography with respect to those of Kropotkin, Mary Kingsley, and Elisee Reclus.[25] And yet Boas does not feature at all in his account either.[26]

This is important for our purposes because through his learning and his early Arctic fieldwork, Boas wanted to stress human–environment interactions in geography, and particularly their *mutual* influence. In this, he was specifically influenced by debates in Germany about the 'New Geography', particularly as outlined in the first volume of Friedrich Ratzel's *Anthropo-Geographie*.[27] An example of this in Boas's thinking is provided in the following: 'We will apply these results to the study of geography. Its objects are, the phenomena caused by the distribution of land and water, by the vertical forms of the earth's surface, and by the mutual influence of the earth and its inhabitants upon each other'.[28]

As Boas argued in this landmark statement, the geographical project was to involve the imbrication of human and natural phenomena:

> Our consideration leads us to the conclusion that geography is part of cosmography, and has as its source the affective impulse, in the desire to understand the phenomena and history of a country or of the whole earth, the home of mankind ... Many are the sciences that must help us to reach this end; many are the studies and researches that must be pursued to add new figures to the incomplete picture; but every step that brings us nearer the end gives ampler satisfaction to the impulse which induces us to devote our time and work to this study, gratifying the love for our country we inhabit, and the nature that surrounds us.[29]

My focus on this statement has been important to the argument of this chapter for three reasons. The first is that, for anthropologists, Boas's outline

---

23 Hartshorne, *Nature of Geography*.   24 Livingstone, *Geographical Tradition*, 290–294.
25 Kearns, *Geopolitics and Empire*.
26 For further discussion of Boas's place in the geographical canon, see Powell, "Study of Geography?".
27 Ratzel, *Anthropo-Geographie*.   28 Boas, "Study of Geography", 140.
29 Boas, "Study of Geography", 141.

of "The Study of Geography" was a very important paper that has stimulated debate for nearly a century and a half. Over the past decade or so, it has been recovered by a number of 'neo-Boasian' anthropologists in the United States, who have tried to detect in Boas all sorts of origins of later theoretical concepts.[30] And over the past five years, it has been recovered by anthropologists and social scientists in France following a new French translation.[31]

The second reason is that for Boas himself, "The Study of Geography" was one of his most important papers. He included the paper in his final, major collection of essays, *Race, Language and Culture*, as one of two very general papers that 'indicate the general attitude underlying my later work'.[32] It was the earliest paper included from the sixty-two that made the final selection. Anthropologists often cite this republished 1940 version as the key canonical text for American anthropology, but it is thereby removed entirely from its intellectual context. These relate to the ways in which disciplines have approached issues around the relations between people and their environments.

The third reason is that this focus relocates Boas's fieldwork on southern Qikiqtaaluk (Baffin Island) as central in his intellectual development. This reinforces a central point of my chapter. The consequence of the neglect of Boas by historians of geography, and the neglect of Boasian geography by historians of anthropology, has been that a number of assumptions have been made about the study of the Arctic that have persisted until today. In other work, I have drawn out the implications of this episode for any attempt to conceive of a geographical canon and for related attempts to conceive of disciplinary positioning between the natural and social sciences.[33] I mention this here because, although relatively short, this fieldwork has played a critical role in the history of anthropology.

The conventional narrative goes that Boas-the-geographer was interested in environmental determinism. He went to do fieldwork in Cumberland Sound because this was envisaged as the location where the social-environmental relationship would be starkest. That is, that Inuit Culture and Arctic environments were chosen by Boas as presenting the best possible site to test this hypothesis. The supposed Damascene conversion happened because, during fieldwork, Boas had the revelation that Inuit Culture develops in spite of the environment, rather than because of it. In consequence, Boas was able-to-become-anthropologist. He then resolved to undertake future research

---

30 See, for example, Bunzl, "Franz Boas". 31 Espagne and Kalinowski, eds., *Franz Boas*.
32 Boas, ed., *Race, Language and Culture*, vi. 33 Powell, "Questions on the Canon?", 2–8.

with the peoples of the Pacific Northwest, essentially because the culture was more complicated, owing to the less pervasive environmental influence.

This account is greatly generalized and abbreviated here, but this conventional view seems to have emerged at the behest of some of Boas's graduate students. And of course, it was an easy view to hold, given the development of German geography during the 1920s and 1930s, and the development of Boas's own thinking about the relations between race and culture. But the Boasian conversion myth has always helped the creation myth of anthropology – as the younger, but rapidly superior sibling of geography – which continues to predominate in the United States.[34]

But, as examinations of his field materials from the Arctic show, Boas was working through his readings of Kant and the neo-Kantians, and the relations of the *Naturwissenschaften* and *Kulturwissenschaften*, during his time with the Inuit in Cumberland Sound. In developing this work for publication, as *Baffin-Land* and *The Central Eskimo*,[35] he was using his material to articulate an agenda between these two disciplines. Further reflection on the imbrications of methods and theories between the disciplines in this period will facilitate better understanding. Both disciplines have been criticized for internalist approaches to disciplinary history,[36] and would benefit from further collaboration and cross-fertilization.[37]

For various reasons, Boas's intellectual project evolved over the next decade, such that by the late 1890s he was employed in museology at the American Museum of Natural History. However, the geographical project about the relations between people, environments, and regions was continued by other scholars.

The Regional Concept in Geography and Andrew J. Herbertson's 'Major Natural Regions'

In February 1904, the Oxford geographer Andrew J. Herbertson outlined his vision for the teaching of *systematic geography* before a Research

---

34 Intriguingly then, in its North American incarnation, Boasian anthropology is acutely canonized. This is directly opposed to the memorialization, or even anti-canonization, of Mackinder in British geography.
35 Boas, *Baffin-Land*; Boas, *Central Eskimo*.
36 The point was made for geography by Livingstone, "History of Science"; and for anthropology by Stocking, *Ethnographer's Magic*.
37 A major conference held in September 2020 by the Royal Anthropological Society and Royal Geographical Society (with the Institute of British Geographers) entitled "Anthropology and Geography: Dialogues Past, Present and Future" began to make serious progress in addressing these issues.

Meeting of the Royal Geographical Society.[38] The point of Herbertson's thesis was to outline a system of *natural regions* to aid in the instruction of geography at the universities: 'A natural region should have a certain unity of configuration, climate, and vegetation'.[39] Herbertson envisaged that a geographical novitiate would be taught to use this framework to learn about the different parts of the world, and then might specialize in one or a number of these regions. Herbertson was initially trained as a botanist, and the legacies of this are evident in his depiction of the natural regions.

It is relatively easy to see the precursors of a number of later debates in the published discussion of Herbertson's intervention on systematic geography – even then, *regional geography* was the nomenclature preferred by Mackinder and others present at the reading of the paper in 1904. However, I want to draw attention to this early attempt at delineating, classifying, and cataloguing of the natural regions. As is well known by historians of twentieth-century geography, the study of such delineated regions became the mainstay of geographical education in British universities as it was institutionalized through the early decades of the twentieth century and well into the 1960s. Herbertson was to take Mackinder's former post to become Reader in Geography in 1905, and later became the first Professor (*ad hominem*) of Geography at Oxford in 1910.[40] Indeed, in their history of the discipline in 1933, *The Making of Geography*, R. E. Dickinson and O. J. R. Howarth claimed that '[s]pecial, or, as it is now termed, regional geography, is thus a product of the last forty years. The culminating point, and as many would claim, *the essential aim of modern geography*, is thus the latest phase in the development of the subject.'[41] As the aim of *modern* geography, this view persisted and met little resistance until the advent of the *new* 'New Geography' of Peter Haggett and Dick Chorley in the early 1960s, which aimed to displace the dilettantism of regional geographers and replace it with models, quantification, and experiment[42] – although it must be noted that the trend to dispense with

---

38 Herbertson, "Major Natural Regions". This term never really caught on. Mackinder was opposed to 'systematic geography' and preferred the idea of 'regional geography'. Other geographers in the period preferred the term 'chorography' or 'landekunde'.
39 Herbertson, "Major Natural Regions", 309.
40 At this time, *ad hominem* professorships could be awarded to individuals already in the employ of the university on a competitive basis. In that sense, they were akin to a personal promotion, rather than the statutory professorships appointed by an electoral board after an external application process.
41 Dickinson and Howarth, *Making of Geography*, 233 [emphasis added].
42 Chorley and Haggett, eds., *Models in Geography*.

regions was less evident in some geography departments, not least Herbertson's former home in Oxford. Moreover, the argument for regional expertise within the discipline of geography continues to be seductive – as evidenced in Alexander Murphy's plea for grand regional narratives by geographers to compete with those issued by the likes of Robert Kaplan and Niall Ferguson.[43]

I want to use Herbertson's natural regions as my point of departure for this section of the chapter. I wish to argue that there have been very specific consequences of the idea of the natural region for the study of the polar regions – specifically, that is, for the study of the Arctic or circumpolar north by geographers. There have been a number of consequences of this framing of this area of scholarship. These have influenced both the education of geographers and the understanding of the circumpolar north. The first of these was that the geographers' world was split into regions for the purposes of analysis, but the selection of these and maintenance of academic interest were significantly influenced by geopolitical concerns. Most notably, British imperial interests influenced areas that British geographers specialized in, and this process was repeated by other European, and later American, states and colonial powers. A second consequence was that the idea of a 'natural region' was unevenly persistent for the study of some areas of the world. This is what Hartshorne meant by 'areal differentiation'.[44] Notably, I would argue, the idea of the natural region persisted for the poles. My argument here is that the idea of a 'natural region' has persisted precisely where the geographical imagination has been relatively absent. By this I mean a lack of the general process through which large groups of geographers specializing in a region resulted in understandings to move beyond the 'natural theorizations'. For the circumpolar region, by contrast, the relatively small number of geographers specializing in this area has meant that the 'natural region' framing has remained relatively dominant. A further consequence of the uneven processes of specialization and region-formation has been the impact on the development of theory *from* such regions. Finally, the continuing framing of the 'natural region' has influenced the political imagination and geopolitics of specific regions, but it has had particularly serious ramifications for the peoples and environments of the circumpolar region.

---

43 Murphy, "Advancing Geographical Understanding"; Kaplan, *Revenge of Geography*; Ferguson, *Empire*.
44 Hartshorne, *Nature of Geography*, 244.

The Theory of the Natural Region and Its Consequences

Herbertson wanted every educated geographer to be familiar with the basic outline of the regions. As he put it, detailed knowledge for each area would be acquired as necessary. However, the process of that more detailed learning and description of particular areas, or chorography, in Ptolemy's term, was always uneven. Particular areas and regions were studied more intensively, others less so. An easy, but nevertheless important, observation to make is that the regions given the most attention by British geographers were the areas of British imperial interest in the late nineteenth and early twentieth centuries – parts of Africa, India and the subcontinent, Australasia, southern Canada. Other parts of Europe, Asia, and North and South America were also of wider geopolitical interest and attracted some disciplinary specialists during the first half of the twentieth century.

The *modern* discipline of geography was thus characterized by uneven processes of region creation. And, in turn, analogous processes were taken up across the social sciences – as in the definition of 'culture areas' in (American) cultural anthropology, or in post-1945 area studies. Moreover, particular regions often became tied to the development of particular social theories.

Intellectually though, the issue is that systematic geography was never able to become *systematic*. All areas were equal, but some were more equal than others. I want to argue that this has had consequences in the emergence of critical intellectual traditions and scholarly communities around different areas. For the 'circumpolar studies', this has not happened to the same degree as, for example, African studies or South East Asian studies. Now of course all 'area specialisms' have their dominant disciplines, dominant theories, dominant centres of excellence, and so on. And this leads to proclivities and peculiarities. I simply want to highlight as an example that there are a number of peculiarities of Arctic studies, or Northern studies, as against these other areas. So regions were not constructed in the same way, and neither were the regional specialisms of different geographers.

In recent decades, there have been excellent scholarly investigations of northern imaginations, such as Peter Davidson's *The Idea of North*, or the accounts of Canadian nordicity by Sherrill Grace and Renée Hulan.[45] But there has been a persistence in popular discourse, and a resurgence in some

---

45 Davidson, *Idea of North*; Grace, *Canada*; Hulan, *Northern Experience*. For further discussion of this, see Powell, "Northern Cultures".

academic discourse, in the dominant framing of 'the Arctic as a Natural Region' – that is, a region where the environment dominates culture and cultural formation. Notwithstanding the important critique of nature–culture binaries from science and technology studies, the framing of the Arctic-as-a-natural-region remains heavily influential in the study of Arctic peoples and societies.[46]

The Geographical Imagination and the Circumpolar Region

The basic point that I want to make in this section is that the Arctic region has played a dual role in the constitution of social theory. The circumpolar north was constructed as an intellectual object in the late nineteenth and twentieth centuries, only at, or during, the closing of the Columbian epoch (as Mackinder had it). And, arguably, even then it was subordinate to the imagined destination of the North Pole. However, this meant that the peoples and sites of the circumpolar north played a critical role in the formation of the social sciences. During the geographical exploration of the 1880s and 1890s, the Inuit of central northern Canada were amongst those encountered during the emergence of social theory. The peoples of the Arctic were the first to be included in theorizations of modern social theory as ethnographic evidence of peoples in their 'pre-contact state', as demonstrated canonically in Marcel Mauss's discussion of their 'seasonal variations' and perhaps also Émile Durkheim's notion of altruistic suicide.[47] Claude Lévi-Strauss even used the metaphor of 'cold' societies to refer those that attempt to create institutions that maintain stability rather than historical change – as opposed to the 'hot' societies of the West.[48]

This late nineteenth-century European fascination has led to the persistence of the Inuit as one of, if not the best-known of the world's 'remote peoples'. The common stereotypes are remarkably well-known and persistent, such as the supposed lack of verbosity of Inuit society, in favour of gestural communication; assumptions about partner swapping; and the pervasive and racist notion of the 'happy Inuit'. What has been most problematic is that these stereotypes have become tropes of social analysis, and

---

46 A core aim of my current European Research Council Consolidator Grant research project, "Arctic Cultures: Sites of Collection in the Formation of the European and American Northlands", is to investigate this discursive formation so as to discover how it emerged and to depict what the consequences have been for inhabitants of the Arctic.
47 Mauss, "Essai sur les variations"; Durkheim, Le Suicide.   48 Lévi-Strauss, Savage Mind.

they have transmuted into more serious assumptions about Inuit societies, such as about individual adaptability and wider cultural resilience to change.

At the same time, within anthropology, geography, and more widely in social theory, studies of the Inuit, in particular, have been seen as something of an intellectual backwater since around 1945. This is because, within the framing of the Arctic 'natural region', there has been an enduring legacy of Inuit being understood as critically dependent on their environmental surroundings. When Franz Boas set out to undertake his geographical fieldwork at Cumberland Sound in 1883, he believed that Inuit society and this environmental site provided the best possible opportunity for testing this Ratzelian hypothesis. In doing so, the Inuit of the central Arctic, and their surrounding environment, were to become the *locus classicus* for the late nineteenth-century theory of environmental determinism or, as Boas termed it, geographical determinism.[49]

Consequently, studies of Arctic societies have been positioned by metropolitan scholars as not having contributed much to conceptions of 'the social', in ways that South Asian studies have contributed to understandings of *caste*, or African studies to *kinship*, or Latin American studies to ideas of *indigeneity*. During anthropological debates about hunter-gatherer societies in the 1960s, for example, David Riches argued that theoretical discussions were dominated by kinship, often based on fieldwork in sub-Saharan Africa, with little reference to Arctic societies.[50] Likewise, as British social anthropology became preoccupied with Melanesia during the 1970s and theories of personhood and relationality, there was little concern with any parallels in the circumpolar north.[51]

Moreover, this means that what Arjun Appadurai terms the 'gatekeeping concepts' of the region have been comparatively less clearly defined and pervasive for the North.[52] And critically this has also meant, I argue, that Arctic societies and peoples have been resistant to the overtures of what Quentin Skinner once termed the return of 'Grand Theory' to the social sciences.[53] Perhaps there was never even an initial turn, as pervasive understandings of the circumpolar north remain wedded to a theorization from the 'early Boas'.

There are, of course, many likely explanations for this. There are national differences that have resisted regional classification in Northern studies, just as in other areas of regional geography or area studies. The most important

49 Boas, *Baffin-Land*.   50 Riches, "Force of Tradition".
51 Ingold, "Closing Keynote Speech".   52 Appadurai, "Theory in Anthropology", 357.
53 Skinner, "Introduction", 12.

element here is the centrality of Greenland in the representation of the Inuit, and indeed for Arctic environments more broadly, and through this the influence of Denmark and Danish historiography.[54] It is important to remember that, for specific historical and political reasons that are beyond the scope of this chapter, the conception and construction of the study of Greenland has been closely controlled by Danish scholars. Initially, such scholarship was developed at the National Museum of Denmark, and centralized after World War II at the University of Copenhagen. Often, this Danish field of *Eskimologi* was centred around acquiring skills such as linguistic competence in Kalaallisut (West Greenlandic), but also combining this with a strong focus on demographic and administrative knowledge and expertise. The idea, quite clearly, was that this formulation of Arctic scholarship was focused on providing the administrative and bureaucratic expertise to underpin the Danish governance of Greenland. But this clearly influenced the development of the wider intellectual field of Arctic studies. As the commonplace saying went, 'If you want to learn about the Arctic, then go to Copenhagen'.[55]

The Danish philologist and ethnologist Kaj Birket-Smith, Director of the Ethnographic Department at the National Museum of Denmark from 1940, was a key exponent of the need for investigation of 'the so-called "Eskimo problem"' and was widely accepted as the twentieth-century expert on Inuit Culture.[56] As an aside, Birkett-Smith and Knud Rasmussen, during the preparations for the Fifth Thule Expedition, 1921–24, believed that the Canadian 'barrenlands' were the location of the 'original Inuit'.[57] Birket-Smith's monograph, translated into English in 1936 as *The Eskimos*, became the authoritative source on Inuit Culture through the middle decades of the twentieth century. On reviewing the revised version from 1959 in *American Anthropologist*, Robert Spencer argued that 'no one will disagree with Birket-Smith's prime assumption that here, among the various Eskimo and Arctic groups, is a series of variations of ecological adaptation'.[58] This framing of 'ecological adaptation' continued to be the dominant approach to

---

54 Birket-Smith, *The Eskimos*; Hughes, "Under Four Flags".
55 In Sweden, owing to a different political and scholarly milieu in the 1870s, the Swedish Society for Anthropology and Geography was founded in 1877.
56 Spencer, "Review of *The Eskimos*", 162.
57 The 'barrenlands' referred to the area in the central mainland of northern Canada (from Great Slave Lake and Great Bear Lake in the west to Hudson Bay in the east). This area is now within the Territory of Nunavut and the eastern part of the Northwest Territories in Canada.
58 Spencer, "Review of *The Eskimos*", 162.

comprehend the issue of the origins of Inuit society, based around a relationship between people and their environment.

As I have argued in other work, because this *Eskimologi* tradition has been so closely bound up with *Danish* national identity, it tended towards a rather conservative historiography until the 1980s.[59] Moreover, it is only in the past few years that Danish scholars, such as Astrid Nonbo Andersen, Lars Jensen, Søren Rud, Ulrik Pram Gad, and Lill Rastad Bjørst, have begun to argue for insights from post-colonial studies for the study of Greenland and the Arctic.[60]

Eskimologie was rarely used as descriptor by colleagues in its English translation. The field of Inuit studies/*études Inuit*, which was to emerge from Canada during the 1980s, is now the preferred term to refer to the wider field of studies of the Inuit and their cultures and politics.[61] In the contributions of Canadian scholars, there has been important research on the Canadian Arctic that has worked carefully with insights from post-colonial studies.[62] Pamela Stern and Lisa Stevenson, for example, clearly influenced by contemporaneous developments in Canadian geography, compiled an important intervention for critical Inuit studies over a decade ago.[63] So, it is fair to say that the dominance of the *Eskimologie* tradition in studies of the circumpolar north is now perhaps weaker than it was earlier in the twentieth century. However, there remain concerns for some about the utilitarianism and puzzling paucity of theorization in contemporary Arctic social sciences.

In attempting a history of Arctic studies, it would also be important to note the influence of Russian and post-Soviet scholars and the role they have played in internationalizing the field since around 1989. There is more that could be said about the dominant influence of different states on the intellectual traditions across the circumpolar region, and I will not discuss this further here. Instead, I hope to have used the example of Arctic studies to

---

59 Powell, "Institutions, Resources and Governance".
60 Anderson, "Greenland Reconciliation Commission"; Jensen, "Commemoration"; Rud, *Colonialism in Greenland*; Gad, *National Identity Politics*; Bjørst, "Saving or Destroying".
61 Earlier anthropological research in northern Canada was heavily influenced by the work of Diamond Jenness; see Richling, *In Twilight*. This, perhaps, gave anthropological research a slightly more applied dimension, as it was directly influenced by federal state policy for northern Canada.
62 Wachowich, "Creative Technologies"; Stevenson, *Life Beside Itself*; Kulchyski, *Aboriginal Rights*.
63 Stern and Stevenson, eds., *Critical Inuit Studies*.

exemplify the ways in which states and groups of scholars have framed different natural regions of the globe.

Theory from the South and the Inclusion of the North

To summarize then, these tropes have developed precisely because the geographical imagination has been relatively absent and the notion of the natural region has remained remarkably resilient. Another more recent constraint placed on the development of Arctic studies has been the development of *global* locutions by social theorists. The adoption of the Global North/Global South binary, as depicted by the Brandt Line in the 1980s, was an understandable attempt to change the simplistic East–West framing of the 'First', 'Second', and 'Third Worlds' of the Cold War. Just like problematic notions of the 'developed' and 'developing' worlds, as a northern scholar, I have often found the terms 'North' and 'South' equally problematic, because some of the groups I have worked with in the Arctic are quintessentially 'North', but at the same time very much 'Fourth World' using other typologies. All of these framings are problematic, and many of them result from the sorts of imaginations that Herbertson and his peers were discussing at the start of the twentieth century.

In their thought-provoking *Theory from the South*, anthropologists Jean and John Comaroff note that, although the 'Global South' is inchoate, the closest thing to a common denominator amongst its member states is that almost all were colonies.[64] The states in the 'Global South' did not all follow the same historical path, or were not colonized in the same historical period or epoch, but many suffered from the ongoing legacies of colonialism. But the same is true of the circumpolar north. The peoples of the northern latitudes have undergone internal colonialism, and now, in areas where forms of political independence have been ceded, there are new challenges from Chinese capital and South African mining companies. This remains an overarching consequence of the dividing of the globe into natural regions from colonial centres of knowledge production and cartographic delineation.

But it is in the spirit of the Comaroffs' theory – the idea that urban Euro-America is beginning to anticipate, even repeat, the recent history of sites in South Africa, Nigeria or Brazil – that the North (perhaps even, facetiously, the 'True North') needs to be incorporated. In a commentary on the Comaroffs, James Ferguson notes that South Africa itself is an anomaly – a place where

---

64 Comaroff and Comaroff, *Theory from the South*.

the past and the future, the 'Global South' and the 'Global North' coexist 'cheek by jowl' as Ferguson puts it.[65] Ferguson makes the joke that at last we get 'Theory from the South', and it is written by two white South Africans living in Chicago (both of whom have now moved to Harvard). Likewise, the sociologist Raewyn Connell in her articulation of *Southern Theory* does so from the vantage point of Sydney, Australia.[66]

In order to write back against the grain of the natural region, Tim Ingold has written about the need for 'histories *from* the North', which should be characterized by particular sensitivities to the peoples and environments found in the northern latitudes.[67] And similar arguments can, and have been, made about the Caribbean or southern Africa or West Africa or Latin America, and so on. At the very least, this problematizes simplistic ideas about core/periphery underlying much development theory, but at the same time it should also highlight that post-colonial relations and unequal distributions of power continue to persist at sites all over the world. Moreover, those histories and geographies are interconnected. So a reconstituted Arctic studies will always speak to global understandings as much as defiantly regional ones. This discussion raises issues for the scholarly conversations that 'northernists', in the widest sense, wish to have about 'northern exceptionality'. As Ingold put it, speaking at the conclusion of the International Polar Year, 2007–09:

> The ... challenge is how to avoid the risk of the North appearing to others, to scholars working in other fields, like just another region of the world, on a par with regions such as Melanesia, East and West Africa, Latin America, and so on, as if to say we can each do our own things in our respective regions of specialization. We must avoid this kind of ghettoization. ... [T]he North gives us ways of doing or telling history which are relevant to people anywhere, to scholars and to residents wherever they happen to live.[68]

The Circumpolar North and the Political Imagination

The argument that I have tried to make should be all the more concerning because the idea of a natural region, a region beholden to its environment, may have been partially reconfigured, but it continues to dominate the contemporary imagination about the circumpolar region. Many commentators continue

---

65 Ferguson, "Theory from the Comaroffs". 66 Connell, *Southern Theory*.
67 Ingold, "Closing Keynote Speech", 202. 68 Ingold, "Closing Keynote Speech", 202.

to reduce the Arctic to *ice*. The Arctic Ocean dominates much geopolitical and strategic discussion. Moreover, in scholarly study of the region, practitioners of climate science and ice sheet modelling continue to dominate agendas. Contemporary scholarship on the Arctic fetishizes *interdisciplinarity*, but these are approaches governed by what Barry, Born, and Weskalnys term a 'logic of interdisciplinarity' – an interdisciplinarity that sees little beyond the natural sciences, and in which the role of the social sciences is often reduced to input into models or public communication.[69] In this sense, the study of the Arctic, despite its recent popularity, remains framed by its emplacement as a natural region.

Moreover, these understandings of the North affect contemporary negotiations about land, sovereignty, and economic development. For example, a further element of the 'happy Inuit' stereotype, noted by Hugh Brody back in 1973, is the idea of the relative lack of political organization of Inuit society.[70] This trope has heavily influenced attempts at resource development in the contemporary Arctic, particularly in Greenland and parts of Siberia. There have been attempts by scholars to undermine these tropes. The Danish anthropologist Kirsten Hastrup, for example, has written sensitively about the idea of ice as argument.[71] I have written elsewhere about the ways in which expertise is proclaimed about the new Arctic.[72] A cottage industry of private consultants, civil servants, energy economists, and NGO practitioners has emerged since 2007, and collectively focuses precisely on Arctic region formation.

These governance and policy debates also impact on how different disciplines continue to understand and 'construct' different parts of the world, or regions. The geographers' world has remained split into regions, but only some of these have been deemed worthy of continuous concern. In other work, for example, I argue that this regional mentality has been particularly influential in the study of the polar regions. Each region was important, but the scholarship they inspired was variegated. This has had consequences in the emergence of critical intellectual traditions and scholarly communities around these different areas of the globe.

There have therefore also been legacies for understandings of Arctic geography – the environments and the cultures of the circumpolar region have become seen as easy to understand, and certain environmentally

---

69 Barry et al., "Logics of Interdisciplinarity", 25. 70 Brody, "Eskimo Politics".
71 Hastrup, "Ice as Argument".
72 Powell, "Configuring an 'Arctic Commons'?"; Powell, "Lines of Possession?".

determinist understandings of geography, from Andrew Herbertson to Robert Kaplan, have continued to dominate geographical and political imaginaries of the Arctic to this day. The long-term, historical deconstruction of this framing is the central objective of my current research.

Conclusion

As the writings of Boas and Herbertson, and more recent interventions by Alexander Murphy,[73] James Sidaway,[74] and Tariq Jazeel show,[75] geographers, like anthropologists, have always been fascinated by, and complicit in, the construction of regions.[76] More recently, scholars from emergent fields in critical international relations and global history have begun to interrogate the intellectual construction of geographical areas. Work in 'global history', such as that by Alison Bashford and David Armitage, has successfully begun to map the creation of circum-Pacific histories.[77] What I hope to have done here is begun to develop an intellectual history of geographies, theories, and narratives about the circumpolar north, and to use this to reveal the importance of nature, environment, and region to historical scholars. Stories of the exceptionality of the North and the Arctic, I argue, are less about the particularity of peoples and environments and more about the development of disciplinary traditions and practices. These narratives are places where the geographical imagination has been absent for too long. Consequently, the idea of a natural region in the North, and across the globe, has been all too pervasive. The consequences for the inhabitants of northern regions have been stark. As we continue to study the Arctic, there is a pressing need for the continuing investigation and reconstruction of such framings for the peoples, lands, and environments of the North.

Bibliography

Andersen, Astrid Nonbo, "The Greenland Reconciliation Commission: Moving Away from a Legal Framework," *Yearbook of Polar Law* 11 (2020).

Anderson, Amanda, and Joseph Valente, "Discipline and Freedom," in Amanda Anderson and Joseph Valente, eds., *Disciplinarity at the Fin de Siècle* (Princeton, NJ: Princeton University Press, 2002), 1–15.

---

73 Murphy, "Advancing Geographical Understanding".
74 Sidaway, "Geography, Globalization".   75 Jazeel, "Between Area and Discipline".
76 Powell et al., "Interventions".   77 Armitage and Bashford, eds., *Pacific Histories*, 6.

Appadurai, Arjun, "Theory in Anthropology: Center and Periphery", *Comparative Studies in Society and History* 28 (1986): 356–361.
Armitage, David, and Alison Bashford, eds., *Pacific Histories: Ocean, Land, People* (Basingstoke: Palgrave Macmillan, 2014).
Barnes, Trevor J., "Lives Lived, and Lives Told: Biographies of Geography's Quantitative Revolution", *Society and Space: Environment and Planning D* 19 (2001): 409–429.
Barr, William, "Geographical Aspects of the First International Polar Year, 1882–1883", *Annals of the Association of American Geographers* 73 (1983): 463–484.
Barry, Andrew, Georgina Born, and Gisa Weszkalnys, "Logics of Interdisciplinarity", *Economy and Society* 37 (2008): 20–49.
Birket-Smith, Kaj, *The Eskimos*, revised edition (London: Methuen, 1959).
Bjørst, Lill Rastad, "Saving or Destroying the Local Community? Conflicting Spatial Storylines in the Greenlandic Debate on Uranium", *The Extractive Industries and Society* 3 (2016): 34–40.
Boas, Franz, *Baffin-Land: Geographische Ergebnisse einer in den Jahren 1883 und 1884 ausgeführten Forschungsreise* (Gotha: J. Perthes, 1885).
Boas, Franz, "The Study of Geography", *Science* 9 (1887): 137–141.
Boas, Franz, *The Central Eskimo* (Washington, DC: Bureau of Ethnology to the Secretary of the Smithsonian Institution, 1888).
Boas, Franz, ed. *Race, Language and Culture* (New York: Macmillan Company, 1940).
Brody, Hugh, "Eskimo Politics: The Threat from the South", *New Left Review* I (1973): 60–68.
Bunzl, Matti, "Franz Boas and the Humboldtian Tradition: From Volksgeist and Nationalcharakter to an Anthropological Concept of Culture", in George W. Stocking Jr, ed., *Volksgeist as Method and Ethic: Essays on Boasian Ethnography and the German Anthropological Tradition* (Madison: University of Wisconsin Press, 1996), pp. 17–78.
Chorley, Richard J., and Peter Haggett, eds., *Models in Geography* (London: Methuen, 1967).
Cole, Douglas, *Franz Boas: The Early Years, 1858–1906* (Seattle: University of Washington Press, 1999).
Cole, Douglas, and Ludger Müller-Wille, "Franz Boas' Expedition to Baffin Island, 1883–1884", *Études/Inuit/Studies* 8 (1984): 37–63.
Comaroff, Jean, and John L. Comaroff, *Theory from the South: Or, How Euro-America Is Evolving Toward Africa* (Boulder, CO: Paradigm, 2012).
Connell, Raewyn, *Southern Theory: The Global Dynamics of Knowledge in Social Science* (Cambridge: Polity, 2007).
Davidson, Peter, *The Idea of North* (London: Reaktion, 2005).
Davis, William M., "The Study of Geography", *Science* 10 (1887): 131–132.
Dickinson, Robert E., and O. J. R. Howarth, *The Making of Geography* (Oxford: Clarendon, 1933).
Durkheim, Émile, *Le Suicide: Étude de Sociologie* (Paris: F. Alcan, 1897).
Espagne, Michel, and Isabelle Kalinowski, eds., *Franz Boas: Le travail du regard* (Paris: Armand Colin, 2013).
Ferguson, James, "Theory from the Comaroffs, or How to Know the World Up, Down, Backwards and Forwards", *Theorizing the Contemporary, Fieldsights* (25 February 2012), no pagination, https://culanth.org/fieldsights/theory-from-the-comaroffs-or-how-to-know-the-world-up-down-backwards-and-forwards (accessed 16 April 2021).
Ferguson, Niall, *Empire: How Britain Made the Modern World* (London: Allen Lane, 2003).

Gad, Ulrik Pram, *National Identity Politics and Postcolonial Sovereignty Games: Greenland, Denmark, and the European Union*, Meddelelser om Grønland/Monographs on Greenland, Man and Society (Copenhagen: Museum Tusculanum, 2016).

Grace, Sherrill, *Canada and the Idea of North* (Montréal, Kingston, Buffalo, London: McGill-Queen's University Press, 2001).

Hartshorne, Richard, *The Nature of Geography: A Critical Survey of Current Thought in the Light of the Past* (Lancaster, PA: Association of American Geographers, 1939).

Hastrup, Kirsten, "The Ice As Argument: Topographical Mementos in the High Arctic", *Cambridge Journal of Anthropology* 31 (2013): 51–67.

Heffernan, Michael, "Mapping Schmitt", in Stephen Legg, ed., *Spatiality, Sovereignty and Carl Schmitt: Geographies of the Nomos* (London, New York: Routledge, 2011), pp. 234–243.

Herbertson, Andrew J., "The Major Natural Regions: An Essay in Systematic Geography", *Geographical Journal* 25 (1905): 300–312.

Hughes, Charles C., "Under Four Flags: Recent Culture Change among the Eskimos", *Current Anthropology* 6 (1965): 3–69.

Hulan, Renée, *Northern Experience and the Myths of Canadian Culture* (Montréal, Kingston, Buffalo, London: McGill-Queen's University Press, 2002).

Ingold, Tim, "Closing Keynote Speech", in John P. Ziker and Florian Stammler, eds., *Histories from the North: Environments, Movements, and Narratives* (Boise, ID: Boise State University, 2011), pp. 198–210.

Jazeel, Tariq, "Between Area and Discipline: Progress, Knowledge Production and the Geographies of Geography", *Progress in Human Geography* 40 (2016): 649–667.

Jensen, Lars, "Commemoration, Nation Narration, and Colonial Historiography in Postcolonial Denmark", *Scandinavian Studies* 91 (2019): 13–30.

Kaplan, David, *The Revenge of Geography: What the Map Tells Us About Coming Conflicts and the Battle Against Fate* (New York: Random House, 2012).

Kearns, Gerry, *Geopolitics and Empire: The Legacy of Halford Mackinder* (Oxford: Oxford University Press, 2009).

Kropotkin, P., "What Geography Ought to Be", *Nineteenth Century* 18 (1885): 940–956.

Krupnik, Igor, ed., *Early Inuit Studies: Themes and Transitions, 1850s–1980s* (Washington, DC: Smithsonian Institution Scholarly Press, 2016).

Kulchyski, Peter, *Aboriginal Rights Are Not Human Rights and Other Essays on Law, Politics and Culture* (Winnipeg, MB; Arbeiter Ring, 2013).

Lévi-Strauss, Claude, *The Savage Mind* (Chicago: University of Chicago Press, 1962).

Liss, Julia E., "Patterns of Strangeness: Franz Boas, Modernism, and the Origins of Anthropology", in Elazar Barkan and Ronald Bush, eds., *Prehistories of the Future: The Primitivist Project and the Culture of Modernism* (Stanford: Stanford University Press, 1995), pp. 114–130.

Livingstone, David N., *The Geographical Tradition: Episodes in the History of a Contested Enterprise* (Oxford: Blackwell, 1992).

Livingstone, David N., "The History of Science and the History of Geography: Interactions and Implications", *History of Science* 22 (1984): 271–302.

Mackinder, Halford J., *Democratic Ideals and Reality: A Study in the Politics of Reconstruction* (London: Constable, 1919).

Mackinder, Halford J., "The Geographical Pivot of History," *The Geographical Journal* 23 (1904): 421–437.

Mackinder, Halford J., "On the Scope and Methods of Geography", *Proceedings of the Royal Geographical Society and Monthly Record of Geography*, New Monthly Series 9 (1887): 141–174.

Mauss, Marcel, "Essai sur les variations saisonnières des sociétés eskimo: Étude de morphologie sociale" (avec la collaboration de H. Beuchat), *l'Année Sociologique* IX (1904–05).

Müller-Wille, Ludger, *The Franz Boas Enigma* (Montréal: Baraka, 2014).

Müller-Wille, Ludger, ed., *Franz Boas among the Inuit of Baffin Island 1883–1884: Journals and Letters*, trans. William Barr (Toronto: University of Toronto Press, 1998).

Müller-Wille, Ludger, and Bernd Gieseking, *Inuit Whalers on Baffin Island through German Eyes: Wilhelm Weike's Arctic Journal and Letters (1883–84)*, trans. William Barr (Montréal: Baraka, 2011).

Murphy, Alexander B., "Advancing Geographical Understanding: Why Engaging Grand Regional Narratives Matters", *Dialogues in Human Geography* 3 (2013): 131–149.

Postel-Vinay, Karoline, "European Power and the Mapping of Global Order", in Kalypso Nicolaïdis, Berny Sèbe, and Gabrielle Maas, eds., *Echoes of Empire: Memory, Identity and Colonial Legacies* (London, New York: I.B. Tauris, 2015), pp. 323–336.

Powell, Richard C., "Configuring an 'Arctic Commons'?", *Political Geography* 27 (2008): 827–832.

Powell, Richard C., "Echoes of the New Geography? History and Philosophy of Geography I", *Progress in Human Geography* 36 (2012): 518–526.

Powell, Richard C., "Institutions, Resources and the Governance of Postcolonial Greenland", in Dawn A. Berry, Nigel Bowles, and Halbert Jones, eds., *Governing the North American Arctic: Sovereignty, Security, and Institutions* (London: Palgrave Macmillan, 2016), pp. 200–216.

Powell, Richard C., "Lines of Possession? The Anxious Constitution of a Polar Geopolitics", *Political Geography* 29 (2010): 74–77.

Powell, Richard C., "Northern Cultures: Myths, Geographies and Representational Practices", *Cultural Geographies* 12 (2005): 371–378.

Powell, Richard C., "Notes on a Geographical Canon? Measures, Models and Scholarly Enterprise", *Journal of Historical Geography* 49 (2015): 2–8.

Powell, Richard C., "Questions on the Canon?", *Dialogues in Human Geography* 2 (2012): 338–340.

Powell, Richard C., "The Sirens' Voices? Field Practices and Dialogue in Geography", *Area* 34 (2002): 261–272.

Powell, Richard C., "The Study of Geography? Franz Boas and His Canonical Returns", *Journal of Historical Geography* 49 (2015): 21–30.

Powell, Richard C., Ian Klinke, Tariq Jazeel, et al., "Interventions in the Political Geographies of 'Area'", *Political Geography* 57 (2017): 94–104.

Ratzel, Friedrich, *Anthropo-Geographie oder Grundzüge der Anwendung der Erdkunde auf die Geschichte* (Stuttgart: Englehorn, 1882).

Riches, David, "Force of Tradition in Eskimology", in Richard Fardon, ed., *Localizing Strategies: Regional Traditions of Ethnographic Writing* (Edinburgh: Scottish Academic Press, 1990), pp. 71–89.

Richling, Barnett, *In Twilight and in Dawn: A Biography of Diamond Jenness* (Montréal, Kingston, Buffalo, London: McGill-Queen's University Press, 2012).

Rud, Søren, *Colonialism in Greenland: Tradition, Governance and Legacy* (London: Palgrave Macmillan, 2017).

Sidaway, James D., "Geography, Globalization, and the Problematic of Area Studies", *Annals of the Association of American Geographers* 103 (2013): 984–1002.

Skinner, Quentin, "Introduction: The Return of Grand Theory", in Quentin Skinner, ed., *The Return of Grand Theory in the Human Sciences* (Cambridge: Cambridge University Press, 1985), pp. 1–20.

Spencer, Robert F., "Review of *The Eskimos* by Kaj Birket-Smith", *American Anthropologist* 63 (1961): 161–162.

Stern, Pamela, and Lisa Stevenson, eds., *Critical Inuit Studies: An Anthology of Contemporary Arctic Ethnography* (Lincoln, NE, London: University of Nebraska Press, 2006).

Stevenson, Lisa, *Life Beside Itself Imagining Care in the Canadian Arctic* (Oakland, CA: University of California Press, 2014).

Stocking, George W., Jr, *The Ethnographer's Magic and Other Essays in the History of Anthropology* (Madison: University of Wisconsin Press, 1992).

Stocking, George W., Jr, "From Physics to Ethnology: Franz Boas' Arctic Expedition as a Problem in the Historiography of the Behavioral Sciences", *Journal of the History of the Behavioral Sciences* 1 (1965): 54–66.

Trindell, Roger T., "Franz Boas and American Geography", *Professional Geographer* 21 (1969): 328–332.

Wachowich, Nancy, "Creative Technologies: Experimentation and Social Practice in Arctic Societies", *Études/Inuit/Studies* 34 (2010): 13–19.

13

Britain's Polar Empire, 1769–1982

DANIELLA MCCAHEY

Introduction

In 2012, Britain's National Environmental Research Council (NERC) proposed a 25 per cent budget cut for the British Antarctic Survey (BAS), the organization responsible for science and administration in the British Antarctic. When BAS Director Nicholas Owens learned of these proposed cuts, he ignited a political maelstrom by taking the matter straight to the Foreign Office, sidestepping NERC Director Duncan Wingham. In response, Prime Minister David Cameron pledged support for BAS and ordered the funding dispute resolved. Then the crisis worsened when Owens was suspended and temporarily replaced by Ed Hill, the director of the National Oceanographic Centre. Possibly drawing on the close association between British polar and ocean studies, Wingham then proposed merging BAS and the National Oceanography Centre later that year, with the new institute to bear the name 'the NERC Centre for Marine and Polar Science'.[1] This move caused an immediate uproar among both scientists and policymakers. Robert Culshaw, BAS's former deputy director, testified that 'merging BAS with the National Oceanography Centre ... would expose British nationals in the British Antarctic Territory and the adjacent maritime region (including South Georgia) to greater risk. It would also pave the way to weakening the British presence in this strategically important area.'[2]

Wingham was called before the House of Commons to answer for these administrative changes and castigated 'for failing to justify the move on cost or scientific grounds; for failing to consult properly, and not taking into account the survey's geopolitical role in the South Atlantic'.[3] This incident

---

[1] Juniper, "'Axing the British Antarctic Survey'".
[2] Written evidence submitted by Robert Culshaw (MS34), Written Memoranda, Proposed merger of British Antarctic Survey and National Oceanography Centre, UK Parliament Web Archive.
[3] Carrington and McKie, "Research Boss Wingham".

13 Britain's Polar Empire, 1769–1982

reified BAS's origin when it was established in 1945 as the Falkland Islands Dependencies Survey before changing its name in 1962, for which 'the basic purpose ... is political, namely to maintain our title to the U.K. Sector by acts of occupation and "administration"'.[4] Over time, the political imperative of BAS, as BAS supporter John Richard Dudeney asserted, 'far from fading away, remains an overriding issue'.[5] Shortly after Wingham's chastisement, NERC dropped the merger plan.

While the above episode demonstrates how the British Antarctic Survey remains a geopolitical tool in the Southern Atlantic, ironically, Wingham's idea to create a centre dedicated to both the oceans and the poles makes sense, considering Britain's historical imperial strengths. The role of the Antarctic within the context of Britain's vast territorial empire has been covered extensively by many historians.[6] Most of this work tends to focus on Britain's land claims in the region. Likewise, there has been work on the centrality of the sea to the history of Antarctica, but this work unevenly addresses the role of the sea in imperialism, with the exception of work done on Antarctic whaling in this period.[7] The British Empire's presence in the Antarctic has traditionally been considered to be a land-based exercise, but this conception diminishes the primacy of sea power and marine management programmes critical to British exploration and the British justification of sovereignty claims in the Antarctic.

Even given the challenges of defining where ice ends and land begins, the terrestrial focus of studies of British imperialism in polar regions is not surprising. Generally, studies focusing on the histories of geopolitics and the acquisition of territory have focused on land.[8] How can you colonize uninhabitable spaces such as air, ice, or water?[9] This chapter narrates the history of British imperialism in the Antarctic, arguing that a sea-focused history of Antarctica not only explains both the initial British interest in the region and its continuing attempts to maintain sovereignty, but also complicates the idea of empire and imperialism more broadly.

---

4 Letter from J. S. Bennett to Miles Clifford, 10 May 1950, SPRI Archives, MS 1326 Stanley Office Proposal of the TAE Box 3.
5 Written evidence submitted by John Richard Dudeney OBE (MS33), Written Memoranda, Proposed merger of British Antarctic Survey and National Oceanography Centre, UK Parliament Web Archive.
6 See, for example, Dodds, *Pink Ice*; Howkins, *Frozen Empires*; Maddison, *Class and Colonialism*.
7 See, for example, Antonello, "Southern Ocean"; Benson and Rozwadowski, *Extremes*; McCann, *Wild Sea*.
8 Peters et al., "Introduction". 9 Carroll, *Empire of Air*.

The chapter will briefly discuss the maritime expeditions of James Cook and James Clark Ross, which were motivated by suppositions that Antarctic exploration could contribute to Britain's maritime trade and economy and aid in the dominance of the Royal Navy in international waters. The chapter then turns to the start of the twentieth century, a time of increasing land-based exploration in the Antarctic, which also ushered in massive industrial exploration of this region by whaling ships. These whalers were managed and operated under the purview of the Colonial Office, which licensed and taxed the whalers hunting in the Southern Ocean, and also embarked on a major resource management programme in the region, known as the Discovery Investigations. As the United Kingdom continued to maintain claims in the Antarctic, even after the 1959 Antarctic Treaty, many of these claims continue to involve concerns over the fisheries, access of tourist cruise ships, and sea power. Examining the history of imperialism in Antarctica with a sea-based perspective shows that the British understanding of Antarctica was never based on the land, but has always involved the region as a whole: the surrounding sub-Antarctic islands, continental land, ice, airs, and sea.

New Waters: Antarctica and Empire in the Eighteenth Century

Historically, the British Empire strongly identified itself with its mastery of the oceans. This is largely a product of geography; as an island nation, it was forced to build a strong relationship with the sea.[10] British navigators were among the first to explore the Antarctic Ocean during the eighteenth century, driven in part to discover the long-hypothesized *Terra Australis Incognita*, a massive undiscovered southern continent. The Scottish hydrographer Alexander Dalrymple published his *Account of the Discoveries made in the South Pacific Ocean* (1769), arguing for the existence of such a continent and detailing the reasons that Britain should seek it. Dalrymple stressed that 'there can be no object more important than discoveries in the South Sea; discoveries, not merely for the *figure of the lands*; not with a view of colonizing; not with the view of conquest; but of an amicable intercourse for mutual benefit'.[11] Any country that opened trade with such a new land, Dalrymple predicted, would certainly be the greatest power in the world. His vision of empire was not concerned with land expansion; in fact, he even argued that the 'East-India

---

10 Reidy and Rozwadowski, "Spaces in Between".
11 Dalrymple, *Historical Collection*, xxviii.

Company are much too engaged in territorial dominion', and recommended focusing on economic and maritime power.[12]

Prompted in part by Dalrymple's urging, in 1772, the Royal Society and the Admiralty collaborated to send an expedition led by naval officer James Cook to explore the Southern Oceans and find a southern continent. In January 1773, Cook became the first documented explorer to cross into the Antarctic Circle. Cook did not make it as far as the continent, coming within 160 km of the Antarctic mainland, when, hindered by the dangerous sea conditions, he wrote that the continent, 'if it actually exists, must lie within the polar circle, where the sea is so encumbered with ice, that the land is rendered inaccessible'.[13] Though this voyage did not result in the discovery of Antarctica, it did result in the vast expansion of the British Empire, through Cook's discovery and claims to regions including Australia, New Zealand, and the sub-Antarctic islands of South Georgia and the South Sandwich Islands. However, Cook's estimation of South Georgia and the South Sandwich Islands cast serious doubts on any value that the land in the Antarctic could yield:

> Lands doomed by Nature to perpetual frigidness; never to feel the warmth of the sun's rays; whose horrible and savage aspect I have not words to describe. Such are the lands we have discovered; what then may we expect those to be which lie still farther to the south? ... If any one should have resolution and perseverance to clear up this point by proceeding farther than I have done, I shall not envy him the honour of the discovery; but I will be bold to say, that the world will not be benefited by it.[14]

Cook's attempts to discover an unknown southern continent on behalf of the British government echoed a similar 1773 expedition to the Arctic, fruitlessly searching for the Northwest Passage. And although Cook did not discover the southern continent, British whalers and sealers continued to be active in the marine and sub-Antarctic islands he discovered. In 1820, three different parties made the first documented sightings of the Antarctic continent, including that of Royal Naval officer Edward Bransfield, investigating, surveying, and claiming for Great Britain the newly discovered South Shetland Islands. Although none of these expeditions resulted in landing on the Antarctic continent, in the mid-twentieth century the United Kingdom used Cook and Bransfield's respective sea voyages to argue for sovereignty based on the rights of discovery.

12 Dalrymple, *Historical Collection*, xxvi.   13 Quoted in Wright, *Seventh Continent*, 58.
14 Cook, *Voyage*.

The Royal Navy, Science and Empire: Antarctica in the Nineteenth Century

In the mid-nineteenth century, the British interest in the Antarctic was primarily related to the Magnetic Crusade (1841–57). Described as 'by far the greatest scientific undertaking the world has ever seen',[15] this was a major international data-collecting enterprise which established geomagnetic observatories in British imperial territories around the world.[16] National interest in geomagnetic explorations came in part from fears of foreign investigations of geomagnetism, a field which was viewed as a British domain.[17] These included major contemporary American and French expeditions to the Antarctic, where their respective scientists collected geomagnetic data.

One major focus of the Magnetic Crusade was organizing expeditions to locate the magnetic poles, the two opposite foci of the Earth's magnetic field.[18] Spurred by the advocacy of Edward Sabine, a prominent member of the Royal Society and a scientific advisor to the Admiralty, the Royal Navy and the Royal Society organized an expedition, led by James Clark Ross, and comprising HMS *Erebus* and *Terror*, to travel to the Antarctic in order to amend 'the deficiency, yet existing in our knowledge of terrestrial magnetism in the southern hemisphere'.[19] Ross had previously led an expedition to the Arctic in search of the magnetic pole.

The Ross Expedition's main purpose was to be a

> naval expedition expressly directed to [geomagnetic] observations in the antarctic [sic] seas ... Identifying the existence and accessibility of two points of maximum intensity in the southern as in the northern hemisphere ... is regarded as a first and, indeed indispensable step to the construction of a rigorous and complete theory of terrestrial magnetism.[20]

After departing Europe in August 1839, in January 1841 the expedition 'shaped our course directly for the Magnetic Pole ... [but] the land interposed an insuperable obstacle to our direct approach.'[21]

Although the Ross expedition did not visit the magnetic South Pole, it 'had approached the pole some hundreds of miles nearer than any of our predecessors; and from the multitude of observations that were made in so many directions from it, its position may be determined with nearly as much

---

15 Quoted in Cawood, "Magnetic Crusade", 493.   16 Goodman, "Follow the Data".
17 Cawood, "Magnetic Crusade".   18 Good, "Follow the Needle", 163.
19 J. S. Herschel, "Introduction", in Ross, *Voyage of Discovery*, vi.
20 Herschel in Ross, *Voyage of Discovery*, viii–xvi.   21 Ross, *Voyage of Discovery*, 182–188.

accuracy as if we actually reached the spot itself'.²² From these observations, the scientists could infer the Pole's position from measurements taken from the sea, resulting in the first definitive charts of magnetic declination, magnetic dip, and magnetic intensity. These magnetic charts contributed to the Royal Navy's ability to manoeuvre through the oceans, supporting Britain's imperial prosperity and security. The *Terror* and the *Erebus* were famously later lost during John Franklin's 1845 voyage to the Arctic, where the crew also recorded magnetic data, understanding that such information could aid in navigation.

Ross's Antarctic expedition was crucial to the nineteenth-century imperial regime. First, it served as a continuation of British exploratory expeditions that linked the production of scientific knowledge with the power and structure of the Royal Navy. Additionally, its geographical scope, focusing on geomagnetism and tidology, demonstrates that a large-scale commitment was needed to produce usable charts, not only in these fields, but other burgeoning disciplines such as meteorology.²³ As a result, every colonial outpost in the British Empire became a potential research site for large-scale data collection. The more territory that they controlled, the more potential for understanding the behaviour of the Earth. And the better that they understood magnetism, wind and sea currents, weather, and so on, the more efficient their military and commercial effects at sea. And so it became that knowledge, in this case knowledge of the oceans, and the imperial project were inextricably linked.

The British Empire and the Heroic Age of Antarctic Exploration

On 27 November 1893, the pioneering Scottish oceanographer John Murray (1841–1914) read an address to the Royal Geographical Society, making a case for the 'Renewal of Antarctic Exploration'.²⁴ Murray, who had served on the globe-crossing *Challenger* Expedition (1872–76), framed his call for greater British involvement in the Antarctic both as an imperial necessity and as a natural calling for a maritime nation; Antarctic exploration would be 'an undertaking worthy of the maritime position and the scientific reputation of this great empire'.²⁵ Referencing the maritime expeditions of Cook and Ross, among others, Murray queried his listeners: 'Is the last great piece of

---

22 Ross, *Voyage of Discovery*, 246.   23 Reidy, *Tides of History*, 285.
24 Murray, "Renewal of Antarctic Exploration".
25 Murray, "Renewal of Antarctic Exploration", 27.

maritime exploration on the surface of our Earth to be undertaken by Britons, or is it to be left to those who may be destined to succeed or supplant us on the ocean?'[26]

Murray was certain that this exploration, which he framed largely as a maritime one, 'should be undertaken by the Royal Navy ... [since] the prestige of the navy does not alone consist of its powers of defence and attack. It has in times of peace made glorious conquests over the powers of Nature'.[27] Additionally, in contrast to the ultimate goals of multiple British expeditions undertaken in the wake of this speech, he posited that 'A dash at the South Pole is not, however, what I now advocate.' Instead, Murray argued that the British Empire should commit to 'a steady, continuous, laborious, and systematic exploration of the whole southern region'.[28] Not long after Murray's address to the Royal Geographical Society, plans were under way to send expeditions to Antarctica.

Even though the first two decades of the twentieth century are better known for their land-based expeditions on the surface of the continent, these were all extremely dependent on the sea. Until 1955, the sea was the only way to travel to Antarctica. Much of the personnel of these expeditions, including the famed explorers Robert Falcon Scott and Ernest Shackleton, had served in either the Royal Navy or the Merchant Navy. British explorer Apsley Cherry-Garrard noted that in the cases of both the *Discovery* and *Terra Nova* Expeditions, 'The executive officers and crew were Royal Navy almost without exception.'[29] This reliance on the sea in expeditions ostensibly meant to show British imperial dominance over the Antarctic interior is particularly clear in the case of the Imperial Trans-Antarctic Expedition, an unsuccessful effort to traverse the continent. The perilous voyage proved that British sea-based successes did not translate to efforts on land. Indeed, the only thing that saved the crossing party from death was the fact that South Georgia, owing to the richness of marine life in the Southern Ocean, was populated by both whaling stations and British administration. Ernest Shackleton's unlikely rescue of his men, which was widely praised, should also be credited to the navigation skills of Frank Worsley, whose success in navigating from Elephant Island to South Georgia showed, among other qualities, a mastery of seafaring. Ultimately the party was rescued by a Chilean naval vessel.

26 Murray, "Renewal of Antarctic Exploration", 2.
27 Murray, "Renewal of Antarctic Exploration", 25–26.
28 Murray, "Renewal of Antarctic Exploration", 25.
29 Cherry-Garrard, *The Worst Journey*, xxxiii–xxxiv.

The Riches of the Ocean: South Atlantic Sealing and Whaling

In the early nineteenth century, Antarctica and many of the sub-Antarctic islands became popular destinations for mostly British and American sealers, driven largely by burgeoning fur seal trade with China.[30] In this period, seal hunting followed a boom-and-bust cycle. Sealers would descend on an island, kill all the fur seals that they could find, and move on. Because of this unrestrained harvesting of local seal populations, by the mid-nineteenth century, fur seals on South Georgia had been hunted almost to extinction. In fact, one visiting British naturalist commented as early as 1838 that 'This beautiful little animal was once most numerous here, but was almost exterminated by the sealers, at the time these islands were first discovered.'[31] Not long after, sealers targeted Antarctic and sub-Antarctic islands seeking the blubber of elephant seals, a practice that officially ended with the Antarctic Treaty System's Convention for the Conservation of Antarctic Seals in 1972. But for most of the nineteenth century, the most active and continuous human presence in the region made no claims to the massive land frontier; they were only interested in chasing the maritime resources.

While sealing continued through the nineteenth and halfway through the twentieth centuries, starting in the early twentieth century the Southern Ocean became an important region for the harvesting of whales. Although whalers were present in the Antarctic throughout the nineteenth century, systematic and large-scale hunts in the region began by the early twentieth century. In 1904, British-Norwegian whaler Carl A. Larsen applied for whaling leases at the British Legation in Argentina for his new enterprise, the Compañía Argentina de Pesca. Shortly afterward, the government of the Falkland Islands issued Ordinance No. 3 of 1906, which made it illegal to hunt whales in this region without a licence and created a tax for each whale harvested. This ordinance was amended by further whaling and sealing restrictions passed in subsequent years. Larsen's first whaling venture paid a 70 per cent dividend in the first year, and by 1911, eight whaling companies operated seven stations at South Georgia.

Over the next fifty years, vast numbers of whales were hunted extensively in the Southern Ocean. Whale oil was a valuable commodity, used in

---

30 Basberg and Headland, "Economic Significance".
31 Fanning, *Voyages to South Seas*, 209.

lubricants, lamp fuel, explosives (adding another geopolitical dimension to whaling at the outbreak of World War I), and, starting in the twentieth century, in margarine in the face of a global fat shortage.[32] It was within this context that Britain made its first territorial claim to Antarctica, a claim that included the waters which were then yielding such a large profit. In 1908, the United Kingdom extended its territorial claim beyond the Falkland Islands and declared sovereignty over 'South Georgia, the South Orkneys, the South Shetlands, the Sandwich Islands, and Graham's Land, situated in the South Atlantic Ocean and on the Antarctic continent to the south of the 50th parallel of south latitude, and lying between the 20th and the 80th degrees of west longitude', a region to be administered through the Colonial Office.[33] This claim was shortly followed by claims from New Zealand and Australia in the Ross Dependency and the Australian Antarctic Territory, respectively, effectively placing most of the continent, as well as its surrounding islands and waters, under British imperial rule. These actions demonstrated a clear intention for the British Empire to acquire as much Antarctic territory as possible. To quote a 1920 memo from Leopold Amery, Under-Secretary of State for the Colonies: 'It is desirable that the whole of the Antarctic should ultimately be included in the British Empire.'[34]

Similarly, in 1930, Antarctic explorer and geologist Thomas Griffith Taylor tied Antarctic territorial claims very strongly to Antarctic whaling, writing, 'In Antarctica ... the flag follows the trade. No nation made any definite claim to Antarctica until the development of whaling in southern waters showed that, however poor the land might be, here was a very valuable territory.'[35] He later added that Antarctica as a whole represents 'Land covered by ice, hard to discover, valueless for commerce, but surrounded by richly endowed seas and touched with mystery and the romance of the unknown.'[36]

It was during this period that the British Empire began the first large-scale and sustained scientific research programme for the region, although it was largely a veneer for justifying taxation of the whaling industry.[37] In 1918, the Colonial Office organized the Discovery Committee which, beginning in 1924, conducted investigations to provide the scientific background to stock management of the commercial Antarctic fishery, the most lucrative in the

---

32 Tønnessen and Johnsen, *History of Modern Whaling*.
33 Quoted in Christie, *The Antarctic Problem*, 301.
34 Quoted in Beck, "International Relations in Antarctica", 112.
35 Taylor, *Antarctic Adventure and Research*, 220.
36 Taylor, *Antarctic Adventure and Research*, 231.   37 Roberts, *European Antarctic*.

world by the end of the decade. In 1925, the British government established a small marine laboratory for the Discovery Investigations, located at King Edward Point, the 'capital' of South Georgia. Despite the centrality of South Georgia as a home base for these research programmes, the primary reason for its existence was for the exploration of the sea and management of maritime life. Thus, as 'A picture of life in an ocean depends upon a knowledge of its relationships to its physical basis – the water', over the years the Royal Research Ships *Discovery*, *William Scoresby*, and *Discovery II* 'crossed and recrossed the waters of the Falkland Sector of the Antarctic', as well as venturing to New Zealand and its Antarctic waters.[38] The investigations continued until 1951 and resulted in thirty-seven reports on whale migration, diet, and behaviour, published between 1929 and 1980.

Whaling in the Southern Ocean was somewhat slowed in 1946 because of the International Whaling Convention (IWC), adopted to 'provide for the proper conservation of whale stocks and thus make possible the orderly development of the whaling industry'.[39] Shore-based whaling at South Georgia ended in 1965, driven by decreasing stocks, fears of overfishing, and cultural shifts regarding marine mammals. When the IWC issued a moratorium on the practice in 1982, whaling in the Southern Ocean largely ceased, with the notable exception of Japanese whaling programmes, which continued to operate under the guise of scientific legitimacy.[40]

Competing Claims: Argentina, Chile, and the British Empire

During the 1940s, the British claim to the Falkland Islands Dependencies was challenged by competing claims from Argentina and Chile, claims largely stemming from frustrations about the involvement of Britain in the Southern Cone's economics and politics more generally. Worried about German incursions in the region, the Colonial Office and the Admiralty collaborated on a secret wartime mission to Antarctica. Alarmed at evidence of Argentine visits to the area, Operation Tabarin, as it was known, resulted in the establishment of three British stations, Deception Island, Port Lockroy, and Hope Bay.[41] In 1945, Operation Tabarin was succeeded by the Falkland Islands Dependencies Survey (FIDS), and by 1955, the British had built ten permanent meteorological stations on the Antarctic Peninsula. In the same

---

38 John, "Second Antarctic Commission". 39 *International Whaling Convention, 1946*.
40 McCahey and Cole, "Human(e) Science?". 41 Taylor, *Two Years*.

period, Chile built five and Argentina built nine, all also on the Peninsula. The scientific data gathered at these stations was a by-product of the political standoff among these countries.[42] Argentina and Britain engaged in acts of gunboat diplomacy to advertise their claims, most intensely in a 1952 incident at Hope Bay when shots were fired, though the situation was quickly defused.[43]

In 1955, in response to the 'illegal claims of these two countries to and encroachments on, British territory in Antarctica', the United Kingdom filed applications against Argentina and Chile in the International Court of Justice.[44] To justify their claim, the United Kingdom offered several pieces of evidence that they believed should sway the court in their favour. The first was through right of discovery; many of the earliest noted sightings of Antarctica and the sub-Antarctic islands came from British maritime expeditions. But more strongly than this assertion, the British application focused extensively on its management of the region's maritime resources.

This application argued that while there had been comparatively little human activity in Antarctica in the second half of the nineteenth century, the revitalization of the region 'called for a corresponding exercise of State authority in the Antarctic'.[45] Since the United Kingdom had instituted several ordinances requiring that whalers obtain licences and pay taxes in order to hunt in the region, it had performed the necessary role of the state in order to manage the populations of whales and whalers. These laws, for which the 'chief object ... was the conservation of stocks', the application argued, 'provide convincing proof of the effectiveness of Great Britain's display and exercise of sovereignty.'[46]

Not only did this application identify the British state's administration of this territory, but it also pointed to the Discovery Investigations, highlighting its focus on marine research and hydrographic exploration: 'Numerous voyages among the principal territories of the Dependencies were made by these ships on each commission, and detailed surveys were made of their coasts and coastal waters.'[47]

With these, among other activities, 'Great Britain alone undertook the responsibilities of sovereignty and performed the functions of a state',[48] and 'has at all times taken all such steps as were open to it in the circumstances to

42 Howkins, "Weather". 43 Dodds, "End of a Polar Empire?".
44 Letter from G. G. Fitzmaurice to Register of International Court of Justice, 31 August 1955. *Antarctica (United Kingdom v. Argentina)*, International Court of Justice.
45 Application Instituting Proceedings, *Antarctica (United Kingdom v. Argentina)*, 13.
46 Application Instituting Proceedings, *Antarctica (United Kingdom v. Argentina)*, 16.
47 Application Instituting Proceedings, *Antarctica (United Kingdom v. Argentina)*, 29.
48 Application Instituting Proceedings, *Antarctica (United Kingdom v. Argentina)*, 27.

assert and maintain its title',[49] despite the frequent incursions of Argentine naval vessels. With this application, the United Kingdom submitted to the judgement of the International Court of Justice. However, Argentina and Chile did not respond or otherwise consent to the Court's jurisdiction, so it had no authority to issue a binding resolution of the dispute.

The IGY and the British Polar Empire

Despite being 'justified in taking strong measures to put an end to Argentina's encroachment',[50] the United Kingdom shifted focus from its ICJ claim to the impending International Geophysical Year (IGY), an international collaboration to collect geophysical data from around the world. Not everyone in the British polar community was pleased with the idea of the IGY. Foreign activity in the Antarctic continent could disrupt British territorial claims in the region, but also there was a general fear that the 'world will more easily forget our work in Antarctica, overshadowed by present spectacular operations by Russia and America'.[51]

At the 1954 meeting of the Special Committee of the IGY, delegates of various member nations discussed the geographical distribution of research stations around the world, noting gaps in the proposed network of Antarctic stations. Based on these gaps, the committee made recommendations to establish an additional station, near 77° S 35° W, near the Vahsel Bay region of the Weddell Sea. In response, in 1955, the Argentine Navy set up a base on the Filchner Ice Shelf. But later that year, the British delegation announced their own plans for a base in the same area. It was immediately clear that this base's construction was not just for the cooperative scientific aims of the IGY, but at least 'in part to support its assertion to sovereignty over the region'.[52]

The plan to establish a base at Vahsel Bay did not benefit from universal support among the British scientific or polar communities. In fact, even after Argentina announced its plan to build its base, many still doubted the value of an additional British station in the region. Building at such an inaccessible site would be extremely expensive and would pull resources from other British stations on the Antarctic Peninsula. For example, since the United Kingdom did not own an icebreaker, building in this area could necessitate the purchase of such a ship, a costly investment. Otherwise, if the scientists ran into

---

49 Application Instituting Proceedings, *Antarctica (United Kingdom v. Argentina)*, 30.
50 Application Instituting Proceedings, *Antarctica (United Kingdom v. Argentina)*, 35.
51 Copy of Meeting Minutes SPRI MS1308/51/7 CC Brian Roberts IGY Great Britain.
52 Sullivan, *Assault on the Unknown*, 294.

trouble, the United Kingdom could face major political embarrassment if its personnel needed to be rescued by an Argentine icebreaker. But the announcement of the Commonwealth Trans-Antarctic Expedition, organized by Vivian Fuchs, essentially forced the Royal Society and the British government into making some sort of permanent station in the Weddell Sea, even if it was not universally thought a good idea, because 'any withdrawal now would leave the Argentines in possession of a base in the area and would greatly weaken our title to the eastern portion of the United Kingdom sector'.[53]

However, the lack of an icebreaker continued to raise questions about the British capacity for maintaining itself in the Antarctic. In 1956, Miles Clifford, former Governor of the Falkland Islands, wrote to the Royal Society of his concerns that if the United Kingdom did not acquire an icebreaker 'it would be indefensible to contemplate the establishment of a permanent base at Vahsel Bay or anywhere in that vicinity', unless 'we are to relinquish this most southerly and scientifically important outpost to Argentina which is not, presumably, contemplated'.[54] David Martin, the secretary of the Royal Society, passed Clifford's warning onto the Duke of Edinburgh, writing about the need for an icebreaker, since 'If we are to maintain our claim to the position of a section of Antarctica, it appears to me that we must visit it regularly.'[55] The United Kingdom even tried to secure promises from the United States for use of one of their icebreakers, but the muddy geopolitics of the Fuchs expedition made the United States hesitant to involve their ships.

In December 1955, the Royal Society sent an Advance Party aboard the MV *Tottan*, led by Royal Navy officer Surgeon Lieutenant-Commander David Dalgliesh, to establish a base at a site located on a nunatak in the Vahsel Bay, avoiding the ice shelf if possible. Initially, Dalgliesh was supposed to receive advice from Fuchs, in addition to aerial reconnaissance when selecting a base site. Unfortunately, Fuchs's ship, the MV *Theron*, was unable to help when it became temporarily trapped in the ice. Without this support, Dalgliesh noted the difficulties with finding a base site that would also comply with the Royal Society's desires. He eventually established Halley Bay, some 241 km north of

---

[53] Cabinet Office, "International Geophysical Year", 31 March 1955, Royal Society Archives, ARF 1094 Box 23B IGY/SCAR.
[54] Miles Clifford, "Need for an Ice-Breaker", 12 January 1956, Royal Society Archives, ARF 1089 Box 9A Antarctic General.
[55] Letter from David Martin to Michael Parker, 22 March 1956, Royal Society Archives, ARF 1089 Box 9A Antarctic General.

Vahsel Bay. But rather than on land, he built a research station on ice floating on the edge of the bay. Not long after the IGY, the value versus the expense of operating such a remote station in such a hostile environment was debated by members of the British polar community. But it was concluded that the base must stay open, since its abandonment would be interpreted as abandoning the United Kingdom's Antarctic claims.[56] This short account of the early history of Halley Bay demonstrates the centrality of the sea to British Antarctic claims. They ultimately built a base established by a Royal Navy officer, on floating ice, and despite the problems that it presented for geophysical fieldwork and the expense of such an extreme environment, continued to maintain a base in this region. Additionally, much of their early hesitation to build in this region came from their worries that they lacked the sea-power to operate this base in the long term.

The Falklands War: Continuing Imperialism in the Antarctic

While the 1959 Antarctic Treaty generally saw the end of gunboat diplomacy in the region, tensions between Argentina and the United Kingdom have remained. For example, the sheltered bay at Deception Island has made it a valuable strategic point in the region, and Argentina, Chile, and the United Kingdom all sustained research stations there through 1967, when the island's unpredicted volcanic eruption drove a full evacuation. The three nations seemed eager to claim sovereignty not just of the land and water, but also of the airwaves, as 'Argentine authorities have an arrangement whereby an office in Buenos Aires issues these QSL cards for amateurs on Antarctic bases'. As such, in 1967, the radio operator at this base suggested that Britain do the same, since 'I assume that it is desirable for British personnel to help promote our claims to this part of the world'.[57] Even today, the United Kingdom only has research stations in the territory that it claims.

Theoretically, the Antarctic Treaty System, established in 1959, rendered the idea of a British polar empire moot. However, in common with other claimant nations, Britain has continued to press its sovereignty in the region, both in terms of their internal policies on the continent, and also through

56 McCahey, *Laboratories*.
57 N. S. McLaren, "Communication Report-Deception Island-1967", British Antarctic Survey Archive Services (BASA) AD6/2B/1967/W.

continued conflict with Argentina in the Southern Ocean. This conflict erupted into a naval and amphibious war in 1982, with the outbreak of the Falklands War, a conflict which included an Argentine invasion of the sub-Antarctic islands of South Georgia and the South Sandwich Islands.

In the period leading up to the war, Argentina was experiencing wide-scale economic problems, as well as civil unrest after the 1976 *coup d'état* resulting in a military junta in Argentina. The new government also meant that military and security objectives achieved higher priority and the Argentine navy grew in geopolitical importance. Additionally, within the context of growing worldwide interest in marine resources and the accompanying interests in charting maritime boundaries and territorial claims, beliefs grew that the southern territories and its offshore waters were in fact resource-rich.[58] In light of the poor economic situation in Argentina, the idea of rich fisheries in the waters surrounding the Falklands and South Georgia, as well as possibilities of offshore oil deposits in these waters, gave the Southern Atlantic islands immense strategic and political value.

Several writers have explored the geopolitical issues surrounding the Falklands War, both connecting the conflict to Antarctica and categorizing it as imperial in nature.[59] This war, the last major naval war of the twentieth century, was a conflict over both the past and future of the British Empire. But it was also, albeit indirectly, a war about Antarctica and who should be there. While South Georgia is not covered under the Antarctic Treaty, this island played a major role in several historical episodes involving the British Antarctic, both land and waters. During the Falklands War, the sub-Antarctic island of South Georgia became a major site of the war. In fact, according to historian Ezequiel Mercau, 'the landing of the *Bahia Buen Suceso* at the abandoned whaling station at Leith Harbour ... is generally acknowledged as one of the catalysts for war'.[60] After the invasion of South Georgia, also known as the Battle of Grytviken, Robert Headland, a member of the BAS staff on the island, condemned the Argentine lack of interest in science: 'The Argentine forces were purely military and had no interest in the scientific station as such.'[61] Implied is the idea that the United Kingdom's dedication to science on this island legitimized their presence in a way that Argentina could not.

But while Headland condemns the Argentine interruption to science on the island, only a few pages later he expounds on South Georgia's economic

---

58 Hepple, "Geopolitics of the Falklands/Malvinas", 226.
59 Dodds, *Pink Ice*; Mercau, *Falklands War*.   60 Mercau, *Falklands War*, 74.
61 Headland, *Island of South Georgia*, 248–249.

possibilities, such as 'possibilities of fishing both krill and fin fish ... the re-establishment of sealing' and, for the growing tourism industry, 'Provision of commercial accommodation'.[62] These opportunities for economic exploitation in the region, mostly stemming from marine resources, represented one of the driving factors in Argentina's invasion to begin with. Ranulph Fiennes's Transglobe Expedition (1979–82), originally meant to emulate the Heroic Expeditions from the early twentieth century, took on new meaning, as this initially little-noticed expedition suddenly became a point of national pride, and one tied to the war.[63] The Royal Navy and Marines in the South Atlantic and the polar explorers, braving both land and sea, thus became, in this moment, each other's mirror.

Conclusion

In this chapter, I have argued that through the study of British maritime activities in the Antarctic, one can see a narrative of imperialism where land takes equal or even secondary focus compared with the sea. Yet it is important to note that the seas around Antarctica took on several different, if sometimes overlapping, meanings for those involved with the British Antarctic. First, the sea was, and to a certain extent remains, the primary way to visit, explore, and administer the land within the polar regions. Since it was through sea voyages that Antarctica was first discovered, mapped, studied, claimed, and even defended, the sea holds an unparalleled role, not just for Antarctica, but for all British overseas territory. Even today, the vast proliferation of cruise ships, especially prevalent on the Antarctic Peninsula, means that most visitors to the region still travel over water. The centrality of ship travel to the Antarctic also means that the Royal Navy, foundational to the expansion of the British Empire around the world, plays a major role in the Antarctic. Not only was the Royal Navy involved in the earliest expeditions to Antarctica, despite the demilitarized nature of modern Antarctica it still maintains an Antarctic patrol.

Besides being a vector for transportation, the sea has been a source of intensive scientific study. As the British Empire often used the ability to gather knowledge as a justification for imperial activities, through studies of the sea, not only did the British Admiralty and merchant shipping gain tactical advantages, but the British government used their rigorous dedication to scientific research to justify its global imperial presence.[64] During the Cold War, when

62 Headland, *Island of South Georgia*, 255.
63 "Britain's Other Expedition", *Newsweek* (26 April 1982).
64 Clarke, "Technocratic Imperial State?".

scientific activities took on a particular geopolitical prestige, 'international activities were ... motivated by domestic concerns about preserving Britain's position as a scientific "Mecca"'.[65] Therefore, for the British Empire, obtaining better and more accurate knowledge, both scientific and geographic, of the polar marine worlds, contributed to their ability to govern not just these regions, but their other colonies elsewhere in the world, still impacted by the weather pattern, tidal flows, and whale/fish populations.

The waters of Antarctica have also been the primary source of wealth in this region. Whaling and sealing (and now fishing) in this territory were historically regulated through the Colonial Office and now, in the more than 1 million km² of the South Georgia Maritime Zone, through the Government of South Georgia and the South Sandwich Islands. In fact, the government's website boasts that it is 'home to some of the best managed, most sustainable fisheries in the world'.[66] As the United Kingdom continues to claim the land of these mostly uninhabitable outcroppings in the Antarctic and sub-Antarctic, it has garnered far more wealth from the marine zones that accompany land sovereignty. It is partially due to this wealth that the United Kingdom first established a major scientific programme in these regions, with the creation of the Discovery Investigations, but also partially why it has faced regular incursions from Argentina and Chile, who contest their presence in the region.

While several scholars have in fact argued that Antarctica should be examined with an eye to colonialism, the focus has generally remained on Antarctic lands, icy or otherwise.[67] The characterization that for the British Empire exploration was largely conceived as a land-grab is extremely tempting for many reasons. The United Kingdom's territorial claims in Antarctica remain its largest territorial claim by far, much larger than even the British archipelago. Many of the more emblematic moments in the history of British polar exploration, such as Ernest Shackleton saving his men from death on Elephant Island or Robert Falcon Scott's traverse to the South Pole or the successful crossing of Antarctica during the Commonwealth Trans-Antarctic Expedition in 1958, all seem to focus on land. Indeed, the British Australian and New Zealand Antarctic Research Expedition (BANZARE), 1929–31, has even been described as an 'acquisitive exploratory expedition'; essentially a land-grab which declared vast land

65 Goodacre, "Representing Science".
66 "Fisheries Overview", *Government of South Georgia & the South Sandwich Islands*.
67 See, for example, Dodds, "Post-colonial Antarctica"; Hains, *Ice and Inland*; Howkins, "Appropriating Space".

territories for Australia.[68] But a re-examination of these moments shows that many attempts at asserting dominance over the land were failures, even embarrassments, for the British Empire, whereas its successes in these moments were extremely dependent on and closely related to its assertions of imperial dominance at sea.

For example, Scott's expedition to the South Pole is largely remembered for his failure to reach it before a Norwegian Party arrived first; Scott and the other members of his South Pole party all died. Shackleton's goal had been to cross the Antarctic continent – but circumstances meant that the entire party spent most of their time shipboard and, once the ship sank, camping on the ice above the frozen Weddell Sea. The Commonwealth Trans-Antarctic Expedition (1955–58) was meant to help the United Kingdom 'gain prestige and at the same time contribute to the solidarity of Commonwealth interests'.[69] But its successful crossing of the continent was a lukewarm victory, since its leader, Vivian Fuchs, was beaten to the South Pole by the New Zealand support party, led by Edmund Hillary, and therefore, this expedition was framed in many ways as another race that the British lost.[70] Though the BANZARE expedition was essentially intended to acquire as much land as possible, with Mawson proclaiming British sovereignty at each point of landfall, most of this expedition was spent at sea; in fact, they were often prevented from landing at all. Further, the BANZARE expedition is notable for producing vast quantities of ocean research and mapping much of the coastline.[71]

Attempts to achieve geographic firsts are of course important in the contexts of imperial claims. After all, first discovery, first landing, and so on are often undertaken with the understanding that to go somewhere first is to claim it in one's country's name. However, without logistical networks, bureaucracy, administration, and enforcement, arguably there is no empire. In the case of the British Empire, while it is true that its stated goals were to acquire more land or at least land-based geographical achievements, not only were these goals only possible through its control of the seas, but even when their expeditions failed, the British Empire maintained dominance in polar regions because of their efforts in the ocean. Therefore, through using the history of Antarctica as a lens, it is possible to see that Britain's characterization as a maritime empire should not just be applied to the eighteenth, and

---

68 Collis, "Proclamation Island".
69 Vivian Fuchs, "Plans for a Trans-Antarctic Journey", 1953 University of Canterbury Library Antarctic Collection.
70 McKenzie, *Opposite Poles*.   71 Roberts, *European Antarctic*, 44.

maybe nineteenth centuries, as dictated by popular historiography; the British Empire has always been and continues to be an oceanic empire.

First, in the post-World War II era, Britain continued to invest heavily in science, technology, and the military.[72] Second, it was in the twentieth century that great exploration and mapping of the sea rapidly accelerated, and just as in Antarctica, imperial powers were eager to fill in blank spaces on the maps and use their newly gained knowledge of the sea both to enforce imperial claims elsewhere and to demonstrate their ability to 'conquer nature' and demonstrate the masculine prowess of their subjects.[73] In fact, the 'knowability' of the ocean, also like the Antarctic, is dependent on vast scientific, military, administrative, technological, and commercial structures, linking the possibilities for discovery to the greatness of one's empire. In fact, the focus of traditional maritime history military and commercial efforts on the surface of the ocean, rather than delving into its depths, has led to several scholars advocating for a turn to 'oceanic history', which considers the special entanglements of humans with oceans both above and below the surface of the water.[74]

As such, through focusing on the sea, historians can see the British Empire continuing from the eighteenth century through the present day. As they returned their land possessions throughout twentieth-century decolonization movements, Great Britain still maintained and sometimes even expanded their reaches over the sea. In fact, returning to the 2012 political conflict at BAS that started this chapter, the creation of a Centre for Marine and Polar Science can be interpreted to be a formal acknowledgement of the centrality of the sea to British imperial efforts in the Antarctic.

Taking a sea-based view of imperialism could also be applied elsewhere in the British Empire. While there has been work on various naval conflicts through the most recent century, they are mostly tied to the histories of specific wars, rather than seen as emblematic of the nature of the British Empire more generally. Additionally, considering the outposts of empire that still exist around the world in the form of land that is very small territory-wise, but strategically valuable for maritime control, a sea-based view of empire would help to explain how British imperialism functions in the modern world.[75]

Additionally, applying a sea-based approach to empire seems a ready fit for the growing issues of climate change around the world. We can see,

---

72 Edgerton, *Warfare State*.
73 See Howkins, *Frozen Empires*, for an analysis of 'conquering nature' in Antarctica, but the literature on this concept is vast.
74 Bashford et al., eds., *Oceanic Histories*.   75 Winchester, *Outposts*.

especially in the Antarctic, that a binary division of land and sea when discussing empire is impossible. Not only is it always to a certain extent both, but what constitutes land and sea is constantly shifting. Ice is, after all, frozen water. When it melts, it becomes the sea. For example, take the research station at Halley Bay; it is a site imagined as land – its founders even use the verb 'landing', but as a floating ice shelf, it is literally the sea. This is compounded by the fact that the ice on which it originally rested has long calved away into the ocean. The latest major calving of the Brunt Ice Shelf, in February 2021, had been predicted by the British Antarctic Survey, which shifted the location of the Halley VI Station (built on skis) in 2016 in anticipation of this event.[76] But although the boundaries between land and sea are very often liminal and indeterminate,[77] it is in Antarctica, where much of the land is permanently covered by (frozen) water, that this binary becomes especially problematic. In fact, one of the greatest threats of climate changes comes from the rising sea levels as the Antarctic ice cap essentially flows into the ocean.

None of this means that the British Empire was uninterested in land claims in any imperial context, including in Antarctica. Indeed, the multiple attempts to be first to plant the British flag at the South Pole, both the successful and failed attempts to be the first to conduct an overland crossing, the continuous occupation of the Peninsula since 1943, the many land-traverses through the twentieth century, and mapping/charting/naming geographic features with an eye towards justifying British sovereignty or promoting the British Empire all speak to the importance of land in the Antarctic. However, most of the territory that Britain both claims and has access to in the Antarctic is not land at all. It is the ice and the sea. And it is in its maritime endeavours that Britain has been most successful and most shown itself to be a Polar Empire.

Bibliography

Archives

British Antarctic Survey Archive Services (BASA), Cambridge, UK
Thomas H. Manning Archives, Scott Polar Research Institute (SPRI), Cambridge, UK
Royal Society Archives, London, UK
UK Parliament Web Archive, London, UK

76 Freedman, "Iceberg".   77 Bashford, "Terraqueous Histories".

Printed Material and Secondary Sources

Antonello, Alessandro, "The Southern Ocean", in Alison Bashford, David Armitage, and Sujit Sivasundaram, eds., *Oceanic Histories* (Cambridge: Cambridge University Press, 2017), pp. 296–318.

Application Instituting Proceedings, *Antarctica (United Kingdom v. Argentina)*.

Basberg, Bjorn L., and Robert K. Headland, "The Economic Significance of the 19th Century Antarctic Sealing Industry", *Polar Record* 49 (October 2013): 381–391.

Bashford, Alison, "Terraqueous Histories", *Historical Journal* 60 (June 2017): 253–272.

Bashford, Alison, David Armitage, and Sujit Sivasundaram, eds., *Oceanic Histories* (Cambridge: Cambridge University Press, 2017).

Beck, Peter J., "International Relations in Antarctica: Argentina, Chile, and the Great Powers", in Michael A. Morris, ed., *Great Power Relations in Argentina, Chile and Antarctica* (London: Palgrave Macmillan, 1990), pp. 101–130.

Benson, Keith, and Helen Rozwadowski, *Extremes: Oceanography's Adventures at the Poles* (Sagamore Beach, MA: Science History Publications/USA, 2007).

Carrington, Damian, and Robin McKie, "Research Boss Wingham in Trouble over British Antarctic Survey Claim", *The Guardian* (3 November 2012).

Carroll, Siobhan, *An Empire of Air and Water: Uncolonizable Space in the British Imagination, 1750–1850* (Philadelphia: University of Pennsylvania Press, 2015).

Cawood, John, "The Magnetic Crusade: Science and Politics in Early Victorian Britain", *Isis* 70 (1979): 493–518.

Cherry-Garrard, Apsley, *The Worst Journey in the World: Antarctic 1910–1913* (New York: George H. Doran, 1922).

Christie, E. W. Hunter, *The Antarctic Problem: An Historical and Political Study* (London: George Allen & Unwin, 1951).

Clarke, Sabine, "A Technocratic Imperial State? The Colonial Office and Scientific Research, 1940–1960", *Twentieth Century British History* 18 (1 January 2007): 453–480.

Coleman-Cooke, John, *Discovery II in the Antarctic: The Story of British Research in the Southern Seas* (London: Odhams, 1963).

Collis, C., "The Proclamation Island Moment: Making Antarctica Australian", *Law Text Culture* 8 (2004).

Cook, James, *A Voyage towards the South Pole and Round the World* (1777).

Dalrymple, Alexander, *An Historical Collection of the Several Voyages and Discoveries in the South Pacific Ocean* (1770).

Dodds, Klaus, "The End of a Polar Empire? The Falkland Islands Dependencies and Commonwealth Reactions to British Polar Policy, 1945–61", *Journal of Imperial and Commonwealth History* 24 (September 1996): 391–421.

Dodds, Klaus, *Pink Ice: Britain and the South Atlantic Empire* (London, New York: I.B. Tauris, 2002).

Dodds, Klaus, "Post-colonial Antarctica: An Emerging Engagement", *Polar Record* 42 (January 2006): 59–70.

Edgerton, David, *Warfare State: Britain, 1920–1970* (Cambridge, UK, New York: Cambridge University Press, 2005).

Fanning, Edmund, *Voyages to the South Seas, Indian and Pacific Oceans, China Sea, North-West Coast, Feejee Islands, South Shetlands, &c.: With an Account of the New Discoveries*

13 Britain's Polar Empire, 1769–1982

Made in the Southern Hemisphere, between the Years 1830–1837: Also, The Origin, Authorization, and Progress of the First American National South Sea Exploring Expedition... (New York: W. H. Vermilye, 1838).

"Fisheries Overview", *Government of South Georgia & the South Sandwich Islands* (accessed May 2021).

Freedman, Andrew, "Iceberg Larger than New York City Breaks Off the Brunt Ice Shelf in Antarctica", *Washington Post* (26 February 2021).

Good, Gregory, "Follow the Needle: Seeking the Magnetic Poles", Walter Kupsch, ed., *Earth Sciences History* 10 (5 November 2007): 154–167.

Goodacre, Jennifer Rose, "Representing Science in a Divided World: The Royal Society and Cold War Britain", PhD diss. (University of Manchester, 2013).

Goodman, Matthew, "Follow the Data: Administering Science at Edward Sabine's Magnetic Department, Woolwich, 1841–57", *Notes and Records: The Royal Society Journal of the History of Science* 73 (20 June 2019): 187–202.

Hains, Brigid, *The Ice and the Inland: Mawson, Flynn, and the Myth of the Frontier* (Melbourne: Melbourne University Press, 2002).

Hardy, Sir Alister, *Great Waters: A Voyage of Natural History to Study Whales, Plankton and the Waters of the Southern Ocean* (New York: Harper & Row, 1967).

Headland, Robert K., *The Island of South Georgia* (Cambridge: Cambridge University Press, 1992).

Hepple, Leslie W., "The Geopolitics of the Falklands/Malvinas and the South Atlantic: British and Argentine Perceptions, Misconceptions, and Rivalries", in Philip Kelly and Jack Child, eds., *Geopolitics of the Southern Cone and Antarctica* (Boulder: Lynne Rienner, 1988), pp. 223–236.

Howkins, Adrian, "Appropriating Space: Antarctic Imperialism and the Mentality of Settler Colonialism", in Tracey Banivanua Mar and Penelope Edmonds, eds., *Making Settler Colonial Space: Perspectives on Race, Place and Identity* (London: Palgrave Macmillan, 2010), pp. 29–52.

Howkins, Adrian, *Frozen Empires: An Environmental History of the Antarctic Peninsula* (Oxford: Oxford University Press, 2017).

Howkins, Adrian, "Weather, Climate and the Contest for Antarctic Sovereignty, 1939–1959", *History of Meteorology* 4 (2008): 27–40.

John, D. Dilwyn, "The Second Antarctic Commission of the R. R. S. Discovery II", *Geographical Journal* 83 (1934): 381–394.

Juniper, Tony, "'Axing the British Antarctic Survey Would Mean the End of Scott's Legacy'", *The Guardian* (9 September 2012).

Maddison, Ben, *Class and Colonialism in Antarctic Exploration, 1750–1920* (Milton Park: Routledge, 2014).

McCahey, Daniella, *Laboratories at the Bottom of the World: Imperialism, the International Geophysical Year, and the Making of Modern Antarctic Science* (Cambridge, MA: Harvard University Press, in press).

McCahey, Daniella, and Simon Cole, "Human(e) Science? Demarcation, Law, and 'Scientific Whaling' in Whaling in the Antarctic", *Journal of Philosophy, Science & Law* 15 (May 2015): 37–51.

McCann, Joy, *Wild Sea: A History of the Southern Ocean.*(Kensington, NSW: University of New South Wales Press, 2018).

McKenzie, Douglas, *Opposite Poles* (London: Robert Hale, 1963).
Mercau, Ezequiel, *The Falklands War: An Imperial History* (Cambridge, UK, New York: Cambridge University Press, 2019).
Murray, John, "The Renewal of Antarctic Exploration", *Geographical Journal* 3 (1894): 1–27.
Peters, Kimberley, Philip Steinberg, and Elaine Stratford, "Introduction", in Kimberley Peters, Philip Steinberg, and Elaine Stratford, eds., *Territory Beyond Terra* (London, New York: Rowman & Littlefield, 2018).
Reidy, Michael S., *Tides of History: Ocean Science and Her Majesty's Navy* (Chicago: University of Chicago Press, 2009).
Reidy, Michael S., and Helen M. Rozwadowski, "The Spaces in Between: Science, Ocean, Empire", *Isis* 105 (1 June 2014): 338–351.
Roberts, Peder, *The European Antarctic: Science and Strategy in Scandinavia and the British Empire* (New York: Palgrave Macmillan, 2011).
Ross, James Clark, *A Voyage of Discovery and Research in the Southern and Antarctic Regions, during the Years 1839–43* (London: J. Murray, 1847).
Sullivan, Walter, *Assault on the Unknown: The International Geophysical Year* (New York: McGraw-Hill, 1961).
Taylor, Andrew, *Two Years Below the Horn: Operation Tabarin, Field Science, and Antarctic Sovereignty, 1944–1946*, ed. Daniel Heidt and Whitney Lackenbauer (Winnipeg: University of Manitoba Press, 2017).
Taylor, Thomas Griffith, *Antarctic Adventure and Research* (New York: Appleton, 1930).
Tønnessen, Johan Nicolay, and Arne Odd Johnsen, *The History of Modern Whaling* (Berkeley, CA: University of California Press, 1982).
Winchester, Simon, *Outposts: Journeys to the Surviving Relics of the British Empire* (New York: Harper Perennial, 2004).
Wright, Helen S., *The Seventh Continent: A History of the Discovery and Explorations of Antarctica* (Boston: R.G. Badger, 1918).

14

Canada and the High Arctic Islands, 1880–1950

JANICE CAVELL

Introduction

Of all the north circumpolar lands, only Greenland extends farther towards the top of the globe than the uppermost reaches of the Arctic Archipelago. Politicians and media commentators regularly extol Canada's identity as a northern nation, yet this area's official name since 1954 – the Queen Elizabeth Islands – is not widely known or often used, and most citizens' knowledge of High Arctic geography is rather vague. Only the military station at Alert on the north coast of Ellesmere Island, about 800 km from the pole, stands out clearly amid the general blur.

The High Arctic region's southern boundary is Parry Channel, the major east–west waterway through the archipelago, in latitude 74° north. Parry Channel also divides the islands where Indigenous people have lived continuously for millennia from those that were abandoned during the harsh climatic conditions of the Little Ice Age (which lasted roughly from 1300 to 1850 AD). In other words, literary and visual representations of the far north as a sublime, unpeopled landscape are not – as writers from other nations sometimes suggest – mere convenient figments of the colonizing gaze.[1] Indeed, when the government moved Inuit from northern Quebec to the High Arctic in the 1950s, they experienced it as an empty, alien place. Describing their first impressions decades later, some of the relocated people used the words 'desolate', 'barren', and 'harsh'.[2]

The opinions expressed in this chapter are the author's and do not represent the official position of the Government of Canada.

1 For example, see Craciun, *Writing Arctic Disaster*, 8–12. A more nuanced assessment is provided in Routledge, *Do You See Ice?*, ch. 3.
2 Inuit testimony before Royal Commission on Aboriginal Peoples, 5–8 April 1993, www.bac-lac.gc.ca/eng/discover/aboriginal-heritage/royal-commission-aboriginal-peoples/Pages/introduction.aspx. Despite Ottawa's concerns about the lack of population in the High Arctic, the relocation was not carried out for sovereignty purposes. See Cavell, "Consolidation and Control", especially 118–119, 129, 135–136.

Currently, scholarly interest is concentrated on the history of white relations with Inuit, but except for the High Arctic relocations, such history is almost entirely limited to the islands south of the dividing line. Yet for well over a century, the vast uninhabited areas north of Parry Channel have posed unique challenges, both politically and culturally. These challenges are in many ways specifically Canadian, but they are also relevant to wider studies of the polar regions.

Canada, created by the union of former colonies in 1867, assumed the role of an imperial power in relation to the archipelago and took settler colonialism to an extreme in which there was state authority, but almost no actual settlement. The Antarctic claims of Australia, New Zealand, Argentina, and Chile have produced somewhat similar situations, but the element of geographical contiguity is more attenuated. On maps, these polar territories do not appear as integral parts of the states that claim them, nor are they central to the respective imaginaries involved.

The Arctic Archipelago, in contrast, is firmly enclosed by the boundary lines on national maps and supposedly a key to the Canadian identity, yet in many ways its northern half remains almost unattainably distant, with very little human presence to mediate its strangeness. For southern Canadians, the High Arctic evokes great pride, yet also great anxiety because of its enduring near-emptiness. It has long been common for Canadians to wonder whether sovereignty over these islands is at risk. The region is not even particularly well-storied through the narratives of white explorers. Among the three great epics of Arctic discovery – the quest for the Northwest Passage, the search for Sir John Franklin's missing expedition, and the race to the North Pole – only the Franklin search did much more than touch its fringes.[3]

Canada's relationship with its northernmost islands accordingly provides a case study in the ongoing complexities of interactions between states and the uninhabited polar regions to which they lay claim. This chapter focuses on both the political aspect and the cultural ramifications. On one side, in the early twentieth century there was a surprisingly early conviction that the High Arctic was geopolitically important, accompanied by innovative and broadly successful strategies to gain international acceptance for Ottawa's sovereignty claims, despite criticism from influential American legal theorists. On the other side, however, the story is far more complicated. Ironically, cultural factors led to a widespread sense of insecurity on sovereignty matters that persists long after any possible foundation for such anxieties vanished.

---

3 The best summary of exploration in this region is, rather typically, a solid but unexciting reference work (Taylor, *Geographical Discovery*).

14 Canada and the High Arctic Islands

High Arctic Exploration Before 1870

The first known Europeans to venture into the region were William Baffin and Robert Bylot in 1616. They charted the main outlines of Baffin Bay and noted the three great sounds that open off it – Lancaster Sound, between Baffin Island and Devon Island; Jones Sound, between Devon Island and Ellesmere Island; and Smith Sound, between Ellesmere Island and Greenland. At the time, it seemed possible that these were all dead ends, and that the North American mainland was connected to Greenland.[4]

Three centuries later John Barrow, the second secretary of the British Admiralty, decided that Lancaster Sound must be the gateway to the Northwest Passage, and in 1818 he sent out two ships under John Ross to prove it. Ross failed to do so and claimed that the sound was a cul-de-sac ending in mountainous land. Barrow quickly organized a new expedition, led by Edward Parry. Parry sailed triumphantly over the location of Ross's supposed mountains and continued on through the channel that now bears his name as far as Melville Island, where he spent the winter of 1819–20. The illustrations in his published narrative, memorably featuring his ships surrounded by ice under a magnificently starry sky, created a taste for what has since been dubbed the 'Arctic Sublime'.[5]

Parry realized that the ice around Melville Island was heavy enough to form a permanent barrier. The search for the Northwest Passage shifted to more southerly latitudes, where progress was blocked by the Melville and Boothia Peninsulas and by the maze-like quality of the various narrow straits within the archipelago. In 1845 Barrow decided to try the northern approach once more. Sir John Franklin's expedition sailed through Lancaster Sound in the *Erebus* and *Terror* and never came out again.

Franklin had turned southward, only to become trapped in the ice near King William Island. During the prolonged search for the missing expedition, however, it was considered possible that he might have gone north instead when attempting to avoid the Melville Island ice. Supposedly, there was a 'pole of maximum cold' near Melville Island, and conditions to the northward would therefore be more moderate, with abundant animal life, navigable waters, and perhaps even an open polar sea. The open sea theory, which dated back to the sixteenth century and was revived by Barrow in 1817–18, had been given scientific credibility by the Russian explorer Ferdinand von Wrangell and the Scottish physicist David Brewster in the early 1820s. It was

---

4 This was Baffin's own belief; see Markham, *Voyages*, 150.
5 Loomis, "Arctic Sublime", 101–102.

further upheld by the German geographer August Petermann and the American hydrographer Matthew Fontaine Maury in the 1850s.[6] As a result, public interest in the High Arctic was intense.

During the search era, which extended from 1848 to 1859, the islands on the north side of Parry Channel – Devon, Cornwallis, Bathurst, and Melville – were charted and new lands were found beyond them, extending nearly to 78° N latitude. No ships succeeded in advancing as far west as Parry's had done, but sledge parties travelled in various directions from bases in Parry Channel. The most notable among these were led by Frederick Mecham and Leopold McClintock, who reached Eglinton, Emerald, and Prince Patrick Islands.[7]

In the central area, the main route was Wellington Channel, which leads northward between Devon and Cornwallis Islands and through which ships could pass. Here the hopes of finding an open sea were particularly strong. An American expedition commanded by Edwin De Haven joined in this part of the search and discovered what De Haven called Grinnell Land in honour of his expedition's patron (this was the Grinnell Peninsula at the northwest end of Devon Island). In an attempt to ascertain whether there was another route to this area, Horatio Austin made a brief foray into Jones Sound. Next, Edward Inglefield set out to make a more thorough investigation at the northern end of Baffin Bay. Inglefield went far enough into Smith Sound to prove that there was no connection with Greenland, and he named the western side Ellesmere Land. In Jones Sound he received the impression that the Ellesmere coast soon trended northwest. Inglefield was convinced that both sounds offered routes to very high latitudes, and so, perhaps, to an open sea.[8]

Another Briton, Edward Belcher, proceeded by ship through Wellington Channel and sent out sledge parties that reached as far north as Cornwall Island. Elisha Kent Kane, a veteran of De Haven's expedition, outdid both his former commander and Belcher by choosing Smith Sound as his entry point for a new American search. Kane proceeded up the channels between Ellesmere Island and Greenland. One of his sledge parties reported an impressive farthest north of 81° 22′ N. Kane's party, and a later one led by

---

6 Brewster, "Observations"; Sabine, preface to Wrangell, *Narrative*, vii–viii; Petermann, "Notes on the Distribution", 125; Kane, *Open Polar Sea*; Kane, *U.S. Grinnell Expedition*, 492; Maury, *Physical Geography*, 146–149.
7 Neatby, *Search*, is a good basic introduction to the various attempts to locate Franklin, based mainly on published sources.
8 Inglefield was much more enthusiastic about Jones Sound as a route in his report to the Royal Geographical Society than he was in his narrative. By the time he wrote the narrative, he had been influenced by the more realistic opinions of another Franklin searcher, Peter Sutherland; Inglefield, "Return of the Isabel", 143; Inglefield, *Summer Search*, 119–121.

his countryman Isaac Israel Hayes, made geographical discoveries on the western side, on what appeared to be a new island, separate from Ellesmere. They too used the name Grinnell Land.[9]

Kane's two published narratives, written with great literary flair, did almost as much as Parry's to popularize the extreme north as a setting for heroic adventures.[10] British publishing endeavours, however, fell short. Mecham and McClintock wrote no books about their High Arctic exploits, while Belcher's volume was a critical and commercial failure.[11] After traces of Franklin were found well south of Parry Channel, all the High Arctic ventures except Kane's were largely forgotten. Instead, McClintock owed his enduring fame to his 1857–59 expedition's discovery of a Franklin cairn on King William Island. The next explorer in the High Arctic was an American, Charles Hall, who took the Smith Sound route in 1871, hoping to reach the North Pole. A decade later came yet another US expedition, largely scientific in purpose, led by Adolphus Greely. When its relief ship failed to arrive, the result was a widely publicized tale of Arctic hardship, starvation, and cannibalism. American stories accordingly dominated popular culture.

The Question of Sovereignty and the Transfer of the Archipelago to Canada, 1854–1880

Canada originally consisted only of four former colonies: Canada East and Canada West (present-day southern Quebec and southern Ontario), Nova Scotia, and New Brunswick. In 1870 the young nation gained a vast internal empire through the transfer of Rupert's Land and the North-Western Territory from the United Kingdom. Rupert's Land, formerly the exclusive domain of the Hudson's Bay Company (HBC) under its 1670 royal charter, was defined as the area whose rivers drained into Hudson Bay. The North-Western Territory, much more vaguely, consisted of everything else under British dominion that was not part of any colony.[12]

Canadians easily might have considered the Arctic islands discovered by British explorers as part of the transfer. Instead, their expansionist visions went

---

9 The Grinnell Peninsula (then thought to be an island) appeared on the 1852 British Admiralty chart as Albert Land, owing to confusion about the first discovery. See Kane, *U.S. Grinnell Expedition*, 200–209. The error was corrected on the 1855 chart, but Kane was not aware of this rectification when he gave Grinnell's name to his own expedition's new territory.
10 Kane, *U.S. Grinnell Expedition*; *Arctic Explorations*.   11 Belcher, *Last of the Arctic Voyages*.
12 British Columbia, Prince Edward Island, and Newfoundland joined in 1871, 1873, and 1949 respectively.

no farther than the northern continental coastline.[13] Reasonably enough, the focus was on settlement in the agricultural lands of the western prairie region. North of this region, the HBC continued its fur-trading business in regions that Canadian administration barely touched.[14] The islands even farther north were a distant realm of British heroism and adventure, but also a realm where American explorers had staked an enduring claim in the popular imagination.

De Haven had merely sighted his Grinnell Land from a distance, and it was later explored by Belcher. Hayes, however, had raised the American flag on the other Grinnell Land – an act with the potential to create future political difficulties, even though as the leader of a privately funded expedition he did not have authority to make territorial claims.[15] Moreover, American whalers had begun to frequent northern waters, sometimes overwintering in the more accessible parts of the archipelago.

The question of sovereignty was first brought forward by Scottish whaler William Penny, with the result that in 1854 the British ambassador in Washington asserted a claim to 'the several groups of islands which lie to the northward of Hudson strait'.[16] How far north of Hudson Strait this claim was intended to apply is unclear; most likely, officials were thinking only of the whaling grounds on the east coast of Baffin Island (which was then believed to be several separate islands).

Twenty years later an inquiry from an American entrepreneur, William Mintzer, led to a more thorough consideration of the matter in London. The Colonial Office decided that the islands should be transferred to Canada to discourage any possible American expansionism, and that the limits of the transferred territory should be only vaguely defined. The purpose of the vagueness was to avoid addressing the status of Kane's Grinnell Land. The US government had shown no disposition to follow up Hayes's claim; British officials did not want to provoke action from Washington by explicitly claiming the area themselves, but neither did they want to irrevocably renounce it.[17]

Before the transfer was finally carried out by an imperial order-in-council in 1880,[18] a British naval expedition under George Nares followed the same route as Kane, Hayes, and Hall, reaching the northern coast of Ellesmere Island. Hall had previously glimpsed, but not landed on, this part of the island, which was named Grant Land in honour of President Ulysses S. Grant; on some maps it was shown as separate from Grinnell Land. The Nares

13 *Report of the Delegates*, 27.   14 Zaslow, *Opening*, 53–63.   15 Hayes, *Open Polar Sea*, 351.
16 Edmund Hammond to Herman Merivale, 12 April 1854, and enclosures, TNA, CO 6/21.
17 On the transfer, see Cavell, *Arctic 1874–1949*, docs. 3–39.
18 Order-in-council, 31 July 1880, *Canada Gazette* (9 October 1880), 389.

expedition proved that the two were in fact connected; its findings also struck a fatal blow to the open polar sea theory. A party led by Albert Markham ventured out over the frozen ocean and encountered exceptionally heavy ice. Markham's party attained a record-setting latitude of 83° 20′ N, but only at the cost of great labour and suffering.[19]

One British memorandum specifically noted that Nares had secured rights extending well to the north of any area that might potentially be claimed by Washington.[20] Yet without the open sea and relatively moderate climate that theorists had predicted, the value of such rights did not appear impressive. Markham's narrative (published in 1878) was popular with readers, going through several editions, yet its picture of the High Arctic was unlikely to inspire northern expansionism among Canadians.

The 1880 transfer placed Canada in an unprecedented situation for a country that had been created fewer than fifteen years before and contained only 4.3 million people. The 1854 British sovereignty claim and the 1870 transfer of Rupert's Land and the North-Western Territory involved mainly regions that were, or seemed likely soon to be, of some economic value. But the 1880 transfer made Canada the second-largest state in the world while adding almost nothing that its citizens considered worth having, except the sheer imperial grandeur of such size.

The result was not surprising: Canadians generally ignored the islands except to note that their resources might be exploited in the far-distant future. There was enough to do in settling and developing the lands acquired in 1870; the archipelago could wait. That it waited less than two decades owed far more to developments outside Canada than to those within it.

Canadian Claims and Foreign Exploration, 1895–1902

In 1895 Canada made a claim to the entire archipelago on its own behalf through a new order-in-council. The motives for this claim remain obscure because the relevant government file has gone missing. It may have been intended to override the potential American claim to Grinnell Land once four decades had gone by since the discovery without any action by Washington, or it may simply have been a matter of dividing the country's Sub-Arctic and Arctic territories into districts for greater administrative

19 Markham, *Great Frozen Sea*.   20 Cavell, *Arctic 1874–1949*, doc. 30.

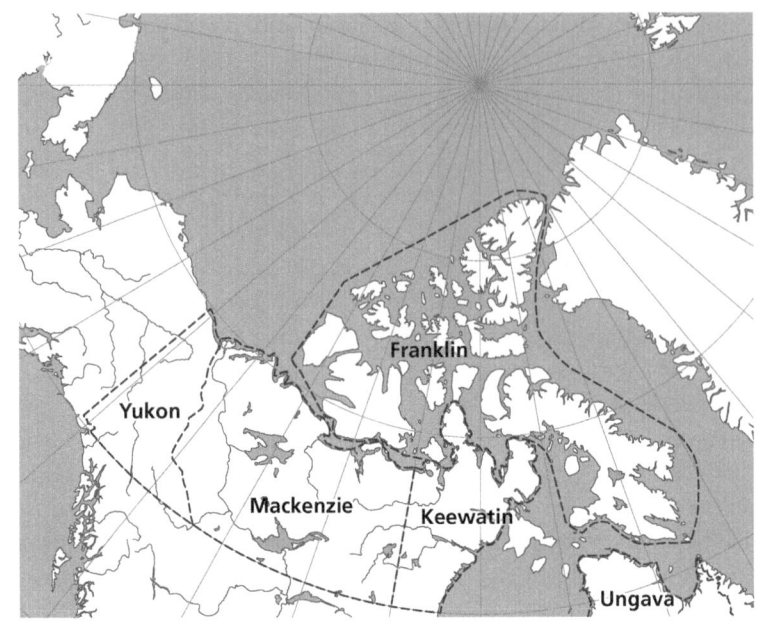

Figure 14.1 Districts in northern Canada, 1895.

convenience. The name District of Franklin was assigned to the archipelago, and the boundary formed an irregular line around the islands (Figure 14.1).[21]

In the late 1890s, the attention of politicians and bureaucrats in Ottawa was drawn gradually northward by such factors as the Yukon gold rush, which reinforced the idea that the Arctic contained valuable mineral resources; the presence of American whalers in Davis Strait, Hudson Bay, and the Beaufort Sea; and the dispute with the United States over the Alaska–Yukon boundary, which was finally resolved through a 1903 arbitral decision.[22]

None of these developments involved the High Arctic islands, but one other factor did: the international quest to reach the North Pole. The two dominant figures in the race were a Norwegian, Fridtjof Nansen, and an American, Robert Peary. Nansen's chosen method was to enter the pack in a small ship constructed to withstand ice pressure, and to drift in the transpolar current from Siberia to the North Atlantic.[23] Peary, however, preferred what he liked to call 'the American route' through Smith Sound

---

21 Order-in-council, 2 October 1895, *Canada Gazette* (19 October 1895), 683–685.
22 Penlington, *Alaska Boundary Dispute*.
23 Nansen, "How Can the North Polar Region Be Crossed?".

and the channels north of it, which were relatively protected from the heavy Arctic ice. After making a base as far north as possible, he intended to sledge the rest of the way to the pole.[24]

Peary had a flair for publicity and the support of several prominent Americans. His activities in the High Arctic were carefully noted by some Ottawa officials, including George Dawson, director of the Geological Survey of Canada. Peary announced his North Pole plans in January 1897. That summer, a government expedition, instigated by Dawson, set out to uphold Canadian sovereignty over Baffin Island and Hudson Bay, and Dawson pushed for yet more action, including regular northern patrols.[25]

The commander of the 1897 expedition, William Wakeham, inadvertently began a new tradition when he raised the flag and made a proclamation on Baffin Island. His action garnered some international press commentary, and a London newspaper asked why it was considered necessary on an island that had long been British. Wakeham rather defensively explained to his superiors that he had been instructed to affirm Canadian sovereignty but not precisely how this should be done. Under the circumstances, he thought hoisting the flag was 'the simplest and most official way', without any implication that he was taking possession 'de novo'.[26]

A few months later, Dawson formulated an innovative method of asserting sovereignty over the High Arctic despite the lack of any actual Canadian presence there. He was familiar with the 1867 treaty between the United States and Russia, which defined the Alaska–Siberia boundary through a meridian line that continued north into the Arctic Ocean without a specific end point. He proposed enclosing the islands claimed by Canada within two such lines – an early version of the sector theory. The change was made through a new order-in-council (Figure 14.2).[27] It would have a major impact on future polar claims not only by Canada but by several other nations. However, Dawson had failed to consider the question of possible unknown islands within the limits set out by the 1897 order.

In 1898 a Canadian declared his intention to join in the race for the Pole. Nansen's own attempt during the *Fram* expedition of 1893–96 had fallen short, but Joseph-Elzéar Bernier – a merchant captain who had become obsessed by the Arctic – believed that a drift starting from a more easterly point on the

---

24 "Transactions of the Society", 117–121.   25 Cavell, *Arctic 1874–1949*, docs. 70, 77, 79.
26 Cavell, *Arctic 1874–1949*, doc. 83.
27 Dawson to Édouard Deville, 2 December 1897, RG 45, vol. 96; order-in-council, 18 December 1897, *Canada Gazette*, 14 May 1898, 2613. For a more detailed account of the sector theory, see Cavell, "Sector Theory".

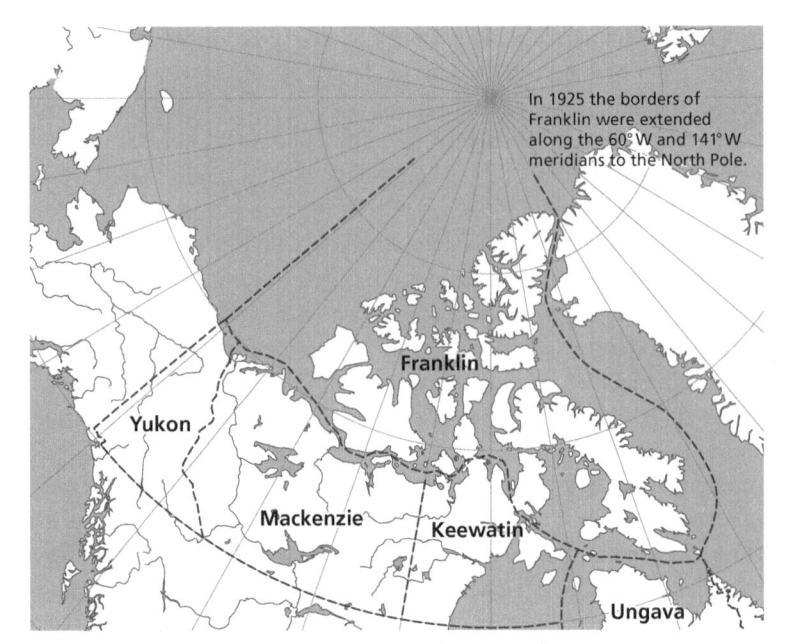

Figure 14.2 Districts in northern Canada, 1897.

Siberian coast would succeed. He submitted his plan to Prime Minister Wilfrid Laurier, who requested Dawson's advice. Dawson evinced little interest, since Bernier's proposed route lay far from the Canadian archipelago. Nevertheless, Bernier launched a public fundraising campaign that won support from scientific organizations, contributing to a belief that Canada ought to be more active in the far north.[28]

In the same year, a new Norwegian expedition set out in the *Fram* under Otto Sverdrup, who had served as ship's captain during Nansen's drift. Sverdrup initially intended to take the Smith Sound route, establish a base on the north coast of Greenland, and then continue eastward with the aim of circumnavigating the island. Allegedly, there was no idea of trying for the Pole, but Sverdrup was given a free hand regarding his route.[29] Such a programme could easily be extended northwards if circumstances allowed, and Peary and his supporters were quickly up in arms.[30] Ice conditions in Smith Sound proved unexpectedly bad, so Sverdrup turned

---

28 On the campaign, see Saint-Pierre, *Bernier*, 153–170.   29 Sverdrup, *New Land*, Vol. 1, 1–2.
30 Hurlbut, "Mr. Peary's Plan".

his vessel to Jones Sound, where no other explorer had ventured since Austin and Inglefield.[31]

Jones Sound, however, proved to be a dead end for extensive discoveries by ship. Sverdrup was intensely disappointed to find that the Ellesmere coast did not turn north until well past the point where Inglefield had reported it appeared to do so. At the far western end of the sound, narrow Cardigan Strait led to the area already explored by Belcher. The only water route north into the unknown was through a passage that the frustrated Norwegians dubbed Hell Gate. Navigating it was impossible, and Sverdrup took the only remaining course. From bases on southern Ellesmere, he sledged north. By the time their expedition ended in 1902, Sverdrup and his men had mapped almost all the previously unknown coasts of Ellesmere and discovered several new islands to the west (Axel Heiberg, Amund Ringnes, Ellef Ringnes, and King Christian).

Strangely, even though its discoveries were so impressive, the Norwegian expedition does not seem to have caused any great anxiety or even interest in Canada. Sverdrup himself was not a charismatic figure, and his various sledge journeys had not been aimed at reaching any particular geographical point. His published account, though it contained much interesting matter, lacked the narrative tensions provided by the drive towards a clear goal, and it made little impression on the reading public.

As for sovereignty, Sverdrup himself was extremely keen for his country to claim his new land. Prudently, he said nothing about this aim when he gave a lecture to the Royal Geographical Society in London, but the assembled British Arctic veterans, including McClintock, seemed to consider it a matter of course that the new discoveries were Norwegian.[32] Their attitude is hardly surprising, for no one at the time saw much value in territory so far to the north. Since Canada had most of the islands, what would it matter if a few others in the archipelago's remotest part went to a small, friendly nation such as Norway?

In Ottawa, at least one official saw things differently. Dawson had died in 1901, but his colleague James White vigorously took up the nascent sector idea and was determined that the entire archipelago must be Canadian. Formerly a member of the Geological Survey, White became the Department of the Interior's chief geographer in 1899 and thus was in a position of considerable influence. However, the implementation of his

---

31 Sverdrup was evidently influenced more by Inglefield's report than by his narrative.
32 Sverdrup, "Second Norwegian Polar Expedition".

ideas was complicated by a new northern impetus in Canada's policy that began in late 1902.

Sovereignty Initiatives, 1903–1911

The Laurier government, in office since 1896, had always demonstrated more interest in the far north than previous administrations. In particular, the powerful minister of the interior, Clifford Sifton, was adamant that Canada must not yield on the Alaska boundary question. Sifton based his arguments on the terms of the 1825 treaty between the United Kingdom and Russia. Laurier, however, was eventually convinced by worried British officials that, because the Americans had occupied the disputed territory since they purchased Alaska from Russia in 1867, Canada's case was poor. Laurier agreed to place the matter before an arbitral tribunal, which under the circumstances amounted to an admission of defeat.

Sifton was enraged, yet he had to acknowledge that international law had evolved over the past century, making effective occupation the key to sovereignty. As a result, Sifton became increasingly concerned about the Arctic islands. The title transferred from Britain, although valid as far as it went, had not conferred full territorial rights. Instead, it was what was called an inchoate or imperfect title, based on discovery and exploration alone. 'Imperfect' did not mean that the title was flawed or worthless, but rather that actual occupation was still required to complete the process of taking possession. It was accepted by theorists of international law that, depending on the nature of the particular territory and other circumstances, a considerable period might pass before occupation began. However, if nothing was done within a reasonable time, or if no protest was made against occupation by another state, the inchoate title would lapse.[33]

Sifton accordingly pushed for action in all parts of the Canadian Arctic where American whalers and traders were known to operate. As a result, in 1903–04 the North West Mounted Police established posts at Herschel Island off the Yukon coast and at Fullerton Harbour, Hudson Bay.[34] The High Arctic was not included in the original programme, but visits to Lancaster Sound and Smith Sound were added at the behest of Albert Low, co-leader of the Hudson Bay expedition in SS *Neptune*.[35]

---

33 Hall, *Treatise*, 107–109.
34 Morrison, *Showing the Flag*, chs. 6 and 7; Cavell, "More Latitude", 295–299.
35 Cavell, "More Latitude", 298.

Although Low was not instructed to do so, he imitated Wakeham and made formal sovereignty proclamations on Devon Island, Ellesmere Island, and Somerset Island (which, though south of Parry Channel, was also uninhabited). As he explained when submitting copies of these documents to the authorities in Ottawa, Low did not consider a proclamation necessary on Baffin Island because there it was possible to affirm Canada's jurisdiction through the concrete act of collecting customs dues on foreign traders' goods.[36] His letter pointed to a serious dilemma: it was not too difficult to display sovereignty in places where the activities of foreigners and Inuit could be regulated, but how, exactly, could effective occupation be established on islands that were completely uninhabited and seemed likely to remain so?

White had developed an answer, but the government was not yet prepared to accept it. He reasoned that the archipelago was a unified geographical entity and that the standard of occupation developed in temperate zones could not be applied to the Arctic. Therefore, Canada must carry out as much occupation as it could, wherever it could, and this action by the state would assure its title to all the islands. The 1897 boundaries conveniently outlined the area to which Canada laid claim, and within which it intended to establish as much of a state presence as was practicable. Meanwhile, government representatives must refrain from proclamations and other such ceremonies, which might be interpreted as meaning that Ottawa did not have confidence in the inchoate title transferred from Britain.[37]

These were cogent arguments. However, White was on less certain ground when he insisted first, that the sector lines must be prolonged until they met at the North Pole, and second, that the Sverdrup Islands had been included in the 1880 transfer because they were contiguous to islands discovered by British explorers, and therefore the fact of their discovery by Norwegians was irrelevant. White wanted the government to make a formal claim as far as the Pole, explicitly including Sverdrup's discoveries. But Prime Minister Laurier – whose main concern was always the potential American threats south of Parry Channel – preferred 'the policy of having the northern waters patrolled by our people, and our jurisdiction quietly extended to every island'.[38]

White likely conceded that it was best to establish occupation before openly addressing the Sverdrup Islands question. However, he took certain other measures on his own. Sifton had asked for a general report on northern

---

36 Cavell, *Arctic 1874–1949*, doc. 153.   37 Cavell, "Sector Theory", 1172–1173.
38 Cavell, *Arctic 1874–1949*, docs. 156, 157.

sovereignty from the government's chief astronomer, William King.[39] This report required maps, which White prepared, and which (unlike the report itself) were made publicly available. They not only showed the sector lines, but showed them extending to the Pole.

Nor was this White's only tactic. The Geographic Board of Canada had begun the task of selecting official northern place names in 1901. White was of course a member of this body, and he ensured that the names given by Sverdrup were considered along with the rest. Since only the state with sovereignty over an area had the authority to give official names, this move encouraged a belief that the land was already Canadian.[40] The names Axel Heiberg Island and Ringnes Islands were accepted, but White believed that Sverdrup's King Christian Island had already been seen by British explorers and given the name Findlay Island. Accordingly, the British name remained on official Canadian maps.[41]

Among his other feats, Sverdrup had proved that Kane's Grinnell Land and Inglefield's Ellesmere Land were not divided by a strait. Combined with the Nares expedition's finding that Grinnell Land and Grant Land were connected, this discovery meant that there was a single large island just west of Greenland. White seized his opportunity and had the whole landmass named Ellesmere.[42] He thus made the American names Grinnell and Grant far less prominent on maps; later, they were dropped entirely. Sverdrup had called the part of the island that he himself was the first to explore King Oscar Land, after the ruler of Sweden and Norway. This designation, too, was overwritten.

The British name Ellesmere reinforced the perception that the entire island was Canadian territory. White thus indirectly but quite effectively undercut the possibility of a Norwegian sovereignty bid. Because it was not possible to reach Sverdrup's new islands by ship, a Norwegian base on southwestern Ellesmere would be essential. Norway, which gained its independence from Sweden in 1905, was anxious to have Britain's goodwill, and a challenge over King Oscar Land would be far riskier than a claim to the newly discovered

39 King, *Report*.
40 The United States Hydrographic Office accepted this premise and followed the Geographic Board's decisions on its maps. See Thomas Washington to Deputy Minister of Marine and Fisheries, 20 January 1916, LAC, RG 42, vol. 226, file 26152 part 2.
41 See correspondence and lists of names, 1901–19, in LAC, RG 21, vol. 153, file 41. As it later turned out, King Christian Island was smaller than Sverdrup's chart indicated and farther to the northeast. It was, therefore, obviously not the same as Findlay Island, and the Geographic Board added it to Canadian maps in 1919.
42 Cavell, *Arctic 1874–1949*, doc. 137.

islands alone – yet a claim to the new islands alone would be virtually impossible to uphold if the only access to them was through Canadian territory. Despite Sverdrup's urging, no official Norwegian claim was ever made.[43]

Bernier, meanwhile, had little to show for his North Pole fundraising efforts since 1898. In 1901, evidently having learned about White's sector theory, he tried to make his plan more attractive to Canadians by suggesting that when he arrived at the Pole – the apex of the sector lines – he could proclaim his nation's sovereignty over the entire archipelago to the south. Bernier had support among some members of parliament, who promoted this idea, while others, seemingly briefed by White, contended that all the islands were already Canada's.

Through a complicated chain of events, Bernier was hired by the Department of Marine and Fisheries as captain of its newly purchased vessel, DGS *Arctic* (formerly the German Antarctic research ship *Gauss*). Laurier's intention was to establish more police posts. Bernier, however, unsuccessfully tried to turn *Arctic*'s first northern voyage into an attempt on the Pole. The police, finding him exceptionally difficult to work with, managed to separate their sovereignty programme from that of Marine and Fisheries.[44]

In 1906 the government passed an act requiring foreign whalers in Canada's northern territorial waters to purchase licences; the act specifically declared that all of Hudson Bay was under Canadian jurisdiction. The main purpose of Bernier's next voyage was to enforce this act, which he successfully did, marking an important step forward in effective occupation.[45] However, Bernier himself preferred a more old-fashioned style of sovereignty assertion, following the examples set by Wakeham and Low. Personal glory had always been among his aims, and the practice of raising the flag and making proclamations allowed Bernier to keep the spotlight on himself.

During his 1906 cruise through Lancaster Sound, Bernier carried out several flag-raising ceremonies. In 1907 he proceeded to Jones Sound and made a sweeping claim that, in accordance with the sector principle, included the Sverdrup Islands, and indeed Bernier reported to Ottawa that it extended 'as far as ninety degrees north'.[46] The first set of activities was permitted by his orders (which had been revised, possibly without Laurier's knowledge, to suit Bernier's views); the Jones Sound sector claim was not. The government

43 On Sverdrup's campaign, see Thorleifsson, "Sverdrup Islands Question", 14, 17, 63.
44 Cavell, "More Latitude", 299–302.   45 Cavell, "More Latitude", 302, 304.
46 Cavell, *Arctic 1874–1949*, doc. 179.

did not publicize the sector aspect of this claim, but Bernier carried out a similar act in 1909, after wintering at the same harbour on Melville Island where Parry had anchored almost a hundred years before. He recorded this second sector claim on a plaque affixed to the prominent landmark known as Parry's Rock.[47]

Bernier, knowing that Peary was still determined to reach the Pole and that he himself would never do so, had apparently come to see a claim extending to the Pole as a reasonable substitute. In 1909 the government might again have refused to endorse his action, if not for the fact that Peary claimed to have finally succeeded, and to have taken possession of both the Pole and the area around it for the United States. In a state of panic, Laurier abandoned his gradualist approach. He declared that Canada's territorial rights did indeed extend to 90° north – even though Canadian occupation in the High Arctic was still non-existent.

After President William Howard Taft made it plain that he would not follow up Peary's sovereignty proclamation and Norway issued no protest against Canada's claim, Laurier neither developed nor repudiated the sector idea. The election of a new Conservative government under Robert Borden brought an end to Bernier's voyages, and since the northern whaling industry was in decline, Arctic issues faded into the background.[48]

Stefansson and the Arctic Continent

The next phase of Canadian policy began in 1913, with an approach from the explorer Vilhjalmur Stefansson to Borden. Stefansson intended to search for an Arctic 'continent' (as it was usually called) in the Beaufort Sea region. According to the theory put forward by Rollin Harris of the United States Coast and Geodetic Survey, this landmass lay west of the Canadian archipelago, beginning not far from the Alaska and Yukon coasts and continuing north almost to the Pole.

Peary was an enthusiastic believer in Harris's idea, and he claimed to have glimpsed part of the continent, which he called Crocker Land, from the Ellesmere coast.[49] His former subordinate Donald MacMillan had organized

---

47 On Bernier's various sovereignty-related actions and claims, see Cavell, "More Latitude", 301–305; Cavell, "Sector Claims", 296–300. On the revision to the 1906 orders, see Cavell, "More Latitude", 303. The account of Bernier's 1907 voyage to Jones Sound in Cavell, "Sector Claims", 296–298, 307 n.2, adds important details not discussed in Cavell, "More Latitude" or any other secondary works.

48 On the responses to Peary's sovereignty proclamation in Ottawa and Washington, see Cavell, "More Latitude", 304–305.

49 Peary, *Nearest the Pole*, 202, 207.

an expedition to search for Crocker Land from a base in Greenland, while Stefansson planned to approach the unknown area from the western Arctic, starting on Prince Patrick Island. Both men had the backing of American institutions. Stefansson wanted more money than his US sponsors were willing to provide, and he made Borden an offer. If Canada contributed funds and he found the land, he would not claim it for the United States, but rather would leave the question of sovereignty to be settled by negotiation between the two countries. Instead, Borden took over the entire venture.[50]

Stefansson had initiated a long Canadian tradition of invoking – and stoking – sovereignty fears as the most effective way to promote official action in the far north. His Canadian Arctic Expedition (1913–18) cost the government over $500,000, far more than Stefansson's initial estimate of $85,000. However, Borden considered the money well spent. Though Stefansson failed to discover a new continent, he did find the last major unknown islands in the archipelago: a cluster northeast of Prince Patrick Island and another south of Ellef Ringnes Island, plus Meighen Island in the northern part of the Sverdrup group. All these new lands were claimed for Canada. Moreover, Stefansson corrected Sverdrup's chart at several points. On Ellef Ringnes, he found a note from MacMillan, who also journeyed extensively in the Sverdrup Islands, though without adding anything new to the map.[51]

Stefansson was unquestionably the most talented author to explore the archipelago since Kane. His narrative, *The Friendly Arctic*, not only recounted his adventures among the northernmost islands, it promoted the ideas that living there need involve no hardships and that the area's resources promised great economic benefits for Canada in the near future. His next book, *The Northward Course of Empire*, repeated these themes. Stefansson also wrote prolifically for newspapers and magazines and had a talent for garnering headlines. MacMillan's rival narrative, *Four Years in the White North*, had little public impact compared with Stefansson's writings.

Despite Stefansson's high public profile, his standing in Ottawa quickly deteriorated. His great ambition was to lead another government-funded

---

50 See Cavell, "Arctic Atlantis". White had never accepted Harris's theory, but it is unlikely that Borden consulted him about Stefansson's offer. If the land had indeed existed where Harris believed it did, much of it would have been outside the sector lines. It is not clear whether Borden realized this, but if he did, his decision was an implicit rejection of the sector principle.
51 Stefansson, *Friendly Arctic*, 506–507, 525–536.

quest for the continent, which he now believed lay closer to Asia than to North America. Stefansson wanted to secure possession of Wrangel Island off the Siberian coast as a base for his new explorations. His focus, accordingly, was on convincing politicians and civil servants to discard what he saw as the irksome limitations of the sector theory and take an expansionist course that, reluctant bureaucrats warned, might set off a dispute with Russia. Stefansson argued that because the Russians had never occupied Wrangel Island and it lay outside the standard 5.5 km limit for territorial waters, it was a *terra nullius* or no-man's-land.[52]

To promote a greater sense of urgency on sovereignty matters in general, Stefansson once again tried the scaremongering tactics he had first employed in 1913. In 1920 he alleged that the Danish explorer Knud Rasmussen was planning to invade the High Arctic islands and colonize them with Greenlanders, thus negating Canada's inchoate title. Rasmussen had written a personal letter to Stefansson that clearly showed he had no such intention. Yet Stefansson insisted that to meet the Danish threat, he must lead a new Canadian expedition to the High Arctic, which could then be turned to Wrangel Island and the new continent north of it.[53]

Unscrupulous though Stefansson's actions were, they provided a forceful and much-needed reminder that occupation was essential. In part because of White, who had become the minister of justice's special adviser on boundary issues, Stefansson's scheme was thwarted and other steps were taken to safeguard Canada's High Arctic title. The purpose of these steps was occupation alone, without any accompanying search for the supposed continent. Ottawa inaugurated annual ship patrols and established several police posts on the islands, including two on Ellesmere Island and one on Devon Island. The post on Ellesmere's Bache Peninsula, erected in 1926, was then the most northerly government station on the planet.[54]

Stefansson's contention that the Arctic was friendly and open to whites and their activities did not impress many Canadians in this decade, but other factors did. Through the efforts of Oswald Finnie, director of the Department of the Interior's new Northwest Territories and Yukon Branch, films, photographs, official publications, and newspaper stories informed the public about government activities. Two of Canada's best-known artists, A. Y. Jackson and Lawren Harris, accompanied the patrols in the late 1920s and produced many

---

52 Cavell, *Arctic 1874–1949*, docs. 221, 271, 272.
53 Cavell and Noakes, *Acts of Occupation*, ch. 2; Cavell, *Arctic 1874–1949*, doc. 220.
54 See Cavell and Noakes, *Acts of Occupation*, especially 84–87, 164–169, 204–209, 219, 235–238, 242–244.

Arctic paintings.⁵⁵ These images and narratives did much to make Canadians see the Arctic as their own.

On the political side, sovereignty concerns were heightened by another foreigner, whose goal – unlike Rasmussen's – was indeed to undermine Ottawa's claim to the far north. This episode brought about the first official Canadian sector claim. Again, the belief in a large unknown Arctic landmass was the catalyst that transformed Canada's northern policy.

The 1925 Sector Claim and the Sverdrup Islands Settlement

Stefansson took no further active part in the quest for the mythical continent, but it was carried on by other enthusiasts, mostly American. After efforts by ship and sledge had failed repeatedly, they turned to aviation. This development had far more effect on Canadian officials than did the search in itself. Stefansson's many publications on the future geopolitical importance of transpolar air routes had already made them aware that even the remotest Arctic location might sooner or later become a foreign base. Therefore, as one civil servant wrote in 1921, possession of any island by another nation could pose an actual danger: 'Such a condition would have always been undesirable but it would be particularly so now in view of the development of aircraft and submarines.'⁵⁶

Just four years later MacMillan, in partnership with aviator Richard Byrd, planned an air search for the continent from a base on Axel Heiberg Island. The alarm in Ottawa was considerable, but the matter was effectively handled. An interdepartmental body, the Northern Advisory Board, was formed to coordinate the response; among the members were Finnie, White, and O. D. Skelton, who had recently been appointed undersecretary of state for external affairs (deputy foreign minister).⁵⁷

Both publicly and through diplomatic correspondence with Washington, the Liberal government of William Lyon Mackenzie King made a formal claim to the entire archipelago, utilizing White's version of the sector theory.⁵⁸ Since the process of High Arctic occupation was well under way, there was a far more satisfactory basis for such an act than there had been in

---

55 On Jackson and Harris, see Ladon, "Art of Arctic Sovereignty".
56 James Harkin to William Cory, 7 April 1921, LAC, MG30 E169, vol. 1.
57 Cavell and Noakes, *Acts of Occupation*, ch. 8; Cavell, *Arctic 1874–1949*, docs. 337, 346, 349, 350, 352.
58 Cavell, *Arctic 1874–1949*, docs. 363, 366, 371, 375, 377, 380, 387.

1909. Officials in the US State Department were reluctant to admit that the establishment of government authority without actual permanent settlement met the criteria for effective occupation. However, neither were they prepared to deny that it did so.

This response – or rather lack of response – was particularly significant because leading American legal theorists had long insisted that it was impossible to occupy the polar regions, and therefore the only possible solution lay in an internationalist approach.[59] In 1924, State Department official Lawrence Martin had proposed that Canada, the United States, and Norway should have equal rights in the archipelago, using the 1920 Spitsbergen (Svalbard) Treaty as a model.[60] Once Martin's superiors learned that Canada was in fact taking steps to occupy even the northernmost islands, no more was heard of this plan. In the North American Arctic, nationalism rather than internationalism prevailed.

MacMillan was personally very hostile to Canadian sovereignty claims, and despite Washington's non-confrontational stance an unpleasant situation might have developed on Ellesmere Island in 1925. However, the Americans experienced difficulties with their planes, and no attempt to establish a base in the archipelago was actually made. Finnie was well aware that MacMillan might cause more problems in the future. He therefore arranged for an ordinance requiring foreign explorers and scientists to secure Canadian permits and to make reports on their work to Ottawa. MacMillan did his best to evade these requirements, but he was forced to comply before he set out on his next expedition.[61]

The Sverdrup Islands question was also resolved to Canada's satisfaction. Norway finally raised the issue through a diplomatic communication in 1925.[62] Canadian officials suspected from the outset that the Norwegians did not really intend to assert their own sovereignty at such a late date, and indeed Oslo's intention was first, to arrange compensation for Sverdrup himself, and second, to secure certain economic rights in the islands, again using the Spitsbergen Treaty as a model.[63]

By the time negotiations began in 1929, sledge patrols by the Mounted Police had been extended to Axel Heiberg and the other islands in the

---

59 Scott, "Arctic Exploration"; Balch, "Arctic and Antarctic Regions".
60 Martin to Alfred Haupt, 21 March 1924, NACP, RG 59, microcopy M-1406, roll 3, file 857.014/7. On the Spitsbergen Treaty, see Roald Berg's Chapter 15 in this volume.
61 Cavell, *Arctic 1874–1949*, docs. 355, 411, 412.   62 Cavell, *Arctic 1874–1949*, doc. 339.
63 Thorleifsson, "Sverdrup Islands Question". The Norwegians later described the Canadian title as already valid before their recognition. See Permanent Court of International Justice, *Legal Status*, series C, no. 64, 1416.

Sverdrup group. These patrols, which gave added substance to the Canadian claim, began in 1926 and continued annually. Inspector Alfred Joy's 1929 journey from Devon Island west to Melville Island and then back east on a more northerly line through the Sverdrup Islands to the Bache Peninsula post was particularly noteworthy.

The Canadians were willing to provide a moderate payment to Sverdrup as a friendly gesture. However, Finnie opposed special economic privileges for Norway, in part because with the development of aviation, such a concession was bound to be 'prolific of misunderstandings and disputes in the future'. Skelton agreed that any 'qualification on full sovereignty' was unacceptable. The Norwegians, having first softened their demand, finally dropped it. They insisted that their recognition of Canadian sovereignty was not based on the sector principle, but since Ottawa had achieved its main goal, Canadian officials took the pragmatic view that the Norwegian reservation did not matter.[64] 'Canada's title to sovereignty in the Canadian Arctic sector is now perfect', proclaimed an official in the Department of External Affairs.[65] A year later, the Norwegian writer Gustav Smedal approvingly described the Canadian patrols as models of 'how to take effective possession of polar areas'.[66]

The 1930s: Sovereignty Achieved

Fifty years after the sovereignty transfer from the United Kingdom, Canada had gone far towards integrating the High Arctic into the nation, at least in the legal and political senses. The government had defined the region as essential to the national interest and substantially increased the personnel and budget for northern administration. It had forestalled possible foreign challenges and rejected expansionism outside the sector limits, balancing nationalism with due concern for peace and international stability.

Canadian successes included an expedition that made the last major geographical discoveries in the High Arctic; the first systematic occupation programme in the polar regions; and the sector theory, which was officially taken up by the Union of Soviet Socialist Republics in 1926. The theory would gain further recognition from Australia, France, Chile, and Argentina in the 1930s and 1940s. The United States never accepted it, but neither did

---

64 Cavell, *Arctic 1874–1949*, docs. 494, 505, 509, 524, 527.
65 Cavell, *Arctic 1874–1949*, doc. 522. The author may have been future prime minister Lester Pearson.
66 Smedal, *Acquisition*, 35.

Washington ever publicly oppose it, despite Norwegian efforts to secure such a statement.[67]

In 1933, White's contention that traditional standards of effective occupation should not be applied in the polar regions was endorsed by the Permanent Court of International Justice (PCIJ) through its decision in the Eastern Greenland case. Norway had challenged Denmark's title to the an uninhabited part of Greenland's east coast on the grounds that Denmark had not occupied the entire island. However, the court found in Denmark's favour.[68] Peter Kikkert has argued that the Eastern Greenland decision was not a turning point for Canada and other nations making polar claims because it did not remove all uncertainty about how much occupation was sufficient.[69] However, it is not the purpose of legal decisions to provide definitive guidance for every future case. Rather, they offer general principles, and the particular circumstances of each dispute must always be taken into account. Yet even considering this fact, Canadian activities clearly more than met the criteria set out in the 1933 decision.[70]

Among themselves, American officials began to soften their stance on occupation. Later in 1933, the State Department's influential geographer, Samuel Boggs, admitted that the polar regions 'may require a special adaptation of political and legal rules and considerations' and he argued that the exercise of jurisdiction was enough to establish a title.[71] Canada unquestionably did exercise as much jurisdiction as was possible. For example, the German geologist Hans Krüger, who set out on a journey through the

67 See Cavell, "Sector Theory", 1181, citing Hugh S. Cumming Jr, memo for Pierrepont Moffat, 28 July 1938, NACP, RG 59, decimal files 1930–39, box 4520, file 800.014 Antarctic/126.
68 See Permanent Court of International Justice, *Legal Status*, series A/B, no. 53.
69 Kikkert, "Grasping for the Ends", 46, 285–286, 289; Kikkert, "In Search", 29–31. Kikkert further suggests that in the 1930s and 1940s it seemed possible that the Eastern Greenland outcome would have little or no impact on future judicial decisions, and therefore officials remained uncertain about sovereignty requirements. "Grasping for the Ends", 263, 288–290; Kikkert, "In Search", 29. However, one prominent writer noted in 1938 that although some legal scholars would still have preferred more stringent requirements, 'everybody agrees that ... [the decision] is of the highest importance for the development of the law of international occupation'; Kunz, "Review of Haver", 207. Many of the government documents Kikkert quotes refer to Antarctica, where exploration was ongoing, rival claims abounded, and even the limited state activities possible in the High Arctic were often not feasible, leaving would-be claimants to fall back on such gestures as dropping proclamations from aeroplanes. In this context, the significance of the Eastern Greenland case was certainly more difficult for policymakers to determine.
70 See Auburn, *Antarctic Law*, 22.
71 Boggs, *Polar Regions*, 2, 31–32. This book reproduces a document dated 21 September 1933; the original is in NACP, RG 59, decimal files 1930–39, box 4522, file 800.014 Arctic/31.

northernmost islands in 1930, complied with all Canadian regulations, including payment of customs duty on his supplies at the Bache Peninsula post. When he did not return, the police carried out extensive searches.[72]

The 1940s: Resurgence of Sovereignty Fears

In 1938, Cabinet minister Thomas Crerar was asked in the House of Commons whether he could reassure the nation about northern sovereignty. He stated that Canada's claim was secure on the basis of international recognition, occupation, and the sector theory. Crerar added confidently that, in his own view, 'our supremacy there is established to a point where it could not be successfully challenged'.[73] Why, then, do so many Canadians still doubt their nation's sovereignty over the High Arctic?

Strangely, the Eastern Greenland decision was not well-publicized in Canada, and until recent years historians gave it little if any weight in their analyses of sovereignty issues. Skelton, who served as deputy foreign minister until his death in 1941, followed the case closely and appears to have considered High Arctic sovereignty secure thereafter, provided that Canada continued to exercise as much state authority as was practicable. When wartime conditions forced a temporary withdrawal, Skelton did not worry.[74] His confidence was justified. It took decades for the Eastern Greenland precedent's importance to be fully proved through rulings in such cases as the Western Sahara dispute (International Court of Justice, 1975). Yet as early as 1946, the author of an internal US government report concluded that because of the PCIJ's decision, 'the Canadian claim to sovereignty over the entire American Arctic would be sustained by an international judicial body.'[75] Unfortunately, Skelton never wrote a definitive memo on the subject, and after he died there was no clear guidance for his successors in the wartime and immediate post-war periods.

Many Canadians, both inside and outside the government, were fixated on the fact that the United States did not endorse the sector theory, preferring a 'glass half-empty' mindset that ignored the endorsements from other

---

72 Cavell, *Arctic 1874–1949*, doc. 406; Barr, "Career and Disappearance".
73 Canada, House of Commons, *Debates*, Vol. 216, 3080–3081.
74 See Cavell, *Arctic 1874–1949*, Introduction, xxxiii, and doc. 548.
75 "Problems of Canadian-United States Cooperation in the Arctic", 29 October 1946, printed in Grant, *Sovereignty or Security*, Appendix G, 307–308. In 1949 the first Canadian government study to take the Eastern Greenland outcome fully into account stated unequivocally that 'Canada has fulfilled the various requirements imposed by International Law'; Cavell, *Arctic 1874–1949*, doc. 572.

nations. Both Bernier and Stefansson considered themselves badly treated by the government, and they contributed to this trend by frequently suggesting that Ottawa had never done enough in the north.[76] There was little to outweigh such pronouncements. The publicity surrounding the Eastern Arctic Patrols became scantier after government cutbacks in the Depression era, and the accomplishments of the 1920s patrols were almost forgotten. The Arctic paintings by Jackson and Harris remained extremely popular, and indeed they gained the status of national cultural icons. However, they gradually became detached from their original context, and since most of them depict scenes of lonely grandeur, they reinforced the perception of the far north as a no-man's-land.

The major factor, however, was the American presence in the region in the 1940s. During World War II, this presence extended no farther north than the more accessible parts of the Eastern Arctic. Moreover, the Americans dutifully requested Ottawa's permission before establishing themselves in the southern part of Baffin Island and on the northern coast of Quebec. The purpose was to facilitate the air ferrying of American-made planes to Britain via Greenland and Iceland, as part of the 1941 Lend-Lease Agreement. Permission was granted without any handwringing about possible sovereignty consequences.[77]

Then in 1946, as the Cold War intensified, Washington proposed a range of joint northern projects, including High Arctic weather stations. US diplomats offered assurances that Canadian sovereignty would be respected. Nevertheless, given the lack of any significant white or Inuit presence north of Parry Channel and Washington's continuing public adherence to a high standard for occupation, many in Ottawa responded in a manner that involved more emotion than reliance on the historical or legal facts. For example, General Daniel Spry declared that Canada had previously done almost nothing in the archipelago. Its title, he insisted, was therefore 'at best somewhat tenuous and weak'.[78] Such alarmist documents may have been intended to ensure that nothing would be taken on trust during the negotiations, but they have given later readers an inaccurate picture of the Canadian legal case. Further protests, also loaded with rhetoric about sovereignty dangers, came from the Department of Mines and Resources, which had long hoped to establish scientific stations in the

---

76 For example, see Bernier, *Master Mariner*; "Stefansson Says". Stefansson continued with his theme of official neglect throughout the 1940s. For example, see "Stefansson Raps".
77 See Cavell, *Arctic 1874–1949*, docs. 549–553. 78 Page, *Documents*, doc. 913, enclosure.

far north under its own auspices. Here, issues of departmental turf appear to have played a part.[79]

Spry and others seemed to fear that the American assurances were no more than diplomatic trickery, but in 1947 Washington readily agreed to a range of conditions, including the important proviso that US personnel would be subject to Canadian laws.[80] This arrangement was in itself an important de facto acknowledgement of Canadian sovereignty. Nevertheless, the general belief that Canada's shaky title was seriously endangered through joint activities with the United States persists. In the minds of many Canadians, the mere image of Americans against a backdrop of emptiness still creates anxiety.

Conclusion

The many episodes of unnecessary panic in Ottawa over supposed external threats demonstrate that a purely political analysis can never capture all the factors at play in state endeavours to possess polar territory. Canadian insecurities on this matter endured in defiance of even the most reassuring facts. In 1969, Washington publicly denied any intention of ever challenging Ottawa's sovereignty over the entire Arctic Archipelago, while at the same time insisting that the Northwest Passage is an international strait.[81] The statement about the islands went all but unnoticed amid the nation-wide uproar about the passage, and it was quickly forgotten. When US Secretary of State George Schulz visited Canada in 1985, a reporter asked him whether it might be a good idea for the Americans to recognize the Canadian title. 'Of course, we recognize [it],' replied Schulz.[82] Again, it made no difference; alarmism about the High Arctic had become a Canadian reflex.

The Canadian story is unique in many ways, owing to such colourful and outspoken non-state actors as Stefansson and to the many political ramifications of the erroneous Arctic continent theory. Yet while other nations may

---

79 Page, *Documents*, doc. 912. On the campaign to establish scientific stations, which began in 1937, see LAC, RG 85, vol. 884, file 9137 part 1.
80 Canadian note, 13 February 1947, and Saul Rae to Lester Pearson, 28 February 1947, LAC, RG 25, vol. 3347, file 9061-A-40 part 1.
81 "No Claim". The same American official, Undersecretary of State U. Alexis Johnson, made a similar statement in 1970; see "Arctic Pact". In 1975 a *Toronto Star* reporter was allowed to view official files, where he found a US diplomatic note that acknowledged Canada's title to the islands. In a long article, he mentioned this fact only in passing, while focusing on the disagreement over Arctic waters; Crane, "Oil Hunt".
82 "Secretary Visits", 46.

not experience the same degree of anxiety over issues of polar sovereignty, the question of how to claim and manage uninhabited regions is a matter of great concern elsewhere in the Arctic and virtually everywhere in the Antarctic. James White's formulation of the sector principle, Ottawa's refusal to abolish the sector boundaries and claim Wrangel Island, the Sverdrup Islands negotiations, and issues of Canada–United States cooperation in the 1940s all have significance for polar historians and policymakers around the globe.

Bibliography

Archival Sources

Library and Archives Canada (LAC), Ottawa:
 RG 21 (Department of Energy, Mines and Resources)
 RG 25 (Department of External Affairs)
 RG 42 (Department of Marine and Fisheries)
 RG 45 (Geological Survey of Canada)
 MG 30 E 169 (James Bernard Harkin Papers)
National Archives [of the United States] (NACP), College Park, Maryland:
 RG 59 (Department of State)
The National Archives of the United Kingdom (TNA), London:
 CO 6 (Colonial Office, British North America)

Canadian Government Publications

Canada Gazette
Debates of the House of Commons

Books and Articles

"Arctic Pact Sought by U.S. and Canada", *New York Times* (22 March 1970): 88.
Auburn, F. M., *Antarctic Law and Politics* (Bloomington: Indiana University Press, 1982).
Balch, T. W., "The Arctic and Antarctic Regions and the Law of Nations", *American Journal of International Law* 4 (1910): 265–275.
Barr, William, "The Career and Disappearance of Hans K. E. Krüger, Arctic Geologist, 1886–1930", *Polar Record* 29 (1993): 277–304.
Belcher, Edward, *The Last of the Arctic Voyages*, 2 vols. (London: Lovell Reeve, 1856).
Bernier, J. E., *Master Mariner and Arctic Explorer: A Narrative of Sixty Years at Sea from the Yarns and Logs of Captain J. E. Bernier, F.R.G.S., F.R.E.S.* (Ottawa: Le Droit, 1939).
Boggs, Samuel Whittemore, *The Polar Regions: Geographical and Historical Data for Consideration in a Study of Claims to Sovereignty in the Arctic and Antarctic Regions* (Buffalo: William S. Hein, 1990).

Brewster, David, "Observations on the Mean Temperature of the Globe", *Transactions of the Royal Society of Edinburgh* 9 (1823): 201–225.
Cavell, Janice, "'A Little More Latitude': Explorers, Politicians, and Canadian Arctic Policy during the Laurier Era", *Polar Record* 47 (2011): 289–309.
Cavell, Janice, "Arctic Atlantis", *Canada's History* 100 (2020): 20–27.
Cavell, Janice, "'Consolidation and Control of All Eskimo Income': The Motive for the 1953 High Arctic Relocation", *Journal of Canadian Studies* 55 (2021): 114–147.
Cavell, Janice, "Sector Claims and Counter-claims: Joseph Elzéar Bernier, the Canadian Government, and Arctic Sovereignty, 1898–1934", *Polar Record* 50 (2014): 293–310.
Cavell, Janice, "The Sector Theory and the Canadian Arctic, 1897–1970", *International History Review* 41 (2019): 1168–1193.
Cavell, Janice, and Jeff Noakes, *Acts of Occupation: Canada and Arctic Sovereignty, 1918–22* (Vancouver: UBC Press, 2010).
Cavell, Janice, ed., *Documents on Canadian External Relations: The Arctic, 1874–1949* (Ottawa: Global Affairs Canada, 2016).
Craciun, Adriana, *Writing Arctic Disaster: Authorship and Exploration* (Cambridge: Cambridge University Press, 2016).
Crane, David, "Oil Hunt Showed We Didn't Control Northern Waters", *Toronto Star* (13 October 1975), A6.
Grant, Shelagh, *Sovereignty or Security? Government Policy in the Canadian North, 1936–1950* (Vancouver: UBC Press, 1988).
Hall, William Edward, *A Treatise on International Law*, 4th edition (Oxford: Clarendon, 1895).
Hayes, I. I., *The Open Polar Sea: A Narrative of a Voyage of Discovery Towards the North Pole, in the Schooner "United States"* (New York: Hurd and Houghton, 1867).
Hurlbut, George C., "Mr. Peary's Plan and Capt. Sverdrup", *Journal of the American Geographical Society of New York* 29 (1897): 453.
Inglefield, E. A., "Report on the Return of the Isabel from the Arctic Regions", *Journal of the Royal Geographical Society* 23 (1853): 136–145.
Inglefield, E. A., *A Summer Search for Sir John Franklin; with a Peep into the Polar Basin* (London: Thomas Harrison, 1853).
Kane, Elisha Kent, *Access to an Open Polar Sea, in Connection with the Search after Sir John Franklin and His Companions* (New York: Baker, Godwin, 1853).
Kane, Elisha Kent, *Arctic Explorations: The Second Grinnell Expedition in Search of Sir John Franklin, 1853, '54, '55*, 2 vols. (Philadelphia: Childs and Peterson, 1856).
Kane, Elisha Kent, *The U.S. Grinnell Expedition in Search of Sir John Franklin: A Personal Narrative* (New York: Harper, 1854).
Kikkert, Peter, "Grasping for the Ends of the Earth: Framing and Contesting Polar Sovereignty, 1900–1955", PhD diss. (Western University, 2015).
Kikkert, Peter, "In Search of Polar Sovereignty, 1900–1959", in Wilfrid Greaves and P. Whitney Lackenbauer, eds., *Breaking Through Understanding Sovereignty and Security in the Circumpolar Arctic* (Toronto: University of Toronto Press, 2021), pp. 25–44.
King, W. F., *Report upon the Title of Canada to the Islands North of the Mainland of Canada* (Ottawa: Government Printing Bureau, 1905).

Kunz, Josef L., "Review of Wolfgang Haver, *Wurde Ostgrönland durch Dänemark in dem Zeitraum von 1921 bis 1931 Okkupiert?*", *American Journal of International Law* 32 (January 1938): 207–208.

Ladon, Agnes, "The Art of Arctic Sovereignty: Towards Visualizing the North as Canadian, 1927–1974", PhD diss. (Queen's University, Kingston, 2017).

Loomis, Chauncey C., "The Arctic Sublime", in U. C. Knoepflmacher and G. B. Tennyson, eds., *Nature and the Victorian Imagination* (Berkeley: University of California Press, 1977), pp. 95–112.

MacMillan, Donald B., *Four Years in the White North* (New York, London: Harper and Brothers, 1918).

Markham, Albert Hastings, *The Great Frozen Sea: A Personal Narrative of the Voyage of the 'Alert' During the Arctic Expedition of 1875–6* (London: Daldy, Isbister, 1878).

Markham, Clements, ed., *The Voyages of William Baffin, 1612–1622* (London: Hakluyt Society, 1881).

Maury, M. F., *The Physical Geography of the Sea* (New York: Harper and Brothers, 1855).

Morrison, William R., *Showing the Flag: The Mounted Police and Canadian Sovereignty in the North, 1894–1925* (Vancouver: UBC Press, 1985).

Nansen, Fridtjof, "How Can the North Polar Region Be Crossed?", *Geographical Journal* 1 (1893): 1–22.

Neatby, Leslie, *Search for Franklin* (Edmonton: Hurtig, 1970).

"No Claim to Islands", *Globe and Mail* (Toronto) (28 June 1969): 11.

Page, Donald, ed., *Documents on Canadian External Relations*, Vol. 12 (1946) (Ottawa: Department of External Affairs, 1977).

Peary, R. E., *Nearest the Pole: A Narrative of the Polar Expedition of the Peary Arctic Club in the S. S. Roosevelt, 1905–1906* (New York: Doubleday, Page, 1907).

Penlington, Norman, *The Alaska Boundary Dispute: A Critical Reappraisal* (Toronto: McGraw-Hill Ryerson, 1972).

Permanent Court of International Justice, *Legal Status of Eastern Greenland*, Series A/B (Collection of Judgments, Orders and Advisory Opinions), no. 53 (Leyden: A.W. Sijothoff, 1933).

Permanent Court of International Justice, *Legal Status of Eastern Greenland*, Series C (Pleadings, Oral Statements and Documents), no. 64 (Leyden: A.W. Sijothoff, 1933).

Petermann, Augustus [August], "Notes on the Distribution of Animals Available as Food in the Arctic Regions", *Journal of the Royal Geographical Society of London* 22 (1852): 118–127.

Report of the Delegates Appointed to Negotiate for the Acquisition of Rupert's Land and the North-West Territory (Ottawa: Queen's Printer, 1869).

Routledge, Karen, *Do You See Ice? Inuit and Americans at Home and Away* (Chicago: University of Chicago Press, 2018).

Saint-Pierre, Marjolaine, *Joseph-Elzéar Bernier: Champion of Canadian Arctic Sovereignty, 1852–1934*, trans. William Barr (Montreal: Baraka, 2009).

Scott, James Brown, "Arctic Exploration and International Law", *American Journal of International Law* 3 (1909): 928–941.

"Secretary Visits Canada", *Department of State Bulletin* 86, 2106 (January 1986): 42–46.

Smedal, Gustav, *Acquisition of Sovereignty over Polar Areas* (Oslo: Jacob Dybwad, 1931).

14 Canada and the High Arctic Islands

Stefansson, Vilhjalmur, *The Friendly Arctic: The Story of Five Years in Polar Regions* (New York: MacMillan, 1921).

Stefansson, Vilhjalmur, *The Northward Course of Empire* (New York: Harcourt, Brace, 1922).

"Stefansson Raps Failure to Settle Arctic Regions", *Globe and Mail* (Toronto) (1 April 1948): 4.

"Stefansson Says Canada Asleep to Importance of Arctic; Praises Russia", *Winnipeg Evening Tribune* (19 May 1937).

Sverdrup, Otto, *New Land: Four Years in the Arctic Regions*, 2 vols., trans. Ethel Harriet Hearn (London: Longmans, Green, 1904).

Sverdrup, Otto, "The Second Norwegian Polar Expedition in the 'Fram', 1898–1902", *Geographical Journal* 22 (1903): 38–69.

Taylor, Andrew, *Geographical Discovery and Exploration in the Queen Elizabeth Islands* (Ottawa: Department of Mines and Technical Surveys, 1964).

Thorleifsson, Thorleif, "Norway 'Must Really Drop Their Absurd Claims such as that to the Otto Sverdrup Islands'. Bi-polar International Diplomacy: The Sverdrup Islands Question, 1902–1930", Master's thesis (Simon Fraser University, 2006).

"Transactions of the Society, January–March 1897", *Journal of the American Geographical Society of New York* 29 (1897): 114–122.

Wrangell, Ferdinand von, *Narrative of an Expedition to the Polar Sea, in the Years 1820, 1821, 1822, & 1823*, ed. Edward Sabine (London: James Madden, 1840).

Zaslow, Morris, *The Opening of the Canadian North, 1870–1914* (Toronto: McClelland and Stewart, 1971).

Online Sources

"Royal Commission on Aboriginal Peoples". Library and Archives Canada, www.bac-lac.gc.ca/eng/discover/aboriginal-heritage/royal-commission-aboriginal-peoples/Pages/introduction.aspx.

15

The Genesis of the Spitsbergen/Svalbard Treaty, 1871–1920

ROALD BERG

Introduction

The Spitsbergen/Svalbard Treaty of 1920 recognizes Norway as the 'full and unqualified' sovereign of the previously *terra nullius* Spitsbergen archipelago, including Bear Island, an area twice the size of Belgium, although with a much smaller population (currently 2,500 people) and no Indigenous residents.[1] Despite Norway's sovereignty, the Treaty gives the citizens of the signatory powers the same economic rights and right of access to the resources of the archipelago. Furthermore, the Treaty guards the users of Spitsbergen's resources against heavy tax burdens, as it confines the tax levels to cover the costs of ruling it.[2] Additionally, the Treaty, according to Michael Byers, 'effectively demilitarizes the archipelago', as it prohibits naval bases, fortifications, and any use 'for warlike purposes'.[3]

---

1 Byers, *International Law*, 17.
2 For the Treaty, see Ulfstein, *The Svalbard Treaty*; a short and good summary of the treaty is given in Pedersen, "Security Issues"; see also the commemorating book, Dahl and Jensen, eds., *Svalbardtraktaten 100 år*.
3 Byers, *International Law*, 21; see also on the treaty Berg, "The Svalbard 'Channel'", especially on the question of demilitarization, which is quite controversial in Norwegian historiography and especially in Norwegian official foreign political research. Torbjørn Pedersen adds to this disagreement that the *Russian* understanding of the demilitarization clause is based on linguistic indistinctness, as the English phrase of the demilitarization clause (Article 9) refers to prohibiting measure for 'warlike purposes', while the official French text refers to '*but de guerre*', which in the Russian translation has become '*v vojennykh tseljakh*' or *all* 'military purposes'. See Pedersen, "Security Issues", 273. Recently, Rolf Tamnes, the leading Norwegian expert on the militarization of the High North during the Cold War, delivered a new close reading of the Treaty, including the demilitarization clause, which deviates from my interpretation of it. See Tamnes, "Sikkerhetspolitiske". Morten Ruud, retired secretary general in the Ministry of Justice (the de facto polar politics department of Norway), concludes his interpretation of the demilitary clause that the treaty does not claim 'complete demilitarization' ('*fullstendig demilitarisering*'), but 'on the contrary' ('*tvert imot*') that the Treaty imposes Norway as the sovereign state to defend the sovereignty, 'if necessary even with military means'. See Ruud, "Svalbardtraktaten i norsk", 67.

15 Genesis of the Spitsbergen/Svalbard Treaty

The non-discriminatory and demilitarization provisions in the Treaty led one Norwegian diplomat, Thor von Ditten, to conclude that the Treaty placed Norway in 'vassalage' to the great powers.[4] Some Norwegian historians seem to agree. For instance, in the leading account of Norway's foreign politics during the interwar period, the historian Odd Bjørn Fure characterizes sovereignty in the Spitsbergen Treaty as restricted (*begrenset*) owing to its 'multilateral arrangement'.[5]

While the 'multilateralization' of the Treaty has been successful, since forty-four states have ratified it,[6] it was originally signed by nine states when concluded at the Paris Peace Conference, 1919–20. Britain, France, and the United States played the leading roles, and the Americans had the last word on the outcome of the Spitsbergen question at the Conference. This chapter will discuss why the Conference solved the sovereignty question of Spitsbergen in connection with a war in which Norway had not even participated, as well as why this question was raised in the first place in 1871, when Sweden aired diplomatically the idea of claiming sovereignty of the Spitsbergen islands for its union partner, Norway.

Between 1814 and 1905, Norway and Sweden were associated in a two-state union after the Danish king had renounced his Norwegian provinces.[7] The union with Sweden was established by the election of the Swedish king to the Norwegian throne. As King of Norway, he had his own government, parliament, and even armed forces, but the King of Norway and of Sweden naturally had only one foreign minister – the Swedish one – as the two union states certainly could not have different foreign policies. This reasonable coordinating arrangement has led some Norwegian historians to conclude that the foreign politics of the two states were detrimental to Norway's interests.[8] The 1871 airing of the sovereignty question of Spitsbergen demonstrates that such simplistic phrases fail to grasp that Norway had its specific foreign interests during the union period of 1814–1905, and that Norwegian interests were heard and also satisfied.[9]

The genesis of the Spitsbergen/Svalbard Treaty has both a Norwegian/Scandinavian and an international side. Both are interconnected in its naming, as the Norwegian parliament replaced Spitsbergen with 'Svalbard' in 1925 as the political name of the archipelago. Geographical names have been

---

4 Berg, *Norge på egen hånd*, 289. 5 Fure, *Mellomkrigstid 1920–1940*, 76, 109.
6 Pedersen, "Security Issues", 272.
7 Berg, *Norsk utanrikspolitikk*, 20–26; Glenthøj and Ottosen, *Experiences of War*, 208–256.
8 Kaartvedt, "1814–1905. Unionen med Sverige", 239 and passim.
9 Berg, "Norway's Foreign Politics".

political anywhere and anytime in the history of European expansionism,[10] and maps have been 'loaded with political significance'.[11] Svalbard was an old Norse name intended to be interpreted as a reminder of the Norse Norweigan sea empire including Greenland, Scotland, Iceland, and the Faroe Islands. This ancient greater Norway was reshaped, linguistically and cartographically, in 1876 as Norwegian oceanographers renamed the North Ocean as 'The Norwegian Sea'.[12] Spitsbergen/Svalbard was part of the dream of re-establishing a lost past in the atmosphere of European imperialism, and the Spitsbergen question 1871–1920 must be regarded in the light of European colonialism in the decades prior to the Great War, when oceanographers as well as polar scientists were 'harbingers of imperialism'[13] and embodiments of nationalism.[14] The history of the Spitsbergen Treaty is a good example of the political entanglements of science,[15] heroism, and economic earnings.

Its start in 1871 was a diplomatic attempt to seize Spitsbergen for Norway in order to serve both scientific and financial interests. From 1905 to 1920, American financial interest, supported by engagement in international law, was allied to Norwegian national interests in both polar expansion and the development of international law for serving small state interests. The Norwegian-American engagement in the development of international law served to camouflage nationalism both in the advancing new world power and for Norway after the dissolution of the union with Sweden in 1905. The main problem to be discussed in the chapter is thus how nationalism and internationalism amplified both small and great powers in international political competition over Arctic empire building.[16]

While the Norwegian history of the development of Norway's Spitsbergen programme is treated in many historical publications,[17] the international history of the treaty has been touched upon in few historical accounts.[18]

10 Wråkberg, "Politics of Naming".   11 Short, *Representing the Republic*, 15.
12 See Berg, "From 'Spitsbergen' to 'Svalbard'", www.tandfonline.com/eprint/bybBVu PE2zaJUyXQAHCt/full#.UrRLGPTuL7M.
13 Evans, *Pursuit of Power*, 634.   14 Frängsmyr, *Vetenskapsmannen som hjälte*, 167.
15 Frängsmyr, *Vetenskapsmannen som hjälte*; see Elisabeth Crawford's concept 'scientific nationalism', discussed more closely in Li, *Forskning og teknologi*, 37.
16 On the general connection between international law and the rise of imperialism, see Koskenniemi, *Gentle Civilizer of Nations*.
17 For example, Mathisen, *Svalbard in International Politics*; Dahl and Jensen, eds., *Svalbardtraktaten 100 år*; Skagestad, *Norsk polarpolitikk*; Berg, *Norge på egen hånd*; Berg, "From 'Spitsbergen' to 'Svalbard'"; Arlov, *Svalbards historie*; Drivenes, "Ishavsimperialisme"; Drivenes and Jølle, eds., *Into the Ice*.
18 Singh, *The Spitsbergen (Svalbard) Question*; Berg, "Norway, Spitsbergen, and America"; Rossi, *Sovereignty and Territorial Temptation*; Vylegzhanin and Kilanov, *Spitsbergen*. See further the reference list in Berg, "The Svalbard 'Channel'", 318–321 (which undoubtedly is uncomplete).

This scarcity of international research is one reason why the chapter focuses on the international frames for the Spitsbergen Treaty. More important, though, is the 'international turn' in historical research after the Cold War,[19] which has widened the traditional research focus in international political studies by elevating the interplay between great powers and minor states to the principal framework of analysis.[20] In the Spitsbergen question, this implies a closer look at the relationship between Norway and the emerging global great power, the United States, who were the leading actor behind the development of international law from the entrance of the twentieth century[21] and dominated the transformation of Spitsbergen from *terra nullius* to a land under Norwegian sovereignty. The US Secretary of State, Robert Lansing, was the architect of the Treaty and therefore the instigator of its core content: the combination of sovereignty and internationalism, or national interests as internationalism in disguise. The background was the development of international competition on natural resources, globally as well as in Spitsbergen.

Guano Bonanza with Diplomatic Entanglements

Although Spitsbergen had no Indigenous population, there is a historical continuity of European political and commercial involvement and utilization on the islands since the discovery of the Spitsbergen islands in 1596.[22] Competition and clashes of interest between European states have contributed to numerous conflicts. The shifting international legal situation of the islands even influenced the development of international law.[23] The dogmas of the legal scholars Grotius and Selden, the *mare liberum* doctrine and the *mare clausum* assertion respectively, were even forged as political tools in the whaling competition between Denmark and Britain around the archipelago.[24] The location of the islands at the entrance to northern Russia lurked in the thoughts of the great power circles from the beginning to the present.[25] During the whaling period in the seventeenth century,

---

19 Sluga, *Internationalism in the Age*, 11f.   20 Sluga and Clavin, *Internationalism*, XIII.
21 Shinohara, *US International Lawyers*, 12–36.
22 The question of the original discovery of Spitsbergen is subject to strong disagreement, especially between Norwegian and Russian archaeologists and historians. See Arlov, *Svalbards historie*, 76; Berg, *Norge på egen hånd*, 170 on Norwegian claims; Vylegzhanin and Kilanov, *Spitsbergen* on Russian claims; Ulfstein, *The Svalbard Treaty*, 34 on a British claim.
23 Rothwell, *Polar Regions*, 4–9 and passim.   24 Ulfstein, *The Svalbard Treaty*, 35.
25 See Berg, "The Svalbard 'Channel'".

hundreds of whalers and dozens of whaling stations established Spitsbergen as a 'frontier in a global struggle between governing European empires'[26] until the whale and walrus populations had been exterminated.[27] A handful of Norwegian and Russian hunters used the archipelago during the nineteenth century, working in a harsh climate with a six-month-long polar night,[28] conditions that did not prevent them being joined by guano diggers, coal diggers, and even tourists.

During the 1860s, Sweden established its position as the leading Spitsbergen power, driven by 'purely scientific motives' according to historian of science Tore Frängsmyr.[29] Sverker Sörlin concludes, in contrast, that Sweden's polar science supported political wishes that the 'Swedish North grew larger by including the Arctic'.[30] Geir Hestmark underlines that *Norwegian* polar science had 'a more political feature than almost all other research in Norway'.[31] Internationally, Beau Riffenburgh finds that polar scientific programmes were always bearers of publicly agitated nationalism.[32]

Led by the polar scientist Adolf Erik Nordenskiöld, Swedish scientific expeditions to Spitsbergen in the 1860s had motivations that were both political and economic.[33] Nordenskiöld discovered guano deposits on the islands. His financial sponsor, the prominent businessman Oscar Dickson, quickly realized the possibility of utilizing these natural resources as fertilizers for European agriculture.[34] This was the reason that Nordenskiöld applied to the king in 1871 to seize sovereignty of the islands for his Norwegian realm in order to protect this enterprise; the revenue generated from guano extraction could obviously fund further scientific expeditions.

The king acted accordingly by ordering his foreign minister to air the question diplomatically with the interested states. The Russian tsar rejected any idea of changing the international status of the islands and insisted on maintaining Spitsbergen as *terra nullius,* open to anyone and ruled by none.

Thus far, the historians are in agreement. But the consensus ignores the fact that Nordenskiöld's initiative had an international context, namely the industrial, commercial, and communications revolutions that reached

---

26 Degroot, *Frigid Golden Age,* 76.
27 Avango et al., "Between Markets and Geopolitics", 30–32.
28 See Nielsen, ed., *Russland kommer nærmere,* 90f.
29 Frängsmyr, "Swedish Polar Exploration", 178, 181.
30 Sörlin, "Rituals and Resources", 104.
31 Hestmark, "Kartleggerne", 10; Ekholt, "Glans og Hæder", 85.   32 Riffenburgh, *Myth,* 198.
33 Frängsmyr, "Swedish Polar Exploration".
34 Wråkberg, *Vetenskapens vikingatåg;* Wråkberg, "A.E. Nordenskiöld"; Arlov, "Maps and Geographical Names", 8.

the northern periphery of Europe and beyond during the middle of the nineteenth century, which explains why Spitsbergen returned to international consciousness exactly at the turn of the 1860s. It was about guano in a huge international market in the century of globalization.[35]

The nineteenth-century 'guano age'[36] had started with panic in North American agriculture. Before the breakthrough of its chemical production at the beginning of the twentieth century, the lack of organic fertilizer stimulated an intense search for guano deposits, considered as the 'enormous, untapped sources of wealth and power' in the unexplored regions of the planet, particularly in South America.[37] This led to a 'guano island mania',[38] a worldwide search for guano islands which even echoed in Norway. In 1873, Norwegian newspapers reported that several ships were on their way to Spitsbergen, Greenland, or the Varanger fjord to build a guano factory.[39]

In 1856, the United States Congress voted for the so-called Guano Act, empowering the American president to lay temporary territorial claim to uninhabited guano islands, and leading to the seizure of more than sixty minor islands and skerries.[40] Other powers followed suit in this 'scramble in the Pacific'.[41] The Franco-German war of 1870–71 sparked an international arms race that led to a further boom for the nitrate contained in guano.[42] The guano deposits in South America were gradually emptied.[43] One of the consequences was 'one of the largest armed conflicts ever fought in the Americas', the War of the Pacific (1879–84) between Chile, Bolivia, and Peru, over the control of the nitrate fields of the Atacama Desert.[44] Nordenskiöld followed such news in the modern mass media, and recognized the relationship between the international guano demand and the Spitsbergen beds when he proposed to establish a station to process Spitsbergen guano. This extractive activity could then fund a meteorological observation station, as well as scientific activities,[45] and further polar research. To Dickson, the industrialist, it was an investment that complemented his work as a philanthropist who supported Swedish polar research. The underlying idea was that Norwegian sovereignty of the islands could protect a Swedish camp for science and business activities.

35 Wenzlhuemer, *Connecting the Nineteenth Century*, 257.
36 Cushman, *Guano*, 23 and passim.   37 Cushman, *Guano*, 27.
38 Rossi, *Sovereignty and Territorial Temptation*, 157.
39 Barthelmess, *Die Deutschen Interessen*, 33, 123, note 100; *Finmarkens Amtstidende* (5 February 1873); Solhaug, *De norske fiskeriers historie*, 20.
40 Cushman, *Guano*, 82.   41 Cushman, *Guano*.   42 Cushman, *Guano*, 69.
43 Wråkberg, *Vetenskapens vikingatåg*, 290f.   44 Cushman, *Guano*, 73.
45 Mathisen, *Svalbard in International Politics*, 21f.

While the guano bonanza was the general background for Nordenskiöld's proposition in 1871 to seek Norwegian sovereignty, it also shaped the international *response* to the Swedish-Norwegian king's diplomatic airing. The Russian response to the idea of Norwegian sovereigny – blunt refusal – is traditionally referred to as 'the Russian veto' to Norwegian sovereignty of Spitsbergen.[46] It has been overlooked that Russia was not the only power that opposed the 'Swedish plan for Colonization' of 1871, as Trygve Mathisen calls the diplomatic airing to bring an end to the *terra nullius* regime on Spitsbergen and to introduce Norwegian sovereignty there.[47] The proposal was vetoed by the majority of the European great powers of the time[48] as it did not include explicit guarantees that the traditional open access to fishing and shipping in the territories in question should be continued.[49]

Norway's government also vetoed Nordenskiöld's proposals for establishing a colony on Spitsbergen, protected by Norway. In other words, Norway declined a proposal from its union partner to seek enhancement of the Norwegian realm. This seemingly paradoxical situation is not as strange as it seems. It is a consequence of the structure and history of the Swedish-Norwegian union, and given these circumstances, it was unsurprising that the Norwegian government 'showed no enthusiasm for the idea', as Mathisen notes sardonically. Norwegian acquisition of Spitsbergen would involve expenses for the Norwegian Exchequer and possibly disputes with foreign powers. Norway's interests on the islands were fully satisfied with the status of the islands as *terra nullius*, open for anybody.[50] Thus the Norwegian reaction was in accord with the Russian reply to the diplomatic note from the Swedish king, namely that the Russian government wanted Spitsbergen to be, by tacit agreement, a territory with an undecided status, open to all states *(par un accord tacite entre les Governments [...] ce group d'isles* [should in the future as hitherto be] *comme un domaine indécis, accessible à tous les Etats dont les nationaux, cherchent à en exploiter les ressources naturelles)*.[51]

In Russian historiography, it has been claimed that these diplomatic phrasings prove that the Norwegian and Russian governments entered into an

---

46 Wråkberg, *Vetenskapens vikingatåg*, 45f.; Kaartvedt, "1814–1905. Unionen med Sverige", 320f.
47 Mathisen, *Svalbard in International Politics*, 20.
48 See Berg in Bones and Jølle, eds., *Norsk polarpolitikks 1870–2020*, for details on the responses from the other powers.
49 Mathisen, *Svalbard in International Politics*, 24f.; Berg in Bones and Jølle, eds., *Norsk polarpolitikks 1870–2020*.
50 Mathisen, *Svalbard in International Politics*, 23.
51 Ulfstein, *The Svalbard Treaty*, 36f., n 53 Kaartvedt, ed., *Den politiske korrespondansen*, Vol. VI, 680.

'intergovernmental agreement' by the diplomatic note exchange in 1871, supplemented by another exchange in 1872.[52] It has been called 'a bilateral treaty between Russia and Sweden-Norway' on establishing a Russo-Norwegian *condominium* on the islands.[53] Such understandings have spread to Western historiography, as Christopher Rossi refers to the 'Agreement of 1872' that 'established a different kind of no-man's land' and 'a special kind of condominium' that closed any future discussion on Norwegian sovereignty of Spitsbergen.[54] Jørgen Holten Jørgensen, a Norwegian expert on Russian Spitsbergen politics, refers to the 'agreement between Russia and Sweden (and therefore Norway) from 1871 and 1872', in which the two states 'through an exchange of diplomatic notes' 'clarified that none of them should claim sovereignty over Spitsbergen'.[55]

The myth of the existence of a Swedish-Norwegian-Russian *agreement* on Norwegian acceptance of predominant Russian interests on Spitsbergen disregards the wordings of the diplomatic exchanges of 1871, followed up in 1872. More importantly, it ignores the fact that the Swedish initiative was discussed by the Norwegian government and promptly dismissed. Its rejection of any attempt to assert sovereignty was motivated by fear of future clashes of interests, *in casu* with the adjacent Russian great power, which dominated both the Norwegian and Swedish perceptions of threats during the nineteenth century.[56] But, first and foremost, Norway had no interest in the sovereignty of Spitsbergen to serve *Swedish* interests. The end of the diplomatic exchanges of 1871–72, as concluded by the American international lawyer James Brown Scott in 1909, was that 'the two governments agreed formally that the region should remain as it had been, no man's land (*terra nullius*)'.[57] Last but not least, the majority of the powers that were involved in the 1871 exchanges of notes agreed to continued free access to the islands and their resources for all nationalities.

There was an important addendum to the Norwegian dismissal in 1871–72. The Norwegian government added several times that 'both location and the general circumstances – *inter alia* the Norwegian fisheries – require that Spitsbergen – if any suggestions should be raised for its inclusion into the system of state sovereignty – should be placed under the sovereignty of Norway'.[58] Above all, it would challenge 'the Norwegian national feeling' if Norwegian hunters, who had been the sole harvesters of the resources of the islands 'during the latest

---

52 Vylegzhanin and Kilanov, *Spitsbergen*, 81 and passim.
53 Vylegzhanin and Kilanov, *Spitsbergen*, 10.
54 Rossi, *Sovereignty and Territorial Temptation*, 151, 158f.   55 Jørgensen, "Barentsburg", 25.
56 Berg, "Russofobiens røtter 1820–1855"; Åselius, *The 'Russian Menace'*.
57 Cited from Rossi '"A Unique International Problem"', 117. Rossi disagrees with Brown.
58 Kaartvedt, ed., *Den politiske korrespondansen*, 480.

period', should meet alien state sovereignty there. Therefore, the Norwegian government concluded its treatment of the Nordenskiöld/Dickson case that 'when the question of sovereignty of Spitsbergen occurs, it should be seen to that the sovereign state becomes Norway' due to 'the geographic position of the islands'.[59]

Failed Polar Imperialism, 1892–1914

The introduction of parliamentary representation in Norway in 1884 strengthened popular political influence, and thus nationalism. Internationally, the Berlin conference of 1884–85 led to the breakthrough of an expansionist variant of nationalism, namely the European colonialism by introducing international legal rules for the occupation by a 'civilized' power of 'uncivilized' land and people, such as the Belgian Congo. The Norwegian-Swedish union participated at the conference, supported the establishment of the Congo as a 'free state', and generally embraced European colonial expansion.[60] Thus, the Scandinavian states were active participants during the peak of what Eric Hobsbawm has named the 'Age of Empires',[61] though the minor states recognized their place in the shadow of the major powers in the 'race for resources and prestige'.[62] They shared the worldview and employed 'their own strategies of imperialism and colonialism', first and foremost the commercial part of them.[63] Although in 1892 the Norwegian government founded its potential colony, Wollert Konow, as the minister responsible for Norway's merchant foreign relations, urged the union's foreign minister to seize Spitsbergen for Norway. Konow underlined that several European powers aimed 'to enhance their possessions to distant areas', even in the Arctic. 'The ownerless situation' could not persist.[64]

Konow's claim was the start of a Norwegian polar imperialist programme that ended successfully in 1920. Owing to the conflicts that eventually led to the dissolution of the union in 1905, the foreign minister was passive, but the

59 'naar der overhovedet bliver Spørgsmaal om at henlægge Spitsbergen under nogen Stats Høihed, bør det sørges for, at dette bliver Norges, idet man derfor med Hans Excellence Udenrigsministeren maa erklære sig enig i, at dette Forhold efter Øernes geografiske Beliggenhed er det naturligste', Indredepartementet til Utriksministeren, Christiania (3 May 1891), in Riksarkivet, UD 1902 vol. 308, 7D1 Spetsbergen 1870–1906, Ifrågasatt besittningstagande av Spetsbergen 1870–92; Mathisen, *Svalbard in International Politics*, 24.
60 Makko, *European Small States*, 66f., 187–189.   61 Hobsbawm, *Age of Empire*.
62 Makko, *European Small States*, 1f.   63 Makko, *European Small States*, 1f.
64 'Da flere af Europas stater nu søge at udvide sine Besiddelser til fjerne Egne, og navnlig Fangstfelterne op imod Nordpolen synes at have faaet større Betydning for flere af Landene, er det en nærliggende Tanke, at den herreløse Tilstand, hvori Spitsbergens Øgruppe for Tiden henligger, ikke ret længe lader sig opretholde', cited from Berg, *Norge på egen hånd*, 151.

Norwegian authorities were active. Private investors, supported by government authorities, built a hotel on Spitsbergen.[65] The Norwegian Postal Service established a post office[66] which stamped 'Spidsbergen' on tourists' letters.[67] In 1897, the Norwegian delegate to the international postal congress in Washington proposed that Spitsbergen should be administratively placed under the Norwegian postal authorities. The International Postal Union in Bern placed Spitsbergen under Norwegian rule,[68] despite protests from Russian delegates, international lawyer F. F. Martens warning that any 'approval [...] of the Swedish-Norwegian right to run a postal office at Spitsbergen might most probably become the strongest justification for the right to occupy the archipelago in the future'.[69]

After newly independent Norway established its own foreign office in 1905, the government invited the interested powers to diplomatic conferences in Norway's capital Kristiania – in 1910, 1912, and 1914 – to negotiate the establishment of some kind of rule, preferably (disguised) Norwegian, over the Spitsbergen islands. This, however, did not come about, as neither Russia nor Sweden accepted any Norwegian expansionist ambitions. Swedish opposition was motivated by reasons of prestige after the humiliating Norwegian secession from the union. Russia had historical as well as strategic reasons for opposing any foreign control of the sea entrance to its north. In 1899, the Russian navy had even sent a warship to Bear Island to prevent a German occupation.[70] In response to Norway's suggestions, a Swedish-Russian alliance launched the idea of a Swedish-Norwegian-Russian condominium. Norway, the obvious junior partner in such an arrangement, disliked the idea intensely. Nothing emerged from even a great power conference in 1914.[71]

American 'Imperialism of Idealism', and Successful Norwegian Polar Imperialism

The reason that the question of sovereignty over Spitsbergen reopened in 1919 was the intrusion of the United States into European (and world) politics at the

---

65 Kolltveit, "'Deckchair Explorers'", 357; Spring, "Cruise Tourists", 41.
66 Arlov, *Svalbards historie*, 232; Nielsen, ed., *Russland kommer nærmere*, ch. 10; Berg, *Norge på egen hånd*, 152.
67 Arlov, *Svalbards historie*, 233.   68 Nielsen, ed., *Russland kommer nærmere*, 432.
69 Nielsen, ed., *Russland kommer nærmere*, 432.
70 Barthelmess, *Die Deutschen Interessen*, 432.
71 For the three conferences, see Rossi, *Sovereignty and Territorial Temptation*, 160; Singh and Saguirian, "The Svalbard Archipelago", 58–60, 64f.; Mathisen, *Svalbard in International Politics*, 75–88, 91–93.

peace conference in Paris. American engagement with Spitsbergen had begun in 1905 after the appearance of a new source of profit following the guano age: coal. John Munroe Longyear, a wealthy mining investor, stumbled across the twentieth century's new guano when visiting Spitsbergen as a tourist in 1901.[72]

Longyear embodied the entrance of upper-class Arctic tourism, which started in 1893 when the first luxury voyage departed from Lübeck to Spitsbergen with some 70 guests onboard a steamer chartered from the German East Africa Line. Some of them did – as in Africa – big game hunting as they hunted polar bears from the deck.[73]

Longyear did not hunt. He observed. In his deckchair aboard the cruise ship, *Auguste Victoria*, he noted at Bellsund that

> '[t]he rock in the glacier debris seemed [...] like gold country. There was a small vessel in the Sound and our pilot told me that the men were prospecting for coal. Spitsbergen now belongs to no country, and if coal or gold are found here some nation will hasten to colonize it.'[74]

Two years later, Longyear returned for an 'exploratory visit'. Samples, analysed back home, proved to be of first-class quality.[75] In 1906, he founded the Arctic Coal Company in Boston. During the preceding summer, he had already recruited twenty-five Norwegian workers to dig coal on Spitsbergen.[76] The year 1905 was the year of Norwegian independence. It was, thus, also the first year of the American age at Spitsbergen – with Norwegian miners, though even British, Dutch, and Russian coal companies established coal mines at Spitsbergen[77] in order to participate in this new, international mining bonanza. Most gave up after a winter or two in the harsh climate.

Nevertheless, the polar islands quickly became almost crowded, compared with previously. There were hunters and tourists, in addition to roughly 100 workers all year around.[78] 'The land is free. Anybody is free – as far as his rifle

---

72 Berg, "Norway, Spitsbergen, and America", 25f.
73 Kolltveit, "'Deckchair Explorers'", 355.   74 Reilly, *Greetings from Spitsbergen*, 135.
75 Shearer, *Olaus Jeldness*, 15. Longyear's original plan was to invest in a huge iron ore project at the Norwegian-Russian border. The Norwegian government hindered these efforts by demanding that the projected mining company should be staffed exclusively by Scandinavian-speaking workforces in the border district to great Russia. Thus, no American engineers could be recruited as work leaders. He then redirected his investment strategy to Spitsbergen with the plan of extracting coal to fuel the iron mines on the mainland; see Marquette Regional History Center, J. M. Longyear Research Library, Longyear Records, A. Spitsbergen Papers. 1. Correspondence 1913–1918, Jeldness, Contract 9 January 1903; Dole, *America in Spitsbergen*, 196f.; Berg, "Norway, Spitsbergen, and America", 28.
76 Hartnell, "Arctic Network Builder", 66.
77 Nielsen, ed., *Russland kommer nærmere*, 443f.   78 Berg, *Norge på egen hand*, 153.

reaches', the newspaper *Finmarken* noted.[79] Certainly, therefore, conflicts followed between hunting tourists and professional Norwegian hunters, and between tough Norwegian miners and rough American foremen.

The main problem for the Americans was the recurrent strikes due to the brutal treatment of their miners. Therefore, Longyear mobilized his political contacts, and they acted. In 1910 the United States Senate voted for an amendment to the Guano Law of 1856 to annex the American mining sites at Spitsbergen. The House of Representatives vetoed the amendment as it clashed with the Monroe doctrine, according to which American foreign policy was limited to the western hemisphere.[80] Instead, during the time of President Taft (1909–13), famous as the instigator of 'Dollar Diplomacy',[81] the State Department hired the outstanding international lawyer Robert Lansing to draw up a cheap and simple ruling regime at Spitsbergen.[82] In 1915 Lansing advanced to the post of Secretary of State. In this capacity, he was given a free hand to solve the 'unique international problem' of Spitsbergen, as he would call it in an article in the *American Journal of International Law* in 1917. Three years later, the Spitsbergen Treaty was the result.[83]

The Treaty was drawn up on the basis of Lansing's 1917 article and his original idea, presented in a State Department memo in 1911, of 'distinguishing political sovereignty [...] from territorial sovereignty', which was to solve the need for rule and continue the *terra nullius* principle of free access to extract resources from the islands. Thus, 'the exclusive exercise of sovereignty' should be introduced 'without regard to the place of such exercise'.[84] By this kind of modification of the Westphalian principle of 'one rule for one state', the need for political and social order could be accommodated without damaging the economic freedom for investors – regardless of nationalities – to harvest profits from the islands.[85] The consequence was the prevention of high taxation, the securing of profits, and the preclusion of production disturbances from striking workers, or any temptation from the ruling state to introduce vacations, working time regulations, or the like. The sovereign

---

79 ACC, file "Arctic Coal Company", in Norwegian Polar Institute, notebook: "A/S Bergen-Spidsbergen"; *Finmarken* (26 September 1903).
80 Berg, *Norge på egen hånd*, 167f.; Singh, *The Spitsbergen (Svalbard) Question*, 36–80; see also Rossi, 'A Unique International Problem', 122–128, for a far more elaborate discussion than here.
81 Veeser, *World Safe for Capitalism*; Rosenberg, *Financial Missionaries*.
82 Berg, "Norway, Spitsbergen, and America", 30f.
83 Lansing, "A Unique International Problem".
84 Rossi, *Sovereignty and Territorial Temptation*, 155.
85 Berg, "Norway, Spitsbergen, and America", 31.

state would, on the other hand, be obliged to force any strikers back to the mines and generally to secure law and order.

In 1920, the principle of 'cleaved sovereignty',[86] or even 'shared sovereignty',[87] was fully developed in the Spitsbergen Treaty. The political sovereignty of Norway was combined with continued access to the resources for citizens of any state that signed the Treaty, as had existed during the *terra nullius* status of the islands before 1920.

But why was Norway selected to undertake the ruler's job?

American interests for future international politics were summed up in President Wilson's fourteen points from 1918, of which the most important was 'the establishment of an equality of trade conditions among all the nations'.[88] At Spitsbergen, the American mines were sold to Norwegian investors in 1916, financed by shares in the new Norwegian mining company that succeeded the American mines.[89] Thereby Longyear became the largest stockholder of the new Norwegian coal company.[90] Consequently, American financial rule on Spitsbergen continued independently from the new Norwegian ownership. This basic precondition for the Treaty of 1920 has been ignored in previous research, though it is self-evidently of great importance to explain why Longyear and his associates – even Lansing (known for serving 'financial and industrial interests')[91] – were inclined to support Norwegian sovereignty. The fact that the American mining business at Spitsbergen never became an economic success is a completely different story.

In September 1918, Lansing proposed to the President that one of the minor goals for the peace conference should be: 'The sovereignty of ... Spitzbergen to be granted to Norway'.[92] In February 1919, he informed the Norwegian envoy in Paris of this, but added that Norwegian sovereignty must be combined with continued access to the resources at Spitsbergen for international investors.[93] The Norwegian workforce should be ruled by the Norwegian state as long as the Americans ruled the profits by the help of the creative development of international law. Lansing's habitus as a strong

---

86 Rossi, *Sovereignty and Territorial Temptation*, 155; Rossi even discusses its relationship to the classical principle of the Westphalian sovereignty concept and to Grotius's defence for *mare liberum*.
87 Byers, *International Law*, 22.
88 https://avalon.law.yale.edu/20th_century/wilson14.asp (11 August 1920); Link, *Woodrow Wilson*, 83.
89 Berg, *Norge på egen hånd*, 174f.   90 Arlov, *Svalbards historie*, 262.
91 Smith, *Lansing and American Neutrality*, III.   92 Lansing, *The Peace Conference*, 190f.
93 Berg, "Norway, Spitsbergen, and America", 32.

adherent to international law combined with his call for serving his country's economic interests. As with his predecessor as Secretary of State, the peace preacher William Jennings Bryan, he believed international law to be a variant of 'the imperialism of idealism'.[94]

The United States fostered a large number of leading international jurists from the 1890s up to World War I, parallel to the first waves of American foreign expansionism in South America and the Philippines, and thus the dawn of the century of worldwide American dominance. The legal profession was a leading 'ideological actor' during the steps towards world leadership,[95] as the development of international law promoted American interests.[96] Internationalism was a disguise for national interests, whether it dealt with intervention into Panama, the Philippines, or Spitsbergen.

Internationalism was also the foundation for foreign political reasoning in Norway.[97] Consequently, Norway was a net deliverer of competent personnel for staffing the international organizations that rapidly grew during the globalizing nineteenth century. The young Norwegian lawyer, Gregers Gram, is a typical example. In 1875 he was recruited as a judge at the international court of justice in Egypt, a court that protected colonial interests.[98] From 1899 until his death in 1929 he served as a member of the permanent arbitration court of international law in The Hague. In 1893 he joined an arbitration court for a seal-hunting dispute in the Bering Sea between Great Britain and the United States. Here, he cooperated closely with Lansing, at the time a young international lawyer assisting the American envoy to the court.[99] The case had particular interest for Norway, as it dealt with marine harvesting areas under disputed sovereignty. The United States acted as defender of responsible nature management, while the British government insisted on free hunting. (Britain won the case in principle, but the American interests were the long-term victors.)[100]

The Bering Sea conflict concerned questions of common use of vast resources in an isolated area far away from any sovereign state, visited by

---

94 Kazin, *A Godly Hero*, 229.   95 Coates, *Legalist Empire*, 49–58.
96 Coates, *Legalist Empire*, 177–183.
97 Berg, *Norsk utanrikspolitikk*, passim; Berg, *Norge på egen hånd*, 91–97; Leira, *Utenrikspolitikkens opprinnelse*, 171.
98 On the court of Egypt, see Makko, *European Small States*, 60–62; Cannon, "Reassessment of Judicial Reform". On Gregers Gram's international carrier, see Bull, "Gram, Gregers", in *Norsk Biografisk Leksikon*, Vol. IV, 529–536.
99 Riksarkivet, PA 596 Gram, "De næste to aar. Beringshav-tvisten, oplevelser i Paris 1893", typewritten manuscript by Gram; Gay, *American Fur Seal Diplomacy*, 91, n 13 (on Lansing).
100 Gay, *American Fur Seal Diplomacy*, 73–94; Sellheim, *The Seal Hunt*, 119–124; Berg, "Norway, Spitsbergen, and America", 30; Bull, "Gram, Gregers", 531f.

competing hunters from states whose only common interest was to hunt down the mammals. No state authority was responsible for sustainable use. The same situation characterized the fishing situation in the ocean between the Norwegian and the British territorial borders, in the Barents Sea, in the Arctic Ocean, and in the *terra nullius* of Spitsbergen.

Lansing was therefore familiar with questions of sovereignty in territories, on land as well as offshore, and with natural resources such as fish or coal. As a member of the Norwegian government in the 1890s, Gram was well-informed about the Nordenskiöld–Dickson episode in the 1870s and on the Norwegian governmental suggestion in 1892 to seize sovereignty of Spitsbergen.

When Lansing advanced to Secretary of State and proposed to eradicate the lawless *terra nullius* situation on Spitsbergen, in Gram he had a key ally in Norway, who in all probability had been his discussion partner on the solution of the 'unique international problem' in the European Arctic. The solution was that the Spitsbergen islands, like some Bering Strait islands many years before, would be regulated by international law and order without preventing international harvesting of the resources or potential over-exploitation.

Between Nationalism and Internationalism

As Joachim Weber has observed, Norwegian 'arcticness' has become a dominant feature in the self-image of Norwegians.[101] Historically, this idealization of the wintry[102] has been some kind of Norwegian exceptionalism as, according to the Norwegian historian Åsa Elstad, 'neither the Americans, the English, the Swedes or the Danes emphasize polar connections as part of their national identity the way Norwegians do'.[103] American polar heroes, such as Peary, are remembered by polar enthusiasts with some doubts over their credibility. The British commemorate Scott and Shackleton as tragic heroes. Even Sweden has a tragic hero, the balloonist Salomon Andrée. The Norwegian hero Amundsen's triumph of seizing the South Pole in 1911 is nationally celebrated to the extent that the Prime Minister was flown in by aircraft to the South Pole during the centenary in 2011 of the victory over Scott.

The official 'arcticness' of Norway originated from the Swedish initiative in 1871 to claim Spitsbergen for Norway. While the Norwegian government

---

101 Weber, "Preface", in Weber, ed., *Handbook on Geopolitics*, vii; see also Hønneland, "Norway's High Arctic Policy", 249.
102 Ekholt, *Glans og Hæder*, 11. 103 Elstad, *Polar Norway*, 51; Ekholt, *Glans og Hæder*, 11.

15 Genesis of the Spitsbergen/Svalbard Treaty

turned down any suggestions of political expansionism that could lead to clashes with competing powers, it concluded that if anybody should take on the burden of ruling the islands in the future, it should be Norway. Up to 1920 this was solely a dream, as no other power could accept the risk that Norway, as the ruler of Spitsbergen, should be authorized to limit the principle of free international access to utilize the resources in Spitsbergen.[104]

The entrance of Longyear into Spitsbergen in 1905, and the engagement of the United States at the Paris Peace Conference of 1919–20, changed both the geopolitical and the financial preconditions for altering the international status of Spitsbergen from *terra nullius* to Norwegian sovereignty. Norway achieved sovereignty on Spitsbergen on the condition that it respected certain restrictions 'as the *quid pro quo* for international recognition of it[s] rule', summed up in the two concepts 'non-discrimination' and 'equal enjoyment'. Citizens and companies from all treaty nations should enjoy the same right of access to the islands and its territorial waters. Taxes should never be collected beyond the amounts required to administer the islands. Last but not least, in order to remove a potential source of future clashes of interest, the archipelago was to be demilitarized.[105] In short, Norway was the steward of the common interest, although Lansing, who designed the Treaty, first and foremost had American interests in mind.

Dag Avango has demonstrated that natural resource exploitation has been the dominant driving force behind international interests in Spitsbergen from 1600 to the present.[106] For most of this period, the states agreed tacitly to keep it as a *terra nullius*. Lansing developed this arrangement by changing the international status to Norwegian sovereignty while keeping international access to its resources through splitting the concept of sovereignty from the frames for resource extraction, disguised behind the principle of common use, and by forcing this new state sovereignty concept through at the peace conference in Paris. Thus, the international community of industrial investors could continue the commercial development of Spitsbergen, shielded from onerous state taxation or discrimination in favour of the citizens of the sovereign state. What happened in Paris in 1920 was the introduction of a form of quasi- or

---

104 In fact, the Norwegians had a well-founded reputation for 'national protectionism' against foreigners who were unable to speak Norwegian, personally experienced by Longyear, as he was denied access to investing in Norwegian mines in 1903 owing to the linguistic defence against foreign investors: Berg, *Norsk utanrikspolitikk*, 41 (Eva Jakobsson's expression).
105 Rossi, *Sovereignty and Territorial Temptation*, 144; Berg, "The Svalbard 'Channel'", 307f.
106 Avango et al., "Between Markets and Geopolitics".

proto-condominium, as Rossi has observed,[107] not a kind of incomplete state sovereignty. The foundation for this new alliance between what became the ruler of the world and little Norway was that both the great state and its small partner shared the fundamental interest of liberal internationalism, combined with a strong belief in national expansionism and a self-image as good governors of the world, or at least of Spitsbergen.

There was also a pecuniary explanation for the new bond between Norway and the United States. The Norwegian chief negotiator in Paris argued that Norway must have Spitsbergen 'as payment' for its services to the Allies.[108] Covered by the official neutrality policy, the Norwegian merchant shipping fleet, one of the largest fleets in the world, had served as the carrier fleet between the Allies. Therefore, it had been hunted by German submarines. Two thousand Norwegian seamen had perished in service of the Entente during Norway's 'neutral alliance'.[109] Thus, from the Norwegian point of view, the fulfilment of the polar imperialist programme from 1892 was achieved at the cost of the torpedoed seamen in service for the belligerent Western powers during the war.[110] Furthermore, the 1920 Treaty served American economic interests, although they were administered by Norwegian owners.

Concluding Comments and Perspectives

The Spitsbergen Treaty, as formulated eloquently by the Norwegian international lawyer Geir Ulfstein, became a 'package deal': 'Norway got the sovereignty, but had to accept equal treatment by other states'.[111] Thus, the Spitsbergen question was in harmony with a long and durable line in Norway's foreign politics after the dissolution of the union, labelled 'national internationalism' by political scientist Tore Nyhamar, to grasp the close relationship between real-political state interest and dependency on the great powers, and on international law.[112]

As Glenda Sluga has emphasized, national and international communities are closely entwined.[113] Such is the case in the European international rivers, flowing through sovereign states, regulated in international agreements that were negotiated between traditionally hostile states, such as France,

107 Rossi, *Sovereignty and Territorial Temptation*, 133, 163.
108 Berg, *Norge på egen hånd*, 256.   109 Riste, *The Neutral Ally*, 226.
110 Rossi, 'A Unique International Problem', 93–136, 129–131.
111 Ulfstein, "Svalbardtraktaten – fortid og framtid", 6.
112 Nyhamar, "Norsk utenrikspolitikk", 149–153.
113 Sluga, *Internationalism in the Age*, 156, n 18.

15 Genesis of the Spitsbergen/Svalbard Treaty

Germany, and the Habsburg Empire, or between the allegedly peace-loving Scandinavians. In 1905, during the fierce crisis that ended with the dissolution of the union, the secession states negotiated a reciprocal guarantee of the continued free flow of the border rivers between them.[114] Thus, the Norwegian separatists accepted that their new-found sovereignty was combined with liabilities that established servitudes upon Norwegian territory in the same manner as the Spitsbergen Treaty established Norwegian sovereignty with servitudes.[115] The Spitsbergen Treaty, thereby, became a 'vassalage treaty'; and the same was said about the river agreement in 1905.

The system of international states, however, is full of equivalent treaties that guarantee common use of resources.[116] Oran Young regards the Spitsbergen Treaty as a distinguished expression of an international 'regime' that has contributed to prevent 'use of the archipelago for warlike purposes'.[117] On the Spitsbergen Treaty, he adds that

> '[i]ts success stands as a monument to the propositions that state sovereignty need not constitute a barrier to effective international cooperation when individual states ... are willing to accept explicit restrictions on the exercise of their sovereign authority'.[118]

In the end, internationalism rather than nationalism decided the Spitsbergen question and even the durability of the Spitsbergen Treaty. However, its roots must be traced back to the American self-interest that overlapped with the Norwegian geopolitical and even military interests at the entrance of the belligerent twentieth century, rooted in networks of international lawyers during the 1890s. The Spitsbergen Treaty was a fortification of international law as well as of the close cultural and economic bonds that established a Norwegian-American '*communis*' at Spitsbergen in which Norway was the ruler and the Americans harvested the profits.

The *communis*, however, was short-lived. In the 1930s, it was replaced by peaceful coexistence between the Norwegian mining towns and a few Russian mining settlements. Though the peace continued, there were countless minor and several grave political crises between the sovereign Norway and the self-confident Soviet settlements during the Cold War. The Norwegians distrusted their neighbours at the archipelago, and they still do, while the Russians

---

114 Berg and Jakobsson, "Nature and Diplomacy".   115 Berg, *Norge på egen hånd*, 40.
116 Berg and Jakobsson, "Nature and Diplomacy", for some examples.
117 Young, in Young and Osherenko, eds., *Polar Politics*, 5f.; see also Rothwell, *Polar Regions*, for a comparison.
118 Young, in Young and Osherenko, eds., *Polar Politics*, 6.

sometimes act as if they hardly respect Norwegian sovereignty. However, the Spitsbergen Treaty, and thus Norwegian sovereignty, was only once openly and formally challenged, when in 1944 Stalin's foreign minister demanded a Norwegian-Russian condominium over the Spitsbergen islands and the cession of Bear Island from his Norwegian colleague. After some nervous hesitation, the claims were dismissed three years later and have not been repeated since.[119]

The Spitsbergen Treaty has proven to be as strong as the European river agreements; multilateral treaties are hard to reinvent without force or endless negotiations,[120] though there have been occasional predictions of its demise. China has recently made moves that incite political alarmism. Towards the end of 2020, the leading North Norwegian newspaper carried news that China was interested in buying a huge private coalfield (134,293 hectares) close to Longyearbyen and would thereby become 'a great power in the Arctic' that threatened Norway's sovereignty.[121] From the other side of the globe, the Trump administration in Washington in 2019 offered to buy Greenland from Denmark, an offer that created considerable distress in a leading Norwegian newspaper that '[n]ext time it might be Norway that is challenged by Trump'. The paper certainly had the Spitsbergen Treaty in mind.[122]

Thus far, there have hardly been any indications that either the West or the East have other aims than to secure the same fundamental values steering the American Spitsbergen politics that concluded with the 1920 Treaty, namely internationalism (free trade, free access, and free business opportunities) under Norwegian stewardship. Internationalism was and still seems to be the most appropriate guide to take care of national interests on Spitsbergen.

Bibliography

Archives

Marquette Regional History Center, J. M. Longyear Research Library, Longyear Records, A. Spitzbergen Papers.
Norwegian Polar Institute, ACC, file "Arctic Coal Company".
Riksarkivet (National Archives of Norway), UD 1902, Vol. 308, 7D1.
Riksarkivet, UD 1906, P-13-O.
Riksarkivet, PA 596 Gram.

---

119 Berg, "The Svalbard 'Channel'", 310–312; Tamnes, "Sikkerhetspolitiske", passim.
120 Bailes, "Spitsbergen", 36.
121 *Nordlys* (29 December 2020), www.nordnorskdebatt.no/kina-i-arktis-en-elefant-pa-vei-inn-i-porselensbutikken/o/5-124-97385.
122 *Dagbladet* (23 August 2019); Berg, "The Svalbard 'Channel'", 316.

15 Genesis of the Spitsbergen/Svalbard Treaty

Published Sources

Arlov, Tor Bjørn, "Maps and Geographical Names as Tokens of National Interests: The Spitsbergen vs. Svalbard Case", *Nordlit* 45 (2020): 4–17.

Arlov, Tor Bjørn, *Svalbards historie 1596–1996* (Oslo: Aschehoug & Co., 1996).

Åselius, Gunnar, *The 'Russian Menace' to Sweden: The Belief System of a Small Power Security Elite in the Age of Imperialism* (Stockholm: Almqvist & Wiksell International, 1994).

Avango, Dag, Louwrens Hacquebord, Ypie Aalders, et al., "Between Markets and Geopolitics: Nature Resource Exploitation on Spitsbergen from 1600 to the Present Day", *Polar Record* 47 (2011): 29–39.

Bailes, Alyson, "Spitsbergen in a Sea of Change", in D. Wallis and S. Arnold, eds., *The Spitsbergen Treaty: Multinational Governance in the Arctic* (Helsinki: Conexio Public Relations, 2011), pp. 34–37.

Barthelmess, Klaus, *Die Deutschen Interessen am moderne Walfang vor 1914* (Cologne: Universität Köln, Historisches Seminar, 1989).

Berg, Roald, *Norge på egen hånd 1905–1920. Norsk utenrikspolitikks historie*, Vol. 2 (Oslo: Universitetsforlaget, 1995).

Berg, Roald, *Norsk utanrikspolitikk etter 1814* (Oslo: Samlaget, 2016).

Berg, Roald, "Norway, Spitsbergen, and America, 1905–1920", *Diplomacy & Statecraft* 28 (2017): 20–38.

Berg, Roald, "Norway's Foreign Politics during the Union with Sweden, 1814–1905: A Reconsideration", *Diplomacy & Statecraft*, 31 (2020): 1–21.

Berg, Roald, "Russofobiens røtter 1820–1855", in Fredrik Fagertun et al., eds., *Det farefulle nord. Trusler og trusseloppfatninger knyttet til Nord-Norge gjennom tusen år* (Tromsø: Universitetet i Tromsø 2001), pp. 53–66.

Berg, Roald, "From 'Spitsbergen' to 'Svalbard': Norwegianization in Norway and in the 'Norwegian Sea'. 1820–1925", *Acta Borealia* 30 (2013): 154–173.

Berg, Roald, "The Svalbard 'Channel', 1920–2020: A Geopolitical Sketch", in Joachim Weber, ed., *Handbook on Geopolitics and Security in the Arctic: The High North Between Cooperation and Confrontation* (Kiel: Springer Nature, 2020), pp. 303–321.

Berg, Roald and Eva Jakobsson, "Nature and Diplomacy: The Struggle over the Scandinavian Border Rivers in 1905", *Scandinavian Journal of History* (2006): 270–289.

Bones, Stian, and Harald Dag Jølle, eds., *Norsk polarpolitikk 1870–2020* (Oslo: Universitetsforlaget, 2023).

Bull, Jens, "Gram, Gregers", in *Norsk Biografisk Leksikon*, Vol. IV (Oslo: Aschehoug, 1929).

Byers, Michael, *International Law and the Arctic* (Cambridge: Cambridge University Press, 2013).

Cannon, Byron D., "A Reassessment of Judicial Reform in Egypt, 1876–1891", *International Journal of African Historical Studies* 5 (1972): 51–74.

Coates, Allen, *Legalist Empire: International Law and American Foreign Relations in the Early Twentieth Century* (Oxford: Oxford University Press, 1916).

Cushman, Gregory T., *Guano and the Opening of the Pacific World: A Global Ecological History* (Cambridge: Cambridge University Press, 2013).

Dagbladet (23 August 2019), www.dagbladet.no/kultur/a-le-avtrump-er-lettsindig-han-matas-pa-alvor/71515978.

Dahl, Irene, and Øystein Jensen, eds., *Svalbardtraktaten 100 år. Et jubileumsskrift* (Bergen: Fagbokforlaget, 2020).

Degroot, Dagomar, *The Frigid Golden Age: Climate Change, the Little Ice Age, and the Dutch Republic, 1560–1720* (Cambridge: Cambridge University Press, 2018).

Dole, Nathan Haskell, *America in Spitsbergen: The Romance of an Arctic Coal Mine*, Vol. 1, (Boston: Marshall Jones Co., 1922).

Drivenes, Einar Arne, "Ishavsimperialisme", in Einar Arne Drivenes and Harald Dag Jølle, eds., *Norsk polarhistorie*, Vol. 2: *Vitenskapene* (Oslo: Gyldendal, 2004).

Drivenes, Einar Arne, and Harald Dag Jølle, eds., *Into the Ice: The History of Norway and the Polar Regions* (Oslo: Gyldendal, 2006).

Ekholt, Thea Kristine, Glans og Hæder over sit Land. Nasjonsbygging i norsk pressedekning av Roald Amundsens Gjøa-ekspedisjon (1903–1906), MA thesis (Oslo: Universitetet i Oslo, 2020).

Elstad, Åsa, *Polar Norway: The White Adventure* (Tromsø: Statsarkivet, 2005).

Evans, Richard J., *The Pursuit of Power: Europe 1815–1914* (London: Allen Lane, 2016).

Finmarken (26 September 1903).

Finmarkens Amtstidende (5 February 1873).

Frängsmyr, Tore, "Swedish Polar Exploration", in Tore Frängsmyr, ed., *Science in Sweden: The Royal Swedish Academy of Science 1739–1989* (Canton, MA: Science History Publications, 1989), pp. 177–198.

Frängsmyr, Tore, *Vetenskapsmannen som hjälte* (Stockholm: Norstedt, 1984).

Fure, Odd Bjørn, *Mellomkrigstid 1920–1940, Norsk utenrikspolitikks historie*, Vol. 3 (Oslo: Universitetsforlaget, 1996).

Gay, James Thomas, *American Fur Seal Diplomacy: The Alaskan Fur Seal Controversy* (New York, Bern, Frankfurt am Main, Paris: Peter Land, 1987).

Glenthøj, Rasmus, and Morten Nordhagen Ottosen, *Experiences of War and Nationality in Denmark and Norway, 1807–1815* (Basington: Palgrave Macmillan, 2014).

Hartnell, Cameron C., "Arctic Network Builder: The Arctic Coal Company's Operations on Spitsbergen and Its Relationship with the Environment", PhD diss. (Houghton: Michigan Technological University, 2009).

Hestmark, Geir, "Kartleggerne", in Einar Arne Drivenes and Harald Dag Jølle, eds., *Vitenskapene. Norsk polarhistorie*, Vol. 2 (Oslo: Gyldendal, 2004), pp. 9–102.

Hobsbawm, Eric, *The Age of Empire, 1875–1914* (London: Weidenfeld and Nicolson, 1987).

Hønneland, Geir, "Norway's High Arctic Policy", in Robert W. Murray and Anita Dey Nuttall, eds., *International Relations and the Arctic* (Amherst, NY: Cambria Press, 2014), pp. 235–261.

Jørgensen, Jørgen Holten, "Barentsburg: Et lite stykke Russland i møte med norsk forvaltning", in Irene Dahl and Øystein Jensen, eds., *Svalbardtraktaten 100 år. Et jubileumsskrift* (Bergen: Fagbokforlaget, 2020), pp. 81–108.

Jørgensen, Jørgen Holten, *Russisk svalbardpolitikk. Svalbard sett fra den andre siden* (Bergen: Fagbokforlaget, 2010).

Kaartvedt, Alf, "1814–1905. Unionen med Sverige", in Narve Bjørgo, Øystein Rian, and Alf Kaartvedt, eds., *Selvstendighet og union. Norsk utenrikspolitikks historie*, Vol. 1 (Oslo: Universitetsforlaget, 1995).

Kaartvedt, Alf, ed., *Den politiske korrespondansen mellom Frederik Stang og Georg Sibbern 1862–1971*, Vol. VI (Oslo: Riksarkivet, 1990).

Kazin, Michael, *A Godly Hero: The Life of William Jennings Bryan* (New York: Anchor, 2007).

Kolltveit, Bård, "'Deckchair Explorers': The Origin and Development of Organised Tourist Voyages to Northern and Southern Polar Regions", *International Journal of Maritime History* 18 (2006): 351–369.

Koskenniemi, Martti, *The Gentle Civilizer of Nations: The Rise and Fall of International Law 1870–1960* (Cambridge: Cambridge University Press, 2001).

Lansing, Robert, *The Peace Conference: A Personal Narrative* (New York: Houghton Mifflin, 1921).

Lansing, Robert, "A Unique International Problem", *American Journal of International Law* 11 (1917): 763–771.

Leira, Halvard, *Utenrikspolitikkens opprinnelse. Norge og verden* (Oslo: Universitetsforlaget, 2020).

Li, Tore, *Forskning og teknologi for fedrelandet. Nasjonal prestisje som drivkraft for myndighetenes engasjement i forskning og utvikling* (Oslo: Kolon, 1919).

Link, Arthur S., *Woodrow Wilson: Revolution, War, and Peace* (Arlington Heights, IL: Davidson, 1979).

Makko, Aryo, *European Small States and the Role of Consuls in the Age of Empire* (Leiden, Boston: Brill, 2020).

Mathisen, Trygve, *Svalbard in International Politics 1871–1925: The Solution of a Unique International Problem* (Oslo: Brøggers Bogtrykkeris, 1954).

Nielsen, Jens Petter, ed., *Russland kommer nærmere. Norge og Russland 1814–1917* (Oslo: Pax, 2014).

Nordlys (29 December 2020).

Nyhamar, Tore, "Norsk utenrikspolitikk: Nasjonal internasjonalisme?", in Jon Hovi and Raino Malnes, eds., *Anarki, makt og normer. Innføring i internasjonal politikk* (Oslo: Abstrakt, 2007), pp. 144–165.

Pedersen, Torbjørn, "Security Issues in the Svalbard Area", in Gunhild Hoogensen Gjørv et al., eds., *Routledge Handbook of Arctic Security* (London, New York: Routledge, 2020), pp. 270–294.

Reilly, John T., *Greetings from Spitsbergen: Tourists at the Eternal Ice 1827–1914* (Trondheim: Tapir Academic, 2009).

Riffenburgh, Beau, *The Myth of the Explorer: The Press, Sensationalism, and Geographical Discovery* (London: Belhave, 1994).

Riste, Olav, *The Neutral Ally: Norway's Relations with Belligerent Powers in the First World War* (Oslo: Universitetsforlaget, 1965).

Rosenberg, Emily S., *Financial Missionaries to the World: The Politics and Culture of Dollar Diplomacy, 1900–1930* (Cambridge, MA: Harvard University Press, 2003).

Rossi, Christopher R., *Sovereignty and Territorial Temptation: The Grotian Tendency* (Cambridge: Cambridge University Press, 2018 [first published 2017]).

Rossi, Christopher R., "'A Unique International Problem': The Svalbard Treaty, Equal Enjoyment, and Terra Nullius: Lessons of Territorial Temptation from History", *Washington Global Studies Law Review* 15 (2016): 93–136.

Rothwell, Donald L., *Polar Regions and the Development of International Law* (Cambridge: Cambridge University Press, 1996).

Ruud, Morten, "Svalbardtraktaten i norsk og internasjonal Svalbardpolitikk", in Hallvard Tjelmeland and Ketil Zachariassen, eds., *Inn i riket. Svalbard, Nord-Norge og Norge* (Tromsø: Institutt for historie, Universitetet i Tromsø, 2003), pp. 59–68.

Sellheim, Nikolas, *The Seal Hunt: Cultures, Economics and Legal Regimes* (Leiden, Boston: Brill Nijhoff, 2018).
Shearer, Ronald A., *Olaus Jeldness* (Vancouver, BC: Shearer, 2013), https://static1.squarespace.com/static/5b11caa631d4df0138d9dfdb/t/5b731e024fa51ab1083d584b/1534271136970/Olaus+Jeldness+Version+6+-+Ronald+A.+Shearer.pdf.
Shinohara, Hatsue, *US International Lawyers in the Interwar Years* (Cambridge: Cambridge University Press, 2012).
Short, J. R., *Representing the Republic: Mapping the United States 1600–1900* (London: Reaktion, 2001).
Singh, Elen C., *The Spitsbergen (Svalbard) Question: United States Foreign Policy, 1907–1935* (Oslo: Universitetsforlaget 1980).
Singh, Elen, and Artemy A. Saguirian, "The Svalbard Archipelago: The Role of Surrogate Negotiators", in Oran R. Young and Gail Osherenko, eds., *Polar Politics: Creating International Environmental Regimes* (Ithaca, NY, London: Cornell University Press, 1993), pp. 56–95.
Skagestad, Odd Gunnar, *Norsk polarpolitikk. Hovedtrekk og utviklingslinjer 1905–74* (Oslo: Dreyers, 1975).
Sluga, Glenda, *Internationalism in the Age of Nationalism* (Philadelphia: University of Pennsylvania Press, 2013).
Sluga, Glenda, and Patricia Clavin, eds., *Internationalism: A Twentieth-Century History* (Cambridge: Cambridge University Press, 2017).
Smith, Daniel M., *Robert Lansing and American Neutrality, 1914–1917* (Berkeley, Los Angeles, CA: University of California Press, 1958).
Solhaug, Trygve, *De norske fiskeriers historie 1815–1880* (Oslo: Universitetsforlaget, 1976).
Sörlin, Sverker, "Rituals and Resources of Natural History: The North and the Arctic in Swedish Scientific Nationalism", in Michael Bravo and Sverker Sörlin, eds., *Narrating the Arctic: A Cultural History of Nordic Scientific Practices* (Canton, MA: Science History Publications, 2002), pp. 73–124.
Spring, Ulrike, "Cruise Tourists in Spitsbergen around 1900: Between Observation and Transformation", *Nordlit* 45 (2020): 39–55.
Tamnes, Rolf, "Sikkerhetspolitiske utfordringer og militær virksomhet", in Irene Dahl and Øystein Jensen, eds., *Svalbardtraktaten 100 år. Et jubileumsskrift* (Bergen: Fagbokforlaget, 2020), pp. 135–184.
Ulfstein, Geir, *The Svalbard Treaty: From Terra Nullius to Norwegian Sovereignty* (Oslo, Copenhagen, Stockholm, Boston: Scandinavian University Press, 1995).
Ulfstein, Geir, "Svalbardtraktaten – fortid og framtid", *Ottar* 2 (2020): 6–10.
Veeser, Cyrus, *A World Safe for Capitalism: Dollar Diplomacy and America's Rise to Global Power* (New York: Columbia University Press, 2002).
Vylegzhanin, Alexandr N., and Vjaceslav K. Kilanov, *Spitsbergen: Legal Regimes of Adjacent Marine Areas* (Utrecht: Eleven International, 2007).
Weber, Joachim, "Preface", in Joachim Weber, ed., *Handbook on Geopolitics and Security in The Arctic: The High North Between Cooperation and Confrontation* (Kiel: Springer Nature, 2020), pp. v–xi.
Wenzlhuemer, Roland, *Connecting the Nineteenth Century World: The Telegraph and the Globalization* (Cambridge: Cambridge University Press, 2012).

15 Genesis of the Spitsbergen/Svalbard Treaty

Wråkberg, Urban, "A. E. Nordenskiöld in Swedish Memory: The Origin and Uses of Arctic Heroism", *Acta Borealia* 36 (2019): 66–182.

Wråkberg, Urban, "The Politics of Naming: Contested Observations and the Shaping of Geographical Knowledge", in Michael Bravo and Sverker Sörlin, eds., *Narrating the Arctic: A Cultural History of Nordic Scientific Practices* (Canton, MA: Science History Publications, 2002), pp. 155–198.

Wråkberg, Urban, *Vetenskapens vikingatåg. Perspektiv på svensk polarforskning 1860–1930* (Stockholm: Kungl. Vetenskapsakademien, 1999).

Young, Oran R., and Gail Osherenko, eds., *Polar Politics: Creating International Environmental Regimes* (Ithaca, NY, London: Cornell University Press, 1993).

16

Industrial Whaling in the Arctic and Antarctic

BJØRN L. BASBERG AND LOUWRENS HACQUEBORD

Introduction

Compared with many other regions of the world, the polar regions have not been areas with much industry. The few exceptions, both north and south, have mostly been associated with resource exploitation: fur-hunting, sealing, whaling, mining – and also tourism. Therefore, in economic-geographical publications, the polar regions have usually been described as Resource Frontier Regions.[1] Considering both the Arctic and the Antarctic, whaling stands out in terms of the very long time period in which it has continuously been undertaken – and in terms of its scale.

In the polar regions, the whaling industry always took place in or close to open waters or as far into the ice as navigation permitted. So it seldom took place in the very High Arctic, or along the inner shores of the Antarctic coast. Some of the whaling grounds were within what is normally defined as the polar regions: in the north, whalers from the early seventeenth century exploited the Arctic Sea – the coastal waters of Spitsbergen, Greenland, Baffin Island, and later the sea north of the Bering Strait. In the south, they later exploited the sea around the South Shetland Islands, the Ross Sea, and the sea along the ice all around the Antarctic continent. However, whaling also took place in seas *surrounding* the high polar regions. In the northern hemisphere, the whalers exploited the coastal waters of Finnmark, Iceland, Newfoundland, and Labrador, and waters south of the Bering Strait. In the southern hemisphere, they exploited the whaling grounds around the peri-Antarctic islands, such as South Georgia and Kerguelen – indeed most of the

[1] Sugdon, *Arctic and Antarctic*; Hacquebord and Avango, "Settlements"; Avango et al., "Industrial Extraction".

Southern Ocean.² In the following analysis, we will take a broad and flexible view of the polar regions to be able to include such whaling, which in many ways was inseparable from that part of the industry that took place in the very high north or south.³

Whaling has long taken place in most areas where whales migrate. The extensive whaling industry of the nineteenth century, for example, was a global phenomenon covering the entire Atlantic, Pacific, and Indian Oceans. But even these aspects of the whaling industry had polar connections. Many whale species migrated between temperate and polar waters. Many whalers also chased whales into the Southern Ocean or the Arctic Sea.

The whalers themselves rarely used the term 'polar' about the areas they were working. They might refer to the Arctic and the Antarctic, but typically referred more precisely to the geographical region where the whaling took place, like Baffin Bay or the South Shetlands. Or, to the contrary, the geographical reference could be very imprecise. British eighteenth- and nineteenth-century whalers used the terms Southern and Northern Whale Fisheries to refer to anywhere south or north of the British Isles.⁴ Arctic and Antarctic whaling grounds were included in these terms.

In this chapter we will discuss whaling as an *industry* – whaling undertaken as a commercial enterprise of some scale. We will not deal with subsistence or Indigenous whaling. Historically, this was the way whaling in most areas had taken place, with the exception of the Antarctic, where there were no Indigenous people. In the Arctic region, the Indigenous peoples in Siberia, Alaska, Canada, and Greenland have hunted whales for centuries as a subsistence activity, and many still do.⁵ Subsistence whaling is fundamentally different from industrial whaling, with the latter run by enterprises most often owned and managed elsewhere and driven by prices and demand in a global market. Industrial whaling expanded and developed through huge technological improvements and with very limited concern for the

---

2 The Arctic Sea and the Southern Ocean have recently been explored as concepts by Sverker Sörlin, "The Arctic Ocean", and Alessandro Antonello, "The Southern Ocean", in Armitage et al., eds., *Oceanic Histories*, 267–318.
3 This way of defining the Antarctic as an economic region is discussed in Basberg, "Perspectives on Economic History". In the Arctic, the economic and political role of whaling was discussed in Avango et al., "Between Markets and Geo-politics".
4 Jackson, *British Whaling Trade*.
5 For historical accounts of Indigenous whaling in the Arctic region, see for example Ellis, *Men and Whales*, 272–298; Caulfield, *Greenlanders, Whales and Whaling*; Faegteborg, "Inuit Organisation"; and Stevenson et al., eds., *Anthropology*.

sustainability of whale stocks. The whaling industry is therefore an example of an exploitative industry with significant ecological consequences.

We will discuss Arctic and Antarctic whaling separately and mainly in chronological order. The Arctic was exploited much earlier than the Antarctic. For more than three centuries, industrial whalers were entirely focused on the northern hemisphere. They were hunting the same whale species, the slow-swimming Greenland right whale or bowhead (*Balaena mysticetus*). Halfway into the nineteenth century, technological developments made whaling on the fast-swimming rorquals (*Balaenopteridae*) possible. From then on, whaling took place in both north and south, but relatively speaking, Antarctic whaling dominated.[6]

The First Arctic Industry

There are some indications that people in prehistoric times used whales. Mostly, whales were washed ashore, but sometimes they were driven to the beach. In the eleventh and twelfth centuries, people around the Bay of Biscay hunted the noordkaper or northern right whale (*Eubalaena glacialis*). From historical sources we know that these whales were chased with rowing boats, captured with hand-thrown harpoons, and towed to the beach near the settlements where they were processed. This technology formed the basis of commercial whaling in the Arctic. In fact, the Basques were the first whalers producing whale oil for a growing market in western Europe. This commercial whaling most likely caused the decline in the number of right whales in the Bay of Biscay.

The Grand Bay Whaling

In the first half of the sixteenth century, Basque cod fishermen discovered the grounds on the northeast coast of Canada (the Grand Bay) and two whale species that could be harvested: the northern right whale, and the Greenland right whale or bowhead.[7] It is not known precisely when whaling started

---

6 The history of whaling throughout all its phases has been extensively researched and also chronicled in numerous broader works. This includes whaling more specifically in the Arctic and Antarctic for obvious reasons, these being the core areas of the industry. We do not intend to review this extensive literature, but will highlight a few fundamental and broad contributions to the main aspects of the development. Arctic whaling in the eighteenth century: Scoresby, *Account of Arctic Regions*; Arctic whaling in the nineteenth century: Starbuck, *History*; Webb, *On the Northwest*; twentieth-century Antarctic whaling: Tønnessen and Johnsen, *Den moderne hvalfangsts historie*, and an abridged version in English by Tønnessen, *History of Modern Whaling*.

7 Turgeon, "Pêches basques"; Ducéré, *Recherches historiques*; Proulx, *Basque Whaling*.

there, but it flourished between 1550 and 1600. According to written sources, the Basques outfitted an average of fifteen ships a year, but at least thirty to forty ships participated in the exploitation during peak years.[8] They caught approximately 300 whales every year. More were killed but lost.

Archaeological research in Red Bay (Labrador) – the centre of this industry – shows furnaces where the blubber was melted (try-works), cooperages, small living quarters, lookouts, and a cemetery. The structures functioned as an extension of the ship and had a very temporary character.[9] The whales were most likely processed alongside the ship, and the blubber was towed ashore where it was boiled to produce oil.[10]

Basque whaling declined at the beginning of the seventeenth century, when merchants in England and the Dutch Republic started whaling in Spitsbergen. They hired many Basque whalers as experts, and this must have influenced the Basque industry. At the same time the Basques lost control of the whale oil market. In addition to these economic factors, climate change may have led to a general shift of the whales to the north. By the 1580s, catches were already beginning to decline, and ships were returning half-empty. Although the Basques continued whaling until the middle of the seventeenth century, it was an industry in decline.

The Spitsbergen Whale Fishery

After the discovery of Spitsbergen in 1596 and Henry Hudson's voyage in 1607, several years elapsed before whaling commenced. Then high prices for grain resulted in the stagnation of the production of vegetable oils and fats, and caused a switch to animal oils and fats. But only when the supply of whale oil from the Basques in Labrador dried up did the English and Dutch merchants launch into whaling in 1611 and 1612. They needed whale oil as raw material for the manufacture of soap and candles and as lubricant in the cloth and leather industry.[11]

In the first years in Spitsbergen, keen competition among whalers of different nationalities thrived – especially between the English and the Dutch. In 1614 it led to the foundation of the Dutch *Noordse Compagnie* (1614–42).[12] Unlike the Muscovy Company, a trading company controlled by a small band of London merchants and excluding merchants from other English towns, the Dutch company was an association of independent enterprises from several Dutch ports. The *Noordse Compagnie* was, in effect,

---

8 Proulx, *Whaling in North Atlantic*.   9 Hacquebord, *De Noordse Compagnie*.
10 Tuck and Grenier, *Red Bay*.   11 Hacquebord, "Smeerenburg".
12 Hacquebord, *De Noordse Compagnie*, 29.

a cartel of whaling enterprises in which agreements were made fixing catches and prices. The Dutch whaling trade was thus a reasonably well-organized enterprise, with ten to twenty ships and an annual catch of approximately 300 whales. Both English and Dutch companies had a charter from their governments which they could use to limit catches and manage the prices. In this way, the first whaling period in Spitsbergen was what we now should call a sustainable hunt.

On Amsterdam Island in northwest Spitsbergen, the Dutch established a whaling settlement that they called Smeerenburg (Figure 16.1). The

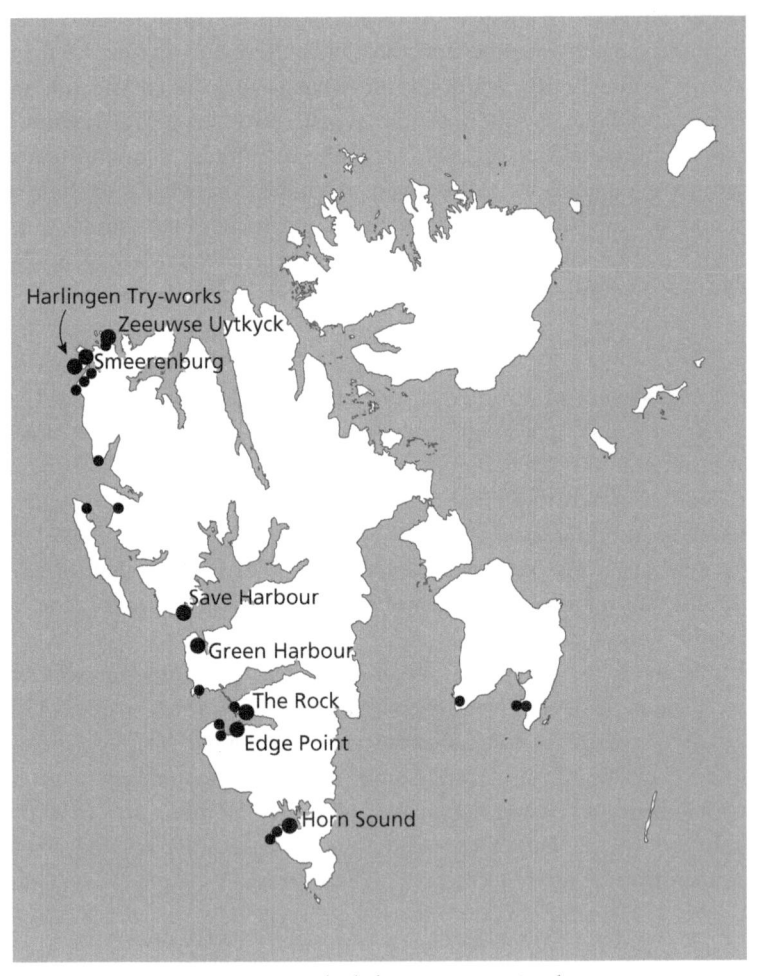

Figure 16.1 Historical whaling stations in Spitsbergen.

settlement consisted of try-works, dwellings, cooperages, storehouses, a smithy, a bottling-room, and a small fortress to protect the settlement against opponents.[13] Whales were hunted with rowing boats in the bays. Winches were used to haul the whales on the beach, cut the blubber of the animal (flensing), and turn the whale over. From 1620 to 1650, about 200 to 250 men worked and lived in this semi-permanent settlement in the summer. In the 1630s, two attempts were made to winter in the settlement to colonize the region. The first attempt was successful, but when the second failed and all winterers died, no new attempts were made.

After the Dutch discovery of the Arctic island of Jan Mayen in 1614, Dutch whaling concentrated there for several years, and only a few Dutch ships sailed on for the west coast of Spitsbergen. A big advantage was that around Jan Mayen there was no competition from the English whalers. Whaling stations were built, and new techniques were employed. Whales were hunted on the high seas with single-masted ships that brought the dead whales ashore to be processed.[14]

At the beginning of the 1630s, the Dutch company experienced its heyday because of high whale oil prices. During this period, the Dutch fleet was divided into two parts: one for Jan Mayen and one for Spitsbergen. At Spitsbergen the *Noordse Compagnie* had to accept competitors (*interlopers*) on its whaling grounds because, owing to a change in the position of the ice edge that the bowhead related to for food, they shifted to the high seas in the north. Under pressure from these competitors and because of internal conflicts, no new extension of the charter was requested in 1642. Whaling then became accessible to every Dutch ship-owner, which meant the end of the controlled whale hunt there.[15]

Many commanders and harpooners formerly serving the *Noordse Compagnie* now voyaged to the Arctic seas on their own account. Part-ownership took over the Dutch trade, and whaling entered a new phase of development. Many families became involved in whaling, and a tradition developed in small ports in the country and on the islands along the northern coast of the Netherlands and Germany. The annual average number of ships

---

13   Excavations of Dutch and Norwegian archaeologists from 1979 to 1981. Hacquebord and Vroom, eds., *Walvisvaart*.
14   Hacquebord, "Jan Mayen Whaling Industry". Almost no remains were found during three archaeological surveys (1983, 1988, and 2014). In the *Zuidbaai* (Titeltbukta) some remains were found from the whaling period, but no calculation could be made of the number of try-works.
15   Bruijn and Hacquebord, *Een Zee van Traan*, 104.

fitted out from Dutch ports increased from 50 between 1642 and 1665 to 126 in the years from 1665 to 1700.[16]

While Dutch whaling prospered, English whaling declined. The English settled in the southern bays of Spitsbergen (like Bell Sound and Horn Sound) and inadvertently drove the foreigners to the better northern whaling grounds.[17] Moreover, the English Muscovy Company was organized like a monopoly, and the company spent a great deal of time, money, and energy fighting English interlopers from London, Hull, and Great Yarmouth. Not until 1670 was English whaling free for everyone; but by then the industry had wound up.[18]

When the price of whale oil started to rise in the 1640s, merchants from German ports such as Hamburg and Bremen also became interested in whaling. Their early activities were so successful that they soon maintained a fleet of forty ships, whaling in the Spitsbergen bays.[19] With so many ships and people in a limited number of sites, maintaining whaling stations became increasingly difficult. The working season was also made shorter by climate change that caused the Spitsbergen bays to freeze for longer periods.

The Dutch, soon followed by the Germans, moved to the whaling grounds along the edge of the west ice between Spitsbergen and Iceland. They even followed the whales into the sea ice and processed the whales alongside the ships or even on an ice floe. The blubber was put into barrels and boiled in the home ports. Many ships were wrecked in the ice.

Until the Fourth Anglo-Dutch war (1780–84), Dutch whalers dominated European whaling. France and England were buying the bulk of their whale products in the Dutch Republic in the second half of the seventeenth and the first half of the eighteenth century. In this period, the English government tried to revive its whaling by placing a duty on imported whale oil and allowing foreigners to work on English whaling ships.

In the second half of the eighteenth century, owing to changed sea ice conditions and extensive whaling, the number of bowhead whales decreased to such an extent that profitability dropped severely. Altogether, the English, German, and Dutch whalers caught about 110,000 bowhead whales in the North Atlantic Ocean between 1612 and 1800. About 65 per cent were taken by Dutch whalers.[20]

---

16 Bruijn and Hacquebord, *Een Zee van Traan*, 102–103.
17 Hacquebord et al., "English and Dutch Whaling".   18 Jackson, *British Whaling Trade*.
19 Oesau, *Schleswig-Holsteins Grönlandfahrt*; Oesau, *Hamburgs Grönlandfahrt*.
20 Bruijn and Hacquebord, *En Zee van Traan*, 333.

Greenland and Davis Strait Whaling

Although some written sources suggest that the Dutch were already trading and hunting in the Davis Strait in the last decade of the seventeenth century, whaling there began in earnest in 1719. In the 1720s, an average number of sixty-seven Dutch whaling ships were sailing annually to this whaling ground. The fishery lasted throughout the eighteenth century, reaching its peak in 1732 before declining rapidly in the 1780s, although the last Dutch whaling voyage to the Strait is recorded in 1826.[21] During the period of Davis Strait whaling, operations also took place east of Greenland, but the popularity of the Davis Strait whaling was most likely stimulated by the potential of trading with the Indigenous Greenlandic hunters.[22]

In addition to the Dutch, Germans hunted in Davis Strait until 1826. German whalers from Hamburg and Bremen had close contact with their Dutch colleagues, often sharing catches and losses. High whale oil prices and encouragement by the authorities also brought Danish whalers to the Davis Strait. From 1749 to 1758, the Danish sent four ships to Spitsbergen and Davis Strait annually: from 1775 to 1788, they made 200 voyages from Denmark to both whaling grounds.[23]

The British followed the Dutch and Germans not only into the west ice near Spitsbergen but also to Davis Strait. Although British whalers were heavily subsidized, their revived whaling trade was not very successful. Only in 1749, when higher bounties coincided with increasing prices for whale products did the British whaling fleet grow. From the 1770s, whalers from Hull and Whitby sailed to Davis Strait on a regular basis. In 1786, Britain outfitted 168 ships for whaling east and west of Greenland.[24] The following year this number increased. Scotland was also active, but at a lower scale. By the 1780s, the British whaling industry was so well-established that the government could reduce the bounties.[25] Altogether, the international whaling fleet killed about 10,000 bowhead whales on these grounds between 1719 and 1800.[26]

In the Napoleonic wars, whalers from Hull made use of the absence of the Dutch whalers to make good profits.[27] After the war, ship-owners in the

---

21 Bruijn and Hacquebord, *Een Zee van Traan*, 135–140.
22 Leinenga, *Arctische walvisvangst*, 139 ff.
23 De Jong, *Geschiedenis*, Vol. 2, 385–387; Vaughan, "Historical Survey".
24 Jackson, *British Whaling Trade*, 265.
25 Jackson, *British Whaling Trade*, 76. See also Sanger, *Scottish Arctic Whaling*; Watson, *The Dundee Whalers*.
26 Leinenga, *Arctische walvisvangst*, 194–196, 198–199; Bruijn and Hacquebord, *Een Zee van Traan*, 157.
27 Scoresby, *Account of Arctic Regions*, Vol. 2, 86 ff.

Netherlands tried to start up bowhead whaling again. They sailed to the old whaling grounds on both sides of Greenland but found that the bowhead population had been over-hunted.

The most extensive British whaling east and west of Greenland took place up to the end of the 1820s. In the ice east of Greenland, whalers complained about the reduced size of the whales.[28] The Davis Strait whaling was more successful, especially when a new whaling ground was discovered in Pond Inlet and Lancaster Sound. More than 2,400 voyages to Davis Strait from 1820 to 1910 have been recorded, mostly undertaken by British whalers.[29] However, half the voyages took place during the first twenty years of this period, and by the mid-1830s, the first signs of depletion were already being noticed here too. The number of British whale ships gradually declined in the decades that followed.

In 1840, whalers from New England and Scotland established land-based whaling in Cumberland Sound (Baffin Island) that lasted until 1860 when the number of whales declined. The Americans and some Scottish whalers moved to Hudson Bay, where they started operations based on wintering and cooperation with the natives. This predominantly American whaling lasted only a few years.

Whales gradually became scarce in the Greenland whaling grounds. Simultaneously, the market for whale products declined. However, the winding-up of the Davis Strait whaling was slow. Whalers from Peterhead and Dundee in Scotland and New England remained active up until 1917.[30]

American Arctic Whaling

Evidence suggests that North American offshore whaling started as early as the first half of the seventeenth century.[31] The first New England settlers were familiar with the economic value of blubber and baleen, but it is not clear how they had learned whale-hunting techniques. They may have brought a knowledge of whaling with them from England, but they more likely learned it from the Dutch colonists around New Amsterdam.

The Indigenous people of New England were already whaling before the first British settlers arrived. The colonists may have followed the basic approach of the Indigenous residents, which was similar to the whaling technique used by the Basques and the Dutch. A combination of Indigenous knowledge and European technology and capital may explain

---

28 Scoresby, *Account of the Arctic Regions*, Vol. 2, 140.   29 Ross, "Annual Catch".
30 Sanger, *Scottish Arctic Whaling*, 110ff.
31 De Jong, *Geschiedenis*, Vol. 2, 275; Starbuck, *History*, 4ff.

the success of North American whaling.³² At any rate, by about 1650, offshore whaling began in New England. European settlers hired Indigenous Americans as oarsmen and lookouts while the colonists provided the capital. In the 1680s, offshore whaling had spread to all the main communities along the New England coast. From the turn of the century, Nantucket Island off Cape Cod, Massachusetts, became the centre.³³

In 1712, the Nantucket captain Christopher Hussey killed the first sperm whale (*Physeter macrocephalus*). Although the hunting of right whales continued, sperm whaling took over, causing a rapid growth in the industry. Because the sperm whales had to be chased on the high seas, voyages lasted longer, and larger vessels were necessary. New hunting methods and technologies were developed. This eventually led the New England whalers to polar waters.

Early American whale ships had to return to the port for flensing and cooking. Eventually the blubber was stripped from the whale alongside the ship on the high seas.³⁴ In the 1760s, boiling the oil on board ships was introduced in the same way as the Basques (and probably also the Dutch) had done it. American whaling now expanded over all oceans in the world searching for new whaling grounds. On a whaling voyage in 1835 the *Ganges*, commanded by Captain Barzillai Folger from Nantucket, discovered right whales off the northwest coast of America.³⁵ In the next six years, the American fleet doubled, and by the mid-1800s, the American fleet comprised 75 per cent of the world's whaling fleet.³⁶ The ships also grew considerably larger in order to complete these long voyages.

The northwest whaling trade started off the coast of Kamchatka and moved to the Sea of Okhotsk, where right and bowhead whales thrived. Within two decades, both whale populations were exterminated in this region. During the period from 1847 to 1867, mostly Americans made 1,391 voyages to the Sea of Okhotsk. During the first decade of this period, 8,240 bowheads and 3,600 northern right whales were killed.³⁷ From 1848 to 1910, as many as 2,712 voyages were made to the Bering Strait and the Chukchi and Beaufort Sea, again, mostly by American whale ships.³⁸

In 1855, a drastic decline in bowhead catches led to the abandonment of whaling efforts north of the Bering Strait. However, declining catches in the Sea of Okhotsk led the whalers back north three years later. Of the original

32 Proulx, *Whaling in North Atlantic*, 60.
33 Starbuck, *History*, 19ff.; Vickers, "First Whalemen of Nantucket"
34 Starbuck, *History*, 53ff.   35 Webb, *On the Northwest*, 35; Spence, *Harpooned*, 99.
36 Webb, *On the Northwest*, 82; Spence, *Harpooned*, 113.   37 Kugler, "Historical Survey".
38 Kugler, "Historical Survey", 153.

population of approximately 30,000 bowheads, whalers killed about 18,600 in the first twenty years.[39] This dramatic depletion shows how newly discovered whaling grounds led to intensive hunting, resulting in a rapid reduction of the whale population.[40] It also made whaling less profitable and less attractive, and too risky for American capital investment.[41] Competition with other investment possibilities like the cotton industry was also increasing in North America.

Because the US transcontinental railway, which opened in 1869, shortened the distance between the western whaling grounds and the market in the east, cargo vessels were no longer needed, and San Francisco rose in importance as a whaling port. On the west coast the American whalers also experienced loss of crew during the gold mining rush there.

There were also other challenges to the industry. The American Civil War greatly affected whaling. The fleet was reduced from 514 to 263 ships in 1866. At the same time, mineral oil was discovered in Pennsylvania, and soon the market for traditional whale products like sources for lighting and various industrial uses collapsed.

Whaling in the Arctic was moving from one whaling ground to another. The whalers initially hunted only two species of whales: the northern right whale and the bowhead. Both animals were seen as easy prey. The northern hemisphere whaling started in the Bay of Biscay, moved to Labrador and from there to Spitsbergen and Davis Strait, later to Hudson Bay, the Sea of Okhotsk, the Bering Strait, the Chukchi Sea, and the Beaufort Sea. With the possible exception of the early days of chartered whaling at Spitsbergen, an unlimited hunt followed the discoveries of new whaling grounds. Within a few years, the whale population was completely exterminated, and the whalers moved to another ground.

Whaling technology was transferred from one country to another, starting with the Basques. They passed on the technology by hiring themselves out to the English and Dutch whaling companies. Some decades later, Dutch whalers did the same by hiring themselves out to the English and the Germans.

The North Atlantic and Arctic Rorqual Hunt: The Origin of a New Whaling Era

A fundamental change and new development of the whaling industry occurred during two decades from the 1860s and is closely associated with

39 Bockstoce and Bodkin, "Historical Status".   40 Kugler, "Historical Survey", 156.
41 Davis et al., *In Pursuit of Leviathan*.

16 Industrial Whaling in the Arctic and Antarctic

the Norwegian whaling entrepreneur Svend Foyn and his employment of new whaling technology at the coast of Finnmark (Norway). Foyn built the *Spes & Fides*, a small iron-hulled steamboat, and equipped it with a grenade harpoon of his own design. This powerful new technology could be used to chase the rorquals – blue whales (*Balaenoptera musculus*) and fin whales (*Balaenoptera physalus*).[42]

Protected by patents, Foyn was able to keep the Finnmark whaling grounds for himself for some years, but from the 1880s a number of whaling companies, mainly from the county of Vestfold in southern Norway, established shore stations and employed the new 'high tech' steam whale-catcher boats along the Finnmark coast, making Norway the world's leading whaling nation. The Norwegian whalers ignored the dramatic effect on the stock of whales, and soon few whales remained within a certain distance of the shore stations. Some companies moved to Iceland, and the first whaling station there was established at Onundarfjordur in 1889.[43]

The extensive whaling at the Finnmark coast worried the fishermen in northern Norway, who believed that it adversely affected the fisheries. They blamed the whaling companies for the reduction of their catches, believing that the whales drove the fish closer to the coast. Therefore in 1904, the Norwegian government prohibited whaling in the waters of northern Norway for ten years.[44] Although the industry declined locally, Finnmark whaling was of crucial importance for the further development of the industry, both in the Arctic and in the Antarctic.

When whaling was prohibited in Finnmark, whaling companies, as we have seen, had already started to move, and continued their trade outside the coastal waters of Northern Norway. Eight companies from Finnmark moved their activities to the coastal waters of Spitsbergen and Bear Island. Some were operating from shore stations, while others used factory ships. Two whaling stations were established: one at Finneset in Green Harbour, Spitsbergen, and one at Walrus Bay, Bear Island. However, because of the distance between the hunting grounds, whaling stations, and markets, the operational costs were high, and the hard environmental conditions with sea

---

42 Tønnessen and Johnsen, *History of Modern Whaling*, 25ff. As was the case in most periods of transition, there were also other inventors who struggled to solve the same problems. One of Foyn's contemporaries was Thomas W. Roys; see Schmitt et al., *Thomas Welcome Roys*; Niemi, "Svend Foyn i Vadsø".
43 Tønnessen and Johnsen, *History of Modern Whaling*, 75–83.
44 Tønnessen and Johnsen, *History of Modern Whaling*, 61–68.

ice, storms, and fogs made whaling difficult. Most whaling companies therefore soon terminated their activities in Spitsbergen and Bear Island.[45]

Norwegian stations were also established at the Faroes, the Hebrides, and Newfoundland. Within eight years from the ban in 1904, Norway established in this way eighteen whaling stations in the Arctic region.[46] At Iceland, the consequences of whaling were dramatic. In 1902 alone, thirty catcher boats killed 1,305 whales (Figure 16.3). The Icelandic government imposed drastic measures to save the whales, and in 1913 it initiated a ban on all whaling from 1915 that would remain in effect for ten years.

The technological development that started with Svend Foyn at Finnmark and spread throughout the North Atlantic and the Arctic region eventually reached the Antarctic. This era of whaling history has been described as 'modern whaling'. The origin of this concept is not clear, but the terms 'old' versus 'modern' were used in contemporary accounts by Norwegian historians describing the transformation of the industry associated with Svend Foyn.[47] The concept was adopted internationally, used for example by Karl Brandt in his study of aspects of the development of the industry.[48] He identified how modern whaling 'differs radically' from earlier whaling in term of species, regions, equipment both for hunting and processing, and new uses for the whale products. The concept was further discussed and defined explicitly by Tønnessen and Johnsen in the introductions to their seminal four-volume work *Den moderne hvalfangsts historie* (The History of Modern Whaling).[49] They especially emphasized technology and scale. While most old-style whaling was very much a craft, modern whaling was a global processing industry. Finally, the whaling companies became larger and more vertically integrated, being involved (as owners) in the fat industry.

Modern whaling now has a 150-year history, and it might be time to rethink the use of the concept. It is obviously not so modern anymore, and the organization of the whaling industry in relation to technology has also gone through significant changes since the days of Foyn. If an alternative

---

45 Gustafsson, "Icebound Frontiers".
46 Tønnessen and Johnsen, *History of Modern Whaling*. The new whaling methods also spread to the North Pacific. In 1898, the Russian Pacific Whaling Company started whaling using Norwegian equipment. The results surprised the traditional Japanese net whalers, and from that same year the Japanese Ocean Whaling Company also began to use Norwegian equipment and methods. Later, the Japanese company even hired Norwegian harpooners. The Japanese-Russian war of 1904–05 ended the Russian Whaling Company, but the Japanese expanded their industry because of an increasing demand for whale meat for human consumption.
47 Risting, *Av hvalfangstens historie*; Aagaard, *Den gamle hvalfangst*.
48 Brandt, *Whale Oil*, 57ff.   49 Tønnessen and Johnsen, *History of Modern Whaling*, 3–15.

concept should be applied, it might instead be 'industrial large-scale whaling'. This describes well the kind of whaling that is associated with the twentieth century in Antarctic waters – the culmination of this industry.

Antarctic Large-scale Industry

From North to South: A Long Transition

During the eighteenth century, the Southern Ocean, islands, and the Antarctic coastline were gradually explored and identified by European expeditions like those of Bouvet, Kerguelen, and Cook. They had scientific and political motivations, but they also brought back knowledge that would lead to commercial exploitation.[50] Observations of whales and seals were noted, and the knowledge from Cook's second expedition (1772–74) was especially important for the further development. The abundance of seals observed at several sub-Antarctic islands were quickly picked up, in particular by the United States and British sealing communities, and a new industry soon developed. Sealing, therefore, was the first Antarctic industry. Whales were also observed, and one of Cook's scientists, George Forster, correctly predicted that whalers one day would come to the Southern Ocean, but only when stocks elsewhere had been depleted.[51]

One consequence of these new discoveries was the establishment of the British Southern Whale Fisheries in 1786, promoted by the Government. British whalers were encouraged to explore new grounds to replace the declining northern trade. The Government also sponsored exploration. One such expedition in the 1790s reached Staten Island (close to Cape Horn), and a whaling base there was considered together with possible whaling even further to the south. When the South Shetland Islands were discovered around 1820, they immediately became a centre for the sealing industry, but it was also suggested that British whaling should get a foothold there.[52]

The national expeditions that explored Antarctic waters in the 1840s primarily had scientific aims. But they were also instructed to look for opportunities for the whaling fleets. Most important in this respect was James Clark Ross's British naval expedition. During the circumnavigation

---

50 The importance of the eighteenth-and nineteenth-century expeditions for the development of Antarctic industry is elaborated in Basberg, "Commercial and Economic Aspects".
51 Forster, *Voyage Round the World*, 533.
52 Colnett, *Voyage to South Atlantic*, 20; Campbell, ed., *Discoveries*, 60.

of the continent and the penetration into what was named the Ross Sea, abundant whales were sighted, and Ross reflected on the potential for a revival of the British whaling industry. Several whaling entrepreneurs were motivated by his observations – although in the beginning with limited success. Charles Enderby initiated the Southern Whale Fishery Company, and in 1850 one of his ships was dispatched from the Auckland Islands to search for whales further south. It reached the Balleny Islands at about 70° south but returned with no results.[53] This was probably the first whaling attempt that was undertaken in the very deep Antarctic region. In 1874 the Gray Brothers – whaling company owners in Peterhead, Scotland – published a pamphlet titled *Report on New Whaling Grounds in the Southern Seas*. Once more, references were made to Ross. The pamphlet was widely circulated and became well-known in the whaling communities in Scotland and abroad. That included the Norwegian whalers. Together with the Scots, they were the next to explore the opportunities. This happened in the early 1890s.

The reasons that the Scots and the Norwegians were keen to explore the southern whaling grounds were at least to some degree similar. They both, as we have seen, faced challenges on the northern whaling grounds. So, in the early 1890s, several expeditions sailed south. A Scottish expedition from the old whaling port of Dundee was organized in 1892, and a fleet of four ships explored the coasts of the Antarctic Peninsula. This speeded up Norwegian planning. Sponsored, among others, by the Sandefjord ship-owner Christen Christensen, the *Jason*, captained by Carl Anton Larsen, explored the same area. *Jason*, with two more ships, still with Larsen as the expedition leader, also made a second voyage in 1893–94. At that time yet another Norwegian vessel set sail, the *Antarctic* – sponsored by the Finnmark whaling pioneer Svend Foyn. This expedition explored the Ross Sea area.[54]

Once again, the expeditions returned from the Antarctic without any whales caught. One reason for this was the same that explained the disappointing earlier adventures. The expeditions were all equipped to hunt right whales, but they were not found in large numbers. So, at least to some extent, they must have misinterpreted Ross's reports – or Ross himself had given imprecise information. The Norwegians and the Scots observed rorquals, but were not able to chase them from their slow-moving vessels. Svend Foyn had

---

53 Fotheringham, "Southern Whale Fishery Company".
54 Tønnessen and Johnsen, *Den moderne hvalfangst historie*, Vol. II, 229ff.; Watson, *The Dundee Whalers*, 138ff.; Bull, *Cruise of the Antarctic*. See also Baughman, *Before the Heroes Came*, where these whaling voyages are put in the broader context of the Antarctic explorations at the time.

obviously invented a new system of whaling that had successfully been adopted in Finnmark, but the steam chaser boats with their grenade harpoons were still too small to be taken the whole way to the Antarctic. Jackson, in his analysis of this early explorative phase, put it this way: 'The fact is that at the same time the Norwegians, just like the Scots, were chasing an old dream in new waters'.[55]

It still took a few years, and some increase in size, before the first steam whale-catcher boat of the new era was brought to the southern hemisphere. In 1903, the Norwegian Adolf A. Andresen started a whaling operation based in Punta Arenas. The catcher boat was not used further south than in the Strait of Magellan, but only a year later the new whaling era finally reached Antarctic waters.

Founding an Antarctic Industry

On the second *Jason* expedition, Larsen visited South Georgia. He also returned in 1902 when he was captain on the *Antarctic* with the Swedish Antarctic Expedition (1901–03) led by Otto Nordenskjöld. They visited a sheltered cove that they named Grytviken (literally 'Pot Bay') after some try-pots that they found there – relics from the first Antarctic industry that was active along the shores of South Georgia in the early nineteenth century.[56] At this point in time, Larsen had conceptualized his plans for a whaling operation. When he reached Buenos Aires after the dramatic ending of the Nordenskjöld expedition when their vessel was crushed by ice and sunk, he was able to get financial support from businessmen there to establish a whaling company based in South Georgia. *Compañía Argentina de Pesca*, established in early 1904, became the first Antarctic whaling company.[57] After a quick trip back to Sandefjord in Norway to make practical preparations for the venture, Larsen, with a group of Norwegian whalers, a cargo vessel, and, most importantly, the small steam whale-catcher boat *Fortuna*, arrived in Grytviken in December 1904. They immediately started the construction of the whaling station, and as early as January the catcher boat brought in the first whale to the processing plant.

Larsen was very soon followed by other Norwegian whaling entrepreneurs who also were looking for new opportunities. One of these was

---

55 Jackson, "Why Did the British?", 117.
56 Nordenskjöld et al., *Antarctica*. A chapter on the expedition's visit to South Georgia is only included in the original Swedish edition.
57 The history of C. A. Larsen and how Compañía Argentina de Pesca was established is recorded in many publications, in most detail in Hart, *Pesca*.

Christen Christensen, who had been cooperating with Larsen in the 1890s. Christensen was at the time a well-established businessman involved both in whaling and in shipbuilding. This may explain the fact that he advocated for a new organization of the whaling operations. He rebuilt a vessel into a so-called floating factory ship. After trying this method briefly at Finnmark, Bear Island, and Spitsbergen, in 1905 he sent the *Admiralen* together with two catcher boats to the Falkland Islands. In the early months of 1906 the expedition proceeded to the South Shetland Islands and thus introduced the new whaling era there.[58] Together with South Georgia, the South Shetlands became the centre of world whaling for almost two decades (Figure 16.2).[59]

At South Georgia, six whaling stations were built over the next few years. The companies were of several nationalities (Argentina, Norway, Britain, South Africa), but the majority of the whalers were recruited in Norway. Factory ships were employed independently or working in cooperation with

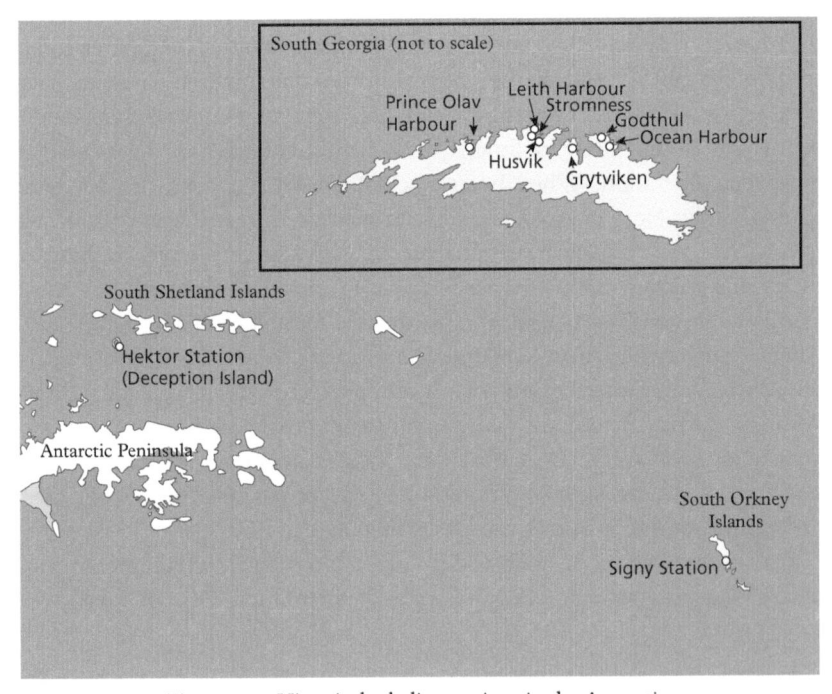

Figure 16.2 Historical whaling stations in the Antarctic.

58 Adie and Basberg, "First Antarctic Whaling Season".   59 Hart, *Whaling*.

the whaling stations.[60] In the South Shetlands, the first to follow Christensen was Adolf Andresen of Punta Arenas, who brought a factory ship to Deception Island in 1906. A whaling station was also set up by the Norwegian company Hektor in 1912.[61] Many more followed and explored also further south along the Antarctic Peninsula. When whaling peaked before World War I, twelve floating factory ships with their catcher boats operated in the South Shetland whaling grounds.

When whaling started in South Georgia and in the South Shetland Islands, the sovereignty of the region was still unresolved. However, the whalers applied for licences from Britain from the very beginning, accepting de facto British rule. The young (becoming independent in 1905) and small Norway had every reason to be on good terms with the British Empire. In 1908, the Falkland Islands Dependencies were formally declared, establishing a regime that became important for the whaling operations there for as long as the industry was active. It clearly demonstrated a link between whaling and geopolitics that became even more apparent in the years to come when whaling expanded into other regions of the Antarctic.[62]

The whaling industry expanded worldwide in the decade leading up to World War I, stimulated by increased demand for whale oil that, owing to new knowledge on hydrogenation, could be utilized as an edible fat.[63] Everywhere it was led by Norwegian technology, entrepreneurs, and whalers. They reached the Canadian east and west coasts, the coasts of southern Africa, Chile, New Zealand, and Australia. The operations were based both at shore stations and factory ships. In the Antarctic region, shore stations were also established at Signy Island in the South Orkneys, Kerguelen Island, and Campbell Islands.[64] However, the peak of Antarctic whaling was still to come, and was not limited to the islands and bases ashore.

---

60 An account of the history of these stations and an analysis of the technological aspects of shore station whaling based on surveys of the remains of the stations can be found in Basberg, *Shore Whaling Stations*.
61 Hart, *Whaling*, 104; Hacquebord, "Hector Station".
62 Hart, *Whaling*, 19ff. See also Roberts, *European Antarctic*; Burnett, *Sounding of the Whale*.
63 Tønnessen and Johnsen, *History of Modern Whaling*, 231ff.
64 The operations varied in size, and none of them was as extensive as the shore stations at South Georgia. But they had in common that steam whale-catcher boats were used for the actual hunting. At Campbell Island, only one catcher boat was employed (from 1910); Elser, *Whaling and Sealing*, 85ff.; Hacquebord and Avango, "Industrial Heritage Sites".

Pelagic Bonanza

During the 1920s, a major transformation took place in Antarctic whaling. The South Georgia and South Shetlands whaling grounds were already being exhausted. Any expansion within the Falkland Island Dependencies was also restricted because of British sovereignty and requirements of leases and concessions that put a limit on number of whaling stations, factory ships, and whale catchers. The further development was closely connected to the factory ships. So far, these vessels had been operating in sheltered bays at the peri-Antarctic islands and especially in the South Shetlands and subject to British regulations. The year 1923 marked the beginning of a new whaling era. In December that year, the factory ship *Sir James Clark Ross*, with C. A. Larsen as expedition leader, made its way together with its fleet of five catcher boats into the Ross Sea. They operated independently of any sheltered waters. The whaling company A/S Rosshavet had been established some months earlier, and Larsen and his colleagues had already applied for a whaling licence in autumn 1922. But it was only in July 1923 that the Ross Sea, together with surrounding coasts, the ice shelf, and landmasses stretching all the way to the South Pole, were defined by British order as the Ross Dependency, under the administration of the New Zealand Government. Again, this indicated a strong connection between the development of whaling and the British imperial ambitions in the Antarctic region.[65]

The *Sir James Clark Ross* returned to the Ross Sea for several whaling seasons. Others followed, and in 1929–30 five factory ships with catchers were operating in this region. However, the Ross Sea whaling became an intermezzo in the development of Antarctic whaling. A/S Rosshavet was the only company that operated with a licence. The others operated in the northern parts of the Ross Sea and challenged the power of Britain to regulate Antarctic whaling. That they could do this is entirely explained by technological changes that made it possible for the expeditions to move operations further into the open ocean and thus beyond the area covered by national jurisdiction and licences. Prime among these technological changes was the so-called slipway.

Early factory ships could not haul whales aboard, meaning they had to be flensed alongside the ship, in much the same way as in previous centuries.

---

65 The foundation of A/S Rosshavet, the development of whaling in the Ross Sea, and the establishment of the Ross Dependency are analysed in various publications and from various perspectives: Tønnessen and Johnsen, *History of Modern Whaling*, 346ff.; Barr and Watt, "Pioneer Whalers"; Auburn, *Ross Dependency*; Templeton, *Wise Adventure*.

This limited the productivity as compared to the shore stations. Many attempts were made to find ways to get the whole whale on board for processing. A technological solution was found with the slipway, invented and patented in Norway by Petter Sørlle and adopted on the floating factory *Lancing* in 1925. Whales could be winched onto the deck through a hole in the stern and flensed and processed on board – in much the same way as on the shore stations of the same era. The solution became an instant success. Other factory ships had slipways installed, and the size of factory ships increased. Typically, they were rebuilt steamers, but in 1928 a purpose-built factory ship was launched at a Belfast yard for the Norwegian ship-owner Anders Jahre. The company and the vessel were named *Kosmos* – reflecting the ambitions of the enterprise. With its 17,801 gross register tons, the vessel was one of the largest at the time. It became a model – a dominant design – for how whaling ships were going to look.

The new-style factory ships, together with larger and more powerful catcher boats, made the whaling operations truly pelagic, independent of sheltered bays or any shore facilities. From the late 1920s, the fleets operated all around the Antarctic continent. The industry reached a peak in 1930–31. More than forty factory ships along with about 200 catcher boats were in Antarctic waters, killing more than 40,000 whales (Figure 16.3). A record 29,410 blue whales were killed.

Whaling, geopolitics, science, and exploration were closely connected in the Antarctic in these years, with British imperial policy and Norwegian whaling interests at centre stage. In many ways, it was a continuation of the earlier development in the Falkland Islands Dependencies and the Ross Dependency.[66] In the mid-1920s, the attention moved to the still unclaimed coastlines between these regions. Instrumental in this development was Lars Christensen (son of Christen Christensen). His whaling fleet had earlier been operating in the Falkland Islands Dependencies and elsewhere, but from the 1920s moved to the coastlines along the ice, especially south of the South Atlantic Ocean. For several consecutive whaling seasons, Christensen sponsored expeditions that explored new whaling grounds, mapped islands and coastlines, and claimed territory for Norway.[67] Bouvetøya was claimed in 1927, Peter I Øy in 1929, and Dronning Maud Land in 1939. These claims, however, never became really important for the whaling operations, as most

---

66 For a detailed analysis on the relationship between whaling and imperial policy in this period, see Roberts, *European Antarctic*, 31ff.
67 Christensen's own account from these years: Christensen, *Such Is the Antarctic*.

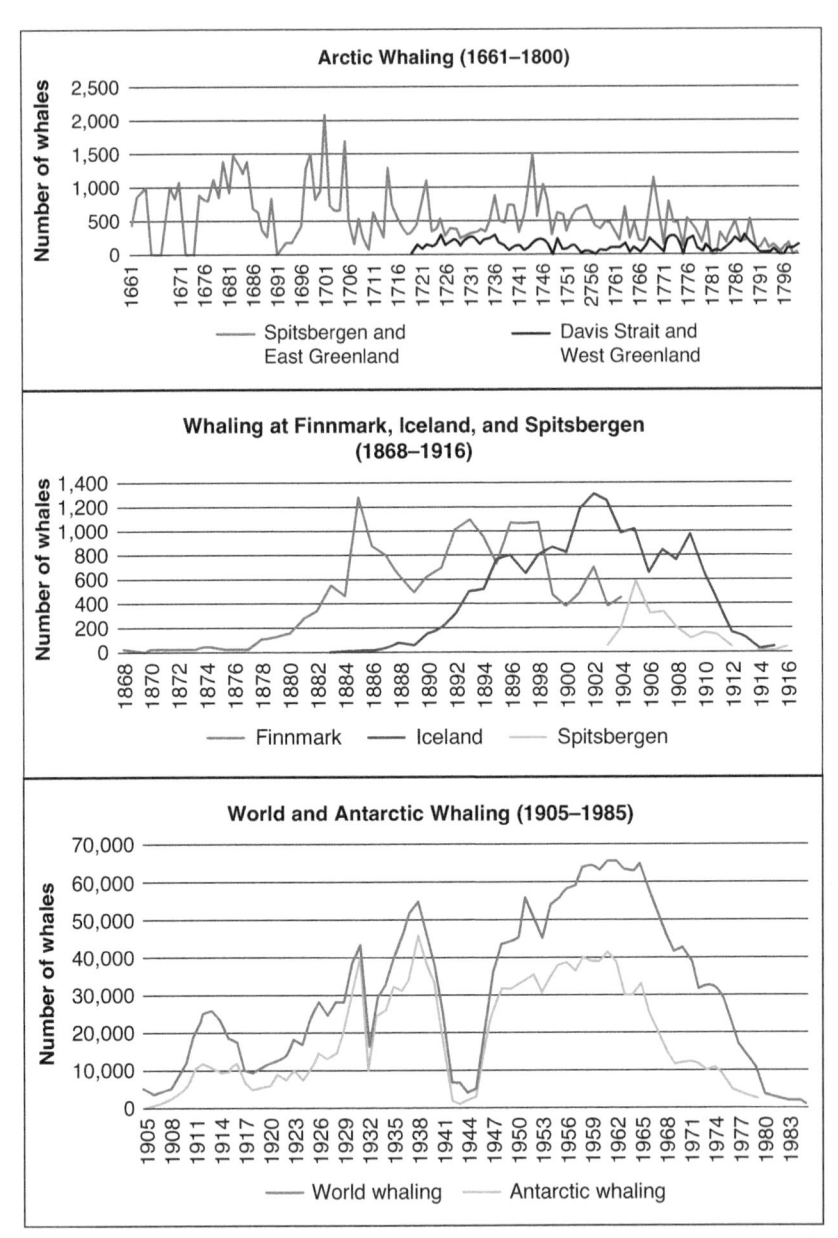

Figure 16.3 Trends in Arctic, Antarctic, and global whaling. (Sources: Leinenga, *Arctische walvisvangst*; De Jong, *Geschiedenis*, part 3; van Sante, *Alphabetische naam-lyst*; International Whaling Statistics.)

whalers – Norwegians and other nationalities – by then operated in international waters.

The huge expansion came at a cost. The record high production of whale oil could not be met by the demand on the world market. Escalated by the general economic downturn of the early 1930s, prices dropped – and the whaling industry faced a severe crisis that peaked in 1931 and 1932. Some Antarctic shore stations were closed and never reopened. Whaling vessels were left in their home harbours, and some never returned to work.[68]

The industry was restructured, with both governments and many whaling companies agreeing that regulations had to be imposed. In the early days of Antarctic whaling when hunting primarily had taken place in the Falkland Islands Dependencies, the licensing system had to some extent prevented uncontrolled growth. When pelagic whaling took off in the 1920s, this system was evaded and further increased the over-exploitation of the industry. After the crisis of the early 1930s, Britain and Norway, the leading whaling nations at the time, negotiated quota agreements between the companies. However, these agreements were voluntary. When both Germany and Japan in the late 1930s established Antarctic whaling, killing again peaked (Figure 16.3).

A Predicted Decline

Critical voices had been raised about the insufficient regulation in Antarctic whaling from the early years. Nevertheless, hunting increased and whale stocks decreased rapidly. A political climate for change and international cooperation only emerged after the almost complete halt to the business during World War II.

To be able to continue commercial whaling, but within a regulatory regime, the International Whaling Commission (IWC) was established in Washington in 1946. From then on, the whaling industry had to follow restrictions on catches, length of the whaling season, and limitation on catching areas. An annual global quota was imposed. But restrictions were challenged, and the history of the IWC has been marked by constant tensions between the whaling industry, the scientific community, and politicians about estimates of stocks and how they could or should be interpreted.[69]

---

68 Tønnessen and Johnsen, *History of Modern Whaling*, 386ff.
69 Several historical analyses of the establishment and operation of the International Whaling Commission have been written that show the many difficulties in making this organization work. See Tønnessen and Johnsen, *History of Modern Whaling*, 499ff. For recent studies, see Heazle, *Scientific Uncertainty*; Burnett, *Sounding of the Whale*; Dorsey, *Whales and Nations*. For a broad review: Basberg, "Regulating Natural Resources".

The early post-war world also saw an increased demand for fats, especially as a raw material for the margarine industry, and the whaling industry in several countries expanded – stimulated by government policy.[70] Norway and Britain tried but failed to regain control of Antarctic whaling. Japan rebuilt their industry, to some extent motivated by US reconstruction policy.[71] The Netherlands, which had not been active in whaling for almost a century, restarted its whaling business.[72] New nations entered the stage, most significantly the Soviet Union, and the Soviet Antarctic whaling fleet soon outnumbered those of other nations.

Despite regulations and quotas negotiated in the IWC, the number of whales killed in Antarctic waters peaked as late as 1960 (Figure 16.3). Whereas peaks in the 1920s and 1930s were composed mainly of large blue whales, the main species caught were now fin whales, along with the much smaller sei whales (*Balaenoptera borealis*), and eventually even minke whales (*Balaenoptera acutorostrata*). The declining size of the whales reflected the declining economic value of the industry, and British and Norwegian companies gradually wound up from the mid-to late 1950s. Together with the Dutch company Nederlandse Maatschappij voor de Walvisvaart, they withdrew from all Antarctic whaling during the 1960s.[73]

The Japanese and Soviet fleets were thus left alone on the Antarctic whaling grounds. Their operations were based on different justifications to the European whalers. The Japanese used the whale meat for human consumption and not primarily for the oil, while the Soviet whaling fleet was a state industry and not concerned with profits in a capitalist sense. Japanese and Soviet whalers in this period also explored whaling grounds in the North Pacific Ocean close to the Arctic, thus compensating for the declining stocks in the south. While Antarctic whaling had completely dominated world whaling for several decades, its absolute as well as relative importance was now declining (Figure 16.3). Industrial Soviet and Japanese Antarctic whaling ceased in the late 1970s.

International efforts to protect the whale population gained momentum from the 1970s. The anti-whaling movement had a strong voice in various

---

70 One exception may be Australia. From advocating Antarctic whaling already in the 1890s, the country had never really entered this industry. Renewed plans both in the 1930s and after World War II were very much opposed by Britain and Norway; Wolfe, "Australian Whaling Ambitions".
71 Basberg, "Convergence or National Styles?".
72 Bruijn and Hacquebord, *Een Zee van Traan*, 255ff.
73 Basberg, "Crisis That Never Came"; Bruijn and Hacquebord, *Een Zee van Traan*, 330.

international environmental organizations. Their work was instrumental for the creation of the United Nations Environment Programme (UNEP) in 1972, where the protection of whales was among the important issues. A strategy was also to increase the number of non-whaling countries in the IWC to influence the decision-making.[74]

Until the mid-1980s, some illegal and unreported hunting took place as in many other exploitative industries – now and in times past. Some whaling operations circumvented the regulations that were gradually imposed. But in 1982, the IWC finally passed a moratorium on whaling (in effect from 1986), putting an end to at least the extensive international industry. However, whales in polar waters have not been left in complete peace. Some Indigenous whaling continues in the Arctic, and Japan has in recent years continued limited whaling in Antarctic waters under the banner of 'scientific' whaling. The operations have been under constant attack from the anti-whaling movement for undermining and evading the moratorium.[75] But for all practical purposes, commercial *large-scale* whaling in Antarctic waters – industrial whaling – had come to an end. The decline was long and foreseeable. Despite attempts at voluntary agreements, national controls, and international regulations, Antarctic whaling was allowed to carry on to the point where whale numbers were massively reduced, preventing any basis for a viable industry.

Conclusions

The historical phases of whaling in polar areas possess several dimensions. One relates to the nations involved, another to the hunting grounds. Distinctions can also be made according to the main species that were targeted. There is of course also the fundamental difference between subsistence whaling and commercial whaling. The very earliest forms of whaling were for subsistence, and this form of whaling has persisted in some communities. But large-scale whaling was always commercial in the sense that the whalers sold their production as raw material for industrial use. Indeed, market conditions, prices and government economic policy have throughout the centuries been vital for the development of the industry, in polar areas and elsewhere.

---

74 Tønnessen and Johnsen, *History of Modern Whaling*, 673ff.; Dorsey, *Whales and Nations*, 207ff.
75 A review of the anti-whaling movement and developments in the decade after the moratorium: Ellis, *Men and Whales*, 434ff.

Another important distinction is between whaling that was land-based (shore whaling) and that which was ship-based (bay whaling and pelagic whaling). These two forms existed in parallel and also replaced each other as the predominant form at least twice. When the first whalers ventured into Arctic waters, the whaling was mostly land-based. Flensing and cooking took place ashore. Shore stations that functioned as annexes to the ships were erected on many places along the coasts of Spitsbergen (most notably *Smeerenburg*), Jan Mayen, and Labrador. From the mid-seventeenth century, following the ice edge and the whales, whaling moved further away from the coast and became ship-based. Flensing took place alongside ships, and cooking took place in home ports.

A main element of Svend Foyn's way of organization was to employ a shore station to process the whales brought in from his steam whale-catcher boats. This model was directly transferred to the south and became a standard set-up at the peri-Antarctic islands. Factory ships were introduced at Spitsbergen in 1903 and in Antarctic waters in 1905, and operated in combination with the shore stations. The operations of these factory ships resembled bay whaling of earlier eras. The whales were still flensed alongside. A main difference, however, was that the actual hunting was much more efficient than before, by steam-powered whale chasers with a harpoon cannon and not by small whaleboats with oarsmen and hand-held harpoons.

In the early transition period from north to south, the shore stations were already an established pattern, while the floating factories were still very much in the experimentation stage and much less efficient. 'Shore factories are superior to floating ones', remarked the British government matter-of-factly in 1912 when discussing further whaling licenses at South Georgia.[76] However, a new transition phase occurred in the 1920s. Technological advances paved the way for the last era of pelagic whaling. In this period, from the late 1920s and as long as industrial large-scale whaling lasted, it became the predominant way of organization. In this era, where catches reached an all-time high, whale oil was more than ever a global commodity integrated in a complex international market economy.

With the possible exception of the chartered whaling in the early seventeenth century, this industry was never conducted in a sustainable way. For most of its years, the industry was more concerned with market conditions and profitability than with sustainability and the future of the whale stocks.

---

76 Dispatch from Secretary of State, London to the Colonial Secretary, Stanley, 16 November 1912 (MS 1228/4/3, Scott Polar Research Institute, Cambridge).

Commercial whaling was an exploitative industry with adverse ecological consequences. It not only depleted the whale stocks but also changed the whole polar ecosystem. This behaviour finally led to the end of world whaling.

Bibliography

Aagaard, Bjarne, *Den gamle hvalfangst* (Oslo: Gyldendal, 1933).
Adie, Susan, and Bjørn L. Basberg, "The First Antarctic Whaling Season of Admiralen (1905–1906): The Diary of Alexander Lange", *Polar Record* 45 (2009): 243–263.
Armitage, David, Alison Bashford, and Sujit Sivasundaram, eds., *Oceanic Histories* (Cambridge: Cambridge University Press, 2018).
Auburn, F. M., *The Ross Dependency* (The Hague: M. Nijhoff, 1972).
Avango, Dag, Louwrens Hacquebord, Ypie Aalders, et al., "Between Markets and Geo-politics: Natural Resource Exploitation on Spitsbergen from 1600 to the Present Day", *Polar Record* 47 (2011): 29–39.
Avango, Dag, L. Hacquebord, and U. Wråkberg, "Industrial Extraction of Arctic Natural Resources Since the Sixteenth Century: Technoscience and Geo-economics in the History of Northern Whaling and Mining", *Journal of Historical Geography* 44 (2014): 15–30.
Barr, W., and J. P. C. Watt, "Pioneer Whalers in the Ross Sea, 1923–33", *Polar Record* 41 (2005): 281–304.
Basberg, Bjørn L., "Commercial and Economic Aspects of Antarctic Exploration: From the Earliest Discoveries to the 'Heroic Age'", *The Polar Journal* 7 (2017): 205–226.
Basberg, Bjørn L., "Convergence or National Styles? The Japanese Challenge to the British-Norwegian Hegemony in the Twentieth Century Whaling Industry", in David J. Starkey and Gelina Harlaftis, eds., *Global Markets: The Internationalization of the Sea Transport Industries since 1850*. Research in Maritime History no. 14 (Liverpool University Press, 2018), pp. 259–283.
Basberg, Bjørn L., "A Crisis That Never Came: The Decline of the Antarctic Whaling Industry in the 1950s and 1960s", *The Mariner's Mirror* 99 (2013): 196–211.
Basberg, Bjørn L., "Perspectives on the Economic History of the Antarctic Region", *International Journal of Maritime History* 18 (2006): 285–304.
Basberg, Bjørn L., "Regulating the Natural Resources in the Antarctic Region: A Historical Review", in Andreas R. D. Sanders, Pål T. Sandvik, and Espen Storli, eds., *The Political Economy of Resource Regulation: An International and Comparative History, 1850–2015* (Vancouver: University of British Colombia Press, 2019), pp. 259–276.
Basberg, Bjørn L., *The Shore Whaling Stations at South Georgia: A Study in Antarctic Industrial Archaeology* (Oslo: Novus, 2004).
Baughman, T. H., *Before the Heroes Came: Antarctica in the 1890s* (Lincoln, London: University of Nebraska Press, 1999).
Bockstoce J. R., and D. B. Bodkin, *The Historical Status and Reduction of the Western Arctic Bowhead Whale Population by the Pelagic Whaling Industry*. Final Report to the National Marine Fisheries Service (New Bedford: 1980).

Brandt, Karl, *Whale Oil: An Economic Analysis* (Stanford: Food Research Institute, 1940).
Bruijn, J. R., and L. Hacquebord, *Een Zee van Traan. Vier eeuwen Nederlandse Walvisvaart 1612–1964* (Zutphen: WalburgPers, 2019).
Bull, Henrik J., *The Cruise of the Antarctic to the South Polar Regions* (London: Edward Arnold, 1896).
Burnett, D. G., *The Sounding of the Whale: Science and Cetaceans in the Twentieth Century* (Chicago: University of Chicago Press, 2012).
Campbell, R. J., ed., *The Discoveries of the South Shetland Islands 1819–1829* (London: Hakluyt Society, 2000).
Caulfield, R. A., *Greenlanders, Whales and Whaling: Sustainability and Self-determination in the Arctic* (Hanover, London: University Press of New England, 1997).
Christensen, Lars, *Such Is the Antarctic* (London: Hodder & Stoughton, 1935).
Colnett, J. A., *Voyage to the South Atlantic and Round Cape Horn into the Pacific Ocean* (New York: Da Capo, 1968; a facsimile of the first edition, 1798).
Davis, L. E., R. E. Gallman, and K. Gleiter, *In Pursuit of the Leviathan: Technology, Institutions and Profits in American Whaling 1816–1906* (Chicago: University of Chicago Press, 1997).
De Jong, C., *Geschiedenis van de oude Nederlandse walvisvaart*, Vol. 2 (Johannesburg: privately published, 1978).
Dorsey, K., *Whales and Nations: Environmental Diplomacy on the High Seas* (Seattle: University of Washington Press, 2013).
Ducéré, E., *Recherches historiques sur les corsaires de Saint-Jean-de-Luz: La tradition au Pays Basque* (Donostia: Elkar, 1982).
Ellis, Richard, *Men and Whales* (New York: Alfred A. Knopf, 1991).
Elser, Lloyd, *Whaling and Sealing in Southern New Zealand* (Invercargill: Craigs, 2014).
Faegteborg, Mads, "Inuit Organisation and Whaling Policies", *North Atlantic Studies* 2 (1990): 124–129.
Forster, George, *A Voyage Round the World, in His Britannic Majesty's Sloop, Resolution* (London: B. White et al., 1777).
Fotheringham, Brett I., "The Southern Whale Fishery Company, Auckland Islands", MPhil diss. (Scott Polar Research Institute, University of Cambridge, 1995).
Gustafsson, Ulf, "Icebound Frontiers of Exploitation: Networks for Whaling in the Polar Regions, 1904–1931", PhD diss. (University of Groningen, 2019).
Hacquebord, L., "Hector Station on Deception Island (South Shetland Islands, Antarctica): An Environment Assessment Study of a Whaling Station", *Circumpolar Journal* 7 (1992): 72–97.
Hacquebord, L., "The Jan Mayen Whaling Industry: Its Exploitation of the Greenland Right Whale and Its Impact on the Marine Ecosystem", in Stig Skreslet, ed., *Jan Mayen Island in Scientific Focus* (Dordrecht, Boston, London: Kluwer Academic, 2004), pp. 229–238.
Hacquebord, L., *De Noordse Compagnie* (Zutphen: WalburgPers, 2014).
Hacquebord, L., "Smeerenburg, Het verblijf van Nederlandse walvisvaarders op de westkust van Spitsbergen in de 17de eeuw", PhD diss. (University of Amsterdam, 1984).
Hacquebord, L., and D. Avango, "Industrial Heritage Sites in Spitsbergen (Svalbard), South Georgia and the Antarctic Peninsula: Sources of Historical Information", *Polar Science* 10 (2016): 433–440.

Hacquebord, L., and Dag Avango, "Settlements in an Arctic Resource Frontier Region", *Arctic Anthroplogy* 46 (2009): 25–39.

Hacquebord, L., and W. Vroom, eds., *Walvisvaart in de Gouden Eeuw* (Amsterdam: De Bataafsche Leeuw, 1988).

Hacquebord, L., F. Steenhuisen, and H. Waterbolk, "English and Dutch Whaling Trade and Whaling Stations in Spitsbergen (Svalbard) before 1660", *International Journal of Maritime History* XV (2003): 117–134.

Hart, Ian B., *Pesca: A History of the Pioneer Modern Whaling Company in the Antarctic* (London: Aidan Ellis, 2001).

Hart, Ian B., *Whaling in the Falkland Islands Dependencies 1904–1931* (Newton St Margarets: Pequena, 2006).

Heazle, Michael, *Scientific Uncertainty and the Politics of Whaling* (Seattle: University of Washington Press, 2006),

Jackson, G., *The British Whaling Trade* (London: A&C Black, 1978).

Jackson, Gordon, "Why Did the British Not Catch Rorquals in the Nineteenth Century?", in Bjørn L. Basberg, Jan E. Ringstad, and Einar Wexelsen, eds., *Whaling and History: Perspectives on the Evolution of the Industry*. Publication no. 29 (Sandefjord: Com. Chr. Christensen's Whaling Museum, 1993), p. 117.

Kugler, R. C., "Historical Survey of Foreign Whaling: North America", in H. K. Jacob, K. Snoeijing, and R. Vaughan, eds., *Arctic Whaling* (Groningen: University of Groningen, 1984), pp. 149–157.

Leinenga, J. R., *Arctische walvisvangst in de achttiende eeuw. De betekenis van Straat Davis als vangstgebied* (Amsterdam: De Bataafsche Leeuw, 1995).

Niemi, E., "Svend Foyn i Vadsø – fra helt til skurk?", *Varanger Årbok* (1987): 110–127.

Nordenskjöld, Otto, Johan G. Andersson, and Carl J. Skottsberg, *Antarctica or Two Years Among the Ice of the South Pole* (London: Hurst and Blackett, 1905 [reprinted London: Hurst, 1977]).

Oesau, W., *Hamburgs Grönlandfahrt* (Glückstadt, Hamburg: J. J. Augustin, 1955).

Oesau, W., *Schleswig-Holsteins Grönlandfahrt auf Walfischfang und Robbenschlag* (Glückstadt, Hamburg, New York: J. J. Augustin, 1937).

Proulx, J. P., *Basque Whaling in Labrador in the 16th Century. Studies in Archaeology, Architecture and History* (Ottawa: Parks Service Environment, 1993).

Proulx, J. P., *Whaling in the North Atlantic from Earliest Times to the Mid-19th Century* (Ottawa: Parks Canada, 1986).

Risting, Sigurd, *Av hvalfangstens historie*. Publication No. 2 (Kristiania: Cappelen, Publikasjon nr. 2 fra Kom. Chr. Christensens Hvalfangstmuseum, 1922).

Ross, W. Gillies, "The Annual Catch of Greenland (Bowhead) Whale in Waters North of Canada, 1719–1915", *Arctic* 32 (1979): 91–121.

Sanger, Chesley W., *Scottish Arctic Whaling* (Edinburgh: John Donald, 2016).

Schmitt, Frederick, Cornelis de Jong, and Frank H. Winter, *Thomas Welcome Roys: America's Pioneer of Modern Whaling* (Charlottesville: University Press of Virginia, 1980).

Scoresby, William, *An Account of the Arctic Regions with a History and Description of the Northern Whale-Fishery*, 2 vols. (London: Constable, 1820 [reprinted Redwood, 1969]).

Spence, B., *Harpooned: The Story of Whaling* (Greenwich: Conway Maritime Press, 1980).

Starbuck, Alexander, *History of the American Whale Fishery* (Secaucus: Castle, 1989).

Stevenson, M., A. Madsen, and E. Maloney, eds., *The Anthropology of Community-Based Whaling in Greenland* (Edmonton: Canadian Circumpolar Press, 1997).

Sugdon, D., *Arctic and Antarctic: A Modern Geographical Synthesis* (Oxford: Blackwell, 1983).

Templeton, Malcolm, *A Wise Adventure: New Zealand in Antarctica 1920–1960* (Wellington: Victoria University Press, 2000).

Tønnessen, Joh N., and Arne O. Johnsen, *Den moderne hvalfangsts historie*, 5 vols (Sandefjord: Norges Hvalfangstforbund, 1959–1971); abridged version in English by Joh N. Tønnessen, *The History of Modern Whaling* (London: Hurst, 1982).

Tuck, J., and R. Grenier, *Red Bay, Labrador: World Whaling Capital A.D. 1550–1600* (St John's: Atlantic Archaeology Ltd, 1989).

Turgeon, L., "Pêches basques en Atlantique Nord: XVII–XVIII siècle; étude d'économie maritime", PhD diss. (Centre d'Études Canadiennes Bordeaux, 1982).

van Sante, G., *Alphabetische naam-lyst van alle de Groenlandsche en Straat-Davissche commandeurs. die zedert 1700 op Groenland en zedert het jaar 1719 op Straat-Davis voor Holland en andere Provincien hebben gevaren* (Haarlem: Joh. Enschede, 1770).

Vaughan, R., "Historical Survey of the European Whaling Industry", in H. K. Jacob, K. Snoeijing, and R. Vaughan, eds., *Arctic Whaling* (Groningen: University of Groningen, 1984), pp. 121–134.

Vickers, D., "The First Whalemen of Nantucket", *William and Mary Quarterly* 40 (1983): 561–583.

Watson, Norman, *The Dundee Whalers* (East Linton: Tuckwell, 2003).

Webb, Robert L., *On the Northwest: Commercial Whaling in the Pacific Northwest 1790–1967* (Vancouver: University of British Columbia Press, 1988).

Wolfe, Adam, "Australian Whaling Ambitions and Antarctica", *International Journal of Maritime History* 18 (2006): 305–322.

17
A Historical Archaeology of the First Antarctic Labourers (Nineteenth Century)

MELISA A. SALERNO, M. JIMENA CRUZ, AND
ANDRÉS ZARANKIN

Introduction

The history of commercial sealing and sealers' lives can be understood within the context of capitalism. Sealing was traditionally carried out by different socio-cultural groups over time, mainly as a low-scale activity that attempted to meet the needs of specific communities (some examples including sealing by hunter-gatherers from Alaska and Tierra del Fuego, among others).[1] In the late eighteenth and early nineteenth centuries, sealing acquired new features within the context of modernity, as it was transformed into a large-scale activity with a trading purpose. Commercial sealing responded to a market logic, and it helped to connect different contexts where the exploitation of resources, the manufacture of products, and trade in raw materials and industrial goods took place.[2]

The focus of exploitation was on seals and elephant seals. While the former were hunted for their skins and/or for their oil (fur seals being well-known for the quality of their dense underfur), the latter were sought for their blubber, as their skins were considered to be useless.[3] Skins and blubber were used in the production of a wide range of articles (see below). Commercial sealing, which we refer to simply as sealing from now on, emerged during the second half of the eighteenth century with the fall of the sea otter skin trade, when sea otters were almost driven to extinction due to over-exploitation. Furthermore, it was

---
1 Salerno, "Persona y cuerpo-vestido".
2 Stackpole, *Voyages*; Richards, *Commercial Exploitation*; Richards, *Sealing*; Berguño, "Shetland del Sur. Primera parte"; Berguño, "Shetland del Sur. Segunda parteñ".
3 Cooper Busch, *War Against the Seals*; Dickinson, "History of Sealing".

connected with the growth of commercial whaling, with which it shared some features, such as the exploitation of animal resources in overseas territories, the simultaneous presence of seals and whales in some areas, and the existence of similarities in some of the tools and techniques used for hunting and/or processing resources.

From a global perspective, the exploitation of seals and elephant seals involved the participation of different nations. However, the United Kingdom and the United States played a leading role in terms of the number of vessels involved, the geographical range of the operations, the amount of resources obtained, and the proceeds from the sale of the products.[4] The United Kingdom had a long seafaring tradition. Meanwhile, the United States actively engaged in the maritime trade from the late eighteenth century.[5]

Seals and elephant seals were harvested at a range of islands in the Southern Ocean, including Desolation and Heard Islands as well as those around Patagonia, the Antarctic Peninsula, and South Georgia.[6] Sealing companies preferred to work in distant lands where states had no means to ensure effective control over exploitation. When sealers found a new hunting ground, they tried to keep its location secret to avoid competition. The secret still tended to leak out, and other sealers would arrive at the recently discovered hunting ground in the following seasons. This incentivized rapid exploitation with no regard to the long-term survival of animal colonies, killing animals of all ages and sexes, regardless of the breeding cycle. Within a few years, the logic of competition and over-exploitation made any given location no longer profitable, encouraging a constant search for new hunting grounds.[7]

Sealers could sell their raw materials to different markets. One of the first trading ports for the sealing industry was Canton (today known as Guangzhou). Chinese merchants wanted sealskins for the manufacture of coats, suitcases, and trunks. In exchange, sealers could receive money or commodities such as tea and china (which were later sold in the West at a profit). As time went by, both London and New York became centres for consumer products, where sealskins were used for clothes and hats for the

---

4 Basberg and Headland, "Economic Significance"; Headland, *Chronological List*; Stackpole, *Voyages*.
5 Putney, *Black Sailors*; Mayorga, "Actividad lobera temprana".
6 Clark, "Antarctic Fur-Seal"; Cooper Busch, *War Against the Seals*; Richards, *Commercial Exploitation*; Smith, *New Zealand Sealing Industry*; Pearson, "Charting the Sealing Islands".
7 Zarankin and Senatore, *Historias de un pasado*; Senatore et al., "Historias bajo cero".

fashion industry. In all cases, the creation and spread of new technologies (including the separation of the underfur from the stiffer outer hairs, and the possibility of transforming the fur into felt and the skin into leather) were crucial to increasing demand for sealskins.[8] Meanwhile, the oil extracted from elephant seal blubber was frequently sold at European or American home ports, as a good substitute for whale oil. It was odourless and produced no smoke, and could be used for lighting, producing lubricants for machinery, wool softener, and other purposes.[9]

The sealing industry employed a substantial workforce. A sealing port could have a fleet of several sealing vessels, each with a sealing crew of ten to twenty-five men, depending on the size of the vessel and the number of boats taken.[10] Although there were multiple reasons for a man to join the industry, the promise of fortune and the desire to visit exotic lands were relevant. Being a sealer demanded specific skills as a sailor and hunter.[11] The job could be physically strenuous, and living conditions harsh, torn between the vessels and the hunting grounds. A sealing voyage from the United Kingdom or the United States to the South Seas could last a year or more. Sealers spent most of the time on board the vessels. Meanwhile, the time spent in the sealing grounds could represent one-third of the length of the voyage. Attention to both of these contexts is necessary to understand sealers' lives.

At the end of the eighteenth century, sealers were already operating on the coasts of South America.[12] The discovery of the South Shetland Islands (the closest region of Antarctica to the American continent) took place in the early nineteenth century. News of the abundant marine resources on the islands attracted a large number of sealers in the next summer season, and sealing continued in three distinct cycles (Figure 17.1).[13] The first was the shortest, lasting from 1820 to 1825, but it was the most intense in terms of both numbers of ships and volume of catch. The second and the third sealing cycles were longer – the second taking place between the 1830s and the 1850s,

---

8 Cooper Busch, *War Against the Seals*; Smith, *New Zealand Sealing Industry*; Burton, "From Shoes to Shawls".
9 Cooper Busch, *War Against the Seals*; Maddison, *Class and Colonialism*; Pearson, "Charting the Sealing Islands".
10 Clark, "Antarctic Fur-Seal"; Cruz, "Memórias".
11 Stackpole, *Voyages*; Salerno, "Persona y cuerpo-vestido".
12 Cooper Busch, *War Against the Seals*; Silva, "La pesca"; Mameli, "La gestión"; Caviglia, *Malvinas*; Mayorga, "Actividad lobera temprana"; Salerno et al., "Explorando bitácoras".
13 Martinic, "Navegantes norteamericanos"; Berguño, "Shetland del Sur. Primera parte"; Berguño, "Shetland del Sur. Segunda parte".

Number of Vessels

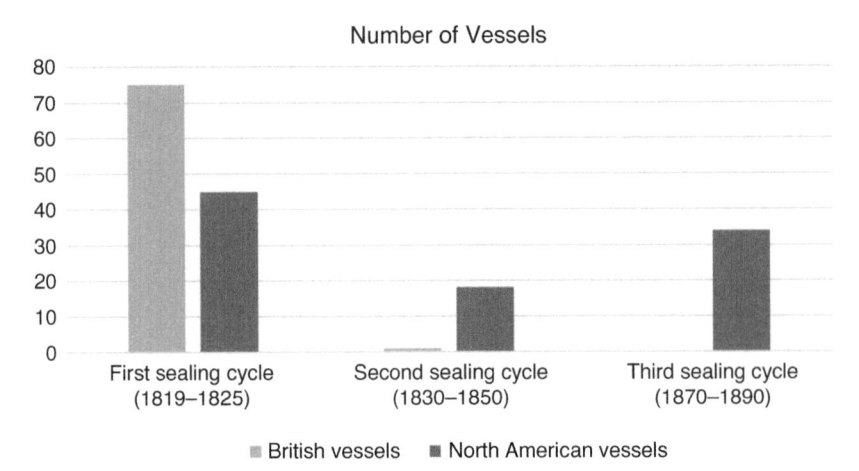

[Bar chart showing number of sealing vessels:
- First sealing cycle (1819–1825): British vessels ~75, North American vessels ~45
- Second sealing cycle (1830–1850): North American vessels ~19
- Third sealing cycle (1870–1890): North American vessels ~34

Legend: British vessels, North American vessels]

Figure 17.1 Number of sealing vessels bound to the South Shetland Islands per sealing cycle and nationality. (Chart based on information provided by Headland, 2018.)

and the third between the 1870s and the 1890s. Each period involved a smaller number of vessels, and a smaller amount of resources taken than in the previous cycle.[14] The time space between one cycle and the next was essential for animal colonies to start recovering. However, the impact of the first cycle was so great as to make it impossible for the population of seals and elephant seals to reach their original figures. The exploitation was also influenced by fluctuations in the global demand for sealing products over time.

Sealers were the first group of people to visit the South Shetland Islands, contributing to the exploration, charting, and description of the region.[15] They represented the dominant presence in the archipelago for almost a century. Between the 1820s and the 1890s, more than 180 sealing vessels are estimated to have sailed to the South Shetlands. Considering that each sealing crew was made up of an average of twenty men, then more than 3,600 sealers could have visited the region during the period (although some people could have sailed to the islands more than once). Notwithstanding, historical research has particularly focused on Antarctica's Heroic Age, when explorers supported by national powers sought to extend the geographical and scientific knowledge of the region between the late nineteenth and the early twentieth centuries. Moreover, when historical researchers have examined

---

14 Basberg and Headland, "Economic Significance". 15 Pearson, "'Knowing'".

17 Historical Archaeology of Antarctic Labourers

the presence of sealers on the South Shetland Islands, their interest has primarily been on the circumstances surrounding the discovery of the archipelago, the actions carried out by some sealing captains, the chronology of the voyages to the region, or the length and productivity of the sealing cycles.[16] Although there could be multiple reasons for ordinary sealers to be made invisible, one reason could be a certain lack of interest in anonymous groups.[17]

The 'Landscapes in White' research project is an international research programme interested in learning more about the early incorporation of Antarctica into modernity.[18] Focusing mainly on historical archaeology, the project discusses how the South Shetland Islands were integrated into capitalism through sealing exploitation. Antarctica has particular features, including that it never had a native population, with climate and weather conditions that are extreme for human presence. Viewing Antarctica through the lens of capitalism gives us a chance to see the continent not as absolute 'otherness', nor as a place completely different and bearing no comparison to others.[19] Furthermore, it allows us to think about its multiple connections with other regions of the world. Sealing vessels came to Antarctica from other continents, the resources taken from the South Shetland Islands were sold in distant markets, and the sealers who worked in the archipelago were hired by private companies.

Much can be learned through the use of historical archaeology, with contributions from other disciplines such as history, anthropology, and heritage conservation. Historical archaeology can be defined as the study of people's lives within the context of modernity. The discipline takes into consideration the material aspects of existence, focusing on the dialogue between information provided by documentary records and archaeological remains.[20] Although historical sources on sealing were rarely written by ordinary workers, some of these documents contain references to life on the South Shetland Islands. However, without a doubt the great majority of

---

16 O'Gorman, "Return"; Smith and Simpson, "Early Nineteenth Century"; Harrowfield, "Archaeology on Ice".
17 Senator and Zarankin, "Widening the Scope"; Zarankin et al., "From the Antarctic".
18 Zarankin and Senator, "Arqueología en Antártida"; Zarankin and Senator, "'Estrategias y tácticas'"; Zarankin and Senator, "Archaeology in Antarctica"; Zarankin and Senator, *Historias de un pasado*; Senator and Zarankin, "Arqueología histórica y expansión"; Zarankin et al., "Paisagens em Branco".
19 Pena, "Negociando gêneros".
20 Johnson, *Archaeology of Capitalism*; Orser, *Historical Archaeology*; Hall, *Archaeology of Modern World*; Wilkie, "Documentary Archaeology".

source material is archaeological traces, which could be produced by all people who worked and lived at the sealing sites, regardless of their rank and skills.[21] Therefore, the remains of structures and objects provide an opportunity for researchers to access previously unknown details on workers' stories.

In this chapter we will discuss who the ordinary sealers were who made up the workforce of Antarctic sealing exploitation, and how these people led their lives within the framework of the capitalist system in which they worked. With that aim in mind, in the first section of this work we will look at the recruitment and composition of the sealing crews, and the organization of their subsistence and work on board the sealing vessels. Although the ports of departure and the vessels were not part of the Antarctic territory, what happened at these locations is relevant to understanding these people's existence during the voyages bound for Antarctica as a whole. In the second section we will examine the organization of sealers' subsistence and work on the hunting grounds of the South Shetland Islands. For the sealing vessels and the Antarctic hunting grounds, we will consider the analysis of specific sets of practices involving work and subsistence, such as sailing, killing, and processing; and habitation, feeding, and clothing. Special attention will be paid to the degree of control that capitalist companies could have exercised over sealers' practices.

Sealing Crews and Life on Board the Vessels

The sealing vessels that operated on the South Shetland Islands came from different corners of the world. Despite sharing some general features, the crews of sealing vessels could have presented specific characteristics concerning the recruitment of the men, the composition of the groups, and subsistence and work on board the vessels. Therefore, in this section we will focus on the case of the American fleet (given its importance in the exploitation of Antarctic resources during the entire nineteenth century). Shipping articles, crew lists, and logbooks of sealing voyages that were bound to the South Shetland Islands, and that were preserved by American institutions, will provide significant information, as will published narratives.

According to information provided by logbooks, most of the crew of these vessels were hired in the ports of departure, while a smaller portion of the

---

21 Zarankin and Senatore, "Arqueología en Antártida"; Zarankin and Senatore, "Archaeology in Antarctica"; Senatore and Zarankin, "Arqueología histórica y expansión".

men could have been recruited in intermediate locations on the way southwards. Some of these places corresponded with well-established and organized ports of call like the Azores. In other places, like Patagonia and Tierra del Fuego, sealing captains could have taken advantage of an Indigenous workforce, considering that native people were traditionally skilful in hunting seals.[22] In the United States, the owners of the companies (that is to say, the people who provided the initial capital for the sealing voyages – including the vessels, the hunting and processing equipment, the advance payment for the sealers, etc.) resorted to agents to facilitate recruitment. As in the case of the whaling industry, agents were in charge of advertizing the search for workers both in port towns and in other cities located in the interior of the country. The agents selected the men who made up the crews. Furthermore, they offered some sort of guidance for fitting out for sea (especially in the case of first-time sealers, known as green hands).[23]

Physical appearance could have been important in the selection of the men,[24] as it was thought that 'constitution' could provide relevant tools to define the body's ability to cope with the harshness of the work. The 'constitution' was understood as the particular 'frame or temperament of the human body',[25] and it was supposed to express – among other things – some sort of relationship between height and weight. Surgeons sometimes examined the health of the candidates.[26] As in the case of whaling,[27] most sealing companies expected to hire a larger number of rookies than experienced sailors and hunters because they could be paid far less, were much more obedient, and were less likely to desert than other employees. Even though some other industries of the time might have considered 'complexion' ('the colour of the skin, particularly of the face'[28]) as a significant criterion of recruitment, in the case of the whaling and sealing industries there seems to have existed much more flexibility.[29]

The men who were hired in American ports had to sign shipping articles establishing a contract with the captain of the vessel. These articles stipulated the nature and the length of the voyage, the destination of the vessel, and the money the employee would receive in return for his labour.[30] As in the case of whaling,[31] payment was equivalent to certain 'lays' or 'shares' of the final

22 Stehberg, *Arqueología histórica antártica*.
23 Browne, *Etchings*; Holmes, *Arctic Whalemen*.   24 Salerno, "Persona y cuerpo-vestido".
25 Webster, *American Dictionary*, 219.   26 Davis, *Nimrod of the Sea*.
27 Nordhoff, *Whaling and Fishing*.   28 Webster, *American Dictionary*, 202.
29 Putney, *Black Sailors*; McKissack and McKissack, *Black Hands, White Sails*.
30 Butts, *Every Sailor*; Dana, *Seaman's Friend*.
31 Davis et al., *In Pursuit of Leviathan*; Currie, *Thar She Blows*.

proceeds of the journey, and it varied depending on the rank of the worker – which could go from approximately 1/15th in the case of the captain, to 1/175th in the case of an inexperienced sealer.[32] This system was highly beneficial to sealing companies, as they were not obliged to pay fixed sums of money, and sealers' prospects of receiving larger remunerations sometimes stimulated their productivity. Despite their commitment, the men were usually paid far less than expected. On the one hand, the money that sealing companies paid in advance was eventually deducted from labourers' payment. On the other hand, sealing companies often waited to sell their products in order to get higher profits in the market. As a result, sealers could experience delays in their remuneration, forcing them to engage in a new sealing voyage to survive.

Crew lists were part of a ship's papers, and they consisted of a list describing the name, rank, birthplace, place of residence, and sometimes the complexion and height of each man on board (especially as a means to individualize them). They had to be delivered to the customs office of the port by the captain before departing,[33] and when a vessel returned home, the captain had to account for the men in the list, certifying the whereabouts of those who were not present (for instance, through notes provided by a consular office in cases of sickness, desertion, etc.). As in any other vessel (be it merchant or military), the crew of a sealing vessel was hierarchically organized by ranks, and responded to a clear division of labour.[34] The captains represented the interests of the companies and were the leading authority during the voyages. The officers were in charge of making the men comply with the captain's orders. The carpenter, the cooper, the cook, and some other employees undertook specific tasks. Seamen were the necessary workforce to sail the vessel and carry out the hunting. They were the lower rank in sealing expeditions, and they were generally divided into two groups depending on their experience: 'able seamen' (those who had previously acquired sealing skills) and 'green hands' (those who were new to the business and needed special training).[35]

The crew lists associated with sealing voyages to the South Shetland Islands show other forms of diversity beyond rank and status. Men frequently declared different birthplaces. While many were from the United States, others came from Europe, Africa, or even Oceania. Within the United States, sealers could come from port towns or other locations in the interior of the country. Some sealing crews could have been racially heterogeneous.

32 Putney, *Black Sailors*.   33 Putney, *Black Sailors*; Bolster, *Black Jacks*.
34 Stehberg, *Arqueología histórica antártica*.
35 Salerno, "Persona y cuerpo-vestido"; Salerno, "Sealers".

17 Historical Archaeology of Antarctic Labourers

Crew lists show the presence of sailors and even officers and captains with non-white complexion.[36] Even though racial differences have been studied in the case of the whaling industry,[37] there is still much to discuss in the case of sealing (in particular within the context of nineteenth-century Antarctic exploration and exploitation). Finally, it is worth mentioning that sealing crews also presented differences of age. While most of the men were between fifteen and thirty years old,[38] the youngest workers could have included the cabin boys and the green hands; and the older ones the captains, the officers, and the able seamen.

Before being embarked on the vessels, sealers had to prepare a 'sea-chest' containing personal articles for the voyages. As in the case of whaling, sealing companies made advance payments so that the workers could do some shopping in 'outfitting stores'.[39] The outfitters maintained close relationships with the owners of the sealing companies. In this way, the money paid in advances rapidly found its way back to the owners. Outfitting stores were well-known for selling low-quality products at inflated prices. Their main customers were green hands, who did not know which sort of products were essential for the work.[40] A sealer's sea-chest could have included dark-coloured pants, frocks, and jackets in light or heavy fabrics (such as woollen, canvas, duck, and waterproof materials); plain or striped shirts in different colours and textiles (including flannel, cotton, and bast fibres); undershirts and stockings; shoes, boots, and pumps; hats and caps. Furthermore, it could have contained some other articles such as tin pots, spoons, knives, blankets, needles, and thread.[41]

In American port towns, wholesale stores provided the vessels with provisions and equipment. Specialized journals (devoted to whaling and sealing – such as the *Whalemen's Shipping List and Merchants' Transcript, 1843–1914*) presented advertisements containing references to ship stores and their products.[42] The analysis of these and other historical documents (such as logbooks) shows some degree of standardization in the type of food that wholesale stores supplied to merchant vessels. Sealing companies frequently bought large quantities of industrially produced articles (salted meat, sea biscuits, etc.), as they represented ready-to-eat meals which could be

---

36 Salerno, "Persona y cuerpo-vestido".
37 Putney, *Black Sailors*; McKissack and McKissack, *Black Hands, White Sails*.
38 Cruz, "Memórias".
39 Salerno, "Persona y cuerpo-vestido"; Salerno, "Sealers"; Salerno et al., "Explorando bitácoras".
40 Nordhoff, *Whaling and Fishing*; Holmes, *Arctic Whalemen*; Davis, *Nimrod of the Sea*.
41 Salerno, "Persona y cuerpo-vestido".   42 Salerno, "Persona y cuerpo-vestido".

preserved for a long time. Fresh food (apples, lemons, strawberries, plums, cheese, etc.) and different ingredients (flour, sugar, rice, salt, vinegar, beans, etc.) were also bought in the United States.[43] Products of different qualities and prices were chosen by different sealing companies, perhaps for different ranks on board. Sealing vessels bought fresh fruit and vegetables from the Azores (for preventing scurvy). On the coasts of Patagonia and Tierra del Fuego sealers could hunt, gather, and trade with Indigenous groups, participating in their own system of food supply.[44]

Following a maritime tradition, the sealing captains decided what and how much food would be provided to the crew. On board the vessels, a designated cook prepared the meals, as the rest of the men were supposed to attend to other duties. The cook possibly prepared specific dishes for the captain, the officers and the men (including different types, qualities and amounts of products).[45] Meals were served at specific times, helping to organize the daily routine at sea. While the captain and the officers ate in the cabin, the rest of the men ate in the forecastle.[46] Differences in the ways that meals were prepared, served, and consumed probably reflected hierarchical differences among the crew.

Social differences might also have become evident in clothing. As in other merchant vessels, the captain, the officers and the men who made up the sealing crews could have worn different garments on board. Moreover, each of these ranks might have had access to articles of different qualities and in different quantities.[47] The activities carried out by each rank had a differential impact on people's dressed bodies. Seamen's clothes often became dirty and torn, and it was difficult for men to find new clothes during the voyages. While in some cases they could have bought specific articles in intermediate ports, there was always the 'slop chest' (a stock of merchandise, including clothes and tobacco, which was sold by the merchant companies and the captains). However, as these articles were expensive and later deducted from the lays or shares, the men did everything they could to avoid them. Sewing, patching, and even knitting were abilities that sailors acquired through necessity.

As with all merchant ships, the inner space of sealing vessels was divided into different sections. This segmentation helped to produce and reproduce people's ranks on board[48] (Figure 17.2). While the upper level corresponded to the deck, the intermediate level accommodated the lower deck, and the

43 Cruz, "Incorporando comidas e contextos". 44 Salerno et al., "Explorando bitácoras".
45 Salerno et al., "Inside or Outside Capitalism?".
46 Nordhoff, *Whaling and Fishing*; O'Gorman, "Return".
47 Salerno, "Persona y cuerpo-vestido". 48 Salerno, "Sealers".

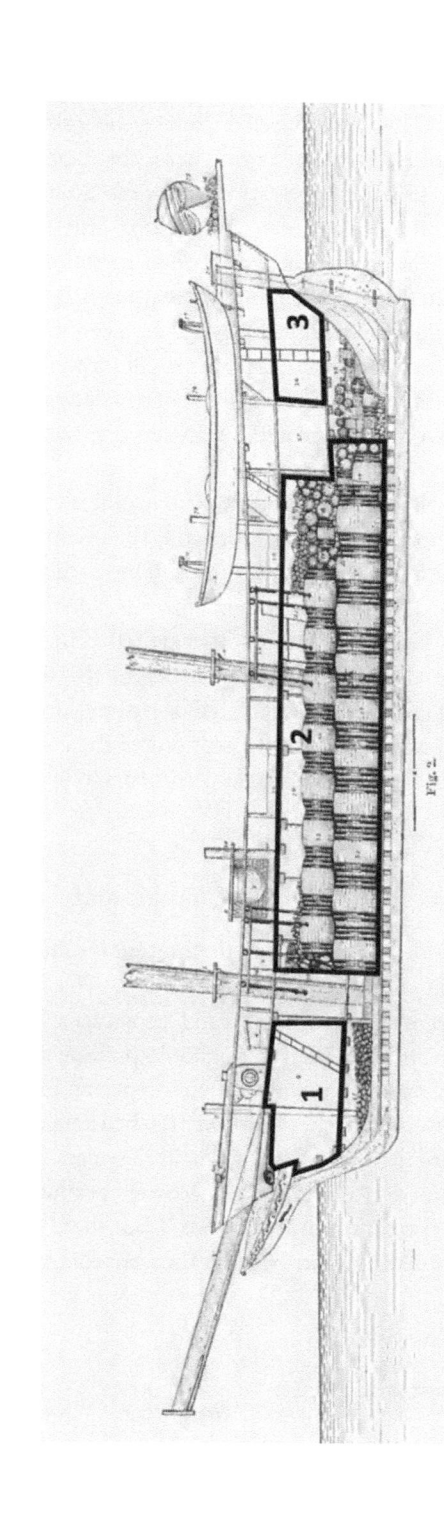

Figure 17.2 Some spaces clearly defined in a nineteenth-century schooner: 1. forecastle, 2. hold, and 3. carbin. (Drawing modified from Clark, "Antarctic Fur-Seal".)

lowest served as the hold. The lower deck included the cabin and the forecastle. The cabin was located in the stern. There, the captain had his own rooms, while the officers had their private state-rooms. Some members of the crew, including the carpenter, the cooper, and so on, sometimes shared a room next to the cabin. The forecastle was located in the bow, and it represented an undifferentiated space where all the seamen had their bunks arranged in rows. This place had no furniture, except for a central table (and the sea-chests which were used as chairs). As it was small for the number of people living there, the forecastle tended to be an over-crowded space, where the boundaries of privacy were transgressed, and everyone shared similar living conditions.

Time on board the vessels was organized through different shifts and watches.[49] During working hours, seamen's duties could be oriented towards navigation or preparation for the hunting grounds. The particularities of these activities became evident during the training process.[50] In the first part of the voyage, the green hands had to learn how to run up the rigging, handle the sails, and help with the cleaning and maintenance of the ship. As the vessels got near the hunting grounds, the green hands had to learn to pull or row (so the men could land and cover specific sections of the coast), and fit the whaleboats with the necessary supplies and instruments to live and work ashore.

Sealers' Lives on the South Shetland Islands

In order to discuss sealers' lives on the Antarctic hunting grounds, we will resort to documentary and archaeological information. The documents considered by the research include logbooks and accounts of American sealing voyages to the South Shetland Islands. Logbooks provide information on sealing strategies, including the landing of men at specific locations for a varied length of time.[51] However, as they were written by captains or mates who often remained on board the vessels, many details of sealers' lives on the archipelago were not described in these sources. Voyage accounts provide a general picture of sealers' presence on the islands,[52] but these documents are few in number, and they usually describe what the narrators found as the

---

49 Butts, *Every Sailor*; Dana, *Seaman's Friend*.
50 Salerno, "Persona y cuerpo-vestido"; Salerno, "Sealers".
51 Stackpole, *Voyages*; Salerno and Cruz, "Between Words and Oceans".
52 See, for instance, Weddell, *Voyage*; Ames, *Mariner's Sketches*; Fanning, *Voyages Round the World*.

17 Historical Archaeology of Antarctic Labourers

most outstanding circumstances surrounding a specific visit to the South Shetlands.

Archaeological work on the South Shetland Islands has shown that most sealing sites identified so far were located on Livingston Island (the second largest island in the region); particularly on Byers Peninsula (at the westernmost tip of Livingston Island). Archaeological findings recovered by the 'Landscapes in White' project[53] on Byers Peninsula include dozens of structures, and hundreds of objects and animal remains, among others (Figure 17.3). They represent the material traces left behind by ordinary sealers while they worked and lived on the archipelago, giving an insight into the diversity of workers' practices and experiences.[54] Archaeological and documentary sources have different natures and need to be approached

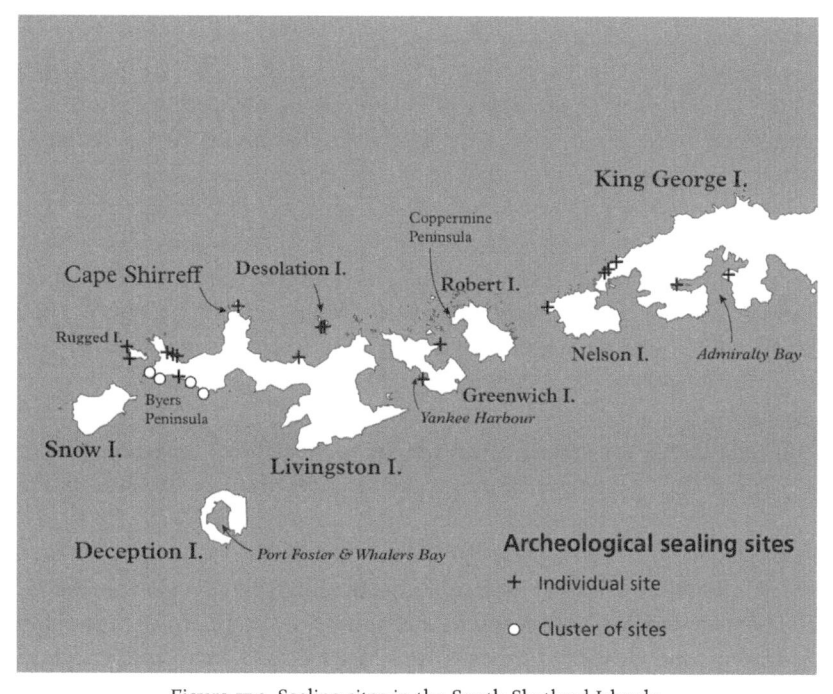

Figure 17.3 Sealing sites in the South Shetland Islands.

53 Zarankin and Senatore, "'Estrategias y tácticas'"; Zarankin and Senatore, "Ocupación humana"; Zarankin and Senatore, "Archaeology in Antarctica"; Zarankin and Senatore, *Historias de un pasado*; Zarankin et al., "Paisagens em Branco".
54 Salerno and Zarankin, "En busca".

through different methods. However, it is possible and relevant to create a dialogue between both lines of evidence.

When sealing vessels arrived at the South Shetland Islands, they immediately started exploration. Even after the first sealing cycle, exploration was essential to understand the distribution and size of animal colonies. When resources were located, the general strategy was to land sealers on specific areas of the shores. According to logbooks, the length of each landing and the decision to establish an encampment depended largely on the abundance of resources. When animals were scarce, the men could have stayed for a couple of hours to a couple of days at a given location.[55] When they found their prey in large quantities, sealers could have spent from days to one or more months at a single place. This affected the organization of the sealers' lives on the islands and produced different archaeological footprints.

When landings only lasted a couple of hours, the men would return to the vessels with the product of their work without building a shelter.[56] For landings of a couple of days, they might shelter from the weather either by resorting to caves (when they were available), or by up turning their boats and sleeping under the wooden structures.[57] However, when they stayed ashore for longer periods, they often found it worthwhile to expend energy on the construction of a shelter. Archaeological evidence suggests that sealers often used outcrops as one side of the structures (an efficient way to reduce work and get protection from weather), and they piled up local stones to build the rest of the walls (Figure 17.4). For the roofs, they often used whale ribs and pieces of wood (occasionally found on the shores from previously wrecked boats). The roofs could be covered with animal skins or old pieces of canvas brought from the vessels.[58]

Sealing camps showed differences in the number, size, and shape of their structures. These were possibly associated with the number and composition of the sealing gangs, the length of the landings, and whether seals or elephant seals were hunted and processed at a specific location.[59] Archaeologists have often distinguished between structures devoted to habitation and to work.[60] The latter had no internal divisions, even though the space was sometimes organized by the presence of hearths and whale vertebrae used as seats.

---

55 Salerno and Cruz, "Between Words and Oceans".
56 Salerno and Cruz, "Between Words and Oceans".
57 Pearson, "Living Under Their Boats".
58 Salerno, *Arqueología de la indumentaria*; Zarankin and Senatore, *Historias de un pasado*; Senatore et al., "Historias bajo cero".
59 Senatore, "Antarctic Historical Sealing".
60 Zarankin and Senatore, *Historias de un pasado*; Zarankin et al., "Paisagens em Branco".

17 Historical Archaeology of Antarctic Labourers

Figure 17.4 Three-dimensional modelling of Cerro Negro sealing site on Livingston Island. Note that the camp consists of four different structures that were built on one of the walls of a rocky outcrop. (Images produced by LEACH-UFMG.)

Material remains associated with food, clothing, leisure time, and so on were found inside them. Shelters possibly devoted to work were smaller. Some enclosures may have served as storage locations for sealskins. Meanwhile, other places dominated by the presence of large hearths may have contained the try-works where the blubber was boiled in order to extract oil.

Even though sealing gangs could have gathered people from different ranks, everybody ended up sharing the same shelter and similar living conditions. As these structures had no internal divisions, there was no room devoted to officers or specific groups of people. The inner space was rather small and, in general, it did not exceed 15 m². The walls were low (approximately 1.2 m tall), owing to limitations in construction materials and the need to keep the structure safe from winds and storms. The shelters were enclosed and dark spaces, dominated by the smoke produced by hearths, and intended to separate the men from weather conditions and constant sunlight. The structures were always crowded, and the boundaries of individual space were easily transgressed by the close presence of others. Within the shelters, everybody was forced to remain kneeling, sitting, or lying down.

Working activities on the South Shetland Islands were devoted to hunting and processing fur seals (*Arctocephalus gazella*) or elephant seals (*Mirounga leonina*). According to documentary sources, the best way to take seals on the shores was to form a lane of men, driving the animals through and knocking them on the head as they huddled together. After the seals were stunned, the men stabbed them in the chest until they were dead.[61] However, as time went by and seals became scarcer and more elusive, sealers resorted to shooting at the seals from a distance (accepting the possibility of damaging the skins). Hunting elephant seals demanded specific techniques. They could be stunned by similar means, but they were killed either with lances, or with gunshots to the head for larger animals.[62]

As hunting took place on the beaches, exposed to the full impact of weather and the ocean, animal carcasses were not often preserved.[63] Moreover, as sealers took care of their hunting tools and did not tend to leave them behind, these artefacts are rarely found. Researchers working on Byers Peninsula have nevertheless been able to recover a series of wooden clubs (some of them with iron rings on the end section to increase the effectiveness of the blows), several pieces of ammunition,[64] leather and wooden sheaths for knives, and an axe with a wooden handle, among others. The variety of these pieces clearly indicates the existence of complex and heterogeneous toolkits.

Historical documents suggest that processing activities started immediately after the seals had been killed. To skin the animals, the hunters cut first around the seal's neck; then down through the chest; and finally around the body, above the flippers. There were different techniques to prepare the skins, and they probably varied through time and considering the demands of specific markets (with the Canton market preferring dried skins, and the American and British markets preferring salted products during the early nineteenth century). If the sealskins were dried, as much blubber as possible was scraped off the skin. Then small holes were made near the edges, and the skins were pegged out on the ground. Drying the skins could take several days, depending on weather conditions. If the sealskins were salted, then some blubber was left on the pelts, and the skins were piled up and left to sweat for a couple of days. Afterwards, they were salted, taking good care to rub the inner surface, and placed in casks or bins.[65]

Processing elephant seals was rather different. First the animals were skinned.[66] Then the blubber was removed and cut into pieces of a given

---

61 Delano, *Narrative of Voyages*; Clark, "Antarctic Fur-Seal".   62 Ames, *Mariner's Sketches*.
63 Cruz, "Memórias".   64 Nolasco, "Pessoas".
65 Delano, *Narrative of Voyages*; Fanning, *Voyages Round the World*; Clarke, *Wreck of the 'Favorite'*.
66 Clark, "Antarctic Fur-Seal".

17 Historical Archaeology of Antarctic Labourers

size, usually called 'horse pieces' (as a machine called the 'horse' – especially popular in the whaling industry – could sometimes be used to carry out this task). These pieces were placed in large trying pots to extract oil. The scraps of blubber were sometimes pressed to get extra product, and they were later used as fuel. The oil was usually stored in wooden casks. On some occasions, the trying pots remained on the vessels, and the men had to transport the pieces of blubber on board (sometimes holding the latter on a 'rafting line' that connected the beach with the vessel).[67] In some other cases, the trying pots were established on the shores, and the men had to find a suitable way of transporting the heavy casks.

Beyond the realm of production, it is relevant to consider the particularities of other social practices on the South Shetlands – such as eating and clothing. Historical documents suggest that sealing gangs often took a limited number of supplies from the vessels.[68] The latter could have included coffee, molasses, alcoholic beverages, sea biscuits, and portions of pork and beef, as also observed in the food remains in sealers' shelters, particularly around the hearths. Historical sources as well as archaeological evidence also show that the men often had to resort to local resources. In particular, they ate the meat of seals and birds,[69] and gathered some eggs. Considering that choices were limited, and that cooking could have been carried out by anyone in the camp, all the men had access to the same meals. Eating food brought from the vessels might have made the men recall their lives in previous contexts, including their hometowns or the ports of departure. In the same way, the incorporation of local resources could have introduced sealers to new flavours and experiences, helping them to become acquainted with the Antarctic territory.[70]

Textile garments and leather shoes have also been found within housing structures (Figure 17.4). Except for occasional findings, textile remains are known only in a fragmentary condition. Most consisted of woven or knitted fabrics.[71] Woven textiles were industrially manufactured from woollen and bast fibres. Most would have been part of exterior garments (such as frocks, jackets, and trousers), and a small proportion could have been interior articles (including shirts and drawers). Following historical documents,[72] these types of fabrics and articles were possibly similar to those sold by outfitters in the ports of departure. Knitted textiles were apparently handcrafted using wool, and they were part of sweaters, gloves, and so on. Some woven fragments

---

67 Clarke, *Wreck of the 'Favorite'*. 68 Goodridge, *Narrative of a Voyage*.
69 Clarke, *Wreck of the 'Favorite'*. 70 Cruz, "Memórias".
71 Salerno, *Arqueología de la indumentaria*. 72 Salerno, "Persona y cuerpo-vestido".

were torn, and others appear to have been intentionally cut. Meanwhile, some other remains presented stitches and patches made with different fabrics.

Most shoes found in sealers' shelters had a standardized appearance. Their construction and style corresponded to nineteenth-century work shoes characteristic of the working classes – including low shoes with an upper section made up of a vamp and quarter. The vast majority of the articles were found complete, although some of the components could have been separated in the archaeological context. A number of shoes presented holes on specific areas of the soles, while others showed signs of extreme damage to the sole stitches (which would have made it impossible to continue wearing them).[73] According to documentary sources, even the strongest nineteenth-century shoes could not withstand conditions on the South Shetland Islands,[74] and some of the men eventually suffered frostbitten feet.[75]

Without a doubt, environmental conditions at the archipelago were particularly harsh, and work and subsistence activities had a profound impact on sealers' clothes and shoes. As it was impossible to acquire new articles, the men had to make do with what they had brought from the vessels. Fabrics obtained from discarded garments (or even from textile bags or old sails) could be recycled as patches.[76] In the case of shoes, the documentary and the archaeological record suggest that the men sometimes used animal skins to wrap their feet and manufacture simple moccasins.[77] All of this could have been true also for the officers who were in charge of the gangs. The shared experience of working and living on the South Shetland Islands could therefore have helped to blur some of the previous social differences in men's appearances.

Final Remarks

Although the transit between different scenarios was part of the dynamics of capitalism and sealers' lives, the relationship between capitalism and the sealing workforce was probably expressed in different ways on board the vessels and in the hunting grounds. From our perspective, labourers' lives on board the vessels and on the South Shetland Islands formed two different aspects of the sealing industry. These aspects were not necessarily contradictory but complementary, as they both served the interests of a capitalist

73 Salerno, "Zapatos rotos"; Radicchi, "Os sapatos lobeiros-baleeiros".
74 Ames, *Mariner's Sketches*, 146.   75 Salerno and Cruz, "Between Words and Oceans".
76 Salerno, *Arqueología de la indumentaria*; Salerno, "Persona y cuerpo-vestido".
77 Salerno, "Zapatos rotos"; Radicchi, "Os sapatos lobeiros-baleeiros".

endeavour in a given space-time context.[78] Sealing was a highly exploitative industry. On the one hand, it attempted to take advantage of animal resources to the maximum possible extent (without paying attention to the consequences of over-exploitation). On the other hand, it attempted to get the most production from labourers at the lowest cost possible, both in economic and practical terms.

In the controlled space of the vessel, and despite the existence of some cracks in the general picture, sealing companies found it useful to make the men respond to discipline, providing them with necessities so they could focus on their work. In the hunting grounds, the companies left the men on their own, and the latter could organize their work and subsistence in different terms. Among other things, the material culture of sealing camps reinforced sharing and a less hierarchical lifestyle,[79] making negotiation between different ranks a necessity. Within this framework, the rhythms of hunting and processing were likely marked by labourers' attempts to increase their own future share.

Sea, earth, vessels, shelters, blood, and seals, among others, are elements that describe the lives of the first Antarctic labourers, whose traces are nowadays the object of study of historical archaeology. Approaching sealers in Antarctica has allowed us to take a closer look at a history without individual heroes, without the direct action of the elites; a history that shows the essence of capitalism as a force that pushes the limits of the world, and transforms the places and the people it touches.

Bibliography

Ames, Nathaniel, *A Mariner's Sketches, Originally Published in the Manufacturers and Farmers Journal* (Providence: Cory, Marshall and Hammond, 1830).
Basberg, Bjørn L., and Robert K. Headland, "The Economic Significance of the 19th Century Antarctic Sealing Industry", *Polar Record* 49 (2013): 381–391.
Berguño, Jorge, "Las Shetland del Sur: El ciclo lobero. Primera parte", *Boletín Antártico Chileno* (April 1993): 5–13.
Berguño, Jorge, "Las Shetland del Sur: El ciclo lobero. Segunda parte", *Boletín Antártico Chileno* (October 1993): 2–9.
Bolster, W. Jeffrey, *Black Jacks: African American Seamen in the Age of Sail* (Harvard: Harvard University Press, 1997).
Browne, John, *Etchings of a Whaling Cruise* (New York: Harper & Brothers, 1846).

---

78 Salerno et al., "Inside or Outside Capitalism?".
79 Zarankin and Senatore, "'Estrategias y tácticas'"; Zarankin and Senatore, "Archaeology in Antarctica"; Zarankin and Senatore, *Historias de un pasado*.

Burton, Robert, "From Shoes to Shawls: Utilization of 'South Seas' Fur Seal Pelts in Late 18th and Early 19th Century England", in Robert Headland, ed., *The Proceedings of the 2016 Historical Antarctic Sealing Industry Conference* (Cambridge: Scott Polar Research Institute, 2018), pp. 87–93.

Butts, Isaac, *Every Sailor His Own Lawyer: The Rights of Seamen* (New York: H. Long and Brother, 1848).

Caviglia, Sergio, *Malvinas: Soberanía, memoria y justicia. Vol II: Balleneros, loberos, misioneros. S. XVIII XIX* (Rawson: Ministerio de Educación de la Provincia de Chubut, 2015).

Clark, Howard, "The Antarctic Fur-Seal and Sea-Elephant Industry", in G. B. Goode, ed., *The Fisheries and Fishery Industries of the United States: Section V – History and Methods of the Fisheries* (Washington, DC: Government Printing Office, 1887), 400–467.

Clarke, W. B., *Narrative of the Wreck of the 'Favorite' on the Island of Desolation: Detailing the Adventures, Sufferings, and Privations of John Nunn; An Historical Account of the Island, and Its Whale and Seal Fisheries, with a Chart and Numerous Wood Engravings* (London: William Edward Painter, 1850).

Cooper Busch, Briton, *The War Against the Seals: A History of the North American Seal Fishery* (Kingston: McGill-Queen's University Press, 1985).

Cruz, María Jimena, "Incorporando comidas e contextos: A alimentação e o corpo nos grupos foqueiros nas Shetland do Sul (Antártica, Século XIX)", MS diss. (Universidade Federal de Minas Gerais, 2014).

Cruz, María Jimena, "Memórias de un mundo congelado: A industria lobeira e as experiencias antárticas no século XIX", PhD diss. (Universidade Federal de Minas Gerais, 2019).

Currie, Stephen, *Thar She Blows: American Whaling in the Nineteenth Century* (Minneapolis: Lerner, 2001 [1960]).

Dana, Richard H., *The Seaman's Friend* (Boston: Thomas Groom, 1851).

Davis, William, *Nimrod of the Sea; or The American Whalemen* (New York: Harper & Brothers, 1874).

Davis, Lance, Robert Gallman, and Karin Gleiter, *In Pursuit of Leviathan: Institutions, Productivity and Profits in American Whaling, 1916–1906* (Chicago: University of Chicago Press, 1997).

Delano, Amasa, *Narrative of Voyages and Travels in the Northern and Southern Hemispheres* (Boston: E. G. House, 1818).

Dickinson, Anthony B., "A History of Sealing in the Falkland Islands and Dependencies 1764 to 1972", PhD diss. (Cambridge University, 1987).

Fanning, Edmund, *Voyages Round the World; with Selected Sketches of Voyages to the South Seas, North and South Pacific Oceans, China etc between 1792 and 1832* (New York: Collins & Hannay, 1833).

Goodridge, Charles, *Narrative of a Voyage to the South Seas, and the Shipwreck of the Princess of Wales Cutter, with an Account of Two Years Residence on an Uninhabited Island* (Exeter: W.C. Featherstone, 1843).

Hall, Martin, *Archaeology of the Modern World: Colonial Transcripts in South Africa and Chesapeake* (London: Routledge, 2000).

Harrowfield, David, "Archaeology on Ice: A Review of Historical Archaeology in Antarctica", *New Zealand Journal of Archaeology* 26 (2005): 5–28.

17 Historical Archaeology of Antarctic Labourers

Headland, Robert, *Chronological List of Antarctic Expeditions and Related Historical Events* (Cambridge: Cambridge University Press, 1989).
Headland, Robert K., "Antarctic Sealing Voyages (1786 to 1922)", in Robert K. Headland, ed., *Historical Antarctic Sealing Industry: Proceedings of an International Conference in Cambridge* (Cambridge: Scott Polar Research Institute, 2018), pp. 171–222.
Holmes, Lewis, *The Arctic Whalemen; or, Winter in the Arctic Ocean (. . .) Together with a Brief History of Whaling* (Boston: Thayer & Eldridge, 1861).
Johnson, Matthew, *An Archaeology of Capitalism* (Oxford: Blackwell, 1996).
Maddison, Ben, *Class and Colonialism in Antarctic Exploration, 1750–1920* (London: Pickering & Chatto, 2014).
Mameli, Laura, "La gestión del recurso avifaunístico por las poblaciones canoeras del archipiélago fueguino", PhD diss. (Universidad de Buenos Aires, 2003).
Martinic, Mateo, "Navegantes norteamericanos en aguas de Magallanes durante la primera mitad del siglo XIX", *Anales del Instituto de la Patagonia, Punta Arenas* 17 (1987): 5–18.
Mayorga, Marcelo, "Actividad lobera temprana en la Patagonia Oriental: Caza de mamíferos marinos", *RIVAR* 4 (2017): 31–51.
McKissack, Patricia, and Frederick McKissack, *Black Hands, White Sails: The Story of African-American Whalers* (New York: Scholastic, 1999).
Nolasco, Raquel, "Pessoas, mamíferos marinhos e objetos: Um olhar simétrico sobre a Antártica do século XIX", MS diss. (Universidade Federal de Minas Gerais, 2018).
Nordhoff, Charles, *Whaling and Fishing* (Cincinnati: Moore, Wilstach, Keys & Co., 1856).
O'Gorman, Fergus, "The Return of the Antarctic Fur Seal", *New Scientist* (1963): 374–376.
Orser, Charles J., *A Historical Archaeology of the Modern World* (New York: Plenum, 1996).
Pearson, Michael, "Charting the Sealing Islands of the Southern Ocean", *Journal of the Australian and New Zealand Map Society* 80 (2016): 33–56.
Pearson, Michael, "'Knowing' the South Shetland Islands: The Role of Sealers' Charts", *Shima* 14 (2020): 108–132.
Pearson, Michael, "Living Under Their Boats: A Strategy for Southern Sealing in the Nineteenth Century: Its History and Archaeological Potential", *Polar Journal* 8 (2018): 68–83.
Pena, Will, "Negociando gêneros com o paralelo 60: Por uma genealogia do prestígio antártico", MS diss. (Universidade Federal de Minas Gerais, 2016).
Putney, Martha, *Black Sailors: Afro-American Merchant Seamen and Whale Men Prior to the Civil War* (New York: Greenwood, 1987).
Radicchi, Gerusa, "Os sapatos lobeiros-baleeiros: Práticas de calçar do século XIX nas Ilhas Shetland do Sul (Antártica)", MS diss. (Universidade Federal de Minas Gerais, 2014).
Richards, Rhys, *The Commercial Exploitation of Sea Mammals at Iles Crozet and Prince Edward Islands Before 1850* (Cambridge: Scott Polar Research Institute, 1992).
Richards, Rhys, *Sealing in the Southern Oceans 1788–1833* (Wellington: Parameta, 2010).
Salerno, Melisa, *Arqueología de la indumentaria: Prácticas e identidad en los confines del mundo moderno (Antártida, siglo XIX)* (Buenos Aires: Del Tridente, 2006).
Salerno, Melisa, "Persona y cuerpo-vestido en la modernidad: Un enfoque arqueológico", PhD diss. (Universidad de Buenos Aires, 2011).

Salerno, Melisa, "Sealers Were Not Born But Made: Sensory Motor-Habits, Subjectivities and Nineteenth-Century Voyages to the South Shetland Islands", in J. R. Pellini, A. Zarankin, and M. A. Salerno, eds., *Coming to Senses: Topics in Sensory Archaeology* (Newcastle-upon-Tyne: Cambridge Scholars, 2015), pp. 77–104.

Salerno, Melisa, "Zapatos rotos: Una aproximación al calzado en arqueología histórica", in E. Cordeu, ed., *VI Congreso Argentino de Americanistas: Sociedad Argentina de Americanistas*, Vol. 2 (Buenos Aires: Dunken, 2009), pp. 369–383.

Salerno, Melisa, and María Jimena Cruz, "Between Words and Oceans: Logbooks and the Antarctic Sealing Industry". Work presented at SC-HAAS Conference 2019 – *Antarctic Connections at the End of the World: Understanding the Past and Shaping the Future*, Ushuaia (2019).

Salerno, Melisa, and Andrés Zarankin, "En busca de las experiencias perdidas: Arqueología del encuentro entre los loberos y las islas Shetland del sur (Antártida, siglo XIX)", *Vestigios* 8 (2014): 131–157.

Salerno, Melisa, Romina Rigone, and Andrés Zarankin, "Explorando bitácoras: Aproximaciones al accionar de los loberos y balleneros en Tierra del Fuego durante el siglo XIX". Work presented at *VII Congreso Nacional de Arqueología Histórica*, Facultad de Humanidades y Artes, Universidad Nacional de Rosario, Rosario (22–26 October 2018).

Salerno, Melisa, María Jimena Cruz, and Andrés Zarankin, "Inside or Outside Capitalism? Sealers' Lives, Food, and Clothing on Board Sealing Vessels and on Antarctic Hunting Grounds", in J. Nyman, K. Fogle, and M. Beaudry, eds., *Historical Archaeology of Shadow and Intimate Economies* (Florida: University Press of Florida, 2019), pp. 158–177.

Senatore, María Ximena, "Antarctic Historical Sealing and Material Culture", in Robert K. Headland, ed., *Historical Antarctic Sealing Industry: Proceedings of an International Conference in Cambridge* (Cambridge: Scott Polar Research Institute, 2018), pp. 61–71.

Senatore, María Ximena, and Andrés Zarankin, "Arqueología histórica y expansión capitalista: Prácticas cotidianas y grupos operarios en Península Byers, Isla Livingston, Shetland del Sur", in Andrés Zarankin and F. Acuto, eds., *Sed Non Satiata* (Buenos Aires: Ed. Tridente, 1999), pp. 171–188.

Senatore, María Ximena, and Andrés Zarankin, "Widening the Scope of the Antarctic Heritage Archaeology and the 'The Ugly, the Dirty and the Evil'", in Susan Bar and Paul Chaplin, eds., *Polar Settlements: Location, Techniques and Conservation* (Oslo: ICOMOS International Polar Heritage Committee, 2010), pp. 51–59.

Senatore, María Ximena, Andrés Zarankin, Melisa Salerno, Valeria Valladares, and María Jimena Cruz, "Historias bajo cero: Arqueología de las primeras ocupaciones humanas en la Antártida", in L. A. Borrero and N. V. Franco, eds., *Arqueología del extremo sur del continente americano* (Buenos Aires: Dunken, 2008), pp. 251–283.

Silva, Hernand, "La pesca y la caza de lobos y anfibios: La Real Compañía Marítima de Pesca en Deseado (1790–1807)", in *Historia Marítima Argentina*, Vol. 4 (Buenos Aires: Departamento de Estudios Históricos Navales, 1985), pp. 507–529.

Smith, Ian, *The New Zealand Sealing Industry: History, Archaeology and Heritage Management* (Wellington: Department of Conservation, 2002).

Smith, R. I., and H. W. Simpson, "Early Nineteenth Century Sealer's Refuges on Livingston Island, South Shetland Islands", *British Antarctic Survey Bulletin* 74 (1987): 49–72.

Stackpole, Edouard A., *The Voyages of the Huron and the Huntress: The American Sealers and the Discovery of the Continent of Antarctica* (Mystic: Marine Historical Association, 1955).

Stehberg, Ruben, *Arqueología histórica antártica: Aborígenes sudamericanos en los mares subantárticos en el siglo XIX* (Santiago: Centro de Investigaciones Diego Barros Arana, 2003).

Whalemen's Shipping List and Merchants' Transcript, 1843–1914 (Mystic Seaport Museum, 2020), retrieved from https://research.mysticseaport.org/reference/whalemens-shipping-list/ (accessed 28 July 2020).

Webster, Noah, *An American Dictionary of the English Language* (Philadelphia: J. B. Lippincott, 1857).

Weddell, James, *A Voyage Towards the South Pole Performed in the Years 1822–24. Containing an Examination of the Antarctic Sea, to the Seventy-fourth Degree of Latitude; and a Visit to Tierra del Fuego, with a Particular Account of the Inhabitants. To which is Added, Much Useful Information on the Coasting Navigation of Cape Horn, and the Adjacent Lands* (Newton Abbot: David & Charles, 1827).

Wilkie, Laurie, "Documentary Archaeology", in D. Hicks and M. Beaudry, eds., *The Cambridge Companion to Historical Archaeology* (Cambridge: Cambridge University Press, 2006), pp. 13–33.

Zarankin, Andrés, and María Ximena Senatore, "Archaeology in Antarctica, 19th Century Capitalism Expansion Strategies", *International Journal of Historical Archaeology* 9 (2005): 43–56.

Zarankin, Andrés, and María Ximena Senatore, "Arqueología en Antártida: Primeras estrategias humanas de ocupación y explotación en Península Byers, Isla Livingston, Shetland del Sur", in *Actas de las Cuartas Jornadas de Investigaciones Antárticas* (Buenos Aires: IAA, 1997), pp. 7–10.

Zarankin, Andrés, and María Ximena Senatore, "'Estrategias y tácticas' en el proceso de ocupación de la Antártida: siglo XIX", in M. Carballo, S. Espinosa, and J. Belardi, eds., *Desde el país de los gigantes: Perspectivas arqueológicas en Patagonia*, Vol. I (Río Gallegos: Universidad Nacional de la Patagonia Austral, 1999), pp. 315–327.

Zarankin, Andrés, and María Ximena Senatore, *Historias de un pasado en blanco: Arqueología histórica antártica* (Belo Horizonte: Argumentum, 2007).

Zarankin, Andrés, and María Ximena Senatore, "Ocupación humana en tierras antárticas: Una aproximación arqueológica", in *Soplando en el viento ... Actas de las Terceras Jornadas de Arqueología de la Patagonia* (Río Gallegos: Universidad Nacional de la Patagonia Austral, 1999), pp. 629–644.

Zarankin, Andrés, and María Ximena Senatore, "Hasta el fin del mundo: Arqueología en las Islas Shetland del Sur. El caso de Península Byers, Isla Livingston", *Praehistoria* 3 (2000): 219–236.

Zarankin, Andrés, Melisa Salerno, and Adrian Howkins, "From the Antarctic to New England: Remembrance of Sealing and Sealers", in Robert K. Headland, ed., *Historical Antarctic Sealing Industry: Proceedings of an International Conference in Cambridge* (Cambridge: Scott Polar Research Institute, University of Cambridge, 2018), pp. 107–121.

Zarankin, Andrés, Sarah Hissa, Melisa Salerno, et al., "Paisagens em Branco: Arqueologia e antropologia antárticas. Avanços e desafios", *Vestígios* 5 (2011): 9–51.

18

Mining and Colonialism in the Circumpolar North

HENRIK KNUDSEN, ARN KEELING, AND JOHN SANDLOS

Introduction

Writing in 1916, shortly after his appointment as 'Geologist in Charge of Explorations', the celebrated Canadian geologist and explorer Charles Camsell reflected on the prospects for development in Canada's 'unexplored' Arctic: 'It is to the mining industry more than any other that we must look for co-operation and assistance in the exploration of our northern regions.'[1] Camsell hailed the prospects for mining to launch the transformation of remote, sparsely populated Arctic and Northern regions into prosperous, modern Euro-Canadian settlement frontiers. Nearly forty years later, reflecting on his geological career and the surge in mineral development activity in Canada's north in the decades around World War II, Camsell confidently concluded, 'To my mind the whole future of the North country depends primarily upon its mineral wealth.'[2] Camsell's visions of mining's capacity for transforming the Arctic both echoes and anticipates the ideology of 'frontierism' characteristic of industry boosters and state agencies around the circumpolar Arctic. The contemporary 'will to drill' for minerals draws on a longstanding narrative of frontier development, linking this history to an imagined sustainable future for Arctic communities based on the exploitation of mineral resources.[3]

Arctic mining (Figures 18.1, 18.2) was a 'frontiering' activity in several senses. Mineral exploration and development took place in regions often remote from major centres of economy and settlement; it promoted the physical and ideological transformation of remote 'wilderness' regions into resources for modern industrial centres; and its exponents advocated for the

---

1 Camsell, "Unexplored Areas", 255. 2 Camsell, *Son of the North*, 242.
3 Dale et al., "The Will to Drill", 213–228. This link between historical and future narratives is echoed in Avango and Roberts, "Heritage, Conservation, and Geopolitics".

18 Mining and Colonialism in the North

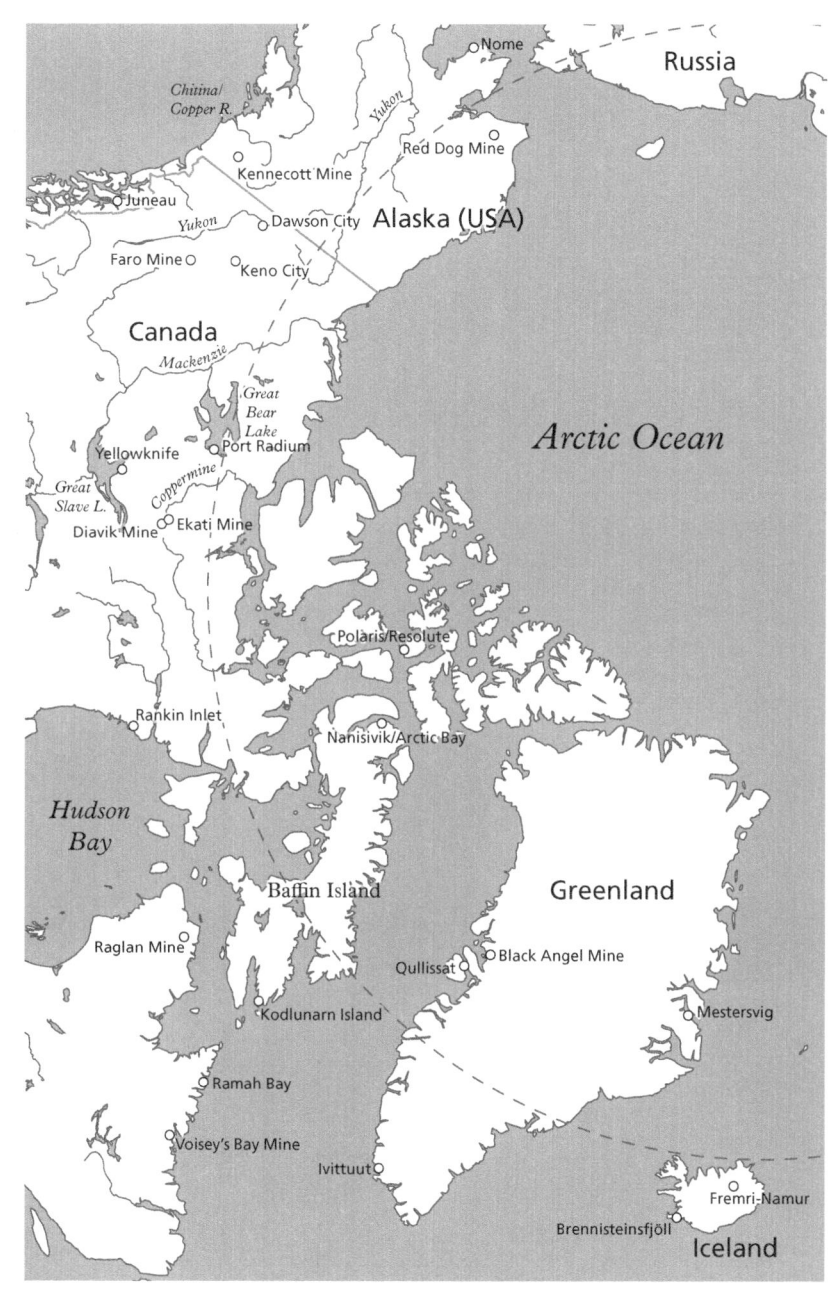

Figure 18.1 Notable mining sites in northern North America and Greenland.

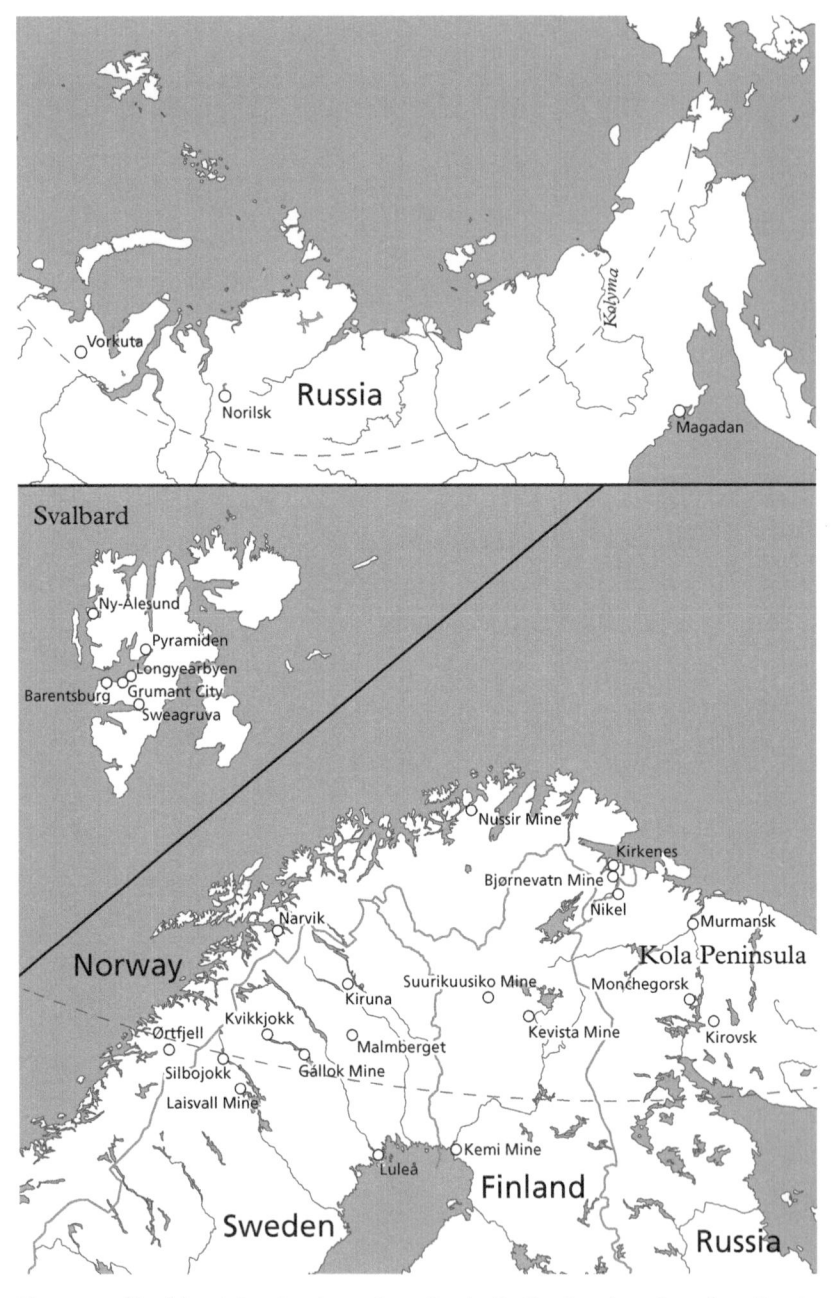

Figure 18.2 Notable mining sites in northern Russia, Svalbard, and northern Scandinavia.

absorption of the Arctic's Indigenous inhabitants into the body politic of the modern state, through mapping, settlement, and the displacement of traditional economies by industrial resource extraction. Whether through the sudden invasions provoked by gold rushes, the establishment of centrally planned industrial settlements by both Soviet and Western governments, or the transformative environmental effects of mineral extraction, mining brought dramatic and often wrenching changes to Arctic peoples and landscapes. As a leading agent of colonial expansion into Arctic territories, mining often left a legacy of economic instability and dependency, as well as a record of environmental degradation that continues to haunt many parts of the region today.[4]

Mining in Arctic North America

Although mining is closely associated with European exploration and colonial resettlement of northern North America, the region's Indigenous cultures had identified and long exploited useful geological materials for a variety of purposes. Soapstone was used for lamps and vessels, other ground and flaked stone for tools, and native copper for weapons, tools, and ornamental purposes. Trade in mineral products ranged extensively within and beyond the Arctic. Around 7,000 years BP, the Maritime Archaic peoples who occupied the northern Labrador coast began to quarry chert, a high-silica quartzite valued for its workability into chipped-stone tools. Chert from the Ramah Bay site was subsequently traded during different periods along vast networks stretching from Ungava Bay and Baffin Island to the north, the Great Lakes region to the west, and the mid-Atlantic coast to the south.[5]

In the central and western Arctic, Inuit and Athapaskan peoples engaged in an extensive copper trade that included both finished products and raw material, as well as sharing production techniques such as annealing and cold hammering. One important sub-network of this trade centred on the

---

4 Although framed primarily around Arctic mining, our account includes mineral developments in more southerly, Sub-Arctic regions, especially where relevant to the northward course of industrialism and settlement. In many cases, mining in the Arctic 'proper', whether understood as the region above the Arctic Circle, above the southern limit of discontinuous permafrost, or encompassing the homelands of Arctic Indigenous peoples, was stimulated by mineral exploration and development in adjacent, more or less remote Sub-Arctic territories.
5 Brake, "R Is for Ramah", www.mun.ca/labradorinstitute/archives/RisforRamahChert.php.

rich deposits of the Copper and Chitina river basins, where Ahtna groups harvested and traded copper both to interior peoples such as the Han and Northern Tutchone, and to coastal groups along the Gulf of Alaska via Tlingit intermediaries.[6] Evidence for copper trade and metallurgy among sequential Arctic coast cultures from the Bering Strait to the Coronation Gulf extends back to at least 4500 BP. The explorer Vilhjalmur Stefansson referred to the Kitlinermiut Inuit as 'Copper Eskimo' because they made their tools and weapons from copper from the Coppermine River area. Rivalry over copper is reputed to have contributed to the notorious Bloody Falls massacre. In July 1771, Hudson's Bay Company explorer Samuel Hearne travelled to the Coppermine River from Fort Prince of Wales on Hudson Bay, accompanied by Dënesųłiné and T'satsąot'inę (the latter also known as 'Copper Indians') guides, searching for rumoured metal deposits. En route the party attacked and killed the inhabitants of an Inuit camp. Hearne's account (and those of subsequent mineral-seekers) at once acknowledged and circumscribed Inuit and Dene relations with and uses of copper, while refiguring the region in terms of its potential for industrial resource extraction.[7]

This incident was neither the first nor the last time that European desire for minerals fuelled both exploration activity and violent conflict. In his ill-fated search for the Northwest Passage, Englishman Martin Frobisher established the first European mining operation in Arctic North America and perpetrated what was probably its first mining fraud. His 1576 expedition included violent clashes and abductions of Inuit from south Baffin Island, who were taken to England along with samples of rock for assay. In spite of poor evidence of silver in the rock, Frobisher and his backers raised funds for a return voyage the following year, which resulted in further violent interchanges with Inuit, as well as producing 200 tons of ore quarried from Countess of Warwick (now Kodlunarn) Island. Following a suspect assay result showing the potential for rich gold and silver deposits, Frobisher led a final expedition to the territory, dubbed 'Meta Incognita', to establish a mining colony. After a long summer's toil his ships abandoned the colony and returned with 1,200 tons of what was subsequently determined to be worthless ore.[8] Like many mining ventures since, Frobisher's gambit resulted in mainly squandered labour, disillusioned investors, and a legacy of conflict with Indigenous people.

6 Pratt, "Copper, Trade, and Tradition"; Franklin et al., *Examination of Prehistoric Copper*.
7 Cameron, *Far Off Metal River*.
8 McGhee, *Arctic Voyages*; Hogarth et al., *Martin Frobisher's Northwest Venture*.

Mining remained a key driver of Euro-American incursions into Indigenous Arctic and northern territories into the modern period. A sequence of gold rushes at the end of the nineteenth century attracted thousands of prospectors to northwest Canada and Alaska, transforming the region. Indigenous knowledge of minerals and mining regions was crucial to the discovery of many of the richest finds, which in turn attracted prospectors, settlers, and mining capital to the North. In 1880, Tlingit Chief Kawa/ēe brought gold samples to a mining engineer in Sitka, Alaska, sparking a gold rush to what would become the city of Juneau.[9] Less than twenty years later, Tagish prospector Keish (Skookum Jim) and his nephew Káa Goox (Dawson Charlie), along with California-born prospector George Carmack and his Tagish spouse Shaaw Tláa (Kate Carmack), discovered gold on a small creek tributary to the Tr'ondëk (Klondike) River, precipitating the Klondike gold rush to Canada's Yukon Territory. A similar 'placer' gold rush followed in late 1898 to Nome, Alaska, where millions of dollars' worth of fine gold flakes were washed from coastal beach sands and, later, adjacent creeks and benches.[10] In the stampedes that followed these and other discoveries, some Indigenous people found work at the margins of the mining economy. But by and large their land-based economies were eroded, their communities were ravaged by introduced diseases, and their sovereignty was replaced by colonial governments.[11]

Gold rushes also spurred the discovery and eventual development of other mines in the western Arctic and Sub-Arctic. Among the richest were the copper mining developments in Prince William Sound and the Wrangell Mountains, centred on the Kennecott mine and mill complex. The region where the Ahtna people had long harvested and traded copper contained a bonanza of remarkably rich ore, up to 85 per cent copper. These deposits, along with previously located copper finds on the coast, were consolidated in 1915 into a massive industrial venture backed by the Guggenheim family and known as the Alaska Syndicate, which included the coastal Beatson mine, the Kennecott mines and mill in the mountains, and railway and steamship companies to export the copper. For a brief period before the 1930s Kennecott was one of the world's major copper developments, thriving on global demand driven by electrification: in total, the company's mines produced more than 0.7 billion kg of copper and over 280,000 kg of silver.[12] The Great Depression and declining ore grades rapidly undermined the

9 Spude, "Overview History", 12.   10 Demuth, "Grounding Capitalism".
11 Spude, "Overview History"; King, "Alaska Natives"; Coates and Morrison, *Land of Midnight Sun*; Haycox, *Alaska*, 209.
12 Hawley, *Kennecott Story*.

Alaska Syndicate's operation, and when Kennecott closed in 1938, its mines, mills, and town were abandoned and the rail tracks torn up. Kennecott Copper survived as a major global mining company with properties in Utah and Chile, but its Alaskan origins reflect the resource colonialism that characterized the industry in the Arctic.[13]

The decades around World War II saw the rapid expansion and intensification of mineral exploration and development across the Canadian Arctic. Government geological surveys and new aviation technologies enabled a pre-war expansion of prospecting activities.[14] In the 1930s, these efforts resulted in two significant operations in the Northwest Territories: a radium mine at Port Radium, on the eastern shore of Great Bear Lake, and the Con Mine, working significant lode gold deposits at Yellowknife on Great Slave Lake. The Port Radium mine, which closed with the collapse of radium prices at the outset of the war, was nationalized along with its parent company Eldorado and reopened in 1942 to produce uranium (previously virtually worthless) for the Allied atomic bomb project. Uranium ore was exported for refining via barges and rail for thousands of kilometres along a route dubbed the 'Highway of the Atom'. The employment during and after the war of Dene men as boat pilots and stevedores not only hastened their transition to a wage economy, but also exposed the workers to radioactive dust without any effective protection or health warnings.[15] A series of other precious metal and base metal mines developed in the Canadian Sub-Arctic during the 1950s and 1960s, ranging from small producers to large-scale open-pit operations.[16]

The post-war period also saw the first efforts to establish mining in Canada's Arctic tundra environments. Spiking nickel prices, driven by US stockpiling efforts and the Korean War, spurred the establishment of the North Rankin Nickel Mine on the Hudson Bay coast in 1957. Although it was a relatively small producer, the company and the Canadian government regarded the mine as an 'experiment' in both underground mining in permafrost environments and the employment of Indigenous labour. Assisted by a federal government keen to promote Arctic development, the mine recruited Inuit to move to the new settlement and take up wage employment, including working alongside southerners as underground miners. The

---

13 Cronon, "Kennecott Journey".   14 Piper, *Industrial Transformation*.
15 Paci and Villebrun, "Mining Denendeh"; Keeling and Sandlos, "Environmental Justice Goes Underground?".
16 For an overview of this mining period, see introduction to Keeling and Sandlos, eds., *Mining and Communities*.

18 Mining and Colonialism in the North

experiment was, however, short-lived: declining ore grades and low nickel prices forced the mine's closure in 1962, and the collapse of the regional economy that followed provided hard lessons on the precariousness of minerals-led development in remote northern regions.[17]

Similarly 'experimental' mining developments followed in the Canadian High Arctic. Lead–zinc discoveries on north Baffin Island led to the establishment of the Nanisivik mine, Canada's first above the Arctic Circle, in 1976. In addition to constructing a mine and purpose-built town approximately 25 km from the Inuit community of Arctic Bay, Mineral Resources International also concluded one of the earliest 'benefits' agreements in Canada, signed with the federal government in exchange for financial support for building costly Arctic infrastructure. The Strathcona Agreement also aimed to ensure industrial employment and training for Inuit workers, but over the twenty-six-year life of the mine, Inuit employees at Nanisivik rarely reached over 20 per cent. The mine's closure and dismantling of the townsite in 2002 sparked bitter reactions by residents of Arctic Bay, who felt excluded from the mine's economic benefits while bearing its local environmental and social impacts.[18] A second High Arctic development, Cominco's Polaris lead–zinc mine on Little Cornwallis Island near Resolute Bay, operated from 1982 to 2002. Operating as a completely 'fly-in, fly-out' mine, Polaris similarly failed to generate significant local economic benefits for Inuit. These experiments in High Arctic mining, lavishly supported by Canada's federal government, contributed to technological and logistical knowledge of extraction in these extreme environments, but provided only limited, short-term economic benefits to regional economies.[19]

Apart from some persistent small producers, mining in Alaska struggled after World War II until a resurgence in the 1970s and 1980s. Large-scale industrial gold production from placer deposits resumed after its nadir in the early 1970s.[20] In the 1980s a series of lode mineral mines producing zinc, lead, and silver opened. The Red Dog Mine in Alaska's North Slope borough, opened in 1989, was significant for its negotiated settlement between the developer, Canadian mining giant Cominco, and the Northwest Alaska Native Association (NANA), title-holders to the lands containing the deposits. One of the first of its kind in the Arctic, this agreement included royalties paid

17 Keeling and Boulter, "Igloo to Mine Shaft"; Boutet et al., "Historical Perspectives on Mining".
18 Rodon et al., "De Rankin Inlet"; Midgley, "Contesting Closure".
19 Bowes-Lyon et al., "Socio-economic Impacts".
20 Cole, "Golden Years"; Spengler, "Overview of Mining".

to NANA's Iñupiat beneficiaries through a regional corporation, employment and training provisions, and joint oversight of the development, including protections for subsistence-based land uses.[21]

Even as industrial mining recovered in 1980s Alaska, it faltered in northern Canada. Volatile prices hit high-cost producers, and several mines experienced production rollbacks, strikes, and even temporary closures. In the early part of the decade, the Asbestos Hill mine (in Arctic Quebec) closed, and the iron mining region in northern Quebec and Labrador suffered rapid contraction. In 1989, a wave of closures hit the Keno Hill and Cyprus-Anvil (Faro) mines in Yukon, and the Pine Point mine in the Northwest Territories (NWT), among the sector's largest northern producers. Low gold prices resulted in production cuts at the Yellowknife gold mines: Giant Mine's operator, Royal Oak Mines, suffered bankruptcy in 1999, and production ceased at both Giant and Con in 2003. The High Arctic mines at Polaris and Nansivik were also shuttered in 2002.

But amidst the industry's difficulties new prospects also emerged. Major new Arctic developments emerged in Nunavik (the Raglan nickel mine) and northern Labrador (the Voisey's Bay nickel mine). Both were established on Inuit territories, which entailed the negotiation of impact and benefit agreements, providing employment benefits and royalty payments to affected communities. Opening in 1996, Raglan's was the first such company–community agreement in Canada, and the mine also helped to consolidate the growing industrial practice of employing workers on a 'fly-in, fly-out' basis rather than establishing purpose-built mining settlements. In the case of the Voisey's Bay mine, the highly contested environmental impact assessment in the 1990s led to the settlement of long-standing land claims between Labrador Inuit and the federal and provincial governments, resulting in the creation of a new, Inuit-governed northern territory, Nunatsiavut.[22]

In the NWT, diamond prospects in the tundra east of Great Slave Lake sparked a staking rush and lured major mining companies to the region in the early 1990s. During the first decade of the new millennium, three mines opened: Broken Hill Proprietary's Ekati Mine; Rio Tinto and Dominion Diamond Corporation's Diavik Mine; and De Beers's Snap Lake project. A short-lived diamond project also opened in neighbouring Nunavut territory, Tahera Diamond's Jericho Mine, which operated sporadically for only six years. The diamond mines boosted the struggling mining sector in the territory, and Yellowknife emerged as a major centre supplying the mines via aircraft and

---

21 Loeffler, "Mining and Communities"; McLean and Hensley, *Mining and Indigenous Peoples*.
22 Rodon et al., "De Rankin Inlet"; Lowe, *Premature Bonanza*; Gibson, "Sustainability Assessment".

ice roads. These developments also included significant economic and employment benefits for some Dene and Métis groups through the impact and benefit agreements concluded between mining companies and Indigenous communities and governments. Still, the negotiation of these agreements created some dissent, depending on which communities were included (or not) in them. Some Dene felt they were rushed through negotiations as they agonized over the opportunities and implications of development on their traditional territories.[23] In addition, the promised secondary employment benefits of diamond cutting proposed for the region collapsed, and after 2008 Canada exported mainly unsorted rough diamonds.

Since the turn of the millennium, the global 'commodities supercycle' has driven considerable exploration and development investment in the North American Arctic. Nevertheless, global volatility in mineral prices continued to interact with the structural challenges of mining in the Arctic, notably high costs and logistical challenges related to remoteness and climate.[24] The early 2000s saw mines open across the region from Alaska to Nunavut, only to close within a few years, although three major operations, the Meadowbank and Meliadine gold mines, and Baffinland iron mine, have since opened. While the industry generated hundreds of millions of dollars in royalties, revenues, and employment in the region, debates continued over whether mineral extraction presented an opportunity for northern territories and Indigenous communities to escape economic dependency on state transfers, or whether mining merely refocused this dependency on uncertain and ephemeral industrial developments.[25] Increasingly, the long-lasting environmental legacies of mining also became apparent: at many sites, the environmental damage wrought by mining left permanent landscape scars and toxic hazards that became public liabilities.[26] Even at operational mines, the long-term impacts and costs of reclamation present considerable concerns, especially in the context of the additional disruptions of climate change.[27]

Greenland

Owing to its sparse infrastructure, remote geography, and environmental challenges, mining in Greenland has been characterized by sporadic

---

23 Bielawski, *Rogue Diamonds*.   24 Carney et al., "Mining and Communities".
25 See, for instance, contributions to Southcott et al., eds., *Resources and Sustainable Development*; Huskey and Southcott, "'That's Where'"; Rhéaume and Caron-Vuotari, "Future of Mining".
26 Dance, "Northern Reclamation in Canada".
27 Pearce et al., "Climate Change and Mining".

development patterns, similar in some ways to the North American Arctic. From 1774, economic management of the Danish settlements in Greenland (referred to as colonies) rested firmly in the hands of the Royal Greenland Trading Department (KGH) – a state trade monopoly largely focused on products from hunting. With the exception of coal and graphite extraction, mining never became a real business priority for KGH, but matters might have been different had there been any easily exploitable resources of precious metals. The histories of Greenland's three biggest, long-lived mining ventures highlight the economic as well as environmental and social challenges that have limited the industry's establishment.

There was reason to believe that mining could be feasible in Greenland, as it had been in neighbouring Iceland. Archaeological and historic evidence suggest that mining of the volcanic island's rich sulphur deposits began in the early Middle Ages. At its peak during the fifteenth and sixteenth centuries, up to 320 tons of raw and processed sulphur were traded out of Iceland annually, normally via Bergen in trading networks controlled by powerful Hanseatic merchants. Sulphur was a commodity of considerable economic and political importance, not least due to the spread of firearms throughout Europe in the late medieval and early modern period. For this reason, the Danish king monopolized the sulphur trade in 1561 and at the same time erected new smelting works in Copenhagen. Sulphur mining was carried out in Iceland until the 1880s.[28]

Commercial interest in Greenland's mineral resources rose in the middle of the nineteenth century after a downturn in hunting livelihoods. But it was British attempts in 1845 to mine graphite from shallow pits at Langø near Upernavik that prompted Danish state action,[29] first to ban the Britons and then to encourage KGH to develop a state-supported graphite industry. These efforts soon ground to a halt as it proved difficult to sell the graphite, and yet they marked the beginning of a mid-century mining mini-boom, with attempts by private companies to mine copper, lead, and cryolite in southwestern Greenland.

Only cryolite became successful, in time developing into a geostrategic resource. Known for centuries by local Inuit in the Arsuk Fjord and used as fishing sinkers, this rare, ice-white mineral was deposited directly on the shore at Ivittuut, a place that was blessed with a wealth of *ammassat* fish (capelin) and used as summer camp by local Inuit. Excavation began in 1853 after Julius Thomsen, a young chemist, obtained a ten-year monopoly on the

---

28 Mehler, "Sulphur Trade".   29 Frandsen, "Grafitminen ved Upernavik".

production of soda and alum from cryolite.[30] The circumvention of the KGH monopoly in this case owed much to the influence of Hinrich Rink, Royal Inspector of South Greenland, and the desire of changing governments to create competition in this area. The first fifty-three barrels of cryolite reached Copenhagen after having been transported out of the fjord on an *umiak* (women's boat). Local Greenlanders were hired during the first seasons until Danish workers arrived in 1856. Although trade and commerce between Danish workers and local Greenlanders were forbidden, the mining company could still employ local labour when needed. Quickly, however, Greenlanders became regarded as an unreliable workforce in the mine – so from an early time the local workforce was limited to a few domestic servants and a kayak pilot.

Mining at Ivittuut made for a hard life. During the harsh winter of 1862–63, fourteen workers (of a total winter workforce of twenty-two) died from scurvy. Ore transport to Europe was another major challenge. From 1856 to 1862, nine chartered ships were wrecked or disappeared in the icy waters. In 1863, only twenty of thirty-one chartered ships made it to Ivittuut. A major deal with Pennsylvania Salt Manufacturing Company in 1865 created a large American market for cryolite, where it was used in the soda industry. Annual production now reached about 10,000 tonnes, with a summer workforce of up to 150 (half that or less during the winters). Ivittuut became the busiest transportation hub in Greenland, with seventeen in- and outgoing vessels each year (average, 1856–1919). During the short, hectic summers, a handful of ships or more would often be seen in the fjord.

Mining brought significant social impacts for nearby Inuit communities. The influx of Danish miners resulted in large numbers of mixed-origin children in the settlement of Arsuk, 16 km away. Gonorrhoea made its first appearance in Greenland at Ivittuut in 1864, and 1872 saw the outbreak of a syphilis epidemic affecting about fifty people during the following years. To contain the disease, strict measures were devised to segregate the population in Arsuk from the mining site, and from the rest of Greenland. Separated traffic and residence zones for mining workers and the locals remained in place until the 1930s. Ivittuut became an isolated company town with its own store and currency to separate its economy from the colonial economy under the KGH monopoly.[31]

---

30 Topp, *Kryolitindustriens Historie*. See also Kragh, "From Curiosity to Industry"; Kruse, "Historical Perspectives".
31 Luckow and Fisker, *Arsukfjorden*, 18–56; Sveistrup, "Ivigtut 1865–1870".

The invention of the Hall–Héroult process in 1886 turned cryolite into an indispensable resource in the aluminium smelting industry. During both world wars, demand surged, driven by the need for light, strong airframes, with global aluminium production rising by a factor of ten from 1916 to 1941. Cryolite became a geostrategic material, almost as indispensable for modern industry and warfare as aluminium itself, and Ivittuut was the only significant and minable source known in the world. The interwar period was a golden age for the mine, with huge profits posted year after year (up to 75 million US dollars in 2020 equivalent). In 1940, just months before Denmark was occupied by German forces, the two companies engaged in cryolite mining and processing were merged and the Danish state took a 50 per cent share in the combined operation. Despite the severing of the Denmark–Greenland connection by Nazi occupation, shipments to the US and Canadian aluminium industries continued throughout the war. Anxious to secure the supply, the United States assumed responsibility for the wartime defence of Greenland and built a naval base in the Arsuk Fjord.[32] Cryolite exports peaked in 1942 at 85,900 tonnes, enabling a rapid buildup of the massive bomber fleets that became a decisive factor in the war against the Axis powers. Competition from synthetic cryolite and resource depletion put an end to mining at Ivittuut in 1962, though reprocessing of old waste rock would continue for another twenty-five years.

Cryolite mining arguably constitutes the best example of resource colonialism in Greenland. Over 135 years, 3.7 million tonnes of cryolite was excavated from the open-pit mine. Up until World War II, taxes on cryolite provided a solid fiscal cornerstone for the Danish colonial project in Greenland – aimed both at protecting the traditional livelihoods and at exploiting the natural resources.[33] Profits from cryolite exports sustained Greenlandic society during the war, giving rise to the idea among Greenlanders that their country could sustain itself from its own resources independently from Denmark. Though it was hailed as Greenland's 'white gold' by geologists and company historians, many Greenlanders have seemed much more ambivalent when talking about cryolite. Some were left with a feeling that their country had been robbed without 'Greenland getting part of the cake' in terms of jobs and development.[34]

A radically different mining community developed at Qullissat on the north-eastern shore of Qeqertarsuaq (Disko Island).[35] Coal for local

---

32 Berry, "Cryolite".   33 Rud, "Governance and Tradition".
34 Petersen, "Kryoliten i Ivittuut", 10.
35 Sørensen, *Qullissat*; Priebe, "A Modern Mine?"; Andersen et al., "Qullissat"; Haagen, "Coal Mine at Qullissat".

consumption had been collected from coal seams exposed on the Disko Bay shores since the 1780s. In 1905 KGH opened a small coal mine on the northern coast of the Nuussuaq Peninsula, and in 1924, mining activities moved to Qullissat where production started up with a workforce of sixteen. With coal seams just 1 m thick, underground mining operations took place in narrow, tilting shafts in temperatures often below freezing. The work was difficult, productivity low, and the coal frequently said to be of inferior quality. Despite these and other challenges, production gradually grew to a level where Greenland's need for coal could be met during World War II. In the 1950s the mine had a permanent workforce of thirty, along with 150–200 casual workers, all of whom were Greenlanders except for management and a few engineers. In this respect Qullissat stood out from nearly all other mining operations in Greenland. The well-paid workforce generated a strong demand for local products, attracting young people from all parts of Greenland. From 300 inhabitants in 1933, Qullissat reached more than 1,400 inhabitants in 1962, making it the sixth largest settlement in Greenland.

Qullissat was unique for Greenland: a settlement dominated by Greenlandic workers, smiths, and carpenters, with a unique and vibrant culture representing a blend of modern industrial society and traditional hunting culture. Qullissat was the first settlement in Greenland to have electric power and a movie theatre. The unique *Vaigat* music style developed here, inspired by American radio and incorporating elements of Hawaiian music.[36] Its mining workforce became the first in Greenland to organize effectively, encouraged by a Danish communist teacher, successfully claiming a 60 per cent pay rise and social security measures, after threatening to strike in 1947.

But the mine was chronically unprofitable, and the policy planners who drafted the post-war industrial modernization plans for Greenland (known as G-50 and G-60) were pessimistic about its future. Post-war economic prospects looked bleak, with traditional hunting livelihoods in decline and the hugely profitable cryolite mine soon depleted. Instead, technocratic planners in Copenhagen envisaged a large-scale modern fishing industry and a population concentrated in larger coastal cities with year-round open ports. By 1949, leading figures in Denmark had concluded that the Qullissat mine would have to close, but rising Cold War tensions and the Korean War once again shifted political priorities towards securing a domestic source of energy. Through the 1950s, the mine would again be praised as 'Greenland's

36 Sejersen, *Efterforskning og udnyttelse*, 45–46.

coal chamber'.[37] With renewed investments, by the early 1960s annual production peaked at about 30,000 tonnes, but increased production only generated accelerating deficits, due to steadily declining coal prices and softening demand in Greenland. The downturn in the European coal mining industry and the general shift to oil made coal mining in Qullissat seem less and less viable. But what mattered even more was the prospect of transferring the large Qullissat workforce to fishing industries elsewhere in Greenland, which formed the foundation and main driving force in the Greenlandic economy.[38]

In 1968, Danish and Greenlandic authorities decided to close the mine. By 1972 Qullissat was abandoned and its 1,100 remaining residents displaced, predominantly to the large west coast cities of Nuuk, Paamiut, Sisimiut, and Ilulissat. The majority moved into hastily built concrete housing blocks. For many Qullissat miners, the poorly communicated closure and displacement became a traumatic experience. Seen from Greenland, the decision looked like a high-handed decision from Copenhagen made without regard for the community. The closure of Qullissat came to symbolize the controversial population concentration policy, Danes' lack of understanding of Greenlandic culture, and the unequal relationship with Denmark. This episode contributed to the growing opposition to Danish rule, eventually leading to the introduction of the Greenlandic Home Rule in 1979. The political consciousness emanating from Qullissat led to a political awakening in Greenland, and rights to underground mineral resources became a core issue for the independence movement.[39]

In 1973 the Black Angel lead–zinc mine began operating further to the north at Maarmorilik in the Uummannaq district, where a small marble quarry had previously operated.[40] After a period of state dominance in the Greenlandic mining sector, this was the first time that the international mining industry took an interest in Greenland – encouraged by the new mining law of 1965. Operations were run by Greenex, a Danish-registered company controlled by Cominco, as part of the company's ongoing Arctic expansion. The Canadian owner brought extensive knowledge about complex sulphide ores and cutting-edge flotation technology and, as noted above,

37 Priebe, "A Modern Mine?", 152. State-driven prospecting activities increased in the early Cold War, e.g. on Greenland's eastern coast (contested since the 1920s), where Danish geologists prospected for uranium and other minerals in order to keep out rival nations, and where the short-lived and unprofitable Mestersvig lead–zinc mine operated 1956–63. See Nielsen and Knudsen, "Too Hot to Handle".
38 Sørensen, Qullissat, 85.   39 Sejersen, Efterforskning og udnyttelse, 46.
40 Dahl, Minedrift i et fangersamfund; Dahl and Lyberth, Grønlandske Migrantarbejdere.

was already active in the North American Arctic. The mine derived its name from a dark stretch in the mountain resembling the shape of an angel. Crushed ore was transported by cable car from the mine entrance, spectacularly located on a near-vertical cliff 600 m above sea level, to processing, storage, and harbour facilities on the other side of the Affarlikassa fjord. When mining stopped in 1990, 11.3 million tonnes of ore had been processed.

Situated in a hunting district, the isolated mining camp was operated as a fly-in, fly-out operation. Company recruitment policy meant that only about 10–15 per cent of the workforce were Greenlanders (the rest being Danes, Scandinavians, and Canadians). The Greenlandic community had expected a much higher percentage. In 1977, the Greenlandic workforce went on strike, protesting a massive wage gap between Greenlandic and non-Greenlandic workers during the first thirty months of employment. Greenlandic workers were also reacting against a host of other discriminatory practices, including the lack of Greenlandic food in the canteen, unequal distribution of living quarters, and the strict measures of social control enforced at the isolated, company-controlled mining camp. They won their pay rise, only to see the number of employees reduced.[41]

The mine had a polarizing effect on the local community. While the municipality of Uummannaq prospered from the influx of taxes, the remote hunting communities near the mine suffered. Noise, dust, and smoke from the site crippled the seal hunt. In 1975, protesting hunters blocked an icebreaker, claiming that springtime icebreaking had adverse economic effects and endangered the lives of hunters on the sea ice.[42] As often the case, the mine generated few long-term social-economic benefits for the local community. Instead, the Black Angel left a toxic environmental legacy. During operations, tailings were disposed directly to the bottom of the fjord, resulting in an annual release of 10–30 tonnes of lead and 30–55 tonnes of zinc, resulting in significant pollution of the marine environment. Other sources of pollution were dust from the ore crusher and concentrator and large waste rock dumps, one of which was located on the shoreline. In the most affected areas, the level of dissolved lead rose by a factor of 3,000 compared with unaffected areas. For many years it was recommended not to collect and eat blue mussels up to 30 km downstream from the site.[43]

Since the closure of the Black Angel mine in 1992, one short-lived gold mine has been operating (2004–13), and, more recently, two small-scale ruby

---

41 Dahl and Lyberth *Grønlandske Migrantarbejdere*, 58–80.
42 Dahl, *Minedrift i et fangersamfund*. 43 Asmund and Johansen, "Short and Long Term".

and anorthosite mining projects have started operations. Yet interest has persisted, and since the establishment of self-government in 2009, governments have viewed revenues from mineral extraction as a route to future prosperity and independence from Denmark.[44] Prospecting activity has increased significantly, focusing, for example, on large unexploited resources of rare earth elements. Whether Greenland should mine its uranium deposits has sparked intense discussion and controversy between Denmark and Greenland.[45] Such issues aside, commercial realities seem fairly bleak.

Svalbard

The Svalbard archipelago, extending roughly between 74 and 81 degrees northern latitude, has been home to several of the world's most northerly mines. Without permanent settlements and regarded as *terra nullius* since its discovery in 1596, Svalbard became a Norwegian possession under the 1925 Spitsbergen Treaty, ending a period of unregulated mining activity. The Norwegian Søren Zachariassen undertook the first coal mining operations in 1899. The first mines were small, seasonal, and short-lived. Nevertheless, strong demand for raw materials in Europe, the promising geology of the archipelago, and resource colonialism all contributed to growing interest from industrialists in Europe and North America. In 1905, a British company established Advent City, the first permanent coal mining settlement. The following year, US industrialist John M. Longyear and his Arctic Coal Company founded the town today known as Longyearbyen. With soaring coal prices and easy access to risk capital, coal mining boomed during World War I. Often supported by foreign ministries, capitalists established new mining towns, including Sveagruvan (Swedish), Ny-Ålesund (Norwegian), Grumant City (Russian-British), and Barentsburg (Dutch). The Spitsbergen Treaty imposed Norwegian sovereignty over these hitherto unregulated ventures, while guaranteeing that citizens of signatory states could operate on equal terms with Norwegian companies.[46]

By 1922 coal prices had dropped to pre-war levels and the boom ended. Only two mines were still in operation in 1926. In the years that followed, a new actor entered the Svalbard mining scene, when the Soviet Union acquired three mining sites – Pyramiden (Swedish), Grumant City, and

---

44 For a critical analysis see Vikström and Högselius, "Cryolite to Critical Metals".
45 Nuttall, *Climate, Society*.
46 Avango et al., "Industrial Extraction"; Avango et al., "Between Markets and Geopolitics"; Hacquebord and Avango, "Settlements".

Barentsburg – and established the company Trust Arktikugol to operate them. By the early 1930s, the Soviet Union dominated Svalbard's mining industry. Seeking to balance the situation, the Norwegian government encouraged the few remaining Norwegian companies to expand. Backed by state subsidies, Norwegian companies such as Store Norske acquired lapsed claims and closed mines to strengthen Norway's position on the archipelago.

From 1934 onwards, only Soviet and Norwegian mining companies operated on Svalbard. In Norway, coal was used for heating, railways, and coke production. The Soviet Union linked its Svalbard coalfields to the Five-Year Plans for the Murmansk region. The Norwegian mines operated with economic deficits and were kept in operation largely to achieve effective occupation and maintain the legitimacy of the Spitsbergen Treaty. The Soviet Union, on the other hand, wanted to keep a foothold in a region strategically located near the military seaport of Murmansk, which became increasingly important as the Cold War progressed.[47] In this way, mining co-produced resource security, territorial sovereignty, and state security.

In 1962, an explosion killed twenty-one miners in Ny-Ålesund, triggering a political crisis that led to the fall of Norway's long-serving Labour Party government. A year later, all mining ended at Ny Ålesund. But the facilities and infrastructure remained in place, and soon Norwegian space research activities began to be moved into the abandoned mining site, followed from 1990 by further research activities within fields like atmospheric, environmental, and climate science. The research stations at Ny-Ålesund secure a continued Norwegian and international presence in the area, tacitly underlining the legitimacy of Norway's sovereignty.

At the end of the Cold War, Russia continued mining at Barentsburg, but in 1998 it closed Pyramiden. The abandoned settlement has since become a destination for tourists interested in industrial ruins and Soviet nostalgia. State-owned Store Norske, by contrast, invested heavily from 1999 to expand and modernize its Sveagruvan operations, becoming the most productive and indeed the only profitable mine in the history of Svalbard. But this golden period was marked by a corruption scandal that saw the company's chief executive jailed. After a collapse in the global coal market following 2014 and massive public bailouts, the Norwegian government finally announced in 2017 that it would permanently close all mining operations except for one small mine in Adventdalen.

---

47 Arlov and Hoel, "Kulldrift i Kald Krig"; Avango, "Remains of Industry".

Fennoscandia

The northward push of mining in Fennoscandia echoed many of the same colonial themes as elsewhere in the Arctic. For political and business leaders, mining promised not only a natural source of wealth, but also an antidote to the 'backwardness' of Indigenous economies (in this case Sámi reindeer herding). If mining represented a pathway to modernization, the Sámi homeland (Sápmi), was a frontier largely empty of human inhabitants. National identity (and destiny) was strongly tied to both northern landscapes and mining.[48] Mining in Fennoscandia, however, should be distinguished from mining in Svalbard, Greenland, and North America because it generally did not occur in remote Arctic outposts, but rather in well-serviced near-Arctic locations that eventually developed into diversified and relatively stable economies.

In early modern Sweden (which encompassed modern-day Finland and parts of Norway), the first northward mining rush began in 1634 with the discovery of silver at Nasafjäll, close to the Arctic Circle. Discovered by a Sámi named Peder Olofsson, the mine spurred the construction of silverworks at Silbojokk, 60 km from the mine. The Swedish Empire was engaged in territorial expansion during the seventeenth century, so it is hardly surprising that the silver mine inspired colonial rhetoric about cultivating Sweden's greatness in a new northern environment (the Norrland region). Nasafjäll was destroyed by a Norwegian-Danish attack in 1659, but new discoveries in Sápmi during the seventeenth century – the silver mines in Kedkevare/ Silpatjåkko and Alkavare, serviced by the Kvikkjokk foundry, and the iron and copper mines that fed the Kengis iron works – created a sustained contact zone between settlers and Sámi.[49]

Swedish historians have tended to view northern colonization as a benign process, but more recent works have pointed to the dire consequences for Sámi during this first wave of mineral-led expansion.[50] Anti-vagrancy ordinances were used to coerce nomadic Sámi to work at the mines, most often tending to reindeer used in the transportation systems linking mines and

---

48 For an overview of northern colonization in Scandinavia, see Sörlin, "State and Resources". For colonial narratives applied to Sámi, see Nyström, "Invisible Histories".
49 For a brief overview of the mines in the Scandinavian Arctic, see Boyd et al., *Mineral Resources*. For a broad overview of resource development on Sámi, see Axelsson et al., "Ethnic Identity".
50 See Lindmark, "Colonial Encounter"; Ojala and Nordin, "Mining Sápmi". For an overview see Kvist, "Racist Legacy".

processing facilities. Mine managers and missionaries imposed a strict disciplinary and moral reform agenda that attempted to stamp out the nomadism and pagan beliefs of the Sámi, imposing mandatory church attendance, banning traditional religious practices, and spatially segregating Sámi workers as a means to better supervise them. Mining administrators and missionaries imposed tough punishments on those who refused to adhere to the new religious and labour orthodoxies, extending the draft that bonded workers to the mining communities or confiscating individual property. Mining thus provided the primary vehicle to extend the power of the early modern Swedish state northward, bringing with it a programme to modernize the culture and economy of the Sámi while simultaneously carting away the natural riches of their homeland.[51]

Sweden's first northern mines were small by modern standards, and it was only in the late eighteenth century that large-scale iron-ore mining began. In 1888 a British firm completed a rail line from Malmberget to Luleå on the Baltic Sea, and by 1903 the government had upgraded the original line and extended it in the opposite direction from Kiruna to the Norwegian port of Narvik, which unlike Luleå was ice-free year-round. With transportation corridors to tidewater and thus markets near and distant, Malmbanen (the Ore Line) spurred a major expansion of mining in northern Sweden. Almost immediately the huge iron deposits at Kiruna and Malmberget accounted for half the iron ore produced in Sweden, and Kiruna remains today one of the largest iron-ore-producing complexes in the world. Many other large mines opened in the following years: the Boliden gold mine, opened in 1924, was one of Europe's largest; the Laisvall mine (1943–2001) was the largest lead mine in Europe, and the Aitik copper mine, opened in 1968, remains one of the largest open-pit copper mines in Europe, producing over 40 million tonnes of ore in 2019.[52]

Norway and Finland also understood mining as a means to vault their northern regions toward modernity. Both countries had a long history of mining in their southern regions, but they began to match Sweden's zeal for Arctic development by the early twentieth century.[53] Norway began with the far northern Bjørnevatn iron mine (and the rail line to the processing centre in Kirkenes) in 1906, one of several iron deposits in the immediate area that have been actively mined up to recent times. Although Norway is more

51 Naum, "Pursuit of Metals"; Naum, "Cultural 'Improvement'".
52 Laruelle, "Three Waves"; Boyd et al., *Mineral Resources*, 56–57; Söderholm and Viklund, "Policy and Business Efforts".
53 Nagel, "Norwegian Mining".

readily identified as an oil producer, there have been significant terrestrial mining projects in the Arctic such as the Kvannevann iron mine at Ørtfjell, established in 1975.[54] Finland's push for a new North was represented symbolically through the ultra-modern architecture and interior design at the community around the Koloski nickel mine, opened in the newly acquired territory of Petsamo in the 1930s.[55] Other important Arctic developments include the Kemi chromite mine (Finland's largest underground operation, which has operated continuously since 1968), and more recently the Kevista nickel mine (2012) and the Suurikuusiko gold mine (2008). In all three Fennoscandian countries, the Arctic has clearly become the most important mining region; in 2016 there were thirty-four operational mines in Finland, Norway, and Sweden, with twenty-four of these located in the north of the Arctic Circle.[56]

The Fennoscandian mining industry's relative economic success can be attributed in part to these countries' tangible infrastructural support for northern mineral development. From the nineteenth century onward, mining in northern Fennoscandia developed simultaneously with strong transportation links, linking core and periphery regions in ways that allowed a less ephemeral mining economy (Sweden's iconic Kiruna and Malmberget mines have operated for more than a century). Finland, Sweden, and Norway's Arctic regions also feature a much larger network of medium-sized urban centres (50–100,000 residents), with diverse economies that have moved away from a sole dependence on mining, featuring manufacturing, education, and services sectors. These Arctic regions can thus be characterized as mature development zones that are no longer dependent on mining, which in 2002 accounted for only 2.5 per cent of economic activity in the Swedish Arctic and 0.8 per cent of GDP in Arctic Norway. Production rates at the older mines in these regions remain stable, and new projects overwhelmingly rely on local populations for skilled labour.[57] This stands in contrast to the less stable frontier regions such as the Northwest Territories and Nunavut, where mining accounted for 36.4 per cent of economic activity in 2004 and where long-distance commuting has limited new mines' contributions to the

---

54 For the most complete overview development in all three Scandinavian countries, see Avango et al., "Constructing Fennoscandia". For Norway, see Ranestad, *Knowledge-Based Growth*.
55 Stadius, "Petsamo". Petsamo was subsequently surrendered to the Soviet Union as part of the terms of peace in 1944.
56 Frederiksen and Kadenic, "Mining in Arctic".
57 Carson et al., "Hot Spots and Spaces".

development or growth of sustainable communities in the region, other than as remote servicing centres.[58]

Mining in the Fennoscandian Arctic has nevertheless featured many of the same political conflicts and environmental problems as in other Arctic regions. For Sámi herders, the landscape-scale impacts of mining-associated infrastructure, particularly railroads, continues to threaten reindeer herds. Although reindeer herding only makes up about 10 per cent of Sámi economic activity, it remains important culturally. As with Indigenous people in other Arctic regions, Sámi political organizations have asserted the right to reject specific mining projects (such as the Nussir copper mine in Norway and the Gállok iron mine in Sweden), as well as to contest state mineral strategies that they feel threaten traditional economic activities, even as they try to negotiate the terms of their own participation in the mining economy.[59]

Pollution has also been an issue for northern Scandinavian mines. Ore processing at Kiruna produced severe sulphur, fluorine, and dust emissions until technological improvements in the 1970s. At Laisvall mine, problems with sediment and heavy metal loading in Lake Laisan and Lake Aisjaure persisted until the implementation of cleanup and control measures in the 1980s.[60] Across the Fennoscandian Arctic, mines historically produced immense amounts of waste rock and tailings, which can contribute to water pollution through heavy metal loading or acid mine drainage. One study in 1999 estimated that mining in Swedish sulphide deposits had produced 300 million tons of tailings and 200 million tons of waste rock, resulting in seventy sites with acute acid drainage issues.[61] In addition, the immense amount of ore removed from larger deposits has also left huge pits and craters throughout the Arctic region, disturbances that geographer Anna Storm has described as post-industrial landscape scars. In some cases, these scars carry dramatic human consequences; both the cities of Kiruna and Malmberget are being relocated, building by building, as mining pits expand to take the iron under settled areas. If mining in Fennoscandian has historically been synonymous with the economic development of Arctic regions (at least for its boosters), like mining everywhere it also carried the seeds of

---

58 Frederiksen and Kadenic, "Mining in Arctic"; Haley et al., "Observing Trends"; Laruelle, "Three Waves".
59 Angell et al., "Industrial Development"; Bjørklund, "Industrial Impacts"; Nygaard, "Indigenous Interests"; Mörkenstam, "Indigenous Peoples"; Nyström, "Invisible Histories"; Persson et al., "What Local People?".
60 Söderholm and Viklund, "Policy and Business Efforts".
61 Gustafsson et al., "Swedish Acid Mine Drainage".

destabilizing cultural change and environmental degradation for the region's original residents.[62]

The Russian Arctic

Mining proved to be a relatively successful pillar of Arctic settlement and development in Russia, though any enthusiasm must be tempered by the scale of human misery and environmental destruction that accompanied the expansion of Arctic mining during the Soviet era.[63] Northward expansion had been an aspirational goal for Russia's rulers during the Tsarist era, resulting in limited settlement for fishing and fur-trading activity, and eventually the construction of transportation links such as the railroad from Petrograd to the year-round northern port of Murmansk by 1917.[64] What had been a tentative northward course of empire in the late imperial period became an obsession of the Soviet regime under Stalin. From 1929, the USSR developed a programme of using prisoners – mainly political inmates but also criminals – to overcome labour shortages and spur development in the Arctic.[65] These workers inhabited the Gulags, prison camps made infamous decades after their establishment by works such as Aleksandr Solzhenitsyn's *The Gulag Archipelago* (1974) and Varlam Shalamov's *Kolyma Tales* (1966). Beginning with Stalin's first Five-Year Plan (1928–32), slave labourers built railroads, highways, mine facilities, and industrial combines (centres that could completely process raw ore, thus ensuring full development of the region rather than the mere exploitation of raw materials). The populations of existing cities such as Murmansk ballooned during this period, while huge prison camps such as Norilsk, Vorkuta, and Magadan eventually developed into important urban areas and administrative centres. The population of the Soviet Arctic increased from 656,000 in 1929 to 1,176,000 a mere six years later.[66] Soviet northward expansion was, in the words of historian Andy Bruno, a form of 'hyper-development', with mining activity leading the industrial charge.[67]

The primary target for mining development during the first Five-Year Plan (1928–32) was the Kola Peninsula. Major apatite deposits (a phosphorus-rich mineral used for fertilizer production) in the Khibiny Mountains supported

---

62 Storm, *Post-Industrial Landscape Scars*.
63 Josephson et al., *Environmental History of Russia*.
64 For an overview, see Eklund et al., "Imageries and Historical Change".
65 Norlander, "Origins of Gulag Capital". 66 Emmerson, *Future History*.
67 Bruno, *Nature of Soviet Power*.

the development of mining and settlement at Khibinogorsk (now Kirovsk) in 1929. The Soviet state also constructed a phosphorus enrichment plant and settlement at Apatity, which became an administrative centre for further regional development. By the mid-1930s Moscow developed a major nickel processing centre in the northwest corner of the Kola Peninsula, with new mining settlements at Monchegorsk and at Nikel (formerly Kolosjoki, re-named after the Soviet Union took possession of the Petsamo region from Finland in 1944). The population of the Kola Peninsula region grew from 32,200 in 1926 to almost 300,000 people by the end of the 1930s, with much of the prison labour force made up of *kulaks* (defined as wealthier peasants). While the apatite industry remained regionally dominant through the 1930s (and still so today), the nickel industry created far more problems with air and water pollution. At Monchegorsk and Nikel, dusty underground environments produced large numbers of silicosis cases among miners, while emissions of nickel, copper, chlorine, sulphuric acid, and carbon monoxide polluted local air and water. Sulphur dioxide pollution from smelter stacks severely reduced vegetation in a broad swathe of territory surrounding nickel production zones (including in neighbouring Norway), an issue that was not addressed adequately until pollution regulations improved in Russia during the late 1990s. By this point, however, mining development had left in its wake an utterly transformed natural environment and settlement geography, changes unparalleled in scale and severity when compared to those in other Arctic nations.[68]

Stalin's second Five-Year Plan (1933–37) devoted half its monetary investment to the expansion of industrial activity to the Far East, including gold mining in the Kolyma River basin (stretching from the Sea of Okhotsk to the Arctic Ocean). Solzhenitsyn claimed that the network of Gulag camps associated with Magadan were among the most infamous in the Stalinist era, with approximately a million prisoners sent here between 1932 and 1956. The notorious Dalstroi organization (the Main Administration for Construction of the Far North) coordinated regional development, managing the arduous construction of a highway to the Kolyma River in 1932 and controlling a vast network of satellite mining camps. The rich gold deposits of Kolyma could be mined through relatively safe placer methods, as miners dug or dredged alluvial ore directly from riverbeds and separated the gold using flumes and sluice boxes. Workers nevertheless died in large numbers from cold, hunger, starvation, or execution for those who attempted escape or had not sufficiently purged

---

68 Bruno, *Nature of Soviet Power*.

themselves of anti-communist sentiment.[69] When Dalstroi expanded its reach north and east to Chukotka in 1939 to mine gold, bauxite, tin, and eventually uranium, prisoners faced underground exposure to silica dust and radiation, in addition to inhumane working conditions and frequent executions that filled mass graves around the camps. For the Indigenous Chukchi, mining brought polluted rivers, damaged reindeer pastures, and sometimes fatal violence from prison workers. As in the Kola Peninsula, Chukotka and Kolyma remained important mining regions long after Nikita Khrushchev wound down the Gulag system in the 1950s, though its network of modern open-cast mining operations has never erased the public memory of the Far East region as home to the worst of all the Gulags.[70]

Many historians have argued that the human and ecological costs of Soviet Arctic expansion resulted directly from the Soviet government's militaristic zeal for modernizing what it saw as a backward region.[71] The human and environmental costs were concentrated in the Kola Peninsula and the Far East, but also spread to other regions. Completed with Gulag labour during the late 1920s, the Norilsk nickel smelter in the central Arctic created extreme pollution problems, and it remains the worst sulphur dioxide emitter in the world.[72] Historian Andy Bruno has questioned the idea that communism was irredeemably more destructive toward nature, suggesting that the Soviet approach to northern development was not fundamentally different from industrial modernization projects in other parts of the world, an argument that has some merit.[73] In Canada, for example, the much lighter impact of mining development in the Canadian Arctic was the product of extreme distances from core markets (and a consequent lack of transportation infrastructure), rather than any lack of desire to exploit the region. Indeed, twentieth-century mining developments in 'near northern' areas such as Sudbury, Timmins, Cobalt, and Rouyn-Noranda carried many of the same environmental impacts as the mines in the Soviet Arctic. But the Soviet mines undoubtedly carried much greater human costs than the Canadian developments, a product of the single-minded zeal with which the Stalinist regime compelled mass migration to the Arctic and imposed a radically new social and ecological order on the region.

69 Norlander, "Origins of Gulag Capital".
70 Demuth, *Floating Coast*; Emmerson, *Future History*; Norlander, "Origins of Gulag Capital".
71 Demuth, *Floating Coast*; Emmerson, *Future History*; Josephson, "Industrial Deserts"; Josephson, "Technology and Conquest"; Josephson, *Resources Under Regimes*; Josephson et al., *Environmental History of Russia*.
72 Nilsen, "Norilsk Tops World's List".   73 Bruno, *Nature of Soviet Power*.

Conclusion

Mining in different parts of the circumpolar Arctic originated from common desires but proceeded along very different historical pathways. Nearly all mining activity in the Arctic was accompanied with a strong rhetorical and practical commitment to colonization, a vision that positioned mining as the surest conduit to modernization and development. For dreamers—the explorers, prospectors, industrialists, politicians, and bureaucrats – mining offered the most viable way to replace the subsistence livelihoods of Arctic Indigenous people and a ready-made economic base to support northward expansion of Arctic frontiers that were invariably hostile to agricultural settlement. One might reasonably argue that the modernization vision attached to northern mining was mere window dressing for the real agenda: acquiring raw materials from hinterland regions to serve the commercial and military objectives of the modern state. Still, there is little reason to doubt the promoters' earnest devotion to their Arctic colonial visions, which had deep historical roots in Europe and North America, and some practical successes (at least from the point of view of the colonizers) across the ideological divides of capitalism and communism. Indeed, mineral development continues to be invoked by some as a catalyst for future Arctic development – including increasingly by many who live in the region.

Despite these common elements, the scale of mineral-led development and colonial expansion varies greatly across the circumpolar Arctic. Certainly the Soviet Union's mass mobilization of forced prison labourers and construction of infrastructure and administrative settlements to support mining stands out for the sheer scale of the effort. While much of the Soviet Arctic mobilization can be understood through the lens of its authoritarian government and its relative freedom from the limits imposed by a capitalist bottom line, Fennoscandian governments also actively promoted Arctic mining and colonization through policy, law, direct investment, and administrative support. Although many of the same calls for Arctic expansion gained a strong following in Canada and the United States, the region's remoteness from viable markets and the cost of building roads and/or rail across extreme distances have prevented all but the most valuable mineral deposits from being developed. Much the same dynamic was evident in Arctic outposts such as Greenland and Svalbard, which remained, with few exceptions, marginal economic prospects at best. There were just too many other, more viable mines outside of the Arctic, in the 'near north' regions of the Canadian Shield, or the relatively more accessible mineral deposits of the European Arctic.

If the history of Arctic mining is one of uneven and often ephemeral development, one common, at times tragic element of these histories is the severe human and ecological costs of northern mining. The scale of such impacts varied by region, but almost everywhere mining occurred, Indigenous peoples faced severe impacts, such as long-term toxic contamination, a depleted ecological base to support their subsistence economies, massive landscape-scale changes to local environments, and profound social and cultural disruption. Although Indigenous groups have more recently taken advantage of the mineral economy through various forms of impact and benefit agreements that guarantee jobs, training, and community investments, their memories of mining's colonial history continues to haunt their encounters with Arctic mineral economies in the present day.

Bibliography

Andersen, Astrid, Lars Jensen, and Kirsten Hvenegård-Lassen, "Qullissat: Historicising and Localising the Danish Scramble for the Arctic", in Graham Huggan, ed., *Postcolonial Perspectives on the European High North* (London: Palgrave Macmillan, 2016), pp. 93–116.

Angell, Elisabeth, Vigdis Nygaard, and Per Selle, "Industrial Development in the North: Sámi Interests Squeezed between Globalization and Tradition", *Acta Borealia* (published online 22 April 2020), https://doi.org/10.1080/08003831.2020.1751995.

Arlov, Thor Bjørn, and Alf Håkon Hoel, "Kulldrift i Kald Krig", in Harald Dag Jølle and Einar-Arne Drivenes, eds., *Norsk Polarhistorie: Rikedomenne* (Oslo: Gyldendal, 2004), pp. 389–441.

Asmund, Gert, and Poul Johansen, "Short and Long Term Environmental Effects of Marine Tailings and Waste Rock Disposal from a Lead/Zinc Mine in Greenland", in *Water & Environment: International Congress* 13–17 September (Seville: IMWA1999), pp. 177–181.

Avango, Dag, "Remains of Industry in the Polar Regions: Histories, Processes, Heritage", *Entreprises et Histoire* 87 (2017): 133–149.

Avango, Dag, and Peder Roberts, "Heritage, Conservation, and Geopolitics of Svalbard: Writing the History of Arctic Environments", in L.-A. Körber, S. MacKenzie, and A. Westerståhl Stenport, eds., *Arctic Environmental Modernities: From the Age of Polar Exploration to the Era of the Anthropocene* (London: Palgrave Macmillan, 2017), pp. 125–142.

Avango Dag, Louwrens Hacquebord, Ypie Aalders, et al., "Between Markets and Geo-politics: Natural Resource Exploitation on Spitsbergen from 1600 to the Present Day", *Polar Record* 47 (2010): 29–39.

Avango, Dag, Jann Kunnas, Maria Pettersson, et al., "Constructing Fennoscandia as a Mining Region", in E. Carina and H. Keskitalo, eds., *The Politics of Arctic Resources: Change and Continuity in the 'Old North' of Northern Europe* (New York: Routledge, 2019), pp. 62–77.

Avango, Dag, Louwrens Hacquebord, and Urban Wråkberg, "Industrial Extraction of Arctic Natural Resources since the Sixteenth Century: Technoscience and Geo-economics in the History of Northern Whaling and Mining", *Journal of Historical Geography*, 44 (2014): 15–30.

Axelsson, Per, Peter Sköld, and Corinna Röver, "Ethnic Identity and Resource Rights in Sweden", in E. Carina and H. Keskitalo, eds., *The Politics of Arctic Resources: Change and Continuity in the 'Old North' of Northern Europe* (New York: Routledge, 2019), pp. 119–139.

Berry, Dawn A., "Cryolite, the Canadian Aluminium Industry and the American Occupation of Greenland during the Second World War", *Polar Journal* 2 (2012): 219–235.

Bielawski, Ellen, *Rogue Diamonds: Northern Riches on Dene Land* (Vancouver: Douglas & McIntyre, 2004).

Bjørklund, Ivar, "Industrial Impacts and Indigenous Representation: Some Fallacies in the Sámi Quest for Autonomy", *Études/Inuit/Studies* 37 (2013): 145–160.

Boutet, J.-S., A. Keeling, and J. Sandlos, "Historical Perspectives on Mining and the Aboriginal Social Economy", in Chris Southcott, ed., *Northern Communities Working Together: The Social Economy of Canada's North* (Toronto: University of Toronto Press, 2015), pp. 198–227.

Bowes-Lyon, Léa-Marie, Jeremy P. Richards, and Tara M. McGee, "Socio-economic Impacts of the Nanisivik and Polaris Mines, Nunavut, Canada", in J. P. Richards, ed., *Mining, Society, and a Sustainable World* (Berlin: Springer, 2009), pp. 371–396.

Boyd, Rognvald, Terje Bjerkgård, Bobo Nordahl, and Henrik Schiellerup, *Mineral Resources in the Arctic: An Introduction* (Geological Survey of Norway, 2016). www.ngu.no/upload/Aktuelt/CircumArtic/Mineral_Resources_Arctic_Mainbook.pdf

Brake, Jamie, "R is for Ramah Chert", in *Encyclopedia of Labrador*, www.mun.ca/labradorinstitute/archives/RisforRamahChert.php (accessed 8 June 2020).

Bruno, Andy, *The Nature of Soviet Power: An Arctic Environmental History* (New York: Cambridge University Press, 2016).

Cameron, Emilie, *Far Off Metal River: Inuit Lands, Settler Stories, and the Making of the Contemporary Arctic* (Vancouver: UBC Press, 2015).

Camsell, Charles, *Son of the North* (Toronto: Ryerson, 1954).

Camsell, Charles, "The Unexplored Areas of Continental Canada", *Geographical Journal* 48 (1916): 249–257.

Carney, Jeanette, Tara Cater, and Arn Keeling, "Mining and Communities", in T. Bell and T. M. Brown, eds., *From Science to Policy in the Eastern Canadian Artic: An Integrated Regional Impact Study (IRIS) of Climate Change and Modernization* (Quebec City: ArcticNet, 2018), pp. 495–507.

Carson, Dean, Lovisa Solbär, and Olof Stjernström, "Hot Spots and Spaces In-between: Development and Settlement in the 'Old North'", in E. Carina and H. Keskitalo, eds., *The Politics of Arctic Resources: Change and Continuity in the 'Old North' of Northern Europe* (New York: Routledge, 2019), pp. 18–37.

Coates, Ken, and William Morrison, *Land of the Midnight Sun: A History of the Yukon* (Montreal and Kingston: McGill-Queen's University Press, 2005).

Cole, Terrence, "Golden Years: The Decline of Gold Mining in Alaska", *Pacific Northwest Quarterly* 80 (1989): 62–71.

Cronon, William, "Kennecott Journey: The Paths out of Town", in William Cronon and Jay Gitlin, eds., *Under an Open Sky: Rethinking America's Western Past* (New York: W. W. Norton, 1992), pp. 28–51.

Dahl, Jens, *Minedrift i et fangersamfund* (Vedbæk: Kragestedet, 1976).
Dahl, Jens, and Karl Johan Lyberth, *Grønlandske Migrantarbejdere i Marmorilik 1973–1978* (Copenhagen: Institut for Eskimologi, Københavns Universitet, 1980).
Dale, Brigt, Ingrid Bay-Larsen, and Berit Skorstad, "The Will to Drill: Revisiting Arctic Communities", in Brigt Dale, Ingrid Bay-Larsen, and Berit Skorstad, *The Will to Drill: Mining in Arctic Communities* (Cham: Springer International, 2018), pp. 213–228.
Dance, Anne, "Northern Reclamation in Canada: Contemporary Policy and Practice for New and Legacy Mines", *Northern Review* 41 (2015): 41–80.
Demuth, Bathsheba, *Floating Coast: An Environmental History of the Bering Strait* (New York: W. W. Norton, 2019).
Demuth, Bathsheba, "Grounding Capitalism: Geology, Labor, and the Nome Gold Rush", in B. Mountford and S. Tuffnell, eds., *A Global History of Gold Rushes* (Berkeley: University of California Press, 2018), pp. 252–272.
Eklund, Niklas, Julia Lajus, Vassily Borovoy, et al., "Imageries and Historical Change in the European Arctic", in E. Carina H. Keskitalo, ed., *The Politics of Arctic Resources: Change and Continuity in the 'Old North' of Northern Europe* (New York: Routledge, 2019), pp. 200–220.
Emmerson, Charles, *The Future History of the Arctic* (New York: PublicAffairs, 2010).
Frandsen, Niels, "Grafitminen ved Upernavik: Et forsøg på minedrift 1845-51", *Grønland*, 60 (2012): 286–295.
Franklin, U. M., E. Badone, R. Gotthardt, B. Willard, and D. Yorga, *Examination of Prehistoric Copper Technology and Copper Sources in Western Arctic and Subarctic North America* (Ottawa: National Museums of Canada, 1981).
Frederiksen, Anders, and Maja Due Kadenic, "Mining in Arctic and Non-Arctic Regions: A Socioeconomic Assessment", ZA Discussion Papers, No. 9883 (Bonn: Institute for the Study of Labor (IZA), 2016), http://ftp.iza.org/dp9883.pdf.
Gibson, Robert B., "Sustainability Assessment and Conflict Resolution: Reaching Agreement to Proceed with the Voisey's Bay Nickel Mine", *Journal of Cleaner Production* 14 (2006): 334–348.
Gustafsson, H. E., T. Lundgren, M. Lindvall, et al., "The Swedish Acid Mine Drainage Experience: Research, Development, and Practice", in J. M. Azcue, ed., *Environmental Impacts of Mining Activities: Emphasis on Mitigation and Remedial Measure* (Berlin: Springer, 1999), pp. 203–228.
Haagen, Birte, "The Coal Mine at Qullissat in Greenland", *Études/Inuit/Studies* 6 (1982): 75–97.
Hacquebord, Louwrens, and Dag Avango, "Settlements in an Arctic Resource Frontier Region", *Arctic Anthropology* 46 (2009): 25–39.
Haley, Sharman, Matthew Klick, Nick Szymoniak, and Andrew Crow, "Observing Trends and Assessing Data for Arctic Mining", *Polar Geography* 34 (2011): 37–61.
Hawley, Charles C., *A Kennecott Story: Three Mines, Four Men, and One Hundred Years, 1887–1997* (Salt Lake City: University of Utah Press, 2014).
Haycox, Stephen, *Alaska: An American Colony* (Seattle: University of Washington Press, 2002)
Hogarth, D. D., P. W. Boreham, and J. G. Mitchell, *Martin Frobisher's Northwest Venture, 1576–1581: Mines, Minerals and Metallurgy* (Ottawa: University of Ottawa Press, 1993).

Huskey, Lee, and Chris Southcott, "'That's Where My Money Goes': Resource Production and Financial Flows in the Yukon Economy", *Polar Journal* 6 (2016): 11–29.

Josephson, Paul, "Industrial Deserts: Industry, Science and the Destruction of Nature in the Soviet Union", *Slavonic and East European Review* 85 (2007): 294–321.

Josephson, Paul, *Resources Under Regimes: Technology, Environment, and the State, New Histories of Science, Technology, and Medicine* (Cambridge, MA: Harvard University Press, 2004).

Josephson, Paul, "Technology and the Conquest of the Soviet Arctic", *Russian Review* 70 (2011): 419–439.

Josephson, Paul, et al., *An Environmental History of Russia* (New York: Cambridge University Press, 2011).

Keeling, Arn, and Patricia Boulter, "From Igloo to Mine Shaft: Inuit Labour and Memory at the Rankin Inlet Nickel Mine", in A. Keeling and J. Sandlos, eds., *Mining and Communities in Northern Canada: History, Politics, and Memory* (Calgary: University of Calgary Press, 2015), pp. 35–58.

Keeling, Arn, and John Sandlos, "Environmental Justice Goes Underground? Historical Notes from Canada's Northern Mining Frontier", *Environmental Justice* 2 (2009): 117–125.

Keeling, Arn, and John Sandlos, eds., *Mining and Communities in Northern Canada: History, Politics, and Memory* (Calgary: University of Calgary Press, 2015).

King, Robert E., "Alaska Natives in the Gold Rush: A Look at Valdez Creek in the Early to Mid-20th Century", in C. H. Spude, R. O. Mills, K. Gurcke, and R. Sprague, eds., *Eldorado! The Archaeology of Gold Mining in the Far North* (Lincoln: University of Nebraska Press, 2011), pp. 274–287.

Kragh, Helge, "From Curiosity to Industry: The Early History of Cryolite Soda Manufacture". *Annals of Science* 52 (1995): 285–301.

Kruse, Frigga, "Historical Perspectives: The European Commercial Exploitation of Arctic Mineral Resources after 1500 AD", *Polarforschung* 86 (2016): 15–26.

Kvist, Roger, "The Racist Legacy in Modern Swedish Saami Policy", *Canadian Journal of Native Studies/Le Revue Canadienne des Etudes Autochtones* 14 (1994): 203–220.

Laruelle, Marlene, "The Three Waves of Arctic Urbanisation: Drivers, Evolutions, Prospects", *Polar Record* 55 (2019): 1–12.

Lindmark, Daniel, "The Colonial Encounter in Early Modern Sápmi", in Magdalena Naum and Jonas M. Nordin, eds., *Scandinavian Colonialism and the Rise of Modernity: Small Time Agents in a Global Arena* (New York: Springer, 2013), pp. 131–146.

Loeffler, Bob, "Mining and Communities", *Economic Development Journal* 14 (2015): 23–31.

Lowe, Mick, *Premature Bonanza: Standoff at Voisey's Bay* (Toronto: Between the Lines, 1998).

Luckow, Ulrik, and Jørgen Fisker, *Arsukfjorden* (Nuuk: Nordiske Landes Forlag, 1977).

McGhee, Robert, *Arctic Voyages of Martin Frobisher: An Elizabethan Adventure* (Montreal: McGill-Queen's University Press, 2001).

McLean, Ron, and Willie Hensley, *Mining and Indigenous Peoples: The Red Dog Story* (Ottawa: International Council on Metals and the Environment, 1994).

Mehler, Natasha, "The Sulphur Trade of Iceland from the Viking Age to the End of the Hanseatic Period", in Irene Baug et al., eds., *Nordic Middle Ages: Artefacts, Landscapes* and Society. Essays in Honour of Ingvild Øye on her 70th Birthday (Bergen: University of Bergen, 2015), pp. 193–212.

Midgley, Scott, "Contesting Closure: Science, Politics, and Community Responses to Closing the Nanisivik Mine, Nunavut", in A. Keeling and J. Sandlos, eds., Mining and Communities in Northern Canada: History, Politics, and Memory (Calgary: University of Calgary Press, 2015), pp. 293–314.

Mörkenstam, Ulf, "Indigenous Peoples and the Right to Self-determination: The Case of the Swedish Sami People", Canadian Journal of Native Studies/Le Revue Canadienne des Etudes Autochtones 25 (2005): 433–461.

Nagel, Anne-Hilde, "Norwegian Mining in the Early Modern Period", GeoJournal 32 (2020): 137–149.

Naum, Magdalen, "Cultural 'Improvement', Discipline and Mining in Early Modern Sápmi", Post-Medieval Archaeology 52 (2018): 102–116.

Naum, Magdalen, "The Pursuit of Metals and the Ideology of Improvement in Early Modern Sápmi, Sweden", Journal of Social History 51 (2018): 784–807.

Nielsen, Henry, and Henrik Knudsen, "Too Hot to Handle: The Controversial Hunt for Uranium in Greenland in the Early Cold War", Centaurus 55 (2013): 321–343.

Nilsen, Thomas, "Norilsk Tops World's List of Worst SO_2 Polluters", The Barents Observer (21 August 2019), https://thebarentsobserver.com/en/2019/08/norilsk-tops-worlds-list-worst-so2-polluters.

Norlander, David J., "Origins of a Gulag Capital: Magadan and Stalinist Control in the Early 1930s", Slavic Review 57 (2008): 791–812.

Nuttall, Mark, Climate, Society and Subsurface Politics in Greenland (London: Routledge, 2017).

Nygaard, Vigdis, "Do Indigenous Interests Have a Say in Planning of New Mining Projects? Experiences from Finnmark, Norway", The Extractive Industries and Society 3 (2016): 17–24.

Nyström, Markus, "Invisible Histories and Stories of Progress: Discourses and Narratives in Decision-Making Institutions in Mining Affairs in Sweden", MA diss. (Uppsala University, 2015), www.diva-portal.org/smash/get/diva2:893936/FULLTEXT01.pdf.

Ojala, Carl-Gösta, and Jonas M. Nordin, "Mining Sápmi: Colonial Histories, Sámi Archaeology, and the Exploitation of Natural Resources in Northern Sweden", Arctic Anthropology 52 (2015): 6–21.

Paci, Chris, and Noeline Villebrun, "Mining Denendeh: A Dene Nation Perspective on Community Health Impacts of Mining", Pimatisiwin: A Journal of Aboriginal and Indigenous Community Health 3 (2005): 71–86.

Pearce, T. D., J. D. Ford, J. Prno, et al., "Climate Change and Mining in Canada", Mitigation and Adaptation Strategies for Global Change 16 (2011): 347–368.

Persson, Sofia, David Harnesk, and Mine Islar, "What Local People? Examining the Gállok Mining Conflict and the Rights of the Sámi Population in Terms of Justice and Power", Geoforum 86 (2017): 20–29.

Petersen, H. C., "Kryoliten i Ivittuut", Atuagagdliutit – AG (4 May 1995): 10.

Piper, Liza, The Industrial Transformation of Subarctic Canada (Vancouver: UBC Press, 2009).

Pratt, K. L., "Copper, Trade, and Tradition Among the Lower Ahtna of the Chitina River Basin: The Nicolai Era, 1884–1900", Arctic Anthropology 35 (1998): 77–98.

Priebe, Janina, "A Modern Mine? Greenlandic Media Coverage on the Mining Community of Qullissat, Western Greenland, 1942–1968", *Polar Journal* 8 (2018): 141–162.

Ranestad, Kristin, *Knowledge-Based Growth in Natural Resource Intensive Economies: Mining, Knowledge Development and Innovation in Norway 1860–1940* (Cham: Palgrave, 2018).

Rhéaume, Gilles, and Margaret Caron-Vuotari, "The Future of Mining in Canada's North", Conference Board of Canada Report (Ottawa, January 2013).

Rodon, Thierry, Francis Lévesque, and Jonathan Blais, "De Rankin Inlet à Raglan, Le Développement Minier et Les Communautés Inuit", *Études/Inuit/Studies* 37 (2013): 103–122.

Rud, Søren, "Governance and Tradition in Nineteenth Century Greenland", *Interventions* 16 (2014): 551–571.

Sejersen, Frank, *Efterforskning og udnyttelse af råstoffer i Grønland i historisk Perspektiv* (Copenhagen: Københavns Universitet, 2014).

Söderholm, Kristina, and Roine Viklund, "Policy and Business Efforts for the Reduced Impact of Mining on Nature When Historical Studies Have Something to Offer Policy Makers", *Technology and Culture* 60 (2019): 192–218.

Sørensen, Søren Peder, *Qullissat: Byen der ikke vil dø* (Frederiksberg: Frydenlund, 2013).

Sörlin, Sverker, "State and Resources in the North: From Territorial Assertion to the 'Smorgasbord State'", in E. Carina and H. Keskitalo, eds., *The Politics of Arctic Resources: Change and Continuity in the 'Old North' of Northern Europe* (New York: Routledge, 2019), pp. 38–61.

Southcott, Chris, Frances Abele, David Natcher, and Brenda Parlee, eds., *Resources and Sustainable Development in the Arctic* (London: Routledge, 2018).

Spengler, Tim, "Overview of Mining in Alaska", Alaska Legislature Legislative Research Report 13.156 (January 2013).

Spude, Robert L., "An Overview History of the Alaska-Yukon Gold Rushes, 1880–1918", in C. H. Spude, R. O. Mills, K. Gurcke, and R. Sprague, eds., *Eldorado! The Archaeology of Gold Mining in the Far North* (Lincoln: University of Nebraska Press, 2011), pp. 274–287.

Stadius, Peter, "Petsamo: Bringing Modernity to Finland's Arctic Ocean Shore 1920–1939", *Acta Borealia* 33 (2016): 140–165.

Storm, Anna, *Post-Industrial Landscape Scars* (New York: Palgrave Macmillan, 2014).

Sveistrup, P. P., "Ivigtut 1865–1870", *Tidsskriftet for Grønland* 2 (1965): 41–80.

Topp, Niels-Henrik, *Kryolitindustriens Historie 1847–1990* (Copenhagen: Kryolitselskabet Øresund, 1990).

Vikström, Hanna, and Per Högselius, "From Cryolite to Critical Metals: The Scramble for Greenland's Minerals", in Robert C. Thomsen and Lill Rastad Bjørst, eds., *Heritage and Change in the Arctic: Resources for the Present, and the Future* (Aalborg: Aalborg University Press, 2017), pp. 177–211.

19

Creating the Soviet Arctic, 1917–1991

ANDY BRUNO AND EKATERINA KALEMENEVA

Introduction

The Soviets liked to build cities. Armed with a worldview that explicitly valorized urban life as a more advanced stage of history, the revolutionary regime that ruled the former Russian Empire from 1917 to 1991 created new settlements throughout its terrain. Part of the thinking was that a predominantly peasant country had to embrace industrial modernity in order to achieve socialism. But the longing extended to places, usually near mineral deposits or in militarily strategic locations, that had few to no rural populations anywhere in the vicinity. With the constant discovery of rich reserves of natural resources, the Soviet north became one of the most rapidly urbanized areas in the USSR. Several hundred industrial cities, towns, and workers' settlements were built from scratch there, often in previously uninhabited territories and by drawing in completely migratory populations. While eleven permanent towns existed in the Soviet far north in 1926, there were already forty-one in 1933.[1] By the 1960s, this number had increased to over 500 big and small industrial settlements.[2]

These permanent towns not only possessed economic and administrative functions, but also served as symbols of having conquered new and distant territories and incorporated them into the particular national, economic, social, and cultural space of the Soviet Union.[3] Scholars have debated the centrality of the notion of 'conquest' in Russia's modern treatment of the north.[4] Whether this commonly evoked idea was the primary organizing

---

1 *Krainii Sever*, 6.   2 "Nauchnyi otchet po teme".
3 Ackermann and Urbansky, "Introduction: Reframing Postwar Sovietization"; Bohn, "'Sozialistische Stadt'"; Crawford, "From Tractors to Territory"; Zarecor, "What Was So Socialist?".
4 McCannon, "To Storm the Arctic"; Richter, "Nature Mastered by Man"; Bolotova, "Colonization of Nature"; Josephson, "Technology and Conquest"; Lajus, "In Search"; Josephson, *Conquest of Russian Arctic*; Bruno, *Nature of Soviet Power*; Chu, "Encounters with Permafrost".

19 Creating the Soviet Arctic, 1917–1991

principle in Soviet development or was joined by other agendas, whether the rhetoric reflected reality or was mere discourse, whether 'conquest' always meant an aggressive analogy of vanquishing an opponent or entailed its own field of divergent meanings, whether the notion stood at odds with more humane and environmentally sensitive strategies of development or was flexible enough to also promote nature preservation and the creation of a good life – all of these questions have elicited different answers from historians studying the Soviet Arctic. However, there is consensus on one point: by hook or by crook, Soviet leaders wanted people to live in its polar region, preferably in urban clusters.

The idea of creating modern settlements in the Arctic was common to many northern countries.[5] Yet the USSR distinguished itself in the priority it placed on developing an urban north. While the twentieth-century Arctic of Canada, Denmark, the United States, Norway, Sweden, and Finland involved science, exploration, exploitation of resources, and mechanisms of defence, none of these countries pursued making the Arctic an area where more people lived with the same stridency as the Soviets. Not only did the Soviet Union possess the longest Arctic coastline of any country in the world, but it also attained the most industrialized and populated northern territory. Placing the USSR's agenda of creating an industrial Arctic where more people would live at the forefront of our vision allows us to better make sense of its tangled past.

The distinctiveness of the Soviet approach can perhaps most vividly be traced with the case of Pyramiden on Svalbard. The desire for acquiring more fossil fuels and maintaining a foothold in the once disputed Norwegian territory inspired the Soviet Union to build three coal mining towns (Barentsburg, Grumant, and Pyramiden). As a signatory to the Svalbard Treaty, the Soviet Union maintained rights to exploit the archipelago's resources, which it exercised in the 1930s under Arktikugol with the goal of fuelling the mainland's rapidly expanding heavy industry.[6] After the death of Soviet leader Joseph Stalin in the early 1950s, the polity turned Pyramiden into a well-stocked, though still miniature, exemplar of a socialist city. Workers received bonuses and enjoyed amenities that were hard to come by in most Soviet cities, and its population grew even as coal supplies dwindled.[7]

---

5 Decker, *Modern North*; Dybbroe et al., "Dynamics of Arctic Urbanization"; Farish and Lackenbauer, "High Modernism"; Hemmersam, "Arctic Architectures".
6 Borovoi, "Deiatel'nost' tresta 'Arktikugol'".   7 Gnilorybov, *Piramida*.

A comparison with the Norwegian town of Longyearbyen is illustrative here. Though only 50 km apart, Pyramiden and Longyearbyen embodied different models of Arctic urbanity. The latter consists of colourful two-storey wooden houses spread over a rather large territory, while the former was built with seemingly similar multistorey brick and has a monument to Vladimir Lenin in the middle of the main street. To a contemporary visitor it may look like a typical socialist town, strangely located in an untypical natural landscape. At the same time, along with several apartment blocks, which were architecturally and technically adapted for the Arctic climate, the built environment of the relatively small settlement of Pyramiden (up to 1,000 inhabitants) included a large Palace of Culture with a cinema theatre and a concert hall, a massive sport complex with a swimming pool and several gyms, a school and a kindergarten, and a pig farm and a greenhouse to supply the settlement. The built structures of Pyramiden represented the ideal of providing urban facilities for the inhabitants of the Arctic.[8] Of course, not all Soviet Arctic towns were as well-equipped as Pyramiden, but nevertheless after the 1960s many of them were imagined, described, and at least planned with the idea of recreating 'a fully developed and normal life', even for small and distant Arctic settlements. Such an urban model reflected an evolution in Soviet policy in the latter half of the twentieth century, even if getting people to the Arctic had been on the agenda from the very beginning.

We contend that the push to people parts of the Arctic sat at the centre of the Soviet Union's approach to its vast polar territories. A good portion of this impulse can be chalked up to settler colonialist and high modernist drives that united empires across the north. But the case of Svalbard, where there had not been an Indigenous population, underscores an even broader lust to transform the north. In its steadfast pursuit to establish the Arctic as a livable space, the USSR stood out. This form of livability entailed certain urbanized and industrialized models of residence, not the expansion of rural and nomadic livelihoods that had been practised in the Arctic for centuries. Indeed, the Soviet version of livability both as a form of socialist modernity and marginalized exile counterposed, if not outright opposed, the lifestyles of many earlier inhabitants. It was the aggressive imposition of industrial realities on non-industrial lifeways that tied the carceral expansion of the Gulag to the enthusiastic flourishing of urban settlements – all at the expense

---

8 Avango et al., "Industrial Extraction"; Avango and Roberts, "Industrial Heritage".

of ways of life that pre-dated the Soviet presence. This orientation also set the Soviet Union apart from the long and influential history of Russia's earlier engagement with the north.

Russia was an Arctic country before it was Russia. In the fourteenth century the principality of Novgorod claimed territories reaching to the shores of the Barents Sea on the Kola Peninsula.[9] Under Grand Prince Ivan III in the late fifteenth century, Muscovy – the Orthodox Christianity-practising, Slavic-speaking polity around Moscow – conquered Novgorod and took nominal possession of its dominions, while vanquishing surrounding principalities into the kernel of the modern Russian state.[10] Orthodox monasteries and hermitages, as well as small groups of traders, migrants, and seasonal fishers appeared amid the Indigenous populations of the far north. This limited presence of agents with some connection to the Muscovite state continued as Russia expanded eastward through Siberia, eventually jumping the Bering Strait over to Alaska.[11]

Though a powerful multi-ethnic and multi-confessional empire by the eighteenth century, Russian control over much of its Arctic lands remained cursory and fragmentary. Near the Bering Strait, the Yupik and Chukchi successfully fended off invading Cossacks in the 1740s and maintained closer ties with visiting Americans through the nineteenth century.[12] Elsewhere tax collectors and missionaries reached inhabitants occasionally, but many native groups spent their lives at some remove from the state.[13] Since serfdom never took full root in the north, and state officials resisted extending the main new institution of local self-governance (*zemstva*), the Great Reforms of the 1860s were less felt in the Russian Arctic than in some other parts of the empire. Migration and modernization schemes became increasingly discussed during the final decades of tsardom, but their implementation remained limited, at least in comparison to what was to come.[14]

Industrializing the Arctic through Stalinism

A key feature of the Soviet project was the push for an industrialized, militarized, scientized, and urbanized Arctic. This process occurred with much brutality, but also with an impulse to make the north a place where

---

9 McCannon, *History of the Arctic*, 69–71.   10 Kollmann, *Russian Empire*, 41–54.
11 Hartley, *Siberia*; Wood, *Russia's Frozen Frontier*; Lincoln, *Conquest of a Continent*; Vinkovetsky, *Russian America*.
12 Demuth, *Floating Coast*, 86–88.   13 Forsyth, *History of the Peoples*.
14 Josephson, *Conquest of Russian Arctic*, 22–29.

many more people would live at least part of their lives. The early Soviet Arctic evokes a kaleidoscope of contradictory images: starvation in Gulag prison camps alongside the heroics of polar aviation; attacks on Indigenous livelihoods alongside sensitive ethnographic studies of northern peoples; constant talk about the beauty of socialist horizons alongside an obsessive focus on violently rooting out counter-revolutionary enemies; disruption of people's material well-being alongside huge projects to build new industrial plants and cities; the establishment of military installations alongside cutting-edge scientific exploration and institution building. Yet an overarching vision of an industrialized Arctic tied these elements together.

The settlement that would become the largest Arctic city in the world came into being with the war that birthed the Soviet Union. After decades of debate, tsarist authorities rushed to build a railroad line to the Murman coast in northwest Russia during World War I. Thousands of prisoners of war served as a primary labour force for this project, many of whom died while facing abysmal deprivations. The terminus of the line became a new city, Romanov-on-the-Murman, quickly renamed Murmansk after the ruling dynasty fell. Unlike Arkhangelsk, which had served as a seaport connection to Europe since the sixteenth century, Murmansk benefited from ice-free coastal waters all year round.[15] After the Bolsheviks took control in late 1917 and the country descended into civil war, foreign troops stationed themselves in the Russian Arctic in hopes of helping to oust the new radical regime.[16] They failed. Soon one of the new Soviet state's earliest Arctic schemes involved turning the Murmansk railroad into a 'industrial-colonization-transportation combine' to self-sufficiently populate and develop the region with its own subsidiary enterprises.[17]

Many people already lived in the Soviet Arctic by the 1920s, of course. Indigenous groups such as the Chukchi, Sakha, Evenki, Nenets, Komi, and Sami had occupied the north for centuries. They engaged in hunting, herding, fishing, and trading, and maintained their own cultural practices and spiritual beliefs. These Indigenous peoples also had plenty of experience with merchants, missionaries, and other state agents (Russian and foreign) but held on to an impressive degree of autonomy over their own affairs. Native northerners frequently saw their own capacity to live on their homelands as being at odds with the transformative agendas of an encroaching state. From their end, Soviet authorities tended to view Indigenous peoples of the Arctic

15 Bruno, *Nature of Soviet Power*, 29–72.   16 Fogelsong, *America's Secret War*.
17 *Proizvoditel'nye sily raiona Murmanskoi*.

as ethnic victims of imperial oppression who nevertheless required modernization to be integrated into the socialist project. The government created a Committee of the North in 1924 and charged it with both gathering information on Indigenous northerners and uplifting them with new Soviet cultural institutions.[18] The ethnographers who dominated this body led the charge in turning a census of the Soviet Arctic into a comprehensive study of native livelihoods.[19] An urge to improve and transform Indigenous ways of life accompanied the sympathy and curiosity of these researchers. When state policy turned aggressive and sought to bring about 'socialism in one country' as quickly as possible in the late 1920s, many once-sensitive ethnographers helped impose violent upheavals on Indigenous communities. The ethnographer Innokentii Suslov penned an intricate account of shamanism among the Evenki while declaring a war on shamans.[20]

The campaign against shamans related to a broader assault on perceived class enemies during the Stalinist revolution of 1928–32. This period of the first Five-Year Plan witnessed a heady push to industrialize, the creation of collective farms, and the liquidation of 'kulaks' (putatively wealthy peasants). These three prongs of Stalinism came together in the Khibiny Mountains. There authorities established a new 'socialist city' above the polar circle, supplied with labour from 'special settlers' (former kulaks who had been exiled to new regions) sent from elsewhere in the country, and created new collective farms both near the industrial works and out in the taiga among Sami reindeer herders.[21] New mining settlements existed throughout the circumpolar north in the 1930s, but the Soviet project in Khibinogorsk/Kirovsk was distinguished by its ambitions to place mining, processing, and a large permanent population in a polar region instead of simply extracting the wealth from the ground with minimal effort. This produced a juxtaposition between the lofty ideological goals of enlivening the north and the brutal circumstances on the ground. Planners dreamed of supplying the 'population with the satisfaction of all the requirements of a normal and cultured existence in the unique conditions of the far north', while those on the ground despaired that 'the contamination of the settlement with garbage, overcrowding, the absence of a basic stock of everyday items, and the

18 Krupnik, *Arctic Adaptations*; Slezkine, *Arctic Mirrors*; Demuth, *Floating Coast*.
19 Anderson, ed., *1926/27 Soviet Polar Census*.   20 Suslov, "Shamanstvo i bor'ba s nim".
21 Bruno, "Industrial Life"; Zaika, "Rehabilitation"; Bruno, "Tale of Two Reindeer".

dirtiness of the area' was creating 'a favourable atmosphere for the development of disease'.[22]

A number of other mid-sized cities popped up in the Soviet Arctic in the Stalinist era, often connected to deposits of coal, metals, or other valuable minerals or energy resources.[23] The biggest of these projects – the nickel mines of Norilsk and the coalfields of Vorkuta – began as prison camps.[24] The Gulag as an institution itself arose in the far north. In the 1920s, authorities set up a prison camp on the Solovestskii islands – home of an old Orthodox Christian monastery – from which grew one of the first construction projects of the Soviet penal system (the White Sea–Baltic Canal).[25] By the mid-1930s, the Gulag supplied labour for almost all northern development projects. As its numbers ballooned with bouts of state repression and terror, the Gulag's putative promise of redemption through labour commonly turned into death by deprivation.[26] These forced labourers built the massive works in Vorkuta and Norilsk. Such compulsion is frequently and rightly taken as a sign of the depravity of the Soviet system. But the concentrated populations that appeared because of the camps also contributed to later campaigns to make the Soviet Arctic livable. As historian Alan Barenberg has shown, deep continuities shaped the transition of Vorkuta from a Gulag town to a company town in the 1950s.[27]

Not only forced labour made the Stalinist Arctic. Scientific expeditions and institution building, polar exploration, and the artistic celebration of the north in film and other media integrated the Soviet Arctic into the country's imagination and identity. Geological prospectors discovered numerous deposits that became sites for Arctic industry, while oceanographers studied Arctic fisheries and their fluctuating stocks.[28] Meanwhile, the predecessor organizations of the current Arctic and Antarctic Research Institute – contemporary Russia's leading body for polar science – came into existence, including under the powerful Main Administration of the Northern Sea Route (*Glavsevmorput*) in 1932. For a period in the 1930s, *Glavsevmorput* exercised authority over much of

---

22 Munts, "Gorod Khibinogorsk", 193; Protocol from a meeting of doctors.
23 Frey, *Arktischer Heizraum*.
24 Barenberg, *Gulag Town, Company Town*; Ertz, "Building Norilsk".
25 Robson, *Solovki*; Kraikovski and Lajus, "'Space of Blue'"; Ruder, *Making History for Stalin*.
26 Barnes, *Death and Redemption*; Alexopoulos, *Illness and Inhumanity*; Bell, *Stalin's Gulag at War*.
27 Barenberg, *Gulag Town, Company Town*.
28 Bolotova, "Colonization of Nature"; Lajus, "'Red Herring'".

the Arctic, sponsoring expeditions, research, and non-Gulag economic operations while also developing sea transport along the northern Soviet coastline. Icebreakers and aeroplanes both angled across the Arctic Ocean and headed toward the North Pole. The feats and follies of these vessels and their crews became fodder for Soviet adventure stories, newspaper tabloids, and documentary films.[29] Soviet filmmakers joined international endeavours to exoticize the north, but also depicted it as part of their homeland.[30]

Another trend in the Soviet era that began in the 1930s was the militarization of parts of the Arctic. As security concerns ramped up during the Great Terror of 1937–38, when the state executed and imprisoned hundreds of thousands of supposed counter-revolutionary 'enemies of the people', the Soviet Navy began to dramatically expand its flotilla on the Murman coast into the Northern Fleet.[31] This military buildup was reinforced when the USSR went to war with Finland in 1939–40 and then Nazi Germany in 1941. During World War II, the Arctic played a key role in transportation. Many citizens evacuated the northwest, and much infrastructure was destroyed. Further east, industrial works under Gulag auspices expanded to meet wartime need. With some territorial gains in the Arctic after victory, including the nickel deposits in the Pechenga region, the Soviet Union rebuilt its industry following similar methods to those employed in the 1930s.[32] The Cold War also enhanced the strategic importance of the Soviet north, especially as it faced two members of NATO – Norway and the United States – one on each end of its Arctic territory.[33]

Making the Arctic Livable

The first decades of Soviet rule had already formed models for industrializing and populating the Arctic. These focused on extensive resource extraction through forced colonization and the exclusive role of central state institutions and industrial ministries in establishing settlements rather than the creation of organic communities in the far north.[34] After Stalin's death in 1953, the political, social, and economic changes known as the 'Thaw' led to significant shifts in Arctic policy.

29 McCannon, *Red Arctic*.   30 Widdis, *Visions*; Kaganovsky et al., eds., *Arctic Cinemas*.
31 Hønneland and Jørgensen, *Integration vs. Autonomy*, 119–120.
32 McCannon, *History of the Arctic*, 223–235; Rowe, *Industry*.
33 Josephson, *Conquest of Russian Arctic*; Demuth, *Floating Coast*.
34 Shirokov, *Dal'stroi v sotsial'no-ekonomicheskom razvitii*.

The closure of most Gulag prison camps and downgrading of the once prominent role of *Glavsevmorput* in the mid-1950s spurred a need to define new principles for the administration of the Soviet Union's vast northern territories. As a result, research into the organization of industry and the creation of settlements in the Arctic became a part of public science in the USSR. This change facilitated increased coordination between local and central scientific institutions, planning organizations, and industrial departments. In the mid-1950s, civil scientific and planning institutes were established in Leningrad, Moscow, Siberia, and the European north, whose duties included elaborating new principles for the economic and urban development of the Arctic.[35] Experts in various disciplines, including economic geographers and geologists, industrial and planning specialists, and architects and sociologists, became concerned with the prospecting and extraction of Arctic resources. Final decisions about further development and construction in the Arctic nevertheless resulted from difficult negotiations between the scientists and planning organizations, local authorities, and industrial ministries.[36]

This new approach often yielded mixed results. The involvement of specialists from different institutions and administrative levels lengthened the process of decision-making and made the issue of final responsibility less clear. Some institutions drew up plans for 'rational' industrial development and the creation of a built environment in Arctic settlements, but other organizations or local construction bureaus did not feel obliged to follow them.[37] Nevertheless, the efforts of design institutes made the creation of suitable built environments in the Arctic an important element of public discourse on various levels from the speeches of officials to local newspaper articles in Arctic settlements.

In the Thaw era of the mid-1950s, Soviet leader Nikita Khrushchev proclaimed a new economic course including active development of natural resources in the north of Siberia and the Far East. Thanks to this initiative, for several decades these territories were turned into a zone of constant construction of new industrial infrastructure and settlements.[38] This policy aimed to discover and exploit 'the natural treasures' of the north and added distant and sparsely populated areas of Siberia and the Far East into visions of an industrialized and urbanized Soviet Arctic. Discoveries of large deposits of gas, oil, diamonds, coal, and other valuable resources in northern Siberia in

---

35 Kalemeneva, "New Socialist Cities".
36 Stas, "Diskussiia"; Kalemeneva, "Smena modelei".   37 Yuzmuhamedov, *Udachnyi*, 87.
38 *20 S'ezd KPSS*, Vol. 1, 80.

the 1950s and 1960s brought new industrial towns.[39] Yet most of the deposits were located in sparsely populated areas with a harsh climate for living and for organizing industrial production, and often distant from the existing transportation networks and economically developed centres, where the main consumers of the resources were concentrated. In this situation, the closure of the Gulag system fundamentally changed migration regimes in the Soviet north, understood as 'policies, practices, and infrastructure designed to both foster and limit human movement'.[40] On the one hand, the Soviet government retained a monopoly over the distribution of all resources, including labour. On the other hand, northern industrial settlements opened to migration flows in the 1950s, and the state had to find new ways to encourage voluntary migration to emerging industrial sites and to facilities previously supported by Gulag prison camps.

Industrialization and urbanization remained based on the recruitment of a non-Indigenous workforce. One tool for attracting new workers to northern industrial sites was the ideological calls for the 'construction of socialism' in distant territories. 'Komsomol appeals' issued by the Central Committee of the Communist Party also sought to 'send the best young fellows' to the construction works in the eastern and northern parts of the country.[41] Just a few weeks after the first appeal in 1956, groups of party and Komsomol activists, as well as other young specialists, arrived at various construction sites in the far north and Siberia.[42]

A state-sponsored system of material privileges for migrants known as 'northern bonuses' became an even more powerful tool of attraction. Newcomers to industrial sites received higher salaries than in other Soviet territories, had longer vacations, and could retain accommodation in their places of origin. The list of territories included in the 'northern bonuses' programme, as well as the list of privileges, changed through the decades. Nevertheless, higher wages and material advantages remained one of the main motivations to move to Arctic industrial towns.[43] For many newcomers, the migration to northern mono-industrial towns was also the only possibility to move within the USSR.[44] Other countries offered incentives for working in the north, but none institutionalized these privileges with the

---

39 Reisser, "Russia's Arctic Cities"; Wilson, "Siberian Oil and Gas Industry"; Hogselius, *Red Gas*.
40 Siegelbaum and Moch, *Broad Is My Native Land*, 3.
41 "Obrashchenie Tsentral'nogo Komiteta", 1.
42 Dolgoliuk, "Rol' kommunisticheskikh partiinykh organizatsii".
43 Emeliantseva Koller, "Negotiating 'Coldness'".   44 Saxinger, "Lured by Oil", 55.

same tenacity and with comparable control over access to goods. As one scholar describes the situation: 'Northerners thus enjoyed luxuries normally reserved for the Soviet nomenclatura: living in the "cognac zone," they flew to Moscow to shop for furs and perfume, took holidays on the Bulgarian coast, and retired in their fifties to custom-built colonies in the Baltics.'[45]

These enticements worked well enough. Already by the late 1960s, more than 90 per cent of the population of some Arctic regions, like the Kola Peninsula, were migrants.[46] But the benefits did not always compensate for the hardships of life in the Arctic. Though migration flows to the newly established Arctic industrial settlements increased annually in the 1950s and 1960s, net out-migration was also very high. As many as 70 per cent left the settlements each year, which remained an important problem in the Soviet Arctic for decades. Sociological surveys showed that the main reason that residents left was their dissatisfaction with living conditions and the lack of developed social and cultural infrastructure.[47]

The newcomers usually had no experience living in the Arctic climate with its long dark winters and light but mild summers. Their migratory status fostered a collective experience. All inhabitants of the emerging industrial towns faced a harsh climate and similar living conditions. Relatively equal motivations for migration helped to create a high level of solidarity and a sense of security in small settlements where everybody knew each other. Strong feelings of connection towards the northern environment often grew, as did a 'euphoria of collectivism' among the builders of the new industries and settlements in the north and Siberia.[48] Moreover, the joint creation of settlements from scratch led to the comparative lack of hierarchy within them. Many felt increased responsibility for collective work and for the future of the town, especially during the first years of construction.[49]

Construction in the Arctic was a challenge for economic planners, architects, and builders. The lack of proper machinery that could operate in cold climates, the isolation from developed industrial centres with necessary building materials, and the difficulties of building on permafrost made any construction in the Arctic much more expensive than in other regions.[50] At the same time, permanent towns in the Arctic also played valuable symbolic

---

45 Thompson, *Settlers on the Edge*, 4.
46 Vaitens, "Sotsial'no-Demograficheskie Osobennosti", 106.
47 Kutsev, *Chelovek na Severe*.
48 Bolotova, "Loving and Conquering Nature"; Bolotova and Stammler, "How North Became Home"; Zhelnina, "'Zhelezo'".
49 Rozhanskii, "'Ottepel' na sibirskom morose".   50 Chu, *Life of Permafrost*.

roles. They were places with concentrated proletarian populations, thus seen as more progressive than peasant regions, and where certain social and cultural models were disseminated.[51] The settlements served the symbolic assimilation of the Arctic through street naming, standard monuments in town squares, neo-classical buildings for local administrations or theatres, as well as in the general planning and architectural schemes.

Northern construction even in former Gulag towns was often led by visiting specialists who had no previous experience of living and working in the polar climate, which led to the frequent use of southern forms in the layout.[52] The lack of theoretical development of construction principles in the Arctic region until the 1960s often affected the built environment of socialist cities. Many smaller settlements did not provide basic amenities and consisted largely of one-storey wooden buildings, which were completely covered with snow during long winters.[53] Even Norilsk and Vorkuta contained only chaotic heaps of barracks and wooden houses beyond the solemnly planned neo-classical centres in the mid-1950s.[54] Many planned towns were at first filled with small wooden houses, barracks, and tents used as workers' dormitories, temporary accommodation that often endured for long periods.

At the same time, the mass housing campaign started by Khrushchev in the mid-1950s moved millions of people out of communal apartments and reshaped socialist urban space with standardized apartment blocks. This campaign had radical effects on the development of the Soviet Arctic. Standardized building practices gave way to specialization oriented toward different climate zones. Like the rest of the country, even small Soviet Arctic towns eventually became home to prefabricated concrete buildings organized in micro-districts with a standard set of communal services like schools, hospitals, houses of culture, and theatres. The new urban experts and architects involved in this campaign adhered to specific principles of 'northern' urban planning that arose in the 1960s.[55] A new social structure of Arctic settlements, as well as the higher level of scientific expertise in their creation, prompted the concept of a 'northern town' with specific social and material features.

Something of a counter-trend emerged in the rural and Indigenous Arctic in this era. Instead of bringing in migrants, non-urban zones lost inhabitants

---

51 Zamyatina, "Igarka as a Frontier".   52 Slabukha, "Zodchie Norillaga".
53 "Obsledovanie naselennykh", list 123.
54 Nazarova, "My, molodye arhitektory", 479–480.   55 Kalemeneva, "New Socialist Cities".

through displacements, resettlements, and the abandonment of villages in areas like the Arkhangelsk province.[56] The erection of industrial and military facilities pushed communities off their homelands. A dramatic example occurred on the island of Novaya Zemlya, which the Soviets turned into a nuclear testing site. As authorities prepared to coat the territory with the residue of mushroom clouds, they forcefully removed Nenets and Russians living there and resettled them on neighbouring Kolguev Island.[57]

Such de-ruralization ultimately served Arctic urbanization. In the middle of the twentieth century, the Arctic became the most rapidly urbanized area in the USSR. By 1966, the population of the far north – a jurisdiction that included Arctic and subarctic territories as well as much of Siberia – was estimated at 5.6 million people, or 2.5 per cent of the total number of citizens in the USSR, and 90 per cent of these people were industrial labourers, which meant that they lived in urban areas.[58] After the reorganization of the Gulag, newly established towns were family-based settlements built without the labour of prisoners. This meant that the social and urban structure of post-Gulag towns differed as they had all the basic elements of 'ordinary life' with various public services and increased expectations from consumer culture in the 1960s.[59]

These new models of urbanization influenced perceptions and representations of the Arctic in Soviet media. While the press avoided mentioning the Gulag past of many northern industrial towns, heroic narratives about Arctic exploration remained a part of official propaganda. The core of these narratives changed in the Thaw era. Whereas in the 1930s the main heroes were often polar explorers and the Arctic itself was represented as an exceptional place, in the 1950s the main focus of numerous articles in the Soviet press was on the creation of normal and 'ordinary life' in the north. The region became described as 'the most romantic place in our country, where people with the most romantic professions work', and as a place of normal life and work for thousands of ordinary Soviet people.[60] The similarity between Arctic settlements and central Soviet cities was often demonstrated through reference to the use of contemporary technologies and the everyday life of citizens.[61] Even Indigenous settlements were often described in the press through modern urban technologies: for example, by pointing out that 'good-quality, insulated houses have long replaced the tents for the Nenets', and by focusing only on the social infrastructure common in Soviet spaces: the

---

56 Berg, "Reform".   57 Arzyutov, "Reassembling the Environmental Archive".
58 Slavin, "Spravka po sovetskomu", list 221.
59 Kalemeneva, "Sovetskaia politika osvoeniia".   60 Rudov, "Arktika bez ekzotiki", 3.
61 "Nasha Arktika", 3.

clubhouse, the school, or the medical centre.[62] Descriptions of new Arctic settlements almost always stressed the vanishing distance between the central parts of the USSR and the newly developed areas of the north.

Living in the Late Soviet Arctic

The last decades of Soviet rule saw the full execution of Thaw-era initiatives at Arctic industrial livability. Political winds famously blew the other way during the late Soviet period, from the mid-1960s to the mid-1980s, as captured by two epithets sometimes used to characterize the premiership of Leonid Brezhnev and his immediate successors: re-Stalinization and stagnation. However, these images of staleness and repression obscure more about the social history of the late Soviet Arctic than they reveal.[63] With the construction process mostly complete, these final decades show the creation of the Soviet Arctic in its fullest form. After all, the Soviet Arctic in this period held the status of the most populated Arctic that has ever existed. In the 1970s and 1980s the quantity of inhabitants in cities and military bases continued to swell, while Norilsk churned out nickel, Vorkuta unearthed coal, and hydrocarbon extraction took off in northern territories of western Siberia. Scientific institutions dedicated to the study of the Arctic existed throughout the north, drawing in educated professionals who often consulted with industry.[64]

Life in urban Arctic settlements in many ways resembled Soviet life more broadly. Prefabricated apartment buildings dotted the terrain, access to consumer goods could be sporadic despite northern bonuses, and residents spent free time on sports, television, music, and drink. Dearth and poverty prevailed, but less so than in the recent past. Stability and boredom captured the atmosphere more than heroic struggles to conquer the north.[65] There were also specific traits, of course. Extreme seasonality and a preponderance of time spent in the cold tied the Soviet Arctic to experiences elsewhere in the circumpolar north. The centralized heating infrastructure of the Soviets inefficiently and erratically compensated for the cold. Most food had to be transported in from distant realms.[66]

All told, it was the combination of hyper-urbanism and Arctic natural conditions that most shaped lived experience in the late Soviet era. Though

---

62 "Arktika dalekaia i blizkaia", 3.   63 Yurchak, *Everything Was Forever*.
64 Josephson, *Conquest of Russian Arctic*, 170–237.
65 Raleigh, *Soviet Baby Boomers*; Ward, *Brezhnev's Folly*.
66 Bolotova, "Conquering Nature"; Emeliantseva Koller, "Negotiating 'Coldness'".

many people only spent stints in the north, migrating away to different climes after a period of time, others made the area a permanent home. Anthropologist Alla Bolotova underscores the attachment to place and affective bonds that many developed for Kirovsk, Apatity, and Kovdor on the Kola Peninsula. Respondents to her interviews cited warmer relations with neighbours and more vivid natural surroundings.[67] Discussing the closed city of Severodvinsk in the Arkhangelsk region, historian Ekaterina Emeliantseva Koller describes how the consumption privileges successfully promoted community cohesion amid the cold. More than doubling in size from a population of about 100,000 in the early 1960s to over 200,000 in the early 1980s, 'Severodvinsk had reached a level of prosperity that today evokes nostalgic feelings by the elderly generation'.[68] One resident even claimed that 'the level of happiness was higher here than anywhere else'.[69] This sense of specialness and contentment extended to Chukotka, where settlers told anthropologist Niobe Thompson that residents were more 'open-hearted' and 'trusting' than in central Russia.[70]

Despite these warm feelings, the main motivation for many migrants to northern industries remained higher wages and other material bonuses. While the continuous growth of new industrial cities with developed urban infrastructure was supposed to 'compensate' for the harsh climate conditions of the Arctic, the level of negative migration remained high even in the 1970s.[71] Indeed, over time the policy of creating permanent Arctic settlements with fully developed social and cultural spheres fell into conflict with economic considerations. The ministries responsible for construction works often saw the new planning and construction principles in Arctic cities as enormously expensive and resisted fully funding projects. Because of this, the built urban environment often failed to create sufficiently comfortable living conditions in the polar environment.[72]

Moreover, new types of extractive industries, such as oil and gas, did not require large settlements with intense concentrations of workers. This called into question the need for expensive social infrastructure with schools or theatres in small Arctic settlements as a mandatory pillar of Soviet Arctic urbanity. As a result, already in the late 1960s some settlements close to new oil extraction sites in western Siberia were designed as rotational camps for

---

67 Bolotova, "Engaging with the Environment".
68 Emeliantseva Koller, "Negotiating 'Coldness'", 257.
69 Emeliantseva Koller, "Privilege of Seclusion", 238.
70 Thompson, *Settlers on the Edge*, 84.   71 Kutsev, *Chelovek na Severe*, 94.
72 Slavin, "Sostoianie stroitel'stva", list 55.

short-term workers.[73] By the 1980s, there were already a few hundred rotational settlements in the Arctic.[74] The main difference between permanent cities and rotational industrial settlements was that the latter contained only basic elements of urban infrastructure, and it was forbidden to arrive there with a family. Yet this policy was applied unevenly: sometimes different bureaucratic institutions considered the same settlements as both permanent and temporary.[75] In addition, some settlements established as rotational camps were transformed into ordinary towns, and vice versa.

If, on the whole, urban migrants to the Arctic, including industrial workers, scientists, military personnel, party functionaries, and families brought along for the ride, found ways to take advantage of the forms of livability promoted by the Soviet state, then how did Indigenous populations fare? Here again we come to the contradictions of socialist settler colonialism. The state's modernizing impulse had hastened the displacement of Indigenous northerners. Some forced relocations occurred because of flooding for hydroelectric dams, exclusion from conservation territories, and evacuations for military installations, but even more occurred as a result of the consolidation of collective farms (*kolkhozy*). Whereas initial collective farms had mostly been set up where Arctic Indigenous peoples had already resided, the agglomeration of them into state farms (*sovkhozy*) from the 1950s to 1970s often required moving to a single regional town.[76] Combined with the practice of sending children to residential schools and isolating occupational activities like reindeer husbandry from domestic life, these changes deeply disrupted native lives.[77] However, it would be a mistake to assume a uniform opposition of Indigenous communities to Soviet modernization. On the contrary, some developed allegiances to the safety net and structures of the late Soviet agricultural economy.[78] Other Indigenous peoples of the Soviet Arctic found themselves residing primarily in the same urban enclaves as settlers and becoming accustomed to such lifestyles.[79]

73 Gavrilova, "Osobennosti sotsial'noi politiki".
74 Kutsev, *Chelovek v Severnom gorode*, 115.
75 Gavrilova, "Osobennosti sotsial'noi politiki", 136.
76 Bruno, *Nature of Soviet Power*, 155–161.
77 Bloch, *Red Ties*; Slezkine, *Arctic Mirrors*, 337–371.
78 Konstantinov, "Reinterpreting the Sovkhoz"; Vladimirova, *Just Labor*; Humphrey, *Marx Went Away*; Vladimirova, "Technologies of Modern Reindeer". On the Sami, also see Luk'ianchenko, *Material'naia kul'tura saamov*; Konstantinov and Vladimirova, "Performative Machine"; Overland and Berg-Nordlie, *Bridging Divides*; Allemann, "Experience of Displacement".
79 Gray, *Predicament of Chukotka's Indigenous Movement*.

Industrial forms of life for human populations in the Arctic also exerted an influence on other lifeforms. Some reindeer populations collapsed amid efforts to increase herd sizes, and whales were almost hunted to extinction in the northern waters.[80] Most visibly, territories surrounding the huge industrial facilities in Norilsk and Vorkuta (and many more throughout the north) became denuded and pockmarked. Forests withered from toxic emissions, waterways lost the ability to house native fish species, and habitats for birds, lichens, and other plants and animals became zones for extracting minerals, metals, and energy. It was precisely in this period of peak human presence in the Soviet Arctic that the perils faced by non-human inhabitants also accelerated and, in some instances, reached their height.[81]

The *perestroika* (reconstruction) period that began after Mikhail Gorbachev came to power in 1985 prompted Arctic aspirations to be voiced in new ways, while also opening the floodgates of critique of the negative impacts on native cultures, the environmental consequences of wanton industrialization, and the inefficiencies of maintaining cities from the stance of the market economy. Gorbachev himself envisaged the northern polar region as an arena for cooperation and argued for putting aside Cold War militarization of the Arctic. But as his project for reform spun out of control, it temporarily empowered Indigenous rights groups and environmental movements that were highly critical of Soviet policy in the Arctic.[82] In the end, though, it was the market fundamentalists who viewed urbanization of the north as a costly mistake who became the most influential voices after the Soviet experiment fell apart in 1991.

Conclusion

If in the Soviet period the country's Arctic was defined by a programme of getting more people to live there, then the collapse of the USSR into fifteen successor states that have abandoned communism witnessed a stark about-face. As human populations worldwide ballooned since 1991, the number of people living in the Russian Arctic shrank. Pyramiden on Svalbard, evacuated in 1998, has become a mausoleum of Arctic communism for visiting tourists.[83]

The massive effort to establish a system of permanent settlements with large-scale industrial activities and communities in the Arctic collided with

---

80 Jones, *Red Leviathan*.   81 Bruno, *Nature of Soviet Power*, 202–213.
82 McCannon, *History of the Arctic*, 266–271.
83 Andreassen et al., *Persistent Memories*; Bykova, "Changing Nature".

the deep country-wide economic crisis of the 1990s. Neoliberal reformers declared that the Soviet Union had over-developed its Arctic and now needed to pay for its poor decision through the privatization of public assets and the abandonment of social incentives.[84] This perspective naturalized the political choices to eviscerate welfare state protections as the harsh medicine that a new capitalist Russia needed, despite any misery it caused. And, indeed, privatization of former state plants and their large infrastructures often harmed the populations of Arctic settlements. Without substantial financial support from the state, the system of privileged benefits and social services accompanying the settlements around northern industries began to fall apart. Within the new market economy, the state and private companies came to see financial bonuses for their inhabitants of Arctic towns and the large urban infrastructure accompanying them – schools and hospitals, theatres and workers' clubs, everything that was earlier considered as a major advantage of Soviet Arctic urbanization – as an unprofitable burden.[85]

As a result of this economic reorientation, the population of the Russian Arctic decreased by almost 20 per cent in the 1990s, mainly owing to migration outflow.[86] While settlements in oil and gas areas still experience population growth, towns in other northern regions have been shrinking. Only with a gradual economic turnaround in the 2000s did the haemorrhaging of population slow down and some counter-currents appear. Legacy industries like Nornickel (Norilsk Nickel) became tremendously rich multinational companies, while oil extraction and exploration – both on land and under the ocean – propped up an economically recovering state.[87] Wealthy businesspeople sponsored local initiatives at renewed modernization in places such as Chukotka.[88]

Yet global warming and other environmental issues have emerged to challenge the possibilities of an Arctic renewal in Russia. Projects to update an aged infrastructure and create new sustainable cities have collided with roadblocks connected to thawing permafrost, seasonal floods, wildfires, and species disappearance.[89] The Arctic is poised to feel the effects of climate change early and potently. In the immediate term these disruptions are likely to interfere with future campaigns to make the Russian Arctic a more livable place for humans. In the medium term one could easily imagine a warmer

---

84 Hill and Gaddy, *The Siberian Curse*.   85 Josephson, *Conquest of Russian Arctic*, 334–339.
86 Sokolova and Choi, "Russian Arctic"; Heleniak, "Out-migration and Depopulation"; Heleniak, "Changing Settlement Patterns".
87 Sellheim et al., eds., *Arctic Triumph*; Laruelle, *Russia's Arctic Strategies*.
88 Thompson, *Settlers on the Edge*.   89 Orttung, ed., *Sustaining Russia's Arctic Cities*.

Arctic attracting migrants as the homelands of billions become scorched and inhospitable. In the long term the future of human life in the Russian Arctic remains as perilous as the existence of *Homo sapiens* overall in the age of the Anthropocene.

The legacies of a Soviet focus on industrial livability have reappeared in rhetoric and vision even as practices of abandonment have played a more defining role since the collapse of communism. On the one hand, the chronological rupture in 1991 underscores the distinctiveness of the Soviet Arctic in ways that are more accurate than unidimensional tropes of carceral torture or gigantomania. With a combination of force and incentives, the Soviet Union sought to overwhelm less numerous rural and Indigenous peoples whom it had deemed 'backward' with urban migrants whom it labelled as modern and socialist. On the other hand, the differences of the Soviet period might more accurately forecast Arctic futures than is often recognized. Despite the widespread alarm about the acuteness of warming in the Arctic, other polar countries might find themselves embracing their own programmes for expanding an urban Arctic as hotter climes of the planet become unlivable.

Bibliography

20 S'ezd KPSS. 14–25 Fevralya [14–25 February] *1956 Goda: Stenograficheskii otchet* [Verbatim record], Vol. 1 (Moscow, 1956), pp. 52–53.

Ackermann, Felix, and Sören Urbansky, "Introduction. Reframing Postwar Sovietization: Power, Conflict, and Accommodation", *Jahrbücher für Geschichte Osteuropas* 64 (2016): 353–362.

Alexopoulos, Golfo, *Illness and Inhumanity in Stalin's Gulag* (New Haven: Yale University Press, 2017).

Allemann, Lukas, "The Experience of Displacement and Social Engineering in Kola Saami Oral Histories", PhD diss. (University of Lapland, 2020).

Andreassen, Elin, Hein B. Bjerck, and Bjørnar Olsen, *Persistent Memories: Pyramiden, A Soviet Mining Town in the High Arctic* (Trondheim: Tapir Academic, 2010).

Anderson, David, ed., *The 1926/27 Soviet Polar Census Expeditions* (New York: Berghahn, 2011).

"Arktika dalekaia i blizkaia", *Smena* (19 November 1967): 3.

Arzyutov, Dmitry, "Reassembling the Environmental Archive of the Cold War: Perceptions from the Russian North", PhD diss. (KTH Royal Institute of Technology, 2021).

Avango, Dag, and Peder Roberts, "Industrial Heritage and Arctic Mining Sites: Material Remains as Resources for the Present – and the Future", in Robert Thomsen and Lill Rastad Bjørst, eds., *Heritage and Change in the Arctic: Resources for the Present, and the Future* (Aalborg: Aalborg University Press, 2017), pp. 127–158.

19 Creating the Soviet Arctic, 1917–1991

Avango, Dag, Louwrens Hacquebord, and Urban Wråkberg, "Industrial Extraction of Arctic Natural Resources since the Sixteenth Century: Technoscience and Geo-economics in the History of Northern Whaling and Mining", *Journal of Historical Geography* 44 (April 2014): 15–30.

Barenberg, Alan, *Gulag Town, Company Town: Forced Labor and Its Legacy in Vorkuta* (New Haven: Yale University Press, 2014).

Barnes, Steven, *Death and Redemption: The Gulag and the Shaping of Soviet Society* (Princeton: Princeton University Press, 2011).

Bell, Wilson, *Stalin's Gulag at War: Forced Labour, Mass Death, and Soviet Victory in the Second World War* (Toronto: University of Toronto Press, 2018).

Berg, Auri, "Reform in the Time of Stalin: Nikita Khrushchev and the Fate of the Russian Peasantry", PhD diss. (University of Toronto, 2012).

Bloch, Alexia, *Red Ties and Residential Schools: Indigenous Siberians in a Post-Soviet State* (Philadelphia: University of Pennsylvania Press, 2003).

Bohn, Thomas, "'Sozialistische Stadt' versus 'Europäische Stadt': Urbanisierung und Ruralisierung im östlichen Europa", *Comparativ: Zeitschrift für Globalgeschichte und vergleichende Gesellschaftsforschung* 18 (2008): 71–86.

Bolotova, Alla, "Colonization of Nature in the Soviet Union: State Ideology, Public Discourse, and the Experience of Geologists", *Historical Social Research* 29 (2004): 104–123.

Bolotova, Alla, and Florian Stammler, "How the North Became Home: Attachment to Place Among Industrial Migrants in the Murmansk Region of Russia," in Chris Southcott and Lee Huskey, eds., *Migration in the Circumpolar North: Issue and Contexts* (Edmonton: CCI, 2010), pp. 193–220.

Bolotova, Alla, "Conquering Nature and Engaging with the Environment in the Russian Industrialized North", PhD diss. (University of Lapland, 2014).

Bolotova, Alla, "Engaging with the Environment in the Industrialized Russian North", *Suomen Antropologi: Journal of the Finnish Anthropological Society* 36 (2011): 18–36.

Bolotova, Alla, "Loving and Conquering Nature: Shifting Perceptions of the Environment in the Industrialised Russian North", *Europe-Asia Studies* 64 (2012): 645–671.

Borovoi, Vasilii, "Deiatel'nost' tresta 'Arktikugol' na Shpitsbergene v usloviiah kratkosrochnogo planirovaniia i ekstremal'nogo klimata, 1934–1941 gg", *Rossiiskaia istoriia* 5 (September–October 2020): 155–166.

Bruno, Andy, "Industrial Life in a Limiting Landscape: An Environmental Interpretation of Stalinist Social Conditions in the Far North", *International Review of Social History* 55 (December 2010): 153–174.

Bruno, Andy, *The Nature of Soviet Power: An Arctic Environmental History* (Cambridge: Cambridge University Press, 2016).

Bruno, Andy, "A Tale of Two Reindeer: Pastoralism and Preservation in the Soviet Arctic", *Region: Regional Studies of Russia, Eastern Europe, and Central Asia* 6 (2017): 251–271.

Bykova, Alina, "The Changing Nature of Russia's Arctic Presence: A Case Study of Pyramiden", *The Arctic Institute* (9 December 2019), www.thearcticinstitute.org/changing-nature-russia-arctic-presence-case-study-pyramiden/.

Chu, Pey-Yi, "Encounters with Permafrost: The Rhetoric of Conquest and Processes of Adaptation in the Soviet Union", in Nicholas Breyfogle, ed., *Eurasian Environments:*

Nature and Ecology in Imperial Russian and Soviet History (Pittsburgh: University of Pittsburgh Press, 2018), pp. 165–184.

Chu, Pey-Yi, *The Life of Permafrost: A History of Frozen Earth in Russian and Soviet Science* (Toronto: University of Toronto Press, 2020).

Crawford, Christina, "From Tractors to Territory: Socialist Urbanization through Standardization", *Journal of Urban History* 44 (January 2018): 54–77.

Decker, Julie, *Modern North: Architecture of the Frozen Edge* (New York: Princeton Architectural Press, 2010).

Demuth, Bathsheba, *Floating Coast: An Environmental History of the Bering Strait* (New York: W. W. Norton, 2019).

Dolgoliuk, Aleksei, "Rol' kommunisticheskikh partiinykh organizatsii v reshenii kadrovyh problem v raionah novogo industrial'nogo osvoeniia Sibiri", in A. Timoshenko, ed., *Deiatel'nost' gosudarstvennykh organov po industrial'nomu osvoeniiu Sibiri v XX – nachale XXI veka*, Vol. 1 (Novosibirsk: Sibirskoe nauchnoe izdatel'stvo, 2009), pp. 161–196.

Dybbroe, Susanne, Jens Dahl, and Ludger Müller-Wille, "Dynamics of Arctic Urbanization: Introduction", *Acta Borealia* 27 (2010): 120–124.

Emeliantseva Koller, Ekaterina, "Negotiating 'Coldness': The Natural Environment and Community Cohesion in Cold War Molotovsk-Severodvinsk", in Julia Herzberg, Christian Kehrt, and Franziska Torma, eds., *Ice and Snow in the Cold War: Histories of Extreme Climatic Environments* (New York: Berghahn, 2018), pp. 253–284.

Emeliantseva Koller, Ekaterina, "The Privilege of Seclusion: Consumption Strategies in the Closed City of Severodvinsk", *Ab Imperio* 2 (2011): 238–259.

Ertz, Simon, "Building Norilsk", in Paul Gregory and Valery Lazarev, eds., *The Economics of Forced Labor: The Soviet Gulag* (Stanford: Hoover Institute Press, 2003), pp. 128–137.

Farish, Matthew, and P. Whitney Lackenbauer, "High Modernism in the Arctic: Planning Frobisher Bay and Inuvik", *Journal of Historical Geography* 35 (July 2009): 517–544.

Fogelsong, David, *America's Secret War Against Bolshevism* (Chapel Hill: University of North Carolina Press, 1995).

Forsyth, James, *A History of the Peoples of Siberia: Russia's North Asian Colony 1581–1990* (Cambridge: Cambridge University Press, 1992).

Frey, Felix, *Arktischer Heizraum: Das Energiersystem Kola zwischen regionaler Autarkie und gesamtstaatlicher Verflechung, 1928–1974* (Vienna: Böhlau, 2019).

Gavrilova, N., "Osobennosti sotsial'noi politiki osvoeniia neftogazodobyvaiushchikh raionov Zapadnoi Sibiri", in A. Timoshenko, ed., *Deiatelnost' gosudarstvennykh organizatsii po industrial'nomu osvoeniiu Sibiri v XX – nachale XXI vv.: Sbornik nauchnyh trudov*, Vol. 2 (Novosibirsk: Sibirskoe nauchnoe izdatel'stvo, 2010), pp. 130–146.

Gnilorybov, N. A., *Piramida – Sovetskii ugol'nyi rudnik na arkhipelage Shpitsbergen (1946–1976)* (Moscow: TsNIEIugol, 1976).

Gray, Patty, *The Predicament of Chukotka's Indigenous Movement: Post-Soviet Activism in the Russian Far North* (Cambridge: Cambridge University Press, 2005).

Hartley, Janet, *Siberia: A History of the People* (New Haven: Yale University Press, 2014).

Heleniak, Timothy, "Changing Settlement Patterns across the Russian North at the Turn of the Millennium", in Vesa Rautio and Markuu Tykkyläinen, eds., *Russia's Northern Regions on the Edge: Communities, Industries and Populations from Murmansk to Magadan* (Helsinki: Kikimora, 2008), pp. 25–52.

Heleniak, Timothy, "Out-migration and Depopulation of the Russian North during the 1990s", *Post-Soviet Geography and Economics* 40 (1999): 155–295.

Hemmersam, Peter, "Arctic Architectures", *Polar Record* 52 (2016): 412–422.

Hill, Fiona, and Clifford Gaddy, *The Siberian Curse: How Communist Economic Planners Left Russia Out in the Cold* (Washington, DC: Brookings Institution Press, 2003).

Hogselius, Per, *Red Gas: Russia and the Origins of European Energy Dependence* (New York: Palgrave Macmillan, 2013).

Hønneland, Geir, and Anne-Kristin Jørgensen, *Integration vs. Autonomy: Civil-Military Relations on the Kola Peninsula* (Aldershot: Ashgate, 1999).

Humphrey, Caroline, *Marx Went Away but Karl Stayed Behind* (Ann Arbor: University of Michigan Press, 1998).

Jones, Ryan Tucker, *Red Leviathan: The Soviet Union and the Secret Destruction of the World's Whales* (Chicago: University of Chicago Press, 2022).

Josephson, Paul, *The Conquest of the Russian Arctic* (Cambridge, MA: Harvard University Press, 2014).

Josephson, Paul, "Technology and the Conquest of the Soviet Arctic", *Russian Review* 70 (July 2011): 419–439.

Kaganovsky, Lilya, Scott MacKenzie, and Anna Westerstahl Stenport, eds., *Arctic Cinemas and the Documentary Ethos* (Bloomington: Indiana University Press, 2019).

Kalemeneva, Ekaterina, "From New Socialist Cities to Thaw Experimentation in Arctic Townscapes: Leningrad Architects Attempt to Modernise the Soviet North", *Europe-Asia Studies* 71 (2019): 426–449.

Kalemeneva, Ekaterina, "Smena modelei osvoeniia sovetskogo Severa v 1950-e gg. Sluchay Komissii po problemam Severa", *Siberian Historical Research* 2 (2018): 181–200.

Kalemeneva, Ekaterina, "Sovetskaia politika osvoeniia Krainego Severa i kritika zhiznennykh uslovii arkticheskikh gorodov v narrativakh khrushchevskogo vremeni", *Quaestio Rossica* 5 (2017): 153–170.

Kollmann, Nancy Shields, *The Russian Empire, 1450–1801* (Oxford: Oxford University Press, 2017).

Konstantinov, Yulian, "Reinterpreting the Sovkhoz", *Sibirica* 6 (Autumn 2007): 1–25.

Konstantinov, Yulian, and Vladislava Vladimirova, "'The Performative Machine: Transfer of Ownership in a Northwest Russian Reindeer Herding Community (Kola Peninsula)", *Nomadic Peoples* 10 (2006): 166–186.

Kraikovski, Alexei, and Julia Lajus, "'The Space of Blue and Gold': The Nature and Environment of Solovki in History and Heritage", in David Moon, Nicholas Breyfogle, and Alexandra Bekasova, eds., *Place and Nature: Essays in Russian Environmental History* (Cambridgeshire: White Horse, 2021), pp. 37–68.

Krainii Sever k 1934 g.: Sbornik materialov po khoziaistvennomu i kul'turnomu stroitel'stvu: prilozhenie k zhurnalu Sovetskii Sever (Moscow, 1934).

Krupnik, Igor, *Arctic Adaptations: Native Whalers and Reindeer Herders of Northern Eurasia* (Hanover: University Press of New England, 1993).

Kutsev, G. F., *Chelovek na Severe* (Moscow: Politizdat, 1989).

Kutsev, G. F., *Chelovek v Severnom gorode* (Sverdlovsk: Uralskoe knizhnoe izdatel'stvo, 1987).

Lajus, Julia, "In Search of Instructive Models: The Russian State at a Crossroads to Conquering the North", in Dolly Jørgensen and Sverker Sörlin, eds., *Northscapes:*

History, Technology, and the Making of Northern Environments (Vancouver: University of British Columbia Press, 2013), pp. 110–133.

Lajus, Julia, "'Red Herring': The Unpredictable Soviet Fish and Soviet Power in the 1930s", in Nina Wormbs, ed., *Competing Arctic Futures: Historical and Contemporary Perspectives* (London: Palgrave Macmillan, 2018), pp. 73–94.

Laruelle, Marlene, *Russia's Arctic Strategies and the Future of the North* (London: M. E. Sharpe, 2014).

Lincoln, W. Bruce, *The Conquest of a Continent: Siberia and the Russians* (New York: Random House, 1993).

Luk'ianchenko, T. V., *Material'naia kul'tura saamov (loparei) Kol'skogo poluostrova v kontse XIX–XX v* (Moscow: Izdatel'stvo "Nauka", 1971).

McCannon, John, *A History of the Arctic: Nature, Exploration, and Exploitation* (London: Reaktion, 2012).

McCannon, John, *Red Arctic: Polar Exploration and the Myth of the North in the Soviet Union 1932–1939* (Oxford: Oxford University Press, 1998).

McCannon, John, "To Storm the Arctic: Soviet Polar Expeditions and Public Visions of Nature in the USSR, 1932–1939", *Ecumene* 2 (January 1995): 15–31.

Munts, O. R., "Gorod Khibinogorsk i ego planirovka", in A. E. Fersman, ed., *Khibinskie Apatity*, Vol. 2 (Leningrad: ONTI VSNKh SSSR Lenzkimsektor, 1932), pp. 192–207.

"Nasha Arktika", *Izvestiya* (1 June 1958): 3.

"Nauchnyi otchet po teme: Eksperimental'nyi zhiloi dom iz aliuminiia i plastmass dlia Noril'ska", Tsentralnyi gosudarstvennyi arkhiv nauchno-tekhnicheskoi dokumentatsii Sankt-Peterburga. Fond 17, opis' 2–2, delo 467, list 7.

Nazarova, Larisa, "My, molodye arhitektory, ne sdavalis' i sviato verili lozungu 'Vse vo imia cheloveka, vse dlia blaga cheloveka'", in G. I. Kasabova, ed., *O vremeni, o Noril'ske, o sebe*, Vol. 5 (Moscow: PoliMedia, 2004), pp. 472–551.

"Obrashchenie Tsentral'nogo Komiteta Kommunisticheskoi partii Sovetskogo Soiuza i Soveta Ministrov SSSR ko vsem komsomol'skim organizatsiiam, k komsomol'tsam i komsomolkam i ko vsei sovetskoi molodezhi", *Pravda* (19 May 1956): 1.

"Obsledovanie naselennykh mest Krainego Severa", Tsentralnyi gosudarstvennyi arkhiv nauchno-tekhnicheskoi dokumentatsii. Fond 17, opis' 2–2, delo 423, list 123.

Orttung, Robert, ed., *Sustaining Russia's Arctic Cities: Resource Politics, Migration, and Climate Change* (New York: Berghahn, 2016).

Overland, Indra, and Mikkel Berg-Nordlie, *Bridging Divides: Ethno-Political Leadership Among the Russian Sámi* (New York: Berghahn, 2012).

Proizvoditel'nye sily raiona Murmanskoi zheleznoi dorogi: Sbornik (Petrozavodsk: Pravlenie Murmanskoi zheleznoi dorogi, 1923).

Protocol from a meeting of doctors in Khibinogorsk, 11 September 1931. Gosudarstvennyi arkhiv Murmanskoi oblasti. Fond R-163, opis' 1, delo 26, listy 8–10.

Raleigh, Donald, *Soviet Baby Boomers: The Oral History of Russia's Cold War Generation* (Oxford: Oxford University Press, 2005).

Reisser, Colin, "Russia's Arctic Cities", in Robert Orttung, ed., *Sustaining Russia's Arctic Cities: Resource Politics, Migration, and Climate Change* (New York: Berghahn, 2016), pp. 1–22.

19 Creating the Soviet Arctic, 1917–1991

Richter, Bernd Stevens, "Nature Mastered by Man: Ideology and Water in the Soviet Union", *Environment and History* 3 (1997): 69–96.

Robson, Roy, *Solovki: The Story of Russia Told Through Its Most Remarkable Islands* (New Haven: Yale University Press, 2004).

Rowe, Lars, *Industry, War and Stalin's Battle for Resources: The Arctic and the Environment* (London: I. B. Tauris, 2020).

Rozhanskii, Mikhail, "'Ottepel' na sibirskom morose: Ustnaia istoriia udarnykh stroek", *Otechestvennye zapiski* 5 (2012).

Ruder, Cynthia, *Making History for Stalin: The Story of the Belomor Canal* (Gainesville: University Press of Florida, 1998).

Rudov, N., "Arktika bez ekzotiki", *Smena* (14 September 1968): 3.

Saxinger, Gertrude, "Lured by Oil and Gas: Labour Mobility, Multi-locality and Negotiating Normality and Extreme in the Russian Far North", *The Extractive Industries and Society* 3 (January 2016): 50–59.

Sellheim, Nikolas, Yulia Zaika, and Ilan Kelman, eds., *Arctic Triumph: Northern Innovation and Persistence* (Cham: Springer Nature, 2019).

Shirokov, Alexandr, *Dal'stroi v sotsial'no-ekonomicheskom razvitii Severo-Vostoka SSSR. 1930–1950-e gg* (Moscow: ROSSPEN, 2014).

Siegelbaum, Lewis, and Leslie Page Moch, *Broad Is My Native Land: Repertoires and Regimes of Migration in Russia's Twentieth Century* (Ithaca: Cornell University Press, 2014).

Slabukha, A., "Zodchie Norillaga (gruppovoi portrel – iz nekotorykh tsifr statistiki)", *Monumentalita & Modernita* 1 Kapitel' (2010): 3.

Slavin, Samuil, "Sostoianie stroitel'stva na Severe SSSR i za rubezhom", Rossiiskii gosudarstvennyi arhiv ekonomiki. Fond 746, opis' 1, delo 136, list 55.

Slavin, Samuil, "Spravka po sovetskomu i amerikanskomu Severu", Rossiiskii Gosudarstvennyi Arkhiv Ekonomiki. Fond 746, opis' 1, delo 135, list 221.

Slezkine, Yuri, *Arctic Mirrors: Russia and the Small Peoples of the North* (Ithaca: Cornell University Press, 1994).

Sokolova, Flera, and Wooik Choi, "The Russian Arctic in the Post-Soviet Period", *Region: Regional Studies of Russia, Eastern Europe, and Central Asia* 8 (July 2019): 197–226.

Stas, Igor, "Diskussiia o stroitelstve gorodov neftannikov zapadnoi Sibiri (po materialam konferentsii 1966 g. v Tiumeni)", *Vestnik SPBGU* 2 (2015): 13–23.

Suslov, I. M., "Shamanstvo i bor'ba s nim", *Sovetskii Sever* 3–4 (1931): 89–152.

Thompson, Niobe, *Settlers on the Edge: Identity and Modernization on Russia's Arctic Frontier* (Vancouver: University of British Columbia Press, 2008).

Vaitens, M. E., "Sotsial'no-Demograficheskie Osobennosti Kol'skogo Severa", in Oleg Ianitskii, ed., *Sotsiologicheskie issledovaniia goroda* (Moscow: 1969).

Vinkovetsky, Ilya, *Russian America: An Overseas Colony of a Continental Empire, 1804–1867* (Oxford: Oxford University Press, 2014).

Vladimirova, Vladislava, *Just Labor: Labor Ethic in a Post-Soviet Reindeer Herding Community* (Uppsala: Uppsala University, 2006).

Vladimirova, Vladislava, "Technologies of Modern Reindeer Breeding as Technologies of Power in Circumpolar Russia: A Study of Selective Breeding of Evenki Reindeer", *Norsk Antropolgisk Tidsskrift* 31 (2020): 249–267.

Ward, Christopher, *Brezhnev's Folly: The Building of BAM and Late Soviet Socialism* (Pittsburgh: University of Pittsburgh Press, 2009).

Widdis, Emma, *Visions of a New Land: Soviet Film from the Revolution to the Second World War* (New Haven: Yale University Press, 2003).

Wilson, David, "The Siberian Oil and Gas Industry", in Alan Wood, ed., *Siberia: Problems and Prospects for Regional Development* (London: Croom Helm, 1987), pp. 96–129.

Wood, Alan, *Russia's Frozen Frontier: A History of Siberia and the Russian Far East, 1581–1991* (London: Bloomsbury, 2011).

Yurchak, Alexei, *Everything Was Forever, Until It Was No More: The Last Soviet Generation* (Princeton: Princeton University Press, 2006).

Yuzmuhamedov, Rishat. *Udachnyi—gorod u poliarnogo kruga: Istoricheskii ocherk* (Moscow: SOREK-poligraphiya, 1998).

Zaika, Yulia, "Rehabilitation of the Northern Home: A Multigenerational Pathway", in Nikolas Sellheim, Yulia Zaika, and Ilan Kelman, eds., *Arctic Triumph: Northern Innovation and Persistence* (Cham: Springer Nature, 2019), pp. 59–80.

Zamyatina, Nadezhda, "Igarka as a Frontier: Lessons from the Pioneer of the Northern Sea Route", *Journal of Siberian Federal University. Humanities & Social Sciences* 5 (2020): 783–799.

Zarecor, Kimberly Elman, "What Was So Socialist about the Socialist City? Second World Urbanity in Europe", *Journal of Urban History* 44 (January 2018): 95–117.

Zhelnina, Anna, "'Zhelezo, sliuda, appatity i rossypi sudeb liudskikh ... ': Proshloe i nastoiashchee v zapoliarnom industrial'nom gorode", in Ol'ga Brednikova and Oksana Zaporozhets, eds., *Microurbanizm: Gorod v detaliakh* (Moscow: Novoe Literaturnoe Obozrenie, 2014), pp. 256–279.

20

Greenland: From Colony to Self-government, 1721–2021

JENS HEINRICH

This chapter considers the historical development of how Greenlanders acquired political participation in their own affairs. As of 2021, most political parties in Greenland see independence as the ultimate goal. The Self-Government Act of 2009 grants the inhabitants of Greenland the right to this independence.[1] My argument here is that a historical view reveals that independence can be seen as the logical next step from the current self-government. This has been attained through continual negotiations between Greenlanders and Danes since the middle of the nineteenth century, and through decolonization and independence processes as seen elsewhere in the world.[2]

Introduction: Learning to Manage Own Affairs

The Thule Culture,[3] the ancestors of present-day Greenlanders,[4] migrated from the Bering Strait region and entered Greenland around 1200 AD. The Thule Culture was primarily based on hunting seals, in addition to other marine and terrestrial mammals, and had little interaction with the Norse settlers in southern and western Greenland. In 1721, on behalf of the Danish-Norwegian Crown, the missionary Hans Egede established a settlement in Kangeq, dubbed 'the Island of Hope', near present-day Nuuk. The settlement moved to Nuuk in 1728. After his hope of finding the descendants of the Norse settlements in the southern part of Greenland proved in vain, Egede

---

1 Act on Greenland Self-Government of 12 June 2009, https://naalakkersuisut.gl//~/m edia/Nanoq/Files/Attached%20Files/Engelske-tekster/Act%20on%20Greenland.pdf.
2 A fully updated history of Greenland in English is not available, but in 2017 a colonial history of Greenland (*Grønland – den arktiske koloni*) was published in the five-volume colonial history of Denmark (*Danmark og kolonierne*).
3 Today the term Inuit (meaning humans) is used by Greenlanders.
4 Seventy-five per cent of the genetic composition of present-day Greenlanders is from Inuit, while 25 per cent is European. Moltke et al., "Uncovering Genetic History".

instead began converting the Greenlanders to Christianity. The Mission in Greenland believed that the Christian belief should be administered in the local language, and this is partly the reason why the Greenlandic language is in a strong position today.[5]

A number of colonial centres were established on the west coast of Greenland during the eighteenth century. The Danish colonial economy in Greenland was based on the production of seal blubber, which was sold in Europe and other places. In 1776, the Royal Greenland Trading Company (Kongelige Grønlandske Handel – KGH) was established, and the company maintained its powerful position until the creation of Grønlands Styrelse – a ministerial department – in 1912. In order to preserve the seal-hunting culture and thereby the basis for the colonial enterprise in Greenland, other nations were prohibited from having contact and dealings with Greenlanders, unless permission was given by the Danish Government. This sealing off of Greenland lasted until after World War II. Nevertheless, during the following century, a deterioration in the society was seen. Famines occurred, along with other social problems, and finally, inspired by the democratic process in Denmark, a form of councils was introduced in Greenland, on a trial basis in 1858 and permanently from 1861. In each colonial centre (thirteen in all) on the west coast of Greenland, Denmark established a Board of Guardians. The inspector Hinrich Rink was one of the proposers to these councils and is one of the most influential persons in nineteenth century Greenland. These boards were administered both by Danish civil servants and local Greenlandic residents. Their responsibilities ranged from relief for the poor and needy and encouragement for productive hunters to functioning as a court for Greenlanders. The idea behind the boards was to educate Greenlanders to manage their own affairs, by promoting self-reliance and responsibility. Danes were to mentor the Greenlanders towards maturity and self-management.[6] This could be seen as the Danish colonial authorities aiming at making themselves redundant, but also as a means to justify their presence. The idea of Greenland gaining a still larger degree of autonomy grew from this initiative.[7]

At the beginning of the twentieth century, parliamentarism was introduced in Denmark, and the colonial administration in Copenhagen began

---

5 Religious beliefs in Greenland are still strong to the present day, and compared with Denmark, Greenlanders are more active churchgoers.
6 Heinrich, *Eske Brun*, 149.
7 This is a point of discussion, but there is no doubt that the Danish authorities supported an increasing Greenlandic autonomy.

a similar process of reform in Greenland. In 1908 the first law concerning the ruling of Greenland was introduced in the Danish parliament.[8] Provincial and municipal councils were to replace the Boards of Guardians. Europeans were excluded from these councils[9] because of their perceived dominance in the Board of Guardians.[10] This move reflected an increasing interest from the Danish authorities in listening to Greenlanders and incorporating their proposals and attitudes in decisions. But the ultimate responsibility for taking decisions remained in Copenhagen, where administrators sought to develop Greenlandic society in a conservative and slow-moving direction, while Greenlandic politicians pushed for a more rapid development.

One of the fronts in this conflict was the use of the Danish language. Many Greenlanders viewed this as a tool to further develop Greenlandic society by giving access to a larger pool of written material, but initially the Danish colonial administration was reluctant to approve the introduction of the Danish language. Danish became a subject in the Greenlandic school system in 1925 thanks to agitation from a group including three Greenlandic members, among them the priest and later member of the provincial council (*Landsråd*) in northern Greenland Mathias Storch. Storch was also an author and had written the first Greenlandic novel *Singnagtugaq: A Greenlander's Dream*.[11] Anthropologist and explorer Knud Rasmussen wrote the preface for the Danish version of the book, describing Denmark as a 'Nation which has assumed the responsibility for raising a primitive society of hunters under new forms'.[12] In Storch's novel, the protagonist, a young Greenlandic man, dreams of a future in which Greenlanders have grown capable of managing their own affairs, and an actual equality with Danes has been reached. In 1931, another novel was published by a young teacher and aspiring politician, Augo Lynge. In his novel, *300 Years Later*, the same political aspiration for

---

8 Until this law, the Instrux of 1782 had been the basis for colonial enterprise in Greenland.
9 The Governors, one for each of the provinces of South and North Greenland, were Chairmen (without voting rights) of the Provincial Councils. Following a revision of the law on the ruling of Greenland in 1925, Danes were again eligible to be members of the councils.
10 Storch, *Strejflys over Grønland*. This, however, is disputed, as Greenlandic members of the Boards of Guardians were actually able to pursue and attain their own interests. This was the case concerning alimony payments from Greenlandic fathers to children born out of wedlock. See the 'white book' on children born out of wedlock, 2011 (Nielsen et al., *Historisk udredning*, in Danish), www.regeringen.dk/media/1227/historisk_udredning_om_retsstillingen_for_boern_foedt_uden_for_aegteskab_i_groenland_i_perioden_1914_til_1963-1974.pdf.
11 The novel was published in 1914 in Greenlandic and in Danish in 1915. In 2016 an English version was published.
12 Rasmussen in Storch, 1914 [own translation].

Greenland is presented.[13] Over time the idea of equality of responsibility and opportunities between Greenlanders and Danes was developed, and played an increasing part in the political struggle in Greenland.

Debates within Greenland over politics and identity were also interwoven with economic and social changes. Seal hunting declined in the early twentieth century, most likely on account of a smaller population of seals, and gradually fishing became the primary occupation of Greenlanders. In the short term this meant a greater dependence on imported goods. Fully fledged industrial fishing came first in the 1950s, partly because investment was hard to obtain, as expenditures could not exceed earnings, but also because of reluctance from the Danish authorities, who feared that too rapid a development could endanger the progress of Greenlandic society. This in turn fed into a debate over who had the right to define Greenlandic identity, or Greenlandic society. Should either occupation (hunting) or language define identity? The debate ended with agreement that if a person felt and saw himself or herself as Greenlandic, then he/she should be seen as such by others – a position that vested the power to define Greenlandic identity (individually and collectively) with Greenlanders themselves.[14]

Yet Greenland remained subject to decisions and conflicts in which Greenlanders had no say. In the late 1920s, a conflict escalated between Denmark and Norway concerning rights to territories in northeastern Greenland. Norway declared sovereignty over a slice of territory that it named Erik the Red's Land, after the Norse adventurer who coined the name Greenland in the late tenth century. Denmark filed a case with the International Court of Justice at the Hague, and in 1933 won a comprehensive victory that sustained Danish sovereignty over the whole of Greenland. The Greenlandic Provincial Councils supported the Danish claim, but more important perhaps was the support of the United States, earned through the sale of the Danish West Indies in 1917.[15] In this case the opinions of Greenlanders, as represented through their councils, coincided with the outcome. But this was not the case in another matter that arguably had more direct consequences. Unable to compete during the 1920s with British fishers in the waters surrounding the Faroe Islands, Faroese fishers lobbied for access to fishing grounds off western Greenland. The Greenlanders feared being unable to use the stocks of fish in their own waters. Their objections were dismissed, and the Faroese fishers operated in Greenland until the 1980s, many from the now-abandoned fishing harbour of Færingehavn (literally

13 Lynge, *Ukiut 300-ngornerat*.   14 Teglbjærg, *Kalâliussuseq*.   15 Heinrich, *Eske Brun*, 28.

Faroese Harbour).[16] Greenlandic politicians were heard, but their wishes were not necessarily granted.

World War II as a Catalyst

World War II proved the decisive turning point in Danish-Greenlandic relations because it ended the isolation from the world that had thus far characterized Greenlandic society. In April 1940, Denmark was occupied by Germany, and the connection to Greenland was cut. The colonial authorities had anticipated the situation by sending supplies to Greenland, in order to avoid any immediate crisis. But it quickly became clear that a new system had to be established. The primary objective of the colonial administration in Greenland, led by Aksel Svane and Eske Brun (respectively the Danish governors of southern and northern Greenland), was to ensure the wellbeing of the population in Greenland and thereby maintain the legitimacy of Danish rule in Greenland. Any shortage of supplies should be avoided, as famines would undermine the colonial project in Greenland. In the absence of connections to Denmark, those supplies were successfully sourced from the United States and Canada, and during the war Greenland did not experience any hardship on account of shortages. The Danish monopoly on connections to Greenland, however, was broken, as the new connections also meant the presence of a US and a Canadian consul in Nuuk to oversee the communication between the administrations of the countries.

The strategic importance of Greenland meant the establishment of US military facilities in various parts of Greenland. On the anniversary of the occupation of Denmark – 9 April 1941 – a defence agreement was signed between the United States and Henrik Kauffmann, the Danish ambassador to the United States who had rejected the government of his occupied country and successfully appealed to be recognized by the United States as the legitimate representative of Denmark.[17] Kauffmann managed to replace the two governors of Greenland by including an article in the agreement allowing the United States a continued presence in Greenland as long as a threat existed towards the North American continent. Initially the US authorities had seen the two governors as the legal authority of Greenland, but they had been outmanoeuvred by the

---

16 Sørensen, *Danmark-Grønland*, 79–82.
17 The Defense agreement of 9 April 1941 was approved by the Danish Freedom Government following the liberation of Denmark in May 1945.

experienced Kauffmann.[18] Between the two governors, there were differences on how to act in the situation. Should Greenland support the Allied forces in the war against the Axis Powers, as Brun argued, or should Greenland take a neutral stance, in accordance with the Danish Government at the time, a view held by Svane? The former position won out, and Svane found himself sidelined in the United States and tasked with maintaining the supply line to Greenland. The biggest facility, the base at Narsarsuaq in southern Greenland, at its maximum housed 6,000 troops. Contact between the local population and US troops was eventually prohibited, as the colonial administration feared that contact could pose a devastating influence on the society, in terms of both cultural integrity and public health. The Greenlandic population occasionally challenged these bans, but on several occasions the protection was justified by events. Initially, when the US troops arrived in Greenland, a proposal had been made by the Americans about having a brothel of local women near the military facilities. This was adamantly rejected by Governor Brun.

Weather forecasts from northeastern Greenland were crucial in the war effort, as these forecasts were used in the preparation for the D-Day landings on 6 June 1944. Brun established a dog-sled patrol to monitor the coast and detect German efforts to establish weather stations. The patrol consisted primarily of Danish members, assisted by Greenlandic sledge drivers.[19] Skirmishes between the patrol and Germans resulted in two casualties, demonstrating their intent to actively contribute to the Allied war effort.[20] Unlike in Denmark, where the government cooperated with the German authorities until 1943, Greenland remained hostile territory for Germans throughout the war.

The war also led to new optimism about Greenland's future in both economic and political terms. The US military's ingenuity and willingness to overcome obstacles in building military bases and landing fields helped make a future based on industrial fishing and fish processing seem more plausible. Such a future would of course require considerable capital investment. But Greenland did have one strong source of income, from the Ivittuut mine in southern Greenland. Important for the production of aluminium

---

18 For an elaboration on ambassador Kauffmann during World War II, see Lidegaard, *I Kongens navn*; Lidegaard, *Uden mandat*; Løkkegaard, *Det danske gesandtskab*.
19 The sledge patrol is still active as the Sirius Patrol, asserting sovereignty in the uninhabited area of Greenland.
20 Howarth, *The Sledge Patrol*.

from bauxite, cryolite was thus crucial to the war effort, and the only known source in the world was at Ivittuut. Earnings from the mine supported Greenland and all Danish activities outside occupied Denmark.

The uncertainty of the wartime situation also increased the demand for news, and in the beginning of 1942 two new media were launched: the newspaper *Grønlandsposten* and Greenland Radio. Greenlanders such as Kristoffer Lynge (editor of the Greenlandic newspaper *Atuagagdliutit*, founded in 1861) conducted the editorial work on the newly founded newspaper and radio alongside the Danish biologist Christian Vibe. These new media broadened the dialogue between the Danes in Greenland and the rest of the population and contributed in delivering information to the public during the war. The number of radios in Greenland grew significantly during the war and enhanced a feeling of being connected to the outside world. Greenlandic-language radio broadcasts contributed to widening the horizons of the population. Inuit groups in Canada were also able to listen to Greenland Radio, resulting in closer contact between different Inuit communities in the Arctic. Danish authorities recognized radio as the perfect medium through which to educate the sparsely and widely populated Greenland through informative presentations from a variety of speakers.[21]

There were also enhanced connections at the political and economic levels. Contact between inhabited places in Greenland was enhanced during the war as supply routes were reorganized. New ports of transits were established, and supplies were thereafter delivered to the smaller settlements. This also made passenger traffic possible along the coast, which supported the feeling of unity amongst the population. And importantly, the war pushed Brun and Svane to ensure the support of the provincial councils for their authority, obtained at a joint meeting of the Greenlandic councils in May 1940. In the following years the provincial councils held further joint meetings, which increased the sense of unity between the regions in Greenland and thereby gave a clearer political direction. At one such meeting in 1943, Brun encouraged members to speculate on how Greenland might be administered after the war's end. His call was motivated by a realization that the pre-war system in Greenland most likely could not be continued. The US presence in Greenland challenged the Danish claim to Greenland, and certain Danes in Greenland feared a Greenlandic desire to be affiliated with the US instead of Denmark. Many Greenlanders reacted positively to the presence of new people and new goods in their homeland. However, the loyalty and

21 Heinrich, *Eske Brun*, 69–164.

devotion of Greenlanders towards Denmark was not challenged by the US presence. As an example, a privately organized collection was made in Greenland to help rebuild Denmark once the war ended, providing a significant amount to be used in Denmark. Brun could ask the council for its suggestions without fear that they would reject Danish presence altogether.

Modernization of Society

When the war ended in the beginning of May 1945 there was genuine joy in Greenland for the liberation of Denmark. But a return to the closed world of the pre-war years was desired by neither Greenlandic politicians nor Danish administrators.[22] The newly formed United Nations demanded annual reports from states with colonial territories on the progress made in the path of those colonies towards independence, a category that included Greenland. The sense that a new administrative structure was needed only grew after a Danish press delegation visited Greenland in 1946 to report on local conditions. The resulting articles raised a critique of the Danish colonial administration, and from several sides the Danish Government was pressured into rethinking how Greenland was ruled.

Change was generally recognized as desirable, but what kind of change? Eske Brun, who had returned to Denmark when the war ended, was brought in as a vice director of the Copenhagen-based Greenland administration with a mandate to oversee and advise on how to proceed. Close cooperation between Brun and the Danish Prime Minister Hans Hedtoft thus began, motivated in part by fear of losing Greenland either to independence or to being taken over by the United States.[23] In August of 1948, the prime minister proposed a reform of the Greenlandic society, which the councils supported. A wide-ranging government Commission[24] was established, and the resulting Commission report (widely known as G-50) laid out a vision for a completely different Greenland. A separate Commission, working on a new Danish constitution, completed the inclusion of Greenland into the Danish realm. As of 5 June 1953, Greenland was no longer a Danish colony, but an equal part

---

22 Heinrich, *Eske Brun*, 69–164.
23 United States proposals to buy Greenland from Denmark have been made a number of times, including in the late 1940s. Denmark rejected the proposals.
24 The Great Greenland Commission of 1948, consisting of Greenlandic and Danish politicians, civil servants, and representatives from different interest groups. See Heinrich, *Eske Brun*, 240–260.

of the Realm, including the right to elect two representatives to the Danish parliament.[25] At the time, Denmark could claim this as a success. It removed the need to report to the United Nations by ending Greenland's status in legal terms as a colony, and the two Greenlandic representatives in the Danish parliament – Augo Lynge and Frederik Lynge – testified to the United Nations that Greenland had willingly chosen to be included in the Kingdom of Denmark. In later years there has been considerable debate over the decision's legitimacy, as it was approved by the Greenlandic provincial council rather than by a referendum, and the council was not fully informed of the alternatives at its disposal.[26]

There is no doubt that despite Danish fears of US influence, the majority of the Greenlandic politicians in the late 1940s and early 1950s saw Denmark as the obvious partner to ensure the modernization of Greenland. The Cold War made Greenland strategically important, given its location between the United States and the USSR, and thus a significant asset for Denmark in its relationship within NATO.[27] Denmark delivered massive funds for the modernization of Greenland, initially focused on improving public health conditions and later for infrastructure improvements, housing, schools, and other facilities that it regarded as characteristic of a modern society.[28] The G-50 report also produced political reforms, with the administration centralized on Nuuk as the capital of Greenland, and the election system was modernized, with voters casting their vote directly for candidates rather than through intermediate councils. Voting rights for women were introduced in 1948, but it was only in 1959 that the first woman was elected to the National Council – the midwife Elisabeth Johansen, who later served a term in office alongside her son Lars Emil Johansen.

Differing views on Greenland's political and economic future began to emerge both in Greenland and in Denmark. Both Augo and Frederik Lynge had been born near Nuuk, but Frederik had moved to the Disko Bay region,

---

25 The election was held in September 1953.
26 Skaale, *Right to National Self-determination*; Kleist, *Kilder til Færøernes*. The Greenlandic Provincial Council was presented with two options – independence or inclusion – but a third option (free association) was not presented. Kleist, *Kilder til Færøernes*. For a view that largely exonerates the Danish authorities, see www.diis.dk/node/18348, published in English as "Phasing Out the Colonial Status of Greenland, 1945–54".
27 Often referred to as the Greenland Card. Greenland was, at least since 1940, seen as strategic important territory, which gave Denmark leverage when dealing on the World stage. See Henriksen, *Grønlandskortet*, https://cms.polsci.ku.dk/publikationer/groenlandskortet/CMS_Rapport_2017_Gr_nlandskortet.pdf.
28 Tuberculosis and other diseases were causing a disproportionately large number of deaths. See Kristiansen, "Tuberkulosebekæmpelsen".

becoming one of the few Greenlanders to hold the position of *kolonibestyrer* (top local official at a town/colonial centre) in the coal mining town of Qullissat in 1947. Augo Lynge represented Southern Greenland and had held teaching positions at the teacher's college (Ilinniarfissuaq) in Nuuk and at a school in Aasiaat. Both men had extensive political experience from being members of the different councils, and through participation in the negotiations between Greenland and Denmark. Frederik Lynge could be characterized as a traditionalist, convinced of the cultural as well as the economic importance of hunting, and cautious about the effects of rapid change. Augo Lynge had been open to developing Greenlandic society politically and economically as far back as the 1930s, with Greenlanders adopting the Danish language in order to open more opportunities for education and economic development. This difference of views also found expression in views on political administration. Frederik Lynge had been critical of the centralization of the administration in Nuuk, fearing that modernization would be a disadvantage for the northern part of Greenland, which retained hunting as the primary occupation. Most of the fishing took place in Southern Greenland, and generally the southern part had a greater focus on the outside world.

Nevertheless, Danish administrators in Copenhagen retained substantial power over economic and social policies in Greenland, including legal reforms. In the 1950s a radically different judicial framework was established in which resocialization instead of punishing offenders was put into effect, although in the 1960s imprisonment was introduced, and the most serious offenders sent to prison in Denmark. Danish and Greenlandic representatives found it difficult to conclude a law on the legal rights of children born out of wedlock, leading to substantial numbers of Greenlanders lacking equal rights, a situation not remedied until 2011.[29] But in Danish eyes, the main obstacle to modernizing Greenlandic society was the scattering of Greenland's population between around 150 often remote and sparsely inhabited settlements.[30] From the late 1940s, the Greenlandic population grew from 22,000 inhabitants to around 40,000 within twenty-five years, mainly owing to improving health conditions. This significant population rise had a clear impact on the plans for developing the society, as housing, schools, and infrastructure quickly became insufficient, and additional funds needed to be approved by the Danish Government. The G-50 Commission proposed a policy that would concentrate the population at fewer places, subsequently launched

29 Nielsen et al., *Historisk udredning*.   30 Heinrich, *Rapport over projekt*.

with agreement from Greenlandic representatives. The National Council established a Population Commission to assess the economic viability of each settlement and determine whether it was worthy of further investment. The same work was done in the newly formed Greenland Department at the prime minister's office in Copenhagen, headed by Eske Brun. However, the recommendations from the Population Commission and the Greenland Department did not always correspond with one another, and the policy was challenged along the way, as critique was raised from within Greenland or also from Denmark. How could people be attracted to leave their home settlements? The official approach from the authorities was to encourage the inhabitants of undesired settlements to move, but in a number of cases the inhabitants felt coerced.[31]

Today, Greenland has seventy-four inhabited settlements, and a trend of people moving to larger places. Larger towns are growing, while smaller settlements are being abandoned, but the question of where to live is an ongoing debate in Greenland linked to questions of identity and culture and often opposed to a Western concept of economic rationality. This is reinforced by language. The majority of the population in Greenland has Greenlandic as their primary language, while, mainly in the bigger towns, a fairly large minority has Danish as their primary language. Some are able to use both languages, but there are groups only able to use either Danish or Greenlandic, and these differences often mirror differences between larger and smaller settlements. This is a legacy of the success of Augo Lynge's position equating adoption of the Danish language to greater economic opportunities – but at a cultural cost, as feared by Frederik Lynge. It is to this process of 'Danification' that I now turn.

Danification

Danification was the cornerstone of post-1945 ambitions to build a modern Greenland. Greenlandic culture and language were deemed unsuited to a civilized and modern society, similar to the Canadian state's belief that Inuktitut and Inuit ways of life were unsuited to the modern world.[32] This approach found support among both Greenlanders and Danes, although some in both countries were skeptical about the scale and the speed of the

---

31 Forchhammer, "Gathered or Dispersed?".
32 The Canadian Truth and Reconciliation Commission among other matters dealt with the Westernization of Inuit children through the boarding school system, http://trc.ca/.

process. The essence of Danification was to alter Greenland into a form of North Denmark.[33]

Danification included conscious attempts to remove Greenlanders from their culture. In 1951, a Danish branch of the international children's organizations Save the Children and the Red Cross proposed to the Greenland administration in Copenhagen to include a number of Greenlandic children in the organization's programme. The Greenland provincial councils approved the proposal, and twenty-two Greenlandic children aged five to seven, either orphaned or with only one parent, were selected. The children were to stay in Denmark for a year, and were to learn the Danish language and Danish culture. Thereafter the children were sent to Nuuk and were placed in a newly built orphanage. The children were only allowed to speak Danish and had minimal contact with their families. The goal of this experiment was to produce standard-bearers for the modernization of Greenland. But the experiment failed and was not repeated. The majority of the children suffered from the loss of their Greenlandic heritage and language and the lack of contact with their families, creating resentment rather than enthusiasm for the project of building a modern Greenland in the Danish image.[34]

The history of the 1951 experiment also poses questions about how much Greenlanders could and did influence social policy in Greenland. In 2020, the Danish government issued an official report on the case on behalf of the Danish and Greenlandic Government. Following the publication of the report, Danish Prime Minister Mette Frederiksen gave an official apology to the six surviving participants in the experiment with the words: 'We can't change what has happened. But we can assume the responsibility and apologize to those we should have taken care of but failed to do so.'[35] Within the Greenland Government, Naalakkersuisut, and the Greenland parliament, Inatsisartut, it was discussed whether Greenland should give an apology, but none has so far been given at the time of writing. It can be argued that the final decision to proceed with the experiment was taken by the Danish Government, but if the Greenland provincial councils had opposed the proposal, most likely it would not have been done. The role of the provincial councils and later the national council was advisory, but they did have an impact on decisions being made in Denmark concerning Greenland. Official Danish policy imposed an

33 Heinrich, "Forsoningskommissionen".   34 Jensen et al., *Historisk udredning*.
35 Prime Minister's office press release, www.stm.dk/presse/pressemeddelelser/undskyldn ing-til-de-22-groenlandske-boern-som-blev-sendt-til-danmark-i-1951/ [own translation].

obligation to hear the representations of Greenlandic politicians.[36] This in turn raises questions, many still not fully answered, about the role of Greenlandic politicians in relation to the modernization of Greenland. Could they, for example, pursue matters in clear violation of Danish interests, or would that have led to a re-evaluation of their own place within the existing power structures?

The impact of the Danification is still apparent in Greenland. The Greenlandic school system came to be organized under the premise that the pupil needed to learn the Danish language in order to obtain an education. The notion of Greenlandic culture and language having been second-rate produced a sense of inferiority and frustration. Language was therefore an important part of the movement for Greenland Home Rule from 1979, which sought to revitalize Greenlandic identity and culture and end the policy of Danification. This Greenlandification of Greenland following the introduction of Home Rule can be seen as a natural reaction to the former Danification. Greenlandification supported Greenlandic culture and language as a vital part of societal development. The Greenland Reconciliation Commission (2014–17) dealt with the legacy of the modernization process, and the aspect of Danification was a major part of the findings of the Commission.

Being Sidelined and Political Mobilization

Danification entrenched the connection between being Danish and being modern within Greenlandic politics and society. The many workers who came from Denmark to Greenland to build and develop the Greenlandic society were both a blessing and a curse. Many Greenlanders felt a sense of inferiority and an inability to influence development, even though Greenlandic politicians were part of major decisions. The idea was to build a modern society in Greenland as quickly as possible; when this was completed, the workers could return to Denmark, and the Greenlanders could assume the responsibility of running the society. This entailed that Greenlanders only needed to be educated to a certain level, as the majority would be fishers and workers at the fishing plants. The inequality between Greenlanders and Danes was most evident in the 'birth criterion' (*fødestedskriteriet*). Under this measure, workers born in Denmark received a bonus for working in Greenland, while workers born in Greenland were

---

36 Heinrich, *Eske Brun*.

paid a lower wage in solidarity with other occupational groups, primarily fishers and hunters. The difference was also justified by arguments that the Greenlandic workforce as a whole was less productive and less educated than the Danish workforce. The criterion was officially not based on ethnicity, as children born of Danish parents in Greenland were also paid the lower salary, if and when the children entered the workforce. The inequality in salaries was only finally abolished in 1990.[37]

While it would not be correct to say that modernization was a process imposed entirely by Denmark against Greenlandic wishes, Greenlandic voices against modernization became stronger in the 1960s and 1970s. In 1970, a two-week-long conference was held in Sisimiut to discuss the future of Greenland. Politicians from Greenland and Denmark, as well as representatives of workers' organizations, students, and the business community participated. Greenlandic students in Denmark formed the Young Greenlanders Council, initially to guide and support students, but soon also to participate in political discussion concerning the development of Greenland. The Council formulated a goal of a Greenland ruled from Greenland, and ruled by Greenlanders.[38] The first Greenlandic rock band Sumé was established by Greenlandic students in Denmark in 1972, and the lyrics of the band's songs gave words to the growing frustrations amongst young Greenlanders.[39]

One of Sumé's songs concerned the closure of Qullissat in 1972, an event that boosted political mobilization in Greenland and continues to be regarded as a major event almost fifty years later. The coal mine had been opened in 1924, and the town over the years grew to be one of the biggest in Greenland. The inhabitants developed a distinct way of life in supplement to the culture of the rest of Greenland – as an example, the workers' movement in Greenland was founded in Qullissat in the 1940s.[40] The mine had experienced economic difficulties for a number of years, due to the lack of local infrastructure and the difficulty of securing export markets for the coal, and finally a decision was made by the Danish Government to close the mine. The Greenland National Council had been heard in the matter, and a majority of the members had supported the closure. Nonetheless, the closure was a traumatic event for the inhabitants, who viewed themselves as having

---

37 Janussen, *Analyse af fødestedskriteriet*.   38 Jensen, "Nyordning og modernisering".
39 A Greenlandic documentary, "Sumé: Mumisitsinerup nipaa" (Sumé; the sound of a revolution), was released in 2014, directed by Inuk Silis Høegh and produced by Emile Hertling Peronard. The meaning of the word sumé is 'where', in the sense of 'Where are we?'
40 Carlsen, "Problemer omkring organiseringen"; Jørgensen, *Moving Archives*.

been overruled by a system and not having any say in regard to their lives. The inhabitants were moved to different towns in Greenland, where they had to rebuild their lives and identities. Today the closure of the mine and the town is still commemorated by the former inhabitants.[41]

In the beginning of the 1970s, a new generation of Greenlandic politicians won seats in the national council and as Greenlandic members of the Danish Parliament. The trio – often referred to as the 'three polar bears' – Jonathan Motzfeldt, Moses Olsen, and Lars-Emil Johansen – came to have an enormous impact on the political course of Greenland. They proposed the idea of a Greenland home rule, and formed the social democratic party Siumut (meaning 'forward'), which dominated politics in the decades after Home Rule. Two members of the trio became leaders of the Greenland Government and the Greenland parliament at differing points in time.[42] Their cause was boosted by the 1972 Danish referendum on membership of the European Community. Seventy per cent of the votes in Greenland had been negative, but as the majority of the Danish votes were positive for the Danish Realm to apply for membership, Greenland automatically gained membership – and with it fears over the loss of control over fisheries to European fishing companies.[43] The control of mineral resources was another sensitive matter in the 1970s. From the time of Hans Egede, Danish authorities had been interested in Greenland's mineral potential, and while there had been few mines in the years since, the success of the cryolite mine at Ivittuut in southern Greenland provided a tempting example.[44] After World War II, a uranium deposit (Kvanefjeldet) was examined near the town of Narsaq, and while it was not developed (thanks in part to Danish concerns over the strategic implications of developing its own nuclear power programme), the project has in recent years been revived with rare earth metals rather than uranium as the primary focus.[45] Despite the controversy over the closure of Qullissat, the Danish government welcomed the Canadian mining company Cominco when it wanted to develop a lead–zinc mine at Maarmorilik, near Uummannaq, which opened in 1973.

During the 1970s, the foundation for Greenland Home Rule was laid. Greenlandic political parties became more clearly defined, and while differences remained within Greenlandic society, a growing consensus emerged that Home Rule was both possible and desirable. Such was the importance of

---

41 Sørensen, *Qullissat*.
42 Jensen, "Nyordning og modernisering"; Jensen and Heinrich, "Fra hjemmestyre til selvstyre".
43 Jensen, "Nyordning og modernisering". 44 Sejersen, *Efterforskning*.
45 Knudsen and Nielsen, *Uranbjerget*.

control over mines and the revenues from them that control over mineral resources became perhaps the most contentious issue in the negotiations, which were finally concluded in 1978. The Danish parliament approved the Act on Greenland Home Rule with a large majority, and a referendum held in Greenland in the beginning of 1979 also produced a large majority for the Home Rule model. Siumut held thirteen out of twenty-one seats in the first elections to the Greenlandic parliament. Atassut (meaning 'attached' [to Denmark]), which as the name suggests wanted to retain a close connection to Denmark, received the remaining eight seats.

When the Home Rule Act came into force in May 1979, Greenland gained competences over domestic administrative matters, with authority from Copenhagen transferred to Nuuk along with money equivalent to the sum previously spent on operating that administrative department from Denmark. The first such responsibilities transferred from Copenhagen were settlements and outer districts, industry and economy, culture and education, and finally welfare. The establishment of a ministry for settlements and outer districts was a direct response to the modernization policy. In 1979, 22 per cent of the population lived in the outer districts but had only received between 3 and 6 per cent of the investments in the preceding twenty years, reflecting their low priority to the Greenland Ministry in Copenhagen. By contrast, the new Greenland Government saw the outer districts as holders of certain traditional cultural qualities, and thereby important for the cultural development of Greenland as a whole, leading to substantially increased investment. With the Home Rule Act, Greenland also had the competence to decide which organizations and community to be part of. In 1982, a referendum on membership of the European Community was held. The result with 52 per cent of the votes meant Greenland left the Community in 1985.[46] While developing new administrative structures posed challenges, the Greenlandic government was able to effectively address certain issues such as alcohol consumption, which peaked in Greenland in 1987, and which through different approaches was lowered to a level that eventually fell below that of Denmark.

Defining Oneself

Following the modernization process and the introduction of Home Rule, emphasis has been put on being able to define oneself, often in opposition to the perceived Danification process.

46 Jensen and Heinrich, "Fra hjemmestyre til selvstyre".

In the 1970s the reintroduction of the traditional summer camps (*aasivik*) acted to reawaken cultural and political energy.[47] In the precolonial era, these aasiviks had brought people from different regions into contact, with goods being traded and family liaisons being forged. Now they also served to strengthen a sense of common political identity in a time of reduced mobility and more settled populations. During the 1970s, relations with fellow Inuit groups across the Arctic region led to the foundation of the Inuit Circular Council (ICC), a non-governmental organization representing 180,000 Inuit of Alaska, Canada, Greenland, and Chukotka.

This emphasis on defining Greenlandic identity was a key reason for cultural and educational institutions being among the first areas to be transferred to Greenland. Being able to express, communicate, and excel from a Greenlandic perspective has been a political priority since the 1970s. New institutions to allow this were established, including Ilisimatusarfik (University of Greenland), Nunatta Katersugaasivia Allagaateqarfialu (Greenland National Museum and Archives), and later the culture house Katuaq. Within the arts, Greenlanders are finding ways to express, to Greenland and the rest of the world, what Greenlandic society, identity, and culture entail. Traditional Inuit tattoos, based on precolonial tattoos, are being reintroduced. The original tattoos most likely were made in order to fight evil spirits, but today the tattoos are signs of Greenlandic/Inuit identity.

Self-government and the Right to Self-determination

By the early 2000s, there was a growing feeling that Home Rule had fulfilled its purpose as a stage on a path from colonial dependency to independence. As in the prelude to the introduction of Home Rule, a Greenlandic Commission started work toward a new agreement, followed by a joint Greenlandic-Danish Commission that delivered a final report in 2008. The resulting Self-Government Act of 2009[48] recognized 'the people of Greenland [as] a people pursuant to international law with the right of self-determination' and said that 'the Act is based on a wish to foster equality and mutual respect in the partnership between Denmark and Greenland'.[49]

---

47 Dahl, *Aasivik*.
48 https://naalakkersuisut.gl/~/media/Nanoq/Files/Attached%20Files/Engelske-tekster/Act%20on%20Greenland.pdf.
49 Preamble of Act on Greenland Self-Government.

While Denmark still retained certain responsibilities in Greenland, the Act transferred responsibility of most areas to Greenland. Importantly, the Act also laid out a pathway to independence, which would be granted if a referendum in Greenland approved a negotiated agreement on independence between the governments of Denmark and Greenland. Independence has remained the long-term goal of all governments in the self-rule era, but with the immediate focus on preparing the road to independence. As with Danification, there has been emphasis on raising education levels and preparing citizens who could lead the way for social and economic progress, but this time without the assumption that the path to modernization runs through Danish language and culture. Subsidies from Denmark, including an annual block grant, have remained essential to the Greenlandic economy and therefore focused political attention on measures that can lead to economic self-sufficiency. Around 90 per cent of export income from Greenland in the years immediately following 2009 came from fisheries, with mining developments either stalled or abandoned, but with hopes invested in increased revenue from tourism. Diversifying the economy and thereby strengthening the economic conditions in Greenland was recognized at the time of self-rule as a prerequisite for an independent Greenland, but that has been difficult to achieve for local as well as global reasons.[50]

The development of Greenland and the relationship with Denmark can in several aspects be considered a success story. Greenland has undergone a radical social transformation in close cooperation with Denmark. And while some groups in Greenland are willing to sever their ties to Denmark, most Greenlanders perceive the relationship with Denmark as a positive one. Most families in Greenland have, to some degree, Danish or European ancestors, and a number of traits in Greenland have been obtained through the connection to Denmark. The Nordic welfare state, with free education, health care, and democratic institutions, as well as developed associations are all directly linked to the connection with Denmark. There is also a high degree of personal fondness among Greenlanders for the Danish monarchy – arguably far more so than for Danish political figures – thanks to their many visits through the years, including Crown Prince Frederik travelling almost 3000 km by dog sled across the northern coast of Greenland.

---

50 Greenland has granted exploitation licences for two mines – Greenland Rubies mine in southern Greenland and Hudson Resources anorthosite mine in Kangerlussuaq. A number of exploration licences could potentially lead to new mines. For further information on mineral resources in Greenland, see Mineral Resources Authority at https://govmin.gl/.

A Greater Say in Foreign Affairs

The strategic importance of Greenland since World War II has meant a continuation of a US military presence in Greenland. A new defence agreement between Denmark and the United States was signed in 1951 and the Thule Air Base established, forcing a relocation of the Inughuit community living near the base to the settlement of Qaanaaq. Most likely the Danish authorities wanted the group moved because they regarded it as being in the group's best interests, but an actual dialogue with the group was not conducted, despite there being a local council since the 1920s.[51] In 1957, the United States began to store nuclear weapons at Thule with what they regarded as the silent consent of Denmark, even though nuclear weapons were prohibited on Danish territory. The question arose again when a B-52 bomber crashed near Thule in January 1968 while carrying four nuclear bombs, leading to a substantial clean-up operation and serious embarrassment. During the 1990s, survivors of the Qaanaaq move organized the association Hingitaq 53 (the displaced from 1953) and sought justice through the Danish judicial system, winning financial compensation and an apology from the Danish prime minister. The full story of the US-Danish discussions became clear in 1995.[52] But security and defence matters in Greenland remain a Danish responsibility. No Greenlandic politicians were included in the early negotiations concerning the defence of Greenland, and while it would be difficult to imagine Denmark acting without consultation, Greenland continues to hold strategic value in Denmark's wider defence policy within NATO.[53]

Greenlandic wishes for full control over foreign and defence policy were initially less strong, as control over domestic issues was prioritized (particularly those related to culture and the economy), but today these affairs are integrated in the political aspirations of Greenland as a means to become an independent country.[54] This is reflected in the Greenland Government being included in the ongoing dialogue between Denmark and the United States, with Greenland having a stronger voice in issues such as service contracts for the Thule Air Base (awarded in 2014 to a US company, with a substantial tax loss for Greenland as a result), and the 2020 establishment of a US consulate in Nuuk. The increasing interest in the Arctic from various countries, including Russia, China, and the United States, will inevitably mean an increase in the

---

51 Brøsted and Fægteborg, *Thule*.   52 Brink, *Thule-sagen*
53 Henriksen and Rahbek-Clemmensen, *Grønlandskortet Arktis' betydning*.
54 Heinrich, "Independence through International Affairs".

possibilities of cooperation for Greenland. This could lead to economic gain for Greenland, but the tension between the countries could also lead to a precarious course ahead for the Greenland Government, especially when Greenland gains independence. Most likely, an independent Greenland would apply for membership of NATO. There are, however, economic considerations to pursue in relation to other countries. Greenland has established Representations in Copenhagen, Brussels, Reykjavik, and Washington, and in 2021 in China, as China is one of the most important markets for Greenland.

Perspective

At the time of writing, in 2021, full political independence from Denmark remains off the immediate agenda, but Greenlanders are increasingly conscious of having a distinct political identity, and a history that is relevant to understanding political and cultural issues today. Following the Black Lives Matter movement in the United States in the spring of 2020, the statue of Hans Egede in Nuuk[55] was painted in red and the word 'decolonize' was written on its base. The perpetrator was later apprehended. Presumably the act was a protest against a man who, in the perpetrator's eyes, had obliterated aspects of Greenlandic culture. In the same summer, a debate was raised following a Danish ice cream manufacturer's abandoning the word Eskimo on one of its products. Both in Greenland and in Denmark, the cases caused heated debates. The history of Greenland and the relationship between the two countries is a crucial part of these debates. In this sense, the history of Greenland is essential in the ongoing political process there. Knowing one's own history is crucial in finding a path forward, and the modern society has been formed as a continuous process containing cultural traits from the Inuit way of life combined with elements from the outside world.

To a still greater degree, the history of Greenland is written by Greenlanders. Discussions on identity and the historical development are part of the society evolving. In this category, the establishment of the Greenland Reconciliation Commission (2014–17) had a mandate centred on raising awareness on the colonial legacy in present-day society.[56] Initially, the

---

55 Danish-Norwegian priest who initiated the colonization of Greenland in 1721. The statue in Nuuk presides on a hill in the old colonial area – the so-called colonial harbour.
56 For an introduction to the Commission, see Thisted, "Greenlandic Reconciliation Commission"; Andersen, "Lessons"; (in Danish) the web magazine *Baggrund*.

Premier of Greenland, Aleqa Hammond, offered an invitation to the Danish Prime Minister, Helle Thorning Schmidt, for Denmark to participate in the reconciliation process, but the invitation was declined.[57] The focus of the Commission, instead of a Danish-Greenlandic perspective, came to be on internal Greenlandic reconciliation. A number of initiatives were started to inform and include the population in Greenland concerning reconciliation: among these were public meetings, historical research projects, surveys, novels, and art projects.[58] At the public meetings, participants were encouraged to express their experiences, either in plenum or via formal interview. A number of themes were brought forward by the public. The Commission saw the work of the Commission as a starting point for the reconciliation process, and the final report from the Commission to the Greenland Government included recommendations on how to continue the process. The Commission underlined the importance of being able to define oneself through history and through different forms of art, as an aspect of building a stronger society. One of the consequences of the reconciliation initiative has been a willingness in the Greenlandic population to deal with difficult themes, such as sexual assaults of children and the high numbers of suicides. There is, however, still a need to raise the level of historical knowledge and awareness in Greenland and in Denmark on the joint historical ties between the two countries.

Recent historical research supports the notion that, to an increasing degree, Greenlandic politicians throughout the past 160 years have had an influence on how Greenland was developed. While their influence has not been in a single direction – there have long been debates over tradition versus modernization, and over the nature of the relationship to Denmark – a clear trend may be detected toward expecting, and exercising, stronger local power over Greenlandic affairs. Greenland is on a path towards independence, even if the timeframe for this independence has not been set, and with it the future relationship between Greenland and Denmark will also eventually be decided.

---

57 The Danish Government, however, is open to dialogue on the historical relationship between Greenland and Denmark, as a number of the 'white books' have been produced over the years. The themes for these white books are decolonization (Dansk Institut for Internationale Studier, *Afvikling af Grønlands kolonistatus*, 2007), Greenlandic children born out of wedlock (Nielsen et al., *Historisk udredning*, 2011), and Greenlandic children undergoing an experiment in the 1950s (Jensen et al., *Historisk udredning*, 2020).

58 https://naalakkersuisut.gl/da/Naalakkersuisut/Departementer/Formandens-departement/Forsoningskommission.

Bibliography

Andersen, Astrid Nonbo, "Lessons from the Greenlandic Reconciliation Process", Justicinfo.net (2020), www.justiceinfo.net/en/43949-lessons-from-the-greenlandic-reconciliation-process.html.

Brink, Poul, *Thule-sagen – løgnens univers* (Aschehoug: Brondum, 1997).

Brøsted, Jens, and Fægteborg, Mads, *Thule – fangerfolk og militæranlæg* (Jurist- og Økonomiforbundets, 1985).

Carlsen, Aksel V., "Problemer omkring organiseringen af en grønlandsk arbejderbevægelse", *Grønlandsk kultur- og samfundsforskning* (2003): 21–44.

Dahl, Hjalmar, *Aasivik – inuit isumasioqatigiiffiat* (Atuakkiorfik, 2005).

Dansk Institut for Internationale Studier (DIIS), *Afvikling af Grønlands kolonistatus 1945–54 – en historisk udredning* (København, DIIS: 2007).

Folketinget, The Constitutional Act of Denmark of 5 June 1953, www.ft.dk/-/media/sites/ft/pdf/publikationer/engelske-publikationer-pdf/grundloven_samlet_2018_uk_web.ashx.

Forchhammer, Søren, "Gathered or Dispersed? Four Decades of Development Policy Debate in Greenland", PhD diss. (Københavns Universitet Institut for Eskimologi, 1997).

Gulløv, Hans Christian, ed., *Grønland – den arktiske koloni* (Gads, 2017).

Heinrich, Jens, *Eske Brun og det moderne Grønlands tilblivelse* (Inussuk, 2012).

Heinrich, Jens, "Forsoningskommissionen og fortiden som koloni", *Baggrund* (28 November 2014), https://baggrund.com/2014/11/28/forsoningskommissionen-og-fortiden-som-koloni/.

Heinrich, Jens, "Independence through International Affairs: How Foreign Relations Shaped Greenlandic Identity before 1979", in K. S. Kristensen and J. Rahbek-Clemmensen, eds., *Greenland and the International Politics of a Changing Arctic Postcolonial Paradiplomacy between High and Low Politics* (Routledge, 2018), pp. 28–37.

Heinrich, Jens, *Rapport over projekt om koncentrationspolitikken i Grønland 1940–2009* (Grønlands Forsoningskommission, 2016).

Henriksen, Anders, and Rahbek-Clemmensen, Jon, *Grønlandskortet Arktis' betydning for Danmarks indflydelse i USA* (Copenhagen: Københavns Universitet Center for Militære Studier, 2017).

Howarth, David, *The Sledge Patrol* (Rowman & Littlefield, 2018).

Janussen, Jakob, *Analyse af fødestedskriteriet – Efterlysning af fuld ligestilling førte til diametralt modsat resultat* (Grønlands Forsoningskommission, 2017).

Jensen, Einar Lund, "Nyordning og modernisering," in Hans Christian Gulløv, ed., *Grønland – den arktiske koloni* (Gad, 2017), pp. 320–371.

Jensen, Einar Lund, et al., *Historisk udredning om de 22 grønlandske børn, der blev sendt til Danmark i 1951* (Statsministeriet, 2020).

Jensen, Einar Lund, and Heinrich, Jens, "Fra hjemmestyre til selvstyre 1979–2009", in Hans Christian Gulløv, ed., *Grønland – den arktiske koloni* (Gad, 2017), pp. 374–421.

Jørgensen, Anne Mette, "Moving Archives: Agency, Emotions and Visual Memories of Industrialization in Greenland", PhD diss. (University of Copenhagen, 2017).

Kleist, Mininnguaq, *Kilder til Færøernes og Grønlands historie – Anden del Kilder angående Grønland* (Thorshavn: Føroya Fróðskaparfelag, 2004), pp. 127–239.

Knudsen, Henrik, and Nielsen, Henry, *Uranbjerget: om forsøgene på at finde og udnytte Grønlands uran fra 1944 til i dag* (Vandkunsten, 2016).

Kristiansen, Paarnannguaq, "Tuberkulosebekæmpelsen i Grønland Udvikling og følger i det offentliges tuberkuloseforanstaltninger i Vestgrønland 1900–1961", MA diss. (University of Greenland, 2004), https://da.uni.gl/media/40894/paarnannguaq-kristiansen.pdf.

Lidegaard, Bo, *I Kongens navn – Henrik Kauffmann i dansk diplomati 1919–1958* (Copenhagen: Samleren, 1996).

Lidegaard, Bo, *Uden mandat* (Gyldendal, 2020).

Løkkegaard, Finn, *Det danske gesandtskab i Washington 1940–1942: Henrik Kauffmann som uafhængig dansk gesandt i USA 1940–1942 og hans politik vedrørende Grønland og de oplagte danske skibe i Amerika* (Gyldendal, 1968).

Lynge, Augo, *Ukiut 300-ngornerat* (Bianco Lunop Nakiteriviane, 1931).

Moltke, Ida, Matteo Fumagalli, Thorfinn A. Korneliussen, et al., "Uncovering the Genetic History of the Present-Day Greenlandic Population", *American Journal of Human Genetics* 96 (2014): 54–69.

Nielsen, Linda, et al., *Historisk udredning om retsstillingen for børn født uden for ægteskab i Grønland i perioden 1914 til 1963-1974* [White book on children born out of wedlock] (Statsministeriet, 2011), www.regeringen.dk/media/1227/historisk_udredning_om_retsstillingen_for_boern_foedt_uden_for_aegteskab_i_groenland_i_perioden_1914_til_1963-1974.pdf.

Sejersen, Frank, *Efterforskning og udnyttelse af råstoffer i Grønland i historisk perspektiv*. Baggrundspapir, Udvalget for samfundsgavnlig udnyttelse af Grønlands naturressourcer (Copenhagen: 2014).

Skaale, Sjúrður, ed., *The Right to National Self-determination: The Faroe Islands and Greenland* (Leiden, Boston: Martinus Nijhoff, 2004).

Søby Kristensen, Kristian, ed., *Greenland and the International Politics of a Changing Arctic: Postcolonial Paradiplomacy between High and Low Politics* (London, New York: Routledge, 2017).

Sørensen, Aksel Kjær, *Danmark-Grønland i det 20. århundrede – en historisk oversigt* (Nyt Nordisk Forlag Arnold Busck, 1983); an updated and revised edition of the book was published in English as *Denmark-Greenland in the Twentieth Century* (Copenhagen: Danish Polar Center, 2006).

Sørensen, Søren Peder, *Qullissat – byen der ikke ville dø* (Frydenlund, 2013).

Storch, Mathias, *Singnagtugaq: A Greenlander's Dream* (Lebanon, NH: University Press of New England, 2014).

Storch, Mathias, *Strejflys over Grønland* (Copenhagen: Levin & Munksgaards, 1930).

Teglbjærg, Kirsten, "Kalâliussuseq – Det at være grønlænder – identitet og etnisk bevidsthed", MA diss. (Københavns Universitet institut for eskimologi, 1978).

Thisted, Kirsten, "The Greenlandic Reconciliation Commission: Ethnonationalism, Arctic Resources, and Post-colonial Identity", in Lill-Ann Körber, Scott MacKenzie, and Anna Westerståhl Stenport, eds., *Arctic Environmental Modernities* (Cham: Palgrave Macmillan, 2017), pp. 231–246.

21

Cold War Environmental Knowledge in the Polar Regions

STEPHEN BOCKING AND PEY-YI CHU

Introduction

In the twenty-first century, scientists and the media track the health of the planet in the polar regions. Shrinking sea ice in the Arctic and Southern oceans, melting ice shelves in Nunavut, Greenland, and West Antarctica, and thawing permafrost in Alaska and Siberia are signals of global warming. This has led people to refer to these regions as a 'canary in the coal mine' or the 'ground zero' and 'epicentre' of climate change.[1] Such metaphors impart an abstract quality to the polar regions, with rising temperatures and loss of ice serving merely as numbers on the dashboard of Spaceship Earth. This view of the polar regions as integral yet neutral – transparent indicators of a global system – has an intellectual and political history. Created by the scientific context of the Cold War, it provides a powerful, panoptic perspective of the planet while obscuring the heterogeneity and pluralism of beings and places.

A striking feature of the Cold War was a great expansion of scientific activity. Stretching from 1947 through 1989, the Cold War was dominated by geopolitical and ideological rivalry between the capitalist United States and the communist Soviet Union, which collapsed in 1991.[2] Tensions between the two so-called superpowers motivated scientific research directed towards strategic and technological imperatives, including the weapons and systems of surveillance and control that became instruments for asserting military and

---

1 "A Canary in the Coal Mine"; Reiss, "Barrow, Alaska"; Almond, "What It's Like"; Kalnins, "Arctic Expedition"; Bergstrom et al., "Antarctica".
2 Following Serhii Plokhy, we date the end of the Cold War to the fall of communism in Europe in 1989. We avoid using 1991 as the conflict's end date because doing so risks promoting a US-centric, triumphalist narrative that assumes the collapse of the Soviet Union to be its endpoint. In actuality, actors at the time, including the George H. W. Bush administration, considered the continued existence of a democratic USSR as desirable. The United States only retrospectively took credit for its breakup. See Plokhy, *The Last Empire*.

ideological superiority. But it also included studies of the global environment, that is, the Earth, its oceans, and atmosphere. While these studies extended around the world, a special focus, particularly in the early years of the Cold War, was on the polar regions. The United States and the USSR asserted leading roles, but polar research also drew scientists from Europe, Asia, Oceania, Africa, and North and South America. Science shaped by Cold War priorities therefore forms a distinctive episode in the history of polar knowledge. The influence of this episode also lingers: research stations, scientific activities, and forms of knowledge that originated during the Cold War still shape our understanding of the polar regions.

This chapter situates polar research within the overlapping histories of the environmental sciences and the Cold War. In recent decades, numerous scholars have examined the history of environmental sciences since World War II. This scholarship has focused on the emergence and evolution of ecology, climate science, and Earth systems science, with explicit attention to the physical environmental sciences.[3] Linking the history of science and environmental history, and informed by post-constructivism and feminist science studies, historians have examined the ideas of nature and 'the environment', notions of catastrophism and abrupt geological change, and the concept of the Anthropocene in relation to the Cold War and its consequences, including radioactive fallout and a potential nuclear winter.[4] Simultaneously, a burgeoning scholarship known as 'the New Cold War History' has expanded perspectives on that historical phenomenon. Scholars have shown that the Cold War was global, extending far beyond relations between the United States and the USSR. It encompassed not only confrontation and competition, but also collaboration and globalization, and was fought not only on strategic and military terms but also in terms of economies and standards of living. Finally, the Cold War was not static: from the 1950s through the 1980s it persisted and evolved, exhibiting national and international shifts and continuities. But while this expanding literature has broken new ground, it has yet to fully incorporate the polar regions.[5]

We argue that the polar regions played central roles in the development of the idea of a global environment during the Cold War. As the polar regions came under surveillance, scientists came to perceive more clearly their

---

3 Doel, "What's the Place?".
4 Dörries, "Politics of Atmospheric Sciences"; Hamblin, *Arming Mother Nature*; Warde et al., *The Environment: A History*.
5 For an authoritative global history of the Cold War that nevertheless all but ignores the Arctic and Antarctica, see Westad, *The Cold War*.

patterns of oceanic and atmospheric circulation and exchange. They also traced interactions between the air and waters of the Arctic and the Antarctic and other parts of the world, such as the effects of polar currents on temperatures elsewhere. Moreover, they detected impacts of distant human activities on the polar regions, including the presence of radioactive elements and industrial chemicals in polar ice, flora, and fauna.[6] Their research provided evidence of connections between the polar regions and the rest of the world. One lasting impact of Cold War polar science was the formation of a global perspective: a view, grounded in international scientific cooperation, of the planet as a single system. Within this view, the polar regions acquired special importance. Yet this panoptic Earth systems perspective also sidelined other views. Most notably, it further marginalized and displaced the knowledge of Indigenous inhabitants of the Arctic. Countering this geophysical view with the insights and transnational agency of voices situated in the polar regions themselves remains an ongoing process.[7]

We begin by discussing the formation of Cold War science in the polar regions. This history of science draws attention to the geographic dimensions of knowledge and action, including the question of whether the polar regions should be considered as the sites of a distinctive relationship between science and the Cold War. Next, we turn to what was learned and not learned about the polar regions. We then consider how the polar regions became defined as distinctive Cold War spaces before concluding with observations regarding the continuing importance of the Cold War to our understanding of the history of environmental knowledge of the polar regions. By situating knowledge about the polar regions in the Cold War, we highlight the capacities and limitations of polar science as well as the need to restore epistemologies that resist the erasure of beings and places.

The Development of Cold War Polar Science

In the context of a global Cold War, the polar regions acquired distinctive strategic significance. The Arctic, situated on the northern frontier of both superpowers and readily traversed by bombers and missiles, was now a zone of confrontation and surveillance, and, in the event of active conflict, of potential sacrifice. The environment of war was transformed by the requirements of

---

6 Murozumi et al., "Chemical Concentrations"; Bocking, "Toxic Surprises".
7 Cameron, "Securing Indigenous Politics"; Cameron, "Climate Anti-politics".

military operations and the need for surveillance of potential adversaries. Aircraft, submarines, satellites, and other technologies created a demand to predict and control the environments in which they operated. Soldiers and technicians, as well as their equipment, had to be able to operate in an environment that was unfamiliar, challenging, even 'hostile' to the inhabitants of more temperate regions. By the late 1940s, the prospect of natural climate change also aroused strategic interest, given its consequences for sea ice and therefore navigation.[8] Ways of manipulating the environment for military advantage – through nuclear, chemical, and biological warfare as well as control of the weather – were also explored.[9] While the Antarctic was not similarly situated at the centre of superpower confrontation, it too had strategic significance, in part because its environment presented similar operational challenges. Overall, therefore, the polar regions became proving grounds: sites for learning how to adapt technologies and bodies to a novel and challenging environment.

The strategic significance of the polar regions implied new requirements for knowledge, with virtually every aspect of their physical environments attracting scientific interest: land, ocean, cryosphere (including sea ice, glaciers, and permafrost), atmosphere, even gravity and magnetic fields. To produce this and other forms of knowledge that strategic priorities demanded, science during the Cold War took the form of 'big science': large-scale research funded and coordinated by the state that addressed questions beyond the capabilities of individual scientists, often employing large instruments or other technologies.[10] While growing out of a longer history of scientific practice, big science developed a distinctive orientation and organization in the Cold War context. On the one hand, it was oriented to military needs. On the other, it was shaped by newly established global institutions and renewed hopes for international cooperation after World War II.[11] These strands – big science, strategic science, and global science – constituted Cold War science, and they made lasting impressions on knowledge of the polar regions.

For this episode in the history of knowledge to be understood, it must be situated within the specific context of the polar regions themselves. Although unprecedented in scale and extent, Cold War research extended an already established role for states in polar science. Studies addressing strategic

---

8 Sörlin, "Narratives and Counter-narratives".
9 Doel, "Constituting Postwar Earth Sciences"; Hamblin, *Arming Mother Nature*; O'Neill and Unger, eds., *Environmental Histories*.
10 Galison, "Many Faces". 11 Selcer, *Postwar Origins*.

priorities were also often tied, particularly in the later decades of the Cold War, to scientific work that addressed other polar issues, including economic development, the assertion of territorial authority, and concern about the state of the environment. This research reflected longer traditions of thinking about the Arctic and its relation to national territories. The history of Antarctic exploration also exhibited aspects of these persistent economic and territorial objectives.

Spurred by Cold War competition, the Soviet state dramatically increased investment in science. Existing institutes expanded, new ones proliferated, and the number of scientists grew rapidly, quadrupling to almost one million between 1955 and 1970.[12] Research into the polar regions benefited. In Leningrad (now St Petersburg), the Arctic and Antarctic Research Institute, whose origins dated to the 1920s, received funding for larger observatories, drifting ice stations, computers, and its own fleet of research vessels. Similarly, the Kola Branch of the Academy of Sciences, founded in 1930, acquired larger budgets and more personnel to investigate mineral resources and their extraction in the Arctic.[13] In 1957, the Soviet government approved the creation of an entirely new branch of the Academy of Sciences, the Siberian Section, based in a specially built suburb near Novosibirsk. Among the Siberian Section's institutes was the Institute of Economics and the Organization of Industrial Production, which developed plans for economic development in the Soviet Arctic.[14] The Siberian Section acquired outposts of its own, including the Institute for Permafrost Science in Yakutsk in 1960, whose programme included solving the engineering challenges of Arctic development.[15] The USSR also established over a dozen year-round research stations on Antarctica.[16]

Soviet scientists also experienced changes in the domestic political and ideological context of science. After Stalin's death in 1953, Soviet leaders undertook reforms in response to the USSR's post-war economic challenges and changed international status. Economically, besides rebuilding after the devastation of war, they asserted the necessity of competing with the capitalist societies of North America and Western Europe. Given Western countries' advantages in technological development, the USSR aimed to modernize its industries so as to 'catch and overtake' (*dognat' i peregnat'*) the United States, its primary rival. Simultaneously, the Kremlin sought to

12 Vucinich, *Empire of Knowledge*, 295.   13 Josephson, *Conquest of Russian Arctic*.
14 Josephson, *New Atlantis Revisited*.
15 Kamenskii, ed., *Akademicheskoe merzlotovedenie v Iakutii*.
16 Baskakov et al., "Arkticheskii i antarkticheskii".

de-escalate geopolitical tensions as a way of serving Soviet interests. Promoting peace and disarmament would not only cultivate a more enlightened image of the Soviet Union among Western audiences; it would facilitate the international trade and investment needed to advance the Soviet economy.[17] The shift in Soviet politics reverberated in science policy. Instead of a narrow focus on specific industrial applications, science administrators re-emphasized fundamental, interdisciplinary research, aided by mathematics and computing, as playing a key role in propelling socioeconomic progress.[18] Bureaucrats and academicians alike embraced an ideology of scientific management, taking an interest in American modernization theory and management science. The shared language of technocracy between the United States and USSR became a basis for transnational scientific cooperation and exchange.[19]

There is a parallel history of state and commercial support of polar science in North America. Centuries of British, American, and eventually Canadian exploration by land and sea mapped territories, travel routes, and resources. After World War I, exploration gave way to more sustained study in Alaska and northern Canada. The Canadian government (including the Geological Survey of Canada and other institutions), private companies, prospectors, and independent scientists surveyed geological and wildlife resources. These activities established the context for Cold War scientific institutions by not only providing a foundation of knowledge of the region, but also making clear how little was known.

After the end of World War II, a variety of efforts were undertaken in response to demands for knowledge to support operations and surveillance in the polar regions. Initial activities included field exercises in which military forces sought operational experience. For example, in 1946, Operation Muskox, a land-borne expedition extending across much of northern Canada, evaluated the mobility of land forces and their equipment. The same year, the US Navy's Operation High Jump, in which several dozen ships conducted operations near Antarctica, provided an opportunity to practise operating in Arctic conditions, but in a region distant enough to not raise tensions with the Soviet Union.[20] These and similar activities exemplified the combination of operational exercises, exploration, and research that were distinctive to the early Cold War era, while also suggesting some interplay between activities in the Arctic and in the Antarctic motivated by similarities in physical environments.

17 Zubok, *A Failed Empire*.   18 Josephson, *New Atlantis Revisited*.
19 Rindzevičiūtė, *Power of Systems*; Gerovitch, *From Newspeak to Cyberspeak*.
20 Dodds, "Assault on the Unknown".

American initiatives included the Arctic Research Laboratory (ARL) at Point Barrow, Alaska (established in 1947, becoming the Naval Arctic Research Laboratory in 1967), and the Snow, Ice and Permafrost Research Establishment (1949), as well as activities in northern Canada and at Thule Air Base in Greenland (including Camp Century, 240 km east of the air base) that examined all aspects of the physical environment, devoting special attention to the engineering challenges posed by permafrost and the polar ice cap. The Danish government established research operations in Greenland, studying the ice, ocean, and ionosphere.[21] In Canada, the Defence Research Board assumed broad responsibility for strategic research, with a special focus on the North, alongside other federal agencies such as the Geological Survey, the Canadian Wildlife Service, and the Fisheries Research Board of Canada. The Polar Continental Shelf Project began operations in 1959, providing facilities for researchers across a range of disciplines. The Arctic Institute of North America facilitated cooperation between the United States and Canada, and to a lesser extent supported scientific activities in Europe.[22] Like the Soviet Union, the United States and other countries established an array of scientific stations across the Antarctic. American scientific activities in Antarctica accelerated after 1959 with the establishment of the United States Antarctic Research Program by the National Science Foundation.

Practices of Cold War Polar Science

Technology was central to Cold War scientific efforts. The use of aircraft, satellites, submarines, and other technologies shaped both research practices and the forms of information collected. It also shaped scientists' relations with polar environments, often distancing them from these environments while encouraging broader, synoptic views. Equipped with aeroplanes, helicopters, and field stations, scientists no longer needed to rely, as had earlier generations of explorers, on Indigenous ways of travel and survival.

Cold War scientific activity made the Arctic and Antarctic outposts of the 'military-industrial-academic complex', linking power and the production of knowledge.[23] Scientists saw themselves as visitors to the polar regions, producing knowledge that could mediate the relation between outsiders and an unfamiliar environment and building the 'terrain intelligence' needed to work with, not against, polar conditions. The polar regions became

21 Doel et al., eds., *Exploring Greenland*; Martin-Nielsen, "'Orgy of Hypothesizing'".
22 van der Watt et al., "Institutions".   23 Leslie, *Cold War*.

strategic 'laboratories' as science shifted towards a more systematic, state-centred model.[24] The metaphor of the laboratory expressed several aspects of how scientists and institutions viewed these regions. Through the application of scientific techniques and technologies they could become sites of experimental analysis. They could also be thought of as pristine, protected by distance from the disruptions of industrial society, lacking their own histories, and therefore, like the ideal of the controlled laboratory, placeless.[25]

Although scientific research responded to strategic goals, there were also opportunities for individuals to exercise agency, particularly by building research programmes through which to pursue their scientific ambitions, negotiating accommodations with their patrons. Research at the ARL that responded to specifically scientific and disciplinary priorities included tracking whale and bird migrations, surveying polar bears and lemmings, and pursuing ethnographic research with Inuit.[26] The Defence Research Board defined its mandate broadly, supporting a variety of projects by university scientists. McGill University scientists conducted studies that combined strategic purposes with ambitions to build new approaches to geographical research.[27] Greenland served as a platform for wide-ranging studies of the physical environment. Throughout the 1950s and 1960s, much polar research expressed a characteristic feature of Cold War science: institutions that were ostensibly focused on military and strategic missions also provided latitude for scientists to pursue, within selected fields, their own ambitions.

Cold War scientific activities commonly combined attention to strategic and non-strategic priorities, such as resource development, weather forecasting, and the assertion of territorial authority. Globally, strategic and civilian research intersected in diverse ways. Satellite images and computer models transformed weather forecasting.[28] Radio tracking technologies originally developed in military contexts were applied to wildlife science.[29] Radionuclides – originally byproducts of the development of nuclear weapons – were applied in biology and ecology.[30] Science therefore served throughout the Cold War to link different areas of activity, including military strategy, assertions of national

---

24 Farish, "Lab and the Land"; Dodds, "Assault on the Unknown".
25 Grevsmühl, "Laboratory Metaphors". 26 Reed and Ronhovde, *Arctic Laboratory*.
27 Bocking, "A Disciplined Geography".
28 Edwards, "Meteorology as Infrastructural Globalism". 29 Benson, *Wired Wilderness*.
30 Creager, *Life Atomic*.

authority, economic development, and environmental protection, on the basis of shared interests in certain features of the environment.

In the early years of the Cold War, much of the research, both strategic and civilian, pursued the effective operation of personnel and equipment in 'hostile' conditions. It aimed to learn how to handle the distinctive challenges of the polar regions, as when petroleum development and strategic activities drew on the terrain intelligence needed to operate on ice and permafrost.[31] Ensuring people and machines would be able to operate in the polar environment required testing human, mechanical, and structural endurance.[32] For example, the Defence Research Northern Laboratory at Fort Churchill studied clothing, equipment, fuels, lubricants, and nutrition. Insects, too, were studied in order to learn how to operate amidst blackfly swarms. The Arctic functioned as a proving ground for both strategic technologies, such as aviation and radio communication, and industrial technologies, such as pipelines and drilling rigs. Surveillance technology was tested and adapted for challenging polar conditions, as experienced, for example, in the Distant Early Warning (DEW) Line.[33] Joint Arctic Weather Stations (JAWS) in northern Canada combined military and civilian agencies, agendas, and cultures; they supported military transport and operations as well as commercial aviation. Both strategic imperatives and resource development demanded knowledge of what lay beneath the ground or ice, illustrating how science in service to Cold War industry pushed the boundaries of resource extraction to the ends of the Earth.

One project demonstrated how strategic and non-strategic scientific priorities could intertwine amidst the unintended consequences of Cold War activities. In 1958, the US Atomic Energy Commission (AEC) proposed Project Chariot: a demonstration, as part of Project Plowshare, of the use of 'peaceful' nuclear explosions to excavate a new harbour at Cape Thompson on the North Slope of Alaska.[34] Project Chariot was eventually cancelled, but not before provoking concerns about human impacts on the Arctic environment and assertions by local Indigenous people of their right to shape decisions that affect their wellbeing. Military and civilian entanglements were also seen in the global distribution of radioactive fallout, which

---

31 Iarocci, "Opening the North".
32 Farish, "Creating Cold War Climates"; Doel et al., "Introduction: Exploring Greenland's Secrets".
33 Farish and Lackenbauer, "Western Electric Turns North".
34 O'Neill, *Firecracker Boys*; Kirsch, "Peaceful Nuclear Explosions"; Cittadino, "Barry Commoner".

21 Cold War Environmental Knowledge in Polar Regions

became concentrated in food sources important to Indigenous people, and the environmental impacts of DEW Line stations and other strategic facilities.

The Cold War provided the context for not only competition and potential conflict but also international cooperation. Mechanisms for transnational exchange were provided by new intergovernmental and quasi-governmental organizations. The United Nations, founded in 1945, and the World Meteorological Organization, founded in 1947, collected economic and geophysical data. Academic societies, such as the International Council of Scientific Unions, organized global research efforts, including the International Geophysical Year (IGY) of 1957–58. Such societies were quasi-governmental: although administratively independent from the state, like the National Academy of Sciences of the United States, they received government funding. Moreover, their members consulted with government officials. In the case of countries in the socialist bloc, academic societies were subject to direct government oversight. Projects such as the IGY were therefore shaped by national interests, including evaluating the scientific capabilities of geopolitical rivals and bolstering territorial claims in places such as Antarctica.[35] By the late 1960s, informal networks had also emerged of scientists, business leaders, and politicians from both East and West, such as the Club of Rome. They dedicated themselves to studying global economic and environmental problems, helping to create international versions of the quintessential Cold War institution, the think tank. While combining academic research and policymaking, they also contributed to international cooperation.[36]

Therefore, another characteristic of Cold War polar science consisted of transnational flows of people and ideas, webs of knowledge production and circulation that responded to both the region's environmental challenges and political and strategic imperatives. These flows were defined partly through national efforts: the United States operated scientifically beyond its borders and cooperated in certain fields, such as meteorology, with other countries, including the Nordic countries. To a limited extent, scientific ties extended across the Cold War frontier. The 'natural affinity' implied by shared environmental challenges spurred interest in technical cooperation between Canada and the Soviet Union. Lester Pearson, the Canadian minister of external affairs, visited Moscow in 1955, and Moira Dunbar, the Defense Research Board's sea ice specialist, learned Russian to access Soviet sea ice

---

35 Needell, "Lloyd Berkner"; Howkins, "Melting Empires?"; Krementsov, *Stalinist Science*.
36 Rindzevičiūtė, *Power of Systems*.

literature.³⁷ From the 1970s, détente took on a distinctive significance in the Arctic, as seen in 1973 with the negotiation of a circumpolar treaty protecting polar bears, and in the late 1980s with the formation of a circumpolar regime of environmental monitoring stimulated by Gorbachev's opening to the West following his 1987 speech in Murmansk.

Cold War Polar Knowledge

Aided by technological advances, perceptions of climate and of the Earth itself shifted during the Cold War. Knowledge of the polar regions played a key role in this process. Whereas climate was previously understood in local and regional terms, by the end of the twentieth century it signified a planetary atmospheric phenomenon.³⁸ This change in perspective resulted from a transformation in scientific approaches to studying climate. Once focused on describing and characterizing the environment of specific places, the study of climate became centred on global atmospheric processes and long-term forecasts. Global and mathematical understandings of climate were developed initially in the nineteenth and early twentieth centuries. But their dominance and application to forecasting were realized only after the advent of electronic computers.³⁹

Starting in the 1950s, meteorologists began generating numerical weather predictions, utilizing electronic computers to more quickly solve the equations that approximated the atmosphere's behaviour.⁴⁰ From predicting local weather, they turned to developing models that encompassed the atmosphere of the entire planet. More accurate global models were created with the help of vast amounts of data collected by a burgeoning network of observation stations and satellites in the 1960s and 1970s. This network encompassed the entire world, including the polar regions, with satellites capable of recording radiation and clouds in the upper atmosphere.⁴¹ Being able to use models to simulate, with computers, the circulation of energy and moisture throughout the entire atmosphere encouraged thinking about the

---

37 On Dunbar, see Thomas, "Woman Scientist". On scientific exchange between the USSR and North America during the Cold War, see also Chu, *Life of Permafrost*.
38 Mauelshagen, "Climate as Scientific Paradigm"; Heymann and Achermann, "Climatology to Climate Science".
39 Edwards, *A Vast Machine*.
40 Heymann and Achermann, "Climatology to Climate Science"; Dalmedico, "History and Epistemology"; Harper, *Weather by Numbers*.
41 Budyko, *Climate and Life*; Edwards, *A Vast Machine*; Weart, "General Circulation Models"; Heymann and Achermann, "Climatology to Climate Science".

Earth itself as an interconnected system. Such an idea was promoted by James Lovelock and Lynn Margulis's 'Gaia hypothesis', which likened Earth to a living system – Gaia – capable of maintaining internal equilibrium.[42] It also motivated calls by scientists such as Soviet climatologist Mikhail Budyko to study interactions between climate and other systems of the earth, including the oceans and snow and ice.[43]

Owing to their massive accumulations of ice and snow, polar regions were not only affected by, but also themselves affected, the Earth's climate. Since the late nineteenth century, climatologists had understood that ice and snow reflected solar radiation back into the atmosphere. The proportion of solar radiation reflected rather than absorbed by a surface is known as albedo. Compared with other surfaces of the Earth (such as the ocean), fields of ice and snow have high albedo. According to theories of climate change that sought to explain past ice ages, under particular circumstances, the high albedo of ice and snow could contribute to hemispheric cooling. Triggered by a variation in the Earth's orbit around the Sun, for example, the reflection of solar radiation would favour the accumulation of ice and snow. More ice and snow meant more reflection, which in turn favoured further expansion of ice and snow cover in a positive feedback mechanism that could produce an ice age.[44]

During the Cold War, scientists studied the influence of polar ice on not only past but also contemporary and future climates of the Earth. Aided by observations from drift stations, aircraft, and satellites, they calculated energy balances in the polar regions, that is, their net gain or loss of heat. Energy balances were estimated for different surfaces and locations – sea, ice, snow, boreal forest, troposphere – as well as for the polar systems (surface and atmosphere combined) as a whole.[45] Comparing energy balances between parts of polar regions with and without perennial ice cover highlighted its importance in decreasing the radiation budget. Studies of energy balance were also used to predict the consequences of climate change for the polar regions. Specifically, scientists took interest in the effect of changes in the concentration of atmospheric carbon dioxide on polar ice. During the 1960s, rising levels of carbon dioxide drew attention to the greenhouse effect,

---

42 Lovelock and Margulis, "Atmospheric Homeostasis".
43 Oldfield, "Mikhail Budyko's Contributions".
44 Brooks, *Climate through the Ages*; Fleming, "James Croll in Context"; Berger, "Brief History"; Krüger, *Discovering the Ice Ages*.
45 Vowinckel and Orvig, "Climate"; Schwerdtfeger, "Climate of the Antarctic"; Ohmura, "Historical Review".

whereby long-wave radiation emitted from the Earth remained trapped in the atmosphere. In 1967, scientists in the United States computed that doubling the amount of carbon dioxide would increase the average air temperature at the earth's surface by 2 °C.[46] Focusing on Arctic ice, Budyko argued that the effects of an increase in carbon dioxide concentration would be amplified by the shrinking of the ice cover. If positive feedback could drive extensive glaciation, then it could also accelerate the disappearance of polar ice. 'A reduction of the glaciated area can promote climate heating', he wrote, 'which in turn will affect further ice cover shrinking'.[47] A picture emerged of the polar regions as both sensitive and unstable, an indicator as well as a driver of climate change.[48]

By the early 1960s, the strategic significance of the polar regions was in decline, as an attack over the North Pole became more unlikely, and the superpowers shifted their attention to Cuba, Berlin, the Middle East, and other flashpoints. As a result, research activities responding to other priorities became increasingly important, even while they built on scientific activities once justified in strategic terms. Since the 1980s, encouraged in part by environmental concerns, there has been a massive expansion of study of the place of the polar regions in global systems, including work in meteorology, climatology, and oceanography.[49] These studies have demonstrated how polar regions do not exist in isolation: studies of global environmental change today rely on studies of the Arctic and Antarctic ice, atmosphere, and oceans undertaken decades ago by the superpowers and their allies.

The 'environmental sciences' in the polar region – meteorology and other atmospheric sciences, geology, seismology, glaciology, and oceanography – together contributed to both the formation of the concept itself of the 'global environment', and to the distinctive place of the polar regions in that environment. The Arctic and Antarctic – ironically, the environments historically considered least affected by human activities – therefore became observatories, constructed on Cold War foundations, of a newly vulnerable global environment. Global environmental monitoring programmes were derived from strategic monitoring systems, and experience with fallout framed studies of environmental contaminants, including persistent toxic chemicals (as Rachel Carson discussed in Silent Spring).[50]

While these disciplines extended globally, they formed distinctive foci and practices in the polar regions, often coalescing around research facilities such as

46 Manabe and Wetherald, "Thermal Equilibrium".   47 Budyko, "Future Climate", 869.
48 Greene, "Arctic Sea Ice".   49 Doel et al., "Strategic Arctic Science".
50 Carson, Silent Spring.

ships and field stations, or natural objects, such as ice and permafrost. Several decades of observations of sea ice, accumulated through satellite, surface, and submarine measurements, have provided a basis for identifying trends over time. The Greenland and Antarctic ice caps provide an archive of changes in the global atmosphere, including increasing carbon dioxide and the presence of traces of centuries of industrial pollution. Models project the amplification of global climate change in the polar regions.[51] Beyond their specific results, these studies have been significant in changing scales of perception, in both spatial terms (encompassing change across the polar regions and their global consequences) and in terms of time (as seen in the notion of ice cores as 'time machines' that enable reconstruction of hundreds of thousands of years of climate history and in projections of future changes in the Arctic and Antarctic).

The Polar Regions as Cold War Spaces

As we have suggested, scientific activities played essential roles in the formation of the polar regions as Cold War spaces. They did so in the context of emerging ideas about the global environment, as geophysical scientists, working amidst strategic imperatives, international political and managerial initiatives, and new images of the Earth from space asserted that the planet must be understood as a single system.[52] This implied a new identity for the polar regions: after being for centuries a focus of political and economic interests, attracting explorers and exploiters alike, they became known instead in geophysical terms. A chief implication of this view was that these regions were perceived as remote and largely separated from the course of human history. Thus, even as Cold War tensions divided East and West, the polar regions were now viewed as neutral spaces. In strategic terms, this meant that the Arctic now served primarily as a buffer zone between the superpowers. In scientific terms, the polar regions were now akin to other neutral, 'placeless' sites, suited to the construction of universal knowledge. Indeed, as we have noted, during the Cold War the polar regions were commonly described as laboratories, in part because they could serve as a stable baseline against which changes in the global environment could be detected and recorded.[53] This view of the polar regions marginalized not only their histories but also those aspects

---

51 Arctic Climate Impact Assessment, *Impacts of Warming Arctic*; Alley, *Two-Mile Time Machine*; Serreze, *Brave New Arctic*.
52 Warde et al., *The Environment: A History*.
53 Grevsmühl, "Laboratory Metaphors". On laboratories as 'placeless sites' see Gieryn, "Three Truth-Spots".

that lacked strategic significance, including species and ecosystems, as well as, in the Arctic, communities and their ways of life, particularly those of Indigenous peoples.

As a laboratory, the Arctic became a site not only for the study of global environmental change, but for experiments that would be considered unacceptable elsewhere. The Arctic joined the American desert, Central Asian steppe, and Pacific islands as a site for testing nuclear weapons. In the Soviet Union, 130 tests were carried out from 1955 through 1990 at Novaya Zemlya, an archipelago that lay less than 150 km from the Eurasian mainland. The Soviet Ministry of Defense initially added Novaya Zemlya to its constellation of test sites in order to execute underwater tests of nuclear torpedoes. From 1957 through 1962, however, the islands also suffered eighty-five atmospheric nuclear tests. These included the most powerful on record, the detonation in 1961 of 'Big Ivan', a 58 megaton nuclear device. After the 1963 Partial Test Ban Treaty, another thirty-nine tests took place underground at Novaya Zemlya, including the Soviet Union's two most powerful underground explosions, in September and October 1973.[54] Although the Arctic was less central to American nuclear testing, the AEC conducted three tests on the Aleutian island of Amchitka from 1965 through 1971.[55] Northern Canada was also briefly viewed as a potential atomic testing ground, and it was proposed that nuclear devices could facilitate exploitation of the Alberta oil sands.

Over time, however, Cold War activities that had been justified by the view of the polar regions as neutral spaces helped, ironically, to erode that identity, particularly in the Arctic. Nuclear tests accelerated the Arctic's transformation into a contaminated space. Fallout from tests at Novaya Zemlya not only spread around the world, but burdened the archipelago with long-term, elevated levels of radiation. An area totaling 100 km^2 surrounding Chernaya Bay along the southern island was especially affected, irradiated by surface and above-water tests in 1957 and 1961. Nor did underground tests spare the environment; radioactive gases produced by subterranean explosions escaped into the air. Such releases differed from underground tests at the Soviet Union's other test site, Semipalatinsk in Central Asia, which were more contained. The difference resulted from the geology of Novaya Zemlya, where moisture-rich rocks generated greater amounts of gas following nuclear explosions and a corresponding buildup of

---

54 Adamsky and Smirnov, "Moscow's Biggest Bomb"; Khalturin et al., "Review of Nuclear Testing".
55 McCannon, *History of the Arctic*, 244.

pressure underground. An accidental venting in 1973 created one of the archipelago's three most radioactive locations.[56] Besides radiation from nuclear explosions, contamination also resulted from the dumping of radioactive waste, including spent fuel, damaged cores, and other equipment from reactors. The Soviet navy, which operated the Novaya Zemlya test site, sank thousands of containers of nuclear waste into the surrounding Kara Sea, as well as nuclear submarines and icebreakers. Liquid waste produced in the Murmansk and Arkhangelsk regions, where nuclear vessels of the Soviet Northern Fleet were built and docked, was discharged into the Barents Sea.[57]

Both practical experience and scientific study indicated that the polar environments, far from being neutral, had in subtle but important ways their own distinctive characteristics. By the 1950s, aviators were noticing haze appearing in what they had assumed were pristine Arctic skies – an apparent effect of processes specific to the polar atmosphere. Radioactive fallout and other contaminants also moved and accumulated in the Arctic in distinctive ways – as became evident in the accumulation of strontium-90 in lichen, caribou, and Inuit.[58] The effects of underground tests at Novaya Zemlya demonstrated the consequences of the distinctive local geology. The biological and physical environmental sciences also began to converge in the polar regions in distinctive ways. For example, study of the ecology of polar bears (especially the role of seals as their chief food source) was combined with analysis of records of long-term trends in sea ice that had been collected originally for strategic purposes.[59] Observations of the effects of human activities also led some to describe the polar regions as distinctively 'fragile', justifying special concern about protecting these environments. Overall, an emerging understanding of conditions in the Arctic implied that this region was not, in biophysical terms, a neutral space, but a place with its own distinctive identity.

The evolving position of the polar regions in the Cold War industrial economy also eroded their status as neutral spaces. Petroleum on the North Slope of Alaska and in northern Canada, as well as uranium and hydroelectric power, encouraged a view of the Arctic as a potential storehouse of energy and other resources. Oil from Alaska promised to reduce American imports from more uncertain parts of the world, especially the Middle East. In

---

56 Khalturin et al., "Review of Nuclear Testing", 16, 19–22, 26–27.
57 Bradley, "Radioactive Contamination"; United States Congress Office of Technology Assessment, *Nuclear Wastes*; Pryde, "Radioactive Contamination".
58 Bocking, "Toxic Surprises". 59 See, for example, Stirling et al., "Long-term Trends".

Canada, some saw northern energy development as the basis for regional economic expansion and a new export industry. Interest in these resources encouraged geological and geophysical surveys as well as engineering research to enable development of the infrastructure of energy – roads, drilling sites and pipelines – in the challenging Arctic environment. The possibility of resources, including uranium, coal, and iron ore, also contributed to interest in the Antarctic during the early Cold War era.[60] However, resource exploitation in both polar regions was constrained by distance, difficult conditions, and cost.

For the Soviet Union, the significance of Arctic resources changed over time, from fueling the country's transformation into an industrial power to satisfying socialist consumption. During the Cold War, the pursuit of material comforts and consumer goods became an ideological battleground. Soviet leaders themselves identified improved consumption as enabling the transition from socialism to communism.[61] Under the leadership of Nikita Khrushchev and Leonid Brezhnev, the USSR pursued international trade, seeking to import both capital goods and consumer products. To obtain global currency the USSR relied increasingly on energy exports, which by the mid-1980s supplied 80 per cent of its currency earnings.[62] A central role in the USSR's energy production was played by the oil and gas fields of western Siberia discovered in the 1960s. They included the largest known gas field at the time, Urengoi, in the far north of Tiumen Province, containing roughly 8 trillion m^3 of proven and probable reserves. North of Urengoi lay additional sizable gas fields on the Taz and Yamal peninsulas.[63] To procure the labour needed to exploit such deposits, the USSR carried out campaigns to encourage voluntary resettlement in the far north. The party-state enticed new workers to harsh Arctic environments by offering wage bonuses, travel to and extended vacations in places throughout the USSR, and well-supplied stores. In an economy where shortages persisted and a society where mobility was restricted, northern settlers could obtain luxuries such as liquor and jewellery, as well as regular flights. For some Soviet citizens during the Cold War, the Arctic could be a space of abundance and opportunity (for more on this, see Andy Bruno and Ekaterina Kalemeneva, Chapter 19 in this volume).[64]

---

60 Dodds et al., "IPY-3".   61 Dunham, *In Stalin's Time*; Reid, "Cold War".
62 Gustafson, *Crisis Amid Plenty*; Sanchez-Sibony, *Red Globalization*; Barenberg, *Gulag Town, Company Town*.
63 Gustafson, *Crisis Amid Plenty*.
64 Thompson, *Settlers on the Edge*; Barenberg, *Gulag Town, Company Town*.

The identity of the polar regions as neutral spaces was further eroded as they became spaces for the assertion of territorial authority. While the United States asserted its capacity to operate or collaborate across the Arctic, including in Canada, Greenland, and Scandinavia, its allies sought both to cooperate with the superpower and to affirm their authority over their national territories.[65] Several nations asserted their territorial authority through support for scientific activity. Science became a kind of political performance, an instrument for asserting a national presence, as seen in Greenland with the Danes, and northern Canada with the Canadians. Research activities were defined as national efforts, as seen in Canada's Polar Continental Shelf Project and Danish studies in Greenland of glaciers, the ionosphere, and other features of its physical environment.[66] During the 1950s, numerous nations asserted authority over portions of the Antarctic, generating, prior to negotiation of the Antarctic Treaty, a series of territorial disputes.[67] Most recently, surveys of the Arctic seabed aimed at delineating national territories have built on knowledge originally accumulated to guide ships and submarines during the Cold War.

Finally, the Arctic was asserted as an Indigenous space. Indigenous people experienced the Cold War in a variety of ways: through Project Chariot in Alaska; the exposure, beginning in the 1930s, of Dene labourers to uranium ore at a mine on Great Bear Lake in northern Canada (an experience that probably resulted in many cases of cancer); the relocation of Inughuit to make way for the Thule air base in Greenland in the early 1950s; and through the effects of DEW Line stations on Inuit settlement and hunting. Indigenous people also played roles in Arctic science as research objects, as in experimental studies of acclimatization.[68] In the Soviet Union, Nenets living on Novaya Zemlya were resettled to make way for the nuclear test site. The islands' inhabitants had been settled there initially in the nineteenth century by tsarist authorities aiming to secure Russian claims over the land. Their displacement during the Cold War therefore extended a history of state intrusions on the autonomy of Indigenous Siberians.[69] After a long struggle, Soviet authorities gradually imposed the planned economy on the Chukchi, turning them from self-organized hunters and herders into disciplined labourers on collective and state farms. The expansion of mining in the Soviet Arctic

---

65 Krige, *American Hegemony*; Heymann and Martin-Nielsen, "Introduction: Perspectives".
66 Knudsen, "Rockets Over Thule?"; Powell, *Studying Arctic Fields*.   67 Dodds et al., "IPY-3".
68 van Wyck, *Highway of the Atom*; Wiseman, "Unlocking the 'Eskimo Secret'".
69 Lukin, "Leaving Novaĭa Zemlĭa"; Krupnik and Chlenov, *Yupik Transitions*.

during the Cold War also dramatically increased the number of settlers in the region while upending the environment.[70]

Cold War interventions reshaped Indigenous ways of life, provoking efforts to assert collective identities and rights of self-determination that continue today. Some Indigenous people in the Soviet Union joined the Communist Party and embraced its modernizing vision, becoming party-state officials and scientists. Sakha leaders of the Soviet republic of Yakutia aimed to turn the capital, Yakutsk, into a centre for science.[71] Indigenous peoples also challenged definitions of knowledge embedded in Cold War scientific activities, demonstrating the potential for other ways of understanding the Arctic environment. Iñupiaq whalers drew upon their observations to demonstrate that the population of bowhead whales, though devastated by industrial whaling, could sustain subsistence hunting. On the basis of their knowledge, the Inuit Circumpolar Conference (later, Council), established in 1977, lobbied the International Whaling Commission to allow Indigenous peoples to continue their historic practices. On both sides of the iron curtain, Arctic Indigenous communities maintained ancestral rituals and beliefs in sentient nature and ethics of kinship and reciprocity.[72]

The distinctive perceptions of the polar regions varied in importance over the decades, exemplifying the character of the Cold War not as a singular episode, but an evolving array of strategic and political circumstances, varying across both time and national contexts.[73] Economic and other priorities became more significant as strategic tensions shifted to other regions of the world. Anxieties about energy supply in the 1970s encouraged attention to Arctic oil and gas. The emergence of environmentalism as a social movement focused attention on the 'fragile' Arctic. Arctic states and Indigenous peoples asserted in different ways their territorial authority and aspirations. In contrast to these circumstances in the Arctic, the entering into force of the Antarctic Treaty in 1961 shifted attention from that region's economic possibilities and territorial claims to its identity as a reserve dedicated to scientific study of the global environment. Contrasting developments reinforced distinctions between the Arctic and Antarctic, producing the divergent Cold War geopolitical histories of these regions. While the Cold War identity of the polar regions as a neutral geophysical space has remained pre-eminent in the Antarctic, in the Arctic this identity now co-exists with a range of other perspectives and priorities.

70 Demuth, *Floating Coast*. 71 Arzyutov, "Environmental Encounters".
72 Demuth, *Floating Coast*, 303–304; McCannon, *History of the Arctic*, 255–256.
73 Doel et al., "Strategic Arctic Science".

Conclusion

More than thirty years after its end, the Cold War still haunts the polar regions. Its traces include, in the Arctic, airfields and other military facilities as well as toxic residues near DEW Line sites, at Camp Century in Greenland, and in abandoned Soviet reactors and submarines. They also include, in Antarctica, active and deserted scientific research stations along the coast and in the interior. The built environments and their debris recall the polar regions' strategic importance as zones of superpower confrontation, surveillance, and operations, as proving grounds for demonstrating national superiority, and as sites of economic development and resource extraction. Accompanying all of these activities was the pursuit of knowledge about the physical environment. Although scientific activities in the Cold War East and West were rooted in different histories of political, economic, and institutional development, they converged in their reliance on digital, nuclear, and aerial technologies and in the organization of big science. The ideas that coalesced of a global environment and of the polar regions as key to understanding the Earth system were shared developments.

The Cold War legacy persists discursively as well. As the loss of sea ice prompts visions of newly accessible natural resources, and as tensions rose in the 2010s between Russia, the USSR's largest successor state, and members of the North Atlantic Treaty Organization, commentators have floated the possibility of a 'new Cold War' in the Arctic. The growing Arctic presence of the People's Republic of China has further spurred such rhetoric.[74] As evidenced by their focus on military exercises, territorial claims, and deposits of fossil fuels, observers invoke the Cold War in order to emphasize geopolitical competition. But outsized attention to competition obscures both the international cooperation that took place during the historical Cold War and the joint responsibility for its environmental consequences. For the Arctic especially, scholars have demonstrated how past assertions of the dawn of a new era have served to legitimate interventions by governments and corporations.[75] Rather than claims to newness, Indigenous thinkers have stressed continuities between the dangers of global warming and a longer history of challenges to Indigenous survival.[76] Cold War environmental

---

74 Oliva, "Arctic Cold War"; Shea, "New Cold War"; Abrahamian, "New Cold War"; Pike, "Cold War".
75 Stuhl, "Politics of 'New North'". The consequences in the Arctic of a new Cold War provoked by Russia's invasion of Ukraine in February 2022 have already become evident in the indefinite suspension of the activities of the Arctic Council.
76 Whyte, "Indigenous Climate Change Studies".

knowledge fostered appreciation of the polar regions as fragile environments requiring protection. But to create livable futures, it will be necessary to listen to other perspectives long silenced or ignored.

Bibliography

Abrahamian, Atossa Araxia, "The New Cold War", *New Statesman* (30 September 2019).

Adamsky, Viktor, and Yuri Smirnov, "Moscow's Biggest Bomb: The 50-Megaton Test of October 1961", *Cold War International History Project Bulletin* 4 (Fall 1994): 19–21.

Alley, Richard B., *The Two-Mile Time Machine: Ice Cores, Abrupt Climate Change, and Our Future* (Princeton: Princeton University Press, 2000).

Almond, Kyle, "What It's Like at the Ground Zero of Climate Change", *CNN.com* (September 2018), www.cnn.com/interactive/2018/09/world/greenland-climate-change-cnnphotos/.

Arctic Climate Impact Assessment, *Impacts of a Warming Arctic: Arctic Climate Impact Assessment* (Cambridge: Cambridge University Press, 2004).

Arzyutov, Dmitry, "Environmental Encounters: Woolly Mammoth, Indigenous Communities and Metropolitan Scientists in the Soviet Arctic", *Polar Record* 55 (May 2019): 142–153.

Barenberg, Alan, *Gulag Town, Company Town: Forced Labor and Its Legacy in Vorkuta* (New Haven: Yale University Press, 2014).

Baskakov, G. A., A. I. Voskresenskii, T. M. Gerasimova, et al., "Arkticheskii i antarkticheskii nauchno-issledovatel'skii institut – tsentr Rossiiskoi poliarnoi nauki", in *Problemy Arktiki i Antarktiki, iubileinyi vypusk 70 (k 75-lettiu AANII)* (St Petersburg: Gidrometeoizdat, 1995), pp. 6–32.

Benson, Etienne, *Wired Wilderness: Technologies of Tracking and the Making of Modern Wildlife* (Baltimore: Johns Hopkins University Press, 2010).

Berger, André, "A Brief History of the Astronomical Theories of Paleoclimates", in André Berger, Fedor Mesinger, and Djordje Sijacki, eds., *Climate Change: Inferences from Paleoclimate and Regional Aspects* (Vienna: Springer 2012), pp. 107–129.

Bergstrom, Dana M., Andrew Klekociuk, Diana King, and Sharon Robinson, "Antarctica: What It Means When the Coldest Place on Earth Records an Unprecedented Heatwave", *The Guardian* (31 March 2020), www.theguardian.com/world/2020/mar/31/antarctica-what-it-means-when-the-coldest-place-on-earth-records-an-unprecedented-heatwave.

Bocking, Stephen, "A Disciplined Geography: Aviation, Science, and the Cold War in Northern Canada, 1945–1960", *Technology and Culture* 50 (2009): 265–290.

Bocking, Stephen, "Toxic Surprises: Contaminants and Knowledge in the Northern Environment", in Stephen Bocking and Brad Martin, eds., *Ice Blink: Navigating Northern Environmental History* (Calgary: University of Calgary Press, 2017), pp. 421–464.

Bradley, D. J., *Radioactive Contamination of the Arctic Region, Baltic Sea, and the Sea of Japan from Activities in the Former Soviet Union* (Richland, WA: Pacific Northwest Laboratory, 1992).

Brooks, C. E. P., *Climate through the Ages: A Study of the Climatic Factors and Their Variations* (New York: R. V. Coleman, 1926).
Budyko, M. I., *Climate and Life*, ed. David H. Miller (New York: Academic, 1974).
Budyko, M. I., "The Future Climate", *Eos* 53 (October 1972): 868–874.
Cameron, Emilie, "Climate Anti-politics: Scale, Locality, and Arctic Climate Change", in Stephen Bocking and Brad Martin, eds., *Ice Blink: Navigating Northern Environmental History* (Calgary: University of Calgary Press, 2017), pp. 465–495.
Cameron, Emilie, "Securing Indigenous Politics: A Critique of the Vulnerability and Adaptation Approach to the Human Dimensions of Climate Change in the Canadian Arctic", *Global Environmental Change* 22 (2012): 103–114.
"A Canary in the Coal Mine", *The Economist* (13 November 2004): 105–106.
Carson, Rachel, *Silent Spring* (New York: Houghton Mifflin, 1962).
Chu, Pey-Yi, *The Life of Permafrost: A History of Frozen Earth in Russian and Soviet Science* (Toronto: University of Toronto Press, 2020).
Cittadino, Eugene, "Barry Commoner and Paul Sears on Project Chariot: Epiphany, Ecology, and the Atomic Energy Commission", *Isis* 109 (2018): 720–743.
Creager, Angela N. H., *Life Atomic: A History of Radioisotopes in Science and Medicine* (Chicago: University of Chicago Press, 2013).
Dalmedico, Amy Dahan, "History and Epistemology of Models: Meteorology (1946–1963) as a Case Study", *Archive for History of Exact Sciences* 55 (April 2001): 395–422.
Demuth, Bathsheba, *Floating Coast: An Environmental History of the Bering Strait* (New York: W. W. Norton & Company, 2019).
Dodds, Klaus, "Assault on the Unknown: Geopolitics, Antarctic Science and the International Geophysical Year (1957–8)", in Simon Naylor and James R. Ryan, eds., *New Spaces of Exploration: Geographies of Discovery in the Twentieth Century* (New York: I. B. Tauris, 2010), pp. 148–172.
Dodds, Klaus, Irina Gan, and Adrian Howkins, "The IPY-3: The International Geophysical Year (1957–1958)", in Susan Barr and Cornelia Lüdecke, eds., *The History of the International Polar Years (IPYs)* (Berlin: Springer, 2010), pp. 239–257.
Doel, Ronald E., "Constituting the Postwar Earth Sciences: The Military's Influence on the Environmental Sciences in the USA after 1945", *Social Studies of Science* 33 (2003): 635–666.
Doel, Ronald E., "What's the Place of the Physical Environmental Sciences in Environmental History?", *Revue d'histoire moderne et contemporaine* 56 (2009): 137–164.
Doel, Ronald E., Kristine C. Harper, and Matthias Heymann, eds., *Exploring Greenland: Cold War Science and Technology on Ice* (New York: Palgrave Macmillan, 2016).
Doel, Ronald E., Kristine C. Harper, and Matthias Heymann, "Introduction: Exploring Greenland's Secrets: Science, Technology, Diplomacy, and Cold War Planning in Global Contexts", in Ronald E. Doel, Kristine C. Harper, and Matthias Heymann, eds., *Exploring Greenland: Cold War Science and Technology on Ice* (New York: Palgrave Macmillan, 2016), pp. 1–22.
Doel, Ronald E., Robert Marc Friedman, Julia Lajus, Sverker Sörlin, and Urban Wråkberg, "Strategic Arctic Science: National Interests in Building Natural Knowledge. Interwar Era through the Cold War", *Journal of Historical Geography* 44 (April 2014): 60–80.
Dörries, Matthias, "The Politics of Atmospheric Sciences: 'Nuclear Winter' and Global Climate Change", *Osiris* 26 (2011): 198–223.

Dunham, Vera, *In Stalin's Time: Middleclass Values in Soviet Fiction* (Durham: Duke University Press, 1990).
Edwards, Paul N., "Meteorology as Infrastructural Globalism", *Osiris* 21 (2006): 229–250.
Edwards, Paul N., *A Vast Machine: Computer Models, Climate Data, and the Politics of Global Warming* (Cambridge: MIT Press, 2010).
Farish, Matthew, "Creating Cold War Climates", in John R. O'Neill and Corinna R. Unger, eds., *Environmental Histories of the Cold War* (Cambridge: Cambridge University Press, 2010), pp. 51–84.
Farish, Matthew, "The Lab and the Land: Overcoming the Arctic in Cold War Alaska", *Isis* 104 (2013): 1–29.
Farish, Matthew, and P. Whitney Lackenbauer, "Western Electric Turns North: Technicians and the Transformation of the Cold War Arctic", in Stephen Bocking and Brad Martin, eds., *Ice Blink: Navigating Northern Environmental History* (Calgary: University of Calgary Press, 2017), pp. 261–292.
Fleming, James Rodger, "James Croll in Context: The Encounter Between Climate Dynamics and Geology in the Second Half of the Nineteenth Century", in André Berger, Marko Ercegovac, and Fedor Mesinger, eds., *Paleoclimate and the Earth Climate System* (Belgrade: Serbian Academy of Sciences and Arts, 2005), pp. 13–20.
Galison, Peter, "The Many Faces of Big Science", in Peter Galison and Bruce Hevly, eds., *Big Science: The Growth of Large-scale Research* (Stanford: Stanford University Press, 1992), pp. 1–17.
Gerovitch, Slava, *From Newspeak to Cyberspeak: A History of Soviet Cybernetics* (Cambridge: MIT Press, 2002).
Gieryn, Thomas F., "Three Truth-Spots", *Journal of History of the Behavioral Sciences* 38 (2002): 113–132.
Greene, Mott T., "Arctic Sea Ice, Oceanography, and Climate Models", in Keith R. Benson and Helen M. Rozwadowski, eds., *Extremes: Oceanography's Adventures at the Poles* (Sagamore Beach: Science History Publications, 2007), pp. 303–329.
Grevsmühl, Sebastian Vincent, "Laboratory Metaphors in Antarctic History: From Nature to Space", in Julia Herzberg, Christian Kehrt, and Franziska Torma, eds., *Ice and Snow in the Cold War: Histories of Extreme Climatic Environments* (New York: Berghahn, 2019), pp. 211–235.
Gustafson, Thane, *Crisis Amid Plenty: The Politics of Soviet Energy Under Brezhnev and Gorbachev* (Princeton: Princeton University Press, 1989).
Hamblin, Jacob D., *Arming Mother Nature: The Birth of Catastrophic Environmentalism* (New York: Oxford University Press, 2013).
Harper, Kristine, *Weather by the Numbers: The Genesis of Modern Meteorology* (Cambridge: MIT Press, 2008).
Heymann, Matthias, and Dania Achermann, "From Climatology to Climate Science in the Twentieth Century", in Sam White, Christian Pfister, and Franz Mauelshagen, eds., *The Palgrave Handbook of Climate History* (London: Palgrave Macmillan, 2018), pp. 605–632.
Heymann, Matthias, and Janet Martin-Nielsen, "Introduction: Perspectives on Cold War Science in Small European States", *Centaurus* 55 (2013): 221–242.

Howkins, Adrian, "Melting Empires? Climate Change and Politics in Antarctica Since the International Geophysical Year", *Osiris* 26 (2011): 180–197.

Iarocci, Andrew, "Opening the North: Technology and Training at the Fort Churchill Joint Services Experimental Testing Station, 1946–64", *Canadian Army Journal* 10 (2008): 74–95.

Josephson, Paul, *The Conquest of the Russian Arctic* (Cambridge: Harvard University Press, 2014).

Josephson, Paul, *New Atlantis Revisited: Akademgorodok, the Siberian City of Science* (Princeton: Princeton University Press, 1997).

Kalnins, Ints, "Arctic Expedition to Investigate 'Epicenter of Climate Change'", *Reuters* (21 September 2019), www.reuters.com/article/us-climate-change-expedition-idUSKBN1W51CZ.

Kamenskii, R. M., ed., *Akademicheskoe merzlotovedenie v Iakutii* (Iakutsk: Institut merzlotovedeniia SO RAN, 1997).

Khalturin, Vitaly I., Tatyana G. Rautian, Paul G. Richards, and William S. Leith, "A Review of Nuclear Testing by the Soviet Union at Novaya Zemlya, 1955–1990", *Science and Global Security* 13 (2005): 1–42.

Kirsch, Scott, "Peaceful Nuclear Explosions and the Geography of Scientific Authority", *Professional Geographer* 52 (2000): 179–192.

Knudsen, Henrik, "Rockets over Thule? American Hegemony, Ionosphere Research and the Politics of Rockets in the Wake of the 1968 Thule B-52 Accident", in Stephen Bocking and D. Heidt, eds., *Cold Science: Environmental Knowledge in the North American Arctic During the Cold War* (London: Routledge, 2019), pp. 217–235.

Krementsov, Nikolai, *Stalinist Science* (Princeton: Princeton University Press, 1997).

Krige, John, *American Hegemony and the Postwar Reconstruction of Science in Europe* (Cambridge: MIT Press, 2006).

Krüger, Tobias, *Discovering the Ice Ages: International Reception and Consequences for a Historical Understanding of Climate*, trans. Ann M. Hentschel (Leiden: Brill, 2013).

Krupnik, Igor, and Michael Chlenov, *Yupik Transitions: Change and Survival at Bering Strait, 1900–1960* (Fairbanks: University of Alaska Press, 2013).

Leslie, Stuart A., *The Cold War and American Science: The Military-Industrial-Academic Complex at MIT and Stanford* (New York: Columbia University Press, 1993).

Lovelock, James E., and Lynn Margulis, "Atmospheric Homeostasis by and for the Biosphere: The Gaia Hypothesis", *Tellus* 26 (1974): 2–10.

Lukin, Karina, "Leaving Novaîa Zemliá: Narrative Strategies of the Resettlement of the Nenets", *Arctic Anthropology* 54 (January 2017): 32–45.

Manabe, Syukuro, and Richard T. Wetherald, "Thermal Equilibrium of the Atmosphere with a Given Distribution of Relative Humidity", *Journal of the Atmospheric Sciences* 24 (1967): 241–259.

Martin-Nielsen, Janet, "'An Orgy of Hypothesizing': The Construction of Glaciological Knowledge in Cold War America", in Julia Herzberg, Christian Kehrt, and Franziska Torma, eds., *Ice and Snow in the Cold War: Histories of Extreme Climatic Environments* (New York: Berghahn, 2019), pp. 69–88.

Mauelshagen, Franz, "Climate as a Scientific Paradigm: Early History of Climatology to 1800", in Sam White, Christian Pfister, and Franz Mauelshagen, eds., *The Palgrave Handbook of Climate History* (London: Palgrave Macmillan, 2018), pp. 565–588.

McCannon, John, *A History of the Arctic: Nature, Exploration and Exploitation* (London: Reaktion, 2012).

Murozumi, M., Tsaihwa J. Chow, and C. Patterson, "Chemical Concentrations of Pollutant Lead Aerosals, Terrestrial Dusts, and Sea Salts in Greenland and Antarctic Snow Strata", *Geochimica et Cosmochimica Acta* 33 (1969): 1247–1294.

Needell, Allan A., "Lloyd Berkner and the International Geophysical Year Proposal in Context: With Some Comments on the Implications for the Comité Spéciale de l'Année Géophysique Internationale, CASAGI, Request for Launching Earth Orbiting Satellites", in Roger D. Launius, James Rodger Fleming, and David H. DeVorkin, eds., *Globalizing Polar Science: Reconsidering the International Polar and Geophysical Years* (New York: Palgrave Macmillan, 2010), pp. 205–224.

Ohmura, Atsumu, "A Historical Review of Studies on the Energy Balance of Arctic Tundra", *Journal of Climatology* 2 (1982): 185–195.

Oldfield, Jonathan, "Mikhail Budyko's (1920–2001) Contributions to Global Climate Science: From Heat Balance to Climate Change and Global Ecology", *WIREs Climate Change* 7 (October 2016): 682–692.

Oliva, Mara, "Arctic Cold War: Climate Change Has Ignited a New Polar Power Struggle", *The Conversation* (28 November 2018), http://theconversation.com/arctic-cold-war-climate-change-has-ignited-a-new-polar-power-struggle-107329.

O'Neill, Dan, *The Firecracker Boys* (New York: St Martin's Griffin, 1994).

O'Neill, John R., and Corinna R. Unger, eds., *Environmental Histories of the Cold War* (New York: Cambridge University Press, 2010).

Pike, Francis, "Cold War: Russia's Bid to Control the Arctic", *The Spectator* (12 December 2020).

Plokhy, Serhii, *The Last Empire: The Final Days of the Soviet Union* (New York: Basic, 2014).

Powell, Richard C., *Studying Arctic Fields: Cultures, Practices, and Environmental Sciences* (Montreal: McGill-Queen's University Press, 2017).

Pryde, Philip R., "Radioactive Contamination", in Maria Shahgedanova, ed., *The Physical Geography of Northern Eurasia*. Oxford Regional Environments Series (Oxford: Oxford University Press, 2002), pp. 448–462.

Reed, John C., and A. G. Ronhovde, *Arctic Laboratory: A History (1946–1966) of the Naval Arctic Research Laboratory at Point Barrow, Alaska* (Washington, DC: Arctic Institute of North America, 1971).

Reid, Susan, "Cold War in the Kitchen: Gender and the De-Stalinization of Consumer Taste in the Soviet Union under Khrushchev", *Slavic Review* 61 (Summer 2002): 211–252.

Reiss, Bob, "Barrow, Alaska: Ground Zero for Climate Change", *Smithsonian Magazine*, (March 2010), www.smithsonianmag.com/science-nature/barrow-alaska-ground-zero-for-climate-change-7553696/.

Rindzevičiūtė, Eglė, *The Power of Systems: How Policy Sciences Opened up the Cold War World* (Ithaca: Cornell University Press, 2016).

Sanchez-Sibony, Oscar, *Red Globalization: The Political Economy of the Soviet Cold War from Stalin to Khrushchev* (Cambridge: Cambridge University Press, 2014).

Schwerdtfeger, W., "The Climate of the Antarctic", in S. Orvig, ed., *Climates of the Polar Regions*. World Survey of Climatology, Vol. 14 (Amsterdam: Elsevier, 1970), pp. 253–330.

Selcer, Perrin, *The Postwar Origins of the Global Environment: How the United Nations Built Spaceship Earth* (New York: Columbia University Press, 2018).

Serreze, Mark C., *Brave New Arctic: The Untold Story of the Melting North* (Princeton: Princeton University Press, 2018).

Shea, Neil, "The New Cold War", *National Geographic* (September 2019): 50–73.

Sörlin, Sverker, "Narratives and Counter-narratives of Climate Change: North Atlantic Glaciology and Meteorology, c.1930–1955", *Journal of Historical Geography* 35 (2009): 237–255.

Stirling, Ian, Nicholas J. Lunn, and John Iacozza, "Long-term Trends in the Population Ecology of Polar Bears in Western Hudson Bay in Relation to Climatic Change", *Arctic* 52 (1999): 294–306.

Stuhl, Andrew, "The Politics of the 'New North': Putting History and Geography at Stake in Arctic Futures", *Polar Journal* 3 (June 2013): 94–119.

Thomas, Campbell, "Woman Scientist the Navy Refused to Take on Board", *The Guardian* (12 January 2000), www.theguardian.com/news/2000/jan/12/guardianobituaries1.

Thompson, Niobe, *Settlers on the Edge: Identity and Modernization on Russia's Arctic Frontier* (Vancouver: UBC Press, 2008).

United States Congress Office of Technology Assessment, *Nuclear Wastes in the Arctic: An Analysis of Arctic and Other Regional Impacts from Soviet Nuclear Contamination* (Washington, DC: Office of Technology Assessment, Congress of the United States, 1995).

van der Watt, Lize-Marié, Peder Roberts, and Julia Lajus, "Institutions and the Changing Nature of Arctic Research During the Early Cold War", in Stephen Bocking and D. Heidt, eds., *Cold Science: Environmental Knowledge in the North American Arctic During the Cold War* (London: Routledge, 2019), pp. 197–216.

van Wyck, Peter C., *The Highway of the Atom* (Montreal: McGill-Queen's University Press, 2010).

Vowinckel, E., and S. Orvig, "The Climate of the North Polar Basin", in S. Orvig, ed., *Climates of the Polar Regions*. World Survey of Climatology, Vol. 14 (Amsterdam: Elsevier, 1970), pp. 129–252.

Vucinich, Alexander, *Empire of Knowledge: The Academy of Sciences of the USSR (1917–1970)* (Berkeley: University of California Press, 1984).

Warde, Paul, Libby Robin, and Sverker Sörlin, *The Environment: A History of the Idea* (Baltimore: Johns Hopkins University Press, 2018).

Weart, Spencer, "The Development of General Circulation Models of Climate", *Studies in History and Philosophy of Modern Physics* 41 (2010): 208–217.

Westad, Odd Arne, *The Cold War: A World History* (New York: Basic, 2017).

Whyte, Kyle, "Indigenous Climate Change Studies: Indigenizing Futures, Decolonizing the Anthropocene", *English Language Notes* 55 (Spring/Fall 2017): 153–162.

Wiseman, Matthew, "Unlocking the 'Eskimo Secret': Defence Science in the Cold War Canadian Arctic, 1947–1954", *Journal of the Canadian Historical Association* 26 (2015): 191–223.

Zubok, Vladislav, *A Failed Empire: The Soviet Union in the Cold War from Stalin to Gorbachev* (Chapel Hill: University of North Carolina Press, 2009).

22

The International Geophysical Year and the Antarctic Treaty System

KLAUS DODDS

The basic objective of the IGY was a mapping of our physical environment. *Just as geographic mapping has its self-evident necessity to man before he can know a region and before he can begin to assess and utilize it, geophysical mapping is a prerequisite to a scientific understanding of the earth and its cosmic environs* ... the fundamental purpose of the IGY was the acquisition of synoptic data – data taken simultaneously on and about the earth in order to get a planetary view of weather, geomagnetism, the ionosphere, the aurora, and the like.[1]

Introduction

During the Cold War, at about the time Ian Fleming was penning *From Russia with Love* (1957), the Soviet Union stunned the world with a successful launch of an artificial satellite, Sputnik. While Western and Soviet spies, real and fictional, were hatching plans to acquire field and signals intelligence, the world's scientific community helped to create their own daring initiative. The International Geophysical Year (IGY) of 1957–58 was audacious in scope and scale – scientists around the world were going to explore and interrogate outer space, the polar regions, and the oceans, and share the ensuing data for the sake of global knowledge generation. Sixty-seven countries pledged their support for the IGY, and what followed was a remarkable example of multidisciplinary and interdisciplinary projects, which involved a mixture of professional scientists and early examples of what would now be termed citizen science. Some of the legacies that have been identified as having an IGY provenance include the 1959 Antarctic Treaty and the discovery of the Van Allen belts.[2]

My sincere thanks to Alessandro Antonello, Adrian Howkins, and Peder Roberts for their excellent comments on an earlier version of this chapter.
1 Hugh Odishaw, "The Meaning of the International Geophysical Year". Remarks by the Executive Director, US National Committee for IGY, before the National Press Club, 4 December 1958 [emphasis added].
2 Korsmo, "Genesis".

The remarks by the Executive Director of the US National Committee for the International Geophysical Year in December 1958 capture something of that ambition by reference to the collection of *synoptic data*. But this does not quite capture the diversity of themes that meander purposefully through this chapter. First, the decade in question, the 1950s, is considered to mark the onset of the 'great acceleration'[3] – a moment when the 'planetary boundaries' associated with the Holocene era (roughly the last 11,700 years) were being reshaped by humanity's impact on the planet. The end result was a recognizable shift in the Earth system that exceeded natural variability.[4] Second, the IGY's mission to collect synoptic data and develop a 'planetary view' was integral to the emergence of the concept of Earth system governance.[5] Third, the IGY and Antarctic Treaty negotiations cannot be divorced from the realities of Cold War global competition and rivalries. While we have scholarship on the 'global Cold War', the polar regions continue to be treated as either exceptional or marginal.[6] The Antarctic, it is argued, complicates Cold War schisms. The Soviet Union and the United States found common cause in the case of the polar continent, which included open and unfettered access to the polar continent and seas.[7] Fourth, the treaty-based regime (the 1959 Antarctic Treaty) drew on the entanglement of science and geopolitics and did so to promote the scientific authority of experts while at the same time enabling the largest scientific power, the United States, to take advantage of data pooling and sharing. Fifth, the changing international politics of the Antarctic coincided with a post-war push for decolonization. While Argentina and Chile accused the United Kingdom of behaving like an old-fashioned imperial power, the treaty itself was nonetheless the product of an 'exclusive club' of twelve parties which included both South American states. Sixth, there was an upsurge in public and scholarly interest in the underworlds of ice, sea, and ground. The IGY was widely framed as an exposé of the inner worlds of the Earth, and television and film (often in colour) were sharing scientific and exploratory findings to global publics.[8] Finally, the treaty negotiations coincided with global legal creep.[9] New governance frameworks were emerging in the 1950s and 1960s designed to address access to the collective resources of global commons such as oceans, outer space, and Antarctica.

3 McNeill and Engel, *The Great Acceleration.*   4 Turney and Fogwill, "Implications".
5 Biermann, *Earth System Governance.*   6 Westad, *Global Cold War.*
7 Gan, "Soviet Antarctic Plans".
8 Della Dora, *Mantle of the Earth.* A good example would be the BBC programme *The Restless Sphere: The Story of the International Geophysical Year* (1957).
9 Collis and Dodds, "Assault on the Unknown".

The narrow period between the IGY and the signing of the 1959 Antarctic Treaty hard-wired a political-legal construct of the Antarctic. The 'treaty-work' legalized obligations, stabilized expectations, institutionalized the power of scientific expertise, and circumscribed Antarctica through a formal zone of application. All this sat uneasily with the planetary and synoptic-based IGY vision of an integrated Earth – the geopolitical and geophysical intersected imperfectly.[10] As the American Geophysical Union reminded its readers, the IGY was supposed to showcase Antarctica as a 'geophysical paradise', but it was never going to be one made in splendid geopolitical isolation.[11]

The Making of Antarctica

Antarctica is the only geographical territory on Earth with an unclaimed sector. There are seven largely unrecognized claims (Argentina, Australia, Chile, France, New Zealand, Norway, United Kingdom), and two semi-claimants in the form of the United States and the Soviet Union (now Russia) that reserve the right to make a claim in the future. While political maps of the Antarctic continent and surrounding ocean in the 1950s did recognize the territorial extent of claims by the claimant states, maps produced in the United States frequently used 'Areas seen only by US explorers' and 'Areas seen by US explorers and by explorers of other countries' to produce a distinct counter-mapping. One example produced in February 1956, entitled "Antarctica exploration and claims", leaves a distinct impression that the US exploratory presence on the landmass encompasses two-thirds of the polar continent.[12] What the map does not distinguish is where the northern boundary of 'Antarctica' might lie. The primary focus was on the landmass of Antarctica and geophysical puzzles such as ice cap thickness.

Was the IGY's cultivation of scientific goodwill and cooperation for the sake of science integral to the Antarctic Treaty? Antarctica's claim to be exceptional has largely rested on either absence and/or a state of abnormality – no Indigenous population, no recognized territorial claims, extreme isolation and climate, no strategic value. Because of this lack and absence, scientific expertise was believed to be decisive in making scientific-technocratic governance possible. The Special (later Scientific) Committee on Antarctic Research (SCAR, 1958) was established to offer advice pertaining

---

10 Howkins, *Frozen Empires*.   11 Kaplan, "International Geophysical Year", 381.
12 Library of Congress, "Antarctica Exploration and Claims", www.loc.gov/item/79692772/.

to 'circumpolar scope and significance'.[13] The polar anthropologist Jennifer O'Reilly identified what she termed an 'epistemic technocracy' at the heart of modern Antarctic governance.[14] Scientific expertise framed Antarctica as a unique 'natural laboratory' (and an 'analogue environment' for outer space) and helped to assemble a medley of advice, formal responsibility, and political capital, which enabled a governance system said to champion not only a spirit of international cooperation and free information exchange, but also informed and enriched by scientific knowledge.[15]

The relationship between scientific expertise and Antarctic governance did not follow what Susan Owens described as a 'technical-rational' model.[16] The IGY's focus on synoptic data collection was tethered to the military-civilian assemblages that made 'big science' possible. As historians of Cold War science and technology have emphasized, the military were major funders of regional and global science, and the polar regions were no exception.[17] Fieldwork was never divorced from prevailing geopolitical sensitivities, with Western scientists rarely granted access to the hinterlands of Russia and China. Even in Antarctica, with its absence of formally recognized borders, the IGY was never free from dramas about unfettered mobility and long-term occupation. For the largest claimant state, Australia, the stated and unstated intentions of the Soviet Union were a perennial source of concern. Would the Soviets become a claimant? Would their scientific stations in Australian Antarctic Territory remain there permanently and was that a possible prelude to something more sinister?

The IGY had to juggle two conflicting tensions which carried with it implications for how Antarctica was considered as a geopolitical space. The acquisition of 'synoptic data' implied that Antarctica was to act as a data repository designed for extraction, processing, and archiving. But thinking and acting globally was hard for some invested polar parties. Claimant states such as Australia and Argentina were being asked to sign up to an IGY that was ready to dispense with political-territorial imaginations in favour of global information sharing, infrastructural collaboration, and data pooling.[18] For claimant states, it was a tough call to accept that other parties, including the two superpowers, were perfectly entitled to establish their IGY Antarctic research stations anywhere in Antarctica. To compound matters further, there was no guarantee that any IGY-established stations would be

---

13 Scientific Committee on Antarctic Research, www.scar.org/.
14 O'Reilly, *Technocratic Antarctic*.   15 Antonello, *Greening of Antarctica*.
16 Owens, *Knowledge, Policy and Expertise*.   17 Herzberg et al., eds., *Ice and Snow*.
18 Jackson, "Antarctica Without Borders".

dismantled in the aftermath. The Soviet Union and United States might decide, reasonably, that their scientific labours were not complete.

When the twelve IGY parties arrived in Washington, DC in October 1959, there was no guarantee that an Antarctic Treaty would materialize. The archival materials pertaining to the treaty conference, which lasted only six weeks, suggest that nothing was inevitable. Buried amongst the diplomatic files, officials in Australia, New Zealand, and the United Kingdom articulated and postulated Antarctic futures and scenarios – as a food resource, as a resource arena, as a missile launch pad.[19] Other sources, such as the personal diary of a member of the UK delegation, provide fascinating insights into a tense negotiating environment. Brian Roberts, the Foreign Office Antarctic expert and researcher at the Scott Polar Research Institute at Cambridge, did not pull his punches.[20] Every polar participant in the IGY would have had their own perspective for continuing their research activity and long-term occupation of Antarctica. Archival-based accounts of American, Australian, New Zealand, UK, Argentine, Chilean, and Soviet histories have affirmed that Antarctic politics and science were deeply entangled with one another.[21]

The Antarctic Problem

In 1951, William Hunter Christie, a staff member at the UK Embassy in Buenos Aires in the late 1940s, published the aptly named *The Antarctic Problem*.[22] Christie astutely recognized that the international politics of the Antarctic was an *affaire géopolitique*. Argentina, Britain, and Chile were rival claimants, and thus it was highly likely that tension would follow if one or more of those parties sought to strengthen their attachments to the Antarctic Peninsula and surrounding islands. Antarctic science was shot through with geopolitical considerations because all three parties recognized that mapping, surveying, and geological research all helped to cement territorial attachments. There was no such thing as politically innocent science for the political administrators in Buenos Aires, London, and Santiago. While polar scientists might not care for geopolitical rivalries per se, their managers and funders were never inattentive to such matters. The British example is a case in point.[23]

19 Dodds, "The Great Game".
20 Beck, "Preparatory Meetings"; and more recently, Heavens and Roberts, *Penguin Diplomacy*.
21 For example, Belanger, *Deep Freeze*.   22 Christie, *The Antarctic Problem*.
23 Dodds, *Pink Ice*.

As a first-hand observer, Hunter Christie was privy to a post-war Argentina eager to project and protect its strategic relationship with the Antarctic and the southwest Atlantic. Both Chile and Argentina sought to define further the geographical extent of their southerly territories in 1940 and 1943 respectively. In essence, they were forced to adopt the legal mechanisms used by the rival claimant state, the United Kingdom. In the midst of World War II, the United Kingdom launched the secret Operation Tabarin, designed to reinforce its territorial and resource interests.[24] The British were adamant that they needed to establish a network of research stations and refuges across the Peninsula to ensure that their presence was permanent and safeguarded. The Falkland Islands Dependencies Survey (FIDS), a direct successor to the naval operation, was charged in 1945 with making that possible, with funding from the UK Colonial Office and tax revenues from Norwegian whaling companies operating in the waters around the Antarctic Peninsula.[25]

In the aftermath of World War II, the US Navy launched two substantial operations, Windmill and High Jump, which brought thousands of naval personnel and their ships and aircraft/helicopters to bear on Antarctica. It was the first such US naval expedition since Charles Wilkes's American expedition of 1838–42.[26] Back in London, plans were afoot to encourage the United States to make a formal claim to the so-called Unclaimed Sector in the Pacific Ocean sector of Antarctica. Other parties such as Chile floated plans to 'internationalize' Antarctica; this gained some traction with the United States and United Kingdom, who favoured a condominium involving the seven claimant states and the United States only. Such plans for limited internationalization collapsed when it became clear that the Soviet Union was not going to accept any arrangement in which it was purposefully excluded. In 1950, a Soviet statement about Antarctica left little room for doubt about the determination of Moscow to ensure its participation in 'any decisions regarding the regime of the Antarctic'.[27]

The 'Antarctic problem' was inevitably a Cold War problem. If the Soviet Union was determined to ensure its full participation in any discussions regarding the future of Antarctica, it was reasonable to assume that there was a danger of a worsening state of affairs on and off the polar ice. And yet the most immediate danger of conflict lay elsewhere. Britain, Argentina, and

24 Haddelsey and Carroll, *Operation Tabarin*.   25 Fuchs, *Of Ice and Men*.
26 Rose, *Assault on Eternity*.   27 Toma, "Soviet Attitude".

Chile were engaged in their own regional power struggle to assert dominance over the Antarctic Peninsula. All three countries were investing resources to map, survey, populate, and evaluate their respective national polar territories. In the main, it was a paper battle involving rival memoranda, maps and charts, and diplomatic statements. Attempts by the UK government to take the dispute to the International Court of Justice in 1955 were rebuffed by Argentina and Chile.[28] Both countries regarded their polar territories as geographically and geologically integral to the nation-state. Moreover, in both countries there was a well-established belief that these most southerly territories were part of an imperial inheritance from Spain. Their formal claims in the early 1940s were, thus, judged to be legal formalities.[29]

The British approach to these remote territories was rooted in collaboration with Commonwealth and other partners, including the United States, Norway, and Sweden. Mindful of the cost and the burden of protecting the disputed sub-Antarctic islands of the Falkland Islands and South Georgia, scientific collaboration and partnership was understood to be supportive of wider geopolitical interests. The Norwegian-British-Swedish Antarctic Expedition (1949–52) was a case in point.[30] The expedition was the first to involve a multinational team with specific disciplinary contributions; the United Kingdom was responsible for geology, Sweden headed glaciology, and Norway led on surveying and meteorology. Several years later, the British helped to fund the privately organized 1955–58 Trans-Antarctic Expedition (TAE), which completed the first mechanized crossing of Antarctica in March 1958. Involving Australian, New Zealand, and South African participants, it also benefited from the support of the US-managed research station at the South Pole. Both expeditions, albeit with different funder and partner models, proved useful in the political and financial cost-burden imposed by Antarctic geopolitics. The United Kingdom was helping, in essence, to build a coalition of partners that could counter-balance any South American polar scheming.

The 'Antarctic problem' identified by Hunter Christie was not necessarily one that could be resolved. For Colonial and Foreign Office officials in London, the very existence of overlapping territorial claims served as a useful foil when colleagues in other departments such as the Treasury questioned the purpose of government spending in Antarctica. The presence

---

28 Hayton, "The 'American' Antarctic". 29 Scott, "Ingenious and Innocuous?".
30 Giaever, *White Desert*.

of persistent counter-claimants Argentina and Chile had its value, and arguably helped to protect funding for FIDS and the wider commitment to Britain's South Atlantic Empire. It encouraged opportunities to work collaboratively with others, and the polar continent proved a useful staging ground for a litany of projects, ranging from the TAE to smaller ventures such as Colonial Office-sponsored support of the Royal Command film *Scott of the Antarctic* (1948). In this multinational affair, with locational filming in Antarctica, Norway, and Switzerland, Ealing Studios worked closely with the Scott Polar Research Institute to ensure that Britain's scientific and expeditionary prowess was being well-represented. In more modern parlance, there was recognition that polar science and exploration offered the country plenty of prestige and soft power potential, all of which was considered welcome at a moment of post-war and post-imperial transition affecting other parts of the world.[31]

However, as others such as Adrian Howkins have considered, the 'Antarctic problem' was not just a British affair. Argentina and Chile were actively buttressing their strategic interests and geopolitical strategies in the Antarctic Peninsula. Adding further piquancy was, in the case of Argentina, the disputed islands of the Falklands/Malvinas and South Georgia. As Howkins notes:

> Whereas Argentine and Chilean interest in Antarctic sovereignty could be viewed as part of the imperial expansion of both states, it was also in direct opposition to British sovereignty claims, which added an anti-imperial dimension. This apparent paradox is critical in explaining the involvement of Argentina and Chile in the IGY. It also provided considerable political impetus to those charged with managing the aftermath of the IGY.[32]

In other words, Argentina and Chile wanted to press their own territorial claims and weaponize accusations that the United Kingdom was acting as an unrepentant colonial power, but do so in a way that did not attract attention from the two superpowers. The most useful thing that both countries achieved in their management of the 'Antarctic problem' was the inclusion of the Antarctic Peninsula region in the area of application attached to the 1947 Inter-American Treaty, which, like Article 5 of the 1948 NATO treaty, committed the United States to the collective defence of the hemisphere.

As the preparations for the Antarctic element of the IGY gathered momentum in the 1950s, there were parts of the continent that were consumed by

---

[31] Dodds, "Filming and Formatting". [32] Howkins, "Reluctant Collaborators", 602.

what Western scholars and political figures had earlier termed the 'Great Game' in Central Asia. Russian writers preferred the term 'tournament of shadows' to convey the plotting, planning, and peddling of influence and spying.[33] Activities such as mapping, surveying, scientific expeditions, base building, even presidential visits (in the case of Chile in 1948) took on heightened importance. All parties were eager to showcase 'effective occupation' of these remote, poorly mapped and poorly understood territories. In 1952, after news broke that an Argentine party had shot over the heads of a British party stationed at Hope Bay, Antarctica, the then Governor of the Falkland Islands, Sir Miles Clifford, warned darkly that Britain might need to put itself on a 'war footing'.[34]

IGY, Antarctica, and Planet Earth

The genesis of the IGY lay in a conversation held at the house of the American geophysicist James Van Allen in April 1950. According to contemporary sources, Van Allen was accompanied by the British scientist Sydney Chapman and the American physicist Lloyd Berkner.[35] The three men were discussing the desirability of conducting a major scientific programme to coincide with maximum solar flare activity. Berkner, however, was also attuned to the importance of science as a form of foreign policy and international diplomacy. Working with the US State Department, he regularly briefed officials about the latest scientific developments and their implications for US standing in the world. Berkner was encouraged by his companions to contact the International Scientific Radio Union and the Mixed Commission on the Ionosphere to declare a third polar year, following earlier iterations in 1882–83 and 1932–33. As it happens, other science bodies responded positively to this initial proposal, including the International Union of Geodesy and Geophysics, and the International Council of Scientific Unions. Within nine months of that initial dinner conversation, major scientific agencies, including the UN's World Meteorological Organization, recommended that the remit be expanded beyond polar environments.

The IGY was not, as it turns out, a third polar year. It was more explicitly global in scope and ambition.[36] Lasting from 1 July 1957 to 31 December 1958, the IGY was described as a 'scientific Olympics'.[37] Involving sixty-seven countries and an estimated 60,000 scientists (including what would now be

33 Meyer and Brysac, *Tournament of Shadows*.   34 Dodds, *Pink Ice*, ch. 4.
35 Needell, *IGY Satellites*.   36 Chapman, "International Geophysical Year 1957–58", 101.
37 Brzezinski, *Red Moon Rising*, 92.

termed citizen science), the Antarctic, and to a lesser extent the Arctic, were nonetheless significant elements in this venture. Later described by the *New York Times* journalist Walter Sullivan as an 'assault on the unknown', the IGY's creation coincided with a marked push towards large-scale investment in the geophysical sciences.[38] Enabled by a Cold War geopolitical dividend, which placed a premium on earthly knowledge and surveillance, glaciology, seismology, and oceanography were beneficiaries of a period when governments and militaries wanted to calculate and understand better the Earth's volume – the role of wind, cold, heat, and moisture in influencing the movement of personnel and the behaviour of materiel.[39] In the Arctic Ocean, for example, travelling safely and discreetly through ice-covered waters was a strategic priority. The secret voyage of the nuclear-powered submarine USS *Nautilus* in the summer of 1958 (Operation Sunshine) was a propaganda coup for the Eisenhower administration after the shock of Sputnik and the public failure of the US satellite system, Vanguard. During the IGY, the United States and the Soviet Union maintained ice drifting stations, with the United States establishing, under Project Ice Skate, stations Alpha and Bravo on the iceberg named T-3 (also known as Fletcher's Ice Island).[40]

Other branches of the military wanted to better understand the curvature of the Earth (the 'Figure of the Earth') and prevailing weather systems, so that calculations about missile and rocket travel might be enhanced.[41] The IGY captured a moment of recognition that there was much to know about the Earth, and multiple possibilities for capitalizing upon those ways of knowing.[42] Historian of science John Cloud has been instrumental in investigating US investment in the CORONA satellite reconnaissance programme. CORONA was underwritten by investment in earth sciences and later satellite-based photography. Distance, gravity, direction, and elemental forces such as wind currents were integral to strategic calculation about the efficacy of bombers, submarines, and later missiles. As Cloud noted, geodesy was a Cold War priority: 'Geodesy is the science of the shape and size of the earth, the "Figure of the Earth", and the precise location of specific points on or near the earth's surface. Geodesy by its nature is global in scope and execution.'[43] An assemblage

---

38 American Geophysical Union, *Antarctica*; Sullivan, *Assault on the Unknown*.
39 Bullis, *Political Legacy*; Hamblin, *Oceanographers and Cold War*; Turchetti and Roberts, eds., *Surveillance Imperative*.
40 Althoff, *Drift Station*. 41 Doel, "Constituting Post-war Earth Sciences" 635–666.
42 Della Dora, *Mantle of the Earth*. 43 Cloud, "Crossing the Olentangy River", 372.

of American and Soviet universities, research institutes, and commercial organizations enriched by military funding patronage were turning to disciplines such as geodesy, geography, geophysics, and geology because they were believed to be essential prerequisites for determining scale, extent, and accuracy.

It is important to acknowledge, therefore, that there were two Cold War pathways for the earth sciences. They intersected with one another, with many US scientists proving perfectly capable of having their work funded by the Office of Naval Research while participating in international enterprises such as the IGY. While the IGY was, at heart, a collective synoptic and simultaneous data collection exercise, sharing data was not problem-free, especially in the realms of the atmosphere and outer space.[44] In the case of the Soviet Union, planning for the IGY was occurring against a complex backdrop where science and scientists were held in high esteem. At the same time, Moscow was eager to ensure that its citizens and those in the 'satellite states' of Eastern Europe were firmly under its control. If data sharing was axiomatic to the IGY, it would have been unwise to assume that the Soviet Union would have accepted this principle straightforwardly. Timing played a major part. As Jacob Hamblin noted with reference to the disciplinary development of oceanography, data-sharing was pushed harder by scientific superpowers such as the United States because they had the facilities and capabilities to harvest and exploit pooled data.[45]

Organizationally, IGY planning involved the leadership of the Special Committee of the IGY (in French, CSAGI: Comité Spécial de l'Année Géophysique Internationale), which met for the first time in March 1953.[46] Initially composed of twenty-three member states, it later grew to sixty-seven.[47] The CSAGI was avowedly non-partisan in character and encouraged scientists and professional scientific bodies to think of programmes of work that were informed by curiosity and cooperation. UNESCO funded the work of the CSAGI, which was divided into fourteen project areas, including oceanographic and glaciological research, ionospheric research, determination of longitude and latitude, seismology, and publication activities.

Empowered by a spirit of scientific internationalism, the IGY offered enticing possibilities for further knowledge about the extent and thickness of the ice sheets, the seafloors around the continent, and global climatic systems, as well as unique opportunities for observation of outer space.[48]

44 Wilson, *IGY*.   45 Hamblin, *Oceanographers and Cold War*.
46 Chapman, *IGY: Year of Discovery*.   47 Greenaway, *Science International*.
48 Launius et al., eds., *Globalising Polar Science*.

22 The IGY and the Antarctic Treaty System

Antarctica's skies were far removed from prevailing patterns of light pollution. The official symbol of the IGY captured what was at stake. As Hugh Odishaw, the executive secretary of the US National IGY Committee noted at the time, 'the Earth is partly light, partly dark – suggesting solar terrestrial relationships', and the symbol depicted 'a satellite and its orbit to indicate IGY interests in the physics of the high atmosphere'.[49] The orientation of the figure of the globe deliberately favours the South Pole, and this was designed to showcase the importance of the geophysical investigation of the polar continent.

The prevailing geopolitics of the Cold War, despite lofty intentions, was not quite so easily contained in the planning and execution of the IGY. The Soviet Union was a dominant player in the IGY Antarctic programme. Its presence was a source of anxiety for many IGY participants, including Argentina, Chile, the United Kingdom, and Australia. Their first base, Mirny, was established in 1956 in what would have been considered in Australia as part of the Australian Antarctic Territory. Others were to follow, such as the Komsomolskaya and Vostok stations. The Soviet IGY research stations brought to the fore a core principle of the IGY, namely 'freedom of scientific investigation'. A so-called Gentleman's Agreement (1955) provided the backdrop for claimant states such as Argentina, Australia, and Chile to engage with the IGY Antarctic programme.[50] Under the terms of the agreement, non-claimant states such as the United States and Soviet Union agreed that their IGY polar activities would not affect the prevailing sovereignty politics of Antarctica. In return, the claimant states had to accept that the other IGY parties had freedom to choose where they wished to locate their scientific stations, irrespective of territorial claims and national boundaries.

The scale and scope of the IGY varied according to logistical capacities and the research station location of the twelve polar parties. Coastal stations were established in 1955–56, and this was deliberately timed so that it was then possible to extend towards the polar interior in 1956–57. The IGY started on 1 July 1957, at the height of the long polar winter in Antarctica. The stations established across Antarctica were a mixture of summer-only and permanent establishments. Over fifty were operational during the IGY, with the United States managing seven, ranging from Wilkes station on the coastline to the South Pole station located in the centre of the continent. The Soviet Union established six stations, all of which were located in the Australian Antarctic Territory. The United States worked closely with New Zealand and

---

49 Odishaw, "International Geophysical Year Symbol", 722.
50 Howkins, *Frozen Empires*, 142.

Australia, and Wilkes was seen as strategically significant as an access point to the interior. Supported by the US Navy, Operation Deep Freeze was a four-year commitment to support the US IGY programme. Tractor traverses of the interior were undertaken by both the United States and the Soviet Union, in conjunction with substantial airlift operations, as part of establishing a logistical network across Antarctica. At the other end of the spectrum, the Belgian base, *Roi Baudoin* Base, housed a small party focusing on atmospheric research (including work on ozone). The base was shut down in 1967.

During the IGY, one of the most notable activities carried out was glacial traverses of the Antarctic ice sheet. US scientist Charles Bentley provided some compelling testimony about IGY science. He spent over two years in Antarctica, and as a seismologist he was part of an expedition that used mechanized Sno-cats to traverse the continent. Starting at another IGY station, Little America, the expeditionary team travelled over 1,100 km to Byrd station in West Antarctica. Criss-crossing the Antarctic ice sheet, Bentley's party was working to discover more about the depth and composition of the ice sheet. Very little was known about the Antarctic as a terrestrial volume rather than simply a planar surface. Using seismic techniques, the party used sound waves (generated by explosives planted in the ice) to measure depth. What the party discovered was that the ice extended in places to some 3,000 m beneath the surface. As Bentley recalled in August 2008 when being interviewed about his IGY research at the University of Wisconsin:

> So, we were doing seismic sounding and other geophysical and glaciological work along the way. And that was when we first discovered that the bed of West Antarctica was so far below sea level. Up until then we had expected that since there were mountains to the north of the route from Little America to Byrd, and there are mountains to the south that there were probably mountains covered by the ice in Central West Antarctica also. So, we were quite surprised when we found that the bed was – we thought after we left the ice shelf where it's floating, of course the bed was well below sea level there, it has to be, but we thought when we got to the grounded ice that the bed would come up underneath. But instead, it went down. And, at first, I wasn't even sure that I was making measurements right.[51]

The very nature of the traverses undertaken by Bentley and colleagues meant that they started in the Ross Dependency (New Zealand) and ended up in the

---

51 Bentley, "Interview with Will Thomas".

unclaimed sector (Pacific Ocean). In other cases, the central location of the South Pole station meant that US colleagues provided logistical support to visiting parties, including the private TAE expedition led by Fuchs and Hillary.

The 1955 Gentleman's Agreement did not resolve the unease on the part of the claimant states, however. In Argentina and Australia, there was plenty of speculation about the future intentions of the superpowers and their collective infrastructural and scientific capacities. While the US South Pole station was emblematic of their capacity to operate across the continent, the Soviets created a scientific presence at the Pole of Relative Inaccessibility (Vostok) and undertook a spectacular mechanized journey to the South Pole in December 1958. For smaller claimant states, the inference was clear. Both countries had the capacity to operate across the polar continent, and glaciological research in particular encouraged a geographical mobility as US and Soviet scientists were eager to develop a more detailed sense of ice sheet thickness and cross-continental profile. Local media in Argentina and Australia speculated about how temporary the IGY bases were going to be.[52] At their most conspiratorial, journalists warned their readers about 'Reds on the ice' and the alarming prospect of secret missile bases across the polar continent. The prospect of Soviet missiles buried under the ice and targeted at cities such as Melbourne, Perth, Santiago, and Buenos Aires were considered a serious, if (it was hoped) an unlikely prospect.

For the claimant states, IGY polar research was conducted in their respective national territories. It made no strategic sense to dilute research endeavour because there was no guarantee with regard to what might happen in the aftermath. The United Kingdom, for example, through the Royal Society, established a new station in what it termed the Falkland Islands Dependencies (FID). The staff attached to the Halley Bay base conducted meteorological, ionospheric, and geomagnetic research. Its location on the Weddell Sea coastline was geopolitically significant in the sense that it was located in a part of the FID that did not have any British research station presence.

The fate of Halley Bay base reveals the tensions implicit in the IGY's commitment to generate synoptic geographies of the Earth. The polar continent had been transformed from a vaguely defined polar desert to a highly complex volumetric space shaped by the intersection of rock, ocean, ice, living material, and air.[53] The development of ice core analysis revolutionized the importance of glaciological research in terms of enhancing

52 Pender, "Red Scare on Ice".   53 Antonello, "Life, Ice and Ocean".

understanding of the history and future of the Earth. Climate became re-framed explicitly as temporal rather than just geographical. Geophysical investigation was the epitome of 'big science', requiring substantial funding, large-scale investment in infrastructure, and an understanding of the elemental entanglements of ice, air, water, and rock. It was a long way from the localized surveying and regional mapping work done by UK governmental agencies like the FIDS, and notably the World Data Centres established by the IGY for collection and processing of IGY-generated materials followed Cold War geopolitical schisms: the Soviet Union was Data Centre A, the United States was declared World Data Centre B, and parts of the rest of the world were World Data Centre C. The claimant states were not selected to be exclusive data centres in the brave new world of IGY 'big science', which perhaps was another sign that imperial powers such as the United Kingdom were junior partners in the pursuit of 'big science'.[54]

The journalist Ronald Fraser noted that the IGY was responding to 'an urge to a new kind of adventure – the scientific exploration of the earth as a planet'.[55] Antarctica benefited from this framing of the Earth as a source of planetary knowledge, and the United States and the Soviet Union were able to use the international division of IGY data labour to reinforce their hegemonic status. While claimant states worried about their marginalization, it is noteworthy that the twelve IGY parties involved in polar research were highly skewed. Apart from Japan, no Asian state was involved in the Antarctic segment. Likewise, South Africa was the sole representative of the African continent. Other countries such as India, which had expressed an interest in the 'question of Antarctica' in 1956 and 1958 at the UN General Assembly, were discouraged from pursuing their lines of enquiry. The Indian government asked in 1956 about the future status of Antarctica, and what would happen to the continent in terms of long-term governance. There was a concerted effort on the part of the United Kingdom and other Commonwealth allies to encourage India to drop its public interest in the far south.[56]

The IGY was a world-making exercise, with the production of synoptic geographies at its heart.[57] Antarctica's status grew accordingly, as the 'assault on the unknown' encouraged some observers to claim that science could and should 'provide a basis for understanding and communication of ideas between people that is independent of political boundaries and ideologies'.[58] The reality of the IGY's Antarctic programme was messier than the spirit of scientific

---

54 Aronova et al., "Big Science".   55 Fraser, *Once Around the Sun*, 24.
56 Howkins, "Defending Polar Empire".
57 Lehman, "Making an Anthropocene Ocean".
58 Kistiakowsky, "Science and Foreign Affairs", 115.

internationalism might have implied. The claimant states were persistent in their preoccupations with sovereignty and the long-term ambitions of the superpowers. The Soviet Union's satellite and rocket plans in the polar regions, including at the Mirny station, added further piquancy to speculation about its intentions. The 'moral panic' manufactured in the United States by the launch of Sputnik in October 1957 no doubt helped to perpetuate a view that the Soviets could not be trusted in places like Antarctica.

Building scientific trust was heightened, however, by the decision to operationalize a Special (later Scientific) Committee on Antarctic Research (SCAR). Created in February 1958, SCAR was empowered to coordinate and support international scientific activity across Antarctica. The focus was resolutely circumpolar and thus the Committee was only too aware that the Antarctic's terrestrial and marine environments could not be partitioned as if they were akin to territorial claims. As an expert body, SCAR's recommendations were and are advisory, but it provided a platform for the IGY's scientific internationalism to beome embedded as the twelve parties headed to Washington, DC in October 1959.

Conferencing Antarctica

When the United States invited the eleven other IGY parties to attend a conference on the future of Antarctica, it was not without intense preparation and reflection. In 1958, officials attached to the Eisenhower administration were well aware that the ending of the IGY brought with it more than simply questions about what to do with all the materials generated during an intense research period of some eighteen months. As with other parties such as Australia and the United Kingdom, there was concern about the long-term intentions of the Soviet Union and a more general consideration regarding the future governance of Antarctica. For all its imperfections, the scientific internationalism of the IGY had created an expectation that polar science and logistics could not be constrained by the political geography of a continent. While the United Kingdom might choose to concentrate its scientific energies in the FID, the United States and the Soviet Union in particular had shown that their work was not going to be constrained by worries about whether they were working in Australian Antarctic Territory, New Zealand's Ross Dependency, and/or Chilean Antarctic Territory. Smaller states such as New Zealand were content to work with the United States during the IGY in shared stations such as Hallett.[59]

59 Quartermain and Markham, "New Zealanders".

By the time the twelve parties agreed upon a conference on the future of Antarctica in October 1959, there had been sixty preliminary meetings with the relevant IGY parties. Seven were claimant states, along with five non-claimant states, ranging in size from Belgium and South Africa to Japan, the Soviet Union, and the United States. What we know of the planning and organization of the conference is in large part thanks to the official records held at various Commonwealth and United States archives. One of the most interesting sources of record, however, is the private diaries of a UK delegate, Dr Brian Roberts. A researcher at the Scott Polar Research Institute at Cambridge University and Foreign Office polar adviser, Roberts was given special permission by the head of the UK delegation, Sir Esler Denning, to keep a contemporaneous record of negotiations. Roberts recorded his thoughts with candour. He described the opening ceremony thus:

> With gay tea-time music, bright lights and a background of potted palm trees and the flag of 12 nations, it seemed more like a prelude to a theatre opening than the opening of an international conference. Sir Esler's entry was accompanied by 'Henry VIII dances'.[60]

But he quickly found himself frustrated by the intransigence of others, especially the counter-claimants Argentina and Chile: 'I find myself wondering how it is that so many adults can hold so many incompatible views. In particular, the interminable Chilean and Argentine speeches about sovereignty show that they still have no real understanding of what we have come here to discuss'.[61]

His diaries also reveal a visceral dislike of the head of the US delegation, Paul Daniels. Roberts's attitude towards Daniels did not improve as the conference proceeded: 'I formed a growing dislike for this arrogant man, who clearly considers that any success the conference may have will be entirely due to his own efforts. He has very little self-control.' What was never entirely clear was whether Roberts was simply struggling to adjust to a new reality – the UK delegation was dancing to a tune composed by the United States and its leading polar authorities, including Laurence Gould. Ambassador Herman Phleger, who led the US delegation and chaired the Conference, was adamant that Gould was integral to its success and not Roberts – or anyone else, for that matter.[62]

---

60 Cited in Dodds, "The Great Game", 45.   61 Cited in Dodds, "The Great Game", 52.
62 United States representative Herman Phleger signed the Antarctic Treaty in December 1959. Phleger sent this photograph to Laurence Gould, an Antarctic explorer credited with shaping US Antarctic policy. Phleger's writing on the photograph reads: 'To Laurence Gould, without whom there would be no Antarctica treaty, with warm

The structure of the conference, which lasted some six weeks, was frantic. Two committees were established to provide structure to the meeting. Committee I considered scientific cooperation and investigation, while Committee II addressed the 'big ticket' items such as Antarctic as a zone of peace, the question of territorial claims and the final provisions of the Treaty. Without scientific cooperation and freedom of investigation being accepted by all the parties, it would have been most unlikely that Committee II would have had much business to conduct. For the non-claimants in particular, the IGY was the catalyst for so much of what was to follow. If freedom of investigation was not embedded within the treaty, there was a real risk that claimant states might think they could exercise some sort of veto, for instance over whether the Soviet Union conducted its research programme in the Australian Antarctic Territory. For Argentina, Australia, and France, as Roberts recorded in his diary, this demand for unrestricted freedom of investigation was anathema.

Resolving these tensions took up much of the final weeks of the conference. The final treaty text reveals political compromise rather than evidence of the IGY scientific results terra-forming the underlying purpose of the conference. Articles I, II, and III on peaceful use, scientific investigation, and cooperation, respectively, were designed to reassure the smaller parties that the superpowers would not turn the polar continent into yet another geographical arena for Cold War competition. As Article I noted:

> Antarctica shall be used for peaceful purposes only. There shall be prohibited, *inter alia*, any measure of a military nature, such as the establishment of military bases and fortifications, the carrying out of military manoeuvres, as well as the testing of any type of weapon.[63]

Article II was designed to reassure the semi-claimants and non-claimants that the underpinning spirit of the IGY would endure:

> Freedom of scientific investigation in Antarctica and cooperation toward that end, as applied during the International Geophysical Year, shall continue, subject to the provisions of the present Treaty.

The scientific legacy of the IGY was not the results per se; rather, it was the underpinning framework that made it possible for scientific stations to be based anywhere.

---

regards, Herman Phleger'. Image available at https://teara.govt.nz/en/photograph/37206/signing-the-antarctic-treaty.

63 The full text of the Antarctic Treaty (1959) is available at www.bas.ac.uk/about/antarctica/the-antarctic-treaty/the-antarctic-treaty-1959/.

Article V, on the prohibition on all forms of nuclear testing, explosions, dumping, and storage, was a diplomatic triumph for Argentina, South Africa, Australia, and New Zealand, who were, as geographically proximate states, the most concerned about the nuclearization of Antarctica. As the Cold War had already revealed, small islands in the Pacific Ocean and thinly populated spaces such as inland Australia and Siberia were already bearing the brunt of militarization and nuclearization.

The pivotal element of the Antarctic Treaty is Article IV. This was the hardest to negotiate because it had to accommodate the interests of seven claimant states (of varying degrees of militancy, according to Roberts' diaries at least) and the two superpowers who reserved their right to make a claim in the future:

1. Nothing contained in the present Treaty shall be interpreted as:
   1. a renunciation by any Contracting Party of previously asserted rights of or claims to territorial sovereignty in Antarctica;
   2. a renunciation or diminution by any Contracting Party of any basis of claim to territorial sovereignty in Antarctica which it may have whether as a result of its activities or those of its nationals in Antarctica, or otherwise;
   3. prejudicing the position of any Contracting Party as regards its recognition or non-recognition of any other State's rights of or claim or basis of claim to territorial sovereignty in Antarctica.
2. No acts or activities taking place while the present Treaty is in force shall constitute a basis for asserting, supporting or denying a claim to territorial sovereignty in Antarctica or create any rights of sovereignty in Antarctica. No new claim, or enlargement of an existing claim, to territorial sovereignty in Antarctica shall be asserted while the present Treaty is in force.

The treaty's area of application circumscribed Antarctica. The treaty applied to all land, sea, and ice shelves below 60 degrees south, which sat awkwardly with the inherent scientific globalism of the IGY. However artificial, the line of latitude selected ensured that the polar continent and substantial portions of the Southern Ocean fell within the purview of the treaty. As the historian of science Aant Elzinga noted, the treaty was highly effective in framing the polar continent as a 'natural laboratory of science'.[64] Strikingly, the treaty text has little to note about the polar environment,

---

64 Elzinga, "Antarctica".

resources, and the more than human communities that inhabit or migrate in and out of the Antarctic.[65]

The area of application had the effect of isolating Antarctica from the mainstream of global politics. The preamble to the treaty noted that: 'Recognizing that it is in the interest of all mankind that Antarctica shall continue for ever to be used exclusively for peaceful purposes and shall not become the scene or object of international discord'. What the treaty parties did, however, was to ensure that it was they who would act as gatekeepers to the Antarctic. While membership was left open to other UN member states, there was a provision added to ensure that only new members who demonstrated 'substantial scientific activity' would be able to apply for voting status as a consultative party. The remainder of the Treaty addressed the mechanisms of cooperation and dispute resolution, the right to carry out inspection, and a series of confidence building measures designed to instil confidence amongst parties. The treaty contained details regarding ratification and entry into force, with a provision for review after some thirty years of implementation. Parties knew, therefore, that there was scope to revisit and revise the provisions of the Antarctic Treaty.

Another theme that the treaty did not consider explicitly was resources. In the 1950s, there was speculation aplenty about the resource value of Antarctica. Journalists routinely wrote newspaper articles exclaiming that the polar continent was filled with strategic minerals like uranium and that there was a good chance that oil, gas, and coal might be commercially exploitable. The treaty parties side-stepped resources for the simple reason that it would have made the business of securing agreement that much harder. Resource exploitation and control had keenly informed early human encounters with Antarctica. By the 1950s, sealing and whaling had had a devasting legacy on Antarctica's marine ecologies, especially around the Antarctic Peninsula. Early explorers had noted the presence of coal and had spotted iron ore staining on rock faces. No one was in any doubt that resources could be exploited in the future. Britain's control of the whaling trade and taxation of Norwegian companies operating in Antarctic and sub-Antarctic waters was integral to polar empire-building. To add the question of resources to the treaty conference would have risked two things: first, exposing further schisms between highly sensitive claimant states and non-claimant parties; and second, drawing unwelcome attention to a continent

---

65 Antonello, *Greening of Antarctica*.

that the United States was eager to manage with the help of a small group of fellow IGY veterans.

By focusing on science and the spirit of the IGY, it was easier to maintain that the twelve delegates were representing the 'interests of mankind', a liberal-rational trope that argues that the world should be ordered on the basis of universal principles and interests such as peace and science. In retrospect, the timing of the conference was highly fortuitous. It is difficult to imagine India and other countries of the global South, alongside China, agreeing to the proposition that twelve largely Euro-American nations should be empowered to decide a treaty-based regime for their desired ordering of the polar continent and surrounding ocean. What the treaty parties did was to find a socio-spatial framework that they hoped appeared virtuous to the wider world (e.g. the principle of governance by consensus) without fundamentally compromising their own political, economic, and strategic interests (including territorial and resource claims). Commercial whaling, as it happens, was under the regulatory mandate of the International Whaling Commission, and there were easier mineral resources to exploit elsewhere.[66] Nuclear testing continued elsewhere in the world until the 1963 partial test ban treaty, and the Arctic bore the brunt of cold weather militarization.[67]

The ratification of the treaty in June 1961 ended an uncertain period after the formal signing of the treaty on 1 December 1959. The United Kingdom was the first to ratify the treaty, and this willingness to act promptly was in part down to two factors. First, Brian Roberts and the British delegation considered themselves pivotal to the development of the treaty. Roberts's diaries, unquestionably, imply that he was a member of the brains trust attached to the treaty.[68] Second, geopolitically and financially the treaty delivered for a Britain buffeted by post-war transition. For the Treasury, the treaty protected the United Kingdom's territorial and resource interests via Article IV of the Treaty. For the Foreign Office, the treaty provided a mechanism for confidence building, demilitarization, and inspection, which helped to reassure those who doubted the intentions of Argentina and Chile. However, the parliamentary ratification process was far rockier in Argentina and Chile, where national representatives and newspapers argued that the

---

66 Fitzmaurice, *Whaling and International Law*, especially ch. 2.
67 Maclellan, *Grappling with the Bomb*.
68 MS 1308/9; BJ. Diaries of Brian Roberts for the Washington Conference, 15 October–1 December 1959; 133 pages and three annexes. Scott Polar Research Archives, University of Cambridge.

countries were 'surrendering' their territorial claims and compromising their territorial integrity.[69]

By eventually ratifying the treaty, all the claimant states were in no sense giving up on their territorial claims. Rather, the seven countries found different ways to remind domestic and international audiences about their claimant status. They were resistant, regardless of distance from those claimed territories, to moves to end their claims in the name of a higher liberal-globalist ideal – a US-dominated vision of global science and explicitly hierarchical world order. This continues to this day, very awkwardly at times.[70]

Conclusions

The development of an Antarctic Treaty System (ATS), after its entry into force in June 1961, was made possible by multiple factors. First, parties were sufficiently motivated to address 'emerging' issue such as commercial fishing, possible mineral exploitation, and environmental protection.[71] They did so because it consolidated the ATS as the dominant ordering mechanism for the polar continent. Second, the underlying rules, norms, and values informing demilitarization, denuclearization, and the promotion of peace and cooperation were largely respected, and nuclear testing displaced elsewhere in the world, such as the Pacific Ocean and Arctic regions. Third, the treaty's membership, informed by consensus-based decision-making, has been able to expand to take into account new members (e.g. China, India, and Brazil) as well as to cope with legitimacy crises surrounding minerals negotiations in the 1980s, and the ongoing membership of apartheid South Africa. Fourth, the ATS faced down accusations that it was elitist, secretive, and reluctant to embrace a wider membership. Finally, for all the scientific achievements of the 2007–08 International Polar Year, no one has claimed that it rejuvenated the Antarctic Treaty System. Seasoned observers such as Alan Hemmings have noted that the ATS parties have not introduced any major governance innovation since the 1991 Protocol on Environmental Protection.[72] The Treaty's consensus style of governance is both its greatest strength and its greatest weakness; parties tend to be cautious with one another lest there is a public breach of that consensus, and a breakdown of the treaty would undermine its ability to represent the international common good.

69 Scott, "Universalism and Title".
70 Dodds, "Awkward Antarctic Nationalism," 16–30.
71 Berkman, *Science Diplomacy*.   72 Hemmings, "Hollowing of Antarctic Governance".

Finally, whatever strategic calculations and geopolitical games are played, the twenty-first-century 'Anthropocene Antarctic' is going to be dancing to a very different tune from that of the 'Geophysical Antarctic' of the twentieth century.[73] Sixty years ago, the IGY was dedicated to investigating the Earth's fabric and underworlds, and the focus was on synoptic data collection. At the same time, however, this desire to poke behind the veil began to reveal some troubling evidence of change. Looking at ice sheets in Greenland and Antarctica, for example, did not just reveal what might lie underneath, but also proved to be an extraordinary guide to Earthly pasts. Ironically, the very region of the world – Antarctica – where we had a parsimonious record of scientific observations, has proven to be the region that, along with the Arctic, is experiencing some of the most extraordinary rates of environmental change. Looking under the 'veil of the Earth' has revealed some ugly truths.

Bibliography

Agar, Jon, *Science in the Twentieth Century and Beyond* (Cambridge/Malden, MA: Polity, 2012).

Althoff, William, *Drift Station: Arctic Outposts of Superpower Science* (Washington, DC: Potomac, 2007).

American Geophysical Union, *Antarctica in the International Geophysical Year* (Washington, DC: AGU, 1956).

Antonello, Alessandro, "Australia, the International Geophysical Year and the 1959 Antarctic Treaty", *Australian Journal of Politics and History* 59 (2013): 532–546.

Antonello, Alessandro, "Life, Ice and Ocean: Contemporary Antarctic Spaces", in K. Dodds, A. Hemmings, and P. Roberts, eds., *Handbook on the Politics of Antarctica* (Cheltenham: Edward Elgar, 2017), pp. 167–182.

Antonello, Alessandro, *The Greening of Antarctica: Assembling an International Environment* (Oxford: Oxford University Press, 2019).

Aronova, Elena, Karen Baker, and Naomi Oreskes, "Big Science and Big Data in Biology: From the International Geophysical Year through the International Biological Program to the Long-term Ecological Research (LTER) Network, 1957–Present", *Historical Studies in the Natural Sciences* 40 (2010): 183–224.

Beck, Peter, *The International Politics of Antarctica* (New York: Macmillan, 1986).

Beck, Peter, "Preparatory Meetings for the Antarctic Treaty, 1958–59", *Polar Record* 22 (1985): 653–664.

Belanger, Diane, *Deep Freeze: The United States, the International Geophysical Year and the Origins of Antarctica's Age of Science* (Boulder: University of Colorado Press, 2006).

Bentley, Charles, "Interview with Will Thomas, 6 August 2008", American Institute of Physics Oral History Interviews, www.aip.org/history-programs/niels-bohr-library/oral-histories/33888-1.

---

73 Leane and McGee, eds., *Anthropocene Antarctica*.

Berkman, Paul, *Science Diplomacy: Antarctica, Science, and the Governance of International Spaces* (Washington, DC: Smithsonian Institute Scholarly Press, 2011).
Biermann, Frank, *Earth System Governance: World Politics in the Anthropocene* (Boston: MIT Press, 2014).
Bocking, Stephen, and Daniel Heidt, eds., *Cold Science: Environmental Knowledge in the North American Arctic During the Cold War* (London, New York: Routledge, 2019).
Briggs, Peter, *Laboratory at the Bottom of the World* (New York: McKay, 1970).
Brzezinski, Mark, *Red Moon Rising* (New York: Times Books, 2007).
Bullis, Harold, *The Political Legacy of the International Geophysical Year* (Washington, DC: US Government Printing Office, 1973).
Chapman, Sydney, *IGY: Year of Discovery* (Ann Arbor: University of Michigan Press, 1959).
Chapman, Sydney, "The International Geophysical Year 1957–58", *Nature* 172 (1953): 101.
Christie, E. W. Hunter, *The Antarctic Problem* (London: George Unwin, 1951).
Cloud, John, "Crossing the Olentangy River: The Figure of the Earth and the Military-Industrial-Academic-Complex, 1947–1972", *Studies in History and Philosophy of Science B* 31 (2000): 371–404.
Collis, Christy, "Critical Legal Geographies of Possession: Antarctica and the International Geophysical Year 1957–1958", *GeoJournal* 75 (2009): 387–395.
Collis, Christy, and Klaus Dodds, "Assault on the Unknown: The Historical and Political Geographies of the International Geophysical Year (1957–8)", *Journal of Historical Geography* 34 (2008): 555–575.
Collis, Christy, and Quentin Stevens, "Cold Colonies: Antarctic Spatialities at Mawson and McMurdo Stations", *Cultural Geographies* 14 (2007): 234–254.
Della Dora, Veronica, *The Mantle of the Earth* (Chicago: University of Chicago Press, 2021).
de Solla Price, Derek, *Little Science, Big Science* (New York, London: Columbia University Press, 1965).
Dodds, Klaus, "The Antarctic Treaty, Territorial Claims and a Continent for Science", in M. Nuttall, T. Christensen, and M. Siegert, eds., *The Routledge Handbook of the Polar Regions* (London: Routledge, 2018), pp. 265–274.
Dodds Klaus, "Awkward Antarctic Nationalism: Bodies, Ice Cores and Gateways in and beyond Australian Antarctic Territory/East Antarctica", *Polar Record* 53 (2017): 16–30.
Dodds, Klaus, "Filming and Formatting the Explorer Hero: Captain Scott and Ealing Studios' Scott of the Antarctic (1948)", in Thomas Freeman and David Smith, eds., *Biography and History in Film* (London: Palgrave Macmillan, 2019), pp. 257–275.
Dodds, Klaus, "The Great Game: Britain and the 1959 Antarctic Treaty", *Contemporary British History* 22 (2008): 43–66.
Dodds, Klaus, *Pink Ice: Britain and the South Atlantic Empire* (London: I B Tauris, 2002).
Dodds, Klaus, "Reflecting on the 60th Anniversary of the Antarctic Treaty", *Polar Record* 55 (2019): 311–316.
Dodds, Klaus, Alan Hemmings, and Peder Roberts, eds., *Handbook on the Politics of Antarctica* (Cheltenham: Edward Elgar, 2017).
Doel, Ronald, "Constituting the Post-war Earth Sciences: The Military's Influence on the Environmental Sciences in the USA after 1945", *Social Studies in Science* 33 (2003): 635–666.
Doel, Ronald, Robert Friedman, Julia Lajus, Sverker Sorlin, and Urban Wrakberg, "Strategic Arctic Science: National Interests in Building Natural Knowledge – Interwar Era through the Cold War", *Journal of Historical Geography* 44 (2014): 66–80.

Drivenes, Einar-A, and Harald Jølle, eds., *Into the Ice: The History of Norway and the Polar Regions* (Oslo: Gyldendal Norsk, 2006).

Elzinga, Aant, "Antarctica: The Construction of a Continent by and for Science", in Elisabeth Crawford, Terry Shinn, and Sverker Sörlin, eds., *Denationalizing Science* (Berlin: Springer, 1993), pp. 73–106.

Fitzmaurice, Malgosia, *Whaling and International Law* (Cambridge: Cambridge University Press, 2015).

Fleming, Ian, *From Russia with Love* (London: Jonathan Cape, 1957).

Fogg, Charles, *A History of Antarctic Science* (Cambridge: Cambridge University Press, 1992).

Fraser, Ronald, *Once Around the Sun: The Story of the I.G.Y.* (London: Hodder and Stoughton, 1957).

Fuchs, Vivian, *Of Ice and Men* (Shrewsbury: Anthony Nelson, 1982).

Gan, Irina, "Soviet Antarctic Plans After the International Geophysical Year: Changes in Policy", *Polar Record* 46 (2010): 244–256.

Gan, Irina, "Will the Russians Abandon Mirny to the Penguins after 1959 . . . Or Will They Stay?", *Polar Record* 45 (2009): 167–175.

Giaever, John, *The White Desert: The Official Account of the Norwegian British Swedish Antarctic Expedition* (London: Chatto and Windus, 1954).

Gould, Laurence, "Antarctica: The World's Greatest Laboratory", *The American Scholar* 40 (1971): 402–415.

Gould, Laurence, "The Polar Regions and Their Relations to Human Affairs". Bowman Memorial Lectures Series 4 (New York: AGS, 1958).

Greenaway, Frank, *Science International* (Cambridge: Cambridge University Press, 1986).

Haddelsey, Stephen, and Alan Carroll, *Operation Tabarin: Britain's Secret Wartime Expedition to Antarctica 1944–46* (Stroud: History Press, 2014).

Hamblin, Jacob, *Oceanographers and the Cold War* (Seattle: University of Washington Press, 2005).

Hayton, Richard, "The 'American' Antarctic", *American Journal of International Law* 50 (1956): 583–610.

Heavens, Steve, and June Roberts, *Penguin Diplomacy. Brian Roberts: Polar Explorer, Treaty Maker and Conservationist* (Cirencester: Mereo, 2020).

Hemmings, A., "The Hollowing of Antarctic Governance", in Prem Goel, Rasik Ravindra, and Sulagna Chattopadhyay, eds., *Science and Geopolitics of the White World* (Cham: Springer, 2017), pp. 17–31.

Herzberg, Julia, Christian Kehrt, and Franziska Torma, eds., *Ice and Snow in the Cold War: Histories of Extreme Climatic Environments* (New York, Oxford: Bergbahn, 2019).

Howkins, Adrian, "Defending Polar Empire: Opposition to India's Proposal to Raise the 'Antarctic Question' at the United Nations in 1956", *Polar Record* 44 (2008): 35–44.

Howkins, Adrian, *Frozen Empires: An Environmental History of the Antarctic Peninsula* (Oxford: Oxford University Press, 2017).

Howkins, Adrian, "Melting Empires? Climate Change and Politics in Antarctica Since the International Geophysical Year", *Osiris* 26 (2011): 180–197.

Jackson, Andrew, "Antarctica Without Borders", *Australian Antarctic Magazine* 22 (2012). www.antarctica.gov.au/magazine/issue-22-2012/antarctic-treaty/antarctica-without-borders/

Kaiser, David, "The Physics of Spin: Sputnik Policies and American Physicists in the 1950s", *Social Research* 73 (2006): 1225–1255.

Kaplan, Joseph, "The International Geophysical Year", *Publications of the Astronomical Society of the Pacific* 68 (October 1956): 381–404.

Kaplan, Joseph, "The Scientific Program of the International Geophysical Year", *Proceedings of the Academy of Sciences* 40 (1954): 926–931.

Kistiakowsky, George, "Science and Foreign Affairs", *Bulletin of the Atomic Scientists* 16 (April 1960): 115.

Korsmo, Fae, "The Genesis of the International Geophysical Year", *Physics Today* (July 2007): 38–43.

Korsmo, Fae, "Shaping Up Planet Earth: The International Geophysical Year (1957–8) and Communicating Science through the Print and Film Media", *Science Communication* 26 (2004): 162–187.

Krige, John, and Kai-Henrik Barth, eds., *Global Power Knowledge: Science and Technology in International Affairs* (Chicago: University of Chicago Press, 2006).

Lajus, Julia, and Sverker Sörlin, "Melting the Glacial Curtain: The Politics of Scandinavia-Soviet Networks in the Geophysical Field Sciences between Two Polar Years, 1932/33–1957/58," *Journal of Historical Geography* 44 (April 2014): 44–59.

Launius, Roger, James Rodger Fleming, and David H. DeVorkin, eds., *Globalising Polar Science: Reconsidering the International Polar and Geophysical Years* (New York: Palgrave Macmillan, 2010).

Launius, Roger, John Logsdon, and Roger Smith, eds., *Reconsidering Sputnik: Forty Years Since the Soviet Satellite* (London: Palgrave Macmillan, 2000).

Leane, Elle, and Jeffrey McGee, eds., *Anthropocene Antarctica* (London: Routledge, 2019).

Lehman, Jessica, "Making an Anthropocene Ocean: Synoptic Geographies of the International Geophysical Year 1957–8", *Annals of the American Association of Geographers* online (16 September 2019).

Leslie, Stuart, *The Cold War and American Science* (New York: Columbia University Press, 1993).

Library of Congress, "Antarctica Exploration and Claims, as of 1 February 1956" (Washington, DC: Library of Congress, 1956).

Maclellan, Nic, *Grappling with the Bomb: Britain's Pacific H-Bomb Tests* (Canberra: Australia National University Press, 2017).

McDougall, William, *The Heavens and Earth* (Baltimore: John Hopkins University Press, 1986).

McNeill, John, and Peter Engel, *The Great Acceleration: An Environmental History of the Anthropocene Since 1945* (Cambridge MA: Harvard University Press, 2014).

Meyer, K., and S. Brysac, *Tournament of Shadows: The Great Game and the Race for Empire in Central Asia* (New York: Basic, 2006).

Naylor, Simon, and James Ryan, eds., *New Spaces of Exploration: Geographies of Discovery in the Twentieth Century* (London: I B Tauris, 2009).

Naylor, Simon, Katrina Dean, and Martin Siegert, "The IGY and the Ice Sheet: Surveying Antarctica", *Journal of Historical Geography* 34 (2008): 574–595.

Needell, Allan A., *Science, Cold War and the American State* (London: Routledge, 2001), 325–355.

Odishaw, Hugh, "International Geophysical Year", *Science* (2 January 1959): 4–25.

Odishaw, Hugh, "International Geophysical Year Symbol," *Science* (27 April 1956): 722.
O'Reilly, Jessica, *The Technocratic Antarctic: An Ethnography of Scientific Expertise and Environmental Governance* (Ithaca, NY: Cornell University Press, 2017).
Oreskes, Naomi, "Introduction", in Naomi Oreskes and John Krige, eds., *Science and Technology in the Global Cold War* (London, Cambridge, MA: MIT Press, 2014).
Owens, Susan, *Knowledge, Policy and Expertise* (Oxford: Oxford University Press, 2015).
Pender, Kieran, "Red Scare on Ice: Antarctica, Australian-Soviet Relations and the International Geophysical Year", *History Australia* 14 (2017): 645–659.
Powell, Richard, "Science, Sovereignty and Nation: Canada and the Legacy of the International Geophysical Year, 1957–1958", *Journal of Historical Geography* 34 (2008): 618–638.
Quartermain, Lawrence, and George Markham, "New Zealanders in the Antarctic", *New Zealand Journal of Geology and Geophysics* 5 (1962): 673–680.
Roberts, Peder, *The European Antarctic: Science and Strategy in Scandinavia and the British Empire* (London: Palgrave Macmillan, 2011).
Roberts, Peder, Lize-Marié van der Watt, and Adrian Howkins, eds., *Antarctica and the Humanities* (London: Palgrave Macmillan, 2016).
Rose, Lisle, *Assault on Eternity; Richard E. Byrd and the Exploration of Antarctica, 1946–47* (Annapolis: Naval Institute Press, 1980).
Ross, Frank, *Partners in Science: The Story of the International Geophysical Year* (New York: Lothrop, Lee and Shepard, 1961).
Scott, Shirley, "Ingenious and Innocuous? Article IV of the Antarctic Treaty as Imperialism", *Polar Journal* 1 (2011): 51–62.
Scott, Shirley, "Universalism and Title to Territory in Antarctica", *Nordic Journal of International Law* 66 (1997): 33–53.
Sullivan, Walter, *Assault on the Unknown: The International Geophysical Year* (New York: McGraw-Hill, 1961).
Toma, Peter, "The Soviet Attitude Towards the Acquisition of Territorial Sovereignty in the Antarctic", *American Journal of International Law* 50 (1956): 611–626.
Turchetti, Simone, and Peder Roberts, eds., *The Surveillance Imperative: Geosciences During the Cold War and Beyond* (London: Palgrave Macmillan, 2014).
Turney, Chris, and Chris Fogwill, "The Implications of the Recently Recognised Mid-20th Century Shift in the Earth System", *Anthropocene Review* online (24 February 2021).
Westad, Odd Arne, *The Global Cold War: Third World Interventions and the Making of Our Times* (Cambridge: Cambridge University Press, 2008).
Wilson, Joseph, *IGY: The Year of the New Moons* (New York: Knopf, 1961).

23

The First Century of US Militarization in Alaska, 1867–1967

MATTHEW FARISH

Almost everything the state has today it owes to military spending.[1]

The constancy of war and its . . . constant erasure is linked intimately to the pursuit and maintenance of an American empire similarly erased.[2]

Introduction

Within the scholarship on 'U.S. state and empire building in the *longue durée*', Alaska plays a surprisingly small role.[3] Past the sizable shelf of studies on World War II, the region also vanishes in the literature on the early years of the global Cold War, despite Alaska's geopolitical prominence and the corresponding effects of additional defence spending, construction, and employment in the period leading up to statehood in 1959.[4] Support for (essentially concurrent) statehood in Alaska and Hawai'i was unquestionably 'entwined with the buildup of both territories as major Cold War defense installations'.[5] To rectify that double oversight, and to draw together periods frequently rendered discrete, this chapter uses the United States (US) military, an institution pivotal to the establishment, expansion, and direction of Alaska as a settler colonial society, to stitch together a century of Alaskan history.

I thank Peder Roberts for his great patience with this document during a very difficult year, and Connie Yang for research assistance and thoughtful comments on a draft. The cancellation of a research visit to Alaska and the inaccessibility of certain library materials are reflected in the shape of the text.

1 Kursh, Harry, *This Is Alaska* (Hoboken: Prentice-Hall, 1961) quoted in Hummel, "U.S. Military", 58.
2 Young, "'I Was Thinking'", 1–2.
3 Blower, "Nation of Outposts", 439. But see Pegues, *Space–Time Colonialism*.
4 To cite one notable case, Alaska is not in the Index of Westad's *Cold War*.
5 Whitehead, *Completing the Union*, 7.

One of the strengths of the historical literature on US imperialism – if also a source of contention – is its emphasis on *territoriality*, from individual 'outpost' landscapes to the making of a 'Greater United States' and a world of war-fighting and fort-building.[6] The 1867 US Purchase of Alaska is surely vital to understanding this long arc of continental, hemispheric, maritime, and finally global ambition: Alaska is where polar and US imperial histories most substantially intersect.

In the polar regions and elsewhere, we ought to consider the 'power and possibility of using military histories to enrich our understanding of the United States and its interactions with the world' – but also our understanding of the making and direction of the United States itself.[7] These sources and repositories, while fraught, are valuable guides to what Catherine Lutz has called 'the military normal': the condition whereby violence, as represented by but not limited to the armed forces, has come to rest at the heart of social life.[8] The processes and practices of militarization, both discursive and material, require careful historicization, and the footprint of the US military was only expanded into its enormous, extant shape during and after World War II. But if the United States is treated as what Aziz Rana calls a 'settler empire', fuelled by a longstanding glorification of 'war and the martial spirit', the example of Alaska, where the Department of Defense (DoD, formerly the Department of War) has been singularly influential, is a reminder of militarization's deep roots and far-flung geographies.[9]

This chapter considers Alaska as a space for transformative and extensive US military activity – activity understood as *suitable*. Although my account concludes in the 1960s, the militarization of Alaska has continued. In recent years Alaska has been home to some 50,000 military personnel and dependants, mostly in the Anchorage and Fairbanks areas; more veterans per capita than any other state; and dozens of active and defunct military sites, from major bases to radar stations.[10] My choice of endpoint stems first from a recognition that Alaska's course changed dramatically in the decade after statehood, particularly owing to the massive Prudhoe Bay oil strike in 1968

---

6 For a start, see Blower, "Nation of Outposts"; Immerwahr, *How to Hide*; Vine, *United States of War*.
7 Heefner, "'Slice of Their Sovereignty'", 52.   8 Lutz, "The Military Normal".
9 Rana, *Two Faces*, 3; Lutz, "Making War at Home", 725. See also Blower, "Nation of Outposts".
10 For military personnel and dependants, see "Special Populations and Areas", https://live.laborstats.alaska.gov/pop/estimates/pub/chap3.pdf (accessed 2 July 2021). For the highest number of veterans per capita, see US Census Bureau, "Percent Veterans By State", www.census.gov/library/visualizations/2015/comm/percent-veterans.html (accessed 2 July 2021).

and the advocacy that led to the signing of the Alaska Native Claims Settlement Act in 1971. These landmarks, both sedimented by older histories, have generated a wealth of scholarship that cannot be synthesized here.

My frame is justified by two additional, seemingly contradictory factors that deserve further contemplation. First, an intensive period of US military interest in the Arctic subsided around 1960, as the DoD, but also the broader public, turned more toward other 'hostile environments'.[11] Second, Alaska's military geography since the early Cold War has been characterized by consistency and recurrence as much as change. This is evident in the continued sway of bases around Fairbanks (Eielson Air Force Base and the Army's Fort Wainwright) and Anchorage (now Joint Base Elmendorf-Richardson), or the enhancement of the Ballistic Missile Early Warning System at Clear Air Force Station (now Clear Space Force Station), southwest of Fairbanks. But it is perhaps most pointed in the persistent presence of two US Army Alaska (USARAK) facilities, the Cold Regions Test Center and the Northern Warfare Training Center, and their use of land around the junction of two essential roads, both military initiatives – the Richardson and the Alaska Highways.[12]

The chapter's four major sections are roughly chronological. I linger first over the early years of Alaska to demonstrate that despite a comparatively modest presence, the Department of War was crucial to Alaska's foundations as a US colony, beginning with the Army's role in attempts to rule parts of Lingít Aaní, the homelands of the Tlingit. Second, the military histories of the long span between the Organic Act of 1884, which introduced a 'rudimentary', settler-focused 'civilian government', and the momentous shifts delivered by World War II, are often overlooked in favour of the events that bookend them.[13] But during this period the Army significantly boosted the burgeoning settler society by supporting expeditions to gain cartographic and ethnographic knowledge, building multiple forts to demonstrate 'order', and above all, leading the push to enhance road and communications infrastructures. Third, in surveying World War II in Alaska, I focus on the military landscapes – but also the military presumptions – that formed the basis for much of what transpired in the fifteen years after the War, an

---

11 See Farish, "Lab and the Land", 28.
12 Additional examples of this recurrence include recent, renewed interest in cold-weather warfare and calls for another generation of Arctic 'early-warning systems'. A more nuanced story of consistency and change since the middle of the twentieth century concerns northern contaminants and the frequently slow environmental violence wrought by militarization.
13 Demuth, "Statehood and Other Events".

extraordinary period in Alaska's history, and the subject of the chapter's fourth section. With a surplus of potential examples at hand, from submarine surveillance to reconnaissance flights and ice islands, I highlight the consolidation of Alaska's role as a site for 'cold weather' operations and related military science.[14] Neither the parts nor the whole are intended to be comprehensive: instead, the chapter is ultimately a rumination on how Alaska's military identity came to be, and how it has endured.

'The Most Careful Vigilance': The Purchase and Its Aftermath

In the morning of 18 October 1867, the Navy warship USS *Ossipee* steamed into Sheet'ká harbour, carrying US Army Brigadier General Lovell Harrison Rousseau.[15] A veteran of both the Mexican-American War and the Civil War, Rousseau was elected to Congress in 1865, where his most notable act was the physical assault of another Representative. Just two years into his Congressional career, he was recalled to the Army and sent to Alaska.[16] In August 1867, Secretary of State William Seward designated Rousseau to 'receive from a similar officer appointed on behalf of the imperial government of Russia, the territory ceded by that government to the United States, pursuant to the treaty of March 30 last'. The list of possessions falling into US hands began with 'all forts and military posts'. Once this 'business' was complete, Rousseau would 'have command in the territory, to be exercised under the orders of the war department'.[17]

Rousseau arrived in San Francisco in September. There, he liaised with Admiral Henry Knox Thatcher, head of the Navy's reconfigured North Pacific Squadron.[18] By late in the month, they were heading north aboard the *Ossipee*, with George Foster Emmons at the helm – a man whose extensive military resumé included the vicious, 'frontier-conquering, empire-building adventure'

---

14 For a straightforward synthesis, see Hummel, "U.S. Military". More work is needed on Cold War radar construction in Alaska, most notably the Distant Early Warning (DEW) Line, a US-led project initiated during the 1950s that stretched to Greenland. In Alaska, DEW and DEW-affiliated sites ran from the Aleutian Islands to the Yukon border, including major stations adjacent to the Iñupiat communities of Utqiaġvik (Barrow) and Kaktovik. See Fritz, "DEW Line Passage".
15 Wherever possible, and with the recognition that I am drawing from several of Alaska's twenty native languages, I have employed the Alaska Native Language Archive's list of "Alaska Native Place Names", www.uaf.edu/anla/collections/map/names/ (accessed 6 July 2021).
16 "Rousseau, Lovell Harrison". 17 "Transfer of Alaska", 83.
18 "Transfer of Alaska", 85.

23 First Century of US Militarization in Alaska

of the US (Wilkes) Exploring Expedition in the Pacific (1838–42), along with the Mexican-American and Civil Wars.[19]

From the 1740s, Russian hunters and traders had brutally exploited the Indigenous peoples and marine mammals of the North Pacific.[20] Driven by demand for fur, and amid a climate of imperial rivalries, Russians claimed outposts in south and southeast Alaska in the last two decades of the eighteenth century. In 1799, under the leadership of Aleksandr Baranov – soon to be named manager of the newly consolidated, monopolistic Russian-American Company – a colonial fort (Mikhailovskii, at Gajaa Héen) was established on Shee (later dubbed Baranov or Baranof Island), in the midst of Lingít Aaní.[21] After incursions, abuses, and murders perpetrated by the Russians, the fort was destroyed by Tlingit in 1802, with Baranov absent.[22] He returned in 1804, bent on revenge and accompanied by a warship. Short on gunpowder, Tlingit residents of Sheet'ká, led by the Kiks.ádi clan, abandoned the 'sapling fort' (Shís'gi Noow) they had built to resist a foretold invasion and embarked on a 'survival march' to an abandoned settlement (Cháatlk'aa Noow, on what the Russians named Chicagof Island).[23] From there, the Tlingit blocked Indigenous maritime trade with the Russians – an action noticed by 'Yankee traders', who set up a rival station nearby.[24]

At Sheet'ká, the Russian colonists destroyed the Kiks.ádi homes on the hill overlooking the ocean (Noow Tlein) and set out to build a fortified settlement: Novo-Arkhangel'sk, which soon became the

---

19 Eperjesi, "Basing the Pacific", 2. Emmons was the father of George Thornton Emmons, who spent time with the Navy in Alaska and then became a Northwest Coast ethnographer and 'expert' on Alaskan matters, part of a longer and broader history of soldiers as collectors and informants on Indigenous life. Jefferson C. Davis (discussed below) 'encouraged this interest in Indian culture among his subordinates'; one Second Lieutenant 'collected specimens and artifacts enthusiastically, even acting as archeologist'. Hughes and Whitney, *Jefferson Davis in Blue*, 386.
20 On this vicious, dynamic history, which also included hunters from the United States and elsewhere, see among other sources Bockstoce, *Furs and Frontiers*; Vinkovetsky, *Russian America*; Demuth, *Floating Coast*.
21 Haycox, *Alaska: An American Colony*, 101; Kan, *Memory Eternal*, 55. See the map, "Traditional Tlingit Country, circa Late Nineteenth Century", based on research by the Tlingit educator Andrew Hope III (Xhaastánch), http://ankn.uaf.edu/Curriculum/Tlingit/Salmon/graphics/tlingitmap.pdf (accessed 6 June 2021). In the summer of 2020, Indigenous activism led to the movement of a statue of Baranov from in front of a Sitka government building to a museum.
22 Urrea, "'Our People Scattered'", 54–58.
23 The 'location' of the fort in 2019 generated substantial media attention. On the march, see Hope, "Kiks.ádi Survival March". For more detail, see Dauenhauer et al., eds., *Anóoshi Lingít Aaní Ká*, which contains Hope's account.
24 The blockade is discussed in Hope, "Kiks.ádi Survival March".

administrative capital of the *Russkaya Amyerika* colony. According to the Tlingit elder Herb Hope, some fifteen years after departing in 1804, the Kiks.ádi returned and 'immediately began to build their new winter quarters right up against the Russian stockade', reminding the residents of Novo-Arkhangel'sk that the forests and mountains beyond were Tlingit land.[25]

Constrained to this and other footholds and preoccupied with extraction, the Russian government nonetheless presumed to negotiate the sale of 1.5 million km^2 of demarcated territory to the United States, which presumed to inherit and possess it, all without consulting Native Alaskans. These multitudinous peoples were present in what was called the Treaty of Cession only to the extent that they were characterized as 'uncivilized tribes' and explicitly excluded from the property rights and protections extended to even lingering Russians.[26] The Tlingit scholar Caskey Russell has written that 'The transaction was symbolic in its ethnocentrism.'[27] And if, in the judgement of one settler historian of the period, the small town named Sitka was, for well over a decade after the Purchase, '*the* American frontier in Alaska', this disproportionality signalled the extent of US imperial hubris.[28]

Once the *Ossipee* arrived at its destination, Rousseau's party, including George Emmons and some 250 soldiers, 'armed and handsomely equipped', landed under the command of Jefferson Columbus Davis.[29] A career soldier in a period of serial violence, during the Civil War Davis had murdered a Major General (for which Davis escaped punishment) and directed a notorious atrocity at Ebenezer Creek, Georgia.[30] After Lovell Rousseau quickly departed, having spent just a week in the north, Davis, who thought little of Rousseau, formally assumed the title

---

25 Hope, "Kiks.ádi Survival March"
26 Quote from Article III of the Treaty, 30 March 1867, www.loc.gov/rr/program/bib// ourdocs/alaska.html (accessed 5 June 2021). See also Kan, *Memory Eternal*, 184.
27 Russell, "Cultures in Collision", 237. See also Arnett, "Between Empires and Frontiers", 32; Banner, *Possessing the Pacific*, 291–292; Jones, "'Search For and Destroy'", 7. On the immediate Tlingit objections to the Purchase, and their longevity, see Russell, "Cultures in Collision", 234–238.
28 Hinckley, "United States Frontier," 57 [original emphasis]. By 1867, Tlingit communities had also suffered from multiple epidemics, especially smallpox, and with the 'population almost at its lowest point during the time of Purchase', the 'appropriation of land and resources began in earnest'. Russell, "Cultures in Collision", 238.
29 "Transfer of Alaska", 86. On the acutely colonial connotations of 'Columbus' and 'Columbia', see Dunbar-Ortiz, *Indigenous Peoples' History*, 4.
30 On Davis and Ebenezer Creek, see Brockell, "Civil War Massacre". On the serial wars of this period, see Vine, *United States of War*, ch. 5.

he had been promised: Commander of the Military District of Alaska.³¹ Novo-Arkhangels'k became Sitka, and Davis replaced Prince Dmitry Maksutov, the last leader of *Russkaya Amyerika* – himself a Navy officer.

As 'peal after peal' of the *Ossipee*'s guns echoed 'in the gorges of the surrounding mountains' and a wharf-based Russian battery responded, the transfer was formalized by a lowering and raising of respective imperial flags on the outcrop renamed Castle Hill, along with a few words, while 'Russian and American citizens' watched. But Rousseau also noted, in passing, the presence of 'some Indians', while a reporter for the *New York Herald* – one of two travelling journalists present – noted 'Creoles and Indians' among the 'eager witnesses'.³² The other reporter, writing for San Francisco's *Daily Alta California*, described Indigenous observers in canoes, stationed 'in the harbor from whence they had a remote but impressive view of the proceedings. Of the nature of the event they had a partial knowledge, and were disposed to regard it unfavorably', owing in part to prior familiarity with 'American whale-ships'.³³

In his report to Seward, which concluded with a note of acquisitive regret that he 'saw very little of the new territory', Rousseau claimed that most of the residents in the Sitka area were 'satisfied with the transfer'. But he additionally quoted an unnamed Tlingit chief: 'True, we allowed the Russians to possess the island, but we did not intend to give it to any and every fellow that came along.'³⁴ (A century later, the Iñupiaq politician William Iggiagruk Hensley gestured precisely to this same principle, along with the absence of any treaties paralleling the Purchase, in a notable speech titled "Why the Natives of Alaska Have a Land Claim".³⁵)

---

31 Hughes and Whitney, *Jefferson Davis in Blue*, 371. The District was converted to a Department of Alaska in March 1868 and folded back into the Department of the Columbia in 1870.

32 "Transfer of Alaska", 90. Byron Adonis, "Alaska", *New York Herald* (13 November 1867), in Allen, ed., *As the Old Flag Came Down*, 9.

33 John H. Goodale ("Del Norte"), "Acquisition of Alaska", *Alta California* (19 November 1867), in Allen, ed., *As the Old Flag Came Down*, 11.

34 "Transfer of Alaska", 89–90. One Navy midshipman, who had been in Sitka for some weeks 'to extinguish a yellow fever outbreak' on his vessel, the USS *Resaca*, referred to this chief as 'Michael Kaukan' (Shchukh, or Mikhail Kukhkan). After mentioning that the same sentiment was held by 'all' the Tlingit in the community adjacent to the Russian fort, Andrew Blair concluded with a line from Epistle I of Alexander Pope's *An Essay on Man* (1734): 'Lo! The poor Indian.' (Pope continued: 'whose untutor'd mind / Sees God in clouds, or hears him in the wind.' Journal of Andrew A. Blair, October 18, 1867, in Allen, ed., *As the Old Flag Came Down*, 8. On Shchukh, see Dean, "'Uses of the Past'".

35 William Iggiagruk Hensley, "Why the Natives of Alaska Have a Land Claim" (1969), reprinted in Williams, ed., *Alaska Native Reader*, 192–201. In 1871, the US Congress stopped any formal treaty-making with Indigenous nations.

A great deal has been written about the Alaska Purchase and the proceedings of 18 October 1867 – events commemorated since 1917 with an official holiday that remains hotly contested in Sitka and elsewhere.[36] Yet this sketch is a reminder that the 'transfer of imperial sovereignty', a swapping of grandiose possessive claims to territory, people, and resources, was fulfilled and extended by the US military, amid an especially violent period of Indigenous dispossession in North America.[37] And until 1884, apart from a two-year interlude when only US Treasury collectors were stationed at several locations across southern Alaska, Rousseau's enormous 'new territory' was the purview – in some places 'more in principle than in practice' – of the Army (until 1877), and then (from 1879) the Navy.[38]

The presence of the military in these early years of the US colony was modest, but it was not insignificant. On a visit to Sitka in 1869 after his retirement, Seward was invited to address the town's settler population. Assuming the necessity of the Purchase and beginning with a grandiloquent description of Alaska's physical attributes, he suggested that the disproportionate ratio of Indigenous people to settlers justified temporary 'military protection', even as he suggested that the 'jealous, ambitious, and violent' Native Alaskans would 'steadily decline in numbers', given that they 'can neither be preserved as a distinct social community, nor incorporated into our society'. They would, Seward stated bluntly, 'merely serve the turn until civilized white men come'.[39] The two presumptions were compatible and came together in a form of colonial geography: if Alaska was enormous, largely inhospitable, and seemingly unsettled, and Natives were on an inevitably declensionist path, the range of US law-making could be limited, principally when it came to land.[40]

Almost a century later, an Army pamphlet described not only 'noble achievement in man's progress', but posited more interestingly that 'the civilian settlement and growth of the Territory was unimpaired by

36 Kwong, "150 Years"; Griffin, "Treaty of Cession".
37 'Imperial sovereignty' is from Soluri, "Fur Sealing", 31. See also Hill, "Imperial Stepping Stone", 80–82.
38 Banner, Possessing the Pacific, 296.
39 The quotes are from of William H. Seward", 10–13. See Hinckley, "Seward Visits His Purchase", 130; Hughes and Whitney, Jefferson Davis in Blue, 387–388.
40 Banner, Possessing the Pacific, 296. Seward and others drew links between Native Alaskans and Asia, situating Alaska firmly 'outside national boundaries, intrinsically as colonial space'. The results certainly 'further hindered sovereignty and facilitated land possession'. Pegues, "Settler Orientalism", 13–14.

a military form of government', crediting Army commanders for this accomplishment.[41] The veracity of this claim is less important than its work as cover for the naturalization of colonialism. We might consider how the *continuing* ability to render Alaska as a 'piece' of the United States is tied to both militarized geographic imaginations and their material manifestations.

In a recent essay Michael Hill has suggested that 'The purchase of Alaska bridged the temporal, physical, and ideological chasm between continental and overseas empire.' It fitted with older visions of westward land acquisition and resettlement while also pointing to and even legitimizing different if complementary forms of possession and rule.[42] This is a simple and substantial but surprisingly uncommon argument. During much of the nineteenth century, the most familiar US euphemism for liberal imperialism was *expansion*, and among its advocates, few were more passionate than Seward, Secretary of State from 1861–69.[43] He and other proponents of the massive Purchase combined focused and ahistorical reasoning to press and justify the case, prophesying, in oft-cited comments, 'a state or many states' while also positioning the Aleutian Islands as 'stepping stones' to Asia.[44] In the debates over the merits of the Purchase, which frequently dovetailed at the racist intersection of 'moral climatology', Seward's geoeconomic aspirations prevailed.[45] They also assumed a more physical shape in the premise of 'support areas which could offer safe havens and resupply stations to American merchant vessels', but additionally 'serve strategic and defense purposes'.[46]

The instructions provided to Jefferson Davis pertaining to 'aboriginal and uncivilized tribes' indicated that 'in the absence of any organized civil Territorial Government', he was to 'act as their general superintendent, protecting them from abuse and regulating their trade and intercourse with our own people'. But to this paternalistic mandate was attached an order that the Indigenous people of the Panhandle were to be approached with 'the

---

41 United States Army, *Building Alaska*.
42 Hill, "Imperial Stepping Stone", 77; also 78–79. See also Hill, "Myth of Seward's Folly", 43–44.
43 As a Senator, Seward was the sponsor of the Guano Islands Act of 1856; by 1863, the United States had claimed fifty-nine islands in the Pacific and Caribbean. This foreshadowed the 'pointillist empire ... built after the Second World War'. Immerwahr, *How to Hide*, 51–56.
44 The first quote is from Arnett, "Between Empires and Frontiers", 32; the second is from Haycox, *Alaska: An American Colony*, 182.
45 Love, *Race Over Empire*, 32–33; Immerwahr, *How to Hide*, 78. On moral climatology, see Livingstone, "Race, Space".
46 Haycox, "Truth and Expectation", 65.

most careful vigilance'. Davis was further advised that 'it may be well to have guns ... always bearing on their village, ready at an instant's warning, to destroy them'.[47] And just a few weeks after the Purchase ceremony, he requested more 'troops designed for this district', citing the 'Indians inhabiting the little village just outside the palisades protecting the town', who 'have the reputation of being very hostile and insolent'. 'They fear the Americans', Davis went on, 'and look with considerable mistrust upon us. Notwithstanding they boast that they can and will whip us some day.'[48] It was not long before he began 'kidnapping Tlingit leaders, hostage taking, imprisoning, bombing villages, and executing Alaska natives'.[49] The violence of expansion was experienced and resisted by Indigenous bodies.[50]

Davis quickly dispatched troops and established forts across southern Alaska, as far west as the Pribilof Islands, where Unangan communities had been traumatically relocated from the Aleutian Islands by Russian traders in the eighteenth century.[51] Although, amid Reconstruction, the Army's Alaskan presence was soon scaled back, and soldiers were sent to other colonial duties in the west, Davis's 'farewell visits' to various Native Alaskan communities in the summer of 1870 signalled the lingering imposition of military 'authority', backed by a defensive mindset, in the US colony. His enthusiastic biographers characterize his Alaskan tenure as that of a 'military caretaker' with limited geographic control sent north by a 'disinterested nation'.[52] Davis's own departing report contrasted the 'docile, honest, and peaceful' Unangan people, 'very nearly approaching a state of semi-civilization', with the 'treacherous' Tlingit, 'who must be ruled by a strong, vigilant, and just government over them'. The Natives living close to his military posts, he claimed, have 'improved wonderfully', 'becoming much more subordinate'.[53]

It is imperative that the scale of the US military's presence in Alaska in the years after the Purchase is not overstated. Maintaining the Army was

47 H. W. Halleck, Head-quarters Military Division of the Pacific, to J. C. Davis, 6 September 1867, reprinted in the *New York Times* (12 December 1867): 2.
48 Jefferson C. Davis to Major John P. Sherbourne, Department of California, 12 November 1867, in Allen, ed., *As the Old Flag Came Down*, 22. Byron Adonis's offensive and patriotically boastful dispatch from Sitka, published in the *New York Herald* on 26 December 1867, captures something of this moment: in Allen, ed., *As the Old Flag Came Down*, 14–17.
49 Jones, "'Search for and Destroy'", 8.
50 Arnett, "Between Empires and Frontiers", 33; Blackhawk, *Violence Over the Land*, 8–9.
51 Haycox, *Alaska: An American Colony*, 183; Jones, *Century of Servitude*.
52 Hughes and Whitney, *Jefferson Davis in Blue*, 392, 395. See also Blower, "Nation of Outposts", 447–450.
53 Report of Colonel J. C. Davis, 20 August 1870, in *Annual Report of the Secretary of War*, 60.

expensive, settler migration to the colony was initially modest, and the hesitant reach of 'policy and law' signalled that Alaska was at the outward edge of the US imperium.[54] Few long-lasting installations were housed there before the 1930s, although the proliferation of heritage sites, landmarks, and 'historic parks' (Fort William H. Seward in Haines, for example) is a reminder of the various afterlives of military initiatives. But from another perspective, classic settler historiographical arguments about neglect are constrained historically and geographically. To treat late nineteenth-century Alaska as largely abandoned by the US government and 'ignored or dismissed' by the US public is mistaken, particularly for Tlingit and other Native communities in southeast Alaska.[55] Moreover, the examples of Davis and other military principals point to the role of Alaska as another destination for the 'colonial careers' of US soldiers, well before many made the move from campaigns on North American Indigenous land to 'overseas' wars and governance in Puerto Rico, Cuba, or the Philippines.[56] In 1873 Davis was pulled out of semi-retirement to attempt what William Tecumseh Sherman, the Commanding General of the Army, called the 'justified ... utter extermination' of the Modoc people in the Klamath Basin (shared by Oregon and California).[57] The troops departing Sitka in 1877 were directed to pursue Nimíipuu (Nez Perce) people across the Pacific Northwest.[58] In its first decades as a US colony, Alaska was tied to broader colonial moves that were often led or assisted by the armed forces.

Occupation and Aspiration

Just a year after the Purchase, and a year before Seward's own trip to southeastern Alaska, Jefferson Davis was visited in Sitka by Major-General Henry W. Halleck, head of the Military Division of the Pacific.[59] Halleck, who had led the Union Army for almost two years during the Civil War, bore considerable responsibility for the (brief) creation of a separate Alaskan Department under his Division. Joining Halleck on the Alaskan tour was the photographer Eadweard Muybridge ('Helios'), who was effectively on

---

54 Arnett, "Between Empires and Frontiers", 33.
55 This counter-argument follows Charlton, "'Our Ice-Islands'", 24. See also Haycox, *Alaska: An American Colony*, 189.
56 Bjork, *Prairie Imperialists*, 4. Of course, Alaska was 'overseas', as well.
57 Hughes and Whitney, *Jefferson Davis in Blue*, 403.
58 See Venn, "Soldier to Advocate", 40; Mighetto and Homstad, *Engineering*, 12.
59 The year 1868 also saw the creation of the Alaska Commercial Company, formed to control sealing on the Pribilof Islands. The result was the rapid slaughter of over 250,000 animals, and the continued 'loss of Unangan political sovereignty'. Soluri, "Fur Sealing", 31.

a military assignment.⁶⁰ From Alaska to Panama, Muybridge was in the midst of an extensive project of 'Indigenous representation'. As Robert Aguirre notes, many of the resulting images 'may be read as briefs for the benefits of U.S. expansion', and the military's employment of Muybridge and his camera 'for the purpose of illustrating the Military Posts and Harbours of Alaska' is telling. Halleck described Muybridge's photographs, some of the first ever taken in the region, in the language of accuracy and latent opportunity: they offered 'a more correct view of Alaska ... than can be obtained from any written description of that country'. That 'correct view', Aguirre suggests, was also a fundamentally colonial one, whereby the trip north was also a journey back in time.⁶¹ As Seward's Sitka words the next year affirmed, this geographic anachronism was an immediate and common impression and imposition, and it soon folded into the popular US vocabulary of 'conquest' and 'extraction' along the Panhandle in the growing tourist traffic of the late nineteenth century.⁶²

Like Muybridge's photographs, the settler contrast between an Indigenous past and a present (and future) associated with the United States was produced in the service of a military occupation.⁶³ And the presumption of a vanishing Indigenous Alaska not only persisted but was also taken up when useful to the military's northern aspirations. It may well have been disturbed by certain forms of military inclusion, but across the century covered in this chapter, the military was also responsible for some of its most focused, cruel manifestations.

Seward arrived at Davis's fortified Sitka near the end of July 1869. Six months earlier, Army troops had 'attacked and surrounded' the adjacent, separated Tlingit village, killing several, and then suggested that the entire community could be destroyed by 'gunship and fort artillery'. In February, the Army's gunship *Saginaw* had fired on a K̲éex̲' Kwáan Tlingit village at the contemporary location of K̲éex̲' (Kake), to the east of Sitka. Soldiers determined that the community had been deserted in advance of their arrival; they were ordered to 'burn the village, destroy canoes, and eliminate the village's winter foodstuffs.' Two other villages were destroyed. What became known as the Kake War – a poor description of a 'one-sided military attack on Tlingit

---

60 Muybridge made his photographic reputation after an 1867 visit to the Yosemite Valley, a 'pristine' place that had been violently cleared of its Indigenous inhabitants in 1851. He was also commissioned by the Army to photograph Davis's vengeful Modoc campaign. See Solnit, *River of Shadows*.
61 Aguirre, "Wide Angle", 59.   62 Campbell, *In Darkest Alaska*, 9.
63 Aguirre, "Wide Angle", 60.

civilian communities' – was followed, at the end of the year, by the shelling of the Tlingit village at Shtax'héen (Wrangell). Criticism of Davis's conduct led Congress to reduce the number of troops in Alaska, and 1870 marked the end of Davis's leadership.[64]

The historian Zachary Jones puts aside lurid, one-sided explanations of the origins of the 'War' and points to three broader causes:

> The Tlingit did not recognize the sale of their ancestral lands to the United States in 1867; the United States and the Tlingit Indians failed to accept each other's legal systems and worldviews; and the Army carried out a policy of using or threatening to use American military technology against Alaska's native peoples with lethal effect.[65]

None of this dramatically changed with the US Navy's entry into Alaskan rule, which corresponded with a growth in the settler population, additional extractive activity, and the stirrings of tourism in southeastern Alaska.[66] In 1880 a Navy ship with a Gatling gun escorted 'five sailboats of armed prospectors' to the waters and lands of the Jilkáat Kwáan (Chilkat) Tlingit: 'The ship's officer explained to the Chilkat chiefs how the gun worked and read a letter to them assuring them that the prospectors would not interfere with their fur trade. The Chilkat chiefs then agreed to open Dyea Pass into Canada to gold hunters.'[67] This scene of coercion precisely captures what Juliana Hu Pegues calls the double obfuscation of 'the historical land ownership of Native peoples and the dispossession that occurred in the clamor for gold'.[68]

Most infamously, in 1882, again following the habits of Army predecessors, Navy weapons levelled the Tlingit community of Aangóon (Angoon), to the east of Sitka on Xootsnoowú (Admiralty Island): storehouses with winter supplies were torched, canoes were destroyed, homes were looted, and six children died from smoke inhalation. As the Tlingit scholar Nancy Furlow writes, these atrocities 'remain in the present through the oral traditions', although the Navy has never apologized for its actions.[69]

---

64 Jones, "'Search For and Destroy'", 1–3.   65 Jones, "'Search For and Destroy'", 7.
66 Poulson, "Legacy".
67 "New Migrants", in Robert D. Arnold et al., *Alaska Native Land Claims* (1978), www.alaskool.org/projects/ancsa/landclaims/LandClaims_Unit3_Ch10.htm (accessed 3 July 2021).
68 Pegues, *Space-Time Colonialism*, 64.
69 Nancy Furlow, "Angoon Remembers: The Religious Significance of Balance and Reciprocity", in Williams, ed., *Alaska Native Reader*, 150. See also the Tlingit anthropologist Rosita Worl's presentation on these entangled incidents: "Tlingit Law, American Justice".

In the years after the Army departed Sitka (and ostensibly Alaska), it nonetheless sent officers such as Frederick Schwatka, William Abercrombie, and Henry Allen on expeditions into the Alaskan interior. Stretching from campaigns in the North American west to Cuba and the Philippines, the biographies of these men are another collective reminder of Alaska's place within increasingly capacious circuits of US empire-building in the period between the Civil War and World War I (in which Allen participated), circuits that extended and gave new shape to the premise of a colonial frontier. Allen's combination of endurance and data-collecting is still celebrated by the Army and others, with occasional acknowledgement of extant Indigenous routes or assistance from Native communities.[70] But it bears stressing that as with earlier Army equivalents in the west, these were military reconnaissance expeditions seeking additional information on lands and peoples, anticipating, as Allen's instructions put it, the arrival of more 'whites who are making their way into the region'.[71]

Indeed, southerners were 'making their way' to Alaska by the thousands in the 1880s and particularly the 1890s, many driven by tales of mineral wealth.[72] The Army took note. In August 1897, weeks after the first steamship laden with Klondike gold had arrived in Seattle, Patrick Henry Ray and Wilds Richardson arrived in Alaska, sent by the Army to report on conditions in communities founded or expanded as a result of the mining boom. Once more, the older Ray was a Civil War veteran who also served in the North American west, Cuba, and the Philippines.[73] In 1881, as part of the first International Polar Year, he had led a two-year expedition, sponsored by the Army's Signal Corps and the Smithsonian Institution, to establish a research base near Utqiaġvik on the Arctic coast of Alaska.[74] A decade and a half later, he and Richardson were in Tachiq (Saint Michael), the location of a Russian trading post on the Bering Sea, and travelled up the Yukon River.[75] Based on what they encountered, Ray

---

70 See Marsett, "Journey Through Wilderness", https://armyhistory.org/5102-2/ (accessed 3 July 2021).
71 Allen, *Report of an Expedition*, 11. See also Schwatka, *Report of Military Reconnaissance*. A fuller discussion of this period would include the work of naturalists who operated weather stations for the Army Signal Service (later the Signal Corps). See Broadhead, "United States Army Signal Service".
72 Already, the community of Juneau (Dzánti K'ihéeni), named after a prospector (who received essential Indigenous assistance, as was so common), had been founded as a mining camp in 1880, during an earlier search for gold to the northeast of Sitka on Tlingit land.
73 See Schneider, "P. H. Ray"; Dumonceaux, "Remaking the Alaska–Yukon Borderlands", 190.
74 Burch, "Smithsonian Contributions".
75 Kuukpak in Inupiaq and Tth'echù in the Hän language, among other Native names for the lengthy waterway.

recommended, among other changes, the reinstatement of a military government in Alaska, and the fostering of 'overland routes from tidewater to the Yukon'.[76] Both suggestions were momentous, even if the former was only locally realized.

Ray's proposals encouraged the Army to establish a series of new posts and camps in the last years of the nineteenth century, echoing the rationale used thirty years earlier: to provide governance where it was perceived to be absent. A fort at Saint Michael, the closest port to the mouth of the Yukon River, was announced late in 1897 and built the following year. For a time, it was the headquarters of the revived Military Department of Alaska.[77] Other forts were erected at Deishú (Haines), Suacit (Valdez), Hohudodetlaatl Denh (Tanana), Tthee T'äwdlenn (Eagle), and Sitŋasuaq (Nome), where Fort Davis, named after Jefferson C. Davis, was established amid another local gold rush.[78] These posts did not last when land and resource rushes subsided, and with the exception of Fort Seward in Haines, all were abandoned by the 1920s. But we might consider Brooke Blower's reminder that forts 'facilitated the growth of other kinds of satellite communities in their orbit'.[79]

The War Department immediately found another justification for many of its Alaskan forts: as stations in a new communications network, the Army Signal Corps' Washington–Alaska Military Cable and Telegraph System (WAMCATS).[80] By 1903, a long stretch linked Nome and St Michael (via the new settler community of Fairbanks) to Fort Egbert at Eagle and across the Yukon border to Dawson City. Another extended from Fort Egbert to Fort Liscum at Valdez, running along a trail that the Army had just built from the Pacific coast between these two sites. An underwater route between Valdez and Seattle was completed in 1904. Signal Corps personnel were transferred from the Philippines to Alaska, and the Army's Chief Signal Officer proclaimed that 'the President or the Secretary of War can now reach, over strictly American lines of telegraph and cable, every important military command from the icy waters of Bering Strait to the tropical seas of

---

76 Schneider, "P. H. Ray", 12; Haycox, *Alaska: An American Colony*, 224–225.
77 *Report of the Governor of the District of Alaska*, 37, 62.
78 David Vine includes Alaskan forts in a striking map of "U.S. Military Bases Overseas" built between 1776 and 1903: *United States of War*, 104–105. For more on the US Army and the Klondike, see Dumonceaux, "Remaking Alaska-Yukon Borderlands"; Haycox, *Alaska*, 225–226.
79 Blower, "Nation of Outposts", 442.
80 The military effort was preceded by Western Union's attempt, in the final years of *Russkaya Amyerika*, to build a telegraph line from San Francisco to Moscow. See Hudson, *Connecting Alaskans*, 10–13.

the Sulu Archipelago'.[81] As the military realm of 'Alaska' was more definitively stitched together, and Alaska was drawn closer – at least for some, in the manner of time–space compression – to the rest of the United States, a Pacific imperial realm was also coming more fully into view. And in Alaska, the military personnel working at WAMCATS often took on multiple roles as 'weather observers, local postmasters, U.S. commissioners, and even U.S. marshals'.[82]

In 1898 and 1899, Abercrombie had been directed by the Army to seek out and more safely render that nationalistic 'all-American' route to the Klondike. From the ocean at Valdez, following and building over long-used Indigenous trails, his team carved out a path for travellers and packhorses, reaching Eagle in 1901. Even as gold fever subsided, or moved on, this trail, dubbed the Trans-Alaska Military Road, became a pivotal piece of settler infrastructure.[83] After Fairbanks experienced another gold boom, the road was diverted there in 1904, opening 'the interior', as the US National Parks Service puts it today, 'to modern civilization'.[84] Under the War Department, the new Board of Road Commissioners for Alaska (or Alaska Road Commission), set up in 1905 and headed by Wilds Richardson, Patrick Henry Ray's former associate, improved what eventually became known as the Richardson Highway. This conduit was eventually used to assist in the construction of another military road, the Alaska (or ALCAN) Highway, which met the Richardson Highway at Delta Junction, near the convergence of the Saas Na' (Delta) and Tth'itu' (Tanana) rivers, and where an Army airfield was established in the 1940s.[85]

The Signal Corps had been active amid war and occupation in both the Caribbean and the Philippines, and the individual most associated with WAMCATS, William 'Billy' Mitchell, then a lieutenant in the Corps, had been on duty in both regions before arriving in Alaska in 1901. It was Mitchell who supervised the surveying and planting of the telegraph line from Valdez to Eagle in 1901 and 1902. After further work connecting the various pieces was completed in 1903, he himself recalled that 'Alaska was open to

---

81 Quoted in Hudson, *Connecting Alaskans*, 18. See also Jessup, "Connecting Alaska", 384–408.
82 Hudson, *Connecting Alaska*, 20. The military did not relinquish control over Alaskan communications infrastructure until 1971.
83 United States Army, *Building Alaska*, 73.
84 "Valdez to Fairbanks Wayside", www.nps.gov/places/valdez-to-fairbanks-wayside.htm (accessed 4 July 2021).
85 The Delta River and others were given English names by Henry Allen. Thomas and Miller, "Post Marks 50th Anniversary", 36.

civilization'. No longer was it possible to 'shut out the white man from the North'.[86] Indeed, as was so common in settler colonial contexts, transportation and communication projects – in this case, both proposed and built by branches of the Department of War – 'opened' space for resettlement, connected communities centred on forts, and laid the literal groundwork for more military land-claiming and land-usage.[87]

Three decades later, stopping in Winnipeg and Edmonton, the Army Air Corps aviator Henry 'Hap' Arnold led ten B-10 bombers from Washington, DC to Fairbanks. These 1934 exploits, and Arnold's recommendations, set the stage for a pronouncement on Alaska's military geography that received lasting popular stature. Leaving his WAMCATS work for a role as a Signal Corps instructor at Fort Leavenworth – another consequential colonial outpost – Mitchell had acquired an interest in the military dimensions of flight, which led in subsequent decades to his role as a prominent US advocate of 'air power'.[88] By the late 1920s, not long after US Army biplanes crossed Alaska on an expedition around the globe, this profoundly cartographic outlook prompted Mitchell to propose that 'Alaska is really the key point to the whole Pacific Ocean'.[89] Following Arnold's flight, as the US Congress debated the construction of outpost airfields, Mitchell pronounced in supportive testimony that Alaska was 'the most strategic place in the world'.[90] His words were backed by a growing chorus of concern for Alaska's military vulnerability.[91] A cold weather testing station for aircraft at Fairbanks was soon authorized, and a site selection team seeking a location for 'what would essentially be . . . a twin city' chose one on the south bank of the Ch'eno (Chena) River, to the east of the town. But it was not until 1939 that Congress provided the funds for what became known as Ladd Field.[92] As Arnold recalled in his memoir, tellingly titled *Global Mission*, in 1940, 'our first air troops arrived, and our first aerial Arctic outpost was established'.[93]

The US Congress had also been persuaded in 1939 to fund the enlargement of a modest naval installation at Sitka and a new one at Sun'aq (Kodiak) – both places with long colonial histories.[94] The same year, civil servant Ernest

---

86 Quoted in Jessup, "Connecting Alaska", 401.
87 See Laduke and Cowen, "Beyond Wiindigo Infrastructure".
88 See Sherry, *Rise of American Air Power*.
89 Mitchell, "America, Air Power". On the 1942 Army flight, see Haycox, *Alaska: An American Colony*, 263.
90 This statement, from an individual familiar with hyperbole and self-embellishment, can be found in many sources. One is Perras, *Stepping Stones to Nowhere*, 30.
91 Haycox, *Alaska: An American Colony*, 277.   92 Price, *World War II Heritage*, 5–6.
93 Arnold, *Global Mission*, 211.   94 Conn et al., *Guarding the United States*, 224.

Gruening had been moved from the Department of the Interior's Division of Territories and Island Possessions to Alaska, as the colonial governor of that specific 'Territory'. He immediately began pressing for additional military assistance. In the intervening two years before December 1941, when Japanese planes appeared in the skies above the Naval Station at Hawai'i's Pearl Harbor – another nineteenth-century US acquisition – various preparations accelerated in Alaska. The War Department's ambition was a 'network of air bases and operating fields', housing 'combat forces'.[95] Early in 1940, after several months of momentum, the Department formally established the Alaska Defence Command (ADC) to oversee this network, and located the ADC's headquarters at Fort Richardson, a recently built Army post with an airfield (Elmendorf) in Anchorage.

Military Connections: World War II

Changes in Alaska's military geographies had been initiated, then, months and years before the Japanese aircraft attack on the military infrastructure and community of Dutch Harbour, on Nawan-Alaxsxa (Unalaska) Island in the Aleutian chain, on 3 and 4 June 1942. On 6 and 7 June, Japanese soldiers landed on the islands of Qisxa (Kiska) and Atan (Attu), respectively. What some call the US 'reconquest of the Aleutians' was an enormous endeavour, supported by 100,000 personnel.[96] Despite the nickname of the 'Forgotten War', this campaign has now generated substantial attention from military historians, and its details are not worth restaging here. The most lasting consequences were felt by the Unangan people of the islands: 881 residents were evacuated from nine villages and sent to crude internment camps called 'duration villages' in southeast Alaska. Dozens perished. At the war's end, some survivors were not permitted to return to their homes and were moved instead to other Aleutian communities.[97]

Even as some Indigenous Alaskans were being relocated and interned, and Indigenous activists were challenging segregation and inequality in Alaska's wartime centres, militarization simultaneously drew in some Alaska Natives, not least in the unpaid Alaska Territorial Guard (ATG), now an iconic feature

---

95 Conn et al., *Guarding the United States*, 224 See also Haycox, *Alaska: An American Colony*, 277–279; Immerwahr, *How to Hide*, 168.
96 Haycox, "Quonsets", 44; Haycox, *Alaska: An American Colony*, 276.
97 Mason, "You Can't Go Home"; Jones, *Century of Servitude*, 107–118. Forty-four residents of Attu, including forty-two Unangax, were captured and interned on the Japanese island of Hokkaido. Seventeen perished. Japanese-descent residents were also incarcerated in Alaska at locations like Fort Richardson, before being transported to prison camps in western states, inland from the coast. Haycox, *Alaska: An American Colony*, 279.

of the state's official military history. By the end of the 1940s, the ATG had been folded into the (paid) Army National Guard system. Along with the specialized Alaska Scouts, where Natives were also prominent, the ATG was still identified, decades after World War II, for its ability 'to live and operate in a harsh arctic environment that usually defeats other soldiers'.[98] Although it was based partially on experience, this characterization pointed to a lingering racialized distinction that was studied with scientific seriousness by the military during the Cold War.

Unsurprisingly, the scholarship on Alaska during World War II is rich, if uneven in emphasis. Some of it is marked by a schism between a 'traditional' past, on the one hand, and a future-facing wartime or post-war state – a modernity delivered from beyond Alaska.[99] The stress on the combination of wilderness, isolation, and the lack of integration is troubling, even as it is undoubtedly correct to assert that 'The war brought fundamental economic change to Alaska', driven by US federal spending. The Department of War disbursed almost $3 billion in Alaska and imported some 300,000 soldiers and other military personnel. Other government branches, from the Geological Survey to the Bureau of Indian Affairs, expanded their activities. Alaska's non-military population almost doubled during the war.[100]

As the Iñupiaq historian Holly Miowak Guise summarizes it, 'war connected the Alaska territory and its people in new ways', and no place was more significant to these connections than the 'increasingly militarized' Anchorage, a railroad town that more than tripled in population during the 1940s.[101] The transformation of Alaska was extraordinary, driven by the military appropriation of 25 per cent of the Territory's land area and the construction of 300 facilities by the War Department, along with associated transportation and logistical activity. Stephen Haycox emphasizes the tens of thousands of Quonset huts, erected first and foremost to address a precipitous housing shortage, but also employed as 'cafeterias, hospitals, and war rooms', as memorable features of these militarized landscapes.[102] In Fairbanks, meanwhile, the use of Ladd Field as a transfer point for the Lend-Lease arrangement with the

---

98 Wright, "Alaskan Scout", 16. See also Guise, "Haycock to Anchorage", 344. The ATG was launched by Gruening in 1939: Haycox, *Alaska: An American Colony*, 278.
99 See, for instance, Haycox, "Quonsets", 31.
100 Haycox, *Alaska: An American Colony*, 283.
101 Guise, "Haycock to Anchorage", 341–342. Guise is also responsible for a superb new website on Native Alaskans and World War II, www.ww2alaska.com. On Anchorage, see also Haycox, *Alaska: An American Colony*, 266.
102 Haycox, "Quonsets", 31–34, 41.

Soviet Union radically changed the site and the attached community: by June 1945, Ladd housed some 4,500 troops and officers.[103]

Some of these facilities, such as Fort Glenn on Umnax (Umnak) Island in the Aleutians, were abandoned soon after the war. Others, like the substantial airfield built on Adaax (Adak) immediately after the Japanese invasion of islands further west, lasted for over half a century, repurposed for an era of nuclear submarines and reconnaissance planes. But perhaps the most substantial landscape feature established in northern North America during the war stretched from British Columbia through Yukon and into eastern Alaska. The massive 'army of occupation', led by the US Army Corps of Engineers, which built the Alaska Highway and other Northwest Defense Projects, may have been 'peaceful' in one sense, but it 'could not help but recast' the region.[104] Such megaprojects transformed human and physical geographies, shattering ecosystems, depleting resources, and introducing diseases. They spurred additional scientific surveys, communication systems, energy extraction, and parallel employment.[105]

Hundreds of cold injuries on Attu in 1943 revealed lingering inadequacies in the Army's field studies of clothing and other equipment for northern combat. The experience of the Aleutians was one factor among many in a global war that led the Army Quartermaster Corps to pursue more formal inquiries on cold-weather warfare.[106] But while Alaska 'seethed with activity' during the war, this research was conducted elsewhere. Its arrival in the north within months of the conflict's conclusion indicates how quickly Alaska was drawn into what became known as the Cold War.[107]

Northern Indoctrination: The Beginnings of the Cold War

In the fall of 1950, the National Academy of Science and the National Research Council hosted the first Alaskan Science conference in Washington, DC. Opened by Ernest Gruening, the event featured an impressive roster of participants, including representatives of various US government departments, the Arctic Institute of North America, and the Smithsonian Institution. Researchers working for or with military agencies were also present, as they were in subsequent Alaskan Science Conferences.[108] The location of the event alone signals the centrality of

---

103 Price, *World War II Heritage*, 7–8.   104 Coates and Morrison, *Alaska Highway*, 8–9.
105 Lackenbauer and Farish, "Cold War", 925–926.   106 Farish, "Lab and the Land", 10.
107 Jenness, *Eskimo Administration I*, 39.
108 *Proceedings of the Alaskan Science Conference*.

Alaska, at mid-century, at the meeting points of government and science. And 'government', in Alaska, still often meant the DoD, which had emerged out of World War II as a major agent of scientific inquiry. The military's history in Alaska, and Alaska's relevance to the nascent Cold War came together to drive a militarization in the late 1940s and 1950s which was as much *conceit* as it was construction.

Alaska is minimally treated in scholarship on the Cold War, at least that which travels beyond northern regions. This absence is striking because 'astonishingly, the level of spending [in Alaska] continued after 1945'.[109] Despite their frequently narrow, uncritical approach, some of the richest reports of this period have been provided by military historians, who take as their starting point the emergence of the region 'as the linchpin of American air atomic strategy'.[110] The ramifications of turning the Arctic into what Arnold's successor Carl Spaatz labelled 'our primary operational objective' were enormous.[111] By 1950, Seward's 'stepping stones' had become the beginning of what another Secretary of State, Dean Acheson, notoriously called a 'defensive perimeter', extending once again to Asia.[112] But Spaatz and the military were also reinventing another nineteenth-century trope, invoking mid-century aeroplanes to urge consideration of a 'new frontier' of 'polar geopolitics'.[113]

Of course, both cartographic premises depended on the prior extension of a US 'perimeter' *to Alaska*. And once again, as the Canadian anthropologist Diamond Jenness reported, World War II and the early Cold War had 'provoked a grave upheaval' in Indigenous communities, as a result of new military establishments that 'restricted movements and activities', but also provided wage-employment, largely for young men.[114]

'Cold areas', a 1949 Army Quartermaster Corps handbook reminded readers, 'can be military hot spots'. For the DoD, in the years after World War II, 'going North' was first and foremost a generic move, or a regional one.[115] As these military manuals proliferated, some of them, in Arnold's words, 'covered only the area around Alaska, but the salient principles held true for all Arctic regions'.[116] Behind this habit was a much older

---

109 Haycox, *Alaska: An American Colony*, 174.   110 Farquhar, "Arctic Linchpin", 36.
111 Quoted in Farish, "Lab and the Land", 10.
112 Acheson, "Crisis in Asia", 116. This was a reprint of Acheson's remarks at the National Press Club on 12 January 1950.
113 "America and Polar Geopolitics".   114 Jenness, *Eskimo Administration I*, 39.
115 *A Soldier's Guide*, 4–5.   116 Arnold, *Global Mission*, 212.

presumption – namely that the military was a suitable, even superior purveyor of geographic knowledge about Alaska, and by extension the Arctic and the poles.[117] But like the back cover of *A Soldier's Guide for Keeping Warm in Extremely Cold Climates*, which featured a rough map centred on the gap of 60 km between the Seward Peninsula and the Soviet Union, the invocation to travel north often steered soldiers to Alaska.

Building on the experiences and challenges of the war, a series of new institutions turned the entire territory into a Cold War laboratory for military-scientific research on 'cold areas', drawing Alaska into a planetary geography produced by and for the DoD that prioritized 'extreme climatic environments'.[118] Collectively, their intimate activities and experiments 'were given urgency by and contributed to a powerful geopolitical logic'.[119]

In the late summer of 1946, some 1,500 soldiers arrived at the Alaskan port of Whittier and boarded a train bound for Fairbanks. The following January, based at Ladd Field and other locations, they participated in the media spectacle of the Army's Task Force Frigid, the sort of exercise that has been staged in Alaska ever since.[120] Notably, amidst this Task Force, the military's unified Alaskan Command (ALCOM) was formalized in January 1947. This 'guaranteed the standing' of both Fort Richardson and Elmendorf Air Force Base – and thus an intensely militaristic character to mid-century Anchorage.[121]

Seeking a site for a yet larger performance after Frigid, officials settled on the Big Delta Army Airfield southeast of Fairbanks, which had been mostly inactive since the war. Exercise Yukon, held in the winter of 1947–48, was hardly the last such operation in Alaska, but it remains decisive for two reasons. First, it was explicitly designed to lay the groundwork for defining still-vague 'doctrines, tactics, techniques and organization for further Arctic operations', with an emphasis on 'methods of training and indoctrination'. Second, it resulted in the creation of a new Army installation, pulled away from Ladd: U.S. Troops, Big Delta, Alaska (a World War II name, revived). Located in the 'extreme' physiographically diverse Alaskan interior, it was

---

117 Farish, "Lab and the Land", 9; Farish, "Canons and Wars", 45.
118 Farish, "Lab and the Land", 4. See also Herzberg et al., eds., *Ice and Snow*.
119 Farish, "Lab and the Land", 6. Another site I do not mention was launched in 1947: the Navy's Arctic Research Laboratory (later the Naval Arctic Research Laboratory), which operated at Point Barrow until 1980. See Reed and Ronhovde, *Arctic Laboratory*.
120 Steward, "Army in the Arctic", 37. Another Task Force, Williwaw, headed to Adak. Farish, "Canons and Wars", 45.
121 Farish, "Lab and the Land", 10.

23 First Century of US Militarization in Alaska

home to a new Arctic Training Center where these same 'methods' would be taught.[122] Within the Center, a Test and Development Section and an Indoctrination School were set up alongside the Training Company.[123] Together, these represent the early manifestations of today's Cold Regions Testing Center and Northern Warfare Training Center, still located at or affiliated with the Big Delta base – renamed Fort Greely in 1955 – and the surrounding lands.[124] For some seventy-five years, as a name like Indoctrination School implies, this swath of Alaska has been a site for the fashioning and circulation of narratives, even if often prosaic, about the north. It is a place where soldiers can experience a kind of purified military Arctic, 'where life – as survival – is a violent proposition'.[125]

In ahistorical prose, one official history concludes that at Fort Greely and in 'winter maneuvers throughout Alaska, men have learned how to live with, not resist', the many 'treacherous' features of the Arctic.[126] Over a century, this language of antagonism had shifted from race to nature. But the human subject research of another Alaskan facility, also founded in 1947, is a reminder of the ways that even during the Cold War, race was also employed as a lens for understanding Arctic nature. Ladd Air Force Base (renamed Fort Wainwright when the Army took it over at the end of the 1950s), was a crucial node for northern air defence, 'strategic reconnaissance', and a modest number of aircraft and equipment tests, but at the Air Force's Arctic Aeromedical Laboratory (AAL), the mission was a different sort of cold-weather experimentation.[127]

For twenty years, before its functions and records were moved to Texas, the AAL pursued research on military bodies, or different bodies that might contrast usefully with military bodies, in Arctic 'climates'. By 1950, it had conducted studies in some twenty-five Alaskan locations, blurring the

---

122 Woodman, *Duty Station Northwest*, 55–59; Thomas and Miller, "Post Marks 50th Anniversary", 37; United States Army, *U.S. Army in Alaska*, 101; Farish, "Canons and Wars", 46.

123 United States Army, *US Army in Alaska*, 101; Thomas and Miller, "Post Marks 50th Anniversary", 37–38. Amid a widespread early Cold War interest in *survival* across the US military, the Air Force ran a similar 'indoctrination' school in Nome, at Marks Air Force Base. See Farish, "Canons and Wars", 46–47.

124 Adolphus Greely's extensive military career included the Civil War and colonial campaigns in the North American west. Concurrent with Philip Henry Ray, Greely also led a notable and unpleasant Army International Polar Year expedition (1881–84) to the far north of Umingmak Nuna (Ellesmere Island), where his team established the military post and research station named Fort Conger. Later, Greely was Chief Signal Officer as telegraph lines were erected across the US empire, including WAMCATS in Alaska.

125 Farish, "Canons and Wars", 47.   126 United States Army, *US Army in Alaska*, 101.

127 Price, *World War II Heritage*, 8.

boundary between laboratory and field, such that Alaska and even the 'Arctic basin' were extensions of the Ladd space on the one hand and proper environments for military inquiry on the other hand. In the same year, the AAL's most notorious project was launched by Kaare Rodahl, the Norwegian head of its Department of Physiology. Seeking more evidence on acclimatization, Rodahl and colleagues conducted tests in Indigenous communities and in some cases flew Native people to Fairbanks for further scrutiny in a cold chamber. Dozens of tracer administrations of the radioisotope iodine-131 were administered without fully informing participants of the risks and purpose of the research. These efforts were persistently characterized by racial categorization – and in the process 'modernized' the colonial distinctions and hierarchies of nineteenth-century Alaska.[128]

When they resurfaced after the Cold War, at an Anchorage conference on Arctic contamination, Rodahl's practices caused widespread outrage, and when the National Research Council was tasked with a formal investigation, a Fairbanks public hearing and interviews in two communities found outrage among Alaska Natives with respect to Rodahl's methods but also to military research beyond Ladd Air Force Base. Just as the acclimatization project was only one thread of inquiry at the AAL, and the AAL was only one of several institutions working in the military laboratory of Cold War Alaska, the generalized resentment was directed at colonialism and its military dimensions.[129] When the Indigenous-run North Slope Borough commissioned their own investigation into the iodine-131 experiments, the approach adopted was broader and drew the narrative forward, connecting the AAL's project to fallout and food chains, waste disposal, and even decaying Russian reactors, in the process offering 'a more comprehensive portrait of Alaskan militarization'.[130]

The clearest corollary to Rodahl's research was conducted by a nominally civilian agency, although in this instance the distinction is unhelpful. During the 1950s, as the United States dramatically increased its stockpile of nuclear weapons and tested them extensively at both its Pacific Ocean and Nevada Proving Grounds, scientists and bureaucrats associated with the programme began to suggest that these destructive devices might have a 'peaceful' use, as tools of 'earthmoving'. By June 1958 this had consolidated into the Atomic Energy Commission's (AEC) portentously named Project Plowshare. Over twelve years, Plowshare conducted twenty-seven nuclear tests – twenty-three

---

128 Farish, "Lab and the Land", 12–13, 15–21.   129 Farish, "Lab and the Land", 3, 19.
130 Farish, "Lab and the Land", 26. Even the title of the report is specious: *Threats to the Health and Environment of Alaska Natives in the Nuclear Age*.

in Nevada and two each in Colorado and New Mexico. None was staged in Alaska, but the new state was the focus of intense AEC attention. Plowshare's Project Chariot proposed multiple detonations to create a harbour and a channel to the ocean at Uivaq Qanitoq (Cape Thompson), on the Chukchi Sea in northwest Alaska. As with other prospective locations for both sudden and slow Cold War violence, Cape Thompson had been explicitly chosen for its 'remoteness', but it was (and is) only about 40 km from the Iñupiat community of Tikigaq (Point Hope). Both before and after a visit from Plowshare representatives, in late 1959 and early 1960 respectively, the village council voted unanimously to oppose Chariot. This and additional criticism led the AEC to end its Chariot efforts in 1962, but not before experimenting with radioactive tracers and bulldozing over contaminated soil.[131]

Conclusion

Nowhere else is the terrain more available, more unrestricted, or more challenging.[132]

If it is instructive to understand US military activity in Alaska after the 1867 Purchase as tied to broader imperial histories, then the military building, exercises, and experiments staged at and supported by Fort Greely, Ladd Air Force Base, and other major nodes of Cold War activity should also be placed into the vast web of US military activity in the middle of the twentieth century, from the North American west to the Marshall Islands. A small portion of this activity, including some of the AAL's work, has generated official reckonings – what Tess Lanzarotta calls 'ethics in retrospect'.[133] More importantly, before, amid, and beyond these retrospectives, the examples of the AAL or Project Chariot point to Alaskan iterations of the relationship between militarization and Indigenous anger and political mobilization. We are still left, though, with vast spans of time and space wherein a many bodies and landscapes have been treated by an enormously powerful institution as expendable in the name of strategic utility.

---

131 Kirsch, *Proving Grounds*, especially 66; Edwards, "Nuclear Colonialism", 110–111; and O'Neill, *Firecracker Boys*, first published in 1994.
132 Kiernan, "Winter Training in Alaska", 10.   133 Lanzarotta, "Ethics in Retrospect".

Bibliography

Acheson, Dean, "Crisis in Asia: An Examination of U.S. Policy", *Department of State Bulletin* 22 (23 January 1950): 111–118.

Aguirre, Robert D., "Wide Angle: Eadweard Muybridge, the Pacific Coast, and Trans-Indigenous Representation", *Victorian Literature and Culture* 49 (2021): 55–72.

Allan, Chris, ed., *As the Old Flag Came Down: Eyewitness Accounts of the October 18, 1867 Alaska Transfer Ceremony* (Anchorage: Alaska Historical Society, 2018).

Allen, Henry T., *Report of an Expedition to the Copper, Tananá, and Koyukuk Rivers, in the Territory of Alaska, in the Year 1885, 'For the Purpose of Obtaining all Information which will be Valuable and Important, especially to the Military Branch of the Government'* (Washington, DC: Government Printing Office, 1887).

"America and Polar Geopolitics", *Army Talk* 173 (26 April 1947): 1–9.

Annual Report of the Secretary of War on the Operations of the Department for the Year 1870, Vol. 1 (Washington, DC: Government Printing Office, 1870).

Arnett, Jessica, "Between Empires and Frontiers: Alaska Native Sovereignty and U.S. Settler Imperialism", PhD diss. (University of Minnesota, 2018).

Arnold, H. H., *Global Mission* (New York: Harper, 1949).

A Soldier's Guide for Keeping Warm in Extremely Cold Climates (Washington, DC: Office of The Quartermaster General, US Army, 1949).

Banner, Stuart, *Possessing the Pacific: Land, Settlers, and Indigenous People from Australia to Alaska* (Cambridge, MA: Harvard University Press, 2007).

Bjork, Katharine, *Prairie Imperialists: The Indian Country Origins of American Empire*. (Philadelphia: University of Pennsylvania Press, 2019).

Blackhawk, Ned, *Violence Over the Land: Indians and Empires in the Early American West* (Cambridge, MA: Harvard University Press, 2006).

Blower, Brooke L., "Nation of Outposts: Forts, Factories, Bases, and the Making of American Power", *Diplomatic History* 41 (2017): 439–459.

Bockstoce, John R., *Furs and Frontiers in the Far North: The Contest Among Native and Foreign Nations for the Bering Strait Fur Trade* (New Haven: Yale University Press, 2009).

Broadhead, Michael J., "The United States Army Signal Service and Natural History in Alaska, 1874–1883", *Pacific Northwest Quarterly* 86 (1995): 72–82.

Brockell, Gillian, "Civil War Massacre Launched Reparations Debate", *Washington Post* (11 September 2014), www.washingtonpost.com/lifestyle/style/civil-war-massacre-launched-reparations-debate/2014/09/11/ab269406-349c-11e4-9e92-0899b306bbea_story.html.

Burch, Ernest S., Jr, "Smithsonian Contributions to Alaskan Ethnography: The First IPY Expedition to Barrow, 1881–1883", in Igor Krupnik, Michael A. Lang, and Scott E. Miller, eds., *Smithsonian at the Poles: Contributions to International Polar Year Science* (Washington, DC: Smithsonian Institution Scholarly Press, 2009), pp. 89–98.

Campbell, Robert, *In Darkest Alaska: Travel and Empire Along the Inside Passage* (Philadelphia: University of Pennsylvania Press, 2008).

Charlton, Ryan, "'Our Ice-Islands': Images of Alaska in the Reconstruction Era", *Journal of Transnational American Studies* 10 (2019): 23–46.

Coates, Kenneth S., and William R. Morrison, *The Alaska Highway in World War II: The U.S. Army of Occupation in Canada's Northwest* (Norman: University of Oklahoma Press, 1992).

Conn, Stetson, Rose C. Engelman, and Byron Fairchild, *Guarding the United States and its Outposts* (Washington, DC: Center of Military History, United States Army, 2000).

Dauenhauer, Nora Marks, Richard Dauenhauer, and Lydia T. Black, eds., *Anóoshi Lingít Aaní Ká: Russians in Tlingit America: The Battles of Sitka, 1802 and 1804* (Seattle and Juneau: University of Washington Press and Sealaska Heritage Institute, 2008).

Dean, Jonathan R., "'Uses of the Past' on the Northwest Coast: The Russian American Company and Tlingit Nobility, 1825–1867", *Ethnohistory* 42 (1995): 265–302.

Demuth, Bathsheba, *Floating Coast: An Environmental History of the Bering Strait* (New York: Norton, 2019).

Demuth, Bathsheba, "Statehood and Other Events: Whales, Alaska Natives, and Perspectives on History", *Process: A Blog for American History* (12 August 2019). www.processhistory.org/demuth-alaska-statehood

Dumonceaux, Scott Drew Cassie, "Remaking the Alaska–Yukon Borderlands: The North-West Mounted Police, the United States Army, and the Klondike Gold Rush", PhD diss. (University of Calgary, 2020).

Dunbar-Ortiz, Roxanne, *An Indigenous Peoples' History of the United States* (Boston: Beacon, 2014).

Edwards, Nelta, "Nuclear Colonialism and the Social Construction of Landscape in Alaska", *Environmental Justice* 4 (2011): 109–114.

Eperjesi, John R., "Basing the Pacific: Exceptional Spaces of the Wilkes Exploring Expedition, 1838–1842", *Amerasia Journal* 37 (2011): 1–17.

Farish, Matthew, "Canons and Wars: American Military Geography and the Limits of Disciplines", *Journal of Historical Geography* 49 (2015): 39–48.

Farish, Matthew, "The Lab and the Land: Overcoming the Arctic in Cold War Alaska", *Isis* 104 (2013): 1–29.

Farquhar, John T., "Arctic Linchpin: The Polar Concept in American Air Atomic Strategy, 1946–48", *Air Power History* 61 (2014): 34–45.

Fritz, Stacey A., "DEW Line Passage: Tracing the Legacies of Arctic Militarization", PhD diss. (University of Alaska Fairbanks, 2010).

Griffin, Kristy, "Treaty of Cession: The Tlingit Knew", *Juneau Empire* (27 June 2017). www.juneauempire.com/life/treaty-of-cession-the-tlingit-knew/

Guise, Holly Miowak, "Haycock to Anchorage: Connecting the Wartime Landscape with Stories from World War II Veteran Holger 'Jorgy' Jorgensen", in Jim Barnett and Ian Hartman, eds., *Imagining Anchorage* (Anchorage: University of Alaska Press, 2018), pp. 340–355.

Haycox, Stephen, "Quonsets, Alaska, and World War II", in J. Decker and C. Chiei, eds., *Quonset Hut* (Princeton: Princeton Architectural Press, 2005), pp. 31–45.

Haycox, Stephen, "Truth and Expectation: Myth in Alaska History", *Northern Review* 6 (1990): 59–82.

Haycox, Stephen W., *Alaska: An American Colony*, 2nd edition (Seattle: University of Washington Press, 2020).

Heefner, Gretchen, "'A Slice of Their Sovereignty': Negotiating the U.S. Empire of Bases, Wheelus Field, Libya, 1950–1954", *Diplomatic History* 41 (2017): 50–77.

Herzberg, Julia, Christian Kehrt, and Franziska Torma, eds., *Ice and Snow in the Cold War: Histories of Extreme Climatic Environments* (New York: Berghahn, 2019).
Hill, Michael A., "Imperial Stepping Stone: Bridging Continental and Overseas Empire in Alaska", *Diplomatic History* 44 (2020): 76–101.
Hill, Michael A., "The Myth of Seward's Folly", *Western Historical Quarterly* 50 (2019): 43–64.
Hinckley, Ted C., "The United States Frontier at Sitka, 1867–1873", *Pacific Northwest Quarterly* 60 (1969): 57–65.
Hinckley, Ted C., "William H. Seward Visits His Purchase", *Oregon Historical Quarterly* 72 (1971): 127–147.
Hope, Herb, "The Kiks.ádi Survival March of 1804" (2000), www.alaskool.org (accessed 18 March 2021).
Hudson, Heather E., *Connecting Alaskans: Telecommunications in Alaska from Telegraph to Broadband* (Fairbanks: University of Alaska Press, 2015).
Hughes, Nathaniel Cheairs, Jr, and Gordon D. Whitney, *Jefferson Davis in Blue: The Life of Sherman's Relentless Warrior* (Baton Rouge: Louisiana State University Press, 2002).
Hummel, Laurel J., "The U.S. Military as Geographical Agent: The Case of Cold War Alaska", *Geographical Review* 95 (2005): 47–72.
Immerwahr, Daniel, *How to Hide an Empire: A History of the Greater United States* (New York: Farrar, Straus and Giroux, 2019).
Jenness, Diamond, *Eskimo Administration I: Alaska* (Montreal: Arctic Institute of North America, 1962).
Jessup, Eric, "Connecting Alaska: The Washington–Alaska Military Cable and Telegraph System", *Journal of the Gilded Age and Progressive Era* 6 (2007): 384–408.
Jones, Dorothy Knee, *A Century of Servitude: Pribilof Aleuts Under U.S. Rule* (Lanham, MD: University Press of America, 1980).
Jones, Zachary R., "'Search for and Destroy': US Army Relations with Alaska's Tlingit Indians and the Kake War of 1869", *Ethnohistory* 60 (2013): 1–26.
Kan, Sergei, *Memory Eternal: Tlingit Culture and Russian Orthodox Christianity through Two Centuries* (Seattle: University of Washington Press, 2014).
Kiernan, Major David R., "Winter Training in Alaska", *Infantry* (November–December 1980): 10–12.
Kirsch, Scott, *Proving Grounds: Project Plowshare and the Unrealized Dream of Nuclear Earthmoving* (New Brunswick, NJ: Rutgers University Press, 2005).
Kwong, Emily, "150 Years in the Making, Kiks.ádi Gather to Commemorate Loss of Land", *KCAW* (17 October 2017), www.kcaw.org/2017/10/17/150-years-making-kiks-adi-gather-commemorate-loss-land.
Lackenbauer, P. Whitney, and Matthew Farish, "The Cold War on Canadian Soil: Militarizing a Northern Environment", *Environmental History* 12 (2007): 920–950.
Laduke, Winona, and Deborah Cowen, "Beyond Wiindigo Infrastructure", *South Atlantic Quarterly* 119 (2020): 243–268.
Lanzarotta, Tess, "Ethics in Retrospect: Biomedical Research, Colonial Violence, and Iñupiat Sovereignty in the Alaskan Arctic", *Social Studies of Science* 50 (2020): 778–801.
Livingstone, David N., "Race, Space, and Moral Climatology: Notes Toward a Genealogy", *Journal of Historical Geography* 28 (2002): 159–180.
Love, Eric T., *Race Over Empire: Racism and U.S. Imperialism, 1865–1900* (Chapel Hill: University of North Carolina Press, 2004).

Lutz, Catherine, "Making War at Home in the United States: Militarization and the Current Crisis", *American Anthropologist* 104 (2002): 723–735.

Lutz, Catherine, "The Military Normal: Feeling at Home with Counterinsurgency in the United States", in Network of Concerned Anthropologists, ed., *The Counter-counterinsurgency Manual: Or, Notes on Demilitarizing American Society* (Chicago: University of Chicago Press, 2009), pp. 23–37.

Marsett, Robert, "Journey Through the Wilderness: Lieutenant Henry T. Allen's 1885 Exploration of Interior Alaska", https://armyhistory.org/5102-2/ (accessed 3 July 2021).

Mason, Rachel, "You Can't Go Home Again: Processes of Displacement and Emplacement in the 'Lost Villages' of the Aleutians", *Alaska Journal of Anthropology* 8 (2010): 17–29.

Mighetto, Lisa, and Carla Homstad, *Engineering in the Far North: A History of the U.S. Army Engineer District in Alaska, 1867–1992* (Missoula, MT: Historical Research Associates, Inc., 1997).

Mitchell, William, "America, Air Power and the Pacific" (1928), from the William Mitchell papers, Library of Congress. www.japanairraids.org/?page_id=4763 (accessed 5 July 2021).

O'Neill, Dan, *The Firecracker Boys: H-Bombs, Inupiat Eskimos, and the Roots of the Environmental Movement* (New York: Basic, 2007).

Pegues, Juliana Hu, "Settler Orientalism", *Verge: Studies in Global Asias* 5 (2019): 12–18.

Pegues, Juliana Hu, *Space–Time Colonialism: Alaska's Indigenous and Asian Entanglements* (Chapel Hill: University of North Carolina Press, 2021).

Perras, Galen Roger, *Stepping Stones to Nowhere: The Aleutian Islands, Alaska, and American Military Strategy, 1867–1945* (Vancouver: University of British Columbia Press, 2003).

Poulson, Rebecca, "The Legacy of Sitka's First Ten Years under the American Flag, 1867-1877", https://alaskahistoricalsociety.org/about-ahs/special-projects/150treaty/150th-resource-library/new-articles/the-legacy-of-sitkas-first-ten-years-under-the-american-flag-1867-1877/ (accessed 3 July 2021).

Price, Kathy, *The World War II Heritage of Ladd Field, Fairbanks, Alaska* (Fort Collins: Center for Environmental Management of Military Lands, 2004).

Proceedings of the Alaskan Science Conference (Washington, DC: National Research Council–National Academy of Sciences, 1951).

Rana, Aziz, *The Two Faces of American Freedom* (Cambridge, MA: Harvard University Press, 2010).

Reed, John C., and Andreas G. Ronhovde, *Arctic Laboratory: A History (1947–1966) of the Naval Arctic Research Laboratory at Point Barrow, Alaska* (Washington, DC: Arctic Institute of North America, 1971).

Report of the Governor of the District of Alaska to the Secretary of the Interior, 1900 (Washington: Government Printing Office, 1900).

"Rousseau, Lovell Harrison (1818–1869)", in *Biographical Dictionary of the United States Congress*, https://bioguide.congress.gov (accessed 26 March 2021).

Russell, Caskey, "Cultures in Collision: Cosmology, Jurisprudence, and Religion in Tlingit Territory", *American Indian Quarterly* 33 (2009): 230–252.

Schneider, William, "P. H. Ray on the Alaskan Frontier in the Fall of 1897" (1985), https://uafanlc.alaska.edu/Offline/UK002H2008-digitalfiles/Library%20Books/PH%20Ray%20on%20the%20Alaskan%20Frontier.PDF (accessed 3 July 2021).

Schwatka, Frederick, *Report of a Military Reconnaissance in Alaska, Made in 1883* (Washington, DC: Government Printing Office, 1885).

Seward, William H., "Speech of William H. Seward at Sitka, August 12, 1869". www.loc.gov/item/48031388 (accessed 30 June 2021).

Sherry, Michael S., *The Rise of American Air Power: The Creation of Armageddon* (New Haven: Yale University Press, 1987).

Solnit, Rebecca, *River of Shadows: Eadweard Muybridge and the Technological Wild West* (New York: Viking, 2003).

Soluri, John, "Fur Sealing and Unsettled Sovereignties", in Kristin L. Hoganson and Jay Sexton, eds., *Across Empires: Taking U.S. History into Transimperial Terrain* (Durham, NC: Duke University Press, 2019), pp. 25–45.

Steward, Hal D., Major, "The Army in the Arctic", *Coast Artillery Journal* (March–April 1947): 37–40.

Thomas, Doris, and Spc. Kim Miller, "Post Marks 50th Anniversary", *Arctic Soldier* (Fall 1992): 36–39.

Threats to the Health and Environment of Alaska Natives in the Nuclear Age (Anchorage: Birch, Horton, Bittner & Cherot, 1997).

"Transfer of Alaska to the United States", *Washington Historical Quarterly* 3 (1908): 83–91.

Urrea, Ian S., "'Our People Scattered': Violence, Captivity, and Colonialism on the Northwest Coast, 1774–1846", MA diss. (University of Oregon, 2019).

United States Army, *Building Alaska with the US Army, 1867–1962*. Pamphlet number 355-5 (Anchorage: Headquarters, United States Army, Alaska, 1962).

United States Army, *The U.S. Army in Alaska* (Anchorage: Headquarters, United States Army, Alaska, 1972).

Venn, George, "Soldier to Advocate: C.E.S. Wood's 1877 Diary of Alaska and the Nez Perce Conflict", *Oregon Historical Quarterly* 106 (2005): 34–75.

Vine, David, *The United States of War: A Global History of America's Endless Conflicts, from Columbus to the Islamic State* (Berkeley: University of California Press, 2020).

Vinkovetsky, Ilya, *Russian America: An Overseas Colony of a Continental Empire, 1804–1867* (Oxford: Oxford University Press, 2011).

Westad, Odd Arne, *The Cold War: A World History* (New York: Basic Books, 2017).

Whitehead, John, *Completing the Union: Alaska, Hawai'i, and the Battle for Statehood* (Albuquerque: University of New Mexico Press, 2004).

Williams, Maria Sháa Tláa, ed., *The Alaska Native Reader: History, Culture, Politics* (Durham, NC: Duke University Press, 2009).

Woodman, Lyman L., *Duty Station Northwest: The U.S. Army in Alaska and Western Canada, 1867–1987*, Vol. 3: *1945–1987* (Anchorage: Alaska Historical Society, 1996).

Worl, Rosita, "Tlingit Law, American Justice and the Destruction of Tlingit Villages" (19 November 2012), https://vimeo.com/53955608 (accessed 6 July 2021).

Wright, Walter E., Captain, "Alaskan Scout", *Infantry* (May–June 1982): 15–16.

Young, Marilyn B., "'I Was Thinking, As I Often Do These Days, of War': The United States in the Twenty-First Century", *Diplomatic History* 36 (2012): 1–15.

24

Petroleum Development and the State in Arctic North America, 1919–1977

PHILIP A. WIGHT

Introduction

The winds howled as the members of the First Combat Intelligence Platoon mushed their huskies through the darkness of an Arctic January day. Temperatures reached −43 degrees Celsius as the men scouted the river valleys and mountain passes of Alaska's Brooks Range. This was no ordinary mission, and these men were no regular infantry. The platoon, comprised of soldiers from the Alaska Territorial Guard (ATG) – a military reserve force of Alaska Natives known as the 'Eskimo Scouts' – was the vanguard of the first reconnaissance survey of a petroleum pipeline from Alaska's North Slope. In the early winter of 1945, three ATG patrols totalling eight men spearheaded a survey of a potential pipeline route from Livengood, north of Fairbanks, to Umiat on the North Slope. The men travelled over 3,200 km by dogsled in the middle of Arctic winter, battling snow deeper than a metre. Here was a moment when traditional Indigenous travel skills and knowledge of the topography proved indispensable for the American war effort and the exploration of Arctic petroleum. ATG members achieved their objective and laid out a feasible pipeline route for the military's petroleum needs. These men were vital for the Navy's petroleum explorations, yet just one small part of the military's unprecedented intervention in the North American Arctic.[1]

The ATG's 1944–45 pipeline survey offers a suggestive window into the hidden and unwritten histories of North American Arctic petroleum exploration. The contribution of these Alaska Native soldiers in ground-truthing the first pipeline survey is almost unknown in Alaska today, despite the centrality of the Trans-Alaska Pipeline System (TAPS) to the state's contemporary political economy. For decades afterwards, private industry – including the

[1] Corbin, *COM ICE PAC Reports*, 125–127. For a full history of the ATG, see Marston, *Men of the Tundra*.

owners of TAPS – used this Native-led survey and related geophysical oil explorations to advance the construction of an Arctic artery. Scholars often use the Prudhoe Bay oil strike in 1968 and the TAPS controversy as shorthand for the beginning of the Arctic oil era, but these developments were the culmination of several decades of intensive military exploration, state-sponsored scientific research, and the construction of novel oil pipelines in the far north.[2] Starting with World War II, the unprecedented intervention of the US government transformed Alaska and northwest Canada into an expansive petroleum province and created the preconditions for development by private industry.

This chapter advances three broad arguments concerning the nature, timing, and political economy of petroleum development in Arctic North America.

First, the exigencies of World War II and the Cold War compelled the US and Canadian federal governments to transform the American Arctic into ground zero for petroleum innovation and production. The state – especially through its military organizations – was the prime mover in the exploration and development of Arctic oil. While private industry made important contributions, scholars must recognize the militarized nature of what historian Paul Sabin evocatively called the 'hydrocarbon frontier'.[3] Between the 1920s and 1950s, US and Canadian federal governments explored and proved out a vast swath of Arctic America, stretching from northwestern Alaska to the Mackenzie River delta. The nature of the north invited robust state intervention. Far from established markets, extraordinarily expensive, and offering daunting environmental challenges, northern development demanded a unique set of resources which made the military uniquely suitable: deep pockets, a wartime social licence, the application of cutting-edge science and technology, and the ability to construct novel Arctic infrastructures without earning a return on investment. In addition to confirming the existence of large oil and gas reservoirs in the region, the US military also constructed the first two Arctic-grade petroleum pipeline systems. Innovating and constructing petroleum transportation systems proved the key to developing hydrocarbons in the American Arctic. While state power proved necessary to overcome the nature of the far north, its frenetic exploration and development of oil left an enduring and indelible impression upon the Arctic environment. Military petroleum efforts helped awaken a burgeoning environmental movement to the hazards of Arctic oil

---

2 Among many examples, see Willis, *Alaska's Place*, and Busenberg, *Oil and Wilderness*.
3 Sabin, "Voices".

development long before the discovery of the continent's largest oil field at Prudhoe Bay.

Second, northern hydrocarbon development was an international project, which sprawled beyond political boundaries and was bound up with the imbricated nature of widespread military infrastructure projects during the war. This trend began in peacetime, when discoveries of oil in Alaska and the Northwest Territories fuelled each other in 1919 and 1920. During the emergency of World War II, the United States and Canada constructed the Northwest Staging Route (NWSR) and the Alaska-Canadian Highway (ALCAN) – petroleum-thirsty infrastructures that necessitated the CANOL (short for Canadian Oil) pipeline system, the first Arctic-grade petroleum supply chain. Historians have too often treated these developments as separate endeavours, but these projects must be viewed holistically.[4] To this end, the NWSR, ALCAN, and CANOL projects are analysed herein as a singular megaproject – the 'Northwest Defense Complex'. At its core, the Northwest Defense Complex constituted a sprawling transportation infrastructure for moving military aircraft and petroleum to and through northwestern America. The complex transformed the region, resulted in the first far north petroleum pipeline, spurred the US Navy to explore the Alaskan Arctic for oil between 1944 and 1953, and paved the way for Cold War petroleum infrastructures throughout the region. Only by seeing the interconnected and far-reaching nature of this project can historians recognize its expansive legacy and the role of the state in northern hydrocarbon development.

Finally, the realization of the militarized hydrocarbon frontier was not simply about national security and defence – it was about how state power would transform these regions for peacetime commercial use. While both the United States and Canadian State adopted various policies oscillating between inducing private investment and reserving promising areas for state-directed production, ultimately both governments played an outsized role in encouraging private oil production. Beginning in the 1920s and culminating between 1942 and 1953, the US military provided 'spadework', to use historian Megan Black's evocative term, that fuelled private oil exploration throughout the region and helped to define the ultimate route for a pipeline from Prudhoe Bay to Valdez. Land surveys, exploration drilling, and the expulsion of Inuit and Iñupiat from ancestral lands helped to incorporate territory for

---

4 Among many examples, see Ramley, *Crooked Road*, and McClure and McClure, *We Fought the Road*.

development and 'twist the earth into a template for capitalist activity', according to Black.[5] The state funded private oil companies such as Standard Oil of California and Imperial Oil to explore the Arctic, provided them surplus equipment, turned over all pertinent geophysical records, offered to sell them oil from restricted government reserves, and conveyed valuable lessons learned in Arctic pipeline construction. This kind of robust federal and military support was a leading way, to use energy historian Paul Sabin's terminology once again, that petroleum abundance was 'made as much as discovered'.[6] Emphasizing the primacy of state power is not intended to deny private industry agency or credit for its contributions, but rather to offer a much-needed corrective to the conventional narrative. Through its military activities, big government primed the pump for big oil to develop petroleum in the far north.

Beginning with a discussion of Arctic oil exploration in the late eighteenth and early nineteenth centuries and the discovery of Norman Wells, this chapter analyses the construction of the Northwest Defense Complex during World War II, the military's discovery of oil in the Naval Petroleum Reserve Number 4, and Cold War petroleum infrastructures in the far north, and concludes with a discussion of the quasi-public nature of TAPS.

A Petroliferous Klondike

Europeans have long viewed the Arctic as a frozen energy frontier. From fisheries and whales to petroleum, the North promised a storehouse of caloric wealth for those willing to coax it from its Arctic environs. Early explorers keenly noted petroleum seeps and other geological formations that might be extracted for profit. In 1789, Sir Alexander Mackenzie recorded deposits of petroleum near Fort Good Hope while exploring for the Northwest Company.[7] Traders from the Hudson's Bay Company discovered multiple petroleum seeps in the Canadian Arctic in the 1830s. Private companies financed early explorations for natural resources in the North American Arctic in the nineteenth century, and as historian Bathsheba Demuth demonstrates, the state followed closely behind.[8]

Both the US and Canadian federal governments oscillated between inducing private investment and withdrawing promising reserves for state-controlled production. The US Army played a pioneering role in the

---

5 Black, *Global Interior*, 8–9.   6 Sabin, *Crude Politics*, 2.   7 Barry, *The Canol Project*, 218.
8 Demuth, *Floating Coast*, 88–89.

production of Arctic environmental knowledge and scientific research with Lt Patrick Henry Ray's International Polar Year expedition between 1881 and 1883. Two years later, a US Navy survey confirmed evidence of oil near Alaska's upper Colville River.[9] The Canadian government similarly encouraged oil prospecting in the Northwest Territories. Dr George W. Dawson, Director of Canada's Geological Survey, called the Mackenzie region 'the most extensive petroleum field in America, if not the world' in 1888. That same year, a Special Senate Committee investigated the 'Great Mackenzie Basin' and recommended over 100,000 km^2 be excluded from public sale and retained as a crown preserve.[10] Based on these promising early reports on both sides of the border, the US Geological Survey (USGS) dispatched multiple parties to investigate the 'arctic prairies' (as naturalist John Muir called the area) in the early 1900s.

Geologist and naturalist Ernest De Koven Leffingwell conducted the most important research and petroleum surveys in Arctic North America in the first decades of the twentieth century. As a member of the Anglo-American Polar Expedition of 1906–08 (funded in part by Standard Oil magnate John D. Rockefeller), Leffingwell explored North America's northernmost continental shelf and stayed behind to continue his surveys until 1914.[11] With assistance from local Iñupiaq peoples, Leffingwell charted the geography and geology of the region, performing groundbreaking Arctic research and identifying the Sadlerochit formation (the main reservoir of Prudhoe Bay). Leffingwell published his findings in 1919 in a USGS report entitled *Canning River Region of Northern Alaska*, which popularized the oil seeps of the North Slope and spurred prospectors to stake claims in the early 1920s in the Cape Simpson area.[12]

Private industry hoped for a petroleum version of the Klondike Gold Rush. Ottawa encouraged oil and gas development by generously postponing royalties on petroleum sales until January 1930. The Canadian government's inducement sent prospector James Kennedy Cornwall to the area, where he followed Alexander Mackenzie's original notes and, with the help of a Dene trapper named Karkasee, secured samples of oil from Norman Wells. Imperial Oil, the Canadian subsidiary of Standard Oil of New Jersey, bought up Cornwall's leases and discovered oil flows in late 1919. In August 1920 Imperial's explorationists tapped into a reservoir, unleashing a gusher 21 m high that flowed at a rate of 1,500 barrels per day.[13] Imperial geologist Ted

---

9 Bleakley, "Policy History of Alaska", 14.   10 Barry, *The Canol Project*, 222.
11 Pratt and Hale, *Exxon: Transforming Energy*, 113.   12 Collins, *On the Arctic Frontier*.
13 Taylor, *Imperial Standard*; Barry, *The Canol Project*, 223–228.

Link told the *Edmonton Journal* in October that Norman Wells was 'the biggest oil field in the world ... it stretched all the way from Fort Norman to the Arctic coast, and the explorer [Vilhjalmur] Stefansson was camped on the end of the same oil vein when he was on Victoria Island'.[14] Drilling at Norman Wells heralded the beginning of oil production in Arctic conditions and presaged both the logistical conundrums of Arctic oil development and states' intense interest in managing northern energy development.

Ottawa enacted new regulations and signed a new treaty to control the burgeoning oil province. In January 1921, Senator Sir James A. Lougheed promulgated a comprehensive and novel set of regulations pertaining to land rentals, production royalties, and exploration requirements. These regulations added barriers to private development and set forth a new system of public ownership, whereby the Crown retained ownership of three-quarters of every new permit issued – the first usage of what would become public or social ownership of petroleum in Canada.[15] The federal government also moved swiftly to gain legal title to promising oil lands. In the summer of 1921, a treaty commissioner facilitated Treaty 11, the last of the numbered treaties, wherein two dozen Dene bands ceded their 'rights, titles, and privileges' in exchange for promises that they could continue hunting and trapping on unoccupied lands. The government also promised annual cash payments, as well as educational, hunting, and medical benefits. Historical evidence is clear that Dene peoples had little idea that they were ceding their traditional territories, whether for widespread oil development or any other colonial endeavour. After private industry discovered less oil than expected, Ottawa failed to uphold its end of the deal, but the treaty nevertheless facilitated continued mineral development of the region.[16]

The frenetic developments at Norman Wells and geological evidence from Leffingwell's surveys encouraged a wave of Alaska survey expeditions by private companies, including Standard Oil of California, in 1920–21. While Standard Oil discovered two modest oil flows, strong petroleum developments in California obviated further development; Arctic Alaska was simply too remote and forbidding to compete with a continent of easily accessible crude. But in an ironic twist, Standard's encouraging findings helped to convince the US government to withdraw the most promising areas from private development.[17]

14 *Edmonton Journal* (16 October 1920).   15 Barry, *The Canol Project*, 236.
16 Page, "Norman Wells", 16–18; McCannon, *History of the Arctic*, 200.
17 Gryc, "National Petroleum Reserve", 12–13.

On 27 February 1923, President Warren Harding ordered 9.3 million hectares of Alaska's North Slope preserved for national security as the Naval Petroleum Reserve No. 4 (NPR-4 or 'Pet Four' as many called it). The US Navy had long recognized the importance of energy and natural resources for American national security and took an early interest in Alaska due to the territory's coal and petroleum reserves.[18] Following the US Navy's transition from coal to petroleum in 1913, the federal government established a series of Naval Petroleum Reserves throughout the nation, including Pet Four in 1923.[19] While the Navy had little idea how much oil lay under Alaska's North Slope (they rejected including Prudhoe Bay as part of NPR-4, believing coastal lands held less promise), government geologists recognized the region's geological potential.[20] Despite promising findings by the US Geological Survey in expeditions undertaken between 1923 and 1926, the oil glut of the late 1920s and 1930s convinced officials to postpone additional surveys.

The discovery at Norman Wells caused a brief flurry of commercial activity in the region. Oil extraction proceeded from 1920 to 1924, but the economics of northern oil production and transportation stymied major growth. Imperial determined the local demand insufficient. While the company considered the construction of a pipeline from Norman Wells to tidewater, the vast distances, extreme climate, and rugged topography added up to a prohibitive cost of $55 million.[21] Without a pipeline, Imperial capped the wells at Norman for the next decade. Only in 1932, with increased mining activity at Great Bear Lake, did Imperial restart production and construct a 1,100 barrel per day refinery in 1935.[22] By 1941, Imperial Oil sold over 9,500 barrels of refined products a year, lowering local prices and helping to fuel northern aviation, exploration, and mining. Despite its local utility, by World War II, 'Norman Wells was still considered by the industry as a white elephant', according to historian R. J. D. Page, 'lost in the northern mists, with little usefulness to Imperial or the nation'.[23] The intensifying drums of war in the late 1930s signalled that Norman Wells and Alaska's North Slope would not be frozen in isolation much longer.

---

18 Schulman, *Coal and Empire*, 6. 19 De Novo, "Petroleum", 656.
20 Bradner, "Our Resources, Our Past", 77.
21 "Empire's Oil Supplies". For the pipeline costs, see Page, "Norman Wells", 17.
22 US Army Corps of Engineers, "Historical Record: CANOL Project". For a broader history of this region and these processes, see Piper, *Industrial Transformation*.
23 Page, "Norman Wells", 18.

The Northwest Defense Complex

World War II precipitated a flurry of defence projects in the far north. With seemingly limitless funds, the Army and its cost-plus civilian contractors built thousands of kilometres of roads and pipelines, constructed dozens of new airstrips, and drilled hundreds of new oil wells throughout northwestern North America. While the public and amateur historians often focus on the famous Alaska–Canada Highway (ALCAN), this was the least important project for wartime needs. The US military constructed the highway primarily as a supply route for a string of strategic airfields, NWSR. The NWSR and ALCAN furthermore promoted the construction of an even larger megaproject that dwarfed the first two: the CANOL pipeline system. Historians have often treated these developments as separate endeavours, with countless books devoted to the ALCAN and few focused on CANOL, but these projects must be viewed holistically as part and parcel of a larger regional megaproject. According to historian Heath Mitchell, they were part of a 'single enterprise, an attempt to ensure that vital wartime supplies could reach Alaska despite the Japanese threat to the sea lanes of the North Pacific'.[24] The NWSR, ALCAN, and CANOL projects are thus analysed herein as the Northwest Defense Complex, a sprawling transportation infrastructure for moving military aircraft and petroleum to and through northwestern America.

The origins of the Northwest Defense Complex stemmed not only from the discovery of oil at Norman Wells, but also from the growing recognition by American and Canadian military officials in the 1930s of the strategic location of Alaska and the northwest. In 1933, US military planners theorized the area between Alaska, Hawaii, and Panama – the 'Pacific Defense Triangle' – as a bulwark for protecting North America and a fortified position to project US power throughout the Pacific Rim.[25] Following the Munich crisis of 1938, Assistant Secretary of State Adolf A. Berle described a 'north–south axis', whereby the United States would strengthen ties with Canada and adopt a 'hemispheric foreign policy'.[26] In 1938 and 1939, in conjunction with a larger military buildup throughout the Pacific, the United States began construction of bases at Sitka, Kodiak, Dutch Harbor, and Fairbanks. In contrast, Canada left its Pacific coast undefended, but did commit to a series of inland airfields.

---

24 Chandonnet, *Alaska at War*, 167.   25 Chandonnet, *Alaska at War*, 3.
26 Conn and Fairchild, *Framework of Hemisphere Defense*, 6.

Recognition of the 'Great Circle Route' connecting the Canadian northwest with Alaska, Siberia, and China invigorated Canadian and American imaginations and led directly to the creation of the NWSR. In 1935 – the same year US Army Air Force General Billy Mitchell famously predicted to Congress that 'He who holds Alaska will hold the world ... it is the most strategic place in the world' – Lt Colonel Henry 'Hap' Arnold led a squadron of B-10 bombers from Washington, DC to Alaska, evaluating and advocating for potential airfield sites.[27] The following year, Canadian Department of Transportation officials performed an aerial surveillance of the region. On the verge of the outbreak of the war, the Canadian federal government authorized a string of airfields, the NWSR, from Grand Prairie, Alberta to Whitehorse, Yukon. The route became operational for daytime flying in late 1941. These airfields took on a new urgency and importance following the extension of the US Lend-Lease Act to the Soviet Union in October 1941, and the decision to ferry thousands of aircraft to Siberia via Alaska.[28]

Following Japan's surprise attack on Pearl Harbor, US and Canadian leaders made several far-reaching decisions that would result in the Northwest Defense Complex and transform Arctic North America. Following a 16 January 1942 request from President Franklin Delano Roosevelt to study the need for an Alaskan highway, a Cabinet committee recommended construction of a road that would connect the NWSR airfields between Fort St John, BC and Big Delta, Alaska. Contrary to common perception, linking these airfields – not simply connecting Alaska to the Lower 48 – was the main justification for the construction of the Alaska Military Highway (or Alaska–Canada Highway, as it would later be called). Moved by the crash of military aircraft on their way to Alaska (due to a lack of infrastructure), on 11 February President Roosevelt approved the Alaska Military Highway.[29]

In the chaotic early days of the war, military planners scrambled to devise adequate petroleum supply chains to fuel the NSWR and Alaska Military Highway – or so-called 'Oil Can Highway' because of the thousands of empty oil drums that littered the hastily constructed road.[30] Navy Commander John C. Reed, who explored for Arctic oil during the war, recalled, 'This was a different kind of war, mechanized beyond previous imagination, and requiring almost unbelievable quantities of petroleum products.'[31] How the military delivered fuel mattered enormously for the war effort, local peoples,

27 Perras, *Stepping Stones to Nowhere*, 30.
28 Coates and Morrison, *Land of the Midnight Sun*.
29 Morrison and Coates, *Working the North*.   30 Garfield, *Thousand Mile War*, 196.
31 Reed, "Exploration", 3.

the Sub-Arctic environment, and the future of northern development. Trucks and aircraft were the least efficient, consuming nearly as much fuel as they delivered. Oil tankships were vastly more efficient, but military planners feared Japanese naval attacks and tankers were in critically short supply because of devastating German U-boat attacks – fifty-five American oil tankers had been sunk in the first six months of the war.[32] Only when Canadian explorer Vilhjalmur Stefansson, Leffingwell's companion on the Anglo-American Polar Expedition of 1906–08, urged consideration of Norman Wells did a pipeline emerge as a military possibility. Since the innovation of long-distance 'trunk' lines in 1878, pipelines had emerged as the time-tested technology for most efficiently delivering oil overland.[33] But no country or company had ever attempted constructing a trunkline in the far north.

With enemies closing in on all fronts, military officials envisaged the CANOL system as an unsinkable oil tanker that could fuel Fortress North America through the crucible of total war. In an April 1942 Cabinet meeting, President Roosevelt emphasized the importance of securing local oil resources for the defence of Alaska and argued the military should spearhead the development of petroleum resources.[34] Later that month, the US War Department approved the first phase of construction of the CANOL Pipeline from Norman Wells to Whitehorse, Yukon. Following the invasion of the Aleutians, military officials speeded up construction, merging soldiers and contractors to expedite the construction of the highway and CANOL system. At the peak of construction in 1943, over 60,000 American and Canadian workers (military and civilian) were employed in constructing the Northwest Defense Complex from Edmonton to Norman Wells, Dawson Creek to Fairbanks. These men constituted an 'Army of Occupation', according to two historians of the far north, which far outnumbered local peoples in Yukon and the NWT.[35]

The CANOL project proved the most expensive, sprawling, and misunderstood infrastructure of the Northwest Defense Complex. While CANOL has traditionally been seen primarily as a crude oil line from Norman Wells to Whitehorse, it was so much more. CANOL eventually constituted two distinct pipeline systems – the 900 km CANOL 1 pipeline from Norman Wells to Whitehorse – and another refined petroleum system from Skagway, across 1,500 km to Whitehorse, Watson Lake, and Fairbanks (CANOL 2, 3, and 4, respectively; Figure 24.1). Furthermore, it also encompassed an

---

32 Williamson, *Age of Energy*, 763.   33 Jones, *Routes of Power*.
34 Dod, *Corps of Engineers*, 319.   35 Morrison and Coates, *Working the North*.

24 Petroleum Development in Arctic North America

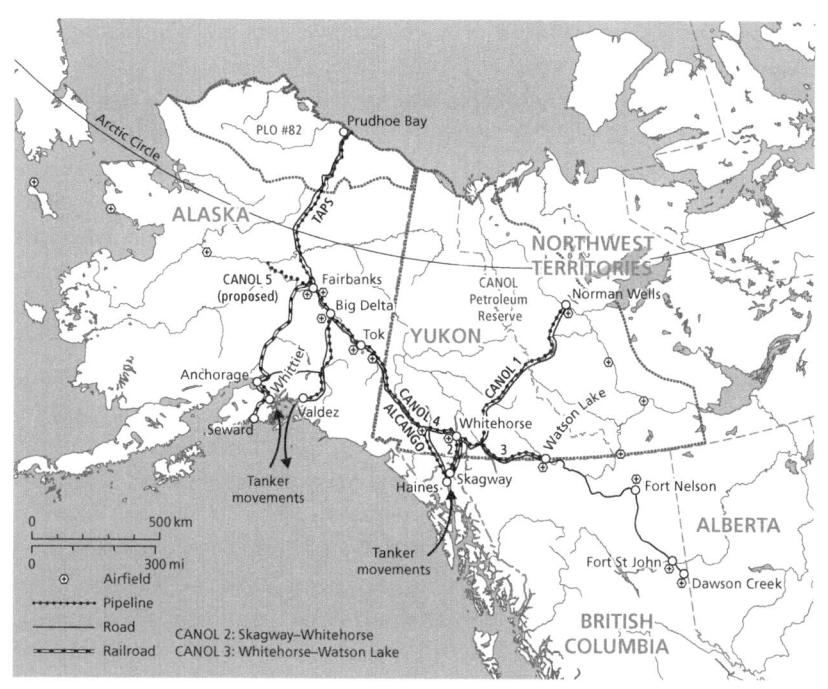

Figure 24.1 Long-distance hydrocarbon pipelines in Arctic and Sub-Arctic North America, 1942–1977.

expansive exploratory drilling programme, 1,000 km of gravel roads, 2,400 km of winter roads, and an entire string of its own aerodromes – a parallel Northwest Staging Route – to supply Norman Wells and potentially ferry aircraft to Fairbanks. CANOL comprised more kilometres of roads and airports than the ALCAN highway. While the general history of CANOL has been offered elsewhere, this inquiry into CANOL will focus on the relationship between the US military and private corporations, the expansive drilling programme under CANOL, and the enduring legacy of this novel energy infrastructure. In the final analysis, CANOL was a state-funded Arctic petroleum development campaign with consequences that endured decades into the future.

To supply CANOL 1 and provide Allied forces with ample quantities of petroleum, the War Department approved an escalating wildcat campaign throughout the Arctic. In July 1942, Imperial oil began a massive state-funded well-drilling programme, sinking fifty-eight new wells at Norman Wells and producing in excess of 4,000 barrels per day by September 1944. Beyond

Norman, the US Army signed an agreement with Imperial Oil to source an additional 20,000 barrels per day from the Arctic Northwest and initiated a sweeping geological and geophysical investigation of the entire region. While Canada established an 80 km 'war zone' around Norman Wells for a CANOL oil reserve, the United States pushed and secured a more expansive 480,000 km² zone that stretched all the way to the Alaska border. In the spring of 1942, the US Army Air Force conducted photogrammetric surveys of the entire Mackenzie Basin, from Edmonton to the Arctic Coast. That summer, the US military even investigated the potential of sourcing oil from the tar sands surrounding Fort McMurray. Eventually, Canadian authorities took over oil exploration activities in the Northwest Territories, with a goal of creating a 'strategic reserve'. After a CANOL meeting, Canadian prime minister Mackenzie King wrote in his diary 'we ought to get Americans out of the further development there and keep complete control in our hands'.[36]

Standard Oil of California and Standard Oil of New Jersey saw far more than patriotism in assisting with the CANOL project. The exigent situation gave these two oil companies a virtual carte blanche to advance their interests throughout the region and their marketing position in the post-war world. According to CANOL expert P. S. Barry, the war between Standard of New Jersey and Standard of California 'was a covert commercial war within the real war'.[37] Regardless of how the oil firms divided up the region and fought for commercial dominance, each profited enormously from their cost-plus contracts and ability to prove out Northwest petroleum supplies with Uncle Sam's funding. Furthermore, Imperial benefited from surplus equipment and drill rigs, which the US government made available for wildcat drilling. The United States paid for the exploration and development of Norman Wells, but retained no ownership rights to the oil following the war.

While exploratory drilling accelerated, CANOL 1 floundered. With no established roads, the worst winter weather in two decades, and soldiers shockingly ill-equipped for the ferocious climate, the project sputtered to an inauspicious start. The logistical challenges of moving millions of tons of freight to a remote portion of the NWT, building a road and novel pipeline across a swath of Sub-Arctic wilderness, and completing the project in a timely manner proved stupefying. These problems with constructing

---

36 Barry, *The Canol Project*, 458–472; Page, "Norman Wells", 19; US Army Corps of Engineers, "Historical Record: CANOL Project", 4–11.

37 Barry, *The Canol Project*, 13.

CANOL 1 only fuelled a dizzying array of supplemental projects and raised numerous questions about the ultimate objectives of the project.[38]

The saving grace and true workhorse of the CANOL project was its petroleum product system. On 20 June 1942, the War Department approved CANOL 2 – a 177 km product pipeline paralleling the White Pass and Yukon railroad from Skagway to Whitehorse. CANOL 2 was quickly built and began moving petroleum products in December 1942. Months later, almost to the day for the original deadline of CANOL 1, the war department approved CANOL 3 to Watson Lake, CANOL 4 to Fairbanks, and CANOL 5 to Tanana (later cancelled) as extensions of the Skagway petroleum product system. These new additions doubled the scope and price of the CANOL project but proved to be the most successful elements of the system.[39] CANOL 2 and 4 endured and continued to operate after the war well into the 1950s.

CANOL 1 proved an ecological and operational disaster, and it was only eleven months after the first oil moved through the line before it was shuttered by the United States and Canada in March 1945. The southern engineers' poor knowledge of the Sub-Arctic environment resulted in chronic problems and often catastrophic consequences. In disturbing the top layer of tundra, workers created a soggy morass that consumed whole vehicles and immobilized construction equipment. Engineers then laid the pipeline directly on the ground without expansion joints or anchors, making the oil conduit vulnerable to rock slides and damage from construction vehicles, as well as thawing permafrost. The hastily built pipeline suffered leak after leak, over 100 in all. Ultimately, 1,164,032 barrels of oil were shipped through the line, but only 975,764 barrels arrived in Whitehorse. While some of the undelivered 188,268 barrels were used to power pump stations and construction equipment, at least 46,000 barrels of crude leaked into the terrestrial and aquatic environment during operations. After shuttering, 50,000 barrels were left in the line, with another 40,000 at the pump stations and in oil tanks. Most of this residual oil eventually spilled into the taiga and tundra. There were oil spills throughout the entire operation – for example an 80,000-barrel tank which collapsed at Norman Wells in early winter 1944 and sent its contents into the Mackenzie River.[40] Journalist Philip Fradkin concluded, 'No energy project in the North before or after was built with less regard for

---

38 For a detailed account of northern exploration and expertise in CANOL 1, see Adcock, *A Thoroughly Modern Enterprise*, forthcoming.
39 US Army Corps of Engineers, "Historical Record: CANOL Project", 30.
40 US Army Corps of Engineers, "Historical Record: CANOL Project", 7, 44, 52.

environmental concerns'.[41] The project left thousands of kilometres of discarded equipment, poisoned soil, and abandoned pump stations – many of which remain enduring environmental hazards.

Ultimately it was not CANOL's environmental harms that doomed the project; it was its economics and optics. After Senator Harry Truman led a Senate investigation into the project in 1943, the US public came to regard CANOL as the epitome of a wartime boondoggle. The pipeline proved more expensive than the ALCAN and, ultimately, the costliest construction project of the entire war. With a cost overrun of 500–600 per cent, the Norman Wells-CANOL 1 system produced oil at $106 per barrel, when California oil products shipped to Whitehorse via CANOL 2 cost only $3.94 per barrel.[42] The Petroleum Administrator for War concluded, 'The cost of this project in terms of critical materials, labor, and money is excessive in the extreme'.[43] One post-mortem report on CANOL's failure went so far as to assert that the project's 'waste in manpower and materials was greater than any act of sabotage by the enemy'.[44] CANOL 1 was sold for scrap and removed in the winter of 1947–48. Thanks in part to his standout performance criticizing CANOL, Senator Truman became Vice President – and within a year, President of the United States.

The legacies of the Northwest Defense Complex are manifold. The project transformed the character, infrastructure, and post-war trajectory of the Northwest. It marked the region's ascendance as an indispensable strategic space and facilitated an intensified militarization of the north in the post-war era. According to historian P. S. Berry, the CANOL project 'overwhelmed nearly one-fifth of Canadian territory for more than three years, leaving a deep imprint on the life in the northwest region and predicating a new era in continental military and economic strategy'. In the wake of the Northwest Defense Complex were dozens of operational airfields, a new road and telephone system linking Edmonton with Whitehorse, Anchorage, and Fairbanks. The 'American Occupation' and these infrastructures proved to be pernicious disease vectors for the region's First Peoples.[45] As historians Bill Morrison and Ken Coates conclude, 'The Yukon had been rediscovered and would never be the same again.'[46]

Finally, the Northwest Defense Complex changed the trajectory of oil exploration for private industry and the state throughout the north. Not only did the state embark on geophysical explorations and wildcat wells

41 Fradkin, *Wanderings*, 61.   42 Page, "Norman Wells", 20.
43 Anchorage Chamber of Commerce, *Study*, 3.   44 Drapeau, "Pipe Dream".
45 Marchand, "Tribal Epidemics".   46 Coates and Morrison, *Land of the Midnight Sun*.

throughout Arctic Alaskan and Canada, the knowledge gained by these operations gave Imperial Oil and Standard Oil of California tremendous capital, opportunity, and political licence to pursue corporate schemes and business opportunities. Thanks to clear geophysical data gained from the war effort, Imperial abandoned further exploratory drilling in the NWT. Imperial determined that the same kind of Devonian geological structures drilled into at Norman Wells existed further south, leading to the development of a significant oil field at Leduc in Alberta in 1947. Imperial bought the CANOL refinery at Whitehorse for a pittance and moved it to Edmonton to profit from the Alberta oil rush. The project also set a new trajectory for the US military's Arctic hydrocarbon exploration beyond the war. The delays and ongoing failures of the CANOL system spurred military officials to find an alternative source of oil for Alaska's defence needs. They focused on the most promising oil prospect in Alaska – the Naval Petroleum Reserve No. 4 on the North Slope.

Proving Out 'Pet Four'

In early 1943, with Japanese troops occupying the Aleutian Islands and engineers struggling to make progress on CANOL 1, President Roosevelt issued Public Land Order 82 and reserved the entire North Slope for military petroleum exploration and development. A memorandum from former USGS geologist Lt W. T. Foran, who had explored the North Slope for oil in 1925, called attention to the oil prospects of the region and encouraged the federal government to explore the region.[47] Alaska's Territorial Governor Ernest Gruening was especially enthused by the economic and military prospects of discovering petroleum in the Arctic, and he coordinated an exploratory survey spearheaded by the Territorial Department of Mines and USGS. In the fall of 1943, guided by local Iñupiaq Simon Paneak from Chandler Lake, the floatplane-equipped survey spent three weeks investigating petroleum seeps and confirmed five oil flows. The survey suggested that the cost of development, including a 1,005 km pipeline from Cape Simpson to Fairbanks via Anaktuvuk Pass, compared favourably with CANOL.[48] The Bureau of Mines sent a report to the Navy, who shared Gruening's enthusiasm. Following the 'CANOL failure by the Department of the Army', several prominent Navy officers and the Director of the USGS argued that the North

47 Gryc, "National Petroleum Reserve", 14.
48 "Oil Seepages".

Slope offered the best chance of fuelling Alaska's future military needs.[49] To this end, the government approved a $2.1 million comprehensive exploration programme of the North Slope by the Navy's Seabees engineering unit in 1944.

The failure of CANOL 1 and the promise of oil reserves in Pet Four focused renewed attention on what one USGS geologist called 'the big question: How the hell do you get oil out of there?'[50] Following his 1924 USGS survey of Arctic Alaska, geologist Philip Smith warned all those who dreamed of extracting and moving Arctic oil: 'the stakes are ... high, and the risks grave and the expenses enormous'.[51] Gruening's 1943 Bureau of Mines survey and private industry came to a similar conclusion. According to economist George Rogers, Standard Oil of California considered exploring for oil on the North Slope (east of NPR-4) during the 1930s, but the daunting logistics and costs ultimately dissuaded private industry. 'It was so difficult to get those resources to market', Rogers recalls, 'they might as well have been on the moon'.[52]

It was in this context that the Navy and the Alaska Territorial Guard commenced their pipeline survey. Between December 1944 and March 1945, the Navy, ATG, Army, and civilian bush pilots investigated the route.[53] Based on this survey, Navy leadership concluded that a pipeline terminating in Fairbanks could supply both military and civilian markets, as well as gain access to the Alaskan railroad, the ALCAN, and the CANOL 4 pipeline. To overcome the challenges, Navy leadership held a conference in Anchorage in 1949 to discuss Arctic pipeline engineering and commissioned a variety of environmental tests in Fairbanks and Barrow to determine its feasibility.[54] By 1950, Navy officials concluded that a pipeline from Umiat to Valdez was the most desirable transportation method if enough oil could be located on the North Slope.[55] These military surveys had direct implications for private industry and local communities. As early as 1946, some Fairbanksans gushed at the prospect of an oil pipeline from Pet Four and a local refinery transforming Fairbanks into an 'oil town'.[56]

The end of the war brought little pause to the effort to prove out Pet Four. The Navy recognized the long-term strategic importance of fuel supplies in

49 "Naval Petroleum Reserves", 290–291.   50 Carey, "Tangled Roots", 28.
51 Smith, "Mineral Resources of Alaska".   52 Carey, "Fred Seaton of Nebraska", 11.
53 McTee, "Alaskan Naval Reserve".   54 Reed, "Exploration", 22, 28, 112, 125.
55 "Fact Sheet on TAPS", October 1973, Series 3, Box 2, Betzi and Lyman Woodman papers, Archives and Special Collections, Consortium Library, University of Alaska Anchorage.
56 Sullivan, "Navy Pushes Hunt".

Alaska, and rising tensions with the Soviet Union provided additional impetus. Nuclear weapons may have been the most terrifying aspect of modern warfare, but petroleum was the unquestionable lifeblood of mechanized combat as every new generation of military technologies consumed ever-greater quantities of oil. Over the next eight years, military contractors and USGS scientists drilled thirty-six core samples and forty-four test wells throughout the North Slope. By 1953, government employees and contractors had thoroughly surveyed the region, photographing 290,000 km^2, testing oil productivity over 155,000 km^2, and mapping another 155,000 km^2. The joint efforts of Arctic scientists and explorationists revealed the modest 70-million-barrel Umiat oil field and two gas fields at South Barrow and Gubik. The expenditure of human and financial capital was at the time, according to historian Andrew Stuhl, 'the largest, most expensive research effort in Northern history'.[57]

The scope and intensity of exploring Pet Four resulted in unprecedented environmental change and damage to the sensitive tundra. Like CANOL, the Navy and its contractors had little experience operating in the far north, and the extreme environmental conditions of the North Slope constantly stymied their efforts. The Navy's 113,000 kg tracked vehicles were incessantly bogged down in the soggy tundra. The tank-like vehicles left indelible scars across hundreds of kilometres of tundra, some resulting in subsidence of nearly 4 m within a year.[58] These tracks remain today. Even when stationary the Navy struggled to adapt to the dynamic Arctic. Building foundations cracked and failed as the permafrost thawed. Access to drinking water proved scarce, and engineers struggled to build effective effluent systems that did not freeze. Government workers overcame these obstacles by dredging enormous quantities of gravel for foundation construction, storing petroleum and human waste in 55-gallon drums and discarding them in massive piles. Bud Helmericks – the only Euro-American homesteader on the North Slope – described how these oil drums were like 'time bombs' that would decimate an acre or two, or even a small lake, when the summer thaw caused the drums to leak.[59] The Navy accumulated so many of these refuse drums that environmentalists coined them the 'Alaskan State Flower'.[60]

Early in their exploration tribulations, the Navy recognized the need for Arctic environmental research. 'Ignorance of permafrost conditions cost the

---

57 Stuhl, *Unfreezing the Arctic*, 93.   58 Mueller, "Alaskan Oil".
59 Bud Helmericks to Fred H. West, 29 April 1969, Folder: TAPS Correspondence, January–June 1969. Wilderness Society Papers.
60 Mr Chafin to David Brower, 4 Sept. 1970. David Brower Papers.

United States millions of dollars during the war', according to John C. Reed.[61] The military feared a repeat of CANOL 1 and enlisted science to avoid another engineering and publicity fiasco. Drilling on the North Slope posed gruelling environmental, logistical, and technical challenges that dwarfed other oil operations. To these ends, in 1947 the government established the Arctic Research Laboratory (renamed Naval Arctic Research Laboratory) in Barrow (now Utqiaġvik). The Laboratory's Arctic research empowered its petroleum exploration throughout the late 1940s and 1950s and would contribute to both private oil development and the construction of the Trans-Alaska Pipeline. Studying nature and exploring for oil had long been conjoined, and the federal government took the lead in pioneering ecological studies and petroleum development in the Arctic.[62]

By the early 1950s, the Navy's $50 million efforts ran afoul of budget-minded Congressmen and corporate oil interests. Representative Leon Gavin (R-PA) compared the Navy's NPR-4 expenditures to the waste of the CANOL pipeline and argued that the price of an Arctic pipeline would be far higher than the Navy's estimate of $100 million.[63] In 1953, the House revoked all future funding for oil exploration in Pet Four. The 1952 election of Dwight D. Eisenhower influenced the decision to stop government-funded exploration. President Eisenhower had close connections with the oil industry, which was increasingly interested in the prospect of Alaskan hydrocarbons and disliked the government's foray into the petroleum business.[64] In a 1944 *Harpers Magazine* article, former Vice President of Standard Oil of New Jersey Wallace Pratt argued that Alaska and the Arctic were destined to be great regions of oil extraction and urged the development of Pet Four.[65] In the 1950s, after the Navy discovered oil, Pratt and oil industry executives wanted the federal government out of the way. Many of the engineers and officers involved in Pet Four drilling were oil men in uniform, and following the war they were eager to privately develop the region. It was as a guest of the Navy during the exploration of Pet Four that Rollin P. Eckis, ARCO's future Executive Vice President, became convinced of the region's enormous value. 'It was then and there that I developed the feeling that there was a tremendous potential for oil on the North Slope', he recalled.[66] Kirby Brant, former counsel and Deputy Director of Office of Naval Petroleum and Oil

---

61 "US Conducts Wide Uranium Hunt in Alaska", *Chicago Daily Tribune* (19 December 1946).
62 Reed, "Story", 177–183; Frehner, *Finding Oil*.   63 "Naval Petroleum Reserves".
64 Mitchell, *Take My Life*, 179.   65 Pratt, "Oil Fields".
66 Sweet, *Discovery at Prudhoe Bay*, 169.

Shale Reserves, argued that the Navy was on the verge of undertaking intensive expansion of exploration in Pet Four in 1953 when President Eisenhower took office and bowed to industry pressure.[67] For some, this became convincing evidence that the military would likely have discovered Prudhoe Bay had the federal government not abandoned exploratory drilling.

Fuelling the Garrison State

The exploration of Pet Four was just one of a flurry of defence projects in post-war Alaska. The Territory boomed as a militarized zone and government-dominated resource frontier. Alaska witnessed an almost seamless transition from federal wartime spending to a Cold War garrison state, and the two conflicts collectively resulted in a profound realignment of the Territory's economy. Government employment spiked from 12 per cent of the employed labour force in 1939 to over 53 per cent in 1950.[68] The threat of long-range Soviet bombers spurred the creation of the 'heartland' concept of defence, whereby military planners deprioritized the Aleutian Islands and committed to a series of military bases throughout Alaska's Interior that would shield continental north America.[69] Congress allotted significant funds in 1946 for Alaskan defence, and the Air Force alone spent $250 million to construct and modernize two air bases outside of Fairbanks between 1950 and 1955.[70] These infrastructural projects built the backbone of the military's garrison state and required enormous volumes of petroleum products as part of the Cold War defence of Alaska.

The Department of Defense constructed two petroleum product lines in the far north during the Cold War, demonstrating technology, learning valuable lessons, and ultimately paving the way for the Trans-Alaska Pipeline System. As early as 1948, military planners began looking to construct a larger oil pipeline, either from Haines or Valdez to Fairbanks, to fuel military needs in interior Alaska, north of the Alaska Range.[71] The CANOL 4 line demonstrated the ability to efficiently move significant volumes of petroleum products overland to Fairbanks, but Cold War military needs required more petroleum products by several orders of magnitude. To this end, in 1950 the Army Corps of Engineers hired the Fluor Corporation of Los Angeles to design a 1,007 km multiproduct pipeline running from Haines to

---

67 Hanrahan and Gruenstein, *Lost Frontier*, 189.   68 Naske, *49 At Last!*, 83.
69 Hunt, *Alaska: A Bicentennial History*, 113. For a full accounting of the militarization of Alaska, see Hummel, "U.S. Military".
70 Carey, "Fred Seaton of Nebraska", 5.   71 "Washington Wire".

Fairbanks that could pump 9,600 barrels of jet fuel daily at a temperature of −29 degrees Celsius. Engineers researched the operational history of CANOL and sought to prevent similar mistakes on the new military fuel line.[72] A consortium of US and Canadian contractors began construction in 1954 and the US Army began operating the new pipeline system, called the Alaska–Canada Gas Oil Fuel Line (ALCANGO) on 12 October 1955.[73]

The pipeline proved an operational success, but like CANOL left an indelible environmental legacy. After tankers unloaded at the deep-water port of Haines, the 20 cm multi-product pipeline moved fuel to Fort Greely, Eielson Air Force Base, and Fort Wainwright. The pipeline carried gasoline, diesel, and aviation fuel, and – most importantly – large volumes of JP4 jet fuel. The new pipeline succeeded in reducing the cost of moving jet fuel from 0.10 cents per gallon by rail to 0.01 cent per gallon by ALCANGO.[74] Not included in these costs were the pipeline's numerous spills. Like CANOL, builders of ALCANGO laid the vast majority of the pipeline above ground. Owing to environmental problems, the military buried additional sections of the line at a cost of over $3 million. Ultimately, the pipeline system cost $38 million and demonstrated the ability to move even more petroleum products over permafrost and under glacial rivers, through mountain passes and sensitive waterways. Years before TAPS, the 'Alaska Pipeline' was a military pipeline for sustaining Cold War readiness.

Alaska's place as the crossroads of military aviation also demanded vast quantities of fuel south of the Alaska Range, and military planners envisioned a pipeline system to Anchorage area bases as early as 1943.[75] Because of the inability of large tankers to utilize the port of Anchorage in winter and heavy snowfall which inhibited oil-by-rail movements, the DoD favoured the construction of a product pipeline from the Deepwater port of Whittier to defence facilities in Anchorage. This route utilized the Portage-Whittier tunnel and Whittier port, constructed in earnest during World War II. The City of Anchorage opposed the pipeline both on economic grounds (estimates showed a $50,000 annual loss to port revenues) and on environmental grounds (the proposed pipeline transited the Campbell Creek drainage, a watershed area where the city sourced drinking water). Military officials

---

72 Hollinger, "Fairbanks–Haines Pipeline", 7.
73 172D Infantry Brigade, "Description of Alaskan Military Facilities".
74 Haines Sheldon Museum, "Haines to Fairbanks".
75 Brush, "Narrative Report 1941–1944", 417.

argued the current situation was untenable, as demand for aviation fuel doubled in 1965 and petroleum logistics bottlenecked. 'Trying to ship our supply by rail', Colonel James Shaver quipped, 'is like trying to fill a bathtub with a teaspoon'. President Johnson's escalation of the Vietnam War amplified the issue, as soon-to-be-commenced C-141 'Starlifter' operations required 432,000 gallons of fuel daily. On 11 March 1966, Congress approved a $13 billion appropriations package for Vietnam operations, which included $5.6 million for the Whittier-Anchorage pipeline. The US Army Corps of Engineers awarded the contract to the Mullens and Dravo Corporation, who commenced construction in the summer of 1966.[76]

Engineers overcame considerable environmental hurdles in the realization of the 98 km pipeline. Construction crews faced harsh weather as they constructed the pipeline through the Chugach mountains and blasted a nearly 4,000 m tunnel through Portage Pass. To mollify local concerns that the line would pollute water supplies, the Army Corps agreed to bury the line over the Campbell Creek drainage near Anchorage, X-ray all welds, and conduct hydrostatic testing of the line before operations. But the dismissal of the X-ray subcontractor and accusations that the Army Corps were not correcting deficient welds rekindled public fears. District Engineer Colonel Clare Farley promised to recheck all 767 welds in the area, necessitating the excavation of 9,100 m of pipe and rewelding several hundred suspect welds. Builders completed the line in October 1967, with the *Anchorage Times* lauding the project as 'the most critically inspected pipeline ever built'. The startup of the line brought 30,000 much-needed barrels per day of jet fuel to Anchorage and heralded a new era of environmental concern surrounding pipelines in the far north.[77]

By the early 1970s, the military's deployment of Minuteman intercontinental ballistic missiles significantly reduced the fuel needs for US Air Force B-52s. This development had the greatest effect on interior Alaska's Strategic Air Command operations and fuel needs. The military mothballed the ALCANGO line in 1971 and the federal government put it up for sale soon afterwards.[78] By the end of the 1970s, as the Trans-Alaska Pipeline began pumping crude, ALCANGO was dismantled and salvaged. Just as quickly as military needs drove the construction of these infrastructures, mission changes (and new sources of petroleum) heralded their demise.

76 Mighetto and Homstad, *Engineering*, 64–68, 211–214.
77 Mighetto and Homstad, *Engineering*, 211–214.
78 Haines Sheldon Museum, "Haines to Fairbanks".

These infrastructures and the torrent of federal spending left a lasting political economic legacy. Post-war Alaska, according to journalist Michael Carey, was a 'federal fiefdom'. Its fiscal politics were dominated by the federal government and the Department of Defense. Slightly more than 20 per cent of Alaska's 228,000 citizens were members of the military.[79] ALCANGO and other military facilities like Fort Greely were major economic drivers and social forces for rural Alaskan communities such as Haines, Tok, and Delta Junction. This federal largesse paved the way for greater participation of Alaskans in their economic affairs. 'Without the influx of new population and prosperity brought in by Military Alaska', political economist and Alaskan constitutional framer George Rogers argued in 1962, 'it is doubtful that Alaska today would be a state'.[80] Private industry hoped that Alaskan statehood would enable greater access to Arctic petroleum reserves.

The combination of soaring US West Coast demand and the spectre of Middle Eastern nationalism (highlighted by the nationalization of the Iranian oil industry in 1951 and the Suez Crisis of 1956) attracted oil firms to re-evaluate Arctic hydrocarbons. These were the historical events driving Richfield Petroleum – whose Vice President had helped prove out Pet Four – to discover the Swanson River oil field on Alaska's Kenai Peninsula in 1957. Richfield's discovery sparked a leasing and exploration boom. Only weeks after proving out Swanson River, Richfield sold half of its Kenai leases to Standard Oil of California for $30 million and invested in what it believed was the real prize – the hydrocarbon frontier and Iñupiaq homeland of the North Slope.

Richfield and other oil firms were armed with recent USGS data and a decade of military Arctic science from Pet Four. In 1954, the Department of Defense opened all records and geophysical data on oil explorations in Pet Four to the petroleum industry.[81] According to Marvis Magnus, who participated in Pet Four expeditions and went to work for Richfield, the data from Pet Four became indispensable for private exploration of the Slope. 'The geological survey and the Navy oil unit set up all the nomenclature and framework for the oil industry when we started taking off in the late 1950s and 1960s', he explained.[82] In 1963, the Sinclair Pipe Line Company prepared a detailed report on a pipeline from the North Slope to Valdez, using government data from the Fairbanks–Haines Pipeline project and the Navy's NPR-4 pipeline surveys.[83] The government further supported the

---

79 Carey, "Tangled Roots", 6, 13; Reed, "Exploration", 183. 80 Rogers, *Future of Alaska*, 63.
81 Stuhl, *Unfreezing the Arctic*, 107. 82 *Katalla to Prudhoe Bay*, 17.
83 Sinclair Pipe Line Company, "Proposed Alaska Pipe Line".

industry by permitting the Navy to sell oil from Pet Four to companies exploring the North Slope.[84]

On 27 December 1967, ARCO's crew felt the roar of natural gas shake the Earth at Prudhoe Bay. A column of white and yellow fire erupted as workers ignited the gas gushing from the test well.[85] The ARCO-Humble team discovered a world-class oil field – an 'elephant' in the lexicon of petroleum geologists. Far from being the beginning of North Slope development, Prudhoe Bay was the culmination of state-sponsored 'spadework'.

'The Largest Privately Funded Construction Effort in History'

On 28 July 1977, the first barrel of Prudhoe Bay crude oil arrived at tidewater in Valdez after flowing through the new $10 billion Trans-Alaska Pipeline System. Alyeska, the pipeline's operator, and its owner companies boasted that TAPS had taken nearly nine years and was 'the largest privately funded construction effort in history'.[86] While TAPS was similar to many other megaprojects like the Panama Canal and Transcontinental Railroad, Alyeska claimed TAPS was exemplary because it was 'totally financed and carried out with private capital'.[87] Ironically, while Alyeska championed its 'private' megaproject, its owners continued to petition for government subsidies and support. Rollin Eckis, then Vice Chairman of ARCO, urged the US government to maintain incentives for Alaskan drilling and mitigate the large risks involved with Arctic exploration.[88] As Eckis knew personally from his time in NPR-4, the state had paved the way for Arctic oil production for decades and continued to offer vital assistance in the 1960s and 1970s.

In 1973, Congress and President Nixon approved TAPS with the justification of national security. The federal government permitted Alyeska priority access to supplies and material under the Defense Production Act of 1950, which mandated that businesses prioritize contracts deemed necessary for national defence. When it came to the design of the pipeline, the USGS and Army Corps of Engineers played a leading role, and much of the science and technology the military utilized in the Arctic went into the construction of TAPS. Under the pretext of the nation's energy security, Congress barred the owners of the pipeline system from exporting their oil abroad and steered the distribution of Alaskan crude throughout the nation. The industry and

84 ISER, "Petroleum Industry in Alaska".   85 Coen, *Breaking Ice*, 11, 24.
86 Exxon Marine, "Alaska".   87 Alyeska Pipeline Service Company, "TAPS".
88 "Oil Executive Sees More Finds".

the pipeline also benefited from massive direct and indirect subsidies. A federal investment tax credit allowed Alyeska's owner companies to write off 10 per cent of the cost of the project. Additionally, federal tax law allowed TAPS owner companies to deduct interest payments from their tax liabilities. Since TAPS was funded with roughly 80 per cent debt, these tax credits added up to billions in state subsidies.[89] The federal government also subsidized the construction of the other half of the system, the largest civilian shipbuilding programme in US history – fifty US-built, US-flagged, and US-crewed oil tankers. Historians have almost totally missed or misunderstood the nature of the system.

Foregrounding neglected and hidden histories of the state in North American Arctic hydrocarbon development offers a new perspective on the timing, nature, and trajectory of these developments. Despite the rhetoric of its owner companies – British Petroleum, Exxon, and Atlantic Richfield – the Trans-Alaska Pipeline System has never simply been a private enterprise. From decades before the discovery of Prudhoe Bay, the federal government played an outsized role in the 'spadework' of Arctic hydrocarbon development – scientific research, pipeline surveys and construction, and the production of geophysical information through an international exploration programme. TAPS was not the end result of a nine-year private effort; it was the culmination of twenty-five years of intensive military and corporate energies. While the US government did not own or operate TAPS, it eagerly assisted in the research, construction, and financing of the system. TAPS should not be known as a 'private industrial project', but rather a state-sponsored project designed for private profit. TAPS and Arctic hydrocarbon development proved a chimera of 'free enterprise'; a project through which the government sustained the nation's petroleum security, even if this supply was delivered by an oligopoly of multinational firms. Private industry stood on the shoulders of the state, but saw the Arctic hydrocarbon frontier as the selfish product of its own creation.

By not seeing the primacy of the state in advancing Arctic hydrocarbon development, historians have abetted a mythology of TAPS and North Slope drilling as a private development story. Such a myopic narrative obfuscates the real engines of history and true political economy of Arctic oil. In Alaska today, large elements of society express the idea that more oil could be produced, 'if only big government would get out of the way'. A more honest accounting of Arctic history demonstrates that decades of military and federal efforts enabled private industry to profit from an underground ocean of oil.

89 Miller, *Little Did We Know*.

By foregrounding the role of the state, scholars can help citizens to see the full public interest stakes of contemporary and future Arctic hydrocarbon development. TAPS and North Slope oil production are not simply private enterprises. They are public-private endeavours with sprawling social consequences and enduring environmental legacies. As the climate crisis accelerates and calls intensify for the managed decline of Arctic hydrocarbon production, citizens and scholars alike would do well to remember the outsized role the state played in creating and sustaining the hydrocarbon frontier.

Bibliography

Archival and Unpublished Sources

172D Infantry Brigade (Alaska), "Description of Alaskan Military Facilities: Pamphlet 360-1 (15 January 1981)", Part 1, Folder 93, Betzi and Lyman Woodman papers, Archives and Special Collections, Consortium Library, University of Alaska Anchorage.

Carey, Michael, "Tangled Roots: The Roots of the Arctic National Wildlife Refuge". Unpublished manuscript. Author's collection.

Carey, Michael, "Fred Seaton of Nebraska and His Friend in Alaska". Unpublished manuscript. Author's collection.

Sinclair Pipe Line Company, "Proposed Alaska Pipe Line Gubic to Valdez" (Sinclair Pipe Line Company, 26 July 1963), British Petroleum Archives, University of Warwick, Coventry, UK.

Published Sources

Adcock, Cristina, *A Thoroughly Modern Enterprise: Exploration in Northern Canada*, forthcoming (Vancouver: University of British Columbia Press).

Alyeska Pipeline Service Company, "TAPS: A Synopsis of Engineering and Cost Factors" (Anchorage, AK: TAPS Owner Companies, 1978).

Anchorage Chamber of Commerce, *A Study of Alaska's 1957 Oil Discovery: Its Strategic Value for the Nation and Land Use in Developing an Oil Field Within a Moose Range* (Anchorage, AK: TAPS Owner Companies, October 1957), Exhibit D.

Barry, Patricia S., *The Canol Project: An Adventure of the U.S. War Department in Canada's Northwest* (Edmonton, AB: P. S. Barry, 1985).

Black, Megan, *The Global Interior: Mineral Frontiers and American Power* (Cambridge, MA: Harvard University Press, 2018).

Bleakley, Geoffrey, *A Policy History of Alaska Oil Lands Administration, 1953–1974* (Pullman, WA: Washington State University, 1996).

Bradner, Tim, "Our Resources, Our Past, Our Future: AOGCC: 50 Years of Service to Alaska" (Alaska Oil and Gas Conservation Commission, 2018), https://www.com

merce.alaska.gov/web/Portals/18/Pub/aogcc50thBooklet.pdf (accessed 20 February 2022).

Brush, James D., Col., "Narrative Report of Alaska Construction 1941–1944" (Anchorage, AK: US Army Engineer District, Alaska, November–December 1944).

Busenberg, George, *Oil and Wilderness in Alaska: Natural Resources, Environmental Protection, and National Policy Dynamics* (Washington, DC: Georgetown University Press, 2013).

Chandonnet, Fern, ed., *Alaska at War, 1941–1945: The Forgotten War Remembered* (Fairbanks, AK: University of Alaska Press, 2007).

Coates, Kenneth S., and William R. Morrison, *Land of the Midnight Sun: A History of the Yukon* (Montreal: McGill-Queens University Press, 2005).

Coates, Peter A., *The Trans-Alaska Pipeline Controversy* (Fairbanks, AK: University of Alaska Press, 1991).

Coen, Ross, *Breaking Ice for Arctic Oil: The Epic Journey of the SS Manhattan* (Fairbanks, AK: University of Alaska Press, 2012).

Collins, Janet, *On the Arctic Frontier: Ernest Leffingwell's Polar Explorations and Legacy* (Pullman, WA: Washington State University Press, 2017).

Conn, Stetson, and Byron Fairchild, *The Framework of Hemisphere Defense* (Washington, DC: Center for Military History, 1989).

Corbin, Harry F., ed., *COM ICE PAC Reports: CBD 1058* (Port Hueneme, CA: U.S. Navy Seabee Museum, 1946)

De Novo, John, "Petroleum and the United States Navy before World War One", *Mississippi Valley Historical Review* 41 (March 1955), 641–656.

Demuth, Bathsheba, *Floating Coast: An Environmental History of the Bering Strait* (New York: W. W. Norton, 2019).

Dod, Karl C., *The Corps of Engineers: The War Against Japan* (Washington, DC: Center for Military History, 1966).

Drapeau, Raoul, "Pipe Dream", *Invention and Technology* 17 (Winter 2002): 25–35.

Edmonton Journal (16 October 1920).

"Empire's Oil Supplies: Exploiting Its Resources", *Times of India* (29 January 1921).

Exxon Marine, "Alaska" (Autumn 1979).

Fradkin, Philip, *Wanderings of an Environmental Journalist in Alaska and the American West* (Albuquerque, NM: University of New Mexico Press, 1993).

Frehner, Brian (*Finding Oil: The Nature of Petroleum Geology, 1859–1920* (Lincoln, NE: University of Nebraska Press, 2016).

Gage, S. R., *A Walk on the CANOL Road: Exploring the First Major Northern Pipeline* (Oakville, ON: Mosaic, 1990).

Garfield, Brian, *The Thousand Mile War: World War II in Alaska and the Aleutians* (Fairbanks, AK: University of Alaska Press, 1995).

Gryc, George, "The National Petroleum Reserve in Alaska: Earth-Science Considerations", US Geological Survey Professional Paper 1240-C (Washington, DC: Government Printing Office, 1985).

Haines Sheldon Museum, "Haines to Fairbanks Military Pipeline and Tank Farm". www.sheldonmuseum.org/vignette/haines-to-fairbanks-military-pipeline-and-the-tank-farm/ (accessed 26 April 2021).

Hanrahan, John, and Peter Gruenstein, *Lost Frontier: The Marketing of Alaska* (New York: W. W. Norton, 1977).

Hollinger, Kristy, "The Fairbanks–Haines Pipeline (Fort Collins: Center for Environmental Management of Military Lands, Colorado State University, 2003).
Hummel, Laurel J., "The U.S. Military as a Geographical Agent: The Case of Cold War Alaska", *Geographical Review* 95 (2005): 47–72.
Hunt, William R., *Alaska: A Bicentennial History* (New York: W. W. Norton, 1976).
Institute of Business, Economic and Government Research (ISER), "The Petroleum Industry in Alaska" (College, AK: University of Alaska, 1964).
Jones, Christopher, *Routes of Power: Energy and Modern America* (Cambridge, MA: Harvard University Press, 2014).
Katalla to Prudhoe Bay: An Entertaining Look at the First 100 Years of the Oil and Gas Industry in Alaska (Petroleum News Alaska, 1997).
Marchand, John F., "Tribal Epidemics in the Yukon", *Journal of American Medical Association* 123 (18 December 1943): 1019–1020.
Marston, Marvin R., *Men of the Tundra: Alaska Eskimos at War* (New York: October House, 1969).
McCannon, John, *A History of the Arctic: Nature, Exploration, and Exploitation* (London: Reaktion, 2012).
McClure, Christine, and Dennis McClure, *We Fought the Road* (Kenmore, WA: Epicenter, 2017).
McTee, A. R., "Alaskan Naval Reserve Pipe Line Prospects", *Oil Weekly* (March 1946).
Mighetto, Lisa, and Carla Homstad, *Engineering in the Far North: A History of the U.S. Army Engineer District in Alaska* (Historical Research Associates, Inc., 1997).
Miller, John R., *Little Did We Know: Financing the Trans Alaska Pipeline* (Cleveland, OH: Arbordale LLC, 2012).
Mitchell, Donald Craig, *Take My Life, Take My Land: The Story of Congress' Historic Settlement of Alaska Native Land Claims, 1960–1971* (Fairbanks, AK: University of Alaska Press, 2001).
Morrison, William R., and Kenneth A. Coates, *Working the North: Labor and the Northwest Defense Projects, 1942–1946* (Fairbanks, AK: University of Alaska Press, 1994).
Mueller, Ernest W., "Alaskan Oil, the Energy Crisis, and the Environment", US EPA Working Paper No. 26 (US Environmental Protection Agency, February 1974).
Naske, Claus-M., *49 At Last! The Battle for Alaska Statehood*, revised edition (Kenmore, WA: Epicenter, 2009).
"Naval Petroleum Reserves", Hearings before the Committee on Armed Services, House of Representatives, 83rd Congress, First Session (1953), 290–291.
"Oil Executive Sees More Finds in Alaska if US Aids in Risks", *New York Times* (30 May 1970).
"Oil Seepages of the Alaskan Arctic Slope", War Minerals Report 258 (Washington, DC: Bureau of Mines, 1944).
Page, R. J. D., "Norman Wells: The Past and Future Boom", *Journal of Canadian Studies* 16 (Summer 1981): 16–18.
Perras, Galen Roger, *Stepping Stones to Nowhere: The Aleutian Islands, Alaska, and American Military Strategy* (Vancouver, BC: University of British Columbia Press, 2003).
Piper, Liza, *The Industrial Transformation of Subarctic Canada* (Vancouver, BC: University of British Columbia Press, 2009).
Pratt, Joseph, and William E. Hale, *Exxon: Transforming Energy, 1973–2005* (Austin, TX: University of Texas, 2013).

Pratt, Wallace E., "Oil Fields in the Arctic", *Harpers Magazine* 188 (January 1944): 108–112.
Ramley, David A., *Crooked Road: The Story of the Alaska Highway* (New York: McGraw Hill, 1976).
Reed, John C., "Exploration of Naval Petroleum Reserve No. 4 and Adjacent Areas, Northern Alaska, 1944–53", US Geological Survey Professional Paper 301 (Washington, DC: Government Printing Office, 1958).
Reed, John C., "The Story of the Naval Arctic Research Laboratory", *Arctic* 22, Proceedings of the U.S. Naval Arctic Research Laboratory, Dedication Symposium (September 1969): 177–183.
Rogers, George, *The Future of Alaska: The Economic Consequences of Statehood* (Baltimore, MD: Johns Hopkins University Press, 1962).
Sabin, Paul, "Voices from the Hydrocarbon Frontier: Canada's Mackenzie Valley Pipeline Inquiry (1974–1977)", *Environmental History Review* 19 (Spring 1995).
Sabin, Paul, *Crude Politics: The California Oil Market* (Berkeley, CA: University of California Press, 2005).
Schulman, Peter A., *Coal and Empire: The Birth of Energy Security in Industrial America* (Baltimore, MD: Johns Hopkins University Press, 2015).
Smith, Philip, "Mineral Resources of Alaska", US Geological Survey (Washington, DC: Government Printing Office, 1924).
Stuhl, Andrew, *Unfreezing the Arctic: Science, Colonialism, and the Transformation on Inuit Lands* (Chicago: University of Chicago Press, 2016).
Sullivan, Walter S., "Navy Pushes Hunt for Oil in Alaska: Residents of Fairbanks Hail Prospects of Becoming a Refining Center", *New York Times* (6 October 1946).
Sweet, John, *Discovery at Prudhoe Bay: Mountain Men and Seismic Vision Drilled Black Gold* (Surrey, BC: Hancock House, 2008).
Taylor, Graham D., *Imperial Standard: Imperial Oil, Exxon, and the Canadian Oil Industry from 1880* (Calgary, AB: Calgary University Press, 2019).
US Army Corps of Engineers, Alaska District, "Historical Record: CANOL Project" (Anchorage, AK: US Army Corps of Engineers, 1950).
"US Conducts Wide Uranium Hunt in Alaska", *Chicago Daily Tribune* (19 December 1946).
"Washington Wire", *Wall Street Journal* (2 January 1948).
Williamson, Herald F., Ralph L. Andreano, Arnold R. Daum, et al., *American Petroleum Industry*, Vol. 2: *The Age of Energy, 1899–1959* (Chicago: Northwestern University, 1963).
Willis, Roxanne, *Alaska's Place in the West: From Last Frontier to the Last Great Wilderness* (Lawrence, KS: University of Kansas, 2010).

25

The Rise of Circumpolar Political Movements

MARK NUTTALL

Introduction

This chapter provides a snapshot of the recent history of Indigenous political movements in the circumpolar north. Over the past six decades or so, Indigenous peoples across the Arctic have pushed forward with political action and initiatives that have aimed to secure national and international recognition of their rights, land claims, the granting of autonomy, and participation in many of the decision-making processes and institutions of governance that affect their lives and homelands.[1] Indigenous peoples' organizations have also become major actors in Arctic environmentalism and international circumpolar affairs.[2]

Circumpolar political movements have arisen largely because of the experiences and legacies of colonization and dispossession, conflicts over land and customary resource use, policies of resettlement enacted by state governments, disruptive social and economic change, residential schools, the social and environmental impacts of extractive industry, and the effects of globalization on Indigenous societies. Indigenous peoples of the circumpolar north share historical and contemporary experiences of living within the administrative and legal systems of nation-states that have attempted to assimilate, marginalize, dispossess, or suppress Indigenous societies, cultures, languages, and livelihoods. This is illustrated by land claims processes, campaigns and struggles for self-government, calls for reconciliation, and action that addresses the legacies of colonialism.[3]

---

1 Examples include Dahl et al., eds., *Nunavut*; Henderson, *Nunavut*; Gray, *Predicament*; Herrmann and Martin, eds., *Indigenous Peoples' Governance*; Mitchell, *From Talking Chiefs*; Wessendorf, ed., *Indigenous Parliament?*; Zellen, *Breaking the Ice*.
2 Nuttall, "Indigenous Peoples"; Semenova, "Political Mobilisation"; Shadian, "Indigeneity".
3 Freeman, ed., *Endangered Peoples*; Howard, *Indigenous Peoples*; Jull, "Politics of Sustainable Development"; Rÿser, *Indigenous Nations*.

Some Arctic states have recognized, to a certain degree, the need for new political arrangements that acknowledge Indigenous rights and have settled land claims or have granted specific forms of self-government.[4] In Alaska, Canada, and Greenland, a number of significant land claims settlements and self-government arrangements have been negotiated between national governments and Indigenous peoples. These include the Alaska Native Claims Settlement Act of 1971, Greenland Home Rule in 1979 (followed thirty years later by Self-Rule), and in Canada, the James Bay and Northern Quebec Agreement (1975), the Inuvialuit Final Agreement (1984), the Nunavut Land Claims Agreement of 1993 (which led to the inauguration of the Territory of Nunavut in 1999), and the Labrador Inuit Land Claims Agreement of 2005, which established Nunatsiavut. These agreements have sought to settle, at least to a certain extent, issues relating to Indigenous rights with respect to traditional territories and resources, and to address self-determination concerning political, cultural and linguistic rights, and well-being.

While the North American Arctic has seen progress with such political settlements, in Norway, Sweden, Finland, and Russia, many land claims issues and Indigenous rights are contested and largely unresolved, although in northern Norway, Sámi now participate in a land management regime.[5] In the case of Russia, legal constraints on the definition of indigeneity and traditional resource use have had implications for the recognition of Indigenous rights and have hindered political movements.[6] However, even when land claims have been agreed in Canada and Alaska, their full implementation can often be a long, drawn-out process, and from an Indigenous perspective achieving a form of political and economic autonomy does not always mean that self-determination has been realized.

Indigenous political movements in the circumpolar north have emerged (and continue to emerge) in the form of Indigenous non-governmental organizations and grass-roots protest in response to specific issues of local and regional concern, such as hydrocarbon projects in Canada and hydroelectric schemes in northern Norway.[7] Indigenous political action has also been mobilized on a global scale in the face of extractive industries, international opposition to traditional hunting practices such as whaling and

---

4 Tidwell and Zellen, eds., *Land, Indigenous Peoples and Conflict*.
5 Wessendorf, *An Indigenous Parliament?*; Spitzer and Selle, "Claims-Based Co-management".
6 See for instance Balzer, "Indigeneity"; Gray, *Predicament*; Semenova, "Political Mobilisation".
7 See for instance Bjørklund, "Industrial Impacts"; Minde, "Challenge of Indigenism"; Paine, *Dam a River*; Nuttall, "Zero Tolerance".

sealing, the long-range transport of contaminants and pollutants, and the impacts of climate change on the Arctic, and in support of circumpolar networks that call for community-based monitoring, conservation, and the establishment of protected areas that incorporate Indigenous knowledge and perspectives.[8]

In the North American Arctic, agreements have been reached between the governments of nation-states and Indigenous people that recognize Indigenous claims and grant Indigenous communities varying degrees of autonomy or self-government.[9] No agreement has yet been so far-reaching as to give an Indigenous group or region full political independence (although the Act on Greenland Self-Government of June 2009 does allow that a decision on independence can be taken by the people of Greenland), but the decentralization of specific administrative functions and responsibilities to local and regional authorities and governments means that some Indigenous peoples now have greater responsibility over their own affairs, as illustrated by comprehensive land claims in Canada and the extensive system of self-government in Greenland. Other forms of participation include co-management models and community-based monitoring that allow Indigenous peoples a certain measure of involvement in decision-making processes and the management of lands, resources, and hunting and fishing.[10] A historical perspective on the political campaigning that has led to such structures, arrangements, and institutions reveals a diversity of approaches and outcomes across the circumpolar north, but also important instances of shared action that speak to the growing agency of Indigenous people and the strength of Indigenous political voices.

Colonization and Change

The Arctic comprises a diversity of homelands for Indigenous peoples such as the Iñupiat, Yup'iit, Alutiit, Aleuts, and Athapaskans of Alaska; the Inuit, Inuvialuit, Athapaskans, and Dene of northern Canada; the Kalaallit, Inughuit, and Iivit of Greenland; the Sámi of Fennoscandia and Russia's

---

8 See for instance Downie and Fenge, *Northern Lights Against POPs*; Lynge, *Arctic Wars*; Nuttall, *Protecting the Arctic*; Herrmann and Martin, eds., *Indigenous Peoples' Governance*; Shadian, *Politics of Arctic Sovereignty*; Wenzel, *Animal Rights, Human Rights*. On the political responses of Indigenous communities to globalization and its pressures see Hall and Fenelon, *Indigenous Peoples and Globalization*.
9 Zellen, *Breaking the Ice*.
10 See for instance Huntington, *Wildlife Management*; Dale and Armitage, "Marine Mammal Co-management".

Kola Peninsula; and a diversity of peoples in the Russian North and Siberia that include Chukchi, Even, Evenk, Nenets, Nivkhi, and Yukaghir. Whether they live as hunters, fishers, or reindeer herders, Arctic peoples have depended for several thousand years on the living resources of land and sea. Today, there is increasing occupational differentiation within Indigenous societies, and people are being drawn to more urban environments, but many Indigenous livelihoods and community economies across the Arctic continue to be based largely on harvesting and using living terrestrial, marine, and freshwater resources. In Greenland, for instance, the most commonly harvested species are marine mammals such as seals, walrus, narwhals, beluga, fin and minke whales; polar bear and land mammals such as caribou, reindeer, and muskox; and fish such as halibut, cod, salmon, and Arctic char. Many of these species provide meat for food, their furs are used for clothing, and other parts, such as bone, are utilized for a range of products, but they are also often key to the formal economic activities and income of households and communities, while fish products are major exports for Greenland's economy.[11]

Indigenous peoples maintain a strong, vital connection to their surroundings through customary resource-use activities, which provide the basis for food production and sustainable livelihoods, in a way that marks them off from non-Indigenous communities. Indeed, one defining attribute of being Indigenous is that it refers to a specific people relating their identity, heritage, and cultural well-being to a particular area and to their traditional cultural and economic dependence on local resources, thus distinguishing them culturally and politically from other peoples and settlers who came to their territories subsequently.[12] Traditional resource-use practices and human–environment relations emphasize reciprocity and remain important for maintaining social relatedness and cultural identity in Indigenous societies. They also reinforce, reproduce, and celebrate relationships between people, animals, and the environment.[13]

From the sixteenth century, voyages of discovery, the gradual colonization of the Arctic, and the exploitation of circumpolar resources through fur trade activities and commercial whaling led to more frequent and prolonged contact between Indigenous peoples and outsiders. This intensified during

---

11 Caulfield, "Political Economy"; Dahl, *Saqqaq*; Kalland and Sejersen, *Marine Mammals*; Nuttall, *Arctic Homeland*.
12 Jentoft et al., eds., *Indigenous Peoples*; Tidwell and Zellen, eds., *Land, Indigenous Peoples and Conflict*.
13 See for instance Anderson, *Identity and Ecology*; Nuttall, *Arctic Homeland*.

the nineteenth and early twentieth centuries. Explorers, whalers, and traders introduced new economic and cultural influences, technologies, and material goods, while unsettling human–environment relations and impacting wildlife populations. Colonial administrators brought northern peoples within the confines of new political institutions and legal systems, while missionaries worked on converting them to Christianity. Over the past 50–100 years in particular, nation-states have enacted policies of resettlement and assimilation, moving nomadic peoples into permanent communities and placing Indigenous children in schools (some of them residential institutions, especially in the case of Canada).[14] The effect has been to transform Indigenous cultures through social, economic, and political changes, to perpetuate social suffering and trauma, to place Indigenous languages under threat, and to erode both the material and cultural bases of customary practices of hunting, fishing, and herding.

In Arctic Canada, for example, Inuit were drawn into situations of economic dependency on Hudson's Bay Company trading posts in the twentieth century. Canadian governments followed a policy of minimalist intervention into the lives of the Inuit, but they were nonetheless affected by economic development as a result of Canada's approach to the Arctic as a hinterland of resources, such as the industrial transformation of the Arctic and Sub-Arctic from mining and the exploration for hydrocarbons.[15] Canada decided on active intervention in the 1950s – partly because of having been shamed internationally by reports of starvation in Inuit nomadic camps – and began to settle Inuit into permanent communities, including for purposes of establishing sovereignty in the High Arctic.[16] Inuit children were sent to school and had to learn a Euro-Canadian curriculum through the medium of English (or French in Quebec). Through education and training, the Indigenous inhabitants of the Arctic were to become modern Canadians, and settlement was aimed at improving their lifestyle options in a new period of economic development on the Canadian Arctic frontier. Government resettlement policies served to undermine traditional Inuit hunting culture further, though, and increased Inuit dependency on the Canadian government and institutions, as well as resulting in far-reaching and long-lasting social

---

14 For a comprehensive analysis, see the final reports of the Truth and Reconciliation Commission (TRC) of Canada, which were published in six volumes in 2015, along with a summary and calls to action. The reports can be read and downloaded at the TRC website, www.trc.ca/about-us/trc-findings.html.
15 See for instance Grant, *Polar Imperative*.
16 Brody, *The People's Land*; Tester and Kulchyski, *Tammarniit (Mistakes)*.

problems.[17] The presence in their settlements of large numbers of southern Canadians as administrators, trade managers, teachers, and construction workers caused considerable resentment among Inuit. Tension and conflict between the Inuit and these incomers, many of whom were transient and seldom remained long in the north, was common.[18]

Many non-Indigenous Canadians regarded Greenland as an admirable example of how northern Canada could be developed and the needs of its Indigenous communities more satisfactorily addressed. Danish colonization of Greenland dates from 1721, when the Lutheran priest Hans Egede established the settlement today known as Nuuk. For over 200 years, the Danes followed an isolationist policy towards Greenland and the indigenous Inuit, controlling trade from 1776 by granting a monopoly to the state-backed Royal Greenland Trading Company (*Det kongelige grønlandske handel*, KGH) and effectively keeping Greenland as a closed country by strictly regulating access to visitors from the outside world. After World War II, Denmark ended this policy and instead pivoted toward a programme of social welfare and infrastructural change as part of a process of modernization of both the country and Inuit society. This was characterized by profound and extensive social, economic, and political change and upheaval. Two Danish government reports, widely known as the G-50 and the G-60 reports after the years in which they were produced, recommended ambitious programmes of investment-driven modernization based on a commercial fishing industry and a rationalization of Greenlandic society, with the closure of small hunting settlements and the concentration of the population in larger towns. Improved health care aided population growth. The aim was to turn Greenlanders into Danish citizens, the Danish language was privileged over Greenlandic, and a number of Greenlandic children were separated from their families and sent to school in Denmark.

During the 1960s, Denmark implemented controversial policies of centralization and urbanization in Greenland. Many people were moved from small, remote settlements and relocated in towns on the west coast, with year-round ice-free, open-water harbours, including Godthåb (Nuuk), Sukkertoppen (Maniitsoq), Holsteinsborg (Sisimiut), and Frederikshåb (Paamiut), where investment in the development of the fishing industry and provision of services was largely concentrated. The number of Danes sent to work in Greenland as administrators, teachers, doctors, nurses, police officers, managers in the fishing industry and other businesses, technicians,

---

17 Brody, *The People's Land*; Henderson, *Nunavut*.   18 Brody, *The People's Land*.

25 The Rise of Circumpolar Political Movements

and construction workers increased significantly. These programmes came with a strong technocratic impulse from Copenhagen, symbolized by the powerful Greenland Technical Organization (GTO), which was charged with building infrastructure and which assumed considerable power over executing Danish policies of development. There were social problems to overcome and solve, but Greenland was in some ways also considered a technical challenge. By the late 1960s and early 1970s, Greenlandic Inuit society had been transformed from primarily small-scale hunting and fishing to a modern, export-oriented economy. As Jens Heinrich has noted in this volume, many Indigenous Greenlanders accepted and even welcomed the changes, and there was Greenlandic participation in the commissions that scoped out the development policy processes.

However, the social changes and upheavals experienced following World War II, and specifically in the 1950s and 1960s, also led to the emergence of Inuit political parties and a heightened sense of Inuit identity. The majority of the Inuit population now lived in the fast-growing west coast towns, a demographic transition which brought its own problems. While life in small settlements had been characterized by and organized around kinship and close social relations, the move to towns disrupted kin-based groups, leading to alienation, social and economic marginality, and discrimination. This was aggravated by ethnic tensions and increasing numbers of Danes living in Greenland because of the need for construction workers, teachers, doctors, and administrators.[19] The coal mining settlement of Qullissat developed a reputation for leftist sympathies, with Indigenous Greenlandic miners finding inspiration in the global workers' movement. The Inuit Party, established in 1963, was the first Greenlandic political party to have wide public support. It was a political reaction to discrimination inherent in Danish policies, such as the 'birthplace criterion' that meant civil servants born in Greenland received 85 per cent of the wages that were paid to civil servants who were born in Denmark. Inspired by Icelandic independence in 1944 and Home Rule in the Faroe Islands in 1948, it advocated for Greenland's complete independence from Denmark, but it failed to maintain momentum on this issue and was dissolved in 1967.

Under the terms of its formal incorporation into the Danish political state in 1953, Greenland elected two members to the Danish parliament, who from the start represented Indigenous interests. In 1969, Knud Hertling, who had been elected a Greenlandic member of the Danish Parliament in 1964 as

---

19 Nuttall, "Greenland".

a Social Democrat, founded the short-lived Sukaq Party (*sukaq* means 'pillar' or 'support'). More enduring was Siumut, which means 'forward', organized as a political movement in 1975 and established as a political party in 1977. Siumut had its origins at the beginning of the 1970s when Greenlandic politicians Moses Olsen (who had been elected a Greenlandic member of the Danish Parliament), Jonathan Motzfeldt, and Lars Emil Johansen (the last two elected to the Greenlandic Council) decided to establish their own political group. Their action was a response to Danish policies enacted in Greenland, especially in the previous two decades, but the beginnings of the Siumut movement can also be traced to a more proximate issue – Greenlandic opposition to membership of the European Community, in part because of concerns over fishing rights, when Denmark joined in 1972. Siumut has taken something of a moderate socialist position since its establishment and has remained the dominant political party in Greenland ever since, even if its periods in power have been as part of coalition government arrangements. At the election of April 2021, however, this dominance was interrupted when the leftist and separatist Inuit Ataqatigiit (IA) party came to power and formed a coalition with the centrist-populist Naleraq (IA had previously been in power from 2009 to 2013, when it formed a coalition government with the Demokraatit party). Originally inspired by radical socialist ideas, IA began as a political movement by Greenlandic students in Denmark in the 1970s. It was established formally as a political party in Aasiaat in West Greenland in 1976 and took an explicit anti-imperialist and anti-colonial stance.[20]

Land Claims and Self-government

Despite social, cultural, and economic transformations and ruptures, many Indigenous communities continue to rely on terrestrial and marine resources, and maintain a strong connection to the environment through these activities. Yet Arctic communities also continue to struggle with the legacies and contemporary realities of colonization and change, of resettlement from small hunting, fishing, and reindeer-herding camps and villages into newly created towns, of increasing urbanization, the effects of globalization, language loss and the erosion of tradition, and a struggle for cultural survival and political autonomy and economic independence. Some of these legacies and

---

20 The forerunner, in a sense, of IA was the Inuit Party. However, the Inuit Party should not be confused with a breakaway group called Partii Inuit, made up of former IA members, that was in a coalition with Siumut and Atassut in 2013–2017.

effects are evident in the poor health situations that are experienced disproportionately by Indigenous populations across the Arctic.[21] Parts of the tundra and boreal environments of Alaska, northern Canada, northern Fennoscandia, and the Russian North have also been disturbed, often in violent ways, by extensive industrial development, such as oil extraction facilities, pipelines and trails from seismic surveys, roads, mining projects (and their toxic legacies), or commercial forestry and clear-cut logging.[22]

For Indigenous peoples globally, the relationships between people and land are indissoluble and so it follows that land rights are inextricably linked to land claims and are often at the heart of Indigenous political movements and Indigenous claims for self-government.[23] Land claims movements – and hence the assertion and reclaiming of land rights – are struggles for self-determination, self-government, autonomy, and justice. Greenland's status as an island with an easily defined border constitutes an important difference from other Indigenous lands in the circumpolar north, where boundaries have been more difficult to draw. In many other cases the protection of Indigenous lands, the recognition of rights to lands and resources, and the settlement of land claims have been seen as essential for the very survival of Indigenous peoples and cultures. Henry Minde shows how the Alta River hydroelectric project in the Sámi heartland of northern Norway in the late 1970s and early 1980s precipitated Sámi political action that changed the dynamic between the state and Sámi as an Indigenous people. Even though the project went ahead, it drew public attention to how Sámi had suffered from a policy of 'Norwegianization' over the previous century, which had not only aimed to assimilate Sámi but had brought customary natural resource use under the administration of the state, and heightened awareness that they were an Indigenous people with distinct rights over lands in northern Norway.[24] A sense of collective Indigenous identity was also strengthened, and Sámi political organization led to the establishment of a Sámi Parliament in 1987 and the constitutional recognition of Indigenous status in 1988. This obligates Norwegian state authorities to create the conditions necessary for the Sámi to protect and develop their language, their culture, and their society.[25]

21 See for instance Møller, "Circumpolar Health and Well-Being".
22 See for instance Herrmann et al., "Effects of Mining"; Keeling and Sandlos, *Mining and Communities*; Sirina, "Oil and Gas Development"; Yakovleva, "Oil Pipeline Construction".
23 Tidwell and Zellen, eds., *Land, Indigenous Peoples and Conflict*.
24 Nilsen, "From Norwegianization"; Minde, "Challenge of Indigenism"; Paine, *Dam a River*.
25 Shadian, "Indigeneity".

The Alta dam controversy was similar to debates in Greenland over resource extraction, including the controversial closure of the Qullissat coal mine and the opening of a lead–zinc mine at Maarmorilik in the early 1970s. But arguably the most significant development in terms of natural resources and Indigenous land rights came in the North American Arctic, where land claims movements in Alaska suddenly gained greater urgency following the 1968 discovery of oil at Prudhoe Bay on Alaska's North Slope. This specific region had long been regarded by government and military authorities as a potential source of oil, but the scale of the Prudhoe Bay strike was unexpected. Concern about such large-scale industrial development and its impacts, which has to be understood within a context of long-standing land use conflicts and threats of expropriation, as well as a history of controversial plans such as Project Chariot (a proposal by the US Atomic Energy Commission in 1958 to use nuclear explosions to create a harbour south of the Iñupiat community of Port Hope), led to the establishment of the Alaska Federation of Natives (AFN) in Anchorage in October 1966. The Alaska Statehood Act of 1958 (Alaska became a state in 1959) had assigned more than 40 million hectares of previously federal land to the new state, and the act required Alaska to select, survey, and patent one-third of the entire land area, which in the process threatened and undermined Native rights to these lands. Encroachment on Indigenous lands continued throughout the 1960s, notably from development, but federal hunting regulations also restricted customary subsistence use. The AFN lobbied the US Congress for the appropriate settlement of Alaskan Native land claims and by 1967 had filed claims for Native title to nearly 150 million of the nearly 152 million hectares of land in Alaska. The discovery of oil at Prudhoe Bay speeded the passage of the Alaska Native Claims Settlement Act (ANCSA) through Congress in 1971. ANCSA did not recognise Indigenous claims to the whole of the state of Alaska, but it did establish twelve regional Native corporations with effective control over one-ninth of the state (a thirteenth corporation was established for Alaska Natives living outside the state). ANCSA extinguished Native claims to the rest of Alaska and awarded $962.5 million in compensation. In effect, ANCSA made Alaska's Native peoples shareholders in corporate-owned land.

Across the border in Canada, Indigenous communities followed developments in Alaska with great interest. Partly, this related to the specific progress made during the ANCSA negotiations, which appeared to indicate a significant level of political recognition, a particularly sore point in Canada given the federal government's controversial 1969 White Paper that proposed to abolish First Nations rights in the belief they prevented full inclusion in Canadian society.[26] Although the White Paper did not cover Inuit, it nevertheless spoke to a wider sense of indifference or even antagonism to Indigenous rights. In 1981, as Yukon First Nations were preparing for negotiations in advance of land claims, a delegation from the Council of Yukon Indians (CYI; now known as the Council of Yukon First Nations [CYFN]) undertook a study tour in Alaska to learn about the social, economic, and political benefits of ANCSA ten years after its implementation. CYI was formed in 1973, and brought together the Yukon Native Brotherhood and the Yukon Association of Non-Status Indians. The resulting report expressed solidarity with Alaska Native people but was critical of the corporate nature of ANCSA and, in particular, the organizational structures and legal regimes within which they now had to move and negotiate. 'One strong impression we were left with', the report's authors wrote, 'was that many Alaskan Natives, particularly the city-based managers and professionals, have forgotten who they are. They adopt organizational goals which are not different from non-Native ones. They are distant from their origins.'[27] The tour and the report influenced the way Yukon First Nations reflected on the nature of what kind of land claim process they would press for and accept.

As Wessendorf points out, regional organizations in the present-day Northwest Territories (NWT), Yukon and Alaska represent a diversity of Indigenous peoples, as compared to Nunavut and Greenland, which have almost entirely Inuit populations, and Sápmi, the Sámi homeland in northern Fennoscandia.[28] Given this diversity, reaching consensus on proposals that all members of a community can agree has frequently been a difficult process. Land claims negotiations have also been hampered by the legacies of historical acts that sought to amalgamate and assimilate such culturally diverse peoples. For example, the Canadian federal government amalgamated separate and distinct First Nations communities in Yukon for administrative purposes in the 1950s. Small communities were brought together into a single band which, while convenient for administrators, only served to undermine cultural values and institutions and created divisions within communities that persisted for generations. David Leas argues that this hindered the development of Indigenous political movements in Yukon, and the development of governance structures, institutions, and constitutions for First Nations governments have often been quite difficult exercises,

---

26 See, for instance, Wheeler, *Making Canadian Indian Policy*.
27 Council for Yukon First Nations, *Land Before Money*, 23.
28 Wessendorf, *An Indigenous Parliament?*, 18–19.

'particularly in those communities that are no longer culturally cohesive due to the influxes of members from other communities'.[29]

In the 1970s, many Indigenous leaders felt a Prudhoe Bay-style oil strike could soon transform the Mackenzie Delta and the coastal regions of the Beaufort Sea. In response the Inuvialuit (whose homelands stretched from the Alaskan border to western Victoria Island) formed the Committee of Original People's Entitlement (COPE) in 1970 to provide an Indigenous voice on issues from resource extraction to housing, with an overriding focus on land rights. In 1971 the Inuit Tapirisat of Canada (ITC) was established as a national voice for Inuit throughout Canada's north, with Tagak Curley as its founding president. Its mission statement foregrounded the negotiation of Inuit land claims and argued that colonization had violated the fundamental rights of Inuit in Canada to govern themselves.[30] Here there were similarities to Greenland, where a new generation of Indigenous activists – many educated in Denmark – couched criticisms of Danish administration in terms of failed colonial projects rather than simply administrative or political mistakes. ITC changed its name to Inuit Tapiriit Kanatami (ITK) in 2001, following the signing of four major Inuit land claims agreements, and it continues to work on issues of importance for the preservation of Inuit identity, languages, culture, and livelihood.

In Greenland, politicians and political activists, organized as the new main political parties of Siumut, Atassut, and IA, began to campaign against Danish governance and advocate for Home Rule in the early 1970s, although IA had initially opposed Home Rule as it felt it would legitimize Danish control over Greenland and argued that the only acceptable political settlement would be independence. During the 1970s the Home Rule debate progressed, within a framework that was comfortably familiar to Danish eyes – political parties, negotiations with authorized representatives, and finally a referendum of the Greenlandic population on 17 January 1979 that decisively voted for the negotiated Home Rule settlement. As with Arctic North America, concerns over who would have the right to control and to derive benefit from oil and gas extraction played a part in the negotiations.

Following the withdrawal of the White Paper in 1970, the Canadian federal government established a policy framework in 1973 for negotiation and settlement of comprehensive land claims by Indigenous people. Canada's 1982 Constitution Act recognized and affirmed the Aboriginal and treaty rights of the country's Indigenous peoples – the Inuit, First Nations, and

---

29 Leas, "Self-government in Yukon", 132.   30 Mitchell, *From Talking Chiefs*.

Métis – and the Inherent Right Policy of 1995 set out how self-government negotiations and arrangements can be considered as part of comprehensive land claims. The federal government also concluded land claims agreements with specific Indigenous groups, often with the looming threat (or promise) of natural resource extraction as a factor. The report of the Mackenzie Valley Pipeline Inquiry of the mid-1970s, for example, which was overseen by Justice Thomas Berger, expressed concerns over the potential impacts of the project and argued that Indigenous people would probably not derive any benefit from pipeline development given the absence of land claims and other legal settlements with the federal government.[31] In 1975, the Inuit and Cree of northern Quebec signed the first comprehensive land claims agreement with the federal government against the backdrop of controversy surrounding hydroelectric development in James Bay. The process of dealing with land claims has been extremely slow in some regions, however. Most agreements made to date have been with Inuit groups in the Arctic and with First Nations in the NWT and Yukon Territory. The Inuvialuit of the western Arctic reached a land claim in 1984, the Gwich'in did so in 1992, the Sahtu Dene in 1994, and the Inuit of Canada's Eastern Arctic were given their own de facto self-governing territory, Nunavut, in 1999. In the NWT, the Tlicho (Dogrib) First Nation signed a land claims agreement with the Canadian government in 2003; at the time of writing, negotiations for land, resource, and self-government rights continue with the Dehcho First Nations and the Akaitcho Dene, while negotiations for self-government are in progress with the Inuvialuit, Gwich'in, and the Sahtu Dene community of Deline. In the Yukon Territory, the Umbrella Final Agreement, reached in 1988 and finalized in 1990, has been used as the framework for individual land claims agreements with each of the fourteen Yukon First Nations. Since then, ten First Nations have signed and ratified an agreement; another two have signed agreements which were not ratified after being defeated in referendums; and two are still being negotiated. In many parts of the northern areas of the provinces of Alberta, British Columbia, Saskatchewan, Manitoba, and Ontario, treaties signed between Indigenous groups and the Crown in the late nineteenth and early twentieth centuries remain in effect.

The specific histories of how colonial states ordered Indigenous communities continue to shape political settlements in the present. In Canada, the Numbered Treaties model set the pattern for Crown-Indigenous relations in the late nineteenth and early twentieth centuries. Accordingly, comprehensive

---

31 Berger, *Northern Frontier, Northern Homeland*.

land claims processes with Indigenous Arctic communities are, in effect, modern treaties with the potential to act as a first step towards self-government. As Irlbacher-Fox states, the negotiating processes are 'compelled by legally recognized aboriginal rights to lands and resources'.[32] The Inuvialuit Final Agreement accorded title to 90,650 km^2 of the NWT to the Inuvialuit, together with financial compensation and other rights (including gas, petroleum, and mineral rights for 12,950 km^2) as a final settlement of territorial claims. The territory of Nunavut (which means 'our land' in Inuktitut), comprises over 2 million km^2 of northern Canada and was inaugurated on 1 April 1999. The population of Nunavut is around 80 per cent Inuit and the government is effectively Inuit-led. While the settlement did not create a new ethnic Inuit region, Canadian territories and provinces have extensive public self-government within the limits defined by the Canadian constitution. Nonetheless, Nunavut has given the Inuit of the eastern Arctic a greater degree of autonomy and self-government than is enjoyed by any other Indigenous group in Canada.[33] The Inuit homeland of Nunavik in northern Quebec is currently subject to negotiations for status as a self-governing region within the province, while following ratification of the Labrador Inuit Land Claims Agreement, the government of Nunatsiavut was established in 2005 to represent the rights of Inuit living in the northernmost areas of the province of Newfoundland and Labrador. It is important to emphasize, however, that land claims settlements do not equate to self-government. For example, while Inuit in Nunavut are beneficiaries of the territory's land claim, government in Nunavut is public government, while the Labrador Inuit land claim agreement was unique in that it included provisions for self-government. Nunatsiavut (which means 'our beautiful land' in Inuktitut) remains part of the province of Newfoundland and Labrador, but the Nunatsiavut government is an Inuit regional government that has authority over areas such as education, health, justice, culture and language, and community matters.

In Greenland, on the other hand, political change at the structural level has been driven by negotiation directly between Danish and Greenlandic representatives, validated by referendums that adjusted the constitutional responsibilities of each side within the territory of Greenland as a whole. On 25 November 2008, 75.5 per cent of the Greenlandic electorate who turned out for a referendum on greater autonomy voted in favour of a new form of self-government called Self-Rule, which was instituted on 21 June 2009. While

---

32 Irlbacher-Fox, "Land Claims".   33 Dahl et al., eds., *Nunavut*; Henderson, *Nunavut*.

Greenland remains a part of the Kingdom of Denmark, the Self-Rule authorities have embarked on an ambitious policy of nation-building and state-formation, with some politicians aspiring to eventual independence (most notably marked in recent years by the drafting of a Greenlandic constitution). Fishing for cod and shrimp is vital to the country's economy, and many small communities still depend on marine mammal hunting, but in recent years Greenlandic political leaders have embarked on policies to develop an extractive industries sector, arguing that the revenues from this would help to facilitate economic and political independence, and a number of mining operations are beginning.[34]

In the Nordic Arctic, Sámi governance differs from Inuit governance in Canada and Greenland in that Indigenous governance in Norway, Sweden and Finland is managed by the state.[35] There have been no treaties between Nordic governments and Sámi, and neither has the land claims model been widely used as a basis for negotiation in Norway or Sweden. However, as in North America, it is resource extraction and development on Sámi lands, as the controversy and events surrounding the Alta-Kautokeino River hydroelectric project in northern Norway in the late 1970s and early 1980s illustrated, that have politicized Sámi issues and rights. While the Sámi Parliaments in Sweden and Norway were established in 1992 and 1987 respectively, the first Sámi Parliament was established in Finland in 1973, and in 1995 the Finnish Constitution recognized 35,000 km^2 of northern Finland as a Sámi homeland, within which Sámi have a right to cultural autonomy.

In Sweden and more recently Norway the Sámi village (*siida*) has been recognized as an administrative unit whose members are entitled to rights over land and resource use, principally reindeer herding, but also hunting and fishing, including for profit. The long-running case between the Swedish state and the Girjas Sámi village over the extent and exclusivity of these latter rights was concluded in 2020 with a victory for the village. In its ruling, the court asserted that the Swedish state bore the burden of proof in proving that Indigenous rights had been extinguished through practice or legislation.[36] The argument bore similarities to rulings in other state contexts, notably the 1973 *Calder v. Attorney-General of British Columbia* case that established the rights of the Nisga'a people over their ancestral lands.

---

34 Nuttall, *Climate, Society*.   35 Shadian, "Indigeneity".
36 Allard and Brännström, "Girjas Reindeer Herding Community".

In Russia, there are complex and unresolved issues that relate to the autonomy and self-determination of Indigenous peoples. Although Indigenous minorities of the Russian North were given certain rights and privileges under the Soviets, these rights have not always been recognized, and many Indigenous groups are demanding forms of self-government and regional autonomy. Russian legislation strictly defines indigeneity.[37] Some forty peoples are legally recognized as 'indigenous, small-numbered peoples of the North, Siberia and the Far East', a status that is tied to the conditions that an indigenous group has no more than 50,000 members, maintains a traditional way of life, inhabits certain remote regions of Russia, and identifies itself as a distinct ethnic community. The Association of the Indigenous Minorities of the Far North, Siberia, and the Far East was founded in March 1990 at the first 'Congress of the Peoples of the North of the Soviet Union' and adopted its current name of the Russian Association of Indigenous Peoples of the North (RAIPON) at its second congress in November 1993. It was incorporated as a public organization within the Russian Ministry of Justice in March 1994.[38] RAIPON was duplicated by the establishment of organizations at the regional level which aimed to influence federal legislation.[39] These organizations worked in cooperation with intellectuals, urban Indigenous élites, and international organizations, and drafted documents that aimed to influence legal thinking about community-based self-government and Indigenous rights.[40] As an example of how intellectuals sought to define Indigenous rights, ethnographer Aleksandr Pika advanced ideas of 'neotraditionalism' based on traditional resource use practices as the basis for self-government.[41] This work contributed to a process that led to changes in legislation and the passing of acts and decrees. Notably, the small-numbered peoples are protected by Article 69 of the Russian Constitution and three federal framework laws that establish cultural, territorial, and political rights, yet the implementation of regulations contained in these laws has been complicated by subsequent changes to natural resource legislation and government decisions on natural resource use in the North. RAIPON and its regional organizations also worked with federal government bodies and municipal government institutions on issues of social and legal problems.

---

37 Balzer, "Indigeneity".   38 Rethmann, "Russian Association".
39 See for instance Crate, "Co-option in Siberia"; Sirina, "Oil and Gas Development".
40 Novikova, "Self-government".
41 Pika, ed., *Neotraditionalism*; Pika et al., eds., *Anxious North*.

25 The Rise of Circumpolar Political Movements

In March 1992, a federal government decree called for a law that would govern the establishment of *obshchinas*, which are organized around family-clan and wider Indigenous community territories, and the transfer of land to them. The law was passed in July 2000 and intended the *obshchina* to be a non-commercial economic and potentially self-governing unit.[42] However, *obshchinas* have no rights to subsurface resources or, for example, to other resources such as timber, and membership of an *obshchina* is limited to those Indigenous peoples who practise 'traditional' subsistence activities. Significantly, non-Indigenous people who hunt, fish, or herd are also entitled to form *obshchinas*. Since the mid-1990s, success in terms of new federal legislation has generally abated as socioeconomic and political problems have increased across Russia. The transition from the Soviet Union to the Russian Federation had an effect on Indigenous political movements, which was strikingly apparent in the reduction of the number of Indigenous representatives in regional and federal legislative bodies.[43] Indigenous peoples in northern Russia have experienced a gradual erosion of rights, and regional and national associations have become increasingly subject to state control. The legislation surrounding traditionalism, nationality, and ethnicity as defining aspects of indigeneity and its influence on Russian approaches to Indigenous rights has been heavily critiqued by scholars such as Balzer and Novikova as allowing the perpetuation of government development discourse and policy that had been a defining feature of Soviet attitudes to Indigenous peoples, and denying any recognition of the right to self-determination.[44]

The common thread running through the cases above is of rights over land being resolved within the context of the overarching state, and not as a precursor to full political sovereignty. Anthropologist Jens Dahl has pointed out the importance of recognizing that, in making land claims and seeking self-government, the Arctic's Indigenous peoples, such as the Inuit, Dene, and Athapaskans, have not been demanding the creation of autonomous ethnic states – rather, they have attempted to assert rights as distinctive peoples within nation states, and to be recognized as having such rights.[45] In most cases, these settlements and new arrangements have transformed the political, social, and economic lives of Indigenous peoples. For Canada, Bone has observed that comprehensive land claims 'provide the means and structure to participate in Canada's economy and society and yet retain a presence

---

42 Fondahl, "Russian Federation Law". 43 Rethmann, "Russian Association".
44 Balzer, "Tension"; and Novikova, "Self-government".
45 Dahl, "Indigenous Peoples", 108.

in their traditional economy and society'.[46] Yet as Irlbacher-Fox points out, the difference between self-determination and self-government may not always be understood by government representatives.[47] While Canada has negotiated land claims and self-government agreements with a number of Indigenous groups, and while they may allow for land ownership, have financial benefits, establish procedures for co-management, address regulations for the environmental review process for industrial projects, and generally give Indigenous communities greater opportunities for participation in decision-making processes, frustrations persist that the right to self-determination continues to be disregarded. Self-government agreements in Canada require Indigenous communities to participate within existing national institutional frameworks and demand an acceptance of Euro-Canadian models of governance, law, property, science, education, and well-being, which fail to recognize self-determination.[48] Irlbacher-Fox argues that self-government is set up to achieve a change 'from being Indigenous to being Indigenous in a way that reconciles Indigenous rights, interests, and being with what conforms to the norms of the Canadian Constitution, democracy and dominant culture'.[49] In this way, she argues, relationships between Indigenous people and the state are not decolonized, but merely modernized, and the institutional status quo remains unchanged.

Political agreements recognizing Indigenous claims and acknowledging rights to self-determination often include significant changes in the ways that living and non-living resources are managed and give importance to the incorporation of Indigenous environmental/ecological knowledge in wildlife management and environmental monitoring. A significant amount of local participation in, and control over, resource management decision-making has been enabled. In some cases, decision-making authority has been transferred to local communities or to Indigenous organizations and institutions at a more regional level, allowing Indigenous ecological knowledge a key role in informing matters of environmental governance. For example, in Nunavut the co-management of wildlife is legislated through the Nunavut Wildlife Management Board (NWMB), a public institution under the Nunavut Land Claims Agreement. It cooperates closely with Inuit hunters' and trappers' organizations, and the incorporation of Inuit *Qaujimajatuqangit* (IQ: Inuit traditional knowledge and ways of being) into its research operations and management principles is particularly strong. IQ has also informed initiatives

---

46 Bone, *Canadian North*, 192.   47 Irlbacher-Fox, *Finding Dahsha*, 160.
48 Coulthard, "Subjects of Empire"; Irlbacher-Fox, *Finding Dahsha*.
49 Irlbacher-Fox, *Finding Dahsha*, 3.

for Indigenous Protected Areas (IPAs) and collaborative environmental governance between Canada's federal government and Inuit communities and organizations for the Tallurutiup Imanga/Lancaster Sound National Marine Conservation Area in northern Nunavut and the Tuvaijuittuq Marine Protected Area in the Arctic Ocean off the coast of Ellesmere Island, Axel Heiberg Island, and other parts of Canada's Arctic Archipelago.

In Greenland, Canada, and Alaska, Inuit groups have outlined and implemented environmental strategies, conservation policies, and community-based monitoring initiatives to safeguard the future of Inuit resource use, and to ensure a workable participatory approach between Indigenous peoples, scientists, and policymakers, to the sustainable management and development of resources. From an Inuit perspective, threats to Arctic wildlife and the environment come not from hunting, but from climate change, and from airborne and seaborne pollutants that enter the Arctic from industrial areas far to the south of traditional Inuit homelands. Threats also come from the impact of non-renewable resource extraction within the Arctic, such as oil, gas, and mining exploration and development, and from increased shipping in northern waters. The expansion of extractive industries in the Arctic and the consequences for Indigenous peoples raise questions of who has rights over subsurface resources and to their development. This is particularly so in areas where Indigenous peoples are fighting for land claims and rights over resources and in places where ownership of subsurface rights is highly contested. In Siberia and eastern Russia, for example, oil and gas extraction and mining ventures have removed significantly large tracts of lands and territories from Indigenous use, and the transport of hydrocarbons across the lands of Indigenous peoples also impacts their traditional activities. Fondahl and Sirina discuss how, for much of the late twentieth century, hydrocarbon development in Russia took place on Indigenous lands, largely in the western Siberian oil fields on Khanty and Mansi traditional territory and the northwestern gas fields on Nenets homelands.[50] In Russia's far east, controversies over the exploitation of Sakhalin Island's oil reserves challenged the territorial rights of the Nivkhi, Evenki, and Uilta. While Russia's Indigenous peoples have received some benefits from oil and gas development, they do not have rights to subsurface resources, and generally the costs and the negative impacts of development on society, culture, environment, and wildlife outweigh whatever positive experiences can be identified and chronicled.

50 Fondahl and Sirina, "Oil Pipeline Development"; Fondahl and Sirina, "Rights and Risks"; see also Murashko, "Protecting Indigenous Peoples' Rights", for a broader discussion.

Indigenous Peoples' Organizations and Circumpolar Affairs

Since the 1970s, Indigenous peoples have emerged as significant actors in circumpolar political affairs. For example, Inuit organizations draw attention to understanding and addressing global forces that erode Inuit rights. Inuit continue to speak out against the animal rights activists still opposing seal hunting, and they are active in the annual meetings of the International Whaling Commission (IWC), working to defend aboriginal subsistence whaling and ensuring Inuit rights are taken into account when the IWC decides on quotas. In the Arctic Council, Indigenous peoples' organizations (IPOs) have argued for the greater inclusion of Indigenous knowledge in Arctic assessment work and in strategies for environmental management and sustainable development, with particular emphasis on the co-production of knowledge between scientists and Indigenous communities. They have played a major role in agenda-setting and political discussion on Arctic environmental issues and governance, and have gained visibility through participation in international fora and initiatives concerned with global sustainability challenges, geopolitics and security.[51]

As Peter Jull has noted, the era of Arctic Indigenous internationalism began with the Arctic Peoples' Conference in Copenhagen in November 1973.[52] Indigenous representatives from northern Canada, Greenland and the Sámi areas of Fennoscandia attended the conference (the Danish government provided Christiansborg, the parliament building, as a venue), which resulted in two resolutions. The first was an emphasis on the need to support and nurture Indigenous cultures and recognize the traditional use and occupancy of, and Indigenous rights to, the lands and waters of Indigenous territories; the second was a proposal to establish a circumpolar-wide body for Indigenous peoples to pursue collective interests. Although this body did not materialize, in some ways the Arctic Peoples' Conference paved the way for an initiative by Inuit leaders who worked on establishing what is now the Inuit Circumpolar Council (ICC).

The ICC represents the rights of Inuit in Greenland, Canada, Alaska, and Chukotka. It was established in Utqiagvik (Barrow), Alaska in 1977 as the Inuit Circumpolar Conference. This meeting of Inuit from across the circumpolar North was initiated by Eben Hopson Sr, who was mayor of the North Slope

---

51 Downie and Fenge, *Northern Lights against POPs*; Nuttall, "Indigenous Peoples"; Shadian, "Indigeneity".
52 Jull, "Politics of Sustainable Development".

Borough and had been involved in the negotiations that resulted in ANCSA. In part, the meeting, which Hopson called the 'First Inuit Circumpolar Pre-Conference', was convened as a response to increased oil and gas exploration and development in the Arctic, such as the expansion of activities on Alaska's North Slope and in the Beaufort Sea. Delegates participated from Alaska, Canada, and Greenland, but there was no representation from the Soviet Union, as members of Siberian Inuit communities (Yuit) were not permitted to travel. One outcome was a resolution that became the foundation for the future work of the ICC, stating that the Inuit of Alaska, Canada, and Greenland were a single indivisible people with a common language and culture, experiences and concerns, living in an Inuit homeland that was separated by the political boundaries of nation states.[53] The ICC held its first General Assembly in Nuuk in 1980 and Hans-Pavia Rosing from Greenland was elected as its first president for a three-year term. Rosing's work included making the ICC a non-governmental organization at the United Nations Economic and Social Council (ECOSOC) in February 1983.

The ICC set about challenging the policies of governments, multinational corporations and environmental movements, and has consistently argued that the protection of the Arctic environment and its resources should recognize Indigenous rights and be in accordance with Inuit tradition and cultural values. Since its formation, the ICC has sought to establish its own Arctic policies and has issued a number of declarations on, for example, Arctic sovereignty and resource development, informed by Indigenous environmental knowledge, that reflect Inuit concerns about development, climate change, pollution, shipping, and conservation, together with ethical and practical guidelines for human activity in the Arctic.

Reflecting its status as an actor in Arctic politics, the ICC played an active role in the development of the work of the Arctic Environmental Protection Strategy (AEPS) in the early 1990s. AEPS was in some ways the forerunner to the Arctic Council, formed in 1996, in which the ICC is a permanent participant alongside the Sámi Council, RAIPON, the Arctic Athabaskan Council (AAC), the Gwich'in Council International (GCI), and the Aleut International Association (AIA). Shadian argues that transnational Indigenous groups challenge traditional assumptions of sovereignty and, in the process, are carving out spaces for alternative sovereignties.[54] For the Arctic's Indigenous peoples, this includes attaining *cultural* sovereignty, rather than

---

53 Fægteborg, "Inuit Circumpolar Conference (ICC)".
54 Shadian, *Politics of Arctic Sovereignty*; Shadian, "Indigeneity".

state sovereignty, affording Indigenous groups a distinct kind of diplomatic authority to participate formally in Arctic regional and global politics.[55] As a pan-Arctic Indigenous peoples' organization, the ICC has also taken a lead in pressing regional and national governments to offset the impact of social, economic, and environmental change and in persuading governments to work on implementing measures for environmental protection, mitigating climate change, and sustainable development. Notable success stories include the organization's central role in the negotiation of the global Stockholm Convention on the Elimination of Persistent Organic Pollutants.[56] Following the negotiations, the ICC lobbied states to ratify the Convention in their national legislatures. The Convention entered into force in May 2003, and the ICC continues to work to ensure that the Convention's obligations are implemented. Inuit leaders argue that systems of environmental management and sustainability policy and practice are only legitimate if they incorporate Indigenous knowledge and allow Indigenous participation.

In 2005, Sheila Watt-Cloutier, the then international ICC chair, submitted a petition on behalf of Inuit living in Alaska and Canada to the Inter-American Commission on Human Rights seeking relief from violations resulting from global warming by greenhouse gas emissions from the United States. Its aim was to draw attention to the behaviour of the United States in terms of fossil fuel consumption and the impact caused by the world's largest industrial economy to the biosphere, and in particular the change wrought on Arctic marine and terrestrial ecosystems, which in turn has consequences for Inuit, including their capacity to move and to hunt on the sea ice. This is also expounded upon in Watt-Cloutier's memoir *The Right to Be Cold*, in which she draws attention to the economic, cultural, and spiritual significance of ice and snow to Inuit Culture and well-being, and describes the impact of a warming Arctic.[57]

In September 2008 in Kuujjuaq, Nunavik, the ICC organized an Inuit Leaders' Summit which resulted in a 'Circumpolar Inuit Declaration on Sovereignty in the Arctic'. It reaffirmed Inuit perspectives on the Arctic as a homeland and emphasized that governments and others with interests in the Arctic should recognize and acknowledge the specific rights of Indigenous peoples. It stressed that, as the world looks increasingly to the Arctic and its resources, and as climate change makes access to circumpolar lands easier, the inclusion of Inuit as active partners is central to national and

---

55 Shadian, "Indigeneity". 56 Downie and Fenge, *Northern Lights against POPs*.
57 Watt-Cloutier, *Right to Be Cold*.

international deliberations on Arctic sovereignty, development, and protection. The declaration emphasized that 'issues of sovereignty and sovereign rights in the Arctic have become inextricably linked to issues of self-determination in the Arctic' and that 'the rights, roles and responsibilities of Inuit must be fully recognized and accommodated' in discussions on matters linked to Arctic sovereignty, including climate change and resource development. This is also reinforced, for example, by the ICC's declaration on principles for resource development, and by recent work emphasizing the importance of protecting and managing Arctic ecosystems such as Pikialasorsuaq (the North Water polynya between the Canadian High Arctic and Northwest Greenland) based on Inuit knowledge, management and monitoring.[58] In April 2021, ICC became the first IPO to be granted observer status within the Intergovernmental Panel on Climate Change (IPCC). In November 2021 it became the first IPO to receive provisional observer status with the International Maritime Organization (IMO).

Indigenous Arctic peoples have also participated actively in the United Nations Permanent Forum on Indigenous Peoples, a body of sixteen representatives, half nominated by Indigenous organizations and half by UN member states, that meets annually to examine Indigenous issues and make recommendations to the UN Economic and Social Council. Arctic Indigenous representatives – particularly Inuit – have played a significant role in the Permanent Forum, demonstrating how global Indigenous movements can find ways of negotiating at international levels and ways of representing and intervening not only in the Arctic as a geopolitical region but also in global debates. Like Indigenous peoples elsewhere in the world, they assert historical and cultural rights to the occupancy and use of lands and resources, and articulate positions that Indigenous peoples are distinct political and cultural communities. But they speak to issues of colonization, self-determination, climate change and the environment, human rights, citizenship, participation, and deliberative democracy that go far beyond the Arctic. This chapter has pointed out that Indigenous political movements – and hence the assertion and reclaiming of land rights – are struggles for self-determination, self-government, autonomy, equity, and justice. Moreover, the protection of Indigenous lands and waters, the recognition of rights to lands and resources, and the settlement of land claims are often seen as essential for the very survival of Indigenous peoples and cultures. As Alfred Kwokwo Barume, a Congolese lawyer known for his global work on Indigenous rights, has put it, land for Indigenous communities

---

58 Inuit Circumpolar Council, *People of the Ice Bridge*.

'is not just for use, but also and more importantly, land sustains their whole livelihood and future'.[59] The rise of circumpolar political movements must be seen within a context of a global Indigenous political history, in which Indigenous voices have expressed how the right to Indigenous homelands is inseparable from human rights.

Bibliography

Allard, Christina, and Malin Brännström, "Girjas Reindeer Herding Community v. Sweden: Analysing the Merits of the Girjas Case", *Arctic Review on Law and Politics* 12 (2021): 56–79.

Anderson, David G., *Identity and Ecology in Arctic Siberia: The Number One Reindeer Brigade* (Oxford: Clarendon, 2000).

Balzer, Marjorie Mandelstam, "Indigeneity, Land and Political Activism in Siberia", in Alan C. Tidwell and Barry Scott Zellen, eds., *Land, Indigenous Peoples and Conflict* (London, New York: Routledge, 2016), pp. 9–27.

Balzer, Majorie Mandelstam, "The Tension Between Mights and Rights: Siberian and Energy Developers in Post-socialist Binds", *Europe-Asia Studies* 58 (2006): 567–588.

Barume, Albert Kwokwo Barume, *Land Rights of Indigenous Peoples in Africa* (Copenhagen: IWGIA, 2010).

Berger, Thomas, *Northern Frontier, Northern Homeland: The Report of the Mackenzie Valley Pipeline Inquiry*, 2 vols. (Ottawa: Department of Supply and Services, 1977).

Bjørklund, Ivar, "Industrial Impacts and Indigenous Representation: Some Fallacies in the Sámi Quest for Autonomy", *Études/Inuit/Studies* 37 (2014): 145–160.

Bone, Robert, *The Canadian North: Issues and Challenges* (Oxford: Oxford University Press, 2009).

Brody, Hugh, *The People's Land: Eskimos and Whites in the Eastern Arctic* (Harmondsworth: Penguin, 1975).

Caulfield, Richard A., "The Political Economy of Renewable Resource Management in the Arctic", in Mark Nuttall and Terry V. Callaghan, eds., *The Arctic: Environment, People, Policy* (Amsterdam: Harwood Academic, 2000), pp. 485–513.

Coulthard, Glen, "Subjects of Empire: Indigenous Peoples and the 'Politics of Recognition' in Canada", *Contemporary Political Theory* 6 (2007): 437–460.

Council for Yukon First Nations, *Land Before Money, Cooperation Before Competition* (Whitehorse: Council for Yukon Indians, 1981).

Crate, Susan A., "Co-option in Siberia: The Case of Diamonds and the Vilyuy Sakha", *Polar Geography* 27 (2002): 85–96.

Dahl, Jens, "Indigenous Peoples of the Arctic", in *Arctic Challenges*, Report from the Nordic Council Parliamentary Conference in Reykjavik, Iceland, 16–17 August 1993.

Dahl, Jens, *Saqqaq: An Inuit Hunting Community in the Modern World* (Toronto: University of Toronto Press, 2000).

---

59 Barume, *Land Rights*, 55.

25 The Rise of Circumpolar Political Movements

Dahl, Jens, Jack Hicks, and Peter Jull, eds., *Nunavut: Inuit Regain Control over Their Lives and Lands* (Copenhagen: IWGIA, 2000).

Dale, Aaron, and Derek Armitage, "Marine Mammal Co-management in Canada's Arctic: Knowledge Co-production for Learning and Adaptive Capacity", *Marine Policy* 35 (2011): 440–449.

Downie, David Leonard, and Terry Fenge, *Northern Lights against POPs: Combatting Toxic Threats in the Arctic* (Montreal: McGill-Queen's University Press, 2003).

Fægteborg, Mads, "Inuit Circumpolar Conference (ICC)", in Mark Nuttall, ed., *Encyclopedia of the Arctic*, Vol. 2 (London, New York: Routledge, 2005), pp. 999–1002.

Fondahl, Gail, "Russian Federation Law on Clan Communes (Obshchinas)", in Mark Nuttall, ed., *Encyclopedia of the Arctic*, Vol. 3 (London, New York: Routledge, 2005), pp. 1802–1803.

Fondahl, Gail, and Anna Sirina, "Oil Pipeline Development and Indigenous Rights in Eastern Siberia", *Indigenous Affairs* 1–2 (2006): 58–76.

Fondahl, Gail, and Anna Sirina, "Rights and Risks: Evenki Concerns Regarding the Proposed Eastern Siberia–Pacific Ocean Pipeline", *Sibirica* 5 (2006): 115–138.

Freeman, Milton M. R., ed., *Endangered Peoples of the Arctic: Struggles to Survive and Thrive* (Westport, CT: Greenwood, 2000).

Grant, Shelagh D., *Polar Imperative: A History of Arctic Sovereignty in North America* (Vancouver: Douglas & McIntyre, 2010).

Gray, Patricia A., *The Predicament of Chukotka's Indigenous Movement: Post-Soviet Activism in the Russian Far North* (Cambridge: Cambridge University Press, 2005).

Hall, Thomas D., and James V. Fenelon, *Indigenous Peoples and Globalization: Resistance and Revitalization* (Boulder, CO: Paradigm, 2009).

Henderson, Ailsa, *Nunavut: Rethinking Political Culture* (Vancouver: UBC Press, 2007).

Herrmann, Thora Martina, and Thibault Martin, eds., *Indigenous Peoples' Governance of Land and Protected Territories in the Arctic* (Cham: Springer, 2016).

Herrmann, Thora Martina, Per Sandström, Karin Granqvist, et al., "Effects of Mining on Reindeer/Caribou Populations and Indigenous Livelihoods: Community-Based Monitoring by Sami Reindeer Herders in Sweden and First Nations in Canada", *Polar Journal* 4 (2014): 28–51.

Howard, Bradley Reed, *Indigenous Peoples and the State: The Struggle for Native Rights* (DeKalb, IL: Northern Illinois University Press, 2003).

Huntington, Henry P., *Wildlife Management and Subsistence Hunting in Alaska* (London: Belhaven, 1992).

Inuit Circumpolar Council, *People of the Ice Bridge: The Future of the Pikialasorsuaq*. Report of the Pikialasorsuaq Commission (Ottawa: Inuit Circumpolar Council Canada, 2017).

Irlbacher-Fox, Stephanie, *Finding Dahsha: Self-government, Social Suffering and Aboriginal Policy in Canada* (Vancouver: UBC Press, 2009).

Irlbacher-Fox, Stephanie, "Land Claims", in Mark Nuttall, ed., *Encyclopedia of the Arctic* (London, New York: Routledge, 2005).

Jull, Peter, "The Politics of Sustainable Development: Reconciliation in Indigenous Hinterlands", in Svein Jentoft, Henry Minde, and Ragnar Nilsen, eds., *Indigenous Peoples: Resource Management and Global Rights* (Delft: Eburon, 2003), pp. 21–44.

Kalland, Arne, and Frank Sejersen, *Marine Mammals and Northern Cultures* (Edmonton: CCI, 2005).

Keeling, Arn, and John Sandlos, eds., *Mining and Communities in Northern Canada: History, Politics, and Memory* (Calgary: University of Calgary Press, 2015).

Leas, David, "Self-government in the Yukon", in Kathrin Wessendorf, ed., *An Indigenous Parliament? Realities and Perspectives in Russia and the Circumpolar North*, IWGIA Document 116 (Copenhagen: IWGIA, 2005), pp. 118–149.

Lynge, Finn, *Arctic Wars, Animal Rights, Endangered Peoples* (Hanover: University of New England Press, 1992).

Minde, Henry, "The Challenge of Indigenism: The Struggle for Sami Land Rights and Self-government in Norway 1960–1990", in Svein Jentoft, Henry Minde, and Ragnar Nilsen, eds., *Indigenous Peoples: Resource Management and Global Rights* (Delft: Eburon, 2003), pp. 75–104.

Mitchell, Marybelle, *From Talking Chiefs to a Native Corporate Élite: The Birth of Class and Nationalism Among Canadian Inuit* (Montreal: McGill-Queen's University Press, 2006).

Møller, Helle, "Circumpolar Health and Well-Being", in Mark Nuttall, Torben R. Christensen, and Martin J. Siegert, eds., *The Routledge Handbook of the Polar Regions* (London, New York: Routledge, 2018), pp. 90–106.

Murashko, Olga, "Protecting Indigenous Peoples' Rights to Their Natural Resources: The Case of Russia", *Indigenous Affairs* 3–4 (2008): 48–59.

Nilsen, Ragnar, "From Norwegianization to Coastal Sami Uprising", in Svein Jentoft, Henry Minde, and Ragnar Nilsen, eds., *Indigenous Peoples: Resource Management and Global Rights* (Delft: Eburon, 2003), 163–184.

Novikova, Natalie I., "Self-government of the Indigenous Minority Peoples of West Siberia: Analysis of Law and Practice", in Erich Kasten, ed., *People and the Land: Pathways to Reform in Post-Soviet Siberia* (Berlin: Dietrich Reimer, 2002), pp. 83–97.

Nuttall, Mark, *Arctic Homeland: Kinship, Community and Identity in Northwest Greenland* (Toronto: University of Toronto Press, 1992).

Nuttall, Mark, *Climate, Society and Subsurface Politics in Greenland: Under the Great Ice* (London, New York: Routledge, 2017).

Nuttall, Mark, "Greenland: Emergence of an Inuit Homeland", in Minority Rights Group, ed., *Polar Peoples: Self-determination and Development* (London: Minority Rights Group, 1994), pp. 1–28.

Nuttall, Mark, "Indigenous Peoples, Self-determination and the Arctic Environment", in Mark Nuttall and Terry V. Callaghan, eds., *The Arctic: Environment, People, Policy* (Amsterdam: Harwood Academic, 2000), pp. 621–637.

Nuttall, Mark, *Protecting the Arctic: Indigenous Peoples and Cultural Survival* (Amsterdam: Harwood Academic, 1998).

Nuttall, Mark, "Zero Tolerance, Uranium and Greenland's Mining Future", *Polar Journal* 3 (2013): 368–383.

Paine, Robert, *Dam a River, Damn a People? Saami (Lapp) Livelihood and the Alta/Kautokeino Hydro-electric Project and the Norwegian Parliament.* IWGIA Document 45 (Copenhagen: IWGIA, 1982).

Pika, Aleksandr, ed., *Neotraditionalism in the Russian North: Indigenous Peoples and the Legacy of Perestroika* (Edmonton: CCI, 1999).

Pika, Aleksandr, Jens Dahl, and Inge Larsen, eds., *Anxious North: Indigenous Peoples in Soviet and Post-Soviet Russia*. IWGIA Document 82 (Copenhagen: IWGIA, 1996).

Rethmann, Petra, "Russian Association of Indigenous Peoples of the North (RAIPON)", in Mark Nuttall, ed., *Encyclopedia of the Arctic*, Vol. 3 (London, New York: Routledge, 2005), pp. 1798–1799.
Rÿser, Rudolph C., *Indigenous Nations and Modern States: The Political Emergence of Nations Challenging State Power* (London, New York: Routledge, 2021).
Semenova, Tamara, "Political Mobilisation of Northern Indigenous Peoples in Russia", *Polar Record* 43 (2007): 23–32.
Shadian, Jessica M., "Indigeneity, Sovereignty, and Arctic Indigenous Internationalism", in Mark Nuttall, Torben R. Christensen, and Martin J. Siegert, eds., *The Routledge Handbook of the Polar Regions* (London and New York: Routledge, 2018), pp. 331–347.
Shadian, Jessica M., *The Politics of Arctic Sovereignty: Oil, Ice, and Inuit Governance* (London, New York: Routledge, 2014).
Sirina, Anna, "Oil and Gas Development in Northern Russia and Indigenous Peoples", in Elana Wilson Rowe, ed., *Russia and the North* (Ottawa: University of Ottawa Press, 2009), pp. 187–202.
Spitzer, Aaron John, and Per Selle, "Claims-Based Co-management in Norway's Arctic? Examining Sami Land Governance as a Case of Treaty Federalism", *Canadian Journal of Political Science* 52 (2019): 723–741.
Tester, Frank, and Peter Kulchyski, *Tammarniit (Mistakes): Inuit Relocation in the Eastern Arctic, 1939–1963* (Vancouver: UBC Press, 1994).
Tidwell, Alan C., and Barry Scott Zellen, eds., *Land, Indigenous Peoples and Conflict* (London, New York: Routledge, 2016).
Watt-Cloutier, Sheila, *The Right to Be Cold* (Toronto: Allen Lane, 2015).
Wenzel, George, *Animal Rights, Human Rights: Ecology, Economy and Ideology in the Canadian Arctic* (London: Belhaven, 1991).
Wessendorf, Kathrin, ed., *An Indigenous Parliament? Realities and Perspectives in Russia and the Circumpolar North*. IWGIA Document 116 (Copenhagen: IWGIA, 2005).
Wheeler, Sally, *Making Canadian Indian Policy: The Hidden Agenda, 1968–1970* (Toronto: University of Toronto Press, 1981).
Yakovleva, Natalia, "Oil Pipeline Construction in Eastern Siberia: Implications for Indigenous People", *Geoforum* 42 (2011): 708–719.
Zellen, Barry Scott, *Breaking the Ice: From Land Claims to Tribal Sovereignty in the Arctic* (Lanham, MD: Lexington, 2008).

26

The History of Polar Environmental Governance

ALESSANDRO ANTONELLO AND JUSTIINA DAHL

Introduction

Over the course of their histories, a range of polities and communities have reached into higher latitudes to control and benefit from polar spaces and resources, enrolling what they thought of as peripheral regions into global geopolitical, legal, and economic systems. In the process they have taken to the poles certain ideas of resource use, value, and humanity's relationship with nature and the environment. With these ideas came practices that disrupted polar ecologies, eviscerated animal populations, polluted landscapes, and undermined Indigenous societies and cultures. From the mid-twentieth century, more extensive national and international frameworks of environmental governance have emerged, including through legislation, treaties, and other conservation practices, to attenuate human impacts and foster some level of ecological productivity and resilience.[1] Only in recent decades have the local and embodied knowledges of Indigenous communities in the Arctic, which have developed over thousands of years, been recognized, along with an acceptance that the effects of climate change seem most intense and immediate at the poles. Environmental governance at the poles has very much developed as a result of global developments and the impositions of elites and publics of the metropoles and temperate regions,

---

This work was supported by an Australian Research Council Discovery Early Career Award (DE190100922) funded by the Australian Government and by the European Research Council under the European Union's Horizon 2020 research and innovation programme (grant agreement no. 716211 – GRETPOL).

1 States and governments are not the only actors in this history, hence the term 'governance', which highlights the part non-government actors – like scientific institutions, corporations, civil society groups, or international organizations – play in framing and tackling environmental problems at all scales. See Jasanoff and Martello, eds., *Earthly Politics*; Lemos and Agrawal, "Environmental Governance".

648

26 History of Polar Environmental Governance

rather than as an organic outgrowth of local ecologies, cultures, and communities.

Ideas, philosophies, ideologies, and projects are central to this history. Any environmental governance framework is tied to larger cultural and geopolitical ideas about what constitutes 'the environment' or 'nature' at any historical moment or by different communities. In the modern era, the polar regions have been characterized in many ways – wasteland, wilderness, remote, empty, fragile, endangered, warming – and these descriptions have animated specific regulatory, diplomatic, or other efforts at instituting polar environmental governance.[2] Modern normative projects of 'improvement' and 'progress' have also animated human–environment relations at the poles. These cultural and geopolitical ideas mean that, despite their outwardly 'rational' scientific and technocratic appearance, structures of environmental governance are political, and deeply normative. Laws, regulations, treaties, and other agreements articulate ideas about the correct relationship between humans and non-human nature, states, and subject peoples, between sovereign states, and even territorial sovereignty and technology.[3] That being said, the history of environmental governance is one of changing intensities, as states and other actors have governed polar environments more intensively at some points and less at others.

The Arctic and Antarctic today each have complex and distinct systems of environmental protection and management. Antarctica is governed through the Antarctic Treaty of 1959 – which freezes but does not resolve disputes over sovereignty – and related international agreements. Since sovereignty and territorial control are essentially settled in the Arctic, environmental governance is more strongly connected to nation-states, but international relations nevertheless play their part, as most environmental issues are transboundary in character. The history leading to these developments is not fully connected or overlapping across both poles: there is not one story but many, and this chapter can only concentrate on a selection. While this chapter makes clear how larger intellectual, geopolitical, and scientific frameworks have informed environmental governance at both poles, only rarely have there been direct and influential connections which link the polar regions *as* polar environments. More often, the poles have been caught up in global stories of the development of states and the associated international

---

[2] In relation to these connections Adrian Howkins has suggested the concept of 'environmental authority': see Howkins, *Frozen Empires*.
[3] Bravo, "Sea Ice Mapping"; Strandsbjerg, "Cartopolitics, Geopolitics and Boundaries".

system, in which competition for space and resources has driven militaries, explorers, scientists and others to move throughout the Earth.

Deep Histories of Environments, States, and Sovereignty

Environmental governance in the polar regions has a deep history, particularly in the Arctic, which European explorers first penetrated at the same time as the international order based on territorial sovereignty was being developed. These past ideas and regulations have created political, legal, and philosophical structures that succeeding generations have contended with. The ecological and landscape effects of past exploitation have also shaped (and continue to shape) the environmental governance of succeeding generations. The Arctic has been permanently inhabited by Indigenous communities for thousands of years, building relationships with the environment and enfolding ideas about appropriate relationships with non-human nature deeply within their cultures. However, Indigenous environmental knowledges were progressively marginalized and undermined by European empires and institutions as they expanded through the Arctic from the sixteenth century. Even if European explorers did inquire about Indigenous environmental knowledges (or even rely on them for survival), they rarely incorporated them into colonial approaches to governing resource extraction.[4] Through the dispossession of land, forced relocation of peoples, and taxation, European empires tried to enfold Arctic environments into emerging Enlightenment rationalities, where land and resources were property within the demands of states and a market economy.[5]

From the sixteenth to the early eighteenth century, as European states and empires expanded northwards in Europe and North America, Arctic environments were often seen as aesthetically sublime but nevertheless backwards spaces that needed to be 'improved' and made profitable.[6] Scientific and commercial activities bound Arctic environments and some of their natural resources to the development of territorial states and international legal ideas, such as effective occupation, territorial and natural borders, colonization, and civilization.[7] Although some activities such as fur trapping and

---

4 Nuttall, *Protecting the Arctic*; Bielawski, "Inuit Knowledge and Science".
5 Jones, *Empire of Extinction*. 6 Sörlin, "Rituals and Resources".
7 Flanagan, "Agricultural Argument"; Fitzmaurice, *Sovereignty, Property and Empire*; Head, "Canadian Claims"; Avango et al., "Between Markets and Geo-politics".

whaling generated a steady revenue stream for states, the newly encountered Arctic environments resisted many other desires of the expanding governments, such as acclimatization of species in Northern Fennoscandia, establishment of farming settlements in Russian America (later Alaska), and mining colonies on *Meta Incognita* (later discovered to be part of Baffin Island).[8]

The expansion of European states and enterprises into polar environments also led to environmental changes that reverberate into the present. The population of bowhead whales (*Balaena mysticetus*) around Spitsbergen, estimated at 46,000 individuals when whaling by Dutch and English companies began around 1600, was essentially destroyed over the next three centuries.[9] Coal burning in North America and Europe in the second half of the nineteenth century spewed toxic heavy metals like thallium, cadmium, and lead into the Arctic, toxins that persist today.[10] The unregulated rush for fur seals in the Antarctic at the start of the nineteenth century killed so many animals that stocks did not recover until the later years of the twentieth century.[11] With these ecological and physical impacts, alongside the deeper histories of environmental knowledges lost and marginalized or political and legal structures and ideas developed, we can appreciate the *longue durée* of environmental governance at the poles.

Resource Rationality and Polar Nature

In the late nineteenth and early twentieth centuries, European and settler colonial societies became increasingly interested in the High Arctic and Antarctica. Male explorers and scientists, both officially representing states such as Norway, the United States, and the United Kingdom, and also acting privately, sought to discover new lands and resources and to understand climate and biogeography at higher latitudes, in spaces largely characterized as 'blank' spots on Western maps. These exploratory impulses, in which performances of masculine heroism were especially valorized, were tied to imperial geopolitics, empires old and new searching for new natural resources to fuel growing industries and populations, as well as newly formed nation-states – like Norway and Canada – seeking to expand or strengthen their territorial borders, resource bases and national identities in times of rapid change.

---

8 Koerner, *Linnaeus: Nature and Nation*; Ruby, *Unknown Shore*; Gibson, *Imperial Russia*; Wood, *Russia's Frozen Frontier*.
9 Hacquebord, "Three Centuries of Whaling".
10 McConnell and Edwards, "Coal Burning". 11 Richards, *Sealing in Southern Oceans*.

Rightful interaction with (and governance of) nature and the non-human environment became central guiding principles at the Paris Peace Conference following World War I in 1919. The newly independent Republic of Finland, having separated from Russia in 1917, demanded territories along the Arctic coastline, which had not been part of its previous territory, to enable economic development. Not only did this expansion bring timber and mineral resources under its sovereignty, but the Finnish negotiators who hoped to solve the coastal border issue in Paris relied partially on geographical determinist narratives, arguing for this expansion by highlighting that 'without this region [Petsamo] a significant proportion of Finnish natural riches cannot reach world trade'.[12]

Although it did not deal with the territorial disputes associated with the Russian Revolution, the Paris Peace Conference also internationalized certain other issues in Arctic environmental governance. In the early years of the twentieth century, British, Russian, Swedish, Dutch, and Norwegian companies had rushed to the Spitsbergen archipelago to establish mining ventures. Unlike whaling in earlier centuries, which had not led to demands for formal international governance, the mining companies demanded that states intervene and establish a more certain legal order over the archipelago to facilitate their investment and guarantee the smooth running of their operations. Around the same time, internationally prominent conservationists, such as the German botanist and conservation official Hugo Conwentz and the Swiss naturalist Paul Sarasin, as well as the *Landsforeningen for Naturfredning i Norge* (the National Association for Nature Protection in Norway), established in 1914, began to call for nature protection in the *terra nullius* of the Spitsbergen archipelago. One proposal was to rotate the administration of the islands among the three countries with strongest ties to it, Norway, Sweden, and Russia. The war interrupted these efforts, and the matter was taken up again at Paris. The resulting Spitsbergen Treaty, signed in 1920, demilitarized the area and recognized Norway's sovereignty over the islands, while permitting citizens of all treaty parties to access the area, and prohibiting Norway (as sovereign) from imposing regulations on economic activity that discriminated against or in favour of a particular state. The treaty also empowered Norway to administer the flora and fauna of the islands and associated waters.[13]

---

12 Dahl, "Seeing Like a State", 200.
13 Wråkberg, "Nature Conservationism"; Avango and Roberts, "Heritage, Conservation, and Geopolitics"; Singh and Saguirian, "The Svalbard Archipelago".

The inter-war period also saw environments in the lower circumpolar latitudes subjected to high modernization through the extraction of resources and modification of landscapes through industrial technologies. The Soviet Union under Joseph Stalin adopted a military vocabulary and declared war on the northern environment. During his first decades of rule, industrializing and urbanizing Russia's northern periphery was seen as an opportunity to prove the supremacy of the new communist state. High modernist megaprojects like the Belomor Canal connecting the Arctic Ocean and the Baltic Sea significantly affected environments and communities while bringing few economic benefits. Extractive industries spawned a chain of monotowns focusing on coal in Vorkuta, metals on the Kola Peninsula and in Norilsk, oil and gas in Ukhta, and diamonds and gold in Kolyma. To advance these extractive industries and achieve this massive environmental reorganization, the Soviet state – encouraged by similar initiatives in the North American and European Arctic in previous centuries – used financial and taxation incentives to encourage the relocation of Soviet citizens. The state also used forced labour from gulags and forcibly relocated Indigenous and local communities to achieve its aims.[14]

In the North American High Arctic, competing conceptions of the Arctic environment were dramatized in a conflict between Roald Amundsen and Vilhjalmur Stefansson. The Norwegian Amundsen portrayed the Arctic as a hostile environment and wasteland and centred himself as its heroic conqueror, even though he used Indigenous knowledge and technologies in the planning of his expeditions.[15] Others like the American geographer Ellsworth Huntington joined in this portrayal, combining his ideas of racial hierarchies and climate determinism to argue that the Arctic caused laziness and sapped people of energy: 'civilization', by his account, was impossible in the high north. On the other hand, the Icelandic-Canadian explorer Stefansson, who spent significant time living in the Canadian Arctic, saw the Arctic and its Indigenous population as a site ripe for development, including the exploitation of untapped resources for the benefit of the state.[16] These debates were part of a longer tradition of understanding, living with, and governing Arctic environments that persisted elsewhere in the Western Arctic after World War II, including discussions about the 'Problem of Northern Norway' that arose in Norway from 1948, and Canadian Prime

---

14 Bolotova, "Colonization and Nature"; McCannon, *Red Arctic*; Ruder, *Making History for Stalin*; Laruelle, *Russia's Arctic Strategies*, 27–28.
15 Elzinga, "Roald Amundsen".   16 Howkins, *The Polar Regions*, 97–98.

Minister John Diefenbaker's 'Roads to Resources' programme, announced in 1957.[17]

While northern polar environments were subjected to re-territorialization, industrialization, urbanization, and increased resource extraction in the first half of the twentieth century, whales in the Antarctic were rationalized as resources and increasingly governed through national and international frameworks. Although some species of penguins and seals on some sub-Antarctic islands were placed under conservation protection in these decades, they were generally – except for the elephant seals of South Georgia – not fully rationalized and exploited as resources at this time. New technologies such as hydrogenation – making oil fats solid – and new technologies for hunting the largest rorquals, plus new markets, made Antarctic whaling a profitable business in the early years of the century.[18] While whaling did occur in many parts of the world ocean, Antarctica was the central site of the global hunt in the first half of the century, and the whale resource was central to conceptions of the Antarctic environment and ideas of environmental governance there in the first half of the century. Within five years of the symbolic first whale kill near South Georgia in December 1904, whale oil production was larger in the south than the north.[19]

Governing the whale resource was not a straightforward task, since the high seas were areas outside state sovereignty. British territorial claims over sub-Antarctic islands and the Antarctic Peninsula were tied to its efforts to regulate and benefit from the whaling industry, which in the first few decades still relied on shore stations to process whales. With the creation of the stern slipway and advances in factory ships, whaling could be conducted entirely on the high seas, and became increasingly a subject of international environmental governance. The discussion of whales in international forums like the League of Nations in the 1930s translated the emerging concern with overharvesting into the idea that whales were resources properly belonging to all peoples, and thus requiring international management. These interwar efforts to govern whaling failed to reduce the catch in any way. During the final stages and immediately after World War II, the United States, motivated by its concerns to ensure 'wise use' of global natural resources and geopolitically ascendant, convened fifteen nations to negotiate and sign the International Convention for the Regulation of Whaling in 1946, which created the International Whaling Commission. The Commission's attempts

17 Bothwell et al., *Canada Since 1945*; Halvorsen and Torgersen, *Problemet Nord-Norge*.
18 Tønnessen and Johnsen, *History of Modern Whaling*, 163.
19 Tønnessen and Johnsen, *History of Modern Whaling*.

to govern whaling in the 1950s were profoundly unsuccessful; whatever the scientists' advice, highly capitalized fleets chased down fewer and fewer whales, nearly pushing stocks to extinction. By the early 1960s, most nations had pulled out of whaling, with whales increasingly seen less as an exploitable resource and more as a sentient, feeling creature demanding protection.[20]

Protecting Polar Animals and Landscapes

The industrial resource rationalities of the first half of the twentieth century held that polar environments, however deficient, could provide for the state and even the global market. These ideas began to change from the 1950s, especially in the Western bloc, through a growing consciousness among scientists and publics alike that humans were harming the environment through pollution and economic development. Polar animals and landscapes were caught up in these global currents, and ecological and ecosystems sciences were central to these ideas.[21] Although the idea of 'rational' or 'wise' use of natural resources – as articulated in the Progressive-era United States in the early twentieth century and which had spread internationally – remained dominant through this era, these decades saw increasing knowledge and realization that industrial pollution and other harms were undermining the natural systems that sustained human life. These new ideas of environmental fragility were global, and were discussed not just in national government institutions, but in new international forums like the United Nations, in international scientific and conservation organizations like the International Union for the Conservation of Nature (IUCN), and in transnational, non-governmental environmentalist groups.[22] The very idea of 'the environment' emerged as a distinct object of research and governance in these post-war years, connected to developing global knowledge and governance institutions.[23]

These ecological and environmental ideas emerged during, and were also inflected by, the early Cold War.[24] The United States and the Soviet Union occupied and militarized the Arctic in previously unimaginable ways, leading to new environmental impacts but also to new environmental knowledge.[25]

---

20 Roberts, *European Antarctic*; Burnett, *Sounding of the Whale*; Dorsey, *Whales and Nations*.
21 Bocking, *Ecologists and Environmental Politics*.
22 Selcer, *Postwar Origins*; Kaiser and Meyer, eds., *International Organizations*; Macekura, *Of Limits and Growth*; Schleper, *Planning for the Planet*.
23 Warde et al., *The Environment: A History*.
24 Doel et al., "Strategic Arctic Science"; Hamblin, *Arming Mother Nature*.
25 Osherenko and Young, *Age of the Arctic*; McCannon, *History of the Arctic*, 236–278.

Building a base to launch missiles in the Greenland ice sheet, for example, demanded glaciological knowledge and laid foundations for later ideas about ice sheet dynamics and climate change. Although the militarization of Antarctica was expressly forbidden under the Antarctic Treaty, environmental ideas, and governance there, were also influenced by the larger Cold War context. The military demands of Cold War competition underpinned a range of technologies that allowed new vision and data about the Earth's environment, whether in the form of satellites and remote sensing, or in the rapid development of ecological sciences because of the needs of nuclear research.[26]

Although the Antarctic Treaty listed the 'preservation and conservation of living resources' as one of its potential areas of action, it was not principally an environmental agreement when signed in 1959. Despite this, the Treaty parties swiftly moved to institute conservation frameworks and measures.[27] The small community of biologists within the Scientific Committee on Antarctic Research (SCAR) started to outline the various environmental effects of human actions in Antarctica and to envisage the continent not simply as a massive ice sheet that was inimical to life, but as a space including animal and plant communities that were susceptible to damage from even localized human activities, like scientific stations. Officials and diplomats from some Treaty parties also saw in conservation an agenda item that might allow them to legitimize the new Treaty. These early efforts led to the Agreed Measures for the Conservation of Antarctic Fauna and Flora (AMCAFF) in 1964, which designated the whole Antarctic as a 'Special Conservation Area' and instituted protections for animals, individually and in communities.[28] The Antarctic Treaty parties saw that governing the environment was good for maintaining ecological relationships as well as geopolitical ones.

Another early and prominent manifestation of the new global environmentalism was concern for whales and seals. In the 1960s and 1970s, both the public and scientists increasingly called for the end to whaling – which seemed a particularly egregious waste of resources driving the stocks to near collapse – and sealing. The International Whaling Commission floundered in its efforts to stop whaling, despite increasing calls from major states and international civil society, including at the 1972 Stockholm Conference on the Human Environment, to ban whaling altogether to allow the

---

26 Bocking, *Ecologists and Environmental Politics*; Turchetti and Roberts, eds., *Surveillance Imperative*.
27 Antonello, *Greening of Antarctica*, 32–37.   28 Antonello, *Greening of Antarctica*, 19–47.

populations to regrow.[29] In the Antarctic Treaty context, protecting seals seemed easy, as there had been no hunting for fur seals since the nineteenth century, and the hunt for elephant seals had ended in the early 1960s. Through the late 1960s, the Treaty parties negotiated the question of seal conservation, eventually signing the Convention for the Conservation of Antarctic Seals in 1972, a comprehensive system for managing the conservation, study, and exploitation of seals.[30] The Canadian seal hunt was central to these changing environmental sensibilities, as the televized killing of a baby harp seal in 1964 scandalized North American and European publics. Although sealing was never banned and catch quotas remained high, in the late 1970s and early 1980s environmentalists, especially the International Fund for Animal Welfare, successfully lobbied European governments and the European Community to ban the import of certain seal products from Canada, an action that profoundly affected the economic livelihood of Indigenous Canadian and Greenland communities who relied on seal hunting for more than subsistence.[31]

As seals and whales were being further protected at both poles, polar bears were coming into the realm of environmental governance in the Arctic. In 1973, Canada, Denmark, Norway, the Soviet Union, and the United States signed the Agreement on the Conservation of Polar Bears, the first major multilateral environmental agreement made for the Arctic and one of the first international environmental agreements based on ecological principles. International concerns over polar bear conservation were first prominently raised at the IUCN's 1954 General Assembly, along with discussions on the conservation of other Arctic marine mammals, although there were divergent ideas about the status of polar bears across the five 'polar bear' states. Populations across the bear's range seemed to be diminished, and while the Soviet Union had banned hunting in 1956 (despite having no scientific count), none of the four other states with bears in their territories considered the species 'endangered' as such. The IUCN's Polar Bear Specialist Group (PBSG), established in 1965 and comprising scientists and environmental managers, worked to coordinate research and data – a necessary precondition of framing and understanding the problem in advance of proposing international solutions.[32]

Between 1968 and 1973 the IUCN and its PBSG laboured to develop protection guidelines for polar bears, while the foreign ministries of

---

29 Dorsey, *Whales and Nations*. 30 Antonello, *Greening of Antarctica*, 49–76.
31 Sellheim, "Legislating the Blind Spot", 81–86; Lavigne et al., "Evolution".
32 Fikkan et al., "Polar Bears", 110–114.

Norway and the United States tried to initiate an agreement. The American government and the IUCN also tried to use the 1973 conference negotiating the Convention on International Trade in Endangered Species (CITES) as another forum for negotiation, without success.[33] The five polar bear states finally agreed to meet in Oslo in November 1973 to discuss the issue among themselves, with the IUCN actively participating. The host country's ambitions for the meeting were initially larger, hoping to reach an agreement on the protection of Arctic wildlife rather than only of polar bears, an aspiration immediately rejected by Canada, the United States, and the Soviet Union.[34] The Agreement they eventually signed covered the polar bear's land and marine habitats. The IUCN hoped the regime would eventually lead to a full international ban on hunting polar bears, with the exception of traditional Indigenous use and scientific and conservation purposes. The agreement, however, retained loopholes for hunting bears in certain circumstances, including the 'management of other living resources', and Canada continued to allow limited trophy hunting, the only state to do so. The PBSG, although not mentioned in the Agreement, has continued to coordinate scientific research, and to establish reliable data to underpin management.[35]

At the same time as Norway attempted to increase multilateralism in Arctic wildlife management, it renewed its attention to Svalbard's environment. In the inter-war years, Norway had incrementally instituted protection for the archipelago's flora, fauna, and landscapes, yet it was not until 1973 that the first national park was established in the region. As American and Soviet interest in Arctic oil increased in the late 1960s and early 1970s, Norway renewed the structures of environmental governance, including the new national parks, to further embed itself as the sovereign of Svalbard.[36] Norway's actions extended further out into the Arctic Ocean: it unilaterally established the Svalbard Fishery Protection Zone (SFPZ) in 1977 and, with the Soviet Union, it formed a joint fisheries commission for the Barents Sea in 1976. Norway asserted that in declaring the SFPZ, it was exercising its exclusive rights to protect and exploit the living and non-living resources of the sea in the area within 370 km of the coast.[37]

33 Larsen and Stirling, *Agreement on Conservation*, 10–11; "Official PBSG Proceedings", IUCN/SSC Polar Bear Specialist Group, http://pbsg.npolar.no/en/references/proceedings.html (accessed 9 February 2021).
34 Larsen and Stirling, *Agreement on Conservation*, 10–11; Fikkan et al., "Polar Bears", 120.
35 Tierney, "Polar Bear Treaty"; Fikkan et al., "Polar Bears", 98, 122.
36 Avango and Roberts, "Heritage, Conservation, and Geopolitics", 134.
37 Hønneland, "Compliance".

Although not created specifically for the polar regions, another notable and long-lasting tool of environmental governance to emerge in the 1970s was the environmental impact assessment (EIA). First created in United States national legislation that came into force in 1970, the practice of assessing a development's effect on environmental quality, and making that assessment public through an environmental impact statement, quickly gained a prominent place at the poles. In Antarctica, by virtue of the strong American position, impact assessment was brought to bear on certain new scientific research programmes as well as the United States's diplomatic positions in relation to Antarctic environmental treaties under negotiation. Other nations also started using EIA in Antarctica. Scientists and civil society, including through SCAR, also began to practise a broadly conceived environmental assessment, for example to frame problems around resource development and other threats to polar environments.[38] In the Arctic, US and Canadian hydrocarbon developments in the 1970s – notably the pipelines required to move oil from the Arctic to southern consumers – were a proving ground for these new assessment practices. The Trans-Alaska Pipeline System was subjected to assessment – although public participation, especially Indigenous participation, was thoroughly curtailed – and despite evidence of its effects, it was approved in 1973. In Canada, the Berger Inquiry into the environmental and social impacts of the proposed Mackenzie Valley Pipeline, through extensive community hearings and participation, including extensive Indigenous participation, found that the environmental harms in many areas would be substantial, and pipelines were therefore delayed.[39] At both poles, the environmental assessments were important not only for articulating and circulating ideas of 'environmental fragility' but also saw extensive discussions over the limits of economic and human development and, in the Arctic, forcefully foregrounding claims for land rights and justice by Indigenous peoples.

Building Comprehensive Regimes for Fragile Polar Ecosystems

As the list of environmental dangers and problems grew, and as polar environments were increasingly seen as interconnected, whole, and fragile ecosystems, the regimes and frameworks of environmental governance in

---

38 Antonello and Howkins, "Rise of Technocratic Environmentalism"; Antonello, *Greening of Antarctica*, 90–105.
39 Stuhl, *Unfreezing the Arctic*, ch. 5.

the polar regions became more comprehensive, overarching, and international. As Antarctic whaling rapidly declined from the mid-1960s, hopes for new resources filled the vacuum. Some companies and states saw in Antarctica a potential source of minerals. Enquiries from mining companies to several Antarctic Treaty party governments around 1969 precipitated diplomatic negotiations and scientific discussions on the question of how to arrange governance of potential mineral resource extraction in the Antarctic region that lasted until the late 1980s.[40] In the same period, fishing in the Southern Ocean also became a source of diplomatic and scientific concern. Soviet experimental fishing voyages for Antarctic krill from the early 1960s raised the prospect of over-harvesting of the main food source of the Antarctic marine ecosystem. Antarctic krill, the most abundant wild animal on Earth by biomass, is consumed by most other Antarctic animals and birds, and over-harvesting might degrade the entire Antarctic marine ecosystem.[41] It was within these scientific and political discussions about mining and fishing that the nature of the Antarctic environment was elaborated and increasingly codified in ideas around ecosystem fragility.

The Antarctic Treaty parties aimed to manage these environmental and resource issues by negotiating new treaties. The Convention for the Conservation of Antarctic Marine Living Resources (CCAMLR), governing Southern Ocean fisheries, was negotiated in the late 1970s and signed in 1980. It was not an orthodox fisheries convention, for its purpose was not only to regulate fishing but to protect the entire marine ecosystem in the Southern Ocean; decisions around catch limits had to be made in consideration of fishing's effects on the whole ecosystem. This was the first fisheries or environmental treaty to centre the ecosystem as such. The Convention balanced pro-conservation and pro-exploitation interests among the Antarctic Treaty parties and other powers with an interest in marine environmental governance, including the European Economic Community. Although part of the larger Antarctic Treaty System, CCAMLR is a standalone agreement, and parties to it need not be parties to the Antarctic Treaty.[42]

From 1982 the Antarctic Treaty parties began negotiating a solution to the more contentious issue of mining in Antarctica. In 1988 they signed the Convention on the Regulation of Antarctic Mineral Resource Activities (CRAMRA). While mineral extraction in Antarctica was a far-off possibility

---

40 Antonello, *Greening of Antarctica*, 77–105.   41 Antonello, *Greening of Antarctica*, 109–126.
42 Antonello, *Greening of Antarctica*, 131–137.

in the 1980s – for both technological and economic reasons – the parties negotiated the treaty because they were worried that the lack of firm law in this area might destabilize their relationships and undermine the Antarctic Treaty, which was effectively allowing for scientific research and cooperation in the region.[43] As they evolved, the CRAMRA negotiations became a significant focus of new global environmentalist action, led predominantly by the Antarctic and Southern Ocean Coalition (ASOC) – an umbrella organization of non-governmental environmentalist organizations headquartered in Washington, DC, formed in the late 1970s – and further pushed by Greenpeace, founded in 1971, which was an ASOC member but nevertheless conducted an independent Antarctic protection campaign. Their campaigns argued that mining activities of any kind were unthinkable for Antarctica, portraying the region as an unspoiled wilderness distant from other harmful human activities. These campaigns had many aspects, including a Greenpeace expedition to, and base in, Antarctica in the late 1980s and early 1990s, as well as significant celebrity power with the world-famous French ocean naturalist Jacques Cousteau.[44] While principally focused on preventing mining, Greenpeace also drew attention to the severe local pollution created by Antarctica's scientific stations. Scientists could no longer escape responsibility for environmental protection.

Despite the years of serious negotiating effort, Australia and France refused to ratify CRAMRA after its signature. In both countries, public opinion responded to the intense global environmentalist campaign, which changed the electoral calculations of governments. Additionally, as both countries were Antarctic territorial claimants, there was some anxiety that, notwithstanding the Treaty's sovereignty freeze, CRAMRA was not sufficiently lucrative for them, even if Antarctic hydrocarbons and minerals were not likely to be exploited for many decades. Instead, Australia and France demanded that mining should be banned. Tense diplomatic negotiations resulted in a comprehensive agreement for environmental governance in Antarctica, the Protocol on Environmental Protection to the Antarctic Treaty (known as the Madrid Protocol).[45] This agreement created a comprehensive system of environmental management with detailed rules and provisions, which permanently bans mining (although the protocol includes a complex and contingent revision clause for this ban) and makes EIA a central management process for all human activities; it also created a Committee for

43 Jackson, *Who Saved Antarctica?*; Andersen, "Negotiating a New Regime".
44 Griffiths, *Slicing the Silence*, 279–289; Shortis, "'Who Can Resist?'".
45 Jackson, *Who Saved Antarctica?*.

Environmental Protection that meets regularly, alongside the Antarctic Treaty Consultative Meetings, to assess activities by all member states. The Madrid Protocol remains the heart of contemporary Antarctic environmental governance.

At the same time as the Antarctic Treaty parties were rushing to replace their abortive minerals convention with an agreement to protect the environment, efforts to protect and manage the Arctic environment through international cooperation and coordination were developing among several Arctic states. As part of their efforts to become Antarctic Treaty consultative parties in the context of the CRAMRA negotiations, Finland and Sweden brought both polar environments into the forums of Nordic cooperation. In regular meetings on polar matters, government officials of the five Nordic states – including Norway, an original Antarctic Treaty signatory and territorial claimant, and the non-signatories Denmark and Iceland – explored issues of economic growth, mineral extraction, environmental protection, and the interchangeability of technology in the polar regions.[46] These meetings and the larger Arctic-focused discussions in the Nordic Council of Ministers and the Nordic Council consciously balanced protection with economic growth, associated principally with extraction and extractive technologies.[47] Later meetings on polar issues among the Nordic states responded to a speech made by the Soviet leader Mikhail Gorbachev in Murmansk in October 1987, in which he presented new ideas for increased Arctic cooperation, including the creation of an integrated energy programme for Europe's north, a joint plan for protecting the north's environment, and increasing scientific exchange. The Finnish Ministry of Foreign Affairs was especially enthusiastic about Gorbachev's overture in the context of Finland's long-standing interests in technology transfer for resource extraction in the Barents Sea and Kola Peninsula.[48]

Ideas about the Arctic environment's 'fragility' became a central element in the bilateral and multilateral negotiations for an Arctic environmental regime that Finland championed, partially inspired by the precautionary principle, the simultaneous CRAMRA negotiations, which intensified

---

46 Signum 13.60: Arktiset alueet: 1988 I; 1988 II; Pohjoismaiset napakysymyksiä käsittelevät kokoukset v.1988 & v.1989; and Signum 13.4. Antarktiset alueet: Etelämannerta koskeva sopimus ja sen soveltaminen; Pohjoismainen yhteistyö napatutkimuksen alalla, Archives of the Ministry of Foreign Affairs, Finland.
47 Nordiska rådet, Nordiska rådets verksamhet, 131.
48 TT-komitea: Arktinen projekti, Signum 13.60 Arktiset alueet 1988 I; 1988 II, Archives of the Ministry of Foreign Affairs, Finland.

following Gorbachev's Murmansk speech.[49] The negotiations initially only included the five Nordic states plus Canada, the Soviet Union, and the United States. However, because of active lobbying, the negotiations were expanded to include non-governmental actors, most notably the Inuit Circumpolar Council. Prominent examples of environmental fragility discussed in these negotiations included the irrefutable evidence of anthropogenic heavy metals and radionuclides in Arctic tundra and lichen, fish, and marine mammals, the oil spill from *Exxon Valdez* in 1989 in Alaska, and the sinking of the Soviet nuclear submarine *Komsomolets* in 1989 in the Barents Sea.[50] The participants, however, differed on how to respond to and govern this fragility. Finland and the Soviet Union argued, as with the CRAMRA negotiations, that economic development (especially mining development) was unavoidable but that it should be accompanied by stringent environmental management with increased research and monitoring.[51] Canada, in contrast, argued that Arctic environmental governance should concentrate on the impacts of large-scale phenomena such as climate change, ozone depletion, Arctic haze, marine pollution, and toxic accumulation in Arctic food chains, a matter of particular importance to Indigenous peoples.[52]

The Finnish-initiated multilateral negotiations led to the signing of the Arctic Environmental Protection Strategy (AEPS) in June 1991. In comparison to the Madrid Protocol, the AEPS is a 'pragmatic' and 'practical' soft law approach which expresses a consensus on protecting the Arctic environment while also taking into consideration the livelihood and health of the Arctic's residents. The topics for action listed in the AEPS balanced Finland's focus on transboundary pollution with Canada's emphasis on Indigenous peoples' relationships with environments. AEPS established four working groups addressing different environmental issues discussed during the negotiations: Conservation of Arctic Flora and Fauna (CAFF), Protection of the Arctic Marine Environment (PAME), an Arctic Monitoring and Assessment Programme (AMAP), and Emergency Prevention, Preparedness and Response (EPRP). As their names indicate, the CAFF and the PAME working groups took inspiration from Antarctica's AMCAFF and CCAMLR.[53] Through the early 1990s, the AEPS working groups, whose membership

49 Young, *Creating Regimes*, 57.   50 Young, *Creating Regimes*.
51 Keskitalo, *Negotiating the Arctic*, 54–56; Tennberg, *Arctic Environmental Cooperation*, 121–123.
52 Signum 13.60 Arktiset alueet: v.1989–1992. Archives of the Ministry of Foreign Affairs, Finland.
53 Tennberg, *Arctic Environmental Cooperation*, 20–21; Keskitalo, *Negotiating the Arctic*, 62–64.

was overwhelmingly comprised of natural scientists, produced reports, guidelines, and strategies such as the CAFF Habitat Conservation Strategy.[54] The eight signatories also established additional task forces to tackle specific environmental and social issues such as the Task Force on Sustainable Development and Utilization.[55]

In 1996 AEPS became integrated into the newly created Arctic Council. Championed by Canada, the Council was a new intergovernmental forum aimed at strengthening security and fostering cooperation in the region between the eight Arctic states and Indigenous Arctic peoples, who gained the status of 'permanent participants' in the forum.[56] Most of the Council's environmental work continued to be done in working groups, which now included a specific Sustainable Development Working Group.[57] Unlike CCAMLR and the Madrid Protocol, the Council does not have a detailed strategy or structure to guide its activities or ascertain that its agreements and goals are being followed and fulfilled – indeed, there has often been a lack of consensus among members about what its priorities should be.[58] Nevertheless, the Council has been successful in providing comprehensive status updates and scientific reports on the state of the Arctic environment as well as negotiating legally binding agreements on search and rescue, scientific cooperation, and marine oil pollution.[59]

Conclusion: Governing the Anthropocene?

At the beginning of the new millennium, with increasing knowledge and certainty about global climate change and a new conception of humanity as a global geological agent ushering in the Anthropocene, the state-centric and human-centred approaches to environmental governance that had grown in the second half of the twentieth century began to be challenged and delegitimized. In December 2005, along with sixty-two other Inuit from Canada and the United States Sheila Watt-Cloutier, chair of the Inuit Circumpolar Council[60] and a seasoned Canadian Inuit politician, petitioned the Inter-American Commission on Human Rights (IACHR) for 'relief from human rights violations resulting from the impacts of global warming and climate

---

54 English, *Ice and Water*, 197.   55 Tennberg, *Arctic Environmental Cooperation*, 80–93.
56 English, *Ice and Water*, 178–251.   57 Bloom, "Establishment of Arctic Council".
58 Barry et al., "Arctic Council".
59 Nord, *Changing Arctic*, 44–46; Nord, ed., *Leadership for the North*.
60 Formerly the Inuit Circumpolar Conference.

change caused by acts and omissions of the United States'.[61] Marshalling their own testimony of living with, and suffering from, diminishing ice and creeping heat, in addition to a cascade of overwhelming scientific evidence summarized in the *Arctic Climate Impact Assessment* of 2004, the petitioners forcefully demanded their 'right to be cold', as Watt-Cloutier would later put it.[62] They were fighting for their rights as Indigenous peoples, communities of elders and young people holding and transmitting knowledge and culture, undermined by the United States which had 'consistently denied, distorted, and suppressed scientific evidence of the causes, rate, and magnitude of global warming'.[63] The Inuit Petition manifested an important development in what is considered environmental governance, that it must necessarily include human rights and justice, and that non-governmental, civil society groups consistently demand that states and international organizations see what they see in the world – that compromised environments make for unhealthy homes.

The IACHR declined to hear the petitioners' case, but in the process a significant question was raised: how to protect ice in the Anthropocene? Although ice is a dominating element of polar environments, it only came under the gaze of national and international environmental governance as the global reduction of the cryosphere was being observed at the turn of the millennium. Apart from rapid decarbonization – achieved, for example, through binding emissions targets and other efforts within the United Nations Framework Convention on Climate Change, signed in 1992 – how does one maintain the cold? Another attempt has been the World Wide Fund for Nature's (WWF) 'Last Ice Area' proposal. Beginning in 2011 as part of larger marine conservation campaigns, WWF called for area protection for the seas north of Canada and Greenland, the area projected to last lose its summer sea ice with future global warming. Called *Similijuaq* by the local Inuit elders, the proposal is meant to protect the animals and people who will rely on that last sea ice; it is action for an ice-deficient future.[64] The move to protect ice – which touches upon the abiotic, inorganic, and geological aspects of the Earth – also moves environmental governance into previously

---

61 "Petition to the Inter American Commission on Human Rights Seeking Relief from Violations Resulting from Global Warming Caused by Acts and Omissions of the United States", 7 December 2005, 1, available at http://climatecasechart.com/non-us-case/petition-to-the-inter-american-commission-on-human-rights-seeking-relief-from-violations-resulting-from-global-warming-caused-by-acts-and-omissions-of-the-united-states/.
62 Watt-Cloutier, *Right to Be Cold*.   63 "Petition", 109.
64 https://arcticwwf.org/places/last-ice-area/. See also Bravo, "A Cryopolitics".

unimagined temporal horizons. If the governance of animals, habitats, and landscapes had previously reckoned with a time span of decades, the effects of climate change and the Anthropocene on ice and the atmosphere move governance onto a timescale of centuries and aeons. The efficacy of this governance will be impossible to judge.

The WWF's Last Ice Area also manifests the global push for marine protected areas (MPAs), which in the Arctic are principally designated through national legal and policy tools. In the Antarctic, the push for MPAs has been a highly visible and contentious issue in CCAMLR. After establishing its ecosystem monitoring programme and the precautionary catch limit for krill by the early 1990s, CCAMLR spent the 1990s trying to deal with illegal, unreported, and unregulated (IUU) fishing and problems such as bird bycatch. After the World Conference on Sustainable Development in Rio in 2002 called for a representative system of MPAs throughout the world ocean, certain states and international environmental NGOs have strongly advocated for Antarctic MPAs, leading to the first high seas MPAs in the world: the first around the South Orkneys in 2009 and the second in the Ross Sea in 2016.[65]

The environmental governance frameworks enacted in earlier times – especially those created in the early 1990s – have continued to operate despite new challenges. At the international level, this governance is regularized, bureaucratized, technocratic, and made in conference and working group settings – whether a dozen people in a committee or thousands at a major United Nations conference. Data is entered, working papers circulate, draft recommendations and policies are debated, and, at the end, new international agreements or actions are taken.[66] Since 1998 the Committee on Environmental Protection meets annually to assess the impact of new developments on the Antarctic continent: all manner of scientific and other infrastructure is now subject to the question of how much it might harm Antarctic ecosystems.

One of the dominant technologies or practices of contemporary environmental governance is the scientific assessment. A deluge of lengthy, dense reports brimming with scientific data, estimates, and projections from a range of national and international bodies has since the 1970s defined the realm of climate and environmental politics. These reports include the assessment reports of the United Nations' Intergovernmental Panel on Climate Change, the Arctic Council's own *Arctic Climate Impact Assessment* of 2004 among

65 Brooks et al., "Reaching Consensus".   66 O'Reilly, *Technocratic Antarctic*.

many others, and SCAR's attempts to force climate onto the Antarctic Treaty System agenda.[67] Physical and social scientists and policymakers have devoted considerable energy to these reports in the hopes of generating political and social change – and governments seem to have been able to defer meaningful action by continually referring major questions to such assessment exercises. Although climate and environmental action has been uneven, these reports have had other effects too. Timo Koivurova has argued that the *Arctic Climate Impact Assessment* of 2004 'established the Arctic as the early warning place of global climate change', partly initiating the contemporary geopolitics of the region.[68] Environmental governance in the Anthropocene continues, therefore, not only narrowly governing human relationships with specific animals or landscapes, but actively creating the very spaces and regions that are subject to geopolitical, ideological, and cultural competition.

Bibliography

Andersen, Rolf Trolle, "Negotiating a New Regime: How CRAMRA Came into Existence", in Arnfinn Jørgensen-Dahl and Willy Østreng, eds., *The Antarctic Treaty System in World Politics* (Houndmills: Macmillan, in association with the Fridtjof Nansen Institute, 1991), pp. 94–109.

Antonello, Alessandro, *The Greening of Antarctica: Assembling an International Environment* (New York: Oxford University Press, 2019).

Antonello, Alessandro, and Adrian Howkins, "The Rise of Technocratic Environmentalism: The United States, Antarctica, and the Globalisation of the Environmental Impact Statement", *Journal of Historical Geography* 68 (2020): 55–64.

Arctic Climate Impact Assessment, *Impacts of a Warming Arctic: Arctic Climate Impact Assessment* (Cambridge: Cambridge University Press, 2004).

Avango, Dag, and Peder Roberts, "Heritage, Conservation, and the Geopolitics of Svalbard: Writing the History of Arctic Environments", in Lill-Ann Körber, Scott MacKenzie, and Anna Westerståhl Stenport, eds., *Arctic Environmental Modernities: From the Age of Polar Exploration to the Era of the Anthropocene* (Cham: Palgrave Macmillan, 2017), pp. 125–143.

Avango, Dag, Louwrens Hacquebord, Ypie Aalders, et al., "Between Markets and Geo-politics: Natural Resource Exploitation on Spitsbergen from 1600 to the Present Day", *Polar Record* 47 (2011): 29–39.

Barry, Tom, Brynhildur Davíðsdóttir, Níels Einarsson, and Oran R. Young, "The Arctic Council: An Agent of Change?", *Global Environmental Change* 63 (2020): 102099.

---

67 Oppenheimer et al., *Discerning Experts*; Wormbs and Sörlin, "Arctic Futures".
68 Koivurova, "Limits and Possibilities", 149.

Bielawski, Ellen, "Inuit Knowledge and Science in the Arctic", in David L. Peterson and Darryl R. Johnson, eds., *Human Ecology and Climate Change: People and Resources in the Far North* (Washington, DC: Taylor & Francis, 1995), pp. 219–228.
Bloom, Evan T., "Establishment of the Arctic Council", *American Journal of International Law* 93 (1999): 712–722.
Bocking, Stephen, *Ecologists and Environmental Politics: A History of Contemporary Ecology* (New Haven: Yale University Press, 1997).
Bolotova, Alla, "Colonization and Nature in the Soviet Union: State Ideology, Public Discourse, and the Experience of Geologists", *Historical Social Research/Historische Sozialforschung* 29 (2004): 104–123.
Bothwell, Robert, Ian M. Drummond, and John English, *Canada Since 1945: Power, Politics, and Provincialism* (Toronto: University of Toronto Press, 1989).
Bravo, Michael, "A Cryopolitics to Reclaim Our Frozen Material States", in Joanna Radin and Emma Kowal, eds., *Cryopolitics: Frozen Life in a Melting World* (Cambridge, MA: MIT Press, 2017), pp. 27–57.
Bravo, Michael, "Sea Ice Mapping: Ontology, Mechanics and Human Rights at the Ice Floe Edge", in Denis Cosgrove and Veronica della Dora, eds., *High Places* (London: I. B. Tauris, 2009), pp. 162–177.
Brooks, Cassandra M., Larry B. Crowder, Henrik Österblom, and Aaron L. Strong, "Reaching Consensus for Conserving the Global Commons: The Case of the Ross Sea, Antarctica", *Conservation Letters* 13 (2020): e12676.
Burnett, D. Graham, *The Sounding of the Whale: Science and Cetaceans in the Twentieth Century* (Chicago: University of Chicago Press, 2012).
Dahl, Justiina, "Seeing Like a State in a Society of States: The Social Role of Science and Technology in the Northward Expansion of the International Society", PhD diss. (European University Institute, 2016).
Doel, Ronald E., Robert Marc Friedman, Julia Lajus, Sverker Sörlin, and Urban Wråkberg, "Strategic Arctic Science: National Interests in Building Natural Knowledge. Interwar Era through the Cold War", *Journal of Historical Geography* 44 (2014): 60–80.
Dorsey, Kurkpatrick, *Whales and Nations: Environmental Diplomacy on the High Seas* (Seattle: University of Washington Press, 2013).
Elzinga, Aant, "Roald Amundsen and His Ambiguous Relationship to Science: A Look at Outcomes of His Six Expeditions", *Journal of Northern Studies* 6 (2012): 53–109.
English, John, *Ice and Water: Politics, Peoples and the Arctic Council* (Toronto: Allen Lane, 2013).
Fikkan, Anne, Gail Osherenko, and Alexander Arikainen, "Polar Bears: The Importance of Simplicity", in Oran R. Young and Gail Osherenko, eds., *Polar Politics: Creating International Environmental Regimes* (Ithaca: Cornell University Press, 1993), pp. 96–151.
Fitzmaurice, Andrew, *Sovereignty, Property and Empire, 1500–2000* (Cambridge: Cambridge University Press, 2014).
Flanagan, Thomas, "The Agricultural Argument and Original Appropriation: Indian Lands and Political Philosophy", *Canadian Journal of Political Science/Revue canadienne de science politique* 22 (1989): 589–602.
Gibson, James R., *Imperial Russia in Frontier America: The Changing Geography of Russian America, 1784–1867* (New York: Oxford University Press, 1976).
Griffiths, Tom, *Slicing the Silence: Voyaging to Antarctica* (Sydney: UNSW Press, 2007).

Hacquebord, Louwrens, "Three Centuries of Whaling and Walrus Hunting in Svalbard and Its Impact on the Arctic Ecosystem", *Environment and History* 7 (2001): 169–185.

Halvorsen, Jahn, and Leiv Torgersen, *Problemet Nord-Norge: statistik økonomisk undersøkelse av Nord-Norges andel i landets nasjonalinntekt i 1939* (Bodø: Bodø Boktrykkeri, 1948).

Hamblin, Jacob Darwin, *Arming Mother Nature: The Birth of Catastrophic Environmentalism* (Oxford: Oxford University Press, 2013).

Head, Ivan L., "Canadian Claims to Territorial Sovereignty in the Arctic Regions", *McGill Law Journal* 9 (1963): 200–226.

Hønneland, Geir, "Compliance in the Fishery Protection Zone Around Svalbard", *Ocean Development & International Law* 29 (1998): 339–360.

Howkins, Adrian, *Frozen Empires: An Environmental History of the Antarctic Peninsula* (New York: Oxford University Press, 2017).

Howkins, Adrian, *The Polar Regions: An Environmental History* (Cambridge: Polity Press, 2016).

Jackson, Andrew, *Who Saved Antarctica? The Heroic Era of Antarctic Diplomacy* (Cham: Palgrave Macmillan, 2021).

Jasanoff, Sheila, and Marybeth Long Martello, eds., *Earthly Politics: Local and Global in Environmental Governance* (Cambridge, MA: MIT Press, 2004).

Jones, Ryan Tucker, *Empire of Extinction: Russians and the North Pacific's Strange Beasts of the Sea, 1741–1867* (New York: Oxford University Press, 2014).

Kaiser, Wolfram, and Jan-Henrik Meyer, eds., *International Organizations and Environmental Protection: Conservation and Globalization in the Twentieth Century* (New York: Berghahn, 2017).

Keskitalo, E. C. H., *Negotiating the Arctic: The Construction of an International Region* (New York: Routledge, 2004).

Koerner, Lisbet, *Linnaeus: Nature and Nation* (Cambridge, MA: Harvard University Press, 1999).

Koivurova, Timo, "Limits and Possibilities of the Arctic Council in a Rapidly Changing Scene of Arctic Governance", *Polar Record* 46 (2010): 146–156.

Larsen, Thor S., and Ian Stirling, *The Agreement on the Conservation of Polar Bears: Its History and Future* (Tromsø: Norsk Polarinstitutt, 2009).

Laruelle, Marlène, *Russia's Arctic Strategies and the Future of the Far North* (Armonk, NY: M. E. Sharpe, 2014).

Lavigne, David M., Victor B. Scheffer, and Stephen R. Kellert, "The Evolution of North American Attitudes Toward Marine Mammals", in John R. Twiss, Jr and Randall R. Reeves, eds., *Conservation and Management of Marine Mammals* (Washington, DC: Smithsonian Institution Press, 1998), pp. 10–47.

Lemos, Maria Carmen, and Arun Agrawal, "Environmental Governance", *Annual Review of Environment and Resources* 31 (2006): 297–325.

Macekura, Stephen J., *Of Limits and Growth: The Rise of Global Sustainable Development in the Twentieth Century* (New York: Cambridge University Press, 2015).

McCannon, John, *A History of the Arctic: Nature, Exploration and Exploitation* (London: Reaktion, 2012).

McCannon, John, *Red Arctic: Polar Exploration and the Myth of the North in the Soviet Union, 1932–1939* (New York: Oxford University Press, 1998).

McConnell, Joseph R., and Ross Edwards, "Coal Burning Leaves Toxic Heavy Metal Legacy in the Arctic", *Proceedings of the National Academy of Sciences* 105 (2008): 12140–12144.

Nord, Douglas C., *The Changing Arctic: Creating a Framework for Consensus Building and Governance Within the Arctic Council* (New York: Palgrave Macmillan, 2016).

Nord, Douglas C., ed., *Leadership for the North: The Influence and Impact of Arctic Council Chairs* (Cham: Springer, 2019).

Nordiska rådet, *Nordiska rådets verksamhet 1971–1986, Översikt över rådets rekommendationer och yttranden* (Göteborg: Graphic Systems, 1988).

Nuttall, Mark, *Protecting the Arctic: Indigenous Peoples and Cultural Survival* (Amsterdam: Harwood, 1998).

Oppenheimer, Michael, Naomi Oreskes, Dale Jamieson, et al., *Discerning Experts: The Practices of Scientific Assessment for Environmental Policy* (Chicago: University of Chicago Press, 2019).

O'Reilly, Jessica, *The Technocratic Antarctic: An Ethnography of Scientific Expertise and Environmental Governance* (Ithaca: Cornell University Press, 2017).

Osherenko, Gail, and Oran R. Young, *The Age of the Arctic: Hot Conflicts and Cold Realities* (Cambridge: Cambridge University Press, 1989).

Richards, Rhys, *Sealing in the Southern Oceans 1788–1833* (Wellington: Paremata, 2010).

Roberts, Peder, *The European Antarctic: Science and Strategy in Scandinavia and the British Empire* (New York: Palgrave Macmillan, 2011).

Ruby, Robert, *Unknown Shore: The Lost History of England's Arctic Colony* (New York: Henry Holt, 2001).

Ruder, Cynthia A., *Making History for Stalin: The Story of the Belomor Canal* (Gainesville: University Press of Florida, 1998).

Schleper, Simone, *Planning for the Planet: Environmental Expertise and the International Union for Conservation of Nature and Natural Resources, 1960–1980* (New York: Berghahn, 2019).

Selcer, Perrin, *The Postwar Origins of the Global Environment: How the United Nations Built Spaceship Earth* (New York: Columbia University Press, 2018).

Sellheim, Nikolas, "Legislating the Blind Spot: The EU Seal Regime and the Newfoundland Seal Hunt", PhD diss. (University of Lapland, 2016).

Shortis, Emma, "'Who Can Resist This Guy?' Jacques Cousteau, Celebrity Diplomacy, and the Environmental Protection of the Antarctic", *Australian Journal of Politics and History* 61 (2015): 366–380.

Singh, Elen C., and Artemy A. Saguirian, "The Svalbard Archipelago: The Role of Surrogate Negotiators", in Oran R. Young and Gail Osherenko, eds., *Polar Politics: Creating International Environmental Regimes* (Ithaca: Cornell University Press, 1993), pp. 56–95.

Sörlin, Sverker, "Rituals and Resources of Natural History: The North and the Arctic in Swedish Scientific Nationalism", in Michael Bravo and Sverker Sörlin, eds., *Narrating the Arctic: A Cultural History of Nordic Scientific Practices* (Canton, MA: Science History Publications, 2002), pp. 73–122.

Strandsbjerg, Jeppe, "Cartopolitics, Geopolitics and Boundaries in the Arctic", *Geopolitics* 17 (2012): 818–842.

Stuhl, Andrew, *Unfreezing the Arctic: Science, Colonialism, and the Transformation of Inuit Lands* (Chicago: University of Chicago Press, 2016).
Tennberg, Monica, *Arctic Environmental Cooperation: A Study in Governmentality* (Aldershot: Ashgate, 2000).
Tierney, James, "The Polar Bear Treaty and the Changing Geography of the High Arctic", *Journal of Animal Law and Ethics* 3 (2009): 141–171.
Tønnessen, J. N., and A. O. Johnsen, *The History of Modern Whaling* (London, Canberra: C. Hurst and ANU Press, 1982).
Turchetti, Simone, and Peder Roberts, eds., *The Surveillance Imperative: Geosciences During the Cold War and Beyond* (New York: Palgrave Macmillan, 2014).
Warde, Paul, Libby Robin, and Sverker Sörlin, *The Environment: A History of the Idea* (Baltimore: Johns Hopkins University Press, 2018).
Watt-Cloutier, Sheila, *The Right to Be Cold: One Woman's Fight to Protect the Arctic and Save the Planet from Climate Change* (Minneapolis: University of Minnesota Press, 2015).
Wood, Alan, *Russia's Frozen Frontier: A History of Siberia and the Russian Far East, 1581–1991* (London: Bloomsbury, 2011).
Wormbs, Nina, and Sverker Sörlin, "Arctic Futures: Agency and Assessing Assessments", in Lill-Ann Körber, Scott MacKenzie, and Anna Westerståhl Stenport, eds., *Arctic Environmental Modernities: From the Age of Polar Exploration to the Era of the Anthropocene* (Cham: Palgrave Macmillan, 2017), pp. 247–261.
Wråkberg, Urban, "Nature Conservationism and the Arctic Commons of Spitsbergen 1900–1920", *Acta Borealia* 23 (2006): 1–23.
Young, Oran R., *Creating Regimes: Arctic Accords and International Governance* (Ithaca: Cornell University Press, 1998).

27
The Antarctic Extension of Latin America

PABLO FONTANA

Introduction

At a global level, the perception of Antarctica has been largely determined by the hegemony of English-speaking accounts and visions, and of central and northern European countries – despite being on the opposite side of the planet – as has been the case with other large regions colonized during the rise of imperialism. Paradoxically, the relationship with Antarctica of the region that is closest to it, and whose main Antarctic countries have the largest and oldest permanent presence on that continent – as well as the strongest sense of belonging – is often ignored or simply interpreted as a simple case of 'territorial nationalism'[1] or even 'Latin *Lebensraum*'.[2] However, the historical and symbolic relationship that these South American nations established with the neighbouring region of the sixth continent is much richer, more diverse, and more dynamic than these interpretations – influenced by views of other geographical and cultural realities – manage to elucidate, and than we can address in these few pages. Undoubtedly a crucial factor in the emergence of the idea of an Antarctica not only Argentine or Chilean, but also as an extension of Latin America, is precisely the existence of strong cultural, idiomatic, historical, and identity ties among Latin American countries.

A general approach to the Antarctic perspective and history of Latin America shows the complex and singular character of this relationship, a relationship that is significantly different from that which other countries have established with Antarctica. It has the distinctive feature of having acquired through Latin Americanism a supranational and regional character, with clear anti-colonialist political meanings. This regional approach to Antarctica, one of a kind, allows us to speak about the Antarctic Extension of Latin America.

[1] Howkins, *Frozen Empires*. [2] Child, "Latin Lebensraum".

Closeness, Continuity

An 'Antarctic Extension of Latin America' pushes us to analyse mainly the cases of Argentina and Chile, since they are the South American countries with the greatest Antarctic presence and history, and it was precisely from the dialogue between these nations that the concept of 'South American Antarctica' arose (Figure 27.1). In the past half-century, other South American states have also been present in Antarctica, and we highlight the cases of Brazil and Uruguay, and to a lesser extent Peru, Ecuador, and

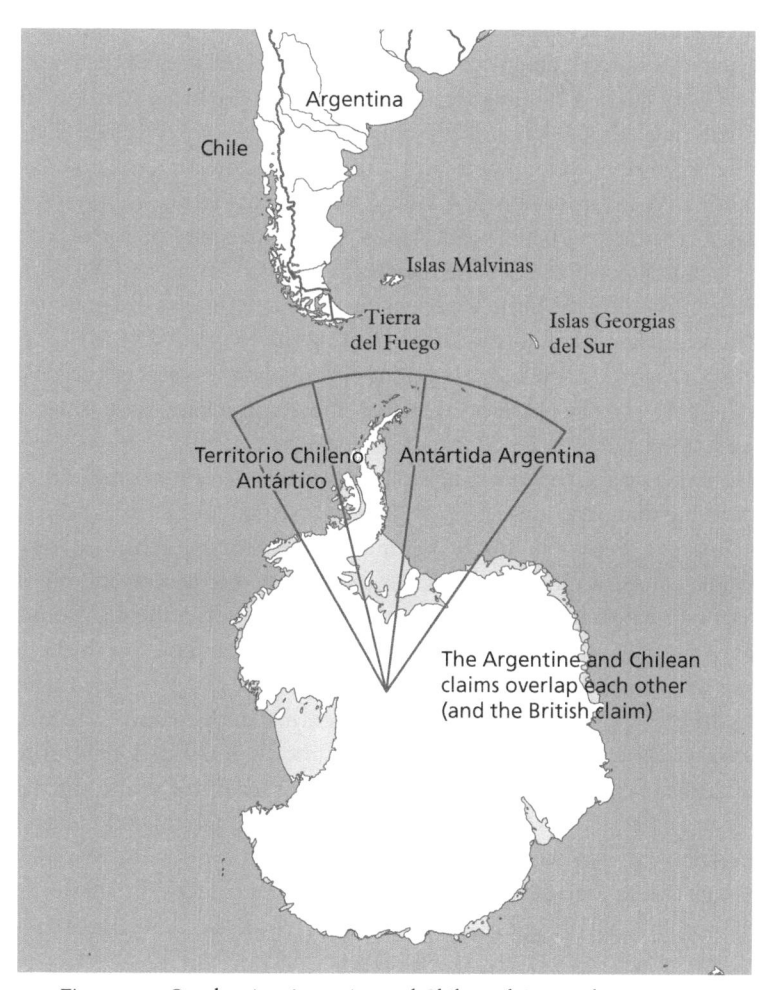

Figure 27.1 Overlapping Argentine and Chilean claims in the Antarctic.

Colombia. Currently, Argentina is the country with the highest number of Antarctic stations (six permanent and seven summer stations), followed by Chile (five permanent and seven summer stations). All bases from both countries are located within their respectively claimed sectors (Argentina 25° to 74° west, Chile 53° to 90° west), which partly overlap (53° to 74° west). Both countries consider themselves to be intercontinental: bicontinental in the case of Argentina (American and Antarctic continents), and tricontinental in the case of Chile (America, Antarctica, and Oceania, due to Easter Island). In this way, the claimed Antarctic territories also define the continental geographic identity of both countries.

Yet there are other factors that justify the centrality of these two countries, and that in turn have determined the force and particularity of their perception of Antarctica, differentiating them from other countries with Antarctic presence or history. They are the only South American countries that are original signatories to the Antarctic Treaty (AT), both with territorial claims, and they have incorporated these claims within provinces or regions of their national territories in mainland America. In the imaginary of both societies, these Antarctic territories are represented as an indivisible part of the national territory.[3] They are the only two countries that have families in Antarctica, in addition to schools and births. In fact, during the toughest COVID-19 quarantine phase in 2020, the only Argentine school open was at Esperanza Base, and the only cinema open was the small theatre in Jubany Base (since 2012 called Carlini Base).

Without a doubt, the most important factor that determines the particular relationship that Argentina and Chile have with Antarctica is the proximity of the Antarctic Peninsula to their American territories, enhanced by the depopulated character of Antarctica at the time of discovering and officially incorporating it to their national territories. No point in Antarctica comes as close to another continent as the Antarctic Peninsula and the South Shetland Islands to South America: only 1,000 km or even less, compared with 2,400 to Australia and New Zealand or almost 4,000 to South Africa. In turn, this proximity reinforced the perception of continuity of the national territory, because the two countries have the southernmost coasts of South America in the Atlantic and Pacific Oceans. This vision of geographical continuity may seem strange to non-South American readers, but it mirrors the relationship of countries like Canada, Norway, or Russia to the islands off their northern coastlines. In addition, these countries have two of the closest gateways to

3 Cardone, "Shaping an Antarctic Identity".

Antarctica: Ushuaia and Punta Arenas, cities from where much of the Antarctic tourism and logistics depart.

Such continuity and closeness have influenced the Argentine-Chilean understanding (shared by certain South American countries) of the British Antarctic claim as a kind of colonialism that survived the boom of European modern imperialism, particularly owing to the remoteness of the 'mother country' from the Antarctic Territory. A parallel can be drawn with the colonial era, when current Latin American countries were colonies of faraway European empires. The introduction of the British Antarctic claim as a 'dependency' of the nearer Malvinas Islands (called the Falklands by the British) only reinforced the perception of this claim as an example of residual colonialism. The British claim would be equivalent to an empire of extreme southern South America occupying islands in the north of Scotland or Norway, expelling their local population, then making some expeditions to the Arctic, and finally claiming a wide territory up to the North Pole as a dependency of those islands that it had occupied earlier, despite the protest of those northern European nations.

Geological continuity is another argument used by both countries to support their Antarctic claim. Beyond its implications in international law, it is interesting here to highlight how this influences the Chilean-Argentine vision. By understanding the Antarctic Peninsula as a continuation of the Andes mountain range, even calling its mountains *Antartandes*, these are two nations that perceive themselves as *Andinos* (Andean) countries of the extreme south of South America, giving rise to the feeling of a 'natural' belonging to that territory, and also that this territory belongs to them, especially if it is uninhabited. Numerous stories from Chilean and Argentine explorers express this feeling, reinforced by landscape similarities with the Andes of the extreme south.[4] In fact, any picture of the southern Patagonian ice field could easily pass as the Antarctic Peninsula.

The Argentine and Chilean projection towards Antarctica can also be considered part of a continuous advance movement towards the south over territories without state control, which were also understood as theirs by inheritance from the Spanish Empire. This continuous advance has certain characteristics that resemble that of the first US American States on the Atlantic coast, which incorporated the central territory and then continued the movement by conquering the American west, with one difference: whereas in Patagonia (and North America) there were Indigenous populations, in Antarctica there was none. The strengthening of the control by both nations

---

4 Vaca, *Antártida, mi hogar*; Cordovez Madariaga, *La Antártida Sudamericana*.

over their Patagonian territories took place at the end of the nineteenth century, and once it was finished, their effective presence in Antarctica began. In fact, in the Argentine Army, the term *Expedicionario al Desierto Blanco* (Expeditionary to the White Desert) is used for those Argentines who winter in Antarctica, drawing a parallel with the name *Expedicionario al Desierto* (Expeditionary to the Desert) used for those soldiers who were sent to Patagonia at the end of the nineteenth century. Even the name *Fortín* (Fort) used to name the first settlement of Argentine families in Antarctica – the *Fortín Sargento Cabral* – belongs to this imaginary, drawing a parallel with the forts established during the incorporation of Patagonian territories.

Another historical 'continuity' in the imaginary of both countries – in particular with the common resistance to the British claim – is that they fought together against a European colonial power in their wars of independence. In the Argentine case this is stronger and has a double character. On the one hand, early patriotic sentiment, as well as the independence revolution (1810–16), arose after repelling English invasions of Buenos Aires in 1806 and 1807. On the other hand, when the British invaded the Malvinas Islands in 1833, this was experienced as a new colonial dominance.

Beyond these issues, it is necessary to analyse the South American Antarctic action throughout the twentieth century, especially that of Argentina and Chile, in order to understand the development of the concept of an *Antártida Sudamericana* (South American Antarctica).

The First Latin Americans in Antarctica (Nineteenth Century)

It is difficult to determine when the South American presence in Antarctica began, since we do not know whether the early inhabitants of Tierra del Fuego ever visited the islands located north of the Antarctic Peninsula. In 1815, during the independence war, two Argentine warships reached a latitude of 65° south, spotting signs of nearby land.[5] Argentine sealers visited the South Shetland Islands at least as early as 1817 or 1818, before the official discoveries of the continent between 1819 and 1821.[6] In 1818, the first piece of legislation from a South American State on Antarctica was approved, when Argentina authorized a sealer to hunt, according to his request, 'in some of the islands that are uninhabited in the vicinity of the South Pole'.[7]

---

5 Quevedo Paiva, *Historia de la Antártida*, 275.   6 Fitte, *El descubrimiento*, 108–112.
7 Capdevila and Comerci, *Los tiempos*, 76.

For the rest of the nineteenth century, the Argentine presence in Antarctica would be limited to sealers, since the country had few resources because of the costs of the independence war and later decades of civil war. Once the national state consolidated in 1880, plans emerged for scientific expeditions to Antarctica with the aim of installing permanent observatories there, but the government decided to focus on strengthening its control of Patagonia, which was largely in the hands of Indigenous peoples, and was threatened by the advance of European empires as well as Chile (whose government followed similar reasoning with regard to not actively engaging Antarctica). These scientific projects preceded by several years those that were planned at the International Congresses of Geography held in London in 1895 and Berlin in 1899, widely viewed by scholars as the start of modern Antarctic exploration. At the same time, there were private Argentine projects for mining in Antarctica. The state authorized them only to explore minerals resources, but these projects did not materialize.

An 'American Antarctica' Is Born (1901–1908)

It was in the early years of the twentieth century when an effective South American state presence began in Antarctica. In 1901, the Argentine State provided material aid to the Swedish Antarctic Expedition of Dr Otto Nordenskjöld, after the arrival of his ship *Antarctic* in Buenos Aires. The expedition was joined by the young sub-lieutenant of the Argentine Navy José María Sobral, who became an integral member of the expedition.[8] Sobral was the first Argentine and Latin American to winter in Antarctica. When the *Antarctic* sank, trapped in the ice, both overwinterers and castaways were rescued in November 1903 by the Argentine corvette ARA *Uruguay*, under the command of Lieutenant Julián Irizar. This rescue would have important consequences for Argentina in Antarctica, since it demonstrated to the State and society that there were human and material resources in place to install and operate scientific bases.

In January 1904, Argentina officially accepted the transfer of the magnetic and meteorological observatory built in 1903 on Laurie Island, in the South Orkney archipelago, by a Scottish expedition under the command of William Speirs Bruce.[9] On 22 February 1904 the first crew under the Argentine flag took possession of the observatory and installed a post office. This is the reason that Argentines commemorate the Argentine Antarctica Day every

8 Sobral, *Dos años*. 9 Capdevila and Comerci, *Cien años de ciencia*.

22 February. The day marks the beginning of the permanent Argentine presence in Antarctica, the first of its kind and the most enduring, as it has continued uninterrupted to the time of writing. It also began a way of populating the Antarctic continent in the permanent and cyclical manner that would later become familiar in that continent, with parties being replaced annually. In 1906 Argentina also became the first country to designate authorities for Antarctic lands, by a decree that appointed commissioners for the South Orkney Islands and for Booth Island, where another observatory was to be installed – which could not be carried out owing to the sinking of the polar ship ARA *Austral*.

The rescue of the *Uruguay* also had an economic consequence for Argentina: in 1904 the *Compañía Argentina de Pesca* (Argentine Fishing Company) was created, the first whaling company of the southern hemisphere. It installed the factory station of Grytviken, which was the first permanent human settlement in San Pedro Island (called South Georgia Island by the British), main island of the archipelago of South Georgia Islands, where in 1905 Argentina also installed a geomagnetic and meteorological observatory.

In 1906 Chile organized an Antarctic expedition that did not take place, owing to the Valparaíso earthquake. However, that same year the *Sociedad Ballenera de Magallanes* (Magellan Whaling Society) was created, based in Punta Arenas, which installed a factory in the Whalers Cove of Deception Island, where a Decree referred to Chilean Antarctic rights.[10] The Argentine government protested the actions of its Chilean counterpart and, in 1906, negotiations began to delimit their Antarctic territories. These can be understood as a continuation of talks that had taken place in the last two decades of the nineteenth century and the first years of the twentieth, when both countries signed a series of documents to peacefully define their American borders (1881, 1888, 1893, 1896, 1898, and 1902), among which stands out the *Abrazo del Estrecho* (Embrace of the Strait) that took place in 1902 between the President of Argentina, Julio Roca, and the President of Chile, Federico Errázuriz Echaurren, in the Strait of Magellan. During conversations in 1906 and 1908, they expressed their intentions to reach an agreement in relation to their Antarctic interests and tried unsuccessfully to define a common border in Antarctica, but the idea of an 'American' (more precisely Chilean and Argentine) Antarctica began to emerge, considering the peninsula an extension of the Andes Mountains. In 1907, Chilean geographer Luis Risco Patrón published a map entitled *American Antarctica*, covering the

---

10 Mancilla González, "Algunos antecedentes".

Antarctic region between 44° and 72° west. A year later he published a book with the same name in which, after reviewing the southern precedents of both countries, he concludes that 'We can designate with the name of American Antarctica the part of the Antarctic lands between the extreme meridians of South America', referring to the Antarctic and sub-Antarctic region between 55° and 90° west.[11]

The lack of agreement over common borders would be exploited by the British Crown, which paradoxically acted as arbitrator in the Argentine-Chilean border negotiations in South America. This was closely linked to the actions of the whaling companies of both South American countries, and the great potential to charge whaling taxes. In 1906 the United Kingdom had already sent a warship that installed officials in San Pedro Island and Deception Island for this purpose. In this context, the British Crown in 1908 claimed an Antarctic territory between 20° and 80° west, south of 50° south, which included what the two South American countries understood as their territory.[12] The document could even be interpreted as including the northernmost Patagonian territories of Chile and Argentina, with the Tierra del Fuego Island, as well as the south of the province of Santa Cruz and the Magallanes Region. It was not until 1917 that the British government modified the chart with a new border that explicitly left these Patagonian territories out, but continued to include the Antarctic, as well as the islands of the South Atlantic.

Meanwhile Chile, through Pilot Luis Pardo Villalón, in command of the ship *Yelcho*, rescued Ernest Shackleton's Imperial Trans-Antarctic Expedition on 30 August 1916. This took place after the failed rescue attempt by Uruguay, with the vessel *Instituto de Pesca No. 1*, under the command of Lieutenant Ruperto Elichiribehety. The rescue of European expeditions by the countries in the extreme south of Latin America, especially those with such ambitious objectives as Shackleton's, could only reinforce this feeling of closeness and belonging to that Antarctic region on the part of the South Americans.

The end of the Heroic Age in Antarctica in the early 1920s meant a clear decrease in fascination for the continent, with a corresponding decline in expeditions. But the advancement of new technologies in those years and their possible applications did not escape the interest of the South American pioneers. In May 1926, a Chilean engineer residing in Argentina, Antonio Pauly, presented a project to the Argentine government to make a flight to

11 Riso Patrón, "La Antártida Americana".   12 *Falkland Islands Gazette*.

the South Pole. The *Instituto Geográfico Argentino* (Argentine Geographic Institute) decided to support him, but the plane – a Dornier Wal – crashed on the way to Argentina, and the expedition was cancelled. The only country that maintained its permanent presence in Antarctica for the next two decades was Argentina, on Laurie Island, where radio communications with South America were established in 1927 and the first Latin American documentary in Antarctica was filmed.[13]

Geopolitical Explosion and Chilean-Argentine Cooperation (1939–1945)

Until the end of the 1930s, the geopolitical situation in Antarctica remained calmer compared with the Heroic Age, but everything changed at the end of that decade, with a growing demand for whale oil. In this climate of tensions and a perceived need to assert claims more actively, the Norwegian government decided to convene in May 1938 an International Polar Conference and Exhibition to be held in Bergen in 1940. Although the meeting never took place owing to the outbreak of World War II, the invitation gave new force to countries with Antarctic histories. Argentina and Chile, the only Latin American countries to be invited, accepted the call. In order to participate, the Argentine President Roberto Ortiz established in July 1939 a provisional Antarctic Commission; one month later Argentina invited Chile to collaborate at the conference, and in September the Chilean Antarctic Commission was created through a presidential decree of Pedro Aguirre Cerda.[14]

The invitation also had unexpected consequences, provoking a geopolitical chain reaction in Antarctica. The Third Reich organized an Antarctic expedition, in order to survey a region and use this for a future territorial claim.[15] When the Norwegian government learned about the expedition, it pre-emptively claimed the territory as Queen Maud Land. Months later, the United States organized its first official expedition in a century, including invited observers from Chile and Argentina.

As might be expected, this chain of events, even in the context of the outbreak of World War II, caused tensions between the three countries that had interests in the Antarctic Peninsula. In August 1940, Argentina responded to a British letter showing its Antarctic claim by issuing a protest to the British embassy and published a map of the Argentine *Instituto Geográfico Militar*

---

13 Fontana, "Between the Ice".   14 Pinochet de la Barra, *Medio siglo*, 36.
15 Ritscher, *Deutsche Antarktische Expedition*, IX.

(Military Geographic Institute) that included the Antarctic sector between meridians 25° and 74° west longitude under Argentine sovereignty. The US Government invited Argentina and Chile to discuss the Antarctic issue with a view to reaching a common position. In turn, the president of Chile, Aguirre Cerda, responded on 6 November 1940 by issuing Decree 1747 that established the limits of the Chilean Antarctic Territory between meridians 90° and 53° west, leaving out the South Orkney Islands. This is the reason that the *Día de la Antártica Chilena* (Chilean Antarctic Day) is celebrated in Chile on that date. However, through diplomatic channels, the Chilean government clarified to Argentina that it meant to prevent Great Britain from 'getting ahead', while respecting Argentine rights.[16]

In the context of this new situation, in March 1941 meetings were held in Santiago de Chile between the Argentine representative Isidoro Ruiz Moreno and the Chilean Julio Escudero Guzmán, in order to establish a boundary between both Antarctic claims, achieving a mutual recognition of rights over 'South-American Antarctica'.[17] Argentina resumed its plan to carry out new expeditions and install more permanent Antarctic stations in 1940–41. Chile also planned an Antarctic expedition, notifying the Argentine government in writing and inviting two Argentine observers. The Argentine expedition took place in early 1942, with the ship ARA *Primero de Mayo*. On this first trip, various sites were explored to install an observatory in the west of the Antarctic Peninsula, scientific studies were carried out, Argentine flags and shields were placed (together with official sovereignty statements), and a lighthouse was built. However, shortly after this, a British ship replaced the Argentine objects with similar ones from the United Kingdom. Argentina asked the Chilean government to send a common expedition to Antarctica, but since they did not have a suitable vessel, they proposed to send Chilean guests on the Argentine vessel the first year, and then reverse the roles the year after. The following summer the same Argentine ship repeated the operation, the objects deposited by the British were removed, and Argentine objects, flags, minutes, and shields were reinstalled. On board, there were three Chilean military guests again, among them the retired Navy officer and member of the Chilean Antarctic Commission Enrique Cordovez Madariaga, who published in 1945 the book *South American Antarctica (La Antártida*

---

16 AMREC, Sección Topográfica C 20 – A (Argentina / Serie 79 – Dirección de Antártida y Malvinas / AH0003/14), Soberanía en tierras antárticas: pretensiones chilenas, Telegrama cifrado No. 1114 de Agilar Lacasa al Ministro de Relaciones Exteriores (7 November 1940).
17 Genest, *Antártida Sudamericana*, 40–41.

Sudamericana), where he described that territory as Chilean and Argentine. In his view, the two 'South American Antarctic countries' should work together to meet the challenges posed by the continent.[18]

The British government decided to oppose these South American actions by installing its own permanent stations through a secret operation called *Tabarin*, under the official facade of countering German presence in Antarctica to keep the Argentine, Chilean, and US governments calm (especially Argentina, whose wheat and meat were central to the British war effort).[19] In February 1944, the first two stations were installed at the same sites selected by Argentina for the same objective, followed by another two in early 1945. This overlap of the three claims, known as 'the Antarctic problem', would lead to a confrontation unmatched in Antarctic history.[20]

The Chilean-Argentine Alliance and South American Antarctica (1946–1956)

An unparalleled Antarctic deployment of the two South American nations began in the context of decolonization processes, especially from the British Empire, and the beginning of the Cold War. In June 1946, Juan Domingo Perón assumed the Argentine presidency with a pro-Latin American, anti-imperialist speech (mostly anti-British), signed a series of bilateral friendship and cooperation agreements with various countries in the region, and started Argentina's most intense period in Antarctica. A year later, he wrote the foreword to a book on Argentine Antarctic rights, published by the Ministry of Foreign Affairs, which described Antarctica as a *magno asunto* (great issue) for Argentina.[21] Under president Gabriel González Videla, Chile also carried out intense Antarctic activity, first under the influence of retired Navy captain Cordovez Madariaga in 1947, and then under General Ramón Cañas Montalva, who had a strong geopolitical vision of Antarctica and was more reticent about the alliance with Argentina, which he saw as a threat. In this context, despite González Videla's caution towards Perón, an alliance between Chile and Argentina in Antarctica was created, reinforced by the threat posed by the British Empire to both nations.[22]

18 Jara Fernández, "Enrique Cordovez Madariaga".
19 Haddelsey and Carroll, *Operation Tabarin*, 28.   20 Christie, *The Antarctic Problem*.
21 Comisión Nacional del Antártico, *Soberanía argentina*.
22 The view that it was the context of the war that led Argentina and Chile to defend their Antarctic interests, as Adrian Howkins maintains, is debatable. There was a long tradition of binational meetings and treaties before the British claim of 1908, and South American interest was renewed in 1938 before the war. It was in the context

In the summer of 1946–47, both countries carried out Antarctic expeditions with guests from the other country. While the Chilean expedition installed its first Antarctic base, the Soberanía (Sovereignty) Meteorological and Radiotelegraphic Station, Argentina built its second Argentine Antarctic base, the Melchior Naval Detachment. Argentine planes and ships scouted the British bases, with exchanges of protest notes. A similar situation occurred between Chilean and British forces, but mutual visits and clear expressions of friendship took place between Argentines and Chileans. Perón issued Decree 8944, which definitely fixed the western limit of the Argentine Antarctic claim, from 68° 34' to 74° west, and published the first bicontinental map of Argentina.

At the same time in Buenos Aires, the Argentine foreign minister sent a diplomatic note to the British ambassador rejecting the United Kingdom's Antarctic claims and stating that in those territories 'the only problem to be solved – with the best will between the parties – is that of the Chilean-Argentine Antarctic border'.[23] Both South American governments agreed to hold an international conference to resolve their claims on Antarctica, and in March 1947 their foreign ministers met to discuss the issue. Although they did not determine any common border, at a second meeting in July they signed a Joint Declaration on 'South American Antarctica', in which they mutually recognized that only Chile and Argentina had 'indisputable sovereignty rights' in this polar zone.[24] With this stance, they arrived in August at the Rio de Janeiro Conference to negotiate the signing of the Inter-American Treaty of Reciprocal Assistance, requesting the incorporation of South American Antarctica within it.

During the following summer of 1947–48, tensions increased to an unusual level, with numerous ships and planes from both nations undertaking surveys, logistics, and activities in Antarctica, in addition to the installation of shelters and the Argentine Naval Detachment *Decepción* and the Chilean station O'Higgins, which has worked without interruption up to the time of writing. On 28 January 1948, the Argentine Foreign Minister sent a note to the British embassy in which he considered the British claim illegitimate and proposed an international conference to determine the region's political legal status. Two days later, the Chilean Foreign Office sent a similar note to the British ambassador in Santiago.

The tensest moment took place in February 1948, when the Argentine Sea Fleet, with its two powerful war cruisers, six destroyers, and other transport

of post-war decolonization that Argentina and Chile escalated the defence of their interests. Howkins, "Icy Relations".
23 Genest, *Antártida Sudamericana*, 101.   24 Genest, *Antártida Sudamericana*, 50.

vessels, visited Deception Island. London quickly sent a cruiser and a frigate. Meanwhile, on 17 February the Chilean President, González Videla, became the first president to visit Antarctica and gave a speech in which, referring to that Antarctic region, he said that 'it constitutes the natural geological extension of our territory, located in the southernmost part and in the extreme south of America', and continued:

> Remnants of old European imperialisms threaten armed violence, snatching Chile and America from possession of these lands of ours ... But America today does not live disarmed and disunited for an aggression to be carried out by an extra-continental power.[25]

In turn, 'South American Antarctica' had its expression in the scientific and academic sphere, with conferences and publications that echoed the concept.[26] Both countries managed to establish, through Joint Declarations, a work plan, in defence of their own interests and, above all, to limit the actions of countries outside the region.[27]

In London, Foreign Secretary Ernest Bevin was questioned on 3 March in the House of Commons where he was required to report on Argentine and Chilean actions in Antarctica. A day later, the Chilean Foreign Minister, Germán Vergara Donoso, and the director of the Argentine Antarctic Commission, Dr Pascual La Rosa, met in Santiago to sign a declaration of joint defence of Argentine and Chilean rights over South American Antarctica. The *Antártida Sudamericana* extended from the eastern Argentine limit to the western Chilean limit, covering all of both claims, and it was expected, according to the third point of the agreement, that before the end of the year the internal borders between the two claims could be defined. A month later, during the Inter-American Conference in Bogotá, the Chilean and Argentine delegates expressed their common position regarding South American Antarctica. Both enjoyed the support of other Latin American nations such as Venezuela, whose Congress affirmed Argentine and Chilean sovereignty over the area, while qualifying British presence as 'remains of colonialism in America' which should be eliminated 'once and for all, forever'.[28]

In the summer of 1948–49, tension eased when the three governments signed a tripartite naval agreement in which they agreed not to send warships larger than a frigate or to make naval demonstrations south of the sixtieth parallel.

---

25 Aramayo Alzérreca, *Historia de la Antártida*, 225.
26 Barreda Laos, *La Antártida Sudamericana*; Mann, *Biología*.
27 Genest, *Antártida Sudamericana*, 54.
28 Arramayo Alzerraca, *Historia de la Antártida*, 225.

Among the reasons were the economic costs that this Antarctic race implied. However, the agreement, renewed annually, did not mean a waiver of sovereignty claims. In 1951 Argentina installed two more stations, and Perón created the *Instituto Antártico Argentino* (IAA – Argentine Antarctic Institute), under the direction of an Antarctic explorer, Colonel Hernán Pujato. Chile, in turn, installed another Antarctic station. It was a delicate balance. At the beginning of 1952, Argentine sailors who were setting up a naval detachment in Esperanza / Hope Bay fired their weapons in a deterrent way to prevent the landing of British forces who wanted to reinstall a station that had caught fire in 1948.[29] Shortly afterwards, in May 1952, President Perón gave a speech in which he stated: 'over these lands, in good faith, no one has rights except Chileans and Argentineans'.[30]

At the beginning of 1953 another serious incident took place when two British frigates landed thirty Royal Marines on Deception Island, capturing two Argentine non-commissioned officers occupying an Argentine hut, which they destroyed, as well as another Chilean shelter.[31] The international press even spoke of an 'open war'.[32] At the time the events were made public, Perón was in Chile visiting General Carlos Ibáñez del Campo, president of that country since 1952, whose anti-colonial ideology was closer to that of Perón (Figure 27.2). On entering Valparaíso the men were received by a crowd with flags of both countries. Together they protested and demanded an explanation and apology for the Deception Island incident. They planned to bring together Navy vessels from both countries to rebuild the facilities, and it was agreed that any aggression by British forces against Chilean or Argentine forces 'would be repelled by both in the most energetic possible way'.[33] While Ibáñez del Campo invoked the Río Treaty on reciprocal assistance, Perón appealed to the Organization of American States. A few days later the prisoners were freed and the shelters were rebuilt. Meanwhile, in Antarctica, the Chilean-Argentine fellowship took hold through rescues and joint patrols. South American activities in Antarctica continued to grow, in particular with Argentina's acquisition of the first icebreaker in Latin America in 1954, and its 1955 installation of the southernmost base at that time in the Weddell Sea. The actions of the United

---

29 Argentina AMREC (Argentina / Serie 79 – Dirección de Antártida y Malvinas / AH0005/18). Incidente Argentino-Británico en Bahía Esperanza. Comunicaciones entre el Ministerio de Marina y el comandante del Grupo de Tareas Antártico.
30 Argentina, Archivo General de la Nación, Audio D985B-02.
31 Argentina AMREC (Argentina / Serie 79 – Dirección de Antártida y Malvinas / 1953 / AH0005/3), Soberanía de Tierras Antárticas. Memorandun de Subdirección y Planificación (19 March 1953).
32 One example was the Italian newspaper *Il Globo*, "Accendi di guerra fredda".
33 Palazzi, *La Argentina*, 318.

Figure 27.2 The President of Chile, Carlos Ibáñez del Campo, is received by the President of Argentina, Juan Domingo Perón, at Buenos Aires Airport during his official visit on 6 July 1953, at the closest moment of the Antarctic alliance between both countries. (Photo: General Archive of the Nation, Argentina.)

Kingdom in Antarctica undoubtedly had the effect of bringing the two South American nations even closer. Thus, when on 4 May 1955 British Prime Minister Winston Churchill submitted a request to the International Court of Justice to initiate proceedings against Argentina and Chile for their 'violations in the British Antarctic territory', the notes were rejected by the two South American governments, who responded that they would jointly carry out the defence of their Antarctic territories.[34]

Parallel Paths (1956–1975)

Although the tension between both South American nations and the United Kingdom had increased for more than a decade, this started to change from late 1955 until the signing of the Antarctic Treaty in 1959, while the Antarctic bond forged between the two nations started to weaken. Among the factors

34 Fontana, *La pugna antártica*, 278.

that influenced this is the withdrawal from power of the two presidents who had maintained a strong defence of their Antarctic territorial claims: Perón in 1955, and Ibáñez del Campo in 1958, although Churchill was also displaced in 1955. The military dictatorship that followed the coup against Perón in 1955 placed less emphasis on Antarctica, and revealed less anti-imperialist sentiment – even less anti-British – and no marked Latin-Americanism, and in fact some incidents occurred in the Beagle Channel between the two countries. However, the Argentine Antarctic Institute continued to publish scientific works that spoke openly of a 'South American Antarctica' or even a 'South American Antarctic Sector'.[35]

The decline of Antarctic whaling reduced the immediate economic interest of the Antarctic seas. But international Antarctic cooperation through science increased with the International Geophysical Year (IGY) in 1957–58. Even in its preparatory meetings, a communion of visions can be observed between the two South American states.[36] The IGY also provided clear information on the impossibility or lack of profitability of an exploitation of Antarctic mineral resources in the short term. The danger of the Cold War approaching the South Pole, as well as the Indian proposal for discussing the 'Antarctic Question' at the General Assembly of the United Nations, drew together countries that until then had been strongly antagonistic, such as the United Kingdom on the one hand, and Chile and Argentina on the other.[37]

During the diplomatic meetings that shaped the AT, both countries' views about the need for an international agreement that would not result in any form of supranational authority prevailed, and guaranteed the political balance that made open access and international cooperation in scientific research in Antarctica possible. While their preferences were situated on a limited access of other countries to the AT, in addition to the original twelve and the recognition of their respective sovereignty, the acknowledgement of the impossibility of reaching such an outcome made them pursue a political balance that could limit the political impact of scientific activity while avoiding escalation in the region.[38] The Chilean proposal for such a standstill agreement was a key element in constituting the political arrangement over which the whole edifice of the AT would eventually be built. Both countries' experiences in the IGY demonstrated that the 'purely scientific' arrangements would not suffice to create a separation from political discord,

---

35 Slaucitajs, *El conocimiento geomagnético*; Frenguelli and Orlando, *Diatomeas y silicoflagelados*.
36 Cardone, *Continent for Peace*.   37 Howkins, "Defending Polar Empire".
38 Cardone and Fontana, "Latin-American Contributions".

and revealed the need for an explicit agreement captured in a formula that could neutralize the political effects of scientific activities. In terms of their initiatives, the Argentine proposal for a nuclear test ban and the Chilean initiative of including environmental protection within the responsibilities of the consultative parties were pivotal to the environmental constitution of the Antarctic regime.[39] Concern about possible nuclear contamination in Antarctica by both countries is not surprising, given their proximity to the continent, and also because the United Kingdom had carried out nuclear tests in Australia and the South Pacific Ocean. Considering the United Kingdom's difficulty in carrying out nuclear tests on its European territory, it could have happened on the Antarctic Peninsula.

A clear difference arose between two groups that further reinforced the closeness of both South American nations. On the one hand Australia, France, New Zealand, Norway, and the United Kingdom mutually recognized their territorial claims, ignoring those of the two South American countries; on the other hand, these southern states only recognized each other's claims, at least where the other's claim did not overlap with their own. The idea of an international agreement instead of any form of supranational administration was proposed and defended by the two South American states and ended up prevailing, as well as the principle of political status quo as a prerequisite for international collaboration in scientific research.

In both nations, there were minority sectors that did not approve of the signing of the AT, which they understood as a betrayal of Antarctic sovereignty, and the trip by Argentine President Arturo Frondizi to Deception Island in March 1961 was precisely to end this resistance and promote its ratification.[40] In parallel paths, both nations ratified the AT and continued to develop their science and their Antarctic presence with the installation of more bases, without strong cooperation. In 1963, the Government of Chile created the *Instituto Antártico Chileno* – INACH (Chilean Antarctic Institute). Meanwhile, the IAA took possession of Ellsworth Station, ceded by the United States in 1959. Almost simultaneously, in 1969 both nations inaugurated aircraft gateways in Antarctica: Chile with the Marsh Martin Airfield at Frei Station and Argentina with the Marambio Base. Years later, on 10 August 1973, a conflict arose when the Argentine provisional president Raúl Alberto Lastiri signed the 'Act of Affirmation of Sovereignty in

---

39 Cardone and Fontana, "Latin-American Contributions", 15; Scilingo, *El Tratado Antártico*.

40 One example of resistance to the AT is Candioti, *Nuestra Antártida*.

Argentine Antarctica' in Marambio.⁴¹ The Chilean government protested and described the act as an 'ostensible violation of Chilean Antarctic sovereignty'.⁴² The situation was overcome in May 1974 in a document on Antarctica signed by Perón and Augusto Pinochet, when the latter visited Argentina, in which they promised to safeguard their respective interests, particularly in relation to the exploration and eventual exploitation of natural resources.⁴³

Dictatorships, Fear, and New South American Actors (1975–1985)

The decade beginning in the mid-1970s was riddled with bloody military dictatorships across Latin America that also set back regional cooperation. Added to this context are the consequences of the global oil crisis, which boosted extractive views of Antarctica, especially in the early eighties, with the negotiation of the Convention on the Regulation of Antarctic Mineral Resource Activities (CRAMRA). According to the Argentine political scientist Miryam Colacrai, this was a period of 'distant competition and coexistence', in which the respective military governments had a 'vision of reductionist and confrontational geopolitics, and transferred that imprint to Antarctic issues'.⁴⁴ While Chile and Argentina increased their number of stations and Antarctic equipment, other South American countries joined the AT, installed stations, and became consultative parties of the Treaty, or began to analyse how to achieve this.

Brazil was the first to do so, given the power that it has in South America, as well as the fact of having south-facing coasts. As early as the mid-1950s, some manifestations of interest in Antarctica had emerged in Brazil, among which the so-called 'defrontaçao (frontage) theory', proposed by the geographer Terezinha de Castro, would end up being the most influential and would even echo in other countries in the region, such as Uruguay, Peru, and Ecuador, also fuelling their interest in claiming an Antarctic sector. It projected the south-facing maritime borders of the national territories toward the South Pole, which resulted in a division of the Chilean and Argentine Claims into six national sectors.⁴⁵ Despite the author's call for Latin American unity, the proposal clearly confronted not only British interests, but also those of Brazil's continental neighbours. This, added to a relative lack of

41 *La Razón*, "Reafirmó la soberanía argentina". 42 *La Opinión*, "El viaje de Lastiri".
43 Moneta, "La política", 93.   44 Colacrai, "Cuando la frontera dialoga".
45 Carvalho and Castro, "A Questão Antártica".

direct interest and an underdeveloped scientific system, meant that this position did not obtain official support, being relegated to influential yet limited sectors among Brazilian elites. In the 1970s, with the oil crisis and the resulting interest in the mineral resources of Antarctica, Brazil began to study the issue more carefully. However, the first private initiatives organized around the *Instituto Brasileiro de Estudos Antárticos* (Brazilian Institute of Antarctic Studies) were held back by the government for fear of negative repercussions on relations with Argentina and Chile. It was a critical moment because Argentina had entered a dispute with Brazil over the Itaipu dam, a project of greater immediate relevance for Brazil. This meant that Brazil's accession to the AT was delayed until 1975, and its first Antarctic campaign until 1982, when said conflict had already been resolved satisfactorily.[46] International factors, including pressure from states in the developing world led by Malaysia for the inclusion of the Antarctic question in the United Nations General Assembly and the operation of India outside the AT, favoured the rapid incorporation of Brazil as a consultative party in 1983, along with India.[47] Those same conditions would also promote and facilitate the entry of other Latin American countries.

Uruguay, with its coasts facing south, and prompted by the actions of its neighbouring countries, especially Argentina, was likely to be next. As early as 1956, a National Commission was formed, reporting to the Ministry of Foreign Affairs, to advise the government on Uruguay's possible rights in Antarctica, but no definite actions resulted from its reports. The origin of Uruguay's Antarctic interest bears some similarities to the Brazilian case, in the sense that it started in the early sixties as a concern of an academic, in this case Professor Julio César Musso, who generated interest and then state action.[48] In fact, it was Musso, author of the book *Antártida Uruguaya* (Uruguayan Antarctica) in 1968, who independently created the *Instituto Antártico Uruguayo* (Uruguayan Antarctic Institute) in the same year; in 1975, the institute was integrated into the state. In 1980 Uruguay ratified the AT; in 1984 it inaugurated the Artigas Antarctic Station. On 7 October 1985 it was accepted as a consultative member of the AT, declared in Uruguay as 'Uruguayan Antarctica Day'; and in 1987 it joined the Scientific Committee on Antarctic Research (SCAR).

In the case of Ecuador, Antarctic interest also stems from a particular individual, Lieutenant Colonel Marco Bustamante, who from 1956 was

46 Rodrigues Gomes Ferreira, *O Sistema do Tratado*, 235.
47 Cardone, *Antarctic Politics of Brazil*, section 3.3.   48 Fontes, *Los aportes*.

equally influenced by the 'frontage theory'. In 1967 this materialized in an official declaration made by the National Constituent Assembly which affirms: 'The Republic of Ecuador has the right to the part of Antarctica intercepted by meridians 84° 30' and 96° 30' west longitude of Greenwich, as it is located on the South American continent', citing the frontage theory.[49] Two decades later, Ecuador would join the AT. Peru joined the AT in 1981 and in 1983 created a National Commission for Antarctic Affairs. Cuba, although it joined the AT in 1984, did not have Antarctic scientific activity but sent doctors to the Soviet Bellingshausen Station for a few years. On the one hand, more South American countries were being included in the AT, by adhering to it and then, in most cases, becoming consultative parties, generally with the prior installation of their own station, all in South American Antarctica. On the other hand, the installation of stations from other non-South American countries in this sector took place. The Soviet Union installed the Bellingshausen Station in 1968, Poland the Arctowski Station in 1977, and China the Great Wall Station in 1985, all on the 25 de Mayo/King George Island. This also led Argentina and Chile to have a more positive view of the presence of other South American countries in that region. This was particularly the case when it came to stations from communist countries, with anti-communist military dictatorships in both countries.

In this framework, Argentina entered a particular period in terms of Antarctic policy, with a double policy: on the one hand, supporting membership of the AT, and on the other hand, with actions of a predominantly 'territorialist' connotation against Chile and the United Kingdom, with a similar attitude on the part of Chile.[50] In this framework of military dictatorships, tensions increased especially between Chile and Argentina in relation to their border differences. The climax of this tension took place in 1978 with a crisis in the Beagle Channel, which was minutes away from unleashing a full-bore war along the extensive border of the two countries. During this crisis, which lasted until 1984, the settlement of Argentine families started in the Esperanza Antarctic Base, the Sargento Cabral Fort. These became the first families to inhabit the Antarctic mainland territory, adding a total of eight births between 1978 and 1983.

War finally broke out between Argentina and the United Kingdom in 1982 over the Malvinas Islands. It was also a conflict with potential Antarctic implications, and it could be considered the first sub-Antarctic war, since it

---

49 Tobar Donoso and Luna Tobar, *Derecho territorial ecuatoriano*, 352.
50 Colacrai, "La política antártica argentina", 45.

began in San Pedro Island and ended in the South Sandwich Islands, when the Royal Marines took over the Corbeta Uruguay Scientific Station of Argentina, later demolishing it–an episode that happened only half a degree from the AT: at 59° 27' south. The help that Chile provided to the United Kingdom during the Malvinas War did not improve the situation, and together with the transfer of a British Antarctic station to Chile in 1984, it marked a period of exception for Chile in terms of the once common position against London. That same year, Chile created *Villa las Estrellas* (Village of the Stars) at the Montalva Base, the second settlement of families in Antarctica, where four births were registered.

Towards a Regional 'South American Antarctica' (1985 to today)

The return of democracy in Argentina in 1983, as well as in Chile in 1990, and in other South American countries with a presence in Antarctica in the mideighties, together with the signing of the Protocol on Environmental Protection to the Antarctic Treaty – known as the Madrid Protocol – in 1991, led to a significant change in regional South American cooperation. These factors meant a profound change in relation to the previous stage, where strong military and territorialist imprint led to talk of a 'Latin *Lebensraum*' in Antarctica.[51] Countries that during those years installed Antarctic stations or began their activities on the continent gained presence, though Argentina and Chile continued to have a leadership role and a stronger presence than the rest, and a renewed bilateral cooperation.[52] This was helped by the resolution of some differences on border issues. The rapprochement began on the Argentine side, with the presidency of Raúl Alfonsín in 1983, who signed the Treaty of Peace and Friendship between Argentina and Chile the following year, a definitive solution in the establishment of territorial borders from the Beagle Channel to the Drake Passage. When democracy was restored in Chile, with the presidency of Patricio Aylwin, the process also received a strong boost from the Chilean side, as expressed in the agreements signed with Argentine President Carlos Saúl Menem in 1991, which solved almost all remaining border disputes along the extensive common border. Both presidents signed a 'Joint Declaration on Antarctica' in August 1990 in Santiago, reaffirming previous binational Joint Declarations (1941, 1947, 1948, 1971, and 1974), and raising the possibility of

51 Child, "Latin Lebensraum", 10.   52 Colacrai, "La cuestión antártica", 321.

establishing a bilateral Antarctic scientific collaboration programme. In the following years, Antarctica would be top of the agenda in their bilateral presidential meetings.[53] At the regional level, the creation of the MERCOSUR (Southern Common Market) in 1991 was an important step, initially made up of Argentina, Brazil, Paraguay, and Uruguay.

In this period, the increase in Antarctic activity in other South American countries also continued. In 1988 Ecuador installed an Antarctic hut to support its scientific work; in 1990 it inaugurated its Pedro Vicente Maldonado summer Antarctic Station and also became a consultative party to the AT. In 1989 Peru founded the Machu Picchu Station and acquired the status of consultative party to the AT. In 1991 the president of Brazil, Fernando Collor de Mello, visited the national Antarctic station. Since 1996, Uruguay has been a member of the Commission for the Conservation of Antarctic Marine Living Resources (CCAMLR), and the following year the British station in Esperanza/Hope Bay was transferred to it by the United Kingdom. Colombia signed the AT in 1989 but has not yet become a consultative party, or established an Antarctic station, although in recent years it has expressed interest in owning one. Finally, Guatemala signed the AT in 1991.

The entry into the Antarctic scene of other South American countries in this new context allowed for the initiation of Antarctic cooperation at the regional level. Argentina played a central role in this new era of Antarctic cooperation, the key figure being Jorge Edgard Leal, a general of the Argentine Army, who led the first Argentine terrestrial expedition to the South Pole in 1965. Leal served as the first director of the *Dirección Nacional del Antártico* (DNA – National Directorate of the Antarctic), created in 1970, holding his position until 1973. His friendship with President Menem allowed him to return to that position between 1989 and 2000, and earned presidential support for several of his ideas and projects, with a strong Latin American vision.[54] Thus, in 1989, the Argentine Antarctic Policy was approved by Decree, which established among its objectives 'within the framework of the National Policy for Latin American Integration, to promote the cooperation with the countries of the region, including the undertaking of joint activities that strengthen common interests', in addition to 'the establishment

---

53 Colacrai, *Continuidades y cambios*, 268.
54 Leal, "La Antártida Sudamericana"; Leal, "Latinoamerica en la Antártida"; Leal, "Latinoamérica en la Antártida: Hacia un futuro posible". In 2001, the DNA also published *La Antártida Sudamericana: Aportes para su comprensión*, by Eugenio Genest, head of the Political Department of the DNA.

of joint facilities with the Latin American parties to the Antarctic Treaty'.[55] That same year Argentina promoted the creation of the *Reunión de Administradores de Programas Antárticos Latinoamericanos* (RAPAL – Meeting of Administrators of Latin American Antarctic Programs) as a forum for coordinating actions in relation to South American Antarctica, which also held its first meeting that year in Buenos Aires. RAPAL meets annually in different cities of Latin America and is composed of the South American states that are consultative members of the AT, with the exception of Colombia and Venezuela, which have participated occasionally as observers, having joined to the AT in 1999. RAPAL has enabled advancement in implementing joint programmes and actions with the other Latin American countries. In Leal's words, it is a forum for reflection, in particular for Antarctic programmes of countries with economic difficulties, a space for cooperation, of neighbouring countries with a common language and interests, and a mechanism for agreement, which harmonizes positions with a shared standpoint. It also became a space for discussing and sharing Antarctic history and scientific projects, and even South American art in Antarctica. Examples include the *Encuentro de Historiadores Antárticos Iberoamericanos* (Meeting of Ibero-American Antarctic Historians) which held its first meeting in 1992 at the Argentine Esperanza Base, the *Encuentro de Historiadores Antárticos Latinoamericanos* (Meeting of Latin American Antarctic Historians), the *Grupo Latinoamericano de Medicina y Biología Humana Antártica* (Latin American Group of Antarctic Medicine and Human Biology), and the *Congreso Latinoamericano de Ciencia Antártica* (Latin American Congress of Antarctic Science).

But the closest cooperation has continued to be between Argentina and Chile. A concrete expression of this is the creation of the *Patrulla Antártica Naval Combinada* (Combined Naval Antarctic Patrol) in 1998, carried out jointly by both countries every Antarctic summer to provide search and rescue and navigation support at sea, and to fight marine pollution. This was later joined by the *Patrulla de Auxilio y Rescate Antártico Combinada Argentino-Chilena* (Argentine-Chilean Combined Antarctic Rescue and Relief Patrol), which is carried out annually by the personnel from the O'Higgins and Esperanza Stations. At the diplomatic level, in 1999 in Ushuaia, the presidents of both countries signed the Antarctic Presidential Declaration, reaffirming their commitment to advocating the common interests of South American Antarctica, in addition to establishing their commitment to

---

55 *Política Antártica Argentina*. Política II.3. and Prioridades III.3.

exploratory and scientific activities aimed at protecting Antarctic ecosystems. In 2003, they signed a declaration on climate change and protection of the ozone layer in the Patagonian and Antarctic regions. The Antarctic issue was at the top of the agenda of the Joint Parliamentary Commission of both countries; it was significantly included in the Maipú Treaty signed in 2009 between the Chilean President, Michelle Bachelet, and the Argentine President, Cristina Fernández de Kirchner. The Presidential Declaration signed in 2012 by the presidents of both nations created an ad hoc committee for coordination of Antarctic policies with the purpose of considering and promoting joint positions at the different forums and regimes pertaining to Antarctica. The Committee consolidated the Antarctic interstate relationship and made it possible to strengthen the bilateral institutional framework, by directly associating the specialized directorates and Antarctic Institutes within both of their foreign ministries, as well as carrying out a dozen joint inspections of foreign stations in Antarctica during three different seasons. Likewise, in 2011, the Binational Parliamentary Commission proposed the establishment of a joint scientific base in Antarctica, which still remains a project under consideration.

At the beginning of the twenty-first century, Latin American Antarctic cooperation had very strong support, with the rise of progressive governments of a strong Latin Americanist ideology. This is the moment when the Hispanic concept of *Patria Grande* (Great Homeland) from the independence era came back with force, a dream of regional unity now extended throughout Latin America. This vision was accompanied by strong initiatives for the development of regional cooperation and integration, led mainly by Venezuela, Brazil, and Argentina, such as the creation in 2008 of the UNASUR (Union of South American Nations), which even considered the possibility of using the Argentine ship ARA *Almirante Irízar* as a joint Antarctic icebreaker. A widely used metaphor in relation to the importance of Argentine-Chilean cooperation for this integration, and in particular to Latin American Antarctic cooperation, is that the regional integration had to start from the south to the north, just like a zipper closes from the bottom up. A clear Antarctic example of integration was the support given to Argentina by the rest of the countries regarding the nomination of Buenos Aires as the location for the headquarters of the Antarctic Treaty Secretariat adopted by the Antarctic Treaty Consultative Meeting (ATCM) in 2003, which was ultimately successful, and began operation in September 2004.

As for the rest of the South American countries present in Antarctica, they also showed an increase in their activity and interest. This was clearly manifested by a series of visits by South American presidents to their Antarctic bases in the early 2010s. The scientific production of Brazil's Antarctic programme began to grow considerably with the initiative of the Ministry of Environment in 2002 and intensified from 2004, with the announcement of the International Polar Year (2007/8), with two new institutes with Antarctic interests being created in 2008. That same year, Brazilian President Luiz Inácio Lula Da Silva visited their Ferraz Station, and the following year the Brazilian Navy acquired the polar ship *Almirante Maximiano*. Also in 2009 activities began on the polar plateau with an expedition to Patriot Hills, and in 2012, in cooperation with the Chilean Antarctic Institute, the *Criósfera 1* (Cryosphere 1) was installed near there – a fully automatic scientific module for data collection on pollutants generated in South America and in Antarctica. The call for financing from the *Programa Antartico Brasileiro* (Brazilian Antarctic Program) was opened in 2009 to joint proposals with other countries, and they began to look for more integrated projects with the rest of Latin America, reaching the signing of an Antarctic cooperation framework agreement with Chile in 2013. A major blow for Brazilian Antarctic science was the fire at Ferraz Station in 2012, but after a few years of reconstruction it was reinaugurated in January 2020, in the presence of the Brasilian Vice President.[56] In 2002, Peru created the *Instituto Antártico Peruano* (Peruvian Antarctic Institute), where research focuses mainly on the study of krill.[57] In 2013, on the twenty-fifth anniversary of the first Peruvian Antarctic expedition, President Ollanta Humala visited the Machu Picchu Antarctic base and announced an increase in the Antarctic budget and the construction of a permanent base further south, which has not yet taken place. In the 2017–18 campaign, Peru expanded its Antarctic activities through the polar oceanographic vessel BAP *Carrasco*, including projects undertaken in cooperation with Argentina. The Ecuadorian government in 2004 created the *Instituto Antártico Ecuatoriano* (Ecuadorian Antarctic Institute) and, in line with the 1967 declaration, the 2008 Ecuadorian Constitution says, 'The Ecuadorian State will exercise rights over the corresponding segments of the geostationary synchronous orbit, maritime spaces and Antarctica'. In 2010, President Rafael Correa visited the Ecuadorian Antarctic station together with the president of Chile, Sebastián Piñera.

56 Cardone, "La apuesta brasileña".
57 Sanchez and Tielemans, "Reinvigorating Peru's Role".

Two years later, he was followed by Uruguayan President José Mujica, who visited the Artigas Base together with the Chilean president. Although these visits were partly due to the fact that they access their bases through the Chilean airfield located on the same island, they are also a manifestation of the prevailing Latin Americanism, as expressed by Mujica in his visit: 'The future must find the entire Latin America united so as to overcome difficulties.' In June 2017, at the ATCM, Uruguayan Albert Lluberas was elected to the position of Executive Secretary of the Antarctic Treaty Secretariat. His mandate was renewed for another four-year term at the 43rd ATCM, organized by France in 2021.

In the mid-2010s, neoliberal centre-right governments in several Latin American countries caused a weakening of regional institutions such as MERCOSUR and UNASUR, and in some cases there was also a decrease in investment in science and technology. However, the Antarctic cooperation between Chile and Argentina remained in place. One of their most prominent joint projects consists of a proposal for the establishment of a Marine Protected Area in the west of the Antarctic Peninsula and South Scotia Arc, as the result of extensive joint work, in particular from the Antarctic institutes and diplomats from both countries. The proposal was presented for the first time in 2018 before CCAMLR. Although it has received very significant support, scientific and diplomatic negotiations are still under way to achieve the required consensus from the twenty-six Commission Member States.

Conclusions

Throughout the twentieth century, the idea of the South American Antarctic quadrant – especially the Antarctic Peninsula – as an extension of Latin America took shape mainly through the two South American countries with the greatest presence and Antarctic history, Argentina and Chile, and later with the inclusion of other states in the region. 'South American Antarctica' emerged conceptually in the mid-twentieth century as an almost exclusively Argentine-Chilean territory, and with a strong anti-colonialist imprint against an extra-continental Antarctic claim, that of the British Empire. It was a rebirth of the concept of 'American Antarctica', born at the beginning of the twentieth century from the dialogue between these two nations, which tried to give meaning to the incorporation of these new unknown and uninhabited lands. Over the past three decades, this idea has reached a more fully Latin American dimension, beyond the territorial claims of Chile and Argentina, but with their leadership and crucial binational cooperation, once the fears and mistakes of the military dictatorships in the region were overcome, and once the extractivist Antarctic fever was deterred by the Madrid Protocol. This Protocol incorporated environmental protection as a new objective to be pursued through scientific cooperation and diplomatic dialogue. With these priorities and under Argentine initiative, an even greater Latin American integration in Antarctica was achieved through the creation of institutions such as RAPAL, also demonstrating the real existence of common interests and visions. This process was boosted at the beginning of the twenty-first century by Latin Americanist governments that imbued these new objectives with an anti-imperialist regional sense. However, there is still a long way to go to achieve a broader, more comprehensive cooperation among the RAPAL countries, creating a full scientific network in that Antarctic region and thus transforming it without doubt into an extension of Latin America.

Bibliography

Archival and Unpublished Sources

AMREC (Argentina / Serie 79 – Dirección de Antártida y Malvinas / 1953 / AH0005/3), Soberanía de Tierras Antárticas. Memorandun de Subdirección y Planificación (19 March 1953).
AMREC (Argentina / Serie 79 – Dirección de Antártida y Malvinas / AH0005/18). Incidente Argentino-Británico en Bahía Esperanza. Comunicaciones entre el Ministerio de Marina y el comandante del Grupo de Tareas Antártico.
AMREC, Sección Topográfica C 20 – A (Argentina / Serie 79 – Dirección de Antártida y Malvinas / AH0003/14), Soberanía en tierras antárticas: pretensiones chilenas, Telegrama cifrado No 1114 de Agilar Lacasa al Ministro de Relaciones Exteriores (7 November 1940).
Archivo General de la Nación, Argentina, Audio D985B-02.

Published Sources

Aramayo Alzérreca, Carlos, *Historia de la Antártida* (Buenos Aires: Editorial Hemisferio, 1949).
Barreda Laos, Felipe, La *Antártida Sudamericana ante el derecho internacional* (Buenos Aires: Linari, 1948).
Candioti, Alberto, *Nuestra Antártida no es tierra conquistada ni anexada: El Tratado Antártico no debe ratificarse* (Buenos Aires: 1960).
Capdevila, Ricardo, and Comerci, Santiago, *Cien años de ciencia argentina en la Antártida: Orcadas del Sur* (Buenos Aires: Dirección Nacional del Antártico–Instituto Antártico Argentino, 2004).

Capdevila, Ricardo, and Comerci, Santiago, *Los tiempos de la Antártida: Historia antártica argentina* (Ushuaia: Editora Cultural de Tierra del Fuego, 2013).
Cardone, Ignacio Javier, *The Antarctic Politics of Brazil: Where the Tropic Meets the Pole* (Cham: Palgrave Macmillan, 2021).
Cardone, Ignacio Javier, "La apuesta brasileña en la Antártida: Trayectoria reciente y perspectivas futuras a la luz de la inauguración de la nueva Estación Antártica Comandante Ferraz", *CUPEA Cuadernos de Política Exterior Argentina* 133 (2021): 29–46, https://doi.org/10.35305/cc.vii33.108.
Cardone, Ignacio Javier, and Fontana, Pablo Gabriel, "Latin-American Contributions to the Creation of the Antarctic Regime", *Polar Journal* 9 (2019), 300–323, https://doi/10.1080/2154896X.2019.1685174.
Cardone, Ignacio Javier, *A Continent for Peace and Science: Antarctic Science and International Politics from the 6th International Geographical Congress to the Antarctic Treaty 1895–1959* (São Paulo, London: University of São Paulo/King's College London, 2019).
Cardone, Ignacio Javier, "Shaping an Antarctic Identity in Argentina and Chile", *Defence Strategic Communications* 8 (2020): 53–88, https://doi.org/10.30966/2018.
Carvalho, Delgado de and Castro, Therezinha de, "A Questão Antártica", *Boletim Geográfico* XIV (1956): 502–506.
Child, Jack, "Latin Lebensraum: The Geopolitics of Ibero-American Antarctica", *Applied Geography* 10 (1990): 287–305.
Christie, Eric William Hunter, *The Antarctic Problem: An Historical and Political Study* (London: Allen & Unwin, 1951).
Colacrai, Miryam, *Continuidades y cambios en la política antártica argentina 1959–2001: Conjugación de factores internos y externos* (Saarbrüken: Editorial Academia Espanola, 2012).
Colacrai, Miryam, "Cuando la frontera dialoga: Singularidades de la relación argentino-chilena en las últimas décadas", *Estudios fronterizos* 17 (2016): 85–99, https://doi.org/10.21670/ref.2016.34.a05.
Colacrai, Miryam, "La cuestión antártica en la política exterior Argentina: Desarrollos recientes y proyección de tendencias", in Alfredo Bruno Bologna et al., eds., *La política exterior argentina 1998–2001: El cambio de gobierno ¿Impacto o irrelevancia?* (Rosario: CERIR, 2001), pp. 307–330.
Colacrai, Miryam, "La política antártica argentina desde 1959", in Ángel Molinari, ed., *La Argentina en la Antártida: 100 años de presencia permanente e ininterrumpida* (Buenos Aires: CARI, 2005), pp. 43–53.
Comisión Nacional del Antártico, *Soberanía argentina en la Antártida* (Buenos Aires: Ministerio de Relaciones Exteriores y Culto, 1947).
Cordovez Madariaga, Enrique, *La Antártida Sudamericana* (Santiago: Nascimiento, 1945).
Falkland Islands Gazette, No. 9, vol. XVIII (1 September 1908).
Fitte, Ernesto J., *El descubrimiento de la Antártida: crónica de los hombres y barcos que exploraron las aguas de las Shetland del Sur* (Buenos Aires: Emecé Editores, 1962).
Fontana, Pablo, "Between the Ice of the Orkney Islands: Filming the Beginnings of the Antarctic Overwintering Tradition", *Polar Journal* 9 (December 2019): 340–357, https://doi.org/10.1080/2154896X.2019.1686811.
Fontana, Pablo, *La pugna antártica: El conflicto por el sexto continente 1939–1959* (Buenos Aires: Guazuvirá, 2014).

Fontes, Waldemar, *Los aportes del Profesor Julio C. Musso al trabajo pionero del Instituto Brasileño de Estudios Antárticos (IBEA)* (2012), https://doi/10.13140/RG.2.1.1732.5603.

Frenguelli, Joaquín, and Orlando, Héctor, *Diatomeas y silicoflagelados del Sector Antártico Sudamericano* (Buenos Aires: Instituto Antártico Argentino, 1958).

Genest, Eugenio, *Antártida Sudamericana: Aportes para su comprensión* (Buenos Aires: Dirección Nacional del Antártico–Instituto Antártico Argentino, 2001).

Haddelsey, Stephen, and Carroll, Alan, *Operation Tabarin: Britain's Secret Wartime Expedition to Antarctica* (Gloucestershire: History Press, 2014).

Howkins, Adrian, "Defending Polar Empire: Opposition to India's Proposal to Raise the 'Antarctic Question' at the United Nations in 1956", *Polar Record* 44 (2008): 35–44, https://doi/10.1017/S0032247407006766.

Howkins, Adrian, *Frozen Empires: An Enviromental History of the Antarctic Peninsula* (New York: Oxford University Press, 2017).

Howkins, Adrian, "Icy Relations: The Emergence of South American Antarctica during the Second World War", *Polar Record* 42 (2006): 153–165, https://doi/10.1017/S0032247406005274.

Il Globo, "Accendi di guerra fredda per il controllo del Polo Sud" (22 February 1953).

Jara Fernández, Mauricio, "Enrique Cordovez Madariaga y su visión de la Antártica Sudamericana a mediados de la década de 1940", *Revista de Historia* 11–12 (2002–2003): 23–26.

La Opinión, "El viaje de Lastiri provoca protestas en Santiago: Discuten nuestra soberanía en la Antártida" (16 August 1973).

La Razón, "Reafirmó la soberanía argentina en la Antártida y destacó la misión de las Fuerzas Armadas el Presidente de la República" (10 August 1973).

Leal, Jorge Edgard, "La Antártida Sudamericana y la Latinoamericana", *Revista Militar* 711 (1983): 14–17.

Leal, Jorge Edgard, "Latinoamérica en la Antártida", *Revista del Centro de Investigación y Acción Social* 501 (2001): 117–126.

Leal, Jorge Edgard, "Latinoamérica en la Antártida: Hacia un futuro posible", *Revista Militar* 718 (1987): 29–35.

Mancilla González, Pablo, "Algunos antecedentes sobre la política antártica chilena, 1892–1917", *Estudios Hemisféricos y Polares* 3 (2012): 137–150.

Mann, Guillermo F., *Biología de la Antártica Suramericana* (Santiago de Chile: Imprenta Universitaria, 1948).

Moneta, Carlos Juan, "La política exterior del peronismo, 1973–1976", in Rubén Perina and Roberto Russel, eds., *Argentina en el mundo 1973–1987* (Buenos Aires: Grupo Editor Latinoamericano, 1988), pp. 220–276.

Palazzi, Ruben Oscar, *La Argentina del Extremo Sur 1810–2004* (Buenos Aires: Editorial Dunken, 2005).

Pinochet de la Barra, Óscar, *Medio siglo de recuerdos antárticos: Memorias* (Santiago de Chile: Editorial Universitaria, 1994).

Quevedo Paiva, Adolfo E., *Historia de la Antártida* (Buenos Aires: Argentinidad, 2012).

Riso Patrón, Luis, "La Antártida Americana", *Anales de la Universidad de Chile* 122 (1908): 243–265.

Ritscher, Alfred, *Deutsche Antarktische Expedition 1938/39* (Leipzig: Koehler & Amelang, 1942).

Rodrigues Gomes Ferreira, Felipe, *O Sistema do Tratado da Antártica: evolução do regime e seu impacto na política externa brasileira* (Brasilia: Fundação Alexandre de Gusmão, 2009).

Sanchez, Wilder Alejandro, and Tielemans, Otto Raul, "Reinvigorating Peru's Role in Antarctic Geopolitics", *Polar Journal* 5 (2015): 101–112, http://doi.org/10.1080/215489 6X.2015.1030164.

Scilingo, Adolfo, *El Tratado Antártico: Defensa de la soberanía y la proscripción nuclear* (Buenos Aires: Hachette, 1963).

Slaucitajs, Leonidas, *El conocimiento geomagnético de la Antártida Sudamericana* (Buenos Aires: Instituto Antártico Argentino, 1957).

Sobral, José María, *Dos años entre los hielos 1901–1903* (Buenos Aires: Tragant, 1904).

Tobar Donoso, Julio, and Luna Tobar, Alfredo, *Derecho territorial ecuatoriano* (Quito: Imprenta del Ministerio de RR.EE., 1982).

Vaca, José María, *Antártida, mi hogar* (Buenos Aires: Troquel, 1957).

28

Moving Muskoxen as an Arctic Resource in the Twentieth Century

DOLLY JØRGENSEN

Introduction

The first written description of the muskox was published in 1744 by Pierre François Xavier de Charlevoix, a French Jesuit and historian, within a description of 'New France' (the French colony of North America) in his multi-volume *Journal d'un voyage*. He describes an animal encountered in the area of Hudson Bay with long, beautiful hair and a musky smell in rutting season – and he gave it the name *boeuf musqué*.[1] Musk was originally a label for the odour from the gland of a male musk deer, a native of Asia, which was used in perfumes, but animals with similar type odours were given musk names, like the muskrat and musk shrew. Charlevoix's original descriptor for the animal stuck: it became muskox in English, *moskusokse* in Norwegian, *myskoxe* in Swedish, *Moschusochse* in German, and stayed *boeuf musqué* in French. The first scientific name of the animal was *Bos moschatus* – an exact translation of *boeuf musqué* – given by George Zimmerman in 1780.[2] In 1816, Henri Marie Ducrotay de Blainville placed the muskox taxonomically into its own genus, *Ovibos*, which represents it as an intermediate between sheep (*Ovis*) and oxen (*Bos*), but retained the musk part as *moschatus*, so that the species is today known scientifically as *Ovibos moschatus*.[3]

When the muskox was encountered and described by Western science, the species was found only in Greenland and Arctic Canada, although fossil evidence shows that during the Pleistocene period (which ended about 11,000 years ago) their range was circumpolar. By 1900, the total number of muskox was limited: extinct in Alaska, a few hundred in mainland Canada, something around 10,000 in Greenland, and an estimated 12,000 in the Arctic

---

1 Charlevoix, *Journal d'un voyage*, 132.
2 Zimmermann, *Geographische Geschichte des Menschen*, 86–88.
3 Blainville, "Sur plusieurs espèces d'animaux".

28 Moving Muskoxen

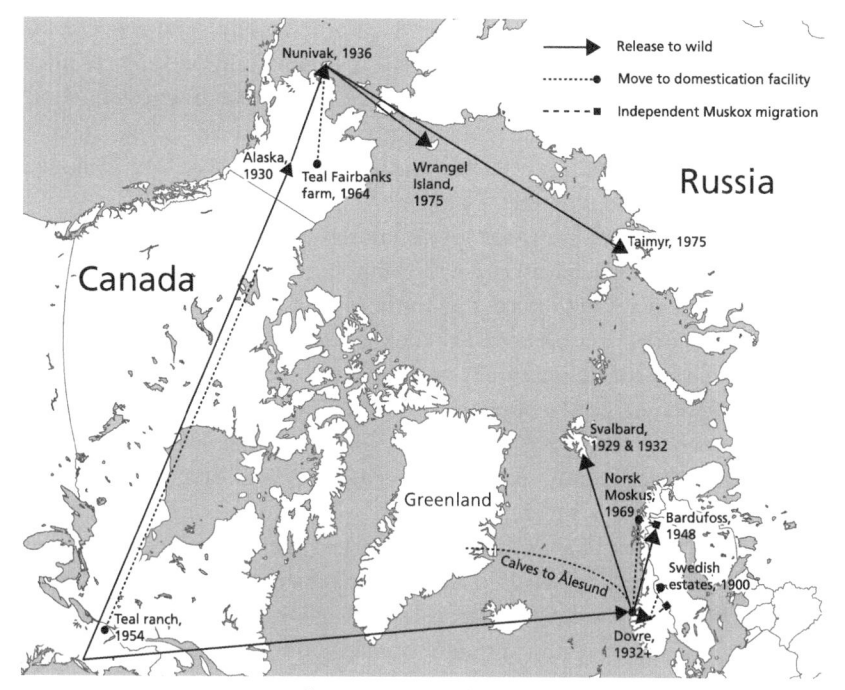

Figure 28.1 Muskox movements discussed in this chapter.

Canadian islands.[4] But if you look at a map of the muskoxen range today, you will find it spread out in small dots across the northern Arctic, including Alaska, far northern Russia, and Scandinavia. This expansion of the muskox in the northern hemisphere did not happen by accident – it was the result of deliberate human choices to move and manage the animal.

In this chapter, I will discuss how muskoxen went from having a small geographical distribution in the 1800s to being spread across the northern reaches of the northern hemisphere by humans in the late nineteenth and the twentieth century.[5] While these movements were never in large numbers, they expanded the muskox's range out across geographies where it had previously become extinct. I will focus on several major muskox populations that have been moved by humans (Figure 28.1), although there are some other movements, such as the transplantation of muskoxen from one part of

---

4 See the estimates in Hone, *Present Status of Muskox*, 7–20; Glover, "Muskox (*Ovibos moschatus*)"; Cuyler et al., "Muskox Status".
5 For an overview of all the known translocated muskox populations, see Cuyler et al., "Muskox Status".

Greenland to another, that also deserve future scrutiny. The movements show us the connected nature of the Arctic both politically and environmentally. Expertise and enthusiasm for muskoxen was shared across national borders. These intentional movements took place with a colonizing, improving, and settling mindset,[6] but as this chapter will show, those lofty ideals did not often translate into success.

In these circumpolar translocations of muskoxen, there are two goals that operate in tension: wilding and domesticating. Sometimes moving muskoxen was envisaged as a way to make the northern landscape more 'wild', returning it to some desired ecosystem. At other times, the move was seen as a way to make the north agriculturally productive through 'domesticating' its animals. These goals often operated in the same geographies, with contrary expectations and conflicting experiences. In my analysis of these muskox movements, I will draw on animal geography scholarship which has attempted 'to discern the many ways in which animals are "placed" by human societies in their local material spaces (settlements, field, farms, factories, and so on), as well as in a host of imaginary, literary, psychological and even virtual spaces'.[7] I will contrast this concept of *emplacement* with animal *movement* and its disruption of human–animal geographies. How do the contradictory goals of wilding and domesticating reflect and shape the emplacement of muskoxen across the Arctic?

As I will show in this chapter, all attempts to move muskoxen to new places around the globe took place within an ideological framework of 'improving' the Arctic. Muskoxen were understood by the historical actors as an untapped resource that could be cultivated, whether as wild animals roaming the landscape freely or as domesticated ones kept in pens. Modern attempts to relocate these animals – to emplace them in new landscapes – were, regardless of the stated wilding or domesticating aim, part of an impulse to 'tame' the Arctic landscape by modifying it to meet a particular colonizing notion of productivity.

The Idea of Muskoxen as a Potential Arctic Resource

Muskoxen encountered in the northern reaches of Greenland turned into a resource for both explorers and commercial hunters. Polar explorations

6 Roberts and Jørgensen, "Animals as Instruments".
7 Philo and Wilbert, "Animal Spaces, Beastly Places", 5.

required tremendous amounts of power in the form of dogs to pull sleds. For the dogs to pull the sleds, they needed calories. In explorer Robert E. Peary's book about his expeditions in Greenland in 1886 and the 1890s, there are detailed descriptions of muskoxen hunts.[8] Although the men consumed some of the muskox meat, it was primarily for the dogs. According to a hunter's account quoted in Elisabeth Hone's *The Present Status of the Muskox in Arctic North America and Greenland* (1934), sled dogs needed nearly a kilogram of muskox meat every day, which, for a team of eight to twelve dogs, meant consuming about ten kilograms a day. In his extensive monograph *Muskoxen and Their Hunters*, Peter Lent estimated that Peary's 1898–1900 expedition took at least 180 muskoxen on Ellesmere Island.[9] Hunts for muskoxen were thus as motivated by the needs of the dogs as they were by the needs of the humans: 'With the utmost eagerness we scanned every new prospect for the coveted animals; for we knew that musk-oxen meant fresh meat for ourselves, and an abundant supply of food for our dogs.'[10] Peary even included a photograph of a 'Royal banquet of my dogs', showing the pack hungrily devouring a muskox carcass.[11] The multi-species entanglements of the Arctic explorations should not be forgotten.

Particularly in the 1920s and 1930s, when the rising value of arctic fox pelts encouraged fox farming in East Greenland, the killing of muskox for meat escalated. In addition to muskox feeding the men and dogs, they were also consumed by the foxes. In one twelve-month span, an estimated 130 muskox were consumed to support an operation raising 60 foxes. Lent estimated that 12,000 muskox were killed in East Greenland between 1924 and 1939.

In 1922, the Arctic explorer and ethnographer Vilhjalmur Stefansson published his book *The Northward Course of Empire* in which he argued that the North had been greatly misunderstood and could become a seat of civilization. After all, he argued, civilization had been moving further and further north into the colder regions over human history. The north, rather than being a barren wasteland devoid of vegetation, was a green space. The trick, Stefansson argued, was to turn the vegetation to productive use:

> The realization kept gradually growing on me that one of the chief problems of the world, and particularly one of the chief problems of Canada and Siberia, is to begin to make use of all the vast quantities of grass that go to waste in the North every year. The obvious thing is to find some domestic

---

8 Peary, *Northward Over "Great Ice"*; see especially chapter 12 which begins with the picture of a muskox skull and includes numerous photographs of dead muskoxen.
9 Lent, *Muskoxen and Their Hunters*, 105.   10 Peary, *Northward Over "Great Ice"*, 332–333.
11 Peary, *Northward Over "Great Ice"*, 341.

animal that will eat the grass. Then when the animal is big and fat it should be butchered and shipped where the food is needed.[12]

Stefansson believed cattle and sheep were not the answer to this problem because of difficulties in feeding and sheltering them during the winter. Traditional crop plants could not withstand the frosts either. Instead, he decided that the solution to this waste was the widespread domestication of reindeer and muskox in the north. With his encouragement, the Canadian Department of the Interior set up a royal commission in 1919 to study the possibilities, and they issued their final report in 1922.[13] The report comes out more in favour of reindeer than muskox because of prior work domesticating reindeer, but it also encouraged further investigation of industrial possibilities for muskox domestication.

Stefansson may have first become acquainted with muskoxen (which he called 'ovibos', based on the Latin name, because he disliked the 'musk' and 'ox' connotations of the regular name) during his time in the Mackenzie Delta of Canada in 1906–07. He had eaten plenty of muskox on his various Arctic expeditions and offered the opinion that 'not one person in ten could even when on his guard tell an ovibos steak from a beefsteak'.[14] He also noted that muskox wool (*qiviut*) was high-quality, although it was difficult to collect and spin because it was mixed with longer hairs. All in all, the muskox was the perfect animal to make the north productive:

> When we sum up the qualities of ovibos, we see that here is an animal unbelievably suited to the requirements of domestication – unbelievably because we are so habituated to thinking of cow and the sheep as the ideal domestic animals that the possibility of a better one strikes us as an absurdity. We have milk richer than that of cows and similar in flavor, and more abundant than that of certain milk animals that are now used, such as sheep and reindeer; wool probably equal in quality and perhaps greater in quantity than that of domestic sheep; two or three times as much meat to the animal as with sheep, and the flavor and other qualities those of beef . . . it appears that they combine practically every virtue of the cow and the sheep and excel them at several points.[15]

Although Stefansson may sound like he is overselling his product, the vision of turning the 'unused' land of the north into a fruitful Arctic was powerful. It encouraged both domestication and reintroduction projects of muskoxen in Sweden, Norway, Alaska, Canada, and Russia over the course of the

---

12 Stefansson, *Northward Course of Empire*, 48.   13 Canada, Royal Commission, *Report*.
14 Stefansson, *Friendly Arctic*, 585.   15 Stefansson, *Friendly Arctic*, 587.

twentieth century. In these projects, muskoxen would be emplaced in new lands and would transform them. The land of snow and ice would be a land of meat and wool.

The First Domestication Experiments

The first attempt to make muskoxen into a domestic species took place in Sweden. In 1899, the Swedish geologist Alfred Gabriel Nathorst led an expedition to Greenland. Nathorst had observed wild muskox herds during the expedition and came to the conclusion that the Swedes should try to import and domesticate the animals. He believed that the muskox would acclimatize perfectly to Sweden and be even more productive than reindeer, since it was more tolerant of mosquitos, less prone to wolf predation, and did not require long-distance migrations over the year to new feeding grounds.[16] Nathorst envisaged that it would be easy to place muskoxen into the Swedish countryside.

This idea of muskox acclimatization was in line with earlier nineteenth-century attempts to transfer animals from one part of the globe to others. Animal acclimatization was based on the idea that these moved species would integrate themselves into similar ecosystems – so camels were taken to the deserts in Australia (where they established wild populations that survive to this day) and the United States (where they did not), rabbits were released in Australia (creating an ecological disaster for indigenous fauna), and house sparrows adapted to North America.[17] By 1900, more than fifty acclimatization societies had been founded, generally operating within a colonizing mindset that saw settled lands as malleable to their own visions of productivity.[18] As Michael Osborne has observed, despite most acclimatization projects failing, the acclimatized animal or plant 'functioned as a symbol of Europe's power over nature and over far-off lands' that 'seemed to confirm that colonization was possible'.[19]

The year after Nathorst's encounter with muskoxen, the Swedish zoologist Gustaf Kolthoff led a Swedish expedition to northeast Greenland sponsored by industrialist Gustaf Emil Broms. Kolthoff was to bring back specimens for the museums (including the Biological Museum in Stockholm) and capture living muskox for domestication, as suggested by Nathorst. After several failed attempts to catch a living individual, the

---

16 Nathorst, *Två Somrar*, 149–150.   17 Ritvo, "Going Forth and Multiplying".
18 Osborne, "Acclimatizing the World".   19 Osborne, "Acclimatizing the World", 151.

expedition was finally successful at capturing a male calf; after another week, they successfully captured a female calf. Unfortunately, bad weather cut the expedition short so only those two animals were captured.[20] These two were taken to Broms's estate near Boden in northern Sweden.[21]

Nathorst was disappointed that only two animals had been brought back, so when he heard that another Norwegian expedition had brought four live calves to Norway, he urged industrialist Karl Fredrik Liljevalch Jr to buy them. Liljevalch bought the two males and two females and moved them to his estate, Medstugan in Jämtland. Nathorst commented in 1900, 'They [the muskox] are kept not here as a curiosity, but are being domesticated, for the benefit of our descendants. One may seriously hope that the experiment will succeed.'[22]

But it did not succeed. One of Liljevalch's males died quickly from a pelvic injury, and one of Broms's calves soon died as well. The remaining Broms calf was taken to Jämtland to join the Liljevalch herd. They lived in a half-hectare pen and were fed on Timothy grass, rutabaga, and carrots. Although Nathorst had predicted that muskox calves would be easily domesticated if around humans, instead they were unruly. According to Henrik Persson, who worked for Liljevalch when the muskox were brought to Medstugan, the animals were uncooperative, and one of the males was consistently charging.[23] By 1904 they had all died.[24]

A quarter of a century later, in 1929, the Icelander Vigfús Sigurðsson applied to the Icelandic parliament for financing to import muskoxen for domestication.[25] The government sponsored the expedition with 20,000 Islandic kroner, and it was successful at taking seven live calves (though they had to kill thirty-four adults to capture them). After being shown off in Reykjavik to the city dwellers, the calves were taken to a farm in Gunnarsholt, about 100 km further east. All except one had died from disease

---

20 Kolthoff, *Til Spetsbergen*. I should note that these were not actually the first live muskoxen calves ever captured in Greenland: in 1899, a pair of calves was captured and sold for exhibition in an English zoo. See Schiött, "Musk Oxen in Captivity".
21 Nathorst, *Två Somrar*, 150.   22 Nathorst, *Två Somrar*, 152.
23 *Svenska Dagbladet*, "Bröderna Printzskölds gamle förare skildrar dödsfärden till Storlien" (18 February 1951).
24 Lønø, *Transplantation of Muskox*, 6.
25 Information about this Icelandic project is taken primarily from Guðmundsson, "Þegar Íslendingar", and a document prepared by NSIU summarizing the Icelandic muskox importations in NP box 166.

within a few weeks. In autumn 1930, another seven calves were purchased in Ålesund from Norwegians who had taken them in East Greenland.[26] Five of those joined the remaining animal in Gunnarsholt, and the other two went to a farm north of the capital in Skorradal. The Icelanders tried to handle the muskoxen like their sheep who were let out for high summer pasture and then brought in for the winter, but the animals all failed to thrive and were dead by 1932.[27]

These early domestication experiments had failed miserably. The idea that one could move muskox calves to another northern location where they would simply acclimatize and thrive in their new environment was enticing. But the reality that the importers faced was that muskoxen were never kept alive in captivity more than a few years, and they never reproduced.

Wild Meat in the Wild Landscape of an Arctic Archipelago

The same year as the calves had been taken to Iceland as domesticates, seventeen young muskoxen were relocated from eastern Greenland to the Svalbard archipelago. This attempt would be quite different than the earlier movements of muskoxen. Svalbard, halfway between continental Norway and the North Pole, had been an early modern whaling station, but the population increased when industrial coal mining started. Longyear City (later Longyearbyen) was established in 1906 on the island of Spitsbergen as a coal company town and became the major settlement of the archipelago. Because of its remote northerly location, there was a constant concern about supplies for the miners. Globally, the early twentieth century had been a time of increasing anxiety about meat. The European-based empires had greatly expanded their dependence on meat imported from colonies and other friendly nations, and during the trade disruptions of World War I, meat

---

26 The Norwegian summary of the Icelandic import in NP box 166 indicates that this second import was in 1931, but this is incorrect. In a letter from farm owner Ársæll Árnason, he says that the calves were bought from Norway in 1930. It is also listed as 1930 in Hoel, "Moskusoksen", unpublished manuscript, no date (before 1933), 15.
27 A veterinarian report on the death of the last muskox in Iceland in June 1932 indicates that it died of a bacterial infection: copy of letter from Niels Dungal to Ársæli Árnason (8 September 1932), NP box 166. Ársæll Árnason, who owned the farm in Skorradal, also had frequent correspondence with Adolf Hoel in 1932–34, asking about the status of muskoxen in Norway.

shortages had been challenging.[28] Norwegian hunters' experience with muskox meat on East Greenland proved a tempting model for providing meat on the hoof in the far north.

Adolf Hoel, founder of the Norges Svalbard- og Ishavsundersøkelser (NSIU), proposed that muskoxen could be introduced to Svalbard to fill the need for meat: 'There is naturally also great importance that such a large meat-producing animal like muskox is found on Svalbard, where it often happens that people are in need and don't have enough food.'[29] The idea was not to raise muskoxen in pens like livestock, but rather to have them wander around Spitsbergen to graze naturally. These would be wild muskoxen harvested when meat was needed, just as wild reindeer were used on the archipelago.[30]

While eating muskox was the eventual goal, killing the new muskoxen introduced in 1929 was strictly prohibited by law.[31] The idea was that the muskoxen should be protected long enough for the population to increase to self-sustaining numbers. The first calves of the herd were observed in 1932; in addition, more animals were relocated from Greenland to Svalbard – another five were set out by NSIU that year.[32]

By the mid-1960s, there were probably about fifty muskoxen on the island of Spitsbergen and hunting was still not allowed. As their numbers grew, muskoxen sometimes journeyed into Longyearbyen. These visits evoked fear and concern. In January 1963, two muskoxen made trouble by grazing in a neighbourhood yard and attacking the local pastor's dog. They were difficult to drive away. 'The animals sauntered around the town houses in Longyearbyen, and parents are afraid to let their children go out on account of the mean muskoxen.'[33] In winter 1972, an old muskox had decided to take up residence near the town's kindergarten.[34] To avoid attacks, the children were kept inside during the school day and were taken to and from school by bus instead of walking there. One woman ended up being chased down the street by the interloper, narrowly escaping through her front door. The local radio was constantly broadcasting the animal's whereabouts and the police tried to shoo it away. In the end, two coal company trucks were used to scare

---

28 Perren, "Farmers and Consumers".   29 Hoel, "Overføring av Moskusokser".
30 Lars Hansen, "Moskusoksens overførsel til Svalbard", *Aftenposten* (19 September 1929), 1.
31 Hoel, "Moskusoksen: Bestand, Jakt, Fangst", 10.
32 "Overføringen av moskusdyr til Svalbard har været vellykket", *Aftenposten* (13 September 1932), 2.
33 "Prestefrue gikk løs på to moskusokser med kostekaftet", *Aftenposten* (4 January 1963), 12.
34 "Moskusokse var farlig for barna", *Aftenposten* (7 February 1972), 15.

the animal out of town. Not only did the muskoxen fail to provide the security of a new meat supply, but rather they offered physical insecurity.

In the late 1970s, alarming reports of declining muskox numbers started coming in. In 1977, only fifteen animals were reported still alive, one of which was 'Atle' who sought shelter in Longyearbyen.[35] The winter had alternated between mild periods and hard freezes, forming ice layers over the ground, which made it difficult for the muskoxen to find food. In 1979, only one lone cow was spotted in the normal muskox feeding grounds near Longyearbyen. Sometime in the early 1980s, this lone individual died, and the muskox was gone from Svalbard.[36]

The dream had been that East Greenland muskox hunting for meat would be reproduced on Svalbard simply by importing the animals. But the Svalbard muskoxen, as wild animals, did not stay in the places that people had intended them to be. The reality was that the herd never grew large enough to support hunting for meat, and on top of that, the animals simply became a nuisance for the inhabitants of Longyearbyen by wandering into town. The muskoxen did not thrive in Svalbard despite the best intentions of NSIU with the 1929 introduction.

Unruly Ornaments in the Norwegian High Mountains

Shortly after the muskoxen were taken to Svalbard, a group of animals was also moved by Hoel and NSIU from East Greenland to the Dovre mountains of central Norway. The mountains have Sub-Arctic tundra vegetation and are home to Norway's only wild reindeer herd. Ten young animals were captured in 1931 and after about a year in captivity in Ålesund, they were taken by train inland and released near Hjekinn railroad station.[37] A few more animals were added to the flock in later years to make up for deaths by disease and injury, including an avalanche that killed three females in 1934. For Hoel, this was 'a scientific investigation' to gain more knowledge of muskoxen biology,[38] although in newspaper coverage, the potential role of the animals as future food became an early headline.[39] By the end of the 1930s, both of these reasons – scientific study and food – disappear from the regular news

35 "Moskus-Atle» har fristed i Longyearbyen", *Aftenposten* (10 March 1977), 15.
36 "Svalbard-moskus dør ut", *Aftenposten* (3 August 1979), 1.
37 Olstad and Tuff, "Innplanting av moskusokser".
38 Hoel, "Moskusoksen: Bestand, Jakt, Fangst", 12.
39 An example of this is the article "Skal moskusdyrene for alvor holde sitt inntog på vårt høifjell?", *Aftenposten* (11 May 1933), which had a subtitle that translates as 'a cheap way to produce meat'.

coverage of the Dovre muskoxen; instead the animals are 'ornaments of the mountains' as an attraction for tourists and animal lovers.[40]

All of the animals had died by the end of World War II. Norway had been occupied by Germany, and after the war, the Germans got the blame for the muskox's disappearance. A headline in *Aftenposten* on 21 November 1945 claimed that 'Germans exterminated muskoxen', although the text of the article makes it clear that some Norwegians, albeit probably collaborators with the Germans, were involved: 'in winter 1943–44 German and "Norwegian" hunters lived in two cabins in the district where the muskoxen stayed. The animals were tame and easy to shoot, and it is possible that it was that winter that the most animals were killed'.[41] Whether or not it was just Germans and collaborators involved in the muskoxen demise, a decision was quickly reached by NSIU to import them from Greenland again. The approximately 300 muskoxen that are currently in the Dovre mountains are descendants of those post-Word War II imports.

From early on, the muskoxen in Dovre showed little fear of being near people. As scientists Olstad and Tuff remarked in 1940, 'one can quite often without difficulty come up within a few metres of the animals'; but they also believed that the muskoxen would become more shy over time.[42] They noted that some of the animals would become aggressive when people approached them, particularly tourists trying to get close-up photographs, but they felt this behaviour was exceptional rather than the rule. Newspaper reports from the 1950s and 1960s reveal regular cases of muskoxen charging tourists who got too close, and wandering into towns. A farmer was even killed in 1963 by a muskox who charged him.[43] As on Svalbard, muskox behaviour was not easily controllable.

The animals often ended up in unwanted locations. Dangerous conditions occurred when they roamed onto the train line or into villages, typically ending with the death of the animal. The railroad line, which had originally facilitated the movement of the muskox to Dovre, proved fatal to them on many occasions, such as the single calf that was struck by a train in 1968 and had to be located and then put down, and the two adults who sought shelter in a train tunnel and were hit by a locomotive in 1978.[44] Animals that wandered into settled areas were sometimes relocated back to the mountains

40 "Dovrefjellenes nyeste prd – Moskusdyreve trives godt", *Aftenposten* (19 October 1940); "Moskuskalver sloppet på Dovre igjen", *Aftenposten* (4 September 1947).
41 "Tyskerne utreddet moskusdyene", *Aftenposten* (21 November 1945).
42 Olstad and Tuff, "Innplanting av moskusokser", 52.
43 For more details about this incident, see Jørgensen, *Recovering Lost Species*, ch. 3.
44 "Moskuskalv på sporlinje måtte avlives", *Aftenposten* (10 June 1968); "To moskuser drept i tunnel", *Aftenposten* (5 September 1978).

with the help of anaesthetics and sometimes simply shot dead. The regional authorities recognized the problem of wild wanderers and set up a conservation plan for muskoxen in 1996 that identified geographically their core area (muskoxen free to roam all year), roaming area (where they could be during the summer migration and movement), and action area (where a decision to remove individuals would be discretionary), leaving everything outside those areas as off-limits for muskoxen (meaning they would be removed/shot immediately).[45] In the next version of the plan, which was issued in 2006, this division was dropped: now there was only the core area (where muskoxen could settle; this area was expanded from the previous version) and non-core.[46] The continuous reports of Dovre muskoxen in the 'wrong' place and the shifting management plans demonstrate that the muskoxen refused to be placed into a set geography – they disrupted the categories that the Norwegians tried to impose on them.

Porous Scandinavian Borders

In summer 1948, ten yearling muskoxen were caught in northeastern Greenland, then released in the wild near Bardufoss in northern Norway.[47] Two of them apparently died shortly after arrival, but the others made themselves at home in the area.[48] In January 1953, NSIU received word that a group of muskoxen had been spotted in Sweden around Kiruna. John Giæver of the NSIU asked the Bardufoss Air Station commander to let him know if they happened to catch sight of the animals. Giæver's characterization of the crossing reveals how the animals were understood to belong to the landscape in which they were placed: 'It is in principle totally natural that it had wandered over to the brother folk [of Sweden] – even if it must be condemned as disloyal.'[49] When he got word that the herd had moved back to the Norwegian side in February 1953, he wrote, 'It is really more loyal.'[50]

---

45 Fylkesmannen i Sør-Trøndelag, *Forvaltningsplan for moskus på Dovre*.
46 Fylkesmannen i Sør-Trøndelag, *Forvaltningsplan for moskusstammen på Dovre*.
47 NP box 244, Letter from S. Bang (NSIU) to Tollkammeret Harstad with attachments (25 August 1948).
48 NP box 244, Letter from Anders K. Orvin (NSIU) to Oberstløytnant John Tvedte (Bardufoss flyplass) (28 July 1950).
49 NP box 244, Letter from John Giæver (NSIU) to Direktør J. G. Jennov (27 January 1953).
50 NP box 244, Letter from John Giæver (NSIU) to Oberst Odd Bull (26 February 1953).

Although the comment might have been a little tongue-in-cheek, by saying that the animal was 'loyal' or 'disloyal' to Norway through its movements, Giæver claimed that the animal should stay in Norway where it had been placed.

The Swedes apparently did not agree. After the Swedish papers reported the sighting on 26 January, the Swedish government listed the animals as protected on the 31st. The Swedish Nature Protection Association wrote to NSIU deputy director Anders K. Orvin that 'The muskoxen's appearance in Lappland is very pleasing and [the Association] will do everything in its power to promote the Scandinavian muskox population's growth.'[51] The Association requested information about the Norwegian reintroduction efforts, particularly those in Bardufoss, since 'the "Swedish" animals must have come from there' (quotation marks around Swedish in the original).

It turns out that the muskoxen did not stay on the Swedish side of the border. By May 1953, they had crossed back. But having the muskoxen, for even such a short time, whetted the appetite of Swedes for the animal. The senior editor of the newspaper *Norrbottens-Kuriren* in Luleå asked the Polar Institute if it would be possible to buy calves for release in northern Sweden.[52] Others from Sweden also wrote in asking for calves. The Institute, however, declined all requests, replying that they were currently only permitted by the Danes to import two calves each year and these needed to be released in Norway to increase the existing Dovre and Bardufoss herds. Director Orvin noted that the Bardufoss muskoxen might decide to cross the border again, and maybe in the future the herd would grow enough to set up a subherd intentionally in northern Sweden.[53] That never happened. The small Bardufoss herd hung on for a while but died out by the late 1950s, so there was no expansion of the Bardufoss herd into Sweden.

Yet muskoxen would again vote with their feet and take up residence on the Swedish side of the Norway–Sweden border, but from a different source: in 1971 a group from the Dovre herd took up residence in the Swedish region of Härjedalen.[54] The immediate public reaction was that the muskoxen might attack people – the earliest article in the local paper *Östersunds-Posten* was run under the headline 'Wild muskoxen in Härjedalen. Warning: They can go on the attack!' But it appears that some Swedish businesses thought the new

---

51 NP box 244, Letter from Sten Dahlskog (Svensk Naturskyddsföreningen) to Direktör Orvin (NSIU) (29 February 1953).
52 NP box 244, Letter from Arvid Moberg (Norrbottens-Kuriren) to NSIU (2 May 1953).
53 NP box 244, Letter from Anders Orvin (NSIU) to Arvid Moberg (Norrbottens-Kuriren) (4 May 1953).
54 For more details about this migration, see Jørgensen, "Migrant Muskox".

muskox residents were a good thing. The local tourist industry in the area quickly latched onto the muskox as a potential draw. Only two days after muskoxen were seen in the area, the Hamrafjället tourist hotel was already advertizing its first expedition to 'Muskoxen land' (Myskoxarnas land) to take place the next morning.[55] The local area was 'invaded by tourists' to see the 'sensation'.[56] The Norwegian wildlife and fisheries department decided not to intervene in the situation, considering it part of 'the animals' natural wandering'.[57]

By 1976, the five animals had become a herd of fourteen, so the time was ripe for a discussion about the animals' future in Sweden. The Swedish environmental protection agency organized a symposium in September 1976 in the town of Fünasdalen up in the mountains to answer questions about the muskoxen that were seemingly going to stay in Sweden.[58] The Sami reindeer herder Bengt Andersson from Tännäs, who was representing the indigenous Sami interests at the meeting, wanted guarantees that no more muskoxen would be allowed in the area. The Sami were worried that the animals would damage cabins and fenced areas, attack their herding dogs, and feed inside the reindeer flocks, making it impossible to herd the reindeer properly. They also objected to the numerous searches that were being conducted by plane, snow scooter, and foot to locate the muskoxen by both tourists and nature conservationists, because they disturbed the reindeer. If the muskoxen were going to be allowed to stay, Andersson said that the Sami wanted compensation for muskox damage. The official policy on muskoxen issued in May 1979, in response to feedback from the meeting and comments received from local, regional, and national authorities as well as scientific experts in 1978, did not, however, include such compensation, nor did it keep the muskox herd from growing.

Although the herd did continue to grow in the 1980s, at the end of the decade the population crashed, probably owing to disease. A few individuals continue to live in the area, and two adults have been released from captivity into the herd to strengthen the herd's reproductive capacity. In Swedish governmental documents, these attempts at keeping the muskox population viable are framed as tourism support, rather than an ecological project, since the muskox is classified as an introduced species ineligible for nature protection.[59]

---

55 "Hel hjord på väg in i Sverige", *Dagens Nyheter* (5 September 1971).
56 "Myskoxar på svensk mark", *Svenska Dagbladet* (8 September 1971).
57 "Moskusoksene blie i Sverige", *Aftenposten* (14 January 1972).
58 Documents about this meeting are found in folder 270–2665–76, Naturvårdsverket archive, Stockholm.
59 Jørgensen, "Migrant Muskox".

The porosity of the Norwegian-Swedish border challenged the intent of those who wanted the muskoxen to stay where they had released them. It also created opportunities for muskoxen to reinhabit a landscape from which they had disappeared several thousands of years before. Muskoxen could never be permanently placed if they were allowed to run free.

Domestication on the Agenda Again: This Time for Wool

In 1954 John Teal, Jr, an Arctic anthropologist, captured some muskox calves in the Thelon Game Sanctuary of Canada and relocated them to his farm in Vermont, which was working as the Institute of Northern Agricultural Research. His vision was that muskoxen would be 'useful not only for Arctic husbandry but also for the many sub-marginal farming areas in our northern states'.[60] His objective was always to produce wool from the animals, which he wanted to breed selectively as domesticates. Teal was encouraged by 'the Norwegian experiment' with muskoxen and was eager to use it as the basis for his new domestication project. Although the Norwegians never framed the Dovre releases as domestication, the knowledge they produced was repurposed by Teal.

In 1964, Teal decided to move his project to Alaska and founded a farm at the University of Alaska Fairbanks. But instead of moving muskoxen from Vermont, new ones were caught on Nunivak Island off the coast of Alaska. The animals caught for this purpose had not been on Nunivak for long. Muskoxen had been extinct in Alaska since the mid-1800s.[61] In 1930, at the request of the Alaskan Territorial Legislature, the US Congress appropriated $40,000 to reintroduce muskoxen to Alaska.[62] The muskoxen were caught in East Greenland, shipped to Norway, then taken to New York. Thirty-six muskoxen were shipped by train from New York to Alaska, where they were put out on University of Alaska property in 1930. The animals stayed there until 1936, when eighteen males and thirteen females were relocated to Nunivak Island, which had been designated as a wildlife refuge. The official purpose of the project was twofold: to contribute to the conservation of the muskox as a species and to re-establish them as wild animals in Alaska.[63] In the

---

60 Teal, "Norwegian Musk-Ox Experiment", 36.
61 Lent, "Alaska's Indigenous Muskoxen".   62 Alaska did not become a US state until 1959.
63 Rouse, "Transfer of Muskoxen". I should note, however, that Vilhjamur Stefansson thought that domestication was the ultimate reason for the Alaskan project: Stefansson, "Farming Without Barns", 56.

1930s, there was widespread scientific concern that muskoxen overhunting in Greenland would lead to its extinction, so establishing viable populations elsewhere was understood as a potential mitigation measure.[64] The idea was that the animals on Nunivak Island would serve as the source population for reintroduction efforts throughout Alaska. Indeed, the numbers took off in the 1950s, so that by 1965 there were 500 animals on the island. With a booming population, in addition to giving some to the Teal farming initiative, the FWS transplanted 158 animals elsewhere in Alaska from 1967 to 1970.[65]

Teal set up the Oomingmak Musk Ox Producer's Cooperative to knit the wool in 1969. Muskox wool (qiviut) was the miracle fibre that would dominate the winter fabric market. Teal's original vision was for Native Alaskan villages to have their own muskox herds and run a cottage knitting industry. Although the cooperative operationalized the knitting part, muskoxen have never been set up as individual farm animals in Alaska. Instead, the muskoxen remained on just one farm ('The Muskox Farm') in Palmer, Alaska. Teal's farm was successful – on a small artisanal scale – and it remains so to this day, selling products through the cooperative. While Teal's farm survived, the ecology and economics of muskox ranching were not particularly favourable. One FWS report from 1967 noted that because of the costs of fencing and feeding, as well as transport of qiviut to market, keeping muskoxen as domesticates on Nunivak would result in a net loss each year rather than a gain.[66] This was the reality that would face the Norwegians who attempted to start their own farm.

When Norwegians began floating the idea of setting up a muskox farm in northern Norway, they called on Teal's expertise because of his extensive experience working with muskoxen in domestic settings. In 1966, Teal visited Tromsø and the town of Bardu to discuss the idea of importing some of his animals to northern Norway. Importation from Alaska ended up not being practical, so instead the Norwegians went to East Greenland, which had been the original source population of those Alaskan muskoxen anyway. Teal continued to play a critical part in the plans for domesticating muskox in

---

64 For discussions of this concern: Roberts and Jørgensen, "Animals as Instruments", 76–77; Jørgensen, *Recovering Lost Species*, 64–66.
65 US Fish and Wildlife Service, Alaska, "Muskox Transplant Program 1967–1970".
66 Lensink, "Muskox Domestication and Husbandry".

Norway. In 1969, Teal once again visited Tromsø as an expert consultant, and he became the official advisor to the farm set up by Norsk Moskus A/S. One newspaper account called Teal 'the father of the idea [of muskox domestication] here in Norway'.[67] What we see is a circular, self-reinforcing relationship: Teal had looked to Hoel and the Norwegian import as an example, Teal set up farm in Vermont and then Alaska, then Norwegian interests in northern Norway looked to Teal.

A proposal to bring muskox to the county of Troms as a domestic wool producer was first raised in 1967 by the parliamentary representative Alfred Henningsen.[68] The idea was that qiviut produced in farms in the northern Norwegian counties of Troms and Finnmark would be processed and shipped to the US where the market price of qiviut was sky high.[69] In January 1969, Henningsen formally asked the Department of Agriculture to support domestication of muskox in Norway. The Norwegian Department of Agriculture had sent the veterinarian Magne Sandbu to Alaska to investigate Teal's operation in May 1968. Sandbu's report cited potential health concerns, especially possible increased parasite loads because of a milder climate in northern Norway than in Alaska, and intense management, including constant work at calming the animals, horn removal, wool collection, and breeding control. Sandbu concluded that with the right controls, risks to people and other animals would be minimized, but he also did not believe that wool production from farmed muskox would 'give a reasonable way of life for folk in northern Norway'.[70] The State declined to give financial support to the project because of these reservations.

Despite this lack of direct support, Henningsen helped found the company Norsk Moskus A/S, which then imported twenty-five calves from East Greenland. In the newspaper coverage around the importation, we can sense the excitement in the air: 'Bardu waits for wool and money from "the muskox adventure"' read one headline.[71] Norsk Moskus A/S tried to build up hype about muskox wool products for the luxury market. In February 1970, the company showed a muskox wool dress at a big agricultural fair. The dress was 'as light as a snowflake and warm', but 'amazingly expensive'.[72] The luxury dress would be expected to fetch a price of over

---

67 "Moskus som husdyr i Norge er ingen drøm", *Aftenposten* (28 November 1970), 6.
68 "Moskusdyr som ullproduserende husdyr i Troms?", *Aftenposten* (3 June 1967).
69 "Plan om moskusullproduksjon i Troms", *Aftenposten* (21 February 1968).
70 Norwegian Parliament, "Sak nr. 5. Spm".
71 "Bardu venter seg ul log penger av moskuseventyret", *Aftenposten* (4 September 1969).
72 "Fnugglett og varmt – og utrolig dyrt!", *Aftenposten* (28 February 1970).

a thousand US dollars (7,000 Norwegian kroner). Fourteen kilos of wool was plucked in 1970, and some was sent to a handcraft association (*Norsk Brukskunst*) to run a design competition to increase interest in the material.[73]

Although the company attempted to build up the hype around qiviut, supplementary income came from public visitors: between January and July 1970, 6,000 people visited the farm, and over 15,000 tourists visited in 1973.[74] At the same time, the new business had to contend with parasitic infections among the animals and several fence breakouts. In summer 1972, eight animals got out of the pens; only three had been recovered after five weeks of looking for them with aeroplane flyovers, and the others were finally captured in October.[75] One animal which got out of the farm in summer 1975 was blamed for the death of a moose hunter.[76]

After struggling for financial survival, Norsk Moskus shut down in 1980. They gave their remaining ten animals to the University of Tromsø for Arctic animal research. The herd was moved onto the island of Ryøya where they could be studied in a controlled, uninhabited environment.[77] The last muskox on Ryøya died in 2018.[78]

The domestication attempts in both North America and Scandinavia did not go as planned. Although both projects envisaged muskoxen as domestic livestock on small farms, muskoxen never became dispersed to smallholders; instead, they were kept only in centralized large operations. While Teal's operation in Alaska survived financially, the Bardu farm folded within ten years; the muskoxen were repurposed from wool producers to scientific objects, and even that lasted less than forty years.

Repopulating Muskox on the Siberian Tundra

There were still plenty of muskoxen on Nunivak, Alaska, available to be relocated even after some had been captured for Teal's farm and others had been moved elsewhere in Alaska. This interested two Russian biologists, Savva Uspensky of the USSR Ministry of Agriculture and Vadim

---

73 "Moskus turistattraksjon. Ull til Brukskunst", *Aftenposten* (11 July 1970).
74 "Uventet mange turister besøker moskus-kalvene", *Aftenposten* (29 July 1970); "Stor økning i besøket til moskusoksfarmen", *Aftenposten* (13 August 1973).
75 "Moskusoksene fra Bardu-farm funnet", *Aftenposten* (3 August 1972); "Moskusoksen jaget jegere ved Bardu", *Aftenposten* (6 October 1972).
76 "Moskus angrep letemannskaper", *Aftenposten* (1 October 1975).
77 Blix et al., "Experiences".
78 Sanna Drogset Børstad, "Nå er det ikke lenger moskus på Ryøya", *Itromso* (13 August 2018), www.itromso.no/nyheter/2018/08/13/Nå-er-det-ikke-lenger-moskus-på-Ryøya-17308683.ece.

Tarkov.[79] The United States had signed an environmental cooperation treaty with the USSR in 1972, in spite of (or perhaps because of) the Cold War.[80] This treaty was just the latest in a series of intergovernmental agreements focused on educational, scientific, and technical exchange beginning in 1958. These were not friction-free exchanges – the science was consistently interpreted within respective political frameworks – but the attempts at bilateral scientific cooperation were genuine.[81] Arctic and Sub-Arctic systems were specifically called out as an area of cooperation in the environmental treaty, and the 'joint development and implication of programmes and projects in the field of basic and applied sciences' were included as possible actions. Under the treaty, a group of Soviet scientists, who had been able to acquire ten muskox calves from Banks Island, Canada, in 1974, asked for a larger transfer from the American Nunivak herd. The Soviets wanted to reintroduce muskoxen to Siberia.

Not everyone was pleased with the suggestion of sending muskoxen to the Russians. It appears from newspaper accounts that the Interior Department had made the agreement sometime before March 1975, but was reluctant to announce it publicly in Alaska for fear of increasing anti-Soviet sentiment there. A letter to the editor in the *Fairbanks Daily News-Miner* criticized the plan, saying, 'If the state is going to release any surplus of musk-oxen to other parties, Alaskans and other Americans should have preference over foreign nations.'[82]

Regardless of the objections, the muskoxen were released to the Soviet scientists. Forty animals, aged one and two years old, caught on Nunivak, were loaded onto a Russian plane in April 1975.[83] Half of the animals were taken to the Taimyr Peninsula to join the ten Canadian animals; the other half were taken to Wrangel Island. The Taimyr Peninsula, which had not had muskoxen for at least two millennia, had become home to an estimated 6,500 animals in 2008; about 800 were on Wrangel Island at the same time.[84] Since these animals were not corralled, but rather released into the wild, it would

---

79 US Fish and Wildlife Service, *U.S.-Soviet Muskox Transplant 1975*.
80 Agreement on Cooperation in the Field of Environmental Protection between the United States of America and the Union of Soviet Socialist Republics.
81 See for example Geltzer, "In a Distorted Mirror"; McDonald, "Scientific Cooperation".
82 Joe La Rocca, "Why Send Musk-Oxen to Siberia?", *Fairbanks Daily News-Miner* (2 April 1975).
83 US Fish and Wildlife Service, *1975 US–USSR Muskox Transplant*. Colour photographs of the expedition were published in US Fish and Wildlife Service, *U.S.-Soviet Muskox Transplant 1975*.
84 Sipko, "Status of Reintroductions".

be easy to think of the Russian project as a rewilding one. But in the 1980s, the intent of letting muskoxen populations go free in these places was to grow their numbers high enough to be able to introduce the animals to other Soviet Arctic regions and set up experimental domestication farms.[85] In the 1990s and early 2000s, some animals from the Taimyr Peninsula and Wrangel Island were indeed relocated to the Yakutia, Yamal, and Magadan regions in northern Russia,[86] although at this point there are no domestication projects.

Conclusion

In 1921 Vilhjalmur Stefansson had remarked that the vast expanses of the Arctic while they might appear desolate at a glance, were teeming with life: 'The arctic land is lifeless except for millions of caribou and of foxes, tens of thousands of wolves and of musk oxen, thousands of polar bears, billions of insects and millions of birds.'[87] Yet this life was believed to be underutilized by humans. Tapping into the abundance of the 'friendly and fruitful' Arctic through the muskox was a path to success: 'We need clothing as well as food, wool as well as meat; and for this and several other reasons I would suppose that the ovibos and not the reindeer will a century hence be the chief domestic animal of the northern half of Canada and the northern third of Asia.'[88] The muskox was an integral element in Stefansson's notion of a 'friendly Arctic'. While the muskox had a limited range at the beginning of the 1900s, they were understood as Arctic animals that could succeed anywhere around the globe; they just needed help to get to those new places.

The flinging of muskoxen between 1900 and 1975 from East Greenland across the planet, from the tundra of Svalbard and the Taimyr Peninsula to the farms of Iceland and Alaska, was an exercise in human hubris. All of the men involved (and I write 'men' intentionally here) were 'improvers' – they wanted to improve living conditions, economic conditions, and even environmental conditions. Whether they tried to domesticate muskoxen for harvest or set them free in the landscape, they thought they were improving on nature, which they found to be wanting. Their improving efforts were challenged by the muskoxen

---

85 Zabrodin and Yakushkin, "Musk-Oxen".
86 Sipko, "Status of Reintroductions".
87 Stefansson, *Friendly Arctic*, 19.   88 Stefansson, *Friendly Arctic*, 6, 589.

themselves: the animals did not stay where they were put, they died of disease, they disrupted human lives. The idea that muskoxen would become standard edible fare across the Arctic has never come to fruition, and qiviut is still the rarest wool on the market. The wild herds in northern Russia and Alaska have grown substantially, but experiences elsewhere show that the populations can crash at any moment. The twentieth-century Arctic 'improvers' discovered that moving and managing were not the same thing when it came to muskoxen. Getting the animals to the desirable place was only the first step in a long journey – one that has more often than not ended in abject failure.

Muskoxen were not the only animal moved around by these kind of improvement projects in the polar region. Just to name a few, reindeer have been taken from Norway to the island of South Georgia; penguins have been captured from the southern hemisphere and released in northern Norway; European bison, North American bison, yaks, and other large herbivores have been released in the Russian tundra to recreate the Pleistocene ecosystem.[89] Some of these acclimatization attempts have had a quick end – the penguins in Norway lasted only about fifteen years – but others have been long-term projects – the reindeer of South Georgia introduced in the 1920s continued to inhabit the island until 2016. In general, all of these projects show the same naive mindset as the muskoxen relocations: a belief that animals are mutable, easily exchanging one polar habitat for another somewhere else in the region, and that they are a vital element to making 'empty' land productive. Yet the practical challenges of these movements have often been obscured through these ideological glasses. The animals themselves, and the necessary ongoing management for their health and wellbeing, have rarely been taken into account.

Whether we look at muskox translocation projects or attempts at turning muskoxen into a domestic livestock species, the projects stem from the same desire to domesticate Arctic and Antarctic spaces. Moving animals to new landscapes was supposed to make them more useful, or valuable, or productive, whether that productivity is measured in terms of mouths fed, sweaters knitted, or biodiversity statistics. These animals were emplaced in physical and imagined spaces tied to Western desires to tame the north.

89 Roberts and Jørgensen, "Animals as Instruments"; Pleistocene Park, https://pleistocenepark.ru/.

28 Moving Muskoxen

Bibliography

Archival Sources

Agreement on Cooperation in the Field of Environmental Protection between the United States of America and the Union of Soviet Socialist Republics, US State Department, Treaties and Other International Acts Series 7345 (23 May 1972).
Folder 270-2665-76, Naturvårdsverket archive, Stockholm.
Fylkesmannen i Sør-Trøndelag, *Forvaltningsplan for moskus på Dovre*, report prepared by Endre Persen (1996).
Fylkesmannen i Sør-Trøndelag, *Forvaltningsplan for moskusstammen på Dovre*, report prepared by Bjørn Rangbru (2006).
Hoel, Adolf, "Moskusoksen: Bestand, Jakt, Fangst, Omplantningsforsøk", unpublished manuscript, no date (before 1933), småskrift collection of Norsk Polarinstitutt library, call number SM-5138.
Lensink, Calvin J., "Muskox Domestication and Husbandry: Its Prospects in Alaska", unpublished memorandum, US Fish and Wildlife Service (19 October 1967), US Fish and Wildlife Service ServCat System, code 49453.
Newspaper archives: *Aftenposten, Dagens Nyheter, Fairbanks Daily News-Miner, Itromso, Svenska Dagbladet*.
Norwegian Parliament, Sak nr. 5. Spm. fra repr. Henningsen om domestisering av moskus i Norge m. v. (29 January 1969), Ordentlige Stortings forhandlinger 1968-29, pp. 2111–2112, in *Stortingstidende* 113.
NP box 166, folder "Moskusokser: Overførsel till Island, Danmark, Sverige, Finnland, USA", National Archives of Norway, Tromsø.
NP box 244, folder 545, National Archives of Norway, Tromsø.
Rouse, C. H., "Transfer of Muskoxen to Nunivak Island – 1936", unpublished report for the US Fish and Wildlife Service dated October 1936, US Fish and Wildlife Service ServCat System, code 49376.
US Fish and Wildlife Service, Alaska, "The Muskox Transplant Program 1967–1970", unpublished report (undated), US Fish and Wildlife Service ServCat System, code 49454.
US Fish and Wildlife Service, *U.S.-Soviet Muskox Transplant 1975*, unpublished report (1975), US Fish and Wildlife Service ServCat System, code 49256.
US Fish and Wildlife Service, *1975 US–USSR Muskox Transplant*, report number FWS-759999 (1975).

Published Sources

Blainville, Henri Marie Ducrotay de, "Sur plusieurs espèces d'animaux mammiferes, de l'ordre des ruminans", in *Bulletin des Sciences par La Société Philomatique de Paris. Année 1816* (Paris: Plassan, 1816), pp. 73–82.
Blix, Arnoldus Schytte, John Ness, and Hans Lian, "Experiences from Forty Years of Muskox (*Ovibos moschatus*) Farming in Norway", *Rangifer* 31 (2011): 1–6.

Canada, Royal Commission, *Report of the Royal Commission to Investigate the Possibilities of the Reindeer and Musk-Ox Industries in the Arctic and Sub-Arctic Regions of Canada* (Ottawa: F. A. Acland, 1922).

Charlevoix, Pierre François Xavier de, *Journal d'un voyage fait par ordre du Roi dans l'Amerique septentrionnale*, vol. 3 (Paris: Nyon Fils, 1744).

Cuyler, Christine, Janice Rowell, Jan Adamczewski, et al., "Muskox Status, Recent Variation, and Uncertain Future", *Ambio* 49 (2020): 805–819.

Geltzer, Anna, "In a Distorted Mirror: The Cold War and U.S.-Soviet Biomedical Cooperation and (Mis)understanding, 1956–1977", *Journal of Cold War Studies* 14 (2012): 39–63.

Glover, R., "The Muskox (*Ovibos moschatus*)", *Oryx* 2 (1953): 76–86.

Guðmundsson, Helga Hrafn, "Þegar Íslendingar stráfelldu sauðnautahjarðir og sýndu kálfana á Austurvelli", *Lemúrinn* (11 December 2013), https://lemurinn.is/2013/12/11/thegar-islendingar-strafelldu-saudnautahjardir-og-syndu-kalfa-hennar-a-austurvelli/.

Hoel, Adolf, "Overføring av Moskusokser til Svalbard", *Norge, Tidsskrift om vårt land* 6 (1930): 15–18.

Hone, Elisabeth, *The Present Status of the Muskox in Arctic North America and Greenland* (Cambridge, MA: American Committee for International Wild Life Protection, 1934).

Jørgensen, Dolly, "Migrant Muskox and the Naturalization of National Identity in Scandinavia", in Susan Nance, ed., *The Historical Animal* (Syracuse: Syracuse University Press, 2015), pp. 184–201.

Jørgensen, Dolly, *Recovering Lost Species in the Modern Age: Histories of Longing and Belonging* (Cambridge, MA: MIT Press, 2019).

Kolthoff, Gustaf, *Til Spetsbergen och Nordöstra Grönland år 1900* (Stockholm: Fr. Skoglunds, 1901).

Lent, Peter C., "Alaska's Indigenous Muskoxen: A History", *Rangifer* 18 (1998): 133–144.

Lent, Peter, *Muskoxen and Their Hunters: A History* (Norman: University of Oklahoma Press, 1999).

Lønø, Odd, *Transplantation of the Muskox in Europe and North-America*, Meddelelser 84 (Oslo: Norsk Polarinstitutt, 1960).

McDonald, Alan, "Scientific Cooperation as a Bridge Across the Cold War Divide: The Case of the International Institute for Applied Systems Analysis (IIASA)", *Annuals of the New York Academy of Sciences* 866 (1998): 55–83.

Nathorst, Alfred, *Två Somrar i Norra Ishafvet, Senare delen, Spanande efter Andrée i Nordöstra Grönland* (Stockholm: Beijers, 1900).

Olstad, O., and P. Tuff, "Innplanting av moskusokser på Dovrefjell", in *Årsmelding om Det Norkse Skogvesen* (Oslo: Skogdirektøren, 1942), pp. 51–55.

Osborne, Michael A., "Acclimatizing the World: A History of the Paradigmatic Colonial Science", *Osiris* 15 (2000): 135–151.

Peary, Robert E., *Northward Over the "Great Ice"*, Vol. 1 (New York: Frederick A. Stokes, 1898).

Perren, Richard, "Farmers and Consumers Under Strain: Allied Meat Supplies in the First World War", *Agriculture History Review* 53 (2005): 212–228.

Philo, Chris, and Chris Wilbert, "Animal Spaces, Beastly Places: An Introduction", in Chris Philo and Chris Wilbert, eds., *Animal Spaces, Beastly Places: New Geographies of Human-Animal Relations* (New York: Routledge, 2000), pp. 1–34.

Ritvo, Harriet, "Going Forth and Multiplying: Animal Acclimatization and Invasion", *Environmental History* 17 (2012): 404–414.
Roberts, Peder, and Dolly Jørgensen, "Animals as Instruments of Norwegian Imperial Authority in the Interwar Arctic", *Journal for the History of Environment and Society* 1 (2016): 65–87.
Schiött, Jul, "Musk Oxen in Captivity", in *Annual Report of the Board of Regents of the Smithsonian Institution for the Year Ending June 30, 1903* (Washington, DC: Government Printing Office, 1904), pp. 601–609.
Sipko, Taras, "Status of Reintroductions of Three Large Herbivores in Russia", *Alces* 45 (2009): 35–42.
Stefansson, Vilhjamur, "Farming Without Barns", *Harper's Magazine* (January 1946): 53–56.
Stefansson, Vilhjamur, *The Friendly Arctic: The Story of Five Years in Polar Regions* (New York: Macmillan, 1921).
Stefansson, Vilhjamur, *The Northward Course of Empire* (New York: Harcourt, Brace, 1923).
Teal, John J., Jr, "The Norwegian Musk-Ox Experiment", *American Scandinavian Review* (1954): 33–36.
Zabrodin, A., and G. D. Yakushkin, "Musk-Oxen", in N. G. Dimtriev and L. K. Ernst, eds., *Animal Genetic Resources of the USSR* (Rome: FAO/UNEP, 1989), pp. 399–407.
Zimmermann, Eberhard August Wilhelm, *Geographische Geschichte des Menschen, und der allgemein verbreiteten vierfüßigen Thiere*, Vol. 2 (Leipzig: Weygand, 1780).

29

Boundaries of Place and Time at the Edge of the Polar Oceans

HAYLEY BRAZIER AND MARK CAREY

Introduction

There is a problem fermenting in the frigid waters of the Beaufort Sea, a portion of the Arctic Ocean north of Canada and the United States. The trouble has its roots in an 1825 treaty signed between Great Britain and Russia, which divided their North American territories into what are now Alaska and Yukon. In that treaty, the two empires drew a north–south boundary along the 'Meridian Line of the 141st degree' that 'in its prolongation as far as the Frozen Ocean, shall form the limit between the Russian and British Possessions'.[1] Nearly 200 years later the inheritors of this agreement, the United States and Canada, are interpreting the phrase 'as far as the Frozen Ocean' in contrasting ways. Canada understands this sentence to mean that the boundary between the two nations extends past the shoreline and into the Beaufort Sea, while the United States argues that the border ends at the coastline where the 'Frozen Ocean' begins. If Canada is correct, the western edge of its Exclusive Economic Zone (EEZ) in the Beaufort Sea runs straight north along the 141st meridian, while the United States contends that its EEZ extends northeast from the angled coastline.[2]

The conflicting interpretations by the United States and Canada of the 1825 treaty have resulted in a section of the Beaufort Sea that both countries claim. This area of the sea might have remained relatively uncontested, however, if not for the dwindling of sea ice. For many decades, the reliability of the

---

Both authors contributed equally to this chapter and are listed alphabetically. Work for the chapter was supported in part by the US National Science Foundation Office of Polar Programs Grant #1543012.

1 Convention between Great Britain and Russia concerning the Limits of Their Respective Possessions on the North-West Coast of America and the Navigation of the Pacific Ocean, Great Britain-Russia, signed 28 February 1825. Oxford University Press database 75 Consolidated Treaty Series 95.
2 Shake et al., "(Un)frozen Spaces", 6–8; Baker and Byers, "Crossed Lines", 70–71.

29 At the Edge of the Polar Oceans

Arctic's annual freeze aligned with the treaty's expectation of an eternally frozen sea. But changing climate and the changing sea ice – which are, after all, always dynamic – have altered the timescale of life in the Beaufort Sea: that supposedly static plane of impenetrable Frozen Ocean is declining, opening more of the sea not only to treaty politics, but also to multinational corporations that have discovered a continental floor rich with the promise of oil and gas.[3] The forever-shifting edge between ocean and ice is reshaping geopolitics, livelihoods, and the political economy of the Arctic Ocean. It turns out that the edges of continents and countries are not as stable or well-defined as many imagined, neither in the past nor the present, and particularly not in the polar regions where ice, sea, and land are so interconnected and where climate change is occurring faster than other parts of the planet.

The Frozen Ocean dilemma is not unique to the Beaufort Sea; nor is the shifting boundary between ocean and ice an altogether novel event. In both the Arctic and Antarctic regions, the ocean–ice edge – the place where the sea laps at the edge of Earth's terrestrial borders – is one of the most dynamic sites in the polar regions. The ice edge has long been characterized by moments of conflict, change, political strife, and geological collisions, as well as biological diversity, economic opportunities, sites for food and sustenance, and homelands. Much of the human history of the polar regions has played out at this ocean–ice interface. For Arctic Indigenous communities, the boundary between sea ice and ocean represents a critical hunting ground, a zone that facilitates human livelihoods, traditions, and survival in a polar environment (Figure 29.1).[4] For American and European imperial ships, the start of the sea ice represented a seemingly impenetrable boundary in both the Arctic and Antarctic, while ice sheets on land often thwarted inland expeditions.[5] In the present day, scientists, tourists, and oil companies increasingly focus their attention on the ice–ocean edge, where rapid changes – from glacier retreat to sea ice thinning – are presenting economic opportunities for some and environmental disaster for others.[6] The preponderance of historical and present-day activity at the edge of this ever-changing ice

---

3 Frey et al., "Divergent Patterns", 33, 39; Shake et al., "(Un)frozen Spaces", 6–8; Baker and Byers, "Crossed Lines", 70–71.
4 Gearheard et al., eds., *The Meaning of Ice*; Hastrup, "The Ice as Argument"; Krupnik et al., eds., *Siku: Knowing Our Ice*; Smith, "'Exceeding Beringia'".
5 Dodds, *Ice: Nature and Culture*; Griffiths, *Slicing the Silence*; Pyne, *The Ice*; Howkins, *The Polar Regions*.
6 Bjørst, "Tip of the Iceberg"; Carey, "History of Ice"; Hastrup, "History of Climate Change"; Sörlin, "Cryo-history"; Lam and Tegelberg, "Dark Tourism".

Figure 29.1 Icebergs and fishing in the Ilulissat Icefjord, Greenland. (Photo by Mark Carey.)

reveals how time, biology, geology, and politics collide – just like they do in the Beaufort Sea. The ocean–ice edge has defined and shaped human history in the polar regions, not only in the Arctic where people have lived for tens of thousands of years, but also in the Antarctic where the edges of ice sheets, sea ice, and icebergs have influenced histories and narratives of science, politics, exploration, whaling, and human–environment dynamics more broadly.[7]

And yet, for all the critical importance of the ocean–ice border, the precise site is often overlooked by social science and humanities researchers who tend to focus either on the ocean or on ice-covered land – not both. Researchers have helped to construct discursive, epistemological, and cultural boundaries between ocean and ice, failing to recognize the fluid interactions that link the sea and the land rather than divide it. The ice edge thus becomes a disciplinary boundary, with ocean scholars on one side and terrestrial researchers on the other. More problematic still is a tendency to construct the ocean–ice, or ocean–land, boundary as static – at least until global warming recently started shrinking ice sheets, thawing permafrost, and thinning sea ice. During the past few hundred years, explorers, political

---

[7] Antonello, "Engaging and Narrating"; Leane and Maddison, "Biography of Iceberg B09B"; Provant et al., "Reframing Antarctica's Ice Loss".

institutions, and environmental managers have not fully recognized just how dynamic the ocean–ice interface actually is. Political borders and laws – not to mention maps and the imagination – have in many cases solidified this boundary as a static, clearly demarcated edge between the ocean and the land.[8] In reality, and as history shows, the ocean–ice boundary has rarely been so clean and clear, and it has never been static or free from politics and societal encounters.[9] Dismantling this constructed barrier between ocean and ice, and between the polar regions and the rest of the planet, requires a lot more than simply recognizing how climate change melts polar ice. Studying the ocean–ice boundary requires that we re-orient our histories of the polar regions to this material and imagined site where solid and liquid water meet, where freshwater and saltwater interact, and where land and ocean are constantly in flux through both space and time.

This chapter examines the rich history of the ocean–ice boundary in both the Arctic and Antarctic regions through a focus on three main types of ice: sea ice, icebergs, and glaciers. The chapter accomplishes four main goals: (1) it demonstrates that ocean–ice boundaries in the polar regions are constantly in flux and dynamic; (2) it shows that while some human societies have recognized and interacted with these dynamic borders, others have tried to concretize and reify the boundaries as static and fixed barriers, which can create conflicts; (3) it illustrates that ice and the sea – and the edge where they meet – are mutually constituted by humans and non-humans; and (4) it argues that we need to approach the polar regions and specifically the ocean–ice boundary through the interplay of both time and space. This ocean–ice edge is a place where Ice Ages meet the present, and where hourly, daily, seasonal, annual, and decadal time periods interface. Spatial and temporal scales must be analysed together if we are to understand how this boundary has mattered in the past, how it matters now, and how it will matter in the future.

Sea Ice

In both geological and human timescales, sea ice is youthful. Sea ice forms seasonally from saltwater that has become too cold to stay in liquid form. Although brine is eventually expelled from the sea ice, if you slid your tongue along newly formed ice you might receive a salty zing.[10] When the Arctic and

---

8 For example, see Steinberg and Kristoffersen, "'Ice Edge Is Lost'".
9 Bravo, "A Cryopolitics"; Cruikshank, *Do Glaciers Listen?*.
10 National Snow and Ice Data Center, "Salinity and Brine", https://nsidc.org/cryosphere/seaice/characteristics/brine_salinity.html (accessed 4 January 2018).

Antarctic experience their seasonal warming a portion of this ice melts, meaning most of it does not often reach more than the age of two or three years. There is also multi-year ice, which endures over time because it does not melt during the summer.[11] Sea ice that is attached to the shore – what scientists refer to as 'landfast' ice, or simply 'fast' ice – stays in one place and does not drift away. Because landfast ice connects to solid ground, it extends the continent's reach into the ocean. Pack ice, or drift ice, floats in sea currents and may move from coastal zones to the open ocean, sometimes travelling dozens or even hundreds of kilometres. Sea ice also fluctuates through time, as both the horizontal and vertical boundaries between land and sea shift over days, years, and centuries. When sea ice contracts, it brings the coastline closer to land. When sea ice thins, it brings the ice surface closer to the water underneath.

The amount of sea ice that annually congregates around the edges of Antarctica causes the continent to balloon to twice its normal size. If you watched a series of Antarctic satellite images, you would see the fluctuation of sea ice continually grow and decline, like lungs rhythmically breathing in and out. Christopher C. Joyner aptly called Antarctica the 'pulsating continent' to describe this seasonal freeze and melt routine.[12] Until recently, sea ice around Antarctica had not shown a clear decline but was actually increasing to the degree of reaching a maximum in 2014. Since then, Antarctic sea ice has contracted, but even so there is significant variation based on the region and the period examined.[13] As the Intergovernmental Panel on Climate Change (IPCC) recently related for Antarctica, 'sea ice extent overall has had no statistically significant trend (1979–2018) due to contrasting regional signals and large interannual variability'.[14] On the opposite side of the globe, however, the sea ice trajectory is clearer. The Arctic Ocean's late-summer sea ice has declined by an estimated 75 per cent, diminishing so visibly that it has become a posterchild for climate change. During the past four decades alone, the amount of multi-year Arctic sea ice (more than five years old) has declined by 90 per cent. In addition to the temporal changes and its shrinkage in area, Arctic sea ice also thinned by 65 per cent between 1975 and 2012, from an average of about 3.5 m thick to 1.25 m, collapsing the vertical ice boundary that once separated air and ocean.[15]

11 For sea ice details and terminology, see www.whoi.edu/know-your-ocean/ocean-topics/polar-research/sea-ice/sea-ice-glossary/ (accessed 10 February 2021).
12 Joyner, "Ice-Covered Regions", 222–223; Griffiths, "Antarctic Marine Biodiversity", 1.
13 Provant et al., "Reframing Antarctica's Ice Loss".
14 IPCC, "Summary for Policymakers", 6.
15 Lindsay and Schweiger, "Arctic Sea Ice Thickness"; IPCC, "Summary for Policymakers", 6.

For Indigenous Arctic residents who have always lived with sea ice, the ice is part of their home and links them to the sea. As Utqiagvik, Alaska resident Wesley Aiken explains, 'I refer to the sea ice as a beautiful garden. Much of our life depends on what our garden provides. I grew up hunting the marine mammals and this time of year (December) I especially enjoyed hunting for seals by setting nets under the ice. I used to go out with my dog team early in the morning and whatever I caught fed my family and the dogs.'[16] The way Arctic residents have interacted with sea ice helps to illustrate the fluidity of ocean–land boundaries and the way continental edges shift and flow (and floe). What is more, the framing of sea ice as home offers a crucial step to undo outsiders' stereotypes of the Arctic and the centuries of colonialism inflicted on Arctic peoples. As anthropologist Janne Flora explains, the Arctic 'is characterized by human activity rather than as one whole untouched and pristine realm'. The latter view, though common among Southerners, is dangerous, notes Flora, because it 'freeze-frames the region and the people who live there'.[17] This freezing of Arctic peoples as both victims of climate change and solely shaped by environmental conditions is deeply problematic, even if changing ice edges do influence residents profoundly.[18] To understand ocean–ice boundaries, then, it is crucial to put societies in their historical and present-day contexts, to consider sea ice and society as mutually constitutive, or assembled, and to recognize that southern narratives of the polar regions often contrast with the ways in which Arctic residents themselves live and interact with Arctic environments.[19]

Showing Arctic residents in their own communities and lives is what the *Siku-Inuit-Hila* (Sea Ice–People–Weather) Project, which ran actively from 2006 to 2010, has done. The project's goal was 'to better understand the dynamics of human–sea ice relationships in the Arctic – that is, how do the people who live with sea ice understand and use it?'[20] The project involved collaborations between researchers and local residents in the three Arctic communities of Qaanaaq (Greenland), Utqiagvik (Alaska), and Kangiptugaapik (Clyde River, Nunavut). In the book titled *The Meaning of Ice*, which resulted from the *Siku-Inuit-Hila* project, participants showed not only how people interact with the ice and their knowledge of it, but also what sea ice means to people

---

16 Gearheard et al., eds., *The Meaning of Ice*, xxxiii.   17 Flora, *Wandering Spirits*, viii.
18 Smith, "'Exceeding Beringia'"; Stuhl, *Unfreezing the Arctic*.
19 Antonello, *Greening of Antarctica*; Dodds and Nuttall, "Geo-assembling Narratives of Sustainability"; Sejersen, *Rethinking Greenland*; Huntington et al., "Climate Change in Context".
20 Gearheard et al., eds., *The Meaning of Ice*, 340.

who live with it. The book categorizes these deeper meanings and relationships into four main categories: home, food, travel, and tools/clothing.

People's physical connection and proximity to the ocean has continuity over time – with sea ice always crucial for life – but their relationship with the ice is constantly changing, both throughout the year and over the decades. At all times, though, sea ice links the ocean and the land; it connects people to places in the ocean and sites on land. In Kangiptugaapik, sea ice generally forms in November. The word for November is *Tusaqtuut*, which essentially means 'news time' because sea ice makes land out of water and facilitates travel, communication, and interaction with other communities along coastlines. As *The Meaning of Ice* explains, 'After months of open water and separation, one could finally hear the news of friends and family from recent months about travels, hunting, births, and deaths. *Tusaqtuut* was the beginning of the sea ice season and a whole new mode of living, traveling, and hunting.'[21] Whereas water divided people, ice united them. Sea ice shifts through seasons, lifting the people above and across the water during winter months – and in the process changing their ways of life at different times of year.

In recent decades, the thinning ice has made it unsafe to hunt, fish, travel, work, and live on the ice in certain regions. As fewer people travel and hunt, it changes their relationship with the sea, too. In one case around Qaanaaq, thinning sea ice in the late twentieth century hindered travel across the previously frozen ocean. Simultaneously, Canadian authorities started to restrict travel across the international border with Greenland. Together, shifting politics and shifting ice combined to limit Qaanaaq residents' access to traditional hunting areas by the early 2000s. Yet the annual shrinking of sea ice should not be considered homogeneously as a loss. After all, again quoting from *The Meaning of Ice*, 'sometimes, the meaning of sea ice is in its absence, as the boundary of open water and sea ice provides critical habitat for marine mammals and a prime hunting ground for local residents'.[22] Sea ice conditions clearly fluctuate not only seasonally but also over years and decades – and all of these changes have far-reaching impacts on Arctic communities.

Icebergs

The fluid linkages between ice and ocean are particularly apparent with icebergs. Icebergs are produced in a process called calving, when glaciers

---

21 Gearheard et al., eds., *The Meaning of Ice*, 16.
22 Gearheard et al., eds., *The Meaning of Ice*, 107.

that flow into the sea shed chunks of glacial ice that float away in the water. Because they calve from continental ice, icebergs are made of freshwater even though they spend their lives travelling in saltwater. Icebergs range in size and are categorized as small, medium, and large. Smaller icebergs fit into almost comical-sounding categories, with 'bergy bits' about the size of a house and 'growlers' only about as large as a grand piano.[23] The largest Antarctic icebergs can rival the size of small countries. Icebergs are enchantingly hazardous: one cannot be totally sure what their next move may be. Bergs break apart, flip, catch on the seafloor, ram into sea ice, and migrate great distances before falling apart – characteristics that make them dangerous to passing ships and tourists in kayaks. And because icebergs release nutrients as they travel through the ocean, their popularity is reflected in the rich biological community that congregates around them.

Most icebergs calve from the Antarctic continent, but icebergs also break from glaciers in the northern hemisphere, especially from Greenland. Icebergs move not only from land to sea but also from polar regions to temperate zones, such as Iceberg Alley off the coast of Newfoundland and Labrador. Yet icebergs travel not only through space, but also time. Icebergs consist of glacial ice that formed from snow buildup on the glacier's surface. Greenland's glacial ice, for example, is more than 100,000 years old, and Antarctica has ice millions of years in age.[24] Icebergs are floating time machines, transporting snow and air of all ages – from the Pleistocene to the Holocene and the Anthropocene. Icebergs link land and sea in additional ways, too, by transporting continental rocks and sediment from land surfaces to the seafloor. Bergs ferry this inland material, called ice-rafted debris (IRD), out to sea (Figure 29.2). As the berg melts, the IRD is left strewn across the bottom of the Atlantic Ocean. During the last Ice Age, Greenland discharged massive iceberg armadas that distributed IRD all the way to the Strait of Gibraltar.[25] Icebergs, then, link North America and Europe, they connect the polar regions to the temperate zones, they join the highest mountains of Greenland with the deepest parts of the Atlantic Ocean seafloor, and they unite the Ice Ages with present-day spectators. These characteristics have helped to turn iceberg tourism into big business from Alaska and Antarctica to Greenland, Norway, and Newfoundland.[26] As

---

23 "Iceberg", *National Geographic*, www.nationalgeographic.org/encyclopedia/iceberg/ (accessed 4 January 2018).
24 On ice cores and the age of Greenland ice, see Alley, *Two-Mile Time Machine*.
25 Bigg, *Icebergs*.
26 Bjørst and Ren, "Steaming Up"; Lam and Tegelberg, "Dark Tourism"; Leane and Maddison, "Biography of Iceberg B09B".

Figure 29.2 Ice-rafted debris embedded in icebergs recently calved from a Greenland ice sheet outlet glacier (Sermeq Kujalleq), which is in the background. (Photo by Mark Carey.)

journalist Joe O'Connor explains, guessing at the age of icebergs, 'It is the iceberg's size, length of journey, age (they are more than 10,000 years old), ever-shifting architecture and inevitable death ... that draws hundreds of thousands of vacationers to Newfoundland each summer to see them'.[27]

Just as tourists travel to the poles to gaze upon icebergs, the bergs have long travelled the world in art and the imagination.[28] Icebergs are present in nineteenth-century art and literature, appearing as characteristic landscapes that present an obstacle to manly conquests and colonial encounters. Artists such as Frederic Church, Edwin Landseer, and William Bradford, among many others, are well-known for their late nineteenth-century Arctic iceberg artworks, exhibited and sold globally.[29] In the twenty-first century, icebergs are quintessential symbols of global warming. Artists and scientists refer to them and invoke them frequently, such as in the Ice Watch exhibits that installed Greenland icebergs in downtown Europe. Artist Olafur Eliasson and geologist Minik Rosing produced these exhibits in Paris in 2014 and London in 2018, so visitors could touch, feel, see, and interact with melting Arctic ice.[30]

27 O'Connor, "Chasing Cold Cash".
28 Bjørst, "Tip of the Iceberg"; Little, "Seeing Icebergs"; Thrush, "Iceberg and Cathedral".
29 Potter, *Arctic Spectacles*.   30 Zarin, "The Artist". Also see https://icewatchlondon.com/.

In 2013, Greenlandic artist Inuk Silis Høegh covered the entire Great Hall of Canada's National Gallery in Ottawa with fifty-six painted panels that, when combined and draped entirely over the building, transformed the National Gallery into an iceberg. The panels were a composite of his father's photographs of actual icebergs. What's more, Høegh installed a soundtrack of iceberg crackling and lapping waves, so anyone near the exhibit could feel that they were interacting with an actual berg.[31]

Icebergs also cross boundaries through commodification, extraction, and consumption of the ice. Since the 1970s, companies have increasingly harvested, packaged, and shipped pieces of Arctic icebergs around the planet. Companies are now selling Iceberg Beer, Iceberg Vodka, and Svalbarði Polar Iceberg Water, among many other iceberg products produced from Canada and Greenland to Scandinavia. They allow people in places as far away as Dubai and New York to drink ancient Arctic precipitation. The companies market their iceberg beverages as pure, pre-industrial iceberg water. Iluliaq water from Greenland says in its marketing that its bottled water 'began as snow, falling from an ice age sky onto what is now the Greenland ice cap. There it remained preserved, untouched and pristine throughout the millennia'. Berg Water is available on amazon.com for just $195 for a twelve-pack. This iceberg water, they say in the product description, is 'harvested from 15,000 year old North Atlantic icebergs'. The slogan on Canada's Iceberg Beer bottle boasts that it is 'Made with pure 25,000 year old iceberg water', while Iceberg Vodka's label says it uses 'the purest water in the world, trapped in icebergs born 12,000 years ago: frozen, untouched, and pristine'.

The assumed purity of iceberg water neglects the ice-rafted debris they ferry out to sea, while the marketing of an empty wilderness erases Indigenous residents from the Arctic and freezes the region in an ancient space and time. Meanwhile, there seems to be a competition over the antiquity of the ice bottled in these beverages, where companies push the age of ice in their beverages back farther and farther in time. Yet the publicized age of ice going into these drinks is a fiction, a guess, a marketing ploy to convince drinkers they are consuming Ice Age 'purity'. Greenland's glacial ice ranges in age from a few decades to 120,000 years old. Dating it requires complex scientific studies that brewers do not even attempt. The precise dates they print on bottles are marketing, not measurements. Nevertheless, ice does move through time and space as the water is distributed globally – in a bottle, into the belly, and in the mind. Companies

---

[31] National Gallery of Canada, "Iceberg".

capitalize on the historical Western imagination of the Arctic as a supposedly pristine wilderness, exotic, the antithesis of civilization and industry, an ancient and empty place rather than an Inuit homeland where vibrant peoples have always lived with, on, and around ice. The marketing thus not only invents the age of icebergs, but also circulates and sells colonial narratives of the Arctic, where a pure, empty, and ancient polar region is the supposed antidote to the problems of European and US industrialization, much as the Arctic was invented for Westerners in the nineteenth century.[32]

There have also been even bigger plans to tap polar icebergs for their water, as entrepreneurs and engineers have for decades fantasized about towing Antarctic and Arctic bergs to distant regions like Australia and South Africa, California and the Middle East.[33] One early proposal came in 1949, when John Isaacs at Scripps Oceanographic Institution suggested they tow an iceberg 30 km in length from the Antarctic to San Diego to help resolve the city's water shortage.[34] The Cold War era further advanced engineering dreams as state leaders focused on the polar regions not only for geopolitical agendas but also for iceberg commodities.[35] The Western Australian Corporation got serious about harvesting Antarctic icebergs as early as 1965, and planning advanced into the 1970s to bring Antarctic water to Perth. RAND Corporation had bigger goals: researchers suggested in 1973 that Antarctic bergs could satisfy annual water needs for four to six billion people worldwide.[36] A few years later, Saudi Arabian Prince Mohammed Al-Faisal suggested that 'an Iceberg project is a better enterprise than oil', so he set up the Iceberg Transport Company to bring Antarctic icebergs to the Middle East.[37] The various schemes and dreams came together in 1977 at an iceberg utilization conference in Iowa, USA, an event sponsored by Prince Mohammed Al-Faisal and the US National Science Foundation. To showcase the tangible possibilities for iceberg transport, they even brought in a 1,133 kg iceberg from Alaska, what a local newspaper dubbed 'the most expensive ice cube in the world'.[38] The conference stimulated several (mostly unrealized) plans and efforts to utilize polar iceberg water far beyond the polar regions, with a notable emphasis on towing Antarctic icebergs to water-starved regions. Ultimately, the conference that built on decades of other

---

32 Bravo, *North Pole*; Wilson, *Spiritual History of Ice*.
33 Winter, "Towing an Iceberg"; Husseiny, ed., *Iceberg Utilization*; Madrigal, "Many Failures"; Ruiz, "Media Environments".
34 Ghosn, "A Flooded Thirsty World". 35 Morgan, "Dry Continent Dreaming".
36 Morgan, "Dry Continent Dreaming". 37 Ghosn, "A Flooded Thirsty World".
38 Newspaper quoted in Ruiz, "Saudi Dreams".

entrepreneurial and engineering fantasies for the frozen substance helped to solidify icebergs as a 'legitimate' natural resource – a resource that could be mined and tapped, mobilized and transported, marketed and consumed all over the world. As Rafico Ruiz explains, the conference 'signaled how state-sponsored institutions could begin to strategically project the emergence of polar resource frontiers'. After all, he concludes, 'the poles have always been the globe's future resource frontiers'.[39] Visions of iceberg towing and consumption illustrate the way governments and companies have historically seen the ocean–ice edge as a site of natural resource extraction through colonial and imperial processes.

Similar to the Beaufort Sea example described at the outset of this chapter, icebergs also generate regulatory and legal riddles as they move across oceans and in beverage containers. On the one hand, some view icebergs as part of the global commons, free for the taking once they float beyond state jurisdiction into international waters. On the other hand, the Newfoundland and Labrador government has regulated and taxed icebergs. In 2016, they imposed a $2,500–5,000 annual fee to harvest Arctic iceberg water along the provincial coast, plus requiring an initial $4,000 water licence.[40] Brewers protested mainly because of the significant financial impact on their small iceberg-tapping businesses, and argued that icebergs do not belong to Canada or Newfoundland because they come from the Arctic and float freely in the ocean. Eventually, the provincial government relented and, in 2018, sharply reduced – but did not eliminate – taxes and fees on iceberg water collection. Questions still linger about who owns icebergs, who can regulate icebergs as property, and where icebergs fall within international law. Do icebergs 'belong' to Greenland, or Antarctica, where they originate, or do they 'belong' to the countries where they end up along the coast?

When the boundaries between land and ocean are blurry and fluid, thorny questions emerge for resources like icebergs. These questions of ownership are not new and first emerged during the heyday of iceberg towing plans in the 1970s.[41] The growing debate around iceberg commodification and taxation – where icebergs are consumed and marketed globally – exists alongside the continued worry about drifting icebergs as a hazard to shipping, submarine infrastructure, and offshore oil platforms. The *Titanic* sank in 1912, but the International Ice Patrol still monitors the North Atlantic Ocean to track every iceberg drifting into the transatlantic shipping lanes south of 48 degrees north.

39 Ruiz, "Saudi Dreams".   40 Maher, "Newfoundland and Labrador Government".
41 Lundquist, "The Iceberg Cometh".

As icebergs separate from their glaciers on land and float out to sea, they can thus be a source of financial ruin for mariners or revenue for beverage companies. Whether bergs drift out of polar regions in ocean currents or are towed behind a fleet of barges, they transcend borders and disrupt boundaries – both real and imagined.

Glaciers and Ice Sheets

Like an extremely thick blanket placed over a bed of rock, the Antarctic ice sheet is the planet's largest ice form, which first materialized some 34 million years ago. Although often referred to as *the* Antarctic ice sheet, it is actually two large bodies of ice, one east and one west, which meet at the centre of the continent. In certain locations, the ice sheets have outlet glaciers that slip off the side of the continent, like streams of ice cream melting down the side of a cone. In other locations, ice sheets spread out from inland mounds toward the ocean, where floating ice shelves extend out into the sea.[42] Ice shelves function just as their name implies: they are thick blocks of ice that expand over the water like a dining room tabletop extends past its legs. Except this tabletop is massive – about 1.6 million km^2, in fact.[43] The Ross Ice Shelf, which stretches off the southeast portion of Antarctica, is alone about the size of Spain. Floating ice shelves are functionally important because they decelerate the movement of inland ice bound for the ocean. In recent decades, climate change has affected the ice sheet and its extending ice shelves, which are decreasing in mass, their meltwater adding to global sea level rise.[44] As the ice shelves melt, the relationship between land, ice, and sea changes – not only globally through sea level rise, but also regionally where ice meets ocean.[45]

Just as the histories of Arctic homelands, exploration, and commodification revolve around the ocean–ice edge, scientists in Antarctica are equally focused, and concerned, about the interaction between ocean and ice. As they extend over the Southern Ocean, ice shelves create a border between the salt water below and the atmosphere above, dividing the fish world from the bird world. Environmental historian Stephen Pyne noted that the

---

42 Joyner, *Antarctica and the Law*, 11, 14–15; Antonello, "Engaging and Narrating", 78–79, 88.
43 DeWeerdt, "Ocean Explorers".
44 Joyner, "Ice-Covered Regions", 225; Rignot, "Is Antarctica Melting?", 324–325, 328–329; Hand, "Polar Scientists", 1070.
45 Provant et al., "Reframing Antarctica's Ice Loss".

ice shelf naturally functions as a 'rampart' that 'segregates hydrosphere from atmosphere'.[46] With a warming ocean, Antarctic scientists – and their instruments – are increasingly attracted to the study of seawater *below* the icy ramparts. To penetrate the ice boundary between surface and seawater, however, is far more difficult than one might assume. Just within the past few decades, innovations in technological instruments have given scientists better access to the waters underneath the ice shelf. Automated underwater vehicles (AUVs), for example, plunge below the ice shelf and collect data as scientists remotely control the submarine's movements. Another approach uses moorings, which are pieces of equipment that scientists install directly onto the seafloor near the ice shelf. Moorings continually collect data over a longer period of time than AUVs, although the data are limited to the mooring's specific location. Scientists can also set up shop on top of the ice shelf and use hot water to bore down through the ice, a difficult drilling process considering that the ice shelves can be hundreds of metres thick. With the bore hole drilled, they can drop equipment into the seawater underneath the ice.

One of the most innovative approaches to accessing the water below the ice boundary, but by no means a new practice, is tagging equipment onto sea animals. As marine animals swim into the dark cavities below the ice shelves, their attached tags collect data about the subsurface water, such as its temperature, and send the information back to scientists' computers on land. Another place for studying ice shelves is in the sky, where planes and satellites provide a broad picture of the ice–ocean boundary. From high above, scientists can use gravity sensors to map the hidden seafloor, which affords a better understanding of water's movement below the ice shelves. Satellites routinely capture images of the ice shelves or employ an altimeter to gauge the ice's depth, which, when compared with previous years, can track the ice's advance or retreat.[47] Using these tools, scientists are discovering that the area below the ice shelf is a place of constant action, change, and in some regions significant ice loss.

As global climate change warms the Southern Ocean and pushes its circumpolar current closer to the ice shelves, scientists worry about the flow of seawater against the underside of Antarctica's ice. Of particular

---

46 Pyne, *The Ice*, 26, 118.
47 DeWeerdt, "Ocean Explorers"; Hand, "Polar Scientists". On the historical manipulation of animals in polar history, see Roberts and Jørgensen, "Animals as Instruments".

interest are the deep watery crevasses that stand between the ice shelf and the seafloor, called 'cavities'.[48] Saltwater continually flows below the ice shelves and into these cavities, sloshing up against the underside and causing a normal amount of glacier melt. But warming seawater is redefining what is normal. This accelerated process of under-the-ice ablation, what scientists call basal melting, could eventually contribute to global sea level rise. Scientists fear that weakened ice shelves will open the floodgates for glacial ice to escape from the continent and rush unabated into the sea. And as Antarctica's continental ice melts into the sea, it pushes more water into the ocean's basins. Ultimately, rising sea levels threaten coastal populations that live along the rims.[49] The weakening of Antarctica's ocean–ice boundary not only affects the Southern Ocean; its consequences are reaching communities the world over, from Miami to Bangkok. Tracking the changing boundary between air, ice, and ocean around the Antarctic continent provides a critical key to understanding the global effects of climate change.

Yet it is not only scientists who are attracted to Antarctica's ocean–ice edge. Once perceived as a wilderness isolated from human populations, Antarctica is now increasingly understood as a place rich with human history and even a site for ethnographic studies.[50] In his 1986 book, *The Ice*, Pyne narrated Antarctica's ice–ocean interface where sea ice and glacial ice meet the ocean as a 'solid-phase boundary', and 'an esthetic no less than a geographic border'.[51] But this edge is not just a barrier. Nowadays, as in the past, it is precisely this boundary between ocean and ice where human activity in Antarctica has concentrated, including whaling, fishing, and exploration.[52] In the twenty-first century, tourists by the tens of thousands increasingly flock to the ever-changing ice edges to snap photographs of penguins gathering on sea ice, to kayak where glaciers plunge into the sea, and to track icebergs for citizen science, recreation, and even national heritage.[53] What's more, the zone where ocean meets ice is also a crucial site for Antarctic conservation policies, given the rich biological diversity where oceans and ice meet. Yet the ocean–ice edge fluctuates through the

---

48 Thompson et al., "The Sleeping Giant", 9, 13, 15.
49 Rignot et al., "Ice-Shelf Melting", 266, 270; Kimura et al., "Ocean Mixing", 8496; Hand, "Polar Scientists", 1071; DeWeerdt, "Ocean Explorers".
50 Antonello, "Engaging and Narrating"; Howkins, *Frozen Empires*; O'Reilly, *The Technocratic Antarctic*.
51 Pyne, *The Ice*, 26, 56.
52 Avango, "Working Geopolitics"; Provant et al., "Reframing Antarctica's Ice Loss".
53 Leane and Maddison, "Biography of Iceberg B09B".

seasons and over decades, just as human trends in Antarctic tourism, conservation agendas, and scientific research practices change over time, too. Clearly, Antarctica is not only a scientific laboratory and driver of distant sea level rise, but also a place where people interact with the ice.

On the other side of the globe, the flow of Greenland's ice sheet toward the sea has created an entirely different kind of concern about ice–ocean linkages: the transit of toxic, thawing remains at Camp Century toward the ocean. Camp Century was a not-so-secret US military base built in 1959 on Greenland's ice sheet, approximately 200 km inland from the coast at an elevation of 1,886 m above sea level. Camp Century was no ordinary base but rather a 'city under the ice'.[54] The military built the camp 1–30 m below the surface of the ice sheet. It accommodated hundreds of soldiers, engineers, and cold-regions scientists, who actually extracted the first polar ice core from surface to bedrock. A small nuclear reactor imported from the United States powered Camp Century, with all its apartments and kitchens, a barber shop and chapel, hospital and recreation centre, and the Research and Development wing where the ice corers drilled into hundred-thousand-year-old glacial ice. Adjacent to the 300 m long 'Main Street' engineers carved a large warehouse into the ice sheet to store weapons, diesel fuel, ploughs, Weasels (tracked vehicles), and everything else it took to run a hidden city below the ice sheet's surface. But from the outset, military personnel and designers failed to understand a key feature of the ice: it moves, and quickly. They started abandoning Camp Century in 1963 because of collapsing tunnels and its overall instability, not to mention the advent of long-range missiles making the site less urgent for US national security. The military had completely deserted Camp Century by 1967.

Unfortunately, they did not clean up their mess – a mess that now threatens humanity because the glacial site is sliding toward the ocean and, more importantly, because the toxic debris left behind could leak into the ice sheet and flow into the sea. Back in the 1960s, Camp Century managers left strewn in the ice huge quantities of garbage, fuel, equipment, construction materials, railways, and everything else the army decided was too expensive to remove. More alarming, they left radioactive waste from coolant for the nuclear reactor, as well as diesel fuel and hazardous chemicals such as polychlorinated biphenyls (PCBs). They also left the biological waste, including sewage and grey water.[55] Now scientists worry that this dangerous dump

---

54 For a history of Camp Century, see Nielsen and Nielsen, *Camp Century*.
55 Colgan et al., "Abandoned Ice Sheet Base".

of toxic debris embedded near the surface of the melting ice sheet is making its way to the ocean, where contaminants will directly affect people and ecosystems around the planet. The debris field at Camp Century is more connected to the ocean than anyone had imagined a half-century ago – even if it is 200 km from and nearly 2,000 m above the ocean.

Camp Century debris is moving toward the ocean through a variety of processes. For one, the ice itself flows toward the edges of Greenland, where outlet glaciers feed ice into fjords surrounding the island. Between 1959 and 2017, the Camp Century site moved approximately 232 m to the west-southwest.[56] Gravity naturally pulls the continental ice from higher to lower elevations and out toward the sea. But in the twenty-first century, atmospheric forces are thawing out Camp Century even faster. Global climate change has reduced the snowpack atop the ice sheet, causing increased surface melting and the overall thinning of Greenland's ice.[57] Experts now worry that this melting could expose the dangerous contaminants left at Camp Century in a matter of decades, probably by the end of this century. Most of the debris is only about 32 m below the surface of the ice sheet. Once exposed, the toxic remnants will act like sediment in a mountain water system, travelling across the ice sheet's topography through streams and rivers that dive into canyons and eventually into moulins, the chute-like cavernous tunnels that bore down through the ice sheet to bedrock. In recent years, scientists have come to understand just how significant these moulins are, not only for transporting water to the base of the ice sheet and then out to sea, but also for lubricating the underside of the ice so it slides toward the ocean even faster.[58] In essence, surface melting of the ice sheet will make the Camp Century contaminants mobile. They will integrate into the vast network of water channels that join the centre of the ice sheet with the sea. The frozen inland areas high on the ice sheet are thus intimately linked to marine ecosystems and human communities along Greenland's coast. Camp Century's flow to the ocean is also an international matter that involves the United States, Denmark, and Greenland, with implications for the planet if radioactive coolant and PCBs reach the ocean's conveyer belt of currents. The scientists studying this toxic debris suggest that 'While Camp Century and four other contemporaneous ice sheet bases were legally established under a Danish-U.S. treaty, the potential remobilization of their abandoned wastes, previously regarded as sequestered, represents an entirely new

---

56 Karlsson et al., "Ice-Penetrating Radar Survey".
57 Colgan et al., "Abandoned Ice Sheet Base".   58 Covington et al., "Moulin Volumes".

pathway of political dispute resulting from climate change.'[59] They suggest that ice change, atmospheric change, and water flows that link the ocean and the ice are already generating political disputes that could worsen over time.

Camp Century is a clear case of intergenerational injustice playing out over decades and centuries, where geopolitics and the US military intersect with slow-moving linkages between ice and ocean. Greenlanders have already suffered from the US presence at Camp Century and the nearby Thule Air Base on the coast. The poet Aqqaluk Lynge explains that US soldiers and ships arrived at Thule and trampled on the graves of the Inughuit. They built military bases and airfields that have – and will continue – to damage Greenlanders. As Lynge concludes:

> From her grave the radar may be glimpsed
> looking out over all the
> Inuit-homeland, half of the earth
> In Qaanaaq, the new Thule, dogs howl
> something is happening
> Is darkness about to descend
> over our country?[60]

It now seems that Camp Century and its wretched chemical debris field is part of that darkness to come.

Conclusion

Studying human relationships with sea ice, icebergs, and glaciers helps to illustrate how the ocean–ice edge is a dynamic boundary that has not only shaped human history, but also reveals how people have valued, studied, imagined, commodified, and politicized this ever-changing border. The ocean–ice interface is mutually constituted as much by biological and geophysical processes as by human history. The edges of continents, the borders of nations, and the boundaries between land and sea are not nearly as fixed and permanent as many imagine – whether the architects of the 1825 treaty for the Beaufort Sea or government authorities collecting taxes on the harvesting of Greenland icebergs. What's more, the ocean–ice edge has human life; it is not simply a geographical or material space, but one produced through time and by multiple social groups. We must unfreeze polar history, to show, in the words of historian Michael Bravo, that these frozen sites 'have a fantastic capacity to be lively and life-giving, holding within them a sense of home,

---

59 Colgan et al., "Abandoned Ice Sheet Base".   60 Lynge, *Veins of the Heart*, 118.

mobility, and temporality stretching from the abrupt change of seasons to organic processes on timescales of centuries and millennia'.[61]

By offering examples of intertwined histories of human and more-than-human forces at the ocean–ice edge, this chapter raises a host of questions about changing ocean–ice dynamics now, in the past, and in the future. Moving forward, we must think about who affects and is affected by the status of the ocean–ice boundary, whose story circulates most widely, and who gets to dominate the decision-making. Local residents in Greenland, for example, have little control over the climate or melting ice that alters their hunting practices or threatens to bring Camp Century's toxic contaminants to their communities and food sources. Again referring to Bravo, then, we must think about cryopolitics in the polar regions – how inequality can unfold at the ocean–ice boundary, whether through political disputes, hunting practices, tourism, or iceberg beverages consumed 6,000 km away from the Arctic. The stark environmental changes that now envelop the Arctic and Antarctic should not define their histories, although historians cannot overlook the significant loss of ice and biodiversity. The mobility, mutability, and temporality of the ocean–ice edge has often complicated society's larger plans to depend upon or organize it, and will continue to do so at increasing rates in the years to come.

Bibliography

Alley, Richard B., *The Two-Mile Time Machine: Ice Cores, Abrupt Climate Change, and Our Future* (Princeton: Princeton University Press, 2000).

Antonello, Alessandro, "Engaging and Narrating the Antarctic Ice Sheet: The History of an Earthly Body", *Environmental History* 22 (2017): 77–100.

Antonello, Alessandro, *The Greening of Antarctica: Assembling an International Environment* (New York: Oxford University Press, 2019).

Avango, Dag, "Working Geopolitics: Sealing, Whaling, and Industrialized Antarctica", in Klaus Dodds, Alan D. Hemmings, and Peder Roberts, eds., *Handbook on the Politics of Antarctica* (Northampton, MA: Edward Elgar, 2017), pp. 485–504.

Baker, James S., and Michael Byers, "Crossed Lines: The Curious Case of the Beaufort Sea Maritime Boundary Dispute", *Ocean Development & International Law* 43 (2012): 70–95.

Bigg, Grant R., *Icebergs: Their Science and Links to Global Change* (New York: Cambridge University Press, 2016).

Bjørst, Lill Rastad, "The Tip of the Iceberg: Ice as a Non-Human Actor in the Climate Change Debate", *Études/Inuit/Studies* 34 (2010): 133–150.

---

[61] Bravo, "A Cryopolitics", 33. Also see Cruikshank, *Do Glaciers Listen?*; Stuhl, *Unfreezing the Arctic*.

Bjørst, Lill Rastad, and Carina Ren, "Steaming Up or Staying Cool? Tourism Development and Greenlandic Futures in the Light of Climate Change", *Arctic Anthropology* 52 (2015): 91–101.

Bravo, Michael, "A Cryopolitics to Reclaim Our Frozen Material States", in Joanna Radin and Emma Kowal, eds., *Cryopolitics: Frozen Life in a Melting World* (Cambridge, MA: MIT Press, 2017), pp. 27–58.

Bravo, Michael, *North Pole: Nature and Culture* (London: Reaktion, 2019).

Carey, Mark, "The History of Ice: How Glaciers Became an Endangered Species", *Environmental History* 12 (2007): 497–527.

Colgan, William, Horst Machguth, Mike MacFerrin, et al., "The Abandoned Ice Sheet Base at Camp Century, Greenland, in a Warming Climate", *Geophysical Research Letters* 43 (2016): 8091–8096.

Covington, M. D., J. D. Gulley, C. Trunz, J. Mejia, and W. Gadd, "Moulin Volumes Regulate Subglacial Water Pressure on the Greenland Ice Sheet", *Geophysical Research Letters* 47 (2020): e2020GL088901.

Cruikshank, Julie, *Do Glaciers Listen? Local Knowledge, Colonial Encounters, and Social Imagination* (Vancouver: University of British Columbia Press, 2005).

DeWeerdt, Sarah, "Ocean Explorers Delve Beneath the Ice", *Nature* 575 (2019): S2–S5.

Dodds, Klaus, *Ice: Nature and Culture* (London: Reaktion, 2018).

Dodds, Klaus, and Mark Nuttall, "Geo-assembling Narratives of Sustainability in Greenland", in Ulrik Gad and Jeppe Strandsbjerg, eds., *The Politics of Sustainability in the Arctic: Reconfiguring Identity, Time, and Space* (London: Routledge, 2018), pp. 1–22.

Flora, Janne, *Wandering Spirits: Loneliness and Longing in Greenland* (Chicago: University of Chicago Press, 2019).

Frey, Karen E., G. W. K. Moore, Lee W. Cooper, and Jacqueline M. Grebmeier, "Divergent Patters of Recent Sea Ice Cover Across the Bering, Chukchi, and Beaufort Seas of the Pacific Arctic Region", *Progress in Oceanography* 136 (2015): 32–49.

Gearheard, Shari Fox, Lene Kielsen Holm, Henry Huntington, et al., eds., *The Meaning of Ice: People and Sea Ice in Three Arctic Communities* (Hanover, NH: International Polar Institute Press, 2013).

Ghosn, Rania, "A Flooded Thirsty World", *Journal of Architectural Education* 74 (2020): 60–69.

Griffiths, Huw J., "Antarctic Marine Biodiversity: What Do We Know About the Distribution of Life in Southern Ocean?", *PLoS One* 5 (August 2010): 1–11.

Griffiths, Tom, *Slicing the Silence: Voyaging to Antarctica* (Sydney: UNSW Press, 2007).

Hand, Eric, "Polar Scientists to Peer Beneath Largest Ice Shelf", *Science Magazine* 348 (5 June 2015): 1070–1071.

Hastrup, Kirsten, "A History of Climate Change: Inughuit Responses to Changing Ice Conditions in North-West Greenland", *Climatic Change* 151 (2018): 67–78.

Hastrup, Kirsten, "The Ice as Argument: Topographical Mementos in the High Arctic", *Cambridge Anthropology* 31 (2013): 51–67.

Howkins, Adrian, *Frozen Empires: An Environmental History of the Antarctic Peninsula* (New York: Oxford University Press, 2016).

Howkins, Adrian, *The Polar Regions: An Environmental History* (Cambridge: Polity, 2016).

Huntington, Henry P., Mark Carey, Charlene Apok, et al., "Climate Change in Context: Putting People First in the Arctic", *Regional Environmental Change* 19 (2019): 1217–1223.

Husseiny, A. A., ed., *Iceberg Utilization: Proceedings of the First International Conference and Workshops on Iceberg Utilization for Fresh Water Production, Weather Modification and Other Applications Held at Iowa State University, Ames, Iowa, USA, October 2–6, 1977* (New York: Pergamon, 1978).

IPCC, "Summary for Policymakers", in H. O. Pörtner et al., eds., *IPCC Special Report on the Ocean and Cryosphere in a Changing Climate* (Geneva: Intergovernmental Panel on Climate Change, 2019).

Joyner, Christopher C., *Antarctica and the Law of the Sea* (Dordrecht: Martinus Nijhoff, 1992).

Joyner, Christopher C., "Ice-Covered Regions in International Law", *Natural Resources Journal* 31 (Winter 1991): 213–242.

Karlsson, Nanna B., William Colgan, Daniel Binder, et al., "Ice-Penetrating Radar Survey of the Subsurface Debris Field at Camp Century, Greenland", *Cold Regions Science and Technology* 165 (2019): 1–13.

Kimura, Satoshi, Adrian Jenkins, Pierre Dutrieux, et al., "Ocean Mixing Beneath Pine Island Glacier Ice Shelf, West Antarctica", *Journal of Geophysical Research: Oceans* 121 (2016): 8496–8510.

Krupnik, Igor, Claudio Aporta, Shari Gearheard, Gita J. Laidler, and Lene Kielsen Holm, eds., *Siku: Knowing Our Ice. Documenting Inuit Sea-Ice Knowledge and Use* (New York: Springer, 2010).

Lam, Anita, and Matthew Tegelberg, "Dark Tourism in Iceberg Alley: The Hidden Ecological Costs of Consuming Iceberg Deaths", in Anita Lam and Matthew Tegelberg, eds., *Criminal Anthropocenes: Media and Crime in the Vanishing Arctic* (Cham: Palgrave, 2020), pp. 145–186.

Leane, Elizabeth, and Ben Maddison, "A Biography of Iceberg B09B", *Australian Humanities Review* 63 (2018): 99–115.

Lindsay, R., and A. Schweiger, "Arctic Sea Ice Thickness Loss Determined Using Subsurface, Aircraft, and Satellite Observations", *The Cryosphere* 9 (2015): 269–283.

Little, J. I., "Seeing Icebergs and Inuit as Elemental Nature: An American Transcendentalist On and Off the Coast of Labrador, 1864", *Histoire Sociale/Social History* 49 (2016): 243–262.

Lundquist, Thomas R., "The Iceberg Cometh? International Law Relating to Antarctic Iceberg Exploitation", *Natural Resources Journal* 17 (1977): 1–41.

Lynge, Aqqaluk, *The Veins of the Heart to the Pinnacle of the Mind* (Montreal: International Polar Institute, 2008).

Madrigal, Alexis C., "The Many Failures and Few Successes of Zany Iceberg Towing Schemes", *The Atlantic* (10 August 2011), www.theatlantic.com/technology/archive/2011/08/the-many-failures-and-few-successes-of-zany-iceberg-towing-schemes/243364/ (accessed 9 June 2017).

Maher, David, "Newfoundland and Labrador Government Thaws Iceberg Tax", *Saltwire Network* (16 August 2018), www.saltwire.com/news/local/newfoundland-and-labrador-government-thaws-iceberg-tax-234191/ (accessed 23 January 2021).

Morgan, Ruth A., "Dry Continent Dreaming: Australian Visions of Using Antarctic Icebergs for Water Supplies", *International Review of Environmental History* 4 (2018): 145–166.

National Gallery of Canada, "An Iceberg in the Heart of Ottawa", *National Gallery of Canada* (19 June 2013), www.gallery.ca/for-professionals/media/press-releases/an-iceberg-in-the-heart-of-ottawa (accessed 27 January 2021).

Nielsen, Kristian H., and Henry Nielsen, *Camp Century: The Untold Story of America's Secret Arctic Military Base Under the Greenland Ice* (New York: Columbia University Press, 2021).

O'Connor, Joe, "Chasing Cold Cash: How Icebergs Became the Field of Dreams for Believers and Schemers", *Financial Post* (21 March 2019), https://financialpost.com/entrepreneur/chasing-cold-cash-how-icebergs-became-the-field-of-dreams-for-believers-and-schemers (accessed 22 January 2021).

O'Reilly, Jessica, *The Technocratic Antarctic: An Ethnography of Scientific Expertise and Environmental Governance* (Ithaca, NY: Cornell University Press, 2017).

Potter, Russell A., *Arctic Spectacles: The Frozen North in Visual Culture, 1818–1875* (Seattle: University of Washington Press, 2007).

Provant, Zachary, Evan Elderbrock, Andrea Willingham, et al., "Reframing Antarctica's Ice Loss: Impacts of Cryospheric Change on Local Human Activity", *Polar Record* 57 (2021): 1–11.

Pyne, Stephen J., *The Ice: A Journey to Antarctica* (Iowa City: University of Iowa Press, 1986).

Rignot, Eric, "Is Antarctica Melting?", *WIREs Climate Change* 2 (May–June 2011): 324–331.

Rignot, E., S. Jacobs, J. Mouginot, and B. Scheuchl, "Ice-Shelf Melting Around Antarctica", *Science* 341 (19 July 2013): 266–270.

Roberts, Peder, and Dolly Jørgensen, "Animals as Instruments of Norwegian Imperial Authority in the Interwar Arctic", *Journal for the History of Environment and Society* 1 (2016): 65–87.

Ruiz, Rafico, "Media Environments: Icebergs/Screens/History", *Journal of Northern Studies* 9 (2015): 33–50.

Ruiz, Rafico, "Saudi Dreams: Icebergs in Iowa", *Arcadia (Environment & Society Portal, Rachel Carson Center for Environment and Society)* 19 (2017), https://doi.org/10.5282/rcc/7900.

Sejersen, Frank, *Rethinking Greenland and the Arctic in the Era of Climate Change* (New York: Routledge, 2015).

Shake, Kristen L., Karen E. Frey, Deborah G. Martin, and Philip E. Steinberg, "(Un)frozen Spaces: Exploring the Role of Sea Ice in the Marine Socio-Legal Spaces of the Bering and Beaufort Seas", *Journal of Borderlands Studies* 22 (2017): 1–15.

Smith, Jen Rose, "'Exceeding Beringia': Upending Universal Human Events and Wayward Transits in Arctic Spaces", *Environment and Planning D: Society and Space* (2020), https://doi.org/10.1177/0263775820950745.

Sörlin, Sverker, "Cryo-history: Narratives of Ice and the Emerging Arctic Humanities", in Birgitta Evengård, Joan Nymand Larsen, and Øyvind Paasche, eds., *The New Arctic* (New York: Springer, 2015), pp. 327–339.

Steinberg, Philip, and Berit Kristoffersen, "'The Ice Edge Is Lost ... Nature Moved It': Mapping Ice as State Practice in the Canadian and Norwegian North", *Transactions of the Institute of British Geographers* 42 (2017): 625–641.

Stuhl, Andrew, *Unfreezing the Arctic: Science, Colonialism, and the Transformation of Inuit Lands* (Chicago: University of Chicago Press, 2016).

Thompson, Andrew, Josh Willis, and Anthony Payne, "The Sleeping Giant: Measuring Ocean–Ice Interactions in Antarctica", unpublished technical report (Pasadena, CA: Keck Institute for Space Studies, December 2015).

Thrush, Coll, "The Iceberg and the Cathedral: Encounter, Entanglement, and Isuma in Inuit London", *Journal of British Studies* 53 (2014): 59–79.

Wilson, Eric G., *The Spiritual History of Ice: Romanticism, Science, and the Imagination* (New York: Palgrave Macmillan, 2003).

Winter, Caroline, "Towing an Iceberg: One Captain's Plan to Bring Drinking Water to 4 Million People", *Bloomberg Businessweek* (5 June 2019), www.bloomberg.com/news/features/2019-06-06/towing-an-iceberg-one-captain-s-plan-to-bring-drinking-water-to-4-million-people (accessed 23 January 2021).

Zarin, Cynthia, "The Artist Who Is Bringing Icebergs to Paris", *The New Yorker* (5 December 2015), www.newyorker.com/culture/culture-desk/the-artist-who-is-bringing-icebergs-to-paris (accessed 29 December 2016).

30

Re-storying from Within: Renewing Relationships Beyond the Shadows of Polar History

JACKIE PRICE, REBECCA MEARNS, AND EMILIE CAMERON

Introduction

At first appearance, asking individuals from and connected to Nunavut, an eastern Arctic jurisdiction of Canada, to contribute to a collection of polar history would seem to be a practical and straightforward request, both for the reader and for the contributors themselves. Yet, as is often the case, the reality of things is not as simple as it first appears.

As most readers are probably aware, many scholars and self-identified experts of polar history do not necessarily live in the polar regions. This is the case for Nunavut. While the contributors to this chapter are well-aware of the extensive expertise, knowledge, skills, generosity of spirit, and critical thinking that exists year-round in the communities that populate Nunavut, this knowledge has not yet found a home in the broader discipline of polar history. Although this community knowledge and experience is present in the disciplines that polar history draws from – anthropology, geography, history, and natural sciences – it is present at different intensities and consistencies.

The space afforded to Arctic communities, specifically their knowledge and experience, becomes more constricted when approached through the lens of the 'polar', which of course includes Antarctica, as in this collection. While ideas of cold, snow, and ice are associated with both regions, and while both regions are subject to intense interest in science and the governance of that science, this is where the similarities abruptly end.

This is only one of many reasons why our entry into this chapter was not straightforward. Although we were able to engage in big conversations where we discussed the weight of polar history and its legacy, pinpointing how we might begin a constructive conversation that focused on developing relationships and creating opportunities instead of creating a bigger gap between ourselves and the discipline proved tricky. Our collective conversations recognized that polar history is more than a retelling of events that are said to have occurred in a cold climate; polar history has shaped much of what is known and understood about the social and physical realities of the polar regions. The different threads of these legacies have been tied together, knotted. What we, as contributors, experienced as knotted was how to tell our story, the way, the method. We understood that even in a small way, our chapter provided us with an opportunity to engage in a different pattern of talking about the north. To do this, we did have to methodically untie our expectations from the expectations of different disciplines, in order for us to write something that reflected the ideas, feelings, and experiences we wanted to share.

This chapter represents one expression of a collective conversation between three women who are friends, and who have each explored life in the north in different ways. While each author has considered these matters in their own way, we each have continually argued for the importance of having these conversations closer to 'home' – wherever that home is, be it the land, the settlement, or the city. Each author understands that what makes home a home is the range of relationships that are held, nurtured, and honoured. The circumpolar, the north, is made up of many networks like this, and offers such diversity, humour, challenges, and love. The authors decided to come together to share these types of stories to broaden how history is told about the north – and to be told for the north.

The conversations that informed this chapter took part over multiple media and over a long period of time. Early on, the decision was made to have this contribution be a group contribution, to mitigate that practice of having an individual be deemed an expert. And none of us wanted to be alone in writing about life in the north from the north. This concern was exaggerated by the concern of being the lone Indigenous contribution. Having engaging conversation seemed like a good idea, and good fun.

Many discussions occurred via email and text, sometimes between two contributors but more often including all three contributors. As Rebecca and Jackie worked in the same location, they were able to engage in casual conversations throughout their time as contributors. We as a trio met through phone calls, or via an online phone app, four times. The first two calls provided an opportunity to meet, catch up, and begin exploring this idea of polar history. A written summary followed up our third call, and a recording and transcript was completed for call four.

The 'within' alluded to in the title of this chapter speaks to a range of landscapes: within the polar, as our collective and individual contributions speak to our dynamics working with and within Nunavut, Canada; within our different communities, be they scholarly, Indigenous, non-Indigenous or actual communities, and all the ways these communities engage, disengage, and imagine; and finally, within ourselves as persons, as human beings. Perhaps it is within this specific 'within' that we see the radical site, the site in which the possibility for adding to the trajectory of how polar history is seen, told, understood, and explored can grow, expand, and encompass a fuller range of experiences and storytelling. This is our hope at least, and this chapter represents one contribution towards that goal.

Notes on this Contribution

There are three notes the authors wish to share. First, both the individual stories shared within this chapter, and the broader story all the voices share, represent the individual contributions of the three authors. The authors share their stories to enlighten readers about the specific experience each author wishes to share. In no way are these experiences being shared to express a broader or singular narrative to be addressed to a specific community, be it Inuit, Indigenous, woman, northern, Canadian, academic. All the authors have their own stories of working within and beyond a single narrative, and do not wish to perpetuate that practice within their own writing. Please enjoy these stories, as they are meant to educate and add to a broader discussion! But also be aware that these points are not the only points to be made.

Second, while our discussions did range across the circumpolar, and sometimes Antarctica, for the majority of this work we focus on Nunavut as north. We recognize that while Nunavut is connected to other northern regions in North America, and across the circumpolar, experiences outside Nunavut are likely to be both similar to and different from what we discuss specifically. While this is the case, we hope that the experiences we share do resonate with those who live in other northern regions. We use 'north' and 'Arctic' interchangeably.

Finally, this chapter will probably not read in the way readers may anticipate a contribution from the north on polar history should be written. As will be explained in the following sections, this contribution is about the north and life in the north. You, the reader, are asked to trust our intent to provide a northern-based contribution to this polar collection. We explore how we experience life in the north; our goal is to share experiences, share our reflections on them, and interrogate the lessons we have gained as a means to illuminate the paths we have taken that have led us to this very experience. In doing this, we are remaining true to our intent, to tell our story in our own way. Telling our story in our way allows us to highlight what is missing, sometimes often, sometimes not, when northerners read polar history: a sense of the vitality of life lived in the north. As the experiences shared in this contribution have already happened, we appreciate that they have happened in the recent past, and the longevity of this past will be determined by when you the reader, read this.

(Polar) History: Sort of Interrupted

In his PhD dissertation "Eskimo Underground: Socio-cultural Change in the Canadian Central Arctic" (1974), Robert Williamson provides a comprehensive and engaging historical overview of the Kivalliq Region in what is now known as Nunavut. His work largely focuses on Rankin Inlet, but other neighbouring communities are also discussed. This thorough work explores the changes with a methodology that is now considered general practice in most academic and literary work about Nunavut and the Inuit experience specifically. It explores the pre-historical aspects of Inuit life at pre-contact, or little contact,[1] that is, limited contact with the outside world and non-Inuit generally, and with Qallunaaq, or the White person, more specifically. He then discusses contact, and then sustained contact,[2] and how these two types of contact changed Inuit

---

[1] Regarding the pre-contact period, Williamson offers significant insight into things such as "The Non-material Culture", including "Concepts of the Soul", "Seniority", and "Respect", but also great insight into "Social Structure and Social Control" and "Socialization and Marriage", both sections offering a wide range of topic-specific discussions such as "The Extended Family", "Ridicule", "Concept of Human Purpose", and "Authority of Grandparents".

[2] In the section titled "The Incursions", Williamson explores the waves of visitors who travelled north, again following a true-to-experience flow of whalers, fur traders, missionaries, and health services. From this general overview, Williamson then moves on to experiences specific to the communities of the Kivalliq Region, providing helpful insights into the development of specific communities, and former trading posts. These histories serve as the foundation for the very settlements that current and future generations of Inuit grow up in and call home – different from the Inuit experience being shared and witnessed by Williamson himself. The introduction and establishment of government, and the formalization of industry and commerce, round off the changes experienced in Rankin Inlet and the Kivalliq Region generally. These changes all lead up to an important examination of how these new forces bring with them new ideas, and more specifically, new ideas about social relations and family trends, which Williamson does with great honesty and respect.

and northern life.[3] Williamson writes with both clarity and certainty. In reading his words, you sense that the reader is benefiting from a respectful, wide-ranging insight into life as experienced by Inuit.

Williamson's PhD is essential reading for anyone interested in understanding the recent history of Nunavut. It allows readers to begin to appreciate the broader narrative of change in the northern, polar, or circumpolar, region. Polar history is a specialized discipline, one that is informed by research completed over the past 100 years. The research completed in this time includes exploration notes/travel narratives, anthropological studies, and a variety of baseline studies looking to establish information on a wide range of topics, including wildlife or economic indicators. More recently, polar history has opened up to include Indigenous oral histories. This information is abundantly available about the north, and covers a relatively short period of time while also covering an impressive range of change and adaptation.

While all contributors appreciate Williamson's contribution to the broader narrative of Nunavut as north and therefore as polar history, it was Jackie specifically who was particularly moved by this book. Jackie first came across Williamson's work while studying at the Scott Polar Research Institute at the University of Cambridge. In her own work she was exploring the history of the settlement – the pace of change in not only the lived experience of Inuit, but also the imagined narrative of change for Inuit. Having grown up in Rankin Inlet herself, though her Inuit familial roots did not come from that community or region, she found that Williamson's book provided her with a wealth of understanding, appreciation and at times, awe. While she understood and appreciated the changes experienced in her community and territory, there is something to be said for looking at such information from so far away from home, as if seeing it with new eyes. It was a feeling that both Rebecca and Emilie appreciated and understood in different, but similar ways.

What was most notable about Williamson's book was its content: the information it shared; the overview of life lived as that life was being changed

---

3 The final section of this book further examines the impact all this change has on Inuit life, exploring topics such as "The Social Protection Response", the "Problem of Language", "Social Shock and Truncation", "Common Human Desires", and finally, the "Non-community". These topics offer readers an appreciation of how significantly this new way of life and being altered the social structure of the community in which Inuit found themselves, and the efforts, challenges, and tensions that Inuit themselves were grappling with in real time, finding new solutions, and getting caught in entanglements of differences and, at times, oppositional principles and responsibilities.

as it was being lived. While this book is now considered historical, at the time that it was written Williamson was writing about contemporary life. In fact, the timeframe between Williamson's arrival in the north and the publication of his book was approximately ten years. This point is both significant, and not. It is significant because it was a period of time when great changes were occurring. Movement into centralized, sedentary life from life lived on the land, where life engages with the rhythm of Sila (or the land, weather, universe) resulted in foundational change in all aspects of Inuit collective and individual life. At this time, spirituality, health, governance, skill development, and intergenerational relations were all shifting – the very foundations that ensured Inuit did more than merely survive in the polar regions, but were fully alive: to thrive, create, imagine, feel, and overcome additional intensities in an already intense environment. This change was seismic, and those present during this transition witnessed these changes, and their implications, in real time. Being present, both physically and critically, to that change is what allows people today, be they Indigenous, northerners, or those from away, to learn about this change (as suggested by Jackie's experience in encountering this text while studying). The changes that Williamson documented in Rankin Inlet are not significant, however, in that the change being witnessed was happening throughout the northern region, and all Inuit in this region at that time were being exposed to these changes. And the truth is, even after this book was written, life continued to change for Inuit. Our point is that history is *lived* ... this truth is not always apparent in written histories of the polar regions.

While the content of Williamson's book has stood the test of time, in the opinion of the contributors, what has started showing its age is the conceptualization of time, history, and periodization used by him (and by others before him) and reproduced since then. The practice of examining Inuit life on a continuum of pre-contact, contact, and post-contact is largely the standard in how life in the north is explored and understood. Although the contributors appreciate that this framework does have a place in how research is conducted by a wide range of scholars, it is necessary to understand this approach to understanding Inuit life within a specific context: when research was being conducted by those new to the north, who were from outside the north, and who were looking to create their own relationship with the north. More significantly, this method works well for those looking to help others understand the north, so they can begin building their own relationship with it, away from it.

What happens then, if the need to have life make sense to those not in the north is not the primary focus? Specifically, what happens when it is those from the north who begin to explain how they see how life is lived, how they see the north? This was also discussed by the contributors, in our wide-ranging conversations. It was early in our discussions that we collectively remembered and discussed an important quote from a respected Elder, Mariano Aupilaarjuk, who lived much of his life in Rankin Inlet, speaking about the works of Knud Rasmussen, the Greenlandic-Danish polar explorer, anthropologist, and writer, credited for foundational work in anthological work on Inuit across Canada and Greenland:

> *I would like to add something. I know that there are mistakes in what Rasmussen wrote. Therefore, I think Inuit should be the ones doing the teaching.*[4]

There are many powerful aspects of this quote that we think are worth noting:

1. The person speaking: for those who are from Nunavut, and many who are not, and who know the high regard in which Aupilaarjuk is held for his interrogation and explanation of Inuit philosophical tradition, his understanding of Inuit *Qaujimajatuqangit*, or Inuit Traditional Ecological Knowledge, and his commitment to sharing his knowledge and experience for the betterment and strengthening of his family, community and Inuit;
2. The recognition of Rasmussen's reputation and authority in defining anthropological practice and tradition, both within the north and beyond;
3. The suggestion that what Rasmussen had written was not correct;
4. The idea that Inuit should be taking greater leadership in teaching ourselves and others about Inuit life, experiences, and knowledges.

It is beyond the scope of this chapter to interrogate each of these points, but we discussed point (4) at particular length throughout our conversations. Each contributor asked what the wide range of sources and disciplines that polar history draws from might look like if told from an Inuit perspective. How would these stories be told? Again, the potential research exploring these specific questions is vast, but for the three contributors connected to this chapter, we concluded that what Aupilaarjuk is saying in this quote is both straightforward and profound: if you change the method, if you change what you are looking at and why, and if you change who is looking, you profoundly change the content of something. Content changes, and how you understand things changes. What it makes you think and feel also changes.

---

4 Aupilaarjuk, quoted in Oosten and Laugrand, eds., *Inuit Perspectives*, 83.

And as it is with most truths that have found voice, the contributors recognize that Aupilaarjuk's simple and profound statement is not only known, but is also embodied within the contributors. While this is the case, it took an exceptionally long time to find the words to express this. We are all thankful that we took the time to really think through things, to question, to connect with, and to wonder collectively, what is it we are trying to say?

The importance of this work is even more impactful when thinking about how researchers from outside the north respond to a quote like this. In fact, Emilie specifically reflects on this point below:

> As I contemplate Aupilaarjuk's words today, I notice the opening that settler scholars are trained to see in the first part of his observation – the claim that Rasmussen made mistakes. If Rasmussen made mistakes, if there is 'another side to the story', then there is an impulse among settler scholars to suggest that someone should gather 'Inuit knowledge' about Rasmussen and his work, in order to set the historical and anthropological record straight. I can imagine that arrangements would be made for conversations with living elders, the hiring of interpreters, the sober presentations to hamlet councils. I can sense the confusion and disappointment of the graduate student when elders fail to answer their questions directly or in ways that are intelligible to the student, when hamlet councilors fail to express great enthusiasm for their important work. And I can see the student continuing on anyways, while the committee of scholars at their home institution eagerly consume their notes from the field.

This is not the only response to Aupilaarjuk's words, but we share this response here as it speaks to institutional and historical patterns that are familiar to all the contributors, and anyone who has experienced speaking truth to power. Instead of getting caught up in the multiple dualities that are structured when functioning within power dynamics (us versus them, Indigenous versus non-Indigenous, northerner versus southerner), the contributors actively decided to tread another path to see where it led them. Thankfully, advice was abundant along the way.

In *Why Indigenous Literatures Matter*, Daniel Heath Justice recognizes the symbolic and physical displacement of Indigenous communities by colonialism and offers multiple compelling and inspirational arguments for how Indigenous literature counters that power. From consistently affirming the presence of Indigenous communities to offer counter-arguments to those made through the colonial lens, Heath argues that the stories we tell, and the stories that are told about us matter as they affirm our humanity to ourselves, our community, and beyond. Justice goes on to write:

> Indeed, I'd go so far as to argue that *relationship* is the driving impetus behind the vast majority of texts by Indigenous writers – relationship to the land, to

human community, to self, to the other-than-human world, to the ancestors and our descendants, to our histories and our future, as well as to colonizers and their literal and ideological heirs – and that these literary works offer us insight and sometimes helpful pathways for maintaining, rebuilding, or even simply establishing these meaningful connections.[5]

In Kim TallBear's chapter of *Critical Indigenous Studies*, "Dear Indigenous Studies, It's Not Me, It's You: Why I Left and What Needs to Change", TallBear offers a creative frame of reference to question adherence to strict disciplinary lines and practices. In sharing the trajectory of her relationship with the Indigenous Studies discipline as an Indigenous scholar, environmental planner, and scientist, she did not anticipate engaging with the discipline of Indigenous Studies. Using the narrative of a romantic interlude, she brilliantly exposes the challenges of building a relationship with a discipline, especially a discipline that one was not trained within. In exploring both the limitations that individual scholars may bring to a new discipline and understanding the undertones the discipline itself may provide to new scholars looking to interact within it, TallBear lays this tension bare, showing how these dynamics limit the growth of both the individual and the discipline itself.

TallBear's offering masterfully examines tensions within a relatively small discipline made up of scholars with a diverse range of origin stories and present localities. The same is true for polar history, specifically circumpolar history, and more specifically, history related to Nunavut. TallBear's writing is familiar, offering practical benchmarks of relationships, such as the honeymoon stage, the recognition of annoying habits, the first fight, and the necessity of taking space away from each other – and for those committed to sustaining a relationship, the unavoidable musings on what needs to change in order to try again.

As all contributors of this chapter have been trained in geography, we heed the advice of TallBear who boldly challenges the Indigenous Studies discipline, and therefore scholars of that discipline and all disciplines, 'to have the courage to conceive theories and projects from a cross-fertilization of radically different fields'.[6] Like TallBear, we recognize that a relationship with polar history must continue to be made, and we appreciate that the discipline itself must also work to build and sustain relationships with those who have a personal relationship with its locality or subject matter. This claim proved interesting to the authors, and Jackie specifically wondered deeply: what is needed to grow this relationship into a respectful,

5 Justice, *Why Indigenous Literatures Matter*, i [original emphasis].
6 TallBear, "Dear Indigenous Studies", 74.

reciprocal, relationship? Is that possible? This chapter takes inspiration from TallBear's method and is one attempt to interrupt the aspect of the relationship that is one-way, supported by unhealthy patterns of preconceived notions and strict adherence to a limited character range or growth. Through this collaboration, ideas on how to build, and hopefully sustain, this healthy relationship emerged. To accomplish this, three practical strategies are employed in this chapter: (1) begin with an appreciation of where the other is coming from and identify some common ground across differences; (2) develop boundaries within the relationships; and (3) be willing to recognize that people come into relationships informed by their past experiences, and be open to understanding how those past experiences determine expectations for current relationships. In following the path laid out by Justice, the contributors recognized that in doing this work, we do it for ourselves and our communities, now and into the future, and doing so connects us to our past.

The Work of Building Relations

Gavin and Stacey is a comedy miniseries produced by the British Broadcasting Company (BBC) that originally ran from 2007 to 2010. This show followed the relationship between a boy (Gavin) from Essex, England, and a girl (Stacey) from Barry, Wales. Through these characters and a network of friends and family, this show poked fun at, while also exploring, ideas of nationalism, and language, cultural, and class difference. Jackie was introduced to the show while studying in the United Kingdom, and quickly became a hard-core fan. The show soon become part of her regular roster; it provided good company, usually while eating a beef black bean takeaway. In no small way, it also provided her with some insight into the cultural politics she was negotiating as a visitor to the United Kingdom.

This show included a very popular Christmas Special that was first aired at Christmas 2009 and on New Year's Day 2010. Jackie enjoyed this episode and made a point of watching it herself on 1 January 2021. She was aware that a second Christmas special was broadcast on Christmas Day 2019, but owing to her intense concern about internet quota, she delayed purchasing it online. But on 2 January 2021, as she fretted about this very chapter, she made the decision to purchase the 2019 Christmas special and watch it. For her, and probably all fans of the show, being able to see the trajectory of the lives of each character and the group as a whole was fun, and it provided an opportunity to marvel at how much could change in ten years.[7]

At the 29:55 mark of the 2019 Christmas special, Stacey passes Gavin a coaster asking him to meet her 'on the island' – Barry Island. She waits for him at the spot where they first declared their love for each other, after meeting for the first time in London following a long-distance relationship of almost six months. In the conversation that follows, Stacey passionately makes the case for Gavin and her to keep working on their relationship, to keep creating new memories, in light of being homeowners and two busy parents to three healthy children. This segment caused Jackie to get quite emotional. As a mom to two children, aged three and four and a half at the time of writing, she understood the stresses of being a parent and in a relationship. She also felt a connection to the show, and thereby to the United Kingdom that she had kept at a distance, as she also navigated a not yet final dissertation for her doctoral programme. And even though these two forces were present, she wondered why she was feeling so emotional.

There were other factors at play with Jackie's emotional response. Jackie had been struggling with finding a structure narrative for this chapter, and as the first contact for this work, she felt both a duty and responsibility to ensure the work got done, and that it reflected the spirit in which the conversations for this chapter had taken place. She was also reflecting on her sobriety birthday. The date 31 December 2020, was either her fourteenth or fifteenth anniversary of becoming sober, and she had been reflecting greatly on her inspiration for sobriety while also replaying bits of that fateful New Year's Eve evening in her head, in part in celebration but also in part in remembrance. While this was the case, she still did not feel she had found a theme in all that she was feeling, and this lack of understanding seemed also to represent the lack of direction for this very chapter.

Her emotional exploration was interrupted with a call from her niece requesting help on a family matter. Jackie's first preference was to stay at home and process all the emotion she was feeling, in the hope of integrating these separate threads into a single narrative that not only made sense, but perhaps led to some peace. Unfortunately, this hope was put on hold to attend to the request at hand. Her tears dried, and she helped out her family.

---

7 By this point, Gavin and Stacey had three kids. 'Neil the baby', son of their friends Nessa and Smithy, was now eleven. Doris the neighbour had passed away, and Gavin and Stacey's family now lived in her home. Nessa and Neil the baby were living with Uncle Bryn. While these were great changes, there were some things that had not changed: Uncle Bryn and Nessa still sang together, Mick and Pamela still lived in Essex and Pamela held on to her gentle and respectable discriminatory views of life in Wales, Dawn and Pete were still together in their way, and Jason still lived in Spain.

On her drive home, taking a route she usually did, she stopped at a four-way stop, common in her community of Iqaluit, Nunavut. Having arrived at the stop before the truck to her right, she knew she had the right-of-way to proceed straight. As she was driving straight, the truck to her right started taking a right turn rather quickly. Aware that the truck and her car were on a collision course, Jackie stopped her car, honked her horn, and looked out her window at the possible trajectory of an accident. Thankfully, the truck stopped, and after giving its front grill a mean look, she carried on to her home.

When Jackie got home, she tried to watch the *Gavin and Stacey* episode again, hoping to recreate the same feelings and experience she had prior to her call from her niece. Of course, in the knowledge of what would happen next, the storyline became predictable, and there was an absence of those initial feelings. She was disappointed that things did not turn out as planned, but she watched the remainder of the show, enjoying the storyline and the cliffhanger ending. Because she had some time, she was able to watch the show one more time in its entirety.

While the glow of the show remained, Jackie was still thinking about her afternoon, and all the emotions she was feeling, all the things she was thinking about: her time in the United Kingdom, the need to get this chapter done, her sobriety, and almost getting hit by a truck. All of these things had to be related, but she was not sure how.

That is, until she was.

It was in the midst of replaying all these points, emotions, and histories that she realized that what she was fighting for was a need to be seen. Needing to be seen came in many different forms. In the case of this chapter – the individual and group feeling of being seen as we wanted to be and not in the shadow of polar history and its expectations. In terms of Jackie's time in the United Kingdom, wanting to be seen and given the freedom to explore her research and herself in her own way, and not in the way the literature of Europe understood Arctic governance. In terms of her sobriety, her need to figure out who she was without the distraction of drinking and all the tangles that came with that. Jackie also realized that in the absence of being seen, she had to make herself seen, as she had when honking her horn at an oncoming, distracted truck driver. For her, and by extension the trio wanting to write this chapter, there was a need to find a structure for making ourselves be seen in our own way. This is what the group conversations were dancing around, and this is what Jackie was experiencing at this time personally.

As graciously argued by Shawn Wilson, research is ceremony. The contributors appreciated that even the research for this chapter provided an opportunity to participate in, learn from, and then share what can be described as a cleansing ceremony. The ceremony, in this case, took the form of a BBC comedy special, old ghosts from the past, and a near-collision that provided the clarity and relationships needed to begin this work.

Re-storying Within: Finding the Patterns

Words have power, and power can be experienced differently. While much thought and consideration can go into a particular word, as a means to understand the source of this power, sometimes it is worth examining the responses to that power to understand it in another way.

While there are many words that are worthy of this kind of examination, a particular word that has an interesting range when thinking of the north, and Nunavut specifically, is *pattern*.

Depending on who you talk to, it can mean many things. If you talk with someone who sews, then they will associate the word with sewing patterns – guidelines that help seamstresses, mothers, aunts, and others make whatever it is they want or need to make, for themselves or for others. If you talk to someone who likes to 'go out on the land', then perhaps they would connect that word to weather patterns, seasonal patterns, animal behaviour. Persons such as these might share a recent trip out on the land, to hunt, gather, or go to a cabin, and the patterns they saw on that trip. Finally, another person may think of a friend or family member, and connect the word pattern with their behaviour, their mannerisms, the way they interact with a person. Perhaps this would be an opportunity to dig in deeper to the ways in which a person interacts with the world, and some of the challenging or helpful aspects that guide this interaction.

For us, the patterns of thoughts, feelings, and expectations evoked by the word 'history' started to gather our attention as the conversations unfolded. We decided to examine the patterns we see when we each think about polar history, and specifically, how we understand history in Nunavut – which is a very specific example of polar history. We did this to understand what patterns we can find amongst ourselves.

Re-storying in Multiple Ways: Tattooing as Patterns, Relations, and Methodology

In her book *Kaandossiwin: How We Come to Know*, Kathleen Absolon centres her work within Indigenous 're-search'. In doing so, she makes the argument that the work of Indigenous scholars, alongside their communities, is to make what was once invisible, visible again. As she writes:

> Colonization has attempted to make our realities invisible and has tried to turn us into the disappearing race ...
> I contest the notion that we are a vanquished race or remnants of the past ... We exist and we are here. Our knowledge is valid, real and concrete. I do not make comparisons with eurowestern methods of searching. There is no need to. There are many pathways to knowledge.[8]

When Jackie approached Rebecca with the idea of co-authoring this chapter, it seemed like a fitting partnership. Having worked with each other for just over a year at the time of authoring this, we have had the opportunity to have many conversations, whether it be about tattooing, our experiences in academia, or our work of the day. When Rebecca thinks of patterns, she thinks of the connections between conversations, like the lines of tattoos that emerge through a tattooing session, coming together to create a beautiful pattern full of thoughts, connections, and meaning.

Below is an excerpt from the fourth conversation held between the contributors. It is an edited transcript of a conversation that discusses the wide-ranging realities facing Inuit looking to do the work of re-storying. The subject matter is Inuit tattooing, a practice that was assumed to be a thing of the past but is now being renewed through the current generation of Inuit women, women who live very different lives from their ancestors who were recorded as having these tattoos prior to the advent of Christianity.

Rebecca Mearns: Part of the challenge that I have experienced in the reclamation of tattooing is that, because the knowledge holders here within our communities, who would have carried this knowledge, so many have passed on. Through colonization and the introduction of Christianity, there was so much that was no longer talked about. What impact does this have on the knowledge that is available and passed down to our generation? What are the challenges we then face to learning and finding more information about tattooing? Often, most of the written information on tattooing has been written by non-Inuit.

This leaves me questioning how this knowledge has been interpreted, through what lens is this interpretation made? It makes me wonder whether we are missing out on details. What could we have learned by engaging directly with those knowledge holders?

---

8 Absolon, *Kaandossiwin*, 12.

Emilie Cameron: So how do you, in your tattooing explorations, how do you handle that feeling of grappling with the idea of what it used to be like? Do you wonder whether you are doing it 'correctly'? In the face of not having some of the information or some of the stories, does that cause you difficulties? How does that work for you?

Rebecca Mearns: I think for me, I have had a few people who have approached me, wanting to receive tattoos, or have messaged me, because they're thinking about getting tattoos, and they are worried they need to learn what it all means before they can get their tattoos. And the truth is, we cannot know everything, and I still have so much to learn about Inuit tattoos. Obviously, there is that gap in knowledge when it comes to tattooing and there is some information out there, and there are Inuit that have done a lot of research into tattooing as well.

I have had many conversations with others about the reclamation of tattooing and how we go about that. We do talk about meaning, but we also acknowledge that we are not going to know everything. Through these conversations, and I do have them with the people I am working with, it is about building the meaning for us, as well as this generation, they're now receiving tattoos, and it's becoming normalized. And it's about reclaiming them and then reclaiming what meaning is and being able to provide our meaning within it. It is also about understanding the beauty and the relationships that are built through tattooing as well. And it is a very different experience to be tattooed by another woman, through the stick and poke method, in their home than it is to walk into a tattoo shop down south and get tattooed by someone who does not know the culture or is using a tattoo machine. These are two very, very different experiences. I do believe that it is part of the reclamation process and journey too, that we are able to build those relationships within our communities, ourselves.

Jackie Price: Which makes total sense, everything you've said makes so much sense, because the one thing I have always appreciated every time you have told me a story about tattooing someone is like how fun it is. You would talk about food or conversation or laughter or the silence and how it is like visiting a friend, visiting a friend in the way that people visit up here, you know, that there is a nice connection. People just being people together.

The process of learning to tattoo, the process of reclaiming this aspect of Inuit Culture, is still ongoing. The experience of understanding and getting tattoos is held close to the heart of those wanting to get tattoos, and those providing them, like Rebecca. Rebecca believes there will be a time and a place to share these stories. For now, it does not feel like those stories should be shared here, at this time, in this contribution. This is an important point to acknowledge. As practices emerge, whether new or regenerative, the re-storying process, the sharing of details, of practices, of rationales and questions will likely be different, if shared at all. It is worth noting explicitly that these experiences are being created as life is being lived, and not everyone wishes to share what they are experiencing with others right away. For some things, people may have to work hard to be privy to them. From the perspective of the contributors, this fact should be respected, as the process of reclamation and re-storying is healing, and healing spaces should be understood as sacred places.

All three contributors appreciate that moving forward under new expectations or dynamics is likely to be uncomfortable for some.

Uncomfortable Patterns

Nancy Wachowich's book *Saqiyuq: Stories from the Lives of Three Inuit Women* explores the changes in Inuit life through the personal stories of three generations of women from the same family. This is an important book, a must-read for anyone wishing to understand how Inuit themselves see their lives and their place amongst all the change. While this book also follows the pattern of speaking first about Inuit life on the land, then into the settlement, then contemporary life, it does so through a relational lens. Each woman is speaking of her own experience, her own questions, and her own understanding of changes experienced in her family and community. Notably, it also discusses the future. Therefore, this book offers a wider range of positionalities, allowing its readers to at least grasp the fullness of life lived continuously, and not only in the past.

This book represents the change that does occur when northerners are provided with the space to tell their stories, either with others or on their own. While this offering is an important benchmark, it is important to note that those looking to engage with polar stories may not be wholly comfortable with the change in conversation. For example, in Sherrill E. Grace's *Canada and the Idea of North*, in her penultimate chapter "Writing, Re-writing, and Writing Back", Grace writes (and it is worth quoting at length) some of her reflections about engaging with a wider range of northern voices:

> *Saqiyuq* is one of the most recent examples of a rapidly emerging tradition of autobiography among the Inuit, Innu, Yukon first Nations, Dene and Cree. Wachowich has reproduced (with minimal editing) the life-stories of three generations of women from one Baffin Island family – a grandmother, Apphia Angalati Awa, her daughter, Rhoda Kaujak Katsak, and Rhoda's daughter, Sandra Pikujak Katsak. For me the most interesting of these

autobiographical narratives is Apphia's, because her voice, like her experience, is so different from those of her modern daughter and young granddaughter. There is a sense in which Apphia invites me to listen to a story (as my own mother might) and to learn about a world I do not know and could not have survived in. I experience a sense of being privileged in listening to her story, which mixes elements of the traditional story with frank accounts of her personal experiences. Rhoda's story, like her English, is much more familiar and terse; she is a modern Canadian – if also an Inuk – and her problems, like her anger, are all too common. It is her attempt to recover a traditional past, erased by Christianity and a southern school curriculum, that most moves me. Sandra's voice is something of a shock because she sounds like a member of the younger generation almost anywhere in North America – a generation I don't really understand or always like. But perhaps that is the (or a) major point and lesson: contemporary voices in English, influenced by the globalized world of the internet, television, email, T-shirts, Coca Cola, American movies and popular culture, do sound much the same. Juxtaposing Sandra with Rhoda and Apphia allows the reader to glimpse (to overhear, as it were) the change and, for me at least, the loss. Sandra, I realize, does not sound northern. Whether she should or not is another matter.[9]

This pattern, this way of understanding the north in a specific way does evoke strong emotions, particularly for those not from the north. This does lead to a funny politic, one that is not explored often, but is necessary to look at. Consider the following reflections from Emilie:

> A significant preoccupation of mine since becoming involved in 'polar' or northern research has been the patterns of relationship and the power structures that frame the whole endeavour. What stands out in my memory is attending my first Inuit studies conference as a graduate student. This was approximately fifteen years ago. I remember being stunned that the conference was largely full of white people talking about Inuit. There were a handful of Inuit there, but most attendees did not seem to know them or talk to them. Everyone seemed to be going about their business, reporting on Inuit lives, culture, and history in little university lecture rooms without a single Inuk present. There was even a session where a white woman was moved to tears in her presentation, talking about the tragic loss of traditional qajaq technology and its replacement with 'ugly plastic' modern boats. To me that moment crystallized the entire conference – a gathering of Qallunaat lamenting the 'lost' traditional Inuit past and warning against present dangers, and many non-Inuit scholars trying to demonstrate their authentic connections with Inuit communities. I remember having this sense that

[9] Grace, *Canada*, 240.

I had stepped into a time warp, that all the political shifts that made a gathering like this almost impossible in other academic realms at that point had somehow skipped over this little pocket of academia. Having been trained in academic programmes that were in the throes of crisis and self-examination around the politics of representation and their own complicity in colonial formations through the 1990s and 2000s, I honestly was shocked that 'Inuit studies' or 'Northern studies' could still exist in this form.

A bit has changed since then, but not as much as you would think. Research in and about the north and about Inuit is still overwhelmingly carried out by Qallunaat. Many more Inuit have entered academia since then and are doing research within or connected to universities and colleges, and many partnerships have developed between Inuit and Qallunaat that are more equitable and meaningful and community-driven. Inuit have been participating more in the Inuit studies conference and making it something different, and also just turning away from this entire realm and creating things for themselves, for their own purposes (as they have always done). But there are still so many entrenched dynamics shaping 'northern research', and still today, the vast majority of research and writing about the north remains driven by priorities that are not 'of' the north in any meaningful way and are grounded in the epistemologies, methodologies, and axiologies of settlers.

So how does one be in relationship with all of this? I have struggled with that question for years. I knew I did not want to reproduce these patterns, but I am aware of the power of inheritances, of structures, and all the ways we reproduce things despite our best efforts and intentions. I have always been wary of claims on the part of Qallunaat to be doing something radically different, to be conducting 'decolonizing' research or research that was grounded in 'true' partnerships; any claims to be exceptional to all this, to have found some kind of safe space within which one might avoid harming others, not be extractive, not be reproducing fundamentally colonial knowledge systems, seemed to me to be its own danger. As a result, I have spent most of my life as 'northern scholar' in a state of deep wariness and angst. Whenever I put on my 'researcher' hat, to ask questions of people or even when observing with that eye, it has always felt yucky. Dangerous. Heavy. Which makes me wonder why I kept doing it! I think for a long time, it felt important to name all of this, to be part of a process of unpacking and unlearning a long history of extractive relations. But more and more, I am seeing the limits of just naming and unpacking old patterns.

Thankfully, not all my relationships and experiences in Nunavut have been about research, and over the years, it is these other relationships that have most provoked me and supported me to develop a different relationship with these heavy patterns. The old patterns are still there, of course. But I am more and more aware of how focusing on the dangers can stifle other possibilities. And keep people fixed in roles that ultimately dehumanize us all. I am interested in what might be possible in the space between unthinking reproduction of colonial relations and a too-wary watchfulness. That is where my attention is these days, anyways. And our conversations have really helped me to imagine and experience this a bit differently.

After this conversation, Emilie heard an interview with Laakuluk Williamson Bathory (whose father is Robert Williamson) on CBC Radio, where she was describing a recent collaborative project called 'Kiinalik: These Sharp Tools'.[10] Laakuluk was asked how the project might contribute to reconciliation efforts in Canada, and her answer was revealing: 'We don't actually talk about reconciliation at all but it's something that we get asked about,' she shared. 'We reject the idea that reconciliation is possible because there are such huge disparities between the group that comes from the colonizing forces and the colonized here in the Arctic.' She and her collaborators instead speak of their work as a form of 'reckoning ... coming right to people and challenging who they are, what their views are', and also as work that is 'unresolved', that sits with the unanswered questions and impossibilities and stakes of what is explored.

Conclusion

In her book *In the Wake: On Blackness and Being*, Christina Sharpe explores the many meanings of 'wake' to challenge the acceptance of black death as a given, both in narration, representation and day-to-day life. In exploring wake as 'the state of wakefulness; consciousness', Sharpe writes:

> It was with this sense of wakefulness as consciousness that most of my family lived an awareness of itself as, and in, the wake of the unfinished project of emancipation.
> *So, the same set of questions and issues are presenting themselves to us across these historical periods. It [is] the same story that is telling itself, but through the different technologies and processes of that particular period.*[11]

We recognize that history left unresolved and uninterrupted does repeat itself in the contemporary. If this is the case, then the contemporary offers as much history as history itself. And yet life also continues beyond the gaze of history. Returning to Williamson, perhaps Jackie's warmest memory of first

---
10 Laakuluk Williamson Bathory interview on "Q" radio show, CBC (September 2020).
11 Patricia Saunders, cited in Sharpe, *In the Wake*, 4 [original emphasis].

coming across his book was in recognizing the very names that Williamson referenced through the book. The Inuit mentioned in the books had names that Jackie recognized, and their families continue to live on, so, while historical in nature, it is contemporary also.

Inuit know that history is often written about them and in their name without their involvement, and generally this is not appreciated or desired. When Inuit voices are included, they are often relegated to the non-academic contribution. But those who call the north home, especially those connected to Inuit Culture, language, and families, think about these big topics. They talk about it, through social media, over a cup of tea, coffee, or wine. They reflect upon it, either quietly or loudly, on their own or with others in their family, town, or beyond. Northern voices are diverse, representing a wide range of experience, interests, and knowledge. To assume a single voice or perspective in the north is incorrect. But it is also incorrect to assume that, because these diverse voices and conversations and reflections do not appear in academic books, they do not exist or do not matter.

You cannot talk about polar history without talking about power and research. It is not an accident that these patterns have come about and continue to reproduce themselves. We have tried to show, here, a different perspective, a different way of sharing knowledge about the north. In so doing, we hope we have opened a space for readers to think about polar history and history-making differently, to step back and query some of the broader relations that shape this field of study, and to consider other possibilities for how we might move forward.

Bibliography

Absolon, Kathleen, *Kaandossiwin: How We Come to Know* (Halifax, NS, Winnipeg, MB: Fernwood, 2011).

Grace, Sherrill E., *Canada and the Idea of North* (Montreal, PQ, Kingston, ON: McGill-Queen's University Press, 2001).

Justice, Daniel Heath, *Why Indigenous Literatures Matter* (Waterloo, ON: Wilfrid Laurier University Press, 2018).

Oosten, Jarich, and Frédéric Laugrand, eds., *Inuit Perspectives on the 20th Century: Inuit Qaujimajatuqangit: Shamanism and Reintegrating Wrongdoers into the Community* (Iqaluit, NU: Nunavut Arctic College, 2002).

Sharpe, Christina, *In the Wake: On Blackness and Being* (Durham, NC: Duke University Press, 2016).

TallBear, Kim, "Dear Indigenous Studies, It's Not Me, It's You: Why I Left and What Needs to Change", in Aileen Moreton-Robinson, ed., *Critical Indigenous Studies:*

Engagements in First World Locations (Tucson: University of Arizona Press, 2016), pp. 69–82.

Wachowich, Nancy, *Saqiyuq: Stories from the Lives of Three Inuit Women* (Kingston, ON, Montreal, PQ: McGill-Queen's University Press, 2001).

Williamson, Robert, *"Eskimo Underground: Socio-cultural Change in the Canadian Central Arctic"*, PhD diss. (Uppsala: Institutionen för allmän och jämförande etnografi vid Uppsala Universitet, 1974).

Wilson, Shawn, *Research Is Ceremony: Indigenous Research Methods* (Halifax, NS, Winnipeg, MB: Fernwood, 2009).

31

Conclusion: Time, and the Future of Polar History

LIZA PIPER AND LIZE-MARIÉ HANSEN VAN DER WATT

Polar history can be seen through four different temporal lenses. There is Deep Time with its geological timescales against which to interpret and understand change. There is the 'golden age' of polar history, approximately 1800 to 1930, which orients the significance of the poles through the perspective of colonial exploration. There is the Anthropocene, our post-Holocene human-dominated epoch, which scholars have dated (not without controversy) to the 1950s and after. The Anthropocene is part of the geological timescale, but in the polar regions it corresponds to a temporality traditionally rooted in geopolitics: the Cold War era of militarization and intensified scientific interest in the polar regions. Lastly, polar temporality is marked by the distinctive rhythms of radical variations in the length of day and night throughout the year. Even as global heating rends the cryospheric fabric of life, these rhythms of light and dark persist in their influence over human social life, work, and culture.

There is a fifth, allochthonous form of polar temporality – on display most recently during the COVID-19 pandemic that began in 2020. This is the view of polar regions and peoples that sees them as out of sync with normative historical timelines. It is a way of linking temporal relations to spatial relations: because polar regions are at a distance from centres of population and power, so too their experience of moments of wider historical significance is sometimes seen as 'delayed'. Early public narratives about COVID-19 and Antarctica characterized the continent as one of the 'last COVID-free places on Earth'. Then the continent became the 'last' place the virus reached.[1] In the circumpolar north, a similar mindset informed the decision of a couple from Quebec who, in March 2020, drove to Whitehorse, Yukon, then flew into the Gwich'in community of Old Crow out of a desire to escape from the pandemic, not realizing that they were more likely to bring the virus to Old

---

1 Minardi, "Antarctica"; Kesling and Dube, "Covid-19 Reaches Antarctica".

Crow with them.[2] To the extent that pandemic relations are forged through networks of social relations, and recognizing that viruses travel, these views of polar environments as remote from pandemic centres reflect an important reality of the coronavirus pandemic. However, they also lend themselves to distorted views of history. The delayed arrival or distance of the poles from the epicentre of the pandemic tell us little about the experience of this historical moment at the poles. More significant features of COVID-19 at high latitudes have been the role of resource and research workers in carrying the virus into polar regions, and the concerns raised about the potential impacts on wildlife – an important reminder of the role of disease in human–wildlife relations. There have also been the ways in which communities, including scientific communities, have responded to the challenges posed by the pandemic. Given the strict biosecurity measures on the continent, concerns for reverse-zoonosis featured high on the agenda of the Antarctic Treaty Consultative Meeting of 2021. The Parties urged Antarctic personnel who tested positive not only to isolate from their colleagues but also to maintain strict isolation from wildlife, even in cases where they had permission to approach.[3] And COVID-19 is far from the only episode where the pressures of normative temporality shape our historical interpretations. The same could be said for the emergent narratives around Arctic and Antarctic climate change – where major effects are being felt 'sooner' than at temperate or tropical latitudes. This is not to suggest that early or late interpretations of polar history relative to normative temporality are better or worse, but rather to clearly identify their exogenous origins – that they are a way in which the poles and their histories are narrated *in relation to* other, distant, and often colonial centres. To focus our attention on the future of polar history means attending to the ways that temporality illuminates the geographies, material, and social relations at work in the polar past.

Deep Time

A Deep Time approach highlights the central significance of climate and climate change in Arctic and Antarctic human histories. Martin Siegert and

---

2 CBC News, "Quebec Couple Fleeing COVID-19".
3 It was the topic of Working Paper 47, "SARS-CoV-2 in Antarctic Species by Way of Reverse Zoonosis", presented by the Scientific Committee on Antarctic Research (SCAR). Concerns for human health were recognized but not discussed. To date, no cases of reverse-zoonoses of SARS-CoV-2 have been found in Antarctica. The paper can be accessed at www.ats.aq.

Andrew Fountain make the point that while geoscientific research in Antarctica has an extremely short history, the continent itself has been pivotal in modulating past climate and sea-level changes, reaching as far back as the ancient supercontinent of Gondwanaland, a Deep Time perspective that long pre-dates human existence. Geoscientific research also challenged the view of Antarctica as a continent 'frozen in time', demonstrating the dynamism of its bedrock geology, and the unexpected and unpredictable interactions between ice-sheet dynamics and ocean warming. Longer timescales illuminate dynamism and change that shape human and other-than-human histories over much shorter periods.

While our present global heating is unprecedented, significant climatic shifts and their environmental reverberations have been a key factor in past human experiences at high latitudes. The presence of refugia during past glaciations, and the opportunities offered by retreating ice, created corridors for the movement of people and other animals in the distant past. The Bering Land Bridge, a product of low sea levels when water was tied up in continental ice sheets, is perhaps one of the best examples of the distinct and consequential interconnections across the circumpolar world that existed in past landscapes. The Bering Land Bridge joined continents, but at the local and regional level there were many other connections and corridors made and then unmade, with marked effects on patterns of movement and occupation. Although many of these climatic changes took place over long periods of time, some occurred much more abruptly. These include dramatic episodes of cooling that followed major volcanic eruptions and the global, albeit transitory, effects of their solar radiation-suppressing dust veils. As Bjarne Grønnow notes in Chapter of this volume, the spread of people in the circumpolar north was 'often an abrupt or discontinuous process'. There were those groups like the Norse who sought settlement in Greenland, and others like the Inuit and pre-Inuit societies whose experiences on the land involved almost constant movement, with social continuity found in the family and the hearth rather than in a specific place. Polar histories, whether of animals in the Antarctic, or of humans and other animals in the Arctic, highlight long experience with climate change, and how it not only created singular opportunities for movement to new places, but also brought about sharp transitions in possibilities for humans or other animals to thrive. In human histories, these transitions included the end of resource-rich societies when ice advanced or communities failed to adapt swiftly and decisively to changing conditions. As we move through the changing climates – local and global – of the present, there is much we stand to learn about living with an unstable Earth in the past.

George Angohiatok pulls our focus into these relationships by describing his life experience. He shows that being on the land is the way to learn from it and to change with it. Angohiatok shares his many lessons from his grandmother in Chapter 2 of this volume. Life spent on the land is combined with learning from previous generations, through stories or by example, to transmit knowledge from one generation to the next. These – experience on the land and learning from Elders – are the core relationships at the root of what scholars in many disciplines call traditional environmental knowledge (TEK) and which has been widely accepted as fundamental expertise in Arctic environments.[4] Bringing this expertise to the fore alongside other forms of scientific knowledge – from ice cores, palaeo-environmental research, and archaeology, to name some examples – allows us to understand how polar environments changed in the deep past and how human societies were affected by and adapted to these changes. Central to this history are relations between humans and non-human animals at high latitudes. Polar history in Deep Time demands that we attend more closely not only to human experiences but also to the changes in the main animal populations – mammoths in the distant past, caribou, whales, muskox, and many others. As Angohiatok, Vandenbrink, Hogg, and McIlwraith observe, 'the land, the animals, and the people are indivisible'. If we take this lesson from George Angohiatok and apply it to our future polar histories, we need to attend much more closely to the pasts we have shared with other species.

Historicizing Indigenous expertise and the ways that knowledge held by communities in the present is tied to Deep Time cannot happen without acknowledging and discerning the ongoing damage of colonialism that has sought to disconnect Indigenous peoples from the land and from their cultural heritage. Carl-Gösta Ojala writes about these processes in his discussion of archaeology and Sámi heritage. Ojala offers but one window into a much larger, circumpolar intellectual history that extends into every discipline – particularly the sciences, which have long viewed polar environments and peoples as laboratories for study. Alongside greater Indigenous participation in archaeological and heritage work, global heating is changing the present and future of archaeology at high latitudes. Some sites are threatened with destruction by rising seas and eroding coastlines; meanwhile, new opportunities for understanding relations with place and other animals are appearing in melting ice patches on mountains and the tundra.[5] Thus the

---

4 For one recent example, see Parlee and Caine, eds., *When the Caribou*.
5 Andrews et al., *Hunters of Alpine Ice*.

methods and practices of different disciplines that shape our knowledge of the distant past at high latitudes will have to continue to change and adapt.

To paraphrase Ojala, every interpretation of the past is political, especially so on lands and among peoples who have experienced the aggressions of colonization. Connections with the land and with past generations, such as those described by Angohiatok, persist in spite of the disruptions of colonialism and must be recognized as part of the resilience of Indigenous cultures. Even if polar history as a field of study was very much born in a crucible of imperialism and exploration, the work presented in this volume also reminds us of the immense value of circumpolar perspectives that point to connections and shared histories that transcend the borders of nation-states – the heirs of a colonial and imperial past. Looking to deeper time helps bring these circumpolar threads into focus.

The 'Golden Age'

Imperialism and colonialism were historical processes that prevailed in the north polar regions from the eighteenth into the mid-twentieth century, and in the south polar regions from the mid-nineteenth century. By the latter half of the twentieth century new geopolitical forces had come to the fore: military, domestic state entities, more powerful Indigenous political bodies (in the Arctic), and eventually circumpolar or at least transnational governance and research organizations. Nevertheless, the power relationships and structures put in place to facilitate exploration and colonialism have had enduring influence in shaping relations between polar and temperate regions. While the nature of the Antarctic Treaty System as a type of colonial regime is the subject of lively debate, largely given its lack of Indigenous or permanent inhabitants, its entanglement with global imperial and colonial politics is well-documented, including in Daniella McCahey's Chapter 13.[6] The two most significant aspects of this larger 'golden age' of polar history (only 'golden' from the vantage point of the metropolis, of course), imperial exploration and settler colonialism, did not proceed in a consistent and uniform fashion, but were marked by windows and geographies of enthusiasm. A centrepiece of imperial exploration, as Russell Potter considers, the lost Franklin expedition created a stimulus for subsequent voyages during a period of good ice conditions in the late nineteenth century (the window of enthusiasm) that created an intense

---

6 See, for example, Scott, "Ingenious and Innocuous?"; Dodds and Collis, "Post-colonial Antarctica"; and Mancilla, "Continent of Whiteness?".

period of activity with consequences for science, colonial relations, and power in the Canadian Arctic.[7] And John Franklin's original focus was on a Northwest Passage (the geography of enthusiasm), one of several hoped-for ice-free corridors in the circumpolar north that could enhance global transportation networks. The race for the South Pole (the geography of enthusiasm, once the North Pole was taken) was a highlight of the so-called Heroic Age, enabled by the commercial resources and national political enthusiasm for polar adventure. The enduring mythical narratives about these feats – and their dominance on polar history timelines – are partly the result of the deliberate construction through diaries written for posterity, as Stephanie Barczewski elaborates on. The inauguration of International Polar Years is another example of windows of scientific enthusiasm that shaped the temporality of polar history in these centuries. Scientific exploration within a larger colonial context persists into the present even as increased Indigenous political power and greater critical awareness of the role of science in society have led to changes in its practice and influence.

As Ryan Tucker Jones, Alexei Kraikovski, and Julia Lajus detail in their chapter, Russia was the first imperial power to wed the process of empire building to the work of science in cold regions. From the eighteenth through to the twentieth century, travel, mapping, the erection of observation and communication systems (such as weather and radio stations), collection of samples and artefacts, and the dissemination of knowledge through imperial networks were all done under the auspices of science.[8] These offered ways for imperial powers to come to terms with unfamiliar people and places, while also using the process of gathering this knowledge, and the knowledge itself, as means to lay claim to these lands without the challenges of attempting settlement in latitudes beyond the reach of viable agriculture. New knowledge was created upon which subsequent exploration, investigation, and eventually colonial settlement and sojourning could then build. Opportunities for 'discovery' and for claiming rights as the 'first' to achieve exploratory or geographical objectives motivated much science, even if the parameters by which such primacy was established were exclusively Western and colonial. Yet polar science was also a consort to resource exploitation. In northern North America, scientists and explorers depended on fur trade transportation networks. In turn, across the polar north, discovery was attuned to prospective resources, as when Alexander Mackenzie, exploring

7 Dunbar, "Effect of Sea Ice".
8 Lindsay, *Science in the Subarctic*; Binnema, *Enlightened Zeal*.

on behalf of a fur trade company, made note of petroleum deposits along the river that would bear his name; or when Adolf Erik Nordenskiöld discovered rich guano deposits on Spitsbergen during a scientific expedition in the 1860s.

Resource exploitation in polar history has been much more clearly marked by the rise and decline of extractive activities, in swings shaped by market demands, technologies, and resource availability. Commercial whaling exemplifies these patterns, with whalers moving into new waters as they 'fished out' other grounds. This pattern of harvesting allowed the industry to thrive for three centuries in northern waters with vessels from competing nations concentrated in the waters around Svalbard, or in Baffin Bay, or the Bering Strait at different times. Although local extirpation propelled the constant search for new waters, and new technologies enabled the move into more challenging regions or in search of new species, the decline of whaling in northern waters arose primarily from shifting market tastes as fossil fuels displaced whale oil and baleen prices plummeted at the turn of the twentieth century.[9] Fur traders similarly took advantage of the natural bounty of animal populations, such as sable in Siberia, sea otter along the Pacific coasts, or beaver in northern North America, but then had to shift to different products as populations could not sustain market demands. Changes in fashion drove harvesting in the fur trade: the rise of silk hats eased pressure on beaver populations, while muskrat, a versatile fur, treated and shaved to make 'Hudson Bay Seal', rose in popularity in the twentieth century.[10] From a temporal perspective, the experimental enthusiasm driving transplantation of muskoxen and reindeer populations, as described by Dolly Jørgensen in this volume, is more akin to scientific and research activity than to the patterns of resource exploitation in high latitudes.

In those polar regions where the fur trade thrived for a long period of time, northern North America and Siberia most notably, colonization efforts were intimately tied to trade geographies. Thus, even as different resource extraction opportunities ebbed and flowed over time, shaping different periods in local histories, infrastructures erected to support resource activities persisted in place well after certain resource opportunities had declined. Christian missionaries had a similar enduring influence in many northern polar regions, arriving in the north during periods of enthusiasm and establishing missions that endured for decades or, in some places, centuries. The history of these missionaries, who shaped colonial relationships in Greenland, Alaska, Russia, Yukon, and the Northwest Territories, and Labrador, remains

9 Bockstoce, *Whales, Ice, and Men*, 252.   10 Ray, *Canadian Fur Trade*, 62.

largely under the purview of what amount to internalist histories, many written by members of the religious orders themselves.[11] Given the role of religious orders in northern voyages and later colonization, greater critical historical attention seems warranted. This is particularly so as the work of many of these men and women overlapped with other imperial and colonial endeavours: some explored, collected, and published research findings; they operated hospitals and schools that served the goals of settler colonialism; and many were motivated by a spirit of adventure, as much as their more secular-minded scientist counterparts. Although the activity of missionaries was largely replaced by that of secular states in the twentieth century, the need remains to reconcile their legacies in future polar histories that grapple comprehensively with colonialism at high latitudes.

If trade and mission posts became nodes in northern geographies in this period, the lines on maps drawn in service to the assertions of sovereignty by nation states have had an equally consequential impact over time. Disputes over polar claims and sovereignty constitute a rich historiographical vein in part because of the importance of boundary moments: those episodes when claims were put forth and lines or 'sectors' agreed to, as Janice Cavell examines, which then went on to shape future relations and conflicts over polar regions. As Roald Berg shows in his chapter on Spitsbergen/Svalbard, the 1920 treaty 'was a fortification of international law as well as of the close cultural and economic bonds that established a Norwegian-American "*communis*" at Spitsbergen in which Norway was the ruler and the Americans harvested the resources'. Canada's nineteenth-century anxieties, as a newly minted nation with aspirations to control its own polar empire – inherited from Great Britain with the transfer of the British Arctic Islands, the North-Western Territory, and Rupert's Land – have now shaped Canada's northern history for over a century. You can see this clearly on a very useful set of maps showing the territorial evolution of the Northwest Territories, found on the website of the Prince of Wales Northern Heritage Centre.[12] The five maps presented there show the evolution of boundaries between 1870 and 1999, with all but one map from the forty-two-year period between 1870 and 1912; and then almost ninety years pass before the final map, from 1999,

---

11 There were, for instance, the memoirs written by Catholic and Anglican missionaries that amount to a genre in and of themselves. One of the most widely cited was by Duchaussois, *Aux Glaces Polaires*, which was translated into six languages.
12 Prince of Wales Northern Heritage Centre, "Territorial Evolution". The North-Western Territory differed from the later Northwest Territories, as the former included what became Yukon Territory.

representing the creation of Nunavut. This sequence encapsulates the political history of boundary making not just in Canada's north, but more broadly in polar regions with Indigenous populations. As Mark Nuttall points out, in the 1970s the Inuit Circumpolar Conference asserted the commonality of Inuit people across northern North America (including Greenland), even as they were 'subdivided by the political boundaries of nation states'. The same relationships can be asserted for other northern Indigenous peoples, including the Gwich'in, Tlingit, and Sámi, whose homelands were partitioned by colonial boundary-making in the nineteenth and twentieth centuries. It was only in the later twentieth century that Indigenous political movements made headway in their assertions of sovereignty and autonomy, but even then these powers have remained in many instances, constrained by the larger nation-states of which these peoples became a part.

Boundary-making and sovereignty have also been crucial in shaping Antarctic history. Antarctic maps have fewer, perhaps simpler geopolitical boundary moments – straight sectoral lines radiating north from the South Pole, partially overlapping on the peninsula, and one sector unclaimed. These were drawn in the span of slightly less than forty years. When the Antarctic Treaty was negotiated, these were neither made permanent nor erased. Overlapping claims and histories of sovereignty disputes continue to lurk in the background of the 'epistemic technocracy' that governs Antarctica, as Klaus Dodds explains in his chapter. While consensus-based decision-making contributed to the Treaty's flexibility and adaptability, these modes of governance also slow down decision-making, a situation that becomes more acute with rapid environmental change and changing geopolitical power balances.

Colonial and imperial histories persist in lines on maps and the possibilities for governance that they enable, in resource and mission geographies, and in the presence or absence of species on land and in the water; they also persist in the ways that broader publics consume and imagine these places. Elizabeth Leane draws our attention to the role of historical fiction in writing histories of polar regions that have enormous cultural power. Although polar historical fiction is by no means confined to the 'golden age' of exploration, it is that period that is disproportionately represented. Leane points to the 'quintessential polar genre of the expedition diary'. Little public attention is given, for example, to the labourers who worked for extractive industries in the polar regions – not least in Antarctica, where science-hero myths pervade. Yet the dominant human presence in Antarctica leading up to the Heroic Age had been labourers in the sealing industry, whose working lives and intimate knowledge of Antarctic environments Melisa Salerno, Jimena Cruz, and Andrés Zarankin consider. Meanwhile, Adriana Craciun's work on the persistent entanglements between Arctic exploration, extractive industries, and geopolitics offers further light on the cultural power of this particular period.[13] It is telling that one of the few works of historical fiction from Canada's north that writes about Christian missionaries is about Emile Pétitot, active in the late nineteenth century, who greatly preferred exploration over his religious responsibilities, and whose published writings have been mined for decades as sources of ethnographic and geographic knowledge.[14] In popular culture, polar history remains a terrain for discovery and exploration more than anything else. Future polar histories need to contend with the weight this creates around the academic historiography and its wider reception.

The Anthropocene

The Cold War and the Anthropocene do not perfectly overlap, although there are important connections between the two periods. The Cold War, moreover, ending as it did with the fall of the Soviet Union, offers a discrete temporalization that is invaluable to historical analysis. Klaus Dodds, Stephen Bocking, and Pey-Yi Chu make important cases for the significance of the Cold War period to polar science. The Anthropocene, by contrast, is ongoing and perhaps only now – in the twenty-first century as global heating and its effects intensify – showing its true features. The open-endedness of the Anthropocene necessarily means that it is more elusive as a coherent temporal and thematic framework for historical analysis. Using the Anthropocene to think about the last seventy years or more of polar history allows us to focus on some of the same key subjects that figure prominently in the Cold War historiography: energy security, the rise of nuclear technologies, polar environments as laboratories, and the manifold effects of militarization. These themes are placed in broader, global context and their origins and effects understood as not uniquely polar, allowing for an otherwise regional area of study to have even greater relevance. In what follows, we examine briefly what polar history looks like through the temporal framing of the Anthropocene. One last important consideration, however, is that neither the Cold War nor the Anthropocene directs adequate attention to

---

13 Craciun, *Writing Arctic Disaster*; see also Craciun, "Franklin's Sobering True Legacy".
14 Haley, *Petitot: A Novel*.

one of the key areas of ongoing historiographical analysis – namely the effects of what scholars have referred to as high modernism on Indigenous peoples in northern colonial contexts. The Anthropocene is most useful for thinking about human relations with the rest of nature, in a period when human interventions and impacts came to dominate in natural systems. We offer some further consideration of this issue below.

Industrial mining operations, commercial fisheries, aviation, and urban settlements all came to northern polar regions before World War II. Andy Bruno and Ekaterina Kalemeneva highlight the priority that the USSR placed on urbanizing the north, with resource towns and cities emerging in the first half of the twentieth century. In northern Canada, the oil strike at Norman Wells in 1921 prompted the signing of Treaty 11, to better secure Canadian title to the resource-rich lands along the Mackenzie River. Oil extracted at Norman Wells was used to make aviation gas, essential to the proliferation of bush planes in the North and integral to wider industrialization. As Henrik Knudsen, Arn Keeling, and John Sandlos describe, industrial mining for coal and other minerals and ores began in Scandinavia, Svalbard, and northern Canada in the early twentieth century, while cryolite mining in Greenland had even longer roots. Many of these older operations continued, expanded, or had effects and influence, including environmental impacts, into the later twentieth century. World War II was a moment of significant change across the polar north, apparent across the region and exemplified in northern North America by what Philip Wight refers to as 'a singular megaproject – the "Northwest Defense Complex"'.

Following this period of transformation, the frame of the Anthropocene draws our attention to these key features of the industrial polar north after 1950: 'extraordinary' energy production and consumption – including nuclear energy – and the proliferation of significant, persistent environmental contaminants at high latitudes.[15] The construction of energy infrastructure continued immediately after the end of the war in the northern polar regions. It accelerated significantly with the Prudhoe Bay oil discovery in 1967. In the decade from the discovery to the delivery of oil to tidewater at Valdez, the politics of oil exploration and development in northern North America shifted dramatically, in what Nuttall characterized as the most 'significant development in terms of natural resources and Indigenous land rights'. Specifically, this period saw the creation of the Alaska Federation of Natives and, in 1971, the Alaska Native Land Claims Settlement Act, and

---

15 Syvitski et al., "Extraordinary Human Energy Consumption".

across the US/Canada border, the Mackenzie Valley Pipeline Inquiry, convened in 1974 with Thomas Berger at its head. The Berger Inquiry was a watershed moment in Indigenous relations with the Canadian state and led directly to the modern land claims settlements of later decades.[16] Conflicts around Indigenous rights and lifeways and oil and gas development persist, most significantly in Gwich'in opposition to drilling in the Arctic National Wildlife Refuge with its effects on the Porcupine caribou herd.[17] Since the 1970s, oil and gas exploration, production, and consumption continued to shape polar lands and waters. As Bruno and Kalemeneva observed from the post-Soviet Arctic, settlements in oil and gas areas were among the only ones that continued to grow after the 1990s. The oil sands in northern Alberta are at the southern edge of the polar region. And, of course, the effects of consuming fossil fuels have been apparent in the Arctic and Sub-Arctic for decades but are now taking on more dramatic form, with ice-free summers, permafrost melting, disappearing lakes and rivers, and massive wildfires.

Alongside the massive expansion of fossil fuel production, there was the concurrent expansion of nuclear research and technologies and uranium production in the northern polar regions – another form of extraordinary energy production and consumption. From 1942 until 1960, the Eldorado mine on Great Bear Lake was a continental supplier of uranium to the Manhattan Project and essential to the assembly of the US nuclear arsenal. Likewise, the Distant Early Warning Line system had significant impacts in bringing the Cold War to Canada's Arctic. Project Chariot in Alaska and Project Cauldron in Alberta proposed the use of nuclear weapons as construction and mining tools respectively. The 1978 re-entry and disintegration of the Cosmos 954 nuclear satellite has been the subject of multiple recent studies.[18] In the Soviet Arctic, as Chu and Bocking describe, Novaya Zemlya was the site of atmospheric and underground nuclear tests into the 1970s, as was Amchitka off Alaska. Polar environments thus served to supply nuclear power, and to test nuclear technologies, and ultimately felt the environmental consequences of the nuclear age, with the elevated radiation at Novaya Zemlya among the most serious, lasting legacies.

Chu and Bocking consider in depth the significance of Cold War priorities in shaping 'a distinctive episode in the history of polar knowledge'. Nuclear technologies and fossil fuels constitute only part of their story. Another part highlights the rising significance of polar ecosystems to studies of the global

---

16 Berger, *Northern Frontier, Northern Homeland.*   17 Dunaway, *Defending the Arctic Refuge.*
18 Rand, "Falling Cosmos"; Dean and Lackenbauer, "A Northern Nuclear Nightmare?", Power and Keeling, "Cleaning up Cosmos".

environment. The 'environment' itself emerged as a distinct object of research and governance during the Cold War, and was connected to global knowledge and governance institutions.[19] One of the measurable criteria of the Anthropocene is pollutants released into the environment since the 1950s. Radioactive fallout constitutes a significant part of these enduring legacies. Bocking has shown elsewhere that contaminants were observed in Arctic environments as early as the late nineteenth century, but only came to be known comprehensively with detailed atmospheric observations in the 1950s.[20] Since the 1950s, contaminants have proliferated and diversified, including not only radioactive fallout, but also persistent organic pollutants (POPs) such as DDT – produced and consumed elsewhere, conveyed by global circulation, and precipitating out at the poles. This history of material circulation and scientific knowledge of POPs culminated in the mid-1980s with research findings that shocked and surprised scientists and Inuit in revealing the extent of contamination of country foods and the human health consequences at high latitudes.

In Antarctictica, the 1980s saw the discovery of another change caused by the global circulation of anthropogenic agents: the ozone hole. Caused in large part by Cold War consumption technologies, its discovery and relatively easily graspable carcinogenic consequences, together with the availability of replacement technology, led to the implementation of the Montreal Protocol that regulates the production and consumption of nearly 100 human-made chemicals referred to as ozone depleting substances (ODS).[21]

The Anthropocene forces us to consider the presence of humans as a force with geological-scale impacts upon the Earth. This power then also casts new light on the vulnerability of other-than-human nature. In this period, moreover, as Justiina Dahl and Alessandro Antonello concluded, Antarctica – once portrayed as forbidding, harsh and inimical to humans – came to be understood and governed as a fragile environment. The original Antarctic Treaty had barely mentioned environmental protection. A series of environmental regulations, frameworks, and protocols followed, not only for the sake of the environment, but also, as Dahl and Antonella explain in Chapter 26, because 'governing the environment was good for maintaining ecological relationships as well as geopolitical ones'. Unlike the northern polar regions, industrial activity in the high southern latitudes (at this point limited to pelagic whaling) crashed, to be replaced by krill fisheries from the 1970s

---

19 Warde et al., *The Environment: A History*.   20 Bocking, "Toxic Surprises".
21 Solomon, "Discovery of Antarctic Ozone Hole".

onwards. Concerns were raised that devastating consequences could follow for whole Antarctic marine ecosystems if krill, also a food source for many marine species, was over-harvested. The potential for mining in Antarctica was explored, but partly owing to pressure from environmental conservation groups, and the wicked problem of Antarctic sovereignty, the environmental framework meant to regulate mining was adapted into an Environmental Protocol that put a moratorium on all mining activities. The north and south polar regions, while coming to be understood as similarly vulnerable places in the global environment, nevertheless faced divergent industrial pressures in the late twentieth century and into the twenty-first.

The Anthropocene directs our attention to the history of extraordinary energy production and consumption in polar regions; to the history of science and technology, including the production of, and contests over, knowledge and expertise; and to the history of contaminants in their material, health, and political effects, and as markers of the interconnectedness of the polar regions with the rest of the globe. The Anthropocene does not, however, direct our attention to colonialism. The period after 1950 saw experimental, high modernist approaches to governing northern Indigenous populations from assertive and expanding bureaucracies. In northern Canada, this included relocation of Inuit populations, projects that were similar to earlier measures in Russia, Greenland, and Alaska.[22] There were also major 'development' initiatives that sought to decolonize the North, while simultaneously extending 'colonialism in another guise – in this case, the northward extension of the liberal order' in Tina Loo's words.[23] The most significant and widespread colonial interventions in northern Indigenous lives in Canada, however, came through the expansion of the residential school system. As Crystal Fraser and the Truth and Reconciliation Commission (TRC) have shown, the federal government took over the school system from the churches in the post-war period.[24] This shift was accompanied by greater recourse to compulsory schooling, the extension of the system to more Indigenous northerners, and the use of school children for medical and nutritional experimentation.[25] Most academic scholarship and the TRC report agree in the assessment that the residential schooling system was genocidal in its intent and

22 Tester and Kulchyski, *Tammarniit (Mistakes)*; Marcus, "Inuit Relocation Policies".
23 Loo, *Moved by the State*, 55; Sangster, *The Iconic North*.
24 Fraser, "T'aih k'ìighe' tth'aih zhit diidich'ùh"; Truth and Reconciliation Commission of Canada, *Canada's Residential Schools*.
25 Mosby, "Administering Colonial Science".

application.[26] In Chapter 20 of this volume, Jens Heinrich emphasizes the similarities between the history of Danification in post-war Greenland and the Inuit experience in Canada in this period. The increased political power of circumpolar Indigenous peoples in the latter half of the twentieth century, while intimately connected to fossil fuel exploitation as noted earlier, also has to be interpreted through this larger history of colonialism and its specific post-war aspects.

The Days and Nights to Come

Polar regions have their own distinctive temporality, just as polar histories can be organized or examined through distinctive temporal lenses: Deep Time, the era of imperial exploration, or the Anthropocene – to draw attention to different, central themes in the polar past. By assessing these temporal frames, we offer alternatives. These alternatives respond to the observation made by Jackie Price, Rebecca Mearns, and Emilie Cameron that there is a need for better conceptualizations of 'time, history, and periodization' than that found in many of the classics of polar historiography. They write about Robert Williamson's work on the Inuit of the Kivalliq Region specifically, but his chopping of time into pre-contact, contact, and post-contact history is a common enough feature of the wider literature where it considers Indigenous histories in the polar North. Elizabeth Leane's Chapter 11 on historical fiction pushes the consideration of temporality even further. Leane uses the Bakhtinian idea of the chronotope to describe the polar regions as 'places that are *about* time'. However, it is the extent of the cryosphere at high latitudes that is primarily responsible for some of this distinctive sense of temporality. Ice, as understood in modern Western culture, holds things in place, frozen in time.

There are countless examples of this cultural construction. Given the pandemic moment in which we find ourselves at the time of writing, we can look to the study of disease for two examples. Much of our current detailed knowledge of the genetics of the 1918–19 pandemic influenza virus comes from samples taken from a young Iñupiat woman buried in the graveyard at Sitaisaq / Brevig Mission, Alaska. In 1951, Swedish microbiologist Johan Hultin retrieved samples of her frozen lungs from the site, with permission from village elders. As the Centers for Disease Control describe

---

26 Woolford, *This Benevolent Experiment*; Powell and Peristerakis, "Genocide in Canada"; Truth and Reconciliation Commission of Canada, *Honouring the Truth*.

this work, 'Hultin believed that within that preserved burial ground he might still find traces of the 1918 virus itself, frozen in time within the tissues of the villagers whose lives it had claimed'.[27] A similar but far more ominous narrative turns frozen polar pathogens from objects of study into novel hazards in a hotter, melted future. Recent outbreaks of anthrax in Siberian reindeer have been attributed to the release of anthrax spores from thawing permafrost.[28] Anthrax can persist in the soil for decades. This has raised the spectre of what other pathogens might be released from our frozen past. Historians are ill-situated to assess the health risks of frozen pathogens. However, we are well-situated to understand that this research and the narratives through which these findings and methodologies are communicated are rooted in culture. In her seminal work, *Do Glaciers Listen?*, Julie Cruikshank looked directly at ice and glaciers, and the experiences of them in a period of encounter between Tlingit, Athapaskans, and Europeans, as sites of cultural contact and divergence. Just as Antarctica's geological history is not held fast by ice, so too the idea of being frozen in time need not guide our future polar histories.

Indeed, how can it? Going forward, global heating will shape new research questions about the past. Polar peoples, like George Angohiatok, have already lived with the experience of warming and its manifold effects on human and other-than-human nature. We need to attend more closely to these past experiences, to look more closely at the phenomenology of life on a warming planet. We should also think about the ways that polar places, people, and pasts will endure even as the cryosphere breaks apart – like the annual breakup of spring, but with the prospect that it will not be remade again come autumn. This possibility should refocus our attention on the significance of cold, snow, and ice in polar histories, but also should push historians to attend to other features, the very long and very short days and nights, the persistence and remaking of communities, that shape life, experience, time, and history at high latitudes.

Bibliography

Andrews, Thomas D., Glen MacKay, and Leon Andrew, *Hunters of the Alpine Ice: The NWT Ice Patch Study* (Yellowknife: Prince of Wales Northern Heritage Centre, 2009).

Berger, Thomas R., *Northern Frontier, Northern Homeland: The Report of the Mackenzie Valley Pipeline Inquiry* (Ottawa: Minister of Supply and Services, 1977).

27 Jordan, "The Deadliest Flu". 28 Stella et al., "Permafrost Dynamics".

Binnema, Ted, *Enlightened Zeal: The Hudson's Bay Company and Scientific Networks, 1670–1870* (Toronto: University of Toronto Press, 2014).

Bocking, Stephen, "Toxic Surprises: Contaminants and Knowledge in the Northern Environment", in Stephen Bocking and Brad Martin, eds., *Ice Blink: Navigating Northern Environmental History* (Calgary: University of Calgary Press, 2017), pp. 421–464.

Bockstoce, John R., *Whales, Ice, and Men: The History of Whaling in the Western Arctic* (Seattle: University of Washington Press, 1986).

CBC News, "Quebec Couple Fleeing COVID-19 'Endangered' Yukon First Nation, Chief Says", *CBC News* (30 March 2020), www.cbc.ca/news/canada/north/quebec-couple-old-crow-yukon-covid-19-1.5514429.

Craciun, Adriana, "Franklin's Sobering True Legacy", *The Ottawa Citizen* (10 September 2014), https://ottawacitizen.com/news/national/adriana-craciun-franklins-sobering-true-legacy.

Craciun, Adriana, *Writing Arctic Disaster: Authorship and Exploration* (Cambridge: Cambridge University Press, 2016).

Cruikshank, Julie, *Do Glaciers Listen? Local Knowledge, Colonial Encounters, and Social Imagination* (Vancouver: UBC Press, 2005).

Dean, Ryan, and P. Whitney Lackenbauer, "A Northern Nuclear Nightmare? Operation Morning Light and the Recovery of Cosmos 954 in the Northwest Territories, 1978", in Susan Colbourn and Timothy Andrews Sayle, eds., *The Nuclear North: Histories of Canada in the Atomic Age* (Vancouver: UBC Press, 2021).

Dodds, Klaus, and Christy Collis, "Post-colonial Antarctica", in Klaus Dodds, Alan Hemmings, and Peder Roberts, eds., *Handbook on the Politics of Antarctica* (Cheltenham: Edward Elgar, 2017), pp. 50–68, https://doi.org/10.4337/9781784717681.00014.

Duchaussois, Pierre, *Aux Glaces Polaires: Indiens et Esquimaux* (Ville La Salle: Noviciat des Oblats de Marie Immaculée, 1921).

Dunaway, Finis, *Defending the Arctic Refuge: A Photographer, an Indigenous Nation, and a Fight for Environmental Justice* (Chapel Hill: University of North Carolina Press, 2021).

Dunbar, Moira, "The Effect of Sea Ice Conditions on Maritime Arctic Expeditions During the Franklin Era", in Patricia D. Sutherland, ed., *The Franklin Era in Canadian Arctic History, 1845–1859* (Ottawa: University of Ottawa Press, 1985), pp. 114–121, https://doi.org/10.2307/j.ctv16pgd.13.

Fraser, Crystal, "'T'aih k'ìighe' tth'aih zhit diidich'ùh (By Strength, We Are Still Here): Indigenous Northerners Confronting Hierarchies of Power at Day and Residential Schools in Nanhkak Thak (the Inuvik Region, Northwest Territories), 1959–1982", PhD diss. (University of Alberta, 2019).

Haley, Susan, *Petitot: A Novel* (Kentville, NS: Gaspereau, 2013).

Jordan, Douglas, "The Deadliest Flu: The Complete Story of the Discovery and Reconstruction of the 1918 Pandemic Virus", *Centers for Disease Control and Prevention* (updated 17 December 2019), www.cdc.gov/flu/pandemic-resources/reconstruction-1918-virus.html.

Kesling, Ben, and Ryan Dube, "Covid-19 Reaches Antarctica, the Last Continent Hit by the Pandemic", *The Wall Street Journal* (22 December 2020), www.wsj.com/articles/covid-19-reaches-antarctica-the-last-continent-hit-by-the-pandemic-11608681353.

Lindsay, Debra, *Science in the Subarctic: Trappers, Traders, and the Smithsonian Institution* (Washington, DC: Smithsonian Institution Press, 1993).
Loo, Tina, *Moved by the State: Forced Relocation and Making a Good Life in Postwar Canada* (Vancouver: UBC Press, 2019).
Mancilla, Alejandra, "A Continent of and for Whiteness? 'White' Colonialism and the 1959 Antarctic Treaty", *Polar Record* 55 (2019): 317–319, https://doi.org/10.1017/S0032247 41900069X.
Marcus, Alan R., *Inuit Relocation Policies in Canada and Other Circumpolar Countries, 1925–60* (Ottawa: Royal Commission on Aboriginal Peoples, 1995).
Minardi, Di, "Antarctica Is the Last Continent Without COVID-19: Scientists Want to Keep It That Way", *National Geographic* (7 August 2020), www.nationalgeographic.com/science/article/antarctica-last-continent-without-coronavirus-covid-scientists-keep-that-way.
Mosby, Ian, "Administering Colonial Science: Nutrition Research and Human Biomedical Experimentation in Aboriginal Communities and Residential Schools, 1942–52", *Histoire sociale/Social History* 46 (2013): 145–172.
Parlee, Brenda L., and Ken J. Caine, eds., *When the Caribou Do Not Come: Indigenous Knowledge and Adaptive Management in the Western Arctic* (Vancouver: UBC Press, 2018).
Powell, Christopher, and Julia Peristerakis, "Genocide in Canada: A Relational View", in Andrew Woolford, Jeff Benvenuto, and Alexander Laban Hinton, eds., *Colonial Genocide in Indigenous North America* (Durham, NC: Duke University Press, 2014), pp. 70–92.
Power, Ellen and Arn Keeling, "Cleaning up Cosmos: Satellite Debris, Radioactive Risk, and the Politics of Knowledge in Operation Morning Light," *The Northern Review* 48 (2018): 81–109.
Prince of Wales Northern Heritage Centre, "Territorial Evolution of the Northwest Territories" (Yellowknife: Prince of Wales Northern Heritage Centre, 2018), www.pwnhc.ca/territorial-evolution-of-the-northwest-territories/.
Rand, Lisa Ruth, "Falling Cosmos: Nuclear Reentry and the Environmental History of Earth Orbit", *Environmental History* 24 (2019): 78–103, https://doi.org/10.1093/envhis/emy125.
Ray, Arthur J., *The Canadian Fur Trade in the Industrial Age* (Toronto: University of Toronto Press, 1990).
Sangster, Joan, *The Iconic North: Cultural Constructions of Aboriginal Life in Postwar Canada* (Vancouver: UBC Press, 2016).
Scott, Shirley V., "Ingenious and Innocuous? Article IV of the Antarctic Treaty as Imperialism", *Polar Journal* 1 (2011): 51–62, https://doi.org/10.1080/2154896x.2011.568787.
Solomon, Susan, "The Discovery of the Antarctic Ozone Hole", *Nature* 575 (2019): 46–47, https://doi.org/10.1038/d41586-019-02837-5.
Stella, Elisa, Lorenzo Mari, Jacopo Gabrieli, et al., "Permafrost Dynamics and the Risk of Anthrax Transmission: A Modelling Study", *Scientific Reports* 10 (2020), 16460, https://doi.org/10.1038/s41598-020-72440-6.
Syvitski, Jaia, Colin N. Waters, John Day, et al., "Extraordinary Human Energy Consumption and Resultant Geological Impacts Beginning Around 1950 CE Initiated the Proposed Anthropocene Epoch", *Communications Earth and Environment* 1 (2020), 32, https://doi.org/10.1038/s43247-020-00029-y.

Tester, Frank James, and Peter Kulchyski, *Tammarniit (Mistakes): Inuit Relocation in the Eastern Arctic, 1939–63* (Vancouver: UBC Press, 1994).

Truth and Reconciliation Commission of Canada, *Canada's Residential Schools: The Inuit and Northern Experience* (Montreal: McGill-Queen's University Press, 2015).

Truth and Reconciliation Commission of Canada, *Honouring the Truth, Reconciling for the Future: Summary of the Final Report of the Truth and Reconciliation Commission of Canada* (Winnipeg: Truth and Reconciliation Commission of Canada, 2015).

Warde, Paul, Libby Robin, and Sverker Sörlin, *The Environment: A History of the Idea* (Baltimore: Johns Hopkins University Press, 2018).

Woolford, Andrew, *This Benevolent Experiment: Indigenous Boarding Schools, Genocide, and Redress in Canada and the United States* (Winnipeg: University of Manitoba Press, 2015).

Index

Introductory Note

References such as '178–179' indicate (not necessarily continuous) discussion of a topic across a range of pages. Wherever possible in the case of topics with many references, these have either been divided into sub-topics or only the most significant discussions of the topic are listed. Because the entire work is about the 'Polar Regions', the use of this term (and certain others that occur constantly throughout the book) as entry points has been restricted. Information will be found under the corresponding detailed topics.

1955 Gentlemen's Agreement, 549

AAC (Arctic Athabaskan Council), 641
AAL (Arctic Aeromedical Laboratory), 585–587
Aangóon, 575
Aasiaat, 496
aasiviks, 503
Abercrombie, William, 576, 578
Absolon, Kathleen, 761
acclimatization, 527, 586, 651, 707–709
Acheson, Dean, 583
activists, Sámi, 115, 117, 119
Adams, Boyd, 231
adaptation, ecological, 292
Adelaide Peninsula, 208, 220
Adélie Land, 191
administration, 165, 302–303, 319, 336, 396, 470, 491, 495–496, 629, 652
administrative capital, 20, 568
administrative functions, 462, 623
administrators, 489, 540, 626–627, 631
Admiralty, 211, 212–214, 305, 306, 311
Admiralty Island, 575
Advent City, 446
adventure, narratives of, 234–235
AEC (Atomic Energy Commission), 518, 524, 586–587
AEPS (Arctic Environmental Protection Strategy), 641, 663–664

aerial radar, 65, 67
Affarlikassa fjord, 445
AFN (Alaska Federation of Natives), 630, 780
Afterlands, 259, 261–262, 267
Agassiz, Louis, 196
Agreed Measures for the Conservation of Antarctic Fauna and Flora (AMCAFF), 656, 663
Agreement on the Conservation of Polar Bears, 23, 657
agreements, 138, 358, 361, 437–439, 622–623, 633, 657–658, 661–662, 678–679, 684–685; *see also* individual agreement titles
    impact and benefit, 438–439, 456
    intergovernmental, 361, 720
    international, 370, 649, 666, 687–688
    land claims, 622, 632–634
agriculture, 133, 144, 146–147, 148, 164, 166, 174, 718–719, 775
AGS *see* American Geographical Society
Aguirre Cerda, Pedro, 680–681
Ahtna, 434, 435
AIA (Aleut International Association), 641
air bases, 516, 565, 580, 584, 585–587, 611–612
    Thule, 505, 516, 527, 743
aircraft, 60, 65, 343, 368, 513, 516, 521, 579, 585, 601–602; *see also* planes
airfields, 529, 579–580, 582, 600–601, 606, 743
Ájtte, 119

789

Index

Akaitcho Dene, 633
Akana, Nellie, 35
Aklavik, 3
Alaska, 84, 85, 86, 87, 434–435, 563, 564, 565, 566, 569–571, 572–587, 600–601, 609–612, 629–631, 640–642, 716–722
  defence, 602, 611
  land bridge to, 84–87
  Natives, 568–570, 572, 580, 586, 593, 630–631, 717
  North Slope, 18, 437, 518, 525, 593, 599, 607–610, 614–615, 616, 630
  northern, 87, 91, 597
  Purchase, 570–571
  Road Commission, 578
  southeast, 567, 573, 575, 580
  US militarization, 563–587
Alaska Federation of Natives (AFN), 630, 780
Alaska Military Highway, 565, 582, 595, 601
Alaska Native Claims Settlement Act *see* ANCSA
Alaska Syndicate, 435–436
Alaska–Canada Gas Oil Fuel Line (ALCANGO), 612, 613–614
Alaska–Canada Highway, 578, 595, 600–601, 603, 606, 608
Alaskan Command (ALCOM), 584
Alaskan Territorial Guard (ATG), 580–581, 593, 608
Alberta, 601, 607, 633, 781
  oil, 524, 607
ALCANGO (Alaska–Canada Gas Oil Fuel Line), 612, 613–614
alcohol, 33, 48–49, 51, 423, 502
ALCOM (Alaskan Command), 584
Aleut International Association (AIA), 641
Aleutian Islands, 571–572, 580, 582, 602, 607, 611
Alexander Land, 190
Alfonsín, Raúl, 692
Alkavare, 448
all-terrain vehicles (ATVs), 35, 47
Allen, Henry, 576
Alutiiq women, 168
Alyeska, 615–616
AMAP (Arctic Monitoring and Assessment Programme), 663
Amazing Adventures of Kavalier and Clay, The, 256
AMCAFF (Agreed Measures for the Conservation of Antarctic Fauna and Flora), 656, 663
Amchitka, 524, 781
American Antarctica, 677, 678–679, 697

American Civil War, 239, 388, 566–567, 573, 576
American Geographical Society (AGS), 1, 9
American interests, 366–367, 369
American Museum of Natural History, 286
American Polar Society (APS), 9–10
American whalers, 330, 332, 336, 386–388, 569
Amery, Leopold, 310
Amund Ringnes Island, 335
Amundsen, Roald, 57, 221, 229, 231, 234–235, 244, 246, 258–260, 263, 267
ancestral lands, 575, 595, 635
Anchorage, 220, 564–565, 580–581, 584, 586, 606, 608, 612–613, 630
ANCSA (Alaska Native Claims Settlement Act), 565, 622, 630–631, 641
Andes Mountains, 675, 678
Andrée, Salomon, 368
Anglo-American Polar Expedition, 597, 602
Anglo-Dutch war, Fourth, 384
Angohiatok
  George, 32–53
  Mabel, 36, 37, 39, 47
  Sam, 34
animal bones, 134, 147
animal colonies, 408, 410, 420
animal populations, 91, 274, 648, 773, 776
animals, 32–33, 36–37, 39–40, 52–53, 140, 419–422, 702–704, 706–709, 710–722, 772–773
  domestic, 130, 134, 147, 705–706, 721
  watching, 40–42
  wild, 660, 704, 711, 716, 722
Antarctic *see* Antarctica
Antarctic and Southern Ocean Coalition (ASOC), 661
Antarctic Circle, 3, 8, 183, 187, 191–194, 198, 305
Antarctic cooperation, 687, 693, 696–697
Antarctic ice sheet, 55, 58, 63–64, 68, 71, 548, 738
Antarctic icebergs, 733, 736
Antarctic labourers, historical archaeology, 407–425; *see also* sealing
Antarctic landscape, 62
Antarctic Peninsula, 60–61, 311, 313, 392, 395, 540–542, 543, 674, 675–676, 680–681
Antarctic problem, 540–544
Antarctic science, 7, 58, 540, 694
Antarctic Treaty, 12, 59–60, 315–316, 527–528, 536–538, 540, 656–657, 660–662, 692, 694
  Consultative Meetings, 662, 697, 771
  negotiations, 26, 537

Index

Secretariat, 695, 697
Antarctic Treaty System (ATS), 7, 15, 244, 315, 536–558, 660, 774
Antarctic whaling, 256, 303, 310, 379–380, 391–401, 654, 660, 687
Antarctica
  above
  American, 677, 678–679, 697
  as 'land of science', 243–247
  biology, 63–64
  blue continent at South Pole, 196–198
  British, 302, 316–317, 686
  claims, 315, 326, 675, 680–681, 683, 697
  coasts, 57, 60, 378
  conferencing, 551–557
  continent, 55–56, 181, 183, 191, 194–196, 197–200, 240, 241, 305, 310
  Cook's continued influence, 193–196
  Cook's legacy, 186–193
  discoverer, 182, 196, 200
  discovery, 181–201, 305
  East, 59, 61–62, 66–67, 68, 197
  expeditions, 18, 56, 59, 197, 200, 239, 246, 678, 680–681, 683
  exploration, 12–13, 19, 25, 56, 229, 241, 258, 304, 307, 514
  explorers, 201, 235, 310, 685
  geology, 60, 70–71
  glacial history, 62–63
  Heroic Age see Heroic Age
  making of, 538–540
  Ocean, 183–186, 304
  overlapping Argentine and Chilean claims, 673
  South American, 673, 676, 682–684, 687, 691, 692, 694–695, 697
  stations, 6, 20, 313, 674, 681, 685, 690, 692–693, 696
  territories, 199, 310, 412, 423, 674, 678–679, 686
  tourism, 675, 741
  vanishing common knowledge about existing mainland in the South, 182–186
  waters, 197, 311, 391, 393, 397, 400–402, 736
  West, 59, 62, 66–69, 510, 548
  whaling see whaling, Antarctic
Antártida Uruguaya, 690
Anthropocene, 480, 511, 558, 664–666, 667, 733, 770, 779–780, 782, 783–784
anthropologists, 17, 50, 279, 284–285, 297, 476, 489, 755
anthropology, 25, 279–297, 411, 749

Arctic, 279, 282–283
  racial, 116
Apatity, 453, 476
Appadurai, Arjun, 291
APS (American Polar Society), 9–10
archaeological evidence, 92, 146, 210, 420, 423
archaeological sites, 79, 80–81, 85, 88, 95
archaeological work, 18, 108, 110–111, 115, 208, 220, 225, 381, 419
archaeologists, 14, 50, 81, 85, 86, 90–91, 106, 112–113, 122, 207
archaeology, Sámi, 106–108, 110–111, 113, 120–122
ARCO, 610, 615
Arctic
  see also Introductory Note above
  Canadian, 32, 50, 91–92, 100, 164, 208, 266, 270, 336, 345
  coasts, 99, 576, 598, 604
  communities, 22, 430, 628, 731–732, 749
  development, 436–437, 449, 455, 514
  hydrocarbon development, 616–617
  mining see mining
  oil development, 594, 598
  Western Canadian, 32–53, 91
Arctic Aeromedical Laboratory see AAL
Arctic anthropology, 279, 282–283
Arctic Archipelago, 325–326, 349, 639, 709
Arctic Athabaskan Council (AAC), 641
Arctic Circle, 3, 7, 153, 157, 437, 448, 450
Arctic climate impact assessment, 665, 666–667
Arctic Coal Company, 364, 446
Arctic Council, 7, 640, 641, 664, 666
Arctic Environmental Protection Strategy see AEPS
Arctic experiences, 262
Arctic governance, 12, 760
Arctic icebergs, 734–735, 737
Arctic Institute of North America, 516, 582
Arctic isotherm, 3
Arctic landscape, 32, 165, 271, 704
Arctic Monitoring and Assessment Programme (AMAP), 663
Arctic Ocean, 7, 90, 167–168, 171–173, 192–193, 198, 653, 658, 726–727, 730
Arctic pioneers, 79–100
Arctic Research Laboratory (ARL), 516–517, 610
Arctic studies, 289, 292–295
arcticness, 368
Arctowski Station, 691

791

area studies, 289, 291
Argentina, 311–312, 315–316, 539–541, 549,
    553–554, 674, 676–678, 679–683,
    686–693, 696–697
  and Chile, 311–313, 541–542, 543, 556, 673–674,
    679–681, 686–687, 689–690,
    691–692, 697
  army, 676, 693
  government, 678, 679, 681
  navy, 316, 677
Argentine Antarctic Institute, 685, 687
Arkhangelsk, 158–159, 161, 165, 170, 172, 466,
    476, 525
Arkhangelsk–Murman steamship
    company, 170
ARL (Arctic Research Laboratory),
    516–517, 610
armed conflicts, 209, 359
armies, 565–566, 570, 572–573, 575–578, 584, 585,
    596, 600, 604, 607–608
Army Corps of Engineers, 582, 611, 613
Army Quartermaster Corps, 582, 583
Arnold, Henry 'Hap', 579, 601
Arsuk, 133, 441
  fjord, 440, 442
artefacts, 19, 79, 80–82, 90, 120, 422, 775
  designs, 81, 97
  lithic, 80, 86
  Norse, 142, 143
artists, 217, 258, 272, 342, 734–735
Asia, 80, 186, 196, 289, 342, 511, 571, 583, 702, 721
  Central, 80, 524, 544
ASOC (Antarctic and Southern Ocean
    Coalition), 661
assertions of sovereignty, 777–778
ATG see Alaskan Territorial Guard
Athapaskans, 623, 637, 785
Atlas of the Pacific Ocean, 190
atmosphere, 55, 253, 259, 356, 468, 475, 511, 513,
    520–522, 738–739
atmospheric carbon dioxide, 63, 521
Atomic Energy Commission see AEC
atrocities, 568, 575
ATS see Antarctic Treaty System
attention, public, 187, 629, 778
ATVs (all-terrain vehicles), 35, 47
Auckland Islands, 392
Auguste Victoria, 364
Aupilaarjuk, Mariano, 755–756
"Auroral Corona with Two Figures", 256
Australasian Antarctic Expedition, 60, 234, 262
Australia, 55–57, 58, 60–61, 64, 538–540,
    547–549, 553–554, 661, 688, 707

Australian Antarctic Territory, 310, 539, 547,
    551–553
autonomy, 466, 488, 527, 621–623, 629,
    634–636, 643, 778
Avango, Dag, 369
average temperatures, 3
Awfully Big Adventure, An, 263
Axel Heiberg Island, 335, 338, 343, 344, 639
Aylwin, Patricio, 692

Bache Peninsula, 342, 345, 347
Bachelet, Michelle, 695
Back, George, 212
Baer, Karl Ernst von, 167–168, 169, 196
Baffin Bay, 211, 327, 328, 379, 776
Baffin Island, 282–283, 285, 327, 330, 333, 337,
    378, 433, 434, 437
Baffin, William, 183, 327
Bainbridge, Beryl, 252–253, 260, 261,
    263–266, 273
Bakhrushin, S. V., 160
Balch, Edwin Swift, 200
baleen, 96, 386, 776
Ballistic Missile Early Warning System, 565
Baltic, 155, 167, 449, 472, 653
Baltic Germans, 167–168
BANZARE (British Australian and New
    Zealand Antarctic Research
    Expedition), 318–319
Baranov, Aleksandr, 567
Bárðarson, Ívar, 144–145
Barents Sea, 89, 156–158, 169, 171–172, 368, 465,
    525, 658, 662–663
Barentsburg, 446–447
Barentsz, William, 192
Baret, Jeanne, 239
Barrett, Andrea, 253, 262, 270–272
Barrow, Sir John, 211, 213–214, 327
BAS see British Antarctic Survey
bases, 6, 156, 157, 231, 313–315, 333, 334–335,
    341–342, 343–344, 505
  military, 475, 553, 611, 741, 743
  naval, 354, 442
  permanent, 59, 90, 99, 314, 696
Basques, 380–381, 386–387, 388
Bathurst Island, 328
bauxite, 454, 493
bay whaling, 402
Beagle Channel, 687, 691–692
Bear Island, 354, 363, 372, 389–390, 394
Beardmore, Sir William, 231
bears, polar, 2, 23, 40, 46, 131, 142, 517, 520, 525,
    657–658

792

Index

Beatson mine, 435
Beattie, Owen, 219, 223
Beaufort Sea, 332, 340, 387–388, 632, 641, 726–728, 737, 743
beaver, 80–81, 776
bedrock, 12, 63, 67, 71, 741, 742
  geology, 71, 772
Beechey Island, 216, 219, 223–224
Belcher, Edward, 328, 330, 335
Belgica, 8
Bellingshausen Sea, 230
Bellingshausen Station, 691
Bellingshausen, Fabian von, 56, 187–190, 191–195, 200
Bellsund, 364
Bentley, Charles, 64, 67, 548
Bergen, 138, 142, 144, 149, 440, 680
Bering Land Bridge, 772
Bering Sea, 173, 367, 576
Bering Strait, 79, 85, 90–91, 97, 100, 163, 167, 378, 387–388, 465
Beringia, 23, 25, 81, 84–87, 99
Bernard Harbour, 34, 45
Bernier, Joseph-Elzéar, 333–334, 339–340, 348
Bertucci, Margaret, 217
beverages, iceberg, 735, 744
Big Delta, 584–585, 601
big game, 46, 82, 364
big science, 15, 513, 529, 539, 550
biological diversity, 727, 740
biology of Antarctica, 63–64
birds, 84–86, 96, 423, 478, 660, 721
Birket-Smith, Kaj, 279, 292
Birthday Boys, The, 252–253, 259–260, 263–266, 273
Biscay, 380, 388
Biscoe, John, 190
bishops, 136–138, 144, 149
bison, steppe, 80–82, 84, 99
Black Angel, 444–445
Blackadder, Jesse, 256
blizzards, 230, 232, 275
blubber, 93, 158, 217, 230, 309, 381–383, 384, 386–387, 407–409, 421–423
blue whales, 389, 397, 400
Boards of Guardians, 488–489
Boas, Franz, 279, 282–286, 291, 297
boats, 35, 45, 47, 233, 242, 409, 420
  skin, 45, 92
Boggs, Samuel, 346
Bolivia, 359
bones, 79, 82, 86, 93, 96–97, 119, 131, 147, 217–219, 223

bonuses, northern, 471, 475
booms, 17, 41–42, 359, 446, 675
Boothia
  Peninsula, 92, 327
  Strait of, 192
Borchgrevink, Carsten, 56, 230
Borden, Robert, 340–341
borders, 108, 110, 113–115, 149, 209, 519, 539, 714, 738, 743
  common, 678–679, 683, 692
  territorial, 651, 692
Bougainville, Louis Antoine de, 239
boundaries, 3–6, 418, 421, 726, 727–729, 732, 735, 737–738, 777–778
  ocean–ice, 729, 731, 744
  of place and time, 726–744
  political, 550, 595, 641, 778
  shifting, 5, 727
Bouvet de Lozier, Jean-Baptiste Charles, 182–183, 391
Bouvet Island, 18
Bowers, Henry "Birdie", 232, 252, 259, 263–264, 265
bowhead whales, 380, 383–385, 387–388, 528, 651
Boyle, Robert, 192
Bransfield, Edward, 56, 187, 200, 305
Bravo, Michael, 8, 23, 743
Brazil, 7, 294, 557, 673, 689–690, 693, 695–696
Bremen, 384–385
Brenton, Howard, 257
Brezhnev, Leonid, 475, 526
Britain *see* United Kingdom
British Antarctic, 302, 316–317, 686
British Antarctic Survey (BAS), 12, 240, 302–303, 316, 320–321
British Antarctic Territory, 302
British Australian and New Zealand Antarctic Research Expedition (BANZARE), 318–319
British Empire, 8, 25, 243, 303, 304–305, 307–308, 310–311, 316–321, 395, 682
British expeditions, 57, 198, 245, 307–308, 312, 330, 391
British explorers, 209, 329, 337–338
British imperial interests, 288–289
British imperialism, 303, 320
British interests, 303, 306, 689
Broken Hill Proprietary, 438
Broken Lands, The, 260
Bruce, William Spiers, 198, 243, 246, 677
Brun, Eske, 491–492, 493–494, 497
Brusilov, Georgy, 172

Index

Buache, Philippe, 182–188, 193
Buchan, David, 211
Budyko, Mikhail, 521
Buenos Aires, 187, 540, 549, 676–677, 683, 694, 695
Buffon, Georges-Louis Leclerc de, 182–183
bull caribou, 42
Bunzl, Matti, 283
bureaucrats, 332, 342, 455, 515, 586
Bush, Vannevar, 11
Bustamante, Lieutenant Colonel Marco, 690
Byers Peninsula, 419, 422
Bylot, Robert, 327
Byrd Station, 65, 548
Byrd, Richard, 9, 16, 241, 343
byres, 134, 135, 140–142

cabins, 416–417, 712, 761
Caesar, Adrian, 260–261
CAFF (Conservation of Arctic Flora and Fauna), 663
California, 209, 573, 596, 598, 604, 607–608, 614, 736
calves, 708–709, 714, 718, 733
 live, 708
 muskox, 708–709, 716, 720
calving, icebergs, 69, 222, 733
Cambridge Bay, 23, 32–35, 38, 42, 45, 47, 50, 52
Cameron, David, 302
Camp Century, 516, 741–744
Campbell Creek drainage, 612–613
camps, 34, 37, 233, 421, 423, 454, 468, 577, 741
 prison, 452, 468; *see also* Gulags
 rotational, 476–477
 summer, 503
Camsell, Charles, 430
Canada, 329–342, 344–347, 437–439, 515–516, 622–623, 632–634, 637–639, 657–659, 663–664, 726
 and Greenland, 99, 379, 622, 635, 641, 665, 735, 755
 and High Arctic islands, 18, 25, 92, 325–350
 1925 Sector Claim and Sverdrup Islands Settlement, 343–345
 Canadian claims and foreign exploration, 1895–1902, 331–336
 Canadian sovereignty achieved, 345–347
 exploration before 1870, 327–329
 resurgence of sovereignty fears, 347–349
 sovereignty and transfer to Canada, 329–331
 sovereignty initiatives, 1903–11, 336–340
 Stefansson, 340–343

Defence Research Board, 516, 517
 government, 436, 515, 597, 625, 633
 northwest, 435, 594
 Parks Canada, 207, 220, 225
 Polar Continental Shelf Project, 516, 527
 sovereignty, 25, 220, 333, 344–345, 348–349
Canadian Arctic, 32, 50, 91–92, 100, 164, 208, 266, 270, 336, 345
 Expedition, 20, 341
 western, 32–53, 91
Canadian High Arctic Research Station (CHARS), 34, 52
Canadians, 326, 329, 331, 333–335, 338–339, 342–343, 344–345, 347–349, 594, 631
Cañas Montalva, Ramón, 682
cannibalism, 212, 217, 223, 329
canoes, 212, 569, 574–575
CANOL, 595, 600, 602–608, 609–612
Canton, 408, 422
Cape Adare, 56, 230, 234
Cape Crozier, 264
Cape Herschel, 214
Cape Thompson, 518, 587
capital, 19, 311, 386–387, 607, 709
capitalism, 17, 407, 411, 424–425, 455
carbon dioxide, atmospheric, 63, 521
Cardigan Strait, 335
cargo vessels, 388, 393
caribou, 34, 37, 41–42, 50, 82, 84, 87, 90–91, 96, 97–99
 bull, 42
caring, 37, 43, 48
Carmack, Kate, 435
carpenters, 414, 418, 443
Carthy, Martin, 222
catcher boats, 389–390, 393–396, 397, 402
Cato, Nancy, 222
cattle, 133, 140, 142, 148
caves, 80, 83–84, 86, 420
CCAMLR *see* Convention for the Conservation of Antarctic Marine Living Resources
central Arctic, 291, 454
Central Asia, 80, 524, 544
central Norway, 88, 112, 711
central Russia, 156, 476
central Siberia, 82, 84
ceremonies, 118, 120, 137, 337, 339, 552, 760
Cerro Negro sealing site, 421
Cháatlk'aa Noow, 567
Chabon, Michael, 256
Challenger expedition, 197
change

794

Index

climate, 53, 55, 320–321, 521–523, 642–643, 663, 664–667, 730–731, 742–743, 771–772
  environmental, 25, 522, 524, 558, 642, 651, 744
  societal, 32, 43–44
changing environment, 38–40, 93
charcoal, 130, 145
Charpentier, Jean de, 196
CHARS *see* Canadian High Arctic Research Station
chartered whaling, 388, 402
Chasing the Light, 256
Cherry-Garrard, Apsley, 252, 262, 308
children, 47, 51, 133, 141, 496, 498, 500, 507, 710, 759
  Greenlandic, 498, 626
Chile, 311–313, 537–538, 540–542, 543–544, 673–674, 676–678, 679–681, 685–686, 688, 691–692
  and Argentina, 311–313, 541–542, 543, 556, 673–674, 679–681, 686–687, 689–690, 691–692, 697
  government, 681, 689
  presidents, 681, 684, 686, 695, 696–697
Chilean Antarctic Commission, 680, 681
Chilean Antarctic Institute, 688, 696
China, 7, 159, 221, 237, 309, 372, 505–506, 529, 556, 557
Chorley, Dick, 287
Christensen, Christen, 392, 394, 397
Christensen, Lars, 13, 397
Christianity, 119, 488, 625, 762, 765
  Orthodox, 156, 465
Christmas, 35, 758–759
chronotopes, 259, 784
Chukchi, 163–164, 387, 454, 465, 466, 527, 624
Chukchi Sea, 388, 587
Chukotka, 84, 90–91, 162, 454, 476, 479, 503, 640
Church, Frederic, 217, 734
churches, 134, 135–138, 141–142, 145, 147, 148, 783
  one-cell stone, 136–137, 146
  small *landnam*, 136, 146
  two-cell, 136–137, 146
Churchill, Winston, 238–239, 687
churchyards, 118–119, 130, 136, 139
circumpolar north, 4, 88, 293–294, 297
  and geographical imagination, 290–294
  and political imagination, 295–297
  initial peopling, 79–100
  mining and colonialism, 430–456

circumpolar region, 288, 290–294, 295–296
circumpolar studies, 289
CITES *see* Convention on International Trade in Endangered Species
cities, 35, 161–163, 413, 435, 451–452, 456, 462, 466, 612, 750
citizen science, 536, 545, 740
citizens, 325, 331, 354, 366, 369, 446, 469, 474, 614, 617
civil servants, 296, 342, 343, 488, 579, 627
civil society, 659, 665
Civil War, American, 239, 388, 566–567, 573, 576
civilian agencies, 518, 586
claimant states, 538, 539, 541, 547, 549–553, 554, 555–557
claims
  Antarctic, 315, 326, 675, 680–681, 683, 697
  imperial, 319–320
Claire Coast, 191
Clarence Island, 233
clashes of interest, 357, 361, 369
climate, 3–6, 9, 142, 146, 167–168, 520–521, 666–667, 744, 770, 771
  change, 53, 55, 320–321, 521–523, 642–643, 663, 664–667, 730–731, 742–743, 771–772
  fluctuations, 84, 90
  harsh, 325, 358, 364, 471, 472, 476
  heating, 4–5, 15, 522
  science, 247, 296, 447, 511
coal, 15, 61, 364, 368, 440, 443, 468, 470, 500, 555
  mining, 22, 444, 446, 463, 496, 627, 709
  prices, 446
coastal erosion, 109, 146
coastal waters, 312, 378, 389, 466
coastlines, 7, 90, 159, 194, 319, 391, 397, 726, 730, 732
coasts, 140–141, 191–192, 387, 389, 402, 416, 418, 492, 493, 689
  Antarctic, 57, 60, 378
  Arctic, 99, 576, 598, 604
  Greenland, 183, 218, 737, 742
  Murman, 158, 169, 466, 469
  Pacific, 99, 187, 577, 600, 776
  Siberian, 170, 334, 342
  Yukon, 336, 340
Coates, Ken, 606
Coats Land, 232
cold areas, 583–584
Cold Regions Testing Center, 585

Index

Cold War, 510–514, 516, 517, 518, 519, 520, 523, 525–529, 536–537, 545–546, 581–584, 594–596, 611, 779
  activities, 518, 524, 587
  competition, 514, 553, 656
  early, 515, 526, 565, 583, 655
  environmental knowledge, 510–530
  polar knowledge, 520–523
  polar regions as Cold War spaces, 523–528
  polar science
    development, 512–516
    practices, 516–520
    priorities, 511, 781
    science, 512, 513, 516–517, 539
  collaboration, 109, 112–113, 141, 171, 173, 286, 511, 539, 542, 758
  international, 65, 155, 171, 281, 313, 688
collective farms, 467, 477
Collor de Mello, Fernando, 693
Colombia, 674, 693–694
colonial administration, 488–489, 491–492, 494
colonial expansion, 116, 433, 455
colonial history, 114, 115–116, 122, 159, 456, 778
Colonial Office, 304, 310–311, 318, 330, 542–543
colonial relations, 767, 775
colonialism, 17, 19, 107, 109, 208, 225, 239, 773–774, 777, 783–784
  and mining, 430–456
  European, 114, 356, 362, 676
  Nordic, 108, 114
  resource, 436, 442, 446
  settler, 326, 464, 563, 651, 774, 777
colonies, 168, 209, 243, 294, 310, 318, 434, 440, 487, 494–495
  former, 235, 326, 329
  mining, 434, 651
  United States, 565, 570, 572–573
colonization, 157, 159, 161, 164, 455, 621, 762, 774, 776–777
  and change, 623–628
Colville River, 597
co-management, 623, 638
Comaroffs, Jean and John, 294
commerce, 7, 154, 168, 213, 226, 310, 441
commercial fishing, 38, 557, 626
commercial sealing *see* sealing
commercial whaling, 18, 26, 380, 399, 401–408, 556, 624, 776
Commerçon, Philibert, 239
Committee of the North, 173, 467
common borders, 678–679, 683, 692
common interest(s), 142, 368, 369, 694, 698

Commonwealth Trans-Antarctic Expedition, 59, 314, 318–319
communications, infrastructures, 6, 565
communis, 371, 777
communism, 22, 454–455, 471, 478, 480, 510, 526, 528, 691
communities, 16–17, 45–46, 225–226, 438–439, 631–632, 648–649, 731–732, 751, 762–764, 772–773
  Arctic, 22, 430, 628, 731–732, 749
  British polar, 313, 315
  human, 555, 742, 757
  Indigenous, 5, 6, 439, 583, 586, 628, 630, 638, 648, 756
  Inuit, 22, 282, 437, 441, 493, 639, 765
  Iñupiat, 587, 630
  permanent, 625
  Sámi, 109, 115, 118, 121–122
  scientific, 70–71, 245, 246, 399, 536, 771
  small, 149, 631, 635, 656
Compañía Argentina de Pesca, 309, 393, 678
companies, 389, 394, 396–399, 411, 413, 414, 442, 444, 718–719, 735–737; *see also* individual company names
  Dutch, 381–383, 388, 400
  mining, 366, 436, 438–439, 441, 652, 660
  Norwegian, 395, 400, 446–447, 541, 555, 652
  private, 440, 479, 515, 596, 598
  sealing, 408, 413–414, 415–416, 425
  whaling, 168, 309, 389–392, 393, 396, 399, 679
compensation, 344, 505, 630, 634, 715
competences, 20, 502
  linguistic, 292
  technical, 9
competition, 237, 244–245, 356–357, 381–383, 388, 408, 441–442, 511, 519, 529
complexities, 70, 118, 122, 160, 263, 326
comprehensive land claims, 623, 632–633, 637
computer models, 65, 517
computers, 514, 520, 739
conferences, 355, 362, 551–553, 556, 658, 666, 680, 684, 736–737, 765
  international, 552, 683
conflicts, 106, 316, 362, 365, 489–490, 688, 690, 691, 727, 729
  armed, 209, 359
  political, 320, 451
  violent, 236, 434
Congress, 359, 566, 575, 579, 601, 611, 613, 615, 630, 636
Connell, Raewyn, 295
conquests, 10, 13, 157, 159, 230, 258, 266, 304, 462–463, 574

Index

Conrad, Joseph, 207, 217, 262
consensus, 70, 223, 245, 358, 463, 501, 556, 557, 631, 663–664
conservation, 22, 311–312, 623, 652, 656–657, 660, 663, 666, 693, 697
Conservation of Arctic Flora and Fauna (CAFF), 663
constitution, 413
construction, 50, 452, 453, 472, 578–579, 594, 599–601, 602, 612, 615–616
  materials, 421, 741
  principles, 473, 476
  workers, 626–627
  works, 471, 476
consultative members, 690, 694
consultative parties, 7, 555, 662, 688, 689–691, 693
consumer products, 408, 526
consumption, 735, 737, 780–781, 782–783
contaminants, 522, 525, 623, 742, 744, 780, 782, 783
contamination, 456, 467, 525, 586, 688, 782
continental ice, 733, 740, 742, 772
continental measurements, 58–60
continental shelf, 226, 597
continuity, 160, 357, 468, 511, 529, 673, 674–676, 732, 772
contractors, 600, 602, 609, 612
contracts, 223, 413, 505, 604, 613
control, 159–162, 165, 466, 472, 501–502, 505, 510, 513, 675, 677
  effective, 408, 630
  imperial, 161, 164, 165–166
  state, 637, 675
Convention for the Conservation of Antarctic Marine Living Resources (CCAMLR), 4, 660, 663–664, 666, 693, 697
Convention for the Conservation of Antarctic Seals, 309, 657
Convention on the Regulation of Antarctic Mineral Resource Activities (CRAMRA), 660–663, 689
Convention on International Trade in Endangered Species (CITES), 658
Cook, Frederick A., 8
Cook, James, 163, 164, 183–190, 192–193, 196, 200, 201, 210, 304–305, 391
cooperages, 381–383
cooperation, 386, 394, 546, 553, 555, 557, 661, 664, 693–694, 696
  Antarctic, 687, 693, 696–697
  international, 60, 155, 171, 226, 245, 371, 399, 513, 519, 529

regional, 689, 692, 695
scientific, 171, 244–245, 512, 515, 553, 664, 698, 720
Cope, John Lachlan, 240
Copenhagen, 116, 292, 440, 443–444, 488–489, 496–498, 502, 506, 627, 640
copper, 434, 435, 440, 453
  mining, 435, 448–449
  native, 433–434
Copper Eskimo, 50, 434
Coppermine River, 210, 212, 434
Corbeta Uruguay Scientific Station, 692
Cordilleran Ice Sheet, 86
Cordovez Madariaga, Enrique, 681
Cornelius, Patricia, 257
Cornwallis Island, 328, 437
Coronation Gulf, 39, 434
COSCO Shipping Corporation, 221
Cosgrove, Denis, 10
cosmography, 283, 284
cosmos, 190
Cosmos 954 satellite, 781
costs, 47, 67, 302, 331, 341, 354, 599, 606–608, 612, 616
  ecological, 454, 456
courts, 367, 488; *see also* individual court titles
COVID-19, 674, 770–771
cows, 147, 706
CRAMRA *see* Convention on the Regulation of Antarctic Mineral Resource Activities
Crerar, Thomas, 347
crevasses, 69, 230, 234, 265, 740
crew lists, 412, 414–415
crews, 149, 271, 307, 308, 388, 412–414, 416–418, 469
  sealing, 409–410, 412, 414–415, 416
Crimean War, 168–169
Crocker Land, 340–341
cruise ships, 221–222, 304, 317, 364
cryolite, 440–443, 493, 501
  exports, 442
  mining, 442, 780
  synthetic, 442
Crystal Serenity, MV, 221
CSAGI (Special Committee of the IGY), 313, 546
Cuba, 522, 573, 576, 691
Culshaw, Robert, 302
cultural changes, 131, 452
cultural heritage, 109, 121, 773
  management, 108, 122
cultural identity, 208, 624

797

Index

cultural resilience, 32, 291
cultural revitalization movements, 106, 120
cultural rights, 106–108, 120, 643
cultural values, 631, 641
culture areas, 289
cultures, 285–286, 497–498, 499–500, 502, 503–504, 505, 629, 639, 641, 648–649
   Danish, 498, 504
   Dyuktai, 83–84, 86
   Greenlandic, 444, 497–499, 506
   Indigenous, 10, 433, 640, 774
   Inuit, 285, 292, 642, 763, 768
   material, 91–93, 95–97, 115, 425
   popular, 329, 765, 779
   Russian, 154, 162, 168
   Sámi, 110, 111
   Saqqaq, 92, 94, 98
   Thule, 487
   Ushki, 84, 86
Cumberland Sound, 218, 282, 285–286, 291, 386
currents, ocean, 59, 168, 738
Curthoys, Ann, 255
Curzon, Lord, 240–241
Cyprus-Anvil, 438

d'Urville, Jules Sebastién César Dumont, 191–192, 196, 200
daguerreotype camera, 216
Dalgliesh, David, 314
Dalrymple, Alexander, 304–305
Danes, 368, 444–445, 487–490, 493, 497, 499, 527, 626–627, 714
Daniels, Joseph, 242
Danification, 497–499, 504, 784
Danilevski, Nikolai, 169
Danish culture, 498, 504
Danish language, 489, 496–497, 499, 626
Danish whaling, 385
Daring Deeds of Polar Explorers, 14
darkness, 79, 92, 100, 593, 743
Darrieussecq, Marie, 259
Dash Patrol, 242–243
data, synoptic *see* synoptic data
David, Edgeworth, 243
Davidson, Peter, 289
Davis Strait, 332, 385–386, 388
Davis, Jefferson Columbus, 568–569, 571–574, 577
Davis, John, 183
Davis, John King, 246
Davis, Paxton, 260
Davis, William M., 282
Dawson Charlie, 435

Dawson City, 577
Dawson Creek, 602
Dawson, George, 333–335, 597
de Fuca, Juan, 209–210
de Gerlache, Adrien, 197, 229–230, 231
De Groot, Jerome, 253–254, 255, 258
De Haven, Edwin, 328, 330
Dead Men, 263
Debenham, Frank, 10, 16, 57
debris
   fields, 742, 743
   ice-rafted, 733–734, 735
   toxic, 741–742
Deception Island, 315, 395, 678–679, 684, 685, 688
declinism, 237–238
decolonization, 106, 108–109, 115, 487, 537
Defence Research Board, 516, 517
Defence Research Northern Laboratory, 518
defence, 155, 524, 564, 595, 607, 611, 614
   projects, 600, 611
Delta Junction, 578, 614
democracy, 638, 692
   deliberative, 643
Denali, 85–87
Dene, 212, 261, 434, 436, 439, 527, 598, 623, 637, 764
   Akaitcho, 633
   Sahtu, 633
Denisovans, 80
Denmark, 149, 292, 346, 442–444, 446, 488–500, 502–507, 626–628, 632, 635; *see also* Faroe Islands; Greenland
   government, 488, 492, 494, 496, 498, 500–501, 516, 626, 640
   National Museum, 98, 292
   Parliament, 489, 494–495, 501–502, 627–628
depopulation, 144–145, 149, 674
deserted settlements, 148–149, 447, 567
determinism, environmental, 285, 291
development, 148, 287–289, 389–391, 396–397, 438–439, 594–596, 602–604, 607, 639–641, 649–650
   economic, 6, 169–170, 296, 451, 514, 518, 625, 652, 655, 663
   gas, 597, 639, 781
   industrial, 439, 470, 629–630
   mineral, 430, 436–437, 455, 598
   northern, 454, 468, 594, 602
   petroleum, 518, 593–594, 598, 610
   private, 598
   rapid, 186, 489, 656
   resource, 296, 517–518, 643, 659

sustainable, 640, 642, 664, 666
technological, 380, 390, 514
whaling, 310, 396
Devon Island, 97–98, 327–328, 337, 342, 345
DEW (Distant Early Warning) Line, 34–35, 45, 50, 267, 269, 518–519, 527
Dezhnev, Semen, 160
diamonds, 439, 470, 653
diaries, 13, 18, 187, 232, 234–235, 241, 265, 552–553, 554, 556
Dickens, Charles, 217
Dickinson, Robert E., 287
Dickson Island, 173
Dickson, Oscar, 173, 358, 359, 362, 368
diplomatic exchanges, 361
discoverer of Antarctica, 182, 196, 200
discovery, 25–26, 187–191, 230–231, 304–305, 335–338, 409–411, 435, 595, 775, 782
 new, 187, 335, 391, 448
 scientific, 55, 57, 60, 71
Discovery Expedition, 56, 241
Discovery Investigations, 304, 311, 312, 318
Discovery of Strangers, A, 261
disease, 146, 163–164, 435, 441, 468, 582, 708, 711, 715, 722
Disko Bay, 94, 131, 142–143, 443, 495
Disko Island, 442
disputes, 85, 313, 332, 342, 345–346, 360, 542, 649, 690, 777
 political, 743–744
 sovereignty, 18, 367, 778
 territorial, 527, 652, 692
Distant Early Warning (DEW) *see* DEW Line
diversity, 22, 24, 71, 96, 106, 110, 414, 419, 623–624, 631
 biological, 727, 740
Do Not Go Gentle, 257
Docker, John, 255
doctors, 19, 218, 241, 626–627, 691
documentary records, 276, 411, 424
documentary sources, 419, 421, 424
documents, 51, 112, 218, 267, 337, 411, 418, 678–679, 689
 historical, 257, 263, 415, 422–423
dog-handlers, 258, 267
dogs, 41, 90, 133–134, 171, 231–232, 234, 265, 705, 715, 731
 teams, 35, 45, 46–47, 731
Dome A, 56
Dome C, 65
domestic animals, 130, 134, 147, 705–706, 721
domestication, muskoxen, 706–708, 716, 718, 719

Dovre, 712, 716
 mountains, 711–712
 muskoxen, 712, 713–714
Drake Passage, 62, 233, 692
Drake, Sir Francis, 210
drama, 12, 256–257, 258, 539
drift ice, 90, 99, 730
driftwood, 90, 93, 96, 133, 135
drilling, 598, 603–604, 610–611, 615, 739, 781
 exploration, 595, 603, 604, 607, 611
 rigs, 518
 sites, 526
Dronning Maud Land, 61, 397
drums, 116, 609
Drygalski, Erich von, 197–198
Dunbar, Moira, 519
Durkheim, Émile, 290
Dutch companies, 381–383, 388, 400
Dutch ports, 381–384
Dutch Republic, 381, 384; *see also* Netherlands
Dutch whaling, 383–384
Dvina, Northern, 153, 155–156, 158
dynamics
 ice sheet, 69, 656, 772
 local, 22
 ocean–ice, 744
 power, 263, 756
Dyuktai Culture, 83–84, 86

Eagle, 577–578
early Cold War, 515, 526, 565, 583, 655
Early Holocene human colonization, 87–89
East Antarctica, 59, 61–62, 66–67, 68, 197
East Greenland, 3, 18, 79, 92–93, 346–347, 705, 709–710, 711, 716–718, 721
Eastern Arctic, 21, 87, 91–92, 94, 100, 348, 634
Eastern Settlement, 130, 134–135, 136–137, 139, 144, 146–147
eastern Siberia, 25, 160, 167
ecological adaptation, 292
ecological costs, 454, 456
ecological knowledge, 593, 773
Economic and Social Council (ECOSOC), 641, 643
economic development, 6, 169–170, 296, 451, 514, 518, 625, 652, 655, 663
economies
 Greenlandic, 444, 504
 subsistence, 79, 134, 148, 456
ECOSOC (Economic and Social Council), 641, 643
Ecuador, 673, 689, 690–691, 693
Edric, Robert, 260

799

education, 235, 288, 496, 499, 502, 634; *see also* individual court titles
effeminization, 237
Egede, Hans, 129, 487, 501, 506, 626
Eglinton Island, 328
Eireki rauða, 130–132, 135
Eisenhower administration, 545, 551
Eismeer, Das, 212
Ekaluktutiak, 32–34, 50–52
Elephant Island, 57, 233–234, 308, 318
elephant seals, 309, 407–408, 410, 420–421, 422, 654, 657
Elias, Amy, 255
Elichiribehety, Ruperto, 679
Ellef Ringnes Island, 335, 341
Ellesmere Island/Land, 92, 325, 327, 328–329, 330, 335, 337–338, 340, 342, 344
Emerald Island, 328
Emmons, George Foster, 566
empire, 153, 161, 164, 166–168, 236, 238, 266, 303–306, 319–321, 650–651
and science, 168, 306
employees, 1, 413–414, 445
employment, 389, 436, 438, 439, 445, 563
benefits, 438–439
industrial, 238, 437
enclosures, 140–141, 421
Enderby Land, 190
endurance, 14, 231, 246, 576
Endurance (book), 260
Endurance (ship), 232–233, 236, 237, 240
energy, 443, 478, 520–521, 525–526, 599, 653
engineers, 443, 582, 605, 607, 609–613, 736, 741
Entdeckung der Langsamkeit, Die, 222
environment
changing, 38–40, 93
global, 511, 522–523, 528–529, 781–783
environmental challenges, 247, 439, 519, 594
environmental changes, 25, 522, 524, 558, 642, 651, 744
environmental contaminants *see* contaminants
environmental determinism, 285, 291
environmental fragility, 655, 659–660, 662–663
environmental governance, 638–639, 648–667
comprehensive regimes for fragile polar ecosystems, 659–664
deep histories of environments, states, and sovereignty, 650–651
governing the Anthropocene, 664–667
protecting polar animals and landscapes, 655–659

resource rationality and polar nature, 651–655
environmental impact assessment (EIA), 659, 661
environmental impacts, 276, 454, 519, 621, 780
environmental knowledge, 5, 17, 512, 529, 597, 641, 650–651, 655
environmental management, 26, 640, 642, 661, 663
environmental monitoring, 520, 638
environmental movements, 478, 594, 641
environmental planners, 757
environmental protection, 12, 518, 557, 642, 649, 661–662, 666, 688, 692, 782
environments, 17–19, 279, 281–282, 285–286, 295–297, 512–514, 516–518, 524–525, 639, 782
extreme, 19, 315, 437
fragile, 529, 782
hostile, 315, 565, 653
natural, 34, 43, 154, 453
northern, 17, 448, 472, 653
physical, 52, 513, 515–516, 517, 527, 529, 536
polar, 516, 518, 649–651, 659, 662, 665, 771, 773, 779, 781
social, 32, 43, 52
equality, 366, 489–490, 503
equipment, 35, 45–46, 141, 209, 513, 515, 518, 525, 739, 741
Erebus Bay, 217, 220
Erebus, HMS, 207–208, 214, 220, 222, 225, 267, 306–307, 327
Erik the Red's Land, 490
erosion, 82, 119, 628, 637
coastal, 109, 146
glacial, 62
Escudero Guzmán, Julio, 681
Eskimologi, 292–293
Eskimos, 217, 292; *see also* Inuit
Central, 286
Copper, 50, 434
Esperanza Antarctic Base/Station, 685, 691, 693, 694
European colonialism, 114, 356, 362, 676
Evans, Edgar, 232, 237, 264, 265–266
Evenki, 466–467, 639
Everland, 253, 259, 262–263, 272–276
Every Man for Himself, 263
evidence, 58, 61, 66, 144–145, 274, 275–276, 281, 434, 553, 558
archaeological, 92, 146, 210, 420, 423
evolution of Antarctic continent and ice sheet, 55–71

Index

excavations, 82, 93–94, 109, 110–111, 117, 118, 119–120, 145, 440, 613
expansion, 91–92, 146–147, 396, 452, 453, 571–572, 574, 639, 641, 651–652
   colonial, 116, 433, 455
   Russian, 153, 157
   territorial, 157, 229, 448
expedition leaders, 13, 260, 392, 396
expeditions, 166–167, 192–197, 209–211, 223–225, 240–245, 260–265, 272–276, 305–306, 391–392, 707–708
   Antarctic, 18, 56, 59, 197, 200, 239, 246, 678, 680–681, 683
   Australasian Antarctic, 60, 234, 262
   British, 57, 198, 245, 307–308, 312, 330, 391
   French, 231, 306
   Japanese, 242
   Norwegian-British-Swedish, 64, 542
   Russian, 171, 186–187
   scientific, 273, 358, 468, 544, 677, 776
   Scottish, 198, 392, 677
   Swedish, 198, 707
   Trans-Antarctic, 314, 542
Expéditions Polaires Françaises, 16
expertise, 9, 33, 111, 122, 154, 159, 292, 296, 704, 749
   scientific, 245, 473, 538–539
experts, 23, 33, 381, 470, 537, 742, 750
exploitation, 89, 111, 114–115, 158, 407–408, 410, 412, 414–415, 687, 689
exploration, 14, 19, 21–23, 240–241, 258, 430, 593–594, 610–611, 774, 778–779
   Antarctic, 12–13, 19, 25, 56, 229, 241, 258, 304, 307, 514
   geographical, 198, 290
   histories, 14, 21, 253, 258, 272
   imperial, 774, 784
   oil, 593, 595, 604, 606, 610, 614, 780
   polar, 8, 9–10, 12, 13–14, 245, 253, 257, 262, 268, 270–271
   Russian, 155, 160
exploration drilling, 595, 603, 604, 607, 611
explorers, 8–9, 11–14, 18–19, 21–22, 224, 234–236, 239, 261–262, 270–272; *see also* individual names
   American, 172, 196, 330
   Antarctic, 201, 235, 310, 685
   British, 209, 329, 337–338
   early, 63, 71, 555, 596
extractive industries, 115, 120, 476, 621, 622, 635; *see also* gas; mining; oil; petroleum
extreme environments, 19, 315, 437
Exxon Valdez, 663

facilities, military, 474, 491–492, 529, 614
factory ships, 389, 394–397, 402, 654
Faeroese, 139
Failing, T. P., 218
failures, 12, 51, 70, 100, 164, 172, 223, 237, 244, 319
Fairbanks, 565, 577–579, 581, 584–586, 600, 602–603, 605, 606, 607–608, 611–612
Fairbanks–Haines Pipeline, 614
Falkland Islands, 309–310, 314, 394, 542, 544
Falkland Islands Dependencies (FID), 311, 395–396, 397–399, 549, 551
Falkland Islands Dependencies Survey *see* FIDS
Falklands War, 237, 315–317
fallout, 511, 518, 522, 524–525, 586, 782
   radioactive, 511, 518, 525, 782
families, 33–34, 41, 43, 45, 47–51, 135–137, 477, 498, 764, 767–768
family members, 33, 37, 43, 262, 266, 761
Farley, Rebecca, 234, 241
farm buildings, 135, 141
farmers, 130, 134, 141–142, 147–148, 712
   Greenlandic, 142, 148
   Norse, 129, 145–146
farms, 130–135, 136, 138–142, 144–145, 146–148, 704, 708–709, 716–719, 721
   collective, 467, 477
   larger, 134, 136, 141
   smaller, 136, 142, 719
   state, 477, 527
   Teal's farm, 717, 719
Faroe Islands, 131, 490, 627
fat(s), 90, 100, 381, 400, 706
fathers, 43–44, 718, 767; *see also* parents
faunal material, 79, 82, 89–90, 96
Fennoscandia, 88, 623, 640
   mining, 448–452
Ferguson Lake, 45
Ferguson, James, 294–295
Ferguson, Niall, 288
Fernández de Kirchner, Cristina, 695
Ferraz Station, 696
Fiction of History, The, 255
fiction, historical *see* historical fiction
FID *see* Falkland Islands Dependencies
FIDS (Falkland Islands Dependencies Survey), 303, 311, 541, 543, 550
field stations, 516, 523
fieldwork, 26, 279, 282, 284, 285, 291, 315, 539
Fiennes, Sir Ranulph, 19–20, 317
figure of the Earth, 545
Filchner, Wilhelm, 244
fin whales, 389, 400

801

Findlay Island, 338
Finland, 7, 106–107, 110, 114–115, 117, 119–120, 121, 449–450, 635, 662–663
    northern, 116, 635
Finnie, Oswald, 342–345
Finnmark, 378, 389–390, 393, 394, 718
    coast, 169, 389
    whaling, 389, 392
Fire on the Snow, The, 257
First International Polar Year, 8, 171, 198, 245, 281, 576
First Nations, 630–633, 764
First World War *see* World War I
Firth Scott, G., 14
fish, 34, 84, 89, 96, 134, 157, 162, 368, 389, 490
fisheries, 211, 304, 339, 385, 389, 501, 504, 596
fishing, 39, 44, 317–318, 623, 625, 627, 628, 635, 660, 666
    commercial, 38, 557, 626
    industrial, 490, 492
    industries, 443–444, 490, 492, 626
fjords, 133–134, 146, 441, 445, 742; *see also* individual fjords
Flag at the Pole, A, 260
flags, 235, 260, 310, 333, 339, 552, 681, 685
    Argentine, 677, 681
Fleming, Ian, 536
flensing, 383, 387, 402
floating ice shelves, 67, 321, 738
fly-in, fly-out operation, 437, 438, 445
food, 42, 43, 45, 93, 95, 231–232, 233, 415–416, 705–706, 710–711
    sources, 163–164, 519, 660, 744, 783
    storage, 99–100
forced labour, 468, 653
forced relocations, 477, 650
forecastles, 416–417
foreign politics, 355, 370
foreigners, 270, 337, 343, 384
former colonies, 235, 326, 329
Fort Churchill, 518
Fort Egbert, 577
Fort Enterprise, 212
Fort Glenn, 582
Fort Greely, 585, 587, 612, 614
Fort Liscum, 577
Fort Richardson, 580, 584
Fort William H. Seward, 573, 577
fossil fuels, 169, 463, 529, 642, 776, 781, 784; *see also* gas; oil
Fourth Anglo-Dutch war, 384
foxes, 41, 46, 131, 705, 721
Foyn, Svend, 389–390, 392, 402

fragility, environmental, 655, 659–660, 662–663
Fram, 231, 334
Framework Convention on Climate Change, 665
France, 16, 58, 64, 65, 190, 231, 232, 345, 355, 661
Frankenstein, 212
Franklin, Lady Jane, 217, 223
Franklin, Sir John, 207–226, 256, 260, 261–262, 327
    expedition, 214, 218, 221–222, 223, 253, 256, 259, 262, 267–268, 270
    route, 215
    future of the past, 225–226
    scholars of disaster, 223–225
    ships, 207, 218–220
    story, 208, 217–218, 219, 221, 224
Franklin's Passage, 222
Franz Josef Land, 171, 173
Fraser, Ronald, 550
freedom, 265, 455, 547, 553, 760
    economic, 365
freshwater, 624, 729, 733
Friedrich, Caspar David, 212
Friendly Arctic, The, 11, 341
Frobisher Bay, 209
Frobisher, Martin, 183, 209, 218, 434
From Russia with Love, 536
Frondizi, Arturo, 688
frontage theory, 7, 691
Frozen in Time, 219
Fuchs, Vivian, 314, 319, 549
fuels, 90, 93, 214, 230, 423, 518, 525, 601–602, 612–613, 651
    fossil, 169, 463, 529, 642, 776, 781, 784
Fullerton Harbour, 336
fur, 46, 131, 157, 158–159, 161, 164, 174, 409, 472, 567
    seals, 309, 407, 651, 657
    trade, 50, 159–160, 163, 309, 575, 624, 776
Fure, Odd Bjørn, 355

Gaia hypothesis, 521
Gamburtsev Mountains, 62, 66
game, 46, 86, 96, 99, 100
    big, 46, 82, 364
    marine, 79, 89, 96, 99
Garðar, 136, 138, 143–144
gas, 615
    development, 597, 639, 781
    exploration, 641, 781
    extraction, 632, 639
    fields, 526, 639

gatekeeping concepts, 291
Gavin and Stacey, 758–759, 760
GCI (Gwich'in Council International), 641
Geiger, John, 219
gender, 11, 71, 258
geodesy, 60, 544–546
geographers, 1, 57, 183, 266, 279, 283, 288–289, 296–297, 346; *see also* individual names
  historical, 154, 279, 297
Geographia Generalis, 182
geographical definitions, 2–7
geographical imagination, 288, 290–294, 297
Geographical Tradition, The, 284
geography, 1, 9–10, 279–297, 703–704, 774–775
  and late nineteenth-century social sciences, 280–281
  circumpolar north and political imagination, 295–297
  conceptions of nature and environment, 281–286
  geographical imagination and circumpolar region, 290–294
  historians of, 281, 283, 285
  history of, 282
  natural region theory, 289–290
  nature of, 284
  new, 282, 284, 287
  physical, 182–183, 186–190, 193, 197, 200–201, 582
  regional, 287, 291
  regional concept, 286–288
  systematic, 286–287, 289
  theory from the South and inclusion of the North, 294–295
geological controls on biology of Antarctica, 63–64
geology, 55, 57, 60, 67, 69, 71, 181, 186, 522, 524
  bedrock, 71, 772
  of Antarctica, 60–62, 70–71
geomorphology, 9, 168
geophysics, 64–66, 186, 544–546
geopolitics, 208, 282, 288, 395, 397, 537, 542, 547, 743, 770
geoscientific research, 55, 71, 772
Germans, 217, 231, 280, 284, 384–385, 388, 492, 682, 702, 712
  Baltic, 167–168
Germany, 58, 232, 283–284, 371, 383, 399, 491, 712
  Nazi, 469
Giæver, John, 713
Giant Mine, 438
Gibbs, George Washington, Jr, 241

Gjoa Haven, 221, 224, 226
glacial ice, 733, 740–741
glaciers, 69–70, 193, 196–197, 274–276, 729, 732–734, 738, 740, 742–743, 785
  outlet, 738, 742
glaciological research, 546, 549
glaciology, 57, 60, 522, 545
Glavsevmorput, 468, 470
global commons, 537, 737
global environment, 511, 522–523, 528–529, 781–783
global history, 297
global knowledge, 12, 536, 782
Global Mission, 579
Global North, 294–295
Global South, 294–295
global warming, 63, 67, 479, 510, 529, 642, 664–665, 728, 734
globalization, 359, 511, 621, 628
goats, 133–134, 140–142, 147–148
gold, 209, 364, 435, 453–454, 575, 653
  rushes, 270, 388, 433, 435, 577, 597
golden age, 442, 770, 774, 778
Gondwana, 55, 61, 772
gonorrhoea, 441
González Videla, Gabriel, 682–684
Goodsir, Dr Harry, 219
Gorbachev, Mikhail, 478, 520
Gore Peninsula, 220
Gould, Laurence, 552
Gould, Rupert Thomas, 200
governance, 556, 557, 573, 577, 638, 640, 655–656, 666, 778, 782
  Arctic, 12, 760
  environmental, 638–639, 648–651, 652, 654, 657–662, 663, 664–667
  institutions, 655, 782
governments, 22–23, 51–53, 159–160, 162, 339–340, 347–348, 360–361, 491–492, 616, 690
  Canadian, 436, 515, 597, 625, 633
  Danish, 488, 492, 494, 496, 498, 500–501, 516, 626, 640
  Greenlandic, 498, 501–502, 505–507
  Norwegian, 360–362, 368, 389, 447, 680
  Russian, 170, 360, 568
  Soviet, 454, 471, 514
  Swedish, 121, 714
  United States, 330, 347, 573, 582, 604, 615, 681, 682
governors, 267, 370, 491–492, 544, 580
Grace, Sherrill E., 764
Graham Land, 190, 229, 233, 240, 243, 310

Index

Grand Bay whaling, 380–381
grandparents, 32, 34, 35–38, 40–41, 44–45, 49, 764, 773
Grant Land, 330, 338
Grant, Shelagh D., 258
grass, 133, 140–141, 147, 705–706
graves, 112, 113, 117–118, 216, 219, 371, 743
Great Britain *see* United Kingdom
Great Circle Route, 601
great powers, 355, 356–357, 361, 363, 370–372
Great Slave Lake, 436, 438
Greely, Adolphus W., 260, 329
Greenland, 129, 130, 131, 132, 133, 134, 135, 136, 137, 138, 139, 144–149, 196–198, 385, 386, 439, 440, 441, 442, 443, 444, 487, 488, 489, 490, 491, 492, 493, 494, 495, 496, 497, 498, 499, 500, 501, 502, 503, 504, 505, 506, 507, 527, 626–628, 640–641, 731–735
and Canada, 99, 379, 622, 635, 641, 665, 735, 755
Boards of Guardians, 488–489
coasts, 183, 218, 737, 742
colonial administration, 488–489, 491–492, 494
colony to self-government, 487–507
Danification, 497–499, 504, 784
East, 3, 18, 79, 92–93, 346–347, 705, 709–710, 711, 716–718, 721
government, 498, 501–502, 505–507
greater say in foreign affairs, 505–506
history, 506
Home Rule, 499, 501–502, 622, 632
Ice Sheet, 146, 196, 656, 734–735
icebergs, 734, 743
independent, 504, 506
learning to manage own affairs, 487–491
mining, 439–446
modernization, 495, 498–499
modernization of society, 494–497
National Council, 495, 496, 498, 500–501
Norse *see* Norse Greenland
Northeast, 92, 490, 492, 707, 713
Northern, 143, 489, 491
Northwest, 211, 643
parliament, 498, 501
perspectivation, 506–507
Population Commission, 497
provincial councils, 489, 493–495, 498
Radio, 493
Reconciliation Commission, 499, 506
self-definition, 502–503
self-government and right to self-determination, 503–504

sidelining and political mobilization, 499–502
South, 92, 133, 441
Southern, 92, 133, 441, 492, 496, 501
Southwest, 129, 130, 140, 440
West, 92, 94–96, 487, 490, 628
whaling, 385–386
World War II as catalyst, 491–494
Greenlanders, 135–139, 142–143, 148–149, 442–443, 487–490, 493–494, 495–496, 497–500, 504, 506
Indigenous, 26, 385, 627
Norse, 129, 139, 145, 147–148
Greenlandic children, 498, 626
Greenlandic councils, 490, 493, 628
Greenlandic culture, 444, 497–499, 506
Greenlandic economy, 444, 504
Greenlandic farmers, 142, 148
Greenlandic identity, 490, 499, 503
Greenlandic politicians, 489, 491, 494–495, 499, 501, 505, 507, 628
Greenlandic population, 492, 496, 507, 632
Greenlandic representatives, 495–496, 634
Greenlandic school system, 489, 499
Greenlandic society, 442, 489–491, 496, 499, 501, 503, 626
Greenlandic workforce, 445, 500
Greenpeace, 661
grenade harpoons, 389, 393
Griffiths, Tim, 260
Griffiths, Trevor, 237
Grinnell Land, 328–329, 330–331, 338
Grollier Hall, 51
Grønlandsposten, 493
grounded ice, 67, 548
growth, 61, 63, 109, 408, 451, 570, 575, 577, 757–758
Gruening, Ernest, 582, 607–608
Grumant City, 446
Grytviken, 234, 316, 393, 678
Guangzhou, 408
guano, 364–365, 776
bonanza, 357–362
Guggenheim family, 435
guides, Indigenous, 212, 258
Guise, Holly Miowak, 581
Gulag Archipelago, The, 452
Gulags, 452, 454, 464–466, 468, 470–471, 474, 653
Gunnarsholt, 708–709
Gwich'in, 633, 770, 778, 781
Gwich'in Council International (GCI), 641

804

Index

Haggett, Peter, 287
Haines, 573, 577, 611–612, 614
Håkon, King, 138
Hall, Charles Francis, 218–220, 260, 267, 329, 330
Halleck, Henry W., 573–574
Halley Bay, 315, 321, 549
Hall–Héroult process, 442
Hamburg, 384–385
Hamelin, Louis-Edmond, 5–6
happy Inuit stereotype, 290, 296
Harding, Warren, 599
hardships, 46, 165, 329, 341, 472, 491
Harper, Stephen, 220
Harper's Weekly, 216, 218
harpooners, 383
harpoons, 89, 95–96, 98–99, 380, 402
  grenade, 389, 393
Harris, Lawren, 342, 348
Harris, Rollin, 340
harsh climate, 325, 358, 364, 471, 472, 476
Haycox, Stephen, 581
HBC *see* Hudson's Bay Company
Headland, Robert, 316, 410
Hearne, Samuel, 210, 434
hearths, 82, 93–94, 97, 100, 111, 114, 420–421, 423, 772
heavy metals, 223, 451, 663
Heighton, Steven, 259, 261–262
hell, 20, 44, 608
Henningsen, Alfred, 718
Herbertson, Andrew J., 286–289, 294, 297
herds, 42, 84, 87, 99, 100, 134, 147, 710–711, 713–715, 719
  muskox, 707, 715, 717
  reindeer, 163, 451, 711
heritage, 106–108, 110, 112–113, 115, 122, 624
  cultural *see* cultural heritage
  issues, 120–122
  management, 106, 108, 120–122
  Sámi, 106, 121, 122, 773
Heroic Age, 18, 20, 25, 56, 57, 229–247, 679–680
  and Antarctica as 'land of science', 243–247
  and British Empire, 307–308
  conventional narrative, 229–234
  defining new forms of Antarctic heroism, 238–242
  evolution of mythology, 234–238
heroism, 236, 238, 266, 330, 356, 651
heroization, 258
Herschel Island, 336
High Arctic, 79, 91, 92–95, 131, 171, 378, 437–438, 625, 651, 653

islands, 18, 25, 92, 325–350
High Arctic, islands
  1925 Sector Claim and Sverdrup Islands Settlement, 343–345
  Canadian claims and foreign exploration, 1895–1902, 331–336
  Canadian sovereignty achieved, 345–347
  exploration before 1870, 327–329
  resurgence of sovereignty fears, 347–349
  sovereignty and transfer to Canada, 329–331
  sovereignty initiatives, 1903–11, 336–340
  Stefansson, 340–343
high seas, 383, 387, 654, 666
Hill, Ed, 302
Hillary, Edmund, 319
Historia Norwegie, 143
historians, intellectual, 280–281
historical documents, 257, 263, 415, 422–423
historical fiction, 25, 252–276, 778–779, 784
  polar expedition novels, 259–263
  post-modern historical fiction and the polar regions, 255–259
  writing the past through history and fiction, 253–255
historical geographers, 154, 279, 297
historical sources, 380, 411, 423
historiography, 253, 254, 257, 258, 270, 292–293, 360–361, 779, 784
History of Polar Exploration, A, 14
Hoel, Adolf, 710, 711, 718
holds, 417
Holt, Kåre, 260
home ports, 384, 402
Home Rule, 501–502, 503, 632
  Faroe Islands, 627
  Greenland, 499, 501–502, 622, 632
  introduction, 499, 502–503
  homelands, 20–21, 129, 131, 466, 469, 474, 480, 621, 623, 642–644
  Inuit, 634, 639, 641, 736, 743
  Sámi, 448, 631, 635
Hope Bay, 311–312, 544, 685, 693
Hope, Herb, 568
horses, 35, 46–47, 80–82, 84–86, 99, 133, 423
hospitals, 473, 479, 581, 741
hostels, 35, 51
hostile environments, 315, 565, 653
House of Commons, 302, 347, 684
houses, 43, 45, 49, 135, 140, 141, 147, 302, 473, 478
  matchbox, 43, 50, 53
  wooden, 464, 473
Howarth, O. J. R., 287

805

Hudson Bay, 210, 329, 332–333, 336, 339, 386, 388, 434, 436, 702
Hudson, Henry, 183, 209, 381
Hudson's Bay Company (HBC), 212, 216, 329–330, 434, 596, 625
Hull, 268, 384, 385
human rights, 120, 643–644, 664–665
Humboldt, Alexander von, 190–192, 283
Hunt, Rebecca, 253, 259, 262, 272–276
Hunter Christie, William, 540–541, 542
hunter-gatherers, 99, 291, 407
hunters, 40, 42, 82, 86, 87, 95–96, 140–141, 409, 413
   Norwegian, 361, 365, 710, 712
   of megafauna, 80
   Russian, 158, 165, 170, 358, 567
Huntford, Roland, 20, 235, 237, 263–264
hunting, 42, 86–87, 131, 147–148, 399, 421–422, 598, 710–711, 731, 732
   grounds, 79, 91, 99, 401, 408–409, 412, 418, 424–425, 727, 732
   northern, 132, 140–141
   muskox, 92, 96
   seals *see* sealing
   societies, 79–80, 89
   modern humans, 81–84
   trips, 142–144
Hurley, Frank, 233, 263
Hussey, Christopher, 387
Hvalsey fjord, 137
hydrocarbon frontier, militarized, 593–617
hydrocarbon pipelines, 603
hydroelectric project, 629, 635

IACHR (Inter-American Commission on Human Rights), 642, 664–665
IASC (International Arctic Science Committee), 15
IASSA (International Arctic Social Sciences Association), 283
Ibáñez del Campo, General Carlos, 685–687
ICC *see* Inuit Circumpolar Council
ice, 38–39, 61–66, 68–70, 181–187, 191–195, 232–233, 548–550, 727, 728, 729, 730, 731, 732, 735–736, 738–744
   ages, 80–81, 86–87, 196–197, 200, 325, 521, 729, 733, 735
   boundaries, 726–744
   caps, 62, 79–80, 82–86, 99
   conditions, 211, 222, 334, 384, 774
   continental, 733, 740, 742, 772
   cores, 523, 773
   drift, 90, 99, 730

   edges, 91, 99, 383, 402, 727–728, 731, 740
   glacial, 733, 740–741
   grounded, 67, 548
   inland, 197–198, 738
   islands, 190, 566
   landfast, 730
   melting, 15, 510, 744, 773
   ocean–ice edge/interface, 727–729, 737, 738, 740, 743–744
   pack, 38, 191, 730
   polar, 130, 193, 259, 512, 521–522, 541
   sea *see* sea ice
   sheets, 55, 58–59, 62–68, 69, 70–71, 546, 548, 558, 727–728, 738–743
      Antarctic, 55, 58, 63–64, 68, 71, 548, 738
      dynamics, 69, 656, 772
      geophysical survey, 64–66
      large, 62, 196, 198
      Laurentian, 86–87
      unstable, 67–70
      West Antarctic, 67, 69
   shelves, 4, 68–70, 314, 396, 548, 554, 738–740
      floating, 67, 321, 738
   streams, 67, 68
   thick, 166, 232
   thickness, 58, 59, 64, 65
iceberg beverages, 735, 744
iceberg water, 735, 737
icebergs, 17, 70, 182–183, 190, 193, 545, 728–729, 732–738, 743
   age, 734, 736
   Antarctic, 733, 736
   Arctic, 734–735, 737
   calving, 69, 222, 733
   Greenland, 734, 743
   towing, 737
Icebergs, The, (painting), 217
icebreakers, 23, 172, 173, 221, 313–314, 445, 469, 525, 685, 695
ice-free corridors, 86, 166, 775
Iceland, 7, 130–132, 133–138, 142, 148, 149, 378, 384, 389, 440
Icelanders, 131–132, 138–139, 709
Icelandic annals, 138, 144, 149
ice-rafted debris (IRD), 733–734, 735
ICES (International Council for Exploration of the Seas), 171
icescapes, 90, 93, 99–100, 257, 259, 276
ICJ *see* International Court of Justice
iconoclasm, 235–236
Idea of North, The, 289
identities, 106–108, 110, 114, 268–269, 273, 490, 497, 524, 527, 528

Index

cultural, 208, 624
Greenlandic, 490, 499, 503
national, 110, 293, 368, 448, 651
Sámi, 110, 114, 116
ideologies, 208, 262, 266, 430, 515, 550, 649
Igaliku fjord, 130, 133
iglus, 37, 43, 45, 49
IGY *see* International Geophysical Year
Illustrated London News, 216, 218
Ilulissat, 143, 444, 728
imagination, 70, 212, 260, 294, 295, 601, 729, 734
  geographical, 288, 290–294, 297
  political, 288, 295
impact and benefit agreements, 438–439, 456
imperial claims, 319–320
imperial control, 161, 164, 165–166
imperial exploration, 774, 784
Imperial Geographic Society, 168
Imperial Oil, 596, 597, 599, 603–604, 607
imperial powers, 169, 320, 326, 550, 775
Imperial Trans-Antarctic Expedition, 57, 308
imperialism, 154, 320, 362, 672, 774
  British, 303, 320
  of idealism, 363–366
inchoate title, 336–337
incompetence, narratives of, 235–236
independence, 93, 338, 446, 487, 494, 503–504, 506, 507, 632, 635
  political, 294, 506, 623, 635
India, 55, 61, 289, 550, 556, 557, 690
Indian Ocean, 146, 198, 240, 379
indigeneity, 106–108, 122, 291, 622, 636, 637
Indigenous archaeology, 108–110
Indigenous communities, 5, 6, 439, 583, 586, 628, 630, 638, 648, 756
Indigenous cultures, 10, 433, 640, 774
Indigenous Greenlanders, 26, 385, 627
Indigenous groups, 108, 416, 456, 466, 623, 633, 636, 638, 642
Indigenous guides, 212, 258
Indigenous knowledge, 6, 17, 109, 386, 435, 623, 638, 642, 653
Indigenous peoples, 434–435, 466–467, 527–528, 570, 629, 632–633, 636–640; *see also* individual peoples
Indigenous peoples' organizations (IPOs), 640–644
Indigenous populations, 235, 357, 464–465, 477, 538, 629, 653, 675, 778, 783
Indigenous rights, 106, 115, 121, 208, 622, 631, 635–638, 640–641
Indigenous Siberians, 160, 162, 164, 168, 174, 527

industrial combines, 452
industrial development, 439, 470, 629–630
industrial employment, 238, 437
industrial livability, 475, 480
industrial mining, 438, 780
industrial pollution, 523, 655
industrial production, 471, 514
industrial settlements, 433, 462, 471–472, 477
industrial towns, 471, 474
industrial whaling, 379, 401, 528
industrialization, 63, 465, 471, 478, 653, 654, 780
industries, 18–19, 378–379, 381, 387–388, 389–391, 397–400, 401–402, 409, 469–470, 615–616
  extractive, 115, 120, 476, 621, 622, 635, 639, 653, 778–779; *see also* gas; mining; oil; petroleum
  fishing, 443–444, 490, 492, 626
  new, 391, 472
  northern, 340, 476, 479
inequalities, 121, 133, 499–500, 580, 744
information, 93, 97, 144–145, 165, 169, 410–411, 412, 418, 753, 762–763
infrastructures, 162, 170, 447, 455, 469, 471, 595–596, 601, 606, 613–614
  communications, 6, 565
  military, 580, 595
  transportation, 595, 600
  urban, 161–162, 476–477, 479
Inglefield, Edward, 328, 335, 338
Ingold, Tim, 295
inland ice, 197–198, 738
insects, 518, 721
institution building, 466, 468
institutions, 116–117, 468, 470, 515, 517, 586–587, 621, 623, 625, 631
  new, 503, 584
  scientific, 470, 475, 515
intellectual historians, 280–281
intellectual histories, 281, 297, 773
Inter-American Commission on Human Rights (IACHR), 642, 664–665
Inter-American Treaty of Reciprocal Assistance, 543, 683
interests, 40, 111, 116, 316, 335–336, 361, 411, 554–556, 679–680, 689–690
  American, 366–367, 369
  British, 303, 306, 689
  common, 142, 368, 369, 694, 698
  national, 345, 356–357, 367, 372, 519
  Norwegian, 355, 360, 397, 718
  public, 214, 328, 550
  resource, 541, 556

807

Index

interests (cont.)
  scientific, 118, 246, 513, 770
  Soviet, 515, 658
  strategic, 513, 543, 556
Intergovernmental Panel on Climate Change, 666
internal waters, 208
international agreements, 370, 649, 666, 687–688
International Arctic Science Committee (IASC), 15
International Arctic Social Sciences Association (IASSA), 283
international collaboration, 65, 155, 171, 281, 313, 688
international conferences, 552, 683
international cooperation, 60, 155, 171, 226, 245, 371, 399, 513, 519, 529
International Council for Exploration of the Seas (ICES), 171
International Council of Scientific Unions, 519, 544
International Court of Justice (ICJ), 312–313, 347, 367, 490, 542, 686
International Geophysical Year (IGY), 14–15, 58–60, 313, 315, 519, 536–558, 687
  Antarctica and Planet Earth, 544–551
  conferencing Antarctica, 551–557
international law, 120, 336, 356, 365–368, 370, 503, 675, 737
  development, 356–357, 367
  fortification, 371, 777
international lawyers, 363, 365, 367, 371
international organizations, 367, 636; see also individual organizations
International Polar Years (IPYs), 58, 171, 192, 295, 557, 696, 775
  First, 8, 171, 198, 245, 281, 576
international politics, 366, 537, 540
International Postal Union, 363
international recognition, 347, 369, 621
international scientific cooperation, 171, 244, 512
international status, 358, 369, 514
international straits, 208, 349
International Union for the Conservation of Nature (IUCN), 655, 657–658
international waters, 304, 399, 737
International Whaling Commission, 399, 528, 556, 640, 654, 656
International Whaling Convention (IWC), 311, 399–401, 640

internationalism, 245, 344, 354, 356–357, 367–368, 370–372
  and nationalism, 171–173, 354–372
  scientific, 546, 551
Inughuit, 211, 527, 743
Inuit, 48–53, 143–145, 220–221, 290–292, 623–626, 631–633, 634, 638–643, 751–755, 764–766
  accounts, 217, 219
  communities, 22, 282, 437, 441, 493, 639, 765
  Culture, 285, 292, 642, 763, 768
  happy Inuit stereotype, 290, 296
  homelands, 634, 639, 641, 736, 743
  knowledge, 40, 643, 756
  leaders, 221, 640, 642
  life, 752, 754–755, 764
  Netsilik, 213, 270
  of Alaska, 503, 641
  of Cumberland Sound, 282
  perspectives, 32–53, 639, 755
  rights, 634, 640
  society, 290–291, 293, 296, 626
  testimony, 208, 217, 218–220, 224
  Thule, 143
  traditions, 33, 50, 53, 641
  women, 762, 764
Inuit Circumpolar Conference, 528, 640, 778
Inuit Circumpolar Council (ICC), 22, 503, 640–642, 663, 664
Inuit Heritage Trust, 208, 221
Inuit *Qaujimajatuqangit* (IQ), 17, 40, 638, 755
Inuit studies, 293, 765–766
Inuit Tapiriit Kanatami (ITK), 632
Inuit Tapirisat of Canada (ITC), 632
Inupiat, 163
Inuvialuit, 623, 632, 633–634
Inuvialuit Final Agreement, 622, 634
Inuvik, 34–35, 48, 51, 266, 269
Ipiirvig, 267–269
IPYs *see* International Polar Years
IQ *see* Inuit *Qaujimajatuqangit*
IRD *see* ice-rafted debris
Irizar, Julián, 677
iron, 143, 148, 170, 448, 451
Iron Age, 111–112
Irony of American History, The, 27
Is History Fiction?, 255
islands, 273–275, 316, 325–326, 330–335, 337–339, 344–346, 357–358, 359–362, 408–410, 580; *see also* individual island names
  ice, 190, 566
  northernmost, 326, 341, 344, 347
  peri-Antarctic, 378, 396, 402

808

Index

small, 90, 142, 274, 554
sub-Antarctic, 304–305, 309, 312, 316, 391, 542, 654
Issaluk, Johnny, 222
Itaipu dam, 690
ITC (Inuit Tapirisat of Canada), 632
ITK (Inuit Tapiriit Kanatami), 632
IUCN *see* International Union for the Conservation of Nature
Ivanov, V., 169
Ivittuut, 133, 440–442, 492–493, 501
ivory, 82, 96–98
IWC *see* International Whaling Convention

Jackson, A.Y., 342, 348
Jahre, Anders, 397
James Caird (boat), 233
James, Cormac, 262
Jämtland, 118, 708
Jan Mayen, 383, 402
Japan, 64, 169, 229, 231, 242–243, 245, 399, 401, 550, 552
JAWS (Joint Arctic Weather Stations), 518
Jenness, Diamond, 583
Joerg, W. L. G., 1, 14
Johansen, Lars-Emil, 501
Joint Arctic Weather Stations (JAWS), 518
Jones Sound, 327, 328, 335, 339
Jones, Max, 237, 245
Jones, Zachary, 575
Jørgensen, Jørgen Holten, 361
Joy, Inspector Alfred, 345
Juneau, 435
jurisdiction, 313, 337, 339, 346, 396, 474
justice, 312–313, 342, 347, 367, 629, 634, 636, 643, 659, 665
Justice, Daniel Heath, 756

Káa Goox (Dawson Charlie), 435
Kaandossiwin: How We Come to Know, 761
Kajganich, David, 222
Kamchatka, 155, 162–163, 164–166, 387
Kamookak, Louie, 221, 224
Kane, Elisha Kent, 196, 272, 328–330, 338, 341
Kangiptugaapik, 731–732
Kaplan, Robert, 288, 297
Kara Sea, 167, 169, 172
Karginsky Interglacial, 81
Karkasee, 597
Kauffmann, Henrik, 491–492
Kearns, Gerry, 284
Kedkevare/Silpatjåkko, 448
Keenleyside, Anne, 217–218, 220, 223

Kéex, 574
Keish, 435
Kekerten, 282
Keneally, Thomas, 262
Kennecott, 435–436
Kennicutt, Chuck, 70–71
Keno Hill, 438
Kerguelen, 195, 198, 378
Kerguelen-Trémarec, Yves-Joseph de, 240, 391
KGH (Royal Greenland Trading Department), 440–443, 488, 626
Khaiyrgas, 83
Khibiny Mountains, 452, 467
Khrushchev, Nikita, 454, 473, 526
Kiernan, David R., 587
Kikkert, Peter, 346
King Christian Island, 335, 338
King George Island, 20, 691
King Oscar Land, 338
King William Island, 214–216, 217, 220, 224, 267, 327, 329
King, William, 338
King, William Lyon Mackenzie, 343
Kingittorsuaq, 142
Kingsley, Mary, 284
kinship, 291, 528, 627
Kirovsk, 453, 467, 476
Kiruna, 449–451, 713
Kirwan, Laurence, 14
Kitikmeot Heritage Society, 50, 51
Kivalliq Region, 752, 784
Klenova, Maria, 240
Klondike, 435, 578
  Gold Rush, 270, 435, 576, 597
  petroliferous, 596–599
Knight, James, 209
knowledge, 17–18, 265, 306–307, 511–512, 513, 515, 527–529, 749, 762, 775
  ecological, 593, 773
  environmental, 5, 17, 512, 529, 597, 641, 650–651, 655
  gaps, 192, 763
  global, 12, 536, 782
  Indigenous, 6, 17, 109, 386, 435, 623, 638, 642, 653
  Inuit, 40, 643, 756
  production, 17, 154, 294, 516, 519
  scientific, 165, 200, 246, 307, 410, 539, 773, 782
  traditions, 17, 25
knowledge-making, 279–297
kochi, 159–160
Kodiak, 579, 600
Koivurova, Timo, 667

Kola, 157, 166, 169
  Peninsula, 106, 113–115, 155, 156–158, 166, 167, 452–454, 456, 472, 476
Kolyma, 84, 153, 453–454, 456, 653
Kolyma Tales, 452
Komi, 466
Kongelige Grønlandske Handel *see* KGH
Konow, Wollert, 362
Korean War, 436, 443
Kovdor, 476
krill, 317, 660, 666, 696, 782–783
Kropotkin, Peter, 282, 284
Krüger, Thomas, 196
Krümmel, Otto, 198
Krusenstern, Adam von, 167, 190
Kugluktuk, 34, 50

laboratories, 517, 523–524, 586, 773, 779
labour, 17, 19, 133, 149, 170, 413–414, 467–468, 471, 474
  forced, 468, 653
labourers, 19, 136, 414, 424–425
  forced, 468
  slave, 452
Labrador, 92, 100, 225, 378, 381, 388, 402, 438, 456, 634
Labrador Inuit Land Claims Agreement, 622, 634
Ladd Field, 579, 581–582, 584
Lady Franklin's Lament, 222
Laisvall, 449, 451
Lake Aisjaure, 451
Lake Laisan, 451
lakes, 32, 44, 111, 133–134, 157; *see also* individual names
  subglacial, 66
Lancaster Sound, 211, 327, 336, 339, 386
lances, 40, 46, 96, 422
Lancing, 397
land, 32–35, 39, 51–53, 182–186, 187–191, 303–306, 315–319, 629–630, 727–730, 772–774
  and sea, 317, 321, 515, 624, 743
  and water, 32, 284, 315–316
  Indigenous, 629, 630, 639, 643
  ownership, 136, 138, 147, 575, 638
  rights, 109, 629, 632, 643, 659
  use, 565, 643
land claims, 321, 569, 621–622, 629, 631, 633, 637, 639, 643
  agreements, 622, 632–634
  and self-government, 628–639
  comprehensive, 623, 632–633, 637
  movements, 629–630

  processes, 621, 634
  settlements, 622, 634
land of science, 243–247
landfast ice, 730
landmarks, 68, 340, 565, 573
landnam, 130, 134–136
landscapes, 133–134, 272, 275–276, 279, 653, 655, 666, 667, 713, 716
  Antarctic, 62
  Arctic, 32, 165, 271, 704
  new, 704, 722
  northern, 448, 704
Landscapes in White project, 18, 411, 419
Landseer, Sir Edwin, 217
Langø, 440
language, 37–38, 139, 285, 490, 497–499, 621, 629, 632, 634, 768
  common, 641, 694
  Danish, 489, 496–497, 499, 626
Lansing, Robert, 357, 365–369
Larsen A Ice Shelf, 70
Larsen B Ice Shelf, 70
Larsen, Carl A., 221, 309, 392–396
Larsen, Henry, 221
Last Ice Area, 665–666
Last Place on Earth, The, 237, 263
Lastiri, Raúl Alberto, 688
Late Palaeolithic, 84, 99, 100
Latin America, 26, 295; *see also* individual countries
  Antarctic extension, 672–698
  birth of 'American Antarctica', 677–680
  Chilean-Argentine alliance and South American Antarctica, 682–686
  dictatorships, fear and new South American actors, 689–692
  first Latin Americans in Antarctica, 676–677
  geopolitical explosion and Chilean-Argentine cooperation, 680–682
  parallel paths, 686–689
  towards a regional 'South American Antarctica', 692–697
Laurentian Ice Sheet, 86–87
Laurie Island, 677, 680
Laurier, Wilfrid, 334, 336–337, 339–340
lawyers, international, 363, 365, 367, 371
Lazarev, Mikhail, 187
lead, 223, 440, 449
leaders, 41, 242, 244, 252, 257–258, 262, 268, 271, 272, 274; *see also* individual names
  expedition, 13, 260, 392, 396
  local, 163, 169
  Soviet, 463, 470, 514, 526, 662

leadership, 155, 169, 172, 190, 197, 236, 239, 266, 526, 546
lead–zinc, 437, 501, 630
Leal, Jorge Edgar, 693–694
Leffingwell, Ernest De Koven, 597, 598, 602
legitimacy, 447, 491, 495, 557
   scientific, 311
Leith Harbour, 316
Lena River, 83, 160–161, 171
Leningrad, 470, 514
Lepekhin, Ivan, 166
Lévi-Strauss, Claude, 290
licences, 309, 396
lichens, 63, 478, 525, 663
lifestyles, 40, 43, 46–47, 50, 464, 477
   hierarchical, 425
Liljevalch, Karl Fredrik, Jr, 708
Lindholm, Otto, 168
liquid waste, 525
liquid water, 66, 729
Liss, Julia, 283
lithic artefacts, 80, 86
Little America, 548
livability, 464, 477
   industrial, 475, 480
livestock, 134, 147, 710, 722; see also individual livestock names
living conditions, 45, 92, 409, 418, 421, 472, 476, 721
living resources, 18, 80, 99, 100, 624, 656, 658
Livingston Island, 419–421
Livingstone, David, 239, 284
Lluberas, Albert, 697
local populations, 117–118, 450, 492, 675
local resources, 139, 158, 423, 624
logbooks, 18, 257, 276, 412, 415, 418–420
logistics, 16–17, 20, 60, 266, 319, 548, 551, 604, 608, 613
Løkvika, 89
Lomonosov, Mikhail, 165–166
long-wave radiation, 522
Longyear, John Munroe, 364–365, 366, 369, 446
Longyearbyen, 20–21, 372, 446, 464, 709–711
Lovelock, James, 521
Low, Albert, 336
Lukács, George, 254
Luleå, 449, 714
Lycksele, 118
Lynge, Aqqaluk, 743
Lynge, Augo, 489, 495–497
Lynge, Finn, 497
Lynge, Frederik, 495–496
Lynge, Kristoffer, 493

Maarmorilik, 444, 501, 630
Macfie, Alexander, 255
Machu Picchu Antarctic base, 696
Mackenzie River, 605, 632, 706, 780
Mackenzie Valley Pipeline, 633, 659, 781
Mackenzie, Sir Alexander, 210, 596, 597, 775
Mackinder, Halford, 280–282, 284, 287, 290
MacMillan, Donald, 340–341, 343–344
Maddison, Ben, 19, 258
Madrid Protocol, 661–662, 663–664, 692, 698
Magadan, 452–453, 721
Magnetic Crusade, 8, 190, 214, 245, 306
magnetic field, 190, 306, 513
magnetic poles, 8, 190, 213, 243, 306
magnetism, terrestrial, 211, 306
Mahon, Derek, 256
Maipú Treaty, 695
Makarov, Stepan, 172
Making of Geography, The, 287
Maksutov, Dmitry, 569
Malaysia, 690
Malmberget, 449–450, 451
Malvinas Islands, 691; see also Falkland Islands
mammals, marine, 9, 85, 89, 157, 162, 311, 567, 624, 731, 732
mammoth, 82, 84, 99, 773
   steppe, 84–85, 99
Man Proposes, God Disposes, (painting), 217
management, 311, 312, 443, 543, 623, 643, 649, 658, 722
   environmental, 26, 640, 642, 661, 663
   heritage, 106, 108, 120–122
Mangazeia, 159
Manhattan, SS, 221
manpower, 141, 147, 167, 606
Māori, 239, 241
maps, 3, 182–186, 198–200, 208, 210, 212, 268–271, 538, 542, 777–778
Margulis, Lynn, 521
marine game, 79, 89, 96, 99
marine mammals, 9, 85, 89, 157, 162, 311, 567, 624, 731, 732
marine protected areas (MPAs), 639, 666, 697
marine resources, 56, 147–148, 316–317, 409, 628
maritime powers, 183, 305
market conditions, 401–402
market economy, 402, 478–479, 650
marketing, 604, 735–736
markets, 19, 157, 386, 388, 389, 408, 414, 422, 717, 722
   global, 159, 379, 399, 447, 655
   global/world, 159, 379, 399, 447, 655
   international, 157, 158

Index

markets (cont.)
  new, 164, 654
Markham, Clements, 9, 197, 241, 244, 331
Marshall, Eric, 231
Martens, F. F., 363
Martin, Lawrence, 344
masculinity, 237–238, 239, 265
matchbox houses, 43, 50, 53
material culture, 91–93, 95–97, 115, 425
Mathisen, Trygve, 360
Maury, Matthew Fontaine, 193, 198, 328
Mauss, Marcel, 290
Mawson, Douglas, 23, 57, 60, 234, 243, 246, 260–261, 262, 319
McClintock, Francis Leopold, 216–217, 220, 223, 328–329, 335
McEwen, Gwendolyn, 222
McGuire, Ian, 256
McMurdo, 16, 23, 57–58, 60
McMurdo Station, 16
Meares, Cecil, 267–269, 270
meat, 90, 100, 134, 423, 682, 705, 706–707, 709–710, 711, 721
  boiling, 94
  muskoxen, 705, 709–711
Mecham, Frederick, 328–329
Medstugan, 708
megafauna, 80–82, 84
megaprojects, 582, 595, 600, 615, 653, 780
Meighen Island, 341
melting ice, 15, 510, 744, 773
Melville Bay, 143
Melville Island, 211, 327, 340, 345
Melville Peninsula, 224, 327–328
Menem, Carlos Saúl, 692
Mercau, Ezequial, 316
merchant vessels, 415–416, 571; *see also* individual ship names
merchants, 157, 158, 381, 384, 408, 414, 440, 466
  Norwegian, 142, 149
MERCOSUR, 693, 697
Meridian Expedition, 171
Mertz, Xavier, 60, 234
Mesolithic, 87–90, 99
  coastal hunters, 89–90
mess attendant, 241
Meta Incognita, 434, 651
meteorological stations, 171, 311, 359
meteorology, 57, 186, 307, 519, 522, 542
Middendorff, Alexander von, 167, 170–171
Middle East, 522, 525, 736
migrants, 85, 465, 471–472, 473, 476, 480
  urban, 477, 480

migrations, 86, 93, 99, 465, 471–472
  bird, 517
  long-distance, 707
Mikkelsen, Caroline, 240
militarism, 155, 242
militarization, 26, 469, 478, 606, 656, 770, 779
  of Alaska, 563–587
militarized hydrocarbon frontier, 593–617
military, 545, 583–584, 593–595, 601–602, 608, 610–611, 613–614, 741; *see also* armies; navies
military bases, 475, 553, 611, 741, 743
military facilities, 474, 491–492, 529, 614
military infrastructures, 580, 595
military officials, 600, 602, 607, 612
military personnel, 477, 564, 578, 581, 741
military planners, 600, 602, 611–612
mills, 217, 435–436
Minds of Winter, 253, 256, 259–260, 261, 263, 266–270
mineral development, 430, 436–437, 455, 598
mineral resources, 115, 170, 332, 430, 501–502, 514, 652, 677, 690
Mineral Resources International, 437
mineral wealth, 430, 576
mines, 348, 366, 435–436, 438–439, 446, 448–451, 454, 501–502, 607
  operational, 439, 450
mining, 430–456, 660–661, 783; *see also* extractive industries
  activities, 115, 443, 446, 452, 455, 599, 661, 783
  Arctic North America, 433–439
  coal, 22, 444, 446, 463, 496, 627, 709
  colonies, 434, 651
  companies, 366, 436, 438–439, 441, 652, 660
  copper, 435, 448–449
  cryolite, 442, 780
  Greenland, 439–446
  history of, 26, 115
  industrial, 438, 780
  industry, 114, 430, 444, 447, 450
  notable sites, 431
  projects, 446, 451, 629
  Russian Arctic, 452–454
  Scandinavia, 448–451
  settlements, 438, 453, 467
  sulphur, 440
  Svalbard, 446–447
  ventures, 434, 639, 652
minke whales, 400, 624
Minuteman, 613
missiles, 143, 512, 540, 545, 549, 613, 656, 741

missionaries, 51, 115–116, 129, 186, 449, 465, 466, 625, 776–777, 779
Mitchell, Billy, 578–579, 601
Mitchell, Heath, 600
mobility, 156, 515, 526, 539, 549, 744
mobilization, political, 499–500, 587
modern whaling, 390
modernity, 407, 411, 449, 462, 464, 581
modernization, 448, 455, 496, 500, 504, 507, 626
  of Greenland, 495, 498–499
  process, 499, 502, 626
Modoc people, 573
monasteries, 156–158, 162, 465, 468
Monchegorsk, 453
money, 16, 41, 46–47, 53, 213, 218, 341, 408, 413–414, 415
monitoring, environmental, 520, 638
Monmonier, Mark, 3
Monroe doctrine, 365
Morrison, Bill, 606
motor-sledges, 232
Motzfeldt, Jonathan, 501, 628
mountains, 2, 81, 91, 115, 168, 196, 233, 548, 711–712, 715
movements
  environmental, 478, 594, 641
  political, 26, 621–622, 628–629, 631, 637, 643–644, 778
MPAs (marine protected areas), 639, 666, 697
Mujica, José, 697
multilateral negotiations, 662–663
multilateralization, 355
multinational corporations, 641, 727
Mundy, Robyn, 263
Murman coast, 158, 169, 466, 469
Murmansk, 173, 447, 452, 466, 520, 525, 662–663
  railway, 173, 466
Murphy, Alexander, 288, 297
Murray, John, 197, 307–308
Muscovy, 159, 465
museums, 109, 112, 116–118, 120–121, 220, 260, 267, 286, 707
muskoxen, 37, 42, 82, 96, 97–99, 702–722, 773
  and porous Scandinavian borders, 713–716
  as potential resource, 704–707
  as unruly ornaments, 711–713
  calves, 708–709, 716, 720
  domestication, 706–708, 716, 718, 719
  for wool, 716–719
  herds, 707, 715, 717
  hunting, 92, 96
  meat, 705, 709–711
  movements, 704

population, 41, 715
  reintroduction, 716, 720
  repopulation on Siberian tundra, 719–721
  wool, 706, 717–719, 722
Musso, Julio César, 690
Muybridge, Eadweard, 573–574
myths, 207–208, 223, 246, 269, 282, 361

Nadasdy, Paul, 17
Nadolny, Sten, 222
NANA (Northwest Alaska Native Association), 437
Nanisivik, 437
Nansen, Fridtjof, 13, 198, 332, 333–334
Nansivik, 438
Nantucket Island, 387
Napoleonic Wars, 166, 186, 385
Napps (character), 273–275
Nares, George, 330–331, 338
narratives, 11, 13–14, 19, 235–236, 239, 258, 260–262, 264–265, 297, 474
  national, 108, 112
  of adventure, 234–235
  of incompetence, 235–236
  of survival, 236–237
  of tragedy, 235–236
Narsaq, 20, 134–135, 501
Narvik, 449
Nasafjäll, 115, 119, 448
Nathorst, Alfred Gabriel, 707–708
National Academy of Sciences, 519, 582
National Council, 495, 496, 498, 500–501
National Environmental Research Council (NERC), 302–303
national identities, 110, 293, 368, 448, 651
national interests, 345, 356–357, 367, 372, 519
National Museum of Denmark, 98, 292
national narratives, 108, 112
National Oceanographic Centre, 302
national security, 595, 599, 615, 741
national territories, 514, 527, 549, 674, 689
nationalism, 213, 242, 244–245, 344, 356, 358, 362, 371, 758
  and internationalism, 171–173, 354–372
  anti-colonial, 237
nationalities, 71, 361, 365, 381, 394, 399, 410, 637
nation-states, 110, 621, 623, 625, 637, 641, 649, 651, 774, 777–778
NATO, 469, 495, 505–506
natural environments, 34, 43, 154, 453
natural gas *see* gas
natural history, 164, 186, 286

Index

natural regions, 280, 287–288, 290–291, 294–296, 297
  theory and consequences, 289–290
natural resources, 114, 157–158, 170, 357–358, 462, 470, 596, 599, 650–651, 655
naturalists, 58, 165, 166, 171, 252, 270, 283
nature
  conceptions, 281–282
  non-human, 649–650
  other-than-human, 782, 785
Nature of Light, 263
naval bases, 354, 442
Naval Petroleum Reserves, 596, 599, 607
navies, 217, 306–308, 566, 570, 575, 599, 607–611, 615; *see also* Royal Navy
navigators, 169, 181–182, 186, 191, 201, 304
Nawan-Alaxsxa, 580
Neanderthals, 80
Nederlandse Maatschappij voor de Walvisvaart, 400
neglect, 155, 283, 285, 303, 573
negotiations, 23, 26, 438–439, 496, 502, 630–635, 641, 642, 658–659, 663
  multilateral, 662–663
Neiden, 118
Nenets, 163, 466, 474, 527, 624
neo-Kantians, 283, 286
NERC (National Environmental Research Council), 302–303
Netherlands, 383, 386, 400; *see also* Dutch whaling
Neumayer, Georg, 195, 197, 198
neutral spaces, 523–524, 525–527, 528
New England, 386–387
New Geography, 282, 284, 287
New Jersey, 597, 604
New South Shetland, 187
New Western History, 11
New Zealand, 56, 58–59, 61, 310–311, 395–396, 538, 540, 547–548, 551, 554
Newfoundland, 3, 134, 378, 390, 634, 733–734, 737
Newnes, Sir George, 230
newspapers, 212, 224, 235, 257, 341, 556, 711–712, 714, 718, 720
nickel, 453, 475
Niebuhr, Reinhold, 27
Nielsen, Nive, 222
Nikel, 453
Nimíipuu, 573
Nimrod expedition, 57, 243
Ninnis, Belgrave Edward, 234
Nome, 435, 577

non-claimant states, 547, 552–553
non-governmental organizations, 503, 622, 641
Noordse Compagnie, 381–383
Noow Tlein, 567
Nordenskiöld, Adolf Erik, 169–170, 358–360, 776
Nordenskjöld, Otto, 198, 393, 677
Nordic colonialism, 108, 114
Nordic Council, 662
Nordic Council of Ministers, 662
nordicity, 5–6
Norges Svalbard- og Ishavsundersøkelser (NSIU), 710–713
Norilsk, 20, 452, 454, 468, 473, 475, 478, 479, 653
Norman Wells, 596, 597–600, 602–605, 607, 780
Norrbotten, 119
Norrland region, 448
Norse artefacts, 142, 143
Norse farmers, 129, 145–146
Norse Greenland, 129–149
  and *Skrælings*, 144–145
  demography, 145–146
  deserted settlements, 148–149
  Eastern Settlement, 130, 134–135, 136–137, 139, 144, 146–147
  ending, 144
  environment, 146
  expansion and withdrawal, 146–147
  hunting trips to north and encounters with *Skrælings*, 142–144
  influence of church and crown, 135–139
  life on farms, 140–142
  livestock, 147
  settlement and subsistence, 133–135
  settlers and motivations, 131–133
  settlers from the East, 130
  Western Settlement, 133–134, 140–142, 144–145, 146–147
Norse Greenlanders, 129, 139, 145, 147–148
Norse settlements, 136, 144–145, 487
Norsk Moskus A/S, 718
North American Arctic, 344, 439–440, 445, 593, 596, 616, 622–623, 630
North Pacific, 159–160, 164, 167, 400, 567, 600
North Pole, 8, 166, 168, 171, 172, 326, 329, 332, 337, 339
North Rankin Nickel Mine, 436
North Slope, 18, 437, 518, 525, 593, 599, 607–610, 614–615, 616, 630
North Water, 92, 256, 643
North West Company, 212
North West Mounted Police, 336

northeast Greenland, 92, 490, 492, 707, 713
northern Alaska, 87, 91, 597
northern bonuses, 471, 475
northern Canadian provincial districts, 332
northern development, 454, 468, 594, 602
Northern Dvina, 153, 155–156, 158
northern environments, 17, 448, 472, 653
northern Greenland, 143, 489, 491
northern industries, 340, 476, 479
northern Norway, 117, 118, 121, 389, 622, 629, 635, 713, 717–718, 722
northern Quebec, 325, 438, 633, 634
Northern Rus', 155
northern Russia, 113, 357, 432, 637, 703, 721, 722
Northern Sea Route, 170, 468
northern Siberia, 79, 99, 153, 174, 470
  Mesolithic coastal hunters, 89–90
Northern studies, 289, 291, 766
northern Sweden, 110–111, 114–116, 121, 449, 708, 714
northern Urals, 153, 157
Northern Victoria Land, 61
Northern Warfare Training Center, 565, 585
Northward Course of Empire, The, 11, 341, 452, 705
Northwest Alaska Native Association (NANA), 437
North-West by South, 222
Northwest Defense Complex, 582, 595–596, 600–607, 780
northwest Greenland, 211, 643
Northwest Passage, 8, 207–226, 231, 326–327
  Barrow era, 210–214
  Franklin era, 214–219
  future of the past, 225–226
  modern era, 219–223
  myths and maps, 208–210
  scholars of disaster, 223–225
Northwest Staging Route (NWSR), 595, 600–601
North-West Territories (NWT), 436, 438, 595, 597, 602–604, 607, 631, 633–634, 776, 777
Norway, 119–120, 148–149, 344–346, 354–363, 366–372, 447–451, 635, 651–653, 657–658, 716–718
  and Spitsbergen *see* Spitsbergen
  central, 88, 112, 711
  governments, 360–362, 368, 389, 447, 680
  northern, 117, 118, 121, 389, 622, 629, 635, 713, 717–718, 722
  sovereignty, 338, 354, 357, 359–361, 366, 369, 371–372, 446–447, 652

Norwegian companies, 395, 400, 446–447, 541, 555, 652
Norwegian hunters, 361, 365, 710, 712
Norwegian interests, 355, 360, 397, 718
Norwegian kings, 129, 138
Norwegian merchants, 142, 149
Norwegian sovereignty *see* Norway, sovereignty
Norwegian whalers, 389, 392–393
Norwegians, 110, 112, 136–137, 344–345, 360, 368, 370–372, 392–393, 446–448, 717
Novaya Zemlya, 167, 170–171, 173, 192, 474, 524–525, 527, 781
novels, 207, 222, 229, 253, 255, 257, 259–260, 262–263, 276
Novgorod, 155–156, 465
Novo-Arkhangel'sk, 567–568
NSIU *see* Norges Svalbard- og Ishavsundersøkelser
nuclear research, 656, 781
nuclear tests, 524–525, 527, 586, 630, 688, 781
nuclear weapons, 505, 517, 524, 586, 609, 781
numbered treaties, 598, 633
Nunatsiavut, 438, 622, 634
Nunavik, 438, 634, 642
Nunavut, 32–34, 631, 633–634, 638, 749, 751–753, 755, 757, 760, 761
  Land Claims Agreement, 622, 638
  territory, 208, 438, 622, 634
Nunivak, 716–717, 719–720
Nuuk, 133, 444, 487, 491, 495–496, 498, 502, 505–506, 626, 641
Nuussuaq Peninsula, 443
NWSR *see* Northwest Staging Route
NWT *see* North-West Territories
Ny-Ålesund, 446–447

Oates' Diary (poem), 256
Oates, Lawrence 'Titus', 232, 252, 256, 264–265, 266, 269
observatories, 171, 306, 514, 522, 677–678, 681
obshchinas, 637
occupation, acts of, 303
ocean currents, 59, 168, 738
Oceania, 414, 511, 674
ocean–ice boundaries, 729, 731, 744
ocean–ice edge/interface, 727–729, 737, 738, 740, 743–744
oceanography, 356, 468, 522, 545, 546
Office of Polar Programs, 16
officers, 212, 214, 221, 256, 258, 414–415, 416–418, 421, 424, 576
  Navy, 569, 607, 681

815

O'Higgins Station, 694
oil, 407–409, 476, 525–526, 594–599, 604–605, 607–610, 615, 616, 639, 780–781; *see also* extractive industries; petroleum
  companies, 604, 727
  development, Arctic, 594, 598
  discovery, 600, 630
  exploration, 593, 595, 604, 606, 610, 614, 780
  extraction, 476, 479, 599, 610
  fields, 595, 598, 607, 609, 615
  production, 595, 598, 599
  spills, 605, 663
  tankers *see* tankers
  whale *see* whale oil
Okhotsk, 162, 168, 387–388, 453
Old Crow, 770
Olofsson, Peder, 448
O'Loughlin, Ed, 253, 256, 259, 261, 266–270
Olsen, Moses, 501
one-cell stone churches, 136–137, 146
open polar sea, 183, 208, 271, 327, 331
open water, 99, 233, 378, 732
Operation Tabarin, 311, 541, 682
oral histories, 50, 51, 753
oral tradition, 22, 239, 258, 575
ordinary life, 474
ore, 434, 445, 449, 451, 780
Orsman, Chris, 256
Orthodox Christianity, 156, 465
Osborne, Michael, 707
Ossipee, 566, 568
otherness, 10–11, 411
other-than-human nature, 782, 785
Ottawa, 220, 326, 332–333, 335, 337, 339, 341–345, 348–350, 597–598, 735
outboard motors, 35, 45
outer space, 536–537, 539, 546
outlet glaciers, 738, 742
over-exploitation, 368, 399, 407–408, 425
overwintering, 8, 230, 270–271, 330, 677
Owens, Nicolas, 302
owner companies, 615–616
owners, 390, 413, 415, 593, 615–616
ownership, 109, 145, 366, 598, 639, 737
  land, 136, 138, 147, 575, 638
  social, 598

Paamiut, 444, 626
Pacific, 157, 161–162, 190, 198, 209–210, 549, 554, 557, 573, 579
  coasts, 99, 187, 577, 600, 776
  North, 159–160, 164, 167, 400, 567, 600
  South, 304, 688

Paigol, 168–169
paintings, 343, 348
Palaeolithic
  Late, 84, 99, 100
  Middle, 80
  Upper, 81–82, 99
Pallas, Peter Simon, 166–168
Palmer, Nathaniel, 56, 200, 717
PAME (Protection of the Arctic Marine Environment), 663
pandemic, 770–771, 784
parents, 20, 32, 35, 45, 498, 710, 759
Paris Peace Conference, 355, 364, 366, 369–370, 652
Parks Canada, 207, 220, 225
Parrett, Favell, 256
Parry Channel, 325–326, 328, 329, 337, 348
Parry, William Edward, 192, 211–212, 213–214, 327–329, 340
Parry's Rock, 340
partial test ban treaty, 524, 556
parties, 57–58, 232, 274–275, 537, 539–541, 544, 548–549, 551–553, 557, 660–661
  consultative, 7, 555, 662, 688, 689–691, 693
  political, 487, 501, 627–628, 632
  treaty, 555–556, 652, 656–657
partnerships, 163, 343, 503, 542, 762, 766
Patagonia, 408, 413, 416, 675–676, 677, 679
patrols, 317, 342, 345, 348, 492, 593, 694
Patrulla Antártica Naval Combinada, 694
Pauly, Antonio, 679
PBSG (Polar Bear Specialist Group), 657–658
PCIJ (Permanent Court of International Justice), 346
Pearson, Lester, 519
Peary Land, 92
Peary, Robert E., 8, 332–334, 340, 368, 705
Pechengsky monastery, 156
Pechora region, 170
Pechora River, 82–84
pelagic whaling, 399, 402, 782
penguins, 2, 63, 233, 654, 722, 740
Pennsylvania Salt Manufacturing Company, 441
peri-Antarctic islands, 378, 396, 402
permafrost, 153, 167–168, 173, 472, 513, 516, 518, 523, 609, 612
  thawing, 479, 510, 605, 728, 785
permanent bases, 59, 90, 99, 314, 696
Permanent Court of International Justice (PCIJ), 346
permanent stations, 314, 682
Perón, Juan Domingo, 682–683, 685–687, 689

Index

persistence, 19, 50, 212, 289–290, 785
Peru, 359, 673, 689, 691, 696
Peruvian Antarctic Institute, 696
Pet Four, 599, 607–611, 614–615
Peter I Island, 190
Peter Pan, 264, 266, 273
Peterhead, 386, 392
Petermann, August, 193–195, 198, 328
Petrograd *see* St Petersburg
petroleum, 525, 595–596, 598–599, 600, 603, 607, 609, 613, 634; *see also* extractive industries; oil
  development, 518, 593–594, 598, 610
  products, 601, 605, 611–612
Petroleum Administrator for War, 606
Petsamo, 450, 652
Philippines, 367, 573, 576–578
Phleger, Herman, 552
physical environment, 52, 513, 515–516, 517, 527, 529, 536
physical geography, 182–183, 186–190, 193, 197, 200–201, 582
Pierce, Robert, 263
Pine Island Glacier, 69
Pine Point, 438
pioneer populations, 85, 89
pipeline surveys, 593, 608, 614, 616
pipelines, 518, 595–596, 599–600, 602, 605–606, 608, 610, 612–613, 614–616, 659
  CANOL, 600, 602, 610
  hydrocarbon, 603
  Mackenzie Valley, 633, 659, 781
  Trans-Alaska, 593, 596, 610, 611–612, 613, 615–617, 659
  Whittier–Anchorage, 613
place names, 33, 56, 338; *see also* individual names
planes, 34, 45, 344, 469, 516, 680, 683, 715, 739
planners
  environmental, 757
  military, 600, 602, 611–612
poems, 165, 256
Point Barrow, 516
Polar Bear Specialist Group (PBSG), 657–658
polar bears, 2, 23, 40, 46, 131, 142, 517, 520, 525, 657–658
polar continent, 537, 543, 547, 549, 553–557
Polar Continental Shelf Project, 516, 527
polar environments, 516, 518, 649–651, 659, 662, 665, 771, 773, 779, 781
polar expedition novels, 259–263
polar exploration, 8, 9–10, 12, 13–14, 245, 253, 257, 262, 268, 270–271

polar history, renewing relationships beyond the shadows, 749–768
polar ice, 130, 193, 259, 512, 521–522, 541
polar regions *see also* Introductory Note above
  as Cold War spaces, 523–528
  as neutral spaces, 524, 527
  definitions, 9
  northern, 182, 478, 776, 780–781, 782
  south, 182, 183–186, 193, 197, 199, 774, 783
polar research, 1–2, 14, 23, 245, 359, 511, 517, 550
Polaris (ship), 218, 267, 437–438
Polaris (mine), 437–438
political action, 22, 621, 622, 629
political aspirations, 489, 505
political boundaries, 550, 595, 641, 778
political conflicts, 320, 451
political crises, 371, 447
political disputes, 743–744
political history, 26, 510, 644
political imagination, 288, 295–297
political independence, 294, 506, 623, 635
political mobilization, 499–500, 587
political motivations, 12, 247, 391
political movements, 26, 621–644, 778
  colonization and change, 623–628
  Indigenous peoples' organizations (IPOs), 640–644
  land claims and self-government, 628–639
political parties, 487, 501, 627–628, 632
political power, 25, 775, 784
political rights, 113, 636
political settlements, 622, 632–633
political sovereignty, 365–366, 637
politicians, 325, 332, 342, 399, 455, 500, 519, 632, 635
  Greenlandic, 489, 491, 494–495, 499, 501, 505, 507, 628
politics, 12, 26, 106–108, 114, 120, 122, 293, 311, 363, 728–729
  foreign, 355, 370
  global, 555, 642
  international, 366, 537, 540
  sovereignty, 547
pollution, 445, 451, 453, 454, 655, 661, 663
  industrial, 523, 655
  water, 451, 453
Pomors, 156–158, 159, 162, 171, 174
popular culture, 329, 765, 779
population, 133, 145, 441, 452–453, 479, 493, 496–497, 651, 657, 709–710
  animal, 91, 274, 648, 773, 776
  Indigenous, 235, 357, 464–465, 477, 538, 629, 653, 675, 778, 783
  local, 117–118, 450, 492, 675

population (cont.)
  pioneer, 85, 89
  reindeer, 478, 776
  Sámi, 111, 113
  whale, 312, 318, 387–388, 400
Population Commission, 497
Porden, Eleanor, 212
Port Radium, 436
Porter, Dorothy, 256
ports, 161, 226, 387, 412–414, 423, 577, 612; see also individual names
  Dutch, 381–384
  home, 384, 402
Posiet, Konstantin, 170
post-colonial studies, 293
Postel-Vinay, Karoline, 280–281
posterity, 234, 252, 265, 274, 775
post-modern historical fiction and the polar regions, 255–259
Potaka, Louis, 241
power
  distributions of, 295
  dynamics, 263, 756
  political, 25, 775, 784
  structures, 499, 765
powers
  imperial, 169, 320, 326, 550, 775
  maritime, 183, 305
Poynter, Charles, 187
practice, power of, 8–16
pre-colonial tattoos, 503
pre-Inuit societies, 79, 90–93, 97, 100, 772
  human remains, 97
  material culture and subsistence, 93–96
  non-material world, 97–98
  prices, 149, 163, 379, 382, 384, 399, 401, 416, 605, 610
  coal, 446
Prince Patrick Island, 328, 341
prison camps, 452, 468
  Gulag, 466, 470–471
prisoners, 452, 453–454, 466, 474, 685
private companies, 440, 479, 515, 596, 598
private development, 598
privatization, 479
privileges, 345, 471, 476, 598, 636
proclamations, 333, 337, 339
production, 158, 401, 407, 423, 425, 438, 441, 443, 780–781, 782–783
  annual, 441, 444
  industrial, 471, 514
  knowledge, 17, 154, 294, 516, 519
  oil, 595, 598, 599

productivity, 397, 411, 414, 443, 704, 707, 722
products, 157, 158, 238, 407–408, 414, 415–416, 420, 454, 772, 776
  consumer, 408, 526
  whale, 384–386, 388, 390
profits, 168, 174, 364, 365–366, 371, 400, 408, 414, 442, 616
progress, 22, 70–71, 210, 224, 231, 233, 327, 622, 630, 633
Project Cauldron, 781
Project Chariot, 518, 527, 587, 630, 781
promyshlenniki, 159, 163
prospectors, 435, 455, 515, 575
prosperity, 446, 476, 614
Protection of the Arctic Marine Environment (PAME), 663
protection, environmental, 12, 518, 557, 642, 649, 661–662, 666, 688, 692, 782
Prudhoe Bay, 594–595, 597, 599, 611, 615–616, 630, 780
Ptolemy, 182, 183, 289
public attention, 187, 629, 778
public interest, 214, 328, 550, 617
pump stations, 605–606
Punta Arenas, 393–395, 675, 678
Purchase, 564, 568–573, 587
Pyramiden, 22, 446–447, 463–464, 478

Qaanaaq, 505, 731–732, 743
Qajaa, 95–96
Qallunaat, 765–766
Qeqertsuaq, 442
Qeqertasussuk, 94–97
Qikiqtaaluk, 282
qiviut *see* muskox, wool
Quebec, 348, 625, 770
  northern, 325, 438, 633, 634
Queen Elizabeth Islands, 325
Queen Maud Land, 680
Qullissat, 442–444, 496, 500–501, 627, 630

Race, The, 260
racial anthropology, 116
racial biological research, 117
racism, 71, 217, 236, 241, 242
radar, 65–66, 743
  aerial, 65, 67
  stations, 564
  synthetic aperture, 68, 694
radiation, 454, 524–525
  long-wave, 522
  solar, 58, 521
radio stations, 173, 775

radioactive fallout *see* fallout
radiocarbon dates, 80–81, 91, 130, 144
radionuclides, 517, 663
Rae, John, 216–217
rail, 170, 174, 435–436, 447, 449, 451–452, 455, 605, 612–613, 615
rain, 38–39, 193
RAIPON *see* Russian Association of Indigenous Peoples of the North
Ranford, Barry, 220
Rankin Inlet, 752–755
RAPAL (Reunión de Administradores de Programas Antárticos Latinoamericanos), 694, 698
Rasmussen, Knud, 51, 292, 342–343, 489, 755–756
Ratzel, Friedrich, 283–284
raw materials, 82, 87, 90, 93, 96, 99–100, 400, 401, 407–408, 452
Ray, Patrick Henry, 576–577, 578, 597
readers, 258–259, 264–265, 269–270, 287, 749, 751–753, 765
realism, 254, 257
reburial, 110, 115, 117–120
reciprocity, 528, 624
reclamation of tattooing, 762–763
Reclus, Elisee, 284
recognition, international, 347, 369, 621
reconciliation, 121, 507, 621, 767, 783
reconstruction, 220, 238, 297, 400, 523, 696
recruitment, 412–413, 471
Red Dog Mine, 437
Reed, John C., 601, 610
referendums, 495, 501–504, 632–633, 634
regional cooperation, 689, 692, 695
regional geography, 287, 291
regional organizations, 208, 631, 636
regional specialisms, 280, 289
region-formation, 281, 288
reindeer, 134, 140, 448, 451, 456, 624, 628, 706–707, 715, 721–722
  herds, 163, 451, 711
  husbandry, 111, 477
  populations, 478, 776
religious orders, 777
relocations, 505, 527, 653
  forced, 477, 650
repatriation, 110, 115–118, 120–121
Report on New Whaling Grounds in the Southern Seas, 392
reporters, 349, 569
reputations, 6, 51, 213, 222, 223, 235, 237–238, 252, 263, 273–274

rescues, 57, 233, 244, 664, 677–678, 679, 685, 694
research, 108–109, 121, 262–263, 279–280, 284–285, 514, 515–518, 753, 760, 766
  activities, 447, 522, 527, 540, 776
  archaeological, 18, 108, 110–111, 115, 381
  geoscientific, 55, 71, 772
  glaciological, 546, 549
  nuclear, 656, 781
  polar, 1–2, 14, 23, 245, 359, 511, 517, 550
  practices, 283, 516
  scientific, 246, 247, 310, 510, 517, 594, 597, 658, 661, 687–688
  stations, 16, 34, 313, 315, 321, 511, 514, 539–541, 542, 547
resettlement, 170, 433, 474, 526, 571, 579, 621, 625, 628
residential schools, 20, 34, 48–49, 50–51, 477, 621, 783
resilience, 50, 161, 294, 648, 774
  cultural, 32, 291
Resolute Bay, 222, 437
resource colonialism, 436, 442, 446
resource development, 296, 517–518, 643, 659
resource exploitation, 96, 369, 378, 526, 555, 775–776
resource extraction, 164, 369, 630, 632–633, 635, 639, 650, 653, 654, 662; *see also* coal; extractive industries; gas; mining; oil; petroleum
  industrial, 433–434
resource frontier regions, 378
resource spaces, 84, 91, 95
resource use, 621–622, 635, 648
  traditional, 622, 624, 636
resources, 92–93, 366, 368–369, 407–408, 410–411, 470–471, 525–526, 555, 642–643, 651–655
  living, 18, 80, 99, 100, 624, 656, 658
  local, 139, 158, 423, 624
  marine, 56, 147–148, 316–317, 409, 628
  mineral, 115, 170, 332, 430, 501–502, 514, 652, 677, 690
  natural, 114, 157–158, 170, 357–358, 462, 470, 596, 599, 650–651, 655
  subsurface, 637, 639
responsibilities, 34, 122, 171, 312, 442, 488–490, 498–499, 502, 504, 623
Reunión de Administradores de Programas Antárticos Latinoamericanos *see* RAPAL
RGS *see* Royal Geographical Society
Richardson Highway, 578
Richardson, John, 216

Index

Richardson, Wilds, 576, 578
Richfield, 614, 616
Richler, Mordecai, 262
rifles, 40, 45–47, 364
right whales, 380, 387–388, 392
rights, 33, 226, 305, 331, 621, 629, 634–639,
    642–643, 681, 685
  cultural, 106–108, 120, 643
  equal, 344, 496
  human, 120, 643–644, 664–665
  Indigenous, 106, 115, 121, 208, 622, 631,
    635–638, 640–641
  land, 109, 629, 632, 643, 659
  political, 113, 636
  self-determination, 503, 528, 637–638
  territorial, 336, 340, 639
Ringnes Island, 338
Rink, Hinrich, 196, 441, 488
Ritter, Carl, 283
rivers, 156–157, 159, 183, 578–579, 776, 781; *see
  also* individual river names
roads, 100, 110, 455, 504, 526, 565, 578, 600–603,
    604, 606
Roberts, Brian, 540, 552–553, 554, 556
Robin, Gordon, 64, 65–67
Roca, Julio, 678
Rodahl, Kaare, 586
Rogers, Stan, 222
romantic explorations, 217, 218
Roosevelt, President, 601–602, 607
Ross Dependency, 310, 396–397, 548, 551
Ross Ice Shelf, 57, 68–69, 738
Ross Sea, 57, 191, 197, 198, 230, 232, 378, 392,
    396, 666
Ross, James Clark, 8, 191–192, 196, 213, 304,
    306, 391
Ross, John, 192, 211, 213, 327
Rossi, Christopher, 361, 370
rotational camps, 476–477
Rousseau, Jean-Jacques, 182
Rousseau, Lovell Harrison, 566, 568–570
Rowley, Graham, 21
Royal Geographical Society (RGS), 14, 197,
    230, 240–241, 245, 282, 287, 307–308, 335
Royal Greenland Trading Department
  see KGH
Royal Navy, 169, 187, 217, 223, 304, 306–308,
    314–315, 317
Royal Society, 192, 305, 306, 314, 549
Ruiz Moreno, Isidoro, 681
Rupert's Land, 212, 329, 331, 777
Rus', Northern, 155
Rusanov, Vladimir, 172

Russia, 113, 154, 155, 164–165, 166–167, 170–173,
    360–361, 452–453, 465, 538–539, 652; *see
    also* Soviet Union
  Academy of Sciences, 166, 167, 173, 514
  as first Arctic empire, 153–174
  Central, 156, 476
  governments, 170, 360, 568
  Imperial Geographic Society, 168
  Imperial Navy, 161, 167, 170
  Indigenous peoples, 637, 639
  internationalism and nationalism, 171–173
  nineteenth-century Arctic, 166–171
  northern, 113, 357, 432, 637, 703, 721, 722
  rise of Eurasian Arctic empire, 157–161
  Russian North
    and origins of Russian Arctic experience,
      155–157
    and Siberia in sixteenth and seventeenth
      centuries, 157–161
  state, 153–156, 163, 170, 465
  Westernization, 161–166
Russian America, 167, 651
Russian Arctic, 155, 169–170, 171–172, 174, 452,
    454, 462–463, 464–465, 466–468,
    475–480; *see also* Soviet Arctic
  mining, 452–454
Russian Association of Indigenous Peoples of
  the North (RAIPON), 636, 641
Russian culture, 154, 162, 168
Russian expansion, 153, 157
Russian expeditions, 171, 186–187
Russian explorers, 159, 165, 327
Russian hunters, 158, 165, 170, 358, 567
Russian North, 153, 161, 170, 173–174, 624,
    629, 636
  and origins of Russian Arctic experience,
    155–157
  and Siberia in sixteenth and seventeenth
    centuries, 157–161
Russian power, 162–163, 165–166
Russian-Finnish Whaling Company, 168
Russians, 153–158, 159–160, 162–164, 168–171,
    173, 200, 293, 466, 474, 567–569
Russkaya Amyerika, 568–569

Sac, John, 241
sacred drums, 115–116
Saginaw, 574
Sahtu Dene, 633
St Petersburg, 161, 165–167, 168–171, 172–174,
    452, 514
Sakha, 466
salt, 157, 158, 416

820

Index

Sámi, 8, 106–108, 109–122, 448–449, 451, 456, 622, 629, 635, 715
  activists, 115, 117, 119
  archaeology *see* Sápmi, archaeology, politics and heritage
  areas, 106, 114–116, 122, 640
  communities, 109, 115, 118, 121–122
  cultural rights and debates on repatriation, 115–120
  Culture, 110, 111
  groups, 106, 112
  heritage, 106, 121, 122, 773
  history, 112, 118
  homelands, 448, 631, 635
  human remains, 116–119
  identity, 110, 114, 116
  origins, 111, 113
  Parliaments, 114, 117, 119–120, 121, 629
  population, 111, 113
  reindeer herding, 448, 467, 715
  sacred drums, 115–116
  skulls, 117, 119
  South, 109, 112
  villages, 112, 635
Sáminess, 107, 114
Samoyed, 163, 168–169
San Francisco, 388, 566, 569
San Pedro Island, 678–679, 692
Sandbu, Magne, 718
Santiago, 21, 540, 549, 681, 683–684, 692
Sápmi, 448, 631
  archaeology, politics and heritage, 106–122
  colonial histories and legacies, 114–115
  historical boundaries, 107
Saqiyuq, 764
Saqqaq Culture, 92, 94, 98
SAR (synthetic aperture radar), 68, 694
Sargento Cabral Fort, 691
satellites, 67–68, 513, 516, 520–523, 547, 656, 739
Scandinavia, mining, 448–451
SCAR *see* Scientific Committee on Antarctic Research
schools, 20–21, 35, 48, 51, 473, 475, 476, 479, 495–496, 625–626
  residential, 20, 34, 48–49, 50–51, 477, 621, 783
Schulz, George, 349
Schwatka, Frederick, 218–220, 576
science, 14–15, 167–169, 182–188, 245–247, 282–283, 316, 511–512, 513–514, 517–519, 775
  and empire, 168, 306
  big, 15, 513, 529, 539, 550
  Cold War, 512–513, 516–517, 539
  global, 513, 539, 557
  history of, 511–512
  Science: The Endless Frontier, 11
  scientific activities, 318, 510–511, 516–517, 522, 523, 527, 528–529, 687–688, 691, 695
Scientific Committee on Antarctic Research (SCAR), 59–60, 70–71, 451, 538, 551, 656, 659, 667, 690
scientific community, 70–71, 245, 246, 399, 536, 771
scientific cooperation, 171, 244–245, 512, 515, 553, 664, 698, 720
  international, 171, 244, 512
scientific discoveries, 55, 57, 60, 71
scientific expeditions, 273, 358, 468, 544, 677, 776
scientific expertise, 245, 473, 538–539
scientific institutions, 470, 475, 515
scientific interests, 118, 246, 513, 770
scientific internationalism, 546, 551
scientific knowledge, 165, 200, 246, 307, 410, 539, 773, 782
scientific research, 246, 247, 310, 510, 517, 594, 597, 658, 661, 687–688
scientific stations, 316, 348, 516, 539, 547, 553, 656, 661
scientists, 9–10, 16, 52–53, 155, 510–511, 516–517, 521–522, 656–657, 738–740, 742
  French, 182, 183
  Russian, 169, 171
  social, 33, 285, 667
Scoresby Sound, 92
Scoresby, William, 192, 211
Scotland, 244, 356, 385–386, 392, 675
Scott and Amundsen, 235, 263
Scott of the Antarctic, 235, 257, 273, 543
Scott Polar Research Institute (SPRI), 9–10, 16, 59, 64–65, 68, 221, 540, 543, 552, 753
Scott, James Brown, 361
Scott, Kathleen, 237
Scott, Robert Falcon, 13, 19, 57–58, 198, 229–232, 234–235, 237–239, 245–246, 252, 260–265
Scott, Walter, 254
Scottish whalers, 282, 386
scurvy, 216, 441
sea ice, 4–6, 32–34, 38, 79, 91, 96, 513, 726–733, 740, 743
  thinning, 727–728, 732
sea levels, 2, 55, 57, 59, 62, 67, 69–70, 548, 738, 740–741
Sea of Okhotsk, 168, 387–388, 453
sea power, 303–304, 315

821

Seadragon, USS, 221
seafloor, 733, 739–740
seal hunting *see* sealing
sealers, 18, 240, 305, 309, 407–415, 676–677
  lives on South Shetland Islands, 418–424
sealing, 17, 19, 148, 309, 317–318, 407, 409, 411, 415, 656–657
  camps, 420, 425
  captains, 411, 413, 416
  companies, 408, 413–414, 415–416, 425
  crews, 409–410
  and life on board, 412–418
  cycles, 409–411
  gangs, 420–421, 423
  historical archaeology, 407–425
  industry, 391, 408–409, 413, 424, 778
  sealers' lives on South Shetland Islands, 418–424
  sites in South Shetland Islands, 412, 419–420
  vessels, 409–412, 414, 416–420
  numbers, 410
  voyages, 409, 412–413, 414
seals, 63, 94, 96, 147–148, 391, 420–423, 425, 488, 490, 656–657
  elephant, 407–408, 410
  fur, 309, 407, 651, 657
  hunting *see* sealing
sealskins, 408–409, 421–422
seasons, 32, 38, 47, 91, 212–213, 226, 232, 732, 741, 744
Seattle, 576–577
Second World War *see* World War II
sector theory, 333, 342, 343, 345–347
security, 307, 469, 472, 505, 664, 711
  national, 595, 599, 615, 741
Sedov, Georgy, 172
Seguin, Louise, 240
seismic surveys, 64–65, 67, 629
seismology, 522, 545, 546
self-determination, 106–108, 503, 622, 629, 636, 638, 643
  rights, 503, 528, 637–638
self-government, 446, 487, 503, 621–623, 643
  and land claims, 628–639
semi-claimants, 538, 553
Semipalatinsk, 524
settlement patterns, 92–93, 111
settlements, 132–134, 144–148, 383, 430–433, 453, 470–473, 476–477, 479, 502, 625–626
  deserted, 148–149, 447, 567
  first/initial, 81, 89, 142, 147, 443, 676
  industrial, 433, 462, 471–472, 477
  mining, 438, 453, 467

Norse, 136, 144–145, 487
  permanent, 6, 344, 446, 478
  political, 622, 632–633
  small, 130, 464, 472–473, 493, 497, 627
  urban, 157, 464, 780
settler colonialism, 326, 464, 563, 651, 774, 777
settlers, 130–131, 132–133, 134, 156, 170, 326, 476, 477, 624, 766
Severodvinsk, 476
Seward Peninsula, 584
Seward, William, 566, 569–571, 573–574, 583
SFPZ (Svalbard Fishery Protection Zone), 658
Shaaw Tláa, 435
Shackleton, Ernest, 57, 198, 201, 229–231, 232–234, 236–238, 243–244, 246, 308, 679
Shalamov, Varlam, 452
shamans, 467
sharing, 49–50
Sharpe, Christina, 767
sheep, 133, 140, 142, 147–148, 702, 706, 709
  and goats, 140, 142, 147–148
  roaming, 141–142
Sheet'ká, 567
Shelley, Mary, 212
shelters, 45, 420–421, 423–424, 425, 683, 685, 711, 712
Sherman, William Tecumseh, 573
shipbuilding, 158–159, 161, 394
ships, 207–211, 213–216, 220–222, 225, 327–328, 381–385, 394–397, 408–410, 412–420, 423–425
  cruise, 221–222, 304, 317, 364
  factory, 389, 394–397, 402, 654
Shirase, Nobu, 242–243
shoes, 415, 424
shore stations, 389–390, 394–397, 402, 654
Shtax'héen, 575
Siberia, 81–82, 97–99, 157–162, 163–164, 165, 168–169, 470–471, 601, 636, 776
  central, 82, 84
  coasts, 170, 334, 342
  eastern, 25, 160, 167
  northern, 79, 89, 99, 153, 174, 470
  western, 84, 160, 475, 476, 526
Siberians, Indigenous/native, 160, 162, 164, 168, 174, 527
Sidorov, Mikhail, 170
Sifton, Clifford, 336, 337
Signal Corps, 577–579
Sigurðsson, Vigfús, 708
Siku-Inuit-Hila project, 731
Silbojokk/Silbbajåhkå, 119, 448
silver, 115, 434–435, 437, 448

Index

Simmons, Dan, 207, 222, 259
Simonov, Ivan, 187
Sinclair Pipe Line Company, 614
Singnagtugaq: A Greenlander's Dream, 489
Sir James Clark Ross (factory ship), 396
Sirius Patrol, 504
Sisimiut, 142, 444, 500, 626
sites, 82–84, 85–89, 92–93, 120, 244, 512–513, 584–585, 681–682, 727–728, 740–741
   archaeological, 79, 80–81, 85, 88, 95
   hearth, 111, 114
   industrial, 471
   test, 524
Sitka, 435, 568–570, 573–575, 579, 600
Siumut, 501–502, 628, 632
Sixth International Geographical Congress, 197
Skagway, 602, 605
Skelton, O. D., 343, 345, 347
skerries, 130, 359
skin boats, 45, 92, 441
Skinner, Quentin, 291
Skolt, 118
Skookum Jim, 435
Skrælings, 142–144
skulls, 117–118
Slavs, 155
sledge dogs *see* dogs
sledge parties, 328
sledges, 90, 92–93, 171, 232, 333, 343
slipways, 396–397, 654
slop chests, 416
Smith Sound, 327, 328–329, 332, 334, 336
Smith, Francis Pettit 'Propeller', 214
Smith, William, 56, 187
Smithsonian Institution, 576, 582
Sno-cats, 548
snow, 45, 63, 146, 193, 231–232, 257, 269, 272, 516, 521
snowmobiles, 33, 35, 45, 46–47
soapstone, 94, 133, 433
Sobral, José María, 677
social environments, 32, 43, 52
social ownership, 598
social sciences, late nineteenth century, 280–281
social scientists, 33, 285, 667
social services, 46, 479
social theory, 290–291
socialist cities, 463, 467, 473
Sociedad Ballenera de Magallanes, 678

societal change, 32, 43–44
sociologists, 17, 470
solar radiation, 58, 521
soldiers, 513, 568, 572–573, 574, 580–581, 584–585, 593, 602, 604, 676
Soldier's Guide for Keeping Warm in Extremely Cold Climates, 584
solidarity, 319, 472, 500
Solomon Gursky Was Here, 262
Solovestskii islands, 468
Solway, David, 222
Solzhenitsyn, Aleksandr, 452
Somerset Island, 214, 337
Sørlle, Petter, 397
sources
   documentary, 419, 421, 424
   historical, 380, 411, 423
   potential, 369, 630, 660
   textual, 111
South Africa, 55, 61, 240, 242, 294, 394, 550, 552, 554, 557
South America, 186–187, 289, 359, 367, 674–675, 679–680, 689, 696; *see also* individual countries
South American Antarctica, 673, 676, 682–684, 687, 691, 692, 694–695, 697
South: An Antarctic Journey, 256
South Atlantic Ocean, 310, 397
South Georgia, 186–187, 232–233, 308–311, 316–318, 393–395, 402, 542–543, 654, 678, 722
South Orkney Islands, 243, 678, 681
South Orkneys, 310, 395, 666, 677
South Pacific, 304, 688
South Pole *see* Introductory Note above
South Pole station, 547–549
South Sámi, 109, 112
South Sandwich Islands, 61, 243, 305, 310, 316, 318, 692
South Shetland Islands, 187–190, 378–379, 391, 394–396, 409–412, 414, 418–420, 421, 423–424, 674
sealers' lives, 418–424
sealing sites, 412, 419–420
southeast Alaska, 567, 573, 575, 580
southern Greenland, 92, 133, 441, 492, 496, 501
Southern Ocean, 18, 21, 304–305, 308–309, 311, 316, 379, 391, 660, 738–740
southwest Greenland, 129, 130, 140, 440
sovereignty, 312–313, 329–330, 335–336, 344–345, 357–358, 361, 365–366, 368–369, 649–650, 777–778

823

sovereignty (cont.)
  assertions of, 777–778
  Canadian, 25, 220, 333, 344–345, 348–349
  claims, 303, 326, 685
  disputes, 18, 367, 778
  Norwegian, 338, 354, 357, 359–361, 366, 369, 371–372, 446–447, 652
  of Spitsbergen, 355, 362, 368
  political, 365–366, 637
  politics, 547
  state, 361, 370–371, 642, 654
  territorial, 365, 447, 554, 649–650
Soviet Arctic, 452, 454–455, 462–480, 526–527, 781; *see also* Russian Arctic
  Committee of the North, 173, 467
  industrializing the Arctic through Stalinism, 465–469
  living in late Soviet Arctic, 475–478
  making the Arctic livable, 469–475
  Thaw era, 470, 474
Soviet Union, 446–447, 462–466, 469–470, 474–475, 514–516, 524–528, 536–539, 546–548, 550–553, 657–658; *see also* Russia
  governments, 454, 471, 514
  leaders, 463, 470, 514, 526, 662
Spaatz, Carl, 583
spadework, 595, 615, 616
Special Committee of the IGY (CSAGI), 313, 546
specialisms, regional, 280, 289
specialists, 289, 470–471, 473
Spencer, Robert, 292
Speranskii, Mikhail, 168
sperm whales, 387
Spes & Fides, 389
spills, oil, 605, 663
Spitsbergen, 170, 171–172, 355–370, 371–372, 381–385, 388, 389–390, 402, 776, 777
  American financial rule, 366
  American 'imperialism of idealism', and successful Norwegian polar imperialism, 363–366
  between nationalism and internationalism, 368–370
  coastal waters, 378, 389
  failed polar imperialism, 1892–1914, 362–363
  guano bonanza, 357–362
  Norwegian Postal Service, 363
  reasons for selection of Norway as ruler, 366–368
  sovereignty, 355, 362, 368
Spitsbergen/Svalbard Treaty, 354–372

Treaty, 344, 355, 356–357, 365–366, 370–372, 446–447, 652
  whale fishery, 381–384
Split Tooth, 256
SPRI *see* Scott Polar Research Institute
Spufford, Francis, 234, 253
stability, 69–70, 290, 475
stagnation, 381, 475
Stählin, Jacob Von, 210
Stalin, Joseph, 372, 452, 453, 653
Standard Oil, 597–598, 604, 607–608, 610, 614
starvation, 163, 210, 212, 329, 453, 466, 625
Starvation Shore, 260–261
state control, 637, 675
state farms, 477, 527
state sovereignty, 361, 370–371, 642, 654
statehood, 563–564, 614, 630
stations, 65, 309, 312, 313, 547, 577, 579, 685, 689, 691; *see also* individual station names
  field, 516, 523
  meteorological, 171, 311, 359
  permanent, 314, 682
  pump, 605–606
  radio, 173, 775
  research, 16, 34, 313, 315, 321, 511, 514, 539–541, 542, 547
  scientific, 316, 348, 516, 539, 547, 553, 656, 661
  shore, 389–390, 394–397, 402, 654
  weather, 492, 518
  whaling, 57, 308, 316, 358, 383, 389, 393–395, 709
statues, 239, 506
status, international, 358, 369, 514
Stefansson, Vilhjalmur, 11, 13, 20, 340–343, 348, 349, 598, 653, 705–706, 721
steppe bison, 80–82, 84, 99
stepping stones, 571, 583
Stevens, Wallace, 269
Stewart, Douglas, 257
Stockholm Conference on the Human Environment, 656
Stocking, George, 283
stones, hot, 93–94
storage, 445, 554
  food, 99–100
  locations, 421
Storch, Mathias, 489
Store Norske (SNSK), 447
storehouses, 172, 383, 575, 596
stories, 222–225, 257–259, 261, 263, 267–268, 270, 274–275, 751–752, 755–756, 763–765
Strait of Boothia, 192
strategic significance, 512–513, 522, 524

Strathcona Agreement, 437
streams, ice, 67, 68
strikes, 365
Stringer Hall, 51
Stroud, Mike, 19
sub-Antarctic islands, 304–305, 309, 312, 316, 391, 542, 654
sub-Antarctic waters, 240, 555
subglacial lakes, 66
submarines, 343, 513, 516, 525, 527, 529, 545, 582
subsistence, 90, 92–93, 133, 379, 401, 412, 425, 609, 657
  activities, 379, 424, 637
  economies, 79, 134, 148, 456
  whaling, 379, 401, 640
subsurface resources, 637, 639
Sukhova, Natal'ya G., 196
Sullivan, Walter, 14, 545
sulphur mining, 440
summer camps, 503
summers, 32, 38–39, 45, 47, 140, 145–146, 190, 192–193, 683–684, 719
summertime, 34, 35–37, 45, 134
superpowers, 510, 512–513, 522–523, 527, 529, 539, 543, 549, 551, 553–554
supremacy, 266, 347, 653
surface melt, 69–70
Surfacing, The, 262
surveillance, 510, 511–513, 515, 529, 545
  aerial, 601
  submarine, 566
surveys
  geographical, 231, 271
  pipeline, 593, 608, 614, 616
  seismic, 64–65, 67, 629
survival skills, 39, 43
survival, narratives of, 236–237
Survivor, The, 262
sustainable development, 640, 642, 664, 666
Svalbard, 20–21, 22, 25, 355–356, 446, 447, 448, 455, 463–464, 709–712, 776, 780
  Archipelago, 446, 709
  mining, 446–447
  Treaty, 463
Svalbard Fishery Protection Zone (SFPZ), 658
Svane, Aksel, 491–492, 493
Sveagruvan, 446–447
Sverdrup Islands, 337, 339, 341, 343, 344–345, 350
Sverdrup, Otto, 334–335, 338–339, 341, 344–345
Swan Point, 86
Swanson River, 614
Sweden, 106–107, 110–112, 114–116, 117–121, 170, 355–356, 449–451, 635, 706–707, 713–715

  central, 113
  northern, 110–111, 114–116, 121, 449, 708, 714
  southern, 111
  state, 114, 119, 121, 635
Swedish-Norwegian-Russian condominium, 361, 363
Swinburne, Algernon Charles, 217, 222
symbols, 97, 115, 220, 462, 547, 707, 734
synoptic data, 536–537, 539
  collection, 537, 539, 558
synthetic aperture radar (SAR), 68, 694
synthetic cryolite, 442
syphilis, 441
systematic geography, 286–287, 289

Tabarin, Operation, 311, 541, 682
TAE (Trans-Antarctic Expedition), 314, 542–543
Taft, William Howard, 340
Tagaq, Tanya, 256
Tagish, 435
taiga, 174, 467, 605
tailings, 445, 451
Taimyr, 172
Taimyr Peninsula, 89, 168, 720–721
TallBear, Kim, 757
Tally, Ted, 257
Tanana, 577, 578, 605
tankers, 221, 602, 612, 616
TAPS *see* Trans-Alaska Pipeline System
tattooing, 503, 761–763
taxes, 138, 149, 168, 309, 312, 369, 442, 445, 737, 743
Taylor, Thomas Griffith, 310
Te Atu, 241
teachers, 44, 220, 443, 489, 496, 626–627
Teal, John, Jr, 716–718
Teal's farm, 717, 719
teams, dog, 35, 45, 46–47, 731
technological developments, 380, 390, 514
technologies, 65, 160–161, 173, 387, 388–389, 390, 513, 516–517, 653, 656
  new, 44, 64, 164, 169, 409, 654, 679, 776
  nuclear, 779, 781
temperate regions/zones, 337, 513, 648, 733, 774
temperatures, 6, 38–39, 62–63, 153–154, 192, 193–194, 200, 443, 510, 512
  average, 3
temporality, 744, 770–771, 775, 784
tents, 93–94, 232, 252, 263, 264, 473, 474
Terra Australis, 182–186, 199–200, 304
terra incognita, 57, 181–182

Terra Nova, 257
Terra Nova expedition, 57, 246, 256, 262, 267, 308
terrain intelligence, 516–518
terrestrial magnetism, 211, 306
territorial authority, 514, 517, 527, 528
territorial claims, 310, 318, 528, 529, 542, 543, 551, 553, 557, 687
territorial disputes, 527, 652, 692
territorial expansion, 157, 229, 448
territorial rights, 336, 340, 639
territorial sovereignty, 365, 447, 554, 649–650
territorial waters, 339, 342, 369
Terror and Erebus (poem), 222
Terror, HMS, 207–208, 214, 220, 222, 225, 260, 267, 306–307, 327, 469
test ban treaty, partial, 524, 556
test sites, 524
tests, 166, 235, 243, 285, 524, 585–586, 615, 754, 781
  nuclear, 524–525, 527, 586, 630, 688, 781
  underground, 524–525
Thatcher, Admiral Henry Knox, 566
Thatcher, Margaret, 237–238
Thaw era, 470, 474
thawing permafrost, 479, 510, 605, 728, 785
thinning sea ice, 727–728, 732
Thomsen, Julius, 440
Thule, 92, 505, 743
  Air Base, 505, 516, 527, 743
  Culture, 487
  Inuit, 143
Thwaites Glacier, 69
tidewater, 449, 577, 599, 615, 780
Tierra del Fuego, 407, 413, 416, 676, 679
Tlingit, 163, 435, 565–568, 572–573, 574–575, 778, 785
Tobolsk, 157, 162
Toll, Eduard von, 172
Totten Glacier, 66
tourism, 226, 378, 504, 575, 744
  Antarctic, 675, 741
tourists, 20, 208, 358, 363–364, 712, 715, 719, 727, 733–734, 740
towns, 35, 41, 43, 45–46, 155–157, 436, 437, 500–501, 626–627, 711–712; *see also* individual town names
  industrial, 471, 474
toxic debris, 741–742
trade, 117, 129, 138, 143, 167, 310, 407, 416, 433, 441
  fur, 50, 159–160, 163, 309, 575, 624, 776

traditional ecological knowledge (TEK), 17, 773
traditional knowledge, 39, 638
traditional resource use, 622, 624, 636
traditional territories, 439, 598, 622, 639
traditions, 8, 12–13, 17, 19, 109, 383, 507, 514, 628, 755
  Inuit, 33, 50, 53, 641
tragedy, narratives of, 235–236
Trans-Alaska Pipeline System (TAPS), 593, 596, 610, 611–612, 613, 615–617, 659
Trans-Antarctic Expedition (TAE), 542–543
Transantarctic Mountains, 57–58, 61, 63, 231
transportation infrastructures, 595, 600
treaties, 354–355, 356–357, 365–366, 369–371, 554–555, 556–557, 648–649, 720, 726, 742–743; *see also* individual treaty titles
  numbered, 598, 633
Treaty of Cession, 568
Treaty of Peace and Friendship, 692
treaty parties, 555–556, 652, 656–657
treeline, 3, 153–154
Tromsø, 717–718, 719
trucks, 602, 760
Trudeau, Justin, 220
Truman, Harry, 606
truth and reconciliation commissions, 51, 121, 783
Tumen', 157
tundra, 79, 81, 87, 91, 99, 100, 436, 438, 605, 609
Tunzelmann, Alexander von, 56
Turney, Chris, 246
Tusaqtuut, 732
two-cell churches, 136–137, 146
Typus Orbis Terrarium, 182
Tyson, George, 261–262

UK *see* United Kingdom
umiak see skin boats
Umiat, 593, 608
umingmak see muskox
Unangan people, 572, 580
UNASUR (Union of South American Nations), 695, 697
underground tests, 524–525
underworlds, 537, 558
UNDRIP (United Nations Declaration on the Rights of Indigenous Peoples), 120–121
Union of South American Nations (UNASUR), 695, 697
United Kingdom, 243–244, 303–305, 311–315, 318–321, 408–409, 540–544, 549–551,

686–688, 691–692, 758–759; see also
  Falkland Islands
and Antarctica in the eighteenth century,
  304–305
and Antarctica in the nineteenth century,
  306–307
and Heroic Age of Antarctic exploration,
  307–308
and International Geophysical Year (IGY),
  313–315
British Antarctic Survey (BAS), 12, 240,
  302–303, 316, 320–321
Colonial Office, 304, 310–311, 318, 330,
  542–543
competing claims from Argentina and
  Chile, 311–313
Falklands War, 237, 315–317
government, 212, 230, 305, 311, 314, 317, 367,
  402, 679, 682
House of Commons, 302, 347, 684
National Environmental Research Council
  (NERC), 302–303
National Oceanographic Centre, 302
polar empire, 302–321
Royal Navy, 169, 187, 217, 223, 304, 306–308,
  314–315, 317
Royal Society, 192, 305, 306, 314, 549
South Atlantic sealing and whaling, 309–311
whaling industry, 385–386, 391–392
United Nations, 58, 495, 519, 655, 687
  Declaration on the Rights of Indigenous
    Peoples (UNDRIP), 120–121
  Economic and Social Council (ECOSOC),
    641, 643
  Environment Programme (UNEP),
    401
  Framework Convention on Climate
    Change, 665
  Intergovernmental Panel on Climate
    Change, 666
United States, 491–492, 537–538, 541–542,
  543–545, 550–552, 563–564, 566–568,
  573–575, 657–659, 726
  AEC (Atomic Energy Commission), 518,
    524, 586–587
  Army Corps of Engineers, 582, 611, 613
  colony, 565, 570, 572–573
  Congress, 359, 365, 566, 575, 579, 611, 613, 615,
    630, 636
  Department of Defense, 564, 611, 614
  Exploring Expedition, 191, 271
  Geological Survey (USGS), 597, 599,
    607, 615

governments, 330, 347, 573, 582, 604, 615,
  681, 682
militarization of Alaska, 563–587
military, 505, 564, 570, 572, 587, 600, 603–604
National Science Foundation, 11, 16, 65, 736
Naval Petroleum Reserves, 596, 599, 607
Signal Corps, 577–579
State Department, 344, 544
Unna Saiva, 120
Unravelling the Franklin Mystery, 220
unstable ice sheet, 67–70
Upernavik, 142, 440
Upper Palaeolithic, 81–82, 99
Upper Volga, 155–156
Urals, 80–84, 159, 162, 168
  northern, 153, 157
uranium, 243, 436, 446, 454, 501, 525–526, 527,
  555, 781
urban centres, 155–156, 157, 160, 450
urban infrastructure, 161–162, 476–477, 479
urban settlements, 157, 464, 780
urbanization, 462, 471, 474, 654
Urengoi, 526
Uruguay, 673, 678, 679, 689, 690, 693
Uruguayan Antarctic Institute, 690
US see United States
USGS see United States, Geological Survey
Ushki Culture, 84, 86
USSR see Soviet Union
Utqiaġvik, 16, 576, 610, 640, 731
Uummannaq, 445, 501

Vahsel Bay, 313–315
Vaigach, 172
Valdez, 577–578, 595, 608, 611, 614–615, 780
values, cultural, 631, 641
Van Diemen's Land, 267
Varenius, Bernhard, 182–183
vegetation, 5, 38, 39, 110, 246, 287, 705
Venetz, Ignatz, 196
Venezuela, 684, 694, 695
Vermont, 716–718
vessels see ships
Vibe, Christian, 493
Victim of the Aurora, 262
Victoria Island, 34, 50, 598
Victoria Land, 197, 200
Victory Point note, 216
Vietnam War, 235, 238, 613
Villa las Estrellas, 692
villages, 218, 474, 572, 574, 580, 587, 628, 635,
  692, 712
violent conflict, 236, 434

viruses, 770–771, 784–785
Vladivostok, 172
Voisey's Bay, 438
Vologda, 156, 158
Vorkuta, 452, 468, 473, 475, 478, 653
Voyage of the Fox in Arctic Seas, 217
Voyage of the Narwhal, 253, 262, 270–272
Voyages of Delusion, 210
voyageurs, 212

Wachowich, Nancy, 51, 764
wages, 471, 476, 627
Wakeham, William, 333, 337, 339
walrus, 90, 99, 131, 138, 140, 142, 149, 163, 358, 624
WAMCATS (Washington–Alaska Military Cable and Telegraph System), 577–579
warming, global, 63, 67, 479, 510, 529, 642, 664–665, 728, 734
Washington–Alaska Military Cable and Telegraph System (WAMCATS), 577–579
waste, 93, 606, 610, 656, 705–706, 741
  liquid, 525
  rock, 442, 451
wasteland, 649, 653, 705
water
  liquid, 66, 729
  open, 99, 233, 378, 732
  pollution, 451, 453
Waterman, Laura, 260–261
wealth, 131, 163, 181, 318, 359, 440, 448, 467, 565, 753
  mineral, 430, 576
weapons, 433–434, 510, 553, 685, 741
  nuclear, 505, 517, 524, 586, 609, 781
weather, 68, 232, 233, 307, 420, 422, 513, 536, 754, 775
  cold, 79, 566, 579
  conditions, 67, 100, 411, 421–422
  forecasting, 492, 517
  patterns, 318, 761
  stations, 492, 518
Weddell Sea, 66, 197, 232–233, 244, 309, 313–314, 319, 549, 685
Weddell, James, 190
weekends, 48–49
Wellington Bay, 39, 45
Wellington Channel, 328
Wells, Erasmus Darwin, 270–272
West Antarctic ice sheet, 67, 69
West Antarctica, 59, 62, 66–69, 510, 548
West Greenland, 92, 94–96, 487, 490, 628

western Arctic, 51, 341, 433, 435, 633, 653
western Canadian Arctic, 32–53, 91
Western Settlement, 133–134, 140–142, 144–145, 146–147
western Siberia, 84, 160, 475, 476, 526
whale oil, 309, 381, 384, 395, 399, 402, 409, 680, 776
  prices, 383, 385
  production, 380, 654
whale products, 384–386, 388, 390
Whalemen's Shipping List and Merchants' Transcript, 415
whalers, 18, 309, 312, 378–380, 381, 385–386, 387–388, 394–395, 398, 401–402
  American, 330, 332, 336, 386–388, 569
  Basque, 381
  British, 385–386, 391
  Danish, 385
  Dutch, 384–385, 388
  Iñupiaq, 528
  Iñupiat, 18
  Norwegian, 389, 392–393
  Scottish, 282, 386
  Soviet, 400
whales, 18, 168, 309, 379–383, 384, 386–392, 397, 400–402, 654–655, 656–657
  blue, 389, 397, 400
  bowhead, 380, 383–385, 387–388, 528, 651
  fin, 389, 400
  minke, 400, 624
  populations, 312, 318, 387–388, 400
  right, 380, 387–388, 392
  species, 379–380, 388
  sperm, 387
  stocks, 311, 379, 399, 402–403
whaling, 309–310, 311, 378–403, 413, 654–655
  American, 386–388
  Antarctic, 256, 303, 310, 379–380, 391–401, 654, 660, 687
  decline, 399–401
  founding of industry, 393–395
  historic sites, 394
  pelagic bonanza, 396–399
  as first Arctic industry, 380
  bay, 380, 402
  chartered, 388, 402
  commercial, 18, 26, 380, 399, 401–408, 556, 624, 776
  companies, 168, 309, 389–392, 393, 396, 399, 679
  Danish, 385
  development, 310, 396
  Dutch, 383–384

828

English *see* whaling, United Kingdom
factory ships, 389, 394–397, 402, 654
Finnmark, 389, 392
Grand Bay, 380–381
Greenland and Davis Strait, 385–386
grounds, 330, 378, 383–388, 392, 397, 400
industrial, 379, 401, 528
modern, 390
North Atlantic and Arctic Rorqual hunt, 388–391
North–South transition, 391–393
operations, 393–395, 397, 401
pelagic, 399, 402, 782
seasons, 396, 399
Spitsbergen whale fishery, 381–384
stations, 57, 308, 316, 358, 383, 389, 393–395, 709
subsistence, 379, 401, 640
United Kingdom, 384, 385–386, 391–392
When the Night Comes, 256
White Sea, 89, 113, 153, 155–158, 161
White, Hayden, 254
White, James, 335, 337–339
White, The, 260
Whitehorse, 601, 602, 605–607, 770
Whittier, 584, 612
Whittier–Anchorage pipeline, 613
Why Indigenous Literatures Matter, 756
Wiebe, Rudy, 261
Wiggins, Joseph, 169
wild animals, 660, 704, 711, 716, 722
Wild, Frank, 231
wildlife, 42, 246, 638–639, 658, 753, 771
wildness, 11
Wilkes Land, 191, 197
Wilkes station, 547–548
Wilkes, Charles, 191, 196, 200, 241, 271, 541, 567
Williams (ship), 187
Williams, Glyn, 210
Williamson, Robert, 752–754, 767–768
Wilson, Edward, 57, 230, 252, 264, 265
Wilson, John, 222
Wilson's Diary, 256
Wingham, Duncan, 302–303
winters, 32–34, 138, 140–142, 259–260, 261, 263, 266–267, 269–270, 710–711, 712
wolves, 41–42, 46, 83, 721

women, 71, 133, 141, 239–241, 261, 495, 750, 764, 777
Alutiiq, 168
Inuit, 762, 764
wooden houses, 464, 473
Woodman, David C., 219
wool, 140, 141, 423, 706–707
muskox domestication for, 716–719
workers, 364–365, 412, 413–415, 436, 438, 441, 452, 453, 462–463, 499
construction, 626–627
workforces, 412–413, 414, 424, 441, 443–444, 445, 500
World Data Centres, 550
World Meteorological Organization, 519, 544
World War I, 173, 236, 237, 310, 367, 395, 446, 466, 515, 576
World War II, 58, 442–443, 491, 541, 563–564, 565, 581, 583–584, 594–595, 626–627
Worsley, Frank, 232–233, 308
Wrangel Island, 20, 342, 720–721
Wrangell Mountains, 435
Wrangell, Baron Ferdinand von, 167, 192, 327
writers, 217, 253, 254–255, 256–257, 261, 265, 270, 316, 325, 755

Xue Long (ship), 221

Yakutia, 153, 168, 528, 721
Yakuts, 159–160, 163
Yakutsk, 160, 167, 514, 528
Yamal, 162, 173, 526, 721
Yana site, 82
Yellowknife, 436, 439
Yenisei Bay, 173
Yenisei River, 169–170
Yermak, 157, 159
Yermak (ship), 172
young people, 33, 40, 44, 49–50, 53, 443, 665
Young, Oran, 371
Yukon, 85, 577, 582, 601, 602, 606, 631, 633, 770, 776
coasts, 336, 340
Indians, 631
River, 576–577
Yupik, 163, 465

Zachariassen, Søren, 446